Poetry
Criticism

Guide to Gale Literary Criticism Series

For criticism on	Consult these Gale series
Authors now living or who died after December 31, 1999	*CONTEMPORARY LITERARY CRITICISM (CLC)*
Authors who died between 1900 and 1999	*TWENTIETH-CENTURY LITERARY CRITICISM (TCLC)*
Authors who died between 1800 and 1899	*NINETEENTH-CENTURY LITERATURE CRITICISM (NCLC)*
Authors who died between 1400 and 1799	*LITERATURE CRITICISM FROM 1400 TO 1800 (LC)* *SHAKESPEAREAN CRITICISM (SC)*
Authors who died before 1400	*CLASSICAL AND MEDIEVAL LITERATURE CRITICISM (CMLC)*
Authors of books for children and young adults	*CHILDREN'S LITERATURE REVIEW (CLR)*
Dramatists	*DRAMA CRITICISM (DC)*
Poets	*POETRY CRITICISM (PC)*
Short story writers	*SHORT STORY CRITICISM (SSC)*
Literary topics and movements	*HARLEM RENAISSANCE: A GALE CRITICAL COMPANION (HR)* *THE BEAT GENERATION: A GALE CRITICAL COMPANION (BG)*
Asian American writers of the last two hundred years	*ASIAN AMERICAN LITERATURE (AAL)*
Black writers of the past two hundred years	*BLACK LITERATURE CRITICISM (BLC)* *BLACK LITERATURE CRITICISM SUPPLEMENT (BLCS)*
Hispanic writers of the late nineteenth and twentieth centuries	*HISPANIC LITERATURE CRITICISM (HLC)* *HISPANIC LITERATURE CRITICISM SUPPLEMENT (HLCS)*
Native North American writers and orators of the eighteenth, nineteenth, and twentieth centuries	*NATIVE NORTH AMERICAN LITERATURE (NNAL)*
Major authors from the Renaissance to the present	*WORLD LITERATURE CRITICISM, 1500 TO THE PRESENT (WLC)* *WORLD LITERATURE CRITICISM SUPPLEMENT (WLCS)*

ISSN 1052-4851

Poetry Criticism

Excerpts from Criticism of the Works of the Most Significant and Widely Studied Poets of World Literature

Volume 65

Michelle Lee
Project Editor

THOMSON
━★━ ™
GALE

Detroit • New York • San Francisco • San Diego • New Haven, Conn. • Waterville, Maine • London • Munich

Poetry Criticism, Vol. 65

Project Editor
Michelle Lee

Editorial
Jessica Bomarito, Kathy D. Darrow, Jeffrey Hunter, Jelena O. Krstović, Thomas J. Schoenberg, Lawrence J. Trudeau, Russel Whitaker

Data Capture
Francis Monroe, Gwen Tucker

Indexing Services
Factiva®, a Dow Jones and Reuters Company

Rights and Acquisitions
Margaret Abendroth, Margaret Chamberlain-Gaston, Jacqueline Key

Imaging and Multimedia
Dean Dauphinais, Leitha Etheridge-Sims, Lezlie Light, Mike Logusz, Dan Newell, Christine O'Bryan, Kelly A. Quin, Denay Wilding, Robyn Young

Composition and Electronic Capture
Kathy Sauer

Manufacturing
Rhonda Dover

Associate Product Manager
Marc Cormier

LIBRARY OF CONGRESS CATALOG CARD NUMBER 91-118494

ISBN 0-7876-8699-9
ISSN 1052-4851

Printed in the United States of America
10 9 8 7 6 5 4 3 2 1

Contents

Preface vii

Acknowledgments ix

Literary Criticism Series Advisory Board xi

Preface

*P*oetry Criticism (*PC*) presents significant criticism of the world's greatest poets and provides supplementary biographical and bibliographical material to guide the interested reader to a greater understanding of the genre and its creators. Although major poets and literary movements are covered in such Gale Literary Criticism series as *Contemporary Literary Criticism (CLC)*, *Twentieth-Century Literary Criticism (TCLC)*, *Nineteenth-Century Literature Criticism (NCLC)*, *Literature Criticism from 1400 to 1800 (LC)*, and *Classical and Medieval Literature Criticism (CMLC)*, *PC* offers more focused attention on poetry than is possible in the broader, survey-oriented entries on writers in these Thomson Gale series. Students, teachers, librarians, and researchers will find that the generous excerpts and supplementary material provided by *PC* supply them with the vital information needed to write a term paper on poetic technique, to examine a poet's most prominent themes, or to lead a poetry discussion group.

Scope of the Series

PC is designed to serve as an introduction to major poets of all eras and nationalities. Since these authors have inspired a great deal of relevant critical material, *PC* is necessarily selective, and the editors have chosen the most important published criticism to aid readers and students in their research. Each author entry presents a historical survey of the critical response to that author's work. The length of an entry is intended to reflect the amount of critical attention the author has received from critics writing in English and from foreign critics in translation. Every attempt has been made to identify and include the most significant essays on each author's work. In order to provide these important critical pieces, the editors sometimes reprint essays that have appeared elsewhere in Thomson Gale's Literary Criticism Series. Such duplication, however, never exceeds twenty percent of a *PC* volume.

Organization of the Book

Each *PC* entry consists of the following elements:

- The **Author Heading** cites the name under which the author most commonly wrote, followed by birth and death dates. Also located here are any name variations under which an author wrote, including transliterated forms for authors whose native languages use nonroman alphabets. If the author wrote consistently under a pseudonym, the pseudonym will be listed in the author heading and the author's actual name given in parenthesis on the first line of the biographical and critical introduction. Uncertain birth or death dates are indicated by question marks. Single-work entries are preceded by the title of the work and its date of publication.

- The **Introduction** contains background information that introduces the reader to the author and the critical debates surrounding his or her work.

- A **Portrait of the Author** is included when available.

- The list of **Principal Works** is ordered chronologically by date of first publication and lists the most important works by the author. The first section comprises poetry collections and book-length poems. The second section gives information on other major works by the author. For foreign authors, the editors have provided original foreign-language publication information and have selected what are considered the best and most complete English-language editions of their works.

- Reprinted **Criticism** is arranged chronologically in each entry to provide a useful perspective on changes in critical evaluation over time. All individual titles of poems and poetry collections by the author featured in the entry are printed in boldface type. The critic's name and the date of composition or publication of the critical work are given at the beginning of each piece of criticism. Unsigned criticism is preceded by the title of the source in which it appeared. Footnotes are reprinted at the end of each essay or excerpt. In the case of excerpted criticism, only those footnotes that pertain to the excerpted texts are included.

- Critical essays are prefaced by brief **Annotations** explicating each piece.

- A complete **Bibliographical Citation** of the original essay or book precedes each piece of criticism.

- An annotated bibliography of **Further Reading** appears at the end of each entry and suggests resources for additional study. In some cases, significant essays for which the editors could not obtain reprint rights are included here. Boxed material following the further reading list provides references to other biographical and critical sources on the author in series published by Thomson Gale.

Cumulative Indexes

A **Cumulative Author Index** lists all of the authors that appear in a wide variety of reference sources published by Thomson Gale, including *PC*. A complete list of these sources is found facing the first page of the Author Index. The index also includes birth and death dates and cross references between pseudonyms and actual names.

A **Cumulative Nationality Index** lists all authors featured in *PC* by nationality, followed by the number of the *PC* volume in which their entry appears.

A **Cumulative Title Index** lists in alphabetical order all individual poems, book-length poems, and collection titles contained in the *PC* series. Titles of poetry collections and separately published poems are printed in italics, while titles of individual poems are printed in roman type with quotation marks. Each title is followed by the author's last name and corresponding volume and page numbers where commentary on the work is located. English-language translations of original foreign-language titles are cross-referenced to the foreign titles so that all references to discussion of a work are combined in one listing.

Citing *Poetry Criticism*

When writing papers, students who quote directly from any volume in the Literary Criticism Series may use the following general format to footnote reprinted criticism. The first example pertains to material drawn from periodicals, the second to material reprinted from books.

Sylvia Kasey Marks, "A Brief Glance at George Eliot's *The Spanish Gypsy*," *Victorian Poetry* 20, no. 2 (Summer 1983), 184-90; reprinted in *Poetry Criticism,* vol. 20, ed. Ellen McGeagh (Detroit: The Gale Group), 128-31.

Linden Peach, "Man, Nature and Wordsworth: American Versions," *British Influence on the Birth of American Literature,* (Macmillan Press Ltd., 1982), 29-57; reprinted in *Poetry Criticism,* vol. 20, ed. Ellen McGeagh (Detroit: The Gale Group), 37-40.

Suggestions are Welcome

Readers who wish to suggest new features, topics, or authors to appear in future volumes, or who have other suggestions or comments are cordially invited to call, write, or fax the Associate Product Manager:

Associate Product Manager, Literary Criticism Series
Thomson Gale
27500 Drake Road
Farmington Hills, MI 48331-3535
1-800-347-4253 (GALE)
Fax: 248-699-8054

Acknowledgments

The editors wish to thank the copyright holders of the criticism included in this volume and the permissions managers of many book and magazine publishing companies for assisting us in securing reproduction rights. We are also grateful to the staffs of the Detroit Public Library, the Library of Congress, the University of Detroit Mercy Library, Wayne State University Purdy/Kresge Library Complex, and the University of Michigan Libraries for making their resources available to us. Following is a list of the copyright holders who have granted us permission to reproduce material in this volume of *PC*. Every effort has been made to trace copyright, but if omissions have been made, please let us know.

COPYRIGHTED MATERIAL IN *PC*, VOLUME 65, WAS REPRODUCED FROM THE FOLLOWING PERIODICALS:

Anglia, v. 113, 1995 for "Sickness unto Death: Crime and Punishment in Henryson's *The Testament of Cresseid*" by Sabine Volk-Birke. Copyright © 1995 by Max Niemeyer Verlag. Reproduced by permission of the author.—*The Chaucer Review,* v. 25, 1991. Copyright © 1991 by Pennsylvania State University. All rights reserved. Reproduced by permission of the Pennsylvania State University Press.—*Children's Literature,* v. 26, 1998. Copyright © 1998 by Hollins College. All rights reserved. Reproduced by permission of Johns Hopkins University Press Journals.—*Children's Literature, Annual of The Modern Language Association,* v. 10, 1982. Copyright © 1982 by Children's Literature, An International Journal, Inc. All rights reserved. Reproduced by permission of Johns Hopkins University Press.—*Cimarron Review,* n. 121, October, 1997 for "Luci Tapahonso, Irvin Morris, and Della Frank: Interweaving Navajo and English in Their Poems and Stories" by Susan B. Brill. Copyright © 1997 by the Board of Regents for Oklahoma State University. All rights reserved. Reproduced by permission of the author.—*Fifteenth-Century Studies,* v. 25, 2000; v. 28, 2003. Copyright © 2000, 2003 by the Contributors. All rights reserved. Both reproduced by permission.—*Forum Italicum,* v. 35, fall, 2001. Copyright © 2001 by Forum Italicum, Inc. Reproduced by permission.—*Genre,* v. 21, spring, 1988 for "The Limerick and the Space of Metaphor" by Ann C. Colley. Copyright © 1988 by the University of Oklahoma. All rights reserved. Reproduced by permission of the publisher and the author.—*Italian Studies: An Annual Review,* v. 37, 1982. Copyright © The Society for Italian Studies 2004. Reproduced by permission.—*Lectura Dantis,* v. 10, spring, 1992 "Dante and Poetic Communio in Zanzotto's Pseudo-Trilogy" by John P. Welle. Reproduced by permission of the author.—*Literary Onomastics Studies,* v. 12, 1985. Copyright © 1985 by Grace Alvarez-Altman. All rights reserved. Reproduced by permission.—*Poesis: a Journal of Criticism,* v. 5, 1984 for "Andrea Zanzotto: From the Language of the World to the World of Language" by Thomas Harrison. Copyright © Contemporary Poetry, Inc., 1983. Reproduced by permission of the author.—*Quaderni D'Italianistica,* v. XX, 1999. Reproduced by permission.—*Scottish Literary Journal,* v. 18, May, 1991 for "Henryson's 'Tragedie' of Cresseid" by Steven R. McKenna. Copyright © 1991 by Association for Scottish Literary Studies and the individual contributors. All rights reserved. Reproduced by permission of the publisher and the author.—*SAIL: Studies in American Indian Literatures,* v. 7, fall, 1995 for "Discovering the Order and Structure of Things: A Conversive Approach to Contemporary Navajo Poetry" by Susan B. Brill. Copyright © 1995 by *Studies in American Indian Literatures.* All rights reserved. Reproduced by permission of the author. / v. 8, fall, 1996 for "The Moon Is So Far Away: An Interview with Luci Tapahonso" by Andrea M. Penner and Luci Tapahonso. Copyright © 1996 by *Studies in American Indian Literatures.* All rights reserved. Reproduced by permission of the authors.—*Studies in Philology,* v. 82, winter, 1985. Copyright © 1985 by University of North Carolina Press. All rights reserved. Reproduced by permission.—*Studies in Scottish Literature,* v. 20, 1985; v. 25, 1990; v. 24, 1996; Copyright © 1985, 1990, 1996 by G. Ross Roy. All rights reserved. All reproduced by permission of the editor.—*Studies in the Age of Chaucer,* v. 12, 1990. Copyright © 1990 by The New Chaucer Society, The University of Tennessee. All rights reserved. Reproduced by permission.—*Unisa English Studies,* v. 25, May, 1987. Copyright © 1987 by the University of South Africa. All rights reserved. Reproduced by permission.—*Victorian Poetry,* v. 26, autumn, 1988 for "Edward Lear's Limericks and the Reversals of Nonsense" by Ann Colley; v. 30, summer, 1992 for "Edward Lear's Anti-Colonial Bestiary" by Ann C. Colley; v. 31, winter, 1993 for "Edward Lear: Deleuzian Landscape Painter" by Kirby Olson. Copyright © 1988, 1992, 1993 by West Virginia University. All rights reserved. All reproduced by permission of the respective authors.

COPYRIGHTED MATERIAL IN *PC*, VOLUME 65, WAS REPRODUCED FROM THE FOLLOWING BOOKS:

Allen, Beverly. From *Andrea Zanzotto: The Language of Beauty's Apprentice.* University of California Press, 1988. Copyright © 1988 by The Regents of the University of California. Reproduced by permission.—Bataille, Gretchen M.

Thomson Gale Literature Product Advisory Board

The members of the Thomson Gale Literature Product Advisory Board—reference librarians from public and academic library systems—represent a cross-section of our customer base and offer a variety of informed perspectives on both the presentation and content of our literature products. Advisory board members assess and define such quality issues as the relevance, currency, and usefulness of the author coverage, critical content, and literary topics included in our series; evaluate the layout, presentation, and general quality of our printed volumes; provide feedback on the criteria used for selecting authors and topics covered in our series; provide suggestions for potential enhancements to our series; identify any gaps in our coverage of authors or literary topics, recommending authors or topics for inclusion; analyze the appropriateness of our content and presentation for various user audiences, such as high school students, undergraduates, graduate students, librarians, and educators; and offer feedback on any proposed changes/enhancements to our series. We wish to thank the following advisors for their advice throughout the year.

Robert Henryson
c. 1420-c. 1505

Scottish poet.

INTRODUCTION

Robert Henryson was a late medieval poet of the Chaucerian tradition whose works have been praised for their realism, humour, and moral seriousness. He is best known for his *Moral Fables* (1569), a collection of thirteen fables based on the Aesopian tradition, and his *Testament of Cresseid* (1593), which some critics consider to be the finest narrative tragedy in medieval and Renaissance Scottish literature.

BIOGRAPHICAL INFORMATION

Henryson was born between 1420 and 1430. Much of what scholars have been able to ascertain about Henryson's life comes from William Dunbar's poem "Lament for the Makars" (c. 1505). In this lament for his fellow poets, Dunbar includes Henryson in a list of about two dozen of his dead predecessors: "In Dunfermelyne he [Death] hes done roune [whisper] / With Maister Robert Henrisoun." This poem as well as other records indicate that Henryson lived in Dunfermline, a market town in western Fife, and was a schoolmaster in the grammar school of the town's wealthy Benedictine abbey. Scholars also believe that like others in such a prestigious position, Henryson was likely a notary public with some legal training, and that he almost certainly had a master's degree. Like the other major poets of his day, Henryson wrote in Middle Scots, the vernacular language spoken throughout the Scottish Lowlands. During Henryson's lifetime, Scotland was undergoing political and social upheaval as the economy transitioned from feudal to mercantile. Political treachery, feuds among the nobility, and civil war erupted, leading to much bloodshed. James I was assassinated in 1437, and James III, who ruled for much of Henryson's life, was killed in 1488. Henryson's *Moral Fables,* written during the 1480s, deals with the social and political disintegration of his day. The plague, a recurring horror in Henryson's lifetime, also killed many people in the fifteenth century. Henryson comments on the devastation of the plague in his "Ane Prayer for the Pest," which scholars believe commemorates the outbreak of 1498-99.

MAJOR POETIC WORKS

Composed during the 1480s, Henryson's *Moral Fables* uses stock types in order to provide moral instruction. Henryson based his fables on a variety of source stories, including Aesopian fables (a Greek literary type), a late-twelfth-century version of Aesop's fables ("Walter the Englishman" ascribed to Gwalterus Anglicus), the mock-epics of Reynard the Fox, and popular, oral Scottish traditions. However, Henryson manipulated and added to the plots of his source materials such that each is a fairly original work. In addition, Henryson's *moralitas*—the generalized, reflective moral statements that follows each fable—are wholly his own invention. As was common in medieval society, Henryson used animals to communicate moral teachings. For example, in "The Cock and the Fox" Henryson uses a cunning and deceitful fox and a vain and gullible cock to warn the readers of the dangers of vanity. In addition to providing moral instruction, critics have also detected political overtones in the fables. In "The Sheep and the Dog" Henryson criticizes the ecclesiastical and the civil courts and makes a plea for the oppressed and the poor.

Scholars are not certain when Henryson penned his longer narratives, *The Testament of Cresseid* and *Orpheus and Eurydice,* both of which were immensely popular in the Middle Ages. *The Testament of Cresseid,* which was not published until long after Henryson's death, is a sequel to Chaucer's tale of *Troilus and Criseyde.* At the end of Chaucer's story, Troilus gives up his life in battle after his lover Criseyde proves unfaithful. In Henryson's sequel, Troilus survives and becomes a wealthy knight. The beautiful and selfish Cresseid, on the other hand, is brought low as her life disintegrates until she is a begging leper. A chance meeting between the estranged lovers changes Cresseid's view on her affliction, and the poem ends with Cresseid on her deathbed giving testament and bequeathing her belongings. She returns a ring to Troilus, who is so surprised and touched to learn of his lost love's fate that he has a statue erected on her grave. Considered to be the most Chaucerian of Henryson's poems, it is written in the rhyme royal of Chaucer's *Troilus and Criseyde.* Like the *Fables, The Testament of Cresseid* views humankind as victimized by the powerful as well as by its own lack of prudence.

Orpheus and Eurydice was published in 1508, shortly after the author's death. Like *The Testament of Cresseid,* this was a well-known, popular, and classic story of the

Middle Ages that recounts the loss and suffering of two famous lovers. Henryson's version of the story is based on Boethius's *Consolation of Philosophy* and modeled as a mythological fable. In the story, Orpheus travels to the underworld to reclaim his wife. He is allowed to return to the land of the living with his wife on the condition that he not look back until they leave the underworld. Orpheus's downfall is his one forbidden glance, which sends Eurydice back to the land of the dead and beyond Orpheus's claim. Like the *Fables, Orpheus and Eurydice* includes a *moralitas*. At 218-lines it is significantly longer than any *moralitas* in the *Fables*, but it serves the same purpose: to explicate the moral instructions of the tale. In addition to his longer narratives, Henryson is known to have written twelve or thirteen short poems. Of these, the most popular is the pastoral ballad "Robene and Makyne." This comical poem, which is often anthologized, relates the tale of a shepherdess who is so overcome with her love for a shepherd that she approaches him with a proposal. The shepherd repeatedly refuses her with lame excuses; however, after she leaves he changes his mind and returns to her with his own offer. But she has changed *her* mind, and this time refuses him. Although it includes considerable wit, the poem also explores the painful reversals and victimization caused by the powerful human appetites.

CRITICAL RECEPTION

Henryson was recognized as a great poet in his own day, as evidenced by William Dunbar's tribute to him in his poem "Lament for the Makars"; however, by the start of the seventeenth century he had been largely forgotten. Only in the last century has his reputation as one of the great figures of Scottish literature been restored. Criticism of Henryson's works has largely been concentrated on the *Moral Fables* and *The Testament of Cresseid*. Many critics point to the upheaval, violence, and disease of late-fifteenth-century Scotland as a driving force behind Henryson's themes and moral statements, particularly such themes as disfigurement, exile, and loss. George D. Gopen contends that "the world of the *Moral Fables* is not a happy one, despite the elegance of the art and the persistence of the humor. As the work progresses, the world of deadly sins, with sadness overcoming joy and depravity overcoming innocence, increasingly dominates. It is filled with persecution, suffering, irresponsible trickery, studied injustice, and sheer gratuitous malevolence." Scholars are also interested in the influence of Chaucer on Henryson's works. Dieter Mehl compares *The Canterbury Tales* with the *Moral Fables*, noting that "Henryson faces the problem of instruction by story-telling more squarely and takes the fable-tradition far more seriously" than Chaucer. In her comparison of Henryson's *The Testament of Cresseid* with Chaucer's *Troilus and Criseyde*, Catherine S. Cox notes that Henryson's version "does not wholly reject the sentimentality of Chaucer's romance, but complicates it, looking at the world of romance with ambivalence and suspicion." Marshall W. Stearns examines Henryson's concern with the plight of the peasantry in his *Moral Fables* and contends that Henryson was a "realist of considerable insight and integrity" whose compassion for the downtrodden made him "a humanitarian in the best sense of the word." Stearns also comments on Henryson's outstanding technique and craftsmanship, noting the "easy flow of his narrative, his metrical fluency and variety, and his skillful creation of tone and atmosphere." Tim William Machan also comments on the serious and genuine nature of Henryson's works, contending that "Henryson's concern for the human condition seems unquestionable, as do the diverse artistry of the *Fables* and the sophistication of its themes."

PRINCIPAL WORKS

Poetry

Here Begynnis the Traitie of Orpheus Kyng . . . [Orpheus and Eurydice] 1508
The Morall Fabillis of Esope the Phrygian [Moral Fables] 1569
The Testament of Cresseid 1593
**The Poems of Robert Henryson* [edited by Denton Fox] 1981

*This modern edition collects all of Henryson's known poetry.

CRITICISM

Marshall W. Stearns (essay date 1966)

SOURCE: Stearns, Marshall W. "The Poet as Humanitarian." In *Robert Henryson*, pp. 106-29. New York: AMS Press, 1966.

[*In the following essay, Stearns discusses Henryson's "championship of the peasantry" in the* Moral Fables.]

In the preceding chapters I have been chiefly concerned with Henryson's times, the origins of his poetry, and the manner in which he made use of his sources. By way of applying some part of this material, I should like to offer a few conjectures on the poet as an individual. It may be that Kinaston's doubtful anecdote about the dying Henryson, rejecting with amused skepticism the suggestion that he employ an incantation to cure his "fluxe," epitomizes the poet. For with fifteenth-century Scotland as a frame of reference, Henryson may be characterized as a realist of considerable insight and integrity, employing a salty wit to expose the shams of his day. His compassion for the downtrodden, however, makes him more than simply an amused skeptic, for essentially he is a humanitarian in the best sense of the word, reserving his satire for minor abuses while thundering with electric wrath at "wrangous" injustice.

The poet's outstanding technique and craftsmanship—the easy flow of his narrative, his metrical fluency and variety, and his skillful creation of tone and atmosphere—have been ably discussed elsewhere.[1] Accordingly, I should like to limit the present chapter to a short exposition of internal evidence in Henryson's poetry which points to a constant factor in the poet's general attitude, namely, his championship of the peasantry.

Fifteenth-century Scotland was an age of transition from a feudal to a mercantile or money economy. Violence was the rule, aided by devastating plagues, an erratic central authority, and the continual changing of land from hand to hand as a result of ceaseless feuds. In this way, many of the less powerful landed gentry were dispossessed upon the reversion of their land to a new overlord. Feudal services were being commuted into money payments, and arable land was being forcibly converted into more profitable sheep pasturage by the feudal lords. To this increasing pool of dispossessed peasants and gentry, the slogan of loyalty, whether feudal or tribal, was beginning to have a hollow ring since it symbolized an arrangement which no longer protected them. Meanwhile, the towns were prospering if the countryside was not, and the merchants and craftsmen, aided by their guilds, were obtaining hitherto unknown economic advantages. On all these facets of the times, Henryson has something to say, and his attitude is both discernible and revealing.

Henryson observed the life around him with a keen, kindly, and sometimes indignant eye. The chief fruits of his observation may be found in his version of Aesop's *Fables*. At the outset, the poet suggests that it is profitable to mingle "merie sport" among earnest subjects, "to light the spreit, and gar the tyme be schort." Not that Henryson cannot moralize with high seriousness and fire when he so desires. But in his *Fables* he relegates most of his moral *sentence* to the end of each story, and it is difficult to escape the impression that he intends his fables to be at least as entertaining as they are instructive.

The poet's treatment of character in the *Fables* sheds light on his general attitude.[2] While he denounces the grasping nobility and the corrupt clergy who prey upon the peasant, the poet's attitude toward the rising townspeople, who were not yet in a position to take advantage of the peasantry, varies from one of chilliness to one of gleeful derision. Henryson's warmth, tenderness, and compassion are reserved for the peasants; nor does his sympathy deteriorate to a mawkish sentimentality, for his "sempill folk" are a sturdily independent lot. When wronged or even patronized, they are most vocal and quick to expose the foul play or affectations of their opponents.

A hint of this prototype may be found in the fable of the **"Cock and the Jewel,"** which tells of a poor Cock who finds a jewel in an ash heap. The Cock is no aristocrat; he realizes at once that the jewel is not for him. He addresses it, however, with the courtesy reserved for his superiors, employing a variation of the time-honored *ubi-sunt* device (ll. 79, 106-10):

> "O gentill Jasp! O riche and Nobill thing!
> . . . . .
> "Quhar suld thow mak thy habitatioun?
> Quhar suld thou dwell, bot in ane Royall Tour?
> Quhar suld thow sit, bot on ane Kingis Croun,
> Exaltit in worschip and in grit honour?
> Rise, gentill Jasp, of all stanis the flour . . ."

Although he frankly prefers corn to jewels, the Cock's courtesy is so great that he suggests that the jewel has reason to despise him for his plebeian tastes (ll. 90-91, 97-98):

> I lufe fer better thing of les availl,
> As draf, or corne, to fill my tume Intraill
> . . . . .
> And thow agane, Upon the samin wyis,
> For les availl may me as now dispyis.

The Cock thereupon deserts the jewel, remaining true to the logic of his station in life, which the poet probably considered fitting and proper.

The humor of the fable is one of situation—a sort of *noblesse oblige* in reverse—but it is impossible not to sense the poet's amused sympathy with the poverty-stricken Cock's airy dismissal of the jewel and his sturdily independent advocacy of the simple way of life. The Cock also makes a very practical point (ll. 104-5):

> For houngrie men may not leve on lukis:
> Had I dry breid, I compt not for na cukis.

By this comment, which breaks right out of the Aesopic context, the poet makes it clear that beneath the surface of the Cock's amusing monologue lies a realistic attitude toward everyday life. The Cock is a poor person of character and integrity.

In the tale of the **"Twa Myis,"** Henryson's sympathetic attitude toward the impoverished peasant becomes more evident in his characterization of the "rurall mous." At the same time, his coolness toward townspeople may be felt in his portrayal of the "burges mous." The very first words that the town Mouse utters can scarcely prejudice the reader in her favor: in a delighted flurry of hospitality at her older sister's visit, the country Mouse has just finished ransacking her cupboard to put together the best meal she can offer; the town Mouse, however, sniffing at her younger sister's rustic banquet of withered peas and nuts, disdainfully inquires, "Sister, is this your dayly fude?" and adds that it is "bot a scorne."

The country Mouse immediately bristles at her older sister's attempt to patronize her. Madame, she says, you are the more to blame; my mother said, Sister, when we were born, that you and I both lay within one womb; I keep the style and custom of my mother by living in poverty, for we have no lands. The town Mouse is unmoved: "My fair sister," she says, "have me excusit."

So the country Mouse switches resourcefully to higher moral grounds (ll. 232-38):

> "Quhat plesure is in the ffeistis delicate,
> The quhilkis ar gevin with ane glowmand brow?
> Ane gentill hart is better recreate
> With blyith curage, than seith to him ane Kow.
> Ane modicum is mair ffor till allow,
> Swa that gude will be kerver at the dais,
> Than thrawin vult and mony spycit mais."

For the first time, the town Mouse is a bit shaken by the moral conviction of her younger sister and sits sadly but quietly at the table, with "littill will to sing." After a short while, however, she can contain herself no longer (ll. 246-49):

> "Lat be this hole and cum into my place;
> I sall to you schaw be experience
> My gude friday is better nor your pace;
> My dische likingis is worth your haill expence."

As an added inducement, the city Mouse announces: "Off cat, nor fall trap, I have na dreid"—an ironic bit of foreshadowing.

The country Mouse is finally persuaded to leave her hovel, but the manner of her assent indicates a characteristic change in her attitude: "I grant," she says laconically; from this point on, she is no longer the gracious hostess but rather the grudging guest. The poet devotes two stanzas to a description of the fine food provided by the town Mouse, who asks her country sister if she notices the difference between this "chalmer and hir sarie nest." The reply of the country Mouse is a strong mixture of dourness and doom: "Ye dame . . . how lang will this lest?"

In spite of her reservations, the country Mouse rapidly learns to enjoy the pleasures of the town. In fact, she is singing "Haill Yule, Haill," when the steward opens the door. The mice flee, as the poet says, without tarrying to wash, but the steward does not notice them. The country Mouse, however, is very much upset, and only the "wordis hunny sweit" of her older sister can persuade her to get up from where she lies "flatling on the ground." At this juncture, the country Mouse is scarcely able to announce that starving in peace is better than a "feist in this dreid and diseis," but her opinions remain unshaken.

Just as the country Mouse has been persuaded to return to the table and drink "anis or twyse," the cat appears. The town Mouse darts to her hole, "as fyre on flint," but her younger sister is caught by "Gib hunter, our Jolie Cat, and her worst fears are realized (ll. 330-33):

> Fra fute to fute he kest hir to and ffra,
> Quhylis up, quhylis doun, als cant as ony kid;
> Quhylis wald he lat hir rin under the stra,
> Quhylis wald he wink, and play with hir buk heid.

(The poet, it may be noted, is writing with his eye on the object.) The country Mouse finally escapes and, pausing only to castigate town life, flees to her rural hovel.

The country Mouse is a real individual with characteristics that are both Scottish and universal. She is poor but proud in the functional sense that she is clever enough to convert her poverty into a source of pride. Her personality is precisely that which would appear in an intelligent person surrounded by the disadvantages of the country. Recognizing her position, she tends to overcompensate in minor ways. Thus, she adopts a few simple and safe convictions about which she is irrepressibly articulate and almost shrill. Hence the reiterated moralizing, the gruff reservations, and the touch of assertiveness. Nor is she above simply making points in an argument. Yet her rural skepticism is capable of rapid readjustment when the advantages are visible and immediate. And through it all glows a canny Scots dourness.

Henryson's keen insight into the character of the country Mouse is exceeded only by his evident affection for her, while his portrayal of the town Mouse, who is not only proud and overbearing but also contemptuous of her younger sister, suggests a mild dislike of the burgesses. As we have seen, the growing prosperity of the towns, with the various privileges available to the townsmen, offered a strong contrast to the poverty of the countryside, and the poet's attitude toward the town is in keeping with his identification of himself with the peasantry, a subject more fully discussed later.

In the fable of **"The Fox, the Wolf, and the Cadger,"** Henryson describes another member of the merchant group, the Cadger, showing less sympathy for him than for the town Mouse. The Fox and the Wolf, it appears, have no doubts about the stinginess of the Cadger as he comes along the road singing, his horse carrying fish-baskets full of herring to market (ll. 2037-39):

> Thocht we wald thig, yone verray Churlische chuff,
> He will not giff us ane hering off his Creill,
> Befoir yone Churle on kneis thocht we wald kneill.

So the Fox resorts to a trick: he plays dead in the middle of the road and waits for the Cadger to discover him.

Coming upon the Fox, the Cadger is highly pleased and very sensibly decides to make "mittennis tway" of the Fox's skin. Henryson describes the ecstatic delight of the Cadger with infectious gaiety (ll. 2060-62):

> He lap full lichtlie about him quhair he lay,
> And all the trace he trippit on his tais;
> As he had hard ane pyper play, he gais.

Further, the Cadger's monologue upon his own good luck is a nice bit of self-characterization (ll. 2063-69):

> "Heir lyis the Devyll" (quod he), "deid in ane dyke.
> Sic ane selcouth saw I not this sevin yeir;
> I trow ye have bene tussillit with sum tyke,
> That garris you ly sa still withouttin steir:
> Schir Foxe, in Faith, ye ar deir welcum heir;
> It is sum wyfis malisone, I trow,
> For pultrie pyking, that lychtit hes on yow."

Again, the Cadger's well-developed sense of property is suggested by his twice-repeated announcement that no peddler is going to steal this skin and ship it to Flanders—the customary port to which furs were exported. He takes the Fox by the heels and "with ane swak he swang him on the creillis," a line which suggests his businesslike zeal.

While the Fox is emptying the creel and the Wolf is collecting the herring, the Cadger walks happily along leading his horse and singing "Huntis up, up, upon hie." He discovers the trick a moment later. At this point in the fable, the reader is presented with a contrasting side of the Cadger's personality, the side that is uppermost when business is bad. The escaped Fox rubs salt into the wound (ll. 2096-97):

> "And sell thy hering thow hes thair till hie price,
> Ellis thow sall wyn nocht on thy merchandice."

The Cadger "trimillit for teyne," and he swears revenge. Nevertheless, with the objectivity of a man who has known responsibility and profited by it, he blames himself for not having a stick in hand to beat such rogues. With characteristic energy, he "lap out over ane dyke, And hakkit doun ane staff . . . That hevie wes and off the Holyne grene."

The Fox now returns to the Wolf and persuades him to try the same trick with tales of a "Nekhering" (the pun is intentional) in the Cadger's creel, too large for the Fox to lift and "callour, pypand lyke ane Petrik Ee." So the Wolf plays dead in the middle of the road and waits for the Cadger. Riding because the load is so light, the Cadger is nursing his wrath. When he spies the Wolf, however, his mercantile caution asserts itself (ll. 2175-76):

> "Softlie," he said, "I wes begylit anis;
> Be I begylit twyis, I schrew us baith . . ."

And the Cadger decides to beat the Wolf without any further investigation.

Henryson's characterization of the Cadger seems to be reasonably fair and true to life. In fact, this Cadger's alternating moods of joy and anger are motivated by sound business reasons. The poet implies that members of the merchant group are proverbially stingy, but he adds other details which are more revealing, such as the practical energy, the responsible self-criticism, and the instinctive caution even in anger. Add to this the flavor and bounce of the verse itself, and the result is a lively characterization tinged with keen satire. Henryson seems to have enjoyed making a cadger the butt of a part of his fable.

Of the few sympathetically described protagonists of the *Fables* who are not peasants, the character of the Fox, in the tale of **"The Fox and the Wolf,"** is of particular interest. In a sense, the "wylie tratour Tod" is out of character as, for the space of one fable, he appears to be simply an imaginative but confused person with an honest impulse to do the right thing. The poet, of course, is occupied with his trenchant criticism of the church, and the fable is Reynardian rather than Aesopic. Nevertheless, the characterization of the Fox has a logic of its own.

At the outset, the Fox studies the planets and is suddenly convinced that he is about to die. Remarking that the lot of "we thevis" is no better than that of the poor, the Fox goes in search of a confessor. He soon encounters "Freir Wolff Waitskaith" (one-who-waits-to-do-injury), and the Fox's complete, immediate faith in the Wolf, whom he traditionally is supposed to outwit, is almost touching (ll. 670-85):

> Seand this Wolff, this wylie tratour Tod
> On kneis fell, with hude in to his nek;
> "Welcome, my Gostlie ffather under God"
> (Quod he), with mony binge and mony bek.
> "Ha" (quod the Wolff), "Schir Tod, for quhat effek
> Mak ye sic feir? Ryse up, put on your hude."
> "Father" (quod he), "I haif grit cause to dude.
>
> "Ye ar Mirrour, Lanterne, and sicker way,

Suld gyde sic sempill folk as me to grace.
Your bair feit, and your Russet Coull off gray,
Your lene cheik, your paill pietious face,
Schawis to me your perfite halines.
For weill wer him, that anis in his lyve
Had hap to yow his sinnis ffor to schryve."

"Na, selie Lowrence" (quod the Wolf), and leuch:
"It plesis me that ye ar penitent."

Above and beyond the amusing description of the Wolf as a pious priest, the novelty of a Fox who not only cannot see through the Wolf's disguise but who also has convinced himself that he is one of the "sempill folk," suggests that Henryson may be diverging again from the beaten path of the Aesopic fabulist.

The conscientious integrity of the Fox during confession is remarkable. When asked by the Wolf if he is sorry for his trespasses, the Fox cannot honestly say that he is. The Wolf seems a little surprised but continues nevertheless, asking if the Fox will "forbeir in tyme to cum and mend." The Fox cannot agree to this, either, pointing out quite seriously that stealing is his means of livelihood, and adding that his social pretensions make it impossible to work (ll. 710-11):

I eschame to thig, I can not wirk, ye wait,
Yit wald I fane pretend to gentill stait.

As a would-be gentleman, the Fox cannot work and he is ashamed to beg. He also adds that he is of "Nature tender," and having reluctantly agreed to give up meat until Easter, he is finally granted full remission.

The Fox then walks to the river honestly bent on catching some fish: "to fang him fisch haillelie wes his intent," but when he sees the water and the stormy waves he is brought up short by the realization of what his penance would mean in actual practice. As he waits, "astonist all still in to ane stair," he notices a flock of goats under a tree, and his mood changes instantly to one of cheerfulness as he steals a little kid. The Fox has not, however, forgotten his penance (ll. 747-51):

Syne over the heuch unto the see he hyis,
And tuke the Kid be the hornis twane,
And in the watter outher twyis or thryis
He dowkit him, and till him can he sayne:
"Ga doun, Schir Kid, cum up Schir Salmond agane!"

By this solution of his difficulties, the Fox's conscience is put to rest as he gorges himself on the "new maid Salmond."

The Fox eats his fill and lies down on his back beneath a bush, stroking his stomach in the heat of the sun. Suddenly he has another fascinating idea: "Upon this wame," he says recklessly, "set wer ane bolt full meit." A moment later, when the keeper discovers him and pins him to the ground with an arrow, the Fox is disgusted but resigned (ll. 768-71):

"Now" (quod the Foxe), "allace and wellaway!
Gorrit I am, and may na forther gang.
Me think na man may speik ane word in play,
Bot now on dayis in ernist it is tane."

He made the remark and it came true—a sort of poetic justice—and the Fox, although quite reasonably irritated by the literal humorlessness of such justice, does not think of questioning it but blames the evil times.

Henryson inherited the chief incidents of the story from earlier authors, but the character of the Fox is his own. The Fox is a consistent realist within a narrow but definite area—the area known to those who are thieves of necessity (ll. 707-9):

". . . how sall I leif, allace,
Haifand nane uther craft me to defend?
Neid causis me to steill quhair evir I wend."

Within this area, the Fox is so honest that he surprises even the Wolf, his Father Confessor. Outside of this area, prodded perhaps by his social pretensions, the Fox seems to be driven to a code of conduct that is confused and desperate, even to the manner of his death.

Why Henryson varied so widely from the traditional characterization of the Fox is a difficult question. The explanation that it was accidental seems inadequate. Perhaps the poet borrowed some of his material, as he did in other cases, from contemporary manners. If so, the key to the character of the Fox may be his marginal social status, for here is a person who speaks of himself as a thief and as one of tender nature, as one of the simple folk and as one who likes to pretend to be well-born—all in a few lines. The evidence is tantalizingly confused and contradictory, yet it does more or less describe a group of people with whom the poet might well have sympathized—the dispossessed gentry.

The dispossessed gentry had suffered the same fate as that of the peasantry who were evicted by the feudal lords, and it was the peasantry's fate, as we shall see, which the poet particularly resented. The landed gentry, especially in the highlands, had been frequently dispossessed by the reversion of lands resulting from ceaseless feuds. Caught between two cultures in a changing society, these former landowners were a confused and desperate lot, of whom Rob Roy, the later guerilla chief, was a direct descendent. Thus, this group makes an interesting parallel to Henryson's Fox: they were notorious thieves who led brief and sometimes courageous lives, and who very definitely looked down upon manual labor and up to the nobility. It would have been quite natural for the poet to be greatly interested in this group and to find qualities that he liked and disliked, as the fable indicates, in these rebellious victims of the unquiet times.

Henryson's favorite protagonist—the sturdily independent peasant—is presented in a variety of ways. In the tale of **"The Lion and the Mouse,"** for example, the poet's heroine, who seems to be demonstrating how a little person can stand up to a king, shares the spotlight with some of Henryson's most outspoken and specific criticism of the treasonable activities of the feudal lords. The story is simple: having captured the leader of a troup of mice who have been playing on his sleeping body, the Lion is eventually merciful and releases her; later, she returns the favor by rescuing the Lion.

The poet devotes much of the fable to the dialogue between the Lion and the Mouse in general and the various arguments of the Mouse in particular. Thus, the character of the Mouse is developed casually in the course of the debate. When the Lion, having caught the Mouse, asks whether she knows that he is "baith Lord and King of beistis all," the Mouse replies with sixteen lines of persuasive reasoning. Consider "my simple povertie" and your "mychtie hie Magnyfycence," she says lucidly, and note that mistakes caused by simple negligence rather than malice and presumption should be forgiven. So far as the mice were concerned (ll. 1440-43):

> "We wer repleit and had grit aboundance
> Of alkin thingis, sic as to us effeird;
> The sweit sesoun provokit us to dance,
> And mak sic mirth as nature to us leird."

Finally, says the Mouse, you lay so low that we thought that you were dead.

The Lion, who is truly royal but by no means the equal of the Mouse in an argument, falls back on the unrealistic statement that even if he had been dead, the Mouse should have fallen to her knees in fear. He thereupon decrees her death for the crime of treason. At this point, the Mouse pleads guilty and throws herself upon the mercy of the Lion. In the course of forty-one lines, she assembles a new defense with an impressive amount of learning, legal and extra-legal. Justice should be tempered with mercy, the triumph of a lion over a mouse would be "lytill manheid," and mouse-meat is especially unhealthful for lions (ll. 1489-95):

> "Also it semis not your Celsitude,
> Quhilk usis daylie meittis delitious,
> To fyle your teith or lippis with my blude,
> Quhilk to your stomok is contagious;
> Unhailsum meit is of ane sarie Mous,
> And that namelie untill ane strang Lyoun,
> Wont till be fed with gentill vennesoun."

The Mouse's final argument is almost as extravagant, although it is traditionally implied if not expressed: she may be able to return the favor some day.

The *moralitas* of this fable, unlike that of many others, is an organic part of the story. The poet adds that the

Lion is the King, who is not without the faults of "lustis, sleuth, and sleip," while the mice are the commons (ll. 1587-93):

> Thir lytill Myis ar bot the commountie,
> Wantoun, unwyse, without correctioun:
> Thair Lordis and Princis quhen that thay se
> Of Justice mak nane executioun,
> Thay dreid na thing to mak Rebellioun,
> And disobey, for quhy thay stand nane aw,
> That garris thame thair Soveranis misknaw.

Thus, Henryson is careful to explain that the common people are restless only because of the bad example set them by their lords and princes. These lords, says the poet, should consider the virtue of "pietie," or clemency, and he proceeds to make his main point (ll. 1616-18):

> I the beseik and all men for to pray
> That tressoun of this cuntrie be exyld,
> And Justice Regne, and Lordis keip thair fay
> Unto thair Soverane King, baith nycht and day.

The weight of the fable is directed against the warring feudal lords, who traffic in treason, while Henryson's sympathies remain clearly with the commons.

Although the Mouse is the heroine of the piece, Henryson does not develop her character beyond the point where she occasionally sounds like an animated roll call of arguments in behalf of the poorer citizenry. Her arguments, however, although many are based on moral and a few on mouselike grounds, are frequently both practical and legal. The result is that it is difficult to escape the impression that the poet intended the Mouse to be an educational vehicle whereby his audience could hear the arguments in favor of the peasantry.

In certain of his fables, Henryson appears to be supplying arguments to combat specific attitudes. Thus in **"The Fox, the Wolf, and the Husbandman,"** the poor Husbandman answers the Wolf's panegyric on loyalty with a very sensible insistence on legality of procedure. In a moment of anger, the Husbandman had sworn that the Wolf could have his team of oxen—an oath which the Wolf and the Fox had overheard. When the Wolf claims the team, the Husbandman, although terrified, answers him with spirit and logic (ll. 2273-79):

> "Schir" (quod the husband), "ane man may say in greif,
> And syne ganesay, fra he avise and se:
> I hecht to steill, am I thairfoir ane theif?"
> "God forbid, Schir, all hechtis suld haldin be!"
> "Gaif I my hand or oblissing" (quod he),
> "Or have ye witnes, or writ ffor to schaw?
> Schir, reif me not, but go and seik the Law!"

In this manner, the Husbandman demands that the procedure be legal and that the Wolf produce some signature, bond, document, or witness.

The Wolf, however, switches the argument to the subject of loyalty as a principle (ll. 2280-86):

> "Carll" (quod the Wolff), "ane Lord, and he be leill,
> That schrinkis for schame, or doutis to be repruvit,
> His saw is ay als sickker as his Seill.
> Fy on the Leid that is not leill and lufit!
> Thy argument is fals, and eik contrufit,
> For it is said in Proverb: 'But lawte
> All uther vertewis ar nocht worth ane fle.'"

Needless to say, this praise of loyalty is not in the Bible, as the Wolf would have the Husbandman suppose. On the other hand, whether or not the Wolf's emphasis on the sacredness of the spoken promise, as well as his praise of loyalty, is essentially a tribal or a feudal point of view or both, it is clear that Henryson has the Husbandman oppose the Wolf by insisting on correct legal procedure (ll. 2287-90):

> "Schir," said the husband, "remember of this thing:
> Ane leill man is not tane at halff ane taill.
> I may say, and ganesay, I am na King:
> Quhair is your witnes that hard I hecht thame haill?"

In effect, although the Husbandman does not question the principle that a man should be loyal, he makes the all-important point that the question of loyalty should be determined legally. A man should not be judged on half of the evidence, says the Husbandman, and the practical result of his reasoning would be to leave the question of loyalty entirely to the courts.

Unfortunately the Wolf has the Fox as a witness, and the poor Husbandman, after a trial that makes a mock of justice, is robbed and terrorized, escaping to his house only to stand and watch the door all night. In his *moralitas,* the poet says briefly that the Wolf is to be likened to a wicked man who oppresses the poor. The Husbandman represents himself, a member of the peasantry, and Henryson makes his point very clearly, showing the Husbandman fighting a one-sided and losing battle. Later in the fable the Fox observes that "God is gane to sleip" and in the same breath feigns a sympathy for the poor in order to trick the Wolf. The irony is bitter and it cuts deeply. It is clear that the poet is skeptical of the value of any appeals to the poor for loyalty.

Two of Henryson's fables appear to be devoted primarily to championing the peasantry. Plot, setting, characterization, even the poet's usually unfailing sense of humor, are subordinated in order to make his point. The *moralitas* assumes great importance, for it is the climax toward which the entire fable builds. On the other hand, the fable proper, perhaps because it does not lend itself so readily as the *moralitas* to the expression of opinion, shrinks until it becomes simply a point of departure, by way of allegory, for the poet's remarks on the contemporary scene.

Thus, the story of the **"Wolf and the Lamb,"** as Henryson presents it, is almost negligible: the Wolf and the Lamb are drinking from the same stream, the Wolf above the Lamb; on the incredible pretext that the Lamb is defiling the Wolf's water, the Wolf kills the Lamb. There is little or no attempt to describe the setting, although the character of the Lamb is developed briefly along the poet's favorite lines, namely, the sturdily independent peasant. Like Henryson's other heroes, the Lamb argues spiritedly in spite of his physical helplessness, and when the ferocious Wolf falsely accuses him (ll. 2637-43),

> The selie Lamb, quaikand for verray dreid,
> On kneis fell, and said: "Schir, with your leif,
> Suppois I dar not say thairoff ye leid;
> Bot, be my Saull, I wait ye can nocht preif
> That I did ony thing that suld yow grief;
> Ye wait alswa that your accusatioun
> Failyeis ffra treuth, and contrair is to ressoun."

For the "selie" Lamb, who is quaking on his knees for very dread, to tell the Wolf that, although he would not dare to say that the Wolf is a liar, he knows nevertheless that the Wolf has no proof and that his accusation is contrary to reason and untrue—such insubordination must have seemed to Henryson's audience as revolutionary as it was futile. For the allegorical surface is never allowed to conceal the fact that the Wolf is rich and powerful and the Lamb poor and weak.

In the one-sided debate that follows, the Lamb adds learning to daring by flourishing the jargon of formal logic ("Ergo . . ."), by quoting Scripture ("halie Scripture sayis . . ."), and by citing the law ("the Law sayis . . ."). In fact, in the course of forty compelling lines, the Lamb has reduced the Wolf to a self-acknowledged monster (ll. 2693-96):

> "Na" (quod the Wolff), "thow wald Intruse ressoun,
> Quhair wrang and reif suld dwell in propertie.
> That is ane poynt, and part of fals tressoun,
> For to gar reuth remane with crueltie."

You would intrude reason where wrong and robbery should dwell, says the Wolf viciously, and to have pity abide with cruelty is treason. Thereupon he kills the Lamb. At this point, Henryson has done everything in his power to show that the Wolf is wrong and the Lamb right: his characterization is simple and unambiguous. With the rhetorical question, "Wes not this reuth?" the poet goes on to the *moralitas* and what is clearly his main objective.

The Lamb, says Henryson, signifies poor people, including all peasants, to whom life is half a purgatory as they attempt by loyalty to earn a suitable livelihood. There are three types of Wolves, the poet says: Lawyers, Mighty Men, and Men of Inheritance; and he proceeds to describe and comment upon the methods of each in a manner which leaves no doubt as to his true attitude. The Lawyer perverts the law. He mingles falsehood with polished terms, pretending that all that he shows is "Gospell," but for a bribe he overthrows the poor man, smothering the right and causing the wrong to win out. Although the poet is aware of exactly how corrupt the law has become, he apparently has lost neither his faith in it nor his capacity for sustained indignation at its abuse. Here he comments (ll. 2721-27):

> O man of Law! let be thy subteltie,
> With nice gimpis, and fraudis Intricait,
> And think that God in his Divinitie
> The wrang, the richt, of all thy werkis wait:
> For prayer, price, for hie nor law estait,
> Of fals querrellis se thow mak na defence;
> Hald with the richt, hurt not thy conscience.

Hell's fire, the poet adds, shall be the reward of such Wolves.

Mighty Men have great plenty but are so greedy and covetous that they will not allow the poor man to live in peace. Although the poor man and his family will starve to death, these Mighty Men take his farm away from him. The poet's comment on this type of Wolf is bitterly resentful (ll. 2735-41):

> O man! but mercie, quhat is in thy thocht,
> War than ane Wolf, and thow culd understand?
> Thow hes aneuch; the pure husband richt nocht
> Bot croip and caff upon ane clout of land.
> For Goddis aw, how durst thow tak on hand,
> And thow in Barn and Byre sa bene, and big,
> To put him fra his tak and gar him thig?

For fear of God, says the poet, how dare you evict a man from his holding and make him beg?

Henryson comments upon Men of Inheritance with considerable fire and fury (ll. 2756-62):

> Hes thow not reuth to gar thy tennentis sweit
> In to thy laubour with faynt and hungrie wame,
> And syne hes lytill gude to drink or eit,
> With his menye at evin quhen he cummis hame?
> Thow suld dreid for rychteous Goddis blame;
> For it cryis ane vengeance unto the hevinnis hie,
> To gar ane pure man wirk but Meit or fe.

It cries a vengeance to the high heavens, says the poet with Carlylesque vehemence, to make a poor man work without meat or fee. Thou shouldst fear the righteous wrath of God!

It becomes increasingly evident that Henryson not only champions the poor but also specifically identifies himself with the poor. The conjecture that the poet was not a court poet would gain convincing support from this internal evidence if from nothing else. In the fable of **"The Sheep and the Dog,"** for example, Henryson speaks in the first person of "we poor people" and expands the moral into a direct, personal plea for the poor.

One of the poet's aims in **"The Sheep and the Dog"** is to criticize both the ecclesiastical and the civil courts—an objective which he admirably accomplishes. At the same time, it is clear that Henryson is building in the course of the fable toward his personal comment in the *moralitas*. As the fable begins, a Dog hales a Sheep into court simply "because that he wes pure." The Sheep is so frightened by the illegal force and talent arrayed against him that he "durst lay na mouth on eird" until he has appeared before the awful judge.

Despite his well-founded fear, the Sheep is so stung by the unjust charge and the flagrantly lawless procedure that he delivers his one and only answer with great spirit. Twice Henryson makes the point that the Sheep is carrying on among many legal complexities without a lawyer—an indication perhaps of the poet's faith in the staying power of the people whom the Sheep symbolizes, and a possible clue to the audience for which he was writing. Finally, in spite of the fact that the court is "corruptit all ffor meid, aganis gude faith, Law, and eik conscience," the fact that the Sheep is a "selie Innocent," and the fact that the decision against him is a "wrangous Jugement," the Sheep is nevertheless convicted, pays his fine by selling the wool off of his back, and returns to the field naked and bare. Henryson makes the tragic conclusion as inevitable as it is swift, and as unjust as it is inevitable.

In the *moralitas,* the poet states at once that the Sheep personifies the poor commons who are oppressed daily by tyrannical men, while the Wolf and his assistants stand for various corrupt court-officials, whose crimes he describes. At this point, however, Henryson departs from his usual treatment and announces that he himself happened to pass by the place where the Sheep lay and heard the Sheep's lamentation (ll. 1286-90):

> "Allace" (quod he), "this cursit Consistorie,
> In middis of the winter now is maid,
> Quhen Boreas with blastis bitterlie
> And hard froistes thir flouris doun can faid;
> On bankis bair now may I mak na baid."

(The poet's very effective use of the winter season to set the tone of the Sheep's lamentation is characteristic.) As he creeps into a hollow, shivering with the cold, the Sheep casts his eyes unto the heavens high and addresses his Maker in no uncertain terms (ll. 1295-98):

> . . . "Lord God, quhy sleipis thow sa lang?
> Walk, and discerne my cause, groundit on richt;
> Se how I am, be fraud, maistrie, and slicht,
> Peillit full bair."

This Job-like plea to God, with its intimacy, moral conviction, and definite trace of irritation, has the force and flavor of a sermon by an old Scots preacher.

Henryson is not satisfied with the Sheep's plea alone, for the poet himself continues in the same vein (ll. 1298-1306):

> . . . and so is mony one
> Now in this warld, richt wonder, wo begone!
>
> Se how this cursit sone of covetice,
> Loist hes baith lawtie and eik Law.
> Now few or nane will execute Justice,
> In falt of quhome the pure man is overthraw.
> The veritie, suppois the Juge it knaw,
> He is so blindit with affectioun,
> But dreid, for micht, he lettis the richt go doun.

In the light of the poet's knowledge of and faith in the legal process, this condemnation of the custodians of the law takes on added weight. It should be noted, however, that the poet tends to blame it on the sin of covetousness. Henryson then makes his own personal plea to God, placing the blame squarely upon the feudal laird (ll. 1307-13):

> Seis thow not (Lord) this warld overturnit is,
> As quha wald change gude gold in leid or tyn;
> The pure is peillit, the Lord [Laird] may do na mis;
> And Simonie is haldin for na syn.
> Now is he blyith with okker maist may wyn;
> Gentrice is slane, and pietie is ago,
> Allace (gude Lord) quhy thoilis thow it so?

In this and the preceding passage, the poet reaches the heights of his criticism of the age. Simony (he says) is held for no sin, and now he is blithe who may gain the most with usury; honorable feeling is slain and pity is gone; the poor are plundered and the laird may do no wrong.

These passages are perhaps the key to Henryson's attitude toward his times. In selecting the "cursed sin of covetousness" in general and usury in particular, the poet is echoing the continual cry of the church long before and after Henryson's day in its tardy adjustment to a developing money economy. By referring to "gentrice" and "pietie," the poet is emphasizing those qualities which the feudal lord should possess in order to make the *status quo* run more smoothly, while the charge of simony was a stock criticism of the church in Henryson's time. All of these criticisms are passionately felt but they are also fairly conventional and typical of the times. The novelty of the poet's comment lies in the fact that he selects the feudal lords rather than any other group as the chief culprits.

In the concluding stanza, Henryson turns sadly to prayer, and it is clear that the poet, as a devout Catholic, feels that this is the only avenue of appeal open to the poor (ll. 1314-20):

> Thow tholis this evin for our grit offence,
> Thow sendis us troubill, and plaigis soir,
> As hunger, derth, grit weir, or Pestilence;
> Bot few amendis now thair lyfe thairfoir.
> We pure pepill as now may do no moir
> Bot pray to the, sen that we ar opprest
> In to this eirth, grant us in hevin gude rest.

Thou sendeth us trouble and sore plagues (says the poet) such as hunger, dearth, great war, or pestilence . . . We poor people at this time may do no more than pray to thee; since we are oppressed on this earth, grant us good rest in heaven. Thus, Henryson's ultimate solution of the problems of his day, above and beyond his particular aversion toward the feudal lords and his compassion for the poor, is probably the same as that of any other intelligent man of good will in his age. It would be ridiculous to expect the poet to be anything else than the product, although an outstanding one, of his own times—times when, due in part to the fact that he lived in a culture steeped in the concept of original sin, no one would readily think of taking direct action to change a world which God had seen fit so to create.

Henryson's championship of the peasantry and his criticism of the feudal lords are two sides of the same coin. It should not be thought that the poet's attitude toward the poor is found only in the *Fables,* for the same note is struck in his minor poems, especially in his **"Want of Wyse Men"** where he declares that the poor "ar all opprest" and that flatterers "pike and pill" the poor, and in his **"Prayer for the Pest"** where he identifies himself once more with the poor, praying God to have mercy "of us, indigent and peure." Nor should it be thought, on the other hand, that the poet's attitude toward the poor was common in his day. In the prologue to the *Fables,* Henryson says that his "author" would not make light of "hie nor low estate," and one can readily understand why an author would not care to antagonize the predatory nobles. The statement that he will not make light of low estate, however, plus the fact that he more than carries out his promise, makes Henryson's verse virtually unique in fifteenth-century literature.

The only parallel to Henryson in English literature is the author of *Piers Plowman,* who is critical equally of church and state, of the nobility, townsfolk, and peasantry. The author of *Piers,* however, treats the demands of the peasants for a rise in the standard of living as evidence of laziness and vagabondage. Henryson never accuses the peasantry of anything worse than justifiably following the bad example of the feudal lords, while his usual attitude, as we have seen, is explicitly to favor the poor. For the poet not only champions the peasantry and identifies himself with the poor, but also assembles a series of significantly *practical* arguments in support of his point of view—a fact which offers another clue to Henryson's occupation and even the audience for which he is writing. At heart, although both would return to an idealized *status quo,* the author of *Piers* is a conformist, writing from a clerical point of view, whereas Henryson is an individualist writing from a humanitarian point of view.

The problem of Henryson's audience is perhaps insoluble. He writes for anyone who wants to read, no doubt, but he is not a court poet—a fact which at once limits his possible audience and sets him apart from the other Scottish Chaucerians. Although the dialect of Middle Scots was never spoken, Henryson's verses, read aloud, would probably have been easily understood by his contemporaries at any social level and, as a schoolteacher, the poet's most obvious audience would have been in his own classroom, a group which could have included the children of the townsfolk, the gentry, and a few perhaps of the peasantry and nobility. Such a conjecture would help explain the pedagogical device of the Aesopic fable as a vehicle for the defense of the peasantry and the criticism of their oppressors.

Henryson was writing, as I have suggested, in a violent age of transition from a feudal to a mercantile economy. As we now see it, the change was inescapable, and the poet, unlike the predatory feudal lords who were paradoxically hastening the decline of feudalism by forcibly dispossessing the peasantry, is passionately condemning the clear and manifold injustices which were an inevitable part of this transition. If asked for his solution to the injustices against which he inveighs, Henryson would doubtless have recommended a return to a more consistent feudalism, although feudalism never actually functioned smoothly and inevitably bred the seeds of its own destruction. Henryson, like Chaucer, is a poet of the Middle Ages. Yet, unlike Chaucer, Henryson is unique among British poets in this respect that, in a literary age devoted to the imitation of foreign models, in an age when poets mentioned the peasantry, if at all, with unquestioned disdain, in an age when the cause of the peasant was not only unheard of but also virtually inconceivable, Henryson speaks out boldly for the poor. In any age, the poet would have been a humanitarian of outstanding insight, integrity, and compassion.

Notes

1. Cf. G. G. Smith, *The Poems of Robert Henryson,* I, xiv ff.

2. In the following discussion of the *Fables,* I have omitted all mention of Henryson's sources, a subject competently treated by G. G. Smith, in *Poems of . . . Henryson,* I, xxix-xlv.

Bibliography

Smith, G. Gregory, ed. *The Poems of Robert Henryson.* 3 vols. Edinburgh and London, Scottish Text Society, 1906-14.

Dieter Mehl (essay date 1984)

SOURCE: Mehl, Dieter. "Robert Henryson's *Moral Fables* as Experiments in Didactic Narrative." In *Functions of Literature: Essays Presented to Erwin Wolff on His Sixtieth Birthday,* edited by Ulrich Broich, Theo Stemmler, and Gerd Stratmann, pp. 81-99. Tübingen, Germany: Max Niemeyer Verlag, 1984.

[*In the following essay, Mehl examines the experimental quality of the* Moral Fables *and claims that Henryson took the fable tradition more seriously than his major literary influence, Geoffrey Chaucer, or his fabulist predecessor John Lydgate.*]

Robert Henryson's **Moral Fables** have often been praised for their humour, their realism, and their moral seriousness. There seems to be a critical tendency to rank them even higher than **The Testament of Cresseid,** which for a long time was the only poem by Henryson to receive any serious critical attention. Douglas Gray, whose account of the **Fables** seems to me by far the most subtle and illuminating, speaks of their "imaginative harmony which is surprisingly impressive, and surprisingly reminiscent in miniature of *The Canterbury Tales.*"[1]

He is not the first to make this comparison, suggested more by the general vitality and variety of the two collections than by any marked similarity in subject-matter or form. The unorthodox range of stylistic devices, the play on different levels of seriousness, the fascinating mixture of realism, humour, rhetorical showmanship and moral commitment—they all contribute to the impression that Henryson was perhaps more influenced by Chaucer's whole attitude towards his own art than by particular works or subjects. Of course, he wrote for a very different audience and in a different cultural climate, however little we can confidently say about his person and his first readers. Chaucer, for instance, does not appear to feel the same urge to justify his literary activity by insisting on its moral purpose and wholesomeness—he leaves that to his Nun's Priest. On the other hand, he often hides behind a narrator whose admitted inexperience and incompetence gives him an excuse for unconventional variety and daring range of tone. Henryson, similarly, seems to try out different voices and narrative strategies and though there is no proper framing device and no change of narrator, except in one or two particular cases, his collection of fables has an experimental quality not unlike that of *The Canterbury Tales.* He uses the animal-world only as raw material, just as Chaucer uses the story-telling device.[2] Henryson is, perhaps, less concerned with the powerful presence of traditions and their validity in the face of actual experience than Chaucer; his main problem is the moral justification of story-telling, the effectiveness of fiction as a means of instruction, or simply the ancient precept of *prodesse* and *delectare,* discussed with a new urgency. The **Moral Fables,** at first sight, seem to be much narrower in range, confined as they are, to the world of animals—and only a handful of animals at that³—but this apparent limitation is transcended by the surprising variety of poetic attitudes, of human situations and estates. If *The Canterbury Tales* are an experimental demonstration of ways of telling stories, the **Moral Fables** could be described as an experiment in fable-telling and fable-moralization. It is this aspect I should like to see more fully explored.

Aesop's fables, in many different versions, were among the most popular of medieval stories, but they do not seem particularly suitable for original and imaginative treatment.⁴ Most of the widely used collections show varying degrees of competence rather than brilliant individuality, and the only major poet before Henryson to attempt an English version, John Lydgate, does not appear to have got very far. Lydgate's *Fables* are usually dismissed as an example of unimaginative routine exercise and they are certainly less exciting than Henryson's. One critic says that they were written "during Lydgate's most mediaeval period", "mediaeval" here being used almost as a term of abuse;⁵ what he means is that they are not particularly original and that Lydgate did not really inform these stories with his own personality. Henryson's handling of his sources, on the other hand, suggests that there was something in these simple tales that appealed to his own poetic temperament and his literary interests. The way he transformed them into new and highly personal narrative poetry is an intriguing subject for closer investigation.

The first thing that is important to note is the way Aesop's fables were practically always treated as a collection rather than as individual tales. Romulus' Latin translation, like most of its medieval derivatives, was a series of brief stories—almost anecdotes—with an equally brief moral attached to each one. "Walter's" version of the first fable, "The Cock and the Jewel" (*De Gallo et Jaspide*),⁶ consists of eight lines, plus another six lines of *moralitas*. The fables in the French *Isopets* are only insignificantly longer and they follow the same pattern. It is not so much the individual story that counts for the translator, but the collection as a whole and it would be pointless to look for subtle differences in the treatment of single episodes. This is confirmed by the well-known fact that in the course of the centuries, more and more stories were added to the original few dozens of genuinely Aesopic fables. Caxton's *Aesop* of 1483, one of Henryson's possible sources, is a comprehensive compilation of quite heterogeneous story-material; some of the items are very far removed from the simple animal fable and the purpose of the book is clearly to provide a large fund of brief tales to be enjoyed and used for moral application by every reader according to his own taste and seriousness.⁷ As "Walter", rather disarmingly, says in his prologue:

> Si fructus plus flore placet, fructum lege; si flos
> Plus fructu, florem; si duo, carpe duo.

This kind of advice is repeated in many prologues to fable-collections and Henryson's prologue, not very different from Lydgate's, is no exception although it has an engaging freshness that makes it sound as if Henryson had been the first to formulate these platitudes of poetic theory. It is more insistent and apologetic, as if directed at an audience that had particularly grave doubts about the use of "feinȝeit fabils of ald poetre".⁸

Henryson's prologue is interesting in another respect too, because it is by no means clear whether it is meant to introduce a single fable or a collection.

Like *The Canterbury Tales,* the **Moral Fables** present teasing problems of unity and overall arrangement. It is not at all evident from the text that, in their present state, they form a unified and deliberately organized collection rather than an unconnected series of individual tales (or groups of tales). There is no definite indication that Henryson had decided on a final order, if indeed he ever planned to include all the fables in a single work.

The textual evidence has been interpreted in conflicting ways. The two most important authorities, separated perhaps only by about three years (1568-1571), give the fables in completely different order. The Bannatyne MS includes, under the general title "Fables", some 15 poems, not all of which can by any stretch of the imagination be classified as Aesopic fables, such as Henryson's own **Orpheus and Eurydice**; neither are they all by Henryson, like Dunbar's *Golden Targe* and *The Thistle and the Rose*.⁹ The compiler obviously did not regard the **Fables** as a self-contained collection, but as individual poems like some of the others he copied for this section. He did, however, recognize two groups: one is a series of six genuine Aesopic fables, introduced by Henryson's own prologue, the other consists of six fox-tales, beginning likewise with a brief prologue and ending with the death of the junior fox. These three fables are linked together by the narrator and it is clear that they form a closelyknit group, evidently inspired by the *Roman de Renart* or related material. Three of the **Moral Fables** are not included in the Bannatyne MS at all.

The Bassandyne print has the great advantage of preserving all the 13 **Fables** and this is the main reason why it has usually been chosen as the basis for modern editions.¹⁰ Its textual superiority is, however, by no means undisputed. The Bannatyne MS (B) does, in several cases, preserve what seems likely to be the original reading whereas the Bassandyne text (Bs) shows clear signs of Protestant expurgation. Mac-Queen's insistence on the superiority of B is very emphatic and though his arguments have not found general acceptance, the authority of B cannot be disregarded altogether.[11] The critical edition by Denton Fox, while using Bs as copytext, incorporates in it many substantive variants from B.

The order of the *Fables* in the Bassandyne print has been championed, rather elaborately, by Roerecke, Fox, Ebin and Spearing.[12] They all recognize a symmetrical pattern in the arrangement and Fox has persuasively argued for the presence of a clear thematic development, from the more light-hearted and humorous tales of the first half to the gloomier and pessimistic tragedies of the second. This is ingenious and some of the evidence is hard to refute, but I still doubt whether it is likely to reflect more than the effort of a later compiler to impose some kind of order on a number of rather disparate tales. In their present form, the *Fables* can hardly have been intended as a collection, as printed in the Bassandyne anthology. If I were to speculate at all, I would assume that Henryson originally meant to translate a series of fables, like "Walter's", Lydgate's, or Caxton's collections, and that in the process he discovered different and more extended treatments suggested by each story.

The chief reason for rejecting or at least questioning the Bassandyne order lies in the astonishing individuality of Henryson's Fables. Some of them appear to defy so openly any inclusion in a series of uniform *exempla* that they lose as much as they gain by being read as part of a series. They are not at all like the stories in Chaucer's *Legend of Good Women* and even less like the Monk's tragedies; they are more like fairly self-contained variations on the tradition of the beast tale and its moral application. The differences between them are more interesting than the common subject and this again connects them, if only in a very general way, with *The Canterbury Tales*.

"The Preaching of the Swallow" and **"The Lion and the Mouse"** are the most obvious examples. Both poems are clearly in the tradition of the dream-vision, complete with prologue, conclusion and their own skilfully balanced structure; they do not depend for their effect on any other poems in the collection. On the contrary, it has been argued that they would have had to undergo extensive revision if they were meant to be incorporated in a series of fables.[13]

This is, I think, supported by the differences in presentation and the poet's attitude towards his story-material. Whereas in most of the *Fables* he just retells the plot, adding his own *moralitas,* he appears to try out two different narrative strategies in these visions. In **"The Preaching of the Swallow"** it is the poet himself who, walking out, becomes the witness of the events narrated in retrospect. He does not actually fall asleep, but the whole situation and the transition from prologue to tale certainly owes something to the dream convention and the experience of listening to the swallow's sermon is not an everyday occurrence, but appears to be in the nature of a revelation. The passing of the seasons is skilfully bridged by the narrator's own involvement as he watches the three stages of the action and these in turn are an illustration of the perennial cycle of the year described in the prologue. Here we are given a different justification for the moral potential of animal fables. The wealth and diversity of God's creation is praised as a manifestation of His power and as an aid to our limited perception. Only through contemplation of the variety of God's creatures can we hope for a glimpse of the Creator himself and of His divine will. The fable that follows is an illustration of this truth: the narrator himself finds instruction in what he experiences in his walks and though the *moralitas* briefly refers to Aesop as the fable's author, it consists for the most part of an application of what the poet has seen and heard, ending with a prayer for grace that includes the reader (or listener) in a congregation addressed by the narrator and, indirectly, by the swallow. There is no need here for the poet to apologize for the story as Chaucer's Nun's Priest does, or for any dissociation from the characters, like "Thise been the cokkes wordes, and nat myne". The completeness of the poem suggests that the author did not rely on its frame or on surrounding fables, but trusted the single story to make its own impact. **"The Preaching of the Swallow"** should not be read as one item in a collection of basically uniform tales, but as an independent poem or as a new beginning within a series of complex and ambitious explorations of a traditional genre.

This bold independence is even more striking in the case of **"The Lion and the Mouse"**. Here again we have an account of the poet's vision, explicitly described as a dream, but the fable itself is not presented as the result of the poet's own observation; it is reported as a specimen of Aesop's own art of fable-telling and fable-moralization. In making Aesop himself appear in a dream, answering the poet's questions and favouring him with a story, Henryson is able to dramatize the relationship between author and audience and to present himself in the role of an ideal listener. Aesop raises the question, which seems to have been very prominent in Henryson's own mind, whether it is any use telling tales if nobody heeds their moral, and the poet's reply to Aesop's objections seems like a modest attempt to justify his own art. It repeats in brief some of the arguments announced in the prologue, but they are given a new urgency by the context of this original dialogue between the modern and the ancient fabulist. The personal authority of the ancient poet is added to the authority of the traditional tales and this is obviously meant to give more weight and immediacy to the poetological argument. Transparent as the fiction may be, it presents a more personal and direct appeal to the reader than merely literary references to the famous name.

The morality, too, is added here at the special request of the narrator and is thus an authentic explication, not, as in all the other fables, the contemporary interpretation of an old story.

The originality of the frame makes it very unlikely that the poet wrote the fable as part of a collection; to justify its place in the Bassandyne-order by pointing out that it stands exactly in the centre of the thirteen tales is tempting, but does not explain the individual character of the tale. The arrangement is more likely to be the afterthought of some ingenious compiler, but it should not be made the basis for elaborate theorizing about the structure of the whole collection. It is, in any case, easy to see why the compiler of the Bannatyne MS placed **"The Lion and the Mouse"** at the end of a series of fables and copied **"The Preaching of the Swallow"** as a separate item away from the other fables.

This question of the unity or disparity of Henryson's **Fables** is not just a minor academic quibble, but is part of the larger problem of the poet's purpose in his use of the tradition of the animal fable for his narrative experiment. This stands in need of some explanation because Henryson evidently did not rely on any precedents in English. Apart from Lydgate's half-hearted attempt, there were, as far as we know, no English collections of fables, such as "Walter's" or the French *Isopets,* unless we assume that he knew Caxton's prose compilation which is quite a different literary enterprise, addressed to a different audience and without the kind of ambition and experimental originality that makes Henryson's **Fables** such a unique collection.[14]

It is quite likely that, when Henryson began his work on the **Fables** he had something like "Walter's" or Lydgate's collections in mind, beginning with a general prologue and continuing with a series of fairly uniform stories. Like "Walter", the French *Isopets,* and Lydgate, he begins with **"The Cock and the Jasp"**, but after that, the order of the **Fables** becomes uncertain, as I have tried to demonstrate, and this suggests that Henryson did not find the traditional pattern very congenial because he treated each story as a new challenge, not only to his narrative skill, but also to his particular concern about the moral justification of telling "feinȝeit fabils". This is why nearly each one of the **Fables** gives the impression of a fresh start, not a repeat performance; each differs, in varying degrees from the others in its handling of sources, in the use of animals as mirrors of human behaviour, and in the application as spelt out in the *moralitas.*

Formally, all the **Fables** follow the same pattern as those in "Walter's" collection and many similar versions in that there is a clear division between the story as such and the moralization. Henryson has used the same formula elsewhere, e.g. in **Orpheus and Eurydice,** but not in **The Testament of Cresseid.** It is an expression of his specific interest in the didactic potential of all his story material and, particularly, in the moral relevance and applicability of seemingly trivial incident. The distinction between chaff and fruit in secular literature or, to use Henryson's words, between the rough nutshell and the sweet kernel, is, of course, a medieval commonplace, but authors differ widely in their practical application of this general concept. Chaucer, I suspect, is often least in earnest when he offers explicit moralizations through some of his Canterbury pilgrims. Relentless moral exegesis has its ridiculous side for Chaucer, as for Shakespeare, and it needs, perhaps, the solemnity of 20th-century medievalists to provide a *moralitas* where Chaucer has wisely omitted it.

Henryson is, on the face of it, not at all a "Chaucerian" in this respect and it seems to me very difficult for the modern reader to know quite how to take his *moralitates.* Whereas earlier scholars tended to ignore them, to dismiss them as irrelevant preaching or even to leave them out in anthologies, modern critics have sometimes gone to great lengths in order to demonstrate the consistency and appropriateness of the *moralitas* in each individual case. It is impossible to be very definite about the author's intentions, but there is certainly no reason to assume that he regarded his *moralitates* as in any way less important than the narrative parts or that there is any discrepancy here between the poet and the preacher. On the other hand, there seems to me every reason to doubt that the *moralitates* are just clear-cut instructions how to read the fables. Rather they demonstrate various possibilities of making such simple stories instructive to the serious reader; some almost read like exercises in ingenious explication.

This is, I think, one of the reasons why the *moralitates* are so different from each other in scope and direction, not only because they belong to such different stories, but because each story can be read and made profitable in more than one way. This is not to claim that an unlimited variety of equally valid interpretations is possible; clearly most of the fables suggest one or two more obvious applications or rather areas of reference. Thus, the story of the Wolf and the Lamb (Fable No XII in Bs) invites a social or political reading more clearly than a theological one. But Henryson is not always concerned with what seems to us the most obvious; he appears to imply that, to derive profit from lightweight tales, some ingenuity may be employed.

To take the first of the **Fables** as an example. It is the shortest and simplest of the series and it looks as if

Henryson still felt more dependent on his source here than in the later tales. Nothing very much happens in this fable: the cock finds a jewel in a dunghill and comments on the fact that it is of no use to him.[15] The traditional moral, as stated by "Walter", is that stupidity has no taste for wisdom. Though Henryson's Cock at first sight is made to seem quite reasonable in recognizing his own limitations, it becomes clear from the *moralitas* that he is by no means held up as an example to be followed by the responsible reader, but as a warning. The reader is made to feel that he has responded to the tale rather prematurely and has misplaced his sympathy. He is alerted to the unexpected directions moralization can take and this should make him more wary in reading the fables. Henryson's *moralitas,* moreover, goes far beyond the traditional interpretation in its range of suggestion. The poet adds a spiritual dimension, referring to the religious properties of the jewel and he compares the cock to all those who never think further than their own stomach. It is a very sophisticated example of what can be done with a simple text, an accomplished little exercise in interpretation, breaking off with a direct appeal to the audience:

> Ga seik the iasp, quha will, for thair it lay.[16]

It would be misguided, here and in the other *Fables,* to look for an exact and detailed correspondence between the tale itself and the moralization, because it seems to me an essential part of Henryson's technique to keep the two quite distinct. He presents the tough nutshell and the wholesome kernel or, to change the metaphor with him, the "merie sport" and the "ernist", each in its own right and this enables him to give a free rein to his poetic imagination and his sense of fun because he will then demonstrate in the *moralitas* how it all can be made to provide material for instruction and reflection. Henryson rarely confuses or even combines the entertaining and the instructive part of the reading process in the way Chaucer and Lydgate do in their own, very different fashions.

It is illuminating to compare Henryson's first fable with Lydgate's version. This confirms not only that "Henryson is forceful, compact and varied, where Lydgate is loose, heavy-handed and monotonous", as Derek Pearsall concludes with some justice, but that their basic methods are quite different.[17] Lydgate does not trust the tale to speak for itself. He can hardly mention any detail without moralizing it; he smothers the plot, never allowing it to come to life, whereas Henryson feels that in literature you cannot have the kernel without the nutshell. Henryson's Cock, on finding the jewel, bursts forth into a delightfully self-confident and pretentious speech about the virtues of the stone and their uselessness to him, a speech that brilliantly combines high and low style, misapplied proverbial lore and commonplace wisdom. Its humour may well owe something to Chau-

cer's Chauntecleer, as Macdonald has suggested,[18] and the narrator does not interfere to point out his folly, so that even a modern critic could be taken in by the cock's high-flown rhetoric. Lydgate's Cock, on the other side, has no chance against the omnipresent narrator, who offers no coherent moral, but makes homiletic capital out of every detail—the cock's watchfulness, his diligence, and his wisdom in knowing what is good for him. Lydgate, not surprisingly, misses the real point of the story completely and loses sight of the fact that, at least in the traditional versions of the tale, the cock is to be despised, not to be admired as a model of Christian behaviour. My point is not that, to quote Pearsall again, "comparison with Henryson is deadly for Lydgate",[19] but to illustrate two different ways of dealing with a story. Both poets agree in considering the simple Aesopic fable a useful vehicle for moral instruction and Lydgate may even have suggested to Henryson his predominantly biblical interpretation, but Henryson spends as much imaginative energy on enlivening the action as on its moralization, whereas Lydgate never seems to be really interested in his characters as such because he often gives us their significance before they even make their first appearance.

This happens, for instance, in Lydgate's second fable, the story of the Sheep and the Wolf. The poet states the moral right at the outset in such a way that the story itself is used only as part of the general argument and is given no reality of its own. Lydgate embarks on wholesale moralizing without a consistent interpretation of the plot; he offers a series of moral commonplaces whose connection with the fable remains rather vague.

Henryson, again, leaves the story to make its own impact. The dialogue between Wolf and Lamb is presented with vivid concreteness and colloquial gusto and the killing of the Lamb is left until the last, quickly moving stanza. There is no interruption or moral commentary by the narrator until the end when the catastrophe has engaged the reader's full emotional sympathy; the effect is heightened by a rhetorical question that has nothing to do with the moral, but is obviously designed to bring home the simple pathos of the situation:

> Wes not this reuth, wes not this grit pietie,
> To gar this selie lamb but gilt thus de?
>
> (2705-6)

It is only then that the poet proceeds to moralize the fable. Again, this is very different from Lydgate's way of handling his story and his audience. To the modern reader, at least, it seems better psychology to engage our imaginative sympathy before insisting on the didactic purpose. Lydgate reminds us rather of Chaucer's Pardoner who can never resist the urge to interrupt the tale with some simple moral whereas Henryson appears more like a critic claiming to discover an abstract message in a text that does not, in so many words, point it out. The *moralitas* does not pretend to exhaust the story or to lay down the only possible interpretation. The proposed application, in this particular instance, is neither religious nor allegorical, but quite specific in its social analysis and pointed accusation. It is possible that it refers to particular grievances in Henryson's own society and it shows that he does not moralize the fables according to some preconceived plan or a fixed exegetic model, but takes each story as a fresh challenge to the ingenuity and wisdom of the serious reader.

This accounts, I think, for the striking differences between the *moralitates*.[20] Some are straightforward social comment and satire, others discuss the fables in terms of biblical parallels, and some propose an elaborate allegorical exegesis. In some instances, at least, it seems evident that Henryson is as much concerned with the technique of moralizing as he is with the details of the application itself. An interesting example is the fable of the Frog and the Mouse. This famous story is told with particular gusto and humour. The Mouse's pretentious discussion of the correspondence between appearance and character and the way she falls an easy victim to the Frog's deceitful sermonizing has more in common with Chaucer's "Nun's Priest's Tale" than Henryson's own version of the Cock-and-Fox story, in its brilliant unmasking of shallow learning and misapplied rhetoric and I do not agree with critics who explain Henryson's additions to the fable with reference to the *moralitas*. Henryson presents a vividly dramatic scene and there is clearly something absurd in an attempt to allegorize it, unless it is done tentatively and with a light touch.

Henryson's *moralitas* is particularly interesting because it falls into two parts. The first three stanzas differ metrically from the rest of the poem, consisting of an eight-line ballad metre with an elaborate rhyme-scheme and a (not very profound) refrain. This kind of variation is used in only one other instance (the fable of the Two Mice). The moralization sounds almost deliberately trite, especially after such a brilliant narrative performance. The tone is more popular than in other *moralitates* and there is a curious discrepancy between the familiar address to the reader as "my brother" and "my friend" and the rhetorical artifice.

The second part of the *moralitas* sets out to allegorize the fable, again in a rather primitive fashion that seems a little incongruous with the wit and subtlety of the tale. Only a somewhat naive reader will be able to take this perfectly seriously; there is a faint suggestion of gentle parody, a humorous self-consciousness about clumsy moralizing and, at the same time, a tentative exploration of the conventional *moralitas*. Just how much, the poet seems to wonder, will the story bear without col-

lapsing under the weight of homiletic ingenuity? The last stanza clearly expresses a certain detachment and shifts some of the responsibility from the author to the reader:

> Adew, my friend, and gif that ony speiris
> Of this fabill, sa schortlie I conclude,
> Say thow, I left the laif vnto the freiris,
> To mak a sample or similitude.

(2969-72)[21]

This has been interpreted in different ways, but I see it as a playful dig at the friars and their excessive moralizing. The poet has given a brief demonstration of what can be done with such a story, but he refuses to do any more "glosynge" although he obviously does not disapprove of the principle as such and might even agree with the Summoner's friar that "Glosynge is a glorious thyng, certayn".[22] It is impossible to be quite certain where serious application ends and parody begins, but we should be careful not to miss the teasing appeal to the reader's judgement and the author's lack of solemn self-assurance.[23] It is difficult to imagine a sophisticated reader not becoming a little uneasy about the kind of allegorization offered by the poet when he equates the mouse with the human soul striving upward while the frog, that is the body, is trying to pull it down. The pretentious triteness of the equation seems a rather dubious demonstration of the moral use of entertaining stories and the contrast to some of the other fables is just clear enough to suggest that Henryson knew what he was doing.

His presentation of the Mouse and the Frog is also remarkable for the subtle and humorous treatment of the characters' animality and here again Chaucer's influence seems likely.[24] Any fable that goes beyond the briefest plot outline has to face the problem of the inherent implausibility of articulate, well-read, and morally responsible animals. It is only at his own peril that a fabulist can try to steer quite clear of comedy, but Chaucer, and Henryson no less, deliberately exploit the comic potential of the fable to achieve a more complex effect and to tease the reader into sensitive cooperation. Like Chaucer's Cock, posing as a servant of Venus, Henryson's Mouse, reflecting on appearance and character, is a pathetic figure who makes it hard for the reader to be quite confident about the author's purpose. There is, of course, a learned tradition behind this debate, as MacQueen has pointed out,[25] but the main point is surely the ludicrous contrast between the natural shape of the Frog and the very human proverb:

> Distortum vultum sequitur distortio morum.

(2832)

The Frog's reply,

> "Thow suld not iuge ane man efter his face."

(2839)

has, of course, a lot to be said for it, as has his argument that his shape was given to him by the almighty Creator, but the apprehension of the Mouse turns out to be more than justified. More important is the obvious irrelevance of human wisdom in the given situation; the whole discussion is made somewhat absurd by the animal reality behind it. No branch of human learning seems less applicable to beasts than physiognomy and this confusion of incompatible categories only serves to illustrate the folly of applying learned commonplaces to complex, real-life situations. It forces the reader to critical reflexion about the principle of the beast-fable and its value as a vehicle for moral instruction. This happens in many of Henryson's fables, though not all of them have the same range of comic learning and ambiguous instruction.

The famous tale of the Town Mouse and the Country Mouse, for instance, derives its effect mainly from the dramatic situation and the contrast between the two sisters and the obvious moral is stated without particular elaboration or any attempt at allegorization, though rhetorically heightened by a change of metre and a refrain. The animal nature of the mice adds comedy to the pretensions of the Town Mouse, but hardly affects the moralization which does not surprise by any ingenuity, but seems almost deliberately conventional.[26] This only goes to illustrate once more that Henryson does not tie himself to any particular pattern, but uses each fable according to what he sees as its specific moral potential. Where the situation implies legal abuses and social oppression he seizes on that aspect with extraordinary intensity as in **"The Wolf and the Lamb"** and **"The Sheep and the Dog"**: the traditional enmity between the wolf and his prey turns into an instance of false witnessing, abuse of the law and corrupt judgement. The two fables are completely without humour; the animals' familiarity with legal procedure and terminology only adds to the pathos of the Lamb's helplessness and brings home to the reader the bestiality of man's oppression of his fellows. Beasts of prey using legal language make us aware of the way men often use the law as a cloak for their predatory instincts. The action of these two fables speaks for itself and hardly needs any moralization, but Henryson's *moralitates* for them are among the longest, not because of any particularly elaborate exegesis, but because of the narrator's personal commitment. The moralization turns into a passionate appeal against the abuse of power and privilege. Explication leads straight into personal exhortation:

> O thow grit lord, that riches hes and rent,
> Be nocht ane wolf, thus to deuoir the pure!
> Think that na thing cruell or violent
> May in this warld perpetuallie indure.
> This sall thow trow and sikkerlie assure:

For till oppres, thow sall haif als grit pane
As thow the pure with thy awin hand had slane.

> (2763-69)

The *moralitas,* which is nearly as long as the fable itself (10:13 stanzas), concludes with a prayer for justice.

Even more emotional is the *moralitas* to **"The Sheep and the Dog"**. The poet begins, as in some other cases, with a tentative interpretation:

> This selie scheip may present the figure
> Of pure commounis, that daylie ar opprest
> Be tirrane men, [. . .]

> (1258-60)

After three stanzas, however, he abandons this traditional approach and returns to the poor lamb whose complaint, he says he overheard "as I passit by Quhair that he lay" (1283-4). This complaint ("cairfull cry") occupies the last five stanzas of the *moralitas*. It is difficult to decide from the text whether, after about two stanzas, the poet takes over to continue the lamentation himself or whether the Lamb's "cairfull cry" goes on right to the end of the poem.[27] The effect, in any case, is an impression of complete identification with the victim: the narrator is no longer a detached commentator who interprets one of Aesop's fables—though Aesop is actually mentioned at the outset; he seems to be completely absorbed by the fate of his character and the reader, too, is made to forget the dividingline between past and present, fable and reality. None of the other *moralitates* uses this method of emotional identification. On the contrary, many of them reflect on the art of moralization and application, as we have seen in the case of **"The Paddock and the Mouse"**, and not all of them are equally serious in their homiletic purpose. Henryson was obviously aware of the fact that he had before him very different kinds of plot and he responded by trying out different didactic procedures. This again argues strongly against the theory of a unified collection.

It is, of course, partly a question of sources and traditions. It is difficult to explain why Henryson, unlike Lydgate, includes in his *Fables* six tales that are not at all Aesopic, but clearly belong to the tradition of the beast-epic; five of them are related to the Reynard-cycle, but there is no agreement as to any precise source.[28]

More important is the observation that these stories are very different in character from the simple Aesopic fables. Most of them have a rather more extended plot, with no very obvious moral undertone. Henryson's *moralitates* clearly reflect this difference; he seems to have felt the problem of moral explication more acutely here and, in consequence, his commentary is more sophisticated, if not strained.

The first group of Reynardian fables, items 3 to 5 in the Bassandyne order, is deliberately linked together by Henryson, without precedent in any previous versions known to us. The Fox makes his appearance in all three tales, first as the father, then as the son, and this changes the character of the fables because they present a series of adventures of the same hero (or his family) whereas the other fables relate completely isolated incidents. The *moralitates,* too, put more emphasis on the significance of the characters and the audience—"worthie folk" (586), "gude folk" (613, 789)—is repeatedly told that they are "typis figurall" (e.g. 584); the reader is compared to a miner who has to separate the gold from less precious metals.[29]

The *moralitas* to **"The Trial of the Fox"** which begins with this simile, is particularly elaborate and the "fabill figurall" is subjected to a somewhat strenuous exercise in moral application. Even the mare's hoof is allegorized as "the thocht of deid" (1125), hardly an interpretation that would have occurred to Henryson's readers without his efforts, and the reference to the "doctouris of deuyne" (1101) in support of his method rather encourages our scepticism because it reminds us of the vain outwitted Wolf whom the Fox mockingly addresses as "new-maid doctour off diuinitie" (1052).

Another group, possibly arranged as a symmetrical counterpart in the Bassandyne collection, consists of two Reynard tales and the story of the Wolf and the Wether;[30] the three fables are not among those collected in the Bannatyne MS and MacQueen suggested that they were written later than the others. They certainly differ from the Aesopic fables again in that they are tales of trickery and deceit rather than anecdotes that offer themselves for obvious moral application. The two adventures of Reynard, in particular, are straightforward examples of the traditional enmity between the Fox and the Wolf. The resourceful Fox cheats the Wolf over and over again and this battle of wits is more in the tradition of the comic folktale than of the animal fable in the original sense. Its main point is ingenious trickery rather than typical human behaviour and entertainment seems more important than instruction. Neither "Walter" or the French *Isopets* nor Lydgate include this type of story in their collections and though later compilers, like Steinhöwel and Caxton are far less discriminating in their choices, it is doubtful whether Henryson was influenced by them. He explicitly refers to Aesop in **"The Fox, the Wolf, and the Husbandman"** and **"The Wolf and the Wether"** and to "myne authour" in **"The Fox, the Wolf, and the Cadger"** and the way in which he expands and dramatizes all the fables helps to make the differences less obvious. At the same time, however, the *moralitates* suggest that he found it a little more difficult to moralize these stories. The moral applications sometimes sound like deliberate exercises: as many details as possible are briefly allegorized, down

to the cheese (2448) and the herring (2213), and some of the conclusions sound more glib and off-hand than the intense and deeply committed *moralitates* to the fables proper. The comic device of the "nekhering", for instance, gives a slightly awkward or intentionally humorous flavour to the final couplet:

> Quhairfoir I counsell mychtie men to haif mynd
> Of the nekhering, interpreit in this kynd.
>
> (2229-30)

The same applies to the ending of the next fable:

> Christ keip all Christianis from that wickit well!
>
> (2454)

It is difficult to know how seriously we are supposed to take this kind of moralization.

The third story in this group is more like the genuinely Aesopic fables, but Henryson brings out the simple comedy of the episode more prominently than any moral implication. The *moralitas,* however, introduces a complete change of tone and begins with a stanza that MacQueen calls "one of the most Lydgatean he ever wrote":[31]

> Esope, that poet, first father of this fabill,
> Wrait this parabole, quhilk is conuenient,
> Because the sentence wes fructuous and agreabill,
> In moralitie exemplatiue prudent;
> Quhais problemes bene verray excellent,
> Throw similitude of figuris, to this day,
> Geuis doctrine to the redaris of it ay.
>
> (2588-94)

It is hardly more "Lydgatean" than the stanza introducing the *moralitas* to **"The Cock and the Fox"**, but in both cases there is a certain self-consciousness and a contrast of tone that is quite unlike Lydgate. After the dramatic speed of the tale itself, heightened by a characteristic use of low style,[32] the elaborate seriousness of the *moralitas* comes as a surprise and the trite homily on presumption, like the slightly pedantic allegorizations in the two prececeding *moralitates,* again suggest that the moralizations do not fit the stories with the same ease and conviction as in the case of the original fables.

It is, perhaps, more a question of degree than of a completely different approach, but it seems clear that Henryson, after adapting the first fables from "Walter", became increasingly more adventurous and experimental, not only in the form he gave to these tales, but also in the choice of material and the methods of explication. Like many authors of beast-epics before and after him, he discovered that a surprising range of emotions, patterns of behaviour, and moral problems can be incorporated in animal stories and this evidently caused him to develop a corresponding variety of didactic strategies.

This unconventionally colourful combination of extended animal-adventure, intense moral appeal and sophisticated exegesis seems to me the supreme achievement of Henryson's *Fables* and though the collection has not the same kind of unity as *The Canterbury Tales* or La Fontaine's fables, it has a range of characters, levels of style, narrative devices and humane wisdom hardly ever equalled in fable or beast-epic before or after, certainly not in English.

For Chaucer, the fable was only one among many narrative traditions. Like Henryson, he finds comedy and instruction in the simple tale of the Cock and the Fox, but he puts the fable into the mouth of the preacher and he is clearly more interested in the tradition of the comic and satiric beast-epic than in Aesopic fables. Henryson faces the problem of instruction by story-telling more squarely and takes the fable-tradition far more seriously. More than Chaucer and even Lydgate, he is concerned with the direct moral application of his art and there is at least a strong likelihood that this reflects a change in the attitude of readers and listeners.[33] Henryson does not cater for a taste in cosmopolitan rhetoric, classical story-material and philosophic debate. He answers the more traditional objection that entertainment has to justify itself, that "feinȝeit fabils" are only acceptable if they can be moralized and that, on the other hand, audiences have to be made to listen if poetry is not to become pointless. Each of his *Fables* is a new appeal not only to our moral awareness, but also to our critical attention as readers and listeners. The doubts and apprehensions expressed in Chaucer's "Retraction" indicate a similar tendency, and the completely altered attitude expressed in Henryson's *Fables* is probably a response to a change in the literary climate rather than just the product of a different poetic temperament. We cannot hope to recover precisely the reservations and preconceptions of Henryson's audience, but they appear to have provoked him to this unique demonstration that explicitly didactic narrative can be, in a variety of ways, highly entertaining and deeply moving.

Notes

1. See Douglas Gray, *Robert Henryson*, Medieval and Renaissance Authors (Leiden, 1979), p. 161.

2. Cf. Robert Sutton, *The Moral Fables of Robert Henryson, The Scots Makar* (Unpublished Diss., University of Massachusetts, 1975), pp. 74-79, on the "frame" of the *Moral Fables*.

3. Cf. *The Moral Fables*, pp. 91-93; Sutton counts "only sixteen different species".

4. See the brief account in the excellent edition of Denton Fox, *The Poems of Robert Henryson* (Oxford, 1981), pp. xli ff. All quotations are from this edition. Cf. also, for the whole tradition of the fable and the beast-epic, Hans Robert Jauss, *Un-*

tersuchungen zur mittelalterlichen Tierdichtung, Beihefte zur Zeitschrift für Romanische Philologie, 100 (Tübingen, 1959).

5. Cf. Alan Renoir, *The Poetry of John Lydgate* (London, 1957), p. 54; see also, *The Minor Poems of John Lydgate,* ed. H. N. MacCracken, Part II, EETS, OS 192 (1934), pp. 566-599.

6. For the text of Romulus in the best-known version by "Walter L'Anglais" see *Recueil Général des Isopets,* ed. Julia Bastin, Société des Anciens Textes Français (Paris, 1930), II, 7 ff.

7. Cf. *Caxton's Aesop,* ed. R. T. Lenaghan (Cambridge, Mass., 1967).

8. On the Prologue see Gray, *Robert Henryson,* pp. 70 ff., and the excellent commentary in the edition by D. Fox.

9. See *The Bannatyne Manuscript,* ed. W. Tod Ritchie, Vol. IV, The Scottish Text Society, N. S. 26 (1930), pp. 117 ff.

10. E.g. *The Poems and Fables of Robert Henryson,* ed. H. Harvey Wood, 2nd ed. (Edinburgh, 1958), and Robert Henryson, *Poems,* ed. Charles Elliott, Clarendon Medieval and Tudor Series, 2nd ed. (Oxford, 1974).

11. See John MacQueen, *Robert Henryson. A Study of the Major Narrative Poems* (Oxford, 1967), pp. 189-199; see also the authoritative account of the textual situation in Fox, *The Poems of Robert Henryson,* pp. 1 ff.

12. The best account (although I do not agree with his conclusions) is by Fox, *The Poems of Robert Henryson,* pp. lxxv-lxxxi; see also L. Ebin, "Henryson's 'Fenyeit Fabils': A Defense of Poetry", *Actes du 2ᵉ Colloque de Langue et de Littérature Ecossaises (Moyen Age et Renaissance)* (Université de Strasbourg, 1978), pp. 222-238, and A. C. Spearing, "Central and Displaced Sovereignty in Three Medieval Poems", *RES [Review of English Studies]*, N.S. 33 (1982), 247-261; on Henryson, pp. 252-257.

13. See the thorough discussion by Sutton, *The Moral Fables,* pp. 97-117; some of his conclusions are similar to mine.

14. Fox, who has made the closest study of Henryson's sources, is very sceptical about Henrysons's knowledge of Caxton's versions; see his edition, p. xlix.

15. Cf. the very perceptive comments in Gray, *Robert Henryson,* pp. 90-92 and 121-123, and Harold E. Toliver, "Robert Henryson: From *Moralitas* to Irony", *ES [English Studies]*, 46 (1965), 300-309.

16. Caxton's brief moral draws a parallel between the jewel and "this fayre and plesaunt book". Henryson is less explicit, but a similar meaning may be implied in his last line.

17. On Lydgate's Fables see Derek Pearsall, *John Lydgate,* Poets of the Later Middle Ages (London, 1970), pp. 192-198; here: 195.

18. See Donald MacDonald, "Narrative Art in Henryson's Fables", *Studies in Scottish Literature,* 3 (1965/66), 101-113. On the use of low style cf. MacQueen, *Robert Henryson,* pp. 107-110.

19. *John Lydgate,* p. 197.

20. The different methods used in the *moralitates* are helpfully discussed in Sutton, *The Moral Fables,* pp. 36-73, and, more briefly, in Gray, *Robert Henryson,* pp. 128-130 and *passim.*

21. See MacQueen, *Robert Henryson,* pp. 110 ff., on the *moralitas* and its relation to the fable, and Fox, *The Poems,* p. 337.

22. Geoffrey Chaucer, *The Canterbury Tales*: The Summoner's Tale (D. 1793).

23. Cf. Gray, *Robert Henryson,* p. 129, for a similar view.

24. On this problem see the excellent study by Jill Mann, "The *Speculum Stultorum* and the *Nun's Priest's Tale*", *The Chaucer Review,* 9 (1975), 262-282, and Gray, *Robert Henryson,* pp. 71 ff.

25. Cf. *Robert Henryson,* p. 120 f.

26. See also Gray, *Robert Henryson,* pp. 76-78.

27. See the note by Fox on line 1298 in his edition, p. 262.

28. Cf. the discussion in Fox, *The Poems,* pp. xlvii ff., and MacQueen, *Robert Henryson,* pp. 208-221; see also Joachim Hildebrand, *Robert Henrysons "Morall Fabillis" im Rahmen der mittelalterlichen und spätmittelalterlichen Tierdichtung* (Dissertation, Hamburg, 1973), pp. 149 ff.

29. See lines 1097-1100 and the note in Fox's edition where he points out that Lydgate makes use of the same metaphor. It is possible that Henryson means the professional interpreter rather than the average reader.

30. On this group cf. MacQueen, *Robert Henryson,* pp. 192 f.

31. *Robert Henryson,* p. 186.

32. Cf. MacQueen, *Robert Henryson,* pp. 185-187.

33. See the interesting article by Richard Bauman, "The Folktale and Oral Tradition in the Fables of Robert Henryson", *Fabula,* 6 (1964), 108-124.

Gregory Kratzmann (essay date 1985)

SOURCE: Kratzmann, Gregory. "Henryson's *Fables*: 'the subtell dyte of poetry.'" *Studies in Scottish Literature* 20 (1985): 49-70.

[In the following essay, Kratzmann studies the "Prologue" to the Moral Fables, *contending that it serves "to alert the attentive reader to some of the rhetorical strategies of the fables which are to follow it."]*

Henryson's **Fables** were once discussed almost exclusively as documents of social realism, or as humorous poems which at their best might be designated "Chaucerian." In an important article in 1962, Denton Fox urged "that it might be helpful to look at the **Fables** from a more severely literary viewpoint, and to examine them as poems"; further, he pleaded the necessity to examine the poems "as wholes," that is, as fables consisting of two carefully related parts, story and moralization.[1] Although there has been some stimulating criticism of the **Fables** during the past twenty years, commentary has been neither as prolific nor as wide-ranging as that directed at **The Testament of Cresseid,** and there is room for more discussion of those two closely-related critical issues raised in Fox's article. This essay has two concerns. The first is to examine the **"Prologue"** to the **Fables** as poetry, to observe how a number of traditional ideas about the nature, purpose and value of allegorical poetry are presented in a way that is both original and challenging. The second is to see what relation the questions about the nature of poetry which are raised in the **"Prologue"** bear to the fables themselves—in particular, to those which are usually considered to be problematic, because the meaning or "doctrine" adduced in the *moralitas* is not what we would have expected from a reading of the tale in naturalistic terms.

Critical commentary on Henryson's **"Prologue"** all too frequently takes the form of paraphrase of the traditional ideas about the nature of poetry which it contains, thereby representing the poetry of the **"Prologue"** itself as little more than a vehicle. Even Denton Fox's notes on the construction of the **"Prologue,"** in his recent meticulous edition of Henryson, underestimate the extent to which vehicle and tenor, style and content, are inseparable in these nine stanzas which are themselves an illustration of "the subtell dyte of poetry" which they introduce.[2] Although the poetry of the **"Prologue"** is not itself allegorical, its highly individual way of proceeding from point to point, and its unexpected changes of tone and emphasis, serve to alert the attentive reader to some of the rhetorical strategies of the fables which are to follow it. Henryson's **"Prologue"** is more than a theoretical statement of a theory of figural poetry: it is an elliptic and ironic "defence" which raises as many questions as it appears to answer, the work of a poet who like Chaucer was more an innovator than a traditionalist.

It is entirely appropriate that the speech of Aesopic animal characters should be described in terms of argument and debate ("And to gude purpois dispute and argow, / Ane sillogisme propone, and eik conclude"). The concessive clause with which the **"Prologue"** opens ("*Thocht* feinȝeit fabils") suggests from the very beginning the presence of a mind which has a keen interest in dialectic, the *pro* and *contra* approach to the establishment of truth. The **"Prologue"** proceeds in the manner of an argument or "demonstracioun," but although its separate parts are all drawn from literary convention, the synthesis is highly individual and thought-provoking. The syntax of the first stanza suggests that the thoughts being presented have a logical or causal relationship ("Thocht . . . ȝit than . . . And als") but the apparent self-assurance and casualness of the narrator constitute a challenge to the reader. Fox's explication of the stanza as a highly compressed introduction to Henryson's aims ("to be *dulce et utile*") and methods ("a highly wrought style, a satirical mode, and a figural technique") is cogent enough, but the dominant impression remains the manner rather than the matter of the stanza. The casual transitions from one major aesthetico-moral topic to another—from the notion of how art can be truthful when its literal basis is fiction, to the capacity which art possesses for giving pleasure, to the conception of the artist as moral and social reformer and from thence to the technique of the figure—direct our attention towards the fundamental and complex question of the relationship between art and truth, and alert us to the possibility of at least one contradiction (can the same work of art be the source of both delight and reproof?). The casual manner, which verges on naiveté, disguises what is indisputably a very exalted view of poetry—of the present poem no less than the "ald poetre" which is the ostensible subject.[3]

The second and third stanzas help to resolve the apparent dichotomy between correction and aesthetic pleasure, but in such a way as to open further questions for the reader. Stanza 2 opens with an apparently conventional simile in which poetry is compared with the bounty of Nature:

> Swa it be laubourit with grit diligence,
> Springis the flouris and the corne abreird,
> Hailsum and gude to mannis sustenence;
> Sa springis thair ane morall sweit sentence
> Oute of the subtell dyte of poetry,
> To gude purpois, quha culd it weill apply.

(ll. 8-14)

The relevant section of Henryson's source, the "Prologue" to the fables of Gualterus Anglicus, might be translated thus:

> This garden brings forth both fruit and flower, and flower and fruit alike give pleasure: the one has beauty, the other savour. If the fruit appeal more than the flower, pick it out: if the flower more than the fruit, gather it: if both please, gather both . . .[4]

Gualterus dissociates himself with graceful irony from the question of interpretation—the reader may do as he pleases, according to his capacity and his interests. His image of the poem as garden expresses the traditional contrast between *dulcis* and *utilis,* although the opposition is not an absolute one, since presumably *fructus* has some of the surface beauty of *flos.* The Henrysonian simile is more complex. No essential difference is implied between the products of nature, the "flouris" and the new shoots of grain: the syntax of lines 10-11 expresses the idea that *both* are "Hailsum and gude to mannis sustenence" (the phrase cannot be satisfactorily read as qualifying only the second of the nouns in line 10). By the repetition of "sweit," the "rhetore" of line 3 is associated with the "sentence" of line 12 (which as Fox rightly indicates is "meaning" here rather than the narrower sense of "moral"[5]). What poetry means is both "morall" and "sweit": the oxymoron expresses the hope of a full and inclusive response more seriously than Gualterus's invitation "take what you can." The pleasure of reading poetry is to be a necessary part of the experience of understanding it, and the reader is left in no doubt about the effort which the "subtell dyte" and its author expect of him. Understanding is to be achieved only after mental and imaginative effort, just as the bringing forth of a crop from "a bustious eird" is made possible only by the physical labor of the husbandman. The repetition of "springis" articulates with fine exactness the sense that meaning, at once moral and sweet, emerges like flowers and grain from the earth—gradually, and only after sympathetic effort. (Denton Fox's note to *ll.* 8-14 seems to give a misleading emphasis, by suggesting that "ane morall sweit sentence" is implied solely by "corne," while "flouris" denotes pleasure.[6] The syntax and logic of the similitude suggest that the associations of both natural objects are present in the "sentence" of allegorical poetry). Poetry, no less than the husbandry of the soil, is seen to have a practical and utilitarian value. "Quha culd it weill apply," placed like an apparent afterthought at the end of the stanza, suddenly introduces the idea that there is a necessary connection between intellectual engagement and moral action. The poem will not have achieved its object unless there is a practical effect on the "misleuing" of mankind, an idea which receives fuller expression in the **"Prologue"** to **"The Lion and the Mouse."**

The second stanza, then, brings into focus a connection between the two aspects of poetry, pleasure and profit, which are juxtaposed in stanza 1: the "sweitnes" which highly-wrought poetry can impart is seen now to be something more than decoration, as an inseparable part of the moral function of letters. The reader is left, however, with the bemusing awareness that what pleases the ear might not be synonymous with what pleases the mind, and perhaps also that since poetry is so "subtell," it may be all too possible to seize upon a "sentence" which is not there at all. In this context, it is worth remarking that Henryson, unlike Gualterus Anglicus and Lydgate (in the Prologue to his *Isopes Fabules*), omits to invoke any divine guidance for his projected "translatioun," thereby depriving the reader of the illusion that there might be a final and ultimate authority for what he is to read.

The third stanza proceeds to emphasize more strongly than the second the priority of the moral element of poetic meaning, through the traditional allegorical image of the nut. This image differs from the natural image of the previous stanza in that a clear distinction is made between its two literal elements: whereas the flowers and corn were both interpreted as parts of poetic "sentence," the shell of the nut is viewed as something dry and ultimately worthless in comparison with the kernel of truth which it contains and preserves. (Some of the witnesses give for *ll.* 15-16 the reading "The nuttis schell . . . Haldis the kirnell, and is delectabill," which if adopted would lead to a very different interpretation of the figure. However, the reading given by the Bannatyne and Makculloch MSS., followed by Fox, is clearly preferable, because it gives a sense which provides a logical relation to the second part of the simile). Although the nut image does not contradict that of the previous stanza, the rhetorical emphasis is clearly different: the shell of poetic fiction, the literal element, is now seen to be worthless in relation to the "doctrine" which it contains. The kernel is described as "sueit," and the logic of the image denies sweetness to the surrounding shell which, being "hard and teuch," would appear to offer no kind of pleasure. After this definition of poetry as an adjunct to Scripture the remainder of the stanza is quite startling, especially as it is offered as having a logical connection with the preceding idea:

> And clerkis sayis, it is richt profitabill
> Amangis ernist to ming ane merie sport,
> To blyth the spreit and gar the tyme be schort.

Although their emphases are different, the images of the second stanza and the first part of the third agree in representing poetry as a serious kind of discourse. There is nothing to prepare the reader for this abrupt change to a much less elevated view of poetry, as pastime or "merie sport," whose profit consists not in any moral function, but rather in recreation from "ernist" matters. This genial and even jocular strain continues into the fourth stanza, as "the mynd that is ay diligent" is now exhorted to take "sum merines" lest it become stale. I. W. A. Jamieson, in a valuable short essay on the poetics of the *Fables,* notes that there is something "decidedly inorganic" about this stanza:

There is no discussion of the effect that "merie sport" might have on the serious material, the "sentence," the "sad materis," the reproof of total misliving. The comment is a little, only a little but the analogy may help, like Harry Bailly's claims, as critical referee for the progress of the *Canterbury Tales,* that doctrine should be followed by mirth.[7]

The dominant effect of this change of mood and the apparent undermining of what has gone before is to challenge the reader's assumptions about the nature of poetry—in particular, about the nature of the "feinȝeit fabils" to follow. Is it possible for poetry to be "merie" and at the same time to make the kind of intellectual demand on the reader which is conveyed by the image of flowers and corn? Is the view of poetry as vehicle for "doctrine" and agent of moral reformation necessarily incompatible with the concept of poetry as entertainment?

These are questions which several of the fables themselves raise, principally through the unusual and unexpected links which are made between their two formal parts, *taill* and *moralitas.* In them, as in the **"Prologue,"** Henryson shows himself to be keenly aware of the way in which his audience is likely to respond, and to make this imagined response an integral part of the dialectic of the poetry. The fourth stanza of the **"Prologue"** gestures towards the authority of "clerkis" by quoting a Latin line from "Esope"—actually, from Gualterus Anglicus—which appears to be a synthesis of the two opposing views, poetry as edification, and poetry as entertainment: *Dulcis arrident series picta iocis.* At the level of theoretical statement this is unexceptionable, but it does not proceed naturally from the thought of the preceding stanzas, which has given emphasis first to one, then to the other aspect of the experience of reading. The **"Prologue"** directs the reader to observe more than this traditional theory of the nature of poetry, the combination of seriousness (*seria*) with mirth (*iocis*). It draws our attention to the question, at once fundamental and complex, of *how* poetry can accommodate and reconcile these divergent impulses. The modesty-topos of stanza 6, with its plea for the beneficent reader's correction where necessary, is a playfully ironic gesture towards the larger questions of involvement and comprehension raised within the **"Prologue."** Henryson leaves us in no doubt about his own commitment to the cause of moral and spiritual reform through the practice of poetry. The final metaphor of the **"Prologue"** is concerned not directly with the nature of poetry and how it is to be comprehended, but rather with the nature of man:

> Na meruell is, ane man be lyke ane beist,
> Quhilk lufis ay carnall and foull delyt . . .

This lament for man's depravity achieves its full force by gathering up echoes of what has preceded it—the function of poetry as reproof (stanza 1), the implicit injunctions to "apply" the fable's "sentence" and "doctrine" (stanzas 2 and 3)—and working them into an urgent and authoritative appeal to the reader. The moral seriousness has an edge of stern wit, in Henryson's reversal of the terms of the traditional beast-fable's metaphor of beast-as-man. Beasts may behave like men for the combined purpose of edification and entertainment in poetic fiction, but this poet insists on a stronger kind of reality. The biblical notion of man-as-beast is commonplace, as Fox notes,[8]—but here the context makes the comparison unexpected and even startling, as the self-disparaging voice of the narrator as servant of his audience gives way to the uncompromising authority of the preacher. One of the effects of this is to raise a further question about the appropriateness of the idea of poetry as recreation—the tone implies that it may well be too late for gentle persuasion. The fact that the fables were written at all would seem to indicate that Henryson's pessimism did not extend so far, although the discussion between the poet-dreamer and the fictional "Aesop" in the **"Prologue"** to **"The Lion and The Mouse"** raises in a more explicit way this question of the possible moral inefficacy of poetry:

> Sa roustit is the warld with canker blak
> That now my taillis may lytill succour mak.

> (*l.* 1396-7)

The final stanza of the **"Prologue"** returns to the mood of quiet reflection on past fable-writing with which the first stanza begins. Here as before the emphasis is upon style ("In gay metir, and in facound purpurate / Be figure wrait his buke"), but now more insistently in terms of audience reception. Fox's note to line 60, which cites a passage from Boccaccio's *Genealogia Deorum* as a parallel, seems to me to distort the sense by claiming that it is "that the *gay metir* will please some readers, and the figure others."[9] The allusion to "Esope's" way of writing seems rather to combine the two social estates of "hie" and "low" into one audience, capable of responding in the same way to both the elegant rhetoric and the figurative technique of the fable. Implicit is a further large claim for this genre of poetry, that it has the potential to reach the widest possible audience through the present poet's skillful use of the resources of his "mother toung."

The prime function of any literary prologue is to attract the reader's interest in what is to follow. Henryson's **"Prologue"** does this in a way which is partially ironic and dramatic in the continued awareness of audience response manifest in it: in this respect it is reminiscent of the rhetorical preliminaries in *The House of Fame* where, as J. A. W. Bennett observes, Chaucer keeps his readers "on the *qui vive* as he quickly shifts from one stance to another."[10] The **"Prologue"** to the *Fables* leaves little room for doubt about its author's belief in the high seriousness of figural poetry, its relevance to

what is perceived to be a state of universal moral decay. In other ways, though, the **"Prologue"** is distinctly open-ended: the reader is made aware that he will need to pay very careful attention to the poetry if he is not to misunderstand it, but at the same time he is reassured that fables offer entertainment and recreation to a mind which is in danger of becoming stale. Douglas Gray, whose structural and stylistic analysis is the most penetrating account of the *Fables* yet written, observes that by the end of the **"Prologue"** "we should expect to find delight in the midst of instruction and morality, and, perhaps, that we should not be surprised to find some 'merie sport' in the moralities as well as in the fables."[11] The first test of the reader's ability to comprehend what proclaims itself as a "subtell" and possible ambiguous art is **"The Cock and the Jasp."** The **"Prologue"** leaves little doubt that this was intended to be read as the first of the *Fables*:

> And to begin, first of ane cok he wrate
> Seikand his meit, quhilk fand ane iolie stone
> Of quhome the fabill ȝe sall heir anone.

Bassandyne's arrangement is in this respect preferable to that of the mid sixteenth-century anthologist George Bannatyne, who appears to have regarded the **"Prologue"** as having an exclusive application to this fable. **"The Cock and the Jasp"** offers, as part of its "sentence," an illustration of what is implied in the **"Prologue"** about the potentialities of the allegorical mode, the peculiar attractions and the peculiar difficulties of the "fenȝeit fabils" which are to follow. In his *moralitates*, it is customary for Henryson to address his audience in a direct and often intimate way, but **"The Cock and the Jasp"** is the only one of the *Fables* to offer the reader what amounts to an open challenge: "Go seik the iasp, quha will, for thair it lay." This, the last line of the fable, has an obvious application to the *moralitas*: the jasp, which is scorned by the Cock, "Betakinnis perfite prudence and conning." John MacQueen's account of the biblical echoes in the *moralitas* supports his view that the "science" praised in the *moralitas* is the knowledge of the way to salvation.[12] But Henryson's challenge to his audience in the line quoted above suggests that the jasp has a secondary and more localized significance, as the "science" to be found within poetry. **"The Cock and the Jasp"** offers an extreme instance of the interpretive difficulties which are to be encountered elsewhere: its meaning (which goes beyond the content of the *moralitas*) depends upon the creation of a tension between actual and ideal, literal and figurative. Here, as in several of the other fables, the reader is confronted in the *moralitas* with an allegorical reading of the *taill* which is at odds—or apparently at odds—with his experience of the *taill* and the kind of allegorical reading which seems natural to it.

It is not that there is a tension between the literal level and allegorical interpretation *per se*: rather, the tension comes into being because of the unexpectedness of the interpretation. The Cock in **"The Cock and the Jasp"** has—even if he is "richt cant and crous"—an appealing kind of commonsense. He recognizes that the gem is valuable ("O gentill Iasp, O riche and nobill thing") but that it is not fitting adornment for one whose needs do not extend beyond mere subsistence. The Cock's language is discussed by both MacQueen and Fox:[13] Both see the abrupt transitions from the extravagant high rhetorical mode to the "low" style appropriate to the farmyard as conveying a sense of moral error—the foolish complacency of bondage to appetitive demands. In terms of the significance given to the Jasp in the *moralitas,* this reading of the Cock and what he stands for is undeniably accurate, but it is necessary to recognize the implications of the irony that the Cock, unlike his critics, had not read the poem. And as we read the *taill* for the first time we are more than likely to respond to him as an exemplar of a reasonable and attractive way of life, especially as he is such a fluent rhetorician. Reading the poem on a literal level, we may even be touched by the Cock's unconcern for market economics: he does not, after all, rush off to sell the "gentill Iasp," but simply bids it "Rise . . . Out of this fen, and pas quhar thow suld be." When we turn to other versions of this fable we are likely to be confirmed in our reaction. His English cousin, the creation of Lydgate, embarks upon an even longer address to the stone. He is even more sententious than his Scots counterpart, and is learned enough to have read in a lapidary that it has more than a material value. Like Henryson's figure, he propounds a philosophy of each to his own, and this system of values is endorsed, without any suspicion of irony, in Lydgate's *moralitas*[14]:

> The cok demyd, to hym hit was more dew
> Small simple grayne, then stones of hygh renoun,
> Of all tresour cheif possessioun.
> Suche as God sent, eche man take at gre,
> Nat prowde with ryches nor groge with pouerte

> (*ll.* 213-17)

If we are called upon to approve Lydgate's rather dreary fowl, then we can hardly be at fault for liking Henryson's, especially as he is without the benefit of a lapidarian's education. What is perhaps most appealing about him is his unfailing deference to the stone: the "apology" to the jasp because of the Cock's preference for worms and snails,

> And thow agane, vpon the samin wyis,
> May me as now for thyne auaill dispyis

> (97-8)

is characteristic of the spirit of high comedy in which Henryson frequently links the animal and human realms,

and not surprisingly it has no counterpart in Lydgate's handling of the fable.

While the critical interpretations of the fable provided by MacQueen and Fox are essentially sound, they give insufficient emphasis to the experience of reading the fable sequentially as a determinant of its "sentence." Although it may seem naive to argue from the standpoint of what the *taill* seems to say at a first reading, it is highly probable that this experience is a calculated element in the way the poetry works. The rhetorical strategy is one of deliberate misleading: we are led to expect one interpretation, the natural one, and instead we are given a highly ingenious interpretation of the Cock as the foolish man,

> Quhilk at science makis bot ane moik and scorne,
> And na gude can; als lytill will he leir—
> His hart wammillis wyse argumentis to heir,
> As dois ane sow to quhome men for the nanis
> In hir draf troich wald saw the precious stanis.

> (*ll.* 143-47)

Henryson begins to manipulate his audience towards the Cock's viewpoint at the conclusion of the **"Prologue,"** where the fable is summarized as being of a cock "quhilk fand ane iolie stone." The subsequent "characterization" of the jasp in the *taill* gives no indication that the stone is to be regarded as anything but a stone (albeit a valuable one). MacQueen finds a direct biblical allusion (to Luke 15:8) in the detail of the "damisellis wantoun and insolent" who sweep away the jewel in their excess of housekeeping zeal, but if this is a biblical allusion it is so muted as to be recognizable till one reads the tale with the information provided by the *moralitas* (where the jasp betokens "perfite prudence and cunning"). In any case, the detail is conducive to a literal understanding of the story. Clark comments that "the cock's early rising and diligence . . . contrast with the idleness and indifference of the hypothetical girls."[15]

Although Fox does not discuss the overall rhetorical strategy of the fable in the way that I am attempting to do here, he is clearly aware of the shock effect of the *moralitas,* "which appears to be as impertinent and mechanical as the moral of an inferior fablieau."[16] The stylistic mode of the *moralitas* is very similar to that of the Cock's peroration upon the jasp, in its modulation between the high style of parallelism and rhetorical question and a simpler, more intimate and particularizing level of language (well exemplified in *ll.* 134-47). The narrator's rhetoric in the *moralitas* is more persuasive than that of the Cock in the *taill*: Henryson speaks with the accents of the Christian moralist, whereas the cock is only a cock on a dunghill. The authoritative voice of the narrator (which now has none of the deference and mock-naiveté which hovers over the **"Prologue"**) compels its audience to return to the *taill,* to attempt to see why and how its central character "may till ane fule be peir." And it is possible to see how the tale will accommodate the allegorical reading which is proposed. Providing that we accept the symbolic identification of the jasp with Wisdom and Knowledge and the metaphorical association between beast and man (and there is no reason we should not), the Cock's failure to recognize the jasp's true value, and his rejection of it in favor of the singleminded quest for physical sustenance, can be seen as the marks of willful stupidity. (In our first reading of the *taill,* where the jasp seems to represent an object of material beauty and value, there is no such pressure to condemn the Cock as a fool, even if his elaborate language does make him look slightly absurd.) The Cock's admission that he loves "fer better thing of les auaill" denotes a certain kind of wisdom according to our first reading—it is attractively honest to admit a greater concern for food and warmth than for a courtier's splendors. But it is not so appealing, I imagine, to hear an admission that learning is of more "auaill" than material satisfaction from one who persists in seeking the latter to the exclusion of all else.

The effect of the *moralitas* in persuading us to review our original comprehension of the *taill* is both witty and complex. The poet has provided a practical demonstration of his proposition that the shell of the nut can indeed be "hard and teuch" to crack, and the "moralitie" about the value of wisdom and learning is made the more memorable because it has come upon us in such an unexpected way. The stern injunction "Ga seik the iasp, quha will, for thair it lay" has the effect of locating wisdom not only in Scripture but also in "the subtell dyte of poetry." Although the voice of the *moralitas* is so magisterial that it might seem impertinent to raise the question, we are surely justified in asking about the final validity of our original response to the *taill* as a lively and amusing exemplum of what is described in **"The Two Mice"** as "blyithnes in hart, with small possessioun." Are we now to forget that we recognized the Cock as a representative of ordinary humanity, perhaps self-important, but basically well-intentioned? Or are we to recognize in the language of the Cock what one Milton critic calls "sin-centred" poetry,[17] claimed to achieve its effects by inducing the reader to assent to attitudes and actions which are then shown to be vicious? This kind of rhetorical descent is surely no more a feature of Henryson's art than it is of Milton's. The theory makes unreasonable assumptions about the naivete of the reader: it disregards the concept of aesthetic distancing entirely, and presupposes an inclination towards empathy. But the *moralitas* is startling nevertheless, and there is every reason for the reader to feel that he has been deceived, probably consciously, by a narrative which has never given an indication that the jewel is meant to be seen as anything other than a jewel.

The assumption has usually been made in criticism of the *Fables* that it is necessary to regard the allegorical interpretation as having priority over the literal sense implicit in the tale, in those fables where there is an apparent collision of meanings. Denton Fox, for example, comments that it is "fairly obvious that the solution to this apparent discrepancy between the fable itself, which appears to approve the Cock, and the *moralitas,* which explicitly condemns him, lies in the fact that Henryson is working on several levels of meaning, or to put it differently, is using a figurative technique."[18] Clark, replying to what he sees as Fox's incorrect emphasis on the harshness of the *Fables,* sees the narrative as being "transformed" by the moralization into an evocation of the difficulty confronting any exercise of freewill.[19] Implicit in both ways of reading is a negation of the reader's initial response to the tale—the necessity for this exists in the minds of the critics rather than in the poetry, which is more flexible than either recognizes. For although in **"The Cock and the Jasp"** there are details of the narrative and the dramatic monologue which can be seen to provide, as it were, a retrospective "justification" for the *moralitas,* the *taill* itself continues to be amenable to the reading which sees the Cock as a figure of the man who is wisely content with his lot. Both interpretations of the fable are finally possible, although in terms of the metaphor in the **"Prologue"** it is the interpretation endorsed by the *moralitas* which constitutes the "kirnell": the "science" celebrated by the *moralitas* is of course superior to the commonsense wisdom represented in the tale. Henryson's distinctive treatment of the traditional story enables it to carry a double "sentence," one part of which is explicit and highly ingenious, the other implicit and eminently natural. Obviously, the kind of double response outlined here depends on our being able to read poetic allegory with the kind of flexibility and sensitivity to paradox which is embodied in the **"Prologue"**'s image of flowers and corn, equally "hailsum and gude to mannis sustenence." Gray observes that Henryson has in this fable "set up a careful, hidden pattern of irony at the expense of the cock, and surreptitiously and wittily has operated the same pattern against us, his readers."[20] He refers to E. H. Gombrich's first example of the impenetrability of pictorial illusion, the trick drawing from *Die Fliegenden Blätter* which is either a rabbit or a duck, depending on how we look at it (*Art and Illusion,* p. 5). The parallel is an illuminating one, providing that we recognize that both areas of allegorical meaning, the "natural" and the "dark," like the illusions in the trick drawing, exist with equal force and validity. (Perhaps an even more appropriate pictorial analogue to the illusion-building in **"The Cock and the Jasp"** might be the kind of Elizabethan perspective painting alluded to in Cleopatra's image of Antony's doubleness— "Though he be painted one way like a Gorgon, The other way's a Mars." This kind of perspective picture usually has a richer surface texture and a greater representational accuracy than the kind of drawings to which Gombrich refers.)

Elsewhere in the *Fables,* it is possible to find a more explicit validation for the kind of double-sided response which **"The Cock and the Jasp"** requires. **"The Paddock and the Mouse,"** probably intended as the concluding fable, is unique in the collection in that it has not one but two *moralitates* at the end of the *taill.* The first of these follows in a natural, organic way from the vividly particular account of how the mouse in her desire to partake of delights on the opposite bank of the stream allows herself to be won over by a suspicious-looking frog, with predictably disastrous consequences—both frog and mouse are seized by an observant kite who is even more greedy than the mouse, and strong enough not to have need of the frog's seductive eloquence. The moral that caution is a necessary part of any personal commitment:

> Be war thairfore with quhome thow fallowis the
>
> (2914)
>
> . . . . .
>
> Grit folie is to gif ouer sone credence
> To all that speiks fairlie vnto the
>
> (2920-21)

is so obvious that it is not necessary for there to be explicit reference to the action of the tale. There follows a second signification, clearly marked off from the first by a change of stanza form and by explicit authorial comment:

> This hald in mynd; rycht more I sall the tell
> Quhair by thir beistis may be figurate.
>
> (2934-5)

The *taill* is now explicated as an allegory of the soul's bondage to the body, swimming "with cairis implicate" through the turbulent waters of the world. The thread which binds together the legs of frog and mouse is life itself, easily and unexpectedly severed by death, *alias* the kite. This interpretation has an ingenious force, not least because of what the figure implies about the desperate and always potentially discordant relationship between spirit and matter.

> The spreit vpwart, the body precis doun;
> The saull rycht fane wald be brocht ouer, I wis,
> Out of this warld into the heuinnis blis.
>
> (2959-61)

The conventional identification of waves with worldly strife acquires new force in Henryson's masterly alliterative colloquialism within the control of an insistently rhetorical form.

> Now dolorus, now blyth as bird on breir;
> Now in fredome, now wardit in distres;
> Now haill and sound, now deid and brocht on beir;
> Now pure as Iob, now rowand in riches;
> Now gounis gay, now brats laid in pres;
> Now full as fishe, now hungrie as ane hound;
> Now on the quheill, now wappit to the ground.
>
> (2941-7)

The allegory works, but only if we are prepared to accept certain inconsistencies between the details of the *taill* and the interpretation which is proposed. (In this respect the *moralitas-taill* link differs from that of **"The Cock and the Jasp,"** because there the particulars of the tale can be accommodated to the allegorical interpretation). The reader who demands complete consistency between figure and interpretation will be hard put to make any theological sense out of the mouse's foolish willingness to join herself to the paddock: the implication that the soul's hunger for "the heuinnis blis" on the other side of life's troubled stream could lead it to accept control by the body is nonsense. So too is the conclusion to which a consistency-conscious interpretation of the kite must lead—namely, that death, which cuts the strife between body and soul, also ends the journey to heaven's bliss. The second part of the *moralitas* depends not only on certain details of the tale itself, but also on the first part of the *moralitas:* the soul is implicitly likened to the mouse who abrogates responsibility. Thus the first three stanzas of the *moralitas* are seen to gain their point not so much by relation to the *taill,* but by their connection with what follows from "rycht more I sall the tell." The folly exemplified in the mouse is, in terms of the final allegorization, the kind which leads to damnation. The kite is evoked with the same kind of savagery as the fiendish churl in **"The Preaching of the Swallow."** Henryson does not make the connection explicit, but the implied link between unprepared death and damnation underlies his quiet prompting towards vigilance and "gud deidis." That the poet's main concern is not with making the terms of the allegory absolutely consistent with the working out of the *taill* is very clearly highlighted by the juxtaposition of two very different, and partly contradictory, *moralitates.* The total effect of the fable is two-fold: a stern reminder of the frailty and unpredictability of earthly things co-exists with a sympathetic and good-humored involvement in the world of transparently human animal creation, an involvement which continually draws attention to itself through the wit and suppleness of the poetic language. The two views of reality are seen, by the end of the fable, to be complementary: the affirmation of life gives depth and poignancy to the warning of its transience. What is advocated, here and in other of Henryson's fables, is understanding rather than rejection of the world. The final stanza illustrates a characteristic and highly appropriate fusion of wit and high seriousness:

Adew, my freind, and gif that ony speiris
Of this fabill, sa schortlie I conclude,
Say thow, I left the laif vnto the freiris,
To mak a sample or similitude.
Now Christ for vs that deit on the rude,
Of saull and lyfe as thow art Saluiour,
Grant vs till pas in till ane blissit hour.

This elaborate fable, the only one of the collection to have two *moralitates,* is not of course ended "schortlie" at all, and the irony is Henryson's way of directing his audience towards the individuality of his achievement. Those whose tastes are for a simple connection between morality and art may find what they seek with the friars.

In **"The Cock and the Jasp,"** a tension between literal and figurative ways of reading is sharply emphasized by the apparent failure of the *moralitas* to answer to the mood of the tale. In **"The Paddock and the Mouse,"** a tension is highlighted by the form of the *moralitas* itself. Each fable achieves its effect by sudden shifts in perspective: the reader is left to find ways of reconciling the intellectual ingenuity of the *moralitas* with the realism which proceeds from a configuration of descriptive detail, plot development, and dramatic speech. The naturalistic mode for which the *Fables* have so frequently been praised should be recognized as only one element, albeit an important one, in a predominantly non-naturalistic poetic. The reader who comes to these poems with the assumption that there should be a logical, organic connection between the two parts of their formal structure will not be disappointed by fables such as **"The Two Mice," "The Cock and the Fox," "The Wolf and the Wether," "The Wolf and the Lamb," "The Sheep and the Dog,"** and **"The Preaching of the Swallow."** One testimony to the intelligence which conceived these poems is that although the moral interpretation proceeds unambiguously from the narrative, it is never trite or anticlimactic. **"The Wolf and the Lamb"** and **"The Sheep and the Dog,"** for example, are bold and topical explorations of injustice: in both fables, the function of the *moralitas* is to bridge the distance between the poetic fiction and the world of the poet and his audience. Here the *moralitates* disturb by the the urgency of the authorial voice as it pleads with God and man for an end to the exploitation of the poor and innocent. In neither of these, nor in the magnificently wide-ranging fable of the swallow and her companions does humor (except of the most dark and bitter kind) play any part. So serious are their moral preoccupations, it would appear, that there can be no disjunction between *taill* and *moralitas,* no room for misunderstanding or evasion of the issues raised. I mention these works here because I do not wish to suggest that the kinds of indirect and witty yoking of the two conventional elements of fable structure are necessarily the marks of a superior kind of poetic composition.[21] All of Henryson's *Fables* are dialectic in structure, but in some of them the oppositions exist between elements within the narrative rather than between narrative and its formal explication.

The expectation that the *moralitas* of a fable "suld correspond and be equiualent" to the logic of the preceding narrative does not arise, usually, in the experience of reading other medieval beast fables. What distinguishes Henryson's works from most of their sources and analogues is the extent of naturalistic detail, physical and psychological, with which the narrative is presented. The mode of the narrative is itself an encouragement to the organic kind of interpretation, but the poet frequently challenges his audience's assumptions about what makes sense. At least once in the *Fables,* there is something close to parody, as an apparently arbitrary link is made between the "moralitee" and a detail of the story. In **"The Fox, the Wolf, and the Husbandman,"** the wolf and the fox are likened, respectively, to a wicked man and the devil, while the husbandman becomes a figure of the godly man, and the woods and the cheese images of worldly riches and covetousness. All of this is ingeniously and enjoyably relevant to the logic of the tale. A comically discordant note is struck, though, by the apportioning of an allegorical value to the husbandman's hens:

> The hennis are warkis that fra ferme faith proceidis:
> Quhair sic sproutis spreidis, the euill spreit thair not
>   speids,
> Bot wendis vnto the wickit man agane—
> That he hes tint his trauell is full vnfane.

(2437-40)

The similitude between hens and good deeds appears ridiculously far-fetched, and even more so the implied need to relate *all* of the major elements of the *taill* to the moralization. There seems here to be some playful mockery of the assumption that poetic allegory involves a patient working out of all the later details. Characteristically, though, Henryson manages to have it both ways, and to give the game a serious edge. For when we return to the *taill* itself, we can see that the allegorization has a kind of relevance, since it is only the husbandman's possession of the hens which saves him from the depredations of the fox and the wolf. (Obviously enough, the allegory will not work if we insist on a strictly literal interpretation, which would have the virtuous man using his good deeds to buy off the devil). The inclusion of this apparently insignificant detail has a similar effect to the omission of apparently important episodes from the *moralitates* of two other fables, **"The Cock and the Fox"** and **"The Two Mice."**

Henryson's delight in the sudden leap from one level of interpretation to another—usually when his reader least expects it—presupposes a high degree of confidence in his audience's powers of assimilation and discrimination. It is unwarranted, I believe, to regard some of the fables as being less successful than others on the grounds that the high-minded admonitions and exhortations of the *moralitates* are not always supported, and in fact are sometimes apparently contradicted, by the approval of clever and self-satisfied worldliness implicit in the texture of the poetry. It is not necessarily the function of the "poesye" to prove or support the "preching" at all, although few readers can have failed to notice how the cleverest representatives of Henryson's human/beast world overreach themselves, usually with disastrous consequences. I agree with Ian Jamieson when he suggests that the **Fables** carry the marks of an experimental essay on the theme of transitoriness, that they illustrate different ways of exploring the question "How shal the world be served?"[22] But I disagree with him about the degree of success which the experiment achieves. He finds something distracting, and ultimately detrimental to the seriousness of the poetry, about the way in which it sometimes presents sin as being funny and even admirable. The poet's identification with the sin-prone natural world is emphasized several times by the dream-vision device of his physical presence as "I," but nowhere with such deliberately startling effect, surely, as in **"The Fox and the Wolf"** and **"The Trial of the Fox,"** where the sober preacher of the *moralitates* represents himself as the pupil of the wily Lawrence (*ll.* 634, 884). One of the effects of the naturalistic, dramatic mode employed in most of the *taillis* is to convey a strong sense of delight in aspects of the fallen world to which the poet and his audience belong.[23] This involvement coexists, however, with an equally strong sense of the world's transience, and its capacity for confusing the unwary and the weak-minded. In **"The Trial of the Fox,"** the lion is presented by the narrative as an impressively just (if somewhat gullible) worldly ruler: the *moralitas,* however, presents a view of the lion which seems disconcertingly at odds with this. He is now "the warld . . . To quhome loutis baith empriour and king" (*ll.* 1104-5), a force to be shunned by "monkis and othir men of religioun." It is noteworthy, though, that what is represented here by the lion is condemned only inasmuch as it has the potential to lead men astray: the lion is dangerous only when the rule of sensuality is adopted,

> As quhen lyke brutall beistis we accord
> Our mynd all to this warldis vanitie.

(1119-20)

"*All* to this warldis vanitie": the effect is not unlike that created by the address to "yonge fresshe folkes" at the conclusion of *Troilus and Criseyde,* where the very terms in which the world is dismissed evoke the sense of its inevitable and legitimate attraction. Henryson's poetry is indeed "Chaucerian" to the extent that it reflects a dualistic perspective on the world—on the one hand delight, and on the other a keen awareness of pain, mortality, and the immanence of divine justice.

This complex viewpoint is implicit in the **"Prologue,"** in its alternation from wittily understated aesthetic theorizing to stern reproof, and in the indirect and sometimes startling connections which are made between narrative and moralization in the fables themselves.

Notes

1. "Henryson's *Fables,*" *ELH,* 29 (1962), pp. 337-56.

2. *The Poems of Robert Henryson,* ed. Denton Fox (Oxford, 1981), p. 187. All quotations are from this edition.

3. In his article, "Henryson and Aesop: the Fable Transformed," *ELH,* 43 (1976), pp. 1-18, George Clark suggests that within the Prologue itself there is an implied contrast between the present work and the conventional Aesopic fable (pp. 2, 5). But this is to underestimate the extent to which Henryson represents the aims and methods of his own work indirectly, in terms of the Aesopic tradition. Clark's comments on the Henrysonian "I" within the fables themselves are, however, very revealing.

4. In Julia Bastin, ed. *Recueil général des Isopets* (SATF, 2 vols., Paris 1929-30), Vol. 2. See also Fox, *Poems,* p. 194.

5. *Poems,* p. 189.

6. *Poems,* p. 189.

7. "'To preue thare preching be a poesye': Some Thoughts on Henryson's Poetics," *Parergon,* 8 (1974), pp. 28-9.

8. *Poems,* p. 192.

9. *Poems,* p. 193.

10. *Chaucer's 'Book of Fame'* (Oxford, 1967), p. 54.

11. *Robert Henryson* (Leiden, 1979), p. 121. Gray's discussion of Henryson's exploitation of the connection between animal and human worlds (pp. 70-117) is particularly helpful. His view of the Prologue does not find in it the degree of ingenuity suggested here, although with his general conclusions I am basically in agreement.

12. *Robert Henryson: A Study of the Major Narrative Poems* (Oxford, 1967), pp. 100-5.

13. MacQueen, *Robert Henryson,* pp. 107-10; Fox, "Henryson's *Fables,*" p. 344.

14. *The Minor Poems of John Lydgate,* ed. H. N. MacCracken (EETS, 1911, 1934), Vol. 2, no. 24.

15. "Henryson and Aesop," p. 7.

16. "Henryson's *Fables*," p. 343.

17. Stanley E. Fish, *Surprised by Sin* (London, 1967).

18. "Henryson's *Fables*," p. 343.

19. "Henryson and Aesop," p. 10.

20. *Robert Henryson*, p. 123.

21. See also Harold E. Toliver, "Robert Henryson: from *Moralitas* to Irony," *ES* [*English Studies*] 46 (1965), pp. 300-9. Toliver does not altogether succeed in illustrating his central proposition that Henryson's *moralitates* "dissolve both sympathy and moral judgment in an ironic solution."

22. "To preue thare preching be a poesye," pp. 31-2.

23. Gray draws attention to what he calls "a suggestion of tentativeness about most of the *moralitates*," in the context of this relativism within the *Fables* (pp. 129-30). His account of the "dark" moralities is particularly stimulating.

George D. Gopen (essay date winter 1985)

SOURCE: Gopen, George D. "The Essential Seriousness of Robert Henryson's *Moral Fables*: A Study in Structure." *Studies in Philology* 82, no. 1 (winter 1985): 42-59.

[In the following essay, Gopen examines the irony and political allegory found in Henryson's Moral Fables.*]*

I. The Seriousness of the *Moral Fables*

The *Moral Fables* has long been underrated, even by its foremost proponents. Lord Hailes, in 1770, thought enough of several of the *Moralitates* to print them, but he left out the corresponding fables.[1] H. Harvey Wood, in his editions of Henryson's complete works (1933, 1958), called the *Fables* "the greatest, and the most original, of Henryson's works," but still referred to it as a "translation," rejoicing that "the moralising, which is admittedly dull, is confined to the postscript."[2] Older criticism tended to confine its praise to the work's charming humor, detailed realism, level-headedness, and careful maintenance of the human/bestial irony. In general, Henryson's major work was dismissed as more or less innocuous, but containing occasional flashes of sensitivity.

Since the 1960's there seems to have been a resurgence of interest in all of Henryson's work. Oxford University Press has issued new editions of all the poetry,[3] the *Moral Fables* has spawned more than a dozen Ph.D. theses, the *Testament of Cresseid* has been called one of the greatest poems in English,[4] and even the minor poems are beginning to receive individual attention.[5]

Concerning the *Moral Fables* in particular, there is a growing sense that something more important than typical fabulizing is at work. George Clark, in his fine article, expresses it well:

> As Henryson recreated them, his Aesopic stories outgrow the artistic and intellectual limitations of their traditional form; comparing one of Henryson's fables to its probable source, the difference seems essentially stylistic, but the development of the style produces narratives whose implications compel our attention and go beyond the explicit moralizations conventionally attached to Aesopic fables.[6]

Denton Fox states with emphasis that "both the *Fables* and the *Orpheus* are, in the end, serious poems about morality."[7] Matthew P. McDiarmid, after years of delighting in the merely pleasant aspects of the poem, has now "become aware of a personality much less at peace, a much more demanding and challenging mind, neither quite at home in his own Christian world nor easily accommodated to the taste of our materialistic one."[8] Nicolai von Kreisler has found the **"Tale of the Lion and the Mouse"** to be "invested with greater authority than the fabulist ordinarily enjoyed,"[9] an opinion of even more significance than he was aware, as I shall try to demonstrate below. Yet even recently we still hear that "a general air of assurance and calm prevails" over the poetry,[10] that the *Moral Fables* was "apparently left incomplete,"[11] and that the fables are "very lively and charming poems which one yet feels like calling *only* charming and lively."[12]

To this point, the "something more important than typical fabulizing" has been identified as the delicate yet forceful nature of Henryson's irony[13] or his alleged use of political allegory.[14] I suggest, however, that Henryson's highly serious and highly cynical message in the *Moral Fables* comes to us through the subtle yet substantially important structure of the poem, which in turn requires the conclusion that the poem is a unified and complete work and by no means "*only* charming and lively" (though indeed most charming and most lively). While we can enjoy Henryson's *Fables* on first reading because of the sheer delight produced by his wit, his humor, his love of language, his sensitive ear, and his keen perception of human nature, a better understanding of the literary aspects of the work, especially its structure, can generate additional appreciation of his fundamental seriousness, his frustration over human weaknesses, his deep sense of pity, and, ultimately, his rather bleak view of human existence (or at least of life in fifteenth-century Scotland). We should allow neither the bright view nor the bleak one to dominate our attention; they are both continually present in the work, and the friction between the two, which produces emotional and intellectual paradoxes at many points, may be the very agent that keeps us captivated, perhaps increasingly captivated, upon many re-readings.

The structure will be discussed below; here let us look at the other signs that the work is no mere humorous entertainment.

Henryson gives us three clues at the outset that the **Moral Fables** will be a work of high seriousness. The first is his choice of stanza form, Rhyme Royal, which Martin Stevens has demonstrated was intended only for elevated poetry dealing with the most solemn of subjects and occasions, perhaps originally limited to public ceremonies at which the monarch was present.

> rhyme royal was the first consciously shaped stanza of high style in English Literature. After Chaucer used it with such great flexibility in the *Troilus,* it set the mode for serious, elevated long poems in the English language until the sixteenth century. There is certainly no doubt that the stanza was the favorite among Chaucer's imitators throughout the fifteenth century.[15]

While Henryson's use of the form by no means guarantees the seriousness of his content, it should at least prepare his readers for the possibility of a solemn literary experience, despite his displays of humor and homeliness.

Henryson gives us the second clue in his **"Prologue"** when he raises the question of how to justify the use of frivolous verse and, simultaneously, warns us that we will have to work hard to extract his deeper meanings. In his opening stanza he defends "feinyeit fabils of ald poetre" (fictitious poetic fables of old) which, although not "al grunded upon truth" (entirely based on truth), still have an important function, "to repreif the haill misleing / Off man by figure of an uther thing" (to criticize man's evil ways through allegory and symbol). He implies that most writing of this sort tends towards the dour and the dull, and therefore he will lighten the task by using his sometimes humorous animals.

> And clerkis sayis, it is richt profitabill
> Amangis ernist to ming ane merie sport,
> To blyth the spreit and gar the tyme be schort.
>
> And scholars say it is most profitable to mix a merry sport in with earnest matters, to lighten the spirit and make the time seem short.
>
> (19-21)[16]

He repeats the thought in the next stanza: "With sad materis sum merines to ming, / Accordis weill" (It makes good sense to mix some merriness with matters that are sober). Note, however, his emphasis: lightness must be *added to* the general solemnity; he writes in earnest and mixes in the merriness. We misunderstand his purpose, then, if we allow his delightful touches to dominate our attention.

We are also warned that these fables are tough nuts to crack (stanza 3) and that we must expect to strain our minds somewhat if we are to make complete sense of the work. This, then, is our second clue: we should not be fooled by the presence of "merriness" into disregarding the essential seriousness of the work. Since fifteenth-century readers considered fables to be literary works of the highest seriousness, we should not hesitate to apply Denton Fox's statement about the tragic poem, **The Testament of Cresseid,** to the **Moral Fables** as well: "Henryson took for granted an audience who would see, because they were looking for it, the evidence that this poem was serious, moral, and Christian."[17] Henryson gives us our third clue by his particular use of the traditional content of the first fable, the **"Tale of the Cock and the Jasper."** Because of its direct applicability to the reader and to the experience of reading fables, this tale has often appeared first in Aesopic collections. While looking for food one morning, a Cock finds a rare gem on a dunghill but passes it by in favor of finding something more digestible. In the usual moral application, the Cock represents the foolish man, and the Jasper, wisdom, an allegorical formula that warns the readers against the folly of disregarding wisdom (i.e., the fables that follow) when it lies before them. Henryson follows this tradition, and in his *Moralitas* he laments the disappearance of moral wisdom in his world ("But now, alas, this Gem is lost and hidden"), urging us to seek it out:

> Go seik the iasp, quha will, for thair it lay.
>
> Go, seek the Jasper, you who will, for there it lies.

"Thair" seems indeed to refer to the fables which follow.

Simultaneously, however, Henryson differs from all previous recounters of this fable, as George Clark points out,[18] by expanding the tale with a great many details which make the Cock's rejection of the Jasper look rather praiseworthy. This bird rises early and sets about his major task with diligence, in contrast to the young girls "wonton and insolent" who have so little regard for their work that they sweep out precious jewels with the trash. The Cock recognizes the nobility of the Jasper immediately, knows its true worth and rightful place (78-84), considers the irony of a lowly animal having found it (85-91), considers his own needs and limitations in life (92-105), rhetorically wishes the Jasper better fortune (106-12), and departs. Clark suggests that Henryson hands us a particularly hard nut to crack by complicating the story with these compelling details.

> If the Cock does not reject the jewel out of arrogance or exclusive preoccupation with bestial appetite but because a real barnyard cock cannot pocket or possess a gemstone, the simplistic moral proposition that the free agent, man, willfully disregards the wisdom that could secure him all the possible benefits of this and the next world gives place to a powerful impression that man, the prisoner of his inescapable limitations, has no plain and easy choice of wisdom and folly.[19]

The third clue, then, is our uneasiness when we discover the Cock was meant to represent the fool who disregards wisdom, instead of the wise man who knows his own limitations and has a sense of relativity.[20]

I believe the clues would awaken us to the seriousness of the poem if we had enough faith in Henryson as a serious writer to begin with; but perhaps because his name has not been adequately respected readers may have regarded the Rhyme Royal form as indicative only of the poem's antiquity, dismissed the warnings of the **"Prologue"** as *pro forma,* and judged the **"Tale of the Cock and the Jasper"** to be a botched job, a fable whose details inadequately prepare the reader for the *Moralitas.* These early promises of high seriousness, however, will be fulfilled by the moral nature of the work as a whole, especially when the reader comes to understand Henryson's structural techniques and their import.

II. The Structure of the *Moral Fables*

Although Henryson entitled his work **The Moral Fables of Aesop the Phrygian,** he took only seven of his thirteen fables from Aesopic sources. The other six come from French tales of the Reynardian tradition and from other sources. In the order that they appear in all but one of the major manuscripts and early prints, they form a neat symmetry according to source.[21]

Figure 1: The Synthetic Symmetry[22]

Aesopic	—	1) The Cock and the Jasper 2) The Two Mice
Reynardian	—	3) The Cock and the Fox 4) The Confession of the Fox 5) The Trial of the Fox
Aesopic	—	6) The Sheep and the Dog 7) The Lion and the Mouse 8) The Preaching of the Swallow
Reynardian	—	9) The Fox, the Wolf, and the Cadger 10) The Fox, the Wolf, and the Farmer 11) The Wolf and the Wether
Aesopic	—	12) The Wolf and the Lamb 13) The Paddock and the Mouse

This symmetry is "synthetic" because it cannot be perceived by the reader during the process of reading. By itself it seems relatively unimportant—order for the sake of order; but considered in conjunction with the other symmetries of the poem, this ordering takes on additional significance. For the moment we should note in particular that it leads us to considering the fables in five groupings according to source and that in this regard tales #6 through #8 form the center of the work.

Medieval poets generally considered themselves craftsmen, builders of literary works, and we should therefore never feel safe in imagining that any of their perceptible structural devices are meaningless. The very word "poet" means "one who makes something" (from the Greek *poiein*), and the Scots in particular refer to their poets as "makars." Such a hidden structural device might be created in imitation of God's creation of the world, using a divine plan that is imperceptible to the mortals who are living through the experience. The structure of many Medieval and Renaissance works of art reflects this concept of creative order (cf. Spenser's *Epithalamion*).

Closer inspection of the *Moral Fables* reveals yet another kind of symmetry, one complex in detail and pregnant with meaning, which could be called the "climactic" symmetry. It also focuses on tales #6-#8 as the center of the work, but unlike its synthetic counterpart it can be sensed by the reader and must be in order for the reader to experience the moral impact of the work as a whole. This symmetry consists of a linear development which continues throughout the work, crescendoing from the first tale to a climax at the mid-point, tale #7, and then subsiding into a decrescendo until the fictional world disintegrates in the thirteenth and final tale.

The entire development depends upon the special nature of the middle fable, **"The Tale of the Lion and the Mouse."** This tale is the work's numerical mid-point not only because it is the seventh in a group of thirteen, but also because it is preceded by precisely 200 stanzas and followed by precisely 200 stanzas.[23] Moreover, the seventh fable stands out from the others in several striking details: only this fable has its own prologue; only this fable is presented in the form of a Medieval dream-vision; only in this fable do characters actually listen to and follow wholesome advice from others; and only this fable ends happily for all of the central characters. We shall see shortly why these facts are significant.

Looking closely at the progression of the fables before and after the seventh fable, we can see the denouements of Henryson's tales increase in harshness as the work proceeds. In the first six tales (those preceding the central fable), none of the "good" characters suffers any permanent damage. The Cock in #1, the City Mouse in #2, and the Mare in #5 suffer no harm whatever; the Country Mouse in #2 and Chanticlere in #3 undergo ordeals but escape intact; and the Sheep in #6 must suffer through a bitter Winter but may survive to grow another coat of wool. Only the Fox in #5, the Wolf in #5 and the Fox in #6 suffer severe physical injury or death, and they, being predators and rogues, have earned only their just rewards. For the most part, everyone receives the fate deserved.

In the six tales that follow **"The Lion and the Mouse,"** however, the relatively sympathetic characters suffer increasingly harsher consequences: the Swallow (#8) is saddened and deprived of companionship; the Cadger (#9) is robbed; the Farmer (#10) is badly frightened and must pay a ransom; the Wether (#11) is shaken to death due to his pride; the Lamb (#12) is eaten despite his innocence and humility; and the Mouse (#13) is flayed alive. The evil characters, on the other hand, fare increasingly well: the Wolves progress from being beaten (#9) to being cheated (#10) to being scared but victorious (#11) to being well fed (#12); the Foxes (#9 and #10) succeed in cheating everyone; and the Kite (#13) encounters no resistance whatever in his murderous attack. Thus Henryson gives us a substantially and increasingly grimmer view of life in the second half of the work than in the first, demonstrating that in a deceitful and sinful world good often falls prey to evil.

All this fits into a symmetrical design that emphasizes the progression away from a world wherein frail men are forgiven or punished by a just God, and towards a world which is dominated by evil and powerful men and from which God has withdrawn.

Along with this climactic development we can perceive yet a third kind of symmetry, which can be called the "concentric" symmetry. Again, fable #7 is the focal point, but this time we can consider the tales in parallel groups receding from the center like ripples around a stone dropped in the water. Figure 2 demonstrates this organization.

The first and last tales are isolated as introduction and conclusion. In each the central characters misuse their power of self-determination; the former escapes harm, but the latter does not. Tales #2 and #12 both concern innocent non-predators (the comparatively innocent Country Mouse and the spotless Lamb, both referred to by Henryson as *sillie*), whose sound reasoning is ignored; the former escapes harm, but the latter does not. Moving still towards the center, #3 and #11 both concern proud non-predators who lack the restraint of reason; the former escapes harm, but the latter does not. The obverse situation occurs in #4 and #10, and in #5 and #9. In the earlier tales the Fox, despite his trickery, suffers death; in the later tales the Fox, despite the immorality of his trickery, succeeds.

This early group (#2-#5), then, pictures a world ruled by divine justice and/or the intervention of Fate:

> To se that selie mous, it wes grit sin;
> So desolate and will off ane gude reid;
> For verray dreid scho fell in swoun neir deid.
>
> Bot, as God wald, it fell ane happie cace:
> The spenser had na laser for to byde,
> Nowther to seik nor serche, to char nor chace,
> Bot on he went, and left the dure vp wyde.

FIGURE 2: THE CONCENTRIC SYMMETRY

1) Cock and Jasper	introduction	misuse of choice no consequences
2) Two Mice		
	non-predators escape harm	
3) Cock and Fox		
		divine justice and/or intervention
4) Confession of Fox	the Fox is killed	
5) Trial of the Fox		
6) Sheep and Dog	God forsakes man	misuse of reason
7) Lion and Mouse	vision of Utopia	proper use of reason
8) Preaching of Swallow	man forsakes God	misuse of reason
9) Fox, Wolf, and Cadger		
	the Fox succeeds	
10) Fox, Wolf, and Farmer		
		human tyranny and lack of divine intervention
11) Wolf and Wether		
	non-predators suffer harm	
12) Wolf and Lamb		
13) Paddock and Mouse	conclusion	misuse of choice fatal consequences

It was a great shame to see that poor Mouse, so desolate and lacking good counsel; for very fear she fell into a swoon, near dead.

But as God willed, a fortunate thing occurred: The Steward had no time to stop, neither to seek nor search, neither to frighten nor to chase, but on he went and left the door wide open.

(299-305 - Tale #2)

> Then spak the cok, with sum gude spirit inspyrit,
> 'Do my counsall and I sall warrand the.'
> . . . . .
>
> This tod, thocht he wes fals and friuolus,
> And had frawdis, his querrell to defend,
> Desauit wes be menis richt meruelous,
> For falset fail eis ay at the latter end.

Then said the Cock, inspired by some good spirit, "Do as I advise, and I shall guarantee you success."
. . . . .

This Fox, though he was false and not to be trusted, and had tricks enough to help him out of a corner, was himself deceived by means most miraculous; for falseness always will fail in the end.

(558-9, 565-8 - Tale #3)

The later group (#9-#12) pictures a world untouched by divine presence and ruled by human tyranny:

> The foxe beheld that seruice quhair he lay,
> And leuch on loft quhen he the volff sa seis,
> Baith deif and dosinnit, fall swonand on his kneis.

The fox observed this happen from where he lay, and laughed aloud when thus he saw the Wolf, both deaf and dazed, fall swooning to his knees.

(2186-8 - Tale #9)

'Ha,' quod the volff, 'thou wald intruse ressoun
Quhair wrang and reif suld duell in propertie.
That is ane poynt and part of fals tressoun,
For to gar reuth remane with crueltie.
Be Goddis woundis, fals tratour, thow sall de
For thy trespas, and for thy fatheris als'.
With that anone he hint him be the hals.

The seli lamb culd do na thing bot bleit:
Sone wes he hedit; the volff wald do na grace;

"Aha," (said the Wolf), "you would be inserting reason where villainy and illdoing should rightly rule. That is an example and instance of false treason, to try to make compassion abide with cruelty. By God's wounds, lying traitor, you shall die for your misdeed, and for your father's, too." With that, at once he grabbed him by the neck.

The innocent Lamb could do nothing but bleat; quickly he was dead. The Wolf would grant him no grace;

(2693-701 - Tale #12)

We therefore have three different conscious arrangements—synthetic, climactic, and concentric—all of which point to tales #6-#8 as forming the core of the work and marking its turning point. The central vision of human justice (#7) is surrounded by the tale of the innocent Sheep who can find no justice (#6) and the tale of the proud flock of birds who ignore wisdom and suffer an unhappy end in which justice is no longer a question (#8).

In tale #6 the Sheep laments the lack of divine intervention in his world:

Quaikand for cauld, sair murnand ay amang,
Kest vp his ee vnto the heuinnis hicht,
And said, "O lord, quhy sleipis thow sa lang?
Walk, and discerne my cause groundit on richt;
Se how I am be fraud, maistrie, and slicht
Peillit full bair, and so is many one
Now in this warld richt wonder wo begone.

Shivering from the cold, lamenting sorely all the while, he cast his eyes up to the heights of heaven and said: "Lord God, why sleep you so long? Awake, and pass judgment on my cause, which is founded on truth; see how I by fraud, corruption, and deception, am stripped full bare;" and so is many a one in this world now, plagued in the extreme.

(1293-9)

The world literally has been God-forsaken. In the central tale, #7, Henryson demonstrates that we could still survive, even without divine intervention, if we only would listen to reason. The Lion, Lord of beasts, literally "awakes and passes judgment" on the Mouse's cause, tempering his personal sense of outrage with reason and open-handed justice:

Quhen this wes said, the lyoun his language
Paissit, and thocht according to ressoun,
And gart mercie his cruell ire asswage,
And to the mous grantit remissioun,
Oppinnit his pow, and scho on kneis fell doun,
And baith hir handis vnto the heuin vpheild,
Cryand, 'Almichty God mot ʒow forʒeild!'

When this was said, the Lion reconsidered his words and let reason rule his thinking, and let mercy assuage his cruel anger, and he granted the Mouse remission. He opened his paw, and she fell down on her knees, and both her hands she held up to heaven, crying "May almighty God requite you!"

(1503-9)

Henryson follows this fable with **"The Preaching of the Swallow,"** which demonstrates by contrast what happens in a God-forsaken world when we do not listen to reason, when we abandon righteous teachings.

Allace, it wes grit hart sair for to se
That bludie bowcheour beit thay birdis doun,
And for till heir, quhen thay wist weill to de,
Thair cairfull sang and lamentatioun.
Sum with ane staf he straik to eirth on swoun,
Off sum the heid, off sum he brak the crag,
Sum half on lyfe he stoppit in his bag.

Alas, it made the heart lament to see that bloody Butcher beating down those birds, and to hear their woeful song and lamentation when they knew well they were about to die. Some with a club he struck to the earth unconscious; he beat the head of some, he broke the neck of others, and some he stuffed into his bag half-dead.

(1874-80)

Henryson uses the symbol of the net to represent human disaster. The Lion is able to escape the hunters' net because his previous use of reason had gained him allies who could bite the cords; but the birds of the following fable are caught fast in the fowler's net because of their having ignored reason beforehand.

The solidity of complex structures of the *Moral Fables* depends to a great extent upon the ability of the central fable to support the weight of its central position and function. In its unique prologue, the narrator walks out into the beautiful fields (representing perhaps the natural goodness of the God-given world), falls asleep, and has a dream-vision. Aesop appears, and after complaining that holy preaching no longer has any effect, consents to tell the following tale. A Mouse, having been captured by a Lion whom he had awakened from a deep sleep, forcefully and intelligently pleads to be released. The Lion is convinced by the Mouse's reasoning and therefore sets him at liberty. Later, when the Lion has been entrapped by villagers' nets, the Mouse summons other mice, frees the Lion, and all happily go on their ways. The narrator then awakens and returns home.

The importance of this tale (and only this tale's) being a dream-vision cannot be underestimated. Nicolai von Kreisler has explained well the general significance of the dream-vision and has suggested its effect on Henryson's fable:

> Abundantly reinforced in the Middle Ages in scriptural and secular writing, the tradition that fostered these strategies was, stated simply, that the most valuable of the ways a man knows truth are the dreams, visions, trances, swoons, ravishings, and ecstacies wherein his soul frees itself from the operation of his body and apprehends truth directly and insensibly, as if it had flown to its own inimitable and immaterial realms. . . . In identifying **"The Lion and the Mouse"** as a dream-vision, therefore, Henryson sought at once to objectify this lesson and to invest it with greater authority than the fabulist ordinarily enjoyed. Specifically, in signifying that his lesson derived from the divine inspiration of the visionary as well as the fabulist's keen worldly observation, Henryson added force to his allegory, for his unmistakable implication was that if "figures" were sensible embodiments or personifications of the truth one could know from the soul's dream-flight as well as symbols of the universal truths knowable in the material world.[24]

Unfortunately, von Kreisler goes on to conclude that all this special emphasis "almost certainly finds explanation in the political implications of his narrative," turning the *Moral Fables* into an allegory of the misrule of James III, and little more. We can see, however, from the effect that the structure of the work has on its meaning, that the significance of the dream-vision reached much further. It gives us Henryson's Utopian vision, presentable only as a dream: a world wherein men listen to each other, allow themselves to be swayed by reason, justice, and mercy, and remember their debts to each other with gratitude. It is a glorious world, in which the Lion can lie down with the Mouse; but unfortunately, it is only a dream, and at its end we must awake and return to the real world.

To underscore this, Henryson repeats the process with significant alterations in the following tale, **"The Preaching of the Swallow."** There the narrator also walks out into the beautiful fields, but this time he remains awake. Again he sees characters reasoning with each other, but in this non-dream world the Swallow's logic is ridiculed and ignored. As a result, the other birds must suffer a bloody death, described in the harshest detail of the work to that point (see 1874-80, quoted above).

The introductory stanzas to **"The Preaching of the Swallow"** turn the reader's attention, at great length, to the presence of a universal order, filled with the beneficence of nature and great promises of personal fulfillment and fruitfulness. Throughout it, as Denton Fox has pointed out, there is "a sturdy progression

towards the natural world of the birds in the fable: the movement is from God to nature, from eternal stability to seasonal mutability, from abstract to general philosophy to concrete specific experience,"[25] leading, I would add, from the world of the dream-vision back towards a world of a most bitter wakefulness. At the beginning of the tale the narrator's visual experience still sounds like the dream-vision of the tale that has just ended; "mouing thusgait, grit myrth I take in mynd, / Off lauboraris to se the besines. . . . In hart gritlie reiosit off that sicht" ("As I wandered thus, I was overjoyed to see the industry of the laborers. . . . My heart greatly rejoicing in that sight") (1720-1, 1728); but by end, sight has become painful: "Allace, it was grit hart sair for to se / that bludie bowcheour beit thay birdis down" ("Alas, it made my heart lament to see that bloody Butcher beating down those birds" (1874-5).

Henryson also makes the transition from the dream world back to the real one in terms of the natural progression of the four seasons, describing two complete cycles[26]: in introducing the tale of the Swallow he begins with Summer (1678) and ends with Spring (1706), but the action of the tale begins in Spring (1713) and ends in Winter (1832). The Summer to Spring cycle suggests a spirit of renewal of a continuing, vigorous, hopeful life; such is the atmosphere of the beginning of this fable, as if the aura of the previous tale had not yet worn off. The Spring to Winter cycle suggests quite the opposite, a dispirited sense of woeful inevitability, a linear progression ending in death, instead of the circular progression ending in renewal of life; such is the "reality" of the world of the Swallow.

Aesop's complaint seems to have been justified: the Swallow's holy preaching had no effect. Henryson never allows the shock of this return from Utopia to die away, and he constantly increases the harshness of the tales' outcomes, saving the most hideous for last. Blindness, appetite, and the ignoring of reason have so completely taken over by then that Henryson dares put the good advice into the mouth of the very character who ignores it. The Mouse recognizes that the frightening physiognomy of the Paddock bodes ill for any alliance between them (2819-32), and even listens to the Paddock decry silken tongues that disguise deceit (2848-50); yet still she allows her appetite to overwhelm her good sense, which results in a most grisly death for her. When the Kite comes to destroy them both, we view an image in little of this world's day of destruction: the Kite (who represents death, we are told in the *Moralitas*) pulls the skin of his victims (who represent the body and the soul) over their heads in one deft motion (*bellieflaucht full fettilie* in Middle Scots), suggesting the ultimate in thoroughness and cold-bloodedness.

Taken individually, these fables most impress the reader with their charm and humor, with their isolated moments of insight into character, and with their technical grace; but when they are viewed in the context of the complex structure of the work as a whole, they have a strikingly different impact. The whole in this case is indeed greater than the sum of its parts. The three symmetries—the synthetic, the climactic, and the concentric—function simultaneously, each with a different effect on the reader, and each making a different contribution to meaning.

The synthetic symmetry

The alternations of Aesopic and Reynardian fables can neither be sensed nor "used" by the reader. They represent mere order, order as a given of the universe, describable neither as static nor dynamic because it is imperceptible. Such an expression of order is symbolic of God's divine plan, to which Henryson pays tribute: "Till understand it is aneuch, I wis, / That God in all his werkis wittie is" (It is enough to understand, I know, that God has a purpose for each of His works).

(1662-3)

The climactic symmetry

The crescendo climaxing in the central fable and disintegrating thereafter may be both sensed and used by the reader. It symbolizes order as a moral force, describable as dynamic because it is available only through the dynamic reading process. It warns directly of worldly dangers and leads through its ups and downs to an ending of worldly despair.

The concentric symmetry

The "ripples" of concentricity can hardly be sensed by the reader, but can be used. They symbolize order as a moral force, describable as static because of the distance, perspective, and careful investigation necessary to perceive it, available only in the static experience of viewing the whole in retrospect. It suggests the possibility of discovering patterns in life, but hints that this knowledge may come too late.

The tension between despair over the future and amusement in the details of the present gives Henryson's work its intriguing quality of restlessness. With the exception of the central dream vision, the world of the *Moral Fables* is not a happy one, despite the elegance of the art and the persistence of the humor. As the work progresses, the world of deadly sins, with sadness overcoming joy and depravity overcoming innocence, increasingly dominates. It is filled with persecution, suffering, irresponsible trickery, studied injustice, and sheer gratuitous malevolence. Some moral indictment is levelled at all the characters except the Sheep, the Swallow, and the Lamb, who instead are subjected to some of the harshest fates in the *Moral Fables.* In each tale but the central one, an animal either is called to obey reason but ignores it, or tries to follow reason but is prevented. The work as a whole charts a progression of

increasing frustration that finally reposes in despair. We move from the admonition to seek out wisdom (in **"The Cock and the Jasper"**) through the discovery of Utopia (in **"The Lion and the Mouse"**) to the finality of universal destruction (in **"The Paddock and the Mouse"**) and we find that Henryson has suggested *through his structure* the common Medieval resolution to the human predicament, the same resolution that he makes explicit in the complaint of the Sheep in tale #6.

'Seis thow not, lord, this warld ouerturnit is,
As quha wald change gude gold in leid or tyn?
The pure is peillit, the lord may do na mis,
And simonie is haldin for na syn.
Now is he blyith with okker maist may wyn;
Gentrice is slane, and pietie is ago.
Allace, gude lord, quhy tholis thow it so?

'Thow tholis this euin for our grit offence;
Thow sendis vs troubill and plaigis soir,
As hunger, derth, grit weir, or pestilence;
Bot few amendis now thair lyfe thairfoir.
We pure pepill as now may do no moir
Bot pray to the: se that we ar opprest
In to this eirth, grant vs in heuin gude rest.'

"Lord, do you not see this world is thrown into chaos, just as some would change pure gold into lead or tin; the poor man is stripped bare, but the great man can do no wrong; and Simony is considered no sin. Now he considers himself the happiest who can win the greatest profit by extortion; kindness is slain, and pity is a thing of the past; alas, good Lord, why do You suffer it to be so?

You suffer this even for our great offense; You send us troubles and sore plagues, as hunger, dearth, great war, and pestilence; and yet this causes few to mend their way of living. We poor people, as of now, may do no more than pray to Thee; since on this earth we are so oppressed, in heaven may God grant us rest."

(1307-20)

Notes

1. Sir David Dalrymple Hailes, *Ancient Scottish Poems, Published from the Manuscript of George Bannatyne,* 1568 (Edinburgh, 1770, rpt. London, 1815), p. 280.

2. H. Harvey Wood, *The Poems and Fables of Robert Henryson,* p. xv. Although Henryson himself states that he is making "ane maner of Translatioun" (32), we should by no means take him literally on this point. All source studies have demonstrated, knowingly or otherwise, how strikingly Henryson differs from whatever previous works he used.

3. *Robert Henryson: Poems,* ed. Charles Elliott, 2nd ed. (Oxford, 1974); *The Poems of Robert Henryson,* ed. Denton Fox (Oxford, 1981).

4. See Jane Adamson's lengthy and spirited article, "Henryson's *Testament of Cresseid*: 'Fyre' and

'Cauld,'" *CR* [*Critical Review*], XVIII (1976), 39-60, and Denton Fox's compelling study in his edition of the poem (London, 1968).

5. Kenneth R. R. Gros Louis, "Robert Henryson's 'Orpheus and Eurydice' and the Orpheus Tradition of the Middle Ages," *Speculum* XLI (1966), 643-55; John Stephens, "Devotion and Wit in Henryson's 'The Annunciation,'" *ES* [*English Studies*], LI (1970), 323-31; Dorena A. Wright, "Henryson's 'Orpheus and Eurydice' and the Tradition of the Muses," *MAE* [*Medium Aevum*], XL (1971), 41-7; Denton Fox, "Henryson's 'Sum Practysis of Medecyne,'" *SP* [*Studies in Philology*], LX (1972), 453-60; Charles A. Hallet, "Theme and Structure in Henryson's 'The Annunciation,'" *SSL* [*Studies in Scottish Literature*], X (1973), 165-74; George S. Peek, "Robert Henryson's View of Original Sin in 'The Bludy Serk,'" *SSL*, X (1973), 199-206; John MacQueen, "Neoplatonism and Orpheus in Fifteenth-Century Scotland: The Evidence of Henryson's 'New Orpheus,'" *ScS* [*Scottish Studies*], XX (1976), 68-89.

6. George Clark, "Henryson and Aesop: The Fable Transfigured," *ELH*, XLIII (1976), 1.

7. Denton Fox, *The Testament of Cresseid*, p. 22.

8. Matthew P. McDiarmid, "Robert Henryson in His Poems," *Bards and Makars: Scottish Language and Literature, Medieval and Renaissance*, ed. A. J. Aitken, M. P. McDiarmid, and D. S. Thomson (Glasgow, 1977), p. 28.

9. Nicolai von Kreisler, "Henryson's Visionary Fable: Tradition and Craftsmanship in 'The Lion and the Mouse,'" *TSLL* [*Texas Studies in Literature and Language*], XV (1973), 395.

10. Maurice Lindsay, *History of Scottish Literature* (London, 1977), p. 38.

11. J. A. Burrow, "Henryson's *The Preaching of the Swallow*," *EIC* [*Essays in Criticism*], XXV (1975), 25.

12. Ian Robinson, *Chaucer and the English Tradition* (Cambridge, 1972), p. 244.

13. See especially David M. Murtaugh's fine article, "Henryson's Animals," *TSLL*, XIV (1972), 405-21.

14. See note 7, above.

15. Martin Stevens, "The Royal Stanza in Early English Literature," *PMLA*, XCIV (1979), 74.

16. The text of Henryson throughout this essay is taken from Denton Fox's edition, *The Poems of Robert Henryson* (Oxford, 1981). All translations are by the present author.

17. Denton Fox, *The Testament of Cresseid*, Introduction.

18. George Clark, "Henryson and Aesop: The Fable Transfigured," *ELH*, XLIII (1976), 1-18.

19. *Ibid.,* p. 10.

20. Several times I have assigned Freshman writing classes the task of deducing a moral from Henryson's "The Tale of the Cock and the Jasper." Not a single student has yet suggested that the Cock might represent a fool, and only a handful have sensed any negative qualities whatever in the portrait.

21. See Howard Henry Roerecke, *The Integrity and Symmetry of Robert Henryson's Moral Fables,* Diss. Pennsylvania State University, 1969. The order differs radically only in the Bannatyne Manuscript. John MacQueen, in his *Robert Henryson: A Study of the Major Narrative Poems* (Oxford, 1967), has made a carefully reasoned argument in favor of the Bannatyne ordering, but the structural relationships I discuss here convince me of the more commonly accepted order.

22. The only work I have seen that treats the *Moral Fables* as a structurally integral whole is Howard Henry Roerecke's unpublished dissertation (see note 37 above). I came to many of Professor Roerecke's conclusions independently, and I support nearly all of his findings and conclusions.

23. Roerecke, p. 126.

24. Nicolai von Kreisler, pp. 393, 395.

25. Denton Fox, "Henryson's Fables," *ELH*, XXIX (1962), 350.

26. George Clark, 13.

Eugenie R. Freed (essay date May 1987)

SOURCE: Freed, Eugenie R. "'Ane Mirour Mak of Me': Robert Henryson's *Testament of Cresseid* as a 'Mirour' of Mortality." *Unisa English Studies* 25, no. 1 (May 1987): 1-6.

[*In the following essay, Freed examines* The Testament of Cresseid *as a tribute and a sequel to Chaucer's* Troilus and Criseyde.]

'Death, thou wast once an uncouth hideous thing,
    Nothing but bones,
   The sad effect of sadder grones:
Thy mouth was open, but thou couldst not sing.

For we consider'd thee as at some six
    Or ten yeares hence,

After the losse of life and sense,
Flesh being turn'd to dust, and bones to sticks.
But since our Saviours death did put some bloud
Into thy face;
Thou art grown fair and full of grace,
Much in request, much sought for, as a good.

For we do now behold thee gay and glad,
As at dooms-day;
When souls shall wear their new aray,
And all thy bones with beautie shall be clad. . . .

George Herbert, *Death*; from *The Temple* (1633)

The art historian Emil Mâle long ago remarked that representations of the dead on thirteenth-century tombs are frequently young, handsome, already transfigured by the artist into the perfection of form in which they would participate in eternal life.[1] By the close of the fourteenth century, sepulchral effigies seem to have regressed from the concept of Death as 'fair and full of grace' to that of the 'uncouth hideous thing'. No longer, in the fifteenth century, is the departed represented as an idealised figure, 'gay and glad' in the 'new aray' in which he or she will come before the throne of God.[2] The 'double tomb', depicting the dead person both as in life and as the artist imagines the remains to look some years after burial, begins to appear. One such tomb is that of Alice de la Pole, Duchess of Suffolk and supposedly a grand-daughter of the poet Chaucer. She died in 1475, and was buried in a fine Gothic tomb at Ewelme, in Oxfordshire.[3] On the lid of her sarcophagus the calm dignity of her sculptured face, depicted as she might actually have looked in late middle age, with a certain severity of feature, is accentuated by graceful, long-fingered hands formally held together in an attitude of prayer, and by the symmetrical folds of sculptured drapery in her head-dress, long cloak and robe, sweeping along the full length of her recumbent body. Though the representation of the face may be realistic, and may even be a portrait, yet the drapery and the tomb itself create a setting which greatly ennobles the figure. Underneath this, visible through the apertures of a screen of stone tracery, the sculptor has placed a second depiction of the Duchess. There she is shown as a rotting corpse, carved in grotesquely realistic detail, the bones emerging from the shrunken form laid out on its shroud, the long hair falling away to reveal the contours of the skull. And this apparently morbid and perverse manner of memorialising the dead was by no means rare in the fifteenth century, although such tombs in Britain never attained the imaginatively repulsive realism of some of the Continent.[4] Why this apparent obsession with the physical facts of the corruption of the flesh? The obvious answer that death was never very far away from the living in the fifteenth century is not altogether adequate, for by modern standards human mortality had always been, and continued to be, high, before, during and after the later Middle Ages: for the overwhelming majority of the population, life was indeed nasty, brutish and short. But an aggravating factor entered in the middle of the fourteenth century in the form of the Black Death—bubonic plague, which spread throughout Europe from about 1347, and brought about such destruction of human life, irrespective of age or rank, as no other disaster had ever equalled. The first visitation of the plague was undoubtedly the worst, but once having come to Europe from the East it remained, flourishing—as we now know—in endemic form amongst the hordes of rodents that democratically shared the living quarters of prince and pauper alike in medieval society. Every ten years or so it would surface again amongst the human population as another epidemic. Robert Henryson, living in Dunfermline in Scotland, expressed its horrors in **"Ane Prayer for the Pest,"** which probably commemorates the outbreak of 1498-99, the worst within living memory of that time. People die, Henryson says, 'as beistis without confessioun, That nane dar mak with uthir residence' (lines 21-2).[5] He describes the manner of their death as 'crewall' and 'suddane', and punningly speaks of the epidemic as 'this byle'—figuratively 'outbreak' and literally 'boil', a graphic reference to the 'bubo', the inflamed swelling that gives its name to bubonic plague. Always lurking in the background of human consciousness, as also in the human environment, even when it was quiescent for some years this 'crewall' and 'suddane' form of death that might virtually wipe out a community in a short time sharpened and emphasised the contrast between, on the one hand, the good things and the joys of living, and, on the other, the agony, both physical and mental, of disease, deformity and a miserable death.

We have no way of knowing whether, after composing this prayer for the preservation of the community from the pestilence, Henryson then succumbed to it, or whether he survived for a few years more. We do know that he died some time before the publication in 1508 of William Dunbar's poem *Lament for the Makars*. To the remorseless drum-beat refrain '*Timor mortis conturbat me*'—'the fear of death confounds me'—Dunbar tells how Death, unsparing of the gifted, whispered in the ear of Robert Henryson and took him off: 'In Dunfermelyne he has done roune / With Maister Robert Henrysoun . . .' (lines 81-2).[6] It was the end of a life of varied achievements, in which poetry played probably only a minor part: unlike Dunbar himself, Henryson was not a professional poet. He was, however, as his poetry demonstrates, a man of great learning. He was a Master of Arts, a canon lawyer in holy orders, and—both by profession and by natural inclination—a teacher.[7] For many years he was attached to the Abbey of Dunfermline in the office of schoolmaster at the Abbey school. One of the duties of the schoolmaster was to make regular visits to the St Leonard's Hospital, a hospice for lepers on the south side of the town. The schoolmaster was probably responsible for the physical and spiritual comfort of the lepers, whose disease was at that time incurable. Henryson might have had ample opportunity to observe there at first hand all the symptoms he ascribed to the unfortunate Cresseid in *The Testament of Cresseid* as the disease ran its full course, unchecked by any effective form of treatment.

Henryson's choice of subject in *The Testament* was undoubtedly made partly in tribute to Chaucer, whom he, no less than Dunbar, Gavin Douglas, and their English predecessors John Lydgate and Thomas Hoccleve, acknowledged as his master in the arts of language.[8] Henryson's poem is a sequel to Chaucer's *Troilus and Criseyde,* taking up the account of the unhappy love affair that forms the principal matter of Chaucer's masterpiece. Chaucer had focussed the conclusion of his work upon the fate of Troilus, and Henryson respectfully indicates that no more need be said of that—

> Of his distres me neidis nocht reheirs,
> For worthie Chaucer, in the samin buik,
> In gudelie termis and in joly veirs,
> Compylit hes his cairis. . . .

> [lines 57-60]

Henryson's narrator therefore turns his attention to the fate of Criseyde (Cresseid, in the Scots version).

Criseyde has not only broken her promise that she would return to Troilus in Troy, but has also broken faith with her devoted lover by entering into a new love-relationship with the Greek warrior Diomede, to whom she has actually given a brooch, a love-token bestowed upon her by Troilus before they were separated. Although Chaucer comments reproachfully upon this last act 'that was litel nede',[9] nevertheless his final words concerning Criseyde are a plea for the reader's compassion for this 'sely womman' who is so 'slydinge of corage':[10]

> . . . if I myghte excuse hir any wyse,
> For she so sory was for hir untrouthe,
> Y-wis, I wolde excuse hir yet for routhe. . . .[11]

We hear no more of Criseyde from the Chaucerian narrator. But the account of Troilus continues: Chaucer allows him to be killed in battle, making it clear that since Criseyde has proved false to Troilus and will never return to Troy, Troilus sets little value on his life. Henryson's sequel, however, necessitates the assumption that Troilus *did* continue to live. The climax of Henryson's work is brought about through a chance meeting of Troilus and Cresseid—he still the handsomest and bravest of knights, she now a leper, a wretched outcast, physically transformed by the disease to a hideous caricature of her former self and reduced in her circumstances to begging 'with cop and clapper', in the company of other lepers, from passers-by. In a moment of tragic irony, the former lovers fail to recognise one another; but Troilus, perceiving something intangible about the poor deformed woman that reminds him of his lost love, throws her a purse full of gold coins. She is told by one of her companions that the giver was Troilus. Cresseid thereupon acknowledges her unworthiness of such steadfast love. She writes out a 'testament' in which she makes bequests of all her remaining possessions, including a ruby ring given to her by Troilus, which she bequeaths to him again; and then she dies. Troilus, receiving the ring and hearing of Cresseid's fate, has a marble monument set upon her grave.

Henryson's narrator claims to find an account of the 'fatall destenie' of Cresseid in an old book taken up by the fireside on a bitterly cold evening. He uses the conventional device of the fictitious 'auctor' also employed by Chaucer in *Troilus and Criseyde.* But it is clear from the outset that Henryson is not merely tying up a loose end left dangling by his master. He approaches his subject from the context of a very different artistic temperament, and in a mode that places its emphasis quite differently from the great Chaucerian work in the tradition of courtly love. Who knows, muses Henryson—'Quha wait gif all that Chauceir wrait was trew?' [l. 64]. It was in another age and climate, in the literal, intellectual, emotional and artistic senses, that Chaucer had, a century before Henryson, taken leave of Criseyde with a plea to posterity that 'for routhe' it 'excuse' her faults committed through weakness and fear. Henryson is fundamentally a moralist, born and raised in a harsher Northern tradition. His vision at times is tinged with a darkness that may have been the heritage of a century and a half of recurrent plague, but was no doubt intensified by his own observations of the misery and indignity caused by incurable disease. Cresseid in Henryson's sequel experiences physical as well as spiritual anguish before her 'wofull end'. She pays for her breaking of faith, and does so in a symbolic manner that juxtaposes the Chaucerian characterisation of Criseyde as a figure of star-like ideal beauty in living human form with its horrible converse, in a manner somewhat analogous to the two adjacent images on the tomb of Chaucer's grand-daughter, the Duchess of Suffolk, or in the vein of grim humour struck by Shakespeare's Hamlet a century after Henryson, when he contemplates the disinterred skull of Yorick the jester in the graveyard and comments: 'Now get you to my lady's chamber, and tell her, let her paint an inch thick, to this favour she must come; make her laugh at that.' (v.)

Henryson opens his work with a description of the season. The sun is in the sign of Aries the Ram, through which it moves from 13th March to 11th April. This is the time of year in which Chaucer set that first moment at the temple of Palladion in Troy when Troilus caught sight of Criseyde and instantly fell in love with her:

> . . . the tyme
> Of Aperil, whan clothed is the mede
> With newe grene, of lusty Ver the pryme,
> And swote smellen floures whyte and rede. . . .
>
> (Bk I, 155-8)

It is also the season of the famous springtime opening of the *Canterbury Tales,* in which the poet describes the renewal of the fertility of the earth and its creatures through the fresh spring rains and the soft south wind, while the 'yonge sonne' runs, like an impetuous lover, through the sign of the Ram. Deliberately counterpointing the opening passage of his work to these famous idealisations of the season, in which the awakening of the earth to renewed vitality is paralleled with the awakening of love, Henryson realistically presents a Scottish springtime, 'ane doolie sessoun'—'a dismal season'—whose freezing blasts dolefully set the scene for his 'cairfull dyte'—his 'tragedie':

> Ane doolie sessoun to ane cairfull dyte
> Suld correspond and be equivalent:
> Richt sa it wes quhen I began to wryte
> This tragedie, the wedder richt fervent,
> Quhen Aries, in middis of the Lent,
> Schouris of haill can fra the north discend,
> That scantlie fra the cauld I micht defend.
>
> [ll. 1-7]

The wintry weather is not exclusively meteorological. The narrator feels also the cold blast of life's winter upon him as he stands shivering in his 'oratur' to view through its glazed windows the setting of the sun and the rising of Venus the evening star. The air is crystal clear, but so cold is the wind that his old bones cannot bear it:

> The northin wind had purifyit the air
> And sched the mistie cloudis fra the sky.
> The frost freisit, the blastis bitterly
> Fra Pole Artick come quhisling loud and schill,
> And causit me remufe aganis my will.
>
> [ll. 17-21]

The narrator explains, with a touch of wistfulness, that he had intended to pray to Venus, 'luifis quene'—Queen of Love—to renew the freshness of his faded heart, but alas, 'for greit cald as than I lattit was' [l. 27]—'the terrible cold prevented me'. And so he is obliged to withdraw to his 'chalmer'—his bedchamber.

Henryson's elderly narratorial figure bears a momentary parallel with Chaucer's Reeve. The Reeve's complaint about the disabilities of age—

> Gras-tyme is doon, my fodder is now forage,
> This whyte top wryteth myne olde yeres,
> Myn herte is al-so mowled as myne heres . . .

is suggested in the vain hope expressed by Henryson's persona that Venus 'wald mak grene' his 'faidit hart'. But where the Reeve is stridently aggrieved at the rav-

ages of time, Henryson's narrator is humorously self-deprecating, and takes practical action in a cheerfully resigned and matter-of-fact manner. He repairs to the fireplace in his 'chalmer', pokes up the fire to warm his frozen limbs, pours himself a drink, wraps up snugly, and reaches for a good book, philosophising:

> Thocht lufe be hait, yit in ane man of age
> It kendills nocht sa sone as in youtheid,
> Of quhome the blude is flowing in ane rage,
> And in the auld the curage doif and deid,
> Of quhilk the fyre outward is best remeid,
> To help be phisike quhair that nature faillit:
> I am expert, for baith I have assailit.
>
> [ll. 29-35]

In contrast to the ideal spring setting of the courtly love-vision, Henryson's frame couples a freezing Scottish Lenten season with the wintry analogue of a narrator whose heart and blood have been chilled by advancing age, who resigns himself to its limitations and to the implied imminence of death. Against this backdrop there begins to unfold the account this persona claims to have found in the book he selected to while away that cold night.

Henryson immediately picks up the thread of Cresseid's life after her departure from Troy and from her heartbroken lover Troilus. She has had her fling with Diomede, who had been sent to escort her from Troy and had made his first overtures to the weeping Cresseid almost before they had ridden beyond the shadow of the city's walls. She had accepted him as her lover after an indecently short interval, and—according to Henryson's succinct account—he had tired of her in just as short a time, and had unceremoniously and unchivalrously rejected her, leaving her 'desolait'. In this situation, the narrator hints, Cresseid became promiscuous:

> Than desolait scho walkit up and doun
> And (sum men sayis) into the court, commoun.
>
> [ll. 76-7]

Chaucer had described Criseyde, dressed in the black widow's habit in which Troilus first saw her at the temple of Palladion, in the following way (BK I, ll 171-5):

> Right as our firste lettre is now an A,
> In beautee first so stood she, makelees;
> Hir godly looking gladede al the prees,
> Nas never seyn thing to ben preysed derre,
> Nor under cloude blak so bright a sterre.

Henryson assumes this idealised beauty as a basis for comparison when he comments upon Cresseid's condition after the defection of Diomede:

> O fair Cresseid, the flour and A per se
> Of Troy and Grece, how was thou fortunait!

To change in filth all thy feminitie
And be with fleschlie lust sa maculait,
And go amang the Greikis air and lait
Sa gigotlike, takand thy foull plesance.
I have pietie thou suld fall sic mischance.

[ll. 78-84]

In the next phase of the story, the spots or blemishes of
fleshly lust marked upon Cresseid's soul by her
'gigotlike' conduct become imprinted on her beautiful
body as well. Cresseid, now 'destitute / Of all comfort
and consolation' [ll. 92-3], makes her solitary way, in
disguise and on foot, back to the home of her father
Calchas the priest. Chaucer had followed the classical
story in making Calchas a priest of Apollo, but Henryson places him in a temple of Love, designating him a
priest of Venus and Cupid. A festival takes place in honour of these deities, to which people flock from far
and wide, just as they did to the festival of Palladion at
which the love of Troilus for Criseyde began. On that
occasion Criseyde had been the cynosure of every eye—
'Hir godly looking gladede al the prees'—but on this,
she flees the sight of other people, taking refuge in 'ane
secret orature / Quhair scho might weip hir wofull
destenye' [ll. 120-1]. Here, all alone, she cries out in
anger against Venus and her son, accusing them of having broken their covenant with her. She claims that they
gave her once 'ane devine responsaill'—a divine assurance—that she would be always 'the flour of luif in
Troy': but that flower has now been withered by the
frost of hard times:

Ye causit me alwayis understand and trow
The seid of lufe was sawin in my face,
And ay grew grene throw your supplie and grace.
Bot now allace that seid with froist is slane
And I fra luifferis left and all forlane.

[ll. 137-40]

Venus and Cupid react with predictable indignation to
Cresseid's blasphemous outcry. Cresseid is immediately
struck down in a trance, and experiences a vision in
which Cupid summons the seven planetary deities to sit
in judgement upon her. The gods who appear are Saturn,
Jupiter, Mars, Phoebus the sun-god, Venus, Mercury
and Cynthia the moon-goddess. They appear as alternately threatening, malevolent or ill-omened, and radiant, life-supporting, or at least apparently benevolent.
The first two, Saturn and Jupiter, father and son, also
have obvious associations with the seasons of the year
and of human life. Saturn embodies the decrepitude of
old age as well as the miseries of the freezing weather
in which the narrator claims to have begun composing
the poem:

His face fronsit, his lyre was lyke the leid,
His teith chatterit, and cheverit with the chin;
His ene drowpit, how sonkin in his heid,
Out of his nois the meldrop fast can rin,

With lippis bla and cheikis leine and thin;
The iceschoklis that fra his hair doun hang
Was wonder greit, and as ane speir als lang.

Atouir his belt the lyart lokkis lay
Felterit unfair, ouirfret with froistis hoir,
His garmound and his gyte full gay of gray,
His widderit weid fra him the wind out woir;
Ane busteous bow within his hand he boir;
Under his girdill ane flasche of felloun flanis
Fedderit with ice, and heidit with hailstanis.

[ll. 155-68]

Saturn is followed by Jupiter, in whose portrait Henryson has concentrated many features implying vitality
and well-being, associated both with the idealised spring
season of love-visions and with the loveliness and radiant health of Cresseid in her former life. Jupiter is handsome and benign; he nurtures all living things, and
wears upon his head a garland of 'flouris fair, as it had
bene in May'. [l. 175] The beauty of youth, health and
vitality is summed up in this figure:

His voice was cleir, as cristall wer his ene.
As goldin wyre sa glitterand was his hair,
His garmound and his gyte full [gay] of grene,
With goldin listis gilt on everie gair. . . .

[ll. 176-9]

Mars and Phoebus follow, likewise opposed to one
another. The glowering visage of Mars, god of 'ire, / Of
strife, debait and all dissensioun' [ll. 183-4] is contrasted
with the life-giving radiance of Phoebus,

. . . lanterne and lamp of licht
Of man and beist, baith frute and flourisching,
Tender nureis and banischer of nicht,
And of the warld causing, be his moving
And influence, lyfe in all eirdlie thing. . . .

[ll. 197-201]

The third couple, whose pairing is somewhat more
subtle, though also antithetic, consists of Venus and
Mercury. Henryson's description of Venus seems to be
indebted in some way to the presentation in *The Kingis
Quair* of the goddess Fortune, whose countenance is
continually changing.[12] The variability of Henryson's
Venus is reflected not only in her facial expression—
sometimes inviting and seductive, then without warning
'angrie as ony serpent venomous' [l. 228]—but also in
her garment, which is half green and half black in token
of the changeability of love: 'Now hait, now cauld, now
blyith, now full of wo, / Now grene as leif, now widderit and ago.' [ll. 237-8] Mercury, who succeeds Venus,
counters her sensuality with his intellectual qualities:
his traditional associations with eloquence and with the
skills of the physician are mentioned. But many of this
god's exploits in classical stories are dishonest and
improper, and he was known as the god of thieves and
liars.[13] Hence Henryson's assertion that Mercury is 'hon-

est and gude, and not ane word culd le' [l. 252] must be made with tongue in cheek. The portrait of Cynthia the moon-goddess, who follows Mercury, is done all in shadowy and negative tones. She seems to reflect not only the characteristics of Saturn, with whom she associates herself in the punishment of Cresseid, but also the malicious and destructive intemperance of Mars and the inconstancy of Venus. Perhaps even the double-dealing and dishonest reputation of Mercury is suggested by the two horns on her head-dress and by the representation upon her breast of the 'Man in the Moon', the 'cherle . . . Quhilk for his thift micht clim na nar the hevin' [ll. 261-3]—a peasant who, according to legend, was thus punished for theft.[14] Cynthia negates in every way the life-sustaining qualities of her brother Phoebus the sun-god, from whom she borrows her light, and also the vitality and beauty of Jupiter. She resembles Saturn in being 'haw as the leid, of colour nathing cleir' [l. 257] and in wearing a grey robe which in her case is 'ful of spottis blak' [l. 260]. This conventional detail, symbolic of inconstancy, associates her both with the soiled character of Cresseid, 'with fleschlie lust sa maculait' [l. 81] and with the figure of Fortune in *The Kingis Quair* (in which Fortune's mantle is of white ermine fur 'degoutit with the self in spottis blake', St. 161).

The synod of the gods hears out the charge of blasphemy levelled against Cresseid by Cupid and Venus, and declares through its appointed spokesman, Mercury, that the punishment to be meted out to her should be assessed by Saturn and Cynthia, the highest and lowest in degree amongst the planets. They sentence Cresseid

> In all hir lyfe with pane to be opprest
> And torment sair, with seiknes incurabill,
> And to all lovers be abhominabill.
>
> [ll. 306-8]

Clearly, the relationship of negation that Saturn and Cynthia respectively have with Jupiter and Phoebus, the two benevolent sustainers of earthly life, is decisive in their being chosen to punish Cresseid. Saturn descends to touch the head of the fallen victim with a 'frostie wand' as he deprives her of her 'bewtie gay, / [Hir] wanton blude, and eik [hir] goldin hair' [ll. 313-4]— that is, he negates those qualities of health and vitality that Cresseid derives from Jupiter. He then proceeds to condemn her in terms of those bodily humours and their effects that were traditionally regarded as 'saturnine'.[15]

> 'I change thy mirth into melancholy
> Quhilk is the mother of all pensivenes.
> Thy moisture and thy heit in cald and dry,
> Thyne insolence, thy play and wantones
> To greit diseis; thy pomp and thy riches
> In mortal neid, and greit penuritie
> Thou suffer sall, and as ane beggar die.'
>
> [ll. 316-22]

Cynthia descends in her turn to complete Cresseid's sentence, adding to the 'saturnine' afflictions the symptoms of leprosy, which Henryson describes with accuracy and in detail:

> 'Fra heit of bodie I the now depryve
> And to thy seiknes sal be na recure,
> Bot in dolour thy dayis to indure.
>
> Thy cristall ene minglit with blude I mak,
> Thy voice sa cleir, unplesand hoir and hace,
> Thy lustie lyre ourispred with spottis blak,
> And lumpis haw appeirand in thy face.
> Quhair thou cumis ilk man sal fle the place.
> Thus sall thou go begging fra hous to hous
> With cop and clapper lyke ane lazarous.'
>
> [ll. 334-43]

Henryson links these manifestations of the disease with the moon-goddess for obvious reasons: coldness and antilife properties are associated with the moon's reflected light and express the negativity of her relationship especially with Phoebus the sun. Crystalline eyes and a clear voice, both common signs of well-being, are mentioned amongst the characteristics of Jupiter; these too Cynthia negates. The discolouration of the skin in dark spots and leaden-coloured lumps reflects the moon's appearance to the naked eye, and with it the traditional corruption which she casts upon all beneath her sphere.[16] The consequent taint of inconstancy and sinfulness is inevitable.

Although it has been asserted that Cresseid's leprosy is venereal in its origin,[17] a recent critic has pointed out that leprosy in the medieval period was rarely regarded as a venereal disease. If Henryson had so regarded it, then his Cresseid would already have contracted the disease by the time she retired to her father's house, and the lengthy passage—amounting to over one-third of this remarkably concise work—in which the leprosy is inflicted upon Cresseid by the gods as a penalty would be undermined in a manner which the poet surely did not intend.[18] Matthew McDiarmid stresses the special association of the disease with the planetary influence of Saturn, requiring in Henryson's work the conjunction of the Moon chiefly because she is 'the planet of swift and sudden change'. He cites the example of the Scottish national hero Bruce, who suffered from leprosy which was not associated at all with promiscuity, but *was* connected with a breach of faith. McDiarmid offers other medieval parallels in which the breaking or dishonouring of a solemn oath brings leprosy upon the perjuror.[19] Cresseid's falseness to Troilus unquestionably contributes to the seriousness of the blasphemy she commits against Venus and Cupid, and emphasises the horrible appropriateness of the punishment that fits this composite crime—an incurable disease that makes her truly the 'unworthie outwaill' she complained of being *before* she was stricken; that casts her, in effect, out of the community of the living, and disfigures her physically so that she becomes not only literally unrecognisable, even to her still-devoted lover Troilus, but actually 'abhominabill' to any lover.

Henryson's device in the remainder of the *Testament* is to juxtapose the former beauty of Cresseid, and the power that it gave her over men and amongst the community, with her degraded and miserable condition now that she has become a leper and one of the living dead.[20] Awakening from the trance during which her terrible sentence was passed by the seven gods, she looks at herself in a mirror and sees the deformity of her face—now an 'ugly lipper face / The quhilk befor was quhite as lillie flour' [ll. 372-3]. Her only desire is to withdraw and to hide herself; the first words actually spoken aloud to another human being by Cresseid in the poem are those she says to her father: 'I wald not be kend.' [l. 380] Her father takes her secretly to the 'spittaill hous' in a nearby village, where she goes unrecognised, 'becaus scho was sa deformait, / With bylis blak ouirspred in hir visage / And hir fair colour faidit and alterait.' [ll. 394-6] In a deliberate contrast to the ice-clear night sky with which the poem begins, 'cloudis blak' cover the heavens as Cresseid faces the reality of her new abode in the leper-house. The setting of Phoebus the sun, once more in implied opposition to the fickle though fair Venus, rising as the sun descends, releases in Cresseid an outpouring of sorrow in which she laments the 'frivoll fortune' that has placed her in her present plight. One recalls the obvious parallels between Henryson's figures of Venus and Cynthia, and the goddess Fortune of *The Kingis Quair*: for all preside over this night of lamentation, Cresseid's first in the leper-house. Abandoned by those who once sought her favours, she compares what she formerly was to what she is now:

> Thy greit triumphand fame and hie honour,
> Quhair thou was callit of eirdlye wichtis flour,
> All is decayit, thy weird is welterit so:
> Thy hie estait is turnit in darknes dour.
>
> [ll. 434-7]

Cresseid comes ultimately to see her fate as emblematic, providing a pattern or model of the vicissitudes of life and of the fate of earthly beauty:

> 'O ladyis fair of Troy and Grece, attend
> My miserie, quhilk nane may comprehend . . .
> And in your mynd ane mirrour mak of me,
> As I am now, peraventure that ye
> For all your micht may cum to that same end.'
>
> [ll. 452-3, 457-9]

She now perceives her present condition, in all its horror, as something that was lurking just below the pleasant surface of her former life, just as her present deformity lay hidden under her former beauty, always implicit in it—the 'skull beneath the skin':

> 'Nocht is your fairnes bot ane faiding flour,
> Nocht is your famous laud and hie honour
> Bot wind inflat in uther mennis eiris.
> Your roising reid to rotting sall retour.
> Exemple mak of me in your memour . . .'
>
> [ll. 461-5]

The image of the flower, repeatedly used both by Chaucer and by Henryson for the beauty of Criseyde/Cresseid, now becomes a withering reminder of mortality; honour and reputation become nothing but wind, vitality and beauty turn to putrefaction.

Cresseid is taken to task by one of her companions, a leper-woman who teaches her the wisdom of acceptance. 'Quhy spurnis thow aganis the wall, / To sla thyself, and mend nathing at all?' [ll. 475-6] demands the voice of common sense. She gives to Cresseid a precious, though hard, nugget of advice: 'I counsall the mak vertew of ane neid, / To leir to clap thy clapper to and fro, / And leif efter the law of lipper leid.' [ll. 478-80] It is a resignation which expresses, in a far more desperate situation, an acceptance of things-as-they-are, in this very imperfect world, which is similar to the opening passages of the work that serve to create its mood.

But Henryson does not leave Cresseid at this point, numbly resigned to the decay of her own flesh in the living death of leprosy. Instead, he leads her into that moving climactic scene in which Troilus comes upon her, and gives her alms in memory of the woman he loved. The disease has so dimmed her eyesight that she cannot clearly see the giver of the 'purs of gold, and mony gay jowall' [l. 521]. But when one of her companions tells her that it was Troilus, Cresseid is enabled to move beyond despair to a kind of self-recognition. Ultimately she is able to appreciate the fineness of Troilus's love for her, and conversely, the vileness of her own breach of faith: 'O fals Cresseid and trew knycht Troylus!' [l. 546] Cresseid's final spoken words do not express self-pity, but self-realisation: 'Nane but myself as now I will accuse.' [l. 574]

Death sets its seal upon Cresseid before she actually takes leave of life: the anti-life properties of the deities who sentence this most beautiful of women to the fate of a leper have assured her of a living death, sealed off from her former life for all the world as though she were already buried. But in allotting to Cresseid this harsh fate of death-in-life, in depicting the rotting away and putrescence of the once lovely face and body as vividly as in the sculptured corpse within the tomb of the Duchess of Suffolk, Henryson allows her at last to attain an integrity that was beyond the grasp of that 'sely womman' of 'slydynge corage' on whose behalf Chaucer had earlier besought the reader's compassion.

Henryson's Cresseid is forced to pay her debts in the fullest measure. But in the growth eventually of true penitence for her faults, and of a new moral perspective and awareness, Henryson suggests that the dimming of her eyesight and the eclipse of her physical beauty through leprosy has been counterbalanced by better moral perception and a greater comeliness of the spirit. Cresseid's own bequest of her 'spreit' to Diana, goddess of chastity [ll. 587-8], goes yet further, hinting that perhaps through the suffering that eventually brought her this insight Cresseid has been purged of her 'fleschlie foull affectioun' [l. 558]. The setting of the poem is pagan, and Henryson explicitly in its final line declines to speak of the fate of Cresseid's soul. Nevertheless, addressing his work to a Christian audience, specifically of 'worthie wemen . . . for your worschip and instructioun' [ll. 610-1], he implies that true beauty lies in integrity, true health in the preservation of good faith.

Notes

1. Emil Mâle, *L'Art religieux de la fin du Moyen Age en France* (Paris: Librairie Armand Colin, 1908; repr. 1925), pp. 347-8.

2. Philippa Tristram discusses Mâle's distinction between thirteenth- and fifteenth-century memorial sculpture in *Figures of Life and Death in Medieval English Literature* (London: Paul Elek, 1976), p. 15.

3. Illustrated and discussed in *The Flowering of the Middle Ages,* edited by Joan Evans (London: Thames and Hudson, 1966), p. 220.

4. Ibid., pp. 220-1.

5. Robert Henryson, *Poems*; selected and edited by Charles Elliott (Oxford: Clarendon Press, 1974). (All quotations from Henryson's works follow this edition. Line numbers from the *Testament* are given thus: [l. 7].)

6. A. M. Kinghorn (editor): *The Middle Scots Poets* (London: Edward Arnold, 1970), p. 126.

7. Documented facts and speculations concerning Henryson's life are assessed by Matthew P. McDiarmid in *Robert Henryson* (Scottish Writers Series; Edinburgh: Scottish Academic Press, 1981), pp. 1-25.

8. Examples of conventional tributes to Chaucer are found in Dunbar's *The Goldyn Targe,* ll. 253-61 and Gavin Douglas's translation of Virgil's *Aeneid,* ll. 339-46. Both are reprinted in Kinghorn, ed. cit.

9. Geoffrey Chaucer, *Troilus and Criseyde* Bk. V, l. 1040; in *Complete Works,* edited by W. W. Skeat (London: Oxford University Press, 1912.); (All citations of Chaucer's works are taken from this edition.)

10. *Troilus and Criseyde* Bk. V, ll. 1093 and 825.

11. Ibid. ll. 1097-9.

12. Kinghorn reprints this passage from *The Kingis Quair* (stanzas 159-66) in *The Middle Scots Poets,* pp. 55-7.

13. Mercury, the traditional 'protector' of thieves and mischief-makers, celebrated the day of his birth, according to legend, by stealing the cattle of Phoebus Apollo and confusing his pursuers with an ingeniously devised false trail. Another instance of his trickery is referred to in Chaucer's *Knight's Tale* (A 1385-92)—his closing of the myriad eyes of Argus. In the *Knight's Tale* he appears to Arcite in a dream to give him an equivocal message, which Arcite misinterprets, with fatal consequences.

14. The complex of legends relating to the 'Man in the Moon' is discussed by O. F. Emerson, *PMLA* xxi, 31-929, and also by R. J. Menner, *JEGP* [*Journal of English and Germanic Philology*] xlviii, 1-14.

15. Elliott (edition cit.) quotes from W. Lilly, *Christian Astrology,* 1647, pp. 57 ff.: 'Saturn is a planet "Cold and Dry . . . Melancholik . . . Masculine, the greater Infortune . . . a contemner of women . . . he signifieth . . . Beggars . . . quartan Agues proceeding of cold, dry and melancholly Distempers, Leprosies." Saturn's "complexion" of melancholy with its predisposing to leprosy replaces Cresseid's "moisture and . . . heit", the sanguine "temperament" of Venus, her former goddess . . . Again, Saturn "causeth Cloudy, Darke, obscure Ayre, cold and hurtfull, black and condense Clouds" (Lilly, p. 60) such as appear when Cresseid enters the leper-house.' Notes to ll. 316-18 and 334-43, pp. 168-9.

16. '. . . [T]he hornes of the fulle mone wexen pale and infect by the boundes of the derke night; . . . the mone, derk and confuse, discovereth the sterres . . .' Boethius, *De Consolacione Philosophiae* IV Met. v, ll. 11-14 (Chaucer's translation). Cf. also *Le Roman de la Rose,* ll.4784-92.

Guillaume de Lorris et Jean de Meun, *Le Roman de la Rose,* Publié par Ernest Langlois. *Societé des Anciens Textes Français* no. 62; 1919-24.

17. Florence H. Ridley, in "A Plea for the Middle Scots", lists several recent scholarly articles and also the edition of Denton Fox (London, Nelson, 1968, pp. 26 ff.) which suggest that leprosy was sometimes considered a venereal disease. Ridley adds: 'In view of Cresseid's sexual misdeeds such an affliction would be logically and thematically appropriate; but of greater significance than its

actual nature is its role as an outward sign of corruption." "A Plea for the Middle Scots", in *The Learned and the Lewed* (Cambridge, Mass.: Harvard University Press, 1974, 175-96; p. 190.)

18. Matthew P. McDiarmid argues the case against the suggestion that leprosy had venereal origins in *Robert Henryson* (op. cit.) p. 100.

19. McDiarmid, op. cit. pp. 105-6.

20. 'When through the Crusades leprosy had been introduced into Western Europe, it was usual to clothe the leper in a shroud, and to say for him the masses for the dead.' Archbishop Richard C. Trench, *Notes on the Miracles of Our Lord,* 1846; x (1862) p. 217, note.

Philippa Bright (essay date 1989)

SOURCE: Bright, Philippa. "Henryson's Figurative Technique in '*The Cock and the Jasp.*'" In *Words and Wordsmiths: A Volume for H. L. Rogers,* edited by Geraldine Barnes, John Gunn, Sonya Jensen, and Lee Jobling, pp. 13-21. Sydney, Australia: Department of English, The University of Sydney, 1989.

[*In the following essay, Bright analyzes "The Cock and the Jasp" as one of Henryson's most often misunderstood fables, asserting that "[t]hrough the cock, who serves as a vehicle for viewing the bestial side of man's nature, we are provided with an illustration of man's blindness in allowing his appetite to override his reason."*]

"The Cock and the Jasp,"[1] Henryson's fable about a cock who finds a precious jewel on a dunghill only to discard it in favour of food, is one of the best known fables in his collection, yet it is also one in which his figurative methods have been consistently misunderstood. Most critics who have discussed the fable have felt that the cock is quite right in rejecting a precious jewel for which he has no use and have been surprised to discover in the *moralitas* that he is explicitly condemned for his folly. To account for the apparent reversal of their expectations they have usually adopted one of two positions: either they have concluded that the *moralitas* is a pious afterthought which has a purely arbitrary connexion with the preceding narrative[2] or else they have argued that the shock of the unexpected interpretation is intentional and an essential part of the meaning of the fable.[3] Both of these positions, however, are untenable since they are based on two quite erroneous assumptions, the first of which is that in the fable we are somehow dealing with a real barnyard fowl on a real dunghill and the second, that Henryson's poetic technique in the narrative causes us to sympathize with the cock's point of view.

Some years ago Denton Fox pointed out that the solution to the problem of the apparent discrepancy between tale and moral in **"The Cock and the Jasp"** 'lies in the fact that Henryson is working on several levels of meaning'.[4] He then went on to explain that in the narrative there are hints which suggest that the cock is to be viewed critically and that he 'symbolizes the man who has abandoned his higher reason and consequently his superior place in the chain of being in favor of animal cunning and selfish common sense'.[5] Fox is correct, I believe, in emphasizing the figurative, rather than the literal, significance of the cock in the narrative, but the only model he offers for understanding the relationship between the literal and figurative levels of meaning in Henryson's fable is that in which one 'thing', in addition to having a significance of its own, also functions as a 'sign' of another 'thing'.[6] In the discussion of the fable which follows, therefore, I will attempt to redress what I see to be the failures of Fox and other critics by re-examining and redefining Henryson's figurative methods.

The immediate source for **"The Cock and the Jasp"** appears to have been Walter the Englishman's 'De Gallo et Jaspide'.[7] Walter's fable is extremely brief and consists of an eight-line narrative detailing the cock's discovery of the jasp and his reasons for discarding it, plus a two-line *moralitas* in which the cock is said to illustrate 'foolishness' and the jasp to represent 'the beautiful gifts of wisdom':

> Dum rigido fodit ore fimum, dum quaeritat escam,
> > Dum stupet inventa jaspide Gallus, ait:
> > Res vili pretiosa loco natique decoris
> > Hac in sorde jaces, nil mihi messis habes.
> Si tibi nunc esset qui debuit esse repertor,
> > Quem limus sepelit, viveret arte nitor.
> Nec tibi convenio, nec tu mihi; nec tibi prosum,
> > Nec mihi tu prodes: plus amo cara minus.
>
> Tu Gallo stolidum, tu Jaspide dona sophiae
> > Pulchra notes; stolido nil sapit ista seges.[8]

In his narrative Walter makes no attempt to characterize the cock beyond giving him the human attribute of speech. Nor does he prepare the audience for the figurative equation of the cock with 'wisdom' or offer any indication that the cock is acting other than sensibly in casting aside a precious jewel for which he has no use. It is only in retrospect and after the jasp has been figuratively equated with 'wisdom' that the cock's action can be seen to be foolish. The narrative in 'De Gallo et Jaspide', therefore, does not have a simple exemplary function but rather has a meaning quite independent of, and even contrary to, the *moralitas*. This situation has been brought about by the fact that Walter is employing more than one figurative mode. While the cock is a metaphoric representative of the human world and functions as a 'sign' only, the jasp functions as both a 'thing' and a 'sign' and is literally a precious jewel in the narrative, and figuratively 'wisdom' in the *moralitas.*

In **"The Cock and the Jasp"** Henryson has considerably expanded Walter's narrative as well as his *moralitas,* and his additions to Walter's version of the fable have significantly altered the nature of the relationship between tale and moral. The first noticeable difference between Henryson's fable and that of Walter concerns the presentation of the cock. Henryson does not merely humanize the cock by giving him the ability to speak but imbues him with a specific personality by mentioning that he is poor and that he is 'Richt cant and crous' (l. 65). The latter phrase, as Denton Fox has stated, is somewhat ambiguous, since it can be used in a heroic or in a humorous sense.[9] Taken in the former sense it would suggest that the cock was brave and bold like a true romance hero, but if *cant* is read as 'lively',[10] and *crous* as 'jaunty' and 'self satisfied',[11] then the implication is that the cock has rather too good an opinion of himself. That Henryson intended the phrase to imply criticism of the cock seems to be indicated by his use of the word *richt* as an intensifier at the beginning of the phrase and by the following statement, 'albeit he was bot pure' (l. 65), which is syntactically anticlimactic. Even if *crous* is not interpreted in a derogatory sense, though, the conjunction of the phrase 'cant and crous' with the detail of the cock's poverty is sufficient to produce a mock heroic effect which in turn serves to underline the cock's self-importance.

As well as introducing details which serve to characterize and to criticize the cock, Henryson, in his portrayal of the cock in the opening stanza of the fable, skillfully combines human and animal characteristics. Not only does he use the word *crous,* which was applied to both animals and humans,[12] to describe the cock, but also, while giving him the human attributes of poverty and pride, he indicates his animal nature by stating that he possesses 'feddram fresch and gay' (l. 64), that he *Fleu* (l. 6) onto a dunghill to obtain his dinner, and that he discovered the jasp while *scraipand* (l. 68) in the dust. Such a deliberate juxtaposition of human and animal characteristics should immediately alert us to the fact that the cock is not to be viewed as a real barnyard rooster but rather serves as a vehicle for observing the bestial aspects of human conduct.

A second important addition that Henryson has made to Walter's fable is his inclusion of a stanza about wanton servant girls who are so anxious to get out to play that they sweep out jewels along with other household rubbish:

> As damisellis wantoun and insolent
> That fane wald play and on the streit be sene,
> To swoping of the hous thay tak na tent

> Quhat be thairin, swa that the flure be clene;
> Iowellis ar tint, as oftymis hes bene sene,
> Vpon the flure, and swopit furth anone,
> Peraduenture, sa wes the samin stone.

(ll. 71-77)

In discussing this stanza Denton Fox has remarked: 'On the one hand the stanza further establishes the tone of barnyard realism by explaining and domesticating the jasp. On the other hand the "Damisellis" provide an excellent parallel to the cock: like him, they pay no attention ("tak na tent," "cair na thing") to a jewel of great value because they are entirely preoccupied with their animal appetites.'[13]

George Clark and Douglas Gray have also commented on the stanza. Clark believes that 'The cock's early rising and diligence, "To get his dennar set was al his cure" (67), contrast with the idleness and indifference of the hypothetical girls',[14] while Gray claims that Henryson 'has teased us . . . by his digression on the wanton damsels (which we read as implying that the cock has a higher estimation of the jewel than they).'[15] Although there is evidence for each of these assertions, none of the three critics mentioned has satisfactorily explained the function of the stanza. The truth is that the girls serve both as a parallel and as a contrast to the cock. Like the cock they are motivated by appetite, but unlike him, and contrary to what might be expected, they have no interest in lost jewels. When the cock begins his address to the jasp in the following stanza, his deference, which is more appropriately human than animal, sets up a comic inversion which extends and develops the mock heroic element of his characterization in the opening stanza and makes it impossible for us to take his subsequent arguments seriously.

Another way in which Henryson has substantially altered Walter's narrative is through the additions he has made to the cock's speech. In Walter's fable the cock justifies his decision to cast aside the jasp by stating that he prefers things that are of less worth. Henryson not only amplifies this statement by rendering it as:

> I lufe fer better thing of les auaill,
> As draf or corne to fill my tume intraill.

(ll. 90-91)

but adds another two stanzas describing the sort of food the cock prefers to the jasp and emphasizing his need to appease his hunger:

> I had leuer go skraip heir with my naillis
> Amangis this mow, and luke my lifys fude,
> As draf or corne, small wormis, or snaillis,
> Or ony meit wald do my stomok gude,
> Than of iaspis ane mekill multitude;
> And thow agane, vpon the samin wyis,
> May me as now for thyne auaill dispyis.

'Thow hes na corne, and thairof I had neid;
Thy cullour dois bot confort to the sicht,
An that is not aneuch my wame to feid,
For wyfis sayis that lukand werk is licht.
I wald sum meit haue, get it geue I micht,
For houngrie men may not weill leue on lukis:
Had I dry breid, I compt not for na cukis.'

(ll. 92-105)

As well as expanding the cock's speech in order to focus attention on his desire for food, Henryson departs significantly from Walter's version of the fable by having his cock adopt the high style. In Henryson's fable, the cock begins his address to the jasp with the eloquent double apostrophe, 'O gentill Iasp, O riche and nobill thing' (l. 79), and concludes it with a series of rhetorical questions linked by repetition and anaphora and culminating in an invitation (involving the use of personification and courtly language) to the jasp to pass out of the filth of the dunghill to its rightfull place:

'Quhar suld thow mak thy habitatioun?
Quhar suld thow duell, bot in ane royall tour?
Quhar suld thow sit, bot on ane kingis croun
Exalt in worschip and in grit honour?
Rise, gentill Iasp, of all stanis the flour,
Out of this fen, and pas quhar thow suld be;
Thow ganis not for me, nor I for the.'

(ll. 106-12)

The cock's eloquence creates the impression that he knows what he is doing in casting aside the jasp, but the incongruity of such eloquence in a barnyard setting undercuts this impression and renders him a pompous, comic figure. Moreover, it quickly becomes obvious that, in his speech, he is using rhetoric to justify his animal appetite. By playing off the style of this speech against the context and by having him ironically defend sensual appetite with a display of reason and eloquence, Henryson does not allow us to take the cock's words at face value but shows him to be an opinionated, deluded creature who is controlled entirely by appetite and who is willing to pervert his reason to its demands—an apt vehicle, in fact, for viewing man's essential animality.

What an examination of Henryson's additions to Walter's narrative has demonstrated, therefore, is that Henryson consciously alienates, rather than engages, our sympathy for the cock. Consequently, the *moralitas,* in which the cock is condemned for his foolishness as he is in Walter's fable, should come as no surprise. Having said this, it is now necessary to look more closely at the nature of the relationship between tale and moral in Henryson's fable and particularly at the methods he uses to establish the relationship.

After concluding the narrative by telling us that the cock went off to seek his food, leaving the jasp lying on the ground, Henryson proceeds to explain the properties of the jasp:

This iolie iasp hes properteis seuin:
The first, of cullour it is meruelous,
Part lyke the fyre and part lyke to the heuin;
It makis ane man stark and victorious;
Preseruis als fra cacis perrillous;
Quha hes this stane sall haue gude hap to speid,
Of fyre nor fallis him neidis not to dreid.

(ll. 120-26)

It is not certain whether the *moralitas* actually begins at line 120 or whether it follows line 126,[16] but it is generally agreed that this stanza, which is not found in Walter's fable, serves as a transition between story and morality. In a recent article on **"The Cock and the Jasp,"** James Khinoy has suggested that in Henryson's fable the jasp is really a jacinth, as in Lydgate's version, since the jasper 'lacks all of the qualities' of the stone found on the dunghill.[17] Khinoy cites a number of authorities in support of his view, but notably absent is any reference to *De proprietatibus rerum* of Bartholomaeus Angelicus.

In his section on jasps, Bartholomaeus describes the jasper stone as follows:

Iaspis est Gemma viridis, smaragdo similis, sed crassi coloris simpliciter est. Eius species sunt septemdecim, dic Isid . . . quamius autem eius color praecipuus sit viridis, tamen multos habet alios intermixtos. Eius virtus est reprimere febres & hydropisim in his, qui gestant ipsum caste. Iuuat etiam parturientem, fugat phantasmata, & inter pericula fecit hominem tutum, interiorem refrigerat ardorem, fluentem compescit sanguinem & sudorem, luxuriam cohibet & impedit conceptum, menstrua constringit & hemorrhoides, si puluerisetur datus cum lacte, vecera inueterata sanat, sordes oculorum purgat, & visum acuit & confortat, maleficiis & incantationibus resistit, efficacior est in argento quam in auro.[18]

If Henryson's description of the jasper stone is compared with that of Bartholomaeus, it will be seen to be very similar. Henryson, like Bartholomaeus, refers to a mixture of colours, and to the capacity of the stone to keep a man safe from danger as well as to check fevers (*fyre,* l. 120) and dropsy (*fallis,* l. 120). Of course, there is no proof that Henryson took his description of the jasper stone directly from Bartholomaeus, but the similarity between the two accounts indicates that he was at least drawing on the same lapidary tradition.

Once Henryson has explained the physical characteristics and virtues of the jasp, he goes on to indicate its spiritual significance:

This gentill iasp, richt different of hew,
Betakinnis perfite prudence and cunning,
Ornate with mony deidis of vertew,
Mair excellent than ony eirthly thing,
Quhilk makis men in honour ay to ring,
Happie, and stark to haif the victorie
Of all vicis and spirituall enemie.

(ll. 127-33)

In equating the jasp with wisdom, Henryson is following the example of Walter, but the parallels he establishes between the physical powers of the jasp and the
spiritual efficacy of prudence and cunning (l. 128) (*i.e.,*
wisdom and learning), show that he is still drawing on
the lapidary tradition in which it was common for gems
and their properties to be given Christian allegorical
and moral significances, as, for instance, in Marbod's
Liber de Gemmis. It is not until the next stanza that any
attempt is made to link the spiritual significance of the
jasp with the precious stone discovered by the cock on
the dunghill.

Like the concluding stanza of the cock's address to the
jasp in the narrative, this stanza opens with a series of
rhetorical questions linked by anaphora:

> Quha may be hardie, riche, and gratious?
> Quha can eschew perrell and auenture?
> Quha can gouerne ane realme, cietie, or hous
> Without science? No man, I ȝow assure.
> It is riches that euer sall indure,
> Quhilk maith, nor moist, nor vther rust can freit:
> To mannis saull it is eternall meit.
>
> (ll. 134-40)

In the praise of *science* (*i.e.,* learning, including
theology) in this stanza there are echoes of the Biblical
praise of wisdom.[19] Furthermore, words such as *riches*
(l. 138) and *meit* (l. 140) call to mind the earthly value
that the cock placed on the jewel and his rejection of it
in favour of food. By redefining such words, by placing
them in a spiritual context, and by means of the other
echoes he sets up in the stanza, Henryson highlights the
false earthly values of the cock and makes the point
that wisdom is the most valuable possession a man can
have. However, although Henryson has established a
number of links between the spiritual significance of
the jasp and the value it has for the cock in the narrative, these lines do not provide a basis for the figurative
reading. This is provided by the stanza which explains
the physical properties of the jasp. For Henryson as for
Walter, therefore, the jasp does not function as a
descriptive symbol or mere 'sign' but is treated as an
interpretative symbol, that is to say as a 'thing' which,
in addition to having a significance of its own, is also a
'sign' of another 'thing'.

The method Henryson uses to uncover the figurative
significance of the cock is quite different. Unlike Walter,
he does not directly equate the cock with foolishness
but claims that he may be *likened* to a fool:

> This cock, desyrand mair the sempill corne
> Than ony iasp, may till ane fule be peir,
> Quhilk at science makis bot ane moik and scorne,
> And na gude can; als lytill will he leir—
> His hart wammillis wyse argumentis to heir,
> As dois ane sow to quhome men for the nanis
> In hir draf troich wald saw the precious stanis.
>
> (ll. 141-47)

It should also be noted that Henryson sets precise terms
of reference for his comparison between the cock and a
fool. The cock is not said to be like a fool in every
respect, but, in preferring corn to the jasp, he is
compared to a fool who scorns learning, yet 'na gude
can' (l. 144). In the narrative, Henryson has exposed
the delusion of the cock in thinking he knows what is
good for him and has shown him misapplying his reason
by using it to defend his sensual appetite. It is thus appropriate that such a creature should, in the *moralitas,*
be compared to a fool who ignorantly believes he has
no use for *science.* As far as the interpretation of the
cock is concerned, there is consequently no evident
disjunction between tale and moral; rather, the two parts
of the fable co-exist in the manner of a similitude.

Critics have had difficulty in relating tale and moral in
"The Cock and the Jasp" because they have failed
both to understand the nature of the connexion between
Henryson's cock and the fool who scorns learning and
to recognize that Henryson is employing more than one
figurative mode. Whereas the jasp is treated as an
interpretative symbol in the *moralitas* and its significance is determined by criteria extraneous to the story,
the cock is treated as a descriptive symbol. Through the
cock, who serves as a vehicle for viewing the bestial
side of man's nature, we are provided with an illustration of man's blindness in allowing his appetite to override his reason. The *moralitas,* in which the jasp is
figuratively equated with 'wisdom' and the cock likened
to a fool, calls attention to such an error and appeals to
those in the audience who will to 'Ga seik the iasp' (l.
161) themselves, that is to say, replace earthly values
with spiritual ones. Not only, therefore, has Henryson
introduced into his fable material which enables him to
avoid the disjunction between tale and moral that is
found in Walter's fable, but he has also extended the
function of Walter's fable by turning it into an *exemplum* which both illustrates and exhorts.

Notes

1. All references to the fable are to the version which
   appears in *The Poems of Robert Henryson,* edited
   by Denton Fox (Oxford, 1981).

2. See, for instance, R. Bauman, 'The Folk Tale and
   Oral Tradition in the Fables of Robert Henryson',
   Fabula, 6 (1963), 117; 'Allegorical', *Times Liter-
   ary Supplement* (10 August 1967), p. 726; D. Mur-
   taugh, 'Henryson's Animals', *Texas Studies in
   Literature and Language,* 14 (1972), 408, note 3.

3. See E. Watson, 'Allegorical', *Times Literary
   Supplement* (31 August 1967), p. 780; H. Roerecke, *The Integrity and Symmetry of Robert Henryson's 'Moral Fables'* (Ph.D dissertation, University of Pennsylvania, 1969), p. 75; M. M. Carens,
   A Prolegomenon for the Study of Robert Henryson

(Ph.D. dissertation, University of Pennsylvania, 1974), pp. 157-58; I. Jamieson, 'The Beast Tale in Middle Scots: Some Thoughts on the History of a Genre', *Parergon,* 2 (1972), 28-30; G. Clark, 'Henryson and Aesop: The Fable Transformed', *English Literary History,* 43 (1976), 8; D. Gray, *Robert Henryson* (Leiden, 1979), pp. 122-23; E. Newlyn, 'Robert Henryson and the Popular Fable Tradition in the Middle Ages', *Journal of Popular Culture,* 14 (1980-81), 11; S. Khinoy, 'Tale—Moral Relationships in Henryson's Moral Fables', *Studies in Scottish Literature,* 17 (1982), 102; G. Kratzmann, 'Henryson's *Fables*: the subtell dyte of poetry', *Studies in Scottish Literature,* 20 (1985), 57-62.

4. Denton Fox, 'Henryson's Fables', *English Literary History,* 29 (1962), 343.

5. Fox, 'Henryson's Fables', p. 344.

6. The terminology I am employing here derives from St Augustine and is explained by J. Chydenius in 'The Theory of Medieval Symbolism', *Societas Scientiarum Fennica: Commentationes Humanarum Litterarum,* 27, 2 (Helsingfors, 1960), 5-8. Fox does not use the same terminology, but in his commentary on Henryson's figurative technique in *The Fables* states: 'Henryson's animals, while remaining animals, signify men, while we are continually reminded that men encompass or fulfil (but sometimes are no better than) animals' ('Henryson's Fables', p. 341) and 'Henryson creates a whole visible world, and the characters and incidents of this world are solid and substantial in themselves, as well as being figures which "show forth the wisdom of the invisible things of God"' ('Henryson's Fables', pp. 347-48).

7. All references are to *Recueil général des Isopets,* edited by J. Bastin, 2 vols (Paris, 1929-30), II (1930), 8.

8. 'The cock, while digging in the dung with his beak, while looking for food, while being astonished after finding a jasper stone, said: "precious object of innate beauty, in a worthless spot, embedded here in the dirt, you have no value for me. If you had been found now by the person who ought to have found you, your glitter, which the muck conceals, would be brought to life by artifice. I am not fitting to you, nor you to me; I am no use to you, nor you to me; I prefer things of less worth." By the cock you should understand foolishness and by the jasp the beautiful gifts of wisdom; such a crop has no appeal for a fool.'

9. Fox, 'Henryson's Fables', p. 344 and *The Poems of Robert Henryson,* p. 196, note to l. 65.

10. For such a reading see *A Dictionary of the Older Scottish Tongue from the Twelfth Century to the End of the Seventeenth,* edited by Sir William Craigie and A. J. Aitken (Chicago and London, 1931-), I, 430, and Fox, *The Poems of Robert Henryson,* p. 196.

11. See *Dictionary of the Older Scottish Tongue,* I, 752, and Fox, *The Poems of Robert Henryson,* p. 196.

12. See *Middle English Dictionary,* edited by Hans Kurath, *et al.* (Ann Arbor, 1954-) p. 722, Charles Mackay, *A Dictionary of Lowland Scotch* (London, 1888), p. 35; *Scottish Dictionary and Supplement,* edited by Dr Jamieson (Edinburgh, 1841), pp. 196-97, 274.

13. Fox, 'Henryson's Fables', p. 342.

14. Clark, 'Henryson and Aesop', p. 7.

15. Gray, *Robert Henryson,* p. 123.

16. See Fox, *The Poems of Robert Henryson,* pp. 197-98, note to ll. 120-26.

17. Khinoy, 'Tale—Moral Relationships in Henryson's Moral Fables', pp. 102-04.

18. Bartholomaeus Angelicus, *De rerum proprietatibus* (Frankfurt, 1601; reprinted, 1964), pp. 742-43. 'Jasper is a green stone similar to the emerald, but of a deeper colour. There are seventeen varieties, as isidore says, and although the colour of the jasper is mainly green, many species nevertheless show a mixture of colours. It has virtue in checking fevers and hydropsy in those who wear it, provided that they live chastely. It also assists women in childbirth, it dispels fantasms, keeps a man safe in the midst of dangers, cools inner heat, tends to inhibit conception, and checks menstrual flow. If powdered and administered in milk it heals old sores, clears the eyes and strengthens the vision, wards off curses and spells, and it is more effective when set in silver than when set in gold.'

19. See Fox, *The Poems of Robert Henryson,* p. 199, note to l. 130.

Philippa M. Bright (essay date 1990)

SOURCE: Bright, Philippa M. "Medieval Concepts of the *figure* and Henryson's Figurative Technique in *The Fables.*" *Studies in Scottish Literature* 25 (1990): 134-53.

[*In the following essay, Bright examines the relationship between the literal and figurative levels of meaning in Henryson's* Moral Fables.]

In the **"Prologue"** which accompanies his collection of thirteen fables Henryson explains that fables teach "be figure of ane vther thing" (*l.* 7),[1] and that Aesop, the author whose work he professes to be translating, wrote "be figure" (*l.* 59) in order to avoid the scorn of those of both high and low rank in society. While such statements clearly imply that Henryson's own fables will employ a figurative technique, there has been considerable disagreement about the nature of this technique and about the kind of relationship that exists between the literal and figurative levels of meaning in his fables. Whereas some critics have stressed the purely arbitrary connection between tale and moral,[2] others have insisted on the essential harmony of the two elements.[3] Others again, while emphasizing the interrelatedness of the two parts, have argued that, in some fables, the *moralitas* is designed to shock and surprise and that the effect thus created is not only intentional, but also an important feature of the meaning of the fable.[4]

In an attempt to answer the questions that such differences of opinion have raised about the nature of Henryson's figurative technique in **The Fables**, a growing number of critics have turned to Erich Auerbach's discussion of figural writing and interpretation in his essay *Figura*.[5] Denton Fox, drawing on Auerbach's assertion that

> Figural interpretation establishes a connection between two events or persons, the first of which signifies not only itself but also the second, while the second encompasses or fulfills the first.[6]

has claimed that

> Henryson's animals while remaining animals signify men, while we are continually reminded that men encompass or fulfill (but sometimes are not better than) animals.[7]

Another Henryson scholar, Robert Gerke, while not wishing to limit the implications of Henryson's use of the term *figure* to the figural method of exegesis as Fox does, has suggested that the figural mode described by Auerbach can help to explain "the particularity and apparent self sufficiency of Henryson's fables"[8] and Stephen Knight, when discussing Henryson's use of the term *figure,* has remarked:

> He is using this word in just the sense in which Auerbach has expounded it in his essay "Figura". That is, the story exists as a pleasant, amusing object, and by figuration it may also have another existence, as a moral analysis.[9]

Douglas Gray, the author of one of the most comprehensive and illuminating recent books on Henryson, has also cited Auerbach's essay as an important source of information about the way Henryson is using the term *figure* in **The Fables**.[10] Moreover, in insisting that the

allegorical or figurative interpretations which contribute to medieval notions of the *figure,* and which form the background to Henryson's fables, "do not imply any dissolution of the literal senses,"[11] Gray presents a view of figurative writing very similar to that of Auerbach.

Although Auerbach has made an extensive study of the term *figure* in his essay, however, such a study has, as far as Henryson's fables are concerned, two major limitations. One is that it is based on Latin writing of the first to sixth centuries and the other, that it focuses on the relationship between the term *figure* and the typological method of writing and interpretation. Auerbach acknowledges that *figure* was also used in conjunction with the more abstract, ethical kind of allegory and that in the Middle Ages "there were all sorts of mixtures between figural, allegoric and symbolic forms,"[12] but he stresses the dominance of the typological mode and does not explore further complexities, such as the fact that although medieval exegetes believed in the historical truth of the events they were interpreting, they often ignored or dissolved historical contexts when uncovering the revealed meaning of such events.[13] If we are to fully understand the implications that Henryson's use of the term *figure* in the **"Prologue"** has for his figurative practice in **The Fables,** we must, then, go beyond Auerbach's essay and examine some of the different figurative contexts in which the term *figure* is used in medieval Latin and vernacular writing and the kinds of meaning with which it is associated in these contexts.[14] Since, as yet, no satisfactory investigation of this type has been undertaken by Henryson critics,[15] such an examination, and the conclusions to be drawn from it, will form the substance of the first part of this article.

One of the most frequent contexts in which the term *figure* occurs in the Middle Ages is the discussion of sacred Scripture. It is often pointed out by medieval theologians that the Bible differs from other kinds of writing since it manifests its sacred truths not only through words, but also by means of the signification of "things".[16] These two modes of meaning are clearly described by St. Thomas Aquinas in the following passage from the *Quaestiones Quodlibetales*:

> However, the manifestation or expression of some truth is sometimes able to be made concerning things and words, in as much as no doubt as words signify things and one thing is able to be a figure of another. Indeed, the author of things is not only able to use words to signify something, but is also able to arrange a thing as a figure of another thing. And in accordance with this, in Sacred Scripture, truth is manifested *doubly*. According to *one way* since things are signified through words: and in this way the literal sense is formed; according to *another way,* since things are figures of other things and in this way the spiritual sense is formed.[17]

> . . . . .

> Manifestatio autem vel expressio alicuius veritatis potest fieri de aliquo rebus et verbis; in quantum scilicet verba significat res, et una res potest esse figura al-

terius. Auctor autem rerum non solum potest verba ac-commodare ad aliquid significandum, sed etiam res potest disponere in figuram alterius. Et secundum hoc in sacra Scriptura manifestatur veritas *dupliciter. Uno modo* secundum quod res significantur per verba: et in hoc consistit sensus litteralis. *Alio modo* secundum quod res sunt figurae aliarum rerum: et in hoc consistit sensus spiritualis.

Aquinas employs the term *figure* in this passage when speaking of the "meaning of things" and, on each of the three occasions on which the term is used, it denotes the kind of symbol which is both a "thing" with a signification of its own and, also, a "sign" of another "thing."[18] The truths which are made manifest by means of this type of symbolism, Aquinas explains, pertain to the spiritual sense, while those expressed by means of words involve only the literal sense.

In a later section of the *Quaestiones*[19] Aquinas distinguishes three kinds of spiritual sense: the moral or tropological, the allegorical or typical and the anagogical. When discussing the allegorical and anagogical senses he employs the term *figure* in the more specialized, typological meaning of "prefiguration" or "foreshadowing". The allegorical sense, he asserts, has its foundation in that mode of figuration in which the Old Testament foreshadows, or is considered to be a prefiguration (*figura*) of, the New Testament, and the anagogical, in the mode of figuration in which the Old and New together signify, or are considered to be a prefiguration (*figura*) of, heavenly things.

Aquinas, though, does not only use the term *figure* when speaking of the symbolic "things" of Sacred Scripture. In the *Summa Theologiae,* in a reply defending the use of metaphors in Holy Teaching, he states:

Dionysius teaches in the same place that the beam of divine revelation is not extinguished by the sense imagery (*figuras sensibiles*) that veils it, and its truth does not flicker out, since the minds of those given the revelation are not allowed to remain arrested with the images (*in similitudinibus*) but are lifted up to their meaning; moreover, they are so enabled to instruct others. In fact truths expressed metaphorically in one passage of Scripture are more expressly explained elsewhere. Yet even the figurative disguising (*occultatio figurarum*) serves a purpose, both as a challenge to those eager to find out the truth and as a defence against unbelievers ready to ridicule it.[20]

. . . . .

Ad secundum dicendum quod radius divinae revelationis non destruitur propter figuras sensibiles quibus circumvelatur, ut Dionysius dicit, sed remanet in sua veritate, ut mentes quibus revelatio fit non permittantur in similitudinibus remanere sed elevet eas ad cognitionem intelligibilium; et per eos quibus revelatio facta est alii etiam circa haec instruantur. Unde ea quae in uno loco Scripturae traduntur sub metaphoris in aliis locis expressius exponuntur. Et ipso etiam occultatio figurarum utilis est ad exercitium studiosorum et contra irrisiones infidelium.

In this passage the term *figure* has a rhetorical sense and refers to the figurative images and comparisons which serve as a protective covering for Divine truths and through which such truths are revealed to mankind.[21]

From what he has to say, both in the *Summa Theologiae* and in the *Quaestiones Quodlibetales,* it is clear that Aquinas considers such comparisons and likenesses to have a single referent only and to involve no more than "the meaning of words" and the literal sense. In the case of figurative expression, he observes in the *Summa,*[22] the literal sense is not the figure of speech itself but what it signifies. To illustrate his point he cites the example of the expression "the arm of God". When Scripture speaks of "the arm of God," he maintains, "the literal sense is not that God has a physical limb, but that he has what it signifies, namely the power of doing and making." In the *Quaestiones Quodlibetales*[23] he expresses a similar point of view. Here he argues that imaginary comparisons such as the goat, by which some people are designated by Christ in Sacred Scripture, have no reality of their own, but are designed solely for the purpose of signifying the things to which they refer. He therefore concludes that they involve only the "historical" (i.e. the literal) sense and distinguishes them from the historical realities of Scripture which signify Christ and His mystical body and which are not mere "signs" of other things, but both "things" and "signs".

Another medieval theologian who uses the term *figure* in more than one sense when discussing the figurative writing and interpretations of Sacred Scripture is Hugh of St. Victor. In his *Allegoriae in Vetus Testamentum* Hugh applies the term to the kind of symbolism whereby Jacob is considered to be a prefiguration of God the Father[24] and Saul, a prophetic foreshadowing of Christ.[25] In *De Scripturis et Scriptoribus Sacris,* on the other hand, he uses it when speaking of the metaphorical expression of Scripture:

If, as they say, we ought to leap straight from the letter to its spiritual meaning then the figures and likenesses of things by which the mind is educated spiritually, would have been included in the Scriptures by the Holy Spirit in vain.[26]

. . . . .

Quod si, ut isti dicunt, a littere statim ad id quod spiritualiter intelligendum est, transiliendum foret, frustra a Spiritu sancto figurae et similitudines rerum quibus animus ad spiritualia erudiretur, in sacro eloquio interpositae fuissent.

Unlike Aquinas, however, who insists that in figurative expression the image has no importance in itself, Hugh stresses that, in figurative speech, what the letter says is just as important as what it signifies:

For even in that which is accepted as having been said figuratively, the letter is not denied to have its own significance, for when we claim that what is said ought not thus, as it is said, to be understood, we assert that very thing to have been said in some other way. Therefore something is said and is signified by the letter, even then when that which is said is not understood just as it is said, but something else is signified by that which has been said. So then in general something is said and is meant by the letter and we must understand first of all that which is meant by the letter, so that what is signified by it can subsequently be understood.[27]

. . . . .

Nam in eo etiam quod figurative dictum accipitur, littera suam significationem habere non negatur, quia cum id quod dicitur, non sic, dicitur, intelligendum esse asserimus, id ipsum aliquo modo dictum esse affirmamus. Dicitur igitur aliquid et significatur a littera, tunc etiam quando id quod dicitur, non ita intelligitur ut dicitur, sed aliud quod per id dictum significatur. Sic igitur omnino aliquid dicitur et significatur a littera, et intelligendum est illud primum quod significatur a littera ut quid per illud significatur, postea intelligatur.

Furthermore, whereas Aquinas claims that the figurative comparisons of Scripture constitute only "the meaning of words," Hugh, following St. Augustine, treats such comparisons as a form of nature symbolism and cites them as an example of the "meaning of things":

That the Sacred utterances employ the meaning of things, moreover, we shall demonstrate by a particular short and clear example. The Scripture says: "Watch because your adversary the Devil goeth about as a roaring lion." Here, if we should say that the lion stands for the Devil we should mean by "lion" not the word but the thing. For if the two words "devil" and "lion" mean one and the same thing, the likeness of the same thing to itself is not adequate. It remains, therefore, that the word "lion" signifies the animal, but that the animal in turn designates the Devil. And all other things are to be taken after this fashion, as when we say that worm, calf, stone, serpent, and others of this sort signify Christ.[28]

. . . . .

Quod autem rerum significatione sacre utantur eloquia, brevi quodam et aperto exemplo demonstrabimus. Dicit Scriptura: Vigilate, quia adversarius vester diabolus tanquam leo rugiens circuit (1. Pet. 5). Hic si dixerimus leonum significare diabolum, non vocem, sed rem intelligere debemus. Si enim duae hae voces, id est diabolus et leo, unam et eamdem rem significant, incompetem est similitudo ejusdem rei ad seipsam. Restat ergo, ut haec vox leo animal ipsum significet, animal vero diabolum designet; et caetera omnia ad hunc modum accipienda sunt, ut cum dicimus vermem, vitulum, lapidem serpentem, et alia hujusmodi, Christum significare.

Not only did medieval theologians sometimes disagree about the way in which the figurative language and imagery of Sacred Scripture signified, but, in their exegesis of Scripture, they also sometimes treated historical realities or "things" as mere "signs." Honorius d'Autun's interpretation of the story of David and Bathsheba (2 Kings 11) is a good example of such exegesis. Honorius expounds the significance of the story as follows:

Whence it is written: *all these things happened to them as a foreshadowing,* (1 Cor. 10). And thus David is a figure of Christ, Bethsabee a figure of the church and Urias a figure of the devil. And just as she, while she bathed in the Cedran fountain, her clothes having been stripped from her, delighted David and was considered worthy of coming to the embraces of the King by whose princely order her husband also was slaughtered, so too, the church, that is the congregation of the faithful, having been cleansed from the dirt of sins through the washing of sacred baptism, is known to have been united with Christ, Our Lord, and the devil is overcome by those who oppose him. And this the names themselves signal. For David is called *the desirable one,* Bethsabee *the well of the testament,* Urias *the glory of my God,* and he designates the devil, who usurped for himself the glory of his God, saying: *I will be like the most high.*

(Isa. 14)[29]

. . . . .

Unde scribitur: *Omnia in figura contingebant illis* (1 Cor. 10). David itaque Christi figuram, Bethsabee Ecclesiae, Urias diaboli imaginem gessit. Et sicut illa, dum in fonte Cedron lavaretur exuta vestibus suis, Davidi placuit, et ad regios meruit venire complexus, maritus quoque ejus principali jussione est trucidatus: ita et Ecclesia, id est congregatio fidelium, per lavationem sacri baptismatis mundata a sordibus peccatorum Christo Domino noscitur esse sociata, et diabolus apostolis impugnantibus est annihilatus. Hoc et ipsa nomina innuunt. David namque *desiderabilis,* Bethsabee *puteus testamenti,* Urias dicitur *gloria Dei mei,* et designat diabolum, qui sibi gloriam Dei usurpavit, dicens: *Similis ero Altissimo.*

(Isa. 14)

In the above passage, Honorius, as is traditional, identifies David, Bathsheba and Uriah as figures (i.e. prefiguring types) of Christ, the Church and the devil respectively.[30] The authority on which he does so is 1 Cor. 10. where it is stated that everything that happened to the Jewish race was a foreshadowing (*figure*) of what would happen to Christian people. On the same authority, he also goes on to find in the adulterous union of David with Bathsheba a foreshadowing of the spiritual union of Christ with the faithful through Baptism. But while Honorius' exegesis of the David and Bathsheba story discovers a typological relationship between the historical realities of the Old Testament and those of the New, the methods by which the relationship is established are anything but historical.[31] In the typological reading of the story the fact that David has been seduced by Bathsheba's physical beauty into committing adultery with her is ignored and, the bathing which gives rise to their adulterous union, removed form its immediate historical context and treated as a mere "sign" of Baptism. In addition, the significance of the historical personages David, Bathsheba and Uriah is located in the meaning of their names, that is to say, in "the meaning of words."

When we turn our attention from Scriptural "figures" to poetic "figures" we find that the situation is just as complex. In the Medieval Latin poetic tradition the term *figure* was not only used to denote various rhetorical figures,[32] but was also applied to the poetic images which served as a covering for hidden truth,[33] as well as to the hidden truths themselves.[34] Similarly, in Middle English poetry the word *figure* is found in such diverse figurative senses as "symbol," "significant sign," "example," "prefiguration," "foreshadowing or foreboding," "parable" and "metaphoric comparison,"[35] while in Middle Scots poetry *figour* is recorded in the sense of "symbol or symbolic representation" and "figure of speech."[36]

Of even greater significance than the fact that the term *figure* was used in a number of different senses in poetic contexts as in Scriptural ones is the fact that, in such contexts, it could also indicate more than one mode of signification and imply more than one kind of relationship between the literal and figurative levels of meaning. The following passages will serve to clarify these points. The first is taken from a twelfth century commentary on the *Thebaid* of Statius. In introducing his work the author of the commentary compares the compositions of poets to a nut:

> . . . the compositions of poets seem not uncommonly to invite comparison with a nut. Just as there are two parts to a nut, the shell and the kernel, so there are two parts to poetic compositions, the literal and the allegorical meaning. As the kernel is hidden under the shell so the allegorical interpretation is hidden under the literal meaning; as the shell must be cracked to get the kernel so the literal must be broken for the allegories (*figurae*) to be discovered;[37]

. . . . .

> . . . non incommune carmina poetarum nuci comparabilis uidentur: in nuce enim duo sunt, testa et nucleus, sic in carminibus poeticis duo, sensus litteralis et misticus; latet nucleus sub testa; latet sub sensu litterali mistica intelligentia, ut habeas nucleum, fragenda est testa; ut figurae pateant, quatienda est littera;

The term *figure* refers in this passage to the allegorical meanings which lie hidden beneath the literal sense of poetry. To obtain these hidden allegorical meanings, it is necessary, according to the author of the commentary, to break open the literal sense and this he does in his commentary by offering ingenious etymological explanations of personal names and details.[38] The mode of meaning that is implied by his use of the term *figure* in the above passage would thus appear to involve no more than the "meaning of words."

In the second passage I have singled out for discussion, namely Boccaccio's interpretation of the myth of Perseus, the situation is quite different. To illustrate his contention that poetic fiction can have more than one sense, Boccaccio gives an example of how the Perseus myth can be read in four different ways:

> Perseus, the son of Jupiter, by a poetic fiction, killed the Gorgon and, victorious, flew away into the air. If this is read literally, the historical sense appears; if its moral sense is sought, the victory of the prudent man against vice and his approach to virtue is demonstrated. If, however, we wish to adopt an allegorical sense, the elevation of the pious mind above those mundane delights which it despises, to celestial things, is designated. Further, anagogically it might be said that Christ's ascent to his Father after overcoming the prince of this world is prefigured (*figurari*) by such a fiction.[39]

. . . . .

> Perseus Iovis filius figmento poetico occidit Gorgonem, et victor evolavit in ethera. Hoc dum legitur per licteram hystorialis sensus prestatur. Si moralis ex hac lictera queritur intellectus, victoria ostenditur prudentis in vicium, et ad virtutem accessio. Allegorice autem si velimus assummere, piementis spretis mundanis deliciis ad celestia elevatio designatur. Preterea posset et anagogice dici per fabulam Christi ascensum ad patrem mundi principe superato figurari.

The fourfold system of interpretation Boccaccio is employing in passage derives from Biblical exegesis, but he is using such a system very loosely, for as Robert Hollander has noted, the second and third senses are essentially the same and their order has been inverted.[40] However, although Boccaccio is not adhering strictly to the rules of exegesis, when he states in the above passage, that, anagogically, Christ's ascent to his Father after overcoming the prince of this world, is prefigured by the story of Perseus, he is using the passive infinitive *figurari* in the typological sense of theological allegory. In doing so he is suggesting that the same kind of relationship exists between the events of the myth and those of Christ's life as exegetes claim holds between the historical events of Scripture and the future glory they adumbrate. It is also noticeable from Boccaccio's comments immediately prior to his fourfold interpretation of the Perseus myth that he does not attempt to restrict the allegories of the poets to the "meaning of words." Such allegories, he observes, are to be discovered in "the things signified through the cortex" and not in the cortex itself.[41]

A comparison of two occasions on which Chaucer uses the term *figure* reveals differences of a similar kind. When, on describing the Parson in *The General Prologue* to *The Canterbury Tales,* Chaucer remarks,

> And this figure he added eek thereto
> That if god ruste, what shal iren do?[42]

> (*ll.* 499-500)

he is employing the term *figure* in the sense of "metaphorical comparison." The primary meaning of words such as *gold, ruste* and *iren* in the above lines is figurative, that is to say, the words function as "signs" only and do not denote "things" which, in turn, signify other "things." This is not the case though, when, in

Book 5 of *Troilus and Criseyde,* Chaucer uses the same term *figure,* in reference to the symbolic boar which Troilus, in his dream, has seen embracing Criseyde and which we are later told, "bitokneth Diomede" (*l.* 513). In acting as a symbol for Diomede the boar functions as both a "thing" and a "sign" and has a separate literal and figurative significance. The two levels of meaning in this instance are equally important; moreover, the relationship between them is one of analogy.

When considering poetic "figures" the point also needs to be made that, by the time Henryson was writing in the fifteenth century, the habit, which had developed over the previous two centuries, of reading poetic fiction in the same way as the theologians read Scripture, was firmly established. In seeking to understand the principles and practices which are implied by his use of the term figure in **The Fables,** it is important, therefore, to look closely at some examples of the kind of overtly Christian interpretations that were supplied for fiction by fifteenth century writers. One fictional work which attracted a good deal of attention through the Middle Ages was Aesop's fables. Walter, the Englishman's twelfth century version of these fables was widely read in medieval schools where its words, constructions and meanings were analyzed and commented upon. It is consequently not surprising to find that a tradition of Latin commentaries exists in which additional allegorical interpretations are offered for Walter's fables. A fifteenth century commentary[43] belonging to this tradition is particularly relevant to the present discussion since it provides additional moralities for Walter's *De Lino et Hirundine* and *De Mure et Rana* which are remarkably close to Henryson's moralizations of these fables.

In dealing with *De Lino et Hirundine,* Walter's fable about the swallow whose warning to other birds to destroy the flax before it poses a threat to them goes unheeded, the fifteenth century commentator first explains the general moral truth that the fable demonstrates:

> Here the author includes another fable of which the lesson is that none should spurn the counsel of another because it often happens that people rejecting the advice of others become ineffectual and so often get into trouble.[44]

>   · · · · ·

> Hic autor, ponit aliam fabulam cuius documentum est quod nullus debet contemnere consilium alterius quia accidit multotiens quod respuentes consilium aliorum inutiles fiunt unde frequenter eis malum evenit.

At the conclusion of the *expositio ad sensum,* which consists of a prose retelling of the fable, he then offers an allegorical interpretation:

> In allegorical terms we can take the birds to mean sinners and the swallow spiritual men who often advise sinners to desist and refrain from their sins, but the sin-

ners, spurning the warnings and the doctrine of the spiritual men, at length are ensnared by the nets of the devil and are delivered over to everlasting fire.[45]

                · · · · ·

> Allegorice per aves intelligere possumus peccatores, per hyrundinem vero spirituales homines qui sepe ammonent peccatores ut desistant et abstineant a peccatis, sed peccatores ammonitionem et doctrinam spiritualium contemnentos tandem per retia dyaboli capiuntur et eterno igno traduntur.

In discovering a parallel between the actions of the swallow and the birds in Walter's fable and those of holy men and sinners the commentator does not treat Walter's animals, which, as vehicles for observing human life and morality, function as descriptive symbols or "signs" in the narrative, as mere "signs" of other "things," but rather as interpretative symbols which are "things" with an identity of their own as well as being "signs" of other "things." As a result the allegorical sense of the fable is an additional level of meaning which co-exists with the literal narrative and preserves literal contexts.

Such was not always the case, however. Very often, Christian interpretations of medieval fictions ignore and dissolve literal contexts and do not easily fit the shape of the narrative. Sometimes, too, more than one interpretation is provided for a particular story. The treatment accorded the story of Focus, the smith, in the Middle English *Gesta Romanorum,*[46] is an excellent illustration of such practices. We are informed in this story that, because he has disobeyed the emperor's command that his birthday should be kept as a holiday, Focus is called before the emperor to account for his disobedience. When he announces that he must earn eight pence every day so that he can yield two to his father, lend two to his son, lose two on his wife and spend two on himself, he is deemed to have given a good account of himself and, instead of being punished by the emperor, is chosen as his successor.

Two separate moralizations accompany the story. In the first of these the emperor is interpreted in a good sense (*in bono*)[47] and equated with "our Lord ihesu crist." Virgil, the philosopher who made the emperor a statue that revealed the names of those who failed to observe his day, is said to represent the "Holy ghost" and the smith, Focus, is identified as "euery goode cristyn man." In addition, an appropriate religious significance is provided for the messengers of the emperor and for each two pence that the smith claims he must yield, lend, lose or spend.

Most of this first moralization corresponds fairly closely with the events of the narrative. The one instance where this is not the case is the interpretation of Focus, the smith, as "euery goode cristyn man." It is stated in the moralization that such a man "owith euery day to worch goode workys, and so ben worthi to be presented to Þhe Emperour of Hevene," but in the narrative the smith is not brought before the emperor on account of his worthiness, but because he has broken a law established by the emperor. In the second moralization that is provided for the story this conflict does not occur. Virgil, the philosopher, and Focus, the smith, are again respectively equated with the "holy ghost" and "every good Christian," but this time the emperor is interpreted in a bad sense (*in malo*) rather than in a good sense and is said to represent the "devil Þe which sterith a man to holde his day, that is to synne, and to wroth god euermor." Since, in this second interpretation, the emperor is equated with "the devil," it is quite fitting that Focus, the smith, who breaks the emperor's law, should be interpreted as "every good Christian." But while one problem has now been solved another has arisen. This new problem concerns the role of the prelate whom it is said the Holy Ghost sets up in the Church "to shewe and pronounce vicis, and allege holy scripturis aʒenst synnerys." By exposing vices and quoting Holy Scripture to sinners the prelate is opposing the devil, yet, in the narrative, Virgil's statue, which has a similar function in that it has been designed to reveal the names of those who break the emperor's laws, acts *for* the emperor by helping him to uphold his law. In the second moralization as in the first, therefore, the figurative reading does not fully co-exist with the literal narrative and does not always preserve literal contexts.

On the basis of the evidence that has been presented, then, two important conclusions can be drawn. The first is that it is likely that Henryson would have understood a good deal more by the phrase "be figure" than the typological mode of writing and interpretation that Erich Auerbach describes as "figural" and the second is that his use of the phrase allows not only for a wide range of figurative practices in his fables but also for more than one kind of relationship between their literal and figurative levels of meaning. I will now briefly examine Henryson's figurative methods in *The Fables* and will attempt to show that such methods are both more varied and more traditional than is usually acknowledged.

If Henryson's fables are classified according to the type of figurative technique he employs in them and the kind of relationship between story and morality that results, they fall, not into two categories, as some critics have suggested,[48] but into three distinct groups including a number of sub groups. To the first group belong such fables as **"The Two Mice," "The Fox and the Wolf"** and **"The Wolf and the Wether."** These fables are typical of most fables belonging to the Aesopic tradition in that the animal protagonists are metaphoric representatives of the human world and have a single referent only and in that the fable narrative concludes with a general moral statement which

either sums up the main idea of the fable (**"The Two Mice"**) or explains what the whole fable illustrates or warns (**"The Fox and the Wolf"** and **"The Wolf and the Wether"**).

The second group of fables is a much larger and more diverse one. In the concluding moralization of each of the fables belonging to this group Henryson follows the exegetical practice of reducing the narrative to a number of parts and of providing one-to-one correspondences for each part. The mode of meaning he employs and the relationship between tale and moral that results, however, are not the same in all fables. In the case of **"The Cock and the Fox"** and **"The Wolf and the Lamb"** the figurative meaning expounded in the *moralitas* is the metaphoric sense of the fable and arises out of what the animal protagonists, as metaphors for human beings, say and do in the narrative. In fables such as **"The Sheep and the Dog," "The Cock and the Jasp," "The Trial of the Fox," "The Preaching of the Swallow," "The Fox, the Wolf and the Cadgea"** and **"The Fox, The Wolf and the Husbandman,"** on the other hand, the meaning expounded in the *moralitas* is an additional sense which co-exists with the literal narrative and extends and complements it thematically.

Sometimes, in explaining this additional sense, Henryson treats details of the literal narrative as interpretative symbols which are both "things" and "signs." The jasp is treated in this way in **"The Cock and the Jasp"** and so also is the mare in **"The Trial of the Fox,"** the fowler, the swallow and the birds in **"The Preaching of the Swallow,"** and the fox, the husbandman, the hens, the woods and the cabok in **"The Fox, the Wolf and the Husbandman."** On other occasions the additional sense is established by means of direct comparisons, such as when in **"The Fox, the Wolf and the Husbandman,"** the wolf is likened to "a wicked man," or when, in **"The Trial of the Fox,"** the lion is likened to "the world," the wolf to "sensuality," the mare's hoof to the "thought of death" and the fox to "temptations." Sometimes, too, Henryson combines direct comparison with metaphorical interpretation (e.g., in **"The Sheep and the Dog"** where the sheep is said to be a *figure* of "the poor common people" while the wolf and the raven are respectively likened to "a sheriff" and "a coroner") or with "the meaning of things" (e.g. in **"The Cock and the Jasp"** where the jasp, which is figuratively equated with "wisdom," is treated as an interpretative symbol,while the cock, which functions as a descriptive symbol, is likened to "a fool who scorns learning").[49]

In fables belonging to the second group, moreover, the additional sense is sometimes based on only one part of the narrative (e.g. **"The Trial of the Fox"** and **"The Preaching of the Swallow"**) and may even conflict with the narrative action. Examples of such a conflict are to be found in **"The Trial of the Fox"** where the mare's absence from the parliament called by the lion is condemned in the narrative but justified in the *moralitas,* and in **"The Fox, the Wolf and the Husbandman,"** where the husbandman, who agrees to bribe the fox in order to resolve his dispute with the wolf, is equated with "ane godlie man" (*l.* 2434) and the hens which are used as the bribe with "warkis that fra ferme faith proceidis" (*l.* 2437). In the case of the latter fable the fact that Henryson's text underwent Protestant revision during the Reformation may well account for such inconsistencies, but, at the same time, it must be remembered that the situation where something is interpreted in a bad sense in the narrative and in a good sense in the allegorical reading was common in scriptural and homiletic exegesis and justified by churchmen such as St. Gregory the Great.[50] The use of association rather than the literal narrative as a basis for forming an interpretation was also common in both traditions and the technique appears to have been employed in the case of Henryson's interpretation of the Husbandman as "ane godlie man," for ploughing is associated with godliness in Langland's *Piers Plowman*[51] and the plough with good example, by Rabanus Maurus in his *Allegoriae in Sacram Scripturam.*[52]

Because of the difficulties that are encountered in relating tale to moral in **"The Trial of the Fox"** and **"The Fox, the Wolf and the Husbandman,"** it has been argued that, in the moralization, Henryson deliberately sets out to surprise the reader and to reverse the readers' expectations.[53] In these fables, though, as in **"The Cock and the Jasp,"** this line of argument seems to me inappropriate, since precedents for Henryson's techniques are to be found in both the exegetical and homiletic traditions. In addition, it should be noted that despite the lack of synthesis of the individual parts of the interpretation, Henryson's allegorical reading of **"The Trial of the Fox"** and **"The Fox, the Wolf and the Husbandman,"** does, in an additive kind of way, form an interpretation of the whole and does, thematically, extend and complement the narrative, for while the narrative of each fable is concerned with worldliness and with greed, the *moralitas* examines the spiritual implications of such behavior.

The third of the three groups into which Henryson's fables can be divided consists of only two fables: **"The Lion and the Mouse"** and **"The Paddock and the Mouse."** Both of these fables combine allegorical interpretation with moral application of a more general nature. In the first part of the *moralitas* which concludes **"The Lion and the Mouse"** individual interpretations are provided for the two animals and for the forest. These interpretations relate to only one part of the narrative and, whereas the forest is treated as an interpretative symbol which is both a "thing" and a "sign," the relationship between the lion and the ruler he is said to signify and between the mice and "the community" is a metaphoric one. In the second part of the *moralitas* the fable is addressed to "lordis of prudence" (*l.* 1594). Here the whole narrative is treated as an *exemplum* which illustrates the virtue of *pietie* (*l.* 1595)[54] and which serves as a guide to others to act in the same way.

A two-part *moralitas* also concludes **"The Paddock and the Mouse."** The first of the two parts is written in ballade stanzas and expounds the metaphorical sense of the fable while the second is written in rhyme royal stanzas and presents an allegorical interpretation of the narrative. Although this allegorical interpretation is based on only one part of the narrative, and although, in the case of the equation of the frog with "man's body," literal contexts have been ignored and dissolved, the allegorical reading relates thematically to the whole fable and is an extension of its literal sense. Furthermore, the frog and the mouse are treated as both "things" and "signs" in the allegorical reading with the result that the relationship between the literal and figurative levels of meaning is one of analogy rather than metaphor.

Owing to the range of material to be covered it has not been possible to examine any of Henryson's fables in detail. Nevertheless, it should be clear from my discussion of his figurative practices that he employs more than one type of figurative technique in *The Fables* and that this results in more than one kind of relationship between the literal and figurative levels of meaning. When Henryson's figurative methods are properly understood, therefore, not only is there no evidence of any tension between theory and practice, but also many of the difficulties critics have had in relating tale to moral cease to exist, for what at first may appear to be discrepancies, turn out, on closer inspection, to be accepted features of the traditions in which he is writing.

Notes

1. All references to Henryson's fables are to *The Poems of Robert Henryson,* ed. Denton Fox (Oxford, 1981).

2. For some statements of this view, see, Richard Bauman, "The Folk Tale and Oral Tradition in the Fables of Robert Henryson," *Fabula,* 6 (1963), 117; "Allegorical," rev. of *Robert Henryson: A Study of the Major Narrative Poems* in *TLS* (10 August 1967), p. 726 and Daniel Murtaugh, "Henryson's Animals" *Texas Studies in Literature and Language,* 14 (1972), 408, n. 3.

3. See, for example, Denton Fox, "Henryson's Fables," *English Literary History,* 29 (1962), 337-56; Anthony White Jenkins, "The mind and art of Robert Henryson," unpub. doct. diss. (University of California, Berkeley, 1967), pp. 2-24; Tom

Scott, "Allegorical," *TLS* (31 August 1967), p. 780; and John Macqueen, *Robert Henryson: A Study of the Major Narrative Poems* (Oxford 1967), pp. 94-188.

4. For a discussion of the function of the apparent dissonance between tale and moral in some fables, see I. W. A. Jamieson, "The Beast Tale in Middle Scots; Some Thoughts on the History of a Genre," *Parergon,* 2 (1972), 28-32 and "To preue thare preching be a poesye: Some Thoughts on Henryson's Poetics," *Parergon,* 8 (1974); M. M. Carens, "A Prolegomenon for the Study of Robert Henryson," unpub. doct. diss. (Pennsylvania State University, 1974), pp. 155-63; George Clark, "Henryson and Aesop: the Fable Transformed," *English Literary History,* 43 (1976), 1-18; Douglas Gray, *Robert Henryson* (Leiden, 1979), pp. 121-138; Stephen Khinoy, "Tale-Moral Relationships in Henryson's *Moral Fables,*" *SSL* [*Studies in Scottish Literature*] 17 (1982), 99-115; Marianne Powell *Fabula Docet: Studies in the Background and Interpretation of Henryson's Morall Fabillis* in *Studies in English* (Odense University), 6 (1983), 112-5 and 152-81; and C. David Benson, "O Moral Henryson," *Fifteenth Century Studies: Recent Essays,* ed. Robert F. Yeager (Hamden, Ct., 1984), 215-35.

5. Translated by Ralph Manheim in *Scenes from the Drama of European Literature,* ed. D. Bethurum (New York, 1959), pp. 11-76.

6. "Figura," p. 53.

7. "Henryson's Fables," p. 341.

8. "Studies in the Tradition and Morality of Henryson's Fables," unpub. doct. diss. (University of Notre Dame, 1968), pp. 37-40.

9. "Some Aspects of Structure in Medieval Literature," *Parergon,* 16 (1976), 11.

10. *Robert Henryson,* p. 120.

11. *Ibid,* p. 120.

12. "Figura", p. 64.

13. For a discussion of the difference between exegetical theory and practice in the Middle Ages see David Aers, *Piers Plowman and Christian Allegory* (London, 1975), pp. 9-32. Aers challenges the assumptions of Auerbach and others about the historical nature of Biblical typology, claiming that the dominant figurative mode in the Middle Ages was one in which figuralists dissolved "events and actions, and with them both the text's images and existential dimensions" (p. 32).

14. Unfortunately, since very little is known about Henryson's life, it is not possible to do more than guess at the sources of his information about the term *figure.* It is only by establishing the concepts and principles with which the term was commonly associated in the Middle Ages, therefore, that we can hope to shed some light on its implications in the Prologue.

15. Some critics have recognized the wide-ranging nature of the term *figure* in the Middle Ages (see, for example, the comments of Robert Gerke, "Studies in the Tradition and Morality of Henryson's Fables," pp. 37-8; Douglas Gray, *Robert Henryson,* p. 120; and Marianne Powell, *Fabula Docet,* pp. 72-3), but they have failed to support their insights, either with any detailed discussion of the term's use, or any analysis of the different kinds of figurative writing and interpretation with which it was associated.

16. On the traditional nature of this type of statement and for further examples see H. de Lubac, *Exégèse Médiévale: Les Quatres Sens de l'Ecriture,* 4 vols. (Paris, 1959-64), vol. 1, pt 2, pp. 496-7.

17. S. Thomae Aquinatus, *Quaestiones Quodlibetales,* ed. P. Fr. Raymundi Spiazzi, O. P. (Taurini, 1949), q. 6 a. 1, p. 146. Unless otherwise indicated, all translations are my own.

18. The distinction Aquinas draws between "the meaning of things" and "the meaning of words" derives from St. Augustine. See *De Doctrina Christiana,* ed. Joseph Martin, *Corpus Christianorum,* 32 (Turnholt, 1962), Bk 2, 10:15, p. 41. For a detailed discussion of Augustine's views and their transmission see also J. Chydenius, "The Theory of Medieval Symbolism," *Societas Scientiarum Fennica: Commentationes Humanarum Literarum,* 27(2) (Helsinki, 1960), pp. 5-39.

19. See *Respondeo,* q. 6, a. 2, p. 147.

20. St. Thomas Aquinas, *Summa Theologiae,* ed. and trans. Thomas Gilby O. P. (Cambridge, 1963), Vol. 1, q. 1, a. 9, r. 2, p. 35.

21. It should also be noted that Aquinas is here speaking about the metaphorical expression of the Bible in much the same way as the poets speak about fiction. On the notion of fiction acting as a veil for truth see Peter Dronke, *Fabula,* (Leiden, 1974), pp. 47-55 and Stephen Manning, "The Nun's Priest's Morality and the Medieval attitude Towards Fables," *Journal of English and Germanic Philology,* 59 (1960), 410-11.

22. Vol. 1, q. 1, a. 10, r. 3, pp. 40-1.

23. *Respondeo,* q. 6, a. 2, p. 147. For a discussion of what Aquinas has to say in the *Quaestiones* about figurative comparisons see J. Chydenius, "The Theory of Medieval Symbolism," pp. 37-8.

24. "In hoc figura, Jacob figurat Deum Patrem," *Patrologiae Cursus Completus,* Series Latina, ed. J.

P. Migne, 217 vols. (Paris, 1844 ff.), vol. 175, col. 686. This work will hereafter be referred to by the abbreviation *PL.*

25. "Secundum aliam figuram Saul (1 Reg. 11) significant Christum." *Ibid,* col. 686.

26. *PL,* 175, col. 14 D.

27. *Ibid,* col. 14. That Hugh's views on figurative expression differ from those of Aquinas is also remarked on by J. Chydenius, "The Theory of Medieval Symbolism," p. 37 and Pamela Gradon, *Form and Style in Early English Literature,* (London, 1971), p. 38.

28. *The Didascalicon of Hugh of St. Victor,* trans., Jerome Taylor, (New York, 1961), p. 122. For the Latin text see *Eruditiones Didascalicae, PL,* vol. 176, col. 790. On the fact that in *The Didascalicon* Hugh makes a spiritual sense of the metaphoric sense of Scripture see, too, H. de Lubac, *Exégèse Médiévale,* Vol. 2, pt. 2, p. 278, n. 4. Hugh, moreover, is not the only medieval theologian who treats the metaphorical expression of Sacred Scripture in this way. Another who does so is Nicholas of Lyre. For a discussion of his views see de Lubac, *Exégèse Médiévale,* Vol. 2, pt. 2, p. 354.

29. *Selectorum Psalmorum Expositio, PL,* Vol. 172, col. 283.

30. On the traditional nature of this type of exegesis see H. de Lubac, *Exégèse Médiévale,* Vol. 1, pt. 2, p. 463.

31. For some examples of the unhistorical nature of typological interpretation, including medieval exegesis of the David and Bathsheba story, see David Aers, *Piers Plowman and Christian Allegory,* pp. 20-32.

32. Geoffrey of Vinsauf, for example, applies the term to the stylistic figures *sinodoche, thapinosis* and *methonomia.* See *Les Arts Poétiques du XIIe et du XIIIe siècle,* ed. E. Faral (Paris, 1924), p. 292.

33. Bernard Silvestris, for instance, points out that *figura* was used as a synonym for *involucrum* (covering or wrapping) and could encompass both historical narrative and fable. For a discussion of Silvestris' views on *figura* see Peter Dronke, *Fabula,* pp. 119-20. See also John of Capua's use of the term in *Directorium Humanae vitae (Les Fabulistes Latins),* ed. L. Hervieux (Paris, 1899; rpt. Hildesheim, 1970), Vol. 5, p. 81; and Pierre Bersuire's statement that "a figure is perceived as an exterior image or form." Bersuire's definition is quoted in full by J. B. Allen in *The Friar as Critic* (Nashville, 1971), pp. 42-3.

34. *Figura* is used in the sense of "inner" or "figurative" meaning in the commentary on the *Thebaid* of Statius commonly attributed to Fulgentius—see

S. Fulgentii Episcopi, *Super Thebaiden* in *Fabii Planciadis Fulgentii V. C. Opera,* ed. R. Helm (Stuttgart, 1898; rpt. 1970), *ll.* 12-20, p. 180, and in the *moralitas* of a fable attributed to Odo of Cheriton (see *Les Fabulistes Latins,* Vol. 4, p. 253).

35. See *Middle English Dictionary,* ed. H. Kurath, S. M. Kuhn and J. Reidy (Ann Arbor, MI, 1952), p. 551.

36. See *A Dictionary of the Older Scottish Tongue,* ed. William A. Craigie (Chicago and London, 1931-), II, 468-9.

37. *Fulgentius the Mythographer,* trans., Leslie Whitbread (Ohio, 1971), p. 239. For the Latin text of the commentary see S. Fulgentii Episcopi, *Super Thebaiden* in *Fabii Planciadis Fulgentii V. C. Opera,* ed. R. Helm, p. 180. Whitbread argues in the introduction to his translation that although the commentary has been commonly ascribed to Fulgentius "it seems safer to speak of an imitator or pseudo Fulgentius as its author," (p. 235). He also notes (p. 236) that a twelfth or thirteenth century date has been proposed for the commentary.

38. On the prevalence of this type of interpretation in the twelfth century see J. B. Allen, *The Friar as Critic,* pp. 14-7.

39. *Genealogie Deorum Gentilium Libri,* ed. V. Romano (Bari, 1951), Vol. 1, iii, p. 19, *ll.* 23-30.

40. See R. Hollander, *Allegory in Dante's Commedia* (Princeton, 1969), pp. 34-5. On the similarities between the allegories of the poets and those of the theologians see also Hollander, pp. 19-24, J. B. Allen, *The Friar as Critic,* passim. and pp. 69-116, and H. de Lubac, *Exégèse Médiévale,* Vol. 2, pt. 2, p. 208.

41. *Genealogie Deorum Gentilium Libri,* Vol. 1, iii, p. 19, *ll.* 19-23.

42. All references to Chaucer's work are to *The Works of Geoffrey Chaucer,* ed. F. N. Robinson (2nd edn., Oxford, 1957).

43. See *Esopus moralisatus cum bono commento* (1492), Bodleian Library. Auct. 5.6.80. For a discussion of this and similar commentaries see Douglas Gray, *Robert Henryson,* pp. 125-8.

44. Esopus moralisatus cum bono commento (1492). There are no folio or page numbers in the MS.

45. *Ibid.*

46. See *The Early English Versions of the Gesta Romanorum,* ed. Sidney J. H. Herrtage (London, 1879), pp. 30-3.

47. The principles behind this type of interpretation are expounded by St. Augustine in *De Doctrina*

Christiana, Bk. 3, 25:36. For some examples in the commentary of Hugh of St. Cher see J. B. Allen, *The Friar as Critic,* pp. 31-3.

48. See, for example, M. M. Carens, "A Prolegomenon for the Study of Robert Henryson," pp. 155-63, and Douglas Gray, *Robert Henryson,* pp. 121-4.

49. For a detailed discussion of Henryson's figurative techniques in *The Cock and the Jasp* see my article, "Henryson's Figurative Technique in *The Cock and the Jasp,*" in *Words and Wordsmiths: A volume for H. L. Rogers,* ed. G. Barnes et al. (Sydney, 1989), pp. 13-21.

50. See D. Aers, *Piers Plowman and Christian Allegory,* p. 24, and H. de Lubac, *Exégèse Médiévale,* Vol. 1, pt. 2, p. 461.

51. See William Langland, *The Vision of William Concerning Piers the Plowman,* ed. Walter W. Skeat, C Text, EETS, O.S., 54 (1873; rpt. London, 1959), Passus 22, *ll.* 260-6.

52. See *PL* 112, *aratrum,* col. 867.

53. See I. W. A. Jamieson, "The Poetry of Robert Henryson: A Study of the Use of Source Material," unpub. doct. diss. (University of Edinburgh, 1964), p. 272 and Douglas Gray, *Robert Henryson,* p. 131.

54. In the fifteenth century the term could mean "faithfulness to duty" as well as "compassion." See, N. Von Kreisler, "Henryson's Visionary Fable: Tradition and Craftsmanship in The Lyoun and the Mous," *Texas Studies in Literature and Language,* 15 (1973), 397-9.

Tim William Machan (essay date 1990)

SOURCE: Machan, Tim William. "Robert Henryson and Father Aesop: Authority in the *Moral Fables.*" *Studies in the Age of Chaucer* 12 (1990): 193-214.

[*In the following essay, Machan contends that by placing Aesop in the* Moral Fables, *Henryson extended "literary authority" to himself.*]

Recent critical discussion of Robert Henryson's *Moral Fables* has emphasized that the fables are not primarily notable for their "delightfully vivid and appealing" descriptions of the animal characters,[1] the terms in which they had been regularly dismissed. Indeed, the serious and genuine nature of Henryson's concern for the human condition seems unquestionable, as do the diverse artistry of the *Fables* and the sophistication of its themes.[2] One of these themes, which Denton Fox

has briefly explored, involves a self-consciousness about authorship which runs throughout Henryson's works. In Fox's words, one of the "profound resemblances" among *Orpheus and Eurydice, The Testament of Cresseid,* and the *Moral Fables* "has to do with the figure of the poet and function of poetry."[3] As contemporary as such a thematic concern might sound, however, it is a concern which emerges largely as a response to specific cultural determinants of fourteenth- and fifteenth-century vernacular poetry which admitted authority and authorship as characteristics only of classical and ecclesiastical writers and texts. The term "auctor" itself was reserved for ancient poets, church fathers, and learned commentators, while a vernacular writer, whatever he may have thought of himself as an artist, was a "makar."[4] The extent to which, indeed, vernacular medieval English writers could think of themselves as artists is problematic, inasmuch as English did not have published, standardized handbooks of grammar or style—the tools, so to speak, for measuring artistry—until the early to middle part of the sixteenth century.[5]

Henryson's interest in "the figure of the poet and the function of poetry" was also very likely contextually conditioned by his respect for Chaucer, who not simply revolutionized vernacular meter, narrative, and characterization but also introduced to English less tangible yet perhaps more revolutionary attitudes toward vernacular writers. But inasmuch as Chaucer wrote with cultural constraints similar to the ones Henryson confronted, the English poet typically toys with the authorial posture at the same time he insists he is only a compiler or translator. In his introduction to the "Canticus Troili" of book 1 of *Troilus and Criseyde,* for instance, Chaucer is careful to deny himself any responsibility for the poem and to impute it all to his author Lollius (1.393-99):

> And of his song naught only the sentence,
> As writ myn auctour called Lollius,
> But pleinly, save oure tonges difference,
> I dar wel seyn, in al, that Troilus
> Seyde in his song, loo, every word right thus
> As I shal seyn; and whoso list it here,
> Loo, next this vers he may it fynden here.[6]

Whether or not Chaucer believed there was an actual historian named Lollius is immaterial here,[7] for the claim that at this particular point in the text there is only a "tonges difference" between Chaucer and his "auctour" is completely disingenuous: Chaucer here intentionally supplements his "source," whatever it was, with one of Petrarch's sonnets. In melding two distinct works, he is thus creating an original text at the very moment he is insisting that he is only translating, and this juxtaposition of incongruent theory and practice bespeaks an awareness of the complex and potentially problematic nature of concepts like literary authority and authorship.

One way to approach the *Moral Fables,* I suggest, is from a perspective which sees Henryson's apparently modern concern with "the figure of the poet and the function of poetry" as a response to the cultural determinants of art in the late Middle Ages. In this vein I would argue that, as a fifteenth-century "makar," Henryson confronted two artistic conflicts. On the one hand, as a follower of Chaucer, Henryson had a well-formed conception of himself as an artist; but on the other hand, as a vernacular writer, he still lacked the cultural status of an "auctor." And again, on the one hand, for poetry to be serious by late-medieval standards it had to be moral and ethical;[8] but on the other hand, for it to be entertaining, it had to be rhetorically "sueit and delectabill" (*Moral Fables* 16). These conflicts, I believe, do not simply inform the *Moral Fables;* they constitute a thematic focus, the theoretical and artistic sophistication of which rivals Chaucer's consideration of the same topic. Accordingly, by means of a close rhetorical reading of the **"Prologue"** to the *Moral Fables* and the fable of **"The Lion and the Mouse"** in particular, I hope to show how Henryson resolves his twofold artistic conflict by articulating his own views of the nature of literary authority and by dramatizing his emergence as a vernacular author. This emergence, in turn, provides insight into the overall structure of the *Moral Fables.*

As Douglas Gray has said, the **"Prologue"** "offers in miniature a defence of poetic fiction, and of the fable in particular, in terms which are not entirely dissimilar from those used later by Sidney."[9] Indeed, if at first glance the **"Prologue"** seems to be only a collection of medieval commonplaces—the fruit and the chaff (line 15) and the bent bow (line 22)—Henryson in effect, by juxtaposing a variety of traditional theories, demonstrates their potentially contradictory nature. Such juxtaposition undermines the absolute authority of any of the traditional positions and consequently provides for Henryson's inscription of his own view that literary authority need not be restricted to the inherited "auctores."

The two central theoretical issues of the **"Prologue"** are the value of poetry and the nature of authority, the first of which is Henryson's initial concern (lines 1-10):

> Thocht feinȝeit fabils of ald poetre
> Be not al grunded vpon truth, ȝit than,
> Thair polite termes of sweit rhetore
> Richt plesand are vnto the eir of man;
> And als the caus quhy thay first began
> Wes to repreif the of thi misleuing,
> O man, be figure of ane vther thing.[10]

In phrasing the distinction between the content and the style of a poem in this fashion, Henryson reshapes traditional concepts in two ways. First, he does not explicitly condemn—and thereby he implicitly accepts—the fact that the "polite termes of sweit rhetore" can be beneficial even if the ideas they express are false; "ald poetre," that is, does not need to be allegorized to be ideologically acceptable, for the rhetoric alone can validate it. Second, he questions the nature of old fables' truth or falsehood, inasmuch as, while he begins by conceding their falsehood, he continues by pointing out that rhetoric can correct evil living; but such would be the case only if the ideas which the rhetoric expresses are themselves true. His initial distinction between "sweit rhetore" and false content is thus blurred if not obviated, for the distinction between absolute truth and falsehood, upon which it depends, is itself implicitly challenged. Priscian and others, by contrast, had defended fables simply on the grounds that, rightly understood, their content, or doctrine, was in fact ethical, and the Aesopic fables in particular were generally recognized to be unambiguously moral.[11]

The second stanza furthers this reshaping of traditional medieval literary theory (lines 8-14):

> In lyke manner as thow a bustious eird,
> Swa it be laubourit with grit diligence,
> Springis the flouris and corne abreird,
> Hailsum and gude to mannis sustenence;
> Sa springis thair ane morall sweit sentence
> Oute of the subtell dyte of poetry,
> To gude purpois, quha cuid it weill apply.

Again, Henryson seems to be employing a thoroughly conventional distinction between the sweetness and beauty of flowers—or rhetoric—and the ethical utility of corn—or content; such, indeed, is how the image is used in the corresponding Latin of Gualterus Anglicus, one of Henryson's sources.[12] Yet Henryson dissolves this very distinction at the same time he makes it, for, as Gregory Kratzmann points out, "The syntax of lines 10-11 expresses the idea that *both* are 'Hailsum and gude to mannis sustenence.'"[13] Moreover, the recurrence of the adjective "sweit" further identifies the "rhetore" of line 3 with the "sentence" of line 12, so that Henryson implies that poetry can be at once ethically "morall" and rhetorically "sweit."

But having thus reinterpreted some traditional distinctions between content and style in a way strongly reminiscent of Geoffrey of Vinsauf's approach in the *Poetria nova,* Henryson proceeds to put into question his own reinterpretation by employing a traditional literary metaphor in an unambiguously traditional way (lines 15-18):

> The nuttis schell, thocht it be hard and teuch,
> Haldis the kirnell, sueit and delectabill;
> Sa lyis thair ane doctrine wyse aneuch
> And full of frute, vnder ane fenȝeit fabill.

Here Henryson asserts that rhetoric is not "plesand" or "sweit" but "hard and teuch" and implies that the real value of fables is the unconditional truth which they contain. And as the reader attempts to hold these contradictory ideas together, Henryson again changes direction (lines 19-21):

> And clerkis sayis, it is richt profitabill
> Amangis ernist to ming ane merie sport,
> To blyth the spreit and gar the tyme be schort.

Henryson thus introduces still another perspective on the nature of truth and falsehood and on the value of rhetoric: he simply circumvents the issues by stressing the physiological benefits of, in a phrase resonant of *The Canterbury Tales,* mixing "ernist" and "sport" by what might be called recreational reading.[14]

This facet of the theoretical discussion continues with the traditional image of the bent bow and reaches an end in the last line of the next stanza, where Henryson quotes the alleged Latin words of Aesop: "Dulcius arrident seria picta iocis" (line 28). Rhetorically, this quotation would seem to have an air of resolution and finality about it: it purports to be the actual words of a genuine "auctor," unlike the rest of the **"Prologue"** it is in the genuine authorial language, and it is followed by a different discussion—of Henryson's own role in the production of the *Moral Fables.* Yet if Aesop's words end the discussion, they do not conclude it. They summarize only the position laid out in lines 19-27, which is itself only one of the viewpoints on poetry and truth which Henryson expresses in the first four stanzas. If one tries to apply Aesop's words to the earlier discussion, it is difficult to see how the distinction between serious and jocund things aligns itself with the other distinctions in any meaningful way. For instance, if the rhetoric of a poem is "hard and teuch," it would seem to be "seria"; but then the "doctrine" it contains becomes jocund diversion, a categorization which is oxymoronic and intellectually indefensible in medieval culture. And again, if some "fenʒeit fabils" are not true, how can their content be either serious or jocund?

Thus the final effect of Aesop's words, according to Kratzmann, is to draw "our attention to the question, at once fundamental and complex, of *how* poetry can accommodate and reconcile these divergent impulses."[15] The **"Prologue"** itself may well be an answer to the very question it poses, however; that is, in exposing these divergent impulses in a coherent, poetic format, Henryson ipso facto accommodates and reconciles them. In any case, the point I wish to stress here is that, in revealing these sometimes contradictory conceptions of poetry, Henryson, as a vernacular writer, assumes the authority to speak in the vernacular about literary matters and thereby abrogates both the exclusivity of the authorial position expressed by Aesop's words and, perhaps, the idea of exclusivity itself. Thus, while the first three stanzas blur the distinctions between truth and falsehood and style and content, the fourth stanza begins to blur that between "auctor" and "makar."

In the subsequent three stanzas Henryson seems to reverse even this position, for he presents himself in one of the common poses of traditional vernacular writers—a humble transmitter of another's texts at the request of a social superior (lines 29-35):

> Of this poete [Aesop], my maisteris, with ʒour leif,
> Submitting me to ʒour correctioun,
> In mother toung, of Latyng, I wald preif
> To mak ane maner of translatioun—
> Nocht of my self, for vane presumptioun,
> But be requeist and precept of ane lord,
> Of quhome the name it neidis not record.

But there is something disingenuous about this posture and something even more disingenuous about his subsequent assertion that (lines 36-38)

> In hamlie language and in termes rude
> Me neidis wryte, for quhy of eloquence
> Nor rethorike, I neuer vnderstude.

As with the use of the humility *topos* by the Franklin at the beginning of his *Tale* (*FranT* 716-27), these remarks are belied by their own context, for Henryson has just finished a very eloquent discussion of his very sophisticated understanding of rhetoric. But to call them simply ironic is imprecise. Superficially, to be sure, Henryson is affirming the authority of his "poete" (line 29) and "author" (line 43) Aesop, but he has also exposed the problematic nature of poetry and of the traditional—authorized—views of it. In now reasserting a portion of that view, he would again seem to be laying it open to questioning. Specifically, he makes the reader ask about the bases for the terms "author" and "translator" and wonder whether a vernacular "makar," especially one as theoretically sophisticated as this one, is not also entitled to be an author; rhetorically, that is, these stanzas have much the same effect as Chaucer's ascription of the "Canticus Troili" to Lollius. In this regard it is significant that Henryson further imputes authority to himself and the poem he is writing by omitting the invocation of divine guidance which appears in the prologues of both Gualterus and Lydgate.[16] It is not the authority of God which Henryson's omission implicitly questions, I would argue, but the need for a vernacular writer to displace authority from himself.

From this perspective on the **"Prologue,"** then, the *Moral Fables* begins with a sophisticated discussion of literary theory which reveals an overriding concern with the value of literature and the nature of literary authority. Far from simply restating an inherited theory, Henryson problematically offers a variety of theories and leads, finally, to the implication that, though he himself is a vernacular writer, he nonetheless may be entitled to speak with authority—to act as an "auctor." In fact, while Henryson maintains that he will write only a translation of his author's text, the stories he composes have a far greater claim to originality.

Indeed, the author's text is itself illusory, for only seven of the thirteen fables are Aesopic.[17] In modern terms, furthermore, fables like **"The Cock and the Jasp"** and **"The Cock and the Fox"** would be considered less translations or retellings than complete reworkings. And, unlike other medieval collections of fables—such as that by Lydgate, who offers only a few fables in no discernible artistic order, or that by Caxton, who translates and extends an already composite collection apparently without thematic organization for the sections or individual tales—the *Moral Fables* bespeaks a coherent thematic design which, while it chronicles Henryson's emergence as a vernacular author, also presents an increasingly bleaker view of the world and of human potential. Of the first five fables, for instance, it is only the last two which end in the death of the central character. And in all of these five it is the foolishness and wickedness of individuals, rather than of society or humanity in general, which is chastised. Indeed, the heraldic icon and elaborate catalogue of animals in the fifth fable, **"The Trial of the Fox"** (lines 873-921), might well be read as confirmation of social order. But beginning with the sixth fable, that of **"The Sheep and the Dog,"** which alleges rampant corruption in the legal system, the tales and "Moralitates" broaden the object of criticism to society and mankind.

The three central fables—**"The Sheep and the Dog,"** **"The Lion and the Mouse,"** and **"The Preaching of the Swallow"**—are particularly important in this alteration in perspective and in Henryson's design for the *Moral Fables* in general. In these fables, as George D. Gopen has noted, the "narrator is at his most prominent,"[18] for here he comments most directly on and participates most fully in the events he is narrating. In **"The Trial of the Fox,"** however, the narrator already begins to emerge as a rhetorical presence in the poem, where without precedent he devotes an entire stanza to admonishing mankind (lines 831-37) and another entire stanza to admonishing one of his characters (lines 971-77). The narrator's presence in his own poem is thus expanded rather than established—an alteration which underscores its own rhetorical significance—in the "Moralitas" to **"The Sheep and the Dog,"** where he claims to have been a viewer of, a participant in, the actual events he narrates (lines 1282-85):

> Bot of this scheip and of his cairful cry
> I sall reheirs, for as I passit by
> Quhair that he lay, on cais I lukit doun,
> And hard him mak sair lamentatioun.

Furthermore, **"The Sheep and the Dog"** is one of the Aesopic tales in the *Moral Fables,* and so by writing himself into the story—by placing the translator as a character in the work he claims to translate—Henryson rhetorically exposes the illusion of his "translatioun" and, at least momentarily, asserts his own independent presence in the creative act. At the same time he begins to valorize his own role in the *Fables,* however, Henryson redirects the tone and import of the collection. As I suggested earlier, no longer do the fables speak of the isolated corruption or stupidity of isolated individuals. Rather, beginning with the lament of the Sheep in this "Moralitas," they address the pervasive ills of society and even, it should be noted, question whether a righteous God is watching over the events of creation (lines 1293-99):

> Quaikand for cauld, sair murnand ay amang,
> Kest vp his [the Sheep's] ee vnto the heuinnis hicht,
> And said, "O lord, qhuy slepis thow sa lang?
> Walk, and discerne my cause groundit on richt;
> Se how I am be fraud, maistrie, and slicht
> Peillit full bair, and so is many one
> Now in this world richt wonder wo begone."

By the end of the sixth fable, then, Henryson has effected two important changes in the nature of the stories he is writing. First, having announced his interest in literary authority in the **"Prologue,"** he has gradually and self-consciously begun to assert his own rhetorical importance in the tales he is telling. Second, he has gradually altered the focus of his concern from the foolishness of one cock to the issue of God's presence in this world.

These contexts of Henryson's increased self-consciousness about his own creative activities and of his heightened social criticism provide a perspective which, I believe, offers new insights into the thematic complexity of **"The Lion and the Mouse."** To be sure, critics have already pointed out a number of the fable's rhetorical qualities which draw particular attention to it and consequently suggest that it was meant to be some kind of thematic climax in the *Moral Fables.* **"The Lion and the Mouse"** is, for example, the central tale of the thirteen *Moral Fables* and thus holds a position which, as A. C. Spearing has shown in his discussion of the "sovereign mid-point," was accorded special significance within late-medieval and Renaissance aesthetics.[19] Moreover, as has often been noted, **"The Lion and the Mouse"** is unique in the *Moral Fables* in a number of ways: it is the only dream vision in the collection; it is the only fable with a prologue; it is the only fable in which the narrator meets and speaks with another character.

Yet the thematic purpose and effect of these qualities gain in coherence from the artistic and social contexts I noted above. Thus the beginning of the **"Prologue"** to **"The Lion and the Mouse"** furthers the creative self-consciousness of the fifth and sixth fables, inasmuch as one of its prominent features is the diversity of well-known medieval literary forms and conceits upon which Henryson draws for the first time in the *Moral Fables.* This cluster of literary conceits, I suggest, seems a self-conscious way for Henryson to draw attention to himself as a writer, just as his presence in the "Moralitas" of **"The Sheep and the Dog"** emphasizes his rhetorical position in and, perhaps, his creative control of the stories he relates. There is the very fact of the **"Prologue"** itself, of course, but also the chronological placement of the story in the conventional "ioly sweit seasoun" (line 1321) of late spring-early summer. It is in this season that the narrator, again conventionally, "rais and put all sleuth and sleip asyde" to go to "ane wod . . . allone but gyde" (lines 1326-27), where he confronts yet another commonplace of medieval literature, the "locus amoenus." The language he uses to describe this literary place is striking (lines 1328-34):

> Sweit wes the smell off flouris quhyte and reid,
> The noyes off birdis richt delitious,
> The bewis braid blomit abone my heid,
> The ground growand with gresis gratious;
> Off all plesance that place wes plenteous,
> With sweit odouris and birdis harmony;
> The morning myld; my mirth wes mair for thy.

While Henryson sporadically employs alliteration throughout the **Moral Fables,** its occurrence here represents, I believe, an especially poetic response to a characteristically poetic situation. The conventional nature of the frame is completed when in this environment the narrator has a "dreme" (line 1347), one of the most distinctive medieval literary experiences.

It is within this patently literary context, then, that Henryson confronts Aesop, whose appearance typically is regarded as only an indication of the "special significance" which Henryson intends for the tale.[20] But for several reasons the details of the dialogue itself would seem to be of thematic importance, and not only for **"The Lion and the Mouse"** but also for the **Moral Fables** in general. First, the meeting between "makar" and "auctor" is unprecedented both in the Aesopic tradition in general and in the **Moral Fables** in particular; even in comparison to generally similar encounters, such as that between Dante and Virgil or Gavin Douglas and Mapheus Vegius (see note 25 below), Henryson's experience is distinguished by the thematic complexity with which the actual meeting is treated. Second, as I have suggested above, Henryson underscores the thematic importance of his unique meeting with Aesop by rhetorically accenting the seventh fable in a variety of ways. Third, in the ancient poet the Scots writer confronts both the specific writer of whom he claims to be only a translator and also, more generally, an emblem of the genuine "auctores" of medieval culture;[21] the meeting itself thus has the potential to be emblematic of a meeting between "auctores" and "makars" in general. All these qualities, then, in conjunction with the theoretical focus of the **"Prologue"**

to the whole of the **Moral Fables,** intimate that Henryson's meeting with Aesop is integral to the developing discussion of "the figure of the poet and the function of poetry."

Indeed, in consonance with this prologue's initial emphasis on literature and literary authority, Aesop is presented as the very emblem of the conventional poet (lines 1356-59):[22]

> Ane roll of paper in his hand he bair,
> And swannis pen stikand vnder his eir,
> Ane inkhorne, with ane prettie gilt pennair,
> Ane bag off silk, all at his belt he weir.

This is not the misshapen Aesop of legend,[23] however, but a distinguished, imperious figure "with ane feirful face" (line 1361). There is thus an immediate contrast between the ancient writer, who confidently advances toward Henryson ("he come ane sturdie pace" [line 1362]), and Henryson himself, who is still reclining "amang thir bewis bene" (line 1346). Significantly, it is Aesop who speaks first (line 1363) and who sits down *beside* Henryson (line 1366), thereby both imaging his superiority once again and also implying a certain familiarity with the Scots writer. The language here is especially striking in this regard. Aesop's first words are "God speid, my *sone*" (line 1363), and it is that "word" (line 1364) which is not only pleasing to Henryson but also well known ("couth") to him. Whether the intended meaning of "word" is "utterance" or "single lexical item," the implication is that Henryson has customarily viewed Aesop as his figurative father, the word with which he initially addresses him ("Welcome, father" [line 1366]) and which he later reprises with a reference to Aesop's "fatherheid" (line 1399); in turn, throughout the **"Prologue"** Aesop refers to Henryson as his "sone" (lines 1370, 1382, 1388).

To be sure, such language might be used between any social or ecclesiastical superior and subordinate, but the wider theoretical context here implies a more specific application: Aesop is Henryson's figurative father in the sense that the genuine "auctores" are the fathers of the vernacular "makars" and nascent authors. Indeed, if the Scots poet presents the ancient as his "father," he also presents him as his "maister" (lines 1367, 1377, 1384), and throughout the dialogue Henryson's language is deferential and includes both rhetorical concessions (e.g., "Displeis ȝow not" [line 1367]) and the invariable use of the honorific plural pronouns "ȝe" and "ȝow." Moreover, the syntax he uses to phrase his final request to Aesop is as elaborately circumspect as that used either by Beowulf or by Sir Gawain for their own respective famous requests (lines 1398-1401):[24]

> "ȝit, gentil schir," said I, "for my requeist,
> Not to displeis ȝour fatherheid, I pray,
> Vnder the figure off ane brutall beist,
> Ane morall fabill ȝe wald denȝe to say."

Given the profound respect which Henryson has for Aesop, it is perhaps not surprising that he conducts himself as an innocent by asking Aesop to declare his "birth . . . facultye, and name" (line 1368). It is surprising, however, that Aesop reveals his "winning is in heuin for ay" (line 1374), inasmuch as the historical Aesop was unambiguously pagan; but in converting Aesop to a Christian now residing in heaven, Henryson eliminates the one potentially complicating aspect of his author's background and in effect provides, through Aesop's eventual acquiescence to Henryson's demands, divine confirmation of his own original theoretical positions. It is also perhaps surprising that Henryson should now, after he himself has clearly recognized the "fairest man that euer befoir" (line 1348) he saw and after this "man" has clearly identified himself (lines 1370-76), further demand that Aesop clarify his literary accomplishments in order to confirm his identity. But Henryson thereby forces himself (and the reader) to pause and consider the qualities and accomplishments of this representative "auctor," and Henryson's questions thus underscore the focus of the passage on literary authority (lines 1379-81):[25]

> Ar ȝe not he that all thir fabilis wrate,
> Quhilk in effect, suppois thay fenȝeit be,
> Ar full off prudence and moralitie?

When Henryson asks of Aesop a composition which meets one set of criteria put forth in the **"Prologue"** to the *Moral Fables*—that the work be both rhetorically pleasing ("ane prettie fabill" [line 1386]) and ethically beneficial ("Concludand with ane gude moralite" [line 1387])—Aesop refuses. But he does so, it must be noted, not because the composition Henryson requests is theoretically impossible—not because poetry cannot be simultaneously rhetorical and ethical, nor because it is impertinent for a "makar" to make such a demand of an "auctor"—but because (lines 1389-90)

> . . . quhat is it worth to tell ane fenȝeit taill,
> Quhen haly preiching may na thing auaill?

As Aesop elaborates this view (lines 1391-97), it becomes clear that from his now divine perspective the corruption and decadence of the world have obviated his ethical "taillis" if not ethical instruction itself. Despite what would seem to be the unchangeable and irrefutable nature of his position, however, the narrator does in fact persuade him to tell a tale, not by the cogency of any further arguments but apparently simply by the power of his own rhetoric (see above). Consequently, during the course of the dialogue Henryson moves from passivity, when he remains reclining to meet Aesop, to activity, when he is not silenced by Aesop's objections but is in fact able to silence them through rhetoric.

In this regard it would seem especially significant that the fable Aesop tells is **"The Lion and the Mouse,"** for this fable and its "Moralitas" offer the most explicit political and social commentary in all of the *Moral Fables*.[26] Henryson may well be "cautious" in having Aesop tell this traditional story of a mouse which, having been freed by a lion, in turn releases the lion from a net in which it has been trapped.[27] But in view of the emphasis which the **"Prologue"** to the fable places on the nature of literary authority, another motivation for this particular tale at this particular point in the *Moral Fables* is possible. That is, in telling a fable which is moralized as an account of the ideal social balance between king and commons, Henryson, through Aesop, confidently assumes what would become the Renaissance role of the adviser to a prince.[28] It is in fact this role which Aesop, in his final paternal and authorial gesture, transfers to the vernacular poet (lines 1615-19):[29]

> . . . My fair child,
> Perswaid the kirkmen ythandly to pray
> That tressoun of this cuntrie be exyld,
> And iustice regne, and lordis keip thair fay
> Vnto thair souerane lord baith nycht and day.

Henryson's unique dialogue with Aesop and the subsequent telling of **"The Lion and the Mouse"** thus enact an usurpation of authorial voice and authority in three ways. First, by drawing Aesop into the *Fables* and directing him to tell a story, Henryson rhetorically questions the authority which he had attributed to Aesop and denied himself in lines 29-42 of the **"Prologue."** That is, up to this point Henryson has feigned to be merely a translator, passing on the text of an "auctor"; there is in the preceding fables the supposition that an "auctor" and an authorial text chronologically and theoretically precede Henryson's production, so that if the stories themselves are fictional, the "auctor" and text are not. But in placing Aesop in the narrative which purports to be the translated text of Aesop, Henryson renders *Aesop* part of the fiction and, consequently, undermines the authority which is imputed to him as an "auctor" and the efficient cause of the fables. In effect, while in the first six fables Aesop is imaged to stand figuratively behind Henryson and speak through him, here Henryson stands behind the ancient and, by claiming to offer direct quotation of him, situates the origin of the author's dialogue and fable in himself. Thus, when Henryson directs himself and the reader to contemplate Aesop as a writer, his own identity as a writer is necessarily also under consideration because he has depicted himself as the creator of Aesop. Second, in silencing Aesop's objections and evidently compelling him to tell a story, Henryson appropriates for himself the dominant role in the dialogue. Since Henryson accomplishes this appropriation through rhetoric rather than argument, and since Aesop does not challenge the theory which justifies "ane prettie fabill . . . with ane gude moralite" or the right of a "makar" to advance such a position, the power of Henryson's own rhetoric and theory, which was initially explored in the **"Prologue"** to the *Moral Fables,* is confirmed. Third, by means of the social criticism which lies at the heart of **"The Lion and the Mouse,"** Henryson, having usurped the rhetorical voice of his "auctor"—that is, authorship—by extension usurps his responsibility for ethical utterance—that is, authority. For these reasons one need not rely on a rigorously Freudian hermeneutic to recognize that in the seventh fable and its **"Prologue"** Henryson represents himself as the child of Father Aesop and his "mother toung" (line 31)—of literary authority and vernacular language—and in this vein it could be said that the seventh fable depicts the replacement of the father with the son: the vernacular author.

Indeed, the Henryson who awakes from the dream of the seventh fable is a changed narrator, as is suggested by the way the next fable, **"The Preaching of the Swallow,"** partly reenacts the events of **"The Lion and the Mouse"** and in this fashion provides a common background against which one can assess the narrator's performance. The narrator is again an active participant in his own narration, and springtime again finds him journeying forth into nature. Thematically, in John Mac-Queen's view, **"The Lion and the Mouse"** and **"The Preaching of the Swallow"** are also quite similar: "The latter offers a general treament of wisdom and providence; the former applies those ideas specifically to the Scotland of James II."[30] Here, in light of my discussion of the seventh fable, I wish to concentrate on the significance of the initial thirteen stanzas, which constitute a kind of prologue and, consequently, another parallel with **"The Lion and the Mouse."** While they have clear thematic links with the fable itself,[31] they may also be regarded as the first authoritative utterances of Henryson the nascent vernacular author.

The first five stanzas (lines 1622-56) dwell on God and his incomprehensible powers; while mankind is discussed, it is so always in terms of its inadequacies in comparison to God's grandeur (lines 1629-32):

> Thairfoir our saull with sensualitie
> So fetterit is in presoun corporall,
> We may not cleirlie vnderstand nor se
> God as he is, nor thingis celestiall.

From this emphasis on God, then, there is a logical progression to his creation (lines 1657-77). Specifically, Henryson begins with the "firmament payntit with sternis cleir" (line 1657) and moves to the creatures on the earth and then to the regular passage of the seasons (lines 1678-1712). This movement is thus a survey of all creation and an affirmation of its harmony, and it thereby constitutes the sort of "moral sweit sentence" which Henryson valorizes in the **"Prologue"** to the *Moral Fables.* But just as the "kirnell" of these stanzas

is "sueit and delectabill," so also is the "nuttis schell," inasmuch as they represent some of the richest description in all of Henryson's works (lines 1664-70):[32]

> Luke weill the fische that swimmis in the se;
> Luke weill in eirth all kynd of bestyall;
> The fouils fair sa forcelie thay fle,
> Scheddand the air with pennis grit and small;
> Syne luke to man, that he maid last of all
> Luke to his image and his similitude:
> Be thir we knaw that God is fair and gude.

In employing a traditional rhetorical set piece like the changing of the seasons, Henryson again could be said to be self-consciously drawing attention to himself as a writer. But in filling "traditional details . . . with new vitality,"[33] in Gray's phrase, and in imbuing the whole with an affirmation of God's power, Henryson fully and confidently comes forth a figurative "sturdie pace" and displays the ability of the vernacular author to be at once rhetorical and ethical; indeed, this fable in its entirety has often been considered among the best in the *Moral Fables.*[34] In the overall structure of the *Moral Fables,* in other words, **"The Preaching of the Swallow"** in part constitutes a forum for Henryson to display his ability to combine pleasing rhetoric and ethical content in what is in effect a demonstration of the legitimacy of his symbolic usurpation of authorial voice in **"The Lion and the Mouse."**

The remainder of the *Moral Fables* lies outside the scope of this discussion, though I wish to suggest how Henryson's emergence as a vernacular author provides insight into the overall structure of the work. Once Henryson dons the mantle of the vernacular author, his view of mankind and its potential as represented in the events of the individual fables grows increasingly bleak, as if to imply the heightened awareness of and concern for the world which are the characteristics of both "auctores" and advisers to princes.[35] In **"The Fox, The Wolf, and the Cadger,"** at the end of which the Wolf is beaten nearly to death, all the characters are interpreted negatively, and the reader is warned of the dangerous flattery of the world. In **"The Fox, the Wolf, and the Husbandman,"** which ends with the certain death of the Wolf, the "Moralitas" again stresses the danger of earthly vanities. In **"The Wolf and the Wether,"** which ends with the death of the Wether, the "Moralitas" admonishes the reader to avoid pride and to seek self-knowledge. In **"The Wolf and the Lamb,"** in which the Lamb is beheaded, the "Moralitas" laments that the poor are suffering at the hands of the noble, landed class. In **"The Paddock and the Mouse,"** in which both protagonists are flayed, the "Moralitas" warns of false intent and of how the soul can be drawn to eternal death by the body.

In short, the structure of the *Moral Fables* further implies Henryson's assumption of Aesop's authority by the way in which the final six fables seem to confirm

Aesop's bleak view of the human condition—a view of which Henryson himself, it will be recalled, had intimations in the sixth fable. Indeed, the transference (or, perhaps, extension) of authority from Aesop to Henryson is also nicely suggested in the "Moralitas" of **"The Wolf and the Lamb,"** where Henryson expresses concerns very much like those expressed by the Sheep in the "Moralitas" of **"The Sheep and the Dog"** (see above) (lines 2770-76):

> God keip the lamb, quhilk is the innocent,
> From wolfis byit and men extortioneris;
> God grant that wrangous men of fals intent
> Be manifest, and punischit as effeiris;
> And God, as thow all rychteous prayer heiris,
> Mot saif our king, and gif him hart and hand
> All sic wolfis to banes of the land.

In the sixth fable it is the Sheep, the rhetorical creation of the "auctor," who wonders about the existence of a righteous God; here Henryson confirms his acquisition of authorial voice by himself articulating these same concerns without the intermediary of the character of the Lamb or, indeed, Aesop.

As Harold Bloom maintains, all writers may labor under the "anxiety of influence," but the anxiety which Chaucer and Henryson faced was in some ways more broadly cultural and linguistic than that confronted by modern writers. Indeed, the anxiety of late-medieval vernacular writers was born of the need both to replace father figures and also, beforehand, to legitimate a familial connection between the antique or patristic fathers and the vernacular sons. And it is this need, I believe, which accounts for Henryson's interest in "the figure of the poet and the function of poetry" in the **Moral Fables** and for his desire not even to attempt to repress his relationship with Aesop but to make it a thematic focus in the work. In the **"Prologue"** Henryson lays out a variety of traditional attitudes about the relations between ethics and rhetoric and in the process accommodates still another attitude, one which accepts the possibility of vernacular authority. Then in the three central fables in particular, Henryson enacts a usurpation of traditional authority and authorship by situating the voice of his "auctor" within himself and demonstrating that the vernacular "makar" can be at once ethical and rhetorical as he surveys the world around him. The whole of the **Moral Fables** can thus be read as an account of Henryson's resolution of the artistic conflicts of the fifteenth century through his emergence as a vernacular author. Such a reading—and such an emergence—is predicated on the cultural determinants within which Henryson worked. Writing at the end of the fifteenth century and in a tradition of vernacular self-consciousness established by Chaucer, Henryson evidently had very forward-looking conceptions of himself as a poet and of the potential for authoritative utterance in the vernacular, but at the same time he

lacked cultural validation of these conceptions. By placing Aesop in the **Moral Fables** and extending literary authority to himself, Henryson dramatizes a moment of profound cultural significance—the creation of vernacular authority.[36]

Notes

1. George Sampson, *The Concise Cambridge History of English Literature,* 2d ed. (Cambridge: Cambridge University Press, 1961), p. 89.

2. Among the important studies in this regard are the following: John MacQueen, *Robert Henryson: A Study of the Major Narrative Poems* (Oxford: Clarendon, 1967); Howard Roerecke, "The Integrity and Symmetry of Robert Henryson's *Moral Fables,* Ph.D. diss., Pennsylvania State University, 1969; Douglas Gray, *Robert Henryson* (Leiden: E. Brill, 1979); Denton Fox, ed., Introduction, *The Poems of Robert Henryson* (Oxford: Clarendon, 1981); Stephan Kinoy, "Tale-Moral Relationships in Henryson's *Moral Fables,*" SSL [*Studies in Scottish Literature*] 17 (1982):99-115; Dieter Mehl, "Robert Henryson's *Moral Fables* as Experiments in Didactic Narrative," in Ulrich Broich, Theo Stemmler, and Gerd Stratmann, eds., *Functions of Literature: Essays Presented to Erwin Wolff on His Sixtieth Birthday* (Tübingen: Max Niemeyer, 1981), pp. 81-99; C. David Benson, "O Moral Henryson," in Robert F. Yeager, ed., *Fifteenth-Century Studies: Recent Essays* (Hamden, Conn.: Archon Books, 1984), pp. 215-35; Gregory Kratzmann, "Henryson's *Fables*: 'The Subtell Dyte of Poetry,'" SSL 20 (1985): 49-70; George D. Gopen, "The Essential Seriousness of Robert Henryson's *Moral Fables*: A Study in Structure," SP [*Studies in Philology*] 82 (1985): 42-59; and Gopen's introduction to his edition *The Moral Fables of Aesop* (Notre Dame, Ind.: University of Notre Dame Press, 1987), which in part synthesizes the SP article. More generally see Louise O. Fradenburg, "Henryson Scholarship: The Recent Decades," in Yeager, ed., *Fifteenth-Century Studies,* pp. 655-92.

3. "The Coherence of Henryson's Work," in Yeager, ed., *Fifteenth-Century Studies,* pp. 276-77.

4. The best discussion of authorship in the Middle Ages remains A. J. Minnis, *Medieval Theory of Authorship: Scholastic Literary Attitudes in the Later Middle Ages,* 2d ed. (Aldershot: Wildwood House, 1988).

5. The rhetoricians Roger Ascham and Thomas Wilson can be mentioned here, as well as the orthographers Sir John Cheke and William Bullokar.

6. The citation is from Larry D. Benson, gen. ed., *The Riverside Chaucer,* 3d ed. (Boston: Houghton Mifflin, 1987).

7. See the good discussion in ibid., p. 1022.

8. See Judson Boyce Allen, *The Ethical Poetic of the Later Middle Ages: A Decorum of Convenient Distinction* (Toronto: University of Toronto Press, 1982).

9. Gray, *Robert Henryson,* p. 70. On Henryson's use (hence awareness) of traditional rhetoric in the Prologue, see Robert L. Kindrick, "Henryson and the Rhetoricians: The *Ars Praedicandi,*" *ScS* [*Scottish Studies*] (Frankfort) 4 (1984):255-70. A collection of Aesopic fables is a particularly appropriate place for the sort of theoretical discussion in which Henryson here engages, since in the Middle Ages the fables were often used to teach rhetorical skills. See Fox, ed., *The Poems,* pp. xlii-xliii.

10. All citations of the *Moral Fables* are from Fox's edition.

11. On the morality of the Aesopic fables see Fox, ed., *The Poems,* p. xlii.

12. Julia Bastin, *Recueil général des Isopets* (Paris: Société des anciens textes français, 1930), 2:7: "Hortulus iste parit fructum cum flore, favorem / Flos et fructus emunt; hic nitet, iste sapit. / Si fructus plus flora placet, fructum lege; si flos / Plus fructu, florem; si duo, carpe duo" (lines 3-6).

13. Kratzmann, "Henryson's *Fables,*" p. 52.

14. See further Glending Olson, *Literature as Recreation in the Later Middle Ages* (Ithaca, N.Y.: Cornell University Press, 1982).

15. Kratzmann, "Henryson's *Fables,*" p. 55.

16. Bastin, *Recueil général,* 2:7: "Ut messis pretium de vili surgat agello, / Verbula sicca, Deus, implue rore tuo" (lines 9-10). Henry Noble MacCracken, ed., *The Minor Poems of John Lydgate,* vol. 2, EETS, o.s., vol. 192 (Oxford: Oxford University Press, 1934), p. 568: "And, as myn auctor doþe at þe cok begyn, / I cast me to folow hym in substaunce, / Fro þe trouþe in sentence nat to twyn, / As God and grace woll yeue me suffysaunce, / Compyle þys lybell for a remembraunce" (lines 50-54).

17. See Fox, ed., *The Poems,* pp. xliv-1. These seven are "The Cock and the Jasp," "The Two Mice," "The Sheep and the Dog," "The Lion and the Mouse," "The Preaching of the Swallow," "The Wolf and the Lamb," and "The Paddock and the Mouse." My discussion in this article supports the arguments which assert that the order of the fables in the Bassandyne print is Henryson's. See Gray, *Robert Henryson,* p. 32; and, for the fullest discussion, Fox, ed., *The Poems,* pp. lxxv-lxxxi. In support of the primacy of the Bannatyne manuscript see MacQueen, *Robert Henryson,* pp. 189-99; and Mehl, "Robert Henryson's *Moral Fables,*" p. 85. For a consideration of the rationale behind the ordering in Bannatyne, see William Ramson, "On Bannatyne's Editing," in Adam J. Aitken, Matthew P. McDiarmid, and Derick S. Thomson, eds., *Bards and Makars: Scottish Language and Literature, Medieval and Renaissance* (Glasgow: University of Glasgow Press, 1977), pp. 172-83. A detailed discussion of the relevant issues lies outside the scope of this article, though I would like to note that the "literary" evidence marshaled in support of the textual evidence of Bassandyne does not at all seem to me inadmissible or beside the point; indeed, such evidence has long been used in arguments about the intended order of *The Canterbury Tales.* The agreement of this evidence seems formidable: it is the Bassandyne order in which Roerecke has demonstrated thematic coherence and symmetrical patterning, Gopen the aesthetic complexity of three "simultaneously functional symmetries," and Spearing an artful utilization of the sovereign mid-point. As A. C. Spearing notes, "It seems unlikely that an organization so ingenious in itself and so appropriate to the meaning of the central tale and of the whole series could have occurred by chance" ("Central and Displaced Sovereignty in Three Medieval Poems," *RES* [*Review of English Studies*], n.s., 33 [1982]: 256). While it is possible that a later redactor and not Henryson himself is responsible for the order, I would argue that such a redactor would have had to have a more sophisticated understanding of authorship and literary structure than Henryson had. And then even if that were the case, this understanding remains a significant statement of vernacular medieval aesthetics.

18. Gopen, ed., *The Moral Fables of Aesop,* p. 12.

19. Spearing, "Central and Displaced Sovereignty," p. 253. The rhetorical importance of the position of "The Lion and the Mouse" is also suggested by the fact that it is seen as a climax in a variety of otherwise differing interpretations of the *Moral Fables.* Thus, in addition to Spearing's commentary, one can mention Gopen's analysis of each of the "three different, simultaneously functional symmetries, all of which taken together demonstrate the unity of the work and its fundamentally serious moral intent"—in this analysis the placement of "The Lion and the Mouse" at the center of the *Moral Fables* is pivotal (Gopen, ed., *The Moral Fables of Aesop,* p. 17); and Roerecke's view that this fable and the two that frame it are "the climactic moral experience of the *Fables*" can also be noted ("The Integrity and Symmetry," p. 160).

20. Gray, *Robert Henryson,* p. 140. In Roerecke's analysis, "Aesop's appearance in the dream vision is another example of Henryson's parody of romance" ("Integrity and Symmetry," p. 164). Nicolai von Kreisler has suggested that "Henryson's guise as an untutored supplicant and the corresponding relationship he sets up with Aesop are especially indicative of his effort to have the strategies of visionary literature serve his own didactic poem" ("Henryson's Visionary Fable: Tradition and Craftsmanship in *The Lyoun and the Mous,*" *TSLL* [*Texas Studies in Literature and Language*] 15 [1973]: 395). And Mehl has maintained that "the poet's reply to Aesop's objections seems like a modest attempt to justify his own art. . . . The personal authority of the ancient poet is added to the authority of the traditional tales and this is obviously meant to give more weight and immediacy to the poetological argument" ("Robert Henryson's *Moral Fables,*" pp. 86-87). It is certainly true that Henryson's response constitutes an "attempt to justify his own art" and that the themes of this Prologue represent a reprise of the themes of the Prologue to the entire collection; but in light of the sophistication which I hope to have shown present in the initial Prologue, the attempt here is not modest, nor, as Roerecke, von Kreisler, and Mehl imply, are its ramifications limited to this fable alone. None of these writers examines the meeting with Aesop in any detail. Moreover, John MacQueen (*Robert Henryson*), Marshall W. Stearns (*Robert Henryson* [New York: Columbia University Press, 1949]), and Robert L. Kindrick (*Robert Henryson* [Boston: Twayne, 1979]) do not comment at all on the thematic significance of Aesop's appearance.

21. On Aesop as an "auctor," see Ernst Robert Curtius, *European Literature in the Latin Middle Ages,* trans. Willard R. Trask (Princeton, N.J.: Princeton University Press, 1973), pp. 49-50; Minnis, *Medieval Theory of Authorship,* p. 161.

22. The transference of authorship from "auctores" to vernacular writers like Chaucer and Henryson—which I am arguing the *Moral Fables* in part dramatizes—is nicely suggested by the Elizabethan writer Robert Greene in his *Vision,* who uses this same traditional iconography for his description of *Chaucer:* "His stature was not very tall; / Leane he was; his legs were small, / Hosd within a stock of red; / A buttond bonnet on his head / From vnder which did hang, I weene, / Siluer haires both bright and sheene: / His beard was white, trimmed round, / His countnance blithe and merry found: / A Sleeuelesse Iacket large and wide, / With many pleights and skirts side, / Of water Chamlet did he weare; / A whittel by his belt he beare. / His shooes were corned, broad before, /

His Inckhorne at his side he wore, / And in his hand he bore a booke: / Thus did this auntient Poet looke" (Alexander B. Grosart, *The Life and Complete Works in Prose and Verse of Robert Greene* [1881-86; rpt., New York: Russell and Russell, 1964], 12:209-10). In his vision Greene dreams that he is "in a faire medowe, sitting vnder an Oake, viewing the beautie of the sunne which then shewed himselfe in his pride" (p. 208), when he sees two individuals who turn out to be Chaucer and Gower. Like Henryson, Greene does not rise to meet his interlocutors, and, like Aesop, Chaucer and Gower "came to me, and sat downe by me, the one of [sic] the right hand, and the other on the left" (p. 209). Again like Henryson, Greene immediately recognizes his interlocutors, though in no small part, one assumes, because he "espyed written on the ones brest *Chawcer* and on the others *Gower*" (p. 209).

23. In Caxton's translation of Rinuccio's *Life,* for instance, Aesop "had a grete hede / large vysage / longe Iowes / sharp eyen / a short necke / corbe backed / grete bely / grete legges / and large feet." *Caxton's Aesop,* ed. R. T. Lenaghan (Cambridge: Harvard University Press, 1967), p. 27.

24. See *Beowulf,* lines 426-32 and *Sir Gawain and the Green Knight,* lines 343-47.

25. In the *Inferno,* in what is perhaps the "locus classicus" of confrontations between vernacular writers and "auctores," Dante also demands the identity of the figure he meets. But there it is clear that Dante, unlike Henryson, does not in fact recognize the figure. It may also be noted that, though Dante, like Henryson, is deferential to his "auctor," he never challenges and overrules him the way the Scots poet does; when Virgil leaves Dante in the Earthly Paradise, it is because the Latin poet himself recognizes the limitations of his knowledge. See *Inf.* 1.61-87 and *Purg.* 27.127-43. Similarly, in the prologue to his translation of Mapheus Vegius's thirteenth book of the *Aeneid,* Gavin Douglas asks about the identity of the "auctor" he meets because he does not know who he is: "I saw зou nevir ayr." This meeting, however, is presented comically: Vegius beats the Scots poet "twenty rowtis apoun [his] rigging" because of Douglas's reluctance to translate the thirteenth book—though Douglas is nonetheless deferential to his "auctor" and acts according to his wishes.

26. Critics have interpreted Henryson's rendition of "The Lion and the Mouse" in a variety of ways, though they all agree on the political nature of the piece. In Fox's reading, the fable "is the only one of the collection that is set firmly in the classical world: the implication is that rhetoric could once compel men to virtue, even if it is no longer so ef-

fective" ("The Coherence of Henryson's Work," p. 277). For Spearing the central stanzas of this central fable constitute "an elegant displacement of sovereignty and triumph in favour of mercy." But sovereignty "here becomes problematic: we are made aware of its negligence, of the potential cruelty of its 'justice,' and of its ultimate dependence on the goodwill of the least of its subjects" ("Central and Displaced Sovereignty," pp. 256, 254). For C. David Benson, on the other hand, the fable suggests "a potential for love in God's creation"; "Although Henryson's sympathy for human suffering and his anger at social abuses are genuine, he, like Langland, finds the only solution to the human condition to lie beyond this world in the love of God" ("O Moral Henryson," p. 227). Gopen sees "The Lion and the Mouse" as "Henryson's Utopian vision, presentable only as a dream: a world wherein men listen to each other, allow themselves to be swayed by reason, justice, and mercy, and remember their debts to each other with gratitude" (*The Moral Fables of Aesop*, p. 22). And the fact that this explicitly social story is framed as a dream is especially significant to von Kreisler, who sees Henryson seeking "at once to objectify his lesson and to invest it with greater authority than the fabulist ordinarily enjoyed" ("Henryson's Visionary Fable," p. 395). Some critics have seen "The Lion and the Mouse" as an allegorical account of the Lauder Rebellion; see Stearns, *Robert Henryson*, pp. 15-18; Kindrick, *Robert Henryson*, pp. 104-105; Matthew P. McDiarmid, *Robert Henryson* (Edinburgh: Scottish Academic Press, 1981), pp. 15-16; and Spearing, "Central and Displaced Sovereignty," pp. 253-54. For an opposing view see Gray, *Robert Henryson*, p. 143; and see Fox, ed., *The Poems*, p. xx, on the general political application of the fables. On the actual events of the Lauder Rebellion see Ranald Nicholson, *Scotland: The Later Middle Ages*, vol. 2 of *The Edinburgh History of Scotland* (Edinburgh: Oliver and Boyd, 1974), pp. 497-514.

27. So Kindrick asserts in *Robert Henryson*, p. 105.

28. See Richard Firth Green, *Poets and Princepleasers: Literature in the English Court in the Late Middle Ages* (Toronto: University of Toronto Press, 1980).

29. Inasmuch as the region in which the *Moral Fables* are imagined to take place is never defined or named, it is tempting to read the unique specificity of "this cuntrie," in light of the possible contemporary allegory which may be inscribed here (see n. 26 above), as a reference to Scotland. If this is in fact the case, then one might argue that here Henryson, through Aesop, breaks down the division between fiction and reality and

thereby underscores the application of what is in effect his own ethical advice.

30. MacQueen, *Robert Henryson*, p. 170; see also pp. 166-68, where MacQueen suggests that Aesop's reference to "haly preiching" at lines 1389-90 "very much looks as if" it "refers specifically to *The Preaching of the Swallow,* to which Henryson intended that *The Lion and the Mouse* should be a sequel" (p. 168). See also Kindrick, *Robert Henryson,* p. 101; and Fox, ed., *The Poems,* pp. lxxviii-lxxix. For an extended discussion of the stylistic and thematic connections of the sixth, seventh, and eighth fables, see Roerecke, "The Integrity and Symmetry," pp. 160-208.

31. MacQueen, *Robert Henryson*, p. 160. For a good discussion of the artistry of "The Preaching of the Swallow," see J. A. Burrow, "Henryson: *The Preaching of the Swallow,*" EIC [*Essays in Criticism*] 25 (1975): 25-37.

32. Cf. Roerecke's observation: "In these stanzas the sweetness of the poetry combined with the sweetness of the *sentence* suggests that we are at the spiritual heart of the poem" ("The Integrity and Symmetry," p. 171).

33. Gray, *Robert Henryson*, p. 111n. On the description of the changing of the seasons as a rhetorical setpiece, see Derek Pearsall, "Rhetorical 'Descriptio' in 'Sir Gawain and the Green Knight,'" MLR [*Modern Language Review*] 50 (1955):129-34.

34. For Roerecke, "The Preaching of the Swallow" "is the most eloquent and beautifully composed of all the fables" ("The Integrity and Symmetry," p. 168). Burrow suggests that it "deserves to be counted as one of the minor masterpieces of medieval English poetry" ("Henryson," p. 25). And McDiarmid judges it the "greatest of the fables, and with *The Testament of Cresseid* one of Henryson's two greatest poems" (*Robert Henryson,* p. 76). To Kindrick, "The Preaching" is one "of the most beautiful and self-consciously rhetorical tales in the Henryson canon" ("Henryson and the Rhetoricians," p. 259). Fox describes it as "one of Henryson's richest and most complex fables" (*The Poems,* p. 274).

35. Cf. Gopen, who suggests that "Henryson gives us a substantially and increasingly grimmer view of life in the second half of the work than in the first, demonstrating that in a deceitful and sinful world good often falls prey to evil" (*The Moral Fables of Aesop*, p. 19). See also Roerecke's extended discussion of this same point in "The Integrity and Symmetry," pp. 89-123. Roerecke suggests that the "first half of the fables shows us creatures

for whom hope of redemption is not past, for they retain their lives" (p. 113), but that "retribution and destruction come to the erring Aesopian creatures of the second half of the *Fables*" (p. 114). In Fox's analysis, in the final six fables "all virtuous persuasions are ineffective, and all evil ones obeyed" (*The Poems*, p. lxxxi).

36. I am happy to acknowledge that this paper has benefited greatly from the comments of my colleague Michael McCanles and of the two anonymous readers for *Studies in the Age of Chaucer.*

David J. Parkinson (essay date 1991)

SOURCE: Parkinson, David J. "Henryson's Scottish Tragedy." *Chaucer Review* 25, no. 4 (1991): 355-62.

[*In the following essay, Parkinson examines* The Testament of Cresseid *as a Chaucerian, medieval tragedy.*]

. . . glengoir missaell leper carles geit scho wes, trocht the quhilk hir fader behuiffit to be stollin all nycht of the towne, and . . . thrie elnis of lynnyng vald nocht fyll the holis was in hir leggis of the lipper.[1]

["syphilitic leprous leper churl's offspring she was, because of which her father had to have her spirited from the town during the night—and three ells of linen would not fill the holes that had formed in her legs because of the leprosy"; insult by Christan Nykquene, an Inverness woman

(1575)]

Henryson's *Testament of Cresseid* may be "a medieval tragedy in the Senecan mode," as well as "unmistakably Chaucerian"; in its attention to debasement and expulsion, though, it is a quintessentially Scottish poem.[2] Here as often elsewhere in Middle Scots poetry, sudden, even violent change dominates: youth into age, honor into shame, spring into winter, the paradisal into the hellish.[3] Rhetorical set pieces herald transitions in which style plummets from the most ornate to the plainest.[4] Without warning or explanation, the protagonist is ejected into painful and disgraceful exile.[5] Things go awry: justice is capricious, eloquence suspect, folly endemic. Given such pessimism, it is the more remarkable that Henryson's protagonist Cresseid should at last aspire towards a haunting vision, however qualified, of hope.

Modern commentators have praised both the vigor and the discipline of Middle Scots verse.[6] There may seem to be a tension between the Scottish poet's ambition to prove mastery of the proper forms and techniques—to claim a central place in the community of polite letters—and the confidence to employ this mastery in a range of topics and genres beyond that of, say, English

courtly verse of the period.[7] Scottish poets frequently test the limits of style and genre. On occasion they seem to break rudely free from the restrictions accepted by that larger community of courtly making.[8] It is appropriate, then, that the narrative and imagery of exile (with their noble antecedents in Old and Middle English poetry) play a crucial part in Middle Scots poetry. In its fascination with boundaries the younger tradition takes strength and claims independence.

Henryson had an abiding interest in the solitary complainer within the desolate wintry scene: his Orpheus, his tardy lover Robin, as well as the Swallow and the fleeced Sheep of his *Fables,* all come to play this role. Nowhere, however, is Henryson so deeply concerned with the course and consequence of punitive suffering as in the *Testament.* This is a poem which is almost too articulate about degrees of exclusion.

Even before narration starts, progress has been thwarted, the aged narrator's springtime world having reverted into winter. There is precedent for taking this as a portent: downturns in the weather often signal the onset of a monitory, even macabre vision.[9] In a topic of medieval art and literature called *The Three Living and Three Dead,* for instance, young princes devoted to pleasure meet their forebears' revenant corpses in a suddenly wintry forest:

The wood of the hunt is . . . at first a cheerful, perfectly mappable place, as the world characteristically is to those in the Pride of Life. . . . With the appearance of the anti-vision, this familiar landscape alters dramatically to a place which, in more senses than one, resembles Dante's *selva oscura*—a state of mind, a landscape of the soul, terrain, in any event, no longer chartable.[10]

Striving to be comfortable despite the cold outside, Henryson's narrator comes upon a "winter's tale" which he proceeds to relate.[11] Despite the horrors outside the window and within the book, he does not seem much disposed toward uncomfortable thoughts about his own mortality: he is a self-indulgent old fellow who is, after all, merely reading and telling this tale to pass time. There is no indication that his wintry experiences will spur him to change his own life.[12]

In the tale itself, the outer world does not revert suddenly from spring to winter. For much of the time, setting is focused upon interiors (the court, the secret oratory, the leper's hospice), within each of which the excluded protagonist Cresseid hides (and is either exclaimed over by the narrator or complains at length herself), and from each of which she must perforce depart. The upset of season in the narrator's preamble corresponds to the moral and then the physical overthrow of the protagonist. In this tale, the forest does not go hoary, the protagonist does.

Being spurned is the first thing to happen to Cresseid in the poem. Having finished with her, Diomede dismisses her; and "than desolait scho walkit vp and doun" (76).[13] At once, the narrator breaks in:

> how was thow fortunait
> To change in filth all thy feminitie,
> And be with fleschelie lust sa maculait.
>
> (79-81)

He will not indulge in "scornefull" or "wickit" language, he insists (86, 91)—having already glanced at her "sa giglotlike takand thy foull plesance!" (83). The level of diction shifting perceptibly, the narrator locates the initial turn from pleasant place to repulsive wilderness inside Cresseid. Alluding to the pollution her behavior brings and to the shunning it earns her from courtly society, the narrator fixes upon Cresseid as a trespasser and rule breaker. The further she goes, the more obvious the danger she poses and the greater the need for further expulsion.

On the other hand, the more obviously polluted Cresseid gets, the more completely she may be purged—a process described by the anthropologist Mary Douglas:

> The attitude to rejected bits and pieces goes through two stages. First they are recognisably out of place, a threat to good order, and so are regarded as objectionable and vigorously brushed away. . . . This is the stage at which they are dangerous; their half-identity still clings to them and the clarity of the scene in which they obtrude is impaired by their presence. But a long process of pulverizing, dissolving and rotting awaits any physical things that have been recognized as dirt.[14]

"Pulverizing, dissolving and rotting" is a fair description of what Henryson has in store for Cresseid. On her path down and outwards, she leaves a trail of the pleasures and advantages her community had allowed her; much later, at the lepers' hospice, her complaint includes a list of these lost things (416-51): *ubi sunt* chamber, bed, cushions, spice and wine, gold and silver cups, saffron sauce, garments, gowns, linen, garden (with all the amenities of springtime; 425-33), fame and honor, singing voice, gracefulness, beauty? For now, though, faded merely from the attentions of the Greek court, Cresseid cannot foresee how far the loss will extend.

Decidedly "destitute" of "comfort and consolatioun", "fellowschip or refute," Cresseid quits the Greeks in disguise and secrecy (92-94). She seeks shelter from disgrace beyond the city walls, at the residence of her father Calchas (here a priest of Venus). Her father's house does not turn out to be a refuge, however; it is instead a way station, the scene of her repudiation of and condemnation by her divine patrons.

"Excludit" by Diomede (75, 133), Cresseid compares her hateful unattached state to the reversion of spring into winter. She casts this reproach particularly at Cupid—her male patron as well as the god "of all thing generabill" (148)—and only secondarily at Venus (to whom Cresseid ascribes Cupid's blindness):

> O fals Cupide, is nane to wyte bot thow
> And thy mother, of lufe the blind goddes!
> 3e causit me alwayis vnderstand and trow
> The seid of lufe was sawin in my face,
> And ay grew grene throw 3our supplie and grace.
> Bot now, allace, that seid with froist is slane,
> And I fra luifferis left, and all forlane.
>
> (134-40)

The metaphor of seasonal reversion refers to what has already befallen Cresseid; she finds in it no warning of harsher lessons to come. When the planetary deities in their "court and conuocatioun" (346) pass judgement on Cresseid's repudiation of Cupid and Venus, however, they take this metaphor as literally predictive. Giving substance to her bitter rhetoric (and to her stained reputation), they punish her with leprosy, a disease they oppose to youth, beauty, and honor (313-40). If Cresseid must lay blame upon her patrons, let her discover what coldness, dryness, and blackness can mean.

The pattern of events here resembles that of the Scottish poet Richard Holland's *Buke of the Howlat* (c. 1450), in which a parliament of birds despoils the overweening owl of their earlier gift of fine feathers and cast him into his ordained solitude in the wilderness.[15] Likewise, the punishment of an intrusive complainer by the deities of love occupies the center of Part One of Gavin Douglas's *Palice of Honour* (1501).[16] Both Holland's Howlat and Douglas's dreamer suffer disfigurement (limited in the case of the latter to a comic staining, despite threats of a direr metamorphosis) because of their rebellious behavior.[17] So does the allegorical personage Reason in William Dunbar's *The Goldyn Targe*: Venus's servant Presence ("physical closeness")

> kest a pulder in his ene,
> And than as drunkyn man he all forvayit.
> Quhen he was blynd, the fule wyth hym they playit
> And banyst hym amang the bewis grene.
>
> (203-06)[18]

Henryson's arrangement of events at the center of the *Testament* would thus seem to contribute to a recurrent topic in Middle Scots poetry, one concerned less with motivation or morality than with the sudden marking out of a troublesome interloper at court.[19]

Like the dreamer of Dunbar's *Goldyn Targe*, Cresseid had assumed that the enclosed garden of polite behavior was paradise; as in *The Goldyn Targe* and *The Palice of Honour,* that garden has revealed itself to be a barren wilderness. Although the imagery of paradise and hell is less explicitly worked out here than in the later poems, Cresseid may still be seen to proceed towards understanding of the hellish consequences of romantic love as she moves further from the heart of her community.[20] Defaced by leprosy now, she again assumes disguise for another departure, this time from her father's house: in "secreit wyse", shrouded in "ane mantill and ane bawer hat," she leaves by "ane secreit ʒet," and goes "wnto ane village half ane myle thairby" (381, 386, 388, 390). As Cresseid discovers new levels to her isolation, she submits to her necessary removal further and further from the center.[21]

What starts out sweetly ends roughly, Cresseid's progress from court to mansion to village "spittaill hous" (391) towards the grave is marked by various losses: love, reputation and courtly company; health, beauty, youth, and the security of kinship; soon, individuality itself.[22] In a florid complaint (as mentioned above), Cresseid itemizes the various properties she has left and is leaving behind; the shallowness of her concern falls into view when, Cresseid herself in full cry of lament,

> Ane lipper lady rais and till hir wend,
> And said, "Quhy spurnis thow aganis the wall
> To sla thy self and mend nathing at all?"
>
> (474-76)

Once again, the presence of the macabre may be felt: like a preaching corpse, the leprous Cresseid alludes to the imminent falls of those fine ladies still exalted in beauty and love (452-69); her appearance and sentiments recall those of the corpse-queen in the northern alliterative romance *The Awntyrs off Arthure*; and yet, despite all this, circumstances do not permit Cresseid her wished-for impressive effect.[23] As the protagonist is called to face stark necessity, so is the reader. Courtliness gives way to bluntness, as it does again when ("for knichtlie pietie" [519]) a homeward-bound Troilus takes jewels and gold "and in the skirt of Cresseid doun can swak; / Than raid away and not ane word he spak" (522-23).[24] Polite consolations and sentiments are now irrelevant. What matters is that Cresseid pass with growing understanding towards her death.

Soon, in her brief testament, Cresseid will name her last few divestitures: her body ("with wormis and with taidis to be rent" [578]); her remaining possessions—an odd conjunction of leper's things ("cop and clapper" [579]) and relics of court (ornaments, gold, a love token [579-83]); and finally her soul, which she commends "to Diane, quhair scho dwellis, / To walk with hir in waist woddis and wellis" (587-88). The outward and downward journey would seem to be proceeding to its expected goal. Cresseid has consigned her body to a hellish but conventional manner of consumption, and exiled her soul to a wilderness.

Seeing that wilderness as the preserve of Diana (not Mars or Saturn), however, Cresseid envisions a chaste refuge for her soul. Diana's forest may not be quite as civilized as the pleasant if shady grove of Elysian myrtle into which Virgil's Dido flits to rejoin her Sychaeus; it will nevertheless be a place of clean exertion and unchanging greenness.[25] At the point Henryson took up her story, Cresseid was walking up and down, desolate. Now she imagines walking (and staying) with a steadfast female protector. Accompaniment, security: with her physical self about to achieve its "true indiscriminable character," Cresseid seeks an end to the polluting forces of memory, emotion, change, and desire.[26] To be amongst those woods and cleansing wells and not to be alone may in Cresseid's dying, reaching vision seem rather like being in heaven.[27]

"Quha wait gif all that Chauceir wrait was trew?" (64), the narrator had asked upon taking up this story. When the poem draws to its conclusion, truth remains in doubt: "we have almost a picture of the poet as liar."[28] Still, one discovery has been wrung out of experience—by the protagonist if not the narrator. Cresseid has found the source to the "greit vnstabilnes" of her life within herself; "Nane but my self as now I will accuse" (568, 574). This is no "gentle, kind" perception, but one that is disillusioned, even austere.[29] Without this accusing self-awareness, such moralizing as the narrator's warning to ladies to "Ming not ʒour lufe with fals deceptioun" (613) is ignorant and worse than useless. Seeking truth, the poet must proceed tersely, ironically; one can only hope for surer understanding beyond this world.

The Middle Scots poets wrote so keenly about disfigurement and exile because these experiences revealed an arbitrary foundation to worldly life. Loss, winter, and old age are to be considered more lasting and substantial than happiness, youth, and spring. Gorgeous style and the pleasant topics to which it is applied (in secular poetry, at least) exist on the surface of this poetry, as pleasure exists on the surface of life; and even the courtliest of these poems contains some reference to the rudeness and roughness about to jut out from beneath the shiny surface.[30] For Henryson and his immediate successors, this awareness presents a dilemma: given its basic inconsistency, how can even the most disiciplined and polished of their secular poems speak with moral authority? By placing this dilemma at the center of a courtly lady's frivolous existence, Henryson attempts to confront it. His narrator tears layer after layer of belonging from Cresseid's life; this savage process manifests a deep pessimism, and has troubled many readers.[31] Still, Henryson has thus gone further than any other Middle Scots poet to liberate his protagonist and his poem from inconsistency. Cresseid's dying aspiration challenged the Middle Scots tradition to take the outcast seriously; it continues to challenge.[32]

Notes

1. *Records of Inverness,* vol. I: *Burgh Court Books 1555-86,* ed. William Mackay and Herbert C. Boyd (Aberdeen, 1906), 243.

2. Douglas Gray, *Robert Henryson* (Leiden, 1979), 166; A. C. Spearing, *Medieval to Renaissance in English Poetry* (Cambridge, Engl., 1985), 168.

3. Priscilla Bawcutt, *Gavin Douglas: A Critical Study* (Edinburgh, 1976), 53; the subject merits further attention.

4. G. Gregory Smith, *Scottish Literature: Character and Influence* (London, 1919), 34-35; A. J. Aitken, "The Language of Scots Poetry", *Scotland and the Lowland Tongue: Studies in the Language and Literature of Lowland Scotland in Honour of David D. Murison,* ed. J. Derrick McClure (Aberdeen, 1983), 46-48; for comparison of this stylistic tendency to aspects of court life in sixteenth-century Scotland, see Jean Hughes and W. S. Ramson, *Poetry of the Stewart Court* (Canberra, 1982), 116-17.

5. Douglas Gray, "Rough Music: Some Early Invectives and Flytings," *English Satire and the Satiric Tradition,* ed. Claude Rawson and Jenny Mezciems (Oxford, 1984), 24-25, 37.

6. See, for instance, C. S. Lewis, "The Close of the Middle Ages in Scotland," *English Literature in the Sixteenth Century Excluding Drama,* vol. 3 of *The Oxford History of English Literature,* ed. Bonamy Dobree and Norman Davis (Oxford, 1954), 68-76; also Denton Fox, "The Scottish Chaucerians," *Chaucer and Chaucerians,* ed. D. S. Brewer (London, 1966), 170, 171, 186; and Wilhelm F. H. Nicolaisen, "Line and Sentence in Dunbar's Poetry," *Bards and Makars: Scottish Language and Literature, Medieval and Renaissance,* ed. A. J. Aitken, Matthew P. MacDiarmid, and Derik S. Thomson (Glasgow, 1977), 65-67.

7. Gregory Kratzmann, *Anglo-Scottish Literary Relations 1430-1550* (Cambridge, Engl., 1980), 17-23, 238.

8. Gregory Smith, 53.

9. Elizabeth Salter and Derek Pearsall, *Landscapes and Seasons of the Medieval World* (London, 1973), 133, 152, 167-68.

10. Philippa Tristram, *Figures of Life and Death in Medieval English Literature* (London, 1976), 165.

11. I do not propose to reopen the question of relations between *Troilus and Criseyde* and Henryson's "vther quair"; this question is summarized in Louise O. Fradenburg, "Henryson Scholarship: The Recent Decades," *Fifteenth-Century Studies: Recent Essays,* ed. Robert F. Yeager (Hamden, Conn., 1984), 70-72.

12. The significance of the unregenerate narratorial stance is discussed in Ian Jamieson, "Some Attitudes to Poetry in Late Fifteenth-Century Scotland," *Studies in Scottish Literature* 15 (1980): 28-42; see also Alicia K. Nitecki, "'Fenʒeit of the New': Authority in *The Testament of Cresseid,*" *Journal of Narrative Technique* 15 (1985): 124-30.

13. In the present essay, all quotations from the *Testament* are drawn from *The Poems of Robert Henryson,* ed. Denton Fox (Oxford, 1981).

14. Mary Douglas, *Purity and Danger: An Analysis of Concepts of Pollution and Taboo* (1966; New York, 1970), 160.

15. For the relevant passage in the most recent edition of the poem, see *Longer Scottish Poems,* vol. 1: *1375-1650,* ed. Priscilla Bawcutt and Felicity Riddy (Edinburgh, 1987), 52-79. See also Felicity Riddy, "The Alliterative Revival," *The History of Scottish Literature,* vol. 1: *Origins to 1660 (Medieval and Renaissance),* ed. R. D. S. Jack, gen. ed. Cairns Craig (Aberdeen, 1988), 44-45.

16. For the relevant passage in *The Palice of Honour,* see *The Shorter Poems of Gavin Douglas,* ed. Priscilla Bawcutt, Scottish Text Society, 4th ser., 3 (1967), 46-51.

17. David J. Parkinson, "Mobbing Scenes in Middle Scots Verse," *JEGP* [*Journal of English and Germanic Philology*] 99 (1986): 494-509.

18. *The Poems of William Dunbar,* ed. James Kinsley (Oxford, 1979), 35.

19. There is a more overt interest in this "marking out" in Dunbar's court satires and his *Flying* with Walter Kennedy.

20. See *The Palice of Honour,* line 2094, and *The Goldyn Targe,* line 215; see also Alicia K. Nitecki, "Gavin Douglas's Yelling Fish: *The Palice of Honour,* Lines 146-48," *N&Q* [*Notes and Queries*] 28 [226], 2 (April 1981): 118-19.

21. See Robert Muchembled, *Popular Culture and Elite Culture in France 1400-1750,* trans. Lydia Cochrane (1978; Baton Rouge, 1985), 112.

22. For a more explicit comparison of the *Testament* to *Everyman,* see John MacQueen, *Robert Henryson: A Study of the Major Poems* (Oxford, 1967), 88.

23. See Spearing, 183.

24. J. A. W. Bennett, "Henryson's *Testament*: A Flawed Masterpiece," *Scottish Literary Journal,* 1; 1 (1974): 14; also Nitecki, 129.

25. See Derek Pearsall's discussion of the properties of Diana's forest in his edition of *The Flower and the Leafe* and *The Assembly of Ladies* (London, 1962), 32; also MacQueen, 86, 90.

26. Mary Douglas, 161.

27. Denton Fox, "The Coherence of Henryson's Work," *Fifteenth-Century Studies,* 278.

28. Ibid.

29. See Götz Schmitz, "Cresseid's Trial: A Revision. Fame and Defamation in Henryson's 'Testament of Cresseid,'" *Essays and Studies,* 32 (1979), 56.

30. Edmund Reiss, "The Ironic Art of William Dunbar," *Fifteenth-Century Studies,* 328.

31. For example, Tatyana Moran, "*The Testament of Cresseid* and the *Book of Troylus,*" *Litera,* 6 (1959): 23.

32. For discussion of some sixteenth-century responses to *The Testament of Cresseid,* see Helena Mennie Shire, *Song, Dance and Poetry of the Court of Scotland under King James VI* (Cambridge, Engl., 1969), 199-200; also R. D. S. Jack, *Alexander Montgomerie* (Edinburgh, 1985), 102-03. The late Denton Fox commented on an early draft of the present essay; like many others, its author shall miss the warmth of his encouragement and the keenness of his advice.

Steven R. McKenna (essay date May 1991)

SOURCE: McKenna, Steven R. "Henryson's 'Tragedie' of Cresseid." *Scottish Literary Journal* 18, no. 1 (May 1991): 26-36.

[*In the following essay, McKenna investigates the nature of Cresseid as a tragic figure in* The Testament of Cresseid.]

There are numerous critical analyses of Robert Henryson's **Testament of Cresseid** which treat the heroine of the poem as a tragic figure and which attempt to define in various ways why the poem and the character are tragic. Douglas Gray, for instance, views the poem in terms of a medieval tragedy—viz., a poem which concludes in disaster.[1] More generally, Thomas W. Craik sees Henryson's poem as a tragic counterpart to Chaucer's *Troilus and Criseyde.*[2] The questions of fate and free will are addressed by E. Duncan Aswell, who argues that divine providence does not exist; rather, the tragedy can be viewed as one where the heroine is a victim of fortune and she must learn how it operates.[3] The inner workings of Cresseid's tragedy are evaluated by Jane Adamson, who sees in Cresseid a tragic tough

ness by which she can eventually view human weakness. Central to this thesis is Adamson's notion that Cresseid's tragedy is the capacity for her to finally understand who and what she has always been.[4]

Illuminating as these studies are, however, none seems to me to do true justice either to Cresseid as a tragic figure or to the more fundamental issue of Henryson's probing of the nature of tragedy itself. Accordingly, I wish to pursue here two closely related questions: What is 'tragic' about Cresseid and her fate? and What, from the answer to this, can we identify as Henryson's theory of tragedy? In attempting to answer these questions, I would like to identify several interrelated characteristics which comprise a highly complex and philosophically elaborate vision on Henryson's part of what tragedy is.

The first, most often noted, and in many ways the most important, overriding concern in Henryson's poem is, broadly speaking, the question of the heroine's identity, particularly as this relates to her own evolving comprehension of herself. We might say that her identity, her true character, and most importantly her progress toward self-understanding form the central mysteries of the poem.[5] Her initial inability, or refusal, to see herself for what she is and was is reflected in her desire to hide in her father's quarters, out of sight of all society, and in her castigation of the gods for her rejection by Diomeid. In taking a slightly different approach than my predecessors to this particular issue in the poem, I wish to suggest that the core of the 'tragic' mystery is best summed up by her question, 'Quha sall me gyde?' (131)[6]—a riddle of the sphinx that forms the central tragic question of the poem, the deciphering of which coincides with the playing out to its resolution of the action of the poem, much as the tragic import of the Sphinx's riddle unfolds as a result of the progress of action in *Oedipus Rex.* Initially, Cresseid sees herself as being *misled* by Diomeid, Venus, and Cupid—a passive, innocent victim of fickle Fortune, whose characteristics appear in the description of Venus. Cresseid imagines the motivating forces of her destiny as being agents over which she has no control—men and gods. Consequently, she does not comprehend her own complicity in the tragic action as it unfolds to and beyond this early episode of the poem. As the action unfolds, so does her own understanding of herself and her situation.

The structural pattern of tragic action, at least according to received opinion, traditionally leads to a catastrophe, a 'downturn', a denouement at the close of a falling action. This movement of tragedy when plotted by Freytag's structural pyramid looks as follows: [see page 74]

This is a fairly standard way of viewing the structure of tragedies, and Henryson's poem can fit neatly within this pyramid. (Indeed, it is the assumed pattern implied in all the commentaries on the poem of which I am

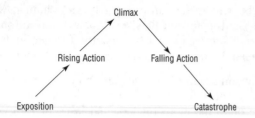

aware.) The Narrator in his exposition of the background sets the scene wherein Cresseid has abandoned Troylus and in turn has been abandoned by Diomeid. The action rises as Cresseid blames Venus and Cupid for her woes and blasphemes them in the process. The action reaches a climax with the parliament of the gods and Cresseid waking with the 'seiknes incurabill' (307). She falls into progressively worse physical health, begins to realise that she has done wrong, and finally has the encounter with Troylus and the subsequent realisation of her own culpability in bringing to pass her tragic misfortune. The pyramid scheme is convenient when viewing the tragedy in this sort of way, and the result is in harmony with the general medieval association of a tragic fall being linked to the cyclical motion of Fortune's wheel: 'Tragedye is to seyn a dite of prosperite for a tyme, that endeth in wrecchidnesse'[7]—*De Casibus Virorum Illustrium.*

However, I would like to suggest here that we can view the scheme of *The Testament of Cresseid* in another, more important structural way, namely with the pyramid structure rearranged and inverted. Thus:

This inversion of the structural pattern brings me to the second characteristic of Cresseid's tragedy in particular and of Henryson's theory in general. Since Henryson so clearly and carefully anchors his own poem in the audience's knowledge of Chaucer's *Troilus and Criseyde,* and particularly in a knowledge of events at the end of Chaucer's poem, we can view the catastrophe in Cresseid's tragedy as having taken place before the action of Henryson's poem begins. In particular, we can point to her rejection of Troilus in Chaucer's poem as the real catastrophe in her story. The action thus falls to a point where at the beginning of Henryson's poem we can view Cresseid at a low ebb, having just been rejected herself and feeling disconsolate, isolated, and utterly alone. From this perspective, the blasphemy of

Venus and Cupid is thus not catastrophic, but rather exposes in symbolic form her initial, catastrophic rejection of Troilus—a blasphemy of courtly love, if you will. This blasphemy of the gods therefore can be seen to function as a catalyst which sets in motion physical and psychological events that help clarify and elucidate the tragic nature of the original catastrophe, the original downturn of her fortune—namely her rejection of Troilus. When viewed in this way, the action in Henryson's poem rises, not falls. Cresseid's blasphemy of the gods reflects the catastrophe, but need not be seen in and of itself as catastrophic or even climatic.

The aftermath of her blasphemy of Venus and Cupid, particularly Cresseid's contraction of the incurable sickness, leads to a third element of Henryson's theory, namely that the tragic figure is the person who must not only discover, but must bear the burden of her own identity—the 'burthen of the mystery' to borrow Wordsworth's phrase. In other words, Henryson shows that the tragic figure is the one who peers behind the veil and in doing so is able to find the answer to the riddle of personal identity, to come to an understanding of the self and reality in all their complexities and bleak horror.[8] Cresseid's realisations about herself, Troylus, and her fate, when coupled with her testament, show that at this final point of the tragic action she has no choice but to bear the burden of knowing who and what she is, paradoxically because at the end she knows that she must also bear the more unbearable burden of knowing who and what she was—'fals Cresseid' (546), the one who abandoned the 'trew knicht Troylus' and brought all the present misery, destitution and destruction down upon herself. By now, the truth for her is unavoidable. This process of her downfall into enlightenment suggests that the heroine is finally tragic not because of some fundamental error of judgement (a view that is all too common in discussions of tragic figures). If her fall were merely the result of error, then she would be a pathetic figure only. Pathetic she no doubt is, but to limit the causal factor of her fall to error ignores the extent to which the tragic act is a matter of volition that carries with it the necessity of guilt. We may want to argue that Cresseid's blasphemy of the gods is an error of judgement, in poor taste, or ultimately an act for which she must bear the punishment. Yet, as my analysis thus far indicates, regardless of Cresseid's blasphemy of Venus and Cupid, her blasphemy of courtly love in rejecting Troylus is the *sine qua non* of her simultaneous movement toward the eventual self-realisation and self-destruction. This act of blaspheming courtly love represents her essential 'criminality'. Henryson carefully frames the criminality of this act in the larger, cosmic criminality of Cresseid's blasphemy of the gods, and here the frame merely echoes the picture. Symbolically, the blasphemy of courtly love assumes cosmic and mythic dimensions, as it must in order to make her a figure of truly 'tragic' proportions. She is no run-of-the-mill adulteress or promiscuous court flirt.

Her tragic progress leads her to a conclusive answer to the riddle she posed at the beginning of the poem, 'Quha sall me gyde?' The answer for her is now what she previously did not know and even denied it had always been: herself, and no one else. Here she acknowledges through her completed self-discovery that she alone bears the responsibility for her fate: neither the gods, nor malicious Fortune, nor the schemings of other mortals are to blame.[9] These are mere projections she once relied on in order to avoid acknowledging her own complicity in her own destruction. She is responsible for the catastrophe and the attendant downfall, as she finally realises, though it is a realisation through retrospection. This progress toward insight is accompanied by the simultaneous movement toward physical blindness, which is nominally a result of her incurable disease. Her final loss of sight suggests that, like Gloucester later or Oedipus earlier, her final insight is not bestowed; rather, it is earned through responsibility for choices and the retrospective realisation of this responsibility. This final disposition of Cresseid as a tragic figure suggests that there is likewise a prophetic element about her as well. She can serve, indeed *does* try to serve, as a warning to other women who can see her and her tragedy as moral exempla.

Related to this prophetic element of her character is a fourth element of Henryson's theory of tragedy. Call it utopian, call it idealised self-realisation if you will. Henryson shows in this tragedy that there is a distinctly human capacity to discover and understand the deepest mysteries and truths about the self *and* to act upon these truths.[10] Cresseid assumes control of her fate at the end by acknowledging her past responsibilities, her culpabilities, and by thus exercising a measure of control over the future via the Testament. Yet even more importantly, implicit in her warning to other women at the end of the poem is the belief that a reorientation of human character is possible, that the tragic figure potentially and paradoxically has the god-like power to help prevent tragedies. In Cresseid's case, this power could in its ideal realisation prevent women from straying onto the tragic path and lead to a greater and grander harmony between the sexes.[11]

This point brings up a fifth element of the tragic vision of this poem that is not nearly as upbeat, prophetic, or utopian. The potential idealised, utopian element of the tragic vision is counterbalanced, indeed neutralised, by the stasis of Troylus and, even more importantly, by the Everyman-like collectivity of the Narrator, who himself functions as a chorus in the drama of Cresseid's progress to destruction. The Narrator acts as a choric figure in a number of ways. He interposes himself between the action and the audience with his moral

commentaries, yet at other times vanishes from sight. As in classical tragedies, he offers the audience and character suggestions and consolation.[12] He is emotionally torn by the complex of feelings evoked by her story, and he attempts to convey these emotions to his audience. Finally, the narrator assumes a pointed moral outlook at the end in his warning to women.

In the end, Troylus and the Narrator and the other lepers shrink away from the painful solitude, the physical and psychological suffering, and, particularly in the Narrator's case, the essential criminality of the tragic heroine. The Narrator-as-chorus specifically warns the women of his audience against such behaviour as has brought Cresseid to her final disposition, cautioning them to shrink from these things too: 'Ming not your lufe with fals deception' (613). The result, therefore, is that the prophetic, visionary truths of tragedy and the tragic figure are doomed to remain secret, mysterious, and ultimately solitary. The chorus, the Narrator, collective humankind can never fully acknowledge that tragic truth without first experiencing it. But as Cresseid and the Narrator both warn, the whole process which leads to the tragic, visionary truth and the accompanying destruction of the self must be avoided if at all possible. And since her case shows the ultimate responsibility of the self for one's fate, tragedy is implicitly avoidable. Access to the tragic wisdom is not deemed worth the cost.

The choric Narrator's view of Cresseid implies that he is looking at reality itself, not at a work of poetic art (the 'vther quair' he picks up after laying Chaucer's *Troilus and Criseyde* aside). This is in part because the Narrator is himself part of the work in question—i.e. Henryson's poem. (If he were to look at Cresseid as unreal, then he himself would become manifestly part of the unreality of Henryson's art.) Thus the Narrator functions more as the ideal witness of the action than as the intermediary between action and audience; he likewise helps keep the action of the poem on the idealised plane which the poetic art must inhabit. The result of this is that the Narrator can frame Cresseid's plight in terms of implicit, yet seemingly absolute, right and wrong—Cresseid as an example of how women should not act, the wrong action being the one that leads to the tragic self-awareness and ruin. Yet the essential quality of Henryson's (as opposed to the Narrator's) tragic vision is a pessimism that exists outside the strictly moral realm, a pessimism in which categories of right and wrong, good and evil, do not always apply. Religion, myth, and their inherent moral orders are the fantasies which the choric Narrator's voice relies upon as the philosophical and psychological barriers that keep the existential horror of tragic reality at bay. Cresseid's 'complaint' and the Narrator's echo of it at the poem's end tacitly imply that there is yet some fundamental meaning to her existence—namely, she is a mirror that can teach by example.[13] The 'testament' portion of the poem, however, and the four stanzas leading up to it, imply the essential futility of everything—the error, guilt, and unspeakable horror of which she is finally aware when all the illusions and rationalisations have broken down. At the poem's end, the Narrator can only *echo* Cresseid's sentiments as voiced in the 'complaint' section, that there is some meaning to all this suffering, that there is a lesson for others to profit from. In the end, however, the Narrator is incapable of touching the dark, existential, and solitary truth of the tragedy. Cresseid seems to understand this aspect of her tragedy in the complaint when she says:

> 'O ladyis fair of Troy and Grece, attend
> My miserie, quhilk nane may comprehend,
> My friuoll fortoun, my infelicitie,
> My greit mischief, quhilk na man can amend.'

> (452-5)

The tragic figure, then, is doomed to remain a solitary figure in two senses, and this brings up a sixth element of Henryson's theory of tragedy. Cresseid's tragedy isolates her from society; or rather, to be more accurate, her tragic condition makes her isolate herself from society—from the court, from other human interactions and, finally, (in the leper colony) from the city itself. There she is unknown, unloved, and free from the watchful eyes she so feared would shame her in the town. A higher principle she discovers in the end is that one need not be among throngs of people to feel the pain of shame that comes with the smite of conscience. The true gauge of her cognitive moral development is her ability to punish herself.

Secondly, and even more significantly, Cresseid as a tragic figure is isolated from Nature as well (as her disease suggests). For the choric Narrator, for collective humanity, Nature is replete with signs and forces that point to the human position in the larger scheme of things, the great chain of being. The Narrator reflects this in a less cosmic, less metaphysical way by responding to the weather, by withdrawing to the fire and his books at the beginning of the poem. Even the lepers, because of their diseases, know their place in the social order if nothing else.[14] However, Cresseid is as much out of place among the lepers as she was out of place in the court after her rejection by Diomeid. For the tragic figure, Nature provides no home, no guides for finding one's place in the scheme of things. The answer to the riddle 'Quha sall me gyde?' is again, and, for the tragic figure, inevitably the self. In this sense, Nature with a capital *N* becomes for the tragic figure nature with a small *n*. Nature can be seen to lose its mythological dimension. The guideposts for existence for the tragic figure are finally not 'out there' (the gods, myths, omens, etc.), but rather are 'in here' (in the self). The struggles of good and evil, right and wrong, fidelity and adultery, and all other existential questions are ultimately internal, solitary, and utterly private. This breakdown of the mythological dimension seems to me to echo a similar philosophical sentiment in the Monk's tragedies in Chaucer's *Canterbury Tales*. In the Monk's tales there is curiously no sense of an ultimate justice at work, thus making the Monk's reported remark in the 'General Prologue' about how the world shall be served not so much ironic as it is a serious existential question. The answer, at least for Henryson's Narrator, is bound up in human love, conducted according to well-defined rules of right and wrong. But for Henryson, as poet, the answer to the question of how the world shall be served is not that simple. The tension created by the disjunction of Narrator and poet leaves the question an open one.

The seventh characteristic of Henryson's tragic vision is a corollary to the sixth. That is, the gods and the god-like tragic heroine finally inhabit estranged realms. Cresseid's final stanzas focus solely on questions of the body and mind and the interplay of the two, which, broadly speaking, is responsible for what she considers to be her fate. When Cresseid leaves her soul to Diane (586), there is no seeming assurance that the goddess of chastity is anything more than a wistful hope and a potential way for Cresseid again to place herself in bigger hands and thus slough off full responsibility of whatever afterlife she may find.

Here it might also be helpful to recall for a moment Henryson's fable of the Sheep and the Dog. The sheep is unjustly charged to pay the dog with five shillings' worth of bread and must therefore sell his wool in the winter in order to pay off the fine. The shivering sheep

> Kest vp his ee vnto the heuinnis hicht,
> And said, 'Oh Lord, quhy sleipis thow sa lang?
> Walk, and discerne my cause groundit on richt;
> Se how I am be fraud, maistrie, and slicht
> Peillit full bair, and so is mony one
> Now in this warld richt wonder wo begone.'

> (1294-9)

The same estrangement holds true for Cresseid. The blasphemy of Venus and Cupid is like the mirror image of a prayer; it is a roundabout plea for understanding and therefore for help in sorting out the mysteries of existence. But for Cresseid, the gods only appear after she swoons, as a dream that vanishes when she wakes. Therefore, I would like to suggest that Cresseid's dream of the gods be taken quite literally as a dream, as happening strictly within her own head as she sleeps, and that the leprosy, whatever symbolic baggage we may choose to attach to it and its relation to the gods, can also be viewed quite literally as a type of venereal disease (as it was perceived to be in Henryson's day).[15] This disease of the body is for its victim an unbearable burden just as the burden of her spiritual disease of the soul and the subsequent knowledge of that disease is also an unbearable one.

So, the progress of the tragic figure, as I have outlined it here, leads to an understanding of an eighth characteristic of Henryson's theory of tragedy, a characteristic alluded to earlier—namely, a potentially god-like human nature. This is manifested in both the heroine's visionary ability to come to an understanding of the self, of how she herself has been responsible for her own disposition, and the equally divine capacity to shape one's own destiny. She realises in the end that she herself is the fickle goddess Fortune whom she blamed initially for her misery. The tragic element of this last point is that Cresseid has all along shaped her destiny without knowing it until she has brought destitution and destruction upon herself; indeed, one of the tragic elements here is that the realisation is born out of personal destruction—that the way down is paradoxically the way up all along. Further, this point is at the heart of the tragic figure's essential criminality; it is in fact the source of the figure's criminality: what the tragic figure comes to understand and acknowledge in the end is that the capacity to shape one's own destiny is really the cause of the catastrophe and all else that results from it. What initially appeared obscure, capricious and confusing, in the end is revealed to be an orderly self-fulfilment of a rational series of causes and effects which she has set in motion.[16]

Lastly, when we take the panoramic view of Henryson's theory of tragedy we see a solitary, isolated human figure who represents what can in theory be an infinitely large conception of what human nature is capable of becoming, but which in practice is only possessed by the tragic heroine. Everyman, in this view, like the choric Narrator himself, is not a tragic hero unless he ceases to be everyman. However, in the collective is conformity, and in conformity there is security. In fact, the explicit moral injunction cautions against such a path that would lead to the tragic, individual truth Cresseid finds at the expense of herself. When myth dies, tragedy dies with it. Therefore, for the Narrator, the tragedy of Cresseid implicitly gives validity to the governing cultural myths of religious and courtly morality. Without such cultural myths, there would be little or no sense for the Narrator or the poem's audience (at least the audience as he conceives it) that the tragic heroine is other than pathetic. Yet the true horror of such a possibility of the loss of all mythic dimension is that the Narrator and the audience would thus come to see reality in the bleak, existential terms that Cresseid finally comes to understand. The choric cultural myths are a way of keeping the tragic truth solitary and secret with the tragic heroine.[17] The hope, if such exists, is in the Narrator's tacit adherence to the cultural myths that give him and his presumed audience the ability to derive a meaningful moral lesson from the horror of Cresseid's fall and her final state of being. 'Quha sall me gyde?' The Narrator hopes the answer his female audience will give is 'Cresseid', but only in the sense that where Cresseid led others will not follow.

Despite the presence of gods in Henryson's poem, Cresseid's tragic movement represents a simultaneous movement toward an intensely isolated, demythologised space. Henryson's conception of tragedy is that the tragic figure does not belong in the world inhabited by collective man. The tragic heroine has violated the codes, has gone beyond the mundane bounds of Everyman. The tragic figure attains, indeed earns, a perspective on mortal existence that no mere mortal can achieve. So, the movement of the heroine to a godlike capacity simultaneously undercuts the mythological dimension of the cosmos. For the tragic figure there are no warm fires burning in the cozy chamber, no comforting drinks that elevate the wintry spirits. In essence, there are no metaphysical roots, no cosmic home.

Notes

1. Douglas Gray, *Robert Henryson* (Leiden, 1979), p. 165.

2. Thomas W. Craik, 'The Substance and Structure of the "Testament of Cresseid": A Hypothesis', in *Bards and Makars,* ed. Adam Aitkin, Matthew McDiarmid, and Derek Thomson (Glasgow, 1977).

3. E. Duncan Aswell, 'The Role of Fortune in *The Testament of Cresseid',* *Philological Quarterly,* 46 (1967), 471-87.

4. Jane Adamson, 'Henryson's "Testament of Cresseid"': "Frye" and "Cauld"', *Critical Review,* 18 (1976), 39-60, especially p. 57.

5. This point is implicit in the analysis by Aswell, who argues that Cresseid has to learn about fortune. Del Chessell, more significally, sees Cresseid's tragedy in terms of her progress toward self-understanding ('In the Dark Time: Henryson's "Testament of Cresseid"', *Critical Review,* 12 (1969), 61-72). Lee Patterson views her tragedy as a movement toward understanding her own faults ('Christian and Pagan in *The Testament of Cresseid', Philological Quarterly,* 52 (1973), 696-714). And Jennifer Strauss argues that the tragedy involves Cresseid's progress toward a sense of responsibility for her fate ('To Speak Once More of Cresseid: Henryson's "Testament" Reconsidered', *Scottish Literary Journal,* 4 (1977), 5-13).

6. All quotations of Henryson's poetry are from *The Poems of Robert Henryson,* ed. Denton Fox (Oxford, 1981).

7. Chaucer's *Boece,* in *The Riverside Chaucer,* 3rd edition, Larry D. Benson general editor (Boston, 1987), 2. pr 2. 70-2. The general theory of tragedy in the middle ages is summed up by Boethius in *De Consolatione Philosophiae* 2. pr 2 and 3. pr 5.

8. This notion anticipates Conrad's Mr Kurtz in *Heart of Darkness,* whose great insight into his and the human condition resolves itself into the stark reiterated words, 'The horror'.

9. As Gray points out (p. 174), Cresseid appears to be a victim of fate, but she can likewise appear, from a different perspective, the agent of fate. Aswell argues that the verb forms used to describe her actions tend to be active forms, suggesting that this indicates responsibility for her fortune. A. C. Spearing, on the other hand, sees her as a victim of the gods' arbitrary and vicious punishment (*'The Testament of Cresseid* and the "High Concise Style"', *Speculum,* 37 (1962), 208-25). (Spearing is one of the most adamant about this particular relation between Cresseid and the gods.) Yet, as Hanna argues ('Cresseid's Dream and Henryson's "Testament"', in *Chaucer and Middle English Studies in Honour of Rossell Hope Robbins,* ed. Beryl Rowland (Kent, Ohio, 1974), p. 295), leprosy in Henryson's day was assumed to be a venereal disease; hence, Cresseid has no one to blame for her disease and fate other than herself. Looking at the matter in more of a classical context, Gray points out (p. 192) the important parallel with ancient tragedy, namely that the gods are omnipotent, but men are given free choice and are thus culpable for their own fates.

10. Adamson points out (p. 57) that this ability to discover the truth about the self is always present, though not realised until the end. Gray notes (p. 205), that at the poem's end Cresseid again becomes an active character by composing the Testament and preparing for death.

11. I should note, however, that this issue side-steps Diomeid's callous treatment of Cresseid. The poem appears to place the burden of harmonising relations between women and men strictly on women's shoulders. We get no indication from Henryson that Diomeid, in rejecting Cresseid, attains the status of a tragic figure. The godlike element of the tragic heroine is graphically illustrated by the segment of the dream in which Saturn and Cynthia condemn Cresseid. When she wakes up she has turned, at least in appearance, into something resembling the two gods as described by the poet in their coming to the parliament: cold, grey and remote (however, Cresseid still is encumbered by her mortality).

12. See Gray, pp. 169-70. Note the Narrator's choric apostrophes at lines 78-91, 323-9, and 610-16.

13. Patterson argues (p. 709) that 'The complaint is thus an attempt to avoid [the process of learning that will come as her life continues] . . . The true Christian optimism of the poem consists precisely in the fact that her experience continues past this attempt to stop its agonizing but necessary crisis'.

14. After Cresseid's complaint, a leper lady tells her:

> 'I counsall the mak vertew of ane neid;
> Go leir to clap thy Clapper to and fro,
> And leif efter the law of lipper leid.'

(478-80)

15. Hanna points out (p. 293) that Cresseid's final thoughts before she falls asleep 'are of the gods and their injustice, and these same thoughts fill her slumber'. The question of responsibility is again raised through the thorny issue of her illness. If we approach the leprosy as a sexually transmitted disease, then we assume that Cresseid is thus responsible. However, the other side of the argument is compelling. Though this is not the place for an adventure into that critical morass, the discussions of her disease and fate given by Hanna, Sidney Harth ('Henryson Reinterpreted', *Essays in Criticism,* 11 (1961), 471-80), Maurice Lindsay (*History of Scottish Literature* (London, 1977)), Craig McDonald ('Venus and the Goddess Fortune in the "Testament of Cresseid"', *Scottish Literary Journal,* 4 (1977), 14-24), John McNamara ('Divine Justice in Henryson's 'Testament of Cresseid"', *Studies in Scottish Literature,* 11 (1973), 99-107), Patterson, Beryl Rowland ('The "seiknes incurabill"', in Henryson's 'Testament of Cresseid"', *English Language Notes,* 1 (1964), 175-7), Spearing, Strauss, E. M. W. Tillyard ('Henryson: "Testament of Cresseid" 1470?' in *Five Poems 1470-1870* (London, 1948), and Harold Toliver ('Robert Henryson: From *Moralitas* to Irony', *English Studies,* 46 (1965), 300-9) will reveal the range and complexity of her relation to the gods and to her own responsibility.

16. On this element of tragedy, see Michelle Gellrich, *Tragedy and Theory: The Problem of Conflict Since Aristotle* (Princeton, 1988), passim and especially p. 40.

17. This point is implied by Spearing, who argues that Cresseid's example 'does not propose any possible remedy for the whole situation. . . . Chaucer, at the end of his poem, repudiating earthly love, offers the love of Christ as an alternative. . . . But in Henryson's poem . . . no positive alternative can be proposed.' (pp. 222-3). From the point of view of her character as she understands it and the situation as the narrator understands it, this is correct.

Rosemary Greentree and Steven R. McKenna (essay date 1992)

SOURCE: Greentree, Rosemary, and Steven R. McKenna. "'The hurt off ane happie the vther makis': Henryson's Construction of His Audience." In *Selected Essays on Scottish Language and Literature: A Festschrift in Honor of Allan H. MacLaine,* edited by Steven R. McKenna, pp. 13-25. Lewiston, N.Y.: The Edwin Mellen Press, 1992.

[*In the following essay, Greentree and McKenna examine the range of methods that Henryson used to get the moral lessons of his* Moral Fables *across to his audience.*]

The words of the lion king in **"The Trial of the Fox"**—"The hurt off ane happie the vther makis" (1065)—cause uproar and laughter in the royal court, ill-natured delight in the agony of the wolf, whose head has been broken by the mare's kick. The lion's sentence derisively restates the Latin maxim feelingly uttered by the fox, when he offers *"Felix quem faciunt aliena pericula cautum"* as his reason for declining to examine the document under the mare's hoof (1033). At a superficial level, the lion could be merely describing the fox's usual response of malevolent enjoyment of the suffering of his dupe; more deeply, he draws the court's attention to the wolf as a figure of fun and an example of foolish behavior. In a wider sense, he expresses the purpose of the **Moral Fables** and reveals their methods.

The closing moments of this fable offer a rare demonstration of successful teaching in the **Fables,** followed by surprising consequences. One animal, the fox, seems to learn prudence from the example of another's misfortune, and he even states the lesson in the formal style of a proverb. The incident is so concisely expressed that it is almost concealed among apparently important distractions such as the assumption of the fox's inheritance and the procession of the beasts; it provokes malicious laughter in the tale and an unexpectedly spiritual lesson in the *moralitas*; it involves the characters who most frequently show aspects of clever and brutal villainy in the **Fables**; and it offers an insight into Henryson's idea of his audience. All of these disparate elements are entirely consistent with Henryson's purpose and methods.

The mare's kick and its consequences exemplify the reversals by which Henryson teaches his audience, jolting them to learn harsh lessons in *moralitates* drawn from tales which often involve vicious comedy and base characters. The violence of the tales hints at the violence of his teaching methods. Brutal instruction makes the wolf "that new-maid doctour" (1092) and qualifies him to act as confessor when the fox is formally executed, a sinister repetition of his comic role

as Freir Volff Waitskaith in **"The Fox and the Wolf."** In a similar way, the poem offers sharp lessons to its audience, and implies the reception of the teaching, in comments throughout the work.

We know that the **Fables** are intended to give pleasure as well as instruction—"[a]mangis ernist to ming merie sport / To blyth the spreit and gar the tyme be schort" (20-21).[1] We know too that medieval comedy is sometimes cruel and unsubtle. We may misguidedly imagine that we can look back from the sophistication of the twentieth century to simple times with primitive amusements. But can any such thoughts prepare us to take moral instruction from such brutal slapstick as the mare's kick? More puzzlingly, do they prepare us to revel in it, as the lion's audience does? To gain some answers, we should look at Henryson's teaching style and at his comments on his audience, from which we may posit his construction of that nebulous entity. Thoughts of the audience may be discerned throughout the **Fables,** when the Narrator refers to those who are taught and in the direct addresses to his own audience: confiding or stern, sharing pleasures and sorrows, moving from formal deference to intimate acquaintance. Particularly telling references come at the beginning, middle and end of the cycle, when it is read in the balanced progression of the order of the Bassandyne Print.

The audience is first acknowledged in **"The Prologue."** The conventional modesty of a conventional narrator is exaggerated to an extreme which undermines the reverence given to those he calls "my maisteris" (29). The familiar metaphors of the nut and bow, the hackneyed request for correction in the translation from his author's Latin to his own "hamelie language and . . . termis rude" (36), the assurance that the work is offered "Nocht of myself, for vane presumptioun / Bot be request of ane lord" (33-34), all make up a leisurely opening, apparently to precede a conventionally decorous work. The audience can hardly be prepared for the directness of the Narrator's comparison of "mony men in operatioun" to "beistis in conditioun" (48-49) and the rigor of the notion of shameless man transformed to "brutal beist." Within the stanzas of **"The Prologue,"** the audience is given both extravagant flattery and harsh condemnation, each implying scant respect. This is an unpromising basis for the relationship of Narrator to audience, quite unlike that of the last stanza of **"The Paddock and the Mouse,"** where the Narrator bids his "freind" farewell.

Such contradictions clash throughout the fable cycle. Members of the audience may be friends or pupils, willing to learn or incorrigible. The least realistic fable, **"The Lion and the Mouse,"** told by Aesop in the Narrator's dream, gives the saddest comment on a narrator's effectiveness in Aesop's question: "quhat is it worth to tell a fenȝeit taill, / Quhen haly preiching may na thing auaill?" (1389-90). Yet the mouse of **"The Lion and the Mouse"** gives a successful demonstration of the preacher's role, perhaps a parody of the fabulist's, when she takes a convincing example from the human world—"oft is sene, ane man off small stature / Reske-wit hes ane lord off hie honour" (1499-1500)—to strengthen her case for being released from the lion's paw. This fable is followed by one full of realistic detail, **"The Preaching of the Swallow,"** which is told through the Narrator's waking experiences. The sentiment which prompted Aesop's question is effectively demonstrated when the birds respond to the swallow's warnings with indifference or derision, and humanity's spiritual blindness and unwillingness to learn are exposed in the grim commentary of the *moralitas*. Comedy is scarce, except in the cheery chatter of the deluded lark, who laughs about the coming of death and speaks more truth than she knows in her ironically ill-chosen proverbs.

The last fable, **"The Paddock and the Mouse,"** encapsulates all Henryson's lessons and gives comment on his audience which is at once acute and affectionate. Both toad and mouse are educated creatures; they exemplify receptive members of an audience, but their learning is sadly misused. The toad augments her instruction with devious cunning to deceive the mouse; the mouse recognizes the evil revealed in the toad's horrid appearance, but is defeated by sophistry and her own failing of greed. We may compare the Narrator's gentle and regretful ridicule of the little mouse with his harsh condemnation of the cock of **"The Cock and the Jasp."** Both characters are led astray by their urgent hunger and longing for food of a particular kind. The mouse yearns for delicacies: "ryip aitis, . . . barlie, peis, and quheit" (2792), but the cock seeks "draf or corne, small wormis, or snaillis" (94), morsels which could alert a medieval audience to his baseness.[2] The cock, "desyrand mair the sempill corne / Than ony iasp, may till ane fule be peir" (141-2), and he is scorned for his lack of perception and enterprise. His pretensions to learning are exposed in his addresses to the jasp, which attempt the high style, but always sink bathetically to the level of his dunghill. The cock is never aware of the lessons about him, and is ruthlessly despised for his complacent ignorance. In contrast, the story of the mouse in the last fable, who is tempted by her educated palate and fails to heed the warnings she perceives, is told with some sorrow. The Narrator deals mildly with her incongruous lack of horse and boat, and his picture of the little creature seems tolerant of her folly.

The cock is an apt figure for erring, unreceptive mankind. He finds the jasp and recognizes it as an object of value, a "riche and nobill thing" (79), but he thinks only of the need for food for his body, "the sempill corne," not comprehending the possibility of enriching his soul, to which the jasp is "eternall meit" (140). He is harshly judged by the Narrator's double standards because he does not see the worth of the jewel—to a human rather than a bird. Recently, some critics have defended him, saying for example that he shows "an appealing kind of commonsense" (Kratzmann 58). (This merely points out that the Narrator's value system, which he assumes to be absolute, is in fact relative.) However contradictory it may seem, this is not satisfactory for the Narrator, who is concerned with the welfare of the soul as an absolute good unto itself. We may contrast his implied admiration for the learning of the little mouse of the last fable, although she ignores the warnings from human physiognomy, perceived in the visible characteristics of the toad, and so is taken by a natural enemy, the kite, in astonishingly unnatural circumstances. We should perhaps not always make too nice an assessment of the Narrator's methods and messages. He appears many times as shortsighted, often overlooking what would seem to be the obvious point raised in a fable. This is not to suggest that he is too inept as a story teller to catch his own meanings. Rather, the selectivity of his vision, particularly in the *moralitates,* reveals certain moral and intellectual biases which are themselves indicative of the Narrator's values and ideological orientation. This does not mean he is wrong in the message he attempts to impart, but instead his essential message reflects certain moral and intellectual limits that for the Narrator imply a monologic value system which he seeks to use as the basis of establishing a community with his intended audience. Implicit in this notion is the idea that whatever is inside (i.e. what the Narrator deems good) is itself good, proper, and right; that which is outside acceptable thought or behavior is thus *ipso facto* bad, improper, and wrong.

The *moralitas* of **"The Paddock and the Mouse"** is directed to an individual, familiarly addressed as "thow," "brother" and "freind." We may compare the disparity of the general, distant conviviality of **"The Prologue"** and the particular closeness (community) of the last *moralitas* with the notion of the implied audience of *Troilus and Criseyde,* described by Dieter Mehl, who discerns both a listening audience at court and a "more solitary and bookish reader" (173). The tone of the *Fables'* concluding stanzas differs from the exaggerated courtesy and harsh moralizing found elsewhere in the work, and implies a genuine regard for each member of the audience rather than general condemnation of the faults of mankind. It is far from being an idealized and uncritical regard, though. The lessons of the *moralitates* preclude any such assumption.

Henryson takes his audience through a harrowing course in moral instruction, in which some comic incidents are quite as violent as the cruel moments of tragedy. In fact, the incidents which we must take seriously are often preceded by comic parallels. We have already mentioned the light-hearted parody of confession administered by the wolf and its gloomy repetition. We may remember too that in **"The Fox and the Wolf"** the fox was shot by the goatherd, after the entertaining confession, ironically and amusingly fulfilling the prediction of his horoscope. The tale of **"The Trial of the Fox"** ends with the judicial execution of the fox, after his formal confession to the "new-maid doctour." There are similar parallels in other fables. The death of the wether comes after the grimly comic chase, and is explained as the punishment due to an upstart who strays from his own territory (and all the tragic transgressions that such an act symbolizes) and tries the patience of lawful authority too far (although, as in **"The Cock and the Jasp,"** the protagonist is shown in the tale to be doing his best by his own inadequate standards).

The wether's expressed concern about guarding the flock because of the absence of the guard dog in **"The Wolf and the Wether"** can be viewed as a noble gesture, particularly since the flock itself is defenseless at the beginning of the fable. However, this motivation on the wether's part is countered by what may indeed be his overarching motive—a will to power over the wolf that is intended to strike terror in the heart of the wolf (2535). As the fable plays out, the wether both literally and symbolically breaks boundaries, and in this action Henryson is showing us the potential for a tragic hubris in the wether's character. The wether, in somewhat arrogant fashion, dons a false identity which might tend to place him higher up on the list of aggressive animals. Further, he also accepts the responsibilities of this action of stepping out of one's place in line: "'All hail the cure I tak it vpon me / ȝour scheip to keip'" he says to the anxious shepherd (2485-6). Initially, the wether sees fun and games in becoming a dog (2577-8). The fun stops, however, when the toy of the play world, his dog skin, tears off and is left behind on a bush as he pursues the wolf. At this point, the wether has no choice but to acknowledge the reality of his own being and, what is even more important, the effects of having tried to evade that reality by trying to become something greater than nature would allow. His transgression of his bounds, though done in a spirit of play, results in a rude shattering of his play sphere.[3] The wolf, when viewed with these matters in mind, can be seen as a necessary corrective that allows for the brutal, tragic education of the wether in his moments before being devoured. The wether is in essence forced to confront the (limited) reality of his own being, as is painfully obvious in his pleadings with the wolf. His claims about never intending to harm the wolf (2558, 2575) are an acute observation *post hoc* on the grim comedy of his actions. Had he ever succeeded in catching the wolf, the wether would very likely have met in the very same fate he faces at the end of the fable. In his case, failure or success can both lead to destruction. The Narrator attempts to drive the point home to us that, for such a character as the wether, no matter if the motive is arrogant or heroic (assuming there's a difference), any attempt to be other than what nature ordains leads inexorably to tragic consequences. A bitter self-awareness may result, but the message seems to indicate clearly that the price paid for such a knowledge is not worth it.

"The Wolf and the Lamb," which follows the tale of the wether, presents the brutal killing of a lamb who ventures to drink from the same stream as a tyrannical wolf, but we cannot laugh about this sacrificial death. We are shocked to find that appeals to truth and the law are ineffective against obdurate malevolence, that there may indeed be no justice operative in the world we inhabit. No gruesome comedy or justified punishment could make us indifferent to the wolf's determined cruelty and the Narrator's sharp exposition in the *moralitas*. A danger presented here, as in **"The Sheep and the Dog,"** is that the cosmos appears at best indifferent to suffering, if not wholly and downright baleful and malignant, and that its claim to justice and respect is dubious. But the Narrator points to a way out of the existential quandary these questions may pose. The *slaughterer* of the innocent lamb, in this case with the emphasis on the flesh and blood of the victim, when viewed from the Christian perspective of sin and damnation the Narrator expects his audience to assume, may be seen as the real self-sacrificial victim. That is, the actions committed by the wolf amount to a presumed sacrifice of his soul at the altar of the collective (Christian) moral order, around which and around *whom* social cohesion is based. The crucifixion is thus the subtext for this fable. In the case of the wolf and the lamb, the poet's construction of an innocent victim (the lamb) is premised on the construction of a victim(izer), the qualities of whom are designed to generate and maintain the desired and dominant socio-religious values in Henryson's audience.[4]

What, we may ask, are the purposes of the frivolous rehearsals of the Narrator's most serious messages? Why should his teachings be perceived and uttered first by the most depraved characters of the **Fables**? We need to consider the audience for whom the lessons were intended and to realize, as our poet did, that the lessons are needed and must be repeated in many ways because humanity is weak and wilful and very unwilling to pay heed and reform. The Narrator must use a range of methods to gain and focus audience attention, and his engagement of audience interest through the grim comedy of the tales is one of these methods. Having given attention to an amusing incident, members of the audience may more readily be shocked by their perception of a similar but tragic happening.

We may consider the first sequence of fox fables, **"The Cock and the Fox," "The Fox and the Wolf,"** and **"The Trial of the Fox,"** noting the progression in violence of behavior and comedy and the preparation for the lessons eventually drawn. We are delighted to find, in **"The Cock and the Fox,"** that the villainous fox escapes without harming his intended victim, "gentill Chantecleir." The brevity of description of characters and setting in this tale implies its familiarity to the audience. Already acquainted with Chaucer's version, they may enjoy Henryson's variations on the theme, such as the short-lived mourning of the hens who would be Chantecleir's widows. The laughter such a tale inspires is untainted by cruel enjoyment of misfortune, since Lowrence is outfoxed by foolish Chantecleir. The enjoyment of the next fable, **"The Fox and the Wolf,"** is caused by some suffering, but there seems to be no need for reproach. The fox is a villainous character, and in the just, fictitious world of the fable he should not succeed. The pleasure we take in the neatly poised ironies of the tale may be disturbed by the austere *moralitas,* which tersely warns of the danger of sudden death for those who are unprepared. This method of teaching is elaborated in **"The Trial of the Fox."** As has been noted, the court is uninhibited in laughing at the wolf's injury, the fox is formally executed, and the *moralitas* deals with a relatively inconspicuous incident. Of course, we share the court's delight. As in the previous fable, calamity has come to a villain. Why should his hurt not make us happy? We can enjoy his deserved misfortune at the level of unthinking, heartless fun, but we may be surprised to think that teaching, to ensure joy for the soul, comes at the expense of the wolf.

If we turn our attention at this point to the fox in this fable, we can see again a process of teaching based on the suffering of one distinct character who is isolated and destroyed. The lion, in regal fashion, proclaims that there will be no preying on lambs and kids in a twenty mile radius. This declaration undoubtedly addresses a noteworthy segment of the population at hand, including himself. In this action, it should be plain that the society, any society, must abridge the wants and desires and in some cases the needs of its members for the sake of social cohesion (in a manner similar to that put forth in Rousseau's "Origin of Civil Society"). So, when the fox has his dinner he in effect breaks the law, and thus incurs the death penalty. The fact that the fox, as the wolf and the lion and presumably many of the other members in the society, is a carnivore indicates that any other such creature in the group could likewise wind up in the position in which the fox finds himself at the end of the fable. What this shows is that the laws which place limits on actions do so for the sake of social and moral order. The very notion that beasts of all sorts can form a parliament as they do in this fable points to the founding principles of such order.

The figure who disrupts the stability of this order, the fox, functions as a kind of scapegoat whose violent removal from the society underscores the importance of social conformity to the law. Individuality in his case— that is, his criminality, for the two are inseparable—is his distinguishing mark, that which separates him from the more or less undifferentiated mass of the rest of the herd. As we also see through his execution, violence and vengeance are not necessarily bad things, provided, of course, that they are carried our by the unanimous consent of the community via its legal system. Violence and revenge are taboo only when carried out by individuals—hence the notion of the criminal. When looking at this through the Narrator's eyes, we can see that conformity to a governing order (legal, ideological, moral, or whatever) forms the basis of avoiding suffering such as the for experiences. What is communal is good, what is individual is bad. The reason for this, as **"The the Trial of the Fox"** and other fables indicate, is that the violator of the "law" through his or her actions calls that very law into question. The violence which raises such questions is in turn answered with violence which, from the Narrator's perspective, renders such questions invalid.[5]

When we shift from the fable world to the human world, we can begin to see the Narrator's didactic intent in terms of crime and punishment. The moral crises that this fox and other foxes in the fables precipitate by violating the rules (sinning, if you will) must be contained in their human manifestations for the human community to survive in a manner that the Narrator deems appropriate. When these foxes are allegorically presented by the Narrator as "temptationis" (1132), "the warld . . . Quhilk makis man to haif na mynd of deid" (2210-1), and "the Feind" (2431), he is pointing out their threat to the moral order and the community built up around it. The punishment of the fox in **"The Trial of the Fox"** clearly communicates the Narrator's belief that transgression of the (moral) law entails anti-social behavior and results in punishment. And it is, after all, the law and its communal stability rather than criminal individuality that the Narrator holds dear. For him, his very identity is bound to the value system he embodies in his outlook on life. His didactic impulse thus becomes an attempt to ensure moral conformity in his audience. He achieves this by isolating a "bad" figure and indicating that "badness" ("otherness") results in pain and death. Even in the bleakest of fables where the bad guys seem to get away with their badness, the overarching Christian value system that informs the fables implies that the get-away is only temporary; an ultimate scheme of justice awaits in the afterlife. (We would stress, however, that this notion stems from the Narrator, not necessarily from the poet himself.)

In short, what the Narrator implies in his teachings is that conformity to the standard notions of moral, ethical, and social behavior keeps the social order from exploding, as **"The Trial of the Fox"** makes abundantly plain. The sense of "the criminal element," "immorality," and "evil" always is embodied in the threatening "other." For this reason, even though this "other" remains a potential representative of "us," it must be removed by way of earthly suffering or the notion of damnation in the hereafter.

Throughout the *Fables* hurt comes to the beasts, with escalation in injustice and severity of physical injury, and in the potential for damage to the soul, culminating in the struggles of the toad and mouse, representing those of the body and soul. The joyous experience of laughter frees us from the restraints which discourage us from examining the viciousness of human nature, just as the cathartic liberation of tragedy frees and purifies the spirit. In Henryson's *Fables* laughter caused by the hurt of a vicious character often precedes sorrow for the victim. Laughter helps isolate the vicious character and unites the laughers around a common enemy, so to speak. The sorrow we are meant to feel for the innocent victims is a key weapon in the Narrator's arsenal of didactic devices. This sort of pity evokes simultaneous sympathy and revulsion—sympathy for the "good" victim and revulsion for the "villain." After such experiences we receive instruction, when our customary defenses of reluctance and resistance to moralizing are in disarray. Such violent treatment is needed by an audience that might show resistance, and the Narrator rarely pictures a receptive audience.

The cohesion the Narrator seeks in his audience comes via the purgation of those values he considers evil. In other words, the improper values must be removed from the human social sphere, and ideally this is what the Narrator has in mind. If the audience takes this lesson to heart, then presumably earthly existence will be more harmonious. The ideological conformity that informs the Narrator's *moralitates* provides for the homogenization and standardization of culture around an unquestioned system of values that provides a guideline for behavior and clear distinctions between good and evil.

The Narrator repeats these lessons, general and particular, throughout the sequence, yet his addresses, whether direct or oblique, imply a growing pessimism about their effectiveness, despite the growing affection for the individuals to whom he speaks. The hurt of Henryson's fabulous creatures can make us "happie" as people who have gained moral instruction, and allows us the experience of cathartic laughter which may make our own hurts more bearable. Any fable exploits the distancing effect of its patently fictitious characters to demonstrate serious issues. The comic rehearsal of the events of some of Henryson's *Fables* distances his audience even further, but paradoxically induces them to be more receptive by engaging their attention and gaining the response of laughter.

Henryson's *Fables* are framed by passages which demonstrate his construction of his audience, in the amiable formality of **"The Prologue"** and the sadly enlightened intimacy of the *moralitas* of **"The Paddock and the Mouse."** In the telling of the tales, there are many glimpses of an audience—the malicious jeerers of the royal court, the unheeding birds, the perceptive fox, the merciful lion, the well-instructed toad and the mouse are some of them. To deal with these there is a range of teachers and methods, and few have any ultimate success. We may wonder if Henryson really expects success. He has no illusions about our aptitude to learn the lessons he teaches. He presents them in ways which are both amusing and tragic, prefiguring the sadly gruesome incidents in grim or gentle jokes, continually using the methods of reversal, shocking those who are unwilling or unable to learn into a fuller understanding, and using the hurts of the body to warn against injury to the soul, hoping that the individuals in his audience may at last enjoy the happiness of Heaven.[6]

Notes

1. On an audience's derivation of pleasure from violent or tragic works, see Packer, Tinsley (esp. 101), and, with particular reference to Henryson's fables, Khinoy (101-102). On the three levels of figural application in verbal art, especially with reference to theories of Plato and Aristotle, see Farrell (11).

2. This is suggested by Denton Fox ("Henryson's *Fables*" 345) and in the note to line 94 in his edition of the *Poems*. The notion is denied by George Clark (8).

3. On the notion of the play spheres, see Johann Huizinga's classic study on the subject, *Homo Ludens*.

4. Social cohesion around a sacrificial victim is an issue discussed at length in Girard's *Violence and the Sacred* and *The Scapegoat*.

5. This consideration of violence owes a debt to Girard's *Violence and the Sacred*.

6. The authors wish to thank Professor Tom Burton of the University of Adelaide for his comments and suggestions on this essay as it evolved.

Works Cited

Clark, George. "Henryson and Aesop: The Fable Transformed." *ELH* 43 (1976): 1-18.

Farrell, Thomas B. "Rhetorical Resemblances: Paradoxes of a Practical Art." *Quarterly Journal of Speech* 72 (1986): 1-19.

Fox, Denton. "Henryson's *Fables*." *ELH* 29 (1962): 337-56.

Girard, Rene. *The Scapegoat*. Trans. Yvonne Freccero. Baltimore: Johns Hopkins UP, 1986.

———. *Violence and the Sacred.* Trans. Patrick Gregory. Baltimore: Johns Hopkins UP, 1977.

Henryson, Robert. *The Poems of Robert Henryson.* Ed. Denton Fox. Oxford: Clarendon P, 1981.

Huizinga, Johan. *Homo Ludens: A Study of the Play Element of Culture.* Boston: Beacon, 1955.

Khinoy, Stephan. "Tale-Moral Relationships in Henryson's *Moral Fables. Studies in Scottish Literature* 17 (1982): 99-115.

Kratzmann, Gregory. "Henryson's *Fables*: 'The Subtle Dyte of Poetry.'" *Studies in Scottish Literature* 20 (1985): 49-70.

Mehl, Dieter. "The Audience of Chaucer's *Troilus and Criseyde.*" *Chaucer and Middle English Studies in Honour of Rossell Hope Robbins.* Ed. Beryl Rowland. London: Allen, 1974.

Packer, Mark. "Dissolving the Paradox of Tragedy." *Journal of Aesthetics and Art Criticism* 47 (1989): 211-219.

Tinsley, John. "Tragedy and Christian Beliefs." *Theology.* March 1982. 98-106.

Sabine Volk-Birke (essay date 1995)

SOURCE: Volk-Birke, Sabine. "Sickness unto Death: Crime and Punishment in Henryson's *The Testament of Cresseid.*" *Anglia* 113, no. 2 (1995): 163-83.

[*In the following essay, Volk-Birke examines* The Testament of Cresseid, *concluding that it is a poem about spiritual emancipation, not crime and punishment.*]

Henryson's *Testament of Cresseid* has been called "perhaps the best, and certainly the most highly praised, narrative poem in English between the works of Geoffrey Chaucer and Christopher Marlowe's *Hero and Leander*".[1] This may be due on the one hand to its artistic qualities, but on the other hand it may also be due to the fascination which the Troilus and Cressida story has had for so many authors in different countries over the centuries. Cressida's infidelity has always been an unalterable fact in their relationship. However, no version before Henryson dealt with her fate after her betrayal of Troilus, whereas the life of the warrior is followed right through to its valiant end in battle and, in Chaucer's version, even to a triumphant apotheosis. In contrast to this careful tying up of the narrative thread, Cressida's story is left hanging in mid-air. It is this deficiency which Henryson's narrator wishes to amend.

At first glance, his continuation of the plot seems simple and straightforward: The heroine who betrayed faithful Troilus and fell for Diomed's wooing in the Greek camp must experience poetic justice. In her turn, she is left by Diomed, thus she suffers herself what she had done before. This leads her, at least according to some rumors, into prostitution. But this is not enough. When she accuses the gods, particularly Cupid and Venus, of breach of promise—the immortals have not kept her in her favourable position as the most beautiful woman in Troy and as the mistress of a powerful warrior—they are deeply offended and retaliate with some fury. Cresseid's blasphemy is punished by leprosy, this most disfiguring as well as terminal illness. Far from inquiring into her own responsibility, Cresseid quarrels with her fate. One day, as she is begging with her clapper and bowl by the side of the road, Troilus rides past. They do not recognize each other, but Troilus is reminded of the Cresseid he loved and he drops a golden girdle, purse, and money into Cresseid's lap before he gallops away, terribly saddened by his memories. When the others lepers reveal his identity to Cresseid, she begins a desperate lament on her faithlessness. She then makes her testament in which she decrees that the ring which Troilus had once given her is to be taken back to him after her death and that he is to be told of the manner of her death. Troilus is deeply moved and he has a marble slab placed on her grave which juxtaposes the two different aspects of her life: "sumtyme countit the flour of womenheid" and "lait lipper".

From our modern point of view we may be inclined to see the story with its moralizing ending, in which the narrator exhorts women to be true and to take Cresseid's fate to heart, as an illustration of a guilt and punishment mechanism which functions with all the severity of the Old Testament precept of an eye for an eye and a tooth for a tooth. John McQueen indeed thinks that "Cresseid's leprosy is to be regarded as the punishment for her lightness in love".[2] E. M. Tillyard saw Cresseid's crime not only in her betrayal of Troilus and the breach of the code of courtly love, but also in her rebellion against Cupid and Venus, which in his opinion corresponds to the sins of *superbia* and *ira*.[3] According to Tillyard, leprosy with its medical and social results is the logical consequence of these sins. The planets who are responsible for the verdict act as instruments of the divine will, in keeping with Chaucer's view of nature as God's "vicaire".

Matthew P. McDiarmid emphasizes a different aspect when he complains that earlier critics were blind in relation to a theme which "no comtemporary reader would have missed, the Boethian theme of patience".[4] In his view, Cresseid rebels against fortune and her unpredictable ways of changing happiness into misery. Cresseid is supposed to learn how to be patient, and in the teaching of this lesson leprosy is not to be read as moral condemnation, it only underlines in a very dramatic manner those changes which have already transformed Cresseid's life: leprosy signifies "exclusion from familial and social life",[5] as Diomed's faithlessness had done before. In McDiarmid's opinion, the rule of fortune over the world constitutes the philosophical centre of the poem, "whatever the heroine's merits or demerits".[6] From here, it is not a great step to Douglas Duncan's position who winds up his critique of Tillyard with the conclusion that Cresseid did not deserve her leprosy, that the reader is entitled to sympathize with her rebellion against the gods, and that Henryson not only evades the moral problem which Cresseid's actions have posed, but that his poem, "far from reposing in orthodoxy", "questions the divine order quite peremptorily".[7]

Can these contradictory interpretations be brought together at all? Why do authors and audiences get so excited about this woman? Why are most of the writers who chose this subject matter, from Boccaccio to Shakespeare, so torn between condemnation and defense? The problem of guilt is certainly central to the story, even if and when there is no mention of any punishment. What makes Henryson of all people decide to have Cresseid die of leprosy when particularly Chaucer left it largely to the audience to judge her? Or does Henryson's version refrain from condemnation, too?

In order to answer these questions, we must ask questions at different levels. First it seems useful to go back behind Chaucer, on whom Henryson relies explicitly, in order to look at the development of the story and the comments made on Cressida's behaviour. Then we must look at Henryson's experience of leprosy and contemporary ways of dealing with it as well as at the treatment which leprosy receives in medieval literature. Equally important seems the attitude of the later Middle Ages towards death and dying. Furthermore, we must ask a few questions concerning Cresseid's motives and psychology, and finally we must follow up the hint which the narrator gives us by describing the genre of the text as "tragedy".[8]

Let us begin with the development of the subject matter. It is of course rooted in the *Iliad,* and the fate of the protagonists is played out before the backdrop of the fall of Troy. The love story, however, does not exist here, there is only Troilus' death in battle.[9] Troilus the lover, and thus the reason for the fascination which the subject matter has exercised over the centuries, is invented and inserted into the story of Troy by Benoît de Sainte-Maure in his *Roman de Troie* as late as around the middle of the 12th century, as a contribution to the new literary tradition of courtly love. Benoît has at once all the important facts: Briseis (not yet called Cressida) is the daughter of the seer Calcas who has defected to the Greeks. He succeeds in making her follow him, after she had begun a love affair with Troilus, which was no secret in Troy. Benoît depicts Briseis' grief about the separation in detail, but at the same time he leaves the reader in no doubt that she finds consolation with Diomed quickly enough after she has entered the Greek camp. She is clearly conceived from the beginning as an unfaithful woman, in keeping with a widespread tradition of antifeminist literature. On the other hand, she has to have attractive features over and above her beauty which could motivate Troilus' love for her. She is therefore one of the few women in the literature of this time who are contradictory and dynamic characters.[10] Briseis is fully conscious of her betrayal. This is made clear by Benoît's commentary ("well she knew she was acting very shamefully") as well as by her great monologue which gives her the opportunity first to analyse her motives and her feelings and then to think about her reputation: "Henceforth no good will be written of me, nor any good song sung. . . . Evil and senseless was my thought, I deem, when I betrayed my lover, for he deserved it not at my hands. . . . Very changeable and faithless is my heart." She considers her situation in a pragmatic manner and comes to the conclusion: "And what avails it to repent? That can never be amended. To Diomede then I will be true, for he is a very worthy and good warrior." Besides, she has no friends and no support in the Greek camp. Had she stayed in Troy, she would certainly have remained faithful to Troilus. Nevertheless, her conscience plagues her, she does not find any rest and is therefore determined, we would say, to repress her qualms: "But I must turn all my heart and mind to Diomede from this time forth, willingly or unwillingly".[11]

Boccaccio, who knew the story from Benoît as well as from the Latin translation by Guido delle Collone (*Historia Troiana,* 1287), does not transfer this monologue into his *Filostrato,* because he stresses the antifeminist element of the story. He allows Criseida a desperate lament about the separation from Troilus and even reproaches and threats to the gods[12] which remind the reader of the accusations by Henryson's Cresseid, but he does not give her the opportunity to reveal her motives to the audience after the betrayal. She simply becomes "base Criseida",[13] representative of female faithlessness, and she is explicitly used by the narrator as a warning to men who should beware of such women who are certainly not worth dying for.

Chaucer in his turn gives Criseyde the opportunity, in parallel to the monologue we find in Benoît, if not to excuse herself, then nevertheless to grieve over her situation. Althought there is no doubt about her weakness and opportunism in listening to Diomed, she does not shirk the recognition that she repays Troilus' faithfulness with betrayal. As in Benoît she knows that she casts a shadow on all women, that is, she considers herself a bad example. But she cannot turn back, therefore she wants to be at least faithful to Diomed. The narrator refuses to endorse the condemnation which Boccaccio insisted on, on the contrary, he tries to excuse her "for routhe", and he tries to give the impression that she hesitated for some time before giving in to Diomed. Her bad reputation should, according to Chaucer, be punishment enough for her guilt.

Henryson, too, is concerned with a bad reputation, pity, and possible excuses in his introduction. In his story, Cresseid is not only accused of unfaithfulness, but of prostitution in the Greek camp after Diomed got rid of her: "And sum men sayis, into the court, commoun." At first, the narrator seems to take this seriously. He breaks out into a lamentation which highlights the difference between Cresseid's former life and its present low in a number of pointed contrasts: from "feminite" to "filth", from "flour and A per se of Troy and Grece" to "fle-schelie lust" and "foul plesance". The influence of fortune ("fortunait", "mischance") is responsible for this fall. The narrator regrets Cresseid's misfortune, which seems to have come over her without any guilt on her part ("and nathing throw the gilt of the") and which is only due to slander, "wickit langage". Does he consider the talk about prostitution only as a rumor then, which wrongs Cresseid? In any case, he will have no truck with the moral indignation about her fickleness ("brukkilnes"). Instead, he stresses his pity and his intention to excuse Cresseid, who has suffered so much from fortune:

> ȝit neuertheles, quhat euer men deme or say
> In scornefull langage of thy brukkilnes,
> I sall excuse als far furth as I may
> Thy womanheid, thy wisdome and fairnes,
> The quhilk fortoun hes put to sic distres
> As hir pleisit, and nathing throw the gilt
> Of the—throw wickit langage to be spilt!
>
> (85-91)[14]

Does this mean that the prostitution is of no importance for Henryson's version? This would be greatly relevant for the interpretation of the text, particularly for the function of the leprosy. Craig McDonald points out that "immorality" was considered as a cause for leprosy in the Middle Ages,[15] Brody also shows that leprosy was often equated with VD,[16] and Schöwerling reads the leprosy as punishment for Cresseid's betrayal of Troilus as well as her sexual incontinence,[17] but Matthew P. McDiarmid disputes this connection for Cresseid.[18] When we look at the function of leprosy in other literary works of the Middle Ages, we can indeed consider an alternative reading which throws a different light on the inexorable mechanism of guilt, that is here unfaithfulness, lust, and blasphemy, and punishment, that is slander, leprosy, and death.

In Hartmann von Aue's *Der Arme Heinrich* as well as in the romance *Amis and Amiloun* leprosy is a punishment, but at the same time it is already atonement and the way to salvation. As soon as Heinrich has learnt his lesson, namely to rely completely on God—something he had failed to do so far—he is healed. Amiloun knows that by perjuring himself he has saved his friend, but fallen into sin himself. He accepts the leprosy as his punishment. It is Amis who must reciprocate his friend's altruistic act, so that Amiloun can be healed. In both cases, leprosy is not an incontrovertible death sentence—God can lift the punishment when it has served its purpose. When we look at this from the narrative point of view, the pattern is as follows: guilt is followed by punishment, so that the wrong which has been done can be identified as such and can be repented. As in the case of Job, repentance is followed by reward, namely the visible acceptance of contrition and atonement in the shape of healing. Leprosy is a particularly appropriate symbol for this narrative and psychological situation. It makes the victim look hideous, that is, it turns the inside out and makes the sin visible. It is thus impossible for the leper to cover up or repress his desparate situation. At the same time, the leper is helpless and has to rely largely on the pity and the charity of others. The disease is certainly terminal, but it progresses very slowly, so that it grants the patient a long time in which to think and to reform. This emphasizes the function of leprosy as a last warning. As it is an incurable disease, the patient can only turn to God, the ultimate healer. Curing leprosy means curing the soul, reward on earth and not only in heaven, proof of God's mercy. In *Der Arme Heinrich* it is made quite clear that Heinrich is not allowed to despair, but that on the contrary it is the leprosy which leads him to a good life on earth according to God's wishes: he does not retreat into a monastry when he has regained his health, but he marries the girl who had wanted to sacrifice herself for him and who has indeed made his healing possible, even if she did so in a different manner than she had planned.

The customs and rituals with which medieval society and church reacted to leprosy support this interpretation of the disease as preparation to redemption. As soon as the illness was diagnosed, the leper was excluded from normal life with a solemn ritual. This had medical, social, and religious reasons. Up until the fifteenth century the belief in the contagiousness of the disease had grown very strong, so the exclusion of the patient from the daily life of the village or town took place for hygienic reasons and was supposed to protect the healthy. The use of clapper or bell can also be explained in this context, it was designed to warn others of the approach of lepers, as even their breath was considered dangerous. The hospitals which gave the lepers board and lodging were supposed to shelter them and guarantee a roof over their heads until they died, so they had the function of quarantine as well as of social security. Furthermore, the hospitals were supposed to provide pastoral care for the patients, as they were expected to interpret their disease as a trial, or as a form of purgatory on earth. Although they were kept apart from society, they were not regarded as outcasts in the religious sense, on the contrary, they could use their malady as a direct path to salvation.

The church gave expression to this fact through the ritual with which it excluded the leper from the community. The rites included elements from the service for the dead and made the link with death quite clear in their non-verbal symbolism. First, mass was celebrated and the patient was allowed a last confession. During the ceremony, he often knelt underneath a black cloth which signified death and the grave. Then the priest sprinkled earth over his feet, which was of course a further reference to his burial, but also to the origin of his body which came from earth. Then the priest explained to the leper that from now on he was dead to the world, but alive to God. He stressed again the significance of the disease: "If in weakness of body by means of suffering thou art made like unto Christ, thou mayest surely hope that thou wilt rejoice in spirit with God. May the Most High grant this to thee, numbering thee among his faithful ones in the book of life. Amen".[19] We can safely assume that Henryson was familiar with these rituals,[20] particularly since Dunfermline, where he had been living since 1465, had a leper hospital on the south side of town. His description of Cresseid's symptoms and outer appearance, which has been confirmed completely by modern medical accounts, also argues for his detailed knowledge of leprosy.

The way in which Cresseid deals with her possessions in her testament is also in accord with contemporary custom and law. The leper had to bequeath part of his fortune to the hospital in order to support his fellow patients, but he was free to dispose of a third of his property in whichever way he liked. However, Cresseid's decrees concerning the alms and the ring do not seem to be sufficient reason for calling the whole of the poem "The Testament of Cresseid", even if her instructions extend to her body and soul, since all this is dealt with in two stanzas only.[21] What can have urged Henryson to put so much emphasis particularly on the testament?

We find a valuable hint in Philippe Ariès' book *Western Attitudes toward DEATH*. He stresses that up until the modern age, every individual who was not killed suddenly, as for example in an epidemic like the plague, knew exactly when death was approaching, took notice of this and made preparations accordingly. Death was not repressed, but given shape, and it was a public event. Relatives, friends, the doctor and the lawyer, as well as the priest were assembled round the death bed. The *artes moriendi* of the 15th und 16th centuries give detailed information about the appropriate ceremonies. Two things happen in this situation. On the one hand there is the trial of the dying person. Good and evil powers take up their positions at the top of the bed.

The dying man will see his entire life as it is contained in the book, and he will be tempted either by despair over his sins, by the "vainglory" of his good deeds, or by the passionate love for things and persons. His attitude during this fleeting moment will erase at once all the sins of his life if he wards off temptation or, on the contrary, will cancel out all his good deeds if he gives way. The final test has replaced the Last Judgement.[22]

Ariès emphasizes the fact that the link between a person's death and his or her biography was certainly seen up until the 15th century: "From then on it was thought that each person's entire life flashed before his eyes at the moment of death. It was also believed that his attitude at that moment would give his biography its final meaning, its conclusion".[23] Everybody has, as Ariès puts it, their own, individual death. This belief is closely linked with another ritual, the testament:

> Until the 18th century, death was a concern for the person threatened by it, and for him alone. Thus it was up to each person to express his ideas, his feelings, his wishes. For that he had available a tool: his last will and testament, which was more than simply a legal document for the disposal of property. From the 13th to the 18th century the will was the means by which each person could express—often in a very personal manner—his deep thoughts; his religious faith; his attachment to his possessions, to the things he loved, and to God; and the decisions he had made to assure the salvation of his soul and the repose of his body.[24]

As the testament was made on the deathbed, it was usually dictated to the priest or to a lawyer. It included the begging for forgiveness to those who were close to the testator, reparations in case of damage or negligence, a recommendation of those present to God and perhaps also instructions about a grave. This was followed by the prayers for the dying and the socalled *commendatio animae,* he was given the absolution and then holy communion, whereupon all he could do was to wait for death in silence.

If we do not interpret the term 'testament' in its narrow modern sense as a disposition over property, but if we include the whole medieval complex of dying with its rituals, considerations and decisions, then a different picture emerges that justifies the title of Henryson's poem. Lament and testament constitute, as I will try to show, the climax of the poem.

The text is divided into a series of transitions which are represented spatially, but which stand for a number of physical, social, and mental transformations, each of which is irreversible. Cresseid experiences herself in these transitions as a passive sufferer, who complains, but who does not act. The first transition takes place in Chaucer: Cresseid is taken to the Greek camp, surrounded by a great entourage. There she laments her infidelity, after she has given in to Diomed's wooing.

She knows that she cannot turn back to Troy now. The second transition happens after the separation from Diomed, when she leaves the Greek camp, this time alone and unobserved. Although she finds refuge with her father, she has lost her social position and cannot show her face in society without shame. Her lament about what she terms her social descent takes the form of blasphemy, which is taken literally by the gods, with well-known consequences. Her glance into the mirror subsequent to her dream reveals to her only her outward appearance, it proves the sentence of the planet gods. The mirror does not have the function of a *speculum,* Cresseid's self-inspection remains narcissistic, even though it is not her beautiful, but her disfigured face which she contemplates.[25] Her third transition is her retreat into the leper colony. She is accompanied by her father this time, but in her new environment she is lonelier than she ever was before. Here follows the greatest of her laments, set apart through stanzaic form and style, characterized by the *ubi sunt* motif, built upon the contrast of past and future. She looks once more now at all her former life and evokes everything that had made her existence so desirable: house and standard of living, the garden in May, fame, honour, physical beauty. In this monologue she does not progress beyond her previous level of self-knowledge, either, but only remembers external things, affluence and luxuries. She does realize that the world is changeable and that this feature now determines her life as well, but she is subject to this condition only because of fortune's caprice. Henryson gives Cresseid's lament some images from the psalms which could have induced the audience to come to their own independent conclusions, but Cresseid only sees her own misfortune, which can merely serve as a warning to the ladies that their beauty is not going to last. Yet even this recognition is completely confined to the here and now and fails to lead to profound analysis, just as the isolation in the leper colony and her impending death failed before. The fourth transition is no longer marked geographically, but by a meeting and an explanation—the encounter with Troilus and the revelation of his identity.

We shall now look at this last part of the story in detail. Cresseid's swoon after the generous knight has been identified, her lament, testament and death form a close-knit unit. Throughout the poem, Henryson depicts the emotional reactions of his heroine in a series of carefully orchestrated steps. In most cases, she only weeps and laments her misfortune. Her heart as the centre of her feelings is mentioned only twice in the text. The narrator refers to it for the first time after she has seen her disfigured face in the mirror, in her first reaction to her leprosy:

> And quhen sho saw hir face sa deformait,
> Gif scho in hart was wa aneuch, God wait!

(349 f.)

The words are chosen deliberately: if she was really sorry, only God knows. This can be interpreted as a rhetorical question, but it can also indicate that the narrator is in doubt, if the disease has had the effect it should have had, namely contrition coming from the depth of the heart. As the continuation of the poem shows, the narrator's doubts are justified. Cresseid's heart, which is the central feature in matters of faithfulness, is only mentioned again when she learns who gave her the alms, but this time the phrasing is unambiguous:

> Quhen Cresseid vnderstude that it was he,
> Stiffer than steill thair stert ane bitter stound
> Throwout hir hart, and fell doun to the ground.

(537-9)

A Christian audience would have been familiar with a pain that pierces the heart like a sword, as this is the traditional image of Mary's emotional reaction to her son's passion. So the metaphor identifies the existential effect of the pain Cresseid suffers now in a place that had seemed invulnerable so far. Her swoon expresses an emotional upheaval which surpasses everything she experienced earlier. It denotes a mental and psychological stress which cannot be born, namely the memory of Troilus' love and fidelity, which Cresseid requited with betrayal. It is highly significant that Troilus has only been mentioned once so far in her laments, in one breath with Diomed, when she accused the gods of having deprived her of her protector. She thus conflates the two men in their function for her, unable or unwilling to differentiate between them. When she describes her fall from fortune's wheel in her lament in the leper hospital at night in all its aspects of loss—social position, beauty, housing, food, drink, friends, lovers—Troilus' love does not figure in it at all. Only at the very end, after the last meeting, she remembers what Troilus was above all: faithful. And only now is she capable of perceiving the wrong she has done to him.

Her swoon is connected with lamentations and self-accusation: "O fals Cresseid and trew knicht Troilus!" The rhetorical device of contrast, which plays a decisive role in the whole of the poem, is here taken to its climax. So far, all the contrasts were defined temporally, they served to distinguish between before and after, past and present. This corresponds to the turning of fortune's wheel. From the peak of beauty, luxury, honour and fame which the past had held she fell by degrees into bad reputation, ugliness, poverty, and the expectation of death which defines her present. This in any case is the interpretation which Cresseid gives to the route she had to take, passively suffering under the influence of fortune and the gods. Her reaction to every new instance of misfortune was lament, weeping over what she had lost, contrasting a positive past with a negative present.

This contrast between past and present comes to an end in her final lament. Cresseid now perceives a contrast which is independent of the passage of time and thus faces the problem head-on. Accordingly, her lament changes into a different category: from the dichotomy between her past and her present which had dominated her thinking so far, she progresses to a dichotomy between a 'you' and her self, that is, she perceives herself as guilty for the first time, but thus also as a responsible, active person and not simply as a passive victim. In other words: the recognition of her guilt brings with it the recognition of her freedom to act, which confirms her individuality. This is what her testament now documents. She disposes of everything she has, on the material, the social, and the spiritual level. In all these spheres she accepts responsibility and acknowledges her freedom to act. Therefore it makes sense for the testament to provide the poem with its title. Cresseid has accepted her fate and places her death deliberately into this context. She has failed in the past, she never was faithful, although she knew that in Troilus she had found somebody who, in contrast to the ways of the world, was completely true. She also perceives the fragility of the world, she realizes that there are only very few lovers who keep their promises. But now she does not use this recognition as an excuse, suggesting that she is only like all the others, but she stresses in the last stanza of her lament explicitly her own individual guilt and responsibility:

> 'Becaus I knaw the greit vnstabilnes,
> Brukkil as glas, into my self, I say –
> . . . Nane but my self as now I will accuse.'
>
> (568-74)

With this utterance she has done something that a Christian audience would identify as corresponding to part of the contemporary death rites, namely the confession of sins. With reference to these lines, the ***Testament of Cresseid*** is often called a "getting of wisdom poem", which means that it describes "the painful revelation to the protagonist of the nature of personal moral responsibility and the possibility of integrity in a world of time".[26] This is certainly true, but does not go far enough. It has already been pointed out that it is not the leprosy which causes Cresseid's change of mind, but Troilus' charity. As we have seen, this statement needs qualification. It is the memory of his love and faithfulness, his chastity, his irreproachable behaviour towards all women, his fulfillment of the chivalric ideal in every respect, and not his generous alms which shocks Cresseid out of her delusion.[27] It is interesting to note that in *Der Arme Hein rich* it is also not the disease as such which leads to a reversal of the hero's priorities, but love, both the self-sacrificing love of the young girl and the love of Heinrich for her and his admiration of her beauty, which are stronger than his wish for health and life. So in Hartmann von Aue's poem the

return to God takes place via the love of a human being. The second step, the return to God, cannot be taken explicitly in Henryson's text. But the first essential move is made, and Henryson strengthens this interpretation of Cresseid's end by means of her testament.

Let us look at Cresseid's last preparations more closely. For the 15th century it is in no way remarkable for her to leave her body to the worms. The transitoriness of the world and the decay of the body were a conventional theme in literature and art, and it was much less frightening than we seem to think today. The rites for the dying reminded everybody explicitly of the fact that the body was made from dust and would revert to this state. Besides, the structure of the testament shows that Cresseid begins with the things she considers least important. Her bequest of her material possessions to the other lepers corresponds to contemporary legal precepts; I think it would be misleading to stress too much her newly found love for others and her charity, although this aspect should not be dismissed out of hand.

The ring for Troilus is certainly more important, as it is not the material value of the object, but its symbolic function which counts. Cresseid wants Troilus to have a token of her love. She cannot revoke her infidelity, but she can make Troilus aware of the fact that she remembered him in her hour of death and that she relates to him, even trusts him with her memory, as he is the only person with whom she wants to establish a contact after and beyond her death. She has this possibility because she dies of leprosy: the disease is the reason why she can hope for his pity, which will allow him to think not only of the wrong she did him, but also of her suffering and perhaps to take her terrible death as an atonement. His reaction proves her right.

Finally Cresseid disposes of the most important item, her soul. The religious rites for the dying include the so-called *commendatio animae*, this is a prayer which recommends the soul which leaves the body to God and asks him to accept it mercifully. One of the agents who are called upon to help the soul is the virgin Mary. Moreover, the soul is not only supposed to be met by a host of angels, it shall also be greeted with songs of jubilation by the choir of virgins.[28] Diana as the virginal goddess thus has a double function in Henryson's poem. On the one hand it seems perfectly reasonable that Cresseid, who repents of her infidelity as well as of her lust, commends her soul to a virgin goddess. On the other hand Henryson's audience is very likely to have associated the virgin Mary and thus the Christian background which can always be seen behind the text.

What does it mean if Cresseid mentions Diomed in her very last words? She does not accuse him, but remembers full of remorse that he was the man to whom she gave the tokens of Troilus' true love. So her final remarks express her insight into her betrayal and her contrition. She holds up a mirror to herself and perceives her sin.

Thus she confirms the path of recogniton which she has taken from the beginning of the poem to its end. What then are we to make of the label "tragedy" which Henryson affixed to his poem? At first glance, it looks as if we were dealing with a tragedy of fortune, as it was defined by Boethius and taken up by Chaucer: Cresseid loses everything that the world can give: social position, love, property, honour, fame, beauty, health, life. The lament, which was considered an important element of tragedy, occurs in several places in the course of the poem and gradually gains in length, detail, and rhetorical brilliance. But Boccaccio already experiments with a question that probes the genre more deeply: Is the fall from the wheel of fortune related to guilt and punishment, or does misfortune hit good and bad alike? Does fortune act according to the decrees of a divine world order or is it at least in harmony with it, or is man helplessly confronted by total arbitrariness and exposed to a cruel and mindless fate? Does he have a free will, or is everything predestined, so that he cannot act in a meaningful way at all? Boethius solved the problem in his own way: he distinguished between material and spiritual goods and thus negated the totality of fortune's power. As she can only take away worldly goods, her scope of action is limited. She can cause painful losses, but she cannot cause tragedy. Reason in the *Roman de la Rose* follows this argument. Misfortune signifies happiness, because it leads to wisdom, whereas happiness leads to misfortune, because it encourages shortsightedness and spiritual blindness. There is no inevitable correlation between a person's character and his fate. Good people can also suffer poverty, need and affliction.

However, if we do not transfer the problem of the connection between guilt and fall on to the philosophical and religious plane, but look for some interplay between fate and character, fortune and free will, as Chaucer has begun to illustrate it in his *Troilus and Criseyde,* then the protagonist must have insight and judgement. Tragedy does not simply arise from sudden misfortune, but from a combination of circumstances and a conscious and free decision taken by a protagonist who accepts full responsibility for his or her actions. The misfortune which arises in this case is neither just punishment nor arbitrary ruin, but something in between, which develops logically from the action but which the protagonist in a sense did not quite deserve.

Where does Henryson come in here? Cresseid perceives herself as passive sufferer. In the beginning, she is full of indignation and interprets her fate ("angerly") only as a tragedy of fortune: "all in cair translatit is my joy"

(130). She considers herself the victim of arbitrary gods, particularly Venus, whom Henryson has given distinct traits of fortune. This view is called blasphemous and punished by leprosy. Cresseid can see a connection between the offense she gave to the gods and their 'revenge', as it seems to her, for her uncontrolled outburst, but the larger context which is at stake still remains hidden to her. Her next interpretation of her fate follows the pattern of the *de casibus* tragedy: she views herself as an example of how the fickleness of the world, which can be observed everywhere, turns a happy and affluent life into its contrary. So she warns the ladies that the same thing can happen to them: "in ʒour mind ane mirrour mak of me" (457). This mirror only refers to the external events, the fall from happiness to misery, as the mirror which Cresseid used after her dream had only shown her outer appearance to her. She does not search for a meaning, a link between herself and her actions and the radical changes which took place in her life; she does not think in the categories of crime and punishment, and is therefore unable to come to an insight into her position.

Only at the very end, after the meeting with Troilus, can she struggle free of her fatalistic world picture. As she achieves self-recognition and manages to act freely and independently, so she proves her sense of responsibility as well as her freedom. Henryson allows Cresseid to parody the medieval concepts of tragedy and to demonstrate how deficient they are as paradigms for human life and actions. I think it has become equally clear that he does not make an example of crime and punishment of Cresseid, which requites infidelity with terminal disease. The poem does not set out to discipline unfaithful women by means of Cresseid as a deterrent. It is concerned, before the dramatic techniques of Shakespeare or of the psychological novel are available, with the possibility of gaining self-knowledge, with the acceptance of responsibility for a sin, and with the possibility of developing the freedom to act independently. Cresseid succeeds in this at the very moment when her life comes to its end and she has nothing left. Chaucer had given Troilus a posthumous chance to come to a detached view of the world from the eighth sphere and had granted him a kind of Christian status by means of his apotheosis—he could do no more for a pagan in Troy. Henryson's continuation of the story of Cresseid is not a contrast to Troilus' end, but needs to be read as a parallel. As he gains in dignity to the very last, so does she.

I would like to close my paper with a provocative hypothesis: Henryson did not write a poem about a crime and punishment mechanism, but a poem about the spiritual emancipation of a woman which begins and ends with a document. Her suffering begins when her fate is decided by a text written by somebody else, that is the letter of separation from Diomed, and it ends when she makes decisions in her own text about her possessions, her body, her memory, and her soul, which embody her coming of age as a socially, morally, and spiritually responsible adult. It is fascinating to see how the end of Henryson's text falls short of this level of consciousness. The writing on the marble plate which Troilus provides for Cresseid stresses again the well-known contrasts of before and after, beauty and ugliness, and of course life and death, and thus falls back on a concept of fortune as the power which rules human fate which has just been invalidated by the whole story of Cresseid—this tells us more about Troilus, however, than about the heroine. The fact that the old and somewhat fussy narrator refers so extensively to the power of fortune, introduces the story as tragedy, and comes to a moralizing conclusion identifies him as the descendant of Chaucer's obtuse narrators, whose story assumes a different meaning than the one he intended.

Notes

1. L. V. Ryan, "A Neo-Latin Version of Robert Henryson's *Testament of Cresseid*", *Acta Conventus Neo-Latini Sanctandreani*, ed. I. D. McFarlane (Binghamton, 1986), pp. 483-491, p. 438.

2. J. McQueen, *Robert Henryson*, (Oxford, 1967), p. 61; cf. also C. McDonald, "Venus and the Goddess Fortune in *The Testament of Cresseid*", *Scottish Literary Journal*, 4 (1977), 14-25, p. 18: "Cresseid's breach of the moral code (her promiscuity) works with the planetary influences to bring about leprosy."

3. E. M. Tillyard, "*The Testament of Cresseid*", *Five Poems 1470-1870*, (London, 1948), pp. 16 f.

4. M. P. McDiarmid, "Robert Henryson in his Poems", *Bards and Makars*, ed. A. J. Aitken, M. P. McDiarmid and S. Thomas (Glasgow, 1977), pp. 27-40, p. 36.

5. Ibid., p. 37.

6. Ibid., p. 38.

7. D. Duncan, "Henryson's *Testament of Cresseid*", *Essays in Criticism*, 11 (1961), 128-35, p. 129.

8. Cf. A. Torti, "From 'History' to 'Tragedy': The Story of Troilus and Criseyde in Lydgate's *Troy Book* and Henryson's *Testament of Cresseid*", *The European Tragedy of Troilus*, ed. P. Boitani (Oxford, 1989), pp. 171-197.

9. Cf. P. Boitani, "Antiquity and Beyond: The Death of Troilus", ibid., pp. 1-19. Boitani points out that Troilus' death represents the end of Troy, it symbolizes the end of the world, which is signified by the fall of Troy. The fact that Troilus dies without offspring is thus a necessary characteristic of his function in the *Iliad*.

10. Cf. R. Antonelli, "The Birth of Criseyde—An Exemplary Triangle: 'Classical' Troilus and the Question of Love at the Anglo-Norman Court", ibid., pp. 21-48, p. 22.

11. Benoît de Sainte-Maure, *Le Roman de Troie, The Story of Toilus,* ed. and transl. by R. K. Gordon (Toronto, 1978), pp. 3-22, pp. 19 f.

12. "Ah, cruel Jove and malicious fortune . . . Harsh and pitiless, you snatch me from the happiness that was closest to my heart . . . It shall not cease from uttering complaints in abuse of you and to your dishonour until I come again to see once more the fair face of Troilus." Boccaccio, *Il Filostrato,* translation in: Gordon, *The Story,* p. 92.

13. Ibid., p. 124.

14. In: R. Henryson, *The Poems,* ed. D. Fox (Oxford, 1987), pp. 111-131; all quotations from this edition.

15. C. McDonald, "Venus and the Goddess Fortune in *The Testament of Cresseid*", *Scottish Literary Journal,* 4 (1977), 14-24.

16. S. N. Brody, *The Disease of the Soul: Leprosy in Medieval Literature* (Ithaca, 1974).

17. R. Schöwerling, "Chaucers *Testament of Cresseid* in der englischen Literatur von Henryson bis Dryden", *Anglia,* 97 (1979), 326-349.

18. M. P. McDiarmid, *Robert Henryson,* 1981, p. 105: "If Cresseid's leprosy had derived from her way of life, there is no reason why Henryson should not have said so. Saturn's special connections with the disease . . . was a commonplace of semi-astrological treatises on astronomy such as that of the universally read Sacrobosco." In relation to the leprosy of the Scottish national hero Bruce, he explains that it is contracted after "his sacrilegious breaking of faith with his rival Comyn, when in a moment of rage he stabbed the latter . . . The curing of the emperor Constantine's leprosy when he adopted the true faith was seen in the same light".

19. P. Richards, *The Medieval Leper and his Northern Heirs* (Cambridge, 1977), p. 123.

20. M. P. McDiarmid assumes that Henryson was a practising lawyer and bachelor in common law, "involved in property and money transactions, testaments, etc.", (*Robert Henryson,* p. 3). R. L. Kindrick, however, thinks there is no definite proof for these activities (*Robert Henryson* (Boston, 1979), p. 17).

21. J. A. W. Bennett, "Henryson's Testament: a flawed masterpiece", *Scottish Literary Journal,* 1 (1974), 5-16, p. 14: "That this brief testament should have given the work its title is inexplicable, and unfortunate."

22. P. Ariès, *Western Attitudes toward DEATH: From the Middle Ages to the Present,* transl. by P. Ranum (London, 1976), p. 36.

23. Ibid., p. 38.

24. Ibid., pp. 63 f.

25. Cf. J. H. M. Taylor, "Un Miroer Salutaire", *Dies Illa. Death in the Middle Ages. Proceedings of the 1983 Manchester Colloquium,* ed. J. H. M. Taylor, Vinaver Studies in French, I (Liverpool, 1984), pp. 29-43. Taylor looks at Guyot Marchant's 1486 edition of the *Dans Macabré* which calls itself "Miroer salutaire" in the sub-title. It is a dance of the dead: "what is presented to the onlooker is a procession of the living, partnered each by his own *mort*" (p. 33). "Thus it becomes the function of the poem and illustrations of the *Danse Macabré* to reveal, as a warning to the living, the essential transience of mortality to which each spectator is subject" (p. 34). Taylor assumes a "widespread association in everyday reality of the mirror and death" (p. 38). She distinguishes between the mirror as reflector, in which the spectator sees only his outward form, and the mirror as transformer, which reveals to the spectator his horrific future self in death. "Everything suggests that this image of the *mirror as transformer* was sufficiently widespread in the Middle Ages to require no gloss, if only, on the most mundane level, because *miroirs de mort* could be bought" (p. 39). Cresseid's warning to the ladies, which concludes her lament in the leper colony, refers simply to the conventional lesson taught by mirrors, namely the transitoriness of the world. The mirror has not made her look into herself, on the individual moral and psychological level.

26. J. Strauss, "To Speak once more of Cresseid: Henryson's *Testament* Re-considered", *Scottish Literary Journal,* 4 (1977), 5-13, p. 5.

27. The gift itself, its material value seems to play only a minor part as far as both Troilus and Cresseid are concerned. It is not his bounty towards the leper but her memory of the beloved, whose affection and fidelity she did not value, which fuels her lament and her tears. What he has given her now, is not important, it is passed on to the lepers in the testament. The token she sends to him after her death is not the girdle or the brooch, but the ring, a symbol of his love from their former days, which seems to be the only one of his gifts that has not found its way to Diomed. Thus she makes it quite clear that she is referring to their love by the token she sends. Troilus is supposed to remember the most beautiful woman in Troy, not the disfigured leper.

28. The Virgin Mary is invoked repeatedly in the *commendatio.* For the virgins, cf. the following: "Commendo te omnipotenti Deo, carissima soror, et ei, cujus es creatura, committo; ut, cum humanitatis debitum morte interveniente persolveris, ad Auctorem tuum, qui te de limo terrae formaverat, revertaris. Egredienti itaque animae tuae de corpore splendidus Angelorum coetus occurrat: judex Apostolorum tibi senatus adveniat: candidatorum tibi Martyrum triumphator exercitus obviet: liliata rutilantium et Confessorum turma circumdet: jubilantium te Virginum chorus excipiat: . . . sancta Dei Genitrix Virgo Maria suos benigna oculos ad te convertat: mitis, atque festivus Christi Jesu tibi aspectus appareant, qui te inter assistentes sibi jugiter interesse decernat." In the *Missale Sarum* (ed. 1492) the *commendatio animae* is clearly part of the *missa defunctorum.* Cf. T. E. Brightman, *The English Rite* (London, 1921). It was still included in the *Book of Common Prayer* of 1549, though it is no longer part of the Order of the Burial of the Dead now.

Catherine S. Cox (essay date 1996)

SOURCE: Cox, Catherine S. "Froward Language and Wanton Play: The 'Commoun' Text of Henryson's *Testament of Cresseid.*" *Studies in Scottish Literature* 29 (1996): 58-72.

[*In the following essay, Cox compares Henryson's* The Testament of Cresseid *with Chaucer's* Troilus and Criseyde, *particularly the treatment of Cresseid.*]

In the ***Testament of Cresseid,*** Henryson's treatment of Chaucer's Criseyde is mediated textually by a voice that is itself a participant in the text; the ***Testament*** narrator may be read as both narrative voice and literary character, the former existing discursively, as a rhetorical construct, and the latter as mimetic reality, having an imagined history and psychology. The narrator embodies Henryson's reading of Chaucer's text as the protagonist of sequences in which he re-reads and re-writes the story of Cresseid's "woefull end." As well, the narrator's central character, Cresseid, further embodies these layers of reading and writing, and thus problematic and compelling parallels exist between the narrator and his construct. Cresseid, we shall see, incorporates the errant text of both the narrator's reading of the "quair[s]" and Henryson's own reading of Chaucer.

What will become apparent also is that the ***Testament*** is a text obsessed with errancy, and, as such, it is a text obsessed with decorum. As the text attends to demarcations of propriety—sexual, discursive—it locates scenes of transgression, places where illusory borders of ideological confinement are confronted. Sexual and discursive errancies, which are manifest thematically in the *Testament*'s treatments of lust, blasphemy, and punishment, coincide with metaphorized representations of gender. These discursive configurations call attention to the narrative's own sense of errancy, its metatextual attention to itself as froward language, as discourse that engages its own "errant notions."[1] Apropos the text's representations of sexual and discursive errancies, my goal in this essay is to reassess Henryson's treatment of cultural and literary decorum in relation to gender.

Cresseid is introduced by the *Testament* narrator as a figure of sexual errancy, an abandoned woman, scorned owing to sexual improprieties, who, as a result of that disdain, further errs:

> Than desolait scho walkit vp and doun,
> And sum men sayis, into the court, commoun.[2]

The phrase "walkit vp and doun" evokes the aimlessness and uncertainty of errancy (*errare,* to wander); Cresseid belongs nowhere and has no place properly of her own. She has been excluded from proper social order owing to violations of decorum, for by becoming the property of everyone she has become the property of no one. Within the immediate context of the story as informed by Chaucer's *Troilus,* Cresseid is left to fend for herself; her body being her only asset, she participates in its exploitation, making it "commoun."[3]

Contextually, the narrative's treatment of Cresseid's sexual errancy in the *Testament* is informed by antifeminist traditions, made evident in part by the narrator's reified sexual perspective: that the feminine is repulsive. Widowed and celibate, Cresseid is described as "fair," a figure of beauty and virtue, but once sexually active, she is described by the narrator as filthy, foul, and tarnished:

> O fair Cresseid, the flour and A per se
> Of Troy and Grece, how was thou fortunait
> To change in filth all thy feminitie,
> And be with fleschelie lust sa maculait,
> And go amang the Greikis air and lait,
> Sa giglotlike takand thy foull plesance!
>
> (*ll.* 78-83)

In medieval Christian theology's antifeminist tenets, "feminine" and "carnal" are linked; all that is perceived as negative and threatening about carnality is ascribed to the feminine: feminine = flesh = corruption, sin, filth. Hence the *Testament* narrator, following Christian antifeminist decorums, links the feminine with the carnal/filth even before Cresseid's leprous transformation: "in filth all thy feminitie," "fleschelie lust sa maculait," "[s]a giglotlike takand thy foull plesance." Indeed the oxymoronic euphemism "foull plesance" is quite telling in the narrator's denigration of the feminine.

And Cresseid *is* her female body; it represents her public identity and, accordingly, her "commoun"

subjectivity. By defining her in this way, the text associates the concepts of promiscuity and errancy thematically; both identify gestures of deviation from some prescribed set of behaviors. The narrator calls attention to Cresseid's "womanheid" first as she represents proper adherence to masculine decorum, and then as a figure of subversive impropriety. The celibate Cresseid represents the feminine carnal subject to masculine control; the "commoun" Cresseid suggests the threat of unleashed carnality, the potential of the feminine to corrupt inherently vulnerable patriarchal decorums. Furthermore, while the *Troilus* narrator has likened Criseyde to the letter "A" by a simile of prioritization—"Right as oure first lettre is now an A" (*l.* 170)—the *Testament* narrator equates the two: Cresseid *is* the Letter, not merely likened to it in primacy. As well, she is the Carnal, with all its negative feminine associations played out in the narrative. For the "carnal" is "literal" in Pauline theology, and hence the feminine, as carnal, is literal; in effect, Woman is Letter, and the Letter is Death. Cresseid, the "A per se," is representative of a twofold feminine threat to Christianity's spiritual man: the carnal Letter and hence carnal Death.[4]

But within the Aristotelian antifeminist tradition, the feminine is "unlimited" as well, and, as such, is always *more than* carnal, always *more than* the letter. According to the Aristotelian/Pythagorean paradigm,[5] epistemological duals—including male and female, one and plural, limited and unlimited—define and schematize meaning. Howard Bloch comments:

> This association translates into what might be thought of as a medieval metaphysics of number, according to which, under the Platonic and Pythagorean schema, all created things express either the principle of self-identity (*principium ejusdem*) or of continuous self-alteration (*principium alterius*). The first is associated with unity, the monad; the second with multiplicity, dyadic structures. Also they are specifically gendered, the monad being male, the dyad female.[6]

The ancient association of the feminine and the unlimited suggests a complex, unpredictable, and mutable feminine nature.[7] Further, as Shari Benstock notes of the feminine, when "[a]ppropriated as a signifier of difference, [it] has been commonly understood to mark difference from a masculine universal."[8] Thus this gendered epistemology contrasts feminine mutability, errancy, and plurality with the stability, consistency, and certainty implied by a masculine universal. Cresseid, "the flour . . . Of Troy *and* Grece" (my emphasis), is mutable and unstable, belonging to neither and yet associated with both.

By unremittingly inscribing anything culturally construed as negative to be feminine, early Christian and medieval patriarchal discourses ensured that the negativity of the feminine would be patristically authorized and culturally perpetual, which was further exacerbated by patronizing assertions of compassion and respect. The negativeness accorded the feminine is manifest in the hierarchical value structure attached to conventional ideologies of gender difference, for the asymmetrical value structure of gendered ideology has conventionally devalued the feminine. Indeed, Toril Moi notes, "It doesn't matter which 'couple' one chooses to highlight: the male/female opposition and its inevitable positive/negative evaluation can always be traced as the underlying paradigm."[9] Medieval antifeminism may indeed be traced to the paradigm of contraries—further distorted by Christianity's applications—and the influence of the underlying antifeminist male/female, superior/inferior paradigm is ubiquitous in the Middle Ages. As Caroline Bynum notes: "*Male* and *female* were contrasted and asymmetrically valued as intellect/body, active/passive, rational/irrational, reason/emotion, self-control/lust, judgment/mercy, and order/disorder."[10] The irreducible difference of masculine and feminine finds the feminine associated with negativeness in both theological and epistemological representations. Both use the feminine to privilege the masculine, though theology pretends, by trumpeting the virtues of virginity, to valorize the feminine by denying what makes the feminine feminine, sexuality. And, as Karma Lochrie argues,

> When virgins are then instructed not to break that which seals them together with God and with themselves, they are being called to enclosure at many levels. The unbroken flesh ultimately means bodily closure and silence.[11]

Hence theological rationales are used to castigate feminine sexuality, just as feminine sexuality fuels patristic exclusion and condemnation—hence, too, codes of decorum are designed to valorize non-sexuality (virginity) and to condemn those who resist constraint.[12]

The contradictory directions in which gender is understood and represented in medieval thought resist reconciliation, and this resistance enables the text to dictate its gendering through conventional, though conflicting, associations and patterns. In evoking a twofold tradition through metaphorized representations of flesh and mutability, Henryson exploits the discrepancies between the two components in relation to language. Cresseid is representative of not only the carnal—the feminine flesh from which further meaning might be conceived—but also the potential multiplicity of meaning that gives rise to the polysemy necessary if language is to transcend literal constraints. This relationship of the feminine to language is articulated in conjunction with a medieval poetics that identifies language in terms of property and decorum. Figurative meaning is imposed, "improper"; such meanings are not the literal, "proper" (*proprium,* one's own) definitions of words (to the extent that a truly literal or proper sense can exist) but rather they are extra-literal, addi-

tions that are neither property nor proper; they are, in effect, "commoun." While the *signum proprium* represents proper association, the *signum translatum* suggests improper, erring senses effected by usurpative, transgressive, and arbitrary transfer.[13] The narrator's description of Cresseid as "A" means that the property of "A"—the first character of the alphabet, the glyph that denotes the capital letter—is transferred to and imposed upon "Cresseid" reflexively, improperly describing her as both primary and literal, and by extension identifying Woman as Letter, as Carnal. As the carnal flesh, the feminine is limited; but as the unlimited *translatio,* the feminine sense of language is its errancy, its extraliteral, improper senses. The feminine *translatio* inscribes the capacity of signification to transcend—or violate—proper decorum in order that multiple senses obtain. The feminine *signa,* as improper, are "commoun"—they are, in effect, promiscuous (mixed, confused, indiscriminate), for they resist constraint and challenge masculine insistence upon ordered decorum.

Cresseid, then, is the errant text, the "commoun" feminine that resists the limitedness of proper masculine stability and inherently challenges the oppressive rigidity of patriarchal propriety. She recuperates the potential of multiplicity to defy decorum and hence to resist control, for the sense of plurality associated with the epistemological feminine finds thematic representation in the errancy/promiscuity alignment attributed to Cresseid by the narrator and his text. There is no *usurpata translatio* without impropriety, and accordingly the "improper" woman is shown to be the subject of masculine scorn. Thus the correspondence of the feminine to language, problematized by the inhering contradiction of theological and epistemological origins, is itself figurative, and hence metaphorized feminine representations are both unstable and destabilizing, for even as the narrator's portrait of Cresseid's feminine promiscuity might arguably reify the patriarchal order that has both created and appropriated prostitutes, the narrator's construction of Cresseid's identity ultimately transgresses his narrative control. But while the female association with "unlimitedness" is largely negative owing to the positive/negative valuation of the pairings, in medieval poetics, with its emphasis on the polysemy of "improper" signification, the unlimitedness of the feminine may be understood as representative of polysemy and hence of poetic language itself, with all its ambiguities and uncertainties and with all its capacity to facilitate the construction of meaning in its necessary errancy. The narrative's emphasis on "commoun" subjectivity and its conjunctive insistence upon sexual errancy as a trope of affronted patriarchal decorum underscore Henryson's attention to his own "feminine" poetics.

The **Testament** elucidates the interconnectedness of the feminine and the "commoun" in its treatment of

Cresseid's offenses and punishments. Cresseid's overt discursive errancy—her blasphemy—corresponds to her insinuated sexual errancy; both are presented as promiscuous behaviors within patriarchal parameters, and hence both challenge decorum. Just as Cresseid's alleged sexual errancy problematically confronts a patriarchal order, so, too, her blasphemous language both participates in and destabilizes a patriarchal decorum of appropriate language, in effect both validating the existence of the patriarchally constructed metaphysical hierarchy of the gods and yet destabilizing that very hegemony by exposing its underlying ideology. Cresseid's offense of blasphemy is described as froward language, a discourse of errancy that violates boundaries of decorum:

> . . . "Lo, quhat it is," quod sche,
> "With fraward langage for to mufe and steir
> Our craibit goddis; and sa is sene on me!
> My blaspheming now haue I bocht full deir."
>
> (*ll.* 351-4)

Cresseid is actually shown to be punished in the ***Testament*** for blasphemy, not for her alleged betrayal of Troilus, though a connection between word and deed is implied:

> "Lo," quod Cupide, "quha will blaspheme the name
> Of his awen god, outher in word [or] deid,
> To all goddis he dois baith lak and schame,
> And suld haue bitter panis to his meid."
>
> (*ll.* 274-7)

Blasphemy, in the context of the narrative, represents Cresseid's unwillingness to accept the consequences of her so-called "fleschelie lust"; that is, her blasphemy articulates her anguish and frustration at finding herself occupying the stigmatized space of the undesired, uncoupled in a social context that recognizes the validity of the feminine only in relation to the superior masculine.[14] In addition, her sexual errancy perhaps qualifies as the "deid" to which Cupid alludes; although Cresseid identifies only her "fraward langage" as the "blaspheming [she has] bocht full deir," the "word" is perhaps prompted by her "deid," that is, her "commoun" behavior. In challenging masculine decorum—in transgressing the boundaries of proper, pious behavior—Cresseid's blaspheming rejects propriety at tremendous personal cost. Blasphemy is treated as a feminine abuse of language that corresponds to a masculine perception of a feminine abuse of sexuality, and hence the punishment is sexualized: "to all louers [Cresseid will] be abhominabill" (*l.* 308).

Sexual and discursive errancy further coincide in the text's emphasis on the interconnectedness of mutability and substitution. Cresseid, feminine *translatio,* has herself been subject to exchange; once transferred to the Greeks, she is proper to them—their property—and yet improper as well, having been purchased, in effect, usurped. Cresseid is shown to be unfixed, mutable, and the ***Testament*** narrator equates mutability and promiscuity. Cresseid substitutes Diomeid for Troilus and validates the exchange through a transfer of emblems—"O Diomeid, thou hes baith broche and belt / Quhilk Troylus gaue me in takning / Of his trew lufe!" (*ll.* 589-91)—but thematically, the circumstances are governed by a decorum of gender: Chaucer's Criseyde has herself been betrayed by the Trojans in their handing her over to the Greeks, but the ***Testament*** narrator suggests that feminine change or feminine agency is, regardless of circumstance and by definition of moral absolutes, negative or wrong. Thus Cresseid is held accountable for the exchange of which she herself is a victim, and she is accordingly scorned by men for her "brukkilnes," her daring to acclimate herself to the alien culture into which she has been sold. Mutability is equated discursively with promiscuity; to confront decorum is to privilege impropriety, to flaunt violations of propriety in a demonstration of "commoun" subjectivity.

Cresseid further substitutes the appropriated yet inappropriate language of blasphemy for the authoritative language of prayer, using a metaphor of mutability—errant change/replacement—as the core of her blasphemous outburst:

> O fals Cupide, is nane to wyte bot thow
> And thy mother, of lufe the blind goddes!
> 3e causit me alwayis vnderstand and trow
> The seid of lufe was sawin in my face,
> And ay grew grene throw 3our supplie and grace.
> Bot now, allace, that seid with froist is slane,
> And I fra luifferis left, and all forlane.
>
> (*ll.* 134-40)

The sexualized imagery of seeds and sowing—one of the ubiquitous medieval fertility images that corresponds to both eros and language, akin to "facound toung" and "pregnant sentence" (*ll.* 268, 270), for instance—describes Cresseid's acknowledgment of divine give-and-take. The sexual gesture of dispensation, "sawin in my face," foreshadows Troilus's sexualized gesture of charity—"And in the skirt of Cresseid doun can swak" (*l.* 522)—and emphasizes the prominent role of exchange in this text. The "seid of lufe," once freely sown and fertile, has given way to sterility—in the sense of wasted potential—and hence Cresseid is "fra luifferis left." Her blasphemy identifies change as the origin of her plaint, and it is this change for which the narrator holds her responsible; undesired change, the narrator asserts, is the fault of women, for replacement entails plurality, and plurality is negatively construed as feminine. Within the textual parameters, then, promiscuity is marked as feminine; it represents the unwillingness of the feminine to respect the proper masculine limits of decorum both sexually and discursively.

The narrative attests that mutability—ideologically inscribed as feminine—not only elicits a fear of the unknown, but provokes a concomitant frustration owing to incapability, ineffectuality, and impotence in response to a lack of control. The anxiety inhering in the text's concern with change is therefore connected to a fear of the feminine Other. (Indeed, the text of Cresseid is the "*vther* quair.") The sense of difference construed as Other adheres to ideological convention in its associations of gender: the feminine Other represents a negative alterity. Images of difference articulated as exchange or replacement may thus be read as narrative indictments of feminine Otherness. Hence the punishment described by Saturn—"I change thy mirth into melancholy, / Quhilk is the mother of all pensiuenes . . ." (*ll.* 316-7)—is articulated in a lexicon of contraries which evokes the Aristotelian/Pythagorean paradigm and suggests that change is itself punishment for change, for feminine errancy/mutability. Hence Cynthia—the Moon, representative of change—has the last word, inflicting illness—"And to thy seiknes sall be na recure / Bot in dolour thy dayis to indure"(*ll.* 335-6)— and mutilation.

As a conventional and ubiquitous feminine representation, the Moon clearly suggests change in her cyclical patterns, instability, and conjunctiveness.[15] Indeed, acting "quhen Saturne past away, / Out of hir sait" (*ll.* 330-31), Cynthia's sadistic punishments effectively illustrate antifeminist conventions of feminine mutability and duplicitousness at their most negative, far more even than the narrator's description of Venus in the same nightmare[16]—"dissimulait," "prouocative," "suddanely changit and alterait," "pungitiue with wordis odious" (225-30). The leprosy itself corresponds metaphorically to Cresseid's twofold feminine crime of errancy; conventionally, leprosy is associated with moral punishment for blasphemy and for sexual wantonness and, as has been well demonstrated, the ***Testament*** clearly draws from conventional etiology in the implicit association of Cresseid's blasphemous or errant behavior/language with her disease. The words of Cynthia ensure that Cresseid will indeed "to all louers be abhominabill" as punishment for her twofold errancy, thereby depriving Cresseid of objectivity in relation to masculine desire in atonement for her violating masculine decorum through sexual and discursive promiscuity.

But that which is "commoun" here defies constraint and instead asserts its discursive promiscuity. Cresseid is not rendered sterile despite being "to all louers abhominabill," "fra all luifferis left," for the errant text is a

fertile text, and it insists upon the capaciousness of its *signa translata*. Promiscuity is thus used by Henryson as an unstable and destabilizing erratic metaphor, and through textual occasions of sexual and discursive promiscuity, Henryson challenges the narrative/ normative presuppositions of decorum. There is an ambivalence inhering in the text's treatment of promiscuity, a sense of inevitable failure in attempting to limit the feminine *signa* coupled with an anxious impulse to pursue the fantasy of umitigated subjection. Henryson's ambivalence apropos the promiscuity of discourse is manifest in the narrative's obvious misogyny, a connection that invites further scrutiny.

In the narrator's initial description of Cresseid, coinciding with Cresseid's suggested sexual errancy is narrative errancy. Each exposes its own subjectivity in relation to violations of decorum, sexual and discursive. With regard to the specific detail of Cresseid's continued sexual errancy, for example, the narrator displaces authority—"sum men sayis"—thereby insinuating that his report is gossip.[17] But the narrator's affected modesty is betrayed as his text unfolds, for while he may claim to abhor gossip, he of course perpetuates it through his own repetition. Hence his profession of concern—

> Ȝit neuertheles, quhat euer men deme or say
> In scornefull langage of thy brukkilnes,
> I sall excuse als far furth as I may
> Thy womanheid, thy wisdome and fairnes,
> The quhi[l]k Fortoun hes put to sic distres
> As hir pleisit, and nathing throw the gilt
> Of the—throw wickit langage to be spilt!

(*ll.* 85-91)

—is undermined by the narrative that contains it. It is with stunning hypocrisy that "sum men sayis" she is "commoun" and that "men deme or say / In scornefull language of [her] brukkilness," for if indeed Cresseid is "commoun" it is because "men" have made her so: she is subject to men's sexual exploitation and, consequently, to their "scornefull langage." By recording the subject of men's language in his own narrative, the narrator implicates himself as the most egregious slanderer of all, for, participating in her condemnation and scorn, the narrator shows himself to be her violator, not her protector. Hence his claim to "excuse als far furth [he] may / [her] womanheid" demonstrates instead arrogant condescension and limitedness; the narrator's introductory remarks suggest that he is not at all prepared to "excuse" her sexual errancy even as he purports to excuse her "womanheid."[18]

Cresseid's textual reality is constructed and manipulated by a narrative voice that seems at once to desire and to detest her.[19] Indeed, the infliction of punishment is described in lingering detail by the narrator, who feigns outrage even as it is his own text that obsesses over

Cresseid's sexualized punishment with an incongruous relish. Further, narrative inconsistencies betray the narrator's futile striving for decorum and show decorum to be betrayed, particularly by way of the narrator's arguably misogynistic voice. Every aspect of Cresseid is condemned by the narrator, even her nightmare, which is described in erotic language as "ane extasie," and Cresseid as "[r]auischit in spreit" (*ll.* 141, 142). In using the language of erotic mystical experience the narrator would seem to be oblivious to the undesirable, unerotic particulars that he is about to describe, but he has already stated that the narrative will "report the lamentatioun / And wofull end of this lustie Cresseid" (*ll.* 68-9), thereby precluding the plausibility of curiosity at specific events as they unfold (hence the after-the-fact labels of "doolie dream" and "uglye visoun" (*l.* 344) serve to maintain narrative illusion).[20] Throughout the narrative Cresseid is subjected to control from both the characters within the story and, more important, from the narrator without; though she is presented as a reality within the parameters of the fiction, she is no more self-determined than any other literary character.

It seems that Henryson uses narrative inconsistency to challenge the illusion of narrative control; just as Cresseid is the narrator's, so the narrator is Henryson's, a textual instrument that reflexively dissects its own processes. Through the construction of narrative voice Henryson betrays the narrative's ideological underpinnings, destabilizing the effect of his own narrative method. For example, the fiction of an inclusive audience—as implied by the first person account of the framing stanzas—is necessarily betrayed by the narrator's *moralitas,* which overtly and directly targets only women:

> Now, *worthie wemen,* in this ballet schort,
> Maid for ȝour worship and instructioun,
> Of cheritie, I monische and exhort,
> Ming not ȝour lufe with fals deceptioun.
> Beir in ȝour mynd this sor[e] conclusioun
> Of fair Cresseid, as I haue said befoir.
> Sen scho is deid I speik of hir no moir.
>
> (*ll.* 610-16, my emphasis)

While the *Troilus* narrator addresses his final remarks to an overtly gendered and inclusive audience: "O yonge, fresshe folkes, he or she"[21] the *Testament* narrator's platitudinous instruction that only women need use Cresseid's "commoun" example as motivation to observe patriarchal dictates of behavior is problematic. Despite his self-deprecating identification of his text as "ballet schort," the narrator's patronizing identifications of his audience as "worthie wemen" and Cresseid as "fair Cresseid"—even as he condemns feminine sexuality—divert attention away from Cresseid and back to her critic. Indeed, as the narrator purports to assert more and more control over the text of Cresseid, he reveals further the text's refusal to submit to such

constraint. The narrator's pretense of respect and closure in the final line likewise calls attention to his inevitable failure, both in its transparent insincerity and in the *reductio ad absurdum* of the deceased body of Woman; the dead Cresseid is not a proper subject of narrative, the narrator insists (though obviously the narrator knows of her death before recounting the text). The narrator shows Cresseid as ventriloquizing this misogynistic narrative voice in her articulation of commonplaces: "O ladyis fair of Troy and Greece, attend / My miserie . . . And in ȝour mynd ane mirrour mak of me" (*ll.* 452-3, 457). Cresseid's lines here are similar in their platitudinous dideacticism to the narrator's own *moralitas,* thereby making her an apparent conspirator in her own misogynistic victimization, and she ostensibly addresses a wholly female audience as well, thereby exposing her own "commoun" subjectivity. But as a textual construct, existing as a reality only within the parameters of an idiosyncratic narrative, Cresseid's words are not only mediated by the narrative voice but produced by it as well. Cresseid and the narrator share a "commoun" voice. As such she seems to lose her "own" voice as the narrative progresses, becoming more and more coincidental with the sanctimonious narrative voice and the limiting postures expressed therein.

For example, Cresseid's absurd descriptions of herself and Troilus after the implausible non-recognition scene work in tandem with the narrative commentary to create the illusion of a redeemed character, who has come to appreciate the narrator's sense of decorum in her apparent privileging of misogynistic fantasy:

> For lufe of me thow keipt continence,
> Honest and chaist in conuersatioun.
> Of all wemen protectour and defence
> Thou was, and helpit thair opinioun;
> My mynd in fleschelie foull affectioun
> Was inclynit to lustis lecherous:
> Fy, fals Cresseid; O trew knicht Troylus!
>
> (*ll.* 554-60)

Indeed Cresseid seems to advocate the repression of the feminine, to deny the feminine both body and voice; her words underscore the coincidence of the sexual and discursive—"Honest and chaist in conuersation"—but privilege a masculine decorum in their desire for feminine chastity (celibacy and silence). These virtues are attributed to Troilus by Cresseid—coincidental with the narrative voice—in order to enhance the narrative's juxtaposition of Good Troilus, Bad Cresseid; Troilus represents all that is masculine and good, Cresseid all that is feminine and bad. The paradigmatic simplicity of the distinction corroborates the text's earlier evocations of antifeminist binary epistemology, and underscores Cresseid's own sexual and discursive errancies, her promiscuous affronts to patriarchal decorum. Otherwise one must wonder at the logic of Cresseid's ascribing to Troilus the label "[o]f all wemen protectour," for *this* is

Cresseid's tragedy—Troilus's failure becomes her blame, and she is scorned for his own ineffectuality. Hence Troilus reiterates this misogynistic conspiracy most egregiously in the superscription—"Lo, fair ladyis . . ." (*l.* 607)—which follows his utterly selfish deflection of blame: "Scho was vntrew and wo is me thairfoir" (*l.* 602).

Returning full circle to the narrator's introduction of the character and her "womanheid," Cresseid's "own" testament echoes the narrator's misogynistic discourse in its disdain for the feminine flesh:

> Heir I beteiche my corps and carioun
> With wormis and with taidis to be rent;
> My cop and clapper and myne ornament,
> And all my gold the lipper folk sall haue
> Quhen I am deid, to burie me in graue.

> (*ll.* 577-81)

Images of filth, debasement, degradation, and passivity are again associated with the feminine as flesh; her body is to be "rent" by "wormis and with taidis," corrupted and violated. The odious sexual metaphor reiterates Cresseid's having been corrupted and violated by men as well; she has been an object of their lust and, accordingly, is a subject of their scorn. Thus while Cresseid's body and language die together—"And with that word scho swelt" (*l.* 591)—the narrative continues; Cresseid's "own" voice is silenced not by death, but by a narrative line that excludes her even as it purports to tell her story. Her testament serves to corroborate a distorted history, for her perceived transgressions are validated by language that vivifies them; her history, in effect, becomes "commoun," taking on a life distinct from the woman who is supposed to have occasioned it.

But there is perhaps a liberating irony in her conclusion, for although Cresseid has no voice of her own, she is depicted as articulating her own wishes via her own testament, and thus the narrative, in effect, gives her the illusion of voice. The broken and dejected Cresseid, then, wills her soul to a place wholly of women—"My spreit I leif to Daine quhair scho dwellis / To walk with hir in waist woddis and wellis" (*ll.* 587-8)—and thus her intended final dwelling place is "waist," uninhabited by "men [who] sayis . . . commoun," and those who "deme or say / In scornefull langage of [her] brukkilness." (77, 85-86)[22] Cresseid's final act of defiance provides the text with a definitive final moment of discursive promiscuity. Cresseid, the embodiment of engendered *translatio,* not only resists narrative constraint but foregrounds that very resistance, thereby insisting upon the value of the (much maligned) feminine in textual poetics and reinforcing Henryson's insistence that the more one strives to control and to purify language through decorum, the more language will foreground its own resistance to that control and

show itself to be promiscuous. Throughout the *Testament* the narrator is exposed as attempting to restrict, reduce, and repress the feminine through conventional tropes of misogyny. He rejects the body of the feminine, yet desires it; he resents his own dependency, and punishes the feminine because his desire cannot be satisfied without her. The narrator's treatment of feminine sexuality in the text corresponds to Henryson's treatment of language; through the narrator, Henryson argues that decorum cannot purify language, that—like Cresseid (the feminine text)—discourse is indeed "commoun."

Metatextual attention to such difference informs the *Testament*'s relationship to Chaucer's *Troilus.* Henryson's "vther quair" is not a sequel but a supplement, an overlapping version of the story's conclusion which presupposes familiarity with the Chaucerian text ("me neidis nocht reheirs" [*l.* 57]). As such, the *Testament* corresponds—or speaks—to the *Troilus*; indeed, a theme of correspondence is framed by the opening lines: "Ane doolie sessoun to ane cairfull dyte / Suld correspond and be equiualent" (*ll.* 1-2), which not only evoke a decorum of association but also foreground the *Testament* as a text both compared and comparing, a text not only of "double sorwes" but of *doubled*—or paired—sorrows. The *Testament* further associates itself with Chaucer through overt comparison:

> Quha wait gif all that Chauceir wrait was trew?
> Nor I wait nocht gif this narratioun
> Be authoreist, or fenзit of the new
> Be sum poeit, throw his inuentioun
> Maid to report the lamentatioun . . .

> (*ll.* 64-68)

In effect the *Testament* competes with the conclusion of the *Troilus,* fulfilling in part the *Troilus* narrator's naive fear that the *Troilus* will itself be corrupted by feminine instrumentality, subject to mutability ("So preye I god that none myswrite the" [V, 1795]). Henryson's handling of the Troilus/Cresseid story demonstrates, through narrative manipulation, the necessary errancy of narrative and text, which will necessarily transgress its own parameters of decorum, and will, in effect, become promiscuous. Indeed, Henryson's appropriation of Chaucer's text demonstrates Henryson's awareness of literary promiscuity; he has made the *Troilus* "commoun," subject and subjective.

Disfigurement operates for Henryson as a destabilizing metaphor of narrative method, a self-referential critique of literary promiscuity manifest in representations of behavior and decorum. And through its images of defacement and infliction, the *Testament* recovers the cruelty and suffering of human existence largely absent from Chaucer's romance. Chaucer's *Troilus* does contain depictions of fear, disappointment, and anguish, and, as Louise Fradenburg has recently demonstrated, the *Troilus* "both participates in, and analyzes, cultural practices of violence in the later fourteenth century."[23] But the *Troilus* privileges the sentiment and nostalgia of romance, and it is primarily through this kind of attention that the *Troilus* articulates its own metatextuality, its awareness of itself as poetry and romance, as a critique of the language of poetry and romance. The *Testament* does not wholly reject the sentimentality of Chaucer's romance, but complicates it, looking at the world of romance with ambivalence and suspicion—"with ane eye lauch, and with the vther weip" (*l.* 231).

Notes

1. Mark C. Taylor, in *Erring: A Postmodern A/theology* (Chicago, 1984) discusses "errant notions" and supplies a lengthy list of the concepts included under this rubric, e.g., transgression, impropriety, subversion, desire (pp. 11-13); I would add to his list promiscuity, which intersects these other notions.

2. Robert Henryson, *The Testament of Cresseid,* ed. Denton Fox (London, 1968), *ll.* 76-7. All subsequent quotations are from this edition; line numbers will be given in the text.

3. Fox glosses "commoun" as "promiscuous" in his edition of the *Testament* (77n). Ridley argues that Henryson's purpose is to reveal the "wrongness" of promiscuity as "violating the natural laws [of God]" a position challenged by the present essay. See Florence H. Ridley, "A Plea for the Middle Scots," in *The Learned and the Lewd: Studies in Chaucer and Medieval Literature,* ed. Larry D. Benson (Cambridge, MA, 1974), p. 183.

4. The association of "carnal" and "literal" derives from St. Paul, esp. 2 Cor. 3.6 and Rom. 8.6.

5. Aristotle, *Metaphysics; Selected Works,* ed. & trans. Hippocrates G. Apostle & Lloyd P. Gerson (Grinnell, IA, 1982), A. 5.

6. R. Howard Bloch, *Medieval Misogyny and the Invention of Western Romantic Love* (Chicago, 1991), p. 26.

7. This epistemology is articulated in contemporary theory by Irigaray in *This Sex Which Is Not One,* (Ithaca, 1985), pp. 23-33 and 205-18. My analysis of the textual feminine corresponds not to an internal privileging of an *écriture féminine* but to a medieval epistemological metaphor of paradigmatic distinction.

8. Shari Benstock, *Textualizing the Feminine: On the Limits of Genre* (Norman, OK, 1991), p. xvi.

9. Toril Moi, *Sexual/Textual Politics: Feminist Literary Theory* (London, 1985), p. 104.

10. Carolina Walker Bynum, *Fragmentation and Redemption: Essays on Gender and the Human Body in Medieval Religion* (New York, 1991), p. 151.

11. Karma Lochrie, *Margery Kempe and Translations of the Flesh* (Philadelphia, 1991), p. 25.

12. See Bloch, pp. 93-112. Shulamith Shahar notes, "In [homiletic and didactic] literature sexual chastity is considered woman's most important quality, together with obedience to her husband." *The Fourth Estate: A History of Women in the Middle Ages,* trans. Chaya Galai (New York, 1990), p. 109.

13. See Augustine, *Contra mendacium* 10.24.

14. Cupid's subject is "he" who would blaspheme the name of "his awin" god; it is curious that Cupid uses the convention of a masculine pronoun sufficing for gender-neutral—which gives a false sense of inclusiveness—when he is in fact speaking of an instance of abuse perpetrated by a woman, whose punishment will be sexualized and therefore gender-specific.

15. Chaucer's Criseyde has pledged loyalty to Troilus by Cynthia (4.1606-10). Henryson follows Chaucer in using *both* Cynthia and Diana, the former overtly identified with the moon, the latter ambiguously aligned with women. It seems appropriate given the texts' concern with mutability and gender that feminine change should be manifest in double(d) representation.

16. The *Testament* is a poem that contains a dream episode rather than a "dream poem" proper. Cresseid's dream would not be considered a formal nightmare (*insomnium*) in medieval dream theory deriving from Macrobius.

17. "Men seyn—I not—that she yaf hym hire herte"; note also the irony of V, 804, where the narrator repeats the men's gossiping about Diomede's being free with his tongue. Criseyde predicts such gossip: "O, rolled shal I ben on many a tonge! / Throughout the world my belle shal be ronge" (V, 1061-2), though she arguably misjudges gender: "wommen moost wol haten me of alle" (V, 1063), a prediction reiterated in C. S. Lewis's condescending and sexist remark that "[t]here have always been those who dislike her; and as more and more women take up the study of English literature she is likely to find ever less mercy," *The Allegory of Love: A Study in Medieval Tradition* (Oxford, 1936), p. 182.

18. The narrator, then, is willing to excuse her for *being* a woman, but not for *acting* like one; Cullen's argument that Henryson's purpose in writing the

Testament is "to vindicate Cresseid's 'womanheid' by showing that her fate was caused, not by promiscuity, but by Fortune and 'wickit langage,' i.e., the blasphemy punished by leprosy" (156) overlooks the narrator's zealous interest in sexual matters. "Cresseid Excused: A Re-reading of Henryson's *Testament of Cresseid*," *Studies in Scottish Literature,* 20 (1985), 137-59.

19. My thinking here has been informed in part by Hansen's chapter on the Wife of Bath—"The Wife of Bath and the Mark of Adam"—which interrogates the majority view of the Wife as "agent, speaker, and, most recently, reader" (26); Hansen argues that while poet and character are similar in their telling of stories, the analogy breaks down because "the Wife's performance demonstrates that Chaucer's Woman . . . disarm[s] the very threat of women's silence and unrepresentability that the poet acknowledges, appropriates, and strategically counters" (39). *Chaucer and the Fictions of Gender* (Berkeley, 1992).

20. See Alicia K. Nitecki, "'Fenȝeit of the New': Authority in *The Testament of Cresseid*," in *Journal of Narrative Technique,* 15 (1985), 120-32.

21. Geoffrey Chaucer, *Troilus and Criseyde* (V, 1835) in *The Riverside Chaucer,* ed. Larry D. Benson, 3rd edn. (Boston, 1987), p. 584. Subsequent reference will be to this edition; book and line number will be given in the text.

22. I am not suggesting that the *Testament* advocates a feminist utopia, but it is, I believe, fitting that a woman who has been so abused by men would seek solace in a place uninhabited by them.

23. Louise Olga Fradenburg, "'Our owen wo to drynke': Loss, Gender and Chivalry in *Troilus and Criseyde*," in *Chaucer's Troilus and Criseyde "Subgit to alle poesye": Essays in Criticism,* ed. R. A. Shoaf and Catherine S. Cox (Binghamton, NY, 1992), p. 88.

John Marlin (essay date 2000)

SOURCE: Marlin, John. "'Arestyus is Noucht bot Gude Vertewe': The Perplexing Moralitas to Henryson's *Orpheus and Erudices*." *Fifteenth-Century Studies* 25 (2000): 137-53.

[*In the following essay, Marlin examines the commonly held critical belief that the* moralitas *in* Orpheus and Eurydice *"deflates the tale's tragic power."*]

Relations between affect and intellect are often uneasy in the act of reading poetry. This tension is inherent in the very act of exegesis, which reorders aesthetic constructs into analytic categories, often by bringing a poem into a relationship with a complex of ideas external to it. Sometimes, however, this tension is also inherent within a literary work itself. As Wesley Trimpi has argued, a poem, when seeking an affective response, will often be at odds with its attempt to engage the intellect if one aim is pursued at the expense of the other, a problem he calls "the ancient dilemma of representation and knowledge."[1] A decorous discursive relationship between affect and reason in a poem requires that these aims be properly balanced.

It is just this balance that is at stake in Robert Henryson's *Tale of Orpheus and Erudices his Queene.*[2] It is a two-part composition, the first part composed of a mostly rhyme-royal adaptation of the story of Orpheus in the Underworld, and the second part offering a 218-line allegorical *moralitas* explicating that story in decasyllabic couplets—thus, an ostensibly self-interpreting work. Henryson stands near the end of a long line of medieval writers who adapted and allegorized Orpheus,[3] and the Middle-Scots Chaucerian is a credit to the tradition. Like other medieval classicists, Henryson conflates and adapts the Orpheus stories of Ovid, Boethius, and Virgil into a composite account; unlike many of his predecessors, he sensitively amplifies the humanity and pathos of Orpheus's plight. In these regards, the first part of Henryson's poem is rivaled perhaps only by *Sir Orfeo,* earning it considerable appreciation from scholars of Henryson and the medieval Orpheus tradition.

Less charitable reviews have been the lot of the *moralitas.* It ostensibly follows Nicholas Trivet's (c. 1265-1334)[4] commentary on Boethius's version of the Orpheus story, found in Book III of *De Consolatione Philosophiae.*[5] Trivet, an English Dominican, wrote a number of theological and historical treatises, as well as a number of commentaries on patristic and classical works. His commentary on Boethius, surviving in 38 manuscripts, was one of the most widely disseminated treatments of *De Consolatione* in the late Middle Ages;[6] it would have been known not only to Henryson, but to any of his readers schooled in the liberal arts. Trivet's allegorization follows closely the spirit, and even the letter of the long medieval tradition of Orpheus commentary; indeed, it has been called "almost plagiarized" from Guillaume of Conche's twelfth-century commentary on Boethius.[7] To the extent Trivet varies from Guillaume, it is to lay a coat of Aristotelian varnish over Guillaume's Platonism, the sort of revision that might be expected near the end of the age of scholasticism. Trivet also incorporates some minor concepts that seem to be derived from the works of the Second and Third Vatican mythographers and Bernardus Silvestris.[8] Guillaume's commentary, in turn, elaborates and extensively revises earlier commentaries by Notker of Labeo (11th c.) and Remigius of Auxerre (10th c.).

At the core of all of these allegorizations is the moral Boethius himself draws from the Orpheus story in *De Consolatione Philosophiae*: "This fable applies to all of you who seek to raise your minds to sovereign day. For whoever is conquered and turns his eyes to the pit of hell, looking into the inferno, loses all of the excellence he has gained."[9] Boethius uses the Orpheus story to illustrate and amplify the *Consolatio*'s thesis, that man's happiness depends on his rational faculties ruling him, not his appetite for the temporal gifts of a blind, unjust Fortune. Hence, Guillaume and Trivet allegorize the story as the progress of a bifurcated soul: Orpheus represents some form of the intellect, and Eurydice some form of the appetites ("natural concupiscence" in Guillaume; the "affections of man" in Trivet). In this scheme, when the intellect masters the appetites or affections, the soul is rightly ordered and can ascend to genuine beatitude. But when love of concupiscence overpowers the intellect, as represented by Orpheus's look back, the disordered soul becomes re-enslaved to *temporalia* and forfeits its bliss.

Following this line, Henryson's allegory figures Orpheus as the "part intellectiue" of the soul (428) and Erudice as "oure affection / Be fantasy oft movit vp and doun" (431-2). Erudice's death is caused by the affection's flight from virtue and toward worldliness. Orpheus's ascent through the planets, Henryson's original contribution to the tale, signifies contrition for misdirected appetites (446), and his descent into the underworld signifies the intellect's attempt to recover sovereignty over the affections. The poet's musical performances in the underworld represent "quhen reson and perfyte sapience / Playis apon the harp of eloquens, / And persuadis our fleschly appetyte / To leif the thoct of wardly delyte" (507-510). The reunion of Orpheus and Erudice marks "Quhen oure desire wyth reson makis pes" (617); Orpheus's fatal backward glance, is, predictably, a return to worldliness and sin (624-6).

Typical of the *moralitas* detractors is Douglas Gray, who writes that it "does its best to drag [the poem] down into the mass of poems which are simply typical of their age."[10] While this judgment stems from a general perception that the *moralitas* deflates the tale's tragic power, a good part of what disturbs readers is a perplexing contradiction between the poem and the *moralitas* with respect to the character Aristaeus. In classical antiquity, Aristaeus appears only in Virgil's version of the myth,[11] and is responsible for Eurydice's death. Medieval adapters regularly brought him into their conflations of the story's several versions; in his, Henryson casts him as a "bustuos" herdsman:

> And whan he saw this lady solitar,
> Barfute, with shankis quhytar than the snawe,
> Prikkit with lust, he thocht withoutin mar
> Hir till oppres—and till hir can he drawe.
>
> (98-102)

Fleeing him, she steps on a venomous serpent, is bitten, dies, and is carried to the Underworld. In allegorizing this passage, the *moralitas* states, surprisingly: "Arestyus, this hird that couth persewe / Erudices, is noucht bot gude vertewe" (435-6).

Unlikely as it seems to have a ravisher "prikkit with lust" signifying virtue (and Henryson and his sources clearly refer here to morality and not potency), the poet seems to be merely following Trivet's and Guillaume's commentaries, both of which figure Aristaeus the same way; hence, Nicholas: "aristeus qui interpretatur virtus" (Aristaeus, who is interpreted as virtue), and Guillaume: "Aristeus ponitur virtute: *ares* enim est virtus" (Aristeus is set down for virtue, for "ares" [a contraction for the Greek "aretes," moral excellence] is virtue).[12] But such tension between tale and allegory is not evident in their versions, as their Aristaeus is merely a name, a flat or abstract type; indeed, he doesn't even appear as a character in the version of the tale they are allegorizing, but is brought into their commentaries through longstanding tradition.[13] In adapting his sources, Henryson depicts the herdsman as an individual with personality, mannerisms and real desires, even to the idiosyncrasy of a foot fetish. He likewise deviates from his classical source material: Virgil's Aristaeus is not explicitly "bustuous"; any lecherous intent on his part is at best understated.[14] Further, the *moralitas*'s "Arestyus . . . / is noucht bot gude vertewe" expresses a certainty about the herdsman's signification—almost the certainty of a bluff—not so evident in Trivet's "Aristaeus qui interpretatur virtus." It is as if Henryson purposely adapted his sources at this point to drive the tale and its *moralitas* in opposite directions.

This dissonance between tale and allegory has generated some critical consternation. Friedman observes somewhat modestly that "relations between the story and the *moralitas* are uneasy, with the *moralitas* sometimes contradicting the fable itself."[15] Louis puts it more bluntly: "Henryson apparently forgot his moral when he was writing the actual poem."[16] MacQueen creatively attempts to reconcile the discrepancy by considering Aristaeus' role as a beast-keeper[17] (line 98) allegorically equivalent to moral virtue's role in keeping control over the carnal passions—the beastly part of man.[18] The text frustrates this reading, however, as the "bustuous" herdsman (Henryson used this same word to describe the natural inclination of the bear in his *Morale Fabiles*) is as much one of the herd as he is over it: he desires "to oppres" Eurydice, rather than bring her into the flock.[19] Despite this problem with Aristaeus, readers see the *moralitas* as the key to the tale's meaning, at least to a degree. MacQueen's reading of the poem is thoroughly grounded in the *moralitas*; McDiarmid believes that "Henryson expects the clerkly reader to recognize the moral meaning in the tragedy that will follow, to reconsider the story once he has read the concluding *moralitas* and still feel it as a tale of human beings, and not merely abstractions."[20] Dorena Wright attempts a mean between accepting and rejecting the allegory, speculating that "either Henryson has wavered uneasily between an allegorical and a non-allegorical method, or (as I prefer to believe) he intended the *moralitas* to provide an optional and added level of meaning, not the obligatory key to the entire poem."[21]

Regardless of their stance on the *moralitas's* role in explicating the myth, the critics almost universally declare it a poetic failure, a great letdown after the sensitive and expressive pair of stanzas that end the tale. Barron writes, "there is a paucity of invention in its application to the narrative, a lack of zest in the plodding couplets which make it difficult to accept as the poet's primary interest" in the poem.[22] The dissonance between the two parts of the work render it "a defective expression of what the poet has to say," according to McDiarmid.[23]

These arguments over the function and poetic worth of the *moralitas* hinge on two critical assumptions, both arising from its explicit claims. The first is that the *moralitas* is supposed to be a harmonious decoding of the tale: after all, it is rather long, translates characters into allegorical figures, and states that the tale's "doctryne and gude instruction" are "hid vnder the cloke of poesie" (418, 420).[24] The second assumption is that the *moralitas* is, as it claims to be, a careful rendering of Nicholas's commentary. Even McDiarmid, who observes some discrepancies between the *moralitas* and its sources, believes Henryson "would not have wished to differ from [the commentary's] analysis or been conscious of the differences of meaning that he does introduce."[25]

Reasonable as these assumptions seem at first glance, they deserve a second, and not merely because adopting them dooms the poem aesthetically. Henryson was a Chaucerian poet who was probably a schoolmaster, practicing lawyer, and well-traveled humanist;[26] most likely he understood all too well the discrepancies introduced into a text through translation. Hence, a more satisfying understanding of the poem might stem from suspending these assumptions and examining whether the tale and its *moralitas* might be reconciled through irony. Such a reading must begin with not a little critical circumspection and justification; due to the privilege irony receives in New Criticism and more recent theoretical schools, questionable ironic considerations of medieval poets and especially of Chaucer have proliferated in recent years. In his biography of Chaucer, Derek Pearsall aptly remarks that readings based on an ironic narrator often "substitute for the enigmatic and elusive intentions of the author the only too obvious intentions of the critic. The cult of the [Chaucerian fallible] persona has thus become a technique for

systematically ironizing the text and appropriating it to the service of particular kinds of programmatic interpretation."[27] How then, might we ascertain the presence of irony in this poem without merely asserting it at those points where the literal text inconveniences our theoretical preconceptions?

A useful if conservative approach would be to consider what irony meant to medieval writers and readers. Rhetorical theorists and encyclopedists of the period generally defined irony as a verbal structure that says one thing but "means" its opposite (or at least means something else), and that opposition is signaled verbally or vocally. Representative of this definition is Isidore of Seville's *Etymologies,* which states, "Ironia est sententia per pronunciationem contrarium habens intellectum" (Irony is a statement having, through the manner in which it is uttered, a contrary meaning).[28] Hence, it is a deliberate act on the part of the author; it "presupposes conscious intention (of a character in the work or the poet) and cannot arise fortuitously."[29] This sense of intentionality differentiates irony in medieval exegesis from the discovery of unconscious verbal or conceptual contradictions that characterizes many contemporary psychoanalytic and poststructuralist treatments of poetry. The role of authorial intention in explicating poetry is, to say the least, a problematic issue amongst modern critics—to many it is anathema—but to medieval readers uncovering the writer's intended meaning was a normal part of literary interpretation. Hugh of St. Victor, for instance, argued in his *Didascalion* that readers should try to determine "quod potissimum scriptor senserit" (what, above all, the author meant) as well as the "voluntas scriptoris" (the inclination of the author).[30] Hence, in developing an ironic reading of the text we might first look for signs of "conscious artistry with which the poet imposes his view of things on the material handed down to him,"[31] through adaptation or re-rendering. Further, we must consider whether the poem's most likely original audiences would have recognized the presence of a set of ironic signifiers, that is, Isidore's *per pronunciationem,* as irony presupposes an audience of initiates that can see the intended reversal of the literal sense.[32] We might also inquire into whether irony is a characteristic or common practice in the larger body of the poet's works, or the tradition within which he normally writes, although these alone cannot confirm that any particular work is to be taken ironically. Finally, we should ascertain whether the proposed ironic reading plays back into the poem's announced thematic concerns.

Conscious artistry seems to be at work in the numerous points of tension between the main parts of the poem. As noted earlier, both the character of Aristaeus in the tale and his symbolic value in the *moralitas* have been meaningfully altered from the form in which they appear in the original sources in such a way as to intensify their incompatibility. Aristaeus represents but one of many conflicts between the tale and the *moralitas* that have been heightened through such adaptation. From the outset, differences in style and manner drive the poem's parts against each other. By developing Orpheus's psychology and subjectivity beyond what one finds in the classical renditions of the story, Henryson's tale achieves a heightened emotional intensity, most notably in Orpheus's *planctus* (135-183) and in his despair at seeing Eurydice's beauty corrupted in hell (352-356). This amplified *pathos* marks all the more strongly the vocal shift at the beginning of the *moralitas,* signaled by the prosodic shift from rhyme royale to couplets, as well as by the direct address, "Lo, worthy folk" (415): this change in *pronunciatio* invites the audience to adopt a new mode of reading, to leave the world of realized, sympathetic characters and enter the world of analytic commentary. Further, the *moralitas* reduces the tale's more rounded human characters to one-dimensional personifications of intellectual qualities, such that the experience of moving from Orpheus's tragic discovery to the moral's propositional discourse is quite jarring. It is a shift from affect to reason—the integration of which is the theme of the *moralitas.*

These vocal and methodological tensions between commentary and tale echo through their substantive dissonances. A slight rupture occurs early in the *moralitas,* where it identifies Calliope as eloquence (426). That this is a traditional interpretation there is no doubt;[33] but it is noteworthy that the tale associates Calliope purely with music (43-5, 68-70) while assigning eloquence to Mercury (213), the classical god of rhetoric. In other words, the poem recognizes music and rhetoric as distinct arts with their own methods. While this is a slight distinction—after all, in medieval allegory the same quality can be indicated by different figures[34]—it does suggest that the poem and the *moralitas* might be working out of different interpretive schemata. Yet the most important substantive discrepancies are those which occur in the *moralitas*'s allegory of plot. Although Orpheus's descent from Phoebus and Calliope (61-3) mark him as an apt figure of the intellect, his thorough characterization as a courtly lover undercuts that figuration.[35] His "accord" (84) with Eurydice is not an image of reason controlling the desires, but of "myrth, blythnes, gret plesans, and gret play," (88). His long complaint at Eurydice's passing shows "His hart was sa apon his lusty quene" (149), and when he petitions the planets for her return, he confesses to Venus that "I am your avin trewe knycht" (206). When Orpheus recognizes Eurydice in the deepest part of Tartarus, he bemoans the loss of "thy rude as rose with chekis quhite, / Thy cristall eyne with blenkis amorouse, / Thi lippis red to kis diliciouse" (354-6). Returning from the Underworld the couple are "talkand of play and sport" (385), underscoring Orpheus's consistent motivation to recover the "warldlie ioye" (89) they

once had. Throughout, the hero wants to indulge, not redeem, his desires: he, not Eurydice, seems a proper figure of the affections. The conventions of courtly romance that Henryson imports into the traditional story strain those of the moral and theological allegory customarily attached to it, and this juxtaposition of traditions creates an instance of the "generic instability" Fyler finds characteristic of both Chaucerian and Ovidian irony, that is, the practice of extablishing one set of generic expectations, only to undermine them by shifting genre.[36]

Orpheus's cupidity wedges tale and moral apart at other points. The *moralitas* equates the hero's long and moving lament on his queen's death with when "parfyte reson wepis wondir sare, / Seand oure appetite thusgate mys-fare" (445-6), ostensibly an expression of contrition for misplaced desire. But in the actual complaint Orpheus regrets only the loss of "plesance and play" (154); he repeatedly cries, "Quhar art thou gane, my luf Erudices?" (143). Here again the gap between tale and allegory widens from the poet's adaptations of his sources. While Orpheus's lament in the woods is stock in both classical and medieval versions of the story, it is rarely developed in the courtly and unambiguously cupidinous terms Henryson deploys. And while Nicholas's commentary mentions the intellect weeping for the affect, he figures it not as a sign of contrition; rather, he holds the intellect culpable: "et ideo [intellectus] non debet flectere aspectum ad [a]effectum" (ll. 76-7). Indeed, Henryson's tale reflects Nicholas's commentary better than his *moralitas,* which follows a logic of its own. A similar disjunction occurs in the *moralitas*'s rendering of the journey to the spheres, which ostensibly symbolizes repentance and a turn to spirituality: Orpheus "passis vp to the hevvn belyue, / Shawand till us the lif contemplatyve" (447-448). Yet in the tale, no such repentance occurs. Orpheus's only motive for visiting the heavens is his desire to recover Eurydice: his pleas to Jupiter, Apollo and Venus all make this plain. Orpheus here may be a figure of praying amiss, but not of "the lif contemplatyve."

This exegetical discord continues in the *moralitas*'s account of Orpheus's five concerts in hell (the classical sources depict only one, another case of Henryson's crafting his material, gaining emphasis through repetition). The *moralitas* figures the cessation of punishments in Hades following Orpheus's songs as a reordering of the soul—that reason, combined with eloquence, are quieting the desires:

> Bot quhen oure mynd is myngit with sapience,
> And plais apon the harp of eloquence;
> That is to say, makis persuasioun
> To draw oure will and oure affection
> In ewiry elde, fra sin and foule delyte,
> This dog our saule has no power to byte.
>
> (469-74)

But again, this is not what happens in the poem. Orpheus plays the music of the spheres, which he discovers as if by accident in his trip to heaven (218-246), not to quell his desires, but in response to either fear of the tormentors or pity for the tormented—perhaps the same misplaced pity for which Virgil chastises Dante in the Inferno.[37] In essence, his eloquence helps him gratify his desire, rather than subordinate it. Moreover, the moral effects of his music are dubious. While Cerberus and the furies doze off to Orpheus's lullaby, Ixioun "out of the quhele can crepe / And stall away" (272-3) presumably to continue his "hardy and curageouse" lechery. Similarly, Tantalus steals a sip from the river (286-8), and Tithyus, while still bound, gains lasting relief from the ravenous grip (300-2). If the tormented represent wrong desires, Orpheus's music actually quiets the guards that hold those desires in check— exactly opposite to the *moralitas*'s interpretation.[38] Henryson cannot plead that he is merely following his *auctoritees*. In Ovid and Boethius, as well as Nicholas's commentary, when Orpheus plays his harp the furies weep instead of sleep, Ixioun's wheel merely stops for a short spell, Tantalus is so moved by the song that he ignores the waters he could drink, and the eagle tearing at Tityus's bowels pauses a moment instead of flying away.[39] Nicholas's commentary emphasizes the furies' role as avengers of sin ("ultrices," ll. 182-3), and notes that the sapience and eloquence figured by Orpheus's music quiet the desires rather than give them opportunities for release. Once again Henryson's adaptations have created a tension which would not have existed otherwise.

The final discord between tale and moral comes when the *moralitas* announces its thesis: "Than Orpheus has wone Erudices / Quhen oure desire wyth reson makis pes, / And sekis vp to contemplacion" (616-618). Where, exactly, in the tale Orpheus achieves this moment of psychic reintegration is hard to find. Even standing before Pluto, Orpheus mourns Eurydice's loss of beauty, indicating his concern for material rather than spiritual good. And after being reunited, "thai went, talkand of play and sport" (383), hardly an image of the reason seeking "vp to contemplacion," as the *moralitas* figures it to be (618). As with the case of Aristaeus, the character of events throughout the fiction seems at odds with their allegorical figuration. That so many of the discrepancies stem from the way sources have been adapted argues that the cumulative dissonance between tale and moral is designed; and, given the wide dissemination of Nicholas's commentary, not to mention the general popularity of the Orpheus legend in medieval schooling, Henryson's most literate readers would likely have been sensitive to these adaptations.

Given the number of moments at which tale and moral seem in conflict, it seems surprising that anyone accepts the *moralitas*'s claim that it interprets the tale. But

several parts of the *moralitas,* especially in the beginning, are in concord with the poem. For example, Orpheus, given his parentage, seems a good figure of the soul's intellective faculty. Eurydice, in demanding marriage of Orpheus and in her penchant to wander in the meadows, seems an apt figure of human affect. The marriage arrangement, in which Eurydice tells Orpheus "In this province ye sall be king and lord" (83), clearly figures the proper relationship between reason and desire. However, the farther into the *moralitas* one reads, the more the discrepancies compound, creating a wider gap between fiction and interpretation. It is as if the *moralitas* begins on solid premises but then takes on a life of its own, independent of the tale, driven less by the language and context of the poem than by its own conceptual framework. This is not to say that the *moralitas* is intellectually bankrupt. It contains moments of fine insight: the notion of reason making peace with desire is appealing in terms of medieval psychology and spirituality, and the figuring of Orpheus's harp as reason and eloquence quieting the desires is a lovely rendering of the medieval idea of the proper role of rhetoric. Arguably, it reaches the same moral conclusion as the tale it supposedly interprets—that is, that ungoverned affections will take you straight to hell. But when the *moralitas* arrives at such moments, it is by its own methods and pursuing its own purposes, inspired by the tale, but not explicating it.

We perhaps should not be surprised to see such a gap between fiction and allegory in a work by Henryson. His later and more famous work, the **Morale Fables** is full of surprising moralities that deploy unpredictable allegorical values that make the reader dependent upon the commentator. And as in **Orpheus,** throughout the **Fables** the morals routinely upset the expectations set up in the tales. This pattern of reversal works by gaining our emotions for the tales' sometimes mean-spirited, sometimes good-natured characters and evoking a visceral judgement on their black-comedic outcomes, but then examining them in the light of what is often rather stern moral reasoning.[40] The tension between tale and moral evident throughout the fables suggests that the morals do not dictate our understanding of the tale; rather, they temper it. The fables engage our affections; the morals cause us to examine them, just as they cause us to reconsider our moral judgment.[41] The reader is invited to negotiate apparently valid claims to truth from different sources—from affect and intellect.[42]

Does a comparable negotiation occur in Orpheus? An approach to that problem may be found in the poem's Chaucerisms. We could virtually ignore the **Testament of Cresseid** and the Tale of **Chauntecleir** and infer Chaucer's influence on Henryson from **Orpheus and Erudices** alone. Written mostly in rhyme-royale, the stanza form of *Troilus* and several of the *Canterbury Tales,* the poem resonates with Chaucerisms. As Friedman notes, Orpheus's petitions to Jupiter, Apollo and Venus are reminiscent of Palamon and Arcites's prayers in the *Knight's Tale,* and Orpheus's moving complaint (134-183) has echoes of the complaint of the Black Knight in The *Book of the Duchess.*[43] Many of the poem's Chaucerisms are more direct. The poem's naming of Proserpine as the Queen of Faery comes from the *Merchant's Tale* (IV (E) 2236f)[44] (and Proserpine seems to get the last word in Henryson's hell, just as she does in January's garden). Henryson's figuring of Watling Street as the Milky Way (188) derives from the *House of Fame* (935-44); that work may be the source for Orpheus's flight to the spheres, as well.

Henryson borrows not only from Chaucer's material, but also from his manner. Narrating Orpheus is an apologetic persona such as we find in Chaucer's dream poems and a few of the *Canterbury Tales.* After reciting the long list of musical terms, the narrator confesses, "Of sik musik to wryte I do bot dote, / Thar-for at this mater a stra I lay, / For in my lif I coud newir syng a note" (240-3). Naturally, he goes on at a later point to speak of how Orpheus "playit mony suete proporcion / With base tonys in ypodorica, / With gemilling in ypolerica" (played many sweet chords, with bass tones in the Hypodorian mode, with harmony in the Hypolocrian[45] mode) (368-70), somewhat like the Knight and other pilgrims who say they will speak no more on a subject and then tarry on it—albeit to a purpose. Further, Henryson's work is rife with Chaucerian digression. The prolix catalogs of the muses, musical terms, and notables in hell all draw us out of the plot's essential action, and these moments of somewhat tedious erudition and arcana smack just a bit of the pedantic eagle in the *House of Fame.* Finally, bookishness, a Chaucerian concern for *auctoritee,* pervades the poem. The narrator carefully identifies and enthusiastically endorses his sources, and reminds us at points that his commentary comes from the library: "I sall the tell sum part, as I haue red" (490). And as we have seen above, we can trust Henryson to follow faithfully his announced sources about as much as we can Chaucer.

This accumulation of Chaucerisms suggests that we might search for one more: a fallible narrator, fallible because he is naive, self-deceived or self-interested. Positing such a narrator may answer a question many have asked, which is, why does Henryson include the *moralitas* at all? There is lesson enough in Orpheus's reversal and his discovery of the simple but profound truth that the weakness of human love (the look back) undermines its power (to raise the dead); those who want more of a moral might examine the poem's political trappings for lessons on princely conduct. Mac-Queen's notion that a medieval reader would typically see such a commentary at the end of a poem is not persuasive. Whether or not morals might be found at the end of texts is a matter of genre. Middle-English

and Middle-Scots vernacular adaptations of classical mythology did not universally or even characteristically include allegorical commentary: none appear appended to the text of *Sir Orfeo* or the works of Gower, James I and Dunbar.

A fifteenth-century Scottish reader might come across a glossed classical text—like the *De Consolatione* containing Nicholas's commentary—or hear a lector expound upon an ancient myth. In any case, the commentary would be by someone other than the poet, and it seems that this is exactly what Henryson has mimicked in the *moralitas* to **Orpheus and Erudices**; this would have been more evident to an audience hearing an oral performance of the poem than it may be for readers. The shift in *pronunciatio* signaled by the change in meter and verse form is accompanied by a shift in address: the third-person narration that dominates the tale gives way to a direct address to the reader—"Lo, worthy folk" (415)—suggesting a fictive rhetorical situation wherein a lecturer addresses several auditors. Throughout the *moralitas* the speaker identifies with his audience: he refers to "our affection" (431), "oure myndis" (436), "our myndis ee" (453), "the feruent lufe / We suld have" (449-50), "oure appetit" (445), and "oure desyre" (455). The *moralitas* becomes personal and communal, with a tone more of speaking than of writing (another deviation from Nicholas's commentary, which remains impersonal and expository entirely in the third person, with the pronoun *nos* occurring only once near the end). Hence, we might examine the speaker of the *moralitas* as a character as individuated and idiosyncratic as Orpheus or Aristaeus, a character whose interests and weaknesses influence our reading of the poem.

This speaker is pedantic and bookish, and, while not quite the ostensible bore of the House of Fame's eagle, he is verbose and confident in his sources. Like Chauntecleir, he exudes confidence for the "olde bookes" that buttress his argument, which is "Rycht full of frute and seriositee" (424). Significantly, his presentation is marked by moments where he loses logical and rhetorical control of his material, perhaps suggesting personal enthusiasms. For instance, with respect to the crimes of Tantalus he translates two clauses of Nicholas ("Tantalus avarum significat . . . quia non sustinet in necessitatibus suis ea [diuicias] expendere, quia delectatus uisu peccunie non uult aceruum diminuere" [214-219])[46] into a fourteen line invective on miserliness (531-544); one almost hears the annoyance of the scrivener or barrister who hasn't been paid. He likewise treats Tityus's desire to divine the future, which Nicholas (222-236) handles with dry, scholastic etymologies, with a lengthy (571-599) outburst against divination, witchcraft, and sorcery. Caught up in this diatribe, he omits from his exegesis of Tityus the formula with which he ends that of each of the other monsters—how Orpheus's harp of reason and eloquence stills the inordinate or misplaced desire figured by each creature. As silence is often significant in Chaucer, it is also so in Henryson: could this absence mark the narrator's personal disquiet of mind? The subject of his invective is divination, and he is striving to divine intellective meaning from a poetic text, something which is hardly among "sic maner of thingis / Quhilk vpoun trew and certaine causis hingis" (590-1), self-proclaimed as the proper object of divination. Perhaps he senses at this moment that his own presentation judges itself, and he loses his thread.

With his moralizing, faith in intellection and love of study, full of "doctryne and gude instruction" (417), this narrator stands in marked contrast to the characters of the tale, who are explicitly driven by affection and appetite, the commentator's figurations notwithstanding. As a man who trusts to things discernible "be calcula-tioun" (595), and unwitting of the divide between his own theory and its practice, he fulfills his own picture of Orpheus: a widowed reason (627), an intellect out of touch with its affections. It is revealing that he recognizes affect "Is alway prompt and redy to fall doun" (628), but not intellect. His scheme of the relationship between reason and emotion finds no space even for his own righteous indignation or his own enthusiasm for study and commentary. Indeed, the only affection finding a place in his allegory is contrition—an emotion consequent to moral reasoning and, hence, a validation of his own theory.

There may be other and better ways to psychologize the lapses in logical and narrative control within the *moralitas,* its progressive deviation from the text on which it comments, and its manner of creating expectations only to frustrate them. What matters is that these rhetorical features are present and therefore can be psychologized, that the *moralitas* is colored by the concerns of a subjective narrator; moreover, that coloring falls squarely into the most common medieval *topoi* of irony: feigned praise.[47] The *moralitas* seems to be endorsing Trivet's commentary, but actually presents an instance of the "vatic pretense" that Fyler finds in many of Chaucer's and Ovid's narrators,[48] that is, a narrator who, like the *House of Fame's* persona, promises the profound and the remarkable, but then systematically deflates those promises and undercuts his own authority. So read, the *moralitas* becomes an artful demonstration of how commentary, through the obsessions and personal concerns of its author, takes on a life of its own independent of its literary object. As such, it is also a demonstration, almost a self-satire, of the digressive style, interpretive excesses and personal enthusiasms, all mixed with moments of wisdom, that mark medieval commentary, especially when it emanates from a mind in which reason and desire are at odds. As happens in the *Canterbury Tales,* the tale sets a standard that judges the teller.

By postulating a fallible narrator we might also understand how the poem's two divisions work together as a literary unit. The *moralitas's* announced theme is the right relationship between affect and reason, and its ideal is a harmony between the two—the balance about which Trimpi writes. Achieving that balance is the problem Henryson's work explores. The tale, with its narrative structure driven by discoveries and reversals, its poetic diction and decoration, and its affect-seeking hero himself "be fantasy oft movit vp and doun" (432) engages our affect and seeks an emotional catharsis. The *moralitas,* with its ratiocinative narrator insisting to the point of self-validation on the primacy of the intellect, depicts a widowed reason, an intellect out of touch with, or at least operating independent of, its affections. As in the morals to the *Fabilles,* the commentator insists on his own interpretive authority while drawing our intellect in a direction our affect might resist. Because he pursues a purely intellective aim (Trimpi's "knowledge") at the expense of and ignoring its related affect ("representation"), he soon diverges from the tale and follows his own path to a self-contradictory destination. But following the affective route is no more satisfactory: the tale's Orpheus seeks the object of his affections through heaven and hell and finds in the end that those affections themselves betray him. Hence, in terms of medieval psychology, the will is left to shift anxiously between affective and cognitive impulses, recognizing the potential danger in pursuing either to its ultimate consequences.

The potential for harmonious cooperation between affect and intellect remains problematic. There are points where the tale and *moralitas* find concord, but these are at best ephemeral, similar to what Robert Frost called "a momentary stay against confusion." In the end, the poem is a representation of its stated theme—that is, the inherent tension between the soul's faculties, whose integration can last no longer than Orpheus's and Eurydice's reunion. Perhaps here Henryson reflects the anxieties of his own age, a period of intellectual turmoil, wherein long-standing scientific, political, and religious certainties were in question, and wherein faith in an overarching intellectual order that dissolved all contradictions had long been on the wane.[49] While Henryson may not have been genius enough to devise new poetic forms to express these tensions, he fully recognized and exploited the potential of the Chaucerian tradition. And in grasping the spirit of Chaucer, Henryson has also grasped something of the spirit of that other great ironist, Ovid, whose *Metamorphoses* inspired the medieval Orpheus tradition. Indeed, Henryson's artfully problematic *moralitas* to **Orpheus and Erudices** exposes the dubious wisdom of persistent medieval attempts to fix a stable meaning on a work whose theme is *omnia mutant.*

Notes

1. *Muses of One Mind* (Princeton: Princeton University Press, 1983).

2. All quotations from Henryson are from Denton Fox, ed., *The Poems of Robert Henryson* (Oxford: Oxford University Press, 1981).

3. For a review of the medieval Orpheus tradition, see John B. Friedman, *Orpheus in the Middle Ages* (Cambridge: Harvard University Press, 1970).

4. For more on Trivet's career, see Beryl Smalley, *English Friars and Antiquity in the Early Fourteenth Century* (Oxford: Basil Blackwell, 1960), 58-65.

5. B. L. Addit. MS 19585, ff. 61b-63b, and B.N. MS lat. 18424. Line numbers in this essay refer to the extract of Nicholas's commentary appearing in Fox, 384-391.

6. Friedman, *Orpheus,* 110.

7. Fox, *Poems,* cvi.

8. Trivet's emphasis on Orpheus's eloquence may stem from the Vatican mythographers, who noted the civilizing effect of music. Bernardus used Orpheus's geneology to establish his allegorical value, as do Trivet and Henryson. Friedman, 110, 112. Henryson elaborates this genealogy even further; see lines 1-70 of the poem.

9. Boethius, *The Consolation of Philosophy,* trans. Richard Green (Indianapolis: Bobbs-Merrill, 1962), 74.

10. *Robert Henryson* (Leiden: E. J. Brill, 1979), 240.

11. *Georgicon* IV, 436f.

12. Fox, *Poems,* 385, 1.47; Friedman, *Orpheus,* 108.

13. Aristaeus enters allegorizations of Orpheus as early as the sixth century, in the *Mythologiae* of Fulgentius. Subsequently, he appeared as a matter of course in commentaries on Ovid and Boethius, even when not a character in the primary text: Fox, 415; Friedman, 89. For instance, see the marginal gloss to X. 10 in *The 'Vulgate' Commentary on Ovid's Metamorphoses,* ed. Frank T. Coulson (Toronto: Pontifical Institute of Medieval Studies, 1991), 119.

14. Virgil describes the incident as follows:

> illa quidem, dum te fugeret per flumina praeceps,
> immanem ante pedes hydrum moritura puella
> seruantem ripas alta non uidit in herba.
>
> (457-9)

(This one, indeed, when she fled from you headlong through the river, the fated girl did not see before her feet an observer on the bank, a monstrous serpent in the tall grass.) R. A. B. Mynors, ed., *P. Vergili Maronis Opera* (Oxford: Oxford University Press, 1969), 97. All translations are my own unless otherwise attributed.

15. Friedman, *Orpheus,* 203.

16. Kenneth R. R. G. Louis, "Robert Henryson's Orpheus and Eurydice and the Orpheus Traditions of the Middle Ages," *Speculum* 41 (1966), 654.

17. In the *Georgics,* Aristaeus is a beekeeper. In early medieval commentary, he became a herdsman, so the change in occupation is not Henryson's original contribution. See Friedman, 108f.

18. John MacQueen, *Robert Henryson: A Study of the Major Narrative Poems* (Oxford: Clarendon Press, 1967), 34-5.

19. Friedman writes, "there is little evidence to support [MacQueen's reading] in either the Orpheus tradition or in Henryson's poem, *Orpheus,* (239 n69). Matthew McDiarmid simply states, "I do not understand MacQueen": *Robert Henryson* (Edinburgh: Scottish Academic Press, 1981), 61 n13.

20. McDiarmid, *Robert Henryson,* 55. Gray, *Robert Henryson,* 237, is somewhat less committal; while he sees sufficient points of contact between the tale and the *moralitas* to make the latter something of a guide to the former, he feels the two are in conflict enough that "It would be wrong . . . to force the allegorical reading of the *moralitas* on to every detail of the story."

21. Dorena A. Wright, "Henryson's Orpheus and Eurydice and the Tradition of the Muses," in *Medium Aevum,* 40 (1971), 46-7.

22. William Raymond Johnston Barron, *Robert Henryson: Selected Poems* (Manchester: Fyfield, 1981), 12. Louis, 646, concurs: "He makes his characters and their tragedy so attractive that the *moralitas,* by comparison, becomes dull and ineffectual. His primary interest is clearly not in the *moralitas* at all."

23. McDiarmid, *Robert Henryson,* 59-60.

24. The *moralitas*'s remark that Nicholas "Applyis it [the tale] to gud moralite" might suggest that the *moralitas* is not deployed as an allegorical decoding of the poem, but rather as one moral application of the poem among many potential modes of understanding it. However, "apply" in Middle Scots also meant "to apply by interpretation" (Douglas used it in this sense); hence, the term still carries the sense of exegesis, and probably does in this context. See *A Dictionary of the Older Scottish Tongue,* ed. William A. Craigle (Chicago: University of Chicago Press, 1937), I. 96.

25. McDiarmid, *Robert Henryson,* 43. Fox, *Poems,* clx, echoes this sentiment: "although [Henryson] departs from [Trivet] in some particulars, he does not make any essential changes in Trivet's allegory."

26. See Barron, 9-10; Smith, xxii-xxv; McDiarmid, *Robert Henryson,* 1-23.

27. Derek Pearsall, *The Life of Geoffrey Chaucer* (Oxford: Basil Blackwell, 1992), 86. Cf. Jonathan Culler: "Irony, the cynic might say, is the ultimate form of recuperation and naturalization, whereby we ensure that the text says only what we want to hear." *Structuralist Poetics* (Ithaca, New York: Cornell University Press, 1975), 156.

28. *Etymologiarum,* ed. William Lindsay (Oxford: Clarendon Press, 1911), I:73. Likewise, Augustine, *On Christian Doctrine*: "Now irony indicates by inflection what it wishes to be understood, as when we say to a man who is doing evil, 'You are doing well'"; trans. D. W. Robertson (Indianapolis: Bobbs-Merrill, 1958), 103. For an introduction to the treatment of irony in the medieval encylopediae and rhetorical treatises, see the first chapter of Simon Gaunt, *Troubadors and Irony* (Cambridge: Cambridge University Press, 1989).

29. Dennis H. Green, *Irony in the Medieval Romance* (Cambridge: Cambridge University Press, 1979), 6.

30. Vi.xi *Patrologia Latina,* 176, 808. Likewise, John of Salisbury complains that teachers of philosophy rendered interpretations "contra mens auctoris" (contrary to the mind of the author); *Metalogicon, ii.xvii, PL* 199, 874. In a paper on "Interpretation and Scholastic Method," (Conference on Representation and Interpretation, Canisius College, Buffalo, NY, April 20, 1995), Prof. Jorge Garcia argued that twelfth-century interpreters of Aristotle and other authors routinely claimed that they were attempting to recover the "intellegens auctoris" and even the "intentio auctoris."

31. Green, *Irony,* 6.

32. Green, *Irony,* 3.

33. See Friedman, *Orpheus,* 112.

34. This type of covalence is suggested by Bernardus Silvestris in his *Commentary on the First Six Books of the Aeneid,* ed. E. G. Schreiber and T. E. Maresca (Lincoln and London: Univ. Nebraska Press, 1979), 11.

35. Gray finds the root of Orpheus's characterization in the romance tradition, as does Louis.

36. John Fyler, *Chaucer and Ovid* (New Haven: Yale University Press, 1979), 3, 4-8, 13, 20.

37. There are other allusions to Inferno in the tale, which suggests that Henryson may have had this meaning in mind. For example, the "ferefull strete" that "For slidderiness scant" (305, 307), and the "mony pape and cardinal," "bischopis" and "Abbottis" in hell (338-42) are Dantesque.

38. Incidentally, these features of the text call into question MacQueen's allegorization, in which the figures in hell represent "various dangers which beset the intellectual power in its quest for the appetites. . . . Orpheus overcomes all these obstructions, only to succumb finally when he is on the very brink of complete success."

39. See Ovid, *Metamorphoseon* X, 40-48, and Boethius, *De Consolatione Philosophiae,* L. III m. 12.

40. For a more thorough development of this thesis, see Harold. E. Toliver, "Robert Henryson: From *Moralitas* to Irony," in *English Studies* 46 (1965), 300-9.

41. Toliver finds a similar distance between poem and narratorial commentary at work in Henryson's *Testament of Cresseid,* as does Sydney Harth, "Henryson Reinterpreted," in *Essays in Criticism* 11 (1961), 471-80. It seems the poet's consistent practice.

42. Although Henryson's poems are not definitively dated, most likely the *Fabillis* came later than *Orpheus*. I am suggesting, then, that Henryson adopted this method of ironic distancing earlier in this career than has previously been indicated.

43. Friedman, 199-200. The complaint might also find roots in Lydgate's *Complaint of the Black Knight* or in any number of secular lyrics circulating at the time. Fleeing to the woods and sobbing "farewell" were common tropes in fourteenth- and fifteenth-century lyrics about lost love.

44. In Sir Orfeo the queen and king of faery take Eurydice away, but they are not explicitly identified as Proserpine and Pluto. Friedman notes that "There are, to my knowledge, no other references to Proserpine as queen of the Fairies except by Chaucer" (198).

45. Conjectural translation; Fox notes that there is no evidence of this musical mode being known in Henryson's; it might be a "nonce formation" that might not "make musical sense" (411-12); presumably a knowing audience would see a parody on hyperspecialized musical terminology.

46. "Tantalus symbolizes the avaricious man, who cannot bear to spend those riches for his own necessities, as he, delighted by the sight, does not wish to diminish his heap of money."

47. See Gaunt, 9, and Green, 139-40; feigned praise is the most common example of irony used in

medieval rhetorics; see the example from August-ine, n28 above.

48. Fyler, 22, 43.

49. Hence, Gray, 30: "It is certainly not surprising that in a period when past certainties were being undermined we should find in literature a liking for enigmas, contradictions, and ironies."

Jana Mathews (essay date 2002)

SOURCE: Mathews, Jana. "Land, Lepers, and the Law in *The Testament of Cresseid.*" In *The Letter of the Law: Legal Practice and Literary Production in Medieval England,* edited by Emily Steiner and Candace Barrington, pp. 40-66. Ithaca, N.Y.: Cornell University Press, 2002.

[*In the following essay, Mathews claims* The Testament of Cresseid *is a literary comment on the fifteenth-century political debate about legal personhood.*]

Much of the fifteenth century was, for Scotland, a period of agricultural crisis and depression. Burgh records speak of the exhaustion of marginal lands and over-worked soils, the exploding peasant population and lack of feudal tenures, the sporadic pestilence and famines incurred by flood, drought, and topographical pollution, and the legal conflict between two powerful and contrasting sets of interests: landowner and tenant, overlord and laborer.[1] It is upon this terrain of agrarian waste and socioeconomic ruin that Robert Henryson lays out his most controversial work. *The Testament of Cresseid* opens with a poetic representation of a medieval farmer's worst nightmare: early in the planting season, showers of hail and blasts of wind descend from the north, freezing the ground and destroying any immature seedlings planted there:

Ane doolie [dismal] sessoun to ane cairfull dyte [poem]
Suld correspond and be equiualent:
Richt sa it wes quhen I began to wryte
This tragedie; the wedder richt feruent,
Quhen Aries, in middis of the Lent,
Schouris of haill [gart (began)] fra the north discend,
That scantlie [hardly] fra the cauld I micht defend.

ʒit neuertheles within myne oratur [oratory]
I stude, quhen Titan had his bemis bricht
Withdrawin doun and sylit [concealed] vnder cure [cover],
And fair Venus, the bewtie of the nicht,
Vprais and set vnto the west full richt
Hir goldin face, in oppositioun
Of God Phebus, direct discending doun.

Throw out the glas hir bemis [beams] brast [burst] sa fair
That I micht se on euerie syde me by;

The northin wind had purifyit the air
And sched the mistie cloudis fra the sky;
The froist freisit, the blastis bitterly
Fra Pole Artick come quhisling loud and schill,
And causit me remufe [remove] aganis my will.

(1-21)[2]

The immediate "tragedie" in the first stanza is the "fer-uent" or harsh weather, and with the storm's descent comes the expectation of imminent material loss.[3] The narrator's self-conscious insertion of himself into the sequence—as a figure who is forced to move inside "aganis [his] will"—demonstrates that he is not a detached chronicler of the climatologically induced destruction, but is a literary figure who is metaphori-cally part of the agricultural discourse he describes. Although the text explicitly situates the narrator inside the "oratur," and away from the elements, he is anxiously gazing outside "throw out the glas" (15). The narrator, in essence, looks into a mirror, and thus at himself. What he sees—a ruined landscape—is a reflected image of his own decayed and aging flesh. Each reference to the deterioration of the land in the opening stanzas is matched by a parallel description of the disfigurement of a concordant region of the nar-rator's body: the "feruent" (bitter or sickly) storm is like the narrator's "grene" (bitter) and "faidit hart" (24); the freezing wind that blasts sprouting plants is analogous to the "greit cald" (27) that deadens sexual virility; and the "froist freisit" (19) is associated with old blood that "kendillis nocht sa sone as in ʒoutheid [youth]" (30).[4]

This opening sequence, so rich in agricultural imagery, seems narratively and thematically removed from the main body of the poem. At the end of the introductory monologue, the narrator, frustrated by his losses, leaves his post at the window and sets out to continue Chau-cer's epic story of *Troilus and Criseyde.* Whereas most of the recent criticism of the *Testament* has focused on its relationship with its famous English exemplar, I find that Henryson's poem illuminates a new and complex exchange between fifteenth-century legal discourse and literary language in the Scottish vernacular, demanding that we view its debts to Chaucer through the lens of legal innovation and characterization.[5] Henryson's ver-sion of the legend chronicles the demise of the heroine, who, after engaging in an illicit affair with Diomeid, is summoned to appear before a fictional council compris-ing eight planetary deities. In a hasty trial, the gods find her guilty of the crime of blasphemy and punish her with leprosy. What is so striking about the *Testament* in legal terms is the profoundly altered status of Criseyde/Cresseid herself. Chaucer's powerful widow, who was endowed with enormous authority in *Troilus and Cri-seyde,* has become a leper, a disenfranchised juridical body devoid of legal agency.[6] As we shall see, Henry-son's heroine cannot be completely understood unless we examine the poem's complex legal refiguration of literary character, a revision that I explore here in terms of the poem's literary and political relation to contemporaneous ideologies regarding the law of personhood.

Medieval conceptions of personhood contained various social, religious, and political dimensions, including the idea that an individual was most appropriately defined through his relationship to a superior authority (such as God, a baronial lord, or a king). Situating itself within this tradition, the narrator's monologue links the ***Testament***'s interpretation of identity construction to agricultural tenure, a practice largely governed in medieval Scotland by aristocratic overlords and legal courts. The introduction depicts the forceful conflation of the human body with the land as a juridical act that promotes the blending of identities, a process that inevitably destroys the discernible boundaries between human and territory and renders these bodies indistinguishable. In an era of labor crisis and agricultural ruin, the destruction of land necessarily generates a parallel destruction of the identities of laborers who work on it.

I argue that through its deployment of agricultural terminology, legislation, and formulas, ***The Testament of Cresseid*** stages a literary intervention into the contemporary juridical debate in Scotland regarding the definition of legal personhood. Specifically, the body of Cresseid—which is mapped in the poem as both a physical entity and a material territory—serves as a vehicle through which Henryson can explore the law of sasine (i.e., "seisin," possession of freehold) and its dictation and eradication of the identity of the indentured tenant. Further, an examination of fifteenth-century leper statutes, seignorial accounts, and tenement disputes illuminates the poet's representation of the legally devalued subject as part of a larger discourse of exclusion, a discourse reserved in medieval Scotland for the discussion of beggars and lepers.

Before we turn to the ***Testament*** itself, it will be necessary to examine in some detail the poet's literary and professional connection to the legal practice of agricultural tenure, a system that was nearly extinguished in England by the fifteenth century but had not yet reached its most complete and logical development in Scotland.[7] As we shall see, Henryson's literary representation of aristocratic abuse corresponds to actual "legal dramas" played out in Scottish burghs and recorded in local registries.[8] Yet as much as Henryson's poems function as legal allegories, they are also participants in legal revisionism. Indeed, Henryson's own life records reveal that the poet's personal loyalties were charged with an ambivalence that infiltrates his texts and deeply informs his secular approach to literary character.

HENRYSON AND THE LAW OF LAND

Like his literary alter ego in ***The Testament of Cresseid***, Robert Henryson was deeply connected to his native land.[9] After earning a law degree from Glasgow College in 1462, he returned to his native burgh of Dunfermline, where he served as head schoolmaster, presumably until his death around 1499.[10] Cartulary records from Dunfermline Abbey indicate that he also served as the church's official notary public, a legal office sanctioned by the pope in the early fifteenth century and held almost exclusively by lawyers extensively trained in canon and civil law. Historically, notaries were responsible for drafting, recording, and authenticating provincial legislation, episcopal and capitular acts, testaments, and various land transactions including sasines, annual rents, reversions, leases, and wadsets (mortgages).[11] Henryson's detailed knowledge of agricultural legality is reflected in three surviving charters drafted and signed "Maister Robertus Henrison, notarius publicus" from 1477 and 1478.[12] All deal with the lands of Spittalfields, near Inverkeithing, that were granted by the Abbot of Dunfermline to George de Lothreisk and Patrick Barone, burgess of Edinburgh, and to Margaret, his spouse.

It is safe to assume that Henryson was equally fluent in the language and usage of other documents of land law, given the explicit references to the writ in **"The Sheep and the Dog,"** the brief in **"The Tale of the Wolf and the Lamb,"** and the assize (session of a court charged with the deliberation of civil actions) in **"The Preaching of the Swallow."** These earlier works present a rich catalog of Henryson's consistent thematic investment in the unstable relationship between the emergent and constantly oscillating land laws and the rights of the Scottish laboring class. For example, in **"The Tale of the Fox, the Wolf, and the Husbandman,"** Henryson describes in great detail the many difficulties that beset tenant farmers, including outdated and ineffective farm implements, oxen that "waxit mair reulie," and intolerant and demanding landlords.[13] The *moralitas* to **"The Sheep and the Dog"** illustrates the partiality of Scottish civil courts. The Sheep, a poor husbandman, is attacked by the Wolf, who presides over the assizes of the itinerant Justice-Ayres:

> This volf I likkin to ane schiref [sheriff] stout
> Quhilk byis [buys] ane forfalt [forfeiture] at the kingis hand,
> And hes with him ane cursit assyis about,
> And dytis [indicts] all the pure [poor] men vp on land
> . . .

(1265-68)

The Wolf, who purchases fines from the Crown, uses them to indict impoverished peasants and unlawfully exact payment from them. These literary details correspond to contemporaneous legal statutes which indicate that the Justice-Ayres were notoriously corrupt.[14]

Perhaps the most striking example of aristocratic abuse and tenant subordination in Henryson's works appears in one of his later fables, **"The Tale of the Wolf and the Lamb."** In the culminating *moralitas,* Henryson uses beast allegory to illuminate the ways in which laboring husbandmen are mistreated by lords who are "peruerteris of the lawis" (2715):

> The thrid wolf ar men of heritage,
> As lordis that hes land be Goddis lane [loan],
> And settis to the mailleris [tenants] ane village,
> And for ane tyme gressome [annual rent] payit and
>   tane;
> Syne vexis him, or half his terme be gane,
> With pykit [picked] querrellis for to mak him fane
>   [want]
> To flit or pay his gressome new agane.
>
>   (2742-48)

Cunning wolves, who represent the landed gentry, illegally seize the property and land of unsuspecting lambs—"maill men" (2708) and "lauboureris" (2708)—and use misleading "termis" (2716) and contracts to trick their tenants into working without pay and abandoning their rented pasturage on the pretext of a quarrel. The passage's specific reference to the landlord's stealing of a tenant's "gressome," or annual rent, is probably a topical allusion to the five anti-eviction laws passed by parliament in the second half of the fifteenth century. Although the statutes were surely intended to alleviate tenant burden, their number and repetition testify to their ineffectiveness.[15]

While the beast fables illuminate the social and legal injustices inherent in the Scottish seignorial system, their flatness lies in their inability to imagine any solutions to the socio-legal problems they discuss, as well as in their failure to conceive of a legal order that opposes (or at least challenges) that in which they are situated. An obscure record included among *The Acts of the Lord Auditors of Causes and Complaints* may explain Henryson's persistently ambivalent exploration of feudal abuse. The document, dated March 23, 1481, refers to a charge filed by a group of "Trekware" (Traquair) tenants, including a "Robert Henrisone," on charges that their landlords, identified as George, David, and Margaret Murray, wrongfully demanded double mailrents:

> In the actiouns and causes presewit be george burns James henrisone, Johne Mudy Robert henrisone marione myddilmaist / Adam wilsone Johne hog Robert Mark will pacok James of burns / laurence wod / Wilʒaim henrisone / et Katrine blenkes tennandes of the landes of trekware on ta parte aganis James erle of buchane and margarate of murray george of murray et dauid murray on þe top parte anent [sic] the takin of doubill malis of the saide landes of trekware / The saide tenandes beand present be thar procuratores et the saide lord erle beand personaly present / and the said margarete of murray et dauid murray being peremptorly summond et oft tymes callit et not operit / The lordes Auditores decretes et deliueris that the saides

margarate george et dauid has done wrang in the takin vp of the malis of the saide landes / and ordanis thaim to Restor et geif agane to the saide tennandes same ekle of the malis as thai haue takin vp of the saide landes of the termes of thre ʒeres bigain et part thai haue nane Intrometting þer with in tyme to cum bot [sic] that thai be frely broikit et joisit [sic] be þe saide lord erle efter the forme of his infeftment schewin et producit before the saide lordes et ordanis letres to be writin In dew forme herapon.[16]

The Lord Auditors ruled that the Murrays did "wrang" in demanding excess rent from their tenants and ordered the landlords to return the money to their subjects. The topical evidence contained in the document relating to date and location is compelling, given what we know about Henryson's life.[17] The historical details relating to the poet's alleged victimization are fascinating, but what is perhaps more important to our understanding of Henryson's participation in the Scottish seignorial system is something that is not explicitly stated in the document: the conditions of his tenure. Henryson's education and profession automatically excluded him from the ranks of abject tenancy, and it is likely that he was, in fact, quite wealthy. Thus, while Henryson was legally subject to his baronial landlord—as all tenants regardless of social rank or wealth were—the circumstances of his tenure were vastly more pleasant than those of the subjugated characters depicted in the fables. Henryson's role within his community was thus extremely paradoxical: at the same time that he was championing the rights of the peasant population in his poems, he was, in his professional capacity as a lawyer, creating laws that would be used to subvert their legal rights and alienate them as legal subjects. What is peculiar about Henryson's ambivalence toward peasants—his belief that they should be empowered but also repressed—is that the attitude is naturalized. In other words, such legal contradiction, rather than obstructing Henryson's vision of the world, serves as a lens through which he can view his community—and the competing ideologies fighting for control within it—in a richer way.

LAND LAW AND A LEPER

The Testament of Cresseid (late 1480s-early 1490s) marks Henryson's poetic movement from fable to cultural and natural myth. Cresseid is introduced in the poem as "the flour and A per se" (78).[18] The botanical personification is repeated six times throughout the poem, which describes the heroine in varying stages of anatomical progression (budding, blooming, wilting). Here, Henryson is clearly playing on a trope common to courtly love poetics in which the female body is depicted as a product of human cultivation.[19] The text extends the personification of the garden to include the mimetic processes of agricultural production and sexual reproduction. Casting herself as farmable fauna,

Cresseid tells Venus, "The seid of lufe was sawin in my face / And ay grew grene throw ʒour supplie and grace" (137-38). Cresseid functions as both a mappable space and a cultivable geographic body, yet the image also identifies Troilus as the appropriate and authorized planter of the field. It is with Venus' grace and Troilus' body that Cresseid becomes sexually fertile and develops into a desired and valuable marriageable commodity. The fetus or the "seid of lufe," however, does not properly gestate in the belly, but is sown in the face. It is this improperly planted seed, which we learn later is Diomeid's, that Cresseid laments "with froist is slane / And I fra luifferis left, and all forlane" (139-40). The striking contrast between (re)productive and destructive seeds seems to draw a tight interpretive boundary that the rest of the text ostensibly sustains: Troilus is the authorized lover and can father legitimate offspring, while Diomeid's unsanctioned love must always be abortive. What is most provocative about the analogy, however, is its implicit, generalized anxiety regarding the authority over and ownership of bodies. The paradigm that is introduced and naturalized is one in which the success and failure of respective sexual unions is determined not by the participating bodies but through an external authority (in this case Venus).

Just as Cresseid is relegated to a passive role in regard to her own sexual economy, the *Testament* implies that sovereignty over her agricultural body is equally out of reach. The topic of arable land could not be discussed in fifteenth-century Scotland without reference to the notion of ownership, and the identity of the tenant could not be discussed without mention of his master. In his thirteenth-century treatise on English law, Bracton describes the feudal villein under the power of his lord as civilly "dead."[20] And as Elizabeth Fowler has noted, civil death marks the descent into selflessness, a space where characters are controlled by others.[21] Just as the field tended by the peasant farmer is subject to the peripheral but omnipotent authority of the feudal lord, so the boundaries of Cresseid's body / land are tightly secured within the narrative and legal jurisdiction of the planetary deities.[22] At the beginning of the narrative, Cresseid accuses the gods of having broken their promise to keep her forever attractive to men: "ʒe gaue me anis ane deuine responsaill [reply] / That I suld be the flour of luif in Troy" (127-28). In the courtroom, Cupid replies that he has fulfilled his end of the bargain—"The quhilk *throw me* was sum tyme flour of lufe" (279, emphasis added)—but the heroine, having blasphemed the gods, has not. Cresseid's failure to adhere to her contract enables the gods to assume control over her body, thereby consigning her to the role of a legal subject.

The nature of the gods and their authorial attitude toward their subject is made strikingly clear in what Jill Mann dubs "the planetary sequence." Building on John

MacQueen's classic interpretation of the deities as physical manifestations of the indifferent and involuntary "natural processes of time and change, growth and decay," Mann argues that the planetary gods are legal instruments by which man comes to internalize his position in a world "whose laws are enacted through him and yet irrespective of him."[23] Despite this, the gods are not exactly practitioners of an abstract, cosmic law. Nor do they serve as "perceptive moral arbiters."[24] An obscure reference to Mercury's role in the courtroom suggests that they can be read as representatives of a juridical authority: "Thus quhen thay gadderit war, thir goddes seuin [seven], / Mercurius thay cheisit [chose] with ane assent / To be foirspeikar [chief speaker] in the parliament" (264-66).

It is not surprising that Henryson assigns Mercury the title of "foirspeikar," given the character's traditional representation within mythological convention as a lawyer or civil advocate. The deity's connection to secular legal procedure makes it tempting to read the "parliament" that he oversees not as a generic "meeting" or "assembly" but as a specific juridical congregation and metaphorical governing body of law. Indeed, the structural format of the trial that the gods conduct reflects some of the legal procedures associated with a specific fifteenth-century parliamentary judicial committee with which Henryson would have been familiar: the Lord Auditors.[25] This appointed tribunal, composed of representatives from the three estates, met in Edinburgh between parliamentary sessions and functioned as an adjunct juridical body that heard and ruled on overflow cases assigned to the lower courts (assize, church, burgh). The court exercised the appellate jurisdiction of parliament, which was limited to civil causes. Within this genre of law, however, fell a wide range of crimes and offenses, including borowgang or suretyship, broken marriage contracts, spuilize (theft), and unpaid mailrents.[26]

The most common grounds for action of wrong tried in these courts—and those crimes in which Henryson surely was most fluently versed—were claims of varying degrees of damages to land and feudal tacks, including (but not limited to) molestation, wrongful occupation, and unlawful manuring.[27] Henryson complicates his depiction of the fictional parliament by overlaying this overtly juridical image with a patina of mythological and literary tropes. The poem positions the gods in their traditional mythological elements and endows each with complementary characteristics: Saturn's face, for example, is "fro[ns]it" (155) because he represents a cold humor, while Jupiter's primeval apparel evokes images of pastoral tribunals of love. Similarly, Mars, the god of war, is dressed in armor and carries his conventional battle implements at his side, and Phebus, the god of sapience, is appropriately accompanied by four Ovidian horses. Yet it is precisely by securing the deities within literary convention that the poet can reconceive these images in terms of contemporary legal theory and practice. The clothing worn by the gods and the instruments that they bear clearly identify them as mythological figures, but they also refer to a peculiarity of the Scottish court system: a 1455 parliamentary statute mandated that all parliamentary committee members color-code themselves according to social rank "under the pains of a ten pound fine."[28] Nobles were ordered to wear red mantles; burgesses, blue; and the clergy, their black ecclesiastic robes. It seems that Henryson interpolates these social markers into his poem and uses them to link the deities to the three estates. Mercury is "cled in ane skarlot goun" (250) and matching red hood (244). Mars carries a bloody sword at his side and his face is described as a "reid visage" that "grislie glowrand ene" (191). Saturn, representing a burgess, appears in court with a bluish pallor, and out of his nose run watery "meldrop[s]" (158). The black clerical robes are worn by Venus (221) and Cynthia (255). Significantly, an ecclesiastical image appears on the breast of the latter: a churl, trying to reach heaven, "micht clim na nar" (263) because he has broken the law by stealing a bunch of thorns.

By oscillating throughout the "parliament" sequence between mytho-literary tradition and imposed juridical convention, Henryson is able to redefine courtly and mythological behavior as legal procedure. As a governing body, the gods claim "power of all thing generabill" (148); that is, they declare omnipotent authority over the supernatural world. This trait, however, is matched only by their self-proclaimed ability to "reull and steir" (149). The puns on the legal terms "rule" and "steer" and the verbs meaning "to chart or map" (on a plot of land) and "to direct or arrange a farm implement or animal" (such as a steer) allow Henryson to conflate the notions of governance and plowing.[29] The implications of the compounded allusion are clear: the gods' jurisdiction encompasses both the agricultural and legal realms.

In the fictionalized courtroom scene, the planetary sequence appears where an informed reader would expect the traditional elements of the fifteenth-century Scottish trial to be—including the testimonials of the litigant, defendant, and witnesses. While the deletion of Cresseid's voice only substantiates what we already know—that she is a legal subject—the insertion of the planetary caricatures in this narrative frame suggests that the descriptive sequence represents an important part of the trial proceedings. The portraits of the deities seem to function as testimonies in their own right, both substantiating the gods' authority to accuse and judge and determining the guilt or innocence of a defendant without participating in the laborious hoop-jumping associated with fifteenth-century juridical procedure. At the same time, the caricatures reveal a horrifying reality of the poetic legal system: the gods are endowed with

legal authority but do not use this power to enact earthly forms of justice. The gods' appearance and behavior echo, but do not exactly imitate, common law procedure, and this highlights the terrible recognition that the literary "parliament" evokes the moral objective of temporal law only to defeat it. Thus, the various legal implements and instruments that the gods attach to their clothing or carry at their sides are not material tokens of legal authority, but suggest that earthly law too is inherently ambiguous and mutable.

Just as Henryson relies on literary devices to redefine the function of the deities in the poem, he uses contemporary legal theory to draw a striking parallel between the procedures and protocol of the fictional court and that of its secular counterpart. In doing so, he illustrates the courts' similar ideological agendas of subordination while exposing the gods' intentions as decidedly more severe. After listening to the testimonies of the litigant, defendant, and appropriate witnesses, the Lord Auditors typically retired to a private chamber to consider the evidence and determine a verdict. Nearly all of the judgments recorded in the casebooks of the Lord Auditors between 1466 and 1494 adhered to a prescribed four-point formula aimed at ensuring the validity of the document and definitiveness of the ruling. After a brief summary of the charges filed—which included identification of the legal parties involved and a description of the land in dispute—the document moved to the verdict, and from there to a description of the punishment to be meted out to the guilty party. Consider the following case, filed March 20, 1478:

> In þe actions et causes presewit be thomas Anderson burges of coupir agains alexander of lawthres of that Ilk anenet [sic] þe soume of 1 mark [sic] clamit be þe said thomas to be aucht to him be þe said alexander be his obligations because of þe alienation maid be the said alexander of the landes of the Spittailfelds et certain vþer landes otrar þe tenores [sic] of the said obligation as was allegit / Baith the saide partijs being present be ther procuratores / And ther Richtes Resones et allegacons in þe said mater at lenth herd sene et vnderstandin the lordes Auditores decretes et deliueris that the said alexander sall otent et pay to the said thomas the said somes of 1 mark [sic] efter þe forme of hes obligationes maid to him þeruppon / Becaus it was clerly prevyt befor þe said lordes that he analijt [sic] þe said landes of Spittalefeld et certane vþer landes otrar þe tennor [sic] of þe sam yn And ordanis letres tobe writtin to distreȝe him his landes et gudes herefor.[30]

The court ruled that Alexander was in default in his payment of "obligations" to his landlord, Thomas Anderson, and ordered him to pay the specified sum of money or face the permanent forfeiture of his "gudes."

This case is fascinating for a number of reasons, one of which concerns its staging within a region with which Henryson was intimately connected. The poet was serving as notary public when this case was filed; in fact, one of the surviving charters signed by Henryson—which also deals with Spittalfield—was dated the same month and year. The ownership, holding, and maintenance of the lands of Spittalfield were clearly topics of heated debate in Dunfermline in the 1470s. As the legal practitioner responsible for producing the legal transactions regarding these lands, Henryson may have dealt directly with the conflict between Thomas Anderson and his tenant Alexander. Perhaps the dispute central to this case inspired the poet to include a reference to the region in the *Testament.* After Cresseid is diagnosed with leprosy, her father commits her to the local leper hospital, which the narrator calls "the spittaill hous" (391). In the 1920s, Ebenezer Henderson asserted that this was a topical allusion to St. Leonard's Hospital, a leprosarium outside Dunfermline.[31] Given the poet's professional involvement in the burgh's juridical and legislative arenas, the "spittaill hous" could also be a reference to the courtroom of Henry Spittal, the chief advocate of Dunfermline's assize courts in 1488-89.[32] Although the assize courts were compositionally different from the Lord Auditors (assize courts consisted of non-parliament members), they heard and ruled on the same types of land dispute cases. Assizers were notoriously corrupt and were often suspected of illegal collusion. If the literary "spittaill hous" is a representation of Spittal's legal house, then it is not a locus of safety and security but a site of partiality and privilege. Cresseid's chances of finding redemption as a leper in the "spittaill hous" are just as remote as Alexander's odds of emerging as the victor in a dispute with his overlord regarding the lands of Spittalfield.

A key element of the judgment is the formulaic phrase acknowledging that both Anderson's and Alexander's testimony had been "seen, heard, and understood" by the auditors. By linking sensory perception to a cognitive process, the document exposes a basic ideological principle of Scottish land law: legal understanding comes primarily through firsthand sensory experiences with the law.[33] Those who testify in court participate in this process, and therefore are "understood." By logical extension, legal parties who are absent are excluded from judicial comprehension, and therefore cannot be accurately registered into the legal memory of the court.

The phrase thus denotes a specific fifteenth-century legal problem—that of juridical identification and representation. The casebooks of the Lord Auditors between 1470 and 1490 reveal that court absenteeism was largely limited to a legally marginalized population: indentured tenants. Over half of the cases filed in these two decades indicate that the tenant, who was almost always summoned to court by his landlord on charges of land abuse, was "peremptorly summond" and "oft tymes callit" but "not operit."[34] The notable absence of the tenant in juridical proceedings bore im-

mediate consequences—he was found guilty by default—and points to larger ramifications that bear crucially on the legal fate of Cresseid in the *Testament.*

The sheer quantity of absentee defendants in one court system over such an extended period of time raises the suspicion that perhaps many of the accused were purposely denied a voice in court. Numerous complaints concurrently filed by tenants in the *Acta dominorum auditorum* dispute default court rulings on the grounds that they were summoned at a place where they had no residence, or that they were never summoned at all.[35] The court's silencing of the tenant—whether intentional or incidental—in effect validates the existence of the legally constructed hierarchy of the auditors and yet destabilizes this hierarchy by exposing its underlying ideology. The implicit threat to the authority of the court is, of course, speech. To acknowledge the presence and testimony of a litigant, defendant, and witness in an official legal context is to inscribe on these individuals a legal identity, to establish their claims as juridical authorities. The voices of all those present are not only seen and heard but understood; they are written down and registered as part of the legal memory of the court. To put it another way, not only do the words of courtroom speakers influence the outcome of the trial, but also their very words become law. By preventing the tenant from being seen, heard, and understood in court, the legal system denies him both a legal identity and, perhaps equally important, the right to challenge the law or create his own.

This distinct historical-legal phenomenon of late fifteenth-century Scotland manifests itself in the courtroom scene in the *Testament,* but with an important twist: the deities aim to prevent Cresseid from speaking both inside *and* outside the courtroom. Cupid convenes the court by ringing a silver bell. The same musical instrument also "rauischit" Cresseid "in spreit [spirit], intill ane dreame scho fell" (142-43). The heroine's descent into unconsciousness—a state in which she remains during the entire legal proceeding—marks her transformation from legal subject to legal nonentity. Although she is physically present, clearly Cresseid is not an active participant in the trial. There is no discussion of Cresseid's guilt, then, because her fate is determined before the court even assembles. Cupid's bell is less a symbol of the law than an instrument of destruction, calling the gods together not to dispense justice but to silence their subject and sentence her to death. The panel's conviction of Cresseid on the charge of blasphemy—instead of lechery as we would expect—is a legally important distinction because it identifies Cresseid's verbal insurrection against the gods, rather than the material loss of her body / land resulting from her infidelity, as the greater offense. Cresseid's "greit iniure" (290), as Cupid calls it, is an act of verbal violence that is potentially lethal, for misrepresenting the gods in speech—and undermining their fame and name—is the only way these immortal bodies can be harmed. When she "blaspheme the name / Of his awin god, outher in word [or] deid" (274-75), then, Cresseid participates in a "discourse of errancy," an insurgent language that challenges and violates the decorum of appropriate speech.[36] Through her blasphemous words, Cresseid attempts to regain self-control the only way she knows how: by illegally usurping the legal identity of her superiors and appropriating their juridical authority onto herself. Her speech, I would suggest, is a legal instrument analogous to Jupiter's sash: it is a material token that represents an aspect of the law. In this case, it symbolizes authoritative possibility, the potential of being seen, heard, and understood inside and, by extension, outside a court of law. It is the threat of losing their own privileged rights of personhood to a legal inferior that motivates the gods' hasty and harsh judgment against her.

The "sentence" that is passed down on Cresseid differs in specific ways from the structural format of a temporal land dispute ruling, and these revisions enable Henryson to point to juridical failings in secular procedure and protocol without implicating his text as a participant in them. They also mark specific clauses and phrases as "legal gaps," juridical spaces that can be manipulated, revised, and later reconstituted. These legal spaces are critically important to Henryson's literary project, constituting the formative basis for his ideological rewriting of the law of personhood. The transition from the trial to the judgment phase of the fictionalized court is appropriately marked by the narrator's summary of Cresseid's offenses against the gods and the introduction of Saturn and Cynthia, the appointed deities who will deliver the judgment and assign the punishment:

> Than thus proceidit Saturne and the Mone
> Quhen thay the mater rypelie [thoroughly] had degest
> 　[digested]:
> For the dispyte [offense] to Cupide scho had done
> And to Venus, oppin and manifest,
> In all hir lyfe with pane [pain] to be opprest,
> And torment sair [sore] with seiknes incurabill,
> And to all louers be abhominabill.
>
> 　　　　　　　　　　　　　　　　(302-8)

Despite the gods' anxious attempts to bypass juridical procedure and hasten the conclusion of the trial, this passage reveals that they unwittingly lapse into it. Cresseid's fate is given more than a cursory glance; it is deliberately and willfully ingested into the bodies of the gods, where it is figuratively absorbed, transformed, and digested. That the heroine's physical suffering becomes a food source for the gods testifies to the underlying weakness of the juridical body. If healthy and whole, legal subjects are potentially threatening, for they have the strength to act on their rebellious desires. In order to sustain itself and maintain its legal authority,

the juridical body must debilitate its subjects. Only when its subjects are consumed is the immediate threat of insurrection removed.

The adjective used to describe the way in which legal subjects are metaphorically eaten alive—"rypelie"—serves as the terminological nexus by which Henryson connects the ostensibly disparate ideas of digestion and juridical procedure. The common definition of the term connotes images of mature or "ripe" foodstuff, yet it is perhaps more useful for our purposes to explore the significance of this term as a legal locution (defined by the *Middle English Dictionary* as "with thorough consideration of the facts and evidence at hand").[37] Although the word does not appear in the *Anderson v. Alexander* case, it is employed in numerous contemporary Lord Auditors' rulings to describe the manner in which the court contemplated the opposing testimonies. In a 1476 dispute between John, Lord Carlisle, and John of Maxwell concerning the latter's alleged illegal occupation of "the place of guvane hagges," the Lord Auditors "Ripely avisit decretes et deliueris that because the said Johne grantit in pertinence of thai[m] / that he had na clame nor Richt to the said place nor landes."[38] Cases filed later that year and in 1489 and 1493 conclude in similar ways: "The lordes auditoures Ripely avisit decretes et deliuevers"; "The lord auditores Ripply avist, decrettes et ordinis"; and "The lordes auditores Ripply avist apone the said exceptions."[39] By inserting this term into a legally charged narrative frame, Henryson makes a pointed criticism of the council of deities and their secular exemplars. Although each claims to engage in contemplative legal thought, both fail to provide evidence that they actually do so. The gods "degest" Cresseid—that is, they *consume* her—but do not *consider* her as anything other than an expendable object. This gesture to contemplate Cresseid is completely self-serving: the gods, like the auditors, can only view their subjects in terms of their use-value to themselves.

Once the formulary introductions are appropriately dispensed with, the narrative segues into the actual ruling, which is divided into two parts. Saturn, the "hiest planeit" (297) and "lawest of degre" (298), serves as the panel's mouthpiece and steps forward to deliver the judgment:

> This duleful [sorrowful] sentence Saturne tuik on
> 　hand,
> And passit doun quhair cairfull Cresseid lay,
> And on hir heid he laid ane frostie wand;
> Than lawfullie on this wyse can he say,
> 'Thy greit fairnes and all thy bewtie gay,
> Thy wantoun blude, and eik thy goldin hair,
> Heir I exclude fra the for euermair.
>
> 'I change thy mirth into melancholy,
> Quhilk is the mother of all pensiuenes;

Thy moisture and thy heit in cald and dry;
Thyne insolence, thy play and wantones,
To greit diseis; thy pomp and thy riches
In mortall neid; and greit penuritie
Thow suffer sall, and as ane beggar die.'

(309-22)

Saturn's sentence lists the consequences of the punishment in progressing degress of severity: the heroine's temperament will sour, then her body will disintegrate, and her material wealth will deplete. Finally, Cresseid "suffer sall, and as ane beggar die." That a reversion in social rank is marked as a worse fate than emotional and physical deterioration suggests that the passage's central concern is social rather than moral.[40] Cynthia's judgment echoes this sentiment:

'Thy cristall ene [eyes] mingit with blude I mak,
Thy voice sa cleir [clear] vnplesand hoir [rough] and
   hace [hoarse],
Thy lustie lyre [skin] ouirspred with spottis blak,
And lumpis haw appeirand in thy face:
Quhair thow cummis, ilk man sall fle the place.
This sall thow go begging fra hous to hous
With cop and clapper lyke ane lazarous [leper].'

(337-43)

By positioning the reference to beggary at the end of a list of agonizing corporeal punishments, the passage implies that the sores, welts, and lesions are not themselves the punishments but merely the means to a more horrific end. As a member of "ane rank beggair" (483), Cresseid is relegated to a social position not unlike that of the evicted or misplaced tenant. Homeless and hungry, she is consigned to wander "fra place to place, quhill cauld and hounger sair" (482).

In the *Testament,* the gods' anxiety registers a concern as serious as that of the secular landlord; as representatives of the law, they know that insurrection challenges the existing legal order and threatens to reverse the existing division of power. Nervous that their legal authority is about to be usurped by their own poetically constructed legal subject, they take it upon themselves to eliminate the threat of future insurgency. By "excluding" Cresseid from her body, they render her homeless. Nor do they stop here, for their designs extend far beyond making her "as ane beggar" (322). Indeed, the gods seek to reduce Cresseid to nothingness, eradicating the lingering physical markers of legal identity that she still bears.

The Law of Leprosy

While numerous crimes and offenses necessitated the legal forfeiture of property or sacrifice of life, only one circumstance in fifteenth-century Scotland allowed for the legal revocation of the rights of personhood: a diagnosis of leprosy.[41] By afflicting Cresseid with the

mysterious disease—with the "seiknes incurabill" (307), as Venus calls it—the planetary deities, in essence, sentence her to a death that is both corporeal and legal. In his influential study of medieval leprosy, Peter Richards describes the process of "exclusion," a practice instituted in Scotland in the late twelfth century and not fully abandoned until the nineteenth.[42] Soon after his diagnosis, the leper was led to the local church, where he was encouraged to participate in a final confession and then a "last Mass." During the ceremony he was often required to kneel beneath a black cloth that symbolized the descent into the grave. The priest then revoked the leper's legal rights: he was stripped of his possessions, birthright, and name and was forbidden to talk to non-lepers, appear in town, or touch anything outside the leper colony except with a stick or rod. Finally, in an act meant to represent the burial, the priest led the leper to the parish cemetery and shoveled dirt onto his feet, telling him that he was hereby, forever, and always "dead to the world."[43]

Clearly the symbolic burial of the leper parallels the actual disposal of his legal rights and identity. The assignment of the title "leper" legally negated all other preexisting identities—including that of tenant.[44] Without a discernible self—a body that society identifies as being endowed with human qualities—the leper ceases legally to exist. In this way Cresseid is not "lyke ane lazarous," a walking corpse, because even the dead still have the legal right to bequeath land and property as well as to name heirs through a will. Rather, she is a visible but unrecognizable (and thus unidentifiable) mass of bones and flesh. Her anonymity is clearly elucidated in the "half-recognition" scene, the passage in which a battle-weary Troilus rides by the begging lepers, one of whom is Cresseid, and is moved by her resemblance to his former lover.[45]

Seing that companie, all with ane steuin [voice]
Thay gaif ane cry, and schuik coppis gude speid [good
   speed],
'Worthie lordis, for Goddis lufe of heuin,
To vs lipper [lepers] part of ȝour almous deid!'
Than to thair cry nobill Troylus tuik heid,
Hauing pietie, neir by the place can pas
Quhair Cresseid sat, not witting [knowing] quhat scho
   was.
Than vpon him scho kest [cast] vp baith hir ene [eyes],
And with ane blenk it come into his thocht
That he sumtime hir face befoir had sene . . .

(491-500)

A primary reason why the hero does not fully recognize the heroine is that she is so severely disfigured. Although he can conjure a hazy image of Cresseid in his mind, he is unable—despite persistent attempts—to connect this image to the face that he sees before him.[46] Troilus' lapse of memory—what one critic has called "psychological delusion, a kind of absent-mindedness"—serves as the catalytic mechanism that actualizes the heroine's loss of identity.[47] Cresseid's nonexistence is no longer a theoretical possibility but a material reality. Because her post-leprosy body is not registered in legal memory as human, female, or lover, Troilus cannot identify her as such. When he passes her on the highway, he cannot distinguish the "place" where Cresseid sits from her actual body. Thus, he imagines not "quha" she is, but "quhat scho was": Cresseid is no longer legally a woman, but she once was. Now Troilus can only see Cresseid as a gap once filled with something that he "befoir had sene."

Cresseid's legal exclusion preoccupies the narrator throughout the **Testament**. Early in the poem Diomeid tires of Cresseid and sends her a "lybell of repudie" (74), or bill of divorce. As a result, the heroine is "excludit fra his companie" (75). By using the term "exclude" within this particular context, Henryson implies that the legal consequences of divorce are analogous to the destructive effects of leprosy. By exchanging Troilus' death (which occurs in Chaucer's version of the legend) for Diomeid's divorce, Henryson enacts a similar measure of legal death; for in the Middle Ages, a woman typically lost the legal rights of ownership over her property, land, and moveable goods upon her divorce.[48] Later in the poem, Saturn reiterates the link between legal and corporeal exclusionism. In his condemning speech against Cresseid he says, "Thy wantoun blude, and eik thy goldin hair / Heir I *exclude* fra the for euermair" (314-15, emphasis added). Here, the deity directly refers to the juridical process of exclusion, juxtaposing the physical effects of the disease—disintegrating blood and wilting hair—with their legal consequences. The eradication of a specific legal privilege—the right to one's namesake—is alluded to when Cresseid enters the leper colony. The narrator, explaining the reason behind her agonizing moans, says, "And still murning, scho was of nobill kin" (398). Similarly, the text depicts Cresseid's father as an ecclesiastical "father," the priest who performs this procedure. After being "excludit" (75) from Diomeid's presence, Cresseid rushes to the temple, where her father, Calchas, "wes keiper of the tempill as ane preist" (107). She immediately confesses her sins to him— "Fra Diomeid had gottin his desyre / He wox werie and wald of me no moir" (101-2)—and requests assistance. In accordance with official guidelines governing the law of exclusion, Calchas leads her to a private oratory, where is she is directed to ask for forgiveness from the gods. Knowing "well that thair was na succour" (376) for his daughter, he waits for her to awaken from her dream and then delivers her to the leper hospital outside of town.

The most powerful interpolation of the process of exclusion in the poem occurs in Henryson's description of the lepers themselves. The **Testament** may be the only nonlegal text that adopts the exact terminology used in contemporary law for lepers. Medieval religious and literary references to lepers—including those in Wyclif's sermons, the Bible, and the *Ancrene Wisse*—use only generic terms such as "lepurs," "lepres," and "lepirs."[49] In calling a band of lepers "lipper folk" (526, 580), Henryson explicitly mimics fifteenth-century leper statutes that use the same phrase to describe the community they legally repress. A statute passed by James I in 1427 forbade lepers from entering the burgh on certain days and at specific times: Item That na lipper folk, nouther man nor woman, enter na cum in a burgh of the realme bot thrise in the oulk, that is to say, ilk Monounday, Wednejday and Friday, fra ten houris to twa eftrnoon and quhair fairis and mercattis fallis in thay dayis, that thay leif thair entrie in the burrowis, and gang on the morn to get thair leving.[50] A similar statute passed the same year further restricts lepers from religious spaces: "Item, That na lipper folk sit to thig, nather in kirk na in kirk ȝaird na uther place within the burrowis"; and a 1466 law concludes, "And thairfor na man sall tak on hand to herberie [harbor] lipper folk, under the pane of ane unlaw."[51] As part of the formulaic makeup of a leper statute, the phrase "lipper folk" is really nothing more than a legalistic formula, a linguistic construction so repetitively employed in such similar contexts that it loses its meaning. To the experienced legal reader, then—that is, Henryson's fifteenth-century audience—the physical referents of "lipper folk," the lepers themselves, are equally devoid of meaning. By interpolating this generic term into his text, along with similar constructions such as "lipper man" and "lipper woman," Henryson participates in a literary revisionism of juridical exclusion. His lepers, save Cresseid, are not inscribed with any identity outside their assigned title of "lipper folk." They are anonymous, faceless figures who wander through the narrative but have no significant impact on it.

Although the majority of the leper statutes enacted in fifteenth-century Scotland were designed to make the leper "invisible" by physically excluding him from public spaces, there is one peculiar statute (registered in the *Statutes of the Gild*) that seems to reverse the ideological mechanism of exclusion by deliberately drawing attention to the leprous body:

> Item, It is statute, that na lipper folk enter within the portis of the burgh: And gif ony happinis to enter, he sall incontinent to be cassin furth be the Serjand of the burgh: And gif ony lipper folk dois in the contrare of this our inhibitioun, and usis to enter within the burgh, the cleithing of the bodie sall be takin fra him and brint [burnt], and he beand nakit, sall be put furth of the burgh. It is in like wayis statute, that sum honest men of the burgh sall gader almons, to be gevin and distribute to all lipper folk in ony meit and convenient place without the burgh.[52]

Lepers who unlawfully entered the gates of the city (and refused to leave on command) were stripped of their clothing and "put furth of the burgh." Medieval conceptions of leprosy, which viewed even the clothing of lepers to be contaminants, undoubtedly deemed this behavior medically necessary to preserve the health of the masses. Yet the very act of public removal of clothing from a sick body also constitutes a grotesque spectacle, one that was, curiously enough, sanctioned by the law. For the viewing public, surely the most exciting parts of the naked leper body were not the organs that were now exposed but the parts of the body that were missing—those that had literally fallen off through the destructive machinations of the disease.

We must bear in mind that removing the medieval leper from his habit was surely no small feat. Henryson's representation of Cresseid's apparel, which includes "ane mantill and ane bawer hat / With cop and clapper" (386), is typical of medieval leper garb (the poet most likely found inspiration for his character's clothing in the attire worn by lepers who lived at St. Leonard's). A fourteenth-century marginal painting in the *Exeter Pontifical* provides a particularly complete description of the English leper's uniform, which is assumed to be similar to the Scot's: an ankle-length tunic made of coarse redbrown cloth with sleeves closed to the wrist, a russet cowl, and black cape.[53] The labored process of removing the clothing from the leper's body piece by piece served a specific ideological purpose: it imitated the slow, agonizing effects of the disease itself, which little by little ate away at flesh and tissue until it fell off the bone. As the public watches with horrified yet enraptured gazes as the leper is stripped and revealed for what he is, or at least what the spectators see him to be—a disfigured mass of bones and flesh—the juridical process of exclusion approaches full circle. The leper is excluded by the church, the law, and finally the community. All segments of the process are thus designed with a common goal: to dehumanize the leper in every way possible and emphasize that the diseased body is not the "other" but "another," something that is decidedly devoid of human attributes and thus undeserving of respect by the public or the law.

In the *Testament,* Cresseid is stripped of her metaphorical clothing—her social and legal coverings of respectability and value—through the dehumanizing effects of leprosy. Henryson does not shield this process from the reader's critical gaze but rather highlights the "spectacle" of the heroine's deteriorating body in the poem by cataloguing the various debilitating manifestations of the disease:

> 'My cleir voice and courtlie carrolling,
> Quhair I was wont with ladyis for to sing,
> Is rawk [harsh] as ruik [crow], full hiddeous, hoir [rough] and hace [hoarse];

> My plesand port, all vtheris precelling [excelling],
> Of lustines [delightfulness] I was hald maist conding [worthy]—
> Now is deformit the figour of my face;
> To luik on it na leid now lyking hes [no person now enjoys].
> Sowpit [wearied] in syte, I say with sair siching [sore sighing],
> Ludgeit [dwelling] amang the lipper leid [leper folk], "Allace!"'

> (443-51)

Cresseid's once melodious voice is now raspy; her beauty, once esteemed above all, is hideously "deformit," and her figure, once supple, has grossly decayed. By serving as the agent and voice who describes these disfigurements, Cresseid participates in (and even promotes) the very discourse that has reduced her to nothingness. Devaluing herself and acknowledging the permanence of her corporeal and legal losses, she surrenders the final component of her identity: the belief that she in fact has one.

At this point in the narrative, with Cresseid's body reduced to nothingness and her person devoid of a legal identity, we cannot imagine any fate for the heroine other than a gruesome and torturous death. In fact, courtly tradition demands it. We expect the end to come quickly, but it is curiously suspended for forty-one lines. In this narrative space Henryson fashions a legal text that is profoundly revisionary. The poem's documentary conclusion of the legal narrative that has preceded it disputes the modes of authority governing the law of personhood while actively refiguring Cresseid within it.

Where There's Will, There's a Way

Having just concluded her Complaint, in which she laments the fallen state of her diseased body, Cresseid secludes herself in the leprosarium and "with paper scho sat doun / And on this maneir maid hir testament" (575-76). At first glance, Cresseid's inscriptions seem innocuous. Molded into what she calls "hir testament," they seem to reflect her *voluntas,* her last will. Cresseid, however, should rightly be prohibited from having a "will" (in both senses of the term). As we remember, it is her unrestrained *voluntas* that gets her into trouble with the gods in the first place. Unable (or unwilling) to control her blasphemous speech, she is afflicted by the deities with a punishment designed to prevent her from participating in any legal procedure—including the drafting of a valid testament. By relegating Cresseid to the space of the legally dead, the law seemingly thwarts any possibilities of future rebellion. According to *Black's Law Dictionary,* a legal persona is dependent on a network of social relations: "Persona est homo cum statu quodam consideratus."[54] In a study of the modern identity, Charles Taylor similarly suggests that "a self exists only within 'webs of interlocution.' . . .

[T]he full definition of someone's identity usually involves . . . some reference to a defining community."[55] Having been stripped of her points of social and legal reference, Cresseid is ostensibly "selfless."

Yet the medieval law of exclusion contains a loophole that presented a potential opportunity for the legal effects of leprosy to be reversed. In erasing a subject from legal memory, the law simultaneously released him from the constraints of legal subjectivity. While the leper is not included in the law, then, he is technically not governed by it either. This legal gap allows Cresseid to exist outside the law—to carve a legal space for herself in the narrative that is completely divorced from the feudal court system and set within her own prescribed (and self-controlled) boundaries.

It is into this space that Cresseid inserts her twelve-line testament. The contents of her will clearly delineate her "will" (*voluntas*) regarding the interment of her corpse and dispersal of her goods:

> "Heir I beteiche [bequeath] my corps and carioun
> With wormis and with taidis [toads] to be rent;
> My cop and clapper, and myne ornament,
> And all my gold the lipper folk sall haue,
> Quhen I am deid, to burie me in graue.
>
> 'This royall ring, set with this rubie reid,
> Quhilk Troylus in drowrie [love token] to me send,
> To him agane I leif it quhen I am deid,
> To make my cairfull deid vnto him kend [known].
> Thus I conclude schortlie and mak ane end:
> My spreit I leif to Diane, quhair scho dwellis,
> To walk with hir in waist [uninhabited] woddis and
>   wellis.

(577-88)

As Julia Boffey has noted, Cresseid's testament conforms to the four-point formula characteristic of most fifteenth-century wills.[56] What is peculiar about the heroine's testament is not the way in which property is bequeathed, however, but the discourse of self-exclusion that underlies it. She begins by disposing of her carcass, which is to be buried "in graue." This hackneyed phrase evokes the medieval tradition of bequeathing one's body to the particular church or religious institution that will dispose of it. As a pagan and leper, Cresseid is excluded from this ritual and therefore must dedicate her "corps" to an unconsecrated piece of land—one that is appropriately filled with "wormis" and "taidis." The text's revision of religious tradition is enlarged in the heroine's dedication of her soul. By leaving her spirit to Diana, the mythological goddess of the hunt, Cresseid consigns herself to spend eternity in the "woddis and wellis," a marginalized space well outside the courtly garden and cultivated field with which she is familiar. The use of the phrase "to be rent" within this legal context is also interesting, as it generates inevitable comparisons to two disparate elements of medieval testamentary convention. Taken in its verbal form (as it appears here), the phrase functions as a metaphor for earthly burial. By requesting that her body be "rent," or shredded, by animals and insects, Cresseid acknowledges herself a participant in the organic processes of decay and decomposition. At the same time, however, this phrase evokes the Christian tradition in which a testator likens himself to a husbandman who "rents" his body from the Lord God during his mortal tenure and returns it to him upon his death. Cresseid's leprous body, of course—which does not legally exist—cannot be given to an ecclesiastical lord or a temporal one because it is not recognized as property. It is precisely through her marginalized position within the law and the church structure—the ownership of her body is ambiguous—that she is able to claim her corpse for herself.

Within this bequeathal sequence emerges a striking paradox: Cresseid claims the wasted body as her own only "to obliterate all physical traces of her existence."[57] By burying her body and distributing her goods, Cresseid seems to thrust herself further into the realm of anonymity. Yet perhaps this is precisely the point: for in anonymity, she is a cipher, an empty space inscribed with nothing yet obligated to no one.

By documenting her *voluntas*—and having it carried out after her death—Cresseid turns the law of personhood inside out. She manipulates established law in order to create a new law that in turn enables her to inscribe on herself an identity that no one can repress or eradicate. By including Cresseid's testament within its narrative body, the **Testament** literally writes her into its own poetic will (the narrative after all is a "testament"). Not only does Cresseid participate in authorized legal discourse, but also her illegal will (in both senses of the word) becomes a validated part of this discourse.

The heroine's reemergence as a legal person is consolidated through her reinsertion into legal memory. Immediately after Cresseid's death, an anonymous leper man delivers word of her demise to Troilus:

> Quhen he had hard hir greit infirmitie
> Hir legacie and lamentatioun,
> And how scho endit in sic pouertie,
> He swelt [fainted] for wo and fell doun in ane swoun;
> For greit sorrow his hart to brist [burst] was boun
>   [ready];
> Siching full sadlie, said, 'I can no moir;
> Scho was vntrew and wo is me thairfoir.'

(596-602)

Where once Cresseid is a "blenk" in Troilus' mind, now she is a "legacie," an indelible textual imprint in his memory. Troilus transfers this mental image of his lost love into a physical text, inscribing her story on a marble tombstone. The words carved into the stone—along with the heroine's name—constitute a "ressoun," an explanation for the text. "Lo, fair ladyis," he writes, "Cresseid of Troy [the] toun, / Sumtyme countit the flour of womanheid / Vnder this stane, lait lipper, lyis deid' (607-9). Troilus' words indicate that Cresseid's corpse is not bequeathed to the fair ladies of Troy and, by extension, to the reader, as an exemplum. Cresseid's written "legacy," by contrast, emphatically is.

In her Complaint, Cresseid tells the audience "in ʒour mynd ane mirrour mak of me" (457). Henryson's poetic mirror seems to cast forth an image of hope and restoration. Cresseid, once crippled, is now whole; where once she was invisible, now she can be "seen"—and, by implication, "heard" and "understood"—in both literal and legal senses. Yet if the **Testament of Cresseid** has transformed the legal status of Chaucer's Criseyde beyond recognition, it has also highlighted the author's culpability in the heroine's fate. Henryson keeps his character alive long enough for her to obtain a legal identity, but destroys her before she can exercise her new rights. Thus, the heroine's subjective will is ultimately subordinate to Henryson's own *voluntas,* his desire to express—however implicitly—that Cresseid's words are always his words, and his words are law.

Notes

1. The court registers of Dunfermline, the burgh that Henryson is believed to have lived in for most of his life, contain numerous accounts of agricultural disasters. See Ebenezer Henderson, *The Annals of Dunfermline and Vicinity, 1069-1878* (Glasgow: John Tweed, 1929), 150-82. See also Sir J. D. Marwick, ed., *Extracts from the Records of the Burgh of Edinburgh, 1403-1528* (Edinburgh, 1833), 71-72.

2. Robert Henryson, *The Testament of Cresseid,* ed. Denton Fox (London: Nelson, 1968). All subsequent citations are to this edition and will be given in the text.

3. Walter Scheps reads the *Testament* through the lens of Caledonian climatology, comparing Chaucer's use of weather patterns with Henryson's ("A Climatological Reading of Henryson's *Testament of Cresseid*," *Studies in Scottish Literature* 15 [1980]: 80-87). Included in his essay is a discussion of the Scottish planting season. See also Alasdair A. MacDonald, "Fervent Weather: A Difficulty in Robert Henryson's *Testament of Cresseid*," *Scottish Studies* 4 (1984): 271-80.

4. *Dictionary of Old Scots Tongue,* s.v. "fervent" 3; *Middle English Dictionary,* s.v. "grene" 3a.

5. The classic study of the relationship between Chaucer and Henryson is Marshall Stearns's chapter in *Robert Henryson* (New York: Columbia University Press, 1949), 48-69. More recent studies include David Benson, "Critic and Poet: What Lydgate and Henryson did to Chaucer's *Troilus and Criseyde*," *Modern Language Quarterly* 53 (1992): 23-40; and Robert Kindrick, "Henryson's 'Uther Quair' Again: A Possible Candidate and the Nature of the Tradition," *Chaucer Review* 33 (1988): 190-220.

6. John Finlay discusses the roles of women in Scottish courts in "Women and Legal Representation in Early Sixteenth-Century Scotland," in *Women in Scotland, 1100-1750,* ed. Elizabeth Ewan and Maureen M. Meikle (East Linton: Tuckwell, 1999), 165-75.

7. I. F. Grant, *The Social and Economic Development of Scotland before 1603* (Edinburgh: Oliver and Boyd Publishers, 1930), 200. See also C. D'Ollvier Farran, *The Principles of Scots and English Land Law* (Edinburgh: W. Green & Son, 1958), 17-28.

8. I agree with R. J. Lyall's claim that Henryson's *Fables* are not merely allegories but reflections of contemporary local practices ("Politics and Poetry in Fifteenth-Century and Sixteenth-Century Scotland," *Scottish Literary Journal* 3 [1976]: 5-29).

9. For details of Henryson's life, I am indebted to Denton Fox's biographical summary in *The Poems of Robert Henryson* (Oxford: Clarendon Press, 1981), xiii-xxv.

10. "Anno Domini etc. [M.cccc.] xij die decimo mensis Septembris Incorporatus fuit venerabilis vir Magister Robertus Henrisone in Artibus Licentiatus et Decretis Bachalarius" (*Munimenta alme universitatis Glasguensis,* ed. C. Innes, Maitland Club, no. 72 [Glasgow, 1954], 7:69). The date of Henryson's death is still a much-contested subject. In 1968 Denton Fox placed the poet's death "before 1505." The content of a minor poem attributed to Henryson—"Ane Prayer for the Pest"—suggests a slightly earlier date, around 1499. The poem probably refers to the plague that struck Edinburgh in 1499 and killed many of its citizens. The likelihood that Henryson did not live long after the plague (owing either to illness, old age, or both) is suggested in a passage of the text in which Henryson includes himself among the diseased who seek mercy from God:

> Superne lucerne, guberne this pestilens,
> Preserue and serue that we nocht sterf thairin,
> Declyne that pyne be thy devyne prudens,
> For trewth, haif rewth, lat nocht our slewth ws twyn;
> Our syte, full tyte, wer we contryt, wald blin;
> Dissiuir did nevir, quha euir the besocht

> But grace, with space, for to arrace fra sin;
> Lat nocht be tint that thow sa deir hes bocht!

Cited in Fox, *The Poems of Robert Henryson,* lines 65-72.

11. David Walker, *A Legal History of Scotland* (Edinburgh: W. Green Publishing, 1990), 2:276. For a detailed discussion of the function and usage of notarial instruments in fifteenth-century Scotland, see also Hector MacQueen, *Common Law and Feudal Society in Medieval Scotland* (Edinburgh: Edinburgh University Press, 1993), 94-97.

12. *Registrum de Dunfermelyn* (Edinburgh: Bannatyne Club), MS fol. 63a, 63b, 64a. See also Henderson, 176.

13. Cited in Fox, *The Poems of Robert Henryson,* 2252. All subsequent citations of Henryson's fables are from this edition and will be given in the text.

14. Stearns, *Robert Henryson,* 31.

15. In 1429, King James mandated that barons could not remove "coloni" or "husbandi" from their lands if leases were still valid. See *The Acts of the Parliaments of Scotland, 1127 to 1707. Printed by the Command of His Majesty King George the Fourth in pursuance of an address to the House of Commons of Great Britain,* ed. T. Thomson and C. Innes, 2 vols. (Edinburgh, 1844), 17; hereafter *APS* with volume and page number. The parliament of James II ordered that lords could not evict their leased tenants if the land legally changed hands. The act, passed in 1449, reads: "It is ordained, for the safety and favour of the poor people that labour the ground, that they, and all others that have not taken or shall take lands in times to come from Lords, and have times and years thereof, that, suppose the Lords sell or alienate these lands, the Takers shall remain with their tacks unto the ische [*sic*] of their times, into whosoever hands these lands come, for such male [rent] as they took them for before" (*APS,* 2:35). Identical statutes were passed in 1469 and 1491 (*APS,* 2:96, 2:225). For more information, see Grant, *Social and Economic Development,* 244-64.

16. *Burns v. Buchane,* in *Acta dominorum auditorum: The Acts of the Lord Auditors of Causes and Complaints, 1466-1494* (London: House of Commons, 1807), 96; hereafter *ADA* with participating parties and page references.

17. It must be noted that local documents record a number of individuals bearing the name Robert "Henrisone" or Robert "Henderson" living in the general region of Edinburgh, which of course casts doubt on the ability of scholars or historians to link specific historical documents decisively to the poet. Fifteenth-century Trekware (Trakware, Traquair) was approximately twenty-five miles south of Dunfermline and eighteen miles south of Edinburgh. Historical records place Henryson in Glasgow in 1462 and in Dunfermline in 1477-78. Where the poet resided in the years before, in between, and after these dates is unknown. Given his acclimation toward centers of industry, politics, and law, it is entirely possible that he lived for some time in Traquair. The burgh was a favorite hunting and fishing retreat for James I, II, and III and the castle there was a popular meeting place for the king and his vassals. Sir James Stewart, the Black Knight of Lorn and husband to Queen Joan, the widow of James I, was granted the lands by royal charter in 1439. James of Buchane, Stewart's son, was knighted in 1469 and legitimated twenty years later. For more information, see Peter Maxwell Stuart's pamphlet *Traquair House Guidebook* (Peebleshire, Scotland: Jarrold, 1986), 22.

18. By depicting Cresseid this way, Henryson immediately graphs floral imagery onto Chaucer's more literate comparison in *Troilus and Criseyde*: "Right as our firste lettre is now an A, / In beaute first so stood she makeles" (*The Riverside Chaucer,* ed. Larry Benson [Boston: Houghton Mifflin, 1987], 1.171). Feminist critics have also discussed the female body in terms of these images. Annette Kolodny contends that bodily transgression promotes the simultaneous fracturing and blending of identities, a process that inevitably destroys the discernible boundaries between human geographic territory but at the same time motivates what she calls a "pastoral impulse," the innate legal and psychological desire to create a compromised identity—one that is definable—through the image of the gendered land (*The Lay of the Land: Metaphor as Experience and History in American: Life and Letters* [Chapel Hill: University of North Carolina Press, 1975], 26). For Peter Stallybrass, the conflation of flesh and field is both a literary construction as well as a social reality. The married woman in particular not only becomes a legal discourse in that her legal identity is suspended but also is ideologically configured as "the fenced-in enclosure of the landlord, her father, or husband" ("Patriarchal Territories: The Body Enclosed," in *Rewriting the Renaissance: The Discourses of Sexual Difference in Early Modern Europe,* ed. Margaret Ferguson, Maureen Quilligan, and Nancy Vickers [Chicago: University of Chicago Press, 1986], 123-42). Mikhail Bakhtin identifies the female body as a "locus of class conflict" in which the battle between the haves

and the have-nots is topographically mapped onto physical features. The inevitable consequence is a distorted cartographic image—a map symbolizing the self that is recognizable as neither human nor agrarian (*Rabelais and His World,* trans. Helene Iswolsky [Cambridge: MIT Press, 1968], 26-27).

19. There are also historically specific reasons why Henryson likely represented Cresseid in the manner he did. Chaucer employs the metaphor sparingly, instead resurrecting archaic forms of descriptive comparisons heavily influenced by classical mythology and continental courtly tradition. Thus, Chaucer's notable absence of agricultural terminology afforded Henryson the freedom to explore the issue of bodily duality on the figure of Cresseid without concern for any historical impediment or residual literary influence related to his famous predecessor. In addition, Henryson's "agriculturalizing" of traditional court motifs reflects the pervasive atmosphere of political and economic instability of late fifteenth-century Scotland. In an era four times without a king and with no centralized government, the popularity of the court and its culture was rapidly dwindling. See Louise Fradenburg, *City, Marriage, Tournament: Arts of Rule in Late Medieval Scotland* (Madison: University of Wisconsin Press, 1991), 35-46; and William Ferguson, *The Identity of the Scottish Nation* (Edinburgh: Edinburgh University Press, 1998), 36-75.

20. "Est etiam mors civilis in servo in servitute sub potestate domini constituto" (*De legibus et consuetudinibus Angliae,* trans. Samuel E. Thorne [Cambridge: Belknap Press of Harvard University Press, 1968], 421b). Also cited in Sir Frederick Pollock and Frederic William Maitland, *The History of English Law before the time of Edward I* (Cambridge: Cambridge University Press, 1899), 1:433.

21. Elizabeth Fowler, "Civil Death and the Maiden: Agency and the Conditions of Contract in *Piers Plowman,*" *Speculum* 70 (1995): 768.

22. The narrator, himself a character, is equally confined within the text. His plea to Saturn later in the text—"O cruell Saturne, fraward and angrie . . . / Withdraw thy sentence and be gracious" (323, 327)—demonstrates his own level of subjectivity and, thus, inability to intervene on his heroine's behalf.

23. Jill Mann, "The Planetary Gods in Chaucer and Henryson," in *Chaucer Traditions: Studies in Honour of Derek Brewer,* ed. Ruth Morse and Barry Windeatt (Cambridge: Cambridge University Press, 1990), 96; John MacQueen, *Robert Henryson: A Study of the Major Narrative Poems* (Oxford: Clarendon Press, 1967), 70.

24. Lee Patterson, "Christian and Pagan in the *The Testament of Cresseid,*" *Philological Quarterly* 52 (1973): 700. For an alternative reading of the dream sequence in the poem, see Ralph Hanna III, "Cresseid's Dream and Henryson's *Testament,*" in *Chaucer and Middle English Studies in Honour of Rossell Hope Robbins,* ed. Beryl Rowland (London: Allen and Unwin, 1974), 288-97.

25. For my discussion of the structure and composition of the Lord Auditors, I am indebted to David Walker's research in *A Legal History of Scotland,* Vol. 2, 309-21.

26. For a complete listing of the types of charges brought before the court, see the appendix in *ADA,* 1466-94.

27. The members of the council represented the three estates and were chosen for their practical experience with land law (as landlords) or their specialist knowledge of particular statutes or legislative areas. Between 1478 and 1485, a total of fifty-four men sat as Lord Auditors of causes and complaints for a total of eighty-seven days spread over twelve sessions of parliament; twenty-two were ecclesiastics, fourteen were nobles (two earls and twelve barons), and eighteen were burgesses. Although the exact number of members per council is unknown, it is likely that the court's composition was similar to that of parallel committees—such as the Lords of Session and Lords of Council—which typically contained nine members. For more information, see Walker, *A Legal History of Scotland,* 2:318-19, and *APS,* 2:36, c. 10.

28. *APS,* 2:43, cc. 11-12.

29. *Middle English Dictionary,* s.v. "reule" 9a; "steiren" 1a.

30. *ADA, Anderson v. Lawthres,* 83.

31. Henderson, *The Annals of Dunfermline and Vicinity,* 170.

32. Ibid., 169.

33. For a discussion of the significance of physical tokens and material artifacts in the medieval Scottish legal system, see Walker, *A Legal History of Scotland,* 2:309-10.

34. For examples of cases adhering to this format, see *ADA, Wemys v. Wemys and Malevil,* 101; *Carmichael v. Ramsay,* 103; *Spens v. Forster,* 119-20.

35. *ADA, Ogilvy v. Ogilvy,* 5; *Ramsay v. Boyes,* 41. That the court did not know where the tenant lived is unlikely, given that the litigant was the tenant's landlord (and thus the defendant almost always

lived on his lord's land). It seems more probable, then, that little if any effort was expended by the juridical council to notify tenants of impending court dates or to summon them in ways in which they could respond (e.g., an illiterate farmer could not respond to a writ).

36. Catherine Cox, "Froward Language and Wanton Play: The 'Commoun' Text of Henryson's *Testament of Cresseid*," *Studies in Scottish Literature* 29 (1996): 63.

37. *Middle English Dictionary,* s.v. "ripeli" 1a.

38. *ADA, Carlisle v. Maxwell,* 50.

39. *ADA, Mure v. McLellan,* 50; *Murray v. Buchane,* 134; *Crauford v. Peltegren,* 173.

40. For essays that treat the gods' judgment as a catalyst for the heroine's moral growth, see Mairi Ann Cullen, "Cresseid Excused: A Re-reading of Henryson's *Testament of Cresseid*," *Studies in Scottish Literature* 20 (1985): 137-59; and John McNamara, "Divine Justice in Henryson's *Testament of Cresseid*," *Studies in Scottish Literature* 11 (1974): 99-107.

41. Most individuals who were convicted of a felony forfeited their property, land, and moveable goods to the Crown and were executed. The mentally ill were committed to asylums and hospitals; while the individual was institutionalized, the Crown held legal guardianship over his possessions and property. Upon the individual's release or death, all holdings were returned to him or his heirs (*Regiam Majestatem,* ed. Rt. Hon. Lord Cooper [Edinburgh: Skinner, 1947], 2, c. 40). With his diagnosis, however, the leper lost all of his legal rights. For more information, see Gerard Lee, *Leper Hospitals in Medieval Ireland* (Dublin: Four Courts Press, 1996), 1-72.

42. Peter Richards, *The Medieval Leper and His Northern Heirs* (Cambridge: D. S. Brewer, 1977), 50-51. See also John Comrie, *History of Scottish Medicine* (London: Bailliere, Tindall and Cox, 1932), 193-202; and Christopher Daniell, *Death and Burial in Medieval England, 1066-1550* (New York: Routledge, 1997), app. 1, "Jews and Lepers."

43. Sabine Volk-Birke reads this ceremony through the lens of religious redemption, arguing that the disease spiritually cleanses the body in preparation for divine redemption ("Sickness unto Death: Crime and Punishment in Henryson's *The Testament of Cresseid*," *Anglia* 113 [1995]: 163-83).

44. By using leprosy as the agent responsible for Cresseid's loss of identity, Henryson is surely playing with the term's secondary use; according to the *Middle English Dictionary,* "leprous" (1b) not only referred to a gamut of flesh-eating diseases, but also was used by medieval alchemists and farmers to describe a diseased or corrupted element or plot of land.

45. Thomas Craik, "The Substance and Structure of the *Testament of Cresseid*: A Hypothesis," in *Bards and Makars: Scottish Language and Literature: Medieval and Renaissance,* ed. Adam Aitken, Matthew McDiarmid, and Derick Thomson (Glasgow: University of Glasgow Press, 1977), 22.

46. Ibid.

47. Jane Adamson, "The Curious Incident of Recognition in Henryson's *The Testament of Cresseid*," *Parergon* 27 (1980): 17.

48. Felicity Riddy explores the discourse of exclusion that pervades the *Testament* in "'Abject odious': Feminine and Masculine in Henryson's *Testament of Cresseid*," in *The Long Fifteenth Century: Essays for Douglas Gray,* ed. Helen Cooper and Sally Mapstone (Oxford: Clarendon Press, 1997), 229-48.

49. *Middle English Dictionary,* s.v. "lepre, 1,2,3," "leprous" 1a, and "lepur 1."

50. *APS,* 2:16, c. 8.

51. Ibid., *Leges Burgorum,* c. 62, cited in *The Practicks of Sir James Balfour of Pittendreich,* ed. Peter G. B. McNeil (Edinburgh: Stair Society, 1962), 1:131.

52. *Statutes of the Gild,* c. 16, cited in McNeil, *Practicks of Sir James Balfour,* 131.

53. British Library, MS Lansdown 451, f. 157.

54. "A person is a man considered with reference to a certain status." See Henry Campbell Black, with Joseph Nolan and M. J. Connolly, *Black's Law Dictionary: Definitions of the Terms and Phrases of American and English Jurisprudence, Ancient and Modern* (St. Paul, Minn.: West Publishing, 1979), 1029.

55. Charles Taylor, *Sources of the Self: The Making of Modern Identity* (Cambridge: Cambridge University Press, 1989), 36.

56. Julia Boffey, "Lydgate, Henryson, and the Literary Testament," *Modern Language Quarterly* 53 (1992): 41-56. Traditionally, testators began their wills with a formulary statement in which they dedicated their spirit to God and their bodies to the parish church where they were christened or blessed. Next came the bequests of material items, namely, land and moveable goods such as furniture, jewelry, clothing, and religious books. The

will typically concluded with a formulary statement attesting that the testator was sound in mind and body, ensuring that his *voluntas* was consistent with the content of the will he transcribed. For more information on the structural format of the medieval British will, see Michael Sheehan, *The Will in Medieval England* (Toronto: Pontifical Institute of Medieval Studies, 1963), 163-230.

57. Boffey, "Lydgate, Henryson, and the Literary Testament," 53.

Michael G. Cornelius (essay date 2003)

SOURCE: Cornelius, Michael G. "Robert Henryson's Pastoral Burlesque *Robene and Makyne* (c. 1470)." *Fifteenth-Century Studies* 28 (2003): 80-96.

[*In the following essay, Cornelius demonstrates how "Robene and Makyne" satirizes poetic conventions—particularly the courtly romance, the* pastourelle, *the* carpe diem *poetry, the elegy, and the genre of women wanting control—and maintains that the poem is "a stylistic achievement in the burlesque of both poetry and morality."*]

Robert Henryson's **"Robene and Makyne"** (c. 1470), the earliest surviving pastoral poem recorded in the English language, remains one of Henryson's best known works; "the excellence of this poem has long been recognized even by those who do not appreciate Henryson's other works"[1] notes critic Robert Kindrick, and he is correct in that assessment. The comical story of the shepherdess Makyne's advances towards the reluctant shepherd Robene, and the ensuing reversal of fortune that finishes the work, have delighted audiences for centuries. Well-anthologized and studied often in British literature survey courses, **"Robene and Makyne"** with its pithy nature, uncomplicated structure, comical subject material, and "charming"[2] language, stands as a good example of the work of a poet often considered one of the last great medieval *makars*.

In terms of literary criticism, though, **"Robene and Makyne"** remains largely ignored by Henryson scholars and is considered a minor footnote to this poet's *Testament of Cresseid* and his *Morall Fabillis,* mainly because most critics are not sure how **"Robene and Makyne"** fits into the Henryson canon. Exemplifying the prevalent critical interpretation of the man and his works, Denton Fox labels Henryson a "dour moralist";[3] Henryson's conservatism, though, appears largely at odds with both the burlesque, almost bawdy, subject material of **"Robene and Makyne"** and the accepted *moralitis* (moral meaning) of the poem as found in lines 91-92: "The man that will nocht quhen he may / sall haif nocht quhen he wald"[4] (the man that will not when

he may / shall have not when he would). Henryson's conclusion of a missed sexual opportunity clashes with the seeming ideology of a poet writing so piteously of Cresseid's punishment and moral redemption, or of the heavy-handed fabler whose Aesopic tales often include morals as long as the original stories. More than most medieval authors, Henryson and the body of his work are frequently considered from a universal, almost apostolic perspective, and he is seen as a conservative moralist whose personal ideologies permeate his poems. The question is thus broached: can one reconcile the Henryson we have come to expect from *Cresseid* and the *Fabillis* with the poet of the burlesque **"Robene and Makyne"**?

Most Henryson critics do not ask the question posed here; those who do attempt to place **"Robene and Makyne"** into the "traditional" Henryson canon state that, since no manifest sin occurs within the poem, Henryson is advocating humankind's use of reason over passion and the need to ignore our baser instincts, as Robene first does, despite sexual temptations. Thus, as Fox and others have argued, in contrast to the comic, bawdy nature of the poem, morality perseveres,—and I dislike this reading for two reasons. First, this argument is inherently misogynistic, concluding that, since it is the woman who acts as sexual aggressor, hers is the carnality of women in general, a vice which Henryson wishes to repudiate. In the conventions of this genre, the male acts as sexual aggressor, and it is tenuous to suggest that Henryson, who writes so eloquently of feminine tragedy elsewhere, purposely changes convention to write of feminine carnality. His major poems, while moralistic, do not lack compassion, and the delightfully zealous Makyne hardly seems a character of whose moral compass Henryson sternly disapproves. Secondly, if he had wished to write a moralistic tale about sexual rejection, he could have done so more effectively by utilizing a straightforward approach, matching the genre of the piece to the moral (as he does in *Cresseid* and the *Fabillis*). Further, Henryson's use of the burlesque style in this poem and his lampooning of several poetic conventions suggest that a strict anti-sexual interpretation of the poem is erroneous; moreover, he provides the reader with the perfect maxim or "moral" to summarize the poem in lines 91-92. For us to ignore this maxim—expressed in the poet's own words—and instead impose a stricter interpretation is a faulty position; Henryson's principle establishes that his work must not be read for comedic effect only. To ignore his own words and to choose instead an almost allegorical conservativism is an unjustified stance.

What, then, is Henryson doing in **"Robene and Makyne"** if not moralizing to his audience? Perhaps a clue can be taken from Geoffrey Chaucer. Literary versatility is the watchword of the medieval poet, especially during an era when literary stylistics were heavily influenced by the whims of a sometimes demanding patronage. In his *Canterbury Tales,* Chaucer produces a stirring religious sermon; a bawdy, almost filthy *fabliau*; and a courtly romance. Henryson, who acknowledges his Chaucerian influences in *The Testament of Cresseid,* was almost certainly affected by Chaucer as his poetic predecessor, in both style and subject. It is conceivable that **"Robene and Makyne"** represents a literary experiment of Henryson's, where he utilizes burlesque to explore and satirize popular genres and literary conventions he chooses not to use. A burlesque, as Scots scholar Allan H. MacLaine notes, "is any kind of grotesque imitation or mimicry for purposes of satire, severe or gentle. It can be a means for vulgarizing lofty material, or, conversely, for treating ordinary material with mock dignity."[5] In **"Robene and Makyne"** Henryson in fact satirizes not one, but five, separate genres in his poem: the courtly romance, the *pastourelle,* the *carpe diem* poem, the elegy, and the popular medieval convention of women wanting to rule men.

As I will demonstrate, the sheer number of genres satirized in **"Robene and Makyne"** allows the reader to conclude that Henryson's poem was intended as an overwhelming satirical compilation of popular literary conventions, assembled to be a comic burlesque to end all burlesques. Toward this end, it is important for modern-day readers to remember that the poet's work has no direct analogue. While H. was certainly familiar with such popular burlesques as Chaucer's "The Tale of Sir Thopas," and while his own poem has affinities with Adam de la Halle's *Le Gieus de Robin et de Marion,* among other works, the fact that Henryson chooses to work without a direct source (though his major works *Cresseid* and the *Fabillis* refer to their sources) suggests that he wishes to create something wholly new. As Tom Scott notes, "Henrysoun [sic] seems to have adapted the convention to his own purposes";[6] Scott proposes that **"Robene and Makyne"** breaches both Henryson's conventional poetic style and the modes popular in the late fifteenth century, though Scott never specifies what the poet's literary purposes might have been. By exploring the idea that Henryson's "purposes" extended beyond moralizing and included lampooning the above mentioned genres and conventions, this essay seeks to show the full spectrum of the poet's potential.[7]

THE POEM

The poem is deceptively simplistic in both plot and structure. Robene, a young shepherd, is busy tending his flock when the lovesick maiden Makyne confesses her undying love to him. In fact, she has loved him for the last two or three years, and now, having finally found the courage to confess her desire, the girl tells him that she would surely die, should Robene not return her feelings in kind. Robene, however, remains unim-

pressed, and rejects Makyne out of hand, alleging that, should they indulge in carnal relations, his sheep would certainly not approve:

> The weddir is fair, & I am fane,
> My scheip gois haill aboif;
> And we wald play us in this plane,
> They wald us both reproif.
>
> (29-32)

This seems the poorest excuse any man has ever proffered in turning down the advances of a woman, but Makyne, undaunted, counters with a clarification: not only is she offering her "hairt all haill" but also her "madinhaid." Yet Robene continues to resist, wavering only enough to suggest that Makyne return the next morning, since right now, his sheep are restless. Now here is a man devoted to duty! Nonetheless, Makyne tries one more time, begging Robene at least to talk with her, but he refuses, coldly saying, "Makyne, sum uthir man begyle, / for hamewart I will fair" (63-64).

Disconsolate, Makyne turns towards home. Robene, meanwhile, having settled his sheep for the night, begins to re-think his earlier refusal of the young maid, and sure enough, he changes his mind. Dashing after her, he catches up with her and now professes his love to her, declaring that his sheep will be fine until morning. Makyne, however, has had a talk with herself on the way home, and she, too, has had a change of heart:

> Robene, thow hes hard soung & say,
> In gestis and storeis auld,
> The man that will nocht quhen he may
> sall haif nocht quhen he wald.
> I pray to Jesu every day
> Mot eik thair cairis cauld
> That first preisis with the to play,
> Be firth, forrest, or fawld.
>
> (89-96)

Now Robene pleads and begs, but it is all for naught:

> Robene, that warld is all away
> and quyt brocht till ane end,
> and nevir agane thairto perfay
> Sall it be as thow wend;
> For of my pain thow maid it play,
> and all in vane I spend;
> as thow has done, sa sall I say,
> murne on, I think to mend.
>
> (105-12)

Thus, the tables have turned, and Makyne goes home "blyth annewche," leaving Robene dolefully alone with his sheep. As Henryson sums up the failed relationship, "Scho sang, He sichit sair" (134).

The comedy is both obvious and infectious, and the effect the poem has on the reader is immediate satisfaction; perhaps romance has not been served, but revenge has, and for Makyne (and the sympathetic reader), this is the next best thing. Robene, one surmises, has likely learned his lesson, and the next time a comely young maiden comes calling, one feels that he will be a bit more receptive than the first time around.

Most critics identify the poem's burlesque style and the way it satirizes at least some aspects of other genres; yet they then veer away from this idea, as if to suggest that Henryson, the moralist, could not have meant to be funny intentionally. They ignore the comedic and burlesque principles of the poem, the inversion of convention, and the juxtaposition of the lovers, their reversal of roles. A close examination of how the poet lampoons each of the five conventions—the courtly romance, the *pastourelle,* the *carpe diem* poetry, the elegy, and the genre of women wanting control—reveals much about the design and interpretation of the poem, as well as about the poet who created it.

THE COURTLY ROMANCE

There is no such thing as the typical courtly romance. As Dorothy Everett rightly notes, a courtly romance may be "long or short, verse or prose, a tale of adventure involving brave knights, great kings, and distressed ladies, often motivated by religious themes or sheer love of adventure."[8] While **"Robene and Makyne"** features no knights or kings, it shows one distressed lady, who, while perhaps not seeking adventure, certainly finds her own little drama out in the pasture. Rather than just adapting the plot of the courtly romance, though, Henryson also inverts several of the conventions of the courtly love genre. Perhaps one of the most obvious is the Ovidian "love me or else I shall die" quality familiar to readers of courtly romances everywhere: Troilus manifests this symptom of love in Chaucer's *Troilus and Criseyde,* taking to his bed for some time, the situation seeming quite dark. Henryson uses the convention, but he places the words in the mouth of the woman, Makyne, who talks eloquently of her "dule in dern"—her hidden woe—and the fact that if Robene chooses not to love her, surely, she will succumb to it.

When Robene refuses, miraculously, Makyne does not perish as she had predicted; instead, she persists, and he rebuffs her again, the power to say "yes" or "no" all his, instead of the dame's, as courtly love dictates. When Robene asks, "[Q]uhat is lufe?," Makyne reels off several more courtly love notions, but again, Robene remains (as a proper courtly maiden should remain) unimpressed and inaccessible; to him, Makyne seems to be losing her mind. What the girl is doing is playing the part of the medieval courtly lover, and not very well at that. As Scott notes,

> Makyne clearly has been hearing of romantic lovers and wants to try it [courtly love] out, though it's a

garbled version she has. She imitates the lover rather than the lady, and instead of being aloof and inaccessible, she is all too accessible.[9]

Scott is almost shocked by her accessibility, but he shouldn't be; Robene is the character who needs to remain unconquerable, and, for a while, he does; he is aloof and standoffish, as a correct medieval courtly dame should be. It is only after Makyne leaves and Robene perhaps remembers who he is and what his traditional role should be, that he chases after her. Now he is the aggressor, the man, pursuing the former lover, but when he catches Makyne, he finds her all too willing to adopt her traditional role as the dame, but suddenly, she becomes aloof and inaccessible.

Scott seems to believe that the joke Henryson eschews is the "implied natural ease of country (courtly) love— the green wood is nearby, the passions of the folk are as simple and uncomplicated and innocent as those of the birds and the animals they spend their lives among."[10] Simple? Uncomplicated? Innocent? The wooing between Robene and Makyne is anything but those three words! Their courtship remains complex, an almost ritualistic (though backwards) dance of parry and thrust, very similar to the courtly romances one might have read at that time, except of course, that the roles are reversed, and this, clearly enough, is Henryson's "joke." The poet also suggests that at times it is necessary for the woman to adopt the role of the aggressor before she can take on the mantle of the pursued; here, Makyne must convince Robene to give chase, and when he does, she is no longer interested in him. Has she re-thought her carnality? Or is perhaps Henryson's punchline that the great joy of the courtly romance for the dame falls not in being captured but in being pursued, and that for Makyne, and for women everywhere, to be chased is simply enough, while for Robene, the man, it is ultimately more important to catch, to be the victor? After all, while Robene plays the part of the courtly woman and allows Makyne to woo him, his glib answers betray his enjoyment of both the ritual and the rejection of the courtly lover. It is only after Makyne leaves, and only after some thought on Robene's part, that he realizes what he has done, and that regardless of who pursues and wins whom, the outcome is the same, and it is this all-important outcome—at least to the male—that he loses because of his foolishness. Thus the great "joke" is, as Henryson notes, "The man that will nocht quhen he may / Sall haif nocht quhen he wald" (91-92). Through this inversion of courtly convention, the poet begins to set the ground rules for his burlesque, and by the use of comic reversal, he demonstrates his poetic ability to adjust the rules of tradition for his own purposes.

THE PASTOURELLE

A French pastoral genre, the *pastourelle* is a short narrative poem, often with dialogue, in which a knight or other high-ranking male courts and sometimes seduces a shepherdess (Adam de la Halle's Old French *Le Gieus de Robin et de Marion* is a dramatized *pastourelle*). Fox notes a "clear link" between **"Robene and Makyne"** and "the *pastourelle* tradition,"[11] though of course in this case it is the shepherdess who woos a shepherd.[12] Through **"Robene and Makyne"**'s setting, style, and tone, however, Henryson is clearly burlesquing the common *pastourelle*.

In the *pastourelle* "Era tutta soleta" (She was all alone), an anonymous fourteenth-c. Italian poem, the narrator, a male, spies the object of his desire alone "in un prato d'amore" (in a meadow of love) (2).[13] Complaining of his "dule in dern" ("mi riclose"—unhappy me, he says), he professes his love to her: "Io mi t'arrendo!" (I surrender!—11, 8). Also eschewing the courtly love tradition of the lover's illness after rejection and the method of using mythological comparisons, the narrator then states:

> Non senti mai Achille (Achilles never felt)
> per Pulisena bella (for beautiful Polyxena)
> le concenti faville (the burning sparks)
> quant'io senti' per quella (that I felt for her).
>
> (21-24)

Alas, our lover is eventually abandoned, and this rejection, he notes, is the reason he writes this "canzonetta" (little song—44). Certainly Henryson makes use of the setting and conventions of the *pastourelle*: the green meadow and his own "gude grene hill"; the short, almost abbreviated nature of the romance; and the one-time meeting that leads to painful rejection. All of these can be found in both Henryson and the *pastourelle*—except, of course, that he has again inverted sexual positioning and made the traditional seducer (the male) the seduced. In fact, there are so many correlations between **"Robene and Makyne"** and the *pastourelle* that one might be tempted to state that Henryson's intent in the poem is to burlesque, or even broadly to satirize, the *pastourelle* tradition itself. This interpretation, though, is limiting, to both Henryson and the reader: if the poet had wished to satirize or parody a *pastourelle,* why not send a high-born woman to seduce the shepherd? Likewise, why not have her succeed? If Henryson was merely working with one tradition to burlesque, then I believe he would have adhered closely to the rules of that specific tradition, inverting the sexual roles but remaining true to the nature of the genre being parodied. One of the characteristics of a good parody, after all, is that both what is being satirized and how the satire is accomplished are instantly recognizable to the parody's intended audience. Without effecting in a reader an instantaneous recognition of the fact that these pieces are indeed satires, he/she would indeed be baffled.

Furthermore, it is interesting to note that, while in the *pastourelle* tradition the seduction may or may not be successful, here, there are two attempted seductions, and both are unsuccessful. Robene and Makyne summarily reject and are rejected by one another, but a simple burlesque of the *pastourelle* would only require the woman's being turned down, and not the man's. Hence, this layering of seductive sequences, like the difficulty in identifying a singular literary convention being satirized in **"Robene and Makyne"** works to ratify my thesis that more than one literary convention is being lampooned in the poem. Thus, while the *pastourelle* acts as a framework for Henryson's burlesque, it, along with the courtly romance, is not the do-all or end-all tradition the poet is satirizing.

CARPE DIEM POEMS

After the seduction sequence, however, Henryson turns to other poetic traditions to burlesque in his work. While *carpe diem* poetry also has at its core love, enjoyment, and seduction as basic themes, Henryson's burlesque of this tradition occurs *after* the attempt at love-making, during a conversation between Robene and Makyne.

Lines 91-92, the oft mentioned "The man that will nocht quhen he may / Sall haif nocht quhen he wald," are usually identified as the *moralitis* of Henryson's poem, and as such, hold paramount significance to the piece. These two lines, of course, instantly bring to mind the *carpe diem* tradition, the "seize the day" mentality that concludes Horace's ode to Leuconoe: "carpe diem, quam minimum credula postero."[14] Henryson's critics often seem puzzled that the "moral outcome" of his short poem is an unsophisticated "gather ye rosebuds while ye may" type of plea for sexual immediacy, and have had much difficulty reconciling the moralist with this seemingly amoral pronouncement. The lines, however, make sense when one notices that Henryson is not trying to espouse the "seize the day" mentality but rather to mock it.

"Robene and Makyne" is about sexual opportunity and immediate gratification; however, it is more correct to state that the poem describes the loss of sexual opportunity and reward, at least for Makyne and especially Robene. In a *carpe diem* piece, a woman is usually urged to surrender her favors, and often her maidenhood, to a man, since one can never know what tomorrow may bring. Here, perversely, Makyne avoids that general argument until after the fact; thus, the gender espousing the argument (female versus male) and the time the argument is proffered (after the fact) are inverted. Makyne does not tempt Robene with the *carpe diem* mentality; rather, she chastises him with it. She does not say: "Love me now, for who knows what tomorrow may bring?" In fact, Robene suggests to her that she return tomorrow should she wish to continue courting him, and Makyne pleads only to be allowed to stay and at least talk to him, which of course Robene refuses. It is only after the latter reconsiders her proposal that she taunts him with the *carpe diem*: "You had your chance," she states basically, "and you blew it."

This is a very interesting use of the *carpe diem* admonition; rather than employing it in pursuit of her desire, Makyne decides to punish him after he has refused her. *Carpe diem* is always about love, lust, desire, and the reciprocation of these emotions; here, Henryson inverts these values, in the same manner he has inverted the traditional sexual roles in the *carpe diem*. As he places these words in a woman's mouth instead of a man's, he uses them not to pursue but to punish; thus, "seize the day" becomes not an entreatment but a taunt.

Those critics who cannot reconcile the moral Henryson with the author of **"Robene and Makyne"** should take note. In this work the poet burlesques not one but five traditions, the first three of which often espouse primarily sex and sexuality. While his experiment is a literary success as far as entertainment is concerned, most critics have deemed the poem a moral failure; yet this judgement is not entirely correct. Henryson's lampooning of courtly love, *pastourelle,* and *carpe diem* demonstrates his "gentle" disdain (to use Maclaine's definition of the burlesque) for these genres. I am certainly not suggesting that the poet burlesques the genres to condemn their poetics (for clearly he would recognize the literary merits of each), but rather, that he lampoons them because of the stereotypes they espouse. It is important for readers to remember that neither Robene nor Makyne commits the sin of fornication; rather, each offers love and is rejected. Thus, Henryson shows his disdain for the moral systems associated with the three traditions; he believes in the value of the literary standards of courtly love works, *pastourelles,* and *carpe diem* poetry, but he disapproves of the eventual outcomes. It is a gentle disapproval, almost loving: when he wishes to utilize these conventions, he inverts and burlesques them, not searingly or angrily, but "charmingly" and comically, so that he may disagree with them without offending the traditions the genres represent.

Some critics have maintained that the lack of sexual action in the poem—the fact that both characters are eventually rejected—hints strongly at Henryson's moral fiber, that despite his wish to write *within* these traditions, he can only do so by inverting convention, and that the ultimate deconventionalization of the genres represents the critical thrust of the poem. However, it seems more likely to me that Henryson is not writing within these traditions at all, but rather *at* them, using his language as loaded as a gun. This difference is an important distinction and explains where the burlesque

comes into play. The poet is not writing a *pastourelle,* or a courtly romance, or a *carpe diem* poem; instead, utilizing the conventions and literary traditions of the works, he writes at them by burlesquing them, and by satirizing these texts and their value systems; his goal is not to shame, and not to celebrate, but rather to invert tradition. He does this by allowing the woman to pursue the man, but the final result is that sexual passion loses in the end. Morality is thus saved, but not, as Fox notes, at the expense of poetry.

The Elegy

There are two other traditions that Henryson burlesques in **"Robene and Makyne"** While one, the theme of women wanting power over men, is certainly intentional, his lampooning of some elements of the elegy seems an almost accidental outcome from Robene's responses to Makyne as she pursues him. I say "almost" because I believe that Henryson was fully aware of elegiac convention when he penned this section of the poem, and utilized this genre, as all the others, to add to his burlesque. The result is interesting, and further demonstrates both Henryson's ability as burlesque poet and his desire to invert the conventions.

Still, the elegy marks perhaps the most difficult tradition in which to connect both Henryson and his poem. Stanley B. Greenfield defines an elegy as "a relatively short reflective or dramatic poem embodying a contrasting pattern of loss and consolation, ostensibly based upon a specific personal experience or observation, and expressing an attitude towards that experience."[15] Certainly, in both Robene's refusal of Makyne's company and in his later loss we see elements of the traditional elegy—or, more specifically, in keeping with the pattern of Henryson's use of other poetic genres, we see these elements being inverted.

The poet was probably quite familiar with the elegiac tradition. Firstly, certain themes common to Old English elegies such as *The Wanderer* and *The Seafarer* were probably derived from Boethius, an important influence on Henryson (some critics have deemed that Henryson's own moral structure is essentially Boethian, though this has yet to be thoroughly examined). Like other lyric forms, the elegy never went out of fashion, and in fact, shortly before Henryson, the pastoral elegy, a lament over the death of a young shepherd-poet, was enjoying something of a renaissance in Italy, and both Petrarch and Boccaccio utilized this form. Furthermore, based on biographical evidence gleaned partly from within Henryson's works, John MacQueen has determined that the poet possibly studied for some time in Italy, specifically at the University of Bologna.[16] Thus, Henryson's probable Italian connection and his knowledge of these authors demonstrate that he had considerable cognizance of the elegy. Furthermore, Petrarch had discovered "a motive implicit in the medieval pastoral"[17] and began to use his pastoral elegies as satirical works.

Nonetheless, it is the traditional elegy that Henryson burlesques in **"Robene and Makyne"** The work's bucolic setting necessitates that the poem become a pastoral elegy, but the broader elegiac tradition, better known in fifteenth-c. Britain, is what is being satirized here. Robene's professed desire for solitude, both Makyne's and Robene's great personal loss (of a mate), and Makyne's eventual consolation, all make the poem an interesting spin on the elegiac tradition.

In the beginning of the *The Wanderer,* the anonymous poet writes "Oft him anhaga are gebideð / Metudes miltse" (Often the solitary man enjoys / The grace and mercy of the Lord, 1-2).[18] Certainly, a solitary man such as Robene may know the grace of God; after all, a lonely figure is concordant with the notion of the *peregrinus,* "a pilgrim-hermit who seeks salvation by submitting himself to the trials and loneliness of self-imposed exile."[19] Robene's refusal of Makyne's advances—seemingly incongruous to both the modern and medieval audience—may bring to mind the religious exile, a man who seeks salvation through solitude. There is always some essence of the solitary life from which shepherds and thus pastoral poems cannot escape, and the manner in which this solitude is expressed by the fictive character can lead to some essential conclusions by the poem's audience. In **"Robene and Makyne"** Henryson's shepherd seems, at first, to desire solitude; he rebuffs Makyne's sexual advances and even sends her away, preferring the company of his sheep. Thus, the poet inverts the elegiac tradition of the lonely exile; here, Robene *chooses* to remain alone, with only his flock for company, at least for a while. Then, he regrets his decision, and dashes after Makyne, who has, of course, changed her mind, and in the end, Robene remains a lonely exile, just as he was at the beginning of the poem.

As a convention, the elegy comes into play mainly in the loss both Robene and Makyne endure, as well as in Robene's professed desire for solitude and Makyne's wish for revenge. Both experience the sense of privation that typifies the elegy—in this case, the loss of a companion and potential lover. Of course, the loss is hollow, since neither actually had the other in the first place, and this is another inversion of the elegiac theme, where the privation is more psychological than physical. Nevertheless, both Robene and Makyne reel from this loss; upon departing, Makyne walks home "Full wery eftir cowth weip," while later, after his rejection, Robene is left "in dolour and in cair." Thus, the privation, and the mourning that accompanies it, occur, fulfilling another part of the elegiac tradition.

Consolation comes next, but only Makyne achieves it, and only in the form of revenge, when she is able to reject Robene. The reader of course does not believe that she has lost interest in him, but rather that she acts out of spite and revenge, or as part of her plan, as if she only wanted Robene to chase after her all along (6). Either reading is possible, but nonetheless, consolation comes only to Makyne and in the form of cold revenge; the internal consolation, a spiritual awakening, or the external consolation, a homecoming, conventional to elegiac tradition, are not found here.

Henryson's elegiac inversion lacks the moral outcomes which the inversions of the courtly love poem, the *pastourelle,* and the *carpe diem* poetry have; therefore, the poet's use of elegiac burlesque lacks the weight of his other inversions. However, Henryson also realizes—more than other pastoral poets—the elegiac nature of the shepherd's life, the ease of solitude, and the tenuous character of companionship. His Robene reacts accordingly, as perhaps the oft distrustful elegiac hero would, only later to regret his actions; yet there is no consolation for him, only for the woman he spurned, and thus tradition is inverted once again.

Women Wanting to Rule Men

The fifth literary tradition burlesqued in **"Robene and Makyne"** prevalent in Makyne's final declaration of assertion and independence, is the genre of women wanting to gain control over men, led of course by Chaucer's "Wife of Bath's Prologue and Tale." It surprises me that more has not been done with this avenue of research, especially by medieval feminist critics, who would find Makyne's aggressive advances towards Robene working against the stereotype of the medieval woman. In fact, Makyne is both aggressor and victor in the sexual roundplay without having to lose her maidenhood—a feat that allows her to retain the medieval ideal of virginity while still conquering the male, thus catapulting Makyne over Chaucer's Wife, William Dunbar's Wedo, and Gautier le Leu's Widow, amongst others, who have long ago sacrificed their sexualities in the name of familial power.

The Wife of Bath remains the standard bearer for women of this ilk. A virile, domineering, yet ultimately frank and endearing figure, she declares that "Wommen desire to have sovereynetee / As well over her housbond as her love / And for to been in maistre him above" (1038-40).[20] The Wife of Bath batters her husbands with her sexuality, in order to gain obeisance, and since she does not abhor the act of sex itself (as she notes, "And Jhesu Crist us sende / Housbondes meeke, yonge, and fresh abedde," 1258-59), this domineering does not seem too great a hardship on her. Indeed, many critics have noted that the Wife of Bath's carnality—that which gives her both pleasure and dominion over her husbands—seems to be one of the gap-toothed, wide-hipped Wife's favorite personal qualities.

Yet early in her prologue, the Wife notes the distinct disadvantage she and her like-minded sisters, the Wedo and the Widow, must endure; nothing is more revered in a medieval woman than virginity. Being a wife may have its privileges, but nothing will command respect and attention like being a maid. In her prologue, the Wife rails against this reverence for maidenhood:

> Or where commanded he virginitee?
> I woot as well as ye, it is no drede,
> Th'apostel, whan he speketh of maidenhede,
> Hey seyde that precept thereof hadde he noon.
> Men may conseille a womman to been oon,
> But conseilling nis no commandment.

> (62-67)

It is clear, though, to both the reader and to the Wife, that this is an argument she cannot win; nothing she can say can mitigate the stain of sexuality, even sexuality within the confines of the sacrament of marriage.

Furthermore, second marriages (and in the case of the Wife, her fifth) are ecclesiastically problematic unto themselves. Chaucer presents the example of the Samaritan of the Bible, who had five husbands; Jesus said to her, "'Thou hast yhad five housbondes' quod he, / 'And that ilke man that now hath thee / Is not thine housbonde'" (17-19). The Wife responds "What that he mente therby, I kan not seyn" (20), but to a medieval reader, the message is all too clear, as Juan Luis Vives, a Spanish humanist, notes in his text *The Instruction of a Christian Woman*:

> [T]hat better it is to abstain than marry again, is not only counseled by Christian pureness, that is to say, by divine wisdom, but also by pagans, that is to say, by world wisdom. Notwithstanding, widows lay many causes wherefore they say they must marry again . . . [but] she, enflamed with vicious lust, forgetteth her own womb . . . for none of you taketh a [second] husband but to the intent that she will lie with him, nor except her lust prick her. What a ragiousness is it, to set thy chastity common like a harlot.[21]

This quotation represents the predominant misogynistic mentality that the Wife of Bath is concerned about; in order to achieve mastery over her husband, she must sacrifice both her chastity *and* her reputation. While neither of these attributes seems important to the Wife, the fact that she rails against the Church's constrictive attitudes of chastity and marriage in her prologue indicates her disgust with these views. Furthermore, in the "Wife of Bath's Tale," the loathsome old woman needs only one opportunity at marriage to gain mastery over her dream husband, the handsome young knight; the Wife, though, relates not one but five distinct marriages, and even with the fifth she achieves only a fraction of the type of union she has in mind. Despite numerous attempts, then, the Wife has yet to achieve the complete dominance she seeks.

Makyne, however, does not need to marry Robene to gain mastery over him; she pledges that she will surrender her maidenhood, but he never asks her for it. Instead, the girl needs only to offer and entice, and this is enough to gain her domain. As Scott notes:

> Instead of the maid being the victim of the seducer, here Makyne clearly is the aggressive party, first in rousing the sluggish Robene's interest and then rejecting his advances because they come too late—and, one suspects, because they come at his will instead of her own. There is a parody here of the medieval convention that what woman wanted was to rule man.[22]

If what Scott notes is true, that Makyne is both sexual aggressor and controlling shrew who later rejects Robene, then what, exactly, is the parody at work here? If Makyne uses her sexuality to gain some sense of mastery over the man, then is that not a straight-out portrayal of the genre rather than an inversion of it? How is it that Henryson is burlesquing this fifth literary tradition, itself born in a lampooning of courtly love? Scott never says, but the answer is in what Makyne does after she gains mastery over Robene: she goes home. In other words, though Robene surrenders control to her (and this is what many critics including Scott have suspected she has wanted all along), why doesn't she utilize this control to gain what she wants? After all, if she is playing a type of "control" game, then the prize—her precious maidenhood—could prove costly for her should Robene have accepted when she first offered it to him. If control, and not love, is her intention, then Makyne dangerously gambles with a valuable commodity; true, she wins in the end, but it is an unexpected victory, and in fact, both the audience as well as she must be puzzled as to why Robene turned her down three times in the first place.

I propose that Makyne's decision is born out of revenge and spite (the desire to hurt the man who has previously rejected her), and perhaps, if this poem had further stanzas, she may later regret that decision, too. Thus, a momentary decision, coupled with the desire for revenge, has given to her what years of sexual battery and learning in the romantic arts could not achieve for the Wife of Bath: namely, control and respect, mastery over man without the sacrifice of maidenhood. Yet these rewards are fleeting, and therein lies the nature of the burlesque; Henryson seems to note that the unfortunate woman cannot have both, at least not for long, and must choose one or the other. Given Makyne's ultimate decision to retain her chastity and Henryson's own moralist nature, it is quite likely that we find here another literary convention coming under the humorously disapproving gaze of the moralist *makar*.

ELOQUENCE, MORALITY, AND THE BURLESQUE

In the thirteenth century, St. Thomas Aquinas cautioned against "secular eloquence," stating that

> He who strives principally after eloquence does not intend that men should admire what he says, but strives rather to gain their admiration for himself. Eloquence, however, is commendable when the speaker has no desire to display himself but wishes only to benefit his listeners.[23]

Boccaccio, Boethius, and Chaucer all strove to ensure that morality accompanied their poetry and prose, so that each of their works, to varying degrees, reflected Aquinas's attitudes regarding literature and morality.

Henryson has long been seen as the medieval poet who affirms Aquinas's view time and again, and **"Robene and Makyne"** has often been read in a conservative, moralistic sense. Yet, as I have demonstrated, this traditional interpretation of a moralist Henryson falls short in this burlesque poem, whose zealous and infectious joy and inversion of poetic convention implies a man more concerned with form than substance. Clearly, the poet does not hold faith in the moral implications of these five traditions; however, the fact that carnality is not recognized in the poem, but instead rejected, is not enough to dictate that the poem rejects a carnal reading. Makyne was fully prepared to surrender her maidenhood to Robene; it is only his brief reticence that halts the sexual proceedings, and although Henryson burlesques sexual poetic convention, he does not present a clear moral alternative. There is no high road in **"Robene and Makyne"**; lust and temptation are replaced by revenge, not temperance. Thus, morality is present, but Henryson relates to the reader first and foremost his admiration for firm principles before showing his disapproval of the moral systems some courtly genres express.

I have demonstrated that Henryson's **"Robene and Makyne"** through its inversion of five separate literary traditions—the courtly love poem, the *pastourelle*, the *carpe diem* tradition, the elegiac tradition, and the medieval convention that what women most wanted was to have mastery over their husbands—is a stylistic achievement in the burlesque of both poetry and morality. Henryson's complex, measured comedy lampoons several of the poetic traditions of his time, and while mocking the values they represent, he also demonstrates his respect for the conventions from which they derive. Thus, as Fox notes, poetry is not abandoned for the sake of morality, but rather, inspired poetry works to form a measured if understated morality that goes hand-in-hand with the "sometimes dour" but always even-handed moralist and excellent poet that the Scottish *makar* Henryson has come to be known as today.

Notes

The author wishes to thank Allan Maclaine for his contributions to and guidance toward writing this essay.

1. Robert L. Kindrick, *Robert Henryson* (Detroit: Twayne-G. K. Hall, 1979): 163.

2. I put the word "charming" in quotes not to indicate that it is a direct quote but rather merely to note that perhaps every Henryson critic I have come across uses this word to describe the poem.

3. Denton Fox, *Testament of Cresseid* (London: Thomas Nelson and Sons, 1968): 39.

4. All quoted material comes from Fox, ed. *The Poems of Robert Henryson* (Oxford: Clarendon Press, 1981) and will from now on be marked, ac-

cordingly, within the text of this essay. The earliest surviving copy of *Robene and Makyne* is in the National Library of Scotland, MS 1. i. 6, c. 1568. Most scholars agree that dating the poem is nearly impossible, but when pressed, they place it in the 1470s.

5. Allan H. Maclaine, "Burlesque as a Satiric Method in the Poems and Songs of Burns," *Scottish Literary Journal* 13.1 (1984): 30-46.

6. Tom Scott, "Henrysoun: The Minor Poems," from an unpublished and unfinished work on Scottish literature, part of which is now available through the Robert Henryson Society and Glasgow University's Scottish Teaching and Research Network (STARN), which can be found on the web at: http://www2.arts.gla.ac.uk/COMET/starn/henryson/tscott/minpoems.htm.

7. See also Fox, "The Scottish Chaucerians," 164-200 (179) in *Chaucer and Chaucerians: Critical Studies in Middle English Literature*. Ed. Derek S. Brewer (Tuscaloosa, Alabama: University of Alabama Press, 1966).

8. See Dorothy Everett, *Essays on Middle English Literature* (Oxford: Clarendon Press, 1955): 16.

9. Scott, note 6, above, 1.

10. Scott, 2.

11. Fox, *The Poems of Robert Henryson,* 469.

12. Fox also notes a strong connection between *Robene and Makyne* and the traditional ballad, especially in the poem's alternating tetrameter and trimeter rhyme scheme and in its short narrative style. However, one could hardly argue that Henryson is satirizing a ballad, a form that defies burlesque since it encompasses almost any convention. Nonetheless, it is interesting to note another literary genre that the poet was perhaps including in his work.

13. The poem is taken from William D. Paden, trans. and ed. *The Medieval Pastourelle* (New York: Garland Publishing, Inc., 1987).

14. Seize the day; trust tomorrow as little as possible. As quoted from Eduard Fraenkel, *Horace* (Oxford: Clarendon Press, 1957): iv.

15. Stanley B. Greenfield, *Continuations and Beginnings: Studies in Old English Literature.* Ed. Eric Gerald Stanley (London: Routledge, 1966): 143.

16. For more on this subject, see John MacQueen, *Robert Henryson: A Study of the Major Narrative Poems* (Oxford: Clarendon Press, 1967).

17. Thomas Perrin Harrison, Jr. *The Pastoral Elegy: An Anthology* (Austin, TX: University of Texas Press, 1939): 8.

18. The quoted text from *The Wanderer* is taken from Frederick G. Cassidy and Richard N. Ringler, *Bright's Old English Grammar and Reader* (Fort Worth: Harcourt Brace Jovanovich College Publishers, 1971): 361-71 (371). The translation by Richard Hamer is from Michael Alexander and Felicity Riddy, *St. Martin's Anthologies of English Literature: The Middle Ages* (New York: St. Martin's Press, 1989): 92-99 (99).

19. Cassidy, 330.

20. All text comes from Geoffrey Chaucer, *The Wife of Bath*. Ed. Peter G. Beidler (Boston: Bedford Books, 1996). From now on, the text shall be cited within the essay.

21. Text cited from Kate Aughterson, *Renaissance Women: Constructions of Femininity in England* (London: Routledge, 1995): 73-74.

22. Scott, 1.

23. Quoted text from Thomas Aquinas, *The Selected Writings of St. Thomas Aquinas*. Trans. Robert P. Goodwin (New York: Prentice Hall, 1965): 67.

FURTHER READING

Criticism

Benson, C. David. "Critic and Poet: What Lydgate and Henryson Did to Chaucer's *Troilus and Criseyde*." In *Writing after Chaucer: Essential Readings in Chaucer and the Fifteenth Century,* edited by Daniel J. Pinti, pp. 227-41. New York: Garland Publishing, Inc., 1998.
    Discusses Henryson's and John Lydgate's appropriation of Chaucer's work.

Cullen, Mairi Ann. "Cresseid Excused: A Re-Reading of Henryson's *Testament of Cresseid.*" *Studies in Scottish Literature* 20 (1985): 137-59.
    Addresses criticism of the main character's morality in *The Testament of Cresseid.*

Fox, Denton. Introduction to *The Poems of Robert Henryson,* edited by Denton Fox, pp. xliii-cxxiii. Oxford: Clarendon Press, 1981.
    Provides a detailed overview of Henryson's life and work.

Godman, Peter. "Henryson's Masterpiece." *Review of English Studies* n.s. 35, no. 139 (August 1984): 291-300.
    Refutes claims that *The Testament of Cresseid* is a flawed masterpiece.

Gray, Douglas. "Dunfermline and Beyond." In *Robert Henryson,* pp. 1-30. Leiden, The Netherlands: E. J. Brill, 1979.
    Discusses how the intellectual setting of fifteenth-century Scotland influenced Henryson's writing.

Johnson, Ian. "Hellish Complexity in Henryson's *Orpheus*." *Forum for Modern Language Studies* 38, no. 4 (October 2002): 412-19.
    Examines the use of vernacular language in Henryson's *Orpheus and Eurydice.*

Kindrick, Robert L. *Henryson and the Medieval Arts of Rhetoric.* New York: Garland Publishing, Inc., 1993, 345 p.
    Presents a book-length study on the influence of medieval rhetoric on Henryson's writing.

———. "Henryson's 'Uther Quair' Again: A Possible Candidate and the Nature of the Tradition." *Chaucer Review* 33, no. 2 (1998): 190-220.
    Explores the sources for Henryson's *Testament of Cresseid.*

McDiarmid, Matthew P. "The Shorter Poems and 'Ane Schort Conclusioun.'" In *Robert Henryson,* pp. 117-25. Edinburgh: Scottish Academic Press, 1981.
    Examines Henryson's shorter poems.

Pittock, Malcolm. "The Complexity of Henryson's *The Testament of Cresseid.*" *Essays in Criticism* 40, no. 3 (July 1990): 198-221.
    Analyzes the differing critical interpretations of *The Testament of Cresseid.*

Additional coverage of Henryson's life and career is contained in the following sources published by Thomson Gale: *British Writers Supplement,* Vol. 7; *Dictionary of Literary Biography,* Vol. 146; *Literature Criticism from 1400 to 1800,* Vols. 20, 110; *Literature Resource Center*; and *Reference Guide to English Literature,* Ed. 2.

Edward Lear
1812-1888

(Also wrote under the pseudonym Derry Down Derry)
English poet, artist, and travel writer.

INTRODUCTION

Although a landscape painter by profession, Edward Lear is best known for his "nonsense" poetry. Lear is also credited with popularizing the limerick; his prolific output of limerick-style nonsense verse topped 200 poems. Some of these poems have become classics of children's literature, including "The Owl and the Pussy-Cat" and "The Pelican Chorus."

BIOGRAPHICAL INFORMATION

Lear was born May 12, 1812, to Jeremiah Lear and Ann Skerrett Lear, the twentieth of their twenty-one children. The Lear family lived in Holloway, a suburb of London. When Lear was very young the family suffered extreme financial difficulties. The family home was rented out, and the four-year-old Lear was sent to live with his oldest sister, Ann, whom he stayed with for the rest of his childhood. Around the age of seven he had his first epileptic seizure, one of several health problems that would plague him throughout his life. Lear did not attend school, and he was self-taught in his first vocation as an artist. By the age of sixteen he was supporting himself and Ann by selling his art, primarily anatomical natural history sketches.

In 1832, Lear published his first collection of drawings, *Illustrations of the Family of Psittacidae, or Parrots.* The work was to have far-reaching consequences: Edward Stanley, who would become the earl of Derby, admired the book and asked Lear to draw the animals at his family estate. Lear's relationship with the family provided the inspiration for the nonsense verse that eventually made him famous. He stayed with Stanley's extended family at Knowsley Hall periodically between 1832 and 1837, enjoying the earl's valuable patronage and meeting wealthy aristocrats very far out of his own social class. Eventually, however, Lear's poor health—particularly his asthma—made it necessary for him to leave England. The earl of Derby financed his removal to Rome, where he lived for the next ten years practicing his craft as a landscape painter. While in Rome he also compiled and published his first *Book of Nonsense*

(1846), using the pseudonym Derry Down Derry, as well as the *Gleanings from the Menagerie and Aviary at Knowsley Hall* (1846).

Political tensions compelled Lear to leave Italy in 1848, and he traveled for some months throughout the Mediterranean. In March 1849 he came to Malta, where he met Franklin Lushington, and the two traveled together through Greece. Many biographers believe Lear fell in love with Lushington, a love his friend never requited during their forty-year relationship. He returned to England in June of that year and met the poet Alfred Tennyson and his wife Emily. Lear set some of Tennyson's poetry to music, and Tennyson wrote a poem for Lear. He also became very close to Emily, who remained one of his dearest friends and confidants throughout his life. He began to study painting at the Royal Academy while publishing the journals from his travels, including *Journals of a Landscape Painter in Albania, &c.* (1851) and *Journals of a Landscape Painter in Southern Calabria &c.* (1852).

Eventually, however, the unfriendly English climate took its toll on Lear's health; he cut his studies at the Royal Academy short and returned to the Mediterranean, settling in Corfu in 1855. In Corfu, Lear was close to Lushington, who worked for the government there, but he did not stay long. During this time he traveled extensively throughout the region, visiting England periodically, and occasionally resettling elsewhere. In 1856 he hired a manservant, Giorgio Kokali, who accompanied Lear for the next twenty-seven years, until Kokali died in 1883. Lear published an enlarged edition of the *Book of Nonsense* in 1861, and his sister Ann died that same year. In 1862 his friendship with Gussie Bethell evolved into a romance. The courtship lasted for four years, concluding when Lear considered proposing marriage. Lear consulted Bethell's sister Emma, and at her suggestion he abandoned his plan. He had, by this time, left Corfu for the last time and established himself at Cannes, which served as his base until 1870, when he decided to settle in San Remo, Italy. He named his new home Villa Emily, after Emily Tennyson. He published the last of his travel journals that year, *Journal of a Landscape Painter in Corsica,* as well as a new volume of poems, entitled *Nonsense Songs, Stories, Botany, and Alphabets.* Two years later he published *More Nonsense, Pictures, Rhymes, Botany, Etc.* (1872) before embarking on further travels, including trips through Egypt, India, and Ceylon.

Lear's last collection of poetry, *Laughable Lyrics: A Fourth Book of Nonsense Poems, Songs, Botany, Music, Etc.,* appeared in 1877. He continued traveling while maintaining a home base in San Remo, visiting England for one last summer in 1881. In 1886 he became very ill with bronchitis, and did not ever fully recover. That year he wrote his last poem, the autobiographical nonsense verse "Incidents in the Life of My Uncle Arly." Close friends, including Gussie Bethell and Franklin Lushington, visited him in San Remo while he was ailing, but he died alone January 29, 1888. He was buried in San Remo.

MAJOR POETIC WORKS

Lear published several travel journals and a smattering of natural history illustrations, but his four books of nonsense poetry are the source of his reputation as an author. Lear himself labeled his works "nonsense," but the term was not intended as dismissive so much as an indication that the subject matter and language would stray beyond Victorian propriety and reason. The earlier poems are most often based on the limerick, a verse form that had become popular in the 1820s. Though not yet called "limericks," the poems were distinguished not only by their recognizable rhyme and metric scheme, but also the content, often focusing on a peculiar person from a specific location, such as "the old man from Tobago" or "a fat man from Bombay." The limerick is the chief style of poetry found in Lear's *A Book of Nonsense* and in *More Nonsense.*

Lear distinguished the mere "nonsense" of the limerick books from the *Nonsense Songs* of 1870. These are longer poems with stronger characterization and deeper emotion, and they tend to be Lear's best known and loved. In *Nonsense Songs* Lear published "The Owl and the Pussy-cat," "The Duck and the Kangaroo," "The Jumblies," and similar stories of unlikely traveling companions who seem to be flouting, in various ways, the expectations of their home communities. There are shades of unhappiness in some of the poems from *Nonsense Songs,* either in the discontent that sends the travelers wandering or in the unwanted results of their travels, but many of the characters also evince a sweet and simple happiness.

In *Laughable Lyrics* Lear's nonsense turns darker. "The Dong with a Luminous Nose" revisits the voyage of "The Jumblies," emphasizing the loss experienced by those left behind. "The Courtship of the Yonghy-Bonghy-Bò," a story of lost love, has often been interpreted by biographers and critics as an expression of Lear's sadness over his failed romance with Gussie Bethell. If *Laughable Lyrics* is generally sadder than Lear's earlier work, it is also more nonsensical, featuring more invented locations and creatures, such as the Quangle Wangle, who lived alone on his Crumpetty Tree. The Quangle Wangle, the Bò, and other nonsense characters reflect the autobiographical aspects of Lear's longer nonsense verse: self-deprecating, at turns playful and melancholy, and driven by wanderlust.

CRITICAL RECEPTION

Though Lear called his work "nonsense," critics have responded to his work seriously, with an appreciation for Lear's facility with language and his varied sense of humor, both verbal and visual. Critics have often used the term "limerick" to describe Lear's short poems. Although William Harmon acknowledges the poet's familiarity with popular limerick books of the 1820s, he argues that Lear was not attempting to write in the limerick mode and that his limerick-type poems plainly deviate from the classic model. The question of Lear's usage of the limerick bears on the social function of nonsense poetry and the purpose it served. Priscilla Ord's study of Lear's limerick-based verse indicates that nonsense verse such as the limerick was often part of extemporaneous games at family parties, not unlike the setting at the Derby estate where Lear started writing. While the place names typically found in the first lines of the rhymes have led some critics to suggest that the verses were learning aids for the earl's children while studying geography, the common social venue for the limerick, and Lear's own insistence that they were pure nonsense, suggest otherwise. Even so, according to John Rieder, the verses function on behalf of children, opening an imaginative space for children to be free from rules and parental expectations.

Thematic studies of Lear's work have naturally tended to focus on the longer poems. Scholar Ina Rae Hark has identified loss, especially loss of love, as a dominant theme in the longer poems; as Hark explains, the characters of the longer poems are open to a psychological complexity not available to characters in Lear's four-line nonsense verse. In her study of such poems as "The Owl and the Pussy-cat," Hark also highlights repressed sexual themes, noting Lear's use of phallic imagery and an undercurrent of sexual ambivalence. Many critics have called for greater attention to Lear's illustrations, which often add another layer of meaning to his poems, through facial expressions and other physical features that underscore or sometimes belie the words of the verses. Kirby Olson notes "[t]he drawings fill out, rather than illustrate, the poems." Lear's poetry has often been compared to the nonsense verse of Lewis Carroll. However, Olson notes that, unlike Carroll, "Lear apparently sought merely to entertain or cheer up his young listeners, and entertain himself in the process, before moving on."

PRINCIPAL WORKS

Poetry

A Book of Nonsense 2 vols. [as Derry Down Derry] 1846; enlarged edition [as Edward Lear], 1861
Nonsense Songs, Stories, Botany, and Alphabets 1870
More Nonsense, Pictures, Rhymes, Botany, Etc. 1872
Laughable Lyrics: A Fourth Book of Nonsense Poems, Songs, Botany, Music, Etc. 1877
Queery Leary Nonsense: A Lear Nonsense Book [edited by Lady Constance Strachey] 1911
The Complete Nonsense Book [edited by Lady Constance Strachey] 1929
The Complete Nonsense of Edward Lear [edited by Holbrook Jackson] 1947
Teapots and Quails, and Other New Nonsenses [edited by Angus Davidson and Philip Hofer] 1953
Lear in the Original: Drawings and Limericks 1975
The Complete Verse and Other Nonsense [edited by Vivien Noakes] 2002

Other Major Works

Illustrations of the Family of Psittacidae, or Parrots (drawings) 1832
Views in Rome and Its Environs: Drawn from Nature and on Stone (drawings) 1841
Gleanings from the Menagerie and Aviary at Knowsley Hall (drawings) 1846
Illustrated Excursions in Italy 2 vols. (drawings) 1846
Journals of a Landscape Painter in Albania, &c. (journal) 1851
Journals of a Landscape Painter in Southern Calabria &c. (journal) 1852
Indian Journal: Watercolours and Extracts from the Diary of Edward Lear (1873-1875) (journal) 1853
Views in the Seven Ionian Islands (drawings) 1863
Journal of a Landscape Painter in Corsica (journal) 1870
Tortoises, Terrapins, and Turtles Drawn from Life [with James de Carle Sowerby] (drawings) 1872
Letters of Edward Lear [edited by Lady Constance Strachey] (letters) 1907
Later Letters of Edward Lear [edited by Lady Constance Strachey] (letters) 1911
Edward Lear in the Levant: Travels in Albania, Greece and Turkey in Europe, 1848-1849 [edited by Susan Hyman] (journals) 1988
Edward Lear: Selected Letters [edited by Vivien Noakes] (letters) 1988

CRITICISM

Holbrook Jackson (essay date 1947)

SOURCE: Jackson, Holbrook. Introduction to *The Complete Nonsense of Edward Lear*, pp. ix-xxviii. London: Faber and Faber Limited, 1961.

[*In the following essay, first published in 1947, Jackson emphasizes the autobiographical aspects of Lear's poetry and remarks on Lear's talent for verbal invention.*]

1

Just over a hundred years ago the children of England (and also many older folk) were surprised into entertainment by the appearance 'out of the blue' of an oblong book of hilarious rhymes and still more hilarious pictures by an author hitherto unknown to the general public. This fantastic collection of rhymes-without-reason was an instantaneous success, and Edward Lear's *Book of Nonsense* had given a local habitation and a name to one of the oldest and most persistent of human faculties. Its author, like an earlier poet, awoke to find himself famous—but in an entirely different branch of art from that by which he sought to earn a living, and he remains its unchallenged laureate. The literature of nonsense has grown in quality as well as quantity during the past century but the whole-hearted abandonment of sense, as formalised by Edward Lear, is still the classical example of this curious and amusing art.

There are several ways of approaching the fine arts and particularly that of an artist so peculiar as Edward Lear, for although the entertainment value of the **Book of Nonsense** and its pendants is obvious, the personality and motives behind that work will repay examination. Such an examination is tempting because Lear was no ordinary writer turning out humorous books for a living, nor were those books his only productions; on the contrary his nonsense began as the sideline of a professional life devoted to the illustration of books, mainly ornithological, and the pursuit of the picturesque for those landscapes which were latterly his main source of revenue. At the same time nonsense was not merely an occasional, still less an idle occupation. What appeared to begin and end in the casual amusement of children was actually a method of amusing, or, better, diverting himself. His excursions into the realm of nonsense were certainly occasional but the occasions were so frequent as to pervade the whole of his life, ultimately becoming a continuous as well as a formal medium of expression. Nonsense was the safety-valve of his consciousness responding to most of his approaches to himself and his environment. It became ultimately a world in itself specially created by him as a refuge from the trials and irritations of life: ill-health, lack of means, and, above all, an over-strung sensibility. Nonsense was thus Lear's Ivory Tower and it was far more accessible than most retreats of the kind and its peace could be enjoyed without fuss or ceremony in most emergencies. It was as though he lived a double life, one in the realm of sense and the other in that of nonsense; and he had the power of transmuting himself from one to the other at will, a gift which he exercised almost continuously as his familiar letters prove. Most of those who know the **Book of Nonsense** and even one or more of the sequels think of Lear solely as writer and illustrator of amusing limericks; but that was only one form of his nonsense. In addition and equally important are his nonsense alphabets and vocabularies, poems and pictures, which comprise nonsense geography, natural history, botany, and anthropology. He depended largely upon his own subconscious promptings for the flora and fauna of this funny cosmogony, but was not averse from annexing birds and animals from nature which happened to approximate to his own nonsensical conceptions. Thus pelicans and parrots, seals and rhinoceroses and other queer creatures associated appropriately with his Dongs and Pobbles and Quangle-Wangles:

Herons and Gulls and Cormorants black
Cranes and Flamingoes with scarlet back,
Plovers and Storks, and Geese in clouds,
Swans and Dilberry Ducks in crowds.

He even nonsensified himself and his cat in verse, and in those humorous drawings which are a characteristic and happy feature of a large number of his letters to intimate friends.

2

There was something preposterous about Edward Lear, amiably preposterous. He might have stepped out of one of his own nonsense books, and he seemed to know it and to make the most of it. He pokes fun at himself even when he is serious, and his letters dance with caricatures of his own plump figure, high-domed brow, and bushy whiskers. By profession he was a painter of birds and landscapes, by habit a wanderer, a humorist and a grumbler. He was, in fact, an artist, and if he had not been forced to fritter away his life in earning a living, he might have been a greater artist in his chosen profession of topographical illustrator. Instead of that he became famous for his side-lines—the sketches in water-colour incidental to his finished paintings, as well as to the nonsense rhymes and pictures which were his quaint lines of communication with his friends and their children, but which were themselves developed from an involuntary need for whimsical expression. Some inner conflict, aggravated by indifferent health and insufficient wealth drove him to cut capers with words and images and ideas. And so, by accident he becomes the laureate of nonsense, objectivising for his own relief and, as it happens, for our delight, that wilfulness which ever kept him a child in a world that was already in its second childhood.

He was born at Highgate on the 12th May 1812, and died in 1888 at San Remo, on the Italian Riviera where he had lived for eighteen years with his Albanian servant, Georgio Kokali, who had served him for nearly thirty years, and his famous cat, Foss, who had predeceased him by a few months at the advanced age of seventeen years.

Lear was the youngest of a family of twenty-one children, most of whom he outlived. Of the twenty-one, thirteen were girls and Edward was brought up by Ann, the eldest, who continued to mother him until her death when he was nearly fifty. His father was a stockbroker of Danish descent who speculated his way from affluence on Highgate Hill to poverty and the King's Bench Prison. His mother came from Durham, and was presumably English. Edward also attributed a liking for Irish character to the influence of a 'Gt.Gt.Gt.Gt.Gt.Gt. grandfather' of Irish blood. So, remembering Hans Andersen, who was a Dane, and the supposed humour of Ireland, one may argue that Danish and Irish blood is a good mixture for the production of that kind of humorous fantasy which he called nonsense. But whatever his descent, Edward Lear possessed many of the characteristics of the more eccentric of wandering Englishmen, and neither he nor his peculiar brand of humour could have been produced anywhere but in England, the birthplace of the *Ingoldsby Legends,* the *Bab Ballads,* and *Alice in Wonderland.*

He never married; there is no evidence that he was attracted to women except as friends, and his works, literary and graphic, are as sexless as the artistic efforts of a child. He occasionally puzzles over the problem of marriage as he puzzles over so many things which are not quite obvious, but when he is in his forty-first year he rebukes any impulse to that end by reflecting that if he married he would 'paint less and less well', and further, this most determined and illustrious entertainer of children puts it on record that the thought of 'annual infants' of his own drives him 'wild'. In the same letter he argues as many bachelors, scared at the idea of a lonely old age, have done before him: 'If I attain to 65, and have an "establishment" with lots of spoons, etc., to offer—I *may* chain myself:—but surely not before. And alas! and seriously—when I look around my acquaintances—and few men have more, or know more intimately, do I see a majority of happy pairs? No, I don't. Single—I may have few pleasures—but married—many risks and miseries are semi-certainly in waiting—nor till the plot is played out can it be said that evils are not at hand.' Fear of matrimony is evidently a recurring whimsy, whose continued presence is revealed ten years later when he is living in Corfu, where he is attracted by a native girl and wishes, playfully, he were 'married to a clever good nice fat little Greek girl—and had 25 olive trees, some goats and a house'. 'But', he adds, 'the above girl, happily for herself, likes somebody else,' and there the matter ended and Edward Lear makes the pilgrimage of life alone, though not without friends, and the friendship of faithful servants, and the seventeen year long companionship of 'Old Foss', the cat, amusingly immortalised in so many of his drawings.

Although his education, according to modern standards, was inadequate, and he was earning a living as a commercial artist at fifteen, he managed to accumulate considerable culture. He could read or talk in at least half-a-dozen languages, including Greek both ancient and modern; and in addition to his skill as a painter of landscapes and his technical exactitude as an illustrator of birds, he composed and sang songs, wrote light verses, kept long diaries, wrote innumerable letters, and gave a new idiom to humorous drawing. He must also have had a gift for communicating his skill for at one time he was the art-master of Queen Victoria.

3

Those nonsense drawings and their attendant verse and prose reveal an invincible boyishness. On one side Lear was as old as the rocks he painted, on another as young as the children he loved or the child he awoke in the adults who loved him. This plump, bewhiskered man with high-domed brow, small, spectacled eyes and loose-fitting clothes was ineradicably childlike, although he must have looked what he would have called an 'old cove' nearly all his life. But in spite of that there was something of him that would not grow up: his peterpan-theism was no pose. There was an unusual physical expression of this fortunate anomaly of prolonged adolescence. At the age of forty-one, the year, it will be recalled, in which the idea of marriage began to puzzle him, he 'cut two new teeth', and, after the attendant discomforts of this event, at first thought to be mumps, there was a renewal of health and spirits which he attributed to the belated infantile phenomenon.

Attempts at portraiture are fortunately unnecessary, for Lear loved self-dramatisation and has left several personal glimpses, both literary and graphic, the best of all that full-length self-portrait in verse which introduces this collection of his nonsense.

4

His varied gifts and dual character were encouraged by the manner of his upbringing, and although we have no cause for complaint, Edward Lear was always conscious of some masculine inadequacy. 'Brought up by women—and badly besides—and ill always,' he had no chance of 'manly improvements or exercise'. Yet, he says, 'I am always thanking God that I was never educated, for it seems to me that 999 of those who are so, expensively and laboriously, have lost all before they arrive at my age (47)—and remain like Swift's Strulbruggs—cut and dry for life,' whereas he seemed always to be on 'the threshold of knowledge'. Much as he loved quietness, inwardly and outwardly, he could not be still. He never lost the restlessness of childhood, and as he could not achieve the inward calm he craved, he denied its existence: 'As for content that is a loathesome slimy humbug—fit only for potatoes, very fat hogs—and fools generally. Let us pray fervently that we may never become such asses as to be contented.'

One of the most surprising things about him is that he managed to combine roving habits and impecuniosity with a considerable social status. It surprise even Lear himself. He cannot understand how 'such an asinine beetle' could have made so many friends. 'The immense variety of class and caste which I daily came in contact with in those days, would be a curious fact even in the life of a fool.' Many of his friends were patricians or 'swells', as he called them, and if he had wished he could have spent much more time than he did in the houses of the great and affluent, but being social rather than gregarious, he hated the 'bustle and lights and fuss of society' and soon tired of being a *flâneur*. Yet, pursued as he was by the demon of boredom, he must have friends as well as work, and contriving to enjoy both he went his grumbling, but, on the whole, cheerful way always rather surprised that 'such a queer beast' should have so many friends, and whimsically resentful at the drudgery which temperament and circumstances imposed upon him.

5

No more diligent artist ever lived. He had the concentration of a beaver and never liked parting with a job once he had started to gnaw it. During fifty years of his busy life, for instance, he made 200 illustrations for Tennyson's poems, but did not live to see any of them published.[1] Sometimes he suspected this laboriousness although he looked upon a 'totally unbroken application to poetical-topographical painting and drawing' as the 'universal panacea for the ills of life'.

The number of drawings he turned out on a sketching tour was astounding. In one year alone (1865) his 'outdoor work' comprised, '200 sketches in Crete, 145 in "the Corniche", and 125 at Nice, Antibes and Cannes.' He goes to India and in six months despatches to England 'no less than 560 drawings, large and small besides 9 small sketch books and 4 journals'. He was then sixty-two and described himself, with some justice, as 'a very energetic and frisky old cove'. When not travelling in search of the picturesque or working up his sketches, he is holding exhibitions of drawings and paintings from the sale of which he lived, or writing to his friends and patrons about work in progress and the attendant economic problems which were never entirely absent, and any spare time was devoted to the diaries which he kept for years, and those travel books[2] which he illustrated with some of his best drawings.

He lived to draw and paint and drew and painted to live, pretending to hate the necessity of having to go on day after day 'grinding' his 'nose off'. But although he talked little of art as such, and affected to belittle his own inspiration, his artistry was more than technique and it is a criticism of criticism that his drawings, particularly those in black and white and water-colours, should have been sidetracked rather than assessed. His habit of under-statement, as in the case of Anthony Trollope, is responsible for some of the posthumous neglect of his graphic work. His trick of looking upon himself as a recorder and 'topographer' rather than a creator, has been taken too literally. Self-depreciation was not a pose. Lear was as puzzled about his gifts as he was about marriage, or, indeed, about life. Conscious of 'being influenced to an extreme by everything in natural and physical life, i.e. atmosphere, light, shadow, and all the varieties of day and night', he wondered whether it was 'a blessing or the contrary', but decided, wisely enough, that 'things must be as they may, and the best is to make the best of what happens'. Like Pangloss he concludes that all is for the best in the best of all possible worlds and he certainly makes the best of this sensitiveness before the picturesque, grumbling much but demanding little beyond 'quiet and repose' so that he could get on with his work.

His idea of heaven is a place of charming landscapes without noise or fuss. 'When I go to heaven, if indeed I go—and am surrounded by thousands of polite angels—I shall say courteously "please leave me alone:—you are doubtless all delightful, but I do not wish to become acquainted with you;—let me have a park and a beautiful view of sea and hill, mountain and river, valley and plain, with no end of tropical foliage:—a few well-behaved cherubs to cook and keep the place clean—and—after I am quite established—say for a million or two years—an angel of a wife. Above all let there be no hens! No, not one! I give up eggs and roast chickens for ever".'

6

Uncertainty of income (for even the patronage of rich friends does not stabilise his finances) predisposes him to wish for a sinecure, and when, in 1863, Greece took to herself a king, Lear requests his friend Fortescue (afterwards Lord Carlingford) to 'write to Lord Palmerston to ask him to ask the Queen to ask the King of Greece to give' him a 'place' specially created, the title to be 'Lord High Bosh and Nonsense Producer . . . with permission to wear a fool's cap (or mitre)—three pounds of butter yearly and a little pig,—and a small donkey to ride on'. Before that, rumour having raised Mr. Gladstone to the Hellenic throne, Lear had threatened to 'write to Mr. G. for the appointment of Painter Laureate, and Grand Peripatetic Ass and Boshproducing Luminary' to the Greek Court.

The problem of finance was a constant irritant, and his wish to stabilise his income, though couched in the Learian nonsense idiom, was none the less a reality. But although he was chronically short of cash, he was never actually destitute or even poor. It was the lack of regular income rather than poverty which gave him a permanent feeling of insecurity. He was thus forced by circumstances to think unduly about money. Such a condition might have made him thrifty, which is often the first step to miserliness; but he was as generous as he was poor and continually helped the still poorer members of his family and others less closely related. 'I only wish for money to give it away,' is no idle boast, as we know from the records of many generous acts. His books contribute little to his variable income and it is to his landscapes that he turns for subsistence. He becomes a travelling showman of his own works, for at Corfu or Valetta or San Remo, he holds exhibitions, and in his later years there was a small permanent show of his pictures at Foord's Gallery in Wardour Street. But customers are shy and they do not always pay promptly. The position would have been still worse but for the support of regular patrons. His old friends are ever ready to help and to enlist the help of their friends, but even then there are lean periods, for, alas, 'private patronage must end in the natural course of things, but eating and drinking and clothing go on disagreeably continually.' Like William Blake he began his career as an illustrator of the works of others, and it was as a delineator of birds for the ornithologist John Gould that he attracted the attention of Edward Stanley, thirteenth Earl of Derby, the Whig statesman and scholar, known to literature as Bulwer Lytton's 'Rupert of debate'. Lord Derby engaged him to illustrate a book on the menagerie which was then a show-piece of the Stanley demesne at Knowsley near Liverpool. This commission was momentous, for it earned him the lifelong patronage of the noble family which has done many more serviceable things than lend its name to the most famous horse race in the world, not least the befriending of the quaint 'cove' whose work has already outlived the fame of his first kindly and illustrious patron. Edward Lear worked for no less than four successive Earls of Derby—but, more important still, he worked or rather played for the children in the household of his first patron, and by so doing achieved immortality. The first **Book of Nonsense** was composed to amuse the grandchildren, nephews and nieces of the thirteenth earl, to whose 'great-grandchildren, grand-nephews and grand-nieces', it is dedicated.

7

If ever a gifted man worked for a living it was Edward Lear, and, although he joked about his journeys, they were not jaunts but professional expeditions in search of the picturesque, with the object of turning it into marketable landscapes. He is in fact a pictorial merchant: a later Dr. Syntax—in search of a living. Scenery is the raw material of his trade. When trekking across Albania he is glad to leave the district of Peupli for Akhrida, where he hopes the scenery will be 'more valuable'. He is, as he declares in his *Corsican Journal,* a 'wandering painter—whose life's occupation is travelling for pictorial and topographic purposes'. But although he always makes a virtue of necessity, work is life to him. He fears idleness because it exposes him to boredom, and if he is capable of enduring the prophylactic of drudgery, he has no liking for the sedentary side of painting: 'No life is more *shocking* to me than sitting motionless like a petrified gorilla as to my body and limbs hour after hour—my hand meanwhile, peck peck pecking at billions of little dots and lines, while

my mind is fretting and fuming through every moment of the weary day's work.'

He craves for movement as though his curiously active mind needed the companionship of an active body, for 'after all one isn't a potato', so perhaps it is better 'to run about continually like an ant'. It was nothing for him even when past his prime to walk fifteen and twenty miles a day, and to do an amount of sketching as well. The trade of landscape-painter was perhaps, after all, only the excuse for those laborious journeys in Albania, Greece, Corsica, Malta, Crete, Egypt, Corfu, Switzerland, Calabria and other parts of Italy, the French Riviera, and India. There are indications that he relished travel for its own sake and was always planning jaunts to ever more distant lands. It is probable, also, that he found in travel a means of relief from that mental stress which, as we shall see, was an underlying cause of his jocularity. The craving for movement is like a chronic desire to run away from himself. 'The more I read travels the more I want to move,' and he playfully invited his friend Fortescue to go with him to 'New Zealand, Tasmania and Lake Tchad'. As he grew older he believed that a sedentary life, after moving about as he had done for more than half a century, would 'infallibly finish' him 'off suddenly'. And although, he reflected, he might 'with equal suddenness be finished off if he moved about', he believed that 'a thorough change' would affect him 'far better rather than far worse. Whereby', he concludes, 'I shall go either to Sardinia, or India, or Jumsibobjigglequack this next winter as ever is.'

8

This restlessness was no doubt due to a nervous defect, for although Lear lived for well over seventy years, he always, and with reason, looked upon himself as an invalid and could not understand why he continued to survive after he was fifty. There was reason for these fears, whimsically as he often stated them, for he was an epileptic, and suffered also from chronic asthma and bronchitis, from which he ultimately died. But in spite of these defects, he had varying spells of comfortable health, and his ailments did not interfere with his love of wandering in strange lands, and of working continuously, and, on the whole, happily, at high pressure. At one time he is advised 'to take things easy' as he has 'the same complaint of the heart that my father died of', but there is no evidence that he took the advice. Asthma and bronchitis would have driven him to warmer and drier climates even if he had not been otherwise predisposed to travel. Some of his irascibility may be attributed to physical and nervous defects, but much of it is a normal if exaggerated love of grumbling, to which he invariably gave the characteristic Lear touch of nonsense. He is, however (after the manner of men who explode over trifles), inclined, like Walter Savage

Landor, to congratulate himself on his composure. An instance occurs after a sunstroke in Italy: 'I often thank God', he said, 'that although he has given me a nature easily worried by small matters, yet in such cases as this I go on day after day quite calmly, only thankful that I do not suffer more.'

9

He has also numerous aversions, such as noises, crowds, hustle, gaiety, fools and bores, which are doubtless valetudinarian. Once he confesses that 'barring a few exceptionals', all human beings seem to be 'awful idiots'. Yet he is neither prig nor curmudgeon, and inclined to gently scan his brother man, but he enjoys company rather than 'society'. He is a worker but not a team-worker. 'Always accustomed from a boy to go my own way uncontrolled, I cannot help fearing that I should run rusty and sulky by reason of retinues and routines.' He repudiates the term Bohemian, but has 'just so much of that nature as it is perhaps impossible the artistic and poetic beast can be born without'.

Noise is the annoyance which comes in for the full blast of his whimsical invective, and it is the misplaced sounds of children, cats, poultry and music which annoy him most. He humours this sensitiveness all over Europe. In Paris: 'all the Devils in or out of Hell! four hundred and seventy-three cats at least are all at once making an infernal row in the garden close to my window. Therefore, being mentally decomposed, I shall write no more.' At a Swiss hotel the greatest drawback is the noise of children: 'the row of forty little ill-conducted beasts is simply frightful.' At Rome: all manner of things irritate him; among them the conversion of so many to the Roman Catholic faith and Manning preaching 'most atrocious sermons . . . to which nevertheless, all heaps of fools go'. But of all objectionable noises unwanted music inspires the fullness of his powers of vituperation. In Rome 'a vile beastly rotten-headed foolbegotten pernicious priggish screaming, tearing, roaring, perplexing, splitmecrackle, crachimecriggle insane ass of a woman is practising howling below-stairs with a brute of a singing master so horribly, that my head is nearly off'. And some few years later at Corfu he is 'much distressed by next door people who had twins babies and played the violin: but one of the twins died, and the other has eaten the fiddle—so all is peace'. As usual he compensates himself for these worries with a dose of nonsense, as, for example, the thought of ultimate calm among choice friends 'under a lotus tree a eating of ice creams and pelican pie, with our feet in a hazure coloured stream with the birds and beasts of Paradise a sporting around us'.

10

These irascibilities which play so large and so amusing a part in his letters, are mere whimsies when compared with his pecuniary anxieties. Money, always in 'short supply', is a stock subject of his letters, and at times, and much against the grain, he is forced to become a borrower. He is inclined to be thrifty but does not succeed in saving more than £300 until he is past fifty, and rejoices in the thought that henceforward he will be 'entitled annually to £9'. The labour of 'hopelessly endeavouring to get in subscriptions' for one of his books, is so great that 'I abhor the sight of a pen, and if I were an angel I would immediately moult all my quills for fear of their being used in calligraphy'. He dislikes the financial aspect of his work, but in spite of a large circle of friends and acquaintances and growing reputation both as artist and humorist, the task of earning a living remains a problem and a cause of anxiety. He has long been an artistic lion, one of the 'sights' of Cannes, Valetta, Corfu—or whereever he may have pitched his studio, but his numerous visitors seem more inclined to sponge on his personal charm than to buy his pictures, and he dislikes being lionised at any time. At Malta he was 'dubbed a mystery and a savage' because he fled from the crowd of visitors who would have thronged his rooms without dreaming of spending £5 on a drawing. In a whole season he 'only got £30 from the rich Cannes public'. He had a bad winter in 1878 at San Remo, having sold but one drawing for £7, and would have 'come to grief' had it not been for two friends who bought some of his smaller oil paintings. In addition to these fluctuations in turnover, he suffers from the failure of his publisher, and his troubles are increased when the tenants of his villa at San Remo abscond owing him nearly £100.

11

He broods less upon these material worries than upon the evanescence of life and of all those things, friendship and the beauty of the earth, which are his real attachments. He is capable of consoling himself for the shortage of material possessions with a quip, but his acute sense of the shortage of time is not so easily assuaged. He attempts to soothe his temporal anxieties by resort to those apologetics which are common to all who are sensitive to evanescence. 'The fact is,' he argues, 'time is all nonsense,' and he inclines to leave it at that, resolving the incomprehensible by invincible pursuit of his chosen craft. His pictures give permanence to memories and impression and thus create a desirable illusion of timelessness. Yet the possession of a keen sense of fact will not permit him to be more than temporarily soothed by such arguments. He cannot bluff himself. He knows he is walking in the 'dusty twilight of the incomprehensible' and instinctively seeks to escape through the door of nonsense. 'I wish I were an egg and going to be hatched,' he sighs, summing up his desire for Nirvana.

12

Lear's nonsense is no mere tissue of quips and jokes. It is a thing in itself in a world of its own, with its own physiography and natural history; a world in which the nature of things has been changed, whilst retaining its own logical and consistent idiom. He expresses a nonsensical condition which is peculiar to himself and necessary to his serenity, and it may be that this fantastic world gratifies for him a desire which we all share to some extent, probably more than we are willing to admit, and which he seems to share, by anticipation, with the surrealists of our own time.

The authentic brand of nonsense is rarely absent from his letters, if no more than the fantastic spelling of a word. The art perfected in the *Nonsense Books* is here seen in the rough. It is not surprising, for instance, that the far-fetched hope of selling his Tennyson illustrations for the large sum of £18,000 should set him off. In that unlikely event, he will buy a 'chocolate coloured carriage speckled with gold, driven by a coachman in green vestments and silver spectacles wherein sitting on a lofty cushion composed of muffins and volumes of the Apocrypha', he will 'disport himself all about the London parks to the general satisfaction of all pious people, and the particular joy of Chichester, Lord Carlingford and his affectionate friend Edward Lear'. Here we have nonsense combined with humour, and there are many similar passages in the letters. In one of them he threatens to go to Darjeeling or Para and 'silently subsist on Parrot Pudding and Lizard Lozenges in chubbly contentment'. Lear is not a good sailor and once he writes from Folkestone that if the sea is rough he will hire, somewhat inconsistently, 'a pussilanimouse porpoise, and cross on his bak'. He records that one of his frequent coughs shakes off one of his toes, '2 teeth and 3 whiskers,' and he is so irritated by the doctor's concern that he orders 'a baked Barometer for dinner and 2 Thermometers stewed in treacle for supper'.

13

Lear is an adept at the game of monkeying with words. Like Rabelais and Swift and Joyce he has a genius for fantastic verbal adventures, but often they do little more than play tricks with established spelling. The more familiar the words the more he is tempted to tamper with them. The habit is ingrained, the result not alone of a natural love of the whimsical and an indomitable sense of fun, but it is also, as he himself is aware, an instinctive effort to bridge a gap between idea and expression. 'Proper and exact "epithets" always were impossible to me,' he says, 'as my thoughts are ever in advance of my words.' And here also we may discover a key to his nonsense, or 'nonsenses', as he calls them, which are perhaps ahead of rather than behind his senses.

In the first of his published letters to Fortescue, whom he likes to address as '40scue', he recounts the names of the distinguished foreigners at Rome, in 1848, as:

'Madame Pul-itz-neck-off and Count Bigenouf—Baron Polysuky, and Mons. Pig.' He is afraid to stand near the door, lest the announced names should make him grin. In his letters as well as his books he rattles off strings of queer examples with familiar gusto. A projected journey to Egypt makes him 'quite crazy about Memphis and On and Isis and crocodiles and ophthalmia and nubians and simoons and sorcerers and sphingidos'.

It is natural that Lear should have fallen, as we should now believe, into the then widespread vogue of punning. But he is no slavish imitator of Lamb and Hood. Even his puns have a style of their own which often trips over the boundaries of humour into his own rightful realm of nonsense. Here is an example from a letter of 1865:

'This place (Nice) is so wonderfully dry that nothing can be kept moist. I never was in so dry a place in all my life. When the little children cry, they cry dust and not tears. There is some water in the sea, but not much:—all the wet nurses cease to be so immediately on arriving:—Dryden is the only book read—the neighbourhood abounds with Dryads and Hammerdryads: and weterinary surgeons are quite unknown.'

A trip to the Ionian Islands induced a punning declension of archipelago: 'v.a. Archipelago, P. Archipelament, P. P. Archipelagore.' In the same manner he has 'German, Gerwomen and Gerchildren', and such constructions as 'geraffino' for a young Giraffe, and 'hippopotamice' as an improved plural for hippopotamus.

Elsewhere he performs a different trick with an undertone of Learian irony:

'I went into the city to-day; to put the £125 I got for the *Book of Nonsense* into the funds. It is doubtless a very unusual thing for an artist to put by money, for the whole way from Temple Bar to the Bank was *crowded* with carriages and people—so immense a sensation did this occurrence make. And all the way back it was the same, which was very gratifying.'

14

But as he is not content with being a punster, he quickly enters into the fun of any verbal trick new or old, and when Charles Dickens popularises Wellerisms, Lear becomes an easy convert to that once fashionable kind of humour: 'On the whole, as the morbid and mucilaginous monkey said when he climbed up to the top of the Palm-tree and found no fruit there, one can't depend upon dates.' The vocabulary of Sam Weller is also exploited in 'viddy' for 'widow', and 'wurbl' for 'verbal', and among other Cockneyisms such mispronunciations as 'chimbly' (chimney) and 'suddingly', recall Mrs. Gamp.

Phonetic spelling plays a considerable part in many of his nonsense words, and often a complete effect is obtained by this process as in 'yott' (yacht), 'rox' (rocks), 'korn' (corn), and 'toppix' (topics). He is better, however, in distortions like 'buzzim' (bosom), 'omejutly' (immediately), 'pollygise' (apologise), 'spongetaneous (spontaneous), 'mewtshool' (mutual), 'gnoat' (note), 'fizzicle' (physical), 'fizziognomy' (physiognomy), and 'phibs' (fibs).

He weds the 'n' or 'an' with the next word, as 'a narmchair', 'a nemptystummuk', 'a noppertunity', 'sill kankerchief', and indulges in the superfluous aspirate, as 'hempty'. Sometimes he translates whole sentences into nonsense-spelling, as 'I gnoo how bizzy u were', or 'witch fax I only came at granuously', or 'phits of coffin' or 'sombod a nokking at the dolorous door', or 'vorx of hart', and reports that he has 'become like a sparry in the pilderpips and a pemmican on the housetops', which reads like an excerpt from *Finnegans Wake!* He likes an absurdity such as 'sufficient unto the day is the weevil thereof', and in 'Mary Squeen of Cots' he anticipates the verbal inversion known later as a Spoonerism. The fun reaches a climax when inflation is added to distortion and his imagination bodies forth a portmanteau-word of no less than thirty-one letters like *splendidophoropherostiphongious,* to express his satisfaction with a dinner-party.

It is none of these verbal adventures, however, that reveal Edward Lear at his best as a word-maker. In the examples I have given he is doing little more than amusing himself and his friends by following a fashion of the moment for that sort of thing, although his success indicates both a natural gift for word-building and a need for that kind of expression. His inventiveness is extraordinary and what nearly always begins as fun often ends in an extension of the boundaries of expression. His imagination is always at its best when it has some concrete form or idea for its objective. This is proved by the nomenclature of his nonsense creatures. In this realm he has only one peer—Lewis Carroll. But where the creator of *Alice* has some half dozen masterpieces to his credit such as the *Jabberwock, Bandersnatch, Snark* and *Boojum,* Lear has a whole zooful of distinguished creatures many of which, like the *Pobble* and the *Quangle Wangle,* have become common objects of the popular imagination.

15

This busy and distracted man wrote and illustrated, or illustrated for others, a score of volumes, and left in manuscript many more, including diaries, letters and, as he called them, 'nonsenses'. In addition, his landscapes in oil and water-colours, his realistic representations of parrots and other creatures, and his masterly nonsense drawings in black-and-white, which often anticipate Phil May's style and economy of line, would fill a fair-sized gallery; and he had some considerable fame among his large circle of friends as a composer of songs, particularly with Tennyson's words, which he would render with great expression in a thin tenor voice, often reducing his select audiences to tears.

16

This collection of the Nonsense of Edward Lear forms a complete reproduction of the four volumes of nonsense published during the author's lifetime, together with a few hitherto unpublished pieces included in the selection called *Nonsense Songs and Stories,* edited by Sir Edward Strachey, in 1895. In this collection there appeared for the first time the characteristic self-portrait in verse reproduced in the present volume.

I was at first tempted to re-arrange the various items in some sort of classification, but remembering that this collection is for entertainment I decided to follow the Lear tradition by arranging the sections in chronological order. The reader may thus roam about and pick and choose at will—which, after all, is the pleasantest way to know Mr. Lear. Another advantage of this method is that all the illustrations are placed where Lear intended them, and as integral to his art of nonsense. I have included specimens of his music and of his handwriting, and also a pictorial record of Old Foss, the cat, and on the title page an example of his epistolary caricatures of himself from an autograph in my possession.

The early nonsense books are not readily accessible as most of them were very properly used up, or eaten up, by the children for whom they were written. The original editions of *The Book of Nonsense* (1846), as well as *Nonsense Songs, Stories, Botany and Alphabets* (1871), *More Nonsense* (1872) and *Laughable Lyrics* (1877), are all scarce. It is easier to find a *First Folio Shakespeare* than a first edition of *The Book of Nonsense*: even the British Museum Library has to content itself with a copy of the third edition (1861). The popularity of that book has been continuous and progressive for a hundred years. During the author's lifetime there were many editions, and scarcely a year has since passed without a reprint.

I am obliged to Mr. George Macy of New York for the courtesy of permission to use as the basis of this Introduction the study of Edward Lear written originally for his bibliographical review, *The Dolphin,* and I am indebted to the following sources for biographical details: *The Letters of Edward Lear* (1907) and *Late Letters of Edward Lear* (1911), both edited by Lady Strachey; Mr. Angus Davidson's *Edward Lear: Landscape Painter and Nonsense Poet* (1938); and *Edward Lear on My Shelves,* the monumental folio by which Mr. William B. Osgood Field, the distinguished American bibliophile, has celebrated Edward Lear and his own unique collection of Lear manuscripts and first editions.

Notes

1. A selection of these illustrations was published in 1889, the year after his death, with a Memoir by his old friend Franklin Lushington.

2. *Views in Rome.* (1841); *Excursions in Italy* (1846); *Excursions in Italy, Second Series* (1846); *Journal of a Landscape Painter in Albania and Illyria* (1841); *Journal of a Landscape Painter in Southern Calabria* (1852); *Views in the Seven Ionian Islands* (1863); *Journal of a Landscape Painter in Corsica* (1870).

William Harmon (essay date 1982)

SOURCE: Harmon, William. "Lear, Limericks, and Some Other Verse Forms." *Children's Literature* 10 (1982): 70-6.

[*In the following essay, Harmon compares Lear's work to the traditional form of the limerick, arguing that Lear's limerick-type poems differ from the classic model.*]

The limerick—in its familiar, five-line form with a rhyme scheme of *aabba*—was neither invented by nor perfected by Edward Lear, who wrote, in fact, very few verses that qualify technically as limericks. Lear's "nonsenses" share the limerick's general metric and rhythmic scheme: two lines of anapestic trimeter, two lines of anapestic dimeter, a fifth line of anapestic trimeter; but Lear's usual rhyme scheme and his arrangement of the lines do not meet the standards of the perfect limerick.

It is not that he lacked a model. Perfect limericks existed before Lear's birth in 1812, and he is known to have been familiar with volumes that appeared in the early 1820s: *The History of Sixteen Wonderful Old Women* (1821) and *Ancedotes and Adventures of Fifteen Gentlemen* (c. 1822).[1] To the latter Lear gave credit for his first introduction to the form, and he singled out one verse for particular attention, even drawing three sketches in illustration (the text and drawings in the original volume are anonymous, but the artwork has been attributed to Robert Cruikshank):

> There was a sick man of Tobago
> Liv'd long on rice-gruel and sago;
>   But at last, to his bliss,
>   The physician said this—
> "To a roast leg of mutton you may go."[2]

The verse was printed as five lines, and it is rhymed perfectly; that is to say, it is a classic limerick in form. Never, to my knowledge, did Lear even attempt this exact format. He did, it is true, keep to the habit of ending his first line with a place-name (customarily a

provincial or colonial place), but he seems never to have construed the stanza as one of five lines. Even in his sketches for "There was a sick man of Tobago," Lear combined the third and fourth lines as one, a practice followed quite consistently in his **Nonsense** books. Along with the adherence to the four-line format (sometimes in Lear's sketches reduced to three or two), Lear followed the format of *some* of the verses in the volumes from the 1820s, whereby the last line, instead of rhyming, merely varies the first line and still ends with the same word. All the verses that I have seen from *The History of Sixteen Wonderful Old Women* do this:

> There was an old woman of Leeds
> Who spent all her time in good deeds;
>   She worked for the poor
>   Till her fingers were sore,
> This pious old woman of Leeds.[3]

Of the verses in *Ancedotes and Adventures of Fifteen Gentlemen,* some rhyme perfectly (as we have seen in "There was a sick man of Tobago," which formally resembles "A tailor, who sailed from Quebec"), but others fall back on variation and repetition:

> As a little fat man of Bombay
> Was smoking one very hot day,
>   A bird called a snipe
>   Flew away with his pipe,
> Which vexed the fat man of Bombay.[4]

Lear drew an illustration for a variant of this verse. It shows a very fat little man, but the caption (written as two long lines) calls him simply "an old man of Bombay."[5]

Lear published about two hundred and ten of his four-line nonsenses, and in the overwhelming majority he keeps to a single rhyming practice and ends his first and fourth (last) line with the same word. In its most characteristic form, the verse begins with a line of anapestic trimeter in which a general type of character (old or young person, man, woman, or lady) is presented, with an indication of place, either general (a garden or a station, say) or specific. The second line, also of anapestic trimeter, rhymes perfectly or comically with the first and, as a rule, sets forth some eccentricity of the person presented in the first line. The third line is anapestic tetrameter with an internal rhyme linking the second and fourth stressed syllable. The fourth line returns to the trimeter and ends with the same word as the first line. Since this format differs so much from the true limerick, and since Lear himself is not known to have used the word *limerick,* I propose that we return to his usage and call these peculiar verses *nonsenses,* as he did. He did not invent the form but he did perfect it.

By my tally, fourteen of Lear's two hundred and ten nonsenses depart from his usual scheme of rhyme and repetition, and all but two of these are in his first *Book of Nonsense* (1846). All are printed as four lines. In ten variants, the last line repeats the end of the *second* line, as here:

> There was a Young Lady of Hull,
> Who was chased by a virulent Bull;
> But she seized on a spade, and called out—"Who's
>   afraid!"
> Which distracted that virulent Bull.[6]

In one of these variations, the line-break is eccentric:

> There was an Old Man who said,
> "How,—shall I flee from this horrible Cow?
> I will sit on this stile, and continue to smile,
> Which may soften the heart of that Cow."[7]

And only four of Lear's nonsenses, all in the volume of 1846, satisfy the rhyme scheme of the perfect limerick. One has to do with a general place (**"There was an Old Man of the Coast"**); the remaining three stand out as peculiarly unusual and also, I think, peculiarly distinguished:

> There was an Old Man who supposed,
> That the street door was partially closed;
> But some very large rats, ate his coats and his hats,
> While that futile old gentleman dozed.
>
> There was a Young Lady whose eyes,
> Were unique as to color and size;
> When she opened them wide, people all turned aside,
> And started away in surprise.
>
> There was an Old Lady whose folly,
> Induced her to sit in a holly;
> Whereon by a thorn, her dress being torn,
> She quickly became melancholy.[8]

On this subject, I must disagree somewhat with the judgment of Herman W. Liebert in two particulars. He says that "Lear made the limerick widely popular,"[9] but it is clear that Lear was dealing in a different form, although the proper limerick was available and possibly popular even before his birth. What remains popular is a form of verse that Lear, with his own utterly eccentric genius, altered beyond easy recognition—a form of verse, moreover, that seems to have survived or escaped Lear's adjustments of its essential nature. "Since Lear," Liebert continues, "the limerick has become a vehicle for wit rather than for nonsense. The *witty* limerick naturally demands a 'punch' in the last line. But Lear was writing nonsense, and rightly preferred, for his last line, an altered repetition of the first."[10] We are all in Liebert's debt for his sensitive and sympathetic annotations of *Lear in the Original,* but I must differ with virtually every idea in the sentence I have just quoted. The distinction between wit and nonsense is by no means prismatic. By "nonsense" Lear seems to have meant "trifle" rather than something illogical, contradic-

tory, or meaningless. And, whatever Lear meant, I do not think that we can get away with aligning wit and punch on one side and nonsense and no-punch on the other. Besides, Lear wrote verses with three kinds of last line, and one seems as nonsensical as another.

Lear's greatness comes from other kinds of verse, especially the longer lyrics and haunting songs: **"The Owl and the Pussy-Cat," "The Dong with a Luminous Nose," "The Pelican Chorus," "The Pobble Who Has No Toes,"** and perhaps a half-dozen others. His nonsenses are much less witty and much less "nonsensical," and they are certainly much less important in the history of children's verse or light verse in general.

His apparent belief that the four-line format is proper remains interesting, however, and I want to conclude by both coming forward into the present and going back into the centuries before Lear. Since his death in 1888, only two new verse-forms related to the limerick have enjoyed any celebrity. The earlier of the two is the clerihew, invented by Edmund Clerihew Bentley (a distinguished lawyer who also invented *Trent's Last Case*), almost as though in perpendicular opposition to the general trend of the limerick. In the limerick, we find an imaginary person put into a rhyme-word place and more or less chastised by a regular verse form. In the clerihew, we normally find a real person whose name forms the rhyme word for some deliberately irregular verses, which rhyme *aabb* but should not follow a metrical scheme. Here is an attempt of my own:

> Cesare Borgia
> Would have preferred the situation in Georgia
> Before the Emancipation
> Proclamation.

In their classic forms, both the limerick and the clerihew involve a rhyme with a proper name—a place in the former, a person's name in the latter. I do not know why should this be the case, except that both verse-forms seem aimed at the exposure of ridiculous or eccentric behavior, a kind of "singular" conduct displayed in language by names (the notion of the "singular name" has been explored by John Stuart Mill in a sober work on logic and by T. S. Eliot in a frivolous poem about cats). Whatever the causes of this persistent name-concentration, it is found in yet another light-verse form, the delightful double dactyl invented by John Hollander and Anthony Hecht. This form consists of two four-line stanzas, each made up of four lines of dactyllic dimeter with a rhyme between the fourth lines of the two stanzas (these lines are slightly truncated, lacking the two final unstressed syllables). The first line is usually two dactyllic nonsense words (as in the title of the definitive collection, *Jiggery Pokery*); the second line is a name, like "Benjamin Harrison," that scans as two dactyls.

Some later line, normally the second or third of the second stanza, must consist of a single six-syllable word that scans as two dactyls. In the best double dactyl that I know, George Starbuck's "Monarch of the Sea," two of these demanding requirements are doubled: the name consists of *four* dactyls, and there are *two* six-syllable dactyllic words in the second stanza:

> "Jiminy Whillikers,
> Admiral Samuel
> Eliot Morison,
> Where is your ship?"

> "I, sir, am HMS
> Historiography's
> Disciplinarian.
> Button your lip."[11]

Here we have another departure from the limerick model—perpendicular in a dimension other than that of the clerihew, one might say. Here, as in the clerihew, we rely on a real person's name, but, as in the limerick, there is strict regularity of rhythm and meter. The dactyl, we should note, is the opposite of the limerick's favored anapest. Each in its own way, Lear's nonsense, Bentley's clerihew, and the double dactyl varies the basic limerick format.

Despite the different styles of printing, I believe that the fundamental and original form is a matter of four lines. The rhythm may be anapestic, dactyllic, or anomalous, but, as in virtually all English poetry since the fourteenth century, the primordial foot is iambic. Furthermore, as in almost all musical forms, the four lines each contain space for four stresses, although the inclusion of a pause or rest can reduce the number of stresses to three. I speculate that a number of changes have been suffered by the primal form, but it persists in its original shape in such poems as Blake's "London," which is four stanzas of four lines each, with each line containing four stresses. This is the syllabic form called "8.8.8.8" or "long measure" in hymnals. In the 8.6.8.6 form it is called "common measure" and is very close to the standard "ballad measure" and the "fourteeners" of the sixteenth century. In the 6.6.8.6 form ("short measure"), it is the same as the "poulter's measure" that was the most popular verse-form in English for some years in the sixteenth century; it seems to be the original of certain nursery rhymes ("Hickory Dickory, Dock," for example) and for limericks as well. It may seem treacherous to suggest such a thing, but any nonsense or limerick can be sung to a short-measure tune like that of "Blest Be the Tie that Binds."

> The limerick's story is clear;
> It only begins to seem queer
>   If you worry betimes
>   About the sad rhymes
> Of that runcible gentleman, Lear.

Notes

1. See Iona and Peter Opie, eds., *The Oxford Dictionary of Nursery Rhymes* (Oxford: Clarendon, 1952), pp. 91, 267, 329, 400, 407-08.

2. Opies, p. 407 and plate XIX. See also Herman W. Liebert, *Lear in the Original: Drawings and Limericks by Edward Lear for his "Book of Nonsense"* (New York: Kraus, 1975), pp. 17, 52-55.

3. Opies, p. 267.

4. Ibid., p. 91.

5. Liebert, pp. 36-37. Liebert does not note that this is very close to a verse in *Anecdotes and Adventures of Fifteen Gentlemen.*

6. *The Complete Nonsense of Edward Lear,* ed. Holbrook Johnson (New York: Dover, 1951), p. 39.

7. Ibid., p. 38.

8. Ibid., pp. 16, 17, 31.

9. Liebert, p. 17.

10. Ibid., p. 18.

11. *The Oxford Book of American Light Verse,* ed. William Harmon (New York: Oxford University Press, 1979), p. 517. A slightly different version may be found in Starbuck's *Desperate Measures* (Boston: Godine, 1978). The poem is copyright © 1978 by George Starbuck, reprinted by permission of David R. Godine, Publisher, Inc.

Ina Rae Hark (essay date 1982)

SOURCE: Hark, Ina Rae. "The Longer Poems." In *Edward Lear,* pp. 52-100. Boston: Twayne Publishers, 1982.

[*In the following essay, Hark traces the development of Lear's longer poems, suggesting that they are more autobiographical and darker than his short poems. Hark gives special attention to themes of sexuality and loss, finding in Lear's verse intimations of loneliness and anxiety about his sexuality.*]

GENERAL CHARACTERISTICS

If, as the writer for the *Spectator* who reviewed Lear's nonsense books asserted, nonsense requires "a power of joyous rebellion against sense—of vital rebound from it,"[1] then the Lear of the longer poems was writing inferior nonsense, for his vital powers of joy and rebellion were certainly diminishing. And if, as Elizabeth Sewell believes, nonsense is a game that the forces of order in the mind play with the forces of disorder so that they may hold disorder in abeyance, then Lear was losing the emotional detachment necessary for playing the game.[2] Although it is going too far to say that Lear's longer poems do not qualify as nonsense, they do represent nonsense of a different kind. While many limerick protagonists choose to act eccentrically or to take on appearances that deviate from the expectations of society, a majority of the characters in the nonsense songs would love to fit into the crowd, only to have fate prevent them from doing so. Like Arnold's speaker in "Dover Beach," they stand on the shore and hear "the eternal note of sadness" coming in. Limericks that deal with catastrophes generally end as soon as the boom falls; the songs often begin with the catastrophe and explore the protagonist's attempts to adapt to reduced circumstances.

The "plots" of the nonsense songs do not vary as widely as do those of the limericks. Two themes, wandering and loss, predominate. Autobiographical parallels are clear. Lear had begun the limericks, and set their pattern, while still working at Knowsley, with many possibilities before him; the longer nonsense springs from the middle of his *Wanderjahre,* when the paradoxical contours of his trap had become all too familiar. But although the general mood of the longer poems is far more melancholy than that of the limericks, Lear still examines his themes from all possible angles. Poems about journeys describe either characters who escape an unsatisfactory status quo to seek freedom, adventure, and/or love or those whom the travelers have left behind. The poems scrutinize both those who leave and those who are left because Lear could alternately identify with each of these positions. He had escaped the confining atmosphere of England only to find himself deserted by the Lushingtons, Fortescues, and Congreves who could return home while he had to remain an exile. The losses that the poems portray may be either explicit loss of love and companionship or metaphorical deprivations of physical abilities, clothing, food, or mobility that express the poet's sense of his own imperfection and incompleteness.

In the longer poems the geography and the inhabitants of the nonsense world also differ somewhat from those in the limericks. While the limericks often verge on fantasy, Lear never whole-heartedly commits himself to it. All the places mentioned can be found on a map, the protagonists are all human beings (if outlandish ones), and animals do not talk. These conditions change in the nonsense songs. Some take place in the known world, but many of the travelers eventually arrive at the Great Gromboolian Plain or the Hills of the Chankly Bore, lands of Lear's invention. These lands do not belong to a separate fantasy universe, unrelated to our world, since, for example, the pelicans' daughter in **"The Pelican Chorus"** can fly there from a point of departure on the Nile. However, they represent a country—one might call it "nonsense land"—that Lear never discov-

ered for all his journeying, an uncharted realm where contentment impossible in one's familiar surroundings may sometimes, although not always, be found. Its features recur from poem to poem, for the nonsense songs together constitute a related body of myth-making. Each separate verse explores a facet of nonsense land, and characters who have a central role in one poem occasionally play a subsidiary role in another.

In keeping with the more fantastic setting, the characters rarely qualify as humans, in even the dubious sense of humanness represented by the limerick protagonists. These poems feature either anthropomorphized animals, personified inanimate objects, or "humanoid" members of nonsense species such as the Dong, Jumblies, Yonghy-Bonghy-Bò, Pobble, and Quangle Wangle. The Discobboloses seem human enough, despite their name, until Lear mentions in the sequel to their poem that Mrs. Discobbolos is "octopod." Of all the longer poems humans appear only in two minor verses, **"The New Vestments"** and **"The Two Old Bachelors,"** in the person of the Bó's beloved Lady Jingly Jones, and as Lear himself in the autobiographical poems **"How Pleasant to Know Mr. Lear"** and **"Incidents in the Life of My Uncle Arly."** All in all, the longer poems have far closer links to the traditional nursery rhyme and fairy tale than do the limericks, which create a specific atmosphere of nonsense for which previous analogs do not exist.

These changes that occur as one moves from limericks to nonsense songs possibly compensate for the loss of emotional distance in the latter. The limericks reflect the paradoxes of Lear's life just as strongly as do the other poems, but the presentation is abstract and symbolic, and the disengagement of the poetic voice keeps troublesome feelings under control. In the songs, however, the parallels to Lear's actual experience cause him to separate himself from his characters by dehumanizing them and setting them in an imaginary landscape. The two groups of poems complement one another and once more reflect the duality of Lear's art. They stand in relation to one another as do the nonsense drawings to the landscapes—the same world portrayed from two different perspectives. It is quite fitting, therefore, that the volumes that contain Lear's limericks do not include any nonsense songs, and the volumes that contain the longer poems, *Nonsense Songs* (1871) and *Laughable Lyrics* (1877), contain no limericks.[3]

Nonsense Songs

Changes also occur between these two volumes of longer verse, for in *Nonsense Songs* the geography of nonsense land is sketchy, glimpsed from afar, and although the poems contain talking animals and animate household objects, only one, **"The Jumblies,"** portrays any imaginary creatures. The loners who dominate the limericks and recur in some of the *Laughable Lyrics* do not appear here; except for the deserted "me" in **"Calico Pie,"** all the poems feature pairs or groups of creatures setting out on journeys together. These verses explore Lear's need to travel, rather than emphasize the loneliness he often felt while traveling. In fact, as a group these first nonsense songs share a greater consistency of theme than any other related group of Learian verses. Each one concerns protagonists who become dissatisfied with life at home and set off for new surroundings. Then Lear, in his typical multiplicitous manner, examines in turn all the variables such a basic situation might entail.

The three most closely connected poems, **"The Owl and the Pussy-cat," "The Duck and the Kangaroo,"** and **"The Daddy Long-Legs and the Fly,"** had previously appeared together in the American journal *Young Folks* in 1870. Each describes two disparate creatures coming together as travel companions and details their journeys. The motivations for the travel differ in each case, however. The owl and the pussy-cat go on a courtship voyage; they change rapidly from companions to lovers to husband and wife. The kangaroo seems a wonderer by profession, and the duck joins him out of boredom with its home pond. The daddy long-legs and the fly have become misfits in formerly comfortable surroundings and flee to nonsense land as companions in misfortune, creating a new life in reduced circumstances. So in the three poems the mood at journey's end changes from festive happiness to less ecstatic contentment to resigned sadness.

"The Owl and the Pussy-cat," probably Lear's best known poem, is also one of his happiest.[4] Along with **"The Jumblies"** it illustrates those occasional miracles that every now and then replace the disasters that the arbitrary and paradoxical fortune of Lear's universe usually brings on. The title pair, to be sure, do not hurl themselves recklessly at fate as do some of the limerick characters. They prudently set out well-provisioned and financed: "They took some honey, and plenty of money, / Wrapped up in a five-pound note."[5] They also pay attention to social proprieties. Pussy exclaims: "O let us be married! too long we have tarried," but because a proper wedding requires a ring, they tarry another year and a day in search of one. The "too long we have tarried" is itself ambiguous. Does Pussy mean that two lovers should not sail for very long together in a "beautiful pea-green boat" without benefit of clergy? Or does "married" mean "consummated," synonymous in a respectable Victorian vocabulary? Have they restrained their passion for too long? The time spent searching for the ring implies commitment to social duty on the one hand and further damage to reputation and further frustration of passion on the other—Lear's typical paradoxical trap.

However, the difficulties disappear when the lovers finally leave our world and arrive at "the land where the Bong-tree grows." A pig with the desired ring in his nose miraculously appears, willing to sell it for only one shilling of the substantial sum wrapped up in the five-pound note. And a "Turkey who lives on the hill" is immediately at hand to perform the marriage ceremony. Since the sharing of food always cements loving relationships in Lear, the poet details the contents of the wedding feast, "mince and slices of quince," eaten with a "runcible spoon," bearing one of Lear's favorite nonsense adjectives. Then comes the epiphany:

> And hand in hand, on the edge of the sand,
>   They danced by the light of the moon,
>   The moon,
>   The moon,
>   They danced by the light of the moon.

Here the positive values of song and dance transfer over from the limericks; such scenes will occur again and again in the longer poems.

The shore and moonlight also figure prominently and frequently in the settings of nonsense land, for both encompass the contradictions of that land. The shore mediates between settled ground and wandering sea; it is a place from which one embarks, upon which one starts a new life, and where one may be left behind by love. Moonlight combines brightness with darkness, may suggest magic or melancholy. In this poem, and many of the others, it is certainly magic, with the joy of owl and pussy-cat emphasized by the energetic finale of the refrain in which "moon," like the words that end each of the other stanzas, is repeated four times.

Trouble never enters the world of **"The Owl and the Pussy-cat,"** but its absence may result because Lear looks only at the culminating miracle and not at the origins of the two creatures' love or the causes of their setting out on their voyage. "The Owl and the Pussy-cat went to sea / In a beautiful pea-green boat"; this is all we know. Could their love perhaps not flourish on land? Did some equivalent of "them" decide that owls and pussy-cats should not mate (as indeed they do not in nature)? Moreover some sexual confusion occurs in the poem, since Lear never denotes either owl or pussy-cat by a male or female pronoun,[6] although he describes the pig as definitely male, "with a ring at the end of *his* nose" (italics mine). Subconsciously, perhaps, Lear is leaving the lovers' respective sexes ambiguous, and making them of different species, in order to portray his conflicting desires for both the security of conventional marriage and, the deeper need, for love from his closest male friends.

In the limericks one never thinks to question the motivations of the protagonists; they all live quite beyond the pale of psychology. The longer poems, however, while portraying a nonsensical lack of logic in the causation of events, deal with character in a more realistic fashion. Because Lear in most of the other travel poems describes precisely what set the characters off on their journeys, the lack of such information in this poem creates at least a suspicion that if the information had not been suppressed, it might have compromised the joyous tone of **"The Owl and the Pussy-cat."**

Lear's second pair of travelers, the duck and the kangaroo, do not actually set off on their travels until four lines from the end of the poem. If Lear reveals very little about the reasons and preparations for the voyage of the owl and the pussy-cat, he devotes this verse to little else. The journey itself seems almost anticlimactic. **"The Duck and the Kangaroo"** primarily expresses the theme of symbiotic cooperation in adapting to circumstances that characterizes several of the longer poems, but that **"The Owl and the Pussy-cat"** touches on only briefly. The relationship of the two companions differs substantially from that of the owl and the pussy-cat, in that the respective attributes of duck and kangaroo complement a lack in the other, while the owl and the pussy-cat, equal partners in love, seek from outside help in meeting a shared need. The duck and the kangaroo need each other's aid in much the same way that both owl and pussy-cat need the aid of the pig and the turkey.

The duck is the thinker of the pair, the prime mover in their adventure, who gives direction to the aimless wanderings of the kangaroo. Although the poem is structured as a dialogue, with each stanza beginning either "Said the Duck" or "Said the Kangaroo," the duck originates and dominates the conversation. It—once again the sex of the characters is not specified—has an expansive imagination that has been frustrated because of its confinement to "this nasty pond" where "my life is a bore." The kangaroo, on the other hand, has the physical capability to "hop! / Over the fields and the water too, / As if you never would stop!"[7] So the duck asks for a ride, promising to "sit quite still, and say nothing but 'Quack,' / The whole of the long day through!"—although the aggressive, voluble confidence it displays throughout the poem casts doubt on how well it might keep such a promise. And directly following its promise of reticence, it proceeds to set the itinerary: "And we'd go to the Dee, and the Jelly Bo Lee, / Over the land, and over the sea."

Although the kangaroo is a timid, old-maidish sort—another side of Lear, the hypochondriacal traveler—who stands to gain little from the partnership, it graciously tells the duck that its companionship "might bring me luck." However, the prospect of the duck's "unpleasantly wet and cold" feet on its back does not

delight the kangaroo, and it fears that rheumatism may result from their touch. But the seemingly impulsive duck has in fact figured everything out carefully in advance:

> Said the Duck, 'As I sate on the rocks,
> I have thought over that completely,
> And I bought four pairs of worsted socks
> Which fit my web-feet neatly.
> And to keep out the cold I've bought a cloak,
> And every day a cigar I'll smoke,
> All to follow my own dear true
> Love of a Kangaroo!'

So they leave "all in the moonlight pale" for another Learian epiphany:

> So away they went with a hop and a bound,
> And they hopped the whole world three times round;
> And who so happy,—O who,
> As the Duck and the Kangaroo?. [*sic*]

It is rather a shock to hear the duck, who has approached their joint trip as a prudently conceived business proposition, suddenly declare his or her passion for "my own dear true love of a Kangaroo." Indeed, the sexual content in this poem differs far more from conventionalized courtship than does the romance of the owl and the pussy-cat, which is nonsensical only in the difference of their species and the uncertainty about their respective genders. **"The Duck and the Kangaroo"** shares these confusions, but it adds some more ambiguous Freudian undercurrents. The poem contains no masculine or feminine pronouns at all. Since the duck makes all the plans and advances and wears a cloak and smokes cigars, it would seem to be masculine. Yet Byrom asserts that the duck is female and that "the joke is: how funny to have a timid kangaroo and a bossy duck."[8] He provides no evidence for making the assumption, but one imagines the illustrations may have influenced him. With the duck straddling it, the kangaroo's tail, formerly trailing limply on the ground, juts out straight and erect; the visual phallic suggestions are quite strong. And the kangaroo's fears of the unpleasantly wet and cold feet of the duck likewise suggest a sexual image, this time one of aversion in which the kangaroo seems female rather than male. It feels safe to proceed only after the proper prophylactic precautions have been taken. But whatever its indications of Lear's uneasiness about physical sexual contact and his ambivalence about sexual identity, **"The Duck and the Kangaroo"** does not concern itself primarily with romance. It deals with the need to escape dull routine and the various compromises and adaptations that are the price of freedom. Even more than the owl and the pussy-cat, the duck and the kangaroo depart from the impulsive model of the wilder limerick protagonists to become the prudent tourists abroad. They doubtless closely resemble Lear and Giorgio on a painting expedition.

The third verse of this group, **"The Daddy Long-legs and the Fly,"** has nothing to do with the need for romance or adventure. Since love is not at issue here, Lear makes both characters decidedly male; he gives both the title "Mr." and uses "he" frequently to refer to both. The poem is the first of several describing the loss of joys once possessed, of happy days that are no more. The two companions, despite a long sea voyage "far, and far away . . . across the silent main" to the great Gromboolian plain, end as they began, playing battlecock and shuttledoor. No magic moonlight bathes the cold, dreary shore upon which they meet or the vast empty plain to which they flee.

Technically the verse advances beyond the simple rhyme schemes, thumping rhythms, and childish diction—the nursery-rhyme quality—of **"The Owl and the Pussy-cat"** and **"The Duck and the Kangaroo."** Here the stanza form is longer, the pace slower, and the rhyme scheme for each stanza a complex *a b c, b d e f e, g g, h h*. These changes combine to create a subdued and sadder mood. As the action comes back around to the initial situation, so the poetic structure is generally symmetrical. A first narrative stanza is followed by five dialogue stanzas that alternate between the two speakers, as in **"The Duck and the Kangaroo."** The sixth stanza varies from the pattern by beginning with four lines of narration and continuing with eight lines of dialogue spoken by the two insects in unison. A seventh narrative stanza, parallel to the first, concludes the poem.

Lear may have made that sixth stanza structurally distinct from the others because it contains the heart of his message, to which he wants to call attention:

> So Mr. Daddy Long-legs
>   And Mr. Floppy Fly
> Sat down in silence by the sea,
>   And gazed upon the sky.
> They said, 'This is a dreadful thing!
> The world has all gone wrong,
> Since one has legs too short by half,
>   The other much too long!
> One never more can go to court,
> Because his legs have grown too short;
> The other cannot sing a song,
> Because his legs have grown too long!'[9]

Unlike the previous travelers, and those that succeed them in *Nonsense Songs,* the daddy long-legs and the fly have not become discontented with life at home and so sought greener pastures; life has, so to speak, become discontented with them and has arbitrarily altered them so that they no longer fit into a formerly comfortable existence—the world *has* all gone wrong. The poem portrays a situation in which nothing quite fits together. The two insects meet at an awkward time ("it was too soon to dine") of day, upon a summer's afternoon when,

however, "the wind was rather cold." None of the many colors mentioned in the poem match. The daddy long-legs is dressed in brown and gray, the fly in blue and gold, the king and queen of the court in red and green. The sails of the companions' boat are pink and gray, not the "pea-green" of the sails in Lear's poems that tell of happier voyages. Even the mutual pastime they can still share and engage in, a game of badminton, has had its name scrambled from battledore and shuttlecock to "battlecock and shuttledoor." Most tragically, although the afflictions of each would work to the advantage of the other, they have no way to exchange them. They cannot form a symbiotic unit as can the duck and the kangaroo. So their resort to nonsense land "with one spongetaneous cry" in a providentially appearing boat is an act taken by exiles rather than seekers. The silent timelessness evoked in the closing lines suggests a limbolike, purgatorial existence:

> They sailed across the silent main,
>   And reached the great Gromboolian plain;
> And there they play for evermore
>   At battlecock and shuttledoor.

In a poem whose prevailing mood is one of estrangement, the game itself is one that separates the players with a net.

The subdued tone of **"The Daddy Long-legs and the Fly"** prefigures the melancholy strains of the misnamed *Laughable Lyrics*[10] such as **"The Dong with a Luminous Nose,"** **"The Pobble Who Has No Toes,"** and **"The Courtship of the Yonghy-Bonghy-Bò."** And even the two preceding, happier voyage poems lack the exuberant, devil-take-the-hindmost nonconformity that often appears in the limericks. But Lear had not quite finished with the limerick spirit of nonsense, which returns in two of the *Nonsense Songs,* **"The Jumblies,"** and **"The Nutcrackers and the Sugar-Tongs."**

"The Jumblies" could serve as a compendium of the many sides of the relationship between "them" and the limerick protagonists. The poem begins with a spirited disregard for conventional wisdom:

> They went to sea in a Sieve, they did,
>   In a Sieve they went to sea:
> In spite of all their friends could say,
> On a winter's morn, on a stormy day,
>   In a Sieve they went to sea!
> And when the Sieve turned round and round,
> And every one cried, 'You'll all be drowned!'
> They called aloud, 'Our Sieve ain't big,
> But we don't care a button! we don't care a fig!
>   In a Sieve we'll go to sea!'[11]

It is as if several Old Persons had banded together in a type of corporate eccentricity, impossible in the fragmented "real" world of the limericks, but achievable in the "far and few" lands where the Jumblies live and where even normal people have green heads and blue hands. The Jumblies' friends embody the concerns "they" frequently express for both Philistine propriety and the genuine dangers that the eccentric braves:

> 'O won't they be soon upset, you know!
> For the sky is dark, and the voyage is long,
> And happen what may, it's extremely wrong
>   In a Sieve to sail so fast!'

Erika Leimert remarks that the friends' warnings resemble those given to most explorers and that the Jumblies themselves represent "aller derer, die unbekümmert um das Urteil der anderen, sich in das Unbekannte hinauswagen, unerschrocken das scheinbar Unmögliche versuchen" (all those who, unconcerned with the judgments of others, set forth into the unknown, unafraid to attempt the seemingly impossible.)[12] Lear, however, realizes that the friends have a good deal of sense on their side when they forecast shipwreck for a leaky sieve. For the Jumbly vessel is not a magic sieve that does not take in water. Lear pushes his paradox to its limits when he reports "The water it soon came in, it did, / The water it soon came in."

The Jumblies perceive the water as threatening only to make their feet wet, not to sink them. So they wrap their feet in pinky paper and climb into a crockery jar for the night. And in this poem faith and ingenuity carry the day; their feet stay dry and the sieve illogically stays afloat. The Jumblies successfully sail to the distant Western Sea. Lear parallels their nonsense view of the adventure, characterized by the elevation of individual instinct over all other considerations, with the previously cited sense of the friends:

> And each of them said, 'How wise we are!
> Though the sky be dark, and the voyage be long,
> Yet we never can think we were rash or wrong,
>   While round in our Sieve we spin!'

In **"The Jumblies"** all the potential catastrophes that inform the Learian universe miraculously vanish, just as the voyagers' seemingly ineffective methods for dealing with the incoming water prove to be just the thing. The singsong of the refrain has an incantatory quality that keeps all harm away.

The Jumbly voyage is so magical that they reach their epiphany before reaching their destination. Moonlight and song accompany the very first night of their travels:

> They whistled and warbled a moony song
> To the echoing sound of a coppery gong,
>   In the shade of the mountains brown.
> 'O Timballo! How happy we are,
> When we live in a sieve and a crockery-jar,
> And all night long in the moonlight pale,
> We sail away with a pea-green sail,
>   In the shade of the mountains brown!'

The final element of Learian communion, food, appears when they land and purchase

> . . . an Owl, and a useful Cart,
> And a pound of Rice, and a Cranberry Tart,
>   And a hive of silvery Bees.
> And they bought a Pig, and some green Jack-daws,
> And a lovely Monkey with lollipop paws,
> And forty bottles of Ring-Bo-Ree,
>   And no end of Stilton Cheese.

The enumeration of incongruous items, a characteristic of nonsense,[13] suggests the limericks once more. One almost hears "There was an Old Man with a Cart, who purchased a Cranberry Tart" or "There was an Old Person of Dawes, who had a monkey with Lollipop paws."

Most of the travelers in the limericks, and in Lear's other poems, either leave home for good to find happiness (or at least lessening of pain) or return home defeated in some way. But the Jumblies, after twenty years or more, all come back in triumph, having grown tall and conquered "the Lakes, and the Torrible Zone, / And the hills of the Chankly Bore." Lear then incorporates into the conclusion of the poem another, and the rarest, facet of the limericks: the coming together of romantic nonconformists and careful society. For upon the Jumblies' return the friends display no bitterness at seeing their gloomy prophecies refuted; rather they make an offering of food. Instead of adhering rigidly to their prosaic principles, they convert enthusiastically to the Jumbly philosophy:

> And they drank their health, and gave them a feast
> Of dumplings made of beautiful yeast;
> And every one said, 'If we only live,
> We too will go to sea in a Sieve,—
> To the hills of the Chankly Bore!'

Although the "if we only live" darkens the ending somewhat, implying that the friends either retain some doubts about the safety of the voyage or, more likely, have waited too long to trust in themselves and throw off conventional restraints, **"The Jumblies"** nevertheless stands as one of Lear's most optimistic and joyous works. Because, however, Lear could always see the dark side of happiness (and conversely the lighter side of disaster) he does not leave the euphoria of the poem uncontradicted. Therefore, in *Laughable Lyrics,* as we shall see, he uses the Jumbly chorus and the Jumbly voyage in **"The Dong"** to reveal that their triumphal return does not represent an unalloyed happy ending for everyone.

"The Nutcrackers and the Sugar-Tongs" does not even attempt to realize the communal joy of **"The Jumblies,"** but it shares with the former poem a reversion to the limerick conflict between "them" and eccentrics who fly in the face of conventional behavior for their kind. The heroes here are inanimate table accessories, who, like the duck, detest a boring and circumscribed existence:

> 'Must we drag on this stupid existence for ever,
> 'So idle and weary, so full of remorse,—
> 'While every one else takes his pleasure, and never
> 'Seems happy unless he is riding a horse?'[14]

Since their long legs, unlike those useless limbs of the daddy long-legs and fly, are "so aptly constructed," they decide to join "everyone else" for a ride. When the nutcracker, who has originated the plan, experiences a moment of doubt ('Shall we try? Shall we go? Do you think we are able?'), the tongs settles the matter with a decisive "Of course!" As in **"The Jumblies,"** faith in one's ability to accomplish a goal generates the ability to accomplish it. In an instant the adventurers leave the house, enter the stable, mount up, and ride away. Of course, "they," the respectable kitchen accessories, voice their disapproval, in a passage that echoes the nursery rhyme "Hey Diddle Diddle":

> The whole of the household was filled with amaze-
>   ment,
>   The Cups and the Saucers danced madly about,
> The Plates and the Dishes looked out of the casement,
>   The Saltcellar stood on his head with a shout,
> The Spoons with a clatter looked out of the lattice,
>   The Mustard-pot climbed up the Gooseberry Pies,
> The Soup-ladle peeped through a heap of Veal Patties,
>   And squeaked with a ladle-like scream of surprise.

Despite their intention to join everyone else, mobility and freedom so exhilarate the nutcrackers and the tongs that they leave the mundane world behind by galloping away to—where else in Lear?—the "beautiful shore." They decide, "We will never go back any more." As their snapping and cracking fade away, the poet reports, "And they never came back."[15] The emphatic finality of the escape resembles that of the inhabitants of Basing and Rimini in the limericks:

> There was an Old Person of Basing,
> Whose presence of mind was amazing;
> He purchased a steed, which he rode at full speed,
> And escaped from the people of Basing.[16]

> There was an old person of Rimini,
> Who said, 'Gracious! Goodness! O Gimini!'
> When they said, 'Please be still!' she ran down a hill,
> And was never more heard of at Rimini.[17]

Such might have been Lear's mood as he left England on the first trip to Rome.

Lear does not wait for a later volume to explore an unhappier side of the situation portrayed in **"The Nutcrackers and the Sugar-Tongs."** In the poem that directly follows it in *Nonsense Songs,* **"Calico Pie,"** the triumphant exclamation, "And they never came back," becomes a lament "They never came back to me." While all the preceding poems deal with a small group of adventurers who run away from the conventional crowd, this song, one of the few works Lear wrote in the first person, portrays a "me," an individual of unspecified age, sex, or species, whom the whole animal kingdom, and by implication, the whole world, has abandoned. Each of the four stanzas has precisely the same structure, beginning with "Calico" combined with a monosyllable, then describing in turn "little Birds," "little Fish," "little Mice," and "Grasshoppers," who engage in their normal forms of locomotion, perform some other activity, and then never return to the speaker, e.g.:

> Calico Jam,
>   The little Fish swam,
> Over the syllabub sea,
>   He took off his hat,
>   To the Sole and the Sprat,
>   And the Willeby-wat,—
> But he never came back to me!
>   He never came back!
>   He never came back!
> He never came back to me![18]

The rhymes are lively, and the refrain with its fourfold repetition resembles that of **"The Owl and the Pussy-cat,"** but the poem describes desertion and isolation rather than union. Although the other songs reflect Lear's restlessness with settled domesticity, **"Calico Pie"** delineates the wanderer's loneliness. Because he makes it a converse of his travel poems, one might conclude that Lear sees his loneliness resulting from his decision to wander. The "me" may also represent those he had left behind in England, particularly his sister Ann, and he perhaps feels his loneliness is a punishment for running out on them. In any event, his sympathies were shifting, and in *Laughable Lyrics* his attention leaves the voyager to look at the individual who "starts in a paradise, isolated, only to end up in a paradise, doubly deserted."[19]

In the remaining three poems in *Nonsense Songs,* however, Lear takes a look at those who willingly live settled domestic lives and whose travels involve only afternoon excursions. **"Mr. and Mrs. Spikky Sparrow"** represents Lear's one attempt to portray a happy family in which mother, father, and children live together in an atmosphere of mutual concern and affection; the Sparrows inhabit a wish-fulfillment household Lear had never had and would never have. Touching in its naive assumptions about what constitutes domestic happiness, the poem nevertheless represents a failure of imagination on Lear's part because such a situation was totally outside his emotional experience. It is the only Lear poem that is cloying in the same way as much inferior Victorian children's literature, particularly the refrain with its "Twikky wikky wikky wee, / Wikky bikky twikky tee" and other "ikky" variations. The tetrameter couplets are technically uninspired.[20]

As her husband sits on a nearby branch, Mrs. Sparrow is "A-making of an insect pie" and singing to amuse "her little children five / In the nest and all alive"[21]—unlike the majority of the twenty-one little Lears. But Mrs. Sparrow is concerned about her husband's coughing and sneezing, brought on by his failure to wear a hat. Mr. Sparrow takes no umbrage at her wifely nagging; on the contrary, he thanks her effusively:

> Mr. Spikky said, 'How kind,
> 'Dear! you are, to speak your mind!
> 'All your life I wish you luck!
> 'You are! you are! a lovely duck!

And now that the subject has come up, the husband remarks that her health too has been suffering from lack of a bonnet.

Mrs. Sparrow's wording of her concern, however, indicates that the pair want to wear hats for reasons beyond the simple warding off of colds and neuralgia: "No one stays out all night long / Without a hat: I'm sure it's wrong!" "Wrong" here has the same double meaning, of both unhealthy and socially improper, something "no one" does, that it has when the friends of the Jumblies use it. Therefore, the two birds decide to dress in the height of fashion in order to "look and feel / Quite galloobious and genteel!" Lest they be too extravagant, though, they choose to buy second hand in "Moses' wholesale shop." They return to the excited compliments of their offspring:

> Their children cried, 'O Ma and Pa!
> 'How truly beautiful you are!'
> Said they, 'We trust that cold or pain
> 'We shall never feel again!
> 'While, perched on tree, or house, or steeple,
> 'We now shall look like other people.'

This rejoicing over conformity puts the Sparrows light years away from the Jumblies or the limerick eccentrics in their bizarre outfits. Lear never really approves of the values that "they" hold, and that the Sparrows wish to emulate, but he realizes that one can avoid much heartache—"cold or pain"—by going along with "other people." In **"Mr. and Mrs. Spikky Sparrow,"** a poem oozing contentment, he for once gives "them" their due.

The poet casts a more cynical eye at cozy domesticity in the two verses that conclude *Nonsense Songs,* **"The Broom, the Shovel, the Poker, and the Tongs"** and **"The Table and the Chair."** These return to the world of household implements introduced in **"The Nutcrackers and the Sugar-Tongs."** The former begins as a courtship poem like **"The Owl and the Pussy-cat."** As two couples, Mr. Tongs and Mrs. Broom, Mr. Poker and Miss Shovel, take a coach ride in the park, all four sing a song, generally a sign of loving togetherness in Lear. And the Poker's serenade, which combines an offer of food with song, reinforces the impression of a love poem:

> 'O Shovely so lovely!' the Poker he sang,
> 'You have perfectly conquered my heart!
> 'Ding-a-dong! Ding-a-dong! If you're pleased with
> my song,
> 'I will feed you with cold apple tart![22]

But the third stanza, sung by the tongs, turns into a lament. Mrs. Broom "doesn't care about me a pin." He suspects that she objects to his thinness and long legs, characteristics unavoidable in a pair of tongs. While the sugar-tongs found its shape advantageous for making a mounted escape, the long legs of this pair of fireplace tongs are a liability, as were the elongated limbs of the daddy long-legs, and, his self-caricatures reveal, as Lear thought his own lanky legs to be. The tongs addresses his love bitterly:

> 'Ah! why don't you heed my complaint!
> 'Must you needs be so cruel, you beautiful Broom,
> 'Because you are covered with paint?
> 'Ding-a-dong! Ding-a-dong!
> 'You are certainly wrong!'

Here "wrong" carries none of the ambiguity of its use in **"The Jumblies"** and **"Mr. and Mrs. Spikky Sparrow"**; it is a heartfelt protestation against injustice.

The response of the two ladies ends any speculation about the song being a love poem:

> Mrs. Broom and Miss Shovel together they sang,
> 'What nonsense you're singing today!'
> Said the Shovel, 'I'll certainly hit you a bang!'
> Said the Broom, 'And I'll sweep you away!'

The broom and the shovel significantly repudiate nonsense itself. At this point the coachman, "perceiving their anger with pain," quickly drives them home. There, no doubt on the hearth where they perform their household duties, "they put on the kettle, and little by little, / They all became happy again." The poet then suddenly intrudes with "there's an end of my song," even though the previous songs in the poem had been specifically attributed to the characters. Perhaps he identifies himself with them at the end in order to make the reader accept the validity of the dubious reconciliation. Even if one does believe that the four become "happy" again, their happiness can surely comprise only an absence of overt strife, not the joy achieved by the owl and the pussy-cat or the Jumblies. The reversals of symbols of joy from the happier poems reveal that love may flourish in nonsense land but not on the homely hearth.

The first two stanzas of **"The Table and the Chair"** contain a statement made by the table to the chair and the chair's reply, a dialogue structure similar to that of **"The Duck and the Kangaroo"** and **"The Daddy Long-legs and the Fly."** Like the duck, the table finds life confining and proposes travel as a cure:

> 'You can hardly be aware,
> 'How I suffer from the heat,
> 'And from chilblains on my feet!
> 'If we took a little walk,
> 'We might have a little talk!
> 'Pray let us take the air!'[23]

And like the kangaroo the chair demurs; it moreover believes the plan impossible of execution:

> 'Now you *know* we are not able!
> 'How foolishly you talk,
> 'When you know we *cannot* walk!'

As in several of the preceding poems, however, faith in oneself can work miracles; the table persuades its companion that "it can do no harm to try." Although "slowly" and with a "cheerful bumpy sound," they succeed in walking around town, to the amazement of all.

Up to this point, **"The Table and the Chair"** closely resembles **"The Nutcrackers and the Sugar-Tongs."** But these adventurers do not, like the nutcrackers and tongs, disappear over the horizon, nor do they go around the world three times like the duck and kangaroo. As in **"The Broom, the Shovel, the Poker, and the Tongs,"** Lear reverses a pattern established in other poems, for the table and chair become hopelessly and helplessly lost. They finally must pay a duck, mouse, and beetle to guide them home. These creatures serve the same function as the coachman in the preceding poem and illustrate the characters' loss of control over their own destinies. Once safely home, the table and chair stage a Learian epiphany with food and dancing:

> 'What a lovely walk we've taken!
> Let us dine on Beans and Bacon!'
> So the Ducky, and the leetle
> Browny-Mousy and the Beetle
> Dined, and danced upon their heads
> Till they toddled to their beds.

None of Lear's other successful adventurers ever cuts his festivities short to "toddle" off to bed. The quality of the dash for freedom has diminished radically. As Byrom notes: "They are really strays and belong at home. When the animals rescue them, they congratulate each other like tourists who have been badly frightened but do not care to admit it to each other."[24] Their flying in the face of probability has far more mixed results than in the other nonsense songs and in the limericks. And in his later long poems Lear would abandon this reckless attitude or else show it having dreadful consequences.

The eccentric spirit of the limericks has its last gasp in a little-known poem, **"The New Vestments."** The protagonist is an "old man in the Kingdom of Tess / Who invented a purely original dress." With their designation of an old man from a specific locality who did something out of the ordinary, these first two lines strongly suggest the opening of a limerick. The "original dress," which combines dead mice, rabbit skins, and other skins of uncertain origin ("but it is not known whose") with garments composed of all manner of edible substances, resembles the outlandish costumes of many limerick protagonists. One thinks in particular of the old man of Blackheath:

> Whose head was adorned with a wreath,
> Of lobsters and spice, pickled onions and mice,
> That uncommon old man of Blackheath.[25]

But this poem, with five stanzas and forty-three lines of heroic couplets, provides far more space for detailed reflection on the phenomenon of bizarre dress than does the brief, prescribed limerick verse form. Although the fate of the new vestments parallels that of the spinach shawl worn by the young lady of Greenwich: "But a large spotty Calf, bit her shawl quite in half, / Which alarmed that young lady of Greenwich,"[26] the emotional effects of the incidents, and their magnitude, differ completely. The young lady merely suffers through an alarming experience, while the old man of Tess undergoes a harrowing, nightmare variation on **"The Emperor's New Clothes"**:

> He had walked a short way, when he heard a great noise,
> Of all sorts of Beasticles, Birdlings, and Boys;—
> And from every long street and dark lane in the town
> Beasts, Birdles, and Boys in a tumult rushed down.
> Two Cows and a half ate his Cabbage-leaf Cloak;—
> Four Apes seized his Girdle, which vanished like smoke;—
> Three Kids ate up half of his Pancaky Coat,—
> . . . . .
>
> He tried to run back to his house, but in vain,
> For Scores of fat Pigs came again and again;—
> They rushed out of stables and hovels and doors,—
> They tore off his stockings, his shoes, and his drawers;—
> And now from the housetops with screechings descend,
> Striped, spotted, white, black, and gray Cats without end,
> They jumped on his shoulders and knocked off his hat,—
> When Crows, Ducks, and Hens made a mincemeat of that;—
> . . . . .
>
> They swallowed the last of his Shirt with a squall,—
> Whereon he ran home with no clothes on at all.[27]

It is easy to forget that the attackers are only eating up the food-constituted clothes; the episode suggests both rape and cannibalism. The old man seems about to be devoured himself by a horde of ravening predators, who suggest all those grotesque limerick gluttons. This time, however, the gluttons do not choke or become ill but completely rout the milder eccentric. Due to the overall absurdity of the situation, the piling up of details, and the impossible magnitude of the attack force, the poem generates considerable humor. (It closely resembles a Dr. Seuss story in rhythm, content, and form.) But it combines the humor with equal amounts of horror. The dreadful experience certainly teaches the old man his lesson: "And he said to himself as he bolted the door, / 'I will not wear a similar dress any more, / Any more, any more, any more, never more!'" With this emphatic finality Lear renounces the devil-may-care nonconformity and adventure for adventure's sake that infuse his previous work. He would return to them "never more."

Laughable Lyrics, the volume that contains **"The New Vestments,"** appeared in 1877, the last of Lear's nonsense books to be published during his lifetime. Its contents display a maturity befitting a last work. The altered tone may reflect the settled, travel-weary poet, who has learned that voyages of adventure rarely result in miraculous happiness. Or, given Lear's many-sided perspective on things, it may reflect just another way of looking at situations he had formerly treated lightly or optimistically. One can pair several poems in this volume with counterparts in *Nonsense Songs* and observe illuminating contrasts. In general, *Laughable Lyrics* contains no animated inanimate objects, fewer animals, and more nonsense creatures unique to Lear. The poetic diction is less childish and the poetic structure more complex. The songs in the *Lyrics* do not evoke the world of fairy tale and nursery rhyme as strongly as do those in *Nonsense Songs*. And rather than stress escape from an unsatisfactory existence, they focus on the characters' attempts to compensate for loss or loneliness without simply evading them as the daddy long-legs and the fly had attempted to do. These poems have a distinct Darwinian strain: adapt or perish. Characteristically, though, Lear does not settle decisively on either alternative as preferable. Most of the adaptive mechanisms the characters employ have a touch of the ludicrous and the self-delusive. It is difficult to tell whether Lear approves of them as saving illusions or uses them to ridicule all those rationalizations by which people convince themselves that an absurd planet is the best of all possible worlds.

One poem that raises this question is **"The Dong with a Luminous Nose,"** the only one in the volume that Lear composes as an overt companion piece to a previous verse, **"The Jumblies."** **"The Dong"** qualifies the universal happiness achieved in that poem by showing the devastating effect the Jumblies' voyage has had on the Dong, a native of those far off lands they reach in their sieve:

> Long years ago
> The Dong was happy and gay,
> Till he fell in love with a Jumbly Girl
> Who came to those shores one day.[28]

During the Jumblies' sojourn the Dong knows communal as well as romantic love, as he joins in their celebration with its familiar elements of music, dance and moonlight:

> Happily, happily passed those days!
>   While the cheerful Jumblies staid;
> They danced in circlets all night long,
> To the plaintive pipe of the lively Dong,
>   In moonlight, shine, or shade.

But then the Jumblies sail home. Instead of the triumphal reception the earlier poem describes as resulting from their return, **"The Dong"** portrays the desolate lover:

> . . . left on the cruel shore
> Gazing—gazing for evermore,—
> Ever keeping his weary eyes on
> That pea-green sail on the far horizon.

The Dong will not accept the loss and resolves to wander over "valley or plain . . . lake and shore / Till I find my Jumbly Girl once more!" He stubbornly refuses adaptation, in the form of resignation to the unalterable. And yet he adapts quite well to the difficulties of his new role as seeker for his lost love. To facilitate his night searches, he designs as a lantern a "wondrous Nose" made from the bark of the Twangum Tree:

> A Nose as strange as a Nose could be!
> Of vast proportions and painted red,
> And tied with cords to the back of his head.
>   —In a hollow rounded space it ended
>   With a luminous Lamp within suspended,
>   All fenced about
>   With a bandage stout
>   To prevent the wind from blowing it out;—
>   And with holes all round to send the light,
>   In gleaming rays on the dismal night.

This amazing apparatus, as well as the "plaintive pipe," announces the Dong's sexual frustration with a crude phallic symbolism that none of Lear's other long noses begins to approach in obviousness. Although the Dong does not adjust sensibly to his abandonment by his love, he does find a purpose in life and a symbolic way to express, and perhaps externalize, his grief.

But is the reader to admire the Dong or to laugh at him? The opening stanzas, which introduce his nightly peregrinations with an aura of Byronic brooding and Gothic mystery, qualify as some of the best poetry Lear ever produced:

When awful darkness and silence reign
Over the great Gromboolian plain,
   Through the long, long wintry nights;—
When the angry breakers roar
And they beat on the rocky shore;—
    When Storm-clouds brood on the towering heights
Of the Hills of the Chankly Bore:—

Then, through the vast and gloomy dark,
There moves what seems a fiery spark,
   A lonely spark with silvery rays
    Piercing the coal black night,—
   A Meteor strange and bright:—
Hither and thither the vision strays,
   A single lurid light.
Slowly it wanders,—pauses,—creeps,—
Anon it sparkles,—flashes and leaps;
And ever as onward it gleaming goes
A light on the Bong-tree stem it throws.[29]

Nevertheless one senses a touch of parodic exaggeration in these lines, particularly in the accumulation of adjectives and the juxtaposed verbs in the sequence from "wanders" to "leaps." As the Dong transforms himself into this rather ludicrous Wandering Jew of nonsense land and sets out on his quest, he himself remarks, "What little sense I once possessed / Has quite gone out of my head!" But since the Dong inhabits a nonsense world, could this loss of sense not indicate the attainment of a higher wisdom? Is he an uncompromising Romantic idealist or a lovesick fool? The poet informs us in the concluding stanza that the Dong's quest is hopeless: "While ever he seeks, but seeks in vain / To meet with his Jumbly Girl again." He leaves open the question of whether his perseverance in a lost cause should be considered noble or idiotic. Lear perhaps created his nonsense world in order to avoid answering questions like these.

He does at least explore the matter further in **"The Courtship of the Yonghy-Bonghy-Bò,"** which shares with **"The Dong"** the theme of love found and then snatched away.[30] While **"The Dong"** may express Lear's feelings of rejection and loneliness symbolically, **"The Yonghy-Bonghy-Bò"** comes much closer to the actual details of his life. Commentators agree that the Bò is Lear himself, Lady Jingly Jones is Gussie Bethell, and the poem is a fictionalization of their abortive romance.[31] Several other details from Lear's experience find their way into the poem. Noakes believes that the name of the Yonghy-Bonghy-Bò was inspired by a southern Italian muleteer Lear employed during his travels in Calabria who "to Lear's delight . . . finished every incomprehensible sentence with the refrain 'Dighi Doghi Dà.'"[32] The name might equally well derive from a musical evening supplied by some Albanian gypsies while Lear was visiting that country in 1848: "The last performance I can remember to have attended to, appeared to be received as a capo d'opera: each verse ended by spinning itself out into a chain of rapid little Bos, ending in chorus thus: 'Bo, bo-bo-bo, BO!—bo, bobobo, BO!'"[33]

Moreover, throughout the poem the nonsense world and the "real" world come into closer proximity than usual. "The Coast of Coromandel / Where the early pumpkins blow" sounds like a fitting nonsense location, from which one could easily proceed to the Gromboolian plain or the Hills of the Chankly Bore. But in fact it is situated on the Bay of Bengal in southeastern India; Lear had visited this region during his last great excursion in 1873. The Bò is a nonsense creature who also appears in one of the alphabets; Lady Jingly is a human being from England. Because this poem deals with his own experience so closely, Lear sets it in a twilight zone between the worlds of sense and nonsense.

The lonely Yonghy-Bonghy-Bò is materially poor: "Two old chairs, and half a candle,—/ One old jug without a handle,—/ These were all his worldly goods."[34] With these worldly goods he would gladly endow Lady Jingly. He can in addition offer an abundance of food ("Fish is plentiful and cheap"), Lear's pervasive symbol of caring, and an inexhaustible supply of love: "As the sea, my love is deep!" Although the lady returns his love, the proposal comes too late. She has already bound herself to one of "them": "Handel Jones, Esquire, & Co." Jones's corporate connections suggest money and respectability; his first name may connote the pompous religious orthodoxy Lear despised. (*Handel* also means "trade" or "business" in the language of the Germans the poet detested.) The full name "Handel Jones" also clearly puns with inverse alliteration on the Bò's "old jug without a handle." For the Bò, like Lear himself, does lack a "Handel," an aristocratic name and all the material advantages (and perhaps sexual potency as well) that Jones can bestow upon his wife. However, the relationship between the Joneses appears solely materialistic. He sends Dorking Hens with delight, but does not come to join her on the Coromandel Coast. Nevertheless, Lady Jingly cannot break with loveless convention, and she responds in her husband's manner to her would-be lover: "I can merely be your friend! /—Should my Jones more Dorkings send, / I will give you three, my friend!" She then banishes the Bò from her company, and he responds to his loss, like so many Learian characters—and Lear himself—by running away.

Lear of course has altered the facts somewhat and telescoped the events of his drawn-out romance with Gussie. Unlike Lear, the Bò does propose only to have his love reject him because she is already married. Gussie may have married Adamson Parker because Lear never got around to proposing to her. So the poet is painting himself in a more sympathetic light than the actual circumstances would seem to warrant. He had, however, experienced sister Emma's discouragement of his proposal and Gussie's later marriage as rejections, and the rearrangement of the events in **"The Yonghy-Bonghy-Bò"** strengthens the poem's fidelity to his emotions. And by including two wretched lovers in the poem, in contrast to a single deserted Dong, Lear also allows himself to express both sides of his conflicting feelings about marriage. When the Bò mounts a turtle, who appears fortuitously like the pig in **"The Owl and the Pussy-cat"** and the boat in **"The Daddy Long-legs and the Fly,"** he sails away "with a sad primaeval motion," but he can still muster a song. He seems likely to adapt to a solitary existence on "the sunset isles of Boshen." The Bò's reaction may reflect Lear's anxieties that marriage might restrict his freedom.

But the poem concludes with Lady Jingly, who can neither throw off conformity, like one of the eccentrics, in order to follow the Bò, nor resign herself to her former life. Like the Dong, she is trapped in a self-made purgatory, and she sits paralyzed (by guilt?), incapable of even his pitiable attempts to regain happiness:

> From the Coast of Coromandel,
>   Did that Lady never go;
>   On that heap of stones she mourns
>   For the Yonghy-Bonghy-Bò.
> On that Coast of Coromandel,
>   In his jug without a handle
>   Still she weeps, and daily moans.

This situation rather strangely reverses that in the **"Dong"**; for here it is the faithful male lover who sails away and it is the rejecting female who, left on the "cruel shore," laments forever the loss of love. It would, I think, be inconsistent with Lear's personality and his continuing affection for Gussie to see this gloomy portrait of Lady Jingly sobbing over her lost opportunity as a wish-fulfillment punishment of Gussie for having married someone else. By the end of the poem Lady Jingly no longer stands for Augusta Bethell but has turned into an image of Lear's loneliness, reflecting not only his loss of Gussie but all the separations of his life, from Lushington, from Fortescue, from his mother. Because Lady Jingly creates her own predicament by rejecting commitment to love, one suspects that Lear felt himself both victim and cause of all the abandonments he had suffered over the years.

Lady Jingly's fate further comments on the question of adapting to loss that Lear presents so ambiguously in **"The Dong."** In **"The Yonghy-Bonghy-Bò,"** and perhaps, in retrospect, in the former poem as well, the question of whether one ought to resign oneself to circumstances or defy them becomes moot. Often adaptation depends more on capability than volition. No matter how necessary Lear may have believed adaptability to be, he senses that for many it is simply impossible. Lady Jingly and the Dong, miserable as they are,

may therefore be seeing life clearly and seeing it whole. And two other poems in *Laughable Lyrics*, **"The Pobble Who Has No Toes"** and **"Mr. and Mrs. Discobbolos,"** which portray characters who accept loss cheerfully and make the best of it, do not add any additional certainty; for in each case the characters' methods of adapting can be read either as pragmatically sensible or as blindly self-deluding.

While the two poems that portray a failure to resign oneself to loss concern an unsuccessful quest for love, the two that depict acceptance of loss do not involve courtship.[35] They reflect the settled domestic world of the Sparrows rather than the romantic wanderings of the owl and the pussy-cat. The plot of **"The Pobble"** in fact carefully reverses the pattern of the journey poems. Like **"The New Vestments,"** it also represents the victory of the spirit of "them" over the carefree recklessness of the eccentric. The poem opens in limerick fashion with an exchange between the Pobble and "they":

> The Pobble who has no toes
>   Had once as many as we;
> When they said, 'Some day you may lose them all,'—
>   He replied,—'Fish fiddle de-dee!'[36]

However, because the first line informs us that the Pobble had indeed lost his toes, the nonsense reply to "their" meddlesome solicitousness does not carry the sense of triumph it does in a limerick such as

> There was an old person of Sestri,
> Who sate himself down in the vestry,
> When they said 'You are wrong!'—he merely said
>   'Bong!'
> That repulsive old person of Sestri.

The Pobble lives with his Aunt Jobiska, a fussy mother-figure whom Lear may have drawn on the model of his sister Ann. The welfare of his toes is her principal concern in life. She doses him with medicinal "lavender water tinged with pink" because "The World in general knows / There's nothing so good for a Pobble's toes!" When she sends him on an errand, to swim the Bristol Channel to catch fish for her cat, she has him wrap his nose in scarlet flannel because

> . . . 'No harm
> 'Can come to his toes if his nose is warm;
> 'And it's perfectly known that a Pobble's toes
> 'Are safe,—provided he minds his nose.'

But the Pobble does not mind his nose carefully enough. A porpoise carries away the flannel, and the toes mysteriously disappear:

> And nobody ever knew
>   From that dark day to the present,
> Whoso had taken the Pobble's toes,

In a manner so far from pleasant.
Whether the shrimps or crawfish gray,
Or crafty Mermaids stole them away.

"They" must now bring the prostrate Pobble home to "his Aunt Jobiska's Park." Her reaction to the catastrophe is rather puzzling. She does not chide the Pobble for his carelessness, or bewail the loss of his toes, but without batting an eye assures him that "It's a fact the whole world knows, / That Pobbles are happier without their toes." While such a statement does not technically contradict Aunt Jobiska's earlier pronouncements—they had all concerned the welfare of the toes, not the benefits or drawbacks of possessing them—it certainly does represent an abrupt about-face in attitude. Is she a hypocrite, like the fox with the grapes? Is she determined, like Pangloss, to prove that whatever is is for the best? Is she simply telling her nephew a consoling lie? Or is she a fatalist who knows that one must accept the blows of life and continue on bravely? Again Lear displays an extremely ambivalent attitude toward adaptation to circumstance.

The poem becomes even more ambiguous when one realizes that although the Pobble takes all the risks and suffers the loss, the verse concentrates mainly on the reactions of his aunt. Except for his opening "Fiddle de-dee," he never speaks in the poem. He is a passive character who constantly has things done to him. Aunt Jobiska "made him drink" the lavender water. She sent him to swim the channel. The porpoise and the undetermined assailant stripped him of flannel and toes without his even being aware he had been attacked. He had to be placed in "a friendly Bark," rowed home, and "carried up." The poet even reports his request for food indirectly, and as "an earnest wish." What defect has rendered this creature so powerless? And why should his life always have revolved around the condition of his toes?

Having examined Lear's works up to this point, one finds the answer fairly obvious, given the intimate connection between nose and toes. The Pobble has been emasculated.[37] The poem deals with a losing struggle to maintain potency, in all senses of the word. Raised in a smothering, effeminate atmosphere, the Pobble is symbolically castrated the moment he sets out into the world to do a man's job. The reverse echoes of **"The Owl and the Pussy-cat,"** the closest thing to a conjugal poem that Lear ever wrote, serve to illustrate the Pobble's incapacity for such affairs. The Pobble goes to sea alone and on a domestic errand in the Bristol Channel, not with a lover and with an exotic land as his destination. His poem contains a "pussy-cat" also, Aunt Jobiska's "Runcible Cat with crimson whiskers"; but the Pobble does not share a feast with it. He must instead provide the food for the "runcible" creature, not enjoy his own food with a "runcible spoon" as do the

protagonists of **"The Owl and the Pussy-cat."** If his function is analogous to that of any creature in the previous poem, it is to that of the pig who must surrender its ring, as the Pobble surrenders his toes. And the pig was at least paid a shilling! The owl and the pussy-cat make their nuptial voyage in a pea-green boat; the porpoise who carries off the flannel is "sea-green."[38] The fowl and the feline row their own boat; the Pobble must be rowed home by "them." While both poems conclude with a meal ("And she made him a feast at his earnest wish / Of eggs and buttercups fried with fish"), one celebrates a wedding and is followed by a dance, while the other provides much-needed nourishment for a weakened traveler. In each case the Pobble's situation provides an impotent variation on a positive action by the two lovers.

One might, therefore, read Aunt Jobiska as a representative of all the women in Lear's life, from his mother, to Ann, to Gussie, and as a focus for all his negative feelings about them. Under a guise of solicitousness and conformity with social wisdom—Mrs. Sparrow springs immediately to mind—women emasculate a man, then expect him to cope with a virile world of "sailors and admirals."[39] And when the experience totally incapacitates him, they blandly cook supper and assure him that he will be much happier as a eunuch. One doubts that Lear consciously composed **"The Pobble"** to express such hostilities, but they do lurk beneath its surface. Even with the Freudian perspective retained, however, an alternative reading, as is usual in Lear, suggests itself. His sexuality caused Lear so much distress that he may have agreed wholeheartedly with Aunt Jobiska that Pobbles (people?) really are better off without their "toes."

On the other hand, abandoning the sexual symbolism, one can read the poem as another expression of the theme of safe but limiting domesticity that begins with **"Mr. and Mrs. Spikky Sparrow"** and **"The Table and the Chair"** and continues in **"The New Vestments."** All these poems deny the faith that travel can bring transcendent happiness that the journey poems, particularly **"The Jumblies,"** endorse. In **"The Pobble,"** it becomes dangerous to venture outside the door. **"Mr. and Mrs. Discobbolos"** continues this theme. At the same time it stresses the reduced quality of life that avoidance of danger—one form of adaptation to the precarious nature of Lear's universe—may necessitate. In form the poem returns to the exchange-of-dialogue stanza structure and stanza-ending refrain of the *Nonsense Songs*. Its title suggests that of **"Mr. and Mrs. Spikky Sparrow,"** and, in fact, **"Mr. and Mrs. Discobbolos"** uses the anxious concern of its title couple for one another's welfare, expressed through conventional circumlocutions and traditional terms of endearment, to parody the cozy married bliss that Lear had portrayed so unconvincingly in **"Mr. and Mrs. Spikky**

Sparrow." Now he sees clearly that cowardice and self-deception often lie at the root of such "happy" domesticity.

Mr. and Mrs. Discobbolos set out one day on a seemingly innocuous sightseeing picnic:

> Mr. and Mrs. Discobbolos
>   Climbed to the top of a wall.
> And they sate to watch the sunset sky
> And to hear the Nupiter Piffkin cry
>   And the Biscuit Buffalo call.
> They took up a roll and some Camomile tea.[40]

As most Lear characters are when sharing food, they are "as happy as happy could be." But then fear seizes the wife. She imagines that during their descent they might "fall down flumpetty / Just like pieces of stone!" With an equation of good health and proper clothing analogous to that made by Mrs. Sparrow, she inquires of her husband:

> 'What would become of your new green coat?
>   'And might you not break a bone?
> 'It never occurred to me before—
> 'That perhaps we shall never go down any more!'

She then engages in a clever bit of marital blame-passing, inquiring disingenuously of "my own darling Mr. Discobbolos": "What put it into your head / To climb up this wall?"

Her husband cannot dispel her fears, or deny his responsibility for their plight. But after a brief period of embarrassment, during which his ears turn "perfectly pink," he decides that their apparent predicament is actually a blessing in disguise. Just as Aunt Jobiska asserts that Pobbles are happier without their toes, he declares:

> 'But now I believe it is wiser far
> 'To remain for ever just where we are.'

So despite their fear of falling both Discobboloses stand up on the wall and declare in a song that they have stumbled into paradise:

> 'Far away from hurry and strife
> 'Here we will pass the rest of life,
>   'Ding a dong, ding dong, ding!
> 'We want no knives nor forks nor chairs,
> 'No tables nor carpets nor household cares,
>   'From worry of life we've fled—
>   'Oh! W! X! Y! Z!
> 'There is no more trouble ahead,
> 'Sorrow or any such thing—
>   'For Mr. and Mrs. Discobbolos!'

Few efforts at rationalizing away ill fortune could be more complete.

Again the question of how Lear views such adaptability to disaster returns. On the one hand, a passage from a letter to Fortescue shows that Lear sometimes shared the Discobboloses' view that it is better to escape the hurry and strife of earthbound life: "Going up and downstairs worries me, and I think of marrying some domestic henbird and then of building a nest in one of my own olive trees, where I should only descend at remote intervals during the rest of my life."[41] On the other hand, Lear knew that one could not escape life so easily, and he must intend us to see that the Discobboloses have to go through considerable mental gymnastics in order to turn calamity into blessing. And if their contentment at the end of the poem seems to justify the self-deception, Lear typically turns the tables once more by writing in 1879, at Wilkie Collins's request, a second part to the poem that quite literally blows up the complacency of Mr. and Mrs. Discobbolos.

The sequel finds them still on their wall after twenty years. They are happy, healthy, well regarded by their neighbors, and the parents of twelve fine children. But Mrs. Discobbolos becomes anxious about the children's isolation from normal social life. So she inquires: "Did it never come into your head / That our lives must be lived elsewhere, / Dearest Mr. Discobbolos?"[42] It is a fatal quesion. Declaring his wife a "runcible goose," Mr. Discobbolos slides down from the wall, digs a trench, fills it with dynamite and gunpowder, and blows himself and his family "In thousands of bits to the sky so blue." Does this awful destiny punish the wife's desire to tamper with an idyllic personal existence for the sake of social conformity; or does it illustrate that adaptation to ill fortune can become so complete that one refuses to take advantage of other opportunities when they come along? (The husband's mission of destruction ironically demonstrates that the family could have come down safely from the wall at any time.) Lear is noncommittal:

> And no one was left to have said,
>   'O, W! X! Y! Z!
>   'Has it come into anyone's head
> That the end has happened to all
>   Of the whole of the Clan Discobbolos?'

Despite the sadness and the many calamities in the *Nonsense Songs* and *Laughable Lyrics,* no one dies in any of them except here. Byrom suggests that by blowing up this family Lear is having revenge for his unhappy childhood, destroying socially respectable domesticity and denying that he has lost anything worthwhile in lacking it as a child or parent: "In this splendidly riotous death joke there is a great deal of relief. The home that smashed the child's spirit has itself been smashed. The delusive hopes that misled the grown-up's spirit have at last been dashed."[43]

Certainly the poem travesties the cloying, bourgeois family togetherness of Mr. and Mrs. Sparrow. Both poems contain a domestic establishment on a high perch, a nagging wife, and concern with what society views as proper. But birds at least belong in trees, if not in fashionable clothes, while "octopod" Discobboloses are only living an illusion of happiness and belonging on that wall. And once social reality "comes into" Mrs. Discobbolos's head, her formerly adoring and agreeable husband turns into "terrible Mr. Discobbolos," a suicidal/homicidal maniac, a dynamite-wielding nihilist.

In fact, all of the family's problems materialize only at the instant in which they "come into [someone's] head," a phrase used in seven of the nine choruses. Thus there is irony in the final refrain, in which no one is left to have the realization of the final destruction come into his head. Initially the couple fearlessly climbs the wall until the fears of falling come into Mrs. Discobbolos's head. She assumes that the idea for the excursion was "put into" her husband's head. Likewise, it suddenly comes into his head that they will never get down. Her decision that the children must go into society also comes into her head, and she chides her husband because the idea never came into his. Then the situation turns around, and suddenly Mr. Discobbolos raises the accusing voice: "What has come to your fiddledum head!" However, the idea of blowing up his family does not "come into" his head; he simply acts. Nor does his wife's "We shall presently all be dead" "come into" her head. She simply knows; for now both are going on instinct, not reason. So perhaps what Lear uses his nonsense to attack here is not the bourgeois family per se, but the world of sense to which such families belong. After all, where would the Jumblies have been if it had suddenly come into their heads that their sieve was dangerously full of holes? In most of the *Laughable Lyrics* the defiant spirit of the Jumblies and the limerick protagonists has proved powerless against fate. In **"Mr. and Mrs. Discobbolos"** Lear can grant that spirit no positive achievements, but he can at least allow it to blow up all those sensible stay-at-homes who fool themselves into believing that, no matter what losses they suffer, they will be happy if they only do what everyone else approves of.

If **"Mr. and Mrs. Discobbolos"** refutes the domestic conformity of the Sparrows by utterly annihilating it, another poem, **"The Pelican Chorus,"** merely mocks it with sympathetic humor. Once again Lear is taking a basic situation and viewing it from many perspectives. The two verses about bird families share several surface similarities, paramount among them the fact that they both do describe families of birds. Lear carries over from the limericks a disinclination to portray nuclear families of humans and a compensating fondness for portraying familial establishments composed of birds. In addition the pelicans, like the Sparrows, admire fashionable attire, as their detailed description of the "grandly dressed" King of the Cranes demonstrates. Both poems employ couplets and a refrain couched in nonsense bird language, although in the **"Pelican Chorus"** the annoying "twikky wikky wee" of the Sparrows is replaced by one of Lear's most charming musical effusions:

> Ploffskin, Pluffskin, Pelican jee!
> We think no Birds so happy as we!
> Plumpskin, Ploshkin, Pelican jill!
> We think so then, and we thought so still![44]

However, the domestic milieux of the two poems differ substantially. **"Mr. and Mrs. Spikky Sparrow"** portrays a comfortable but economy-minded middle-class establishment; the pelicans are king and queen of their kind. And the major event they recollect in flashback in the poem, the "coming out" of their daughter Dell and her subsequent courtship with and marriage to the King of the Cranes, takes place in the midst of the highest of high society. Lear's emotional associations with middle-class domesticity were all negative and intense, so that the attempt to picture the happy sparrow family rings false. But he knew the aristocracy quite well without having any emotional investment in its mores. Therefore he could detach himself to satirize its foibles without malice and depict its joys without envy.

King and Queen Pelican assume their superiority to other birds with the unthinking assurance that so often accompanies birth into a noble station:

> No other Birds so grand we see!
> None but we have feet like fins!
> With lovely leathery throats and chins!
> . . . . .
> Wing to wing we dance around,—
> Stamping our feet with a flumpy sound,—
> Opening our mouths as Pelicans ought,
> And this is the song we nightly snort.

Through incongruous word choice such as "leathery," "flumpy," and "snort" Lear suggests that such assumptions of superiority are often ludicrous, with little basis in objective fact. The poem also depicts the gala society gatherings where "Thousands of Birds in wondrous flight / . . . ate and drank and danced all night," and the concealed taints of blood: "And a delicate frill to hide his feet,—/ (For though no one speaks of it, every one knows, / He has got no webs between his toes!)." No doubt many of Lear's society friends could see themselves underneath the feathers.

While serving as a parody of a fashionable entertainment, Dell's debut represents at the same time still another of those communal feasts, like those that the Dong reflects upon, that the Jumblies celebrate in their sieve and repeat with their friends when they return, that the owl and the pussy-cat partake in after their marriage. All the elements of the Learian epiphany appear: singing and dancing; the sharing of food as a symbol of love ("For the King of the Cranes had won that heart, / With a Crocodile's egg and a large fish-tart"); the color of the crane's "pea-green trowsers"; the shore in the moonlight. But for the first time in one poem Lear combines the happy journey to nonsense land with the portrayal of those whom the travelers leave behind on the cruel shore. **"The Pelican Chorus"** is both **"The Jumblies"** and **"The Dong,"** both **"The Nutcrackers and the Sugar Tongs"** and **"Calico Pie."** So in the last stanza the tone changes from one of bois-trous humor, more characteristic of the *Nonsense Songs,* to the familiar melancholy of *Laughable Lyrics*:

> And far away in the twilight sky,
> We heard them singing a lessening cry,—
> Farther and farther till out of sight,
> And we stood alone in the silent night!
> Often since, in the nights of June,
> We sit on the sand and watch the moon;—
> She has gone to the great Gromboolian plain,
> And we probably never shall meet again!
> Oft, in the long still nights of June,
> We sit on the rocks and watch the moon;—
> —She dwells by the streams of the Chankly Bore,
> And we probably never shall see her more.

The synthesis allows Lear to accommodate his ambiva-lence about families, love, and society better than in any other single poem. "We probably never shall see her more" echoes "And they never came back to me," but the "probably" cancels out total despair. Unlike the Sparrows, whose children are not ready to leave the nest, the pelican family must split up. Dell flies off to begin her own family, and the king and queen, while "alone in the silent night"—and *silent* is a negatively charged word for Lear—are not really alone. They still have each other and their subjects.

Nevertheless, King and Queen Pelican have been excluded from the world of miracles. They must remain in the real world, on the existing Nile in the actual month of June, while their daughter has entered the timeless nonsense landscape of Gromboolian plain and Chankly Bore. Like the other protagonists in *Laugh-able Lyrics* they have suffered loss and must reconcile themselves to it. Thus, when they repeat the refrain for the last time, one notices that they "think" no birds as happy as they. Their happiness is not real; they have only convinced themselves that they possess it, just like Aunt Jobiska and Mr. Discobbolos in the first part of his poem. The confused verb tenses of "We think so then, and we thought so still" show the strain of maintaining that no difference exists between genuinely joyful past and forlorn present. Like all successful adapters in the poems, the pelicans delude themselves, but because their loss is the least severe, in this poem their rationalizations sound the least desperate.

Although the mood of the *Nonsense Songs* was gener-ally cheerful, Lear introduced elements of melancholy

in **"The Daddy Long-legs and the Fly"** and **"Calico Pie."** Conversely, *Laughable Lyrics* is a generally melancholy volume, but Lear, true to his multifaceted approach to life, does not fail to include one poem whose happy ending is unqualified. **"The Quangle Wangle's Hat"** exactly reverses the situation of **"Calico Pie,"** the token unhappy poem in *Nonsense Songs,* and comments as well on those deserted protagonists of *Laughable Lyrics* like the Dong and Lady Jingly Jones. It narrates the reversal of fortune of a lonely being with whom a whole flock of diverse nonsense creatures comes to live. The "me" of **"Calico Pie"** watches all the creatures of land, sea, and air desert him, and the poem ends with him left alone. The Quangle Wangle, concealed beneath an enormous Beaver Hat as he sits on the top of a Crumpetty Tree, begins in a solitary state:

> 'But the longer I live on this Crumpetty Tree
> 'The plainer than ever it seems to me
> 'That every few people come this way
> 'And that life on the whole is far from gay!'[45]

However, his hat proves as attractive to those seeking shelter as do similar types of headgear in the limericks.[46] After an initial inquiry from Mr. and Mrs. Canary about establishing a home on the hat's 102-foot width

> . . . to the Crumpetty Tree
>   Came the Stork, the Duck, and the Owl;
> The Snail, and the Bumble-Bee,
>   The Frog, and the Fimble Fowl;
> (The Fimble Fowl, with a Corkscrew leg;)
> And all of them said,—'We humbly beg,
> 'We may build our homes on your lovely Hat,—
> Mr. Quangle Wangle, grant us that!
>   Mr. Quangle Wangle Quee!'
>
> And the Golden Grouse came there,
>   And the Pobble who has no toes,—
> And the small Olympian bear,—
>   And the Dong with a luminous nose.
> And the Blue Baboon, who played the flute,—
> And the Orient Calf from the Land of Tute,—
> And the Attery Squash, and the Bisky Bat,—
> All came and built on the lovely Hat
>   Of the Quangle Wangle Quee.[47]

"Calico Pie" is a centrifugal poem, with all elements flying away from a central void; this is a centripetal poem, with all elements converging on the central character. The parade resembles that of the animals in **"The New Vestments,"** but these creatures come to build, not to devour.

The poem ends with the familiar Learian epiphany, now taking place in a blissful present rather than an ir-recoverable, remembered past:

> And at night by the light of the Mulberry moon
> They danced to the Flute of the Blue Baboon,

On the broad green leaves of the Crumpetty Tree,
And all were as happy as happy could be,
    With the Quangle Wangle Quee.

With this poem the changing moods associated with the unpredictability of the nonsense universe from the limericks through *Nonsense Songs* and *Laughable Lyrics* comes full circle. If the arbitrary mutability of the world Lear portrays means that one can never be sure of retaining happiness, love, or a place in a community, it also means that isolation and loneliness may vanish just as suddenly as joy. The presence on the hat of two of the more miserable characters from the *Lyrics,* the Pobble and the Dong, as well as others identifiable with the happier *Nonsense Song* protagonists (an owl, a duck, and a married pair of small birds that suggests the Sparrows), underscores the ongoing revolutions of fortune in nonsense land. Lear's poems teach us to guard against complacency, since disaster may lurk around the corner; they just as firmly teach us to guard against despair because hope may drop out of the sky tomorrow.

Lear dwells repeatedly on the same problems and examines them from many possible angles, but he gives no final answers. Had he really wished to come to some firm conclusion about adapting to loss and loneliness, he would not have chosen to write the kind of poetry he did. Its ambiguity allows for multiple interpretations and is calculated to prevent any arrival at logical conclusions. Lear did not try to make sense out of life; he regarded such an effort as hopeless. So he made nonsense of it instead.

Two Poetic Autobiographies

Lear wrote two longer poems that never appeared in any of the volumes of verse he published during his lifetime, although he circulated copies of them widely among his friends. Overtly rather than covertly autobiographical, as is characteristic of their author, they view his life from two different perspectives. The first, an untitled collaborative effort with a young friend, Miss Bevan, written in 1878, has become known by its first line, **"How pleasant to know Mr. Lear!"** It is a descriptive poem, painting a word picture of the appearance, habits, and surroundings of a "crazy old Englishman, oh!" It proceeds through a series of nonsequiturs, using details accurate in themselves but often juxtaposed without logical connectives:

He reads but he cannot speak Spanish,
    He cannot abide ginger beer.[48]

It also displays the self-deprecating humor about his physical appearance that marks Lear's self-caricatures:

His mind is concrete and fastidious,
    His nose is remarkably big;

His visage is more or less hideous,
    His beard it resembles a wig.

His body is perfectly spherical,
    He weareth a runcible hat.

The nonsense songs reveal that these jokes conceal genuine pain, but this verse stays on the external level, with the poet commenting dispassionately upon himself in the third person. The poem thus avoids expressing any of Lear's more disturbing emotions. How seriously can a reader take his description of himself weeping on seashore and hilltop when he immediately follows it with a nonsense menu: "He purchases pancakes and lotion, / And chocolate shrimps from the mill." Although one suspects a self-mocking irony in the phrase "How pleasant," joined in the final two lines to a suggestion of impending death,[49] the poem probably offers a fair approximation of the image Lear presented to the world—a jolly, lovable old eccentric.

The second autobiographical poem, **"Incidents in the Life of My Uncle Arly,"** the last nonsense poem Lear ever wrote, is not a description but a history. It is narrated in the first person, the only poem besides **"Calico Pie"** to be so, and its melancholy is only partially distanced. True, the poem concerns not "Mr. Lear" but "Uncle Arly," and the first-person speaker is not this figure, but his nephew (or niece). The disguise, however, is paper-thin. Lear freely acknowledged that the poem was about him; including a draft in a letter to Fortescue in June 1884, he remarked, "I shall send you a few lines just to let you know how your aged friend goes on."[50] As Byrom observes, we soon "spot Lear hiding 'unclearly' in "UncLE ARly," and we recognize "the 'Adopty Duncle' of his many 'little folks.'"[51] All the incidents and items mentioned in the poem serve as symbolic nonsense equivalents of events and objects in Lear's life.

"Uncle Arly" begins with a tableau:

O my agèd Uncle Arly!
Sitting on a heap of Barley
    Thro' the silent hours of night,—
Close beside a leafy thicket:—
On his nose there was a Cricket,—
In his hat a Railway-Ticket;—
    (But his shoes were far too tight.)[52]

By following its use through the songs, one recognizes "silent" as a code word for unhappiness.[53] The leafy thicket may represent the garden at San Remo, or simply the natural scenes that Lear painted. The nose, of course, is the physical feature that stands out. The cricket, most critics agree, represents Lear's nonsense muse.[54] The railway ticket symbolizes the long years spent in wandering. And what about the parenthetical tight shoes? In the letter to Fortescue, which emphasizes this line by adding "Too! too! far too tight!" to it, the distress is quite literal, as Lear follows the stanza with: "By the 15th. May, I was just able to get away from here on my journey of discovery; I was frightfully pulled down by my illness—with swollen feet; and unable to walk."[55] But surely the pinching shoes also suggest the painful limitations of his nature—epilepsy, homosexuality, depression.

The poem then proceeds to relate in flashback how Uncle Arly arrived at the state the first stanza describes. In youth he "squander'd all his goods away" and had to embark on a life of wandering and diverse subsistence jobs:

> Like the ancient Medes and Persians,
> Always by his own exertions
>   He subsisted on those hills;—
> Whiles,—by teaching children spelling,—
> Or at times by merely yelling,—
> Or at intervals by selling
>   Propter's Nicodemus Pills.

Then on a fateful day

> . . . in his morning rambles
> He perceived the moving brambles—
>   Something square and white disclose;—
> 'Twas a First-class Railway-Ticket;
> But, on stooping down to pick it
> Off the ground,—a pea-green Cricket
>   Settled on my uncle's Nose.

Although chronologically out of sequence, since it follows the account of several years of wandering, this stanza must refer to the Knowsley years; for it was at Knowsley that Lear received his "ticket" to travel among "first-class" patrons abroad and at Knowsley that he first began writing nonsense. (The application of his favorite nonsense color, "pea-green," to the cricket reinforces its identification with his poetry.)

Uncle Arly travels for three-and-forty winters—not *years,* since Lear often went home to England in the summers—exactly the amount of time that elapsed from his first leaving England to his settling at San Remo. By this time the shoes are "worn to splinters," although still, paradoxically, "too tight." As the nonsense surely must have, so the cricket provides comfort during the weary and painful travels:

> Never—never more,—oh! never,
> Did that Cricket leave him ever,—
>   Dawn or evening, day or night;—
> Clinging as a constant treasure,—
> Chirping with a cheerious measure,—
> Wholly to my uncle's pleasure,—
>   (Though his shoes were far too tight.)

The cricket possibly represents as well the loyal, and constant, companionship Lear had been doomed never to experience with anyone. Perhaps this explains its perching on the phallic nose.

At long last Uncle Arly settles at "Borley-Melling, / Near his old ancestral dwelling." Byrom remarks of these lines that "here Lear seems to prefer fiction to life, for he has Uncle Arly settle not in a nonsense San Remo but in Borley-Melling, a nonsense village near his ancestral home. Lear, of course, had no ancestral home, and those he visited he mostly disliked."[56] I believe, however, that Borley-Melling is indeed a nonsense San Remo and that Lear is using the phrase "ancestral dwelling" with bitter irony. The home he built from the ground up in San Remo and then had to rebuild *was* an ancestral dwelling for a man who felt himself born parentless, who had spent his prime homeless, and who would leave no descendants, only nieces and nephews widely scattered in New Zealand and America. Since Lear was his own sole ancestor and heir, why should he not call the Villa Tennyson an ancestral dwelling? The distance between the commonly assumed meaning of such a term and Lear's private joke expresses succinctly the sense of isolation that dominated his emotional life.

In the first stanza of the poem, Uncle Arly, sitting on his heap of barley with his cricket, resembles Lady Jingly Jones, sitting on her "heap of stones" with her Dorking hens. Doubtless Lear means the image to evoke the same feeling of despair. Unlike Lady Jingly, however, Uncle Arly is allowed by his creator to escape from his misery at last:

> On a little heap of Barley
> Died my agèd uncle Arly,
>   And they buried him one night;—
> Close beside the leafy thicket,—
> There,—his hat and Railway-Ticket;—
> There,—his ever-faithful Cricket;—
>   (But his shoes were far too tight.)

Nevertheless, he is ignominiously buried by "they," not "we," as the first-person narration might lead one to assume. And the constricting shoes follow him even to the grave, as do all the few constants of his life.

When "they," the strangers in San Remo, buried Lear, they had carved on the stone an inscription he had left for them: "In Memory of Edward Lear. Landscape painter in many lands. Born at Highgate May 12, 1812. Died at San Remo January 29, 1888. Dear for his many gifts to many souls." It was followed by some lines from Tennyson's poem addressed to Lear, "To E. L., on his Travels in Greece." Had "they" been truly wise, they would have disregarded Lear's instructions and used the last stanza of **"Uncle Arly"** as his epitaph instead.

Notes

1. *Spectator,* December 23, 1871, p. 1571. The reviewer did in fact prefer the limericks to the longer poems.

2. *The Field of Nonsense* (London, 1952), passim. Sewell does consider the nonsense songs as departures from pure nonsense.

3. The arrangement was not, however, intentional. Lear had intended to include limericks in his second volume of poems, but his publisher, Bush, persuaded him to reserve them for a subsequent volume. Perhaps the publisher detected the appropriateness of such a separation.

4. But see Byrom, p. 160, for some darker undercurrents in the poem.

5. The text of "The Owl and the Pussy-Cat" appears in *Complete Nonsense*, pp. 61-63.

6. See Byrom, p. 159, on the sexual confusion. In an unfinished sequel, "The Children of the Owl and the Pussy-Cat," Lear does make it clear that the owl is the father and the cat the mother.

7. The text of "The Duck and the Kangaroo" appears in *Complete Nonsense*, pp. 64-66.

8. Byrom, p. 164.

9. The text of "The Daddy Long-Legs and the Fly" appears in *Complete Nonsense*, pp. 67-70.

10. Lear had wanted to call the book "Learical Lyrics," which, considering the autobiographical resonances of the poems it contains, would have been far more apt. See Noakes, p. 272.

11. The text of "The Jumblies" is found in *Complete Nonsense*, pp. 71-74.

12. "Die Nonsense-Poesie von Edward Lear," *Neueren Sprachen* 45 (1937): 371.

13. See Sewell, pp. 61-80.

14. The text of "The Nutcrackers and the Sugar-Tongs" appears in *Complete Nonsense*, pp. 75-77.

15. The line contrasts with "They all came back" in "The Jumblies," although *never* is to be the rule in most of Lear's poems.

16. *Complete Nonsense*, p. 21.

17. Ibid., p. 190.

18. The text of "Calico Pie" appears in *Complete Nonsense*, pp. 78-80.

19. Byrom, p. 174.

20. Here I disagree strongly with Byrom, who states that "Mr. and Mrs. Spikky Sparrow" is "a bright, flinty poem, made of tough, trochaic, tetrameter couplets," p. 194.

21. The text of "Mr. and Mrs. Spikky Sparrow" appears in *Compete Nonsense*, pp. 81-84.

22. The text of "The Broom, The Shovel, The Poker, and The Tongs" appears in *Complete Nonsense*, pp. 85-86.

23. The text of "The Table and the Chair" appears in *Complete Nonsense*, pp. 87-89.

24. Byrom, p. 172.

25. *Complete Nonsense*, p. 168.

26. Ibid., p. 194.

27. The text of "The New Vestments" appears in *Complete Nonsense*, pp. 245-46.

28. The text of "The Dong with a Luminous Nose" appears in *Complete Nonsense*, pp. 225-28.

29. The mention of the Bong Tree identifies the Dong's home as the same land as that to which the owl and the pussy-cat travel.

30. Both poems therefore provide an alternative view of the happy courtship of the owl and the pussy-cat.

31. See Noakes, p. 220; Byrom, p. 182; Davidson, p. 197; and Philip Hofer, "The Yonghy-Bonghy-Bò," *Harvard Library Bulletin* 15 (1967): 229-37.

32. Noakes, p. 79.

33. Ibid., p. 95.

34. The text of "The Courtship of the Yonghy-Bonghy-Bò" appears in *Complete Nonsense*, pp. 237-41.

35. There is an unpublished version of "The Pobble" in which the Pobble gives away his toes as a wedding gift to Princess Bink of Jampoodle (printed in Davidson, pp. 241-43). But this version becomes a straightforward love poem. When he decided to stress the loss, Lear eliminated the romantic interest, for loss of love seems to have been the one deprivation Lear could not let his characters convince themselves is for the best.

36. The text of "The Pobble Who Has No Toes" appears in *Complete Nonsense*, pp. 242-44.

37. See Edmund Miller, "Two Approaches to the Nonsense Poems of Edward Lear," *Victorian Newsletter* 44 (1973): 5-8, for his Freudian reading of both versions of "The Pobble."

38. "Sea-green" is the Homeric epithet that Lear adapted as his "pea-green." The use of the original term once again implies that the magic of nonsense land eludes the Pobble.

39. "And all the Sailors and Admirals cried, / When they saw him nearing the further side,—/ 'He has gone to fish, for his Aunt Jobiska's / Runcible Cat with crimson whiskers!'"

40. The text of "Mr. and Mrs. Discobbolos" appears in *Complete Nonsense*, pp. 247-48.

41. Quoted in Noakes, p. 252.

42. The text of "Mr. and Mrs. Discobbolos, Second Part" appears in *Complete Nonsense*, pp. 249-51.

43. Byrom, p. 203. He also notes the parallels between this poem and "Mr. and Mrs. Spikky Sparrow."

44. The text of "The Pelican Chorus" appears in *Complete Nonsense*, pp. 232-35.

45. The text of "The Quangle Wangle's Hat" appears in *Complete Nonsense*, pp. 252-54.

46. See Byrom, p. 214, for the pertinent examples from the limericks.

47. This list resembles a catalogue of arriving birds in "The Pelican Chorus," but in that verse the departure of the flock also occurs, since that poem describes both coming together and desertion.

48. The text of "How pleasant to know Mr. Lear!" appears under the heading "Self-Portrait of the Laureate of Nonsense" in *Complete Nonsense*, pp. vii-viii.

49. The final lines read: "Ere the days of his pilgrimage vanish / How pleasant to know Mr. Lear!"

50. *Later Letters*, p. 283.

51. Byrom, pp. 219-20.

52. The text of "Incidents in the Life of My Uncle Arly" appears in *Complete Nonsense*, pp. 275-76.

53. The phrases "the silent main" ("Daddy Long-legs"); "thru the silent-roaring ocean" ("Yonghy-Bonghy-Bò"); "When awful darkness and silence reign" ("The Dong"); and "we stood alone in the silent night" ("Pelican Chorus") all occur in passages describing the protagonist's unhappiness. It is an odd equation, in view of the fact that Lear hated noise.

54. See Noakes, p. 307; Byrom, p. 223.

55. *Later Letters*, p. 283.

56. Byrom, p. 224.

Selected Bibliography

PRIMARY SOURCES

Laughable Lyrics, a Fourth Book of Nonsense Poems, Songs, Botany, Music, etc. London: Bush, 1877.

The Complete Nonsense of Edward Lear. Edited by Holbrook Jackson. London: Faber, 1947; rpt. New York: Dover, 1951.

Later Letters of Edward Lear. Edited by Lady Strachey. London: T. Fisher Unwin, 1911.

SECONDARY SOURCES

Byrom, Thomas. *Nonsense and Wonder: the Poems and Cartoons of Edward Lear.* New York: Dutton, 1977.

Davidson, Angus. *Edward Lear: Landscape Painter and Nonsense Poet (1812-1888).* London: John Murray, 1938.

Hofer, Philip, and Thompson, Randall. "The Yonghy-Bonghy-Bò: I. The Poem. II. The Music." *Harvard Library Bulletin* 15 (1967): 229-37.

Miller, Edmund. "Two Approaches to Edward Lear's Nonsense Songs." *Victorian Newsletter* 44 (1973): 5-8.

Noakes, Vivien. *Edward Lear: the Life of a Wanderer.* London: Collins, 1968; rev. ed. London: Fontana, 1980.

Sewell, Elizabeth. *The Field of Nonsense.* London: Chatto and Windus, 1952.

Priscilla A. Ord (essay date 1985)

SOURCE: Ord, Priscilla A. "'There Was an Old Derry Down Derry, Who Loved to Make Little Folks Merry': A Closer Look at the Limericks of Edward Lear." *Literary Onomastics Studies* 12 (1985): 93-118.

[*In the following essay, Ord examines Lear's nonsense verse in the context of the social history of the limerick. The critic also discusses the purpose of Lear's verse, considering the claim that many of the verses were written to teach geography to children.*]

Edward Lear, whom most know as a writer and illustrator of nonsense rhymes and verses, as well as nonsense songs, stories, alphabets, recipes, and botany, predominantly for children, was also an accomplished illustrator, landscape painter, and poet. Born May 12, 1812, in Holloway, a suburb north of London, Edward, the twentieth of twenty-one children of Ann Clark (née Skerrit) and Jeremiah Lear, was prone to petit mal epileptic seizures, which he referred to as the "Terrible Demon" in his diary, and suffered from attacks of chronic asthma and bronchitis that were later to make it impossible for him to live in England in the winter.

When his father, a well-to-do stockbroker, went bankrupt in 1816, following several unwise business speculations, the family was dispersed, and Edward, who was but three at the time, was placed in the care of his eldest sister Ann where he remained even after the family debts had been paid and his father was released from King's Bench Prison. Being too frail to attend school, Edward was tutored by Ann, who also gave him lessons in drawing and painting. He studied natural history on his own, wrote poetry, and began to earn his own way by making sketches, preparing illustrations, and executing anatomical and disease drawings for doctors and surgeons. Still in his teens, he began a serious study of the parrots at the London Zoological Gardens in Regent's Park that ultimately resulted in the publication, in 1832, of a series of folios, entitled *Illustrations of the Family Psittacidae,* the first complete volume of colored drawings of birds on so large a scale to be produced in England, equal to the well-known studies of Audubon and Barraband. He also undertook a similar study for *Tortoises, Terrapins, and Turtles* (1872).

It was, however, the previous volume on parrots that brought him to the attention of Lord Stanley, an amateur naturalist who was later to become the 13th Earl of Derby. After seeing his expert illustrations and observing him at work, Lord Stanley commissioned him to illustrate a volume based on the unique, private menagerie at Knowsley Hall, his family's estate in Lancashire. Lear spent the major portion of the next five years, 1832-1837, sketching and preparing the illustrations for the book. The resulting volume, titled *Gleanings from the Menagerie and Aviary at Knowsley Hall,* was published privately in 1846.

While working at Knowsley, two things occurred which were to direct the course of Lear's life from that point onward. First his eyesight began to fail, and his attacks of asthma and bronchitis became more severe. This prompted him to abandon the exacting, extremely detailed work that was necessary to draw and paint natural history specimens from life. Instead he became a landscape painter, which permitted him to travel and avoid the harsh English winter weather that aggravated his health.

Secondly, Lear and others began to recognize his ability to entertain children, as well as adults, with extemporaneous nonsense verses accompanied by quick sketches for illustrations.

> Shortly after Lear arrived, the Earl noticed that the grandchildren and great-grandchildren would leave the dinner table as soon as they politely could and dash off below stairs. Inquiring, the Earl learned that they were gathering in the steward's dining room where the new zoological artist was entrancing them with ridiculous rhymes and improbable drawings about "a young lady of Portugal, whose ideas were excessively nautical," who drew people who looked like owls and vice versa, who meted out poetic injustice by bringing good people to bad ends, and who was always making fun of big noses, like that Old Man's "on whose nose, / Most birds of the air could repose; / But they all flew away, at the closing of day, / Which relieved that Old Man and his nose." . . .
>
> Instead of declaring the steward's quarters off limits the Old Earl [Lord Stanley's father] brought the star attraction upstairs to dine and socialize with the family.

Edward Lear became not just a retainer at Knowsley but a guest and good friend. The friendship lasted through several successions to the title. "Fancy," Lear wrote some 50 years later, "having worked for 4 Earls of Derby."

(Kastner, p. 110)

It is ironic that Edward Lear, who considered himself a "topographical landscape painter," was sought after, even in his own time, for his detailed watercolor sketches instead of the larger oil paintings that required more of his time and efforts. The further irony is that, although the value of his artwork, as might be expected, has increased considerably since his death, he is known almost exclusively at the present time for his limericks and several of his longer nonsense poems, including **"The Owl and the Pussycat,"** written in 1868 for three-year-old Janet Symond, the daughter of one of Lear's friends, **"The Courtship of the Yonghy-Bonghy-Bò,"** **"The Pobble Who Has No Toes,"** **"The Akond of Swat,"** and **"Incidents in the Life of My Uncle Arly."**

Edward Lear did not, as many have assumed, invent the rigid rhymed and metered poetic form that is known today as the limerick. While it has, over the years, come to be closely associated with him, the origin of the verse form, as well as the derivation of its appellation, is uncertain. To be sure, however, his fondness for and extensive use of this form of nonsense poetry undoubtedly contributed significantly to its development, its acceptance, and its popularity.

At least three popular books containing verses of the limerick form were published a quarter century before Lear's in the early 1820's. The first, *The Adventures of Fifteen Young Ladies,* and its sequel, *The History of Sixteen Wonderful Old Women, . . . Their Principal Eccentricities and Amusements,* were published in London in 1821 by John Harris. (Byrom, p. 50) A year later, John Marshall published a toybook, *Annecdotes and Adventures of Fifteen Gentlemen,* attributed to R. S. Sharp, a grocer, poet, and author of several other books for children. *Fifteen Gentlemen* is considered by some to be a parody of the two volumes that preceded it, and its colored woodcut illustrations appear to be the work of Robert Cruikshank, a caricaturist and the elder brother of George Cruikshank, a well-known illustrator of children's book. Included in this volume were "a fat man of Bombay," "a poor man of Jamaica," "a tailor who sailed from Quebec," and "a sick man from Tobago," who turned out to be an inspiration for not one but two 19th century authors.

> There was a sick man of Tobago
> Liv'd long on rice-gruel and sago;
> But at last, to his bliss,
> The physician said this—
> "To a roast leg of mutton you may go."

(Opie, p. 406)

There was an old man of Tobago
Who lived on rice, gruel, and sago;
Till, much to his bliss,
His physician said this—
To a leg, sir, of mutton you may go.

(Opie, p. 407)

While at the Villa Emily in San Remo in August 1871, Lear wrote the following in the introduction to *More Nonsense Pictures, Rhymes, Botany &c.* (1872).

> Long years ago, in days when much of my time was passed in a country house, where children and mirth abounded, the lines beginning, "There was an old man of Tobago," were suggested to me by a valued friend, as a form of verse lending itself to limitless variety for rhymes and pictures; and thenceforth the greater part of the original drawings and verses for the first *Book of Nonsense* were struck off with a pen, no assistance ever having been given me in any way but that of uproarious delight and welcome at the appearance of every new absurdity."

(Lear, *The Complete Nonsense Book,* p. 21)

Coincidently, it is the same verse about the "sick man of Tobago" to which Charles Dickens refers, through the character of Eugene, in the second chapter of *Our Mutual Friend* (1864).

Neither Lear nor his immediate successors called the verses limericks. In fact, the word is first cited in the *Oxford English Dictionary* (*O.E.D.*) in 1898, ten years after Lear's death, and it is defined as "A form of 'nonsense verse.'" The final citation is taken from Rudyard Kipling's *Stalky and Co.* (1899) as follows: "Make up a catchy Limerick, and let the fags sing it." "By then," as John Byrom points out in *Nonsense and Wonder: The Poems and Cartoons of Edward Lear,* "it [the limerick] had lost not only its respectability, but also its final refrain, in favor of the novel and epigrammatic tail-line which it almost invariably has today." (Byrom, p. 50) Lear's limericks, as Joseph Kastner points out in his article on Lear in *Smithsonian,* "were often violent and uncharitable, but they were always chaste." (Kastner, p. 110)

As to the derivation of the word, the *O.E.D.* indicates that it is

> Said to be from a custom at convivial parties, according to which each member sang an extemporized "nonsense-verse," which was followed by a chorus containing the words, "Will you come up to Limerick?"

Angus Davidson states that

> It is possible that these extemporized nonsense-verses were in the limerick form and took their name from the words of the chorus, though the latter are not themselves in the limerick metre.

(Davidson, p. 18)

There were two separate volumes in which the bulk of Lear's limericks appeared: *A Book of Nonsense* (1846) and *More Nonsense Pictures, Rhymes, Botany &c.* (1872). The first collection was compiled in 1845 from those verses that had amused the children at Knowsley, as well as several written in the interim for the children of friends in whose homes he had stayed and even the children of strangers whom he encountered during his travels. Emery Kelen believes that the first volume might, quite likely, have been encouraged by those former children for whom Lear was an "Adopty Duncle" and who, now parents themselves, wished to have copies of the rhymes that they remembered. (Kelen, p. 35) Thus,

> On February 10, 1846, Thomas McLean, who had brought out his [Lear's] *Views in Rome* in 1841, published *A Book of Nonsense* in two volumes at 3s. 6d. There were seventy limericks in all; Lear chose the *nom de plume* "Derry Down Derry" and placed on the title page a limerick explaining how the book had come about:

> There was an old Derry down Derry
> Who loved to see little folks merry;
> So he made them a Book,
> And with laughter they shook
> At the fun of that Derry down Derry!

(Byrom, p. 9)

From all reports the book was an immediate success, and it was reprinted and republished frequently, running into nearly thirty editions in his lifetime. Early editions were literally "read to pieces." Curiously it was not until Routledge, Warne and Routledge reissued the book in 1861 that Lear affixed his name to the work, perhaps fearing originally that his association with a book of nonsense for children might "damage" his reputation as a landscape painter. (Kelen, p. 35-36) The dedication not only identified Lear as the author of the verses, but it stated that the book itself was for the children of his original audience at Knowsley.

TO THE
GREAT-GRANDCHILDREN, GRAND-NEPHEWS, AND GRAND-NIECES
OF EDWARD, 13TH EARL OF DERBY,
THIS BOOK OF DRAWINGS AND VERSES
*(The greater part of which were originally made and composed
for their parents.)*
Is Dedicated by the Author,
EDWARD LEAR
London, 1862.

In form, the limerick consists of two three-beat lines, followed by two two-beat lines, sometimes written as one, concluding with a single three-beat line that rhymes with the first two lines in an $a^3a^3b^2b^2a^3$ rhyme scheme. Originally the subject matter was humorous by presenting a nonsensical argument or statement.

Lear's limericks were printed in three lines with an almost German system of capitalization, that included most nouns and all proper names, in the early editions. The 1854 edition, however, featured the limericks in the five-line italic form with capitalization reserved for proper nouns only. The greater portion of the limericks, 184 out of the total 229, or 80%, introduce an old or young man, lady, girl, person—either male or female, the clues being derived from subsequent pronoun usage, the figure in the illustration, or a combination of the two—or, in but one case, a sailor from some specific geographical location or a named topographical feature or direction. In all but one case, limerick #227 being the exception, these persons existed at some time in the past. Almost following a formula, the first line reads:

                              man
                              lady
There was / is an old / a young person (m or f) of /
    in. . . .
                              girl
                              sailor

The second line, then, is a relative clause, referring to the subject of the first line and ending with a word that rhymes with and provides a pronunciation guide to the placename, topographical feature, or direction named in that line. There are, however, several foreign place-names ending in -*a* where, no doubt reflecting his own pronunciation, the rhyming word ends in -*er*, such as:

96.	Corsica	saucy-cur
108.	Janina	fanning her
110.	Sparta	daughter
112.	Buda(pest)	ruder
114.	Aôsta	lost her
115.	Anacona	no owner
116.	Apulia	peculiar
119.	Ischia	friskier
121.	Lucca	forsook her
123.	Parma	calmer
124.	Pisa	please her
133.	Russia	hush her
136.	Majorca	walker
145.	Calcutta	butter
153.	Smyrna	burn her
159.	Iowa	stow her
163.	Jamaica	Quaker
166.	Columbia	some beer

Also, with British and popular pronunciation prevailing, it is difficult for present-day readers to accomplish a complete rhyme with the following items:

30.	Dorking	walking
45.	Hull	Bull
91.	Prague	plague

92.	Prague	vague
97.	Marseilles	veils

The third and fourth lines rhyme or, if they are written as one, have internal rhyme. The final line is frequently a repeat or refrain of the first line, often in the form of a relative clause or an exclamation about the subject of the limerick, featuring an unusually descriptive if not outlandish adjective or verb. For example,

> There was an Old Person of Gretna,
> Who rushed down the crater of Etna;
> When they said, "Is it hot?" He replied, "No, it's not!"
> That mendacious Old Person of Gretna.

> There was an Old Person of Ewell
> Who chiefly subsisted on gruel;
> But to make it more nice, he inserted some mice,
> Which refreshed that Old Person of Ewell.

The last line almost invariably ends with the same word as the first line. (Hark, p. 28)

> The refrain effect . . . distinguishes Lear's limericks from those that have subsequently evolved, for later limerick writers generally aim at a clever twist for the last rhyme to serve as a kind of punch line.
>
> (Hark, p. 29)

A cursory look at the list of adjectives that Lear has used, particularly in his final line—including a few he invented, such as *borascible* (2), *abruptious* (76), and *ombliferous* (107)—are some indication of the range of vocabulary that is necessary to fully understand and appreciate Edward Lear's humor. Other adjectives that he coined, and for which he will be remembered, include *meloobious,* referring to a sound; *runcible,* modifying, at one time or another, the words *cat, goose, hat, spoon, state of mind,* and *wall*; and *scroobious,* applied to conduct and movements.

The subject matter of these limericks is far from serious. They describe the existence of

> an individual who is in the literal sense remarkable, i.e. something about his or her appearance, behavior, or circumstances is worthy of remark. . . . They engage in eccentric and often impossible behavior; their heads are too small, their noses and legs too long, their eating habits and ideas of fashion strange. They fall victim to terrible calamities. They come into conflict with neighbors, the infamous *they* of Lear's world, and with the animal kingdom, but they also on occasion develop satisfying symbiotic relationships with both.
>
> (Hark, p. 23)

The verse form may be confining and conventionalized, but the people and the situations in which they find themselves are far from those that would be considered conventional.

Just as an ailing old man from Tobago served as the inspiration for Lear's first limericks, a simple statement in a recent article on children's play and games in the Victorian Era prompted the present study of Edward Lear and those limericks. Following a brief description of the illustrated alphabets—similar to the one that Lear composed for Lord Tennyson's sons Hallam and Lionel, "A was an ape, / Who stole some white tape, / . . . ."—that different families commissioned Lear to devise to aid their children's learning, the author of the article states, "Lear also created geographical limericks to teach place names and countries." (Nadel, p. 31) Three examples, the **"Young Lady of Tyre,"** the **"Old Man of Coblenz,"** and the **"Old Man of Vesuvius,"** respectively, are presented as examples, but no further information or proof for this statement is provided.

Most studies of children who lived during the Victorian Era indicate that their play and games were meant to be instructive, as well as healthful, and that their literature was decidedly didactic. In writing his limericks, was Edward Lear's real motive to teach Victorian children, especially that collection of cousins, the grandchildren and great-nieces and great-nephews of the Earl of Derby, who all lived together and were tutored at the estate, their geography? An article in an edition of *The Cornhill Magazine* from 1908 includes an account of how Lear came to write the limericks and appears to substantiate a didactic purpose.

> It would almost seem that at this time he [Lear] was trying, in his kindly way, to instruct the youthful mind in the rudiments of geography, for he draws his heroes and heroines from such unsuspected places on the earth's surface. It is true that the idea of composing such rhymes was suggested to him by a friend at Knowsley, who in an unguarded moment uttered the pregnant words, "There was an old man of Tobago." That was enough for Lear, and he ransacked the index to the atlas of the world to find the names of places from which "an old man" or "an old lady" might (or might not) have come—always, as I believe, with the idea of education in disguise. Thus he commandeered Smyrna, Ischia, Columbia, Madras, and Moldavia to serve his purpose. . . ."
>
> (Malcolm, p. 26-27)

Was this really Lear's purpose or what a later author has assumed it might have been? His biographers have correctly identified the source of his inspiration as the "man from Tobago" from *Fifteen Gentlemen.* Lear, as has been noted, acknowledges this fact himself in his introduction to *More Nonsense.* Nowhere, however, including material that has been published to date from his private correspondence and diaries, has anyone been able to determine with certainty his reasons for writing the limericks or, more specifically, what prompted his preference for providing his heroes and heroines with a specific geographical locus in the majority of his verses. Although we are free to speculate, I doubt that his motives were anywhere near as serious as Sir Ian Zachery

Malcolm purports them to be. The definitive answer may yet lie in one of Lear's diaries, which have been deposited in the Houghton Library at Harvard, along with a substantial collection of his watercolors.

It is unfortunate that it is impossible to determine the exact time or place of composition for any of the limericks since Edward Lear did not date any of his verses or their accompanying illustrations. Several facts are known, however, and some conclusions may be based on them. The 212 limericks that were published in Lear's lifetime appear in two separate volumes. These are, as mentioned before, *A Book of Nonsense,* published originally in 1846, containing 112 limericks, and *More Nonsense Pictures, Rhymes, Botany &c.,* published in 1872, containing 100 more limericks. In the tables that follow, these volumes have been designated "a" and "b," respectively. Additional limericks that have been discovered and subsequently published include ten in *Teapots and Quails* (1953), designated "c," and seven in *Lear in the Original* (1975), labeled "d."

Of the limericks in the present study, 175, or 76% of them, incorporate the name of a specific geographical place. Considering only the limericks from Lear's two original collections, the result is remarkably consistent; 160 of the 212 limericks (76%) exhibit placenames. By narrowing the field even further to include just the limericks from the 1846 volume, the majority of which had been composed for the children at Knowsley, 80 of the 112 limericks (71%) contain geographical locations. A greater percentage, however, refer to geography—80 of 100 (80%)—in the 1872 volume that is a collection of limericks that Edward Lear wrote after leaving Knowsley in 1837.

The greatest number of limericks devoted to any one geographical region, a total of 86, commemorate places in the United Kingdom—England, Scotland, Wales, and Northern Ireland—and the Republic of Ireland, places that one would assume were fairly familiar to the Knowsley children. Interestingly enough, only 29 of these 86 appear in the 1846 volume. The remaining 57, including all eight of the limericks that refer to London and its environs, were published later and were probably written for children whom Lear met in his travels rather than for his attentive audience at Knowsley.

Turning to the 51 limericks that designate places in Europe, they do name major countries and cities that the Earl's heirs would have been expected to know. The 31 that appeared in the 1846 volume, with a few possible exceptions, probably figured prominently in their geography lessons. The same is true for the majority of the cities and countries that are named in the limericks from *A Book of Nonsense* from Africa, Asia, North America, and South America, all of which might support some method in the madness of their composition.

It is equally possible, however, that, aside from some of the early limericks that may have been prompted by discussions that followed the children's geography lessons, Edward Lear, instead, wrote many of the limericks to more or less commemorate some of the places to which he travelled or in which he actually lived for some period of time. Leaving England in July of 1837 for his health, Lear travelled through and/or stayed in Bavaria, Luxemborg, Germany, the Alps, Milan, and Florence. Over the years, he made frequent excursions all over the Mediterranean, especially throughout Italy and Greece, and in his later life he had an extended stay in India and Ceylon. A brief outline of his itinerary is as follows:

1842	Sicily
	the Abruzzi
	the Adriatic
1847	Calabria
	Sicily
	Naples
1848-49	Ionian Islands
	Greece, which was perhaps his favorite
	Albania
	Turkey
1854	Corfu
1860's	Arabia
	Egypt
	the Holy Land
	Palestine
	Asia Minor
	Syria
1868	Corsica
1873-74	India
	Ceylon

In 1870 Lear settled permanently in San Remo where he lived, except for brief trips to England, summers in Switzerland and other parts of Italy, and his tour of India and Ceylon, until his death, January 29, 1888.

Geography lessons, commemorative poetry, or nonsense? What would the "laureate of nonsense," as he was dubbed by a critic in *The Spectator* in 1887, think of this serious inquiry? He would probably reply as he did when some suggested that his limericks and drawings contained political symbolism and that the characters were real people, "some of them in public life."

> Lear absolutely denied these reports. "More care," he tells us, "than might be supposed has been given to make the subjects incapable of misinterpretation: *Nonsense,* pure and absolute, having been my aim throughout."
>
> (Davidson, p. 20-21)

That his various forms of nonsense were and still continue to be popular almost goes without saying. In February 1886, forty years after its first appearance and two years before Lear's death, John Ruskin paid Edward Lear an exceptional compliment when he wrote the following:

> "Surely the most beneficent and innocent of all books yet published is the *Book of Nonsense,* with its corollary carols—inimitable and refreshing, and perfect in rhythm. I really don't know any author to whom I am half so grateful, for my idle self, as Edward Lear. I shall put him first of my hundred authors." This praise from a man who was still regarded as the foremost critic in England was deeply satisfying to Lear who, much more perhaps than he was apt to admit, wanted to be recognized as a highly original nonsense-writer at a time when just appreciation of his painting was withheld, and a sense of failure haunted him.
>
> (Lehmann, p. 111)

In the "Introduction" to *The Complete Nonsense of Edward Lear,* Holbrook Jackson further describes the continued popularity of Lear's nonsense.

> The early nonsense books are not readily accessible as most of them were very properly used up, or eaten up, by the children for whom they were written. The original editions of *The Book of Nonsense* (1846), as well as *Nonsense Songs, Stories, Botany and Alphabets* (1871), *More Nonsense* (1872), and *Laughable Lyrics* (1877), are all scarce. It is easier to find a *First Folio Shakespeare* than a first edition of *The Book of Nonsense*; even the British Museum Library has to content itself with a copy of the third edition (1861). The popularity of that book has been continuous and progressive for a hundred years.
>
> (Jackson, p. xxviii)

Bibliography

Byrom, Thomas. *Nonsense and Wonder: The Poems and Cartoons of Edward Lear.* New York: E. P. Dutton, 1977.

Davidson, Angus. *Edward Lear: Landscape Painter and Nonsense Poet, 1812-1888.* London: John Murray, 1938.

Fadiman, Clifton. "How Pleasant To Know Mr. Lear!" *Party of One.* Cleveland: The World Publishing Company, 1955, pp. 411-420.

Hark, Ina Rae. *Edward Lear.* Boston: Twayne Publishers, 1982.

Kastner, Joseph. "The Runcible Life and Works of the Remarkable Edward Lear." *Smithsonian,* 12:6 (September 1981), pp. 106-117.

Kelen, Emery. *Mr. Nonsense: A Life of Edward Lear.* Nashville: Thomas Nelson Incorporated, 1973.

Lear, Edward. *The Complete Nonsense Book.* Edited by Lady Strachey. New York: Duffield & Company, 1929.

———. *The Complete Nonsense of Edward Lear.* Edited by Holbrook Jackson. London: Faber and Faber, Limited, 1947.

———. *Lear in the Original: Drawings and Limericks by Edward Lear for His Book of Nonsense.* Introduction and notes by Herman W. Liebert. New York: H. P. Kraus, 1975.

———. *Teapots and Quails.* Edited and introduced by Angus Davidson and Philip Hofer. London: John Murray, Ltd., 1953.

Lehmann, John. *Edward Lear and His World.* New York: Charles Scribner's Sons, 1977.

Malcolm, Sir Ian Zackary. "Edward Lear." *The Cornhill Magazine,* 97 (1908), pp. 25-36.

Nadel, Ira Bruce. "'The Mansion of Bliss,' or the Place of Play in Victorian Life and Literature." *Children's Literature,* 10 (1982), pp. 18-36.

Noakes, Vivien. *Edward Lear, The Life of a Wanderer.* Boston: Houghton Mifflin Company, 1969.

Opie, Iona and Peter. *The Oxford Dictionary of Nursery Rhymes.* London: Oxford University Press, 1952.

Richardson, Joanna. *Edward Lear.* London: Longmans, Green & Co., Ltd., 1965.

Smith, William Jay. "'So they smashed that old man . . .': A Note on Edward Lear." *Horn Book Magazine,* XXXV:4 (August 1959), pp. 323-326.

The Times Index-Gazetteer of the World. London: The Times Publishing Company, Ltd., 1965.

Ann C. Colley (essay date spring 1988)

SOURCE: Colley, Ann C. "The Limerick and the Space of Metaphor." *Genre* 21, no. 1 (spring 1988): 65-91.

[*In the following essay, Colley contends that the "literalizing impulse" of Lear's limericks effectively strips poetic language down to its barest essentials and provides readers with "a view of metaphor which might otherwise be unavailable."*]

Nonsense literalizes whatever it touches so that what had seemed connected, acceptable, even unremarkable, is no longer so. Dislodged by nonsense's verbatim eye, objects, features, phrases, and events step forward, alone and unsupported by their commonplace accoutrements. It is in Edward Lear's limericks that this literalizing impulse of nonsense is most evident. In **"There was an Old Man of Apulia",**[1] for instance, the words bound along the surface of the text, separated from time and memory. The verse blithely invites the reader to accept the Old Man of Apulia's feeding his sons "nothing but buns" as literal fact, requiring neither motive nor consequence. Lear's drawing accompanying this limerick renders the effect of this literalism even more

explicit, for neither frame, nor setting, nor shadow supplements the illustration. Like the words in the text, the drawn characters press towards the verbatim foreground and, stripped of a dimension, spread out flat across the page. Not even the naming of the specific geographic location in the limerick's first line supplies a background. Each item comes forward without the accustomed boundaries to place it in the expected context.

The literalizing impulse in Lear's limericks, though, does more than single out, expose, and play with the foibles of humanity. It also, perhaps surprisingly, parodies the metaphoric impulse, and in so doing affords a view of metaphor which might otherwise be unavailable. Nonsense strips metaphor of its normal context and reveals the visible and audible spaces which define its structure and which are the source of its power. These insights, available through the pressure of the genre's unique orientation, can help the reader turn to the traditional metaphor with a clearer eye; specifically, they can allow him to make a rather unorthodox leap from the metaphoric velleities of Lear to the actual metaphors of such authors as Ovid and Dante. What Lear's limericks reveal about metaphor can clarify the power of the metaphoric figures in *The Metamorphoses* and the *Divine Comedy,* though it will eventually lead the reader back to the limericks, suggesting ways in which the metaphoric impulse contributes to their distinctive pleasure.

THE LIMERICK

Although Lear's limericks seem intent upon presenting a metonymic perspective and, thus, regarding experience as if it were a shopping list of objects and places, something closer to the opposite is true. At the same time as the verses are letting everything go along serially "by one and one" (Sewell 56)[2] and are separating and isolating elements (butter, plague, pickled onions, and Prague), they are also hastily putting them back together by offering clumsy, quasi-logical sequences among the various segments. For instance, because nobody answers the bell, the hair of the Old Man "who said 'well!'." turns white, and because terrible dreams trouble the Old Person of Rheims, he eats cake to keep awake.

These sequences, which seem to echo mockingly the steps of a syllogism, are familiar. Less obvious is the binding influence of the metaphoric impulse, of which the limerick in its literal mode may be said to be an accidental parody. With this impulse comes a promise to collapse the isolated pieces into one manageable idea, to let a unity emerge between what usually are considered to be distinctly different events or images. The outrageous rhymes in the limericks begin to suggest the metaphoric transference of qualities from one object to another. The shared, approximate sounds of the rhymes draw objects together which normally would have little to say to each other. "Rhodes/Toads" (**"There was an Old Person of Rhodes"**), "Prague/Plague" (**"There was an Old Person of Prague"**), "Coblenz/Immense" (**"There was an Old Man of Coblenz"**) couple in a manner which recalls or parodies the interaction of the "tenor" and "vehicle" of metaphor. Giving an illusion of a metaphoric frame, the rhyme momentarily holds and brackets the separated images. It pretends to make sense of the merely serial.

It is, however, what I choose to call the metaphoric adjectives in the limerick's last line which more readily give the illusion of blending the various pieces. They are larger, longer, and seem to have a rougher texture than the words around them. The examples offer some of Lear's most memorable phrases: **"That intrinsic old man of Peru," "That ombliferous person of Crete," "That mendacious old person of Gretna," "That oracular Lady of Prague,"** and **"You luminous person of Brutes."** Lear gathers all the force of the limerick into the adjectives. Like siphons, they draw off the free-floating pieces into a single container. The adjectives no longer just mockingly qualify their accompanying nouns; they also pretend to justify and combine the disparate elements of the entire verse. For instance, how else would it be possible to understand or unite the facts that the Young Lady of Welling plays the harp and catches carp than to state in the last line that she is an "accomplished young lady of Welling"? Her being "accomplished" gives, at least, a semblance of an essence which binds her acts. Certainly, the illustration does not succeed as well as the word. The drawing hints that the lady is a mermaid and shows her seated in water playing the harp with one hand and fishing with the other, but it neither clasps her separated hands nor otherwise visually evokes an adjectival frame to bracket the distinctions.

Even when the adjective makes little sense and really does not seem to justify the action of the limerick, like **"That intrinsic old man of Peru"** who tears his hair and behaves like a bear, or like **"That ombliferous person of Crete"** who dresses in a sack, "spickle-speckled with black," still Lear throws the weight of the limerick into that final adjective. It draws the preceding lines together and unites them. And, in keeping with the demands of metaphor, this vague and ambiguous adjective creates a gap in which the reader must supply the means of combining or tying together the incongruous details.

In its pretense to pull the verse away from its metonymic singularity, the metaphoric impulse within the limericks also becomes their subject. The literalizing power of nonsense places the metaphoric impulse on display, strips the metaphor of nuances which would otherwise confuse the view, and exposes what is not always

evident—that contrary to what is often suggested, the power of metaphor does not necessarily depend on its faculty to fuse the dissimilar. Instead its potency rotates within its structural spaces. Without the aid of nonsense and its hyperbolic, mocking mode, the reader too swiftly overlooks the spaces between the parts of metaphor and rushes to fuse them, so compelling is the desire to discover coherence, a sense of completion, which is normally absent or unavailable. Lear's nonsense seems to play with this desire, but ultimately fractures the promises of metaphor.

The translucent rhymes of the limericks make it difficult to ignore these spaces. On the one hand the rhymes give the appearance of combining separated elements, but, on the other, they insist on their separateness. Because Lear forces the rhymes into extremes, he compels the reader to consider each singly. No part of the rhyming words blends noiselessly into the other. Each announces itself and its unnatural conjunction. For instance, in spite of the obvious audible correspondence between "Rhodes" and "Toads," "Coblenz" and "immense," or "Prague" and "Plague," the reader remains aware only of the differences between them. In their haste to correspond, these words trip over each other and expose the stumbling blocks of their individuality. The rhyme is at once completed and broken apart.

Illustrations also render the space visible, for no matter how frequently the words of the limericks' verses describe a collision of one object or figure with another, the drawings refuse to carry the intended violence through. A gap always intervenes. Rarely does a figure touch another, and rarely do the instruments of harm reach their victim. Instead, they hang suspended and unconnected. For instance, the knife with which an Old Person of Tartary divides his jugular artery floats blissfully free of his extended finger and his screeching wife's hands; the large stones which "several small children" throw at an Old Person of Chester hang like bubbles over the man's right side, and the oversize puppy which is supposed to snap up an Old Man of Leghorn fails, as if blocked by the intervening space. One figure might stare at another, but none touches, not even when harmony exists between the two. The Old Man of Whitehaven and the raven dance parallel, yet unattached, and the "ecstatic" Old Person of Tring gazes at his mirror image in the moon, through an interval which seems to increase both his desire and his separateness. It is as if the illustrations dismember the illusion of synthesis promised by the verse. The words might vow that the Old Man of Nepaul who is split in two will be mended by "some very strong glue," but the accompanying illustration does not, for it chooses to emphasize the separateness of the man's severed parts. Like the drawings of the Old Man of the Nile's severed thumbs or the Young Person of Janina's decapitated head, the illustrations serialize the body.

The visible absence of connection also characterizes the limericks which claim to unite the animal and the human world. Here there is a half-metamorphosis in which the animals adopt human shapes, and the humans unconsciously assent to display animal forms: the Old Man in the Tree perches and sits staring at a bee that bears his face. His posture imitates the bee's. The Young Lady of Portugal rests in a tree where she literally has a bird's-eye view of the sea she examines. Her face resembles a crow's. The Old Person of Dover extends his arms as if they were wings of the bees in the field. The Old Man who said, "Hush!" looks remarkably like the bird he "perceives" in a bush, while the bird wrily endures some resemblance to him: The man's arms spread like wings, and his baton stretches out behind in the manner of the bird's perky tail. But, even when there are additional hints of metamorphoses from the verses, the transformations are not complete. The human and animal parts sit on top of one another or lie side by side announcing, like the rhymes, their fundamental autonomy.

Although, finally, these fissures in the text seem to deflate the metaphoric adjective's promise of synthesis, they do not obliterate the presence of metaphor. Rather, they literalize it, and in so doing, bring the metaphor's intrinsic character to the surface. To begin with, they expose the first phase of metaphor—the moment involving the anxiety of difference. The puzzling and slightly worrisome associations involved in the limericks parody the unusual conjunctions within the metaphoric comparison which unbalance the reader, and, initially, cause him to be primarily aware of the dissimilarities between the object and what is being identified through it. For instance, the bringing together of the carp and the harp (**"The Young Lady of Welling"**), a hatchet and a flea (**"An Old Man of the Dee"**), and a smile and a voyage on the goose's back (**"The Old Man of Dunluce"**) echoes and exaggerates the more memorable metaphoric conjunctions (e.g., the compass and love in Donne's "A Valediction Forbidding Mourning"). Moreover, the limericks seem to participate in the second phase of metaphor—the resolution of the differences into similarities and congruity. Their concluding metaphoric adjectives mock the reader's impulse to find a resting place in congruity, and in that act remind him of the ever-present audible and visible spaces within metaphor itself. The limericks, therefore, in their accidental role as commentators on metaphor, suggest what is not always evident—that contrary to what is often proposed, the power of metaphor does not necessarily depend on its faculty to fuse the dissimilar. The figure's potency also dwells within its structural gaps. No longer can the reader, therefore, hasten to blend the disparate pieces and hurry to feel the immediate embrace of a moment's closure. Now, the reader must face metaphor, divested

of its illusory coherence, with a memory of its literal structure. And he must acknowledge the gaps and explore the power that resides with them.

OVID AND DANTE

The transition from Lear to Ovid is not as radical as the reader might think, for each captures his subjects at some metamorphic moment between one state and another. Although in Ovid there is nothing of Lear's absolute playfulness, his metamorphoses do have something of the frozen and caricatural quality present in the limericks. In this limited respect, Ovid's work may be said to illustrate an intermediate step between nonsense and metaphor.

At first, the metaphors in *The Metamorphoses* seem to be little concerned with the spaces exposed in nonsense. Rather, they appear to be more involved in eradicating distinctions. As if fashioning metaphor as a miniature to be hung like a pendant from the neck of the text, Ovid sets a particular moment into a pictorial mode and frames it. Within the boundaries of this portrait, experience moves away from the time-bound milieu of the verse and approaches the silent and simultaneous world of the visual where events do not necessarily move to the rhythm of the text. Such a visual "epiphany" is seductive, for it promises respite from the serial demands of time and offers a neat, unified vision. An example of this relief from difference comes in Book Three. Initially, the passage describing how mortals grew from seeds sown by Cadmus progresses step by step to a chronological beat:

> glaebae coepere moveri,
> primaque de sulcis acies adparuit hastae,
> tegmina mox capitum picto nutantia cono,
> mox umeri pectusque onerataque bracchia telis
> exsistunt, crescitque seges clipeata virorum:
>
> (III, 106-110)[3]

> The covered earth broke open, and the clods
> Began to stir, and first the points of spears
> Rise from the ground, then colored plumes, and
>   helmets,
> A very harvest of the shields of warriors. . . .
>
> (III, 106-110)[4]

But then Ovid transposes the passage into a metaphoric mode and disengages the event from the historical measure. He discards all allusions to growth, crops, and harvest, and leaps to an image and a context which exists outside the text's rhythmic movement: The legion grows

> sic, ubi tolluntur festis aulaea theatris,
> surgere signa solent primumque ostendere vultus,
> cetera paullatim, placidoque educta tenore
> tota patent imoque pedes in margine ponunt
>
> (III, 111-114)

So when on festal days the curtain in
the theatre is raised, figures of men
rise up, showing first their faces, then
little by little all the rest; until at
last, drawn up with steady motion, the
entire forms stand revealed, and plant
their feet upon the curtain's edge.[5]

Because the curtain as an interior object alienates itself
from the earthy exterior of the narrative, the metaphor
releases the description of the growing legion from the
text's temporal demands. The inversion transposes the
incident into its own epigrammatic enclosure.

Because the metaphor can offer a place where there is a
possibility of a brief liaison with a self-contained,
enclosed landscape, the reader eagerly clamps the fissures of the rhetorical figure shut. Responding to the
lure of the visual embrace, his consenting eye overlooks
the spaces which divide the metaphor.

These spaces, however, need to be recognized, for the
gaps made visible through Lear's limericks are vital to
the metaphoric structure within the writings of such
serious authors as Ovid and Dante. Most readily this
critical space reveals itself through the comparative
"like" which splits the tenor from the vehicle.[6] The two
parts of the figure stand side by side: "quo se cumque
acies oculorum flexerat, illic / vulgus erat stratum, veluti cum putria motis / poma cadunt ramis agitataque
ilice glandes" (*The Metamorphoses,* VII, 584-586).
("Wherever I looked was a great heap of bodies lying
like rotten apples or wormy acorns.") Within this
comparative frame, rarely does one of the two portions
replace or touch the other. Rather, one repeats the other,
but in another guise. When Dante describes the
departure of the poet Guido Guinicelli ("Purgatory,"
XXVI), he repeats the movement by comparing the
poet's leaving to that of a fish disappearing into the
deep. By reversing the imagery, by turning the fire that
surrounds the poet's departure into the cooling water of
the fish's medium, Dante, however, opens and preserves
the spaces between the tenor and the vehicle: "Poi,
forse per dar luogo altrui secondo / che presso avea,
disparve per lo foco, / come per l'acqua il pesce andando al fondo." ("Then, perhaps to give place to
another following close behind, he vanished through the
flames like a fish that goes through the water to the
bottom") (XXVI, 133-35).[7] As with any repetition
including rhyme, even though one portion by the very
nature of its similarity seems to mirror the other, the
necessity of comparison and its companion anticipation
distorts the reflection. This necessity, for instance,
initiates and continues the rapid volley between the images of the tongue and the serpent in Ovid's chilling
description of Philomela's severed tongue. Hardly a
sustained moment emerges when the two may blend
and stand still in the metaphoric enclosure. Instead, the
images share the space of comparison which separate
them:

ipsa iacet terraeque tremens inmurmurat atrae,
utque salire solet mutilatae cauda colubrae,
palpitat et moriens dominae vestigia quaerit

(VI, 558-560)

the severed tongue along the ground
Lay quivering, making a little murmur,
Jerking and twitching, the way a serpent does
Run over by a wheel, and with its dying movement
Came to its mistress' feet.

In other instances, frequent doubling or serializing of
comparisons fashions spaces in the metaphoric structure.
Earlier in the story of Philomela, Ovid describes her
distress by isolating the pieces of the metaphor and listing them. (The mode almost parallels the serialization
in Lear's limericks.) Philomela recoils

velut agna pavens, quae saucia cani
ore excussa lupi nondum sibi tuta videtur,
utque columba suo madefactis sanguine plumis
horret adhuc avidosque timet, quibus haeserat, ungues.

(VI, 527-530)

As a frightened lamb which a gray wolf has mangled
And cast aside, poor creature, to a safety
It cannot quite believe. She is like a dove
With her own blood all over her feathers; fearing
The talons that have pierced and left her.

A similar impulse is at work in Canto III of "The
Inferno." There Dante conflates the gaps between
metaphors with the gaps within metaphors. He frames
the representation of evil with images that halt the
reader and compel him to consider each separately, as if
walking through a picture gallery. The gaps between the
vignettes are as visible as the individual pictures:

Come d'autunno si levan le foglie
l'una appresso de l'altra, fin che'l ramo
vede a la terra tutte le sue spoglie,
similemente il mal seme d'Adamo
gittansi di quel lito ad una ad una,
per cenni come augel per suo richiamo.

(112-117)

As the leaves fall away in autumn, one after
another, till the bough sees all its spoils upon
the ground, so there the evil seed of Adam:
one by one they cast themselves from that
shore at signals, like a bird at its call.

Spaces, of course, also dwell in those metaphors which
let the animal's movements carry the burden of a
person's suffering. It is, however, not the obvious difference between animals and humans which creates
these gaps. It is, paradoxically, the similarities between
the two which call attention to the distinctions. (The
half-metamorphosed drawings of Lear come to mind.)

The fact that a cowering rabbit or a fierce falcon can sustain and represent human experience directs the reader's focus to the means and, thereby, uncovers difference. Amid this confusion of opposite and identical images, the figure admits intervals where synthesis is desired.

Difference emphasized by comparison is not alone in opening metaphor. Like a lion that swishes his tail behind him, and consequently, eradicates his tracks, sometimes metaphor removes traces of itself as it proceeds, creating space. As the pictorial segments of the figure succeed each other, they leave behind the noise of individual words and scatter the memory of their meaning to the text's margin. Eventually they move farther and farther away from the verbal event that had occasioned the metaphor. When, for example, Dante encounters a troop of damned souls coming alongside a bank, he says:

> ciascuna
> ci riguardava come suol da sera
> guardare uno altro sotto nuova luna;
> e sì ver' noi aguzzavan le ciglia
> come 'l vecchio sartor fa ne la cruna.
>
> ("The Inferno," XV, 17-21)

> each looked at us as men look
> at one another under a new moon at dusk;
> and they knit their brows at us as the old
> tailor does at the eye of his needle.

By the time the reader reaches the figure's conclusion, he must gather and regroup the scattered words and remind himself that Dante is talking about a troop of damned souls. Like a flock of starlings after it flies through the intricate branches of a tree, the words come back together and, in a sudden flurry of activity, move on into the flight of the text: "Così adocchiato da cotal famiglia, / fui conosciuto da un, che mi prese / per lo lembo" (22-24) ("Eyed thus by that company, I was recognized by one who took me by the hem.").[8]

Occasionally when the author places the pictorial image before the tenor, the imprinting of the initial visual element is sufficiently powerful to brush aside the subject matter of the text. Dante, for instance, writes of the movement of the suffering souls by first depicting the flight of the cranes. Although the last word is with the shades, the effect is not, for the straight motion of the singing cranes' flight subordinates the verbal activity below, and in the wings' wake, disperses the immediate concerns of the plot's material:

> E come i gru van cantando lor lai,
>   faccendo in aere di sé lunga riga,
>   così vid' io venir, traendo guai,
>   ombre portate da la detta briga.
>
> ("The Inferno," V, 46-49)

And as the cranes go chanting their
lays, making a long line of themselves in the
air, so I saw shades come, uttering wails,
borne by that strife.

On the whole, the static and consuming nature of metamorphosis, by contrast with metaphor, confirms the essential gaps within the metaphoric structure, and the spaces which Lear's limericks exposed become more intelligible. Throughout *The Metamorphoses,* it is difficult not to be struck by the terrifyingly frozen quality of the transformations. The blithe half-metamorphoses of Lear's nonsense are not possible. For instance, the mild pleasures experienced by the Old Man who sits on a rail next to an owl and drinks bitter ale are unavailable. The Old Man's owl-like face with its flattened features and beaked nose are not at all horrifying; rather, they proffer to both him and the owl the opportunity to understand one another, enjoy their ale, and be "refreshed" together. No such respite is given to those caught in Ovid's transformations. In *The Metamorphoses* the transformations are tragic and complete. Repeatedly the gods and mortals are trapped or literally rooted in the essence from which they seek deliverance. Metamorphosis does not offer escape; rather, it ensures a terrible continuation. Phaethon's sisters find no release from their sorrow. Instead, they remain, sterile, eternally trapped and hardened in their tears:

> Phaethusa, sororum
> maxima, cum vellet terra procumbere, questa est
> deriguisse pedes; ad quam conata venire
> candida Lampetie subita radice retenta est;
> tertia, cum crinem manibus laniare pararet,
> avellit frondes; haec stipite crura teneri,
> illa dolet fieri longos sua bracchia ramos,
> dumque ea mirantur, conplectitur inguina cortex
> perque gradus uterum pectusque umerosque manusque
> ambit . . .
>
> (II, 346-355)

> . . . Phaethusa, the oldest daughter,
> Because, she made complaint, her feet had stiffened;
> Lampetia, the fair one, tried to help her
> And could not move at all, suddenly rooted
> In earth; another sister, tearing her hair,
> Pulled leaves away, and another, and another,
> Found shins and ankles were wood, and arms were
>   branches,
> And as they looked at these, in grief and wonder,
> Bark closed around their loins, their breasts, their
>   shoulders,
> Their hands. . . .

In other instances, metamorphosis permanently entangles its victims and traps their grief. The Theban women who grieve the loss of Ino are allowed no relief. The angered Juno offers neither death nor purge. On the contrary, she hardens and frustrates their mourning by turning them to rock and stone. The rejected Phineus fares just as badly, for he is changed to marble, his supplications "caught and fixed forever" (V, 234-235). Aglauros is caught too. Her transformation seals the envy that eats her away:

> saxum iam colla tenebat,
> oraque duruerant, signumque exsangue sedebat;
> nec lapis albus erat: sua mens infecerat illam.
>
> (II, 830-832)

> Her neck was stone, her features hard as marble.
> A lifeless statue sat there, and the statue
> Was black, not white, dark with her evil spirit.

Not even Daphne escapes. Her metamorphosis traps and roots her, so that there is no freedom from Apollo's passion. Becoming a laurel merely holds her still for his lustful fondling.[9]

The loss of verbal power exacerbates the static quality of metamorphosis. Time and time again, not only does the outward form change but also the voice. Juno takes revenge upon an Arcadian girl loved by Jove by turning her into a bear and by taking her power of speech away:

> neve preces animos et verba precantia flectant,
> posse loqui eripitur: vox iracunda minaxque
> plenaque terroris rauco de gutture fertur;
> mens antiqua manet. (facta quoque mansit in ursa)
> adsiduoque suos gemitu testata dolores . . .
>
> (II, 482-486)

> the power of speech
> Might have been dangerous for her to plead with,
> So that was taken, and her voice became
> An angry threatening growl. Her human feelings
> Were left her in her bear-like form; she moaned. . . .

Actaeon too is trapped without a human voice. His hunting companions call his name; silently, he turns his head towards them and with that silence ushers in his own death. The daughters of Minyas change into bats, but it is not the deprivation of human form which distinguishes their transformation; it is their voicelessness which renders them most impotent: "conataeque loquid minimam et pro corpore vocem / emittunt peraguntque levi stridore querellas" (IV, 412-414) ("They tried to speak, / But the sounds they made were tiny as their bodies, / A squeak of Protest"). The angered Venus emasculates Acmon by denying him a voice in which to respond to his friends: "cui respondere volenti / vox pariter vocisque via est tenuata, comaeque" (XIV, 497-498) ("he tried to answer back, but both his voice and throat / Grew thin"). Few resort like Philomela or Io to images or to writing. Wordless and often voiceless, they are locked into themselves.

In an almost contrapuntal manner, metaphor works against and inverts the sterile, self-revolving form of metamorphosis. It breaks open what the transformation seals. An opportunity to see this contrapuntal arrangement comes in Book XI of *The Metamorphoses* when Ovid describes the way Bacchus binds the women who have murdered Orpheus. After Bacchus has attached their feet to roots and thrust them deep into the earth, each one

> dumque ubi sint digiti, dum pes ubi, quaerit, et ungues,
> aspicit in teretes lignum succedere suras
> et conata femur maerenti plangere dextra
> robra percussit, pectus quoque robora fiunt,
> robora sunt umeri; longos quoque bracchia . . .
>
> (XI, 79-83)

> looked to see their fingers,
> Their toes, their nails, and saw the bark come creeping
> Up the smooth legs; they tried to smite their thighs
> With grieving hands, and struck an oak; their breasts
> Were oak, and oak their shoulders, and their arms. . . .

The passage hardens and narrows as it proceeds. The repetition of "robora" ("oak") tightens Bacchus' binding. But when Ovid summons a metaphor to describe the women's struggle, there is a move in the opposite direction which momentarily opens up both the text and the women's fate, as if metaphor were their last opportunity to reach beyond themselves. He writes:

> utque suum laqueis, quos callidus abdidit auceps,
> crus ubi commisit volucris sensitque teneri,
> plangitur ac trepidans adstringit vincula motu:
> sic, ut quaeque solo defixa cohaeserat harum,
> exsternata fugam frustra temptabat, at illam
> lenta tenet radix exsultantemque coercet . . .
>
> (XI, 73-78)

> As a bird struggles
> Caught in a fowler's snare, and flaps and flutters
> And draws its bonds the tighter by the struggling,
> Even so the Thracian women, gripped by the soil,
> Fastened in desperate terror, writhed and struggled,
> But the roots held.

Although the intent of the passage is to depict the inevitability of the women's destiny, the effect is not quite so, for the bird's motions push away from the trap. The struggle extends outwards, away from the fowler's snare. Even though death must come, in the metaphoric figure, at least, a force rages against mortal closure and desperately attempts to grasp an alternative, to create a space, a difference between itself and what holds it down. Deprived of the metaphor, the Thracian women are unable to move out. They can only cast down their eyes and smite their thighs as if affirming the closure and pressing towards their own enclosure.

Their downward, grieving motion is contradicted by the contrapuntal, upward exertions of the trapped bird. The possibilities which the metaphor admits into the text through the bird's movements are also rendered visible because the image of the snared bird comes to it from a context which does not necessarily depend upon what precedes and follows in the narrative. The image alights from a place outside. And once it arrives, like the motion of the bird's wings, it continues to refer to something beyond itself. In this way, metaphor saves itself. On the other hand, metamorphosis has nothing but its own essence. The oak tree's bark and the aniaml's aspect signify and seal the transformed image's character. No space comes between the interior and the exterior. No middle exists. Inextricably, the two are one and one is two. They have consumed each other.

But acknowledging the openings within metaphor is not sufficient, for spaces alone do not distinguish the figure. The activity within these intervals also articulates metaphor. A digression to Chapter Nineteen in *The Adventures of Huckleberry Finn* offers an instance of this principle. In the beginning when Huck describes the panoramic view of "t 'other side of the river," he inadvertently depicts the landscape of metaphor. By speaking not only of the objects to be viewed but also of the gaps between them, he marks the figure's spatial character. The spaces he sees become objects in their own right:

> . . . then for about an hour there wouldn't be nothing to hear nor nothing to see—just solid lonesomeness. Next you'd see a raft sliding by, away off yonder, and maybe a galoot on it chopping, because they're almost always doing it on a raft; you'd see the axe flash and come down—you don't hear nothing; you see that axe go up again, and by the time it's above the man's head, then you hear the *k'chunk!*—it had took all that time to come over the water.

> (178)

Huck, however, does more than recognize the intervals between events. He also shows a sensitivity to the activity within those spaces. For instance, when he notices the gaping holes among the stacked wood ("piled by cheats"), he remarks, "you can throw a dog through it anywheres" (177). Such is the possibility of metaphor, for his comment implies that the observer propels his own fantasies into these gaps. It is inside these openings that metaphor licenses the play of desire, the pursuit of something beyond itself, and condones the quest for synthesis, the yearning to merge with another. Ovid's myths are, of course, replete with such quests. His rendition of "Echo and Narcissus," in particular, involves the play of desire and offers a narrative analogue to its role in the metaphoric structure. The myth also continues to elucidate the distinctions between metaphor and metamorphosis.

From the very opening of Ovid's narrative, Echo is associated with desire, for Ovid informs the reader that it is she who had chosen to delay the suspicious Juno while Jove "was on top of . . . some nymph among the mountains" ("fecerat hoc Iuno, quia, cum deprendere posset / sub Iove saepe suo nymphas in monte iacentis, / illa deam longo prudens sermone tenebat, / dum fugerent nymphae . . ." III, 362-365). When Echo sets eyes on Narcissus, Jove's sexual desires become hers, but because she is unable to do more than "answer in the words she last had heard" ("haec in fine loquendi / ingeminat voces auditaque verba reportat" 368-369), she cannot coax Narcissus to come near her. Eventually, she has the opportunity to disclose her lust, for Narcissus becomes separated from his companions and calls,

> "ecquis adest?" et "adest" responderat
> Echo.
> hic stupet, utque aciem partes dimittit in omnis,
> voce "veni!" magna clamat: vocat illa vocantem.
> respicit et rursus nullo veniente "quid" inquit
> "me fugis?" et totidem, quot dixit, verba recepit.
> perstat et alternae deceptus imagine vocis
> "huc coeamus" ait, nullique libentius umquam
> responsura sono "coeamus" rettulit Echo
> et verbis favet ipsa suis egressaque silva
> ibat, ut iniceret sperato bracchia collo.

> (380-389)

> "is Anybody here?"
>   "Here!" said Echo.
> He looked around in wonderment, called louder
> "Come to me!" "Come to me!" came back the answer.
> He looked behind him, and saw no one coming;
> "Why do you run from me?" and he heard his question
> Repeated in the woods. "Let us get together!"
> There was nothing Echo would ever say more gladly,
> "Let us get together!" And, to help her words,
> Out of the woods she came, with arms all ready
> To fling around his neck. . . .

The remainder of the myth is almost too familiar to recount. Narcissus haughtily rejects Echo, who retreats and languishes until "she is voice only" ("vox manet," 399). Then one day another rejected youth who has suffered from Narcissus' pride raises up his hands and pleads, "sic amet ipse licet, sic non potiatur amato!" (405) ("May Narcissus / Love one day, so himself, and not win over / The creature whom he loves!"). Soon Narcissus comes to a pool to quench his thirst, and, of course, falls in love with his own image. In the end, grieving for what he cannot have, Narcissus dies. That transformation, however, brings no relief. Even in Hell he finds a pool to gaze in where he can watch his image in the Stygian water.

Although both Echo and Narcissus are trapped by their lust, there are differences in their plight which recall the distinctions between metaphor and metamorphosis and which evince the role of desire. Echo's dilemma suggests the structure and activity of metaphor, for throughout the narrative, she longs for Narcissus, something outside of herself. And she craves a blending of their bodies. But, as in the metaphoric structure, spaces intervene and frustrate her sexual fantasy; yet, simultaneously, they keep that desire alive and compel her to reach for something else. Space defines Echo. Because her lust infuses her words with a sensual appetite, her words are not mere repetitions of what precedes. When she repeats, "Let us come together!" ("coeamus," 387), for instance, she transforms Narcissus' request from a piece of passing curiosity into a proposition. By breaking the boundaries of verbatim meaning, she overcomes the trap of repetition. Echo's inability to initiate a conversation is also suggestive of metaphor. Like metaphor which refers to something other than itself, she too must look elsewhere to find her words. Her idiosyncrasy implies that of metaphor— that is, metaphor is an echo of something else; it originates in a thought, a sound, a visual image beyond or behind itself.

The spaces which define Echo's presence are not possible for Narcissus. Because pride and self-love embrace him, he can admit no other. Inextricably bound to himself ("se cupit," 425), he is as trapped as those who are changed into forms which capture and freeze their suffering. When Narcissus sees his reflection, the metamorphosis is complete. For him, no space comes between the interior and exterior. His experience is not that of the "supreme mirror" in which exists the possibility of seeing and touching oneself at the same time. His self feeds off itself until he dies. Echo, on the other hand, can live because she can desire and mourn for something else and can escape her own body. But, for Narcissus who pleads, "o utinam a nostro secedere corpore possem! / votum in amante novum, vellem, quod amamus, abesset" (467-468) ("If I could only / Escape from my own body! If I could only . . . / Be parted from my love"), no intervals intercede to sustain him. His is a life and a death without possibility of dialogue. And his is a fate which compels him to seek the superficial image. As soon as Narcissus dips his eager face into the reflecting water, the image is dispelled and exposes nothing else.

Although Dante in "The Inferno" accused Ovid of never imagining a transmutation so extraordinary that two natures "front to front," "were prompt to exchange their substance" (XXV, 97-102),[10] the myth of Echo and Narcissus contains the potential for such a vision. If Echo's desire to come together with Narcissus had been fulfilled, the result might have been something like that Dante describes in one of the most gruesome cantos of "The Inferno" (Canto XXV), in which a serpent takes hold of a "shade" and blends so completely with him that neither is "two nor one" ("né due né uno"). The necessity for metaphoric space is, perhaps, never so vividly depicted as in this episode. Dante speaks:

> Com'io tenea levate in lor le ciglia,
>   e un serpente con sei piè si lancia
>   dinanzi a l'uno, e tutto a lui s'appiglia.
> Co' piè di mezzo li avvinse la pancia
>   e con li anterïor le braccia prese;
>   poi li addentò e l'una e l'altra guancia;
> li diretani a le cosce distese,
>   e miseli la coda tra 'mbedue
>   e dietro per le ren sù la ritese.
> Ellera abbarbicata mai non fue
>   ad alber sì, come l'orribil fiera
>   per l'altrui membra avviticchiò le sue.
> Poi s'appiccar, come di calda cera
>   fossero stati, e mischiar lor colore,
>   né l'un né l'altro già parea quel ch'era:
> come procede innanzi da l'ardore,
>   per lo papiro suso, un color bruno
>   che non è nero ancora e 'l bianco more.
> Li altri due 'l riguardavano, e ciascuno
>   gridava: "Omè, Agnel, come ti muti!
>   Vedi che già non se' né due né uno."
> Già eran li due capi un divenuti,
>   quando n'apparver due figure miste
>   in una faccia, ov' eran due perduti.
> Fersi le braccia due di quattro liste;
>   le cosce con le gambe e 'l ventre e 'l casso
>   divenner membra che non fuor mai viste.
> Ogne primaio aspetto ivi era casso:
>   due e nessun l'imagine perversa
>   parea; e tal sen gio con lento passo.

(49-78)

While I kept my eyes on them, lo! a serpent with six feet darts up in front of one and fastens on him all over. With the middle feet it clasped the belly, and with its fore feet took his arms, then struck its teeth in one and the other cheek; its hind feet it spread upon his thighs, and put its tail between them, and bent it upwards on his loins behind. Ivy was never so rooted to a tree as the horrid beast entwined its own limbs round the other's; then, as if they had been of hot wax, they stuck together and mixed their colors, and neither the one nor the other now seemed what it was at first: even as in advance of the flame a dark color moves across the paper, which is not yet black and the white dies away. The other two were looking on, and each cried, "Oh me, Agnello, how you change! Lo, you are already neither two nor one!"

Now the two heads had become one, when we saw the two shapes mixed in one face, where both were lost. Two arms were made of the four lengths; the thighs with the legs, the belly and the chest, became members that were never seen before. Each former feature was blotted out: the perverse image seemed both and neither, and such, with slow pace, it moved away.

The episode turns Echo's desire to blend her body with another's and Narcissus' self-bonding into a terrible prospect. So disquieting is the incident that when the passage's metaphors occasionally proffer an alternative to the consuming image of the serpent, the relief normally available through metaphor is immensely magnified. But the respite is brief, for throughout "The Inferno," such deadly blending is not only potent but also repetitive. All the circles of Hell are composed of those who are either irretrievably locked to others or frozen into themselves.

The sterile, rooted metamorphosed figures of Ovid resonate against each other. In the lowest circle, for instance, Dante sees traitors "so close together that they had the hair of their heads intermixed" (XXXII, 41-42) ("sì stretti, / che 'l pel del capo avieno insieme misto"). When he looks at their raised faces, to his horror, Dante notices that "their eyes, which before were moist only within, welled up with tears, which ran down over the lips, and the frost bound each to each and locked them even tighter" (46-48) ("li occhi lor, ch'eran pria pur dentro molli, / gocciar su per le labbra, e 'l gelo strinse / le lagrime tra essi e riserrolli"). Those solidified tears fasten the traitors together—"clamp never bound board on board so strongly" (49-50) ("Con legno legno spranga mai non cinse / forte così").

The fear of these diabolical fusions is reflected not only in the descriptions of the sinners who congregate in Hell but also in the urgency with which the text moves towards Dante's eventual separation from Virgil and, indeed, towards his entrance into Paradise. Throughout "The Inferno," the mode in which Virgil takes hold of Dante and the way in which Dante clings to his master menacingly duplicates or, at least, parallels the locked postures of the various sinners. In Canto XIX, for example, Virgil pulls Dante to his breast, and the two rise body to body. Dante writes, "Però con ambo le braccia mi prese; / e poi che tutto su mi s'ebbe al petto, / rimontò per la via onde discese" (124-126) ("Thereupon he took me in his arms, and when he had me quite on his breast, remounted by the path where he had descended").[11] Even more perilously, their configuration matches the serpent's treacherous hold of Agnel. Repeatedly, Virgil's arms entwine themselves around Dante's body, and the two hold fast in some dangerous imitation of the serpent's deadly embrace. One episode in Canto XXIV describes Virgil's seductive appropriation of Dante:

> come noi venimmo al guasto ponte,
> lo duca a me si volse con quel piglio
> dolce ch'io vidi prima a piè del monte.
> Le braccia aperse, dopo alcun consiglio
> eletto seco riguardando prima
> ben la ruina, e diedemi di piglio
>
> (19-24)

> when we came to the ruined bridge my
> leader turned to me with that sweet look
> which I saw first at the foot of the mountain.
> After taking some counsel with himself, looking
> first well at the ruin, he opened his arms and
> laid hold of me.

In the following canto (Canto XXV), in a continuation of the serpent episode that begins in Canto XXIV, the two watch the horrific coupling of the serpent and Agnel below. Each pair mirrors the other; their mutual reflection binds them in yet another infernal synthesis. Later, in Canto XXXI, Virgil's and Dante's imitation of the embrace is again in view, and more so, for they blend into one: When Virgil beckons to Dante and says, "Come here, that I may take you." (134) ("Fatti qua, sì ch'io ti prenda"), Dante obeys and Virgil takes him so that "of himself and me he made one bundle" (135) ("poi fece sì ch'un fascio era elli e io"). Only their dialogue saves them from the complete metamorphosis. Words which were unavailable to Ovid's victims and which are lost to Agnel (interestingly, the serpent commences to possess Agnel by puncturing his cheeks and covering his mouth) are present for Virgil and Dante. Their verbal exchange replaces the image of their binding embrace and forestalls the fatal, wordless alternative. Their words create spaces through which they may retreat or seek those other than themselves.

The urgency to advance towards Paradise is the haste to relinquish the necessity of Virgil's embrace and enter a landscape which is spacious and emptied of the claustrophobic multitudes and dense darkness of Hell. Throughout the circles of Paradise a clarifying light illuminates a larger view and augments experience, so that when Dante describes his reaction to the sight of the Eternal light, he writes, "più di largo / . . . mi sento ch'i'godo" (XXXIII 92-93) ("I feel my joy increase"). And space as measured by time defines the power of that vision: "Un punto solo m'è maggior letargo / che venticinque secoli a la 'mpresa / che fé Nettuno ammirar l'ombra d'Argo" (94-96) ("A single moment makes for me greater oblivion than five and twenty centuries have wrought upon the enterprise that made Neptune wonder at the shadow of Argo"). In this open landscape, there is a longing to linger and stretch out, a yearning which the metaphors of Paradise honor. And space is crucial to the manner in which Dante beholds and joins with Beatrice. The meeting of their eyes reverses the awful frozen gaze of the bound traitors in "The Inferno," and it contradicts the coupling of the serpent and Agnel. When Dante looks at Beatrice, he sees neither himself nor her. His is not Narcissus' fate nor is it that of those metamorphosed by their lustful attention, for Beatrice's eyes deflect Dante's and direct them to the divine whole. By reflecting the light that shines from God, her sight reaches beyond the two of them and, thus, prevents the space between them from collapsing.

The saving grace of the deflecting gaze in Beatrice's eyes suggests that of metaphor. It recalls metaphor's ability not only to redirect the consciousness to something beyond the immediate experience but also to respect the intervals between the tenor and the vehicle, an act which protects each from closing down over the other. Perhaps one way of understanding metaphor is to think of it as a figure standing between desire and death.[12] The metaphoric difference allows passion and fantasy to live within its structure without fear that such desires, particularly those that involve the merging of bodies, will destroy and transmute its victims into frozen, sterile, self-referential beings. Through its spaces and its deflecting mode, metaphor checks the fantasy of merging one being with another and, thereby, protects itself, the text, and the reader from the stifling embrace that admits nothing else. In its own seductive and paradoxical way, metaphor keeps desire alive, for by promising to merge one image with another, the figure dares itself and the reader to engage the fantasy of synthesis; simultaneously, however, the figure consciously obstructs the destructive elements of the fantasy by looking beyond itself. Occasionally metaphor breaks itself apart, and, like the limericks, deconstructs its own illusions. Metaphor spares what it touches from death just as Lear's nonsense drawings keep the hammer suspended over the victim's head. One never really expects the deadly blow to fall.

The pleasure of the limericks is that their hyperbolic and parodic modes exaggerate and widen the spaces that metaphor admits and let the reader play safely among them. When the limericks enlarge these spaces, they break, more distinctly, away from the enclosures of metamorphosis and the compulsions of desire, and, consequently, free the reader from the anxious tension which characterizes metaphor. The reader can now move easily between each object and event, without the burden of memory or time and without dread of a fearful embrace. The limericks are even further removed than metaphor from the threat of closure. So, for instance, when the Young Lady of Hull is chased by "a virulent Bull," seizes a spade, and calls out "Who's afraid!," her lack of concern is also the reader's. As the accompanying illustration suggests, the Young Lady and the bull will never touch or mingle with each other like Agnel and the serpent. They will always smile delightfully at each other through the space that not only separates them but also protects them from harm. The incongruities of their posture, their words, and their actions keep difference alive and mortal inevitability far away—as far away as the land where the Jumblies live.

And like the Jumblies who go to sea in a sieve, those who read the limericks voyage happily and securely. Ironically, it is the limericks' holes and spaces which keep the reader afloat. They allow the reader to chart experience in a form which removes him from the shadows of memory, time, and enclosure. They place him among the differences or gaps which are an integral, but often, paradoxically, unavailable, part of experience. The power of the limerick seems, finally, to derive from the spaces provided by the metaphoric vehicle.

Notes

1. All quotations and illustrations of the limericks come from: *The Complete Nonsense of Edward Lear.*

   Lear's limericks follow a consistent idiosyncratic pattern. Each of the four-line verses opens with a version of "There was an Old Man (or Young Lady) of . . ." (and a geographic location is named), proceeds to the listing of an isolated characteristic of the limerick's subject, and concludes with a variation of the first line. The variation usually involves the addition of a defining adjective, like that in the line of "There was an Old Man of Apulia": "That whimsical Man of Apulia."

2. Sewell suggests that nonsense sets "before the mind a possible universe in which everything goes along serially, by one and one."

3. Ovid: *Metamorphoses.* (London: William Heinemann Ltd.; Cambridge, MA; Harvard UP, 1960), 2 vols. Subsequent quotations from the Latin text will be taken from this edition.

4. Ovid: *Metamorphoses,* trans. Rolfe Humphries. Subsequent quotations from the translated English text will be taken from this edition.

5. Because the Humphries translation is misleading at this point in the text, I have used the English translation which accompanies the Latin text. See n. 3.

6. For the purposes of this essay, simile will be treated as a form of metaphor. The distinction between simile and metaphor that depends on "like" or "as" has seemed inadequate ever since Roger Shattuck questioned it in the introduction to his translation of Apollinaire.

   Shattuck writes:

   > It is possible to distinguish two uses of imagery: that of illustration and that of transformation. The former employs a figure in order to bring out a certain aspect or meaning of the object. In this process the object is never lost sight of, but is seen in a new light or a new focus. The latter function, transformation, is the use of a figure whose reality is made to be more forceful than that of the object; the resulting new reality obliterates and is substituted for the original. All this is not simply a circumlocution for the terms "simile" and "metaphor." These words partially indicate the distinction I am trying to make but they are not accurate. A simile, although it usually only illuminates, can at times transform if its content is sufficiently vivid. Surprise is the element of this vividness which Apollinaire stressed to good purpose, for surprise obliges one to use all the faculties of the imagination. Likewise a metaphor, although syntactically it does imply a transformation, may be strong enough only to illustrate.

   (31)

7. Dante Alighieri, *The Divine Comedy,* trans. Charles S. Singleton. All subsequent quotations from both the Italian and the English translation will be taken from this edition of *The Divine Comedy.*

8. The wandering similes of Homer are, of course, another case in point.

9.   vix prece finita torpor gravis occupat artus,
     mollia cinguntur tenui praecordia libro,
     in frondem crines, in ramos bracchia crescunt,
     pes modo tam velox pigris radicibus haeret,
     ora cacumen habet: remanet nitor unus in illa.
         Hanc quoque Phoebus amat positaque in stipite dextra
     sentit adhuc trepidare novo sub cortice pectus
     conplexusque suis ramos ut membra lacertis
     oscula dat ligno; refugit tamen oscula lignum

                                              (I, 548-556)

     When her limbs grew numb and heavy, her soft breasts
     Were closed with delicate bark, her hair was leaves,
     Her arms were branches, and her speedy feet
     Rooted and held, and her head became a tree top,
     Everything gone except her grace, her shining.
     Apollo loved her still. He placed his hand
     Where he had hoped and felt the heart still beating
     Under the bark; and he embraced the branches
     As if they still were limbs, and kissed the wood.
     And the wood shrank from his kisses. . . .

10. Taccia di Cadmo e d'Aretusa Ovidio,
         ché se quello in serpente e quella in fonte
         converte poetando, io non lo 'invidio;
     Ché due nature mai a fronte a fronte
         non trasmutò sì ch'amendue le forme
         a cambiar lor matera fosser pronte

                                    ("The Inferno," XXV, 97-102)

Concerning Cadmus and Arethusa let Ovid be silent, for if he, poetizing, converts the one into a serpent and the other into a fountain, I envy him not; for two natures front to front he never so transmuted that both forms were prompt to exchange their substance.

11. This passage was, by order of the Spanish Inquisition, expurgated from copies of the *Divine Comedy* introduced into Spanish territory.

12. Readers familiar with psychoanalytic criticism will recognize some similarity between this concept and the notion of metaphor as a tool by which one copes with reality. Specifically, some readers might recall Jacques Lacan's understanding of metaphor as a necessary construct if one is to synthesize experience and find a means by which to mediate the difference between the self and the other. For instance, if a child is to evolve into an integrated person, that child must break away from complete identification with the Father, see himself as being different, and accept the absence of the phallus. To do this, the child must leave what Lacan speaks of as a metonymic and foreclosed relationship with the Father and move into one which is symbolic or metaphoric. Without this shift, the child runs the risk of becoming schizophrenic. For a clear discussion of this concept, see De Waelhens, pp. 4-19.

In another context, See suggests that without the power of metaphor to recognize and utilize differences, language runs the risk of becoming incestuous and drifts towards its death, to "a dangerous repetition of the same . . ." (72).

Works Cited

Alighieri, Dante. *The Divine Comedy.* Trans. Charles S. Singelton. Princeton: Princeton UP, 1970-1975.

De Waelhens, Alphonse. *Schizophrenia.* Trans. W. Ver Eeche. Pittsburgh: Duquesne UP, 1972.

Lear, Edward. *The Complete Nonsense of Edward Lear.* Ed. Holbrook Jackson. New York: Dover Publications, Inc., 1951.

Ovid. *Metamorphoses.* London: William Heinemann Ltd.; Cambridge, MA: Harvard UP, 1960.

———. *Metamorphoses.* Trans. Rolfe Humphries. Bloomington: Indiana UP, 1968.

See, Fred G. "The Kinship of Metaphor: Incest and Language in Melville's *Pierre,*" *Structuralist Review* I (Winter 1978).

Selected Writings of Guillaume Apollinaire. Trans. Roger Shattuck. New York: New Directions Book, 1971.

Sewell, Elizabeth. *The Field of Nonsense.* London: Chatto and Windus, 1952.

Twain, Mark. *The Adventures of Huckleberry Finn.* Middlesex, England: Penguin Books Ltd., 1974.

Ann Colley (essay date autumn 1988)

SOURCE: Colley, Ann. "Edward Lear's Limericks and the Reversals of Nonsense." *Victorian Poetry* 26, no. 3 (autumn 1988): 285-99.

[*In the following essay, Colley focuses on episodes of animal and human metamorphosis in Lear's poetry.*]

Readers of Edward Lear's nonsense are often surprised to learn that he was a serious artist preoccupied with the subject matter, technique, and even the sale of his work. They are astonished to discover Lear's fine illustrations of animals and birds (his ornithological prints easily rival Audubon's) and to see his topographical landscapes which record his extensive and prolific search for the picturesque. Recently, as if posthumously bestowing the acceptance Lear desired in his lifetime, the Royal Academy of Arts exhibited selections from the entire range of Lear's work.[1] Once more the incongruities between Lear's earnest and humorous pieces bewilder admirers, and they notice, for instance, the differences between his landscapes executed in the manner of Claude Lorrain and any one of his jingling limericks. No correspondence between the two styles easily avails itself. These incongruitites, however, need not be alienating. Rather, their dissimilarity can be a source of clarification, for it helps explicate the topsy-turvy mode of nonsense and, in particular, makes it possible to regard Lear's limericks not only as antitheses of the serious pieces but also as inversions of them. It is as if Lear, when composing his limericks, took his daily "academic" work and turned it upside down and inside out. In a sense, the limericks emerge as reverse images of the paintings.

Lear's way of going about composing the nonsense pieces also reverses his elaborate approach to his academic paintings.[2] When Lear painted his topographies or prepared his landscapes and animal studies for printing, he labored over them endlessly. He was never content to let these compositions alone. Two pictures which he began in 1859 he "finally finished in 1878." In between, Lear candidly acknowledged, he had "altered, & condensed, & resurrected, & reconsidered" them.[3] This proclivity to revise increased during his final years when he was intent upon completing his illustrations of Tennyson's poems. From early morning until night, he was entangled in a process which involved his "penning out," tracing, washing, enlarging, and worrying about the techniques of reproduction—"on and on, 'ad infinitum.'"

No such labor accompanies his nonsense verses and drawings. Abandoning the rigor of his other work, Lear seems to have written and drawn these humorous pieces with the utmost casualness. An 1861 diary entry reflects the difference: "I am unable from constant interruption to work—so I give it up and lead a life of idleness—drawing 'Nonsenses' at times,—but sleeping at others" (March 6). Another entry suggests that the nonsense belonged to some other mode of time or consciousness. On April 5, 1861, Lear remarked, "Quite too dark to work, drew nonsenses." Lear seems to have tucked his nonsense into parts of the day not connected to the labor accompanying sunlight; he often squeezed it into the corners of his correspondence and of the pages of his diaries. For instance, in a letter to Curtis (January 1, 1881) concerning the difficulties of his "poetic series of illustrations," Lear interjected the following riddle:

> In what part of the world are the
> Ears of Donkeys most brittle?
> In Switzerland; because in that
> Country they have Glass ears (glaciers).[4]

And in the midst of a diary entry about his landscape drawings, Lear casually inserted a limerick (one which did not find its way into the nonsense books):

> There was an old man with a ribbon
> Who found a large volume of gibbon
> which he tied to his nose
> and said—'I suppose'
> This is quite the best use for my ribbon

>   (January 2, 1882)

As readers of his letters and diaries frequently discover with pleasure, Lear also added nonsense drawings to the margins of pages. For example, in a postscript to a letter addressed to Wilkie Collins (April 27, 1885), he dashed off a sketch of "The Household of Villa Tennyson," showing, in order, "Edward Lear," "Foss the cat," "Chip, the goldfinch which perches on Foss's tail," and "Koo & Ko ye pigeons."[5] The effortless lines of the caricatures reveal none of the self-conscious attention to detail and correction which characterizes his paintings and studies. The spontaneity which he was not willing to let dominate his serious pieces is permissible and desirable within the field of his nonsense.

Even when Lear was preparing his humorous work for publication and was, therefore, having to adopt a more self-conscious posture, there is sparse evidence of any anxious reworking of the words or images. Certainly, there is some editing, but it is minimal. For instance, Lear made only one emendation to the limerick, "There was an old man on whose nose / The birds of the air could repose." Its accompanying drawing, flowing with the deft strokes of Lear's pen, depicts the old man's extended arms as if he were signaling not only his acceptance of the flock of birds perching on his nose but also the author's willingness to expose his impulsive self. In a like manner the lines of the verse display little interruption. All remain untouched except the last, which Lear altered from "deserted that man & his nose" to "which relieved that man & his nose." Similarly, his corrections of "The Comfortable Confidential Cow" for *Twenty-Six Nonsense Rhymes and Pictures* are slight. Lear fusses a trifle with the position of the cow's horns; otherwise, the images and words sit as contentedly as the cow toasting her bread.

If the reader turns his attention away from a consideration of the differences in the working methods, and places the limericks next to the paintings, the oppositions and inversions suggested by the labor of the serious work, on the one hand, and the casualness and spontaneity of the humorous pieces, on the other, become more explicit, and, in turn, help isolate the qualities which characterize Lear's limericks and fashion the pleasures of nonsense. A comparison of the two styles immediately reveals that the limericks displace and twist the realism of the academic pieces. When Lear executed his bird illustrations and his landscapes, he concentrated upon being true to what he saw. For instance, Lear based his bird prints upon drawings and elaborate color notations taken while observing live birds which a keeper had, somehow, to keep still (Audubon drew his from dead specimens). And when Lear composed his landscapes, he traveled far to paint them on site and worked diligently to make them realistic. It is no accident that he labeled himself a "topographical painter," and it is not surprising that he became enamored with the endeavors of the Pre-Raphaelite Brotherhood to be true to nature—a number of Lear's paintings rendered under the influence of William Holman Hunt ("Daddy Hunt") display that school's minute attention to details.[6]

The limericks, however, upset this realism and partake of a world which represents people and events literally—that is, Lear's animal studies by stretching, approximating, and exaggerating the idiosyncracies of their compositions, let the subjects of those pieces stand verbatim before the reader. In the limericks Lear abandons the homogenizing attention to detail that blurs the subjects of the paintings and actually makes it difficult to tell exactly what they are about. In this manner, the limericks not only magnify, strip, and unhinge Lear's detailed attention to the contours of a landscape or to the exact breadth of a bird's wingspan but also bring to the surface an explicitness which the orientation of realism dismisses. The resulting literalism of the caricatures and hyperbolic images dislodges an ironic and humorous vision from the conventions of the picturesque and the naturalists' classifications. Perhaps the most obvious of these displacements appear in the limericks founded upon Lear's ornithological studies. Take, for example, his "Spectacled Owl," an 1836 watercolor, which meticulously depicts every feather and mark of the owl and which pulls the viewer's attention to the owl's devouring eyes.[7] The watercolor is disturbing, for a human quality lurks within the bird's face. Inside the boundaries of realism, however, that element is hastily swept aside by the measured particulars of the painting. But, when Lear transposes the "Spectacled Owl" from the topographical mode into the literal key of his nonsense drawings, the humanity quickly returns. The carefully rendered details recede into approximation and gather into simplified lines. Notice, for instance, the caricatured versions of the "Spectacled Owl" in **"There was an old person of Crowle."**[8] In the midst of a nest of owls sits this "depressing old person" who wears a hat and suit, has a beard and a mouth, yet resembles the watercolor owl.

His half-human appearance confirms and thus, makes literal the humanity implied in the painting. His eyes glare with human intensity.

In addition to explicating the implicit, the limericks reverse the paintings and literalize experience by pushing aside associations, eradicating shadows and images, and expelling superfluous dimensions. They strip fact of its context. Neither frame, nor setting, nor shadow supplements the drawings accompanying the limericks. None proposes a past or a contrast against which to judge the content. Separated from time and memory, the images press close against the surface of the text and let go of their spatial orientation. In this way, Lear inverts the topographies so that no hint of the Lorrain or Pre-Raphaelite perspectives that informed his watercolors or oils remains. Gone is the picturesque point of view exercised by Lear in his travel journals. A passage from his *Journals of a Landscape Painter in Southern Calabria* (1852) displays the "Romantic" and topographical orientation which he set aside in order to compose his limericks. The passage quoted below follows Lear and his companion as they move from the foreground of the landscape, descend into the middle ground, and raise their eyes to behold the vista of the undulating hills:

> The view of Cánalo from the ravine of the Novito is extremely grand, and increased in majestic wonder as we descended to the stream through fine hanging woods. Having crossed the wide torrent-bed—an impracticable feat in winter—we gradually rose into a world of stern rocks—a wilderness of terror, such as it is not easy to describe or imagine. The village itself is crushed and squeezed into a nest of crags immediately below the vast precipices which close round the Passo del Mercante, and when on one side you gaze at this barrier of stone, and then, turning round, perceive the distant sea and undulating lines of hills, no contrast can be more striking. At the summit of Cánalo stands a large building, the Palazzo of Don Giovanni Rosa.[9]

Because the limericks negate this sense of place, depth, and sublime terror, outlines of images in the nonsense drawings crowd against the exterior of the page, liberated from any context. The human figures which the contours of the landscape once defined and which were, consequently, hard to distinguish from their surroundings come forward. (Although Lear painted portraits of animals, he did not paint portraits of people, and rarely did he make a person the subject of his serious work. Usually he subordinated the human figure and let it be just one more element in the landscape—as if mainly to lend his topographies a sense of scale.[10]) In the limericks, these figures leave behind the elements they were serving and stand on their own. The Old Person of Dutton (p. 41), for instance, stretches out flattened and letter-like against the surface of the page. There is nothing behind him and nothing to put him in his place. His wide-open posture suggests the pleasure of his freedom.

A Young Lady of Hull (p. 39) who distracts a "virulent bull" with a spade is similarly unattached. Both she and the bull spread out across the page and face each other with whimsical delight. Without the picturesque perspective, the danger, or perhaps the sublime terror, of their confrontation never materializes.

On the few occasions when there is a semblance of a background, the figures at the back of the drawing are no more than accordion-like extensions of those in front. Examples include Lear's drawing of the cousins who catch toads for the Old Person of Rhodes (p. 28) and that of the twenty sons who wait for an Old Man of Apulia (p. 24) to feed them buns. Their repeated lines drive the eye's attention forward. In all the illustrations, this preoccupation with the surface strips away a dimension so that the legs of chairs, tables, and people spread out flat across the page. It is as if without a tragic prospect, there is no need to create a backdrop to which to retreat. Not even the naming of the specific geographic locations in the first lines of the limericks (e.g., Prague, Rheims, Coblenz, and Whitehaven) serves to supply a context. Rather, the names of the cities and towns recline on the ornamental edge of the rhymes of the verse. Time defines no place; consequently, the fact of place permits few shadows into the contours of the reader's understanding.

The very action of the limericks also inverts Lear's serious pieces, for it lies on the surface, away from suggestions of the temporal. The drawings and the words are lively, bursting with kinetic energy, yet, paradoxically, unenlightened by either the past or the future. In fact, the action continuously falls back on itself; when events in the limericks appear to be engaging time, they are, in effect, moving neither backwards nor forwards. Like the set opening and closing lines of the verses, they return to themselves, untouched by time. In **"There was an old person of Filey"** (p. 180), the action is continuous, yet strangely static, for the old person's dancing is not structured by a beginning, a middle, and an end. Rather, it is caught in a seesawing present, that, like the illustration accompanying the verse, alternates between the Old Person's high stepping and the other man's stooped ringing of the bell. Each takes its turn and holds the dance in place. The repetitive words also subvert what impulse there might be to indulge in the temporal, even when the action pretends to be defined by chronological limits. For example, **"The Old Man of Dunluce"** returns to its beginning:

> There was an old man of Dunluce,
> Who went out to sea on a goose;
> When he'd gone out a mile, he observ'd with a smile,
> 'It is time to return to Dunluce.'

> (p. 178)

And in another limerick which pretends to involve the reader and the subject of the verse in a progressive sequence, once more the repetition in the last line undercuts that intent:

> There was an old Man of the Hague,
> Whose ideas were excessively vague;
> He built a balloon, to examine the moon,
> That deluded Old Man of the Hague.

> (p. 40)

As I have said, because Lear releases his subjects from the burden of time and memory, the limericks are unoccupied by tragedy.[11] The action and words of the text bound along, blithely inviting the reader to accept a Young Lady's purchasing "some clogs and small spotty dogs" as literal fact, requiring neither motive nor consequence. No slight temptation beckons the reader to consider what happened before or after the event. Because the action floats freely out of context, anything can happen, and nothing matters. So when a door squeezes a Young Lady of Norway flat, and she casually exclaims, "But what of that?" the reader agrees with her. Similarly, no menace girds the Lady of Chertsey as she sinks underground, and none attends the grandmother's threat to burn the Young Person of Smyrna.

In addition to literalizing the realism of the paintings and pushing images and words forward, Lear's nonsense verses and drawings reverse his serious work by opening up what the topographies and prints enclose. Although his landscapes depict the picturesque and, hence, represent sweeping panoramas, they do not finally leave the viewer with a sense of spaciousness. The uniform washes and topographical lines which blend the shapes of the mountains with those of the plains and the pastures, and the groupings of figures which repeat the gatherings of trees and rocks combine to create a landscape which does not admit space. One part either parallels or merges into the other and succumbs to the strictures of the frame of the picture. Paradoxically within a genre dedicated to the prospect of a landscape, the details fail to extend the boundary of the painting. The ubiquitous collections of huddled figures in Lear's topographies confirm its self-referential idiom.

In the limericks, on the other hand, faces of the subjects turn to look out beyond the text, and serialized, sometimes isolated, images frolic on a frameless page, admitting and displaying the gaps that fall between them. These images are responding to the literal quality of Lear's nonsense which separates objects and words and forces the reader to take experience as a shopping list of places, events, and items: butter, plague, pickled onions, and Prague. His limericks celebrate an Old Man who sits in a pew and tears his blue spotted waistcoat into pieces (p. 58)—an activity which duplicates the piecemeal progress of the limerick. One of Lear's unpublished nonsense verses renders the principle of serialization in the limerick even more explicit. The verse lists a variety of objects and animals and lines them up into pairs separated by conjunctions and pauses:

> Thistles & Moles,
> Crumpets & Soles—
> Set it a rolling
> & see how it rolls. (. . .)[12]

The accompanying drawing carries the serialization through, for it depicts two of each named items descending a slope in this metonymic mode. As in the limerick, each isolated pair sets the nonsense in motion.[13]

However, this tendency of Lear's nonsense to turn the topographies inside out by separating what the landscapes merge, needs to be qualified, for, as is often noted, there is a semblance of connection among the various and isolated elements of the limericks. It seems that at the same time as the limericks are inverting and slicing experience, they are also hurriedly putting it back together. Sometimes nonsense pretends to offer a semblance of synthesis by presenting its own mocking form of logic. In **"There was an old person in gray,"** (p. 195) pieces of evidence come together and parody "logical" sequences that reside within the deeper structure of the limerick. At the risk of stretching the association too far, it seems that the first two lines suggest an announcement of the subject matter of a major premise: "There was an old person in gray, / Whose feelings were tinged with dismay." The third offers the particulars associated with a minor premise ("She purchased two parrots, and fed them with carrots"), and the last renders a conclusion based upon the preceding statements—perhaps, even a tacit "therefore" echoes within the concluding line: "Which [therefore] pleased that old person in gray."

More often and more obviously there is some semblance of cause and effect at work. In one limerick, the Old Man of the Nile cuts off his thumbs because he stupidly sharpens his nails with a file (p. 55); in another the Old Person of Rheims eats cake to keep awake because he is troubled with horrible dreams (p. 55). The impulse to think that one event leads to another in these verses recalls the logic of the verses which Lear read and which provided Lear with his first models of the limerick. One of these pieces is

> There was an old Captain of Dover,
> Whom all the physicians gave over;
> At the sound of the drum,
> And "The enemy's come!"
> Up jump'd that bold Captain of Dover.[14]

Another from that book is "There was a sick man of Tobago" to which Lear later added his own set of illustrations:

> There was a sick man of Tobago
> Liv'd long on rice-gruel and sago;
>   But at last to his bliss,
>   The physician said this—
> "To a roast leg of mutton you may go."

Both verses set up a logical sequence of events which Lear's limericks subvert by only pretending to move forward from cause to effect. The originality of Lear's verse is that the last line, by repeating the first, undermines the progressive movement of the 1823 models. The memory of the model, however, is available, but displaced to throw over all the expectations of a connected sequence.

These quasi-logical connections, though, are familiar. Less obvious is the binding influence of the metaphoric impulse of which the limerick seems to be an accidental parody. With this impulse comes a promise to collapse the isolated pieces into one manageable idea, to forge a unity between what usually are considered to be distinctly different events or images. The outrageous rhymes in the limericks begin to suggest the metaphoric transference of qualities from one object to another. The shared, approximate sounds of the rhymes draw objects together which normally would have little to say to each other. "Rhodes / toads," "Prague / plague," and "Coblenz / immense" couple in a manner which recalls or parodies the interaction of the "tenor" and "vehicle" of metaphor. Giving an illusion of a metaphoric frame, the rhyme momentarily holds and brackets the separated images. It pretends to make sense of the merely serial.

It is, however, what I choose to call the metaphoric adjectives in the last lines of the limericks that more readily give the illusion of blending the various elements. Being larger, longer, and having a rougher texture than the words around them, each is distinctive. The examples offer some of Lear's more memorable phrases: **"That intrinsic Old Man of Peru"** (p. 12), **"That ombliferous person of Crete"** (p. 13), **"That mendacious Old Person of Gretna"** (p. 52), **"That oracular Lady of Prague"** (p. 54), and **"You luminous person of Barnes"** (p. 176). Lear gathers all the force of the limerick into the adjectives. Like siphons, they draw off the free-floating pieces into a single container. The adjectives no longer just mockingly qualify their accompanying nouns; they also pretend to justify and combine the disparate elements of the entire verse.

In some cases, the sequence actually has the appearance of plausibility. For instance, how else would it be possible to understand or unite the facts that the Young Lady of Welling plays the harp and catches carp than to state in the last line that she is an "accomplished Young Lady of Welling"? (p. 50). Her being "accomplished" gives at least a semblance of an essence which binds her acts. Certainly, the illustration does not succeed as well as the word. The drawing hints that the lady is a mermaid and shows her seated in water playing the harp with one hand and fishing with the other, but it neither clasps her separated hands nor otherwise visually evokes an adjectival frame to bracket the distinctions. But even when the adjective makes little sense and really does not seem to justify the action of the limerick, like **"That intrinsic Old Man of Peru,"** who tears his hair and behaves like a bear, or like **"That ombliferous person of Crete,"** who dresses in a sack, spickle-speckled with black, still Lear throws the weight of the limerick into that final adjective. Like a magnet, it draws the preceding lines together and unites them. And, in keeping with the demands of metaphor, this vague and ambiguous adjective creates a gap in which the reader must supply the means of combining or tying together the incongruous details.

This final adjective, however, cannot hold the limerick together perpetually. The strain of the pretence coupled with the literalizing force of nonsense breaks open the illusion and exposes the gaps which the "metaphor" promised to close. No longer does the limerick seem to express the continuity and synthesis available in the landscapes, for the bringing together of the carp and the harp (**"The Young Lady of Welling"**), a hatchet and a flea (**"An Old Man of the Dee,"** p. 34), and a smile and a voyage on the goose's back (**"An old man of Dunluce"**) are only parodies of metaphoric comparison.

Among the pressures which keep the serializing or metonymic quality dominant are the translucent rhymes of the limericks. They make it difficult to ignore the spaces between items. On the one hand, the rhymes, like the parallels in the topographies, give the appearance of combining separated elements, but, on the other, they insist on their separateness. Because Lear forces the rhymes into extremes, he compels the reader to consider each singly. No part of the rhyming words blends noiselessly into the other. Each announces itself and its unnatural conjunction. For instance, in spite of the obvious audible correspondences between "Rhodes" and "toads," "Coblenz" and "immense," or "Prague" and "plague," the reader remains more aware of the differences between them. In their haste to correspond, these words trip over each other and expose the stumbling blocks of their individuality. The rhyme is at once completed and broken apart.

Illustrations also render the space visible, for no matter how frequently the words of the verses of the limericks describe a collision of one object or figure with another, the drawings refuse to carry the intended violence through. Always a gap intervenes. Rarely does a figure touch another, and rarely do the instruments of harm reach their victim. Instead, they hang suspended and unconnected. For instance, the knife with which an Old Person of Tartary divides his jugular artery floats bliss-

fully free of his extended fingers and his screeching wife's hands (p. 50); the large stones which "several small children" throw at an old Person of Chester hang like bubbles over the man's right side (p. 51), and the oversize puppy which is supposed to snap up an Old Man of Leghorn fails, as if blocked by the intervening space. One figure might stare at another, but none touches, not even when harmony exists between the two. The Old Man of Whitehaven and the raven dance parallel to one another, yet unattached, and the "ecstatic" Old Person of Tring gazes at his mirror image in the moon, through an interval which seems to increase both his desire and his separateness (p. 36). It is as if the illustrations dismember the illusion of synthesis promised by the verse. The words might vow that the Old Man of Nepaul who is split in two will be mended by "some very strong glue," but the accompanying illustration does not, for it chooses to emphasize the disengagement of the man's severed parts (p. 27). Like drawings of the Old Man of the Nile's severed thumbs or the Young Person of Janina's decapitated head (p. 186), the illustrations serialize the body.

The visible absence of connection also characterizes the limericks which claim to unite the animal and the human world. In these pieces which recall the watercolor studies like the "Spectacled Owl," there is a half-metamorphosis in which the animals adopt human shapes, and the humans unconsciously assent to display animal forms: the Old Man in a tree perches and sits staring at a bee that bears his face (p. 7). His posture imitates the bee's. The Young Lady of Portugal rests in a tree where she literally has a bird's eye view of the sea she examines (p. 10). Her face resembles a crow's. The Old Person of Dover extends his arms as if they were wings of the bees in the field. The Old Man who said, "Hush!" looks remarkably like the bird he "perceives" in a bush, and the bird wryly endures some resemblance to him: the man's arms spread like wings, and his baton stretches behind in the manner of the bird's perky tail (p. 42). But, even when there are additional hints of metamorphoses from the verses, the transformations are not complete. The human and animal parts sit on top of one another or lie side by side announcing, like the rhyme, their fundamental autonomy. The literalism of the limericks has made it possible to recognize and separate out the half-human element buried within the animal studies.

These half-metamorphoses also participate in the reversal in the limericks of Lear's paintings, for they upset his own metaphor of a "metamorphosis" to describe his method of preparing two hundred topographies to compose his illustrations for Tennyson's poems. When Lear revised these sketches, he thought of them as evolving, step by step, from the "eggs" (the original sketches) to the full-grown "chrysalis state" (the drawings ready for printing). In a letter to Underhill, his printer, Lear explained the process:

> The drawings selected for illustration are 200 in number & of all sorts & kinds of scenery—Indian—Turkish—English etc etc etc—and in the first instance all the 200 are *already done* in black & white—but only about 4 inches long. . . . Next to these 200—(which I call the "Eggs"—) I have done the 200 in rough light & shade—the same size as the lithograph I send—& wh—is to be the size of all if eventually published. (This lot I call "newly hatched caterpillars".) After this I went in for the whole lot twice the size—in order to get correct idea of effect—but only extremely rough—(& these I termed "full grown caterpillars"—) 4thly I did & am now doing the same set—finished so far as to be in a state copied by a lithographer—& these are the last or "Chrysalis state—" about a fourth part of the whole 200 being already completed.
>
> (December 27, 1878)[15]

Lear was uneasy until this metamorphosis was complete. During his last fifteen years the fear that his failing health might prevent his bringing the project to its conclusion haunted him. No such anxiety, however, frequents his limericks, for there Lear was content to let the metamorphoses remain unresolved. In fact, the limericks take pleasure in displaying a figure like the old person of Brill who is caught half-way between being a fish and a man (p. 162) or like the old man of Marsh who is happily stuck somewhere between being a man and a frog (p. 165). No force hastens to complete the transformation and sink one form into another. The metonymic mode of nonsense relieves one of that necessity.

Related to this difference between the Tennyson illustrations and the limericks is another which involves the ways in which words and images come together. When Lear prepared his drawings for the Laureate's poems, he did not wish to render the poet's lines in an explicit manner. Rather, he desired to create images which are not tied to the specific setting of the poem but are indebted to the "higher and deeper matters" of them. For instance, Lear selected a piece he had executed in Macedonia to accompany the phrase "A land of streams" from the first line of the second verse of "The Lotos-Eaters," and he chose one of his landscapes of Albania to depict "A place of tombs" from "Morte D'Arthur." Through the medium of his images, Lear seems to gather the selected phrases and move them out of the poem into a realm which is distinct from the text and its function of naming meaning. In a sense, he subjects Tennyson's words to the metamorphoses of his illustrations—that is, the words and their forms evolve and take on another shape. As they move further into the visual field, they discard their sounds and their particularity and gradually adopt a more silent and nameless aspect which more closely reflects the "higher and deeper matters."

The relation between words and images in the limericks, on the other hand, is quite the opposite, for the nonsense drawings stay with and are indebted to the words of the verse.[16] In the manner of their subjects who are half animal and half human, the illustrations of the limericks are caught between the act of writing and drawing. As visual-verbal puns they carry on the dark, bold lines of the words—the very curves of the letters are those of the drawings. Each section of a figure in the drawing reflects a syllable from the words below; consequently, the reader views the details as if he were reading the lines of the verse. His eyes follow the segments spread out across the flat surface of the page while his ear attends to the syllables in the articulated rhythms of the stanza. No longer can the reader sweep his eye over the page, encouraged by the washes that seek to blend the details of Lear's topographies. Rather, he must pause at each portion or letter of the drawing.

Like the other inversions, this one also helps isolate the distinctive qualities of the limerick. The facile, syllabic character of the nonsense drawings reflects the ease with which nonsense resides within a disjointed world. Within the context of the limerick, there is no need to fill in the empty spaces, to join the disparate parts, or come to a metaphoric closure. The limericks mock the reader's impulse to find a resting place in congruity. They remind him of the ever-present and visible gaps in his own experience. But because this reminder comes unattached to time, memory, and even place, the prompting is neither unsettling nor threatening. In the end, it seems that the pleasure of nonsense, like that of being acquainted with Lear (**"How pleasant to know Mr. Lear!"**) is that nonsense removes the reader (and, indeed, its author) from the anxiety of difference and lets him safely explore the gaps between events.

Notes

1. Dates of the exhibition, "Edward Lear," are April 20-July 14, 1985. The exhibit was also shown at the National Academy of Design (New York) from September 10 to November 3, 1985.

2. For a discussion of Lear's career as a landscape painter see Philip Hofer, *Edward Lear as a Landscape Draughtsman* (Cambridge, Massachusetts, 1967). In addition to offering a detailed account of the meticulousness of Lear's technique, the book allows the reader to see numerous reproductions of Lear's landscapes.

3. The Houghton Library, Harvard University has Edward Lear's diaries written between 1858 and 1887. This entry is from February 20, 1878.

4. A. L. S. to Curtis, Houghton Library.

5. A. L. S. to Wilkie Collins, April 19, 1885, Houghton Library.

6. Among the oil paintings executed under the influence of William Holman Hunt are "Quarries of Syracuse" (1852), "Thermopylae" (1852), and "Temple of Bassae" (1854). Also see Ann C. Colley, "Edward Lear and the Pre-Raphaelite Impossibility," *JPRS* [*The Journal of Pre-Raphaelite Studies*] 7, no. 1 (November 1986): 44-49.

7. Reproductions of the "Spectacled Owl" may be seen in Susan Hyman, *Edward Lear's Birds* (New York, 1980), p. 83, and in Vivien Noakes, *Edward Lear 1812-1888* (London, 1985), p. 27.

8. "There was an old person of Crowle" and subsequent limericks quoted in this paper are from *The Complete Nonsense of Edward Lear,* ed. Holbrook Jackson (New York, 1951), p. 195.

9. *Edward Lear's Journals: A Selection,* ed. Herbert Van Thal (New York, 1953), p. 103.

10. Lear painted a watercolor portrait of Robert Burton. In that portrait, however, the face fails to be prominent, for it is overshadowed by the cloth which surrounds it.

11. Ina Rae Hark in *Edward Lear* (Boston, 1982) discusses the idiosyncrasies of Lear's limericks. She, though, when emphasizing their disjunctive quality, discovers tragedy. She explains:

> Lear accentuates the uncertainty of his world by teasing his readers with certainty. Predictable patterns do run through the limericks, e.g. "they" will react hostilely to eccentricity, gluttons will be punished, but just as one becomes confident in making such associations, the poet throws in an exception to upset them. Such final unpredictability is at base very frightening. In the limericks Lear underplays the terror of the situation through restraint of emotion in his presentation. . . . When Lear moved on to less controlled poetic forms, however, the more melancholy aspects of the nonsense world became increasingly apparent
>
> (p. 51)

12. MS of "Thistles & Moles" is at Houghton Library. It is one among others composed in the same mode.

13. Elizabeth Sewell in *The Field of Nonsense* (London, 1952) writes that "the aim of Nonsense is very precise indeed. It is by means of language to set before the mind a possible universe in which everything goes along serially, by one and one" (p. 56).

14. *Anecdotes and Adventures of Fifteen Gentlemen,* 1823 (London, [?1823]), n. p.

15. A. L. S. to Underhill, July 2, 1885, Pierpont Morgan Library.

16. Thomas Byrom in *Nonsense and Wonder: The Poems and Cartoons of Edward Lear* (New York, 1977). His discussion of the limericks emphasizes the discrepancies between the verses and their accompanying illustrations. He opens his discussion, entitled "Picture and Poem Discrepancy," with the statement of his conviction: "A glance through both series [of the limericks] will quickly satisfy the reader that in nearly every picture poem there is a discrepancy" (p. 120). Hofer also notes how, many times, Lear's "cartoons" mollify or seem indifferent to the content of the verse (see pp. 120-150).

Ann C. Colley (essay date summer 1992)

SOURCE: Colley, Ann C. "Edward Lear's Anti-Colonial Bestiary." *Victorian Poetry* 30, no. 2 (summer 1992): 109-20.

[*In the following essay, Colley asserts that while Lear's verse is apolitical, the accompanying illustrations sometimes are not. The critic views Lear's sympathetic renderings of animals as a critique of English efforts to "civilize" natives of non-Western countries.*]

Without a doubt the drawings that Edward Lear dashed off to illustrate his nonsense capture the tenor of the verses they accompany. Exuding a kinetic energy, these illustrations, like the words beneath them, isolate and exaggerate the subject's peculiarities. They authenticate the hyperbolic mode of the verbal text.[1] This tightly woven relation between the words and images, however, is not entirely seamless. As Thomas Byrom observes, there are discrepancies, for the cartoons sometimes subvert or override the words they are supposed to illustrate.[2] These differences, though, are not entirely the result of what Byrom identifies as Lear's "transcendentalism"—they do not merely reflect Lear's sense of "a mysterious happiness" that overpowers his "often sensibly glum view of life" (p. 138).

Many of the significant disparities between the words and images also issue, in part, from the fact that his nonsense—especially his limericks—has an historical background that one does not usually think of attaching to Lear's work. The gaps between the words and images reveal that his nonsense is not as exclusively full of "wonder" or as free of immediate purpose as Byrom or anyone who enjoys the limericks entirely for their fun might believe. In fact, they may often be thought of as reflecting a political attitude.

With a few exceptions the verses of the limericks themselves are not "political." Although there are passing allusions to places and expeditions associated with the expanding British empire, the verses are essentially ahistorical. Their words move along the page unattached to time and even to place—the naming of a city or a country in the first and last lines of the verses never fully situates the subject, for in Lear's nonsense, names offer a rhyme—a mere sound—to play with for its own sake. Not even the naming of specific geographic locations in the limericks (for example, Prague, Rheims, Coblenz, and Whitehaven) serves to supply a context. These names "recline on the ornamental edge of the verse's rhymes. Time defines no place" (Colley, p. 19). Moreover, the surprising conjunctions of words, people, and things in the verses topple the established order of things, and, consequently, seem to liberate their contents from anything outside of themselves. The pleasure of nonsense, of course, often originates in this sense of freedom.

The drawings that accompany these limericks, on the other hand, are not so detached. Indeed, they reflect a "political" agenda. They illustrate more than the words require—as Byrom would say, they "disclose what the verse does not indicate" (p. 135)—for in addition to depicting the topsy-turvy world of nonsense, they refer, quite explicitly, to certain Victorian imperialistic principles with which Lear seems to have had difficulties. The drawings reveal a Lear who is sensitive to the fact that animals—not, it should be emphasized, necessarily people—are being used as emblems of England's dominion over remote territories and nations. In particular, they show his impatience with the practice of "colonizing" the animal world.

Lear and Victorian Imperialism

For those who have read Lear's correspondence and journals written abroad, the suggestion of his criticizing any facet of Victorian imperialism might seem, at first, incongruous. Clearly, Lear was capable of subscribing to the colonial system and its prejudices against the non-English. For instance, he could be patronizing and find humor in a Sikh officer's toilet,[3] and, especially when feeling uncomfortable, could register disgust with such figures as "a big, horrid, vulgar, ill-dressed, gross blacky Indian" (p. 140) or speak of "filthy Arab savages."[4]

More to the point, perhaps, is the fact that Lear depended upon the privileges of imperialism. Throughout his life his acquaintances and closest friends (significantly, they were also his patrons who supported his painting and travels) were those administering the various British protectorates. Among these were Sir Henry Storks (Lord High Commissioner at Corfu), Sir Stratford Canning (Ambassador at Constantinople), and notably, of course, Franklin Lushington (Judge to the Supreme Court of Justice in the Ionian Islands), Chichester Fortescue (Under Secretary for the Colonies and afterwards Chief Secretary for Ireland), and Lord Northbrook (the Governor General of India who arranged and financed Lear's 1873-1875 sojourn in India).

Lear, however, was not entirely uncritical of the colonial system. Writing on April 24, 1864, for instance, he referred to the "insidious" colonial officials who make life difficult for those under their rule (*Letters of Edward Lear,* p. 309). In addition, he often revealed his impatience with the absurdities of "Palace" life (p. 48), the foolishness of certain conventions (see his list of absurd titles, p. 258), and what he labeled the "jealousies & smallnesses & professional quirks" (p. 130) of English society abroad. To his credit he also frequently displayed a genuine interest in the culture of the protectorates he visited. At times he even chastised himself and the English officials for what he perceived as their ignorance concerning the language and culture of a country (*Edward Lear's Indian Journal,* p. 91).

That Lear could periodically express seemingly contradictory sentiments is not out of character. In "The Jew as Victorian Cultural Signifier: Illustrated by Edward Lear," Ina Rae Hark recognizes this typical "Learian paradox," and, in particular, reflects upon the disparities in his discourses concerning Jews—he could regard them as intimate friends, as patrons; he could criticize anti-Semitism, but, on other occasions, he could not get beyond the "hooked-nose" stereotypes dominant in Victorian cartoons. To account for these contradictions Hark explains that Lear both subscribed to and felt distant from the dominant Victorian ideology. She makes the significant point that even though from the age of fifteen on Lear was "befriended by aristocrats and high-ranking civil servants," he was not raised in that class. (Lear's sisters educated him at home.) The result is that "he was both a part of and apart from the imperial power relations in which so many of his friends and patrons engaged."[5]

Undoubtedly this feeling of marginality, of being caught on the outside looking in, helped Lear form an ironic and critical distance between himself and "others" (the infamous "They" of his limericks[6]) and, moreover, exacerbated his sensitivity to the repression of individuality—a reaction that finds expression in the limericks and seems to have been especially strong in the presence of "Popes and Parsons" who "sit on our brains."[7] This feeling, though, did not necessarily result in his fully appreciating the colonial oppression of the non-English. Instead, his "exile" (a term Lear applied to himself) was a circumstance that most often motivated him to turn to the animal world for consolation and caused him to be acutely aware of its importance.[8]

Throughout his life Lear found a pleasant and relatively safe companionship with animals. (He often worried that others found him, in his words, "ill-tempered and queer.") His celebrated attachment to Foss, his cat, is an example. The numerous drawings of him and Foss stepping in an ironic union are, perhaps, testimony enough. Lear's letters are full of these revealing sketches. In addition, Lear was fond of referring to himself as an animal. For instance, when he was working on his parrot studies, he proclaimed, "for the last 12 months I have so moved—thought—looked at,—& existed among Parrots—that should any transmigration take place at my decease I am sure my soul would be very uncomfortable if anything but one of the Psittacidae."[9] Lear almost realized that transformation in his numerous self-portraits in which he depicted himself as a rather stout bird with stubby wings. On other occasions he used animals to portray his state of mind. For example, in the late 1830s when he arrived in Italy to study landscape painting, he exclaimed, "I am extremely happy—as the hedgehog said when he rolled himself through a thistlebrush" (Noakes, p. 58). And almost forty years later he wrote whimsically to Lord Carlingford, "I think of marrying some domestic henbird and then building a nest in one of my own olive trees, where I should only descend at remote intervals during the rest of my life." Accompanying these words is a drawing of a henbird snuggling up in her nest to a stout and resolute Lear—perched far from the complications of human relationships. This empathy sustains the anticolonial motif of his limericks.

LEAR'S ANTI-COLONIAL BESTIARY

That Lear's identification with and sensitivity to animals became entangled with Victorian imperialistic practices is not surprising. Animals, of course, have often carried the burden of political symbolism. In nineteenth-century England they suffered the full weight of that tradition. The amassing of vast collections of wild animal trophies and exotic bird skins, the sudden sprouting of city zoos (in London, Surrey, Birmingham, Liverpool, and Manchester), the creating of private menageries, the interest in natural history books, the producing of animal furniture (elephant foot stools and African antelope hall stands), the popularity of traveling wild animal displays, the breeding of hybrids like "tigons," and the consuming of exotic flesh (elephant trunk soup, roast giraffe, kangaroo hams, and Chinese sheep) were all, in a sense, "patriotic" acts that represented the suppression of the peoples of Africa and Asia (to a lesser extent, those of Australia and Canada). Each act symbolized possession or control.[10] Each, as Harriet Ritvo in her study of this subject suggests, "offered an especially vivid rhetorical means of re-enacting and extending the work of empire."[11]

As those familiar with Lear's biography might recall, Lear was closely connected to many who were in the forefront of these activities. As a young man in the 1820s and 1830s he earned his living drawing birds for lavish books about new and exotic birds. He worked, for instance, with Prideaux Selby and with Sir William Jardine, who had a collection of 6,000 birds skins in his home.[12] Through these connections, at the age of eighteen, he received permission to make drawings of the parrots in the new zoological gardens in Regent's Park (this was the zoo founded by Sir Stamford Raffles, an East India Colonial administrator) and was then asked to contribute illustrations to the visitors' guide book. With the help of patrons he published the first of twelve volumes entitled *Illustrations of the Family of Psittacidae or Parrots* (1830-32). This volume immediately won him a favorable reputation as a natural history illustrator so that he was soon asked to contribute studies to guides, proceedings, and historical series, such as *The Transactions of the Zoological Society, The Zoology of Captain Beechey's Voyage, The Zoology of the Voyage of the HMS Beagle,* several volumes of *The Naturalist's Library,* and Bell's *A History of British Quadrupeds.* He also prepared lithographs for *Tortoises, Terrapins and Turtles,* and worked for Dr. Gray in the British Museum. Moreover, for a number of years, he was employed by John Gould and contributed hundreds of drawings to his elaborate bird volumes, among which are *The Birds of Europe, A Monograph of the Ramphastidae or Toucans,* and *A Century of Birds from the Himalayan Mountains* (a book based on a collection of 100 Indian bird skins). During this time, under Gould's patronage, Lear visited zoos in Holland, Germany, and Switzerland to make drawings of their birds.

Being employed by Gould (who, by the way, before he turned to birds had stuffed the King's pet giraffe) was not easy, for, among other annoyances, he appropriated Lear's work (Noakes, p. 38). As a result, in 1832 Lear was pleased to start working for Lord Stanley, the heir to the Earl of Derby and the President of the London Zoological Society. For the next five years (until 1837) Lear lived at Knowsley Hall, the Earl's one hundred-acre estate outside of Liverpool. His task was to make an illustrative catalogue of the animals and birds in Lord Stanley's private menagerie. (Some of these drawings appeared in *The Gleanings from the Menagerie and Aviary at Knowsley Hall,* 1846.) Of all the menageries and aviaries, the one at Knowsley Hall was the most elaborate. In it were 345 mammals and 1,272 birds. To collect these specimens Lord Stanley was in touch with over twenty agents throughout the world who sent him new species for his menagerie and skins for his museum (the museum contained 25,000 specimens), and he financed expeditions to Africa, Honduras, and the Hudson Bay territories (Hyman, p. 57). Moreover, Lord Stanley kept detailed notes on animal behavior, on classification, identification of new species, adaptation to the English climate, and reproduction (Ritvo, p. 239). Like many of his contemporaries he was interested in breeding these exotics for domestication, eating, and experiments with cross breeding. The lord enjoyed his "Half-bred Produce."[13]

The breeding and collecting of exotics was not the sole means by which those, like Lord Stanley, extended the work of Empire. He and other landed gentry, of course, also took pride in their domestic livestock. For instance, they oversaw the raising of prize cattle and horses so that they might gain prestige from a particular animal's distinguished lineage or enormous size. (Ritvo documents how many "Barons of Beef" raised abnormally large cattle for exhibition.) They made their domestics into emblems of power and class. Similarly dogs and cats found themselves subjected to the pressure of pedigree. Their masters raised and exhibited them to display their own privilege and dominance over those of an inferior rank (Ritvo, pp. 82-121). Like the exotic animals these domestics also became icons of imperialism and its desires.

As readers of Lear's nonsense know, Lear began composing his limericks while at Knowsley Hall, ostensibly to entertain the Earl's children (Noakes, pp. 43-44). Inevitably, his work as a naturalist crept into his nonsense. It is, therefore, not unusual to see the storks, parrots, and owls of his naturalist studies transformed into nonsensical caricatures, and to find many of the limericks concerned with a person's relationship to an animal or a bird. For instance, the "Black Stork" which Lear rendered for Gould's *The Birds of Europe* (Vol. 4) finds its way into the illustration accompanying "There was an Old Man of Dumblane." In the nonsense drawing, even though the context alters, the stork's posture remains distinctly true to its natural self. Its figure then multiplies into the seven storks drawn to illustrate *A History of Seven Families of the Lake Pipple-Popple.*

That Lear would allow the stork to remain true to itself reflects the respect he had for animals and their individuality. He was unusual among natural history illustrators because whenever the conditions permitted it, he insisted on drawing from living rather than stuffed birds.[14] In a sense, his illustrations uncage the birds and animals trapped by imperialistic practices. Instead of dwelling upon the bird's ornamental or "typical" qualities, his drawings capture a fleeting moment from a particular animal's life. Lear refused to define his subject within the lifeless context of "kind." Moreover, unlike those who tended to set their subjects apart so that the birds refer only to themselves and, thereby, exist merely as observable objects, Lear registered the presence of an unspecified "other" that catches the subject's attention and causes the pelican, the toucan, the marsh harrier, the kestrel, or the owl to turn and cast back its own responsive, even critical, eye.[15] In particular, the owl possesses a haunting gaze, for his eyes tenaciously hold the viewer's and reduce the importance of the onlooker. In all these drawings of the birds, though, there is an exchange which protects the

bird's integrity and diminishes the observer's power. The artist and the viewer are "put in their place." Neither can fully violate, objectify, nor possess what is before him.

Lear's inclination to protect his subjects' integrity surfaces in the pictorial commentary he occasionally added to his preparatory sketches. For instance, when he was drawing studies of the Rose-ringed Parakeet, he bordered his page with disparaging drawings of those who gathered around him as he worked (Hyman, p. 20). In one, an enormous parakeet looks down upon the zoo visitors' gaping, inferior faces and easily asserts its authority and nobility.

The illustrations for the limericks express more explicitly Lear's desire to give animals their due and displace people's sense of their own superiority. Through these nonsense drawings he achieves a kind of revenge, on the animals' behalf, against those who attempted to manage, organize, cage, domesticate, and dominate their captives. He mocks what he was seeing while working with ornithologists, zoologists, collectors, keepers, hunters, breeders, and exhibitors and turns their myth of superiority upside down.

Lear had always enjoyed poking fun at the rage to classify and, thus, to control the natural world. His nonsense botany, in which, for instance, he identifies the "Manypeeplia Upsidownia" and draws people like petals hanging upside down on a stem, is an example of how he relished unsettling the order of things. In the drawings accompanying the limericks, this desire to upset the hierarchy and, especially, to topple man's mistaken sense of his own importance, receives even fuller expression. Through these illustrations Lear inverts the "chain of being" so that a cow perches on the branches of a tree and gleefully looks down on the Old Man of Aosta; people inhabit trees and live in nests, and like the Old Man of Dundee and the Old Person of Crowle are regarded scornfully by the birds who surround them.

There is a metamorphic dimension to this displacement. The Young Lady of Portugal who climbs a tree, the Old Man who speaks with a bee, and the Old Person of Crowle unwittingly resemble the birds and the insects they accompany. Like the verses below that remain mute about this transformation, they are oblivious to the changes in their physiognomy. Through these metamorphoses Lear, of course, continues to demolish the order of things. He reverses the metamorphoses in the works of George Cruikshank and J. J. Grandville in which the animals are essentially forgotten and are required to take on man's image. In Lear's illustrations, a man or a woman cannot help but adopt an animal's features. The person gets left behind. For instance, the Old Man who said "Hush!" looks at a bird and has no choice but unconsciously to mirror it. Similarly, the old man of Dover looks like the bees who pursue him. He can outstep neither their image nor their sting. He is the one preyed upon. The old person of Nice who associates with geese and the old man of El Hums who lives on nothing but crumbs must suffer the "tolerant" or amused glances of the birds they unknowingly imitate. As always with Lear, the birds possess the controlling eye. Only occasionally do the verses of the limericks speak of this metamorphosis. For instance, in "There was an old person of Brill" the reader learns how people make fun of the man who has "purchased a shirt with a frill" and who, consequently, resembles a fish. (His shirt has "gills.") Even here, though, Lear's drawing adds its own mocking commentary to the verbal text, for it shows that the man who holds the fish (so that he might laugh at the old person) parallels, without realizing it, the very posture he derides.

As part of their "debunking" of those who wish to dominate, Lear's visual texts often ridicule the imperialistic notions of observation. In the illustrations for the limericks, instead of its being the person who looks or analyzes—as, of course, was the practice of the naturalists, collectors, and breeders—it is often quite the opposite. Externalizing what was already latent within his own natural history studies, Lear's nonsense drawings emphasize the observing animal or bird in such a manner as to disqualify a person's inflated sense of himself. The ass, in spite of its lowly position, disdainfully looks back at the old Man of Madras who attempts to ride him, and the cur with his self-possessed and self-satisfied eye destroys the old Man of Kamschatka's apparently misplaced belief in his own prominence. The illustration disqualifies what the verbal text claims to be true—that the old man "possessed" the cur. In other limericks, the exchange of glances between man and animal contradicts the imperialistic eye that not only negates the animal's regard but also finds it "insignificant."[16] That eye would not admit the visual interplay between the fish and the Old Person of Ems, and the young Lady in white and the "birds in the air." It would not tolerate their mutual regard.

Lear's illustrations ridicule imperialistic practices in other ways. People, not animals, are caged. They are stuck in nests, held by the nose by parrots, or trapped in trees. When men and women attempt to display their ability to dominate or control by riding an animal, Lear's visual text demonstrates their inevitable powerlessness. Even though the old man steers the hare's tail like a rudder or the old person of Ickley dangles a whip in front of a tortoise, neither ultimately is master. Neither determines the course nor sets the speed. In Lear's drawing the hare's twinkling eye and the tortoise's stubborn grimace suggest that each animal is following its own impulse. The hare will run away with the despairing man and the tortoise will render the whip

more feeble that its rider imagines. Similarly, according to the visual text, the old person of Rye and the old man of Boulak are not long in command. One will fall (Lear's drawing reveals how precarious the man's posture on the fly's back really is—he should not look so confident), and the other will be consumed by the crocodile (the crocodile's smiling teeth confirm the ending that the words below suggest merely as a possibility). In fact, the only beings that are masterful are the animals. When, for instance, the enormous grasshopper jumps on the back of the old person in black or the large, menacing beetle runs over the neck of the old Man of Quebec, it is clear from the illustrations that the insects' resolute expressions command and overwhelm the men underneath them. Even the humblest animals—the small birds, the puppies, the crabs—exceed their usual proportions and dwarf the people who stare at them.

Lear also reverses the popular notion that animals exist merely for people's benefit—for their survival and entertainment. In his drawings a calf eats a young Lady of Greenwich's garment, birds "repose" upon an old Man's nose; to make themselves a nest, birds pluck the whiskers from an old man in a tree; "two owls, a Hen, four Larks and a Wren" nest in an old man's beard, and birds sit upon a Young Lady's bonnet. People serve animals. They play the flute for pigs (a wry reversal of the nursery rhymes in which the dog plays the flute for old mother Hubbard), they sing to frogs, ducks and pigs, and fan "overheated fowl." Upon each occasion, Lear's animals show how foolish people are. One fowl raises a contemptuous eye, and the pigs stand with a dainty nobility while they patiently suffer the old person of Bray's aggressive performance.

Indeed, Lear's visual text reveals little tolerance for those who are intent upon domesticating or civilizing animals by training them to act like humans—particularly English humans. The doubtful glance of the owls who are being taught to drink tea because, according to an old Man of Dumbree, "To eat mice is not proper or nice" (5), and the pitiful looks of the expiring fish whom the old person of Dundalk is teaching to walk are examples of Lear's impatience with those who by imposing their own ideas of correct behavior deny others' existence. His drawings are his revenge, for whenever he portrays anyone in the act of "civilizing" an animal, he shows that person turning into the very thing he or she is attempting to reform. For instance, through the twist of Lear's pen, the old man of Dumbree comes forth as a larger version of the "little owls" he instructs. He is not as "civilized" as he would like to think. Similarly, the old Lady of France, who teaches the ducklings to dance and tries to rid them of their inappropriate quacking, turns into a duck. Her hair separates into flowing feathers and her face displays its duck-like features. Even the old person of Dundalk begins to resemble what he unsuccessfully attempts to humanize. These metamorphoses confuse the imperialistic imperative by exposing the "wildness" that is latent within humanity.[17]

Ideally Lear would have liked a more fraternal partnership between man and animal. In a few of his nonsense illustrations he indulges this dream by depicting people and animals moving harmoniously together: coat tails and wings, fingers and webbed feet, and noses and beaks merge and extend themselves as if responding to the same rhythmic pulse. Their sympathetic motions contradict the idea of human domination. In these drawings, animals are no longer tokens of political submission. They are not used, as was the faithful rhinoceros of Lear's tale, as "diaphanous" doorscrapes. The old person of Skye and the bluebottle fly, and the old Man of Whitehaven and a Raven dance contentedly together. Their limbs and their expressions borrow from each other to form a happy union. Such conviviality animates the old person of Bree who travels between land and sea, the tranquil person of Hove who with wrens and rooks studies his books, and the old man and the owl who imbibe to their mutual benefit.

Although the nonsense drawings often celebrate this ideal, the words below sometimes expose what the reality can be when there is a code that frustrates that possibility. They address society's outrage when an individual fails to conform to the expectations of the code. For instance, the people who see the man of Whitehaven dance a quadrille with the raven "smash" him, and the people of Dumblane exile the old man who resembles a crane. Typically, of course, Lear's drawing reveals that one of the outraged citizens, himself, resembles a bird.

With all these illustrations in mind it is difficult to think of the limericks as belonging almost exclusively to the timeless, frivolous world of nonsense and children's entertainment. Although the drawings show their indebtedness to the verse they illuminate, they also follow their own political directive. Their criticism represented by Lear's freely drawn and spreading lines surreptitiously undoes the orderly and formulaic verbal package that the rhymes of the verse neatly tie together.

In making this political commentary, Lear is obviously secure in the safe asylum of nonsense. Significantly, though, Lear seems also to have benefited from an important difference between words and images. That difference grants him a permission he might not have otherwise enjoyed. Although, of course, nonsense words attempt to break out of the restrictions of "sense," they still carry a "responsibility," for they continue to be signs of meaning. No matter how ludicrous their sequence, the words bear the burden of having already been used and, thus, "possessed" by those who have spoken, read, written, or heard them. Words cannot be separated from a social context. I would like to suggest, however, that drawings are another matter. Nonsensical lines belong only to the person who executes them. Although they partially conform to some general mimetic principle, they can freely change their "spelling" and in that liberty to be "mistaken" or to be individualistic find a privacy which shields the creator. Lear's drawings are not already "owned" by those who regard them; consequently, he can play more amply. There is room for a safe ambiguity.

This distinction, perhaps, bears a resemblance to one that the artist Frank Auerbach proposed in a recent conversation with Robert Hughes. Auerbach suggested that in contrast to poetry, painting creates its own "fresh language." In his mind:

> There is no syntax in painting. Anything can happen on the canvas and you can't foresee it. Paul Valery used to say that if the idea of poetry hadn't existed forever, poetry could not be written now. The whole culture is against it because language is always being worn down and debased. But painting is always a fresh language because we don't use it for anything else.[18]

With this kind of freshness Lear's drawings seem to represent what he desired for the animals and birds he portrayed. Each illustration and each animal retains its "ownness" and rebels against being a commodity, a symbol, or an icon for the Sir Stamford Raffles, the Sir William Jardines, the John Goulds, and the Lord Stanleys. Each deflects or confuses the "possessive" gaze; each refuses to be useful. Each catches the eye in a moment between the familiar and the unknown, the public and the private.

Notes

1. For a discussion of the similarities between the visual and verbal texts of Edward Lear's limericks, see Ann C. Colley, "Edward Lear: The Limerick and the Promise of Synthesis," in *The Search for Synthesis in Literature and Art: The Paradox of Space* (Athens, Georgia, 1990), pp. 9-28.

2. Thomas Byrom, *Nonsense and Wonder: The Poems and Cartoons of Edward Lear* (New York, 1977), pp. 120-150.

3. *Edward Lear's Indian Journals*, ed. Ray Murphy (London, 1953), p. 136.

4. *Letters of Edward Lear to Chichester Fortescue, Lord Carlingford and Frances Countess Waldegrave*, ed. Lady Strachey (London, 1907), p. 100.

5. Ina Rae Hark, "The Jew as Victorian Cultural Signifier: Illustrated by Edward Lear," *BuR* [*Bucknell Review*] 34, no. 2 (1990): 87.

6. For a discussion of the "They" in Edward Lear's nonsense, see Ina Rae Hark, *Edward Lear* (Boston, 1982), pp. 29-30.

7. For references to Edward Lear's sensitivity to the repression of individuality see *Letters of Edward Lear,* p. 225, and Hark's "The Jew as Victorian Signifier," p. 91.

8. Perhaps also because Lear was "typically English," he paid considerable attention to the animals he observed during his travels. In his *Journal of a Landscape Painter in Corsica* (1868), for instance, he repeatedly describes the "unmerciful beating of the horses" being used to transport him. See *Edward Lear's Journals: A Selection,* ed. Herbert Van Thal (New York, 1952), p. 199. He seems almost oblivious to the treatment of the people around him.

9. Vivian Noakes, *Edward Lear: The Life of a Wanderer* (Boston, 1969), p. 33.

10. John Berger, in *About Looking* (New York, 1980), p. 19, remarks that, "in the nineteenth century, public zoos were an endorsement of modern colonial power. The capturing of the animals was a symbolic representation of the conquest of all distant and exotic lands."

11. Harriet Ritvo, *The Animal Estate: The English and Other Creatures in the Victorian Age* (Cambridge, Massachusetts, 1987), p. 205.

12. For a complete study of Lear's work with bird illustrations see Susan Hyman, *Edward Lear's Birds,* intro. Philip Hofer (New York, 1980). Interestingly, in her study of Victorian attitudes towards animals, Harriet Ritvo excludes the subject of birds.

13. In *Edward Lear's Birds* Susan Hyman records the fact that "a nineteenth-century catalogue of art works lists as his [Lord Stanley's] contribution many portraits of animals bred successfully at Knowsley and a canvas of epic proportions entitled *Wild Ass, Zebras and Half-Bred Produce*" (p. 57).

14. It was, of course, not unusual for natural history illustrators to draw from dead birds or from other drawings of the bird in question. The American naturalist John James Audubon was typical. He used stuffed birds, skins, and birds "that had been observed in their natural state but which were often killed before being drawn." Lear, on the other hand, worked with live birds in the parrot house in London's Zoological Garden. "While a keeper named Gosse held the birds, Lear carefully measured their wing spans, the size of their beaks and the length of their legs." While there he made "pencil sketches and detailed color notes" (Hyman, p. 20).

15. For examples of illustrations in which the birds refer only to themselves and, thereby, exist only as objects to be observed, see *The Bird Illustrated 1550-1900 From the Collection of the New York Public Library,* intro. Roger Tory Peterson (New York, 1988), pp. 26-27.

16. In *About Looking* John Berger remarks, "Animals are always observed. The fact that they can observe us has lost all significance. They are the object of our ever-extending knowledge. What we know about them is an index of our power, and thus an index of what separates us from them" (p. 14).

17. A number of critics remark on Lear's metamorphoses. Among the most prominent is Thomas Byrom in *Nonsense and Wonder: The Poems and Cartoons of Edward Lear* (p. 75).

18. Robert Hughes, "The Art of Frank Auerbach," *The New York Review of Books,* 37, no. 15 (October 11, 1990): 24.

In a recent discussion Professor Lorrie Goldensohn (Department of English, Vassar College) reminded me that "there is a culturally encoded, frequently traditionally imposed system of interpreting meanings for visual images at least as immediately binding as for verbal ones." I agree that what she suggests is often the case, but believe that on the whole drawings or rather the lines of a drawing do not necessarily impart this encoding. As "sketches" they are freer to dwell in or to create the spaces of ambiguity. They are lines that are in the process of becoming codes—they have not yet reached the definition associated with a code. In that case they are "freer."

Kirby Olson (essay date winter 1993)

SOURCE: Olson, Kirby. "Edward Lear: Deleuzian Landscape Painter." *Victorian Poetry* 31, no. 4 (winter 1993): 347-62.

[In the following essay, Olson considers the nineteenth-century aesthetic theory of the picturesque and sublime as it relates to Lear's visual art and his poetry.]

Whatever else the picturesque may have meant to an earlier generation, to Edward Lear (1812-88) it was a meal ticket, a "line of flight" (in Gilles Deleuze's phrase), and a lifelong aesthetic preoccupation. In this paper, I will attempt to trace Lear's "line of flight"—his peregrinations through the worlds of aesthetics—and his flight into the comic picturesque, an ideal world with strong affinities to the picturesque aesthetic from which it diverges. What I want to explore, therefore, are definitions of the picturesque and to essay a definition of the comic picturesque, as well as to look at one individual within a tradition, and to illuminate how that one individual—Edward Lear—adapted that tradition to his personal predilections.

"Throughout the eighteenth century," Walter Hipple writes, "most aestheticians tended to ignore the ridiculous and risible and to confine themselves to the serious traits—beauty, sublimity, picturesqueness. Only those writers who deal largely with literature, in which the comic element plays a pronounced role, are led naturally to treat of the ludicrous; writers whose concern is with painting and sculpture, and still more those whose chief interest is in gardening, architecture, or external nature itself, tend equally naturally to ignore a quality of such slight importance in their subjects."[1]

But isn't this argument circular? After all, if aestheticians had prized comic topiary shrubbery, or portraits of gypsies hitting each other in the face with lemon meringue pies, such subject material would have become a necessity or at least a possibility for landscape designers and painters—since visual artists follow theory as much as theoreticians follow visual artists.

Hipple adds in an endnote to the above passage, that "it is true, to be sure, that the picturesque has connections with the ludicrous, as in the genre painting of the Dutch school, and that the sublime may be connected with the ludicrous in the mock-heroic. Beauty has never, I think, any but an accidental connection with the ludicrous" (p. 342).

Hipple, then, says that beauty, alone of the three, is totally solemn, but aren't these categories susceptible to slippage? Even in Kant, arguably the most rigorous of the aesthetic philosophers, the categories of the beautiful and the sublime are sometimes very difficult to differentiate. Kant does not deal with the picturesque as a category, but his immediate inheritors in his tradition, Richard Payne Knight and especially Sir Uvedale Price, put a great deal of effort into clarifying the distinctions among the three principal terms. Hipple claims that "his [Price's] works on the picturesque remain the principal monument of picturesque doctrine" (p. 202). William Gilpin, Price's immediate predecessor, had founded the picturesque as an aesthetic term of great importance, but had left the picturesque, as Price put it, "involved in paradox" (Hipple, p. 202). Whereas Gilpin had finally despaired of finding first principles which would allow him to distinguish between the beautiful and the picturesque, and admits his puzzlement,[2] Price attempts to remedy this aporia by categorizing the picturesque as rough and run-down, and associating beauty with smoothness and youth.[3] Although Gilpin had already made such a distinction, he would frequently back off from his definitions, while Price is more dogmatic or forceful in his assertions. Autumn, Price says, is best for the depiction of the picturesque, while spring is best

for the depiction of beauty (p. 138). A partial and uncertain concealment yields the picturesque (p. 69), while beauty is passive and easily experienced. We must actively work at understanding the picturesque. It "excites that active curiosity which gives play to the mind, loosening those iron bonds with which astonishment chains up its faculties," while "in a spot full of the softest beauties of nature," pleasure is "to be received, not sought after; it is the happiness of existing to sensations of delight only—we are unwilling to move, almost to think, and desire only to feel, enjoy." The picturesque is difficult, challenging—it "corrects the languor of beauty," and "seems to be perfectly applicable to tragi-comedy" (p. 98). That which defies the understanding at first glance is picturesque, that which is immediately understood, is beautiful. Shaggy animals such as sheep and donkeys are picturesque, while well-delineated, sleek animals, such as Arabian horses, are beautiful.

Although there is no indication that Edward Lear ever read Sir Uvedale Price or William Gilpin or Immanuel Kant, the great theoreticians of the sublime and picturesque had been writing in the late eighteenth century, and Lear had been born in the early nineteenth. Lear inherited a tradition of the picturesque, writing in his *Journal of a Landscape Painter in Corsica* that a clearing surrounded by the great Corsican forest reminded "me of Robinson Crusoe's settlement as represented in beautiful Stothard drawings, those exquisite creations of landscape which first made me, when a child, long to see similar realities."[4] Lear was influenced by a great number of painters whose reputations, like Stothard's, have slid into near oblivion. In his Corsican book Lear writes that "towards the bridge over the Taravo there are many lovely pictures which would delight the eye, and give work for the pencil of Creswick, who (so it seems to me) is the best portrayer (after Turner) of river and wood scenery combined" (p. 107). Lear's journals are rife with the names of such forgotten painters and illustrators of the sublime and picturesque as Creswick. But Turner was well known, thanks largely to John Ruskin, and Lear revered Turner, though he was also terribly jealous: "Depressed enough already—the glory and beauty of Turners depressed me still more."[5] Lear has Ruskin to thank for his introduction to Turner. In a letter toward the end of Lear's life, Lear writes to Ruskin of "the wonderful Turners [which Ruskin donated], in the Taylor Institution. A treat for which I also may take the pleasure of thanking you, as I often do mentally for having by your books caused me to use my own eyes in looking at Landscape, from a period dating many years back" (Noakes, p. 20). But it is Albrecht Dürer, whose keen observation and rich detail caused Lear's aesthetic weathervane to point in a direction different from the picturesque standard toward the stark simplicity of his drawings for children. In Vienna, he writes, "I had folio after folio of Albert Dürer's drawing all to my blessed self. I never looked at anything else, but passed the whole morning on the old Nurenberger's works, getting a good lesson as to what perseverance & delicate attention to drawing may do. You would have liked to see some of the wonderfully beautiful sketches of weeds—flowers, & birds, which were there—much reminding me of certain hedgehogs, shells, flies, & pole cats etc. etc.—of other days" (Noakes, p. 20).

Landscape is the artistic legacy into which Lear was born, but he explodes in disgust from time to time, writing for example, "How could I ever have looked with delight on Gaspar Poussin, or S. Rosa?" (Noakes, p. 20). Although he was an assiduous worker in the landscape field, he slowly lost interest in the orthodox aspects of it. Lear writes at the age of fifty-nine, to a friend, and possible client, "I am doing a lot of 30£ and 40£ pictures—but with what success I cant tell yet. Some of those of Egypt would delight M. P. (I've got lots of beans up if he comes this way in March)."[6] The mercenary character of much of Lear's art in the landscape tradition is necessitated by the difference between Lear's aesthetic predilection for Dürer's simplicity, against the prevailing preference for intricacy, roughness, and grandeur. Lear loved Dürer. Uvedale Price, however, ridiculed Albrecht Dürer for not possessing the requisite picturesqueness Price admired, but instead producing "dry meagre forms" (p. 79).

Although his aesthetic background is confused, and therefore difficult to trace, Lear is at least aware of the major currents in aesthetic thought in the period just preceding his own, and in some striking ways uses what has been set up by Gilpin, Price, Ruskin, and others as material with which to develop his own aesthetic, especially in the field of nonsense poetry, where he felt most free to combine and utilize what was available in any pattern he thought most likely to amuse. Having sketched the background of the picturesque movement, and set this against Lear's own interest in such nonpicturesque artists as Dürer, I would now like to explore Lear's version of the picturesque, how he is both within this tradition, and outside of it and commenting upon it, and how he forges a new, comic picturesque out of the tension between the picturesque and the comic picturesque.

In *Journal of a Landscape Painter in Corsica,* Lear uses the terms "picturesque," "beautiful," and "sublime" frequently. Although he never explicitly defines these terms, we can look at the kinds of scenery to which they are applied in order to understand what it is that Lear means by them. By far the most frequently used term is "picturesque," which occurs on almost every page of the approximately 250-page journal. Though it would be impossible in a single article to inventory and

define every single variation on the way "picturesque" is used, it seems clear nonetheless that the term refers to old and rundown towns, which were once beautiful; forest scenery that provides roughness and intricacy; quaint or bizarre local outfits; queer personalities; and purely Corsican (because exotic and rare) animals and plants. Clearly, the term has been expanded from Gilpin and Price's definition, which referred almost uniquely to landscape painting. Lear sees cityscapes, too, as picturesque. He writes, "Bastia from this point is picturesque, though not beautiful; no charm of architecture commends it in any way; yet the large masses of building on the edges of cliffs, with caves and coves, slips of sand, and clear water, in deep shadow, and all alive with dabbling and swimming children, make a good picture; . . . the houses are so full of very elaborate detail, and so crowded with peculiarities of Corsican buildings" (pp. 194-195). From this passage, it can be determined that Price's definition of "bustle and animation" (p. 121) as qualities of the picturesque, as well as "deep shadow," which provided intricacy and variety, along with the "large masses of building on the edges of cliffs," the cliffs themselves possessing "caves and coves," make for a "good picture." This last criteria is Gilpin's most important prerequisite.[7]

The "peculiarities of Corsican buildings," which provide the picture with a foreign quality, seem quite important to Lear. The following passage from Price indicates that he, too, found foreignness itself a quality of the picturesque:

> But when some plant of foreign growth appears to spring up by accident, and shoots out its beautiful, but less familiar foliage among our natural trees, it has the same pleasing effect as when a beautiful and amiable foreigner has acquired our language and manners so as to converse with the freedom of a native, yet retains enough of original accent and character, to give a peculiar grace and zest to all her words and actions.

(p. 193)

Price wants assimilation to English character, but not at the expense of a total loss of native origins—in fact, this strangeness can be piquant. For Lear, foreignness has a stronger seduction than for Price. In his later *Indian Journal,* Lear writes that "quite near the pagoda are tents, and a lot of soldiers, horses, camels, and elephant, and all sorts of Indian picturesquenesses."[8] In fact, Anglicization is to Lear almost always a blight on picturesqueness. Later in the *Indian Journal* Lear writes, "Thence to the fort, a very grand building, somewhat like that of Agra, but infinitely inferior in its general interior effect, for most horribly ugly barracks, railings and other hideous British utilities prevent and confound the scene" (p. 96). Delhi has been so contaminated by Anglicization that Lear explodes, "O Delhi! the long contemplated! Verily one hour of Benares or Brindaban is worth a month of thy Britishized beauties which, whatever they once were, please this child very little now" (*IJ*, [*Indian Journal*] p. 98). Compared with Price's foreigner who has been assimilated into England, or compared to John Constable's nationalistic privileging of English and particularly Suffolk country-side over all other, we can see how far Lear has strayed in this regard from the standard. Not only does Lear describe the foreign as picturesque in and of itself, but he has a tendency to see singular things, outside of any pictorial frame, as picturesque. Soldiers, horses, and camels, for example, are so described. Edward Lear's nonsense alphabets, which I will discuss later, are often illustrated by a singular foreign animal or personage. Singularity does find some support as a picturesque quality in one passage in Price, where he indicates that a single tree can be picturesque, if it possesses the same qualities of intricacy and variety as a group of trees (p. 192).

The term "beauty" is employed much less frequently in Lear's aesthetic lexicon. In the above description of Bastia, it seems to be synonymous with "charm." In the following passage, also from the Corsican journal, Lear makes what appears to be a Burkean distinction: "Small were the hills, Latin or Sabine, edging the Roman campagna—small the delicate distances of Argos or Bassae; but all were refined and beautiful. To me these Corsican Alps, like their Swiss brethren, seem generally more awful than lovely" (p. 163). "Lovely," and "beautiful," and "charming" can all be separated from the awful by the terms "delicate" and "refined." Lear sees the picturesque quite often, and the beautiful less often, so there is an implication that Lear prizes the beautiful over the picturesque, since it is more rare, and what is rare is usually more valued than that which is common, though a very thorough study of this valorization might also reveal that Lear is getting what he is looking for—and that he is looking for the picturesque, not the beautiful. At any rate, Price points out that "it seldom happens that those two qualities [beauty and the picturesque] are perfectly unmixed" (p. 105). Lear very rarely uses the term "sublime." In the entire Corsican journal, he employs this term as few as five times, in contrast to the hundreds of times he uses the word "picturesque." It may be that Corsica is simply less sublime than it is picturesque. Lear sometimes substitutes "awful," where others might use the word "sublime." But even this word is rare. Speaking of mountain crags, Lear writes that they are "doubly awful and magnificent now that one is close to them . . . the tops of the huge rock buttresses being hidden, they seem as if they connected heaven and earth" (p. 92).

Aside from their historical interest, Lear's writings on landscape painting are still lively and readable on account of his humor, which often playfully engages standard versions of the picturesque. Christopher Hussey, for instance, says that picturesqueness, according to

Uvedale Price's aesthetic rival and sometime ally Richard Payne Knight, "consisted in a blending and melting of objects together with a playful and airy lightness, and a sort of loose, sketchy, indistinctness."[9] This vagueness led to distancing, an attempt to objectify the other, which is frequently seen as a political goal by contemporary critics of the picturesque movement.[10] Often, the subjects to be objectified consisted of gypsies, the poor, the livestock off which the wealthier classes lived, and sought to control through the freeze-frame of fine art. Lear seems to have fun with this notion in a description cited in *Edward Lear in the Levant*.[11] On September 26, 1848 (the year of one of many uprisings in Paris), Lear is painting near Elbassan, a city in Albania. In a description of a prototypically picturesque landscape, Lear writes that it is

> a town singularly picturesque, both in itself and as to its site. A high and massive wall, with a deep outer moat, surrounds a large quadrangle of dilapidated houses, and at the four corners are towers, as well as two at each of the four gates: all of these fortifications appear of Venetian structure. Few places can offer a greater picture of desolation than Elbassan; albeit the views from the broad ramparts extending round the town are perfectly exquisite: weeds, brambles, and luxuriant wild fig overrun and cluster about the grey heaps of ruin, and whichever way you turn you have a middle distance of mosques and foliage, with a background of purple hills, or southward, the remarkable mountain of Tomhor. . . . No sooner had I settled to draw . . . than forth came the population of Elbassan.
>
> (pp. 85-86)

A Moslem crowd which resented Lear's attempt to vie with creation drove him off with rocks. Instead of the distancing landscape is supposed to create, Lear was literally attacked by the landscape. Through his narrative, it becomes clear that Lear is aware of the political implications of his depictions, and satirizes the landscape mode with a kind of black humor. The Elbassaniotes told him they would not be written down and sold to the Russian Czar, which is precisely what many of their neighbors had had done to them after their last uprising. Many others were slain, drafted, or turned into slaves at Constantinople. Those who were left were "more heavily taxed than before" (p. 86). If there is something comic about this scene, and there is, it is in Lear's initial hilarious merriment at the sound of their speech as they upbraided him, and secondly in his fleeing the barrage of stones, only to hook back up with his bodyguard, who had a whip. While the Elbassaniotes saw Lear as a surveyor and as a sinner against God, saying that "Satan draws!" (pp. 85-86), Lear, while sympathizing with their plight, went blithely on about his own business. Lear can understand the concern of those around him, but his own ideals are unaffected. He is a grudging collector of the picturesque and sublime, and although his ethical concerns are clearly reflected in his journals, he goes on with his profession un-daunted, daily turning out new pictures for the market. How is it that Lear's idealism and understanding are unbroken by all of the horror and suffering that he sees in Albania, in Palestine, along the Nile, in Corsica, and in India? Raimonda Modiano writes in her analysis of Friedrich Theodor Vischer's attempt to create a comic sublime that

> the comic character does not pretend to be above the limitations of the ordinary world. His idealism, then, is from the outset suffused with skepticism and cannot be easily subjected to parody. . . . The comic sublime thus depends on a radical and most exacting form of idealism, one guaranteed by standards which acknowl-edge the dignity of humanity in the midst of the belit-tling circumstances to which individuals are ordinarily exposed.[12]

The sublime, however, with its emphasis on awe and wonderment, turning on that point where understanding ceases and judgment trembles, seems too strong an emo-tion for what Lear wishes to convey. Lear begins with the picturesque—that which is unusual, and spurs on the curiosity—but then he creates instead not an anti-picturesque but a parallel picturesque, which is in no way a sarcastic denunciation of the field of landscape from which it has sprung. Rather, Lear blends almost impossibly high idealism and optimism (traits Modiano sketches throughout her essay) with a mirthful and yet hard-headed understanding of life's realities. He thus begins to chart an area that Gilpin and Price left all but unexplored, though Price does say that "the picturesque is adaptable to the grandest as well as to the *gayest* scenery" (p. 96).

This implication that merriment can be subsumed within the picturesque is typified by Lear's description of an excursion to a picturesque forest just outside of the town of Porte Vecchio in Corsica. In this account, Lear tells of coming upon a "harmless lunatic, . . . [whose] present delusion is that he is king of Sardinia, which explains his magnificent manner." Lear writes that the poor fellow believed that he had swallowed two gendarmes, and he resolutely intended to starve the intruders. After two weeks, the lunatic believed he had accomplished this feat and went back to working and eating (*Corsica*, pp. 68-69). If the picturesque was sup-posed to be an exercise in objectification, what was this? This time Lear has described a poor lunatic, clas-sic picturesque material, but whose interiority contains the external guardians of law and order. If the poor often starved while the rich stuffed themselves, there is a further reversal in this episode in which a poor man starves himself in order to extinguish the imaginary guardians of the rich whom he had somehow mistakenly internalized. Is this criss-crossing of codes a conscious, or perhaps even an unconscious aesthetic subversion on the part of Lear?

We know that Lear read John Ruskin on Turner, from his own letter to Ruskin, which has been previously cited. Perhaps at least in reference to Ruskin, we can see a subversive version of "comic picturesque," one that challenges, rather than extends or parallels the picturesque. In his essay, "Of the Turnerian Pictur-esque," Ruskin writes of the old church of Calais that it epitomized the picturesque because it was "useful still, going through its own daily work,—as some old fisher-man beaten gray by storm, yet drawing his daily nets: so it stands, with no complaint about its past youth, in blanched and meagre massiveness and serviceable-ness."[13]

Is Lear drawing on Ruskin, then, in his Corsican journal, when he features "grasshopper-pigs" (p. 133), so named because Lear finds that the two long pieces of wood attached to their shoulders, which are criss-crossed and which resembled skis, make them look like "vast grasshoppers"? Lear's footnote explains that the pigs have had these odd "wings" attached to them to prevent them from straying into the garden or vineyard. Like Ruskin's account of the Calais church, then, these curiosities are "useful still," and can be seen as possess-ing "serviceableness," and yet Lear positions one pig so that its rear end deliberately faces the viewer full-on. Surely this is a subversion of the notion of the picturesque, as well as a transgression against Victorian decorum?

In Lear's nonsense proper, or improper, he develops a highly refined version of his comic picturesque mode. I say improper because, after reading Lear's nonsense,[14] Ina Rae Hark's commentaries in the Twayne Series,[15] and some 800 pages of biography, I no longer see the poems as nonsensical at all. They appear to me to have a highly precise, if not very recapitulable meaning: they resist meaningful analysis. In this respect, they are much like Price's "picturesque" and Kant's "sublime." Price makes it clear, in his account of the picturesque, that curiosity is a necessary component of the picturesque—the mind follows gaps, and places where shadows have obscured the original brightness (pp. 98, 87). There is also a partial and uncertain concealment, while what is beautiful is obviously and immediately so. We need not work to understand the beautiful, it can be passively received (p. 98). Kant, unlike Price, saw the beautiful as not being immediate.[16] Judgment is stirred by that which initially resists interpretation:

> All stiff regularity (such as approximates to mathemati-cal regularity) has something in it repugnant to taste; for our entertainment in the contemplation of it lasts for no length of time, but it rather, in so far as it has not expressly in view cognition or a definite practical purpose, produces weariness. On the other hand, that with which imagination can play in an unstudied and purposive manner is always new to us, and one does not get tired of looking at it.
>
> (p. 80)

Kant then denounces Marsden's view that it is novelty which produces beauty. For a pepper garden in a forest, Marsden's example, does not retain its novelty after one day. To spin a phrase off Ezra Pound's "Poetry is news which stays news," Kant might have said that "Beauty is news which stays news," as it is found in the "peculiar fancies with which the mind entertains itself, while it is continually being aroused by the variety which strikes the eye" (p. 81). As an example of beauty, Kant give us a rippling brook which can entertain the mind with free play. To illustrate the sublime, he draws a picture of "bold, hanging, and as it were threatening rocks; clouds piled up in the sky, . . . volcanoes in their violence of destruction, the boundless ocean in a state of tumult" (p. 100). We esteem these images in spite of our instinct of self-preservation, because we ourselves can grasp infinity, of which these giant displays of nature are small specks. Still, our understanding momentarily recoils and falls back upon judgment. There seems to be a moment of confusion which is translated into the aesthetic judgment. Without that confusion, whether produced by novelty, and then petering out, or produced by that pattern which presents a beauty so arresting that it stays beauty, there is no aesthetical judgment of either the beautiful or the sublime. Thomas Weiskel, in writing of Schiller, says, "Schiller draws the logical conclusion that *confusion* is the preeminent occasion of the sublime."[17] Weiskel continues, "Somehow the sublime authorizes a translation of absurdity into freedom; lack of connection or *non-sense* [my emphasis] is redeemed" (p. 35). Finding a pattern in what appears to be a resisting chaos is, in other words, the aesthetic act.

In the above passage I am attempting to set up the possibility of judging Lear's nonsense poetry as aesthetic, and in particular as embodying another variant of Lear's comic picturesque as seen in his landscape journals. First, I must revive the idea of comic genius in order to appreciate properly Lear's contribution. Comic genius is incomprehensible to Kant and many others in his era, and as a result, it seemed to many in the period immediately following their critical endeavors and up until our own day that somehow comic poetry is not really poetry at all. Richard Payne Knight, a close friend of Sir Uvedale Price, says in *An Analytical Inquiry into the Principles of Taste* that comedy shows us character after it has been "perverted by the habits, and modified by the rules of artificial society," and that "it exhibits our inconsistencies and incongruities, exhibiting in their junction a perversion or degradation of the natural character of man: such as boasting and cowardice, ignorance and pedantry, dulness and conceit, rudeness and foppery," and finally that the "ridiculous is generally based on the degradation of whatever is exalted."[18] Kant, meanwhile, sees that the comic results in a feeling of health and that laughter is good because "it moves the intestines and the diaphragm" (p. 177), but

that because jokes have a short duration, and end suddenly, they do not fit his previous description of the beautiful as that which stays beautiful: "Laughter is an affection arising from the sudden transformation of a strained expectation into nothing" (p. 177). Therefore, the comic is not beautiful at all. Furthermore, the admittedly intense pleasure of the absurd is not aesthetic because it gives no satisfaction to the understanding. And yet a moment of nonsense accompanies every judgment of the picturesque and sublime (though, for Price at least, "beauty" is immediate). If short duration of intensity is not enough for comedy to be considered as aesthetical, what of comedy that stands up to continual rereading? In her paper on Vischer's comic sublime, Modiano suggests how Vischer valorizes the comic not as a degraded form of tragedy, but as an even higher and more rare art form: "In the end the comic appears as a more desirable and capacious mode than the sublime; it includes the sublime and gives it a more secure foundation than it had on its own" (p. 242).

In his drawings and nonsense verses, Lear combined his love of Dürer's straight line with some aspects of the picturesque to create a hybrid form which immediately swept England and its colonies. "He gave a new idiom to humorous drawing. That deceptively simple line based on a child's view of an absurd adult world set in a style which has infected most modern comic artists and can be found in the current issue of *Punch* or the *New Yorker*."[19] If such a thing as a comic genius is permitted to exist, this was a founding act of genius, one, to paraphrase Kant, which summoned the comic genius in others. But is Lear's nonsense picturesque? I think that Sir Uvedale Price could have been describing one of Lear's drawings which parallel (I do not want to say illustrate, for reasons I will come to later), Lear's limericks, when he wrote, "We are amused and occupied by ugly objects, if they be also picturesque, just as we are by a rough, and in other respects a disagreeable mind, provided it has a marked and peculiar character; without it, mere outward ugliness, or mere inward rudeness, are simply disagreeable" (p. 154). Although "an excess of picturesqueness produces deformity," Price can assert that "lengthening a nose may be considered picturesque" (p. 148). Finally, he writes, "Deformity, like picturesqueness, makes a quicker impression [than ugliness or beauty], and, the moment it appears, rouses the attention" (p. 153). Deformity causes an active response, as opposed to the passive response given to beauty or its corollary ugliness. Some of the above characteristics, as well as the idea of age as a picturesque trait opposed to freshness or youth ("by far the majority of limerick protagonists— 169 of 212—are either Old Men or Persons" [Hark, p. 26]), can be found in the following limerick, one of a hundred that illustrate an obstreperous and deformed though charming old man engaged in an asocial, or antisocial, but not really violent act:

There was an old man of West Dumpet,
Who possessed a large nose like a trumpet;
When he blew it aloud, it astonished the crowd,
And was heard through the whole of West Dumpet.

(p. 181)

The drawing which accompanies this limerick (see fig. 2) shows a prancing character with a nose twice as long as his body, and a group of singularly displeased West Dumpetians, with frowning faces or holding their ears.

The drawings fill out, rather than illustrate, the poems. The poems themselves are fraught with curious lacunae, which sometimes point toward an odd incomprehensibility, which are pushed further into aporia by the drawings. Ann Colley's powerful reading of the limericks offers some clues as to how they cleverly resist reading on the one hand, while offering a kind of sense on the other.[20] Enticed by outrageous rhymes into attempting to make connections where none can exist, and contemplating violence which will never take place, upset in our conventional responses, we relieve out subsequent anxiety in laughter.

Colley's reading of the limericks, in my view, proves their picturesqueness, at least in terms of some of Price's categories (deformity, resistance to interpretation, the disagreeable minds of peculiar characters, etc.); however, to Colley, the limericks reverse the aesthetic Lear practiced in his landscape work:

> In addition to explicating the implicit, the limericks reverse the paintings and literalize experience by pushing aside associations, eradicating shadows and images, and expelling superfluous dimensions. They strip fact of its context. Neither frame, nor setting, nor shadow supplements the drawings accompanying the limericks. None proposes a past or a contrast against which to judge the content. Separated from time and memory, the images press close against the surface of the text and let go of their spatial orientation. In this way, Lear inverts the topographies so that no hint of Lorrain or Pre-Raphaelite perspectives that informed his watercolors or oils remains. Gone is the picturesque point of view exercised by Lear in his travel journals.

(p. 289)

And yet, as I hope I have insistently pointed out, some elements of that picturesque aesthetic remain in the limericks, and some of his longer nonsense poems actually draw on the picturesque tradition for portions of their background imagery. **"The Dong with a Luminous Nose"** (pp. 225-228), for example, opens with a classic description of the towering heights of the Hills of the Chankly Bore, a sublime setting undercut somewhat by an obsessively repetitive rhyme scheme. We also find in Lear's nonsenses "purpledicular crags" (p. 230) among rugged rocks; harmless volcanoes (p. 52), and other fragments of picturesqueness such as the exotic nobodies the Akond of Swat (pp. 257-259), writ-

ten while in the field in India and "The Scroobius Pip."[21] Lear's nonsense alphabets describe singular, foreign, strangely charming, deformed personages who illustrate to a tee Lear's comic but never explicitly stated definition of the picturesque (see fig. 3).[22] Many of the longer poems deal with two or more characters setting off on an interminable voyage into the exotic: the Owl and the Pussycat (pp. 61-63) go to sea (no place special) in a beautiful pea-green boat; the "Table and Chair" decide to stop being passive furniture and run around the town and get lost. In any case these voyages are often a sally into the foreign, very like Lear's own lifelong odyssey.

Most critics, in writing of Edward Lear, concentrate on his loneliness, his epilepsy, and his low self-esteem as the primary conditions for his perpetual flight into the wilds of the unexplored domains of the globe and his refuge in nonsense. I would like to propose that this "line of flight" is instead a very brave, idealistic, and successful attempt to sketch out an existence of his own invention, an attempt that would have been denied to him if he had remained in England. Is it not just this bravery and idealism, the fierce genius for independence, that we respond to in Lear's comic picturesque journals and nonsenses? In contrast to the conventions imposed by Victorian society, in which persons were classed according to their economic or sexual status, Lear successfully fled these distinctions, and in his flight established one of the most picturesque personalities of the Victorian era. Like the boundary-crossing gypsies, tramps, and bandits that the exponents of the picturesque liked to see portrayed on canvas, Lear too fled across boundaries, though they were race, gender, and class, as well as national boundaries. His friendship with his servant, Giorgio, for instance, attained a depth of affection unusual in an employer/employee relationship of this nature. In his *Journals,* Lear often describes him only as "the Suliot," a gentle mockery of the distancing created by such ethnic terminology. In fact, Lear worries constantly about Giorgio's happiness, is disturbed when his family does not write when they are on the trail, and tries to placate him when he is sulky with cigarettes and excellent food. Lear's letters, written to a wide variety of men and women, illustrate very well his capacity to make connections. But he did not care to pin himself down with a family, or connections which would limit his ability at self-definition. As Lear fled one set of connections, or limitations, he nevertheless developed others. Even outside the dimensions of conventional British society, Lear developed bonds of affection. He worried greatly about the horse pulling his coach across Corsica, for example, and constantly took his driver to task on the charge of brutality, finally dismissing him. Lear's cat Foss, who starred in some of his most memorable drawings, was perhaps his closest companion during the last sixteen years of his life, and when the cat died, Lear, like a spouse, himself died a few months later. He avoided conventional adult bonds

of affection such as marriage, but found many friend-
ships with children. Unlike Lewis Carroll, however,
Lear's poems were sometimes written for girls, and
sometimes for boys, and sometimes for an audience of
both. Also unlike Carroll, there seems to be nothing of
the predatory aspect of offering a serial story in
exchange for prolonged contact. Lear apparently sought
merely to entertain or cheer up his young listeners, and
entertain himself in the process, before moving on. His
nomadic existence was clearly his own choice. There
were women who certainly wished to marry him, and
whom he liked. Was he gay? Jean-Jacques Lecercle
claims that Lear was a repressed homosexual, but offers
no evidence.[23] Suffice it to say that after thoroughly
checking through all of Lear's extant biographies, I can
find no substantiation to Lecercle's claim. In his *Indian
Journal,* Lear makes many comments on the beauty or
lack thereof in the local women (p. 122), and his few
clear references to homosexuality are exclusively
limited to complaints about the homosexuality in the local men (p. 117). Although a few biographers do raise
the question, that is all they do. To my mind, Lear defies definition, and any attempt to squeeze him into any
of the sexual typologies currently available (gay,
repressed gay, frustrated heterosexual, homosexual on
the sly, sexual invert, etc.), seem doomed to be
inconclusive. Steven Shaviro's article on Deleuze and
Guattari's theory of sexuality, which thoroughly
scrambles the notion that we can remain within or
represent any one given category of sexuality over any
period of time, expresses well the nomadic sexuality
which seeks to escape the too tight shoes of naming.[24]
Lear was a nomad who crossed borders, and his art is
the clearest expression of this defiant personality who
refused to settle into a category. He describes his own
situation very clearly in the following limerick:

> There was an old man on the Border,
> Who lived in the utmost disorder;
> He danced with the cat, and made tea in his hat,
> Which vexed all the folks on the Border.

> (p. 202; . . .)

Can we judge Lear's path through art? Perhaps a passage by Gilles Deleuze from his essay *"Pensée Nomade,"*[25] on Nietzsche, will help me get Lear into a
conceptual frame in which I would like to have him
judged:

> Schizo-laughter or revolutionary joy, that is what
> emanates from great books, in place of the anguishes
> of our little narcissism or the terrors of our guilt. We
> could call that the "comedy of the *surhumain,*" or even
> the "clown of God." There is always an indescribable
> joy which radiates from great books, even when they
> speak of ugly, desperate, or terrifying things. Every
> great book already enacts a transmutation, making for
> tomorrow's sanity. We cannot not laugh when we burn
> through codes.

> (p. 170; my translation)

Lear's comic picturesque deterritorializes the boundaries
carefully set by Gilpin, Price, Ruskin, and the others,
turning their logic into illogic, their order into disorder,
their sense of desolation into merriment, allowing him a
free space to reinvent himself on the borders of the
Empire.

Notes

1. Walter John Hipple, *The Beautiful, The Sublime,
   And the Picturesque* (Carbondale, 1957), p. 113.

2. William Gilpin, *Three Essays: On Picturesque
   Beauty* (London, 1792), pp. 26-27.

3. Uvedale Price, *An Essay on the Picturesque*
   (London, 1796-98), p. 90.

4. Edward Lear, *Journal of a Landscape Painter in
   Corsica* (London, 1870), p. 141. Hereafter referred
   to as *Corsica.*

5. Vivien Noakes, *Edward Lear* (London, 1985), p.
   20.

6. Vivien Noakes, *Edward Lear: Selected Letters*
   (Oxford, 1988), p. 233.

7. William Gilpin, *Observations on the Western Parts
   of England Relative Chiefly to Picturesque Beauty*
   (London, 1808), p. 328.

8. Edward Lear, *Indian Journal,* ed. Ray Murphy
   (London, 1953), p. 82. Hereafter referred to as *IJ.*

9. Christopher Hussey, *The Picturesque: Studies in a
   Point of View* (London, 1967), p. 16.

10. See "The Politics of the Picturesque," by Alan
    Liu, in his *Wordsworth and History* (Stanford,
    1989), pp. 61-137; and Ann Birmingham, *Land-
    scape and Ideology* (Berkeley, 1986).

11. Susan Hyman, *Edward Lear in the Levant*
    (London, 1988).

12. Raimonda Modiano, "Humanism and the Comic
    Sublime: From Kant to Friedrich Theodor Vis-
    cher," *SIR* [*Studies in Romanticism*] 26 (1987):
    244.

13. John Ruskin, "Of the Turnerian Picturesque," in
    Modern Painters, Works, ed. E. T. Cook and Alex-
    ander Wedderburn (London, 1902-12), 6:11.

14. All quotations from Lear's nonsense writings, un-
    less otherwise noted, are from *The Complete
    Nonsense of Edward Lear* (New York, 1951).

15. Ina Rae Hark, *Edward Lear* (Boston, 1982).

16. Immanuel Kant, *The Critique of Judgment* (New
    York, 1951), p. 20.

17. Thomas Weiskel, *The Romantic Sublime*
    (Baltimore, 1976), p. 35.

18. Richard Payne Knight, *An Analytical Inquiry Into the Principles of Taste* (London, 1805), p. 413.

19. Ray Murphy, intro., *Indian Journal,* p. 16.

20. Ann Colley, "Edward Lear's Limericks and the Reversals of Nonsense," *VP* [*Victorian Poetry*] 26 (1988): 294-298.

21. Not found in the Dover edition, but in the posthumous collection *Nonsense Songs and Stories* (London, 1894), pp. 60-62.

22. *Webster's Unabridged Dictionary* defines the picturesque as "the quality or principle which combines what is unusual or charming in scenes, objects, actions, or ideas without attaining beauty or sublimity," *Webster's Unabridged Dictionary,* ed. William Allen Nelson (Springfield, 1955), p. 1858. Gilpin and Price would have recognized some of this description but "unusual," "charming," "objects," and "actions" are an expansion upon their definitions, an expansion possibly enacted in part by Lear.

23. Jean-Jacques Lecercle, *The Violence of Language* (London, 1990), p. 5.

24. Steven Shaviro, "*À chacun ses sexes*: Deleuze and Guattari's Theory of Sexuality," *Discours Social/ Social Discourse* 1, no. 3 (1988): 287-298.

25. Gilles Deleuze, "*Pensée Nomade,*" *Nietzsche Aujourd'hui* (Paris, 1973), pp. 159-174.

John Rieder (essay date 1998)

SOURCE: Rieder, John. "Edward Lear's Limericks: The Function of Children's Nonsense Poetry." *Children's Literature* 26 (1998): 47-60.

[*In the following essay, Rieder observes that Lear's limericks often portray an adult-like authority figure in a mocking way, thus opening an imaginative space for children to be free from rules and parental expectations.*]

Readers who seek to make sense of Edward Lear's nonsense limericks are in danger of putting themselves into the frustrating position of the people who question Lear's man of Sestri:

> There was an old person of Sestri,
> Who sate himself down in the vestry,
> When they said "You are wrong!"—he merely said "Bong!"
> That repulsive old person of Sestri.
>
> (192)

But if Lear's limericks defy critical interrogation, they do so with a good deal more charm than the repulsive old person of Sestri, because their resistance, unlike his,

does not put an end to conversation. On the contrary, their inscrutability instead raises the crucial question of the difference between the meaning of Lear's nonsense and its function. The question I wish to raise here, then, is not what Lear's nonsense means but rather what it does.[1]

This important distinction appears, for instance, in a comment Lear made in 1871 regarding some of the reviews of his second volume of nonsense writings: "The critics are very silly to see politics in such bosh: not but that bosh requires a good deal of care, for it is a sine quâ non in writing for children to keep what they have to read perfectly clear & bright, & incapable of any meaning but one of sheer nonsense" (*Selected Letters* 228). Lear's point is that his nonsense's irrationality is the result of a painstaking, rational process. To attempt to see past the surface of such verse is to ignore precisely what is most important about it, so that such seeing is a way of being blind to its real artistic merit. Indeed, the tension produced by offering multiple invitations to interpretation within a piece of art that at the same time deliberately resists any attempt to make sense of it has been called the essential feature of literary or artistic nonsense in general (Tigges 27).

Yet Lear's emphasis here is not on the general character of nonsense so much as on its appropriateness to a certain audience. "Writing for children," he says, requires one to keep things "perfectly clear & bright." What purpose does this clarity and brilliance serve, and how is it specific to writing for children? One of the "clear & bright" things about Lear's limericks is his highly predictable handling of the form.[2] The first line usually uses the formula "There was an [old/young] [man/lady/person] of [place name]." Lear frequently echoes this formula in the final line: "That [adjective] old man of [place name]." The middle lines usually describe some sort of eccentric behavior on the part of the subject, often accompanied by a response to it by the people around him or her, as in the oft-repeated formula beginning the third line: "When they said." The "old man of Sestri" limerick is a good example of this basic structure. Sometimes the interaction between the eccentric and "the people" extends into the final line, yielding variations on the basic formula: "They [verb] that old man of [place name]" (e.g., "So they smashed that old man of Whitehaven" [39]) or "Which [verb] the people of [place name]" (e.g., "Which distressed all the people of Chertsey" [7]). Thus the rather chaotic interplay between Lear's eccentrics and "them" is tightly contained within the repetitive form, providing a combination of novelty and familiarity that, like much nonsense verse for children, provides the child with a strictly rule-bound, reliable, and therefore reassuring set of boundaries within which to experience the fantastically extravagant and sometimes threatening contents of the poems (Ede 58-60; Kennedy).

The most distinctive feature of Lear's poetic craft in the limericks is his handling of the final line. Here one often finds whatever frightening or violent material the limericks contain, such as the eccentric protagonist being smashed or killed or drowned or choked. The need to control such threatening possibilities may help to explain the curious restraint of Lear's formal handling of the final rhyme. Unlike most later composers of limericks, and in distinction even from the "sick man of Tobago," which Lear cited as the primary model for his limericks,[3] Lear almost never tries to deliver a witty or surprising rhyme at the end of a limerick. But this is not to say that the final lines contain no surprises. On the contrary, the adjectives that describe the eccentrics are fabulously various. Sometimes they deliver an appropriate description or judgment, but just as often the description or judgment is mildly or strikingly inappropriate, and on a good number of occasions it is entirely mysterious. For instance:

> There was an Old Man of Peru,
> Who never knew what he should do;
> So he tore off his hair, and behaved like a bear,
> That intrinsic Old Man of Peru.

>   (12)

"Intrinsic" neither expresses a judgment nor plausibly describes any of the old man's qualities. It is quite as inscrutable as the man of Sestri's "Bong."

What the use of "intrinsic" achieves, in fact, is precisely the shortcircuiting of interpretation that Lear describes as the "perfectly clear & bright" quality of his verse, that which makes it "incapable of any meaning but one of sheer nonsense." According to one eminent theorist of nonsense, "This is the beginning of nonsense: language lifted out of context, language turning on itself . . . language made hermetic, opaque" (Stewart 3). Nonsense, according to Stewart, is language that resists contextualization, so that it refers to "nothing" instead of to the word's commonsense designation. In this way Lear's wildly inappropriate adjectives are paradigmatic instances of one of the fundamental activities the limericks perform: the world of Lear's nonsense is a playground.[4] It separates itself from the "real" world, letting loose a number of possibilities, including dangerous and violent ones, and at the same time disconnecting those possibilities from the real world, that is, from what goes on after the game is over. Thus Lear's artistry is "repulsive," not quite in the unmannerly fashion of the man of Sestri, but in that, like him, it stakes out a territory where being "wrong" is only a way of rhyming with "Bong."

The insulation of the artistic event from its social context is hardly peculiar to children's nonsense verse, however. We enter similarly playful (and, Huizinga argues, quasi-sacred) spaces when we go into an art gallery or a theater. But the distance from the commonsense world achieved in Lear's limericks is not just that of aesthetic contemplation. Although the language of any verbal artifact can be said to play rather than to work insofar as its readers adopt an aesthetic disposition toward it, Lear's limericks direct themselves to a specific audience and function precisely by actively refusing to work as conventional communication. This is not to say that the language of the limericks falls out of referentiality altogether, but rather that the truncated or suspended referentiality of Lear's nonsense is what makes the limericks peculiarly appropriate for children. And to adapt Lear's own critical vocabulary, the limericks' clear but restricted referentiality also makes them not just playful but festive in a full and complex way.

Lear declared both the limericks' intended audience and their festive character on the title page of his ***Book of Nonsense*** (1846) with this limerick and its illustration:

> There was an old Derry down Derry,
> Who loved to see little folks merry;
> So he made them a book, and with laughter they shook
> At the fun of that Derry down Derry.

The illustration . . . shows the dancing Derry down Derry handing his book to a group of frolicking children. Keeping in mind that most of Lear's limericks were not written with publication in mind, but rather as gifts for specific children, we might ask what relationship between the adult and the children the book is helping to create or mediate. Lear simply calls it "fun" in this limerick, but it is a special kind of fun. The adult dancing amidst the children may be in charge of the situation, since, after all, he wrote the book; or he may be giving up his authority, becoming one of "them," when he hands the book over to the children. The adult's size and dress clearly differentiate him from the children. What is not clear, however, is whether his dancing is a performance for them or an emulation of their excitement, and so, by implication, it remains unclear whether the book is primarily an entertainment for the children or a means of entrance into the children's fun for the adult. The point is not that it is one way or the other, but that both possibilities are offered. The adult's authority is neither protected nor abdicated, but rather suspended, at least for as long as the fun continues.

The suspended hierarchical relation between adult and child suggests social possibilities that move the limericks' fun beyond the formalistic aspects of play as understood by Huizinga and applied by critics such as Sewell and Ede. Instead, their engagement of social convention here resembles the highly charged mode of festivity that, according to Mikhail Bakhtin's classic book on Rabelais, was ritualized in the medieval carnival. Bakhtin argues that the carnival "celebrated temporary liberation from the prevailing truth and the established order; it marked the suspension of all hierarchical rank, privileges, norms, and prohibitions" (10). The relationship between Derry down Derry and the children is indeterminate, it seems to me, in much the way that social rules and hierarchies were set topsy-turvy during carnival. That is, Lear's verses, like a carnival celebration, clear a space for nonsensical fun by creating a hiatus in social rules and hierarchies, so that for a while it may become hard to tell the difference between us and them, high and low, teacher and student, or even adult and child.

But there is also a crucial difference between the spirit of carnival and Lear's nonsense. If the carnival "offered a completely different, nonofficial, extraecclesiastical and extrapolitical aspect of the world" and so "built a second world and a second life outside officialdom" (Bakhtin 6), Lear's nonsense directs its parodic and liberating energies not against the state or the church but rather in less "official" directions. In keeping with the interests of his intended audience, it is the private, domestic realm rather than the public domain that most preoccupies Lear in the limericks. They consistently address some of the most basic social conventions with which children struggle, such as those governing eating, dressing, grooming, and talking. Lear's approach to these conventions is "meta-cultural," in that it manipulates and explores the limits of social codes (Bouissac). Consequently the limericks tend to expose the arbitrariness or artificiality of convention rather than laying down the law. The limericks on eating, for instance, include stories of starvation and of gluttony, of "old men" who sink into alcoholic depression and of others who enjoy pleasantly recuperative snacks, of accidental cannibalism but also of miraculous cures (such as the man who is cured of the plague by eating a bit of butter).

Within this festive frame it remains unclear whether the children receiving these limericks are supposed to identify with the eccentrics or with the people—or with neither. The people react to the protagonists' antics with delight, curiosity, embarrassment, perplexity, astonishment, solicitude, outrage, and sometimes violent retribution. In fact, the range of behaviors exhibited by the eccentrics is matched in its breadth and unpredictability by the range of attitudes expressed toward them by the other characters, and both the behaviors and the attitudes are as portable and transient as carnival masquerades. This similarity tends to undermine the notion, once popular among critics of Lear, that "they" represent an intolerant social normality and that the eccentrics stand for persecuted individualism, or that the limericks deliver a univocal polemic in favor of the ec-

centrics' freedom to be themselves or against the people, who often close ranks against Lear's oddballs (Hark, "Edward Lear").

If the boundaries and hierarchies put into play in Lear's carnival are not reliably congruent with the boundaries between the eccentrics and "them," nevertheless they surely refer to social conformity and the conventions that govern manners and private codes of behavior rather than sacrality or legitimacy. They quite often do this by way of a widely prevalent strategy in children's literature: that of inviting identification between humans and animals. For instance:

> There was an Old Man in a tree,
> Who was horribly bored by a Bee;
> When they said, "Does it buzz?" he replied, "Yes, it does!
> It's a regular brute of a Bee!"
>
> (7)

The old man, not the bee, is the one who is out of his proper place, perhaps invading the bee's territory, so that the word "brute" in the last line puns on the uncertain distinction the limerick sets up between a social animal and an unsociable human. The illustration emphasizes the similarity between the old man and the been in a more broadly comic way, since their faces are nearly mirror images of one another, right down to the pipes in their mouths. Perhaps this hints at some hypocrisy in the old man's attitude, and perhaps it also indicates the interchangeability of roles within the limerick's play space. At the very least, the limerick and the illustration cast serious doubt on whatever kind of authority the old man might have to pronounce the bee a "regular brute."

The social dynamics in this limerick involve a contest over who is occupying whose place and who has the right to say what is "regular." Although the limerick's general tenor is antiauthoritarian, the form of authority being satirized does not resemble that of general society toward the eccentric individual nearly as much as it looks like the interaction of an authoritative adult with a child. Or rather, the adult, like Derry down Derry, has been transformed into a comic entertainer, a clown, who mimics the irrationality and hypocrisy of adult authority in the face of the buzzing, childlike bee's own parodic imitation of him.

I am suggesting that the limericks consistently address themselves to the kind of authority adults exercise over children in general, and, more specifically, that the social institution toward which they are primarily directed is the Victorian family. The limericks offer a panoply of interactions between children and adults that refers, both mockingly and at times far more tenderly, to the family. For Lear himself, we can speculate, nonsense enacted an alternative to the parental relationship that some combination of muted homosexuality and serious health problems made psychologically, if not physically, impossible for him.[5] Lear's nonsense was for him a way of cementing a playful, avuncular relationship with the children he met in his travels. Lear's nonsense persona, Derry down Derry, gives way to **"Uncle Arly"** in Lear's last, most autobiographical poem; and the Lear of the nonsense in general is the one he called an "Adopty Duncle" on the drawings of an alphabet when he presented them, one by one, to a little girl at the hotel they were sharing (Noakes 243-44). The old man in the tree, I would argue, has no less entered into a fantasy of family life than the Lear in the self-portrait illustrating the following passage in a letter of 1871: "I think of marrying some domestic henbird & then of building a nest in one of my olive trees, whence I should only descend at remote intervals for the rest of my life" (*Selected Letters* 236).[6]

Whatever way the limericks may have functioned for Lear, they can be coherently understood as extending to the child reader an invitation to imaginative role-playing. The dramatistic game they open up refers predominantly to basic areas of socialization—eating, dressing, grooming, speaking, and so on—and to the kinds of tensions inherent in familial relationships, that is, ones involving obedience and authority, conformity and individuation, nurturance and independence. The limericks treat these relationships in a carnivalesque fashion, using parodic, grotesque, ridiculous, and subversive strategies of representation. Whether the limericks' overall effect is to rehearse rebellion or to provide a safety valve for antiauthoritarian energies seems to be precisely what the form of nonsense refuses to determine. Instead, the limericks' nonsensical resistance to commonsense interpretation draws a kind of magic circle around them, not only setting loose the extravagant energy and exuberant emotions of the nonsense world but also, at the same time, sealing off this world from "real" consequences. The limericks themselves often allude to and, indeed, theorize this magic circle in a quite detailed and often delightful way. Let me now, without presuming to make sense out of Lear's nonsense, try to trace this circle through a series of limericks.

We can begin with another man in a tree:

> There was an old man in a tree,
> Whose whiskers were lovely to see;
> But the birds of the air, pluck'd them perfectly bare,
> To make themselves nests in that tree.
>
> (191)

The old man in the tree appears to be another comic self-portrait of Lear, and the illustration shows him smiling impishly on his branch while the little birds pluck him bare. Even more explicitly than in the bee limerick, the childlike animals have aggressively set on an adult invading their territory. But this is an unexpectedly tender poem, for it transforms the birds' attack on the old man's "lovely" whiskers into the benevolent activity of nest-building. Thus it rather pointedly reverses the plot of Humpty Dumpty, the nursery rhyme to which the illustration clearly alludes. This is not a cautionary tale about the irremediable consequences of a foolish action. Rather, this poem seems to encourage the child audience's aggressivity in the belief that such comic and aesthetic appropriation of the poem will ultimately have constructive results. The poem represents an adult attitude of optimistic tolerance toward the rambunctious and perhaps unruly children set free to play at nonsense.

At the opposite extreme from this old man's tolerance one finds a didactic adult being subjected to some of Lear's most clear-cut ridicule:

> There was an old man of Dumbree,
> Who taught little owls to drink tea;
> For he said, "To eat mice, is not proper or nice,"
> That amiable man of Dumbree.
>
> (184)

Here the illustration is particularly relevant. In it the old man of Dumbree has lined up the owls in front of him so that he can amiably instruct them to act in a way that goes against their nature. Lear presents this arrangement in such a way as to emphasize the uniformity being imposed on the owls, so that they turn into a faceless series of "proper" students of etiquette. The old man's authoritarian project is rendered thoroughly ludicrous by his own birdlike posture and beaklike nose. Thus this limerick renders quite explicit the antididactic element implied by the "Old Man in a Tree" reversal of Humpty Dumpty. At the same time, it may preserve some of that poem's tolerance by pronouncing the old man of Dumbree "amiable"; or perhaps this hint of tolerance enters the poem simply by way of the indeterminancy and playfulness enjoyed by the adjective in the final line. The fact that there is really no way of telling whether the limerick's sympathy for the man of Dumbree is congenial or nonsensical is, after all, precisely what keeps Lear's parodic strategy from breaking out of the circle of nonsense and turning into full-fledged, allegorical satire.

The emotional counterpart of the limericks' indeterminacy and tolerance is their strong ambivalence. For example:

> There was an old person of Crowle,
> Who lived in the nest of an owl;
> When they screamed in the nest, he sceamed out with the rest,
> That depressing old person of Crowle.
>
> (195)

The person of Crowle seems to exemplify the quality of nonsense that Bakhtin, speaking of carnival laughter, would call its most egalitarian element, its holism: "It is directed at all and everyone, including the carnival's participants. . . . This laughter is ambivalent: it is gay, triumphant, and at the same time mocking, deriding." Unlike the laughter of satire, which places the satirist above and in opposition to the object of laughter, this kind of laughter "expresses the point of view of the whole world; he who is laughing also belongs to it" (Bakhtin 11-12). But this "depressing" old person's egalitarian laughter also has the appearance of an invasion. The price of its liberating effect on the "old person" may be that it threatens the stability of the social relationships inside the nest. The owls in the illustration certainly seem to be of two minds about it. The largest ones, apparently assuming the role of parents, glare coldly at the demented-looking man in their midst, while the smallest ones look quite comfortable and secure in his presence. Thus a hierarchical reception of nonsense dictated by conventional familial roles uneasily resists the egalitarian possibility that nonsense might transform the nest of owls into a family made up entirely of children.

The art of Lear's nonsense is the art of sustaining its ambivalence and indeterminacy; but making the limericks "perfectly clear & bright" also involves providing some form of resolution or at least security for the child audience. Thus Lear's success depends on his ability to balance the eruptive possibilities of the nonsense against a perhaps stronger, more imperative demand for closure. To say that the limericks ultimately satisfy this demand in a purely formal way is not to detract from them, but rather to epitomize much of my argument and bring it, so to speak, full circle. As an illustration let me offer this final limerick:

> There was an Old Man, on whose nose,
> Most birds of the air could repose;
> But they all flew away, at the closing of day,
> Which relieved that Old Man and his nose.
>
> (58)

Although the old man is said to be relieved by the birds' departure, the illustration shows that he is quite happy in their presence. Yet the substitution of the old man's tremendous nose for the various nonsense perches, the trees or nests of the other limericks, confers some additional, strenuous responsibility on him. Even though it is the birds, not the man, who perch themselves on the nose, it is the old man who assumes the posture of a tightrope walker. The effort and the performance are ultimately his, and the birds enjoy it contentedly and seemingly without any awareness of the old man's artistry. Yet what relieves him and makes the balancing act possible is the knowledge that it will end and the birds will depart as surely as "the closing of day." Time

is the partner of poetic form, and will bring about a kind of closure even where meaning remains open. Lear's artistry establishes an interlude where the children in his audience find themselves metaphorically suspended from the conventional world but still secure in the reassurance of the nonsense world's finitude, its balance of imaginative possibility and formal limits, and the certainty that the game always comes to an end.

Notes

1. Unless otherwise indicated, Lear's limericks are quoted from *The Complete Nonsense of Edward Lear.*

2. See Hark, *Edward Lear,* 24-29. The critical literature on Lear's limericks is very concisely and usefully surveyed by Colley, 1-31.

3. On the sources of the limericks and Lear's handling of them, see Hark, *Edward Lear,* 24-29; Byrom, 49-51; and Colley, 25-27.

4. On play in the limericks, see Ede, 58-60; on the marking-off of play space, see Huizinga, 9, 19-20.

5. Lear's most recent biographer states unequivocally that "there is no evidence whatever of homosexuality in [Lear's] life" (Levi 31); Lady Susan Chitty's 1989 biography, in contrast, takes Lear's love for Frank Lushington as the keynote of its interpretation of Lear's life. My argument adheres to the presentation of the problem of Lear's sexuality in Noakes's *Edward Lear: The Life of a Wanderer.*

6. See *Selected Letters,* 236, for the portrait as well, a charming sketch of an expressionless, bird-sized Lear sitting in a nest with his arm around a coyly smiling henbird.

Works Cited

Bakhtin, Mikhail. *Rabelais and His World.* Trans. Helene Iswolsky. Bloomington: Indiana University Press, 1984.

Bouissac, Paul. "The Meaning of Nonsense (Structural Analysis of Clown Performances and Limericks)." In *The Logic of Culture: Advances in Structural Theory and Methods,* ed. Ino Rossi. South Hadley, Mass.: J. F. Bergin, 1982. Pp. 199-213.

Byrom, Thomas. *Nonsense and Wonder: The Poems and Cartoons of Edward Lear.* New York: Dutton, 1977.

Chitty, Susan. *That Singular Person Called Lear: A Biography of Edward Lear, Artist, Traveller, and Prince of Nonsense.* New York: Atheneum, 1989.

Colley, Ann C. *Edward Lear and the Critics.* Columbia, S.C.: Camden House, 1993.

Ede, Lisa. "An Introduction to the Nonsense Literature of Edward Lear and Lewis Carroll." In *Explorations in the Field of Nonsense,* ed. Wim Tigges. Amsterdam: Rodopoi, 1987. Pp. 47-60.

Hark, Ina Rae. *Edward Lear.* Boston: Twayne, 1982.

———. "Edward Lear: Eccentricity and Victorian *Angst.*" *Victorian Poetry* 16 (1978): 112-22.

Huizinga, Johan. *Homo Ludens: A Study of the Play-Element in Culture.* 1950. Reprint. Boston: Beacon, 1955.

Kennedy, X. J. "Disorder and Security in Nonsense Verse for Children." *The Lion and the Unicorn* 13 (1990): 28-33.

Lear, Edward. *The Complete Nonsense of Edward Lear.* Ed. Holbrook Jackson. 1947. Reprint. New York: Dover, 1951.

———. *Selected Letters.* Ed. Vivien Noakes. Oxford: Clarendon, 1988.

Levi, Peter. *Edward Lear: A Biography.* New York: Scribner, 1995.

Noakes, Vivien. *Edward Lear: The Life of a Wanderer.* Boston: Houghton Mifflin, 1969.

Sewell, Elizabeth. *The Field of Nonsense.* London: Chatto and Windus, 1952.

Stewart, Susan. *Nonsense: Aspects of Intertextuality in Folklore and Literature.* Baltimore: Johns Hopkins University Press, 1979.

Tigges, Wim. "An Anatomy of Nonsense." In *Explorations in the Field of Nonsense,* ed. Wim Tigges. Amsterdam: Rodopoi, 1987. Pp. 23-46.

FURTHER READING

Biographies

Chitty, Susan. *That Singular Person Called Lear.* London: Weidenfeld and Nicolson, 1988, 305 p.
    Offers a scholarly biography of Lear.

Levi, Peter. *Edward Lear: A Biography.* London: Macmillan, 1995, 362 p.
    Presents a very colorful and thorough biography of Lear.

Criticism

Colley, Ann C. *Edward Lear and the Critics.* Columbia, S.C.: Camden House, 1993, 119 p.
    Discusses Lear's life and the reception he received in intellectual circles.

Dilworth, Thomas. "Society and Self in the Limericks of Lear." *Review of English Studies* n.s. 45, no. 177 (February 1994): 42-62.
    Examines the relationship between Lear's drawings and his verse and emphasizes themes of repressed anger and sexuality in Lear's works.

Glasgow, Eric. "Edward Lear in Greece." In *Romantic Reassessment,* edited by James Hogg, pp. 63-9. Salzburg, Austria: Institute Fur Anglistik und Amerikanistik Universitat Salzburg, 1981.
    Examines Lear's impressions of Greece as they relate to the cultural relationship between Greece and Britain.

Additional coverage of Lear's life and career is contained in the following sources published by Thomson Gale: *Authors and Artists for Young Adults,* Vol 48; *British Writers,* Vol. 5; *Children's Literature Review,* Vols. 1, 75; *Dictionary of Literary Biography,* Vols. 32, 163, 166; *Literature Resource Center; Major Authors and Illustrators for Children and Young Adults,* Eds. 1, 2; *Nineteenth-Century Literature Criticism,* Vol. 3; *Reference Guide to English Literature,* Ed. 2; *Something About the Author,* Vols. 18, 100; *World Poets;* and *Writers for Children.*

Luci Tapahonso
1953-

American poet and children's writer.

INTRODUCTION

Luci Tapahonso is considered to be one of today's most influential and innovative Native American writers. Her poetry is significantly influenced by Navajo culture and traditions, and is often praised for its versatility and conversive style. Written in both Navajo and English, Tapahonso's poetry speaks to people of all cultures; however, she always maintains her connection to the people, land, and stories of her Navajo roots.

BIOGRAPHICAL INFORMATION

Tapahonso was born on November 8, 1953, to Eugene Tapahonso and Lucille Deschenne Tapahonso in Shiprock, New Mexico. One of eleven children, Tapahonso refers to her family as semi-traditional Navajo and believes that her upbringing, supported by the environment of the Navajo reservation, provided her with considerable respect for and understanding of Navajo culture. She received her primary education from the Navajo Methodist School and Shiprock High School. She began studying journalism at the University of New Mexico in 1976, but after meeting and becoming significantly influenced by Leslie Marmon Silko, a Native American writer and professor at the university, Tapahonso began to take her writing more seriously and switched her field of study to English. She graduated with a bachelor of arts in 1980 and a master of arts in creative writing from the same institution in 1983. In addition to her literary career, Tapahonso has developed a career in academia. She taught at the University of New Mexico from 1987 to 1989 as an assistant professor of English. Tapahonso then moved to the University of Kansas where she taught English from 1990 to 1999. She is currently a professor of American Indian Studies and English at the University of Arizona at Tucson. Tapahonso has two daughters, Lori and Misty, from her first marriage to artist Earl Ortiz; the couple divorced in 1987 and she married again in 1989 to Bob G. Martin, a Cherokee.

MAJOR POETIC WORKS

Tapahonso published her first book of poems, *One More Shiprock Night: Poems,* in 1981. The collection draws on childhood experiences from her upbringing in rural

New Mexico on the Navajo reservation. A majority of the poetry contained in this work reflects the importance of music in the Navajo culture. It also exhibits her ability to use everyday language and speech patterns, both in Navajo and English, to mirror the intimacy found in conversation. In *Seasonal Woman* (1982) Tapahonso alludes to the strength and traditional power of women in Navajo society. The poems also address such topics as racism and violence in the American Southwest. For example, in "Hard to Take" Tapahonso describes incidents of racism against Navajo customers by a cashier at Foodway and sales ladies at Merle Norman. This collection also contains one of her readers' favorite poems, "Hills Brothers Coffee," which is a direct translation from Navajo. *A Breeze Swept Through* (1987), Tapahonso's third book, returns to themes of Navajo culture, focusing on the connection between its mythical past and spiritual present. Many of the works in *Sáanii Dahataal: The Women Are Singing* (1993), a collection of poetry and prose, focus on the pull Tapahonso feels, as an adult living in Kansas, to her New Mexican roots. Critic Gretchen M. Bataille notes that this work "demonstrates her versatility and maturity as a writer and brings together the elements of landscape, tradition, and humour that were evident in earlier works." Her latest book, *Blue Horses Rush In* (1997), is a combination of poetry and stories about the happiness and sadness of ordinary life. The works in this collection embody a recurring theme found in most of Tapahonso's writing: the connection between family, community, ancestry, and the land.

CRITICAL RECEPTION

With the publication of *Sáanii Dahataal: The Women Are Singing* and *Blue Horses Rush In,* both of which received great critical acclaim, Tapahonso secured her position as an influential and innovative Native American writer. In particular, scholars praise the seamless and unique way that Tapahonso's poetry combines Navaho and English; critic Susan B. Brill notes that when Tapahonso "shifts to the Navajo language in her writing, she does so as a means of inviting her listener-readers into the worlds of her stories and poems—thereby enabling her readers to learn and value and understand words, worlds, and peoples from within rather than from without." Bataille compares Tapahonso with such Native American writers as Joy Harjo, Louise Erdrich, and Leslie Marmon Silko, contending that she is "an undisputed important female voice in the American Indian literary landscape."

PRINCIPAL WORKS

Poetry

One More Shiprock Night: Poems 1981
Seasonal Woman 1982
A Breeze Swept Through 1987
Sáanii Dahataal: The Women Are Singing 1993
Blue Horses Rush In: Poems and Stories 1997

Other Major Works

Navajo ABC: A Diné Alphabet Book (juvenilia) 1995
Songs of Shiprock Fair (juvenilia) 1999

CRITICISM

Patricia Clark Smith and Paula Gunn Allen (essay date 1987)

SOURCE: Smith, Patricia Clark, and Paula Gunn Allen. "Earthy Relations, Carnal Knowledge: Southwestern American Indian Women Writers and Landscape." In *The Desert Is No Lady: Southwestern Landscapes in Women's Writing and Art,* edited by Vera Norwood and Janice Monk, pp. 174-96. New Haven, Conn.: Yale University Press, 1987.

[*In the following excerpt, Smith and Allen examine several American Indian stories about the connection between the people and the land, including stories by Tapahonso, Leslie Marmon Silko, and Joy Harjo, and contend that American Indian literature "must be understood in the context of both the land and the rituals through which [American Indian people] affirm their relationship to it."*]

Long before *context* became an academic buzz word, it was a Spider Woman word. It speaks of things woven together, and of understanding the meaning of a thread in terms of the whole piece of goods. For southwestern American Indians, that whole is the land in its largest sense. The land is not only landscape as Anglo writers often think of it—arrangements of butte and bosque, mountain and river valley, light and cloud shadow. For American Indians, the land encompasses butterfly and ant, man and woman, adobe wall and gourd vine, trout beneath the river water, rattler deep in his winter den, the North Star and the constellations, the flock of sandhill cranes flying too high to be seen against the sun. The land is Spider Woman's creation; it is the whole cosmos.[1]

American Indian people—even urban dwellers—live in the context of the land. Their literature thus must be understood in the context of both the land and the rituals through which they affirm their relationship to it. Women and female sexuality are at the center of many of these rituals. The wilderness, American Indian women, ritual, and American Indian women's writing are inextricably woven together. I begin by looking at the relationship between American Indian literature and ritual and then go on to speak of how women and wilderness are part of these.

Like the songs and stories from their ongoing oral tradition, contemporary American Indians' literature is connected with ritual. Even contemporary American Indian jokes often rely on a knowledge of ritual:

> *Q. What's a seven-course dinner on the Sioux Reservation?*
>
> *A. A six-pack and a puppy.*

To get the full savor of the joke (or the puppy), you need to understand that puppy meat was valued more highly than dog, as veal is thought tastier than beef, and the Sioux used to serve puppy only as a special treat on ceremonial occasions. A seven-course dinner, including fine wine or champagne, is a white way of marking a special occasion. But contemporary Indians, for cultural and economic reasons, are more likely to pop the top of a beer can than the cork on a bottle of Dom Perignon. Alcoholism is common on reservations. The joke takes in all of this knowledge, and it is, among other things, a reflection both wry and poignant on a lost richness and a present deprivation. But to make the joke at all is to reaffirm the richness of American Indian life and humor, to recall a connection with ritual, with "the way," at the same time as one acknowledges what one contemporary American Indian woman poet, nila northSun, calls "the way things are."[2] Like the joke, contemporary American Indian literature reflects to a certain degree ritual understandings.

American Indian literature involves ritual; ritual is ceremonial action that reaffirms people's connection with the land. Nontribal people often perceive the land as an object, as something faintly or greatly inimical, to be controlled, reshaped, painted, or feared.[3] Tribal people see it as something mysterious, certainly beyond human domination, and yet as something to be met and spoken with rather than confronted. For them, the land is not just collection of objects you do things *to,* nor is it merely a place you do things *in,* a stage-set for human action. Rather, it is a multitude of entities who possess intelligence and personality. These entities are active participants with human beings in life processes, in thoughts and acts simultaneously mundane and spiritual. People and the land hold dialogue within the structure of ritual, in order to ensure balance and harmony. Ritual is the means by which people, spirits, rocks, animals, and other beings enter into conversation with each other. One major part of people's ritual responsibility is to speak with these nonhuman entities and to report the conversation; American Indian literature records echoes of that ongoing dialogue.

In this literature, that dialogue, the ritual interplay between people and the land, is often presented in sexual terms. Of course, the sexual metaphor for expressing some sort of relationship between people and land is not unique to Native Americans: scholars have remarked the inclination of early European male colonists to speak of the American earth in terms of sexual conquest, envisioning themselves taming and possessing a virgin land or being seduced away from civilization by the wilderness. But as Annette Kolodny has pointed out, imagery that casts the land as a rape victim, a seductress of men, or a compliant virgin ripe for taming by "husbandry" was understandably uncomfortable for colonial women on the Eastern frontiers, even though they, like their menfolk, dreamed of transforming the landscape. Instead of using overtly sexual metaphors, eighteenth-century colonial women wrote about their hopes and plans for sweetly *domesticating* wilderness, for grafting native stock, for planting gardens. Later, when white women found themselves in the open prairies rich with wildflowers, they spoke

enthusiastically of discerning natural parklands and gardens ready to respond gratefully to their care.[4]

Eighteenth- and nineteenth-century women's letters and travel diaries, on the subject of the land, recall certain shared archetypes from popular literature, and it is not only biblical passages about *Judea capta* and Goshen that come to mind. One thinks as well of Pamela and Jane Eyre taming, respectively, the wildernesses in Mr. B———and Rochester; of the Peggottys and their friends reclaiming Little Em'ly and Martha into the family circle—of all the good men and women of the popular literature of the time who cajole and encourage their sexually undisciplined friends into comfortable, useful, temperate domesticity.

Subduing or training a wild landscape into a kitchen garden one can tend and view with satisfaction through the window is much like Jane's assisting at Mr. Rochester's transformation from an unpredictable creature of passionate energy into a loving (if handicapped) husband, upon whose lap she can perch familiarly as she combs the snarls from his "shaggy black mane." Both acts, even though they suppress the wilder aspects of sexuality, are really assertions of sexual dominance; the domesticator proves more powerful than the now tamed wild thing. Productivity and fertility are not necessarily diminished by either act; domesticated plants arranged in orderly rows bear fruit, even as the Rochesters, we are told, produce children.

And yet something is lost. Though fertile and easier to live with, both the tamed Rochester and the domesticated plants are oddly defused of a particular charge of sexual energy that was at once frightening and intoxicating and quintessential. Rochester and the garden-grown plant are no longer completely themselves. Readers and gardeners alike sense that loss, however dimly. (When I first read *Jane Eyre,* Rochester's blindness and humility disturbed me deeply. And even when my family's loamed beds were thick with hybrid June strawberries, my mother and I walked the field beyond the garden, parting the grasses to find the small, sparse wild fruit. The wild strawberries weren't ours the way the garden ones were; we couldn't control their growth, couldn't take them for granted, but they were incomparably sweet.)

* * *

Southwestern American Indian cultures do not approach wilderness as something to be either raped or domesticated, but they do associate wilderness with sexuality. Indeed, they see wilderness and sexuality as identical. In both traditional and contemporary literatures, wilderness often appears not as mere landscape-backdrop, but as a spirit-being with a clearly sexual aura. That being, who always embodies some aspect of the land, may be either male or female. A male being may abduct a human woman, or a female being may seduce a human man, but subjugation is not the dynamic of either event. In the instances of spirit-men abducting human women, what happens is not a Zeus-style rape, not the ravishing of some hapless girl who's had the dubious luck to encounter a swan or a bull with a knowing leer in his not-quite-animal eyes.

In such comings-together of persons and spirits, the land and the people engage in a ritual dialogue—though it may take the human participant a while to figure that out. The ultimate purpose of such ritual abductions and seductions is to transfer knowledge from the spirit world to the human sphere, and this transfer is not accomplished in an atmosphere of control or domination.

In old stories like the Keres Yellow Woman stories, or in Leslie Silko's contemporary "Yellow Woman," based upon them, the human woman makes little attempt either to resist or to tame the spirit-man who abducts her. Nor do men, in stories where they are seduced by spirit women, attempt to control or dominate them. The human protagonists usually engage willingly in literal sexual intercourse with the spirits who simultaneously walk the land and embody it. This act brings the land's power, spirit, and fecundity in touch with their own, and so ultimately yields benefit for their people.

If their full nuances are taken into account, *to have intercourse with* and *to know* convey something of the sense of what really goes on in those bushes beyond the light of the village fires, of what really happens up there, far to the north where the Ka'tsina has taken you. Unlike Yeats's Leda, the human protagonist does, without question, put on both knowledge and power through the sexual act. Furthermore, the act channels the awesome power and energy of our human sexuality—the preserve of wilderness in human beings—into socially useful channels. The coming together of person and spirit may lead to the birth of magical children, the discovery of rich sources of food or water, or the gift of a specific ceremony.

I want to turn now to two Navajo stories about the connections between the people and the land. The great Navajo chant *Beauty Way* deals with a fruitful coming-together of an earth-surface person—a human being—and a spirit; the *Beauty Way* ceremony itself, which incorporates the story, is given to the Navajo people as a consequence of that event. "The Snake-man," a contemporary short story by Luci Tapahonso, a young Navajo writer, movingly echoes elements of the *Beauty Way* story.

Beauty Way concerns the adventures of two sisters, White Corn Girl and Yellow Corn Girl, during the Navajo-Taos Pueblo wars. Corn Man, their uncle, has promised to marry them to the best warriors, but to his dismay the men who prove to be the most skillful in battle are two strange, sickly-looking elders enlisted as volunteers on the Navajo side. Instead of sticking to his promise, Corn Man tells his nieces to choose husbands for themselves at the victory celebration dance. But, as in the stories of many other cultures, promises have a way of keeping themselves once they are made.

At the dance, the Corn Girls grow overheated and stray away from the dance circle into the cool darkness, where they smell a strangely alluring odor, the sweet pipe smoke of two handsome young men encamped at some distance from the Navajo. The men obligingly share their intoxicating tobacco with the Corn Girls, and each sister falls asleep beside one of the strangers. When the sisters awake, they discover to their dismay that they have not been lying with a pair of handsome young warriors after all, but with the two mysterious old codgers to whom they were originally promised. Their relatives track them down but then, in disgust, leave the two women to the elderly husbands they appear to have chosen for themselves. Unbeknownst to either the Corn Girls or their family, the two old ones are actually Big Bear Man and Big Snake Man.

Finding themselves seduced and abandoned by their family, the Corn Girls run away together from their husbands, covering much of the Navajo country in their flight and pursued from afar by Big Bear Man and Big Snake Man. Eventually, at the Rio Grande, the two girls are separated. Here, the myth branches into what will become *Mountain Way* and *Beauty Way*. The former concerns White Corn Girl, Elder Sister, who eventually finds herself among her husband's Bear People. *Beauty Way* follows Yellow Corn Girl, Younger Sister, who finally arrives ragged and thirsty at a pool atop Black Rock, near Canyon de Chelly. There, a handsome stranger offers her sanctuary beneath the earth. She accepts and slips through a crevice to the underground world—the domain of her in-laws, the Snake People.

In the lower world, the Snake People initially appear to Younger Sister in human form. She does not guess their identity at first, even though they address her kindly as "daughter-in-law" and hold target practice with lightning arrows—a sure clue, for the Snake People are closely associated with weather. Younger Sister's adventures now assume a pattern. Her in-laws give her tasks or set her prohibitions which she bungles each time out of ignorance, absent-mindedness, or impetuous curiosity. Each time, when the Snake People confront her with her errors, she puts up a remarkably realistic adolescent defense, presenting herself as a hapless, put-upon innocent stumbling through life, a girl from whom little should reasonably be expected. "I am someone who's just traveling any old place," she says.

Each time they are confronted with this defense, the Snake People reply, with great forbearance and mild sarcasm, "Yes, we can see that." Their treatment of Younger Sister is delightful in its wise restraint. Even though they often suffer more than she does from her irresponsibility, they and other beings always help her out of her predicaments and are satisfied to let her be punished by the natural consequences of her actions, trusting experience to teach her what she needs to know.

For example, on her first night among them, she is warned not to rekindle the fire once it goes out. The Snake People additionally caution her that, should she catch a clear sight of them, she must remember that their ugliness lies only in their shape. Of course she rekindles the fire, and its light reveals her benefactors as a family of snakes. Younger Sister leaps wildly among them in panic before she fearfully resigns herself to bedding down again in their midst. In the morning, the Snake People complain that they're sore from being trampled upon, but all Younger Sister suffers is a case of swollen joints, although she's run away from their kinsman and literally walked all over them. Their continuing care of her is the best evidence of their true nature; Snake People, contrary to the old cliché of the Western matinee, do not speak with forked tongues, and that is the lesson she must begin with.

Younger Sister next is entrusted with jars containing wind, hail, male and female rain, and mist. On successive days, when the Snake People are gone about their business, she disobeys instructions and meddles with each jar in turn, unleashing the different kinds of weather. The Snake People are treated to a week of dust storms, floods, hailstones, and pea-soup fog, but each night they sigh "what can we expect?" and again leave her to care for the jars the following morning.

Younger Sister is being gently and skillfully socialized, learning by example the wisdom and forbearance of the Snake People, learning to respect the power of the elements and the need for great care and scrupulous attention to ritual in their presence. Unlike Ulysses and Pandora, her ancient Greek counterparts who against orders let things out of bags or boxes, Younger Sister is given room to err in order to prepare her eventually to take full charge of the weather.

Off and on during Younger Sister's underworld sojourn among the Snake People, she glimpses a shadowy figure who bears some resemblance to the elderly man she has fled, but Big Snake Man stays in the background, allowing his family to socialize his bride. He does not directly enter Younger Sister's experience again until the end of her time among his people, when she is cautioned not to stray from the Snake People's territory. Of course, her eager curiosity moves her to test those prohibitions, with disastrous results. In this, her last

forbidden venture, she wanders to the north and joins some rock wrens in a rock-rolling game. Younger Sister, a clumsy novice, is crushed beneath the stones. By the time her body is recovered only her bones remain, but Big Snake Man sings over her and restores her to life.

After all her trials and errors, Younger Sister is at last deemed ready to begin learning *Beauty Way* for herself—though in a sense she has been learning it all along. After a four-year apprenticeship, she masters all the songs and prayers and sand paintings and is entrusted with the ritual paraphernalia of the great chant. At the end of that time, Big Snake Man, now revealed as her husband, performs the full nine-day ceremony for her. But she is told that Big Snake Man will no longer be considered her husband, for neither he nor earth-surface people may perform chants for their own kin. (Elder Sister, who has been having parallel adventures all this time among various spirits who live in the mountains, is simultaneously learning *Mountain Way*.)

After her *Beauty Way* ceremony, Younger Sister leaves the Snake People and the two Corn Girls, reunited, go back to their human family long enough for them to sit their younger brother down between them and teach him both *Beauty Way* and *Mountain Way*. When they have passed on the ceremonies, the sisters return to the wilderness—Elder Sister to the mountains, and Younger Sister to the realm of the Snakes—to take their places among the Holy People. Back among the Snake People, Younger Sister is again given charge of the jars of weather.[5]

* * *

It is important to understand this story and similar ones, like the Keres stories of Yellow Woman, as stories about the relationship between human women and the land and its various embodiments.[6] As a consequence of her initial erotic experience, Younger Sister is socialized but not suppressed; she fares far better than most of the European folk-tale heroines who stray away from their families into the forests. Her encounters with the spirits of the land teach her what she needs to know in order to be an adult woman: to live within a family, to understand and respect the forces of nature, and maintain a ritual relationship with them. The preserve of wilderness within her—her energy, curiosity, sexuality—is not forcibly repressed, as if it were shameful and unnatural, but brought into contact with the outer wilderness. Both inner and outer wilderness are natural and beautiful sources of energy and fertile supply, but the outer wilderness is balanced, and it operates in harmony; balance is what Younger Sister must learn from her time among the snakes. Over a long period of experimentation, she learns to draw on her own inner wilderness and to channel it usefully.

In the story, Big Snake Man is indeed threatening at times, and he remains unfathomably mysterious. But even before he comes together with Younger Sister, he appears as an anonymous benefactor of her people. His alliance with her may involve a little deception, but it is hardly rape. When she flees him, he pursues her at a discreet distance—shooing her, so to speak, in the direction she needs to go, allowing her to find her own adventure. Through most of her time in the lower world, he remains a shadowy figure, working his healing magic when it is needed.

The sisters are not a pair of passive princesses badgered into submissiveness by their husbands and in-laws. They are strongly bonded with one another, and each makes choices that, even when they are in error, result in the getting of wisdom and power. In this story, a woman's exploration of her inner wilderness, and her dalliance with an embodiment of the outer wilderness, do not result in expulsion from paradise or in the unleasing of a stinging swarm of evils. Rather, her adventures end in the gift of a healing ceremony, the knowledge to use that ceremony rightly, and the power to pass it on to her own people. It must make a great difference for a child to grow up with the story of Younger Sister, rather than the stories of Eve and Pandora, as part of her heritage, and such a story must strongly shape her visions both of wilderness and of what it means to be a woman.

Younger Sister's story is a beautiful and useful paradigm for the way many contemporary American Indian women writers deal with the theme of women and the land. As Leslie Silko tells us:

> You should understand
> the way it was
> back then
> because it is the same
> even now.[7]

"Even now"—in a contemporary Christian boarding school on the Navajo Reservation—the story goes on. "The Snake-man," by Luci Tapahonso, subtly incorporates aspects of Younger Sister's wilderness experience.[8] *Beauty Way* permeates and enriches this brief and seemingly artless short story about little girls who innocently thwart an institution designed to socialize them out of the Navajo way into the white world. In this gentle tale of resistance, the land, embodied in two spirit-beings, one male and one female, helps the children preserve their Navajo identity against great odds.

Tapahonso's loose, easy narrative unselfconsciously shifts tenses and plot order, recalling the style of much American Indian oral literature and giving a strong sense of nonlinear time to the story. What's happening at a given moment to the little girls is of a piece with what often happens, and what has happened before in old-story time. The tale is at once a piece of psychological and sociological realism; though set in modern times, it is an old story, or part of one.

"The Snake-man" centers on the nighttime doings of homesick little girls quartered in a third-floor dormitory room, allowed to see their families only on weekends, who long wistfully "to go to public school, and eat at home every day." The dorm mother sleeps in a separate room down the hall, and her "mothering" amounts to policing them. She is mostly a nuisance to be circumvented, effective neither as a mother nor as a disciplinarian. The institution, though sterile and isolating, does not wholly strip the children of either family or ritual life, for these little girls create both for themselves. Within their barren room, far away from their families, they mother one another, the big girls taking charge of the smaller ones, and pass on what comfort, philosophy, and knowledge they can to one another. When they grow frightened, "They all [sleep] two-to-a-bed, and the big girls [make] sure all the little girls [have] someone bigger with them."

The calmest and most mature girl is an orphan whose parents are buried in the school cemetery. Each night she sneaks down the fire escape to rendezvous at the edge of the graveyard with her mother's ghost. The other children stand guard at the window during her walks and question her eagerly about her mother when she returns. The child draws strength from her trips to the graveyard and sleeps peacefully once she's back in the dorm. The others huddle together in the dark and enjoy scaring themselves with talk about ghosts and about "what the end of the world will REALLY be like." Their speculations muddle Navajo, Christian, and comic-book eschatology, reflecting their cultural confusions, as they talk of the time when "all the dinosaurs and monsters that are sleeping in the mountains will bust out and eat the bad people—no one can escape, either." When she hears this, the little girl who is nurtured by her dead mother only says quietly, "No one can be that bad."

Apart from the benign mother-ghost, the main spirit-person in the little girls' world is a male figure, the Snake-man, said to live in the attic. "There was a man in there, they always said in hushed voices, he always kept the attic door open just a little, enough to throw evil powder on anyone that walked by. . . . Once they even heard him coming down the attic stairs to the door." The Snake-man isn't visible, "cause he's sort of like a blur, moves real fast and all you can see is a black thing go by"—but he steals jewelry from them and "has a silver bracelet that shines and if he shines it on you, you're a goner."

Once, when the girl is in the graveyard and the others are standing guard, they hear a scratching noise outside. Certain *"he"* is making the sound, they rush to the windows trying to catch sight of him, "to get a description of him in case someone asks them," and they station someone on the fire escape "in case he tries to get up here." When the girl returns from the graveyard, the others hysterically tell her about the lurking presence outside. She calmly suggests it's "probably somebody's father trying to see his daughter." This settles the other children down; eventually, after more discussion, they agree the shadowy visitor is most likely the boyfriend of one of the junior high girls on the lower floor. They return to speculating about the Snake-man and finally drift off to sleep, all but one: "The bigger girls slept with the littler ones, and they prayed that God wouldn't let . . . the snake man come to them, and that the world wouldn't end until after their moms came to visit. As the room got quiet and the breathing became even and soft, the little girl got up, put on her house-coat and slid soundlessly down the fire escape."

The children of Tapahonso's story need to learn how to become Navajo women. They must learn, first, to head complex households; second, to deal with their own sexuality; third, to understand and perform their ritual obligations—the same things the two sisters of *Beauty Way* and *Mountain Way* must learn. Consciously or subconsciously, the children are trying to carry out their learning tasks, even within the sterile enclosure of the dormitory. In "The Snake-man," we see them being socialized toward Navajo womanhood, aided, as their Corn Girl ancestors are, by spirit-people who embody different faces of the wilderness.

The spirit figures, the mother-ghost and Snake-man, surround the dormitory and keep alive the connection between the children and the land. Ironically, the walls of the institution are no walls at all; the children bring the frightening power of wilderness right into the dorm attic, and one of them secretly ventures outside each night to encounter its benign, nurturing presence.

The gentle mother-figure is unusual, in that Navajo ghosts of the sort who manifest themselves around graveyards are generally considered threatening; Tapahonso herself has written a number of poems that deal with the notorious ghosts of accident victims who haunt the shoulders of New Mexico Route 666, inflicting their hostile half-lives on unwary travelers. No sane person deliberately seeks them out.[9]

The unseen spirits of dead relatives, however, can be absorbed back into the natural world and become helping presences in people's lives. In **"A Spring Poem-Song,"** Tapahonso tells her children to go outside early in the morning and greet them:

> They hover waiting
> in front of the house

> by the doors
> above the windows
> They are waiting to give us their blessing
>   waiting to give us protection
> go out and receive them
> The good spirits in the gentle-bird morning
> They hover singing, dancing in the clear morning
> They are singing   They are singing[10]

The mother-ghost of "The Snake-man" is this sort of spirit, taken back into the natural world and seeing to her orphaned daughter's blessing and protection, even though she takes specific visible form. Moreover, she seems to take on aspects of one of the great Mothering spirits of the Navajo world, Changing Woman, perhaps, or Spider Woman. Certainly, she embodies the nurturing powers of wilderness. The little girl describes her mother waiting outside "at the edge of the cemetery by those small, fat trees. She's real pretty. . . . She waves at me like this: 'Come here, shi yashii, my little baby.' She always calls me that. She's soft, and smells so good." There in the dark of the trees, away from the confining walls—a place a child might normally find terrifying—she gives her daughter knowledge of her roots, destiny, and right conduct, talking to her lovingly "about when I was a baby, and what I'll do when I get big. She always worries if I'm being good or not."

Through her daughter's mediation, the mother-spirit's teaching and tenderness extend to the other girls who remain within the dorm. The Mother's stabilizing presence, among other things, enables the children to confront Snake-man and all he represents. A bogeyman in an Anglo story is often said to be a means for children to objectify and confront their sexual fears; indeed, probably Snake-man *does* have a great deal to do with male potency—a phenomenon doubly mystifying to little girls in a sexually segregated boarding school. Like all snakes, he is phallic—not just because he's longer than he is wide, but also because he is capable of astonishing feats of shape-shifting and sneaking up on you. According to the children, he's also intent on "throwing evil powder on you." This detail may be a displaced image of ejaculation, but it may also derive from Navajo stories about skinwalkers of both sexes, who witch people with corpse powder. Certainly, in his physical movements, Snake-man reminds one of archetypal males in many cultures—a back-door man, a dark blur easing out of sight round a dark corner, a Navajo C. C. Rider, or Speedy Gonzales. When the children seek a "rational" explanation for him, they connect him with sexual males; first they think he's a divorced father, and finally they choose the explanation that is most interesting to them—he's the boyfriend of one of the older girls on a forbidden tryst.

Snake-man, then, in part represents the men the little girls must eventually encounter in their lives as women. But Snake-man is more than any Freudian explanation suggests. He is an embodiment of the wilderness, and his sexuality goes beyond the human, although he encompasses it, for he embodies the wilderness outside people as well as within them. As in *Beauty Way,* he is the agent through which the little girls experience the land, or aspects of it. His presence keeps them alive to the awesome and potentially threatening force of wilderness. It is in part through him that they learn the art of being a family, of nurturing, and of being in a ritual community, for the thrilling fear he excites impels them to bond together and to invent as best they can private rituals that keep them safe without reducing his mystery and power.

In this simple and moving story of resistance, the children create their own nurturing community to substitute for the tribal life they have been denied; the one in touch with her dead mother becomes a kind of clan mother to the others. The institutional walls do not shut out the wilderness the children must keep touching if they are to learn to be women. Instinctively, they bring the wilderness inside and go forth to meet it in the spirit-figures who directly and indirectly communicate the knowledge the children need most.

Even a story like "The Snake-man," then, which seems to contain little landscape and says little about the land, may center on the relationship between people and wilderness. Certainly one of the most distinctive themes in contemporary Southwestern Indian literature by women is the retelling of the traditional women-abducted-by-wilderness-spirit stories.

Interestingly, this is a theme that these writers' contemporary male counterparts do not choose to retell. American Indian male writers do use images of the Southwestern land that suggest her as female; they address her as "our mother" and convey a clear sense of land as a living entity. Their poems and stories contain human lovers and mothers, daughters and grandmothers, witches and medicine women. But, despite the wealth of old stories about male heroes encountering spirit-women as lovers or platonic helpers, the tales of Grandmother Spider or Changing Woman giving crucial advice to questing heroes are not the tales contemporary men choose to retell.

The figure from oral literature about whom American Indian men of the Southwest write most fondly is Coyote, who appears frequently as a hell-raising buddy or alter ego, or as the symbol of the dogged will to survive—the continuance, despite the odds, of both the wilderness and the tribes.[11] That symbolism is legitimate and moving. But in the last ten years or so, Coyote seems to have become especially an emblem of *male* bonding, *male* elan, *male* cussedness and creativity and survival. Indian women writers in the Southwest, on the other hand, seem far more open to depicting encounters with spirit-figures of both sexes.

This may simply be a reflection of a present-day uneasiness on the part of men toward powerful women that cuts across cultures; after all, few contemporary Anglo men have written modern versions of *She*; there is no musical about The Blessed Virgin Mary Superstar. It may not be a comfortable time for male writers in any segment of American culture to deal with supernatural women of power. But American Indian women writers in the Southwest continue to center some of their finest work on direct encounters with the land in the form of the spirits who embody it, whether Snake-man or Grandmother Spider, Coyote or the angry entity who has been speaking up lately through Mount St. Helen's voice. These women bring astonishingly varied emphases to that common theme; their diversity is not surprising, given their different tribal affiliations and upbringings, ranging from Tapahonso's traditional reservation family life, to the Hopi poet Wendy Rose's adolescence in 1960s Berkeley, to the military-base childhood of Chickasaw writer Linda Hogan. It is that diversity I want to speak of now, and how the encounter with the land is presented in the works of three women writers—Luci Tapahonso (Navajo), Leslie Silko (Laguna Pueblo), and Joy Harjo (Creek).

Tapahonso is the youngest of the three women and had the most traditional upbringing, as one of eleven children born to Navajo-speaking farming people who still live on the mesa north of Shiprock. Some of her early schooling was off-reservation, at what is now Navajo Academy in Farmington, New Mexico—an experience she draws on for "The Snake-man"—much of her adult life has been spent in urban Phoenix and Albuquerque. As Geary Hobson notes in a recent review, her work often centers on "coming back home to visit . . . or thinking about going back home, or . . . about not being able to go back home, even when one knows that would be the best possible medicine."[12] In her biographical note for her first collection of poetry, she writes, "I know I cannot divide myself or separate myself from that place—my home, my land, my people."[13]

Tapahonso's characters cannot separate themselves from the land, whether they abandon the city, or continually affirm their identity with points west, or simply understand the Albuquerque cityscape as somehow an extension of

> the whole empty
> navajo spaces past
> Many Farms   Round Rock[14]

In the city, they continue to perform ceremonial actions that seal their connections with the land. In the early morning they greet the spirits of relatives, whose presence mingles with the cheerful voices of sparrows on the lawn.[15] They sprinkle cornmeal on the threshold of a daughter's first-grade classroom:

remember now, my clear-eyed daughters,
remember now, where this pollen,
   where this cornmeal is from
remember now, you are no different
see how it sparkles
feel this silky powder
it leaves a fine trail skyward
as it falls
      blessing us
      strengthening us[16]

It is important and restorative for Tapahonso's urban Indians to remember that, beyond the city and within it, beneath and between the pavement, the earth remains herself. After a thunderstorm, a woman expects rainwater to pool in the folds of heavy plastic draped over the family's bikes, but she is pleased instead to see the rain making its way to its natural destination, sliding in streams off the plastic, "absorbed instantly / by the dirt / dirt thirsty in winter."[17]

For Tapahonso, kinship with the land is more than a question of affectionate memory and respect, and it is far more than metaphor. This comes through clearly in **"A Breeze Swept Through,"** about the births of her two daughters, Lori Tazbah and Misty Dawn, who are the earth's daughters as well:

The first born of dawn woman
slid out amid crimson fluid streaked with stratus
  clouds
    her body glistening August sunset pink
    light steam rising from her like rain on warm
    rocks
      (A sudden cool breeze swept through
      the kitchen and Grandpa smiled then
      sang quietly, knowing the moment.)
She came when the desert day cooled
and dusk began to move in
in that intricate changing of time
    she gasped and it flows from her now
    with every breath   with every breath.
    She travels now
      sharing scarlet sunsets
      named for wild desert flowers
      her smile a blessing song.
And in mid-November
early morning darkness
after days of waiting pain,
    the second one cried   wailing.
    Sucking first earth breath,
    separating the heavy fog,
    she cried and kicked   tiny brown limbs.
    Fierce movements as
    outside the mist lifted as
    the sun is born again.
      (East of Acoma, a sandstone boulder
      split in two—a sharp, clean crack.)
    She is born of damp mist and early sun.
    She is born again   woman of dawn.
    She is born knowing the warm smoothness
      of rock.
    She is born knowing her own morning
      strength.[18]

The babies bear a strong family resemblance to the "Navajo spaces" of their mother and, in the case of the younger child, to her father's Acoma spaces as well; their own small bodies at birth echo the land's appearance at that very moment. Their arrivals are acknowledged not only by their human relatives, but by the land herself, who welcomes them as flesh of her flesh with a breeze of annunciation, a rock splitting clearly in two. The children are named for the land, whose power flows through them in the cycles of their breath.

The characters in Tapahonso's poems can easily lose touch with the blood connections they were born knowing; her poems encompass humorous and tragic glimpses of people, on or off reservation, who are divided, uncentered, helpless, and speak unflinchingly of bars and parking lots, alcoholism, abused women, wrecked cars, and abandoned children. But Tapahonso's great theme is the connection with family and land, or the rediscovery of it. In **"Last year the piñons were plentiful,"** she chooses the oldest form of story to talk about that relationship, the story of the erotic coming-together of a woman and the land. "It is the same even now" for this woman as it was in the Corn Girls' time, even though the mysterious male figure who inspires her dreams of "the air heavy with rainscent / sage and rabbitbrush" can use Mountain Bell to awaken her need for wilderness, even though she leaves her clean house and steady husband on a Trailways bus.

Her husband is puzzled at her leaving an apparently happy life, but indeed "happiness [has] nothing to do with it." When she rides with the man on the dark horse toward Two Grey Hills and the Chuska Mountains, it is an old-time ritual wedding with the land she has chosen. Whatever happens after we lose sight of them will result in grandchildren who understand her actions better than her husband does. More immediately, what comes of her elopement is a winter that is all a high-desert winter should be—trees heavy with piñon, deep snow to melt in time and ensure more growth, and icy breathtaking beauty.

A better-known and more sophisticated writer than Tapahonso (though not, I think, a more powerful one), Leslie Marmon Silko is of mixed Laguna, Hispanic, and Anglo ancestry. Many members of her family were educated in Indian schools like Carlisle and Sherman Institute, and as a child she attended a private day-school in Albuquerque. Her work reflects the mixed-blood's sense of dwelling at the edges of communities: "We are . . . Laguna, Mexican, White—but the way we live is like Marmons, and if you are from Laguna Pueblo, you will understand what I mean. All those languages, all those ways of living are combined, and we live somewhere on the fringes of all three."[19] That experience of growing up around Laguna life without being fully immersed in it gives Silko's work a certain doubleness, a flexible narrative point of view. At times there's a distance, an ironic edge, a sense that she is writing *about* a tradition as much as *out* of it. Her narratives are more self-conscious than Tapahonso's in that they call more attention to their sources. In "Yellow Woman," a modern heroine thinks about one of the old-time Yellow Woman stories, even as Silva, the man she has met by the river, makes love to her:

> He touched my neck, and I moved close to him to feel his breathing and hear his heart. I was wondering if Yellow Woman had known who she was—if she knew that they would become part of the stories. Maybe she'd had another name that her husband and relatives called her so that only the ka'tsina from the north and the storytellers would know her as Yellow Woman. But I didn't go on; I felt him all around me, pushing me down into the river sand. . . .
>
> "Do you know the story?"
>
> "What story?" He smiled and pulled me close to him as he said this. . . . This is the way it happens in the stories, I was thinking, with no thought beyond the moment she meets the ka'tsina spirit and they go.
>
> (55-56)

This flexible viewpoint enables Silko to take old tales like the ones of woman-abducted-by-wilderness-spirit and treat them simultaneously, or in successive retellings, with high humor, irony, and reverence. This does not always sit well with her critics, white and Indian alike, some of whom seem to expect all American Indian literature to be as pompously solemn as *Billy Jack* or *Hanta Yo*. But Silko knows that the real stories are large and true enough to contain many stories, to bear many interpretations. In her collection *Storyteller*, Silko juxtaposes a number of pieces that treat very differently the theme of a woman leaving home for the wilderness. "Cottonwood" is a fairly straight retelling of two Yellow Woman stories. In the first, Yellow Woman goes out around the fall equinox to meet the Sun himself:

> She left precise stone rooms
> That hold the heart silently
> She walked past white corn
> hung in long rows from roof beams
> The dry husks rattled in a thin autumn wind.
>
> She left her home
>   her clan
>   and the people
>   (Three small children
>   the youngest just weaned
>   her husband away cutting firewood)
>
> (64)

Her rendezvous with the sun, her willingness to join him, ensures that he will come out of his Sun House; he will not leave the earth locked forever in winter. The second part of the poem deals with her abduction by

Buffalo Man; both the Buffalo People and she herself are finally slain by her jealous husband, Arrow Boy, once he discovers that she does not especially want to be rescued, but the end result is the gift of buffalo meat as food in time of drought,

> all because
> one time long ago
> our daughter, our sister Kochininako
> went away with them.
>
> (76)

Storyteller also contains "Yellow Woman," a masterfully ambiguous story, whose heroine, like Yellow Woman, meets a man by the river, a man named Silva (forest, in Spanish), who may be a Navajo cattle thief or the ka'tsina he laughingly tells her he is—or both. Many details in the story parallel the old Keres tales of Yellow Woman and Whirlwind Man or Buffalo Man. But what is most important in the story is the heroine's awakened consciousness of her own sexuality and her acute sensual awareness of the man, the river, and the mountain terrain they travel: "And again he was all around me with his skin slippery against mine, and I was afraid because I understood that his strength could hurt me. I lay underneath him and I knew that he could destroy me. But later, while he slept beside me, I touched his face and I had a feeling—the kind of feeling that overcame me that morning along the river. I kissed him on the forehead and he reached out for me." (58) In letting herself open to Silva, she lets herself open to wilderness in all its wonder, its threat and vulnerability. The description fits her experience of both the man and the mountain.

"Yellow Woman" ends ambiguously. Silva may or may not get shot by a rancher, and he may or may not be a ka'tsina who will one day return for the heroine. Though she decides finally to tell her family only that she's been kidnapped by "some Navajo," what stays with her—and with the reader—is the lyrical evocation of Silva and his terrain: ants swarming over pine needles, the "mountain smell of pitch and buck brush," the danger and beauty she has experienced on those heights.

The heroine of "Yellow Woman" at times admits that hers is an unlikely story, but on the whole both she and the reader are inclined toward the belief in Silva as mountain spirit. Still, we understand there might be ways, in current parlance, to deconstruct that interpretation. Indeed, Silko does not need a critic to perform that task for her, just as the obscene and irreverent antics of Pueblo sacred clowns in a sense "deconstruct" ceremonies without the help of anthropologists.[20] Her poem "Storytelling" begins with a straight-faced recap of the Yellow Woman and Buffalo Man tale, then proceeds in a rapid verbal montage:

> "You better have a damn good story,"
> her husband said,

"about where you have been for the past
ten months and how you explain these
twin baby boys."

. . . . .

It was
in the summer
of 1967.
T.V. news reported
a kidnapping.
Four Laguna woman
and three Navajo men
headed north along
the Rio Puerco River
in a red '56 Ford
and the FBI and
state police were
hot on their trail
of wine bottles and
size 42 panties
hanging in bushes and trees
all along the road.

"We couldn't escape them," he told police later.
"We tried, but there were four of them and only three
of us."

. . . . .

It was
that Navajo
from Alamo,
you know,
the tall
good-looking one.

He told me
he'd kill me
if I didn't
go with him
And then it
rained so much
and the roads
got muddy.
That's why
it took me
so long
to get back home.

My husband
left
after he heard the story
and moved back with his mother.
It was my fault and
I don't blame him either.
I could have told
the story
better than I did.

(95-98)

Whether deeply moving and ceremonial or slapstick,
whether a woman abandons her water jar or her size 42
panties, whether she goes off with Whirlwind Man or
the good-looking Navajo from Alamo, Silko conveys

the sense that all these stories somehow concern an
inevitable human need to go forth and experience
wilderness—and the sexual wildness that it encompasses.

There is not space here to do justice to Silko's fine,
complex novel *Ceremony*; Paula Allen has already
spoken extensively of its treatment of woman and the
land.[21] But, if male writers have been reluctant to retell
for themselves the old stories of human men and the
spirit-women who embody the land, in *Ceremony* Silko
does it for them. As part of a healing ceremony that
begins long before his birth and his spiritual illness,
Tayo, a half-breed Laguna veteran of World War II,
must "close the gap between isolate human beings and
lonely landscape" brought about through old witchery
that has led not only to Tayo's illness but also to World
War II, strip-mining, nuclear weapons, racism, and a
drought-plagued land. Witchery, not white people, has
set a loveless, fearful, mechanistic, death-bent force
loose in the world.

Silko does a wonderful job of making us see the Laguna landscape as the nexus of all modern history. The
original witches' convention takes place near Laguna;
on Bataan, Tayo sees the remote ancestors of his own
people dying in the jungle mud; Laguna land encompasses the uranium fields; Los Alamos lies to the north
and Trinity Site to the south. Tayo is not a single shell-
shocked veteran suffering from flashbacks but a figure
at the geographic and spiritual center of a cosmic illness.

The ceremony to counter the effects of the witchery
must face the infectious force of people, both Anglo
and Indian, who unbeknownst to themselves are
witchery's victims. These people dismiss all ceremony
and traditions, whether European or American Indian,
as superstition, and they treat the land and one another
as objects. The ceremony turns in large part on Tayo's
coming together with Ts'eh, a beautiful, mysterious
woman he encounters in the mountains beyond the
Pueblo. Ts'eh, she tells him, is a "nickname." We know,
and Tayo eventually figures out, that it is short for Tse-
pi'na—in Keres, "Woman Veiled in Clouds"—the Laguna name for Mount Taylor. She is, she says, "a Mon-
tano," and a member of "'a very close family. . . . I
have a sister who lives down that way. She's married to
a Navajo from Red Lake. . . . Another lives in
Flagstaff. My brother's in Jemez.' She stopped suddenly, and she laughed."[22]

She is a mountain spirit, like her brothers and sisters—
sacred mountains all. Though she and Tayo are lovers,
in scenes among the most erotic in American literature,
her sexuality extends far beyond the act of intercourse—
she is healer, nurturer, plotter, planter, and she schemes
for the good of people and plants and animals. When

she spreads her black storm-pattern blanket, snow falls; she she folds it up again—in time to keep the snow-laden branches of fruit trees from breaking—the sky clears. When she bundles up her blue silk shawl with her damp laundry and seedlings and balances it atop her head, Pueblo style, she is Mount Taylor, its blue summit swathed in clouds. She collects, sorts, and transplants herbs and wildflowers, teaching Tayo something of her lore as she works. "She sat flat on the ground and bent close over the plants, examining them for a long time, from the petals, sprinkled with pollen, down the stem to each leaf, and finally to the base, where she carefully dug the sand away from the roots. 'This one contains the color of the sky after a summer rainstorm. I'll take it from here and plant it in another place, a canyon where it hasn't rained for a while'" (235). When she leaves Tayo, she charges him to help carry on her work, to gather a plant that won't be ready for harvesting before she moves on. At the climax of the novel, after he has resisted a brutal final temptation to perpetuate the witchery, Tayo immediately turns his thoughts to her work: "He would go back there now, where she had shown him the plant. He would gather the seeds for her and plant them with great care in places near sandy hills. . . . The plants would grow there like the story, strong and translucent as stars" (266). From Ts'eh, Tayo learns to nurture; through her, he learns to love the land and to recognize the depth of its love for him.

The Ts'eh and Tayo episodes of *Ceremony* are among the most powerful modern recreations of the old stories of women and the land, just as the novel itself is among the most acute evocations of New Mexico landscape. That landscape can be not only mountain and river bottom, but a barroom floor in Gallup, seen through a child's eyes:

> He lay on his belly with his chin on the wooden floor and watched the legs and the shoes under the tables . . . he searched the floor until he found a plastic bar straw, and then he played with piles of cigarette butts. When he found chewing gum stuck beneath the tables, he put it in his mouth, and tried to keep it, but he always swallowed it. . . . He played for hours under the tables, quiet, watching for someone to drop a potato-chip bag or a wad of gum. He learned about coins, and searched for them, putting them in his mouth when he found them.
>
> (114-15)

This child, or one very like him, will grow up to be Tayo—who knows, even before he meets Ts'eh, how to watch the land with the same intimacy, the same sense of the importance of the small change others might not think worth noticing and treasuring, the same careful regard for the things and creatures others would call trash.

Tayo's sensitivity of eye and heart and his care for the life in things compensate for the precise ceremonial knowledge he has never been given, as a half-outsider.

Even before the war, his illness, and his awareness of the ceremony that centers on him, Tayo knows how to see and understands that ritual means holding intercourse with the land. During the prewar drought he seeks out a spring his uncle has shown him, a spring that never runs dry, even in the dust-bowl years. He does not know the proper Laguna way to pray for rain, but, like the little girls in Tapahonso's "The Snake-Man," he does what he can. He "imagine[s] with his heart" the right rituals and simply shakes pollen over the spring and asks for rain. Then he just sits and watches the pool at the source. What he sees suggests the keenness of his sight and insight, the receptivity of his eye: "The spider came out first. She drank from the edge of the pool, careful to keep the delicate egg sacs on her abdomen out of the water. She retraced her path, leaving faint crisscrossing patterns in the fine yellow sand. He remembered stories about her. She waited in certain locations for people to come to her for help" (98).

Tayo is ready to meet Ts'eh; even before their coming together, he knows that the land is alive and beautiful. She awakens his knowledge that the land is not merely alive but endowed with personality and intelligence and capable of evoking and giving back a love that is infinitely personal.

* * *

At times Tapahonso and Silko skillfully depict the urban Indian experience, but their work seldom strays much farther than Gallup, Albuquerque, or Phoenix.[23] Joy Harjo's particular poetic turf is cities, especially from the point of view of an Indian woman traveling between them. Her poems are full of planes, cars, pick-ups, borders, and white center-lines; she writes not only of the Oklahoma of her childhood and New Mexico, where she's spent many of her adult years, but of Iowa and Kansas, Calgary and East Chicago, Anchorage and New Orleans, and corrugated tunnels in airports, "a space between leaving and staying."[24] Her work traces the modern Pan-Indian trails crisscrossing the country, no longer trade routes in the old way, but circuits—the pow-wow circuit, the academic-feminist lecture circuit, the poetry-reading circuit. The primacy of travel in her works probably makes her, of the three women I've discussed, the most typical of contemporary American Indian writers. In and out of the Southwest, as Paula Gunn Allen remarks, wandering is an old custom among many tribes.[25] This is perhaps especially true of Oklahoma tribal people, whose wanderings have not always been voluntary. In an interview, Harjo said, "maybe the people of Oklahoma always have this sense that somehow we're going to have to move again. . . . Somehow, it's not settled, even though we've all lived there since about 1830."[26]

Harjo is also different from Tapahonso and Silko in two other ways. First, her work is more openly concerned than theirs with feminist themes. Second, she has a strong interest in the occult or metaphysical traditions of cultures besides the American Indian: she is an adept Tarot reader and a visionary.

Harjo does have a strong home-base, an acute sense of the red earth and the red people that the name Oklahoma simultaneously signifies. The literal earth is part of her early memory: "I love language, sound, how emotions, images, dreams are formed in air and on the page," she writes. "When I was a little kid in Oklahoma, I would get up before everyone else and go outside to a place of rich dark earth next to the foundation of the house. I would dig piles of earth with a stick, smell it, form it. It had sound. Maybe that's when I first learned to write poetry, even though I never really wrote until I was in my early twenties."[27]

An early poem, "The Last Song," especially affirms that strong childhood bond with a particular patch of southwestern earth that "has sound," that speaks and nurtures:

> how can you stand it
> he said
> the hot oklahoma summers
> where you were born
> this humid thick air
> is choking me
>
>   . . . . .
>
> it is the only way
> i know how to breathe
> an ancient chant
> that my mother knew
> came out of a history
> woven from wet tall grass
> in her womb
> and i know no other way
> than to surround my voice
> with the summer songs of crickets
> in this moist south night air
>
> oklahoma will be the last song
> i'll ever sing[28]

Here, the land is a mother and a mother of mothers; a singer who gives human singers their songs. This is the poem of a woman who grew up not only playing in the soil, but listening to it. Most of Harjo's poetry does not center specifically on her Creek heritage—or not yet: Geary Hobson speculates that "oklahoma will be the last song / i'll ever sing" may be a promise of the theme Harjo will turn to in time.[29] Meanwhile, the land does not manifest itself in her poetry in spirit-figures out of her particular tribal tradition, like Tapahonso's Snake-man or Silko's mountain ka'tsinas. What does pulse throughout Harjo's work is a sense that all landscape she encounters is endowed with an identity, vitality, and

intelligence of its own. This sense of life and intelligence in the land is quite different from the human emotions an Anglo poet might *project* upon landscape; the life in Harjo's landscapes makes poems written out of the pathetic fallacy indeed seem pathetic by comparison.

"Kansas City" illustrates Harjo's sense of the individual identities of natural things. In that poem, Noni Daylight (a kind of alter ego who appears often in Harjo's works) elects to remain

> in Kansas City, raise the children
> she had by different men,
> all colors. Because she knew
> that each star rang with separate
> colored hue, as bands of horses,
> and wild
>   like the spirit in her . . .[30]

Her children of different colors are comparable, in their beautiful singularity, to the each-ness of stars and horses. Noni's children, Noni's men, and Noni herself are singular and vitally connected with that natural universe of stars and horses. Even though they live in Kansas City, they are not alienated from or outside of nature.

Moreover, in Harjo's poems the land acknowledges its connection to people. In "Leaving," the speaker wakes as her roommate gets up to answer a late-night phone call:

> Her sister was running way from her boyfriend and
> was stranded in Calgary, Alberta. Needed money
> and comfort for the long return back home.
>
> I dreamed of a Canadian plain, and warm arms around
>   me,
> the soft skin of the body's landscape. And I dreamed
> of bear, and a thousand-mile escape homeward.
>
>   (28)

Even the imagined landscape of the Canadian plain, usually considered harsh country and certainly radically different from Harjo's Oklahoma, is like the sisters and friends earlier in the poem who warm and sustain one another. Both the women and the land are soft, comforting, erotic, familiar, associated with the healing and power of the totemic bear, and with home.

Harjo turns to the theme of human erotic connections with spirit figures who embody the land in her many poems about the moon. In them, the moon appears not as symbol and certainly not as background lighting, but as a full, intelligent female person. That the moon should be so important in Harjo's work makes sense given her woman-centeredness and her representation of herself as a woman on the move. The womanness of the moon is in almost all cultures, and she can be there for the wanderer in Anchorage or Hong Kong; like Harjo, she is a traveler too. The moon, that medieval emblem of instability for Western Europeans, is a stable comforter for Harjo; in "Heartbeat," Noni Daylight drops acid and drives through Albuquerque with a pistol cradled in her lap. In the middle of this nighttown horror, "Noni takes the hand of the moon / that she knows is in control overhead." The poem concludes, "It is not the moon, or the pistol in her lap / but a fierce anger / that will free her" (37). Even so, given that Noni has yet to find that anger, the moon is the only entity who remains steady, who reaches out to Noni in a time when "these nights, she wants out."

And yet the comforting moon Harjo knows is also as completely herself and as mysterious as Snake-man or mountain ka'tsinas. Harjo conveys this moon's wildness and independent life beautifully in "Moonlight": "I know when the sun is in China / because the night-shining other-light / crawls into my bed. She is moon." Harjo imagines the other side of the world,

> in Hong Kong, Where someone else has also
> awakened, the night thrown back and asked,
> "Where is the moon, my lover?"
> And from here I always answer in my dreaming,
> "The last time I saw her, she was in the arms
> of another sky."
>
> (52)

What matters most about Harjo's moon is her ability as a living spirit to enter into the sort of dialogue with people that reassures them, no matter where they are, of their own lives and their connection with wilderness. In "September Moon," as Harjo and her children try to cross Albuquerque's Central Avenue in the midst of State Fair traffic, she encounters the moon rising out of the trapped air of the urban Rio Grande Valley:

> I was fearful of traffic
> trying to keep my steps and the moon was east,
> ballooning out of the mountain ridge, out of smokey
>   clouds
> out of any skin that was covering her. Naked.
> Such beauty.
>   Look.
> We are alive. The woman of the moon looking
> at us, and we are looking at her, acknowledging
> each other.
>
> (60)

The land and the person acknowledging each other as living beings, sensate and sensual, their lives inextricably woven together in Spider Woman's web—this is what lies at the heart of American Indian ritual and southwestern American Indian women's writing.

Notes

This chapter was conceived and outlined with Paula Gunn Allen, and we jointly drafted the first few pages. When other commitments made it necessary for Allen

to withdraw from the project, I went on to write the bulk of the essay, and responsibility for errors rests with me. But the ideas here derive from our initial collaboration.

1. I focus here on traditional and contemporary material from southwestern American Indians, but my broader observations about the relations between human beings and wilderness apply to most American Indian cultures. The best book on American Indian religion is Peggy V. Beck and Anna L. Waters, *The Sacred: Ways of Knowledge, Sources of Life,* (Tsaile [Navajo Nation], Ariz.: Navajo Community College Press, 1977). Two good anthologies of essays on the subject are *Seeing with a Native Eye,* ed. Walter Holden Capps (New York: Harper and Row, 1976); and *Teachings from the American Earth: Indian Religion and Philosophies,* ed. Barbara Tedlock and Dennis Tedlock (New York: Liveright, 1975).

2. nila northSun, "the way and the way things are," *diet pepsi and nacho cheese* (Fallon, Nev.: Duck Down Press, 1977), 13.

3. *Often* is, of course, a key qualifying word in this sentence; certainly there are and have been non-Indian people able to perceive the land as something other than an object.

4. See Annette Kolodny, *The Lay of the Land* (Chapel Hill: University of North Carolina Press, 1975), and *The Land Before Her* (Chapel Hill: University of North Carolina Press, 1984).

5. My principle sources for *Beauty Way* are Father Berard Haile, O.F.M., and Lelan C. Wyman, *Beautyway* (New York: Pantheon, 1957); and Clyde Benally, *Diné jí Nákéé' Naahane'; A Utah Navajo History* (Salt Lake City: University of Utah Press, 1982). There are several versions of *Beauty Way,* and this essay contains only a summary of a sacred text of great complexity and beauty.

6. Yellow Woman (Kochinako, or Kochininako), in Keres tradition "the mother of us all," is closely associated with the north, with hunting, and with rain; she is often described as an intercessory figure. In many of the stories, she appears as a human woman who makes alliances with male spirit figures, from whom she obtains gifts that benefit her people. See John M. Gunn, *Schat-Chen: History, Traditions, and Narratives of the Queres Indians of Laguna and Acoma* (Albuquerque, 1917), 184-89; Franz Boas, *Keresan Texts* (New York: Publications of the American Ethnological Society, no. 7, pts. 1-2, 1928), 56-59; Hamilton A. Tyler, *Pueblo Animals and Myths* (Norman: University of Oklahoma Press, 1975), 28-29, 100, 105-06, 213, 227, 229. Of contemporary authors, Leslie Silko draws most often on the Yellow Woman stories.

7. Leslie Silko, "Storytelling," *Storyteller* (New York: Seaver, 1981), 94. Hereafter this volume cited parenthetically in the text.

8. Luci Tapahonso, "The Snake-man," in *The Remembered Earth,* ed. G. Hobson (Albuquerque: University of New Mexico Press, 1981), 308-10.

9.   . . . They say
            you should never pick up
      strangers or injured animals
      on dark reservation roads

      you'll be safe if
      you do not brake for animals
                  on lone moonlight nights
      They say
      the deeds of day
      have no disguise from
                  the darkness of night and truth
      so they say
      never leave the pollen behind and
                  always know a medicineman.

Tapahonso: "This is a warning," in *One More Shiprock Night* (San Antonio: Tejas Art Press, 1981), 90. For other Tapahonso road-ghosts, see "She Sits on the Bridge," in *Earth Power Coming,* ed. Simon J. Ortiz (Tsaile, Ariz.: Navajo Community College Press, 1983), 222; and "They Are Together Now," "A Sense of Myself," 24.

10. Tapahonso, "A Spring Poem-Song," in "A Sense of Myself," 30.

11. See Patricia Clark Smith, "Coyote Ortiz: Canis latrans latrans in the Poetry of Simon Ortiz," *Studies in American Indian Literature,* ed. Paula Gunn Allen (New York: Modern Language Association, 1983), 192-210.

12. Geary Hobson, "Blood Connections," *Contact II* 6, nos. 30-31 (1983-1984), 64.

13. Tapahonso, *One More Shiprock Night,* 94.

14. Tapahonso, "For Earl and Tsaile April Nights," in "A Sense of Myself," 7.

15. Tapahonso, "A Spring Poem-Song."

16. Tapahonso, "For Misty Starting School," in "A Sense of Myself," 27.

17. Tapahonso, "The lightening awoke us," ibid., 12.

18. Tapahonso, "A Breeze Swept Through," ibid., 16.

19. Leslie Silko, "Contributors' Biographical Notes," in *Voices of the Rainbow: Contemporary Poetry by American Indians,* ed. Kenneth Rosen (New York: Seaver, 1975), 230.

20. "The sacred Clowns of North American tribal people are direct evidence that the sacred ways of tribal people are not inflexible, self-important and without humor." Beck and Walters, "Sacred Fools and Clowns," in *The Sacred,* 306. See also Barbara Tedlock, "The Clown's Way," in *Teachings from the American Earth,* 105-18.

21. Paula Gunn Allen, "The Feminine Landscape of Leslie Marmon Silko's *Ceremony,*" in *Studies in American Indian Literature,* 127-33.

22. Leslie Marmon Silko, *Ceremony* (New York: Viking, 1977), 234. Hereafter cited parenthetically in the text.

23. The major exception is Silko's brilliant short story "Storyteller," which grew out of time spent in Ketchikan, Alaska.

24. Joy Harjo, "White Bear," *She Had Some Horses* (Chicago: Thunder's Mouth Press, 1983), 27.

25. Paula Gunn Allen, review of Harjo's *What Moon Drove Me to This?* in *The Greenfield Review* 9, nos. 3-4 (Winter 1981-82): 12.

26. Joy Harjo, in conversation with Paula Gunn Allen, August 1983.

27. Harjo, "Bio-poetics Sketch," *The Greenfield Review* 9, nos. 3-4 (Winter 1981-82): 8.

28. Harjo, "The Last Song," *What Moon Drove Me to This?* (New York: Reed, 1979), 67.

29. Geary Hobson, review of *What Moon Drove Me to This?* in *Greenfield Review* 9, nos. 3-4 (Winter 1981-82): 15-16.

30. Harjo, "Kansas City," *She Had Some Horses,* 33. Hereafter this volume cited parenthetically in the text.

Luci Tapahonso with Joseph Bruchac (interview date 1987)

SOURCE: Tapahonso, Luci, and Joseph Bruchac. "For What It Is: An Interview with Luci Tapahonso." In *Survival This Way: Interviews with American Indian Poets,* pp. 271-85. Tucson: Sun Tracks and the University of Arizona Press, 1987.

[*In the following interview, Tapahonso discusses her work, particularly* Seasonal Woman, *her community, and her culture.*]

The middle one of eleven children, Luci Tapahonso was born in Shiprock, New Mexico, where her family still lives on a farm three miles from the town up on the north mesa. Speaking of her early years in the biographical statement in her first book of poems, ***One More Shiprock Night,*** published in 1981 by Tejas Art Press, she says, "I know that I cannot divide myself or separate myself from that place—my home, my land, and my people. And that realization is my security and my mainstay in my life away from there."

After attending school at the Navajo Methodist Mission in Farmington, thirty miles from Shiprock, she graduated from Shiprock High School in 1971, served in 1974 on the Board of Directors of the Phoenix Indian Center, and took part in a training program for investigative reporting at the National Indian Youth Council. In 1976 she began studying journalism at the University of New Mexico but switched her major to English after studying with Leslie Silko, graduating in 1980. Currently a graduate student at the University of New Mexico, she is pursuing a doctorate in Modern Literature. Married to Earl Ortiz, an artist whose drawings illustrate her first volume, she is the mother of two daughters, Lori and Misty Dawn.

This interview took place at the home of Geary Hobson in Albuquerque, New Mexico.

"Hills Brothers Coffee"

My uncle is a small man
in Navajo, we call him little uncle
     my mother's brother.

He doesn't know English but
     his name in the white way is Tom Jim
     He lives about a mile or so
     down the road from our house.

One morning he sat in the kitchen
drinking coffee
     I just came over, he said
     the store is where I'm going to.
He tells me about how my mother seems to be gone
everytime he comes over.
     Maybe she sees me coming
     then runs and jumps into her car
     and speeds away!
     He says smiling.
We both laugh to think of my mother
     jumping in her car and speeding.

I pour him more coffee and
     he spoons in sugar and cream until
     it looks almost like a chocolate shake
     then he sees the coffee can.
     Oh, that's the coffee with
     the man in a dress, like a church man.
     ah-h, that's the one that does it for me.
     very good coffee.

I sit down again and he tells me
     some coffee has no kick but
     this one is the one.
     It does it good for me.

I pour us both a cup and
     while we wait for my mother,
     his eyes crinkle with the smile

and he says
yes, ah yes, this is the very one,
(putting in more cream and sugar.)

So I usually buy hills brothers coffee
     once or sometimes twice a day
     I drink a hot coffee and

it sure does it for me.

                    —Luci Tapahonso

[*Bruchac*]: *Do you recall when you first started to write poetry or when it began to become an important force in your life?*

[Tapahonso]: I don't remember writing poetry when I was a child, but I remember being fascinated with words and stories, books, at a really early age. I remember taking phrases that I really liked and just sort of memorizing them and repeating them to myself. So it was more a fascination with words than with poetry as a form of writing.

At what time in your life did you make a connection between poetry and the possibility of your own writing?

Not until really late. I was twenty-two or twenty-three. But I had been writing for years before that, since back in high school and I just had all this poetry . . . and I always say that I finally "came out of the closet." (laughter) When I first met Leslie and she taught a class, she was really excited about my poetry. It was really a step for me to show people because it was such a personal thing.

A number of the younger American Indian writers have been influenced by older writers who have encouraged them. You say that Leslie Silko was a big influence in making you take your own work more seriously or making it public?

Yes, yes. And then she helped me. My first short story was published, and it's true I would not have done much probably if I had not met her. I didn't take what I was doing to be something important to the general community.

Memory seems to me to be very important in your work. Can you talk a bit about remembering and its relationship to your poems?

A lot of my poems are memory poems—things that people have told me or memories from my own life, from my parents and from the stories they have told me. And I think that it is really important because the past determines what our present is or what our future will be. I don't think there is really a separation of the three. We have to have the past in order to go on and to survive to draw strength from. You know, a lot of times we think that we are in an awful situation or that this has never happened to someone before. Yet people will tell us of instances where something similar or even worse has happened to someone. Part of the whole thing about story-telling is that it is done in order to draw strength and in order to go on and see ourselves—not as separate from other people in terms of experience and problems and those sorts of things, but to see ourselves in a community and to see a unity with other people, our own family or our relatives, just the community at large.

The idea of community also seems crucial to you as a writer and strikes me as being of great importance to most Native American writers. Yet I see a movement away from community on the part of the European American, a movement inward toward self and personal psychology while American Indian writers are moving in directions which seem to be toward others, their community, the Earth. Why—if you agree with me—is there such a difference between the European American and the Native American poet?

I think that is true, though there are also people going into all kinds of encounter and self-help groups, going to all types of integration training and that sort of thing and that only happens because, maybe, they don't have a community and we're fortunate that we do. We don't see ourselves, I think, as separate. We don't see ourselves alone and, probably, non-Indian poets see themselves as that way—as by themselves—and so they're trying all sorts of things in order to feel secure. We have a whole past, our own history. You know, we *are* our own history, we *are* our own people. We don't see ourselves as separate from that. I think that we're very fortunate in that way because it helps us, it helps the way we think. It's real hard to explain to someone—this whole sense of community because, you know, it's a way of thinking, a way of feeling, actually, and that's hard to explain to someone who doesn't have that.

American poetry—still talking about the European side—seems to be characterized very often by a longing and a loneliness, a sense of being on the edge of a kind of wilderness, a frontier, and trying to force that into a mold which you create on your own. That idea of changing the natural world, of changing everything around you to reflect your image, also seems to be counter to the vision of the American Indian writer. The title of your new book, **Seasonal Woman,** *seems to indicate a strong relationship to natural rhythms. Am I correct in seeing it that way?*

Yes, you are. I also think that this loneliness, this clamoring for some sort of security, leads a lot of people to become "Wannabes," who suddenly decide that this is it, that they're going to be Indian and that sort of thing. That's always struck me as funny, but then it's

sad in a way. I don't know, I can't imagine what it would be like to be in that position. To me, I think it would be like Hell, to be without family, to not know where you came from, not know who your relatives are, and to not be able to have a place and say, "This is, now this is who I am or this is where I came from." I think that it must be really scary.

Geary Hobson told me the story of Adolf Hungrywolf visiting him when Geary was working at the Living Batch bookstore. Adolf Hungrywolf is a German who has been writing about the Blood people. He showed up at the bookstore wearing a huge choker, dressed in buckskins with his long dark hair in braids. I think it was dyed black and his skin was also dyed brown. He greeted Geary with a German accent. (laughter) There are cases like that of people who want to be something they're not. John A. Williams, who is a black American writer, said to me a few weeks ago that nobody in America seems to want to be who they are. Everybody wants to pretend to be somebody else. Yet it strikes me that you are correct—the American Indian writer doesn't want to be somebody else. They may be aware of the mixture of ancestry—a lot of people have both European and Indian ancestry. But I don't feel it is the kind of dividing force that it is for some people.

I think that in Indian cultures when there was first contact with Europeans it was a hard thing to deal with. But then, through the generations, I think that it's become easier to deal with and people have accepted and adjusted. But then it's never really been in any Indian culture to disown one of their own because that's not the way we are. And yet you see that with a lot of Anglo families when the child is, maybe, half black. They can't deal with it. The love they might have for the person who is involved with this person of another race cannot overcome that sort of thing. And yet with Indian families, I think, the family overcomes any division that might occur. I think initially there's always sort of a shock, but that passes and people are accepted and the children, especially, cannot be held to any sort of disgrace because of something somebody else did.

Wendy Rose has a series of poems she calls "Halfbreed Chronicles." She sees it as a very complicated issue. That idea of disowning a person who was of mixed blood or calling them a "halfbreed," which is an insult, is very different from relating to them as one who knows something of two cultures and is able, therefore, to speak between and help people to relate to each other as human beings rather than as separate races. Is a more humane or human relationship to the person of mixed blood truer of the Indian way?

I think so. I think also there's more tolerance within one's tribe or one's family than with somebody of another tribe. So the antagonism Wendy Rose or somebody else has felt has probably come from someone of a different tribe. I think that people who are of mixed ancestry probably value their Indian ancestry more than somebody like me. It becomes doubly important. Sometimes, maybe, that sort of creates a conflict between people who are fullblood and people who are half of different tribes . . .

Many of the people in the "first generation" of American Indian writers in this part of the century who have become well known are people of mixed blood. But there is a new generation, a new wave of American Indian writers coming—let me take you as an example— who are not in that particular category, who are not people who have been pushed out into the world, divided between cultures, and then must work back toward that Indian culture. I wonder why it is that people such as Momaday, for example, who talks of his mixed ancestry in The Names, *or Leslie Silko, or Wendy Rose have been some of the first out there to make those statements?*

I don't know. It's been said that it's a matter of identity. It's a matter of proving their identity. Leslie's book *Ceremony* can be looked at in that way—and in a lot of other ways—that it is a novel of finding one's identity and one's place. But I don't know. It's something that I'll probably have to think about—why that happened. I think that it's a good thing that that happened because it opened the way for the rest of us. I think that I would have been writing anyway because I was into journalism, investigative journalism. So I would have probably been doing a different kind of writing for a living and always doing poetry on the side because I wouldn't stop doing that. But I don't know if I would have ever taken my own poetry seriously.

Then what happens to one person makes it possible for it to happen to another, opens the way?

Yes, there's a whole circuit. There's not really any of that sort of competition.

The idea of song seems central in your writing. Your poem "Listen," begins "Once in high school, a friend / told me: Don't marry a man who / can't sing. There's something / wrong if a man can't sing in Indian." Other poems in **Seasonal Woman** *have song in them, for example "There Have Been Nights," and the last poem "A Prayer."*

With the first one, when she said "Don't . . ." it's like saying, you know there's a saying "Don't trust a man who doesn't like to drink." (laughter) Which is silly, but really being with a man seriously and him not singing is real unstable. It's very sort of crooked, sinister, you know? Because somebody who doesn't sing is, to me, sort of strange. In Navajo, you know it's very

important. There's a song for everything. There are songs for nothing and there are songs for anything. I think it's just natural that it would work itself into the poetry because the poetry, too, is a song—in the sense that it stirs one's mind or that it creates a dance within a person's imagination. It creates movement, so that song is movement not only physical, but spiritually, emotionally. Good poetry is that, is motion and relates to the whole thing of dance and prayer because *they* are all one motion. They are all together. There is no separation.

The poetry is sort of a new extension, a contemporary extension of that sort of thing—for myself, because I'm here, and for my children because they're growing up very differently than I did. At first I used to sort of mourn that. But now I see that it's not really anything that's bad unless we see it that way. That is something I've come to terms with through my writing, I think. I can see how my daughters are growing and I can see how my poetry and the songs and the prayers and their everyday lives are affecting them and how they're changing and so it's a good thing.

The poems in **Seasonal Woman** *seem to be very much linked, to flow from one to the next, to form a sort of cycle. I'm interested in one character who shows up in several poems: Leona Grey. She's in "Her Daughter's Eyes," "Time Flies," and "No Particular Reason." For a time I thought of her as a person like "Noni Daylight" in Joy Harjo's poems who is sort of an extension of Joy herself, another persona. But I wonder about Leona Grey since, though there may perhaps be some paralleling of your own experience in hers, she also ends up being killed in "No Particular Reason."*

That's not for real. I killed her but she's back. I did that in frustration. But what she is, is not really my experience. It is my experience in terms of the way that I know her, but she's several different women that I've known and for a long time I was writing her down as always "she" or "her," giving her names, different names. But then I decided I would put her all together and have her be this real reckless but wise person. So I wanted to pick a name that was sort of real raunchy, so I thought Leona was a good name. I hope I never meet anyone with that name. That would be scary.

And then "Grey"?

"Grey" meaning . . . in terms of that color. Not necessarily something like being a dark person or a gloomy person, not anything like that. I liked that, "Grey." I don't have any particular reasons.

Gray does turn up frequently in the colors of Navajo weaving as one of those transition colors—halfway between dark and light. So it seemed like a very good name for Leona. You say that she personifies a kind of reckless but wise woman? There seems to be a great deal of freedom in the ways women are presented in poems by Native American women as opposed to the ways women live and are presented in poems by many non-Native American women. Have you noticed that?

In fact, gosh, I couldn't sleep last night and it's really strange you should ask me that because I was thinking last night that men are very restricted in our (Navajo) society. Men are very restricted and women aren't. You can do whatever you want and it's all okay because you're a woman and it's the opposite with men.

I like the way you begin this book with the picture of your child, "Misty Dawn at Feeding Time." Was that poem written right after the birth of one of your children?

Misty—that's Misty when she was a few months old, my younger daughter. I always begin my work, no matter what I'm doing, with something for my children. I think it's a good thing to do because I feel good about my children. They're not a hindrance to me and I feel really good about them, so beginning that way I think helps me. It's sort of like assurance that things will go well. So my readings, or whatever I do, I always begin with my children.

Unlike the type of sexuality that occurs within a "typical" American poem, there is a sort of natural and often subtly funny relationship between the sexes. It occurs, for example, in "Raisin Eyes," or "Promise Me a Long Night," or "One More Shiprock Night" from your earlier book. Does that characterize your vision of the relationship between men and women?

I think that it's important to see it for what it is, to be able to see it distinctly and see it aside from any emotions that come along with it. That is important, too, but to be able to see it for what's really going on. You know, people always say love is blind. I think that happens a lot of times. People can't see the situation that they're in. But it's important to see things clearly, with a sense of *clarity* and in simple terms. I think as we grow older a lot of times we lose that perception. We tend to complicate things or read things in or just think that the way a person is looking at you—it means something else. You know, all that sort of thing. But if you can see it for what it is, what's really going on, then it is so much easier.

In some of the poems of Joy Harjo, Leslie Silko, and yourself those events become myth; it becomes like an old story.

Which it is. I think that we were raised with that. How do we know what people generations from now are going to be talking about? It could very well be us. I think

that's true. What we are ties in with stories and the future. We are, you know. Who knows what we are probably repeating . . . and we are repeating what has happened over and over again, not only to us as people. Because people are no different than spiritual beings, I think, and that's the whole key—that we can see things on those different levels. So it ties in with the whole thing of "We are the Earth." At home I remember that people always say, "Oh, she's just being Changing Woman," referring to somebody who is just doing things that are really crazy, then being real serious and acting sane and being the way that this society wants us to function . . .

Or the character of Coyote. Coyote turns up in Joy's poems or Simon Ortiz's poems . . . actually you could make a list as long as your arm. Almost all American Indian writers have a Coyote image or a Coyote story in their work.

Um-humm. And they say things like, "They're just doing that because they're from this clan which is just this certain clan," or, as a joke, "Why, your grandfather was a Bear," and that sort of thing. So there's really not any distinction. I think it works well for us. In stories, a lot of stories I heard when I was growing up, the animals were people and they had done something, something that gave them their animal form. That ties in with not taking things for granted, not saying in a derogatory sense, "You are such an *animal*," or that sort of thing that other people do. Because who are we to say that we are any different?

Violence comes up in a number of your poems. Why is it there?

It goes back to being able to see things clearly or trying to see things clearly for what they are and not, maybe, giving any reasons for it or that sort of thing. It is all part of our everyday lives. We can't really say that it's not. I don't know. I don't know what I'm trying to say. I know what I want to say but I can't put it into words.

There is another kind of conflict I see in some of your poems—between white and Indian. In your poem "Pay Up or Else" a young Indian man is killed because he doesn't pay the ninety-seven cents overdue on the gas he got. How do you relate to that climate of racism on the part of Anglos in the Southwest? What do you, as a poet or a person, do about it?

I don't know how to answer that. I think that first it's important to see that it's here. I know I've experienced it and people close to me have experienced it, even people I don't know have experienced it. It is a familiar feeling to us. It's something that we deal with all the time. And being able to recognize it and to see that it's happened and not to let it frustrate you or let it upset you is important, I think. Maybe that's why I have to write about it because it's important to see things, you know, for what they are—not to mar them or not to cloud them over, to present them simply because it makes us what we are, it's a part of us. I don't know if that explains it.

It seems as if more and more Indian people are reading the poems of American Indian writers and finding something there they need. Do you see your poetry as something of use, as a tool?

I think so, because I consider it a real compliment when people come up to me and say, "I *know*," or "*That* happened to me! I *know* what you mean." So that it's a good thing because young Indian students can relate to literature *finally* and enjoy it and *laugh* and that's very hard to do. When I was going to school, we didn't have that sort of thing. So it's important for them to read this and to really like it and say, "Hey, that's really neat!" or "I could do *that*." It's just such a neat feeling. I have met people who have said that Simon's poems have really helped them deal with certain situations in their lives. So it is a source of strength and it's a source of being able to say, "Well, it's okay." Just being able to relate to poetry because it's *them*.

Is there any poem in particular that you like better than any of the others in **Seasonal Woman**?

No, they're all my babies. (laughter) You probably know how this feels—for a long time I had these poems and they were mine. And then it was finally out in print. Sometimes I think about it and it gets me a little bit depressed because I think a lot of people have this book, a lot of people I know—and I feel good about that—a lot of people I don't know—and so I don't know how my poems are. It's like my kids are running around someplace and I don't know who's taking care of them, something like that. And they're finally out, they're not mine anymore, and I'm sharing them with other people. So that's sort of what I went through with this and I'm still sort of in a slump after this came out. When it came out I was telling Earl, this is just like having a baby.

The postpartum depression.

Yeah. (laughter)

I really like that poem "Hills Brothers Coffee."

It's a translation, a direct translation from Navajo. So that gives it . . . a lot of the words are probably different than if I had written it only in English.

Are any of these others in **Seasonal Woman** *a direct translation from Navajo?*

I think this is the only one in here. Umhum. (looks through book) I think that is the only one that's a direct translation.

Have you written any poems in Navajo?

I'm doing a lot of poetry in Navajo now. In fact, there's a lot of slang for which there's really no translation in English. And if you do translate it, it just sounds kind of flat. So I've been doing poems in Navajo and then not even bothering to translate them and it works really well—at home.

Someone said to me they felt the native language is so important to keep because it is the heart of the people. Do you see the Navajo language as a sort of force for yourself and your poetry?

That's true, I think. They always say at home . . . if you lose, if we lose the language, then we're really not anything anymore. So that is important.

Luci Tapahonso with John F. Crawford and Annie O. Eysturoy (interview date October 1988)

SOURCE: Tapahonso, Luci, John F. Crawford, and Annie O. Eysturoy. "Luci Tapahonso." In *This Is about Vision: Interviews with Southwestern Writers,* edited by William Balassi, John F. Crawford, and Annie O. Eysturoy, pp. 195-202. Albuquerque: University of New Mexico Press, 1990.

[*The following interview, conducted by John F. Crawford and Annie O. Eysturoy in October 1988, provides unique insight into Tapahonso's beliefs about her Native American identity.*]

[*Eysturoy*]: *The question of identity seems to be central to Native American literature in general. Has this been an important question to you as a writer?*

[Tapahonso]: Identity is important, but for me as well as a lot of other Navajo people it's important in terms of what clan we are. My clan is *todikozhi*, because my mother is *todikozhi* and my father is *todich'iin'ii*. To-dikozhi means "salt water" and *todich'iin'ii* means "bitter water." So when I identify myself that's the way I think of myself, first as my mother and then as my father, and then my last name in Navajo which is Tapahonso, "edge of the big water." And so my identity is in terms of the clan, which places the Navajo person in the world and defines one's relationships to other people and one's responsibility. It places me in certain waters. . . . And so my name is already connected to history, and origin, and my relatives. My identity is established; there's no question in my mind about who I am or from what people.

[*Eysturoy*]: *Does that make it easier for you, say, to move between the academic world and your Navajo community?*

[Tapahonso]: Anything that I do just adds to my identity, it doesn't detract; I don't waver. In the creation stories, *todich'iin'ii* is one of the four original clans, and Changing Woman created him from her own body, and this happened at a particular place on the reservation. So as far as my ties with location and place are concerned, this is much more important than the fact that I was born in Shiprock and I was raised there. It has to do with the people and the beliefs and the philosophy and spirituality. And so my sense of place and my sense of the Southwest is a link that has a lot of layers, and the land is only a part of that.

I was born in Shiprock in a comparatively large family. While I wasn't raised in a really strict traditional way, it was semitraditional, which was very common in people of my generation. I learned Navajo first, and then I learned English at home as a matter of necessity. I have always connected English with matters outside my home, and I connect Navajo with the language of my home, and food, and sounds, and descriptions, and people telling me about various things, and just everything that was connected with my upbringing, the way that I was taught, the things that were explained to me, the way I was disciplined. English was always on the periphery.

Then when I began writing, I was fascinated with the English language because you could shape something, you could create whole worlds out of words, and people were always doing that; it was fascinating. So I tried to use words in real complex ways. . . .

[*Eysturoy*]: *Did you try to do this in Navajo as well?*

[Tapahonso]: Not intellectually, the way I did in English. Now I understand that I was fascinated because I already recognized that was possible with any language, whether English or Navajo. But I connected English with the written word, and to this day I can't connect Navajo with the written word. I can't read Navajo well, and I can't write Navajo well. . . . It's agony for me. At one point I could, but now my writing is all in English, and I'm comfortable with that, because of whatever happened with my mental processes as a child. But it's just the writing that is English, and otherwise it's still on the periphery.

So that's how it comes about for me. My reactions and my surprises, everything is always in Navajo first. It takes me a while to cross that space into English, especially if I'm real shocked or something like that. My first reactions are always in Navajo, and when I'm trying to think of how to explain something in English,

I have to go real slow because I have to take care of that process first. It's still a matter of finding the exact way to say it that's as close to Navajo as it can be, but it will never be like Navajo, and that's the real challenge. I really like that searching. It's almost painful to do that, but it's really good because when I find it I know that that was it, and that's the closest I can get. . . .

[*Eysturoy*]: *Do you ever write poems directly in Navajo? I know you have sections of poems written in Navajo.*

[Tapahonso]: I can say poems completely in Navajo, but I can't write them completely in Navajo, because I can't hear all the sounds. When you write in Navajo, you have to hear every sound and I can't. I can't separate the sounds. For instance, if I say *bil dah set'eeh*, which in English means, "They're going so fast, the horse and rider are almost horizontal, and there's dust after them," I can see it in my mind, but if I was to write that in Navajo, I would have a hard time writing that down. It's such a complex thing.

[*Eysturoy*]: *Is the process of translating the oral tradition into a written language difficult?*

[Tapahonso]: It is difficult, but it's also very good; I mean, how else would I do it? And then I'm fortunate, I really do like language, and my knowledge of English is good.

[*Eysturoy*]: *In the process of writing, do you ever compose in Navajo and write it down, and then translate it into English later on?*

[Tapahonso]: No, well, I can do a whole poem in Navajo before I write it in English, depending on the context. . . . For instance, the last poem in my book, **"There is Nothing Quite Like This,"** was all in Navajo to begin with, and then I translated it into English. But there are certain words in English that can't be translated, for instance, how do you say Hills Brothers Coffee? How do you say Tony Lama? So it depends on context.

[*Eysturoy*]: *Have you ever translated poems written in English into Navajo?*

[Tapahonso]: I won't really go any farther in Navajo. There've been poems that I can switch to Navajo from English. But I won't do that much. There's people much more able to do this. They're linguists, and they have a mind with which they can do that. I've accepted pretty much that I can't. But one of my long-term goals is that by the time I'm forty I'll have a working sense of written Navajo.

[*Crawford*]: *I've heard that Navajo is one of the most descriptive languages in the world, because you can do so much with the endings to locate and modify what is going on. English can paint word pictures, but it can't do what Navajo can with such economy. Does that enter into your poetry?*

[Tapahonso]: The language is very visual, and you're right, you can have an entire picture in three or four words, which is hard to do in English. And you have more of a sense of motion, and of placement in Navajo. One of the examples I have of that is that you can define relationships with certain words, including what stage the people are at. If you describe the action of people sitting together as *bil seka,* that means they're living together, therefore they have a serious relationship and are committed to each other, and there's an indication of the time that they have been together, and all that is implied in *bil seka,* a few syllables.

[*Crawford*]: *You've tried to work with mixed audiences, in bringing Navajo culture to Anglos while there are Navajos there listening for special things. How does that work for you?*

[Tapahonso]: It works good, because basically you trust that people are intelligent, and the poetry is much more than just words; it encompasses a lot of other things too. A lot of times I'll read the poetry that I have that's in Navajo, but from the context you can tell what it's about and if the people don't understand what it's about they can still respond to it. The language has a lot of expression in it, so if there's an expression of anger they'll pick it up; it's implied in the tone, so it works well.

Sometimes it kind of calms me to read poems that are real funny in Navajo to an audience and I don't translate or say anything about it, I just do it. And I have a real hard time maintaining a straight face because they don't know that it's funny. Or they might have an idea that it's funny but they don't know how to respond. And that's real funny to me because—it's real funny.

So it generally works real well. It gets the people used to hearing another language rather than just English.

[*Crawford*]: *What do you think of the Anglo writers who for seventy-five years now have gone out to the reservation and tried to interpret what's going on there? I'm thinking of everyone from La Farge to Waters. What problems come out of that kind of excursion?*

[Tapahonso]: Well, I think there's a lot of problems, but to me the most important thing is to point out that anyone's writing is always done out of that person's particular perspective. If you read something and are aware of that, then you're much more careful and more likely not to be wrongly influenced. You know, my writing is certainly filtered through my perspective, so I wouldn't be so bold as to say that I represent the

"Navajo Voice" or anything like that, because I know that I don't. . . . So I think the most important thing writers have to realize is that they're writing through their own perceptions, whether that's a white, or Christian, or male perspective.

We certainly see a lot of European influences in La Farge's work, in the portrayal of his characters, because Laughing Boy is really just a noble savage and sort of untouched and unscathed by anything, so certainly he can't die, while on the other hand the female character deserves to die, because she's so evil by European standards. If you can see all those things, it's real important, but a lot of people don't really think about that; they base their perceptions on what other people have written and don't question the way our culture is formed.

Everything that is authoritative and everything that is documented is somehow substantiated, because, yes, "It is true and we have the records to prove it." And that's where the conflict comes in between oral cultures and written cultures. I think that's real important.

[*Eysturoy*]: *Tony Hillerman has written a lot about the Navajos and uses a great deal of cultural material in his fiction. What is your perception of his work?*

[Tapahonso]: (Laughs) I knew that was coming! (Sighs) Again, it's a matter of perspective. He's so successful, but I think a lot of people don't even stop to realize it is fiction. At some level they might, but when they see Indian people, when they see Navajo people, they think they're knowledgeable because of what they've read. And it's all filtered through Tony Hillerman, bless his heart, his perspective and whatever kinds of intentions that he might have, and whatever sort of confidence he might have in himself as an individual in his knowledge and his ability to write. Now, it would be very unfair, to my mind, for me to pretend or to presume to know so much about white culture or American culture in the Southwest that I would write something akin to "Murder She Wrote" from an Anglo perspective. But that's the difference in the way people are raised, and the way that people believe, and the way that people live. To me, it's a really crucial difference.

[*Eysturoy*]: *Do you see any cultural transgression in his work? Is he in some cases dealing with cultural material which should not be written about, witchcraft for instance?*

[Tapahonso]: I think that he should be very concerned about the kind of things that he's writing about. He makes them out to be something to be very much afraid of, like you're really treading on thin ice. If he feels that way and he tries to get that feeling across to his group, and if in his research and his talking to people he acquired that knowledge, I would be concerned about the place that I was putting myself in in dealing with things like that if I was him. If indeed there is something to be afraid of . . . but apparently he thinks that's trivial. That's the concern I have about that kind of thing. He talks about things that we don't even talk about among ourselves.

On a personal level you're taught the way that people should be, or an individual should be. Then it's just a matter of adhering to that. It's a matter of standards. And it's not "keeping things secret" or it's not that people shouldn't talk about it, or that it's real sacred or anything like that, it's just a matter of standards. It's sort of like people should wash their face every morning, only it's more serious than that.

[*Crawford*]: *What I wanted to ask before was, do you think Anglo writers are getting any better at interpreting Navajos than they were in the past?*

[Tapahonso]: I don't know. That's a real general question. I don't know.

[*Crawford*]: *Let's try this from the other end. The Southwest is becoming more truly multicultural, in that more native people and more Hispanics are writing material that people from all backgrounds are taking seriously. Does that seem to you like a hopeful thing?*

[Tapahonso]: Yes. . . . But we really have to realize that our country is based a lot on the received notion of what it takes to be successful. It takes a long time for minority writers to have a voice. It's hard for people who are not white and male, and so don't fit into the standard category, to be successful writers. But I also think that we've really suffered a setback, and it's directly related to politics, in the last eight years. I hope that with the next administration things'll get a little bit easier. Literature and art are real connected to politics, though they seem like different things.

[*Eysturoy*]: *Did you find it difficult to break through as a Navajo writer when you started writing?*

[Tapahonso]: No, I think I came up when times were ripe, and I thought it was all going to work out in a matter of time. I was published late by some standards, and then I was published quickly. It wasn't by any means by myself, it was by a lot of fellowship and network connections with other people. Leslie Silko had said "You should probably publish," and I thought "Oh, sure." But she kept telling me that, so I finally did. I finally did it myself, but she basically said, "If you don't, I will. I'll submit it for you." So I did, and I was real surprised that it was published. And things just fell into place after that.

My writing was so private, so personal, and I was really shy, I was really afraid of the way things would fit, but it went very well, and people really liked my work when it came out, so it wasn't really difficult for me as a writer; everything really worked out well for me.

[*Crawford*]: *I was talking to people recently from the reservation who want to start a little press there, and what I kept hearing from them was awe of the written word. People are really afraid of using that language or seeing it in print, or are worried about how you do something like that. It seems like every step is a struggle.*

[Tapahonso]: If you know the reservation. . . . I know that if I had stayed in Shiprock I would never have been published. So you have to make compromises, and for me, I had to leave. That's the way that it has to be. You can't live in Shiprock and write and be published and teach at the same time . . . you can't have two things at once.

It's real hard because the connections aren't there, and in this kind of thing almost everything depends on networking and connections and word of mouth. Fortunately our writing circle is so small that everybody knows everybody, and people are wonderful; they're real supportive. In just one or two instances are people being competitive, trying to get each other, but that's real rare. In even that case, people are real forgiving; they just let it be, they don't confront it. We're so few that it's futile to be otherwise.

[*Crawford*]: *You're thinking of Indian writers as a whole?*

[Tapahonso]: No, minority writers.

[*Eysturoy*]: *Do you find it difficult to cross over from the Navajo world to the Anglo world and back again? Is it difficult to bridge the two worlds?*

[Tapahonso]: No, I don't. I think that's really become a cliché. It's untrue for me, because the way that I was raised, my philosophy, is really in me; the way that I think is very much internal. I could go to India or China and still have a sense of who I am.

It's true that one of the compromises that you make when you leave the reservation is that you can't be there for a lot of things that are really important. You can be there for what you can, you can be there when it is absolutely necessary, but you can't be there for all the day-to-day things. But those are the compromises that one has to make. And I realize that, and feel sad over it, but I also realize there's a balance, in my career and my writing, and I meet a lot of people.

Still, my life *is* poorer in a lot of ways because I left. I realize this when my car breaks down, and I get real upset, I get in a quandary, and I don't know who to call. It would have been easier if I was in Shiprock, where somebody would have seen me along the road . . . you know, they would be there. But I could break down on the bridge, and people would, you know . . . it's a matter of compromises. But I think that you do that anywhere in a modern culture.

[*Crawford*]: *The idea of "bridging the two worlds" is an Anglo stereotype, isn't it? It's from the Anglo perspective that of course since our culture is dominant, it's going to be hard for you from the "other" culture to do that. But if you don't start out with our sense of cultural superiority, if you carry your world inside you, it looks completely different. Am I right?*

[Tapahonso]: Yes, I think so. But I think a lot of our people do have difficulty.

[*Eysturoy*]: *You have written mostly poetry, little fiction.*

[Tapahonso]: If I do write fiction, it's short. I don't know how I make that choice. I just get excited about poetry, I just like the challenge of being able to do almost a whole story in a few lines, and thinking about the words I will use, and the words that are most full and vibrant and will encompass what normally ten words can encompass.

[*Crawford*]: *When you write, have you got an idea about how long it will be?*

[Tapahonso]: No, not really, it's not preconceived, I don't think I will start with so many lines . . . but it kind of works that way. But I think that the most important thing in poetry is that one has trouble writing in as few words as possible. Maybe it's that. You try to think in ways it's never been described before, and throw out all the showy things . . .

[*Eysturoy*]: *What is your vision as a poet?*

[Tapahonso]: I think it's real complex. It's the ways I think and the ways I react to all the situations that come to the Navajo people—the way that we talk, the way that we laugh, all those things that are part of the Navajo perspective. But I also know how to function in this world, in the professional and business and academic world . . . a whole different way of functioning. I can chair a meeting, I can organize events, I can raise money. So there's that perspective too. It's really interesting to think about. When I'm writing, it's really me, it's my perspective. But in my perspective there's a lot of different things combined. My viewpoint is fairly typical of the Navajo people. It's real complex.

[*Eysturoy*]: *What projects do you have planned in the future?*

[Tapahonso]: I think having tenure. Here or elsewhere, hopefully here. (Laughs)

[*Crawford*]: *We'll keep that in, just in case anyone's listening.*

[Tapahonso]: And writing more, and devoting more time to writing than I am now. I think that's real crucial, but that means teaching less. Again there's compromises there, but I'd much rather be writing. And my children. My youngest will be a teenager soon, and Lori will be off on her own pretty much. And that they will do well in whatever they do, but will also contribute meaningfully to their community. And going back and building a home. I can see myself having a home that my children and I can go back to, and I can stay at, and I can go to in the summertime. Unless something miraculous happens, I don't see myself living there year round. But finally, when I retire, and I have no more reason to work for money, I'll go back and live there! (Laughs)

Susan B. Brill (essay date fall 1995)

Brill, Susan. "Discovering the Order and Structure of Things: A Conversive Approach to Contemporary Navajo Poetry." *SAIL: Studies in American Indian Literatures* 7, no. 3 (fall 1995): 51-70.

[*In the following essay, Brill proposes that traditional strategies of literary criticism stifle the voices of Native American authors. The critic examines the works of Nia Francisco, Luci Tapahonso, Gertrude Walters, and Esther G. Belin and suggests new strategies of literary analysis that will provide a better understanding of the goals and techniques employed by Native American writers.*]

Contemporary literary analysis provides a range of theories and methods by which critics can interpret, analyze, and evaluate diverse texts. Notwithstanding the plethora of critical approaches in current use, the oppositional linearity upon which these methods and theories are based indicates potential problems in their actual applications towards the literary works of a number of Native authors. It is true that particular strategies have proven more useful than others in critical readings of Native American literatures. The new historicism and cultural criticisms have critiqued earlier methods by which peoples and their histories and literatures have been ignored, marginalized, or even erased from scholarly analysis. Feminist criticism has directed attention to particular Native American literatures and worldviews insofar as they evidence varying degrees of matrifocality which are seen as important contrasts to the predominant phallocentricity of most non-Native cultures. And Bakhtinian informed criticisms have applied notions of dialogism and heteroglossia in explications of the oppositional vocality evident in much contemporary Native writing. However, regardless of the well-intentioned efforts of critics, critical strategies turned towards Native American literatures have all too often distorted or silenced the Native voices within and behind the literatures they intend to illuminate.

Critical methods perpetuate the institutionalization of Native peoples' silence in two serious ways. The first is through a critical privileging that gives precedence to the voice of the critics at the expense of the objectified Native voices present in the literature. To avoid this problem, a conversive critical strategy can enable the critic to work in concert, rather than in competition, with the voices of Native peoples and literatures. In noting this sort of difficulty, Elaine Jahner writes, "Critics need to be aware that conventional approaches and vocabulary are as likely to obscure as to illuminate the ways in which a specific tribal tradition can provide a writer with a set of optional approaches to the form and content of original creative work" ("Critical Approach" 212). This necessitates that critics develop new strategies of literary analysis that will enable critical voices to intermingle with the voices in and of Indian literatures—thereby yielding criticism that is more informed by the voices of the literary works themselves than by the critical voices of scholars.

Arnold Krupat writes, "the Euramerican attempt to think a Native American 'literature' has always been marked by the problem of Identity and Difference, a problem that—as we shall see—marks as well the attempt to develop a written criticism of this 'literature'" ("Identity" 3). Krupat concludes that the substantial differences between critical and Native voices are unavoidable in our critical readings: "While we cannot avoid the explanatory categories of western culture, we can at least be aware of them and beware of them as we approach the 'literature' of other cultures" ("Identity" 10). This paper provides an explicit introduction to the development of a conversive strategy—namely a critical method (as distinct from a critical theory) that is explicitly informed by the voices of those literary texts the method intends to elucidate. Such a conversive and consultative critical strategy provides a new critical method particularly appropriate to the understanding, interpretation, and evaluation of Indian literatures—and insofar as this article is concerned, specifically for the reading of Navajo poetry.

The second way in which Native voices are silenced by contemporary criticism is in the imposition of critical strategies and theoretical approaches that force particular readings upon texts regardless of whether the particular critical orientation is appropriate for the specific text.[1] The underlying grammatical problem (using the term "grammatical" in the Wittgensteinian sense of language game rules) for such endeavors is that both modern and postmodern criticisms are based upon models of linear oppositionality. From the New Critical clashes of opposites reconciled in an eventual forced "harmony" to Marxist informed criticisms that posited the dialectical class struggles of society as manifested in literary works, the modern period explicitly sought in literature the oppositional linearity that modernists erroneously assumed and that we now understand to have been the spurious and problematic assertions of an earlier critical absolutism. As scholars and readers of American Indian literatures know all too well, all literary texts do not manifest the oppositional struggles posited by Western critical strategies—a condition that has functioned to ignore and accordingly devalue those texts that do not fit critical demands. Here I would like to note that American Indian literatures garnered scant attention by literary critics until a number of Native writers of mestiza/o background produced literatures more accessible to Western critical strategies than had been the earlier narratives, stories, chants, and prayers from the oral traditions, which had been available to critics for generations.[2] As Carol Hunter notes, "Contemporary Indian fiction, the novel and poetry, is perhaps more popular among a general audience. It appears to some readers less complex because it conforms with contemporary literary forms and conventions" (84). Of course, the ease with which many readers and critics approach such literary works obscures the actual complexity within those texts.

Postmodern criticisms and theories have attempted to remedy some of the problematic exclusionary effects of modern criticism by offering methods that expand the literary canon through the acknowledgement and privileging of literatures by women, working class, and ethnically diverse writers. Foucault and Lacan pushed the boundaries of earlier historical and psychoanalytic interpretations of texts and of the world and shifted the notion of dialectical class struggles to the more individualized emphasis on discursive analyses that demonstrate the objectification of those individuals denied full subjectivity within the world and within texts. Such analyses also described the processes by which individuals move from subaltern positions of objectivity and into subjective placement. But both dialectical and discursive approaches are based upon a linear oppositionality that assumes inclusion necessarily at the expense of exclusion. Subjectivity, within a linear division, demands a concomitant object against which one's subjectivity is defined. Jeannie Ludlow explains that within a discursive framework, "subjectivity is defined as a (series of) position(s) into and out of which a subject can move, . . . [therefore] a critic should be able to move into and out of subjectivity in order to provide a space within the criticism for the subjectivity of the poet(s)" (26-27). While such a jockeying for and from position can make critical room for Native voices, it does not facilitate the sort of relational conversivity that is evident within the practice of storytelling and which this essay argues and demonstrates is possible within the practice of criticism.

Insofar as the recognition of multiple and diverse subjectivities is concerned, Mikhail Bakhtin's work moved narrative theory further by emphasizing the dialogic heteroglossia extent in human discourse and in the range of discursive structures evident within prose fiction; however, even the greater inclusivity of diverse voices within a Bakhtinian interpretive framework is nevertheless based upon the oppositional linearity inherent to discursive structures. As David L. Moore points out, "dialogic survival, unlike dialectic synthesis, maintains difference within the dynamics of opposition" (17). While the points of opposition are more numerous and more diverse, thereby insuring the inclusion of more and diverse voices, this inclusion is still at the expense of those voices seen to be silent, less significant, or absent—still largely the case for Native American voices (literary and lived). Moore is quite correct in noting that "a dialogic moves toward relationality" (18). Bakhtin's work does move us closer to the relational intersubjectivity achievable through a conversive critical method.

Other Native critics have responded to the possibilities within postmodern criticisms for reading Native American literatures. While Gerald Vizenor hails the arrival of postmodernity, seeing it as a fitting critical position for contemporary mixed-blood trickster writers whom he refers to as "postindian warriors of survivance," Louis Owens points out significant distinctions between a postmodern agenda and the aims of Native writers:

> Ultimately, whereas postmodernism celebrates the fragmentation and chaos of experience, literature by Native American authors tends to seek transcendence of such ephemerality and the recovery of "eternal and immutable" elements represented by a spiritual tradition that escapes historical fixation, that places humanity within a carefully, cyclically ordered cosmos and gives humankind irreducible responsibility for the maintenance of that delicate equilibrium.

(20)

Owens' point is well taken, even though a number of contemporary Native writers such as Gerald Vizenor have experimented with avantgarde postmodern literary styles and aims in order to convey their own mixed backgrounds and multiplicitous perspectives. Vizenor's recent volume, *Manifest Manners: Postindian Warriors of Survivance,* ostensibly postmodern and poststruc-tural, nevertheless demonstrates conversive literary structures in his fluid movements between creative fiction, literary essay, and literary criticism. Throughout the work, diverse voices are interwoven (sometimes comfortably; at other times startlingly, and thereby effectively) in a remarkable postindian trickster discourse.

In a discussion of philosophical method, Ludwig Wittgenstein writes, "In philosophy it is not enough to learn in every case, *what* is to be said about a subject, but also *how* one must speak about it" (*Remarks on Colour* 23e). In other words, rather than focusing on the content of our analyses, often the problem is more deeply rooted within our methods of analysis. Wittgenstein goes on to point out, "One must always be prepared to learn something *totally* new" (23e). In this essay, I provide a brief introduction to a categorically new critical approach that illuminates conversive literary structures in texts and applies a conversive literary critical method. The notion of conversivity emphasizes both the orality of Native American Indian literatures (and which I believe is a part of all literatures, albeit to varying degrees) and the transformative power of language (in the very real sense of conversion, change, a turning from and towards). What is notably new here is that this method is developed through a conversation with the Native texts and traditions themselves. The development and the practice of this method is inherently consultative in that its origins are to be found in a conjoint effort of Western and Native voices—not the forced imposition of Western critical strategies upon Native literatures. The method is directly informed by the method and practice of the oral storytelling tradition.

Points of emphasis include: (1) an intersubjective relationality that privileges relationality and thereby problematizes the self-focused individual, (2) the realization that signs and objects are not divorced from one another (or in other words, a recognition of the presence of signifying objects and objective signifiers), (3) the recognition of subjects and objects in relation to various centering forces (a fact that shifts geometric descriptions away from Euclidean linearity, as in the case of semiotic triangles, and towards non-Euclidean elliptic geometries), (4) the written as an extension of the oral (with varying degrees of orality or conversiveness reflected in any [Native or non-Native] text), (5) the very real transformative power of conversivity, (6) the recognition of individuality and that significance as manifested in varying degrees of relationality, (7) authorial presence asserted through an intentional marginalization that emphasizes the center and privileges self in relation to that center, and (8) the presence and importance of a participatory [audience]—placed in brackets by virtue of the listeners'/readers' active participation.

The necessary brevity of an article necessitates that each of these descriptive elements of a conversive method cannot be discussed in length. Instead, the remainder of this essay will demonstrate the ways in which literary critics can move to work with texts through a conversive method that shifts the critic away from a critical hegemony over literary texts and toward the humbler role of a guide who enables other readers to find their ways to, into, and within the literatures discussed.[3] The literary critic serves very much the same role as a storyteller who relates a story which s/he feels is significant for her or his audience. With each telling, the story changes to maintain its significance for the listener(s). Certain basics, however, do not change. This could be described through Wittgenstein's language game image in which fundamental grammatical rules cannot be changed without altering the game itself; however, on the surface level of play, one can move quite freely and flexibly (albeit within the bounds of the base rules). Insofar as literary criticism is concerned, what this signifies is that one does not alter the essential story, the literature, one does not lie about the text, but rather one must tell the story accurately, honestly and completely. But how we tell that critical story can take many forms based on our audiences, our intentions behind telling our critical stories, and our own interactions with the literatures (interactions that reflect our intersubjective relations with the voices and subjects of the texts).

The conversiveness of Native texts reflects the oral traditions of the writers' particular tribal backgrounds. Anna Lee Walters points out that "the points of reference in oral tradition from which [Navajo writers write] . . . are not recently contrived inventions or devices incorporated into the works here simply for literary purposes or effects" (viii). An example Walters notes is from Della Frank's poem "T'aa Diné Nishli." While a literal translation of the title and ending line of the poem would read, "I am Navajo," the English translation cannot even begin to convey the depth and history signified in the Navajo statement, "T'aa Diné nishli." First of all, the prioritized subjectivity in the English sentence that begins with the first person referent "I" is absent in the Navajo sentence. Rather than first emphasizing herself and then describing herself in terms of her tribal affiliation, Frank's Navajo sentence emphasizes the reality of the tribe and *then* identifies her in terms of the tribe. Within the Navajo sentence, there is no independent first person singular pronoun that refers to the speaker. The reality of the speaker of the sentence is contingent upon her relationship to the tribe, the "sh" first person marker being evident only within the connective relationship noted in the verb. Even in this simple, yet profound, statement, we see the conversive interaction between individual and tribe— the individual speaking her reality as a Navajo, yet that very speech being informed by the reality of the tribe, a

reality that in turn is realized and informed through Frank's utterance and inscription. Elaine Jahner comments on this intertwining of individual and tribe, "most of [today's Native American] writers have established and depend on an especially close relation between the writer, the work, and the traditional community—a relation that determines the contextual semantics of the work and therefore shapes the author's options regarding text structure" ("Indian Literature" 7).

A closer look at several poems by Navajo women writers will demonstrate how they convey within the bounds of the English language (at times switching to the Navajo language where there is no adequate English equivalent) their own worldviews and realities. These writers do not present their perspectives to their readers as outsiders reading and critiquing the poems as poetic objects. Instead, through a conversive engagement between and across events, times, and persons (including the writers of the poems, the persons in the poems, and the readers of the poems), these writers invite their readers into the Navajo worlds of their poems much as a friend would be invited into one's home. And the conversive reading of these poems involves a responsibility on the part of the reader much as any person would have certain responsibilities as a guest in someone else's home (and analogously as the listener of a story would have responsibilities as a participant in a storytelling event).

Conversive structures are evident not only within literary texts. Conversive structural relationships also exist between the different literary works of one writer, between a literary text and its writer, audience, and/or critic, and between different writers and their literary texts. This last conversive relationship can be seen through a pairing of Nia Francisco's poem "Naabeeho Women with Blue Horses" and Luci Tapahonso's poem **"Blue Horses Rush In."** Tapahonso and Francisco grew up together in Shiprock, New Mexico and were friends. They are both familiar with each other's work, and it was Tapahonso who gave the introduction for Francisco when she gave a reading of her poetry at the University of New Mexico in 1988. But regardless of the interpersonal history of Tapahonso and Francisco, the interliterary historicity of their writing is evident within the conversive structures of these two poems. Francisco's poem is the earlier of the two, having appeared in her 1988 volume, *Blue Horses for Navajo Women.*

In the poem, "Naabeeho Women with Blue Horses" (27-29), the image and reality of blue horses are inextricably linked to the capacity of Navajo women to successfully traverse the changes of the world and of their own lives. As Francisco writes, "Devotees of Holy Ones [say] . . . that we Naabeeho women with blue horses must be ready / for the great storms to pass thru our lives during our middle ages / . . . to be the protectors of the younger generations." The blue horses signify the Navajo women's connection with the sacred, their connection with older ways ("the great secret of old women / medicinal ways of knowing") as a means of preparing and empowering them to live in the present and into the future worlds. The second stanza of the poem focuses on the physical, mental, emotional, and spiritual destruction of alcohol. Francisco immediately responds to this stanza with a direct question to other Navajo women and to herself (and, as well, directly to her readers) as she asks, "Are we preparing? getting decorated dressing up young Naabeeho women / for the passing of age no one warned us of. . . ." And as in the oral tradition of storytelling, Francisco's question invites her reader into an imagined listener's vocalized response, "Yes, yes," "Ah yaa ah." Here we see not only Francisco's openly engaging conversive style that speaks directly to her reader, but further, in the open-ended and inclusive first-person plural pronoun "we," Francisco graciously includes her readers with herself and with other Navajo women—not in the sense that a non-Navajo or male reader can read herself or himself into the category "Navajo women," but in the sense that Francisco offers and expects the same responsibility for the future and for future generations—not only of herself and other Navajo women, but also of any reader of this poem. As Leslie Silko reminds us, it is not an omniscient storyteller-narrator who relates the story, but rather the storyteller who serves "to draw the story out of the listeners" or, in a written domain, the readers (57).

The fourth stanza continues the conversive structure of the poem in its direct parallel with the previous stanza's beginning query: "Are we preparing?" The fourth stanza begins, "Must we talk about our tasks or our fastings. . . ." Here, the poem, as in the earlier stanza, responds and converses with itself, with Francisco, with the reader: "let's talk about the tiny piñon nuts [mythically and historically significant for the Navajo with important roles in a number of stories] . . . tell our stories until White Dawn yellow corn meal for female / white corn meal for male in prayer." Traditional oral stories and ceremony conversively engage with the complexities of contemporary poetry and the real world concerns of alcoholism, sexual relationships, Indian religious conflicts with Christian doctrine, and the changing needs of the younger generations. For Francisco, the changes of the world need not be seen in an inevitably discursive, or at the least an unharmonious, relationship. The difficulties and complexities of the world are one-half of a reality that necessarily involves both good *and* evil, both health and disease. The balance of these elements, like the balance between day and night, is crucial to the functioning of societies, peoples, and persons. Francisco notes the non-Navajo oppositionality in her contrast between "fleshy desires or christian woes." But "Naabeeho women with blue horses," women who straddle worlds and who work to conversively interweave those worlds through telling their stories, are those who sleep a "sleep that rested."

Throughout the final stanza, Francisco conversively interweaves these worlds, referring to the mythical and traditional blue horses in the first line, then referring to a woman birthing a new life (her own or that of her child or both)—an image and reality that equally apply to all time (knitting past, present, and future together through a reference that also points to mythic births and mother figures). The third line of this stanza refers to "every woman who selfishly took from her lover's hand . . ."; the reference and diction ("lover's") plant us firmly in the present, but this clause is conversively continued in the subsequent and final line that clarifies that what is taken from the lover's hand is a "brand new / turquoise necklace." In the poem's ending, we've come full circle, with the traditional and mythical significance of turquoise interwoven with a contemporary (and/or mythical) lover and his necklace—an image and story that equally applies today, yesterday, and tomorrow. And in the woman's desire for the turquoise necklace, we see her misplaced longing for the turquoise or blue horses of myth transferred to the materiality of a necklace—the necklace serving as the divorced object of her desire and the sign of her discursive longing for subjective status in relation to the objectified turquoise. While it is not clear that the woman locates her desire for the necklace within the realm of myth, Francisco, however, does so for her readers by conversively intertwining the material desire with the larger and more profound lack of blue horses.

Francisco's conversive tone and structure make it clear that the domain of the sacred which is foundational to the traditional and everyday empowerment of the Navajo (and, insofar as the Navajo are concerned, of any human being) is as real and concrete as a turquoise necklace and blue horses. And as one would expect in a conversational style, the ending is not the linear conclusion of a narrative that begins with a title and first line and extends directly towards its concluding statement or image. Instead the last line of this poem continually points beyond its literary boundaries to a reality and worldview that posits the essential connections between the future and past, both of which necessarily inform the present, and which, for the Navajo, are as real as the present is for Western linear narratives. The poem circles back on itself, showing us the nonlinearity, holism, and welcoming inclusivity of Francisco's Navajo worldview.

Tapahonso's poem, **"Blue Horses Rush In,"** the first poem in her recent volume *Sáanii Dahataał: The Women Are Singing,* demonstrates this conversive style in her poem's continuation of the themes, images, and hopes raised in Francisco's poem and in other nonliterary oral stories. Both Tapahonso and Francisco empha-size the interwoven images of blue horses and women: Francisco in entitling her book *Blue Horses for Navajo Women,* and Tapahonso in beginning her book of sing-ing women with the poem **"Blue Horses Rush In"** (1-2). The poem is dedicated to a very young Navajo woman, "Chamisa Bah Edmo who was born March 6, 1991." Throughout the poem, the image of "horses run-ning: / the thundering of hooves on the desert floor" represents the power and strength of women as they travel through their lives. The "thundering of hooves" and the "sound of horses running" are the prenatal sounds of the little girl's "heart pound[ing] quickly" as "she moved and pushed inside her mother." In a discus-sion of the conflict between "Christianity and tribal religious practices," Kimberly M. Blaeser points out that Native writers "appropriate" Western practices, thereby "investing [them] with a new interpretation" (13, 14). While I do not believe that the term "appropri-ate" conveys the adaptive *and,* at times, welcoming conversive realities of Native transformations of Western traditions, the interpretive newness of the Na-tive semiotics Blaeser alludes to is paramount. We see this sort of transformation as Tapahonso takes the mechanical sounds of a fetal monitor and transforms the sounds into the "thundering of hooves" heralding the arrival of Chamisa Bah Edmo into this world—the world of a hospital room transformed into a world of mythic significance.

The "thundering of hooves," immediately followed by the lines, "Her mother clenched her fists and gasped. / She moans ageless pain and pushes: This is it!," also emphasize that the image of blue horses also represents the power and strength of the mother birthing her baby. The reference to her pain as "ageless" communicates to the reader that this pain is real *and* mythic—a conjunc-tion that serves to underscore the profound significance of her pain, her strength as she pushes through pain, and her/their success, mother, baby daughter, family, tribal community. Tapahonso's conversive style shares this success and joy with her readers. Leslie Silko points out that in storytelling, there is a "kind of shared experi-ence [that] grows out of a strong community base" (57). While the community base within the Navajo tribal community is understandable, storyteller-poets like Luci Tapahonso speak and write to a broader audience, with no less commitment to the storytellers' responsibilities towards their readers' accessibility in/to their poems and stories. As the mother pushes, we read, "This is it!," as the excitement of success is communicated by Tapahonso and directly shared with us all.

In the next stanza, "Chamisa slips out, glistening wet and takes her first breath." This first breath, for the Navajo, signifies the beginnings of her spirit in this world, entering the baby as she inhales for the first time. Tapahonso shares this very personal and sacred

experience with her readers in the conversive style of a sharing between friends:

> Her father's eyes are wet with gratitude.
> He prays and watches both mother and baby—stunned.
>
> This baby arrived amid a herd of horses,
>   horses of different colors.

Tapahonso shares with her readers a father's tears, concerns, and thanks, and also his responsibilities to his wife and daughter as he prays—assisting and watching Chamisa's arrival into this world. This "herd of horses, / horses of different colors" represents the power of all the individuals involved, including the good wishes of family and friends. The different colors point to the dif-ferent directions, and each color is connected with a particular gender. East and yellow represent woman (as evidenced in Francisco's poem, "yellow corn meal for female"); west and white represent man ("white corn meal for male in prayer"). In Tapahonso's poem, we see the father in prayer, read about different horses "thundering" assistance (mechanical, medical, human, familial, mythic, sacred) for the birth. From the father and other men, "White horses ride in on the breath of the wind"—this breath that brings life and spirit to Chamisa.

Tapahonso tells us that horses arrive from each of the four sacred directions, demonstrating the wholeness and sacredness of this birth—a sacredness that is the domain of any birth, but here we see the circle complete with horses arriving from each direction. Each of the direc-tions represents one gender. South and the color blue represent the female: "Blue horses rush in, snorting from the desert in the south. / . . . Bah, from here your grandmothers went to war long ago." Nia Francisco asks in her poem, "Are we preparing?" Tapahonso answers Francisco's question in this poem in which we see the preparations and tasks performed for the baby's first change of life in this world; we hear the baby's pounding heart, her mother's moans and father's prayers; we watch their efforts to insure the strength of Chamisa's beginning. After describing the arrival of the horses from each direction, Tapahonso ends the poem:

> Chamisa, Chamisa Bah. It is all this that you are.
> You will grow: laughing, crying,
> and we will celebrate each change you live.
>
> You will grow strong like the horses of your past.
> You will grow strong like the horses of your birth.

And this strength that is and will be Chamisa's comes not only from the efforts of those in her present world, but also from those who came before, her "grandmoth-ers [who] went to war long ago"—the blue horses of her past, those "Naabeeho women with blue horses." The conversation of life continues across generations and even beyond temporality and into the domain of myth where real historical grandmothers rode mythical blue horses through the journeys of their long lives.

Gertrude Walters notes in her short poem "Shimásání (Grandmother)": "Shimásání, you have traveled a long way—. . . Giving / Love / Protection / Understanding" (Anna Lee Walters 110). And these long travels, carried by the blue horses of myth, faith, and lived history are those which serve to guide and protect the younger and future generations: "Shimásání, . . . / Here I sit / Watching you / . . . / Trying hard to taste your life / Shimásání. . . ." Walters' poem joins the continuing intergenerational conversation of Navajo women explicitly framed in the form of a granddaughter's direct address to her grandmother. While the conversive structures of American Indian, and in this case Navajo, poetry need not take the overt forms of a second person direct address, in "Shimásání" this is the case. The reader is "other" to this poem, overhearing the granddaughter's words (or thoughts) directed to her grandmother and to herself, but shared with the reader, much as a private and personal conversation might be shared with a friend, relative, or trusted acquaintance who happens to be present. Thereby, Walters invites her reader to identify with her and the granddaughter of the poem in their love of, respect for, and gratefulness to *bimásání* (their grandmother).

The poem begins and ends with the same line, "Shimásání, you have traveled a long way—." The dashes that end each of these lines provide a longer pause, much as the storyteller pauses on occasion to allow time for the listeners' responses (vocalized and silent). In an analysis of the interactive aspects of the storytelling process, Susan Pierce Lamb writes, "The interaction between teller and listener is simultaneous, thus reliant on right brain processing" (15). Through the openness and inclusivity of Walters' conversive style, the reader joins the granddaughter in "Trying hard to taste" the long life of "Shimásání." Of course, if the reader happens to be an old woman, then the poem is, as well, conversively directed to her as recipient of the younger woman's descriptive and actual respect and gratitude.

Two other poems focusing on childbirth, by Tapahonso and Esther G. Belin respectively, join in the conversation of these earlier poems, developing and deepening the thoughts, words, and experiences of all the poems. Unlike a discursive or dialogic structure in which each poem or individual asserts its or her own subjectivity and primacy at the expense of others, within a conversive style (both literary and critical), the poems and writers comment upon each other, developing conversations within and beyond the written bounds of each poem. Navajo writers like Tapahonso, Francisco, Walters, and Belin write from and of their own lived experiences, which are informed by their cultural heritages which in turn assume a very real connection with the sacred. For these writers, this connection is manifested in a conversive writing style that points beyond the narrow limits of the writers' lived experiences in this world. The worlds of their poems conversively conjoin the worlds of their lives, the worlds of their people (the tribal reality of the Diné) today, historically, and into the future, and within the timeless world of the sacred. In contrast to the Navajo perception of the interdependency of these worlds, a Western orientation posits sharply delineated distinctions between these worlds, often seen in a competitively fearful framework that opposes individual and group against each other, the temporal material world against a transcendent spiritual world, and a chronological delimitation that either focuses on the present without the recognition of the present's integral interrelationship with both past and future, or recognizes such an interrelationship but privileges the present as the strong vanquisher of a weaker past. Conversely, these poems speak and depict worlds that interact and overlap, not in competition, but in an open engagement unthreatened by the diversity inherent within conversive relations (be those between and among individuals, poems, or worlds). This intermingling of worlds can be seen in Belin's "Bringing Hannah Home" (Anna Lee Walters 18-19).

In the poem, Belin shares with her reader the very private and cultural experience of the burial of a child's placenta. Navajos believe and know that a child will always return to this place that contains the initial source of the child's lifeblood. Belin begins her poem in a very personal conversive style, as if she is sharing the poem and story with a close friend: "we brought hannah home today." Instead of referring to the baby in the objective tone more familiar within Western discourse (e.g., "We brought the baby home today"), Belin personalizes and subjectifies the baby in naming her. And in this naming, and in the first person plural pronoun "we," Belin brings the reader into the personal world of the poem. The reader is expected to know to whom the "we" refers and to know who Hannah is. And even if the reader, by chance and in all likelihood, is not familiar with Hannah nor with those who have brought her home, Belin does not leave the reader in the dark as outsider. After a short first stanza, the very next stanza begins with the needed clarification, "two women with a child and a shovel and a frozen placenta . . . hannah was brought into this world / some say fourth others say fifth / five days before. / before we brought her home." Within Belin's conversive style, reader, speaker, and subjects of the poem are interwoven in a conversation that traverses diverse worlds, times, realities (literary and lived), and persons.

As the two women dig into the ground, the speaker of the poem shares her thoughts and prayers with the reader. In the digging, this woman (aunt, friend, other relative?) remembers another and more difficult digging—that of her father's grave dug into and from the frozen ground of a reservation winter. Within the poem, Belin interweaves the two changes of worlds, Hannah's entry into and a father's departure from this world:

> i thought good thoughts for hannah and her mother
> and prayed for us all
> remembering those who have passed on and those to
>   be born
> and i thought of my children to be born
> and i thought of my father who has passed on.

Even in the immediacy of the burial of Hannah's placenta and her return home (from a hospital or other place of birth), the speaker's prayers (prayers offered by Belin, Hannah's relatives and friends, the poem's persona, and the reader) for Hannah and her mother are also for us all, here now, here before, and here to come. Prayers rooted in the concrete here and now also transcend the limitations of time and space and conversively bespeak an inclusivity inherent within the worldview of the poem. Even in Belin's lack of capitalization, especially in the lower case "i," we see the conversive focus and privileging of the other rather than of oneself.

We converse with, not to, some other person or persons, and within the bounds of a conversation, we speak with the expectation and hope of the "other's" assertion of her or his subjectivity as manifested in a response which in turn points beyond the individual speaking self and to the importance and reality of the listener. This is categorically different from the dialectic, discursive, or dialogic structures that privilege the subjectivity of a speaker with the passive objectivity of the listener who only gains subjectivity through his or her own speech. For the Navajo, activity is acknowledged both within speech and within thought. And within a Navajo conversive style as evidenced in these poems, writers and speakers write and speak in a manner that serves to privilege themselves and their words through the primacy given to their readers and listeners. However, such a conversive style involves the responsibility of the reader or listener to respond in turn and in kind. This is not a reader-response critical approach in which the reader completes the poem (and thereby gains a position of privilege), but a conversive response in which reader/listener continues a conversation that began generations and ages before the actual writing and that will continue into the future—as in the case of the thoughts and prayers "for us all / remembering those who have passed on and those to be born." As Rodney Frey points out, "When a story is being told it is being relived, participated in by those assembled. History unfolds anew" (129). Through the conversive structures present in Belin's poem, her readers actually enter the world and the story of Hannah's homecoming.

Belin ends the poem with Hannah's mother taking "the frozen mass of tissue and blood and life" out of its plastic bag and aluminum foil and placing it in the hole. The poem concludes, "and i felt her heat of tissue and blood and life / squatting with bloodied hands and cold earth / bringing hannah home." The pronoun "her," whose syntactical antecedent is "hannah's mother" but whose "heat of tissue" as well refers to Hannah and also to the female speaker's physical response to the ceremony, presents a conversive ambiguity that in one word, "her," brings the three females together in a homecoming profoundly significant for each: Hannah's arrival in this world and homecoming from the hospital, a mother's new life with her baby daughter ceremonially brought home, the speaker's homecoming with Hannah, Hannah's mother, and her deceased father. This intergenerational and interpersonal homecoming demonstrates the dynamism, fluidity, and inclusivity possible within conversively structured poems.

Tapahonso's **"It Has Always Been This Way"** (17-18) contributes to this conversation, adding her perspective on a Navajo birth. "Being born is not the beginning. / Life begins months before the time of birth"—not only during the baby's life in the mother's womb but also in the lives and generations that precede the baby's life and that inform the lives of both baby and mother. This is explained in the Beck, Walters, and Francisco volume, *The Sacred*:

> In the days before pick-ups, cars and hospitals, the whole process of having a baby was a ritual—with the help of a Hataali (singer or medicine man) and a midwife—there were songs sung, spreading of fresh soil, sprinkling of corn pollen, stretching of the sash belt, and untying of tied knots, and letting hair down. Long ago, childbirth was considered a beautiful real life struggle and it was a ritual with the sacred beings watching on.
>
> (272)

And yet, in the worlds of these poems, the sacredness of new life is respected even within the domain of contemporary hospital rooms. The weight given to the importance of new life also signifies particular responsibilities given to the mother before and after the actual birth, and these responsibilities for the Navajo are neither privatized nor individualistic but involve the participation of extended family and even the larger tribal community, both of which are expected to insure that the mother is enabled to fulfill her responsibilities—which might mean other individuals taking on some of her other chores or jobs.

Tapahonso also explains the burial of the placenta: "It is buried near the house so the child / will always return home and help the mother. / It has been this way for centuries among us." In this burial, we see the significant conjunction of the personal and private with the communal and public, the specific and material with the sacred and the symbolic, and one baby's spatial connection with her mother's home and the love and care of parents and other relatives for a new child. Even the beginnings of life define the circular domain of the conversive for this particular Navajo baby: "Much care is taken . . . to talk and sing to the baby softly in the right way." And the importance of vocalization is emphasized from a child's earliest sounds. The first laugh of the child is conversively responded to by the family members and their celebratory "give-away":

> The baby laughs aloud and it is celebrated with rock
>   salt,
> lots of food, and relatives laughing.
> Everyone passes the baby around.
> This is so the child will always be generous,
>   will always be surrounded by happiness,
> and will always be surrounded by lots of relatives.
> It has been this way for centuries among us.
>
>   (17)

The child's happy vocalized laugh is framed within a conversive engagement in which the emphasis is not on the subjective vocalizing or laughing individual as an objective end; rather, the speech and laughter are viewed as a gift from the child which is offered to those whose response is, in turn, one of giving rock salt and food as gifts to others. With the circularity of a conversive structure, one can only return to one's own point on the circle by going via the other points.

The subjective and self-referential privileging possible within linear oppositions (in which an objective world is defined and understood solely in terms of a subjective and privileged point of orientation) is in sharp contrast to a conversive circularity in which each point is privileged always but never at the expense of any other point. From a Navajo perspective, the devaluation, marginalization, absence, or silence of any person or point on the circle would indicate an incomplete circle and an unfinished and partial conversation. As Robin Melting Tallow, a Native Canadian writer, points out, "the circle has neither beginning nor ending. It has always been. The circle represents the journey of human existence. It connects us to our past and to our future. . . . We are writing the circle" (288). Analogously, a criticism that is not conversively informed by the reality of the text it approaches is, as well, incomplete and partial—a writing that bespeaks more the structure of a monologue than of a multiply voiced conversive critical engagement between text and critic. Dennis and Barbara Tedlock have stressed the importance of "learning directly from the Indian." While their focus is ostensibly on the scholarship of anthropologists, their concerns are well taken in regards to literary criticism as well:

> It is true that anthropologists sometimes describe themselves as students of the Indian; they may indeed

appear to be his students while they are in the field, but by the time they publish their 'results,' it is usually clear that the Indian is primarily an *object* of study.

                                                     (xiii)

A conversive critical strategy places the critic within a conversation that includes critic, writer, text, and the larger context in which the text exists—without the individualized privileging of discursive or dialogic approaches. This involves a very direct interactive engagement between critic and text that in no wise privileges the assumed priority of the critic.

Wittgenstein taught us that a language game is a "form of life" (*Philosophical Investigations* 11). And Paula Gunn Allen echoes Wittgenstein's point when she writes, "Literature is one facet of a culture. The significance of a literature can be best understood in terms of the culture from which it springs" (54). Tapahonso makes this explicitly clear as she begins the final stanza of **"It Has Always Been This Way"**: "It is all this: the care, the prayers, songs, / and our own lives as Navajos we carry with us all the time" (18). The sacred, the communal, the tribal, the personal, the lived, and the living. Blue horses for Navajo women. As Tapahonso ends her poem, "It has been this way for centuries among us." For centuries, and even beyond into the atemporal and nonlinear domain of the timeless and the sacred.

If our aims are to read these poems and to accept the gracious invitations offered by these women poets, then we need to recognize that different words, languages, and worlds require different critical responses. As Jeanne Perreault and Sylvia Vance note in the "Foreword" to *Writing the Circle: Native Women of Western Canada*, "Conventional standards of literary excellence in no way prepare a reader for the complexity of responses the writing contained here will evoke. Readers will discover the limitations of their own reading practices" (xi). Paula Gunn Allen also comments on such difficulties: "The study of non-Western literature poses a problem for Western readers, who naturally tend to see alien literature in terms that are familiar to them, however irrelevant those terms may be to the literature under consideration" (54). Specifically in relation to Navajo poetry, the importance Navajos give to the use of language exhorts the critic to approach the poems and her or his criticism with an analogous degree of respect. As Gary Witherspoon points out, "It is through language that the world of the Navajo was created, and it is through language that the Navajos control, classify, and beautify their world" (7).

For the Navajo, language represents and affects the world—a fact that invites critics to conversively approach the writing of Navajo poets through an intersubjective relationality in which the texts are understood as speaking and, thereby, creative, signifying objects. Arnold Krupat argues for the importance of "an 'indigenous' criticism for Indian literatures" (*Ethnocriticism* 44). One step in that direction is a critical strategy in which Indian literatures are enabled to speak for themselves through a conversive method of criticism. The poems of Nia Francisco, Luci Tapahonso, Gertrude Walters, and Esther G. Belin suggest the value of such alternative critical strategies which enable readers and critics in consciously interactive and intersubjective engagements with the poems—thereby allowing the poems a critical space otherwise denied.[4] As Barney Blackhorse Mitchell says, "The greatest sacred thing is knowing the order and the structure of things" (qtd. in Beck, Walters, and Francisco, 11, 95, 107). Through a conversive criticism, we can come closer to discovering the order and the structures of and within Native literatures.[5]

Notes

1. For a developed discussion of the concept of critical fit or the appropriateness of particular critical approaches towards particular texts, see my volume, *Wittgenstein and Critical Theory*. While this volume specifically addresses the implications and applications of Ludwig Wittgenstein's philosophy for critical theory, the majority of the critical explications refer to Native American literatures.

2. Joseph Bruchac discusses the preponderance of mestizo/a Indian writers in an interview with Navajo poet Luci Tapahonso: "Many of the people in the 'first generation' of American Indian writers in this part of the century who have become well known are people of mixed blood" (Bruchac 278). Both Bruchac and Tapahonso comment on this as a necessary stage for fullblood and more traditionally raised Indians to begin writing and publishing.

3. I discuss this shifting role of the critic at greater length in my book, *Wittgenstein and Critical Theory*.

4. Although this essay specifically focuses on conversive strategies within several poems, the conversive nature of Navajo and other Native American Indian literatures tends to affect the critical process as well. Much of the literary criticism of Native American Indian texts demonstrates the critics' conversive responsiveness to the texts, rather than the critics' extraneous impositions of particular critical theories or methods upon those texts. Here I would suggest that there is much to be learned by the larger audience of critical theorists and literary critics from the actual methods and practice of scholars of Native literatures.

As a final note, I would like to add that a colleague, Jim Sullivan, pointed out the extent to which the tone of this critical essay changes as it begins to converse with the poems. Such shifts, albeit unintentional, are what we would expect and desire within a conversive critical practice.

5. I want to clarify that the reference to the concept of "structures" in no wise signifies the sorts of modernist constructs that poststructuralism rejects. The structures that Navajo elder Barney Blackhorse Mitchell notes are those relational structures that, in fact, exist in the world within and between peoples, other life forms, and things. For Mitchell, there are *real* connections in the world (as opposed to those connections artificially constructed) that can be learned and communicated through life and through stories.

Works Cited

Allen, Paula Gunn. *The Sacred Hoop: Recovering the Feminine in American Indian Traditions*. Boston: Beacon, 1986.

Beck, Peggy V., Anna Lee Walters, and Nia Francisco. *The Sacred: Ways of Knowledge, Sources of Life*. Tsaile: Navajo Community College P, 1992.

Belin, Esther G. "Bringing Hannah Home." Anna Lee Walters. 18-19.

Blaeser, Kimberly M. "Pagans Rewriting the Bible: Heterodoxy and the Representation of Spirituality in Native American Literature." *ARIEL: A Review of International English Literature* 25.1 (1994): 12-31.

Brill, Susan B. *Wittgenstein and Critical Theory: Moving Beyond Postmodern Criticism and Towards Descriptive Investigations*. Athens OH: Ohio U P, 1995.

Bruchac, Joseph, ed. *Survival This Way: Interviews with American Indian Poets*. Tucson: U of Arizona P, 1987.

Francisco, Nia. *Blue Horses for Navajo Women*. Greenfield Center NY: Greenfield Review, 1988.

Frey, Rodney. "Re-telling One's Own: Storytelling Among the Apsáalooke (Crow Indians)." *Plains Anthropologist* 28.100 (1983): 129-35.

Hunter, Carol. "American Indian Literature." *MELUS* 8.2 (1981): 82-85.

Jahner, Elaine. "A Critical Approach to American Indian Literature." *Studies in American Indian Literature: Critical Essays and Course Designs*. Ed. Paula Gunn Allen. New York: Modern Language Association of America, 1983. 211-24.

———. "Indian Literature and Critical Responsibility." *Studies in American Indian Literatures* 1.1 (1977): 3-7. Rpt. in *Studies in American Indian Literatures* 5.2 (1993): 7-12.

Krupat, Arnold. *Ethnocriticism: Ethnography, History, Literature.* Berkeley: U of California P, 1992.

———. "Identity and Difference in the Criticism of Native American Literature." *diacritics* 13.2 (1983): 2-13.

Lamb, Susan Pierce. "Shifting Paradigms and Modes of Consciousness: An Integrated View of the Storytelling Process." *Folklore and Mythology Studies* 5 (1981): 5-19.

Ludlow, Jeannie. "Working (In) the In-Between: Poetry, Criticism, Interrogation, and Interruption." *Studies in American Indian Literatures* 6.1 (1994): 24-42.

Melting Tallow, Robin. Afterword. Perreault and Vance. 288.

Moore, David L. "Decolonializing Criticism: Reading Dialectics and Dialogics in Native American Literatures." *Studies in American Indian Literatures* 6.4 (1994): 7-35.

Owens, Louis. *Other Destinies: Understanding the American Indian Novel.* Norman: U of Oklahoma P, 1992.

Perreault, Jeanne, and Sylvia Vance, comp. and eds. *Writing the Circle: Native Women of Western Canada.* Edmonton: NeWest, 1993.

Silko, Leslie Marmon. "Language and Literature from a Pueblo Indian Perspective." *English Literature: Opening Up the Canon.* Eds. Leslie Fielder and Houston Baker. Baltimore: Johns Hopkins U P, 1981. 54-72.

Tapahonso, Luci. *Sáanii Dahataał: The Women Are Singing.* Tucson: U of Arizona P, 1993.

Tedlock, Dennis, and Barbara Tedlock, eds. *Teachings from the American Earth: Indian Religion and Philosophy.* New York: Liveright, 1992.

Vizenor, Gerald. *Manifest Manners: Postindian Warriors of Survivance.* Hanover: Wesleyan U P, 1994.

Walters, Anna Lee, ed. *Neon Pow-Wow: New Native American Voices of the Southwest.* Flagstaff: Northland, 1993.

Walters, Gertrude. "Shimásání (Grandmother)." Anna Lee Walters. 110.

Witherspoon, Gary. *Language and Art in the Navajo Universe.* Ann Arbor: U of Michigan P, 1977.

Wittgenstein, Ludwig. *Philosophical Investigations.* Oxford: Basil Blackwell, 1984.

———. *Remarks on Colour.* Ed. G. E. M. Anscombe. Trans. Linda L. McAlister and Margarete Schattle. Berkeley: U of California P, 1977.

Luci Tapahonso with Andrea M. Penner (interview date fall 1996)

SOURCE: Tapahonso, Luci, and Andrea M. Penner. "The Moon Is So Far Away: An Interview with Luci Tapahonso." *SAIL: Studies in American Indian Literatures* 8, no. 3 (fall 1996): 1-12.

[*In the following interview, Tapahonso discusses the influence of Navajo oral traditions on her poetry.*]

I first became interested in Luci Tapahonso's work in 1988. At that time, she had three books of poetry to her credit: **One More Shiprock Night, Seasonal Woman,** and **A Breeze Swept Through.** In 1993, when I was writing my thesis on her work, "At Once, Gentle and Powerful: Voices of the Landscape in the Poetry of Luci Tapahonso," the University of Arizona Press had just published **Sáanii Dahataał: The Women are Singing,** a collection of Tapahonso's poetry and prose. That same year, I heard Luci read from that volume at Arizona State University. She was warmly received by the large audience that included many friends and family members. I was impressed by how deeply her words seemed to touch people's emotions; we were moved alternately to tears and laughter as we listened to her poems, songs, and stories. At the two readings I have attended since then, she has had a similar effect on her listeners, although the works read were quite different. Tapahonso's versatility as a poet and writer of short prose, both fiction and non-fiction, is part of what makes her so accessible to a wide audience. Yet she maintains, in all her work, a connection to all that is Navajo: the people, the land, and the stories.

Currently living away from the Navajo reservation where she grew up and still has family, Tapahonso is Associate Professor at the University of Kansas, in Lawrence, where she teaches poetry, both theory and writing, and literature. For the past couple of years, in the spring, Tapahonso has conducted poetry workshops for women in the community, their registration fees benefiting the local Indian Center. This spring she plans to volunteer her time leading poetry workshops at a women's shelter and at a home for troubled adolescents.

Her current writing projects include *Hayoołkaał* (Dawn): *An Anthology of Navajo Writers,* soon to be published by the University of Arizona Press. She is also working on a new volume of poetry and an autobiography.

I recently visited Luci Tapahonso at her home in Lawrence, Kansas. Tapahonso's home is warm and comfortable. There is evidence of "family" everywhere: there are two walls full of family photographs (one in the kitchen, one in the living room) and her grandchildren's art work adorns the refrigerator. As we sat in the kitchen talking, just after I arrived, chicken and dumplings simmered on the stove, country tunes spilled softly from a radio in the corner, and red chile-shaped lights glowed on their cord around the kitchen window. We talked about the University of New Mexico and

University of Kansas English departments, people we both know, classes, students, and our families. We told stories, laughed, and made plans for our brief time together.

The interview recorded here took place the following day, November 4, 1995, after we had spent the morning leisurely breakfasting at the Paradise Cafe (so leisurely, in fact, that we forgot to turn on the tape recorder) and then driving around Lawrence. The driving tour included a visit to Haskell Indian Nations University (formerly, Haskell Indian Junior College). For the actual interview, we sat at her kitchen table and filled up a sixty-minute tape. In transcribing the tape, I deleted most of the conversational and unnecessary additives, such as "you know" and "really." What remains is, for the most part, verbatim.

The University of New Mexico Office of Graduate Studies, through a Research, Project and Travel Grant, provided the funds for my trip, enabling me to conduct this interview as part of my graduate study of Native American literature. I am grateful for their support.

[*Penner*]: *I am particularly interested in the women in your poetry. What is the role of women in matrilineal/ matrilocal culture? Do they participate in storytelling any differently than men?*

[Tapahonso]: The roles of men and women in Navajo culture, in terms of sharing stories, or talking, seem to me to be the same; they're not really different. One way in which the roles might be different would be in ritual or ceremonial contexts in which the man, the *hataałii*, is the central medicine person. There are women who have those roles, too, but it seems like there are more men than women, depending on where you're at. I know on our part of the reservation there are mostly men. Every time we need a medicine person we go to a man. So in that context it might be a little different because they re-enact, or they retell, different parts of the creation story. They are very structured, and very strict about it; there are fixed texts that are never changed. But that's different from when people are just talking and sitting around.

That reminds me of what you were telling me this morning, about how you used to go with your parents for a walk and they would tell stories. Both of them told you stories as you walked at night, under the stars.

Yes, it's valued, equally; like when you're sitting around the table, or going for a long drive. And I think the role of women in matrilineal/matrilocal cultures doesn't mean that women necessarily have a higher status. I think the status is higher than in American society, but I think it's equal to men's roles; both have equal weight. There's a saying in Navajo, on the other hand, that says the home revolves around the woman; beauty extends from the woman. And there's a whole song, there's a whole story, that goes with that in which they say the fire is the center of the home. Everything comes out of the fire. But they also refer to the fire as the woman; from the woman, everything comes. Everything that has to do with the home and the house revolves around her and everybody, the children as well as men, all respect that and hold the woman in high esteem.

In traditional culture, or even like with my own family, my mother is the person who keeps everything together. She's the oldest female, and everybody respects her. Whatever she says goes, and she is in charge of everything. You can go to her for advice, or ask her for help if you need help. On the other hand, you can help her, too. There are people who, the older they get, are seen in these really esteemed and respected roles. My father is very much the same way, but my father, as I was growing up, didn't ever contradict my mother. Everything was always up to my mother. He always said, "Ask your mother. Whatever your mother thinks is okay with me." He went along with whatever my mother said. My brothers are the same way in their marriages, too. And I think, in a sense, with Bob and me it's like that. There are not any major decisions made—I don't think Bob would think of that—without me! If I have to make a decision on my own, he pretty much goes along with what I say. So the roles are equal in that way. Men, I think, in Navajo culture, are much more expected to take part in household, domestic chores than men in American society. It's really looked down upon to have a man sitting watching television while around him people are really working, or doing things; the relatives always say, "Make yourself useful." The man should go outside and find something to do; go chop wood, or rake the yard, or do something, but don't just sit around like you're the king of the house, 'cause you're not! [We both laugh!] That's the case, too, that men are more active in cooking, cleaning, and being really involved in taking care of children. I've seen that with my brothers, my father, and with my marriage, too; it seems natural that the men are really good cooks, and the boys are taught the same way, too. Those are some differences that over the years I've become aware of from talking with friends. I realize that the way we do things is different.

*What about relationships between men and women? I am thinking, in particular, of poems like "**Raisin Eyes,**" in which you talk about single women dealing with relationships. That seems to me to be a recurring theme in your work.*

I don't know if there's really a comment or statement that is being made. Maybe it's just more recognizing the relationships, saying, this is the way things are. There are a lot of women, I mean people who are my own friends, my own relatives, my sisters, that are involved in relationships. The relationships are somehow different than other people's. In some sense they are unique in that they're Indian, and for that reason they're somehow different. It's not really pointing out how that is, or why that is, just that these relationships exist.

Your poetry and fiction often present life the way it is. You seem interested in everyday life.

As for the daily lives of characters, those are probably drawn from my own life, and my sisters'. A lot of my work is really based on and embodied in a whole network of relationships I have.

Are the characters that appear in your work originally someone you know, or knew, and give a different name to?

Sometimes that happens. I always change names. But sometimes the characters evolve on their own. I might notice something, or hear something, and I just begin with that and it turns into something else I'm not aware of at the beginning. I just know there's this idea I want to play with. I remember one time, a long time ago, we were at the Window Rock Fair. It was really crowded, and we were standing in line at the Civic Center, waiting to see George Strait. As we were waiting to go in, everyone was talking to each other, and I remember there were these women in front of us. They were talking about another woman that was with them, and for some reason I was half-listening to them, and half-listening to my sisters. They were mostly talking in Navajo, but every once-in-a-while they would say things in English. One of the things they said in English really struck me, and I took it and began writing about it. They were talking about this girl; her name was something like Sheila, or Shirley, or Sheryl. They were saying, "Oh, that Shirley, she's just like that." Another one said, "Yeah, you got to really be careful what you say around her because she's from Shonto." And then one said, "She's real shy, and you really got to watch yourself around her." Immediately they all agreed and then they turned to something else; and I just thought, for some reason, that alliteration was so neat. "She . . . Shonto . . . Shirley . . . shy . . . ," and so I started with that and then it just evolved into something else completely.

So you hear things, and for some reason you think, "that's really good." That's how I know. I'm really aware of the fact that, just in ordinary language, Navajo people have a real gift for language. They move back and forth between languages, in some cases, not knowing a lot of English, but knowing enough to pick the precise word that they need; knowing enough so it's not all cluttered, they just say exactly what they need to say.

When you hear or see something that strikes you in a particular way, do you say to yourself, "Oh, I need to remember that"? Do you quickly write it down before you forget, or is it the kind of thing you can mentally hold on to?

I remember it, but I do write a lot. I have a journal I write in every day, usually at night, sometimes in the morning, but like this [she shows me her journal] was last night; I write before I go to sleep. Last night I was writing about the moon. Did you see the moon? It was really far away. I thought, the moon is *so* far away. How come it seems far? At home I remember it closer. I was looking at it thinking, it's really far away from us. I was writing about how it seems far, and I was writing about how at home I remember seeing the Yé'ii Bicheii dance, and the moon was just right there. It seems closer there. But last night it was really far away; it's sad. And sometime early this morning I woke up and it was shining into the room; and I was thinking, it's not really that far!

Do you deliberately choose to write "about" certain things?

I don't think I do. If I do it doesn't work. Like this story I was telling you about? [At breakfast that morning, Luci had told me a long story, a composite of another woman's experience and her own; she has been trying to write the story for months.] I wanted to do it; it's not working, so I'm just going to let it go. It's better if I just have a sense of it and go with it. It works out better if I don't know what's going to happen.

Is there a relationship between the stories and the songs that appear in your work?

Do you mean the actual song, or do you mean the mention of songs?

*I hadn't considered the distinction. I suppose I am thinking, for example, about **"The Motion of Songs Rising"**—there are both old stories, and stories that are sung right there.*

Have you heard that, orally? There is a song that goes with that. It's about the Yé'ii Bicheii. It's really about the way that I see the whole concept of ceremony relating to me as an individual. But it's also a mutual outpouring of gratitude from myself for this, but I realize, also, on the other hand, that the Yé'iis, the holy ones, are really old, they're just ageless, so they return and they're happy to see us even though we're real different than the way we were 200 years ago; we're very different, but the essence of who we are, the essence of ourselves, is really still Navajo. And then I understand that—I feel like crying when I think about it—it makes you think about everything that's happened to Indian people, and specifically to Navajo people, everything that they tried didn't work. . . . Every time we go home, probably every three or four months, we always have prayers done for us, or some kind of ceremony, because we've been over here around non-Navajos all the time. So when we go back we always have something done for us. That's what the medicine man always tells us: "the main thing you have to remember is that you're Navajo," he says. "Some people when they get old, sometimes when they're elderly, they don't know why, but they just don't feel right; there's something missing. They can't understand why, but something's not right. So they get mean, they get grouchy, they just strike out and say things to people; something's not settled for them. They know they're at the end of their life and something's gone wrong, but they don't know what it is." He said, "that's what happens, that can happen to a person when they stray away from their original religion. . . . When every person is born, they're given a belief system and a religion to believe in; those two should go together throughout their lives. It makes your life complete to have something to believe in. Everybody," he said, "every person that's born is given that at the beginning of their lives. . . . At the end of your life, if you have stayed to that—you might stray, you might go away for awhile and come back—but as long as you have that," he said, "at the end of your life, whenever it is that you die, you're complete. You don't have any misgivings." He said that's why a lot of old Navajo people and elderly Indian people are always real cheerful; they play jokes, they're real humorous, they're happy, so they have a real good sense of humor. . . . "That's how you want to be," he said. "You were born a Navajo; the path is already there. Everything's there for you; all you have to do is follow it and know about it. . . . Then, that way, no matter what you do, no matter where you go, you always know, you're always clear on who you are."

So they always tell us things like that; we go back for that. But even if I was there I would do the same thing; that's the way my brothers and sisters are. That's really important, that feeling, when something happens that's jarring. Once my sister was driving and all of a sudden something ran out in front of her—she thought maybe it was a dog, a St. Bernard or something—but it ran in front of her and she had an accident. Right away she had something done for her. So when things like that happen, someone breaks into your house, you have something done right away. The ceremony puts your life back into place. So even if I was there I would be doing the same thing. It's because of that sense of the order, the sense of the way things are supposed to be, the right way of doing things, the way life is supposed to be—you know when it's not right—we have a whole myriad of things that can be done about it. You just have to be aware and know how to go about doing it and getting help. I think that of course, then, in doing

that, there are certain songs, prayers. So those come into my work, because they are part of my ordinary life, not a separate kind of thing. That's why, I'm sure, all these things are really important. I feel real fortunate to have that, but at the same time know that I can function in an academic atmosphere, which is really different! It helps to have a base to operate from.

That shows how strong those stories and songs are, to sustain you, even this far away, in such a different environment.

I am really dependent on prayer for everything. I don't do anything without really praying about it first; that's a constant state for me, to always be prayerful. It's really important. And I think I would be like that in another field, too, if I was a writer or not; it's just being immersed. I don't know how it would be not to have that.

Just as the songs and stories you grew up with are woven into the fabric of your life, so the language of oral storytelling, singing, and praying is integral to your poetry. You use certain rhetorical strategies to create the effect of oral language, to replicate not only conversations, but storytelling. Please talk about these strategies—if you can identify them—and how you use them in your work.

It seems that most of my work begins in Navajo; the original ideas are in Navajo. Sometimes they aren't, but most of the time they begin in Navajo. Then, when I write them down, I write them in English. Where it's going to go from there, I'm not clear. Maybe it has to do with the material. I have some work . . . they all kind of begin at the same place, yet as they evolve and as they're being written, one might stay on a certain colloquial level, using ordinary, everyday Navajo syntax. . . . On the other hand, it might move to use English, but a heightened level of English.

More formal?

More formal, but at the same time it's still in a Navajo context. So, how that happens I'm not really sure. Maybe it depends on what I'm writing about, or the emotional quality behind it. I know that in the prose pieces that I've written, they're very much immersed— well maybe except for one or two—in intense emotion. They deal with emotional things that are mostly very painful, and yet they're bounded by order. Even though they're painful, they're redeemed; even though they're painful, they're brought back by extreme love. Those are pieces that can't be poems because the form doesn't allow it; I mean there is too much there to handle. When I begin to write, a lot of times I don't know if it's going to be a poem or prose; it just depends on what happens. Sometimes, when I read them aloud, depending on my audience, I get really involved, too; I relive the whole experience, even though it might not have been mine. But I have—I think, part of what is really important, is to be able to have—empathy for people, to understand the pain of another person, even if you haven't experienced what they have.

So, a lot of my work is clearly not my experience; the act of having written it is not the whole thing, but I have some sense of it. In those instances, it's important that people know about these stories because the person to whom it happened can't, that is, is not in a position to, tell, and so then I realize that part of why people are always telling me stories is because in a sense I have a capacity to tell. It's not that I'm a better story teller, or a better writer than they; it's that I have access that they don't.

The more of those kinds of stories you tell, the more people feel compelled to tell you, because you've entered into their world through what you have already told, through other people's stories. And they know you tell those stories with empathy, so they want to share with you, too, and it keeps going.

Yes. So, the way I see that, I understand that role, and I really have a lot of respect for the stories people tell me; in a way it's sort of odd, wherever I go, I always meet people who are telling me stories, who just tell me all kinds of things. It's amazing to me; and yet, it seems natural. I'll get someone I hardly know who just pours their heart out to me. I kind of know why; I mean, I sort of think there's something behind it, and maybe I'm not clear right now on what it is, but it will become clear to me. It also shows that a lot of people are in pain.

Yes. I find that with my students. They come into my office and tell me these things that are happening in their lives; it's really amazing what they're going through—a lot of pain. That reminds me of something you say in the introduction to **Sáanii Dahataal** *about retaining "the first person narrative voice because it is the stronger voice." Do you still subscribe to that?*

Yes, I do. I have this story—I don't know if you've heard it—it's about a woman who is a grandmother and she loses her grandchild, and the story obviously wasn't mine. But because my mother was from that area and because the woman was a little older, maybe two or three years older than I, I found it really quite easy to move into her voice and tell the story. And I was real familiar with where she lived, the place and everything. But she would never have been able to—she actually didn't even tell me the story herself; it was her niece who told me the story. But I do think using first person is easier, in a sense, and more believable. Because a lot of times when people tell stories they say, "Well, let me

tell you what she told me. This is what she said. She said, 'Last Saturday, when I was in town. . . .'" They assume the voice of that person, so that's really natural. It seems that in my work it's easier to do that than to write in the third person, and to say "Carrie went to town and when she was there she saw this. . . ." There seems to be a distance there. So, it is easier to write in the first person, for me.

How do you bring traditional stories into written text? That is, traditional stories have an original context—a time, place, and circumstance in which they are usually told. What are the effects of separating those stories from their contexts?

What kind of stories?

Stories associated with the Yé'ii Bicheii, or with a ceremony, that somehow become part of your work.

I don't do that. I can write about the ceremony, like the Yé'ii Bicheii, but it's just surface; I won't go beyond that. I think that there are clearly lines; for me, I'm very aware of the boundaries. I would never take like a creation story and rewrite it or re-tell it; I don't think that's my place to do that. A lot of people have done that, but I really don't fool with traditional texts, even though that's very much a part of my experience, now. I think that those are given to us for a particular reason. . . . I think that because of the way I've grown up a lot of things are alluded to, but that's the extent of it. I don't go beyond that.

*So, for example, in your poem **"Blue Horses Rush In"** you speak of the four directions and the colors, but it's not a story that is being retold or appropriated in any way. It's just an allusion, an element.*

Mm hmm. It's like an acknowledgment of certain aspects, it's not a retelling because I wouldn't be able to do that.

Do you see, in your writing, parallels to other contemporary twentieth century work, in general? And to Native American work, in particular?

Mmmm. I think there probably is, but I'm not sure. I don't know if there are parallels, but I know that writers I really like I read over and over. Tillie Olsen? I really like her work. Flannery O'Connor, and James Wright. Scott Momaday, I really like his work, and Linda Hogan. I don't know; there are probably influences but I am not conscious of them, but those are writers I really like. Also, Li-Young Lee, a wonderful Chinese writer, a poet. But I don't know if there are parallels; it's hard for me to make that distinction. In the literary context, there probably are, in the technical aspects, maybe. I see my work as really having begun in Navajo and ending in English; it's hard for me to see how, just on a structural level, someone else's work might be the same. Somebody else might see that, who doesn't have the same kind of baggage that I have; someone who just saw the work by itself. I'm too close to it to see.

Taking a step back from your own work, then, how has the Native American literature "canon" evolved since you first began studying and writing?

I think it has evolved, and it has really been tremendous what has happened in the last, gosh, fifteen years. There's just been an explosion of all kinds of writers. I think one of the really positive things that has happened is that there is more recognition of writers who are writing from their own cultures, who know their own culture, who know their own language, and who are full blood. It seems like, initially, the writing scene was dominated by writers of Native descent, but who weren't full blood, who did not really speak their own languages, did not grow up in their own communities. Maybe a majority of writers are still like that, but, I think it's really good to see writers like Sherman Alexie and Adrian Lewis, Roberta Hill Whiteman, who are full bloods.

Do you know Evelina Lucero?

Yes (smiling); yes, writers like her . . . I think that's been a real important part of what has been happening, to recognize writers like her. That is not to make disparaging remarks about other writers; I think it's been very positive. It's important that people who grew up in the communities, you know, naturally they would have a sense of what those communities are like and not be writing from the outside. So I think in that sense the canon has evolved, and there is just a lot more writing now than there has ever been.

Louis Owens says he used to think he knew of every novel being written by a Native American, but now there are so many.

It is really hard to keep up; you couldn't have said that a few years ago, but now it is really hard to keep current. Especially if you are teaching Native literature and you have to keep on top of things, it is really hard to find the time to do that!

Do you think your own work has influenced younger writers, such as the writers who will be featured in the Navajo writers' anthology you are editing? Have they been influenced by you in any way?

I don't know. I think they would know that. I mean, they would be able to answer that, rather than me. I do a lot of things in schools when I go home, on the reservation. Mostly to show the students that the way they talk is unique; it's really important to have them value themselves. We are inundated by American society; everybody wants to be like everybody else. I think it is really critical that Navajo young people understand they are okay. So I go to the schools and talk to the students about the value of their education, of their culture.

How does writing by Navajo authors differ from literature of other tribes? Do you see a difference in the work that has been submitted for the anthology?

Yes, I do. There's a real strong emphasis on heritage, on clan; people are real aware of their clan.

That's something you don't find in Alexie, for example.

Yes. They are really aware of place, and of clan and family. They are really conscious of their relatives, their grandparents, their aunts. They are conscious of kinship; they are different in that way. They see everyone as somehow being related; there is a sense of heritage in Navajo that I see in this anthology, as well as a sense of history. In a lot of the stories they talk about how different parts of the creation story refer to them. They see themselves as part of the stories, which I think is really neat. I know that in this part of the country [the Midwest] there is not that sense of history.

Are most of these writers living on the reservation?

Yes, most of them are. There are a few that aren't: some people in graduate school, some people teaching, some people in college. So some of them are not, but most of them, including some high school students, are from the reservation. We got a good response, quite varied.

How did you advertise for submissions?

Mostly in the *Navajo Times* and local newspapers. . . . We just kind of plastered the whole reservation with fliers! We sent them out to all the schools, but then a teacher sent in her whole class' work, fourth graders; so I did another call to make it more specific to adults rather than children. I felt bad about that, but it was my own fault for not being clear.

So when you say "we," who else is working on it with you?

Well, actually, it's just me! But I consult a lot with Ofelia Zepeda, because she has done this before, and with my editor, Joanne O'Hare at Arizona, but in the end it's just me. It's like I have all these different hats, so I think of myself as "we"!

So you have mythic proportions, like some of your characters! I am thinking of characters like Lena, Leona, Seasonal Woman, that seem to take on mythic dimensions, or a greater significance than each one's own individual life. Where does that come from?

I think that's the way people talk, the way they say things. Hmmm. Let me think of an example. Like, people might be together at some kind of gathering, and maybe there's a man there, a guy who is kind of tall, and for some reason he is real grouchy, he's in a bad mood, and people say: "How come that guy is getting mad at everybody?" And someone else might say something like, "Didn't you know he was born up there on the mountain, and there's a lot of bears around? One of his clans is bear." They say, "It's real early in the spring; he's not supposed to be awake yet; that's why he's like that." Everybody just sort of laughs, knowingly, and says, "Oh. Well, we'll just let him be the way he is." So they say things like that.

I have just one more question before we conclude. What do you see yourself doing in the future? What shape is your work taking? (I guess that was two questions!)

I would like to continue what I'm doing—publishing, writing. I am not undertaking anything new. I don't really foresee myself doing a lot of new and different things. I want to keep on writing poetry and prose.

We concluded the interview so Luci could get ready for her reading at the Terra Nova bookstore in downtown Lawrence. I had more questions I wanted to ask, and more stories I wanted to hear, but those will have to wait for another time.

The reading at Terra Nova went differently than Luci had planned. She had carefully chosen several selections from her books of poetry, but warned me that if there were a lot of children there, she would probably tell a story, instead. Because the store was promoting her new children's book, *Navajo ABC* (illustrated by Eleanor Schick), several parents brought their children. With them in mind, Luci told a long story about a little Navajo girl named Emma who finds a nickel in the dirt at her Auntie's house and decides to keep it safe in her belly button. Parents, children, and the rest of the audience enjoyed Luci's variety of sound effects and voices. After telling Emma's story, Luci explained the illustrations and words in *Navajo ABC*. Each page prompted a brief story to explain the significance of velvet and quarters, the land and the moon.

From alphabet books to anthologies, from poetry to prose, Tapahonso's work promotes an appreciation and understanding of Navajo culture, in both its traditional and contemporary manifestations. Tapahonso has made a significant contribution to the growing body of Native

American literature. She continues to experiment in her writing, no longer confining herself to the free verse of her early work. We have much to look forward to.

Susan B. Brill (essay date October 1997)

SOURCE: Brill, Susan B. "*Ałk'idáá' jiní* . . . Luci Tapahonso, Irvin Morris, and Della Frank: Interweaving Navajo and English in Their Poems and Stories." *Cimarron Review*, no. 121 (October 1997): 135-53.

[*In the following essay, Brill examines the linguistic interweaving of Navajo and English in the works of Tapahonso, Irvin Morris, and Della Frank, contending that "[f]or them, the interweaving of English and Navajo languages in their writing reflects the everyday interweaving of cultures and languages in the world."*]

Ałk'idáá' jiní . . . A long time ago, they say . . . Navajo stories that begin with these words interweave worlds and times and places and people into the linguistic fabric of the mythic and the historic. Irvin Morris describes these words as "ancient, magical" (225). This beginning of many Navajo stories also serves to connect the storyteller and her or his listeners with the past events of time immemorial. With these words, the listener (reader for written stories) is prepared to hear the words and stories that have been handed down for generations. *Jiní* (they say) shifts the voice away from the actual storyteller and to that of the mythic and/or historic past. With this shift, the storyteller then joins the listeners as they listen together to the story and its events. The shift to these ancient Navajo words transports the listener and storyteller into the storyworld of past and mythic times. Morris explains this experience of listening to a grandmother's stories when he writes, "we drift off into the world of her words" (225). In Morris's writing and in that of other Navajo writers, the Navajo language is used in many of their stories to move their reader-listeners into the Navajo worlds of those stories, even when those stories are predominantly in English. The use of the Navajo language firmly roots the stories within a Navajo world—be that the world of the mythic, the everyday, or, in many cases, both.

There are many different strategies by which this orientation is accomplished, and the incorporation of Navajo language words, phrases, and sentences is one such strategy. Others include the use of repetition, place names that refer to areas within the bounds of *Diné bikeyah* (Navajo homeland), the personification of animals, voice shifts to a second person voice, and formulaic beginnings and endings, among other strategies. And these strategies can also be used to different ends. As Andrew Wiget explains, "writers, including

Native American writers, have employed a number of strategies to illuminate or obfuscate cultural differences as required by their esthetic purposes" (260). The inclusion of Navajo language words and phrases by Navajo writers is a particularly powerful means of evoking a storyworld that is distinctively Navajo. Even one lone word in Navajo can insure that the story's significance must be understood within its tribal lands, context, and history. And such language shifts are especially crucial since, as Luci Tapahonso explains, "There are things that can be said in each one that cannot be said in the other" (qtd. in Baldinger 33).

Writers as diverse as Luci Tapahonso, Irvin Morris, Della Frank, Rex Lee Jim, Nia Francisco, and others use the Navajo language in their writing, a language choice that orients the worlds of their stories and poems within a Navajo framework that points away from the writer's own self-referentiality and more towards the Navajo storyworlds of the poems and stories. Rather than the more self-referential literary models that are the legacy of the past two hundred years of the western literary tradition, these writers offer stories and poems modeled more firmly on their own oral traditions in which the stories told are co-created through the interactive interrelationality between teller and listener rather than by the independent imagination of the writer alone. As Gretchen Bataille notes, "contemporary [Indian] writers, although writing in English and in western genres—the novel and the poem—derive much of their power from the oral literary tradition" (17).

While it is the case that all American Indian writers straddle the worlds between the oral and the literary in diverse ways and to varying extents, especially in their use of their own tribal languages, these Navajo writers demonstrate the extent to which their oral traditions intimately pervade their work from start to finish. For them, the interweaving of English and Navajo languages in their writing reflects the everyday interweaving of cultures and languages in the world that is *Diné bikeyah.* Our understanding of the work of these writers in many ways reflects the power of their bilingualism. In an article that focuses on the biculturalism of Southwestern literatures, Reed Way Dasenbrock reminds us, "The temptations in studying such bicultural writers is to deny their biculturality, to privilege one of their formative cultures in the name of authenticity or the other in the name of universality. . . . [W]e cannot impose our own cultural norms and forms on work with a different cultural context" (317, 314). And one important strategy that situates the work of Navajo writers within the bounds of American literatures, American Indian literatures, and contemporary Navajo literary and oral storytelling traditions is their interweaving of both English and Navajo languages—an interweaving that manifests the diversity and fluidity of peoples, cultures, and lives. As Michael Wilson notes, this is a particular

strength of "the oral tradition [that] constantly weaves relations between old and new stories" (134). And since "it is through language that the world of the Navajo was created, and it is through language that the Navajos control, classify, and beautify their world," as Gary Witherspoon points out, we should expect an especially acute sensitivity to the importance of linguistic choices in the work of many Navajo writers.

Let me take a page or two to briefly explain how the different sorts of strategies involved in writing that is more orally or textually informed manifest themselves in the writing. Then it will be easier to see how language shifts between English and Navajo fit within their writers' oral traditions. Within the western tradition, literary structures reflect the range of dialectic, discursive, and dialogic linear oppositions by which subjects gain presence at the expense of others' objective passivity. As Wiget points out, "Authority, in interactionist terms, is rhetorical: the power to command the floor, compel attention, and manage interest" (259). Within the domain of a discursive oppositionality, particular subjects' assertions of their own subjectivity silence and devalue others whose objectification feeds the subjectifying process. As I note elsewhere, "While such a jockeying for and from position can make critical room for Native voices, it does not facilitate the sort of relational conversivity that is evident within the practice of storytelling . . ." ("Discovering," 53).

Discursive empowerment is definitionally at the expense of some objective disempowerment. And in a world that appears to be increasingly balkanized and embattled, the allure of discursive power often seems more concrete and enduring than it ever really is. N. Scott Momaday makes this point very directly in *House Made of Dawn* in Tosamah's sermon on language and its creative and destructive powers. Tosamah tells his congregation, "In the white man's world, language, too—and the way in which the white man thinks of it—has undergone a process of change. . . . He has diluted and multiplied the Word, and words have begun to close in upon him" (95). The transition that Momaday notes is less a shift from oral to written language, than the shift from conversive (conversational and transformative) to discursive communication. As this paper demonstrates, many writers offer their poems and stories in conversive ways that are much more akin to their respective oral storytelling traditions, even though the words are in written form. When words become texts, then they are discourse, and the static form of discursive texts is not limited to written form. Much of what we see on television and hear in political speeches is discursively driven even though there is an oral component. But it is language that is at the center of discourse—hence Derrida's infamous quote that there is nothing that is not text: *Il n'y a de hors texte.*

Insofar as conversive relations are concerned, while language may be a crucial component of such relationships, it is not its center and base. Language is simply the tool, albeit an essential one. What is at the heart of conversive communication is relationality and love. Within the domain of a conversively relational intersubjectivity, the emphasis is on the connections between subjects (persons—human and nonhuman) rather than on the individuals themselves and their own words, positions, and power. Leslie Marmon Silko explains, "the storytelling always includes the audience and the listeners, and, in fact, a great deal of the story is believed to be inside the listener, and the storyteller's role is to draw the story out of the listeners" (57). "Thus the meaning of the utterance comes from shared intentions based upon prior knowledge, the context of the utterance, and habitual patterns of interaction," notes David R. Olson (261). Conversive empowerment and vocality conjointly serve to empower both the subjectivity of the speaker and listener through a primary emphasis, not on the speaker's own subjectivity, but on the relationship between speaker and listener, between writer and reader, between text and critic.

The conversive emphasis on the relationship between all involved is the communicative paradigm within oral storytelling traditions. As Luci Tapahonso explains, ". . . in Navajo tradition . . . being a part of telling stories is very much a way in which affection is shown . . . And so it's a way to show affection and to be included within either listening to or the sharing of stories" (WCBU Interview). Whereas discursive structures privilege language, subjectivity and positionality, conversive relations emphasize love, relationships and transformation with meaning and significance defined in terms of the connections between subjects (not between subjects and objects, for within a conversive framework, even nonhuman objects take on subjective status as persons in the story).[1]

In their writing, contemporary Navajo writers depict the intersubjective relationality which they present as inherent in all of creation. This is especially the case in these writers' use of their tribal languages. Even when the linguistic and topical focus shifts to *Dinetah* (the traditional Navajo homeland), non-Navajo readers are not necessarily excluded from that world. In fact, the open use of the Navajo language is a means of sharing the Navajo worlds of the writers with their readers— what fits Silko's description of "the boundless capacity of language which, through storytelling, brings us together, despite great distances between cultures, despite great distances in time" (72). For example, when Luci Tapahonso shifts to the Navajo language in her writing, she does so as a means of inviting her listener-readers[2] into the worlds of her stories and poems—

thereby enabling her readers to learn and value and understand words, worlds, and peoples from within rather than from without.

In her poem **"In 1864,"** Tapahonso's occasional shifts to Navajo do not serve to distance the reader nor to make the reader feel other to the poem. In fact, such shifts help move the listener-reader even closer into the Navajo storyworld of the poem. Tapahonso refers to her homeland by the Navajo term, *Dinetah,* glossing the initial use of the term in a footnote at the bottom of the page. Navajo words and other in-group allusions are included with explanations for the non-Navajo reader. Tapahonso's relational techniques welcome her readers into her Navajo world. This enables her readers to become familiar with what might otherwise be unfamiliar (e.g., a reference to "that man, Redshirt, and his army"—glossed as well, "Kit Carson's name was 'Redshirt' in Navajo" [*Sáanii* 9]). Even difficult passages about the horrors of that period of the Long Walk are told in a way that communicates the severity of those times without alienating white readers. Clearly, Tapahonso wants her readers to be able to really hear the horrors of those times and, thereby, to learn from them. Tapahonso shares those times through the voice of her aunt, who tells the story of her own grandmother.

> . . . So many of us were starving and suffering
> that year because the bilagáana* kept attacking us.
> Kit Carson and his army had burned all the fields,
> and they killed our sheep right in front of us.
> We couldn't believe it. I covered my face and cried.
> All my life, we had sheep. They were like our family.
>
> (8)

The attacking *bilagáana* are the white people, and Tapahonso glosses that term accordingly. A footnote at the bottom of the page glosses the word *bilagáana* as "the Navajo word for Anglos" (8). Tapahonso is making great efforts to make her poem and its story accessible to her readers. Throughout the poem, any terms the reader might not know (either Navajo language terms or other in-group allusions) are explained to the reader, much as any storyteller would insure the presence and involvement of her listener in her telling of a story. Even in Tapahonso's gloss of the term *bilagáana,* she refers to white people as "Anglos"—the term commonly used in the Southwest. Here again, Tapahonso's linguistic choices serve to bring her readers even more completely into the regional world of her poem. As Robin Riley Fast notes, "For non-Natives, the contexts in which we've known Indian people, if we have, affect our access to their texts" (516). Hence, the crucial importance of the extra efforts made by these Navajo writers to insure the accessibility of their work to a broad spectrum of possible listener-readers.

Throughout her poem, Tapahonso speaks directly to her listener-readers with all the intimacy of the traditional storyteller, here telling the story of the Navajo's internment at Ft. Sumner through the voices of people described as her own relatives. Even though the majority of her readers, in all likelihood, are *bilagáana,* the intimacy of Tapahonso' conversive style successfully conveys the horrors of 1864 to listener-readers who become part of the storytelling/reading event. Tapahonso speaks *with* her reader in this poem, not *at* a distanced and, thereby, alienated reader. This is particularly evident in Tapahonso's placing of the story of the Long Walk in the voice of her aunt who, in turn, tells the story that had been told to her by her own grandmother. In Tapahonso's telling (the poem), her listener-reader reads/hears the aunt's story along with Tapahonso. Both reader and writer become co-listeners to the aunt's telling. This conjunctive role collapses the distance between reader and writer and moves both closer together in a conversive experience that informs and transforms both. Throughout the poem, Tapahonso's descriptive explanation of the Navajo internment, the telling through diverse perspectives presented in direct second-person voices, and the poet's use of Navajo language all enable the reader to move to, into, and within the poem by traversing such conversive pathways that ease the reader into the Navajo world of the poem.

Within a conversive Navajo telling, the use of the Navajo language welcomes readers into the intimacy of the writers' Navajo worlds, inviting the reader into a closeness unavailable in English. The extent to which Navajo language use moves a writing and a telling more firmly into Navajo worlds can also be seen in Irvin Morris's short story, "The Blood Stone." In this story, Morris relates stories from the Long Walk and his people's interment at Hwééldi (Ft. Sumner). In Morris's version, an old grandmother tells him and his/her reader-listeners the story of her father and her grandparents.

Her grandfather died at Ft. Sumner, and it was there that her grandmother conceived and birthed a red haired baby after having been raped by one of the U.S. soldiers. As she relates, her grandmother kept "two things from that time: a red-haired, blue-eyed child, and a stone pried absent-mindedly from the ground as they sit listening to the discussions about the treaty and the conditions of their release. The stone is red like blood . . ." (227).

Morris's story is told through the interwoven voices of the story's narrator (a Navajo man who is a student out east), his grandmother, great grandfather and other relatives, and these voices are repeatedly returned to their Navajo language origins through linguistic shifts that serve to reorient and further anchor the text in *Dinetah.* As Tapahonso explains, "The place where we're from is really who we are" (Baldinger 32). And as Morris writes about the grandmother's speech in Navajo, "Her words are confident, rich with nasal tones, clicks, and glottal

stops" (225)—distinctive linguistic signs of the Navajo language. The old woman begins the story of her family's history with the traditional beginning that gives the actual historical family events the weight and significance of mythic and ancient times.

> *"Aɫk'idáá' jiní,"* she says. A long time ago, it is said— ancient, magical words. She stops frequently to spit into the can she keeps by her bed. She does this with deliberation, so much a part of the telling. Long silences punctuate her stories, and we drift off into the world of her words.
>
> (225)

And as in the case of Tapahonso's poem, through Morris's inclusion of the Navajo words and phrases of his people and their stories, we listener-readers are invited, as well, into the world of those words. We hear about *Hajíínéí* (the place of emergence) and the Hero Twins who battle with *Yé'iitsoh* (the giants), and we hear about the horrors of *Hwééldi*: *"Nichei yéé áníinee'"*—Your grandfather would talk about those things (226). And when a cat interrupts the story by jumping onto a table, the response is immediate, *"Doo álhályáada, héi!"*— Don't get up on that, hey! (226).

Throughout Morris's story, the Navajo language brings his listener-readers more firmly into the Navajo world of his telling. Whether the words are those of the mythic (*"Hózhó naasha dooleeɫ"*—I will walk in beauty), the everyday (*"Doo' álhalyáada, héi!"*—Don't get up on that, hey!), or the historic (*"Dooda! Dooda!* she pleads with the hairy face looming over her, straining red, breathing liquor in her face"—*"Dooda! Dooda!"*—No! No!), throughout, these Navajo words move us ever closer to *Diné bikeyah,* its beliefs, its people, and its history.

Two poems by Luci Tapahonso and Della Frank demonstrate how only a few words or even just one can powerfully situate a poem firmly within its Navajo framework. Tapahonso's **"For Lori, This Christmas I Want to Thank You in This Way"** is written for her daughter and tells the story of her daughter's birth and first day in this world. This story that begins the poem is juxtaposed with the Christmas nativity story that ends the poem. The final story is told in the daughter's own voice, a shift that interweaves the voices and persons of mother and daughter through their respective storytellings. Tapahonso provides an introductory explanation that alerts her readers to the shift in voice.

> you told the story at seven to your little brothers and
>   sisters:
> "baby jesus—'Awééchí'í born somewhere
> on the other side of the world, far, far away
> some sheep, cows and horses saw him and
> they told other sheep, cows and horses.
> and so they know too.
> all of them and all of us know."
>
> (**Breeze** [*A Breeze Swept Through*] 19)

In the girl's telling, the Navajo framework of the Christmas story is established at the outset. "Baby jesus" is immediately referred to in Navajo—a renaming that orients the story into the world of the Navajo girl and her young Navajo relatives. Here, the lone Navajo term, *'Awééchí'í,* connects the story to the world of the teller and listeners and also to the world of the mythic. The everyday and the mythic are conjoined in a telling/writing that conveys the significance of Christmas for Tapahonso's daughter, for Tapahonso, and for the listeners and readers of the poem-story and its respective tellings.

Language shifts from English to Navajo always serve to place the writing within a Navajo framework. In some cases, the inclusion of the Navajo language connects the writing to the Navajo domain of the mythic and ancient. In other cases, the language shifts bring the writing into a contemporary Navajo world. And often, the occasional use of Navajo terms does both, thereby further welcoming the listener-reader as a visitor to *Dinetah.* Navajo writers include their language in their writing to make the writing, the telling, the story Navajo. When the Navajo language parts are accessible to the listener-reader (either through glosses and translations provided by the writer or through a familiarity with the language), then Navajo storyworlds open themselves up in ways otherwise closed to non-Navajo speakers. However, even if the Navajo is neither translated nor otherwise glossed and if the reader does not know Navajo, the reader is still welcomed into the Navajo worlds of the poems and stories through reading/hearing the sorts of linguistic shifts that one would normally hear among many Navajo people today. Either way, the effect of such linguistic shifts is the interrelational connection that brings listener-readers to the various literary worlds of *Dinetah.*

In many ways, the Navajo language is a language of place, a language that defines its speakers, listeners, writers, and readers as *Diné* people whose existences are inextricably located within the four sacred mountains that define the boundaries of *Dinetah.* As Della Frank writes, "I am that which is: A Navajo person . . . *T'áá' Diné Nishlí*" (Walters 2). Frank defines the reality of *Diné* people as a way of being as expressed in the Beauty Way stories—and this definition is a way of being, not a way of becoming; it is the way of balance and harmony. Frank's use of the Navajo language in her poem "*T'áá Diné Nishli*" establishes the world and words of her writing as firmly *Diné.* This poem expresses the reality that opens itself up to readers whenever Navajo writers write in Navajo. And the reality of being *Diné* is not a discursively subjective reality that privileges the speaker's voice and person, nor is it a dialogically multivocal reality that asserts the primacy of a number of speakers. Rather, the Navajo way as storied in the Beauty Way and as expressed in the writings of diverse contemporary Navajo writers is a con-versively relational reality that privileges the connections that interweave the diverse persons and elements of the world and of story-worlds into an intersubjective privileging, not of the self, but of the other selves in the world with whom we relate. The focus is outward towards others, one's family, clan relatives, and tribal members. This contrasts poignantly with the dominant culture's greater emphasis on individualism and self.[3]

We see this in Morris's volume, as well. When he introduces himself to his readers in the section "*Kééhasht'ínígii* (Where I live)," he does so in relation to his homeland and his people, and he does so first in Navajo and then in English: "*Tóbaahí nishlí, doo Tótsohnii éi báshíshchíín.* That is the proper way to introduce and identify myself. I am of the Edgewater clan, and I am born for the Big Water clan" (47). Although Morris's introduction and Frank's poem identify them as Navajo people, it is important to understand that at the center of their writing is their tribe, not themselves as independent individuals. Their self-identifications as Navajo people do not primarily point inwardly to themselves but outwardly to their families, clans and tribe. The poem begins and ends with the same refrain: "*T'áá Diné Nishli.* / I am that which is: A Navajo Person. / This feeling is around, above, and below me . . ." (1). Frank begins her identification in Navajo, and in her echoing of a refrain in the Beauty Way, she defines her tribal identification within spatial terms. As Irvin Morris explains, "I have seen these landmarks every morning of my life, whether or not I am actually home. These mountains and formations are as real and as alive for me as are the stories that animate them. Better than anything else, they tell me who I am" (41). Luci Tapahonso notes in the Preface to her book *Sáanii Dahataal,* "For many people in my situation, residing away from my homeland, writing is the means for returning, rejuvenation, or for restoring our spirits to the state of 'hozho,' or beauty, which is the basis of Navajo philosophy" (xii). To re-center herself within the framework of *Dinetah,* Tapahonso writes herself back within that place, that philosophy, that way. And, like Frank and Morris, to do so, Tapahonso interweaves the Navajo language throughout her English language poems and stories.

Frank's poem ends with the languages of the above quoted refrain reversed, "I am that which is: A Navajo Person . . . / *T'áá Diné Nishli*" (2). Frank begins and ends the poem in Navajo, thereby using her people's language to firmly root the poem, herself, and her listener-readers in the mythic and everyday world of being *Diné.* And, as Frank framed her poem with a statement in Navajo, Tapahonso ends her preface in Navajo: "*Ahéhee'.*" (Thank you [xii]), and Irvin Morris begins his book with a prayer in Navajo that he, his book, and his readers will go with beauty and goodness.[4]

Since the early sociolinguistic work of Sapir and Whorf, much has been written about the extent to which language use reflects culture and traditions. While bilingualism and code switching are becoming much more common in the writings of many writers, the option of writing in one's own tribal language is less available for many American Indian writers who either do not know their tribal languages at all or, at least, not well enough to write in those languages. This linguistic alienation from one's own tribal history is the outcome of the deliberate attempts on the part of United States government policy to force Indian peoples to assimilate into the dominant white culture, thereby losing languages, traditions, stories, religious ceremonies, and other aspects of traditional tribal cultures. As Beck and Walters explain,

> All over the country children were sent to boarding schools where they were not allowed to speak their own language, where they were disciplined in a totally new and strange way. This was not discipline for survival in the natural environment. It was one that would enable children and succeeding generations, to step more easily into the new mold being created for them for the government and various missionary groups.
>
> (150)

In light of the genocidal and assimilationist historicities of manifest destiny, many Indian writers are not sufficiently proficient in their tribal languages to draw on that linguistic heritage in their own writing. Those Indian writers who do have the facility to bring their own Indian languages into their English language writing tend to be those who have been tribally raised on reservations in which their tribal languages are still widely spoken. However, it is important to note that such linguistic difference is not a determinant of authenticity (often problematically defined in historically and mythically nostalgized terms). As Simon Ortiz makes very clear, the fact that the vast majority of Native writers use "a different linguistic system" (e.g., the various European languages of colonization) in no wise signifies that they "have forgotten or have been forced to forsake their native selves" (10). The differing linguistic capacities of writers reflect the range of their diverse historicities, including tribal backgrounds and affinities, native lands and geographic displacements, and tendencies towards conversive and discursive writing styles.

Insofar as tribal linguistic facility is concerned, many Navajo writers have this capability, and they comfortably bring the Navajo language into their stories and poems in ways that give their language shifts a completely natural feel. These writers grew up with Navajo as a primary language in their everyday lives, so their use of the language reflects an infusion of their own lives and worlds into their writing in ways inacces-

sible for many other Indian writers whose knowledge of their tribal languages is sketchy if existent at all. Language shifts from English to Navajo signal a specific tribal identification that anchors the text firmly within its everyday Navajo context. This can be clearly seen in the titles of the different sections and pieces in Morris's volume. Virtually all of the titles in the first three sections are in Navajo with their translations given parenthetically. Only in the final section of short stories are the titles given first (and only) in English. But even these stories include passages in Navajo—the sorts of language shifts that one would expect to find in the everyday and storied worlds of Navajo people.[5]

For many other Native writers largely unfamiliar with their tribal languages, similar language shifts might signify not only the anchoring of the text within a particular tribal context, but perhaps more importantly, an authorial mooring that re-members the writer back into her or his tribal community—historically, mythically, and imaginatively. As N. Scott Momaday writes, "Once in his life a man ought to concentrate his mind upon the remembered earth, I believe. . . . The journey herein recalled continues to be made anew each time the miracle comes to mind, for that is peculiarly the right and responsibility of the imagination" (*Rainy Mountain* 83, 4). And this re-membering and reconnecting often involves the use of indigenous languages in ways that feel like invocations of peoples, their histories and cultures, often with a sense of nostalgia for past or mythic times.

For example, Momaday begins and ends his novel *House Made of Dawn* with traditional Pueblo terms for beginning a ceremonial story: "*Dypaloh*. There was a house made of dawn. . . . *House made of pollen, house made of dawn. Qtsedaba*" (1, 212). As Susan Scarberry-Garcia explains, "When Momaday opens the novel with '*Dypaloh*' and ends with the word '*Qtsedaba*,' conventional formulaic words used at Jemez Pueblo to frame a story, he is placing his story solidly within oral tradition" (8). For Momaday whose Indian heritage is Kiowa, here and in *The Way to Rainy Mountain*, terms and phrases in Indian languages (Pueblo, Navajo, and Kiowa) point backwards to a nostalgized past ("a time that is gone forever") or a mythicized land ("a landscape that is incomparable") or forwards to an imagined understanding of the writer and his characters in relation to those realities ("the human spirit, which endures") (*Rainy Mountain* 4).

In such cases, the presence of words in Indian languages reflects the writer's own intentional identification with his or her own (or, as in the above quoted example, some other) tribal ancestry. The emphasis is on the writer's connection to that particular Indianness—through ethnicity (as in Momaday's Kiowa ancestry) or through cultural familiarity (as in Momaday's connections to Navajo and Jemez Pueblo cultures having spent much of his childhood years living on those reservations). For example, in *House Made of Dawn,* Momaday has a Navajo character sing part of the Navajo Beauty Way: "*Tségihi.* House made of dawn. . . . May it be beautiful all around me. In beauty it is finished" (146-147). And throughout *The Way to Rainy Mountain,* he includes a number of terms and names in Kiowa. By using the Navajo and Kiowa languages, he anchors his statements and feelings within particular tribal and ancestral languages, thereby giving his expressions historical, cultural, and mythical connections and effects unavailable to him in English. These words serve to connect the writer and his writing with tribal heritages.

These connections differ in significant ways from the case of bilingual Navajo writers whose stories and language switching and personal histories are distinctively Navajo and serve to bring their readers into the contemporary world of Navajo people. While in both cases the language switching connects the present to past and mythic times and places, Momaday's language shifts emphasize the power of the imagination to connect us in the here-and-now with distant peoples and cultures from past or mythic times. In contrast, the work of many Navajo writers most importantly brings their listener-readers into their own everyday Navajo worlds of family gatherings and personal conversations.

For writers like Momaday whose lives and heritages straddle diverse worlds, the linguistic connections made through language-switching demonstrates the processes by which many contemporary Indian people struggle to reconnect with traditions, cultures, and languages from which they have been varyingly distanced. Here, the connective focus is on the writer and his or her tribal reconnecting. This process of tribal and ancestral remembering can be seen in the work of writers as diverse as Momaday, Leslie Marmon Silko, Louise Erdrich, and Louis Owens. The common denominator among these writers is the fact that they are all varingly distanced from their tribal languages and, in some cases, even their tribal communities, traditions, and lands. But regardless of the extent to which Native writers are conversant in their tribal languages, as Simon Ortiz explains, each writer works within the bounds of the colonial languages, transforming them in ways to convey the diverse realities and experiences of Indian America. "Along with their native languages, Indian women and men have carried on their lives and their expression through the use of the new languages, particularly Spanish, French, and English, and they have used these languages on their own terms" (10).

One key to understanding the different identities and intentions behind the use of Indian languages in predominantly English language works of literature is evident in the degree to which those works participate in the language games of their oral traditions or those language games of the western literary tradition.[6] As a rule, I can note that the more literary the work, the greater the emphasis on self and identity (of the writer or some projected persona in the writing) and on the textuality of the writing. The New Critics and poststructural critics point this out clearly. The New Critics rejected any reality beyond the text, and Derrida tells us that there is nothing other than text. As Momaday's statement about the importance of one's imagined identity makes clear, the writings of many Native American writers provide a means of their re-membering themselves as Native American, as individuals connected to indigenous cultures and traditions. While such linguistic re-memberings signify for all Native writers a cultural and ancestral connecting, there are important ways in which such occasional linguistic shifts in the works of Navajo writers such as Morris, Frank, and Tapahonso demonstrate significant distinctions from the analogous strategy in the work of those writers who are unfamiliar with their tribal languages.

For these writers, there is no question at all about their tribal and ethnic identities. They are Indian, Navajo, members of their respective clans and families. These writers do not use their Navajo language as an ostensive means of connecting with a tribal past, a language, or world from which they have been varyingly alienated. For these Navajo writers, their language is not only their ancestral past but also the everyday tribal reality of their own lives. Luci Tapahonso clarifies this point in the Preface to her collection ***Blue Horses Rush In.*** She explains that the interweaving of Navajo and English are a part of her family's world. "We sat for hours— talking, laughing, and sharing family memories and stories. The conversation switched easily between *Diné* and English and, at times, a rhythmic blending of the two" (ix). We see this also in her writing and the writing of other Navajo writers. The focus of their writing is less on self-identity and literariness and more on the content of the story, the relationships between the listener-readers and writer-tellers, and the tribal community in which the story is formed. In following upon their oral storytelling traditions, their use of the Navajo language in their writing establishes their identities and worlds as Navajo, but more importantly, the linguistic shifts define their storyworlds as Navajo and, thereby, facilitate their listener-readers' connections to, entries into, and understandings of *Dinetah.* As Tapahonso explains, "In writing, then, I revisit the place or places concerned and try to bring the reader to them, thereby enabling myself and other Navajos to sojourn mentally and emotionally to our home, *Dinétah*" (***Blue Horses*** xiv).

We can see this in Tapahonso's poem, **"They Are Silent and Quick"**—a poem about Kansas fireflies—insects that serve as signs of her distance from home, from *Dinetah*. In the poem, Tapahonso phones her mother and asks her about the flickering insects: "From far away, she [my mother] says, 'I never heard of such a thing. / There's nothing like that in Navajo stories'" (*Sáanii* 13). For many Native American writers, their occasional use of bits of their tribal languages serves as the sign of both their desired connections to their histories, their ancestries, their traditions, their peoples, but also as the sign of their distance from those desired connections. In contrast, for Tapahonso, it is not the presence of the Navajo language that signifies the desire to bridge a distance, but rather it is the absence of words and stories in her language that signifies distance and alienation.

As Tapahonso considers the reality of fireflies and the fact that she has no words, no stories for those creatures, she writes, "There are no English words to describe this feeling" (14). For her daughter who straddles tribal worlds in her own Navajo / Acoma heritage, the presence of the insects making light is something wonderful. She marvels at the lightning bugs, "'I think that they are connected with magic,' she says, / peering into the darkness. 'Maybe people around here tell stories / about small bits of magic that appear on summer nights'" (13). But at that moment, for Tapahonso, the presence of the alien insects simply magnifies her sense of distance from home. She writes,

> There are no English words to describe this feeling.
> "T'áá 'iighisíí biniinaa shił hóyéé'," I say.
>   Because of it, I am overshadowed by aching.
>   It is a heaviness that surrounds me completely.
> "Áko ayóó shił hóyéé'." We are silent.
>
>   (14)

Tapahonso shifts to Navajo in order to re-center herself and to speak her feelings from a Navajo center, a linguistic shift that serves to relocate herself back home within a world in which there are no fireflies. And yet the poem takes place, not in *Dinetah*, but in Kansas. And in the world beyond *Dinetah*, a sense of comfort and balance in the poem can only be achieved through an interweaving of both worlds (*Dinetah* and Kansas) and languages (Navajo and English). Tapahonso must take her Navajo stories and re-member them in English in order to make room for those "tiny bodies of light." She ends her poem,

> Early the next morning, I awaken from a heavy, dreamless sleep
> and outside the window, a small flash of light flickers off and on.
> Then I recall being taught to go outside in the gray dawn
> before sunrise to receive the blessings of the gentle spirits
> who gathered around our home. Go out, we were told, get your blessings for the day.

> And now, as I watch these tiny bodies of light,
> the aching inside lessens as I see how
> the magic of these lights precedes the gray dawn.
>
>   (14)

Here, Tapahonso takes her people's stories about the significance of the dawn time, and she rewrites (rerights) those stories to fit the reality of the a Navajo woman at dawn in Kansas. And through her interweaving of the languages of Kansas and *Dinetah,* English and Navajo, she bridges the distance that separates her from her home, bringing the fireflies into a Navajo dawn time story and enveloping the events of that morning within the protective bounds of *Dinetah*. As Tapahonso explains in **"A Birthday Poem,"** "Some days, even after great coffee, I need to hear a song / to reassure me that the distance from Dinétah is not a world / away" (*Blue Horses* 79).

Whether it is the flickering lights of the fireflies or the glittering allure of our material culture, writers like Luci Tapahonso and Irvin Morris tell us stories about their struggles to achieve balance in this glittering Fifth World we all share. And one of the most powerful strategies they offer for achieving this balance is through their linguistic interweaving of Navajo and English. For it is through language that the world was initially created, and it is through language that it is recreated and balance is restored. For Tapahonso, Morris, and other Navajo writers, Navajo is not primarily a language of self-identification and self-discovery; it is the language of being, of belonging; it is the language of one's self in relation to . . . ; it is the language of place, of home, of *Dinetah*. As Ofelia Zepeda and Jane H. Hill explain in relation to the importance of indigenous languages for those peoples for whom their languages are still in use: "Each language still spoken is fundamental to the personal, social and—a key term in the discourse of indigenous peoples—spiritual identity of its speakers. They know that without these languages they would be less than they are" (45). Tapahonso makes this very point even more strongly, "They always say at home . . . if you lose, if we lose the language, then we're really not anything anymore" (Bruchac, 285).

For these Navajo writers, it is English that is the language of their historic rupture and re-connection. However, for those Indian writers whose only language of fluency is English, their occasional use of Native terms and phrases poignantly serve as the linguistic signs of rupture and connection. Tapahonso's use of English and Momaday's use of Kiowa are mirror images, opposites yet similars, for both, the languages of rupture and connection, in both cases, languages of self-expression and of personal and cultural historicity, languages that reflect the distances, alienations, and linguistic absences in self and people, the language of discourse, discord, and even dialogue.

Rather than a literary emphasis that focuses primarily on the text, these writers who are closer to their tribal oral traditions emphasize the telling in a conversive means that enables all involved in the telling to participate in the world of the story. Whereas other writers' uses of Indian languages might serve to help us as readers to get to know them and their tribal worlds, if that writing is more textually driven than orally informed, unless we are already part of their worlds, our approach to those worlds is largely from without. But for those writers who bring the oral more completely into their writing, the use of Indian languages further serves to enable both our entry into the storyworlds and, as well, our very real transformations as participants in those written tellings. As David L. Moore notes, "The ways in which readers and writers conceive of culture, self and other, knowledge and experience, past and present, determine different relations between reader and text as well as different readings of literary elements" (7). And Michael Wilson explains, "The combined use of the oral tradition (the cultural 'encyclopedia' of the tribe) and writing is an example of the way American Indian cultures grow and change as they imagine both their relations within the group as well as their relations to outside, sometimes oppressive groups" (132). In the work of Luci Tapahonso, Irvin Morris, and Della Frank, we see how their use of Navajo is an orally informed conversive strategy that brings the storyteller-writers and listener-readers together in a written storytelling relationship.

The difference between textual discourse and conversive relations is whether the focus is more on self, text, and identity, or whether the focus is more on the storyworld, the telling, and relationality. Each writer, story, poem, and novel straddles the line between the oral and written in different ways. The work of some Indian writers is more orally and tribally based, while the writings of other writers is more literarily and textually based. This is a continuum. Literary works range from the more "literary" to the more orally informed. And even different works by the same writer will vary in the mix of oral and textual boundaries. For example, in Morris's volume, the various stories and vignettes straddle this continuum in different ways, some pieces being more openly oral and conversive, while others are more protectively closed and discursive. One marker that indicates these differences in his writing is in the presence or absence of his own tribal language.

The works of contemporary bilingual Navajo writers reflect their oral traditions through their emphases on *Dinetah,* on the interactive and transformative tellings of their writings, and on the very real and concrete connections that define their writing as *Diné.* One strategy by which this is accomplished is their inclusion of Navajo language terms and phrases—a strategy that welcomes us all into their worlds and into the world of *Dinetah.* The distinctive conversivity embodied in the Navajo language portions of these tellings may occasionally serve to discursively distance the reader from the text and the writer, but more often than not, they serve to bridge that distance in the form of conversive pathways that enable the listener-readers to enter the worlds of the stories told.

Notes

1. Within such a Native American conversive semiotics, personhood is an attribution of status, not a delineation of species differentiation. One can have intersubjective conversive relations with other human persons, but also with animal persons, plant persons, and even other persons we would traditionally define as inanimate (e.g., rocks, planets, sun, moon).

2. The term listener-reader (or in some cases reader-listener which gives a different emphasis) is used to convey the reality of a reader who steps into the participatory role of the storylistener responding to and co-creating a story while reading-listening to a story that is in a written form (e.g., short story, poem, novel, play). I'd like to note three other women who have used this (or a similar) term to describe the role of the readers of American Indian literatures: Kate Shanley Vangen in "The Devil's Domain: Leslie Silko's 'Storyteller,'" *Coyote Was Here: Essays on Contemporary Native American Literary and Political Mobilization,* ed. Bo Scholer (Aarhus, Denmark: Seklos, 1984) 117; Lee Maracle in "Oratory: Coming to Theory," *Essays on Canadian Writing* 54 (1994): 9 [This reference is to the "speaker (writer)"]; and Robin Riley Fast in "Borderland Voices in Contemporary Native American Poetry," *Contemporary Literature* 36.3 (1995): 523, 534.

3. For an additional discussion of this topic and poem, see my article "Discovering the Order and Structure of Things: A Conversive Approach to Navajo Poetry," (56).

4. Morris's prayer can be roughly translated as follows: "May this one person go forward in beauty; may this one go forward into the future in harmony and goodness; may this book of mine go off in beauty; may this offering of mine go off in balance and goodness." This is my own translation, so any errors are my own. The original prayer follows:

> *Hózhóogo' éí íishlaa dooleel*
> *Yá'át'éehgo éí íishlaa dooleel*
> *Áyaa dííshjí nizhónígo íishlaa*
> *Áyaa dííshjí yá'át'éehgo íishlaa.*

(Morris ix)

5. For a more complete discussion of the different sections and stories in Morris's volume, see my review essay of the volume in *Studies in American Indian Literatures.*

6. The use of the phrase "language games" refers to Ludwig Wittgenstein's description of any use of language as a game, namely a contingent and contextually driven human construction that has underlying foundational rules that guide individual responses and participation (or "play"). For a more developed discussion of the value of Wittgenstein's philosophical work for literary criticism, see my volume *Wittgenstein and Critical Theory: Beyond Postmodern Criticism and Towards Descriptive Investigations* (Athens: Ohio UP, 1995).

Works Cited

Baldinger, Jo Ann. "Navajo Poet Tapahonso Holds Home in Her Heart." *New Mexico* 70.8 (August 1992): 31-35.

Bataille, Gretchen. "American Indian Literature: Traditions and Translations." *MELUS* 6.4 (1979): 17-26.

Beck, Peggy V., Anna Lee Walters, and Nia Francisco. *The Sacred: Ways of Knowledge, Sources of Life.* Tsaile: Navajo Community College P, 1992.

Brill, Susan. "Discovering the Order and Structure of Things: A Conversive Approach to Contemporary Navajo Poetry." *Studies in American Indian Literatures* 7.3 (1995): 51-70.

————. Review essay on *From the Glittering World: A Navajo Story,* Irvin Morris. *Studies In American Indian Literatures* 9 (1997): forthcoming.

Bruchac, Joseph, ed. *Survival This Way: Interviews with American Indian Poets.* Tucson: U of Arizona P, 1987.

Dasenbrock, Reed Way. "Forms of Biculturalism in Southwestern Literature: The Work of Rudolfo Anaya and Leslie Marmon Silko." *Genre* 21 (Fall 1988): 307-320.

Fast, Robin Riley. "Borderland Voices in Contemporary Native American Poetry." *Contemporary Literature* 36.3 (1995): 508-536.

Momaday, N. Scott. *House Made of Dawn.* New York: Harper & Row, 1989.

————. *Way to Rainy Mountain.* Albuquerque: U of New Mexico P, 1976.

Moore, David L. "Decolonializing Criticism: Reading Dialectics and Dialogics in Native American Literatures." *Studies in American Indian Literatures* 6.4 (1994): 7-35.

Morris, Irvin. *From the Glittering World: A Navajo Story.* Norman: U of Oklahoma P, 1997.

Olson, David R. "From Utterance to Text: The Bias of Language in Speech and Writing." *Harvard Educational Review* 47.3 (1977): 257-281.

Scarberry-Garcia, Susan. *Landmarks of Healing: A Study of* House Made of Dawn. Albuquerque: U of New Mexico P, 1990.

Silko, Leslie Marmon. "Language and Literature from a Pueblo Indian Perspective." *English Literature: Opening Up the Canon.* Eds. Leslie A. Fiedler and Houston A. Baker, Jr. Baltimore: Johns Hopkins U P, 1981. 54-72.

Tapahonso, Luci. *Blue Horses Rush In: Poems and Stories.* Tucson: U of Arizona P, 1997.

————. *Sáanii Dahataal/The Women Are Singing: Poems and Stories.* Tucson: U of Arizona P, 1993.

————. Interview. WCBU-FM. Peoria, Il. 24 April 1996.

Walters, Anna Lee, ed. *Neon Pow-Wow: New Native American Voices of the Southwest.* Flagstaff: Northland, 1993.

Wiget, Andrew. "Identity, Voice, and Authority: Artist-Audience Relations in Native American Literature." *World Literature Today* 66.2 (1992): 258-263.

Wilson, Michael. "Speaking of Home: The Idea of the Center in Some Contemporary American Indian Writing." *Wicazo Sa Review* 12.1 (1997): 129-147.

Witherspoon, Gary. *Language and Art in the Navajo Universe.* Ann Arbor: U of Michigan P, 1977.

Zepeda, Ofelia, and Jane H. Hill. "The Condition of Native American Languages in the United States." *Diogenes* 153 (1991): 45-65.

Gretchen M. Bataille (essay date 1997)

SOURCE: Bataille, Gretchen M. "Luci Tapahonso: A Navaho Voice in the Midwest." In *Native American Women in Literature and Culture,* edited by Susan Castillo and Victor M. P. Da Rosa, pp. 77-86. Porto, Portugal: Fernando Pessoa University Press, 1997.

[*In the following essay, Bataille praises Tapahonso's work, particularly* Sáanii Dahataal: The Women Are Singing, *contending that with this book "Luci Tapahonso joined Joy Harjo, Louise Erdrich, Leslie Marmon Silko, and others as an undisputed important female voice in the American Indian literary landscape."*]

With the publication of her fourth book *Sáanii Dahataal: The Women Are Singing* by the University of Arizona Press, Luci Tapahonso joined Joy Harjo, Louise Erdrich, Leslie Marmon Silko, and others as an undisputed important female voice in the American Indian literary landscape. This book demonstrates her versatility and maturity as a writer and brings together the elements of landscape, tradition, and humour that were evident in earlier works. In this volume, Tapahonso combines poetry and fiction and places herself amid the "foreign" landscape of Kansas, so different from the dry land of Shiprock and the Navajo Reservation where the San Juan and Rio Grande rivers are so quiet compared to the wide and brown waters of the Kaw River in her new Midwestern home.

Born November 8, 1953, in Shiprock, New Mexico, and reared on the Navajo Reservation, Tapahonso knows who she is and that sense of identity comes through her poetry. Unlike many mixed bloods who grew up away from reservation or Indian communities, Tapahonso still calls Shiprock "home." For Tapahonso, Chinle, Lukachukai, Albuquerque, Dulce, and Gallup are not just places on an ancestral map; they are places she has lived and worked and where her extended family has always lived and travelled. The landscape dotted with mesquite, tamarack, and sagebrush, the greasewood and chaparral of the arroyos and buttes of Arizona and New Mexico are where she has gathered piñons, collected firewood, and eaten mutton stew. It is this physical landscape of Arizona and New Mexico that informs and infuses Tapahonso's poetry and short fiction even as she lives among the flat terrain of Kansas. Dinetah, the land of the Diné, is her source of spiritual strength as it has for years physically sustained her people. In 1981 in *One More Shiprock Night,* she wrote, I know I cannot divide myself or separate myself from that place, my home, my land, and my people. And that realization is my security and my mainstay in my life away from there." Later she confirms this view: ". . . the place of my birth is the source of the writing . . ." (*Sáanii,* x).

Navajo is her first language and she was educated at Navajo Methodist School in Farmington, New Mexico, and Shiprock High School on the largest Indian reservation in the United States in both area and population. Tapahonso's clan is Todikozhi (salt water), and her mother Lucille Deschenne is Todikozhi while her father Eugene Tapahonso, Sr., is Todich'ii'nii (bitter water), one of the four original clans. Ironically, for one born in a land of little rain, Tapahonso (in Navajo Tabaaha tsoh) means Big Water Edge or Edge of Big Water.

Tapahonso graduated from the University of New Mexico with a BA degree in English in 1980, taught briefly at San Felipe Elementary School at San Felipe Pueblo, and earned a MA degree in Creative Writing and English from the University of New Mexico in 1982. It was at the University of New Mexico that she was influenced and inspired by Leslie Marmon Silko, then a faculty member at the University, and she began to take her writing seriously.

Tapahonso has taught at the University of New Mexico and Southwestern Indian Polytechnic Institute in Albuquerque. She is an associate professor of English at the University of Kansas where she lives with her husband Bob G. Martin who is Cherokee and president of Haskell Indian Nations University in Lawrence, Kansas. Tapahonso is a commissioner with the Kansas Arts Commission and serves on the Board of Directors for the American Indian Law Resource Centre and the Telluride Institute Writers Forum Advisory Board. In 1989 she was honoured by the New Mexico Commission of Higher Education as a New Mexico Eminent Scholar.

In a public address to members of the Federation of State Humanities Councils, Tapahonso discussed her sense of identity. For her, a proper introduction includes more than her name; it includes her place of birth, her clan identity, and her kinship relationships. Her identity is personal, but it is not singular, for who she is depends on the family, clan, and nation. She acknowledges the importance of these contributors: "This writing, then, is not 'mine,' but a collection of many voices that range from centuries ago and continue into the future" (*Sáanii,* xii). In an interview with Joseph Bruchac (1987) she spoke of the past:

". . . because the past determines what our present is or our future will be. I don't think there is really a separation of the three. We have to have the past in order to go on and to survive to draw strength from" (275). Later in that same volume, she writes in "Just Past Shiprock," "This land that may seem arid and forlorn to the newcomer is full of stories which hold the spirits of the people, those who live here today and those who lived centuries and other worlds ago" (6). Just as her poetry is contemporary but rooted in Diné tradition, her own sense of identity as a Navajo woman includes shopping malls as well as velvet skirts and turquoise necklaces.

In a personal statement, Luci Tapahonso describes herself:

> I was born in Shiprock, New Mexico, where I lived until my early twenties. I grew up in a large, extended household where Navajo was the primary language, and we learned English in later childhood. Though I am now in a predominantly English-functioning environment, I consider Navajo language to be the undercurrent, the matrix which everything in my life filters through. It is the language that soothes, comforts, and cradles for me the extremes of expression, sheer happiness and unbearable grief. Yet I use English to function in American society. This writing is, at times, an exhilarating challenge because I must, as near as possible, find the English version of what are essentially Navajo concepts. It is the beauty of the Navajo language—the sounds, the pauses, the rhythm of songs, prayers, conversation, and oratory that infuses every

aspect of my daily life, and provides sustenance away from the Navajo community. For me, writing is a way of sharing the memories and voices of family and relatives, and a way of surviving. It is, at once, selfish, and it is also a celebration of, and a sharing with others the nurturing sense of equanimity that the traditional Navajo lifestyle is rooted in. As an English professor, my community is made up of students, colleagues, and the city of Lawrence, Kansas; my community is also that of my mother and father's relatives, my siblings' children, my own children and their children, and that of the Navajo people, and the common history and beliefs we represent.

She traces her own identity to the creation of First Man and First Woman and Changing Woman, who represents the uniting of thought and speech and who gave the Navajo their first lessons in childbirth and family relationships. In **"This is how they were placed for us,"** Tapahonso acknowledges the geographical landscape that surrounds the centre of her world on the Navajo Reservation as well as the image of Changing Woman:

> Because of her, we think and create.
> Because of her, we make songs.
> Because of her, the designs appear as we weave.
> Because of her, we tell stories and laugh.
> We believe in old values and new ideas.
>
>   (1)

Traditions such as first-laugh dinners and the importance of the cradle board to Navajo babies can be traced back to the earliest times and stories. The over one hundred clans today are linked to those first four clans created by Changing Woman, clans that established a matrilineal system still guiding contemporary Navajo decisions about marriage and kinship responsibilities. In an interview with Sylvie Moulin, Tapahonso commented, "When I was growing up they used to say that nobody is an orphan, that everybody has a mother and that your mother is the Earth and your father is the Sky" (15). In **"It Has Always Been This Way,"** (*Sáanii,* 17-18) and **"Sháá Áko Dahjiníleh Remember the Things They Told Us"** (*Sáanii,* 19-20) she writes of the importance of remembering the advice of the Holy People about how to rear children and being sure not to break taboos during pregnancy. She remembers to place pollen on her own child's tongue and knows where to bury an infant's belly button.

Tapahonso uses both English and Navajo in her poetry, reflecting the importance of the language of her birth as well as of her formal and informal education. In interviews she has commented that one of many readers' favourite poems, **"Hills Brothers Coffee,"** is a direct translation from the Navajo (Bruchac, *MELUS,* 90). Phrases such as "the store is where I'm going to" and "It does it good for me" mirror Navajo syntax. Tradition appears in her work in the form of important

figures such as yeis or simply through her retelling of the familiar stories. She says in *Sáanii Dahataal,* "To know stories, remember stories, and to retell them well is to have been 'raised right' "(xi). To know the stories and songs is to be wealthy among the People. Such wealth comes from knowing one's identity, for Tapahonso says it is by the knowledge of the stories that "an individual is directly linked to the history of the entire group" (*Culturefront,* 39).

In *Through Navajo Eyes,* Sol Worth and John Adair discussed the importance of walking to the Navajo and the significance the Navajo people place on "moving about" (144-52, 199-207). The documentary films made by Navajos show a silversmith walking to the "old mine," a weaver walking to collect roots for soap, and an elder walking to gather roots and herbs for a ceremony. The Navajo must travel great distances on the reservation, whether to visit relatives, to herd sheep, or to seek vegetation for dyes for wool. This history of walking is represented in the Navajo "Night Chant":

> Happily may I walk.
> Happily with abundant dark clouds may I walk.
> Happily with abundant showers may I walk.
> Happily with abundant plants may I walk.
> Happily on a trail of pollen may I walk.
> Happily may I walk.
> Being as it used to be long ago, may I walk.
>
>   (Bierhorst, 307-8)

In Tapahonso's poetry, the characters travel, walk, or drive from one place to another. According to Tapahonso, the Navajo language itself has a "sense of motion" (Crawford, 198). Navajo history is rooted in travelling. Navajo tradition tells of the movement from three previous worlds before the present fourth world was established and populated by the Earth Surface People. It was only because of the knowledge and wisdom gained by going through earlier worlds that the present world could be established. In more recent history, the Navajo people were forced on the Long Walk in 1864 when more than 8000 Navajo walked to Fort Sumner in southern New Mexico, three hundred miles south of their familiar four sacred mountains. For the Navajo people, the march to Bosque Redondo remains one of the darkest periods of their history; over 2500 died during this period of four years of government captivity. **"In 1864"** is a poem in which Tapahonso relates this historic event to contemporary storytelling: "You are here because of what happened to your great-grandmother long ago" (*Sáanii,* 7). Luci Tapahonso has herself made many journeys from her home—to school and most recently to live in Lawrence, Kansas. She writes frequently of long automobile trips, of her own family members' journeys and of others who have walked great distances. In **"A Prayer"** (*Seasonal Woman,* 51), she writes of driving between Santa Fe and Albuquerque:

I can easily sing
for that time is mine
and these ragged red cliffs
flowing hills and wind echoes
are only extensions
of a never-ending prayer.

(p. 51)

She sees the strength of women in Navajo society and often alludes to that traditional power. The **"Seasonal Woman"** of the title poem in her collection is a "woman of fierce seasons and gentle mornings" (23). Such power is as old as the birth of the world and is linked to the births of her own daughters Lori Tazbah and Misty Dawn. She begins *Seasonal Woman* with **"Misty Dawn at Feeding Time,"** a poem about a mother nursing her baby, but it isn't just any mother, for Misty Dawn is Tapahonso's daughter and it is fitting that this poet who exemplifies in her life and in her poetry her femaleness would write of this most important and intimate activity, a mother nourishing her daughter. For Tapahonso, the sustenance is more than milk; it is the passing on of stories and traditions to her own children, to other Navajo children, and, luckily for her many readers, to a public that reads her words. The last line, "and I will live and live and live," is a testament to the continuance.

In **"A Breeze Swept Through,"** the title poem of her next collection, she begins again with birth, with daughters, and with the relationship between the mythical past and the spiritual present:

The first born of dawn woman slid out amid
crimson fluid streaked with stratus clouds
her body glistening August sunset pink
light steam rising from her like rain on warm rocks

(p. 2)

The poem connects the birth of her first daughter in August with the unusual cool breeze that alerted Grandpa that the birth had occurred. Tapahonso's second daughter was born in mid-November:

She is born of damp mist and early sun.
She is born again woman of dawn.
She is born knowing the warm smoothness of rock.
She is born knowing her own morning strength.

(p. 2)

The first poem of *Sáanii Dahataal* is also about birth. **"Blue Horses Rush In"** is dedicated to the birth of Chamisa Bah Edmo and white, yellow, blue, and black horses from the four directions accompany the birth, blessing it with the balance and wholeness of the Navajo world:

You will grow strong like the horses of your past.
You will grown strong like the horses of your birth.

(p. 2)

In some poems the character of Leona Grey speaks for all women in their various guises. She represents the oral tradition, dialogue in storytelling, and the stories about people the Navajo have known, both traditional stories and contemporary gossip about women who are too wild and drink too much. Leona Grey appears in three poems in *Seasonal Woman.* In **"Her Daughter's Eyes"** the theme of motherhood and generations is expressed:

Leona looked into her daughter's face
knowing they breathe the same memories, the same
  blood—
dark and wet circulating
forever into time and others

(p. 13)

In **"Time Flies"** (13), Leona Grey's baby is born, and in **"No Particular Reason"** (47) Leona is killed by her husband with a beer mug, "ending her nightlife / and life, in general." In **"Light a Candle"** (*Sáanii Dahataal,* 49-50) the character of Leona appears again, or perhaps it is her memory to which Tapahonso asks that a candle be lighted.

Tapahonso's grandmother and mother appear in her poetry, and always her daughters Lori and Misty Dawn are there to represent continuance of the Navajo and of that female line that is traced back to First Woman. She reclaims and reaffirms the experiences of Indian women as mothers and life givers, but also as carriers of traditions and the repositories of knowledge to be passed on to their children. In *One More Shiprock Night,* she writes, "A lot of my writing has to do with my children, about my daughters who are growing up in a totally different way. . . . So my writing has a circular form—it comes back to me through the children and together it becomes a prayer of sorts back to the land, the people, and the families from whence we came originally" (95).

Luci Tapahonso has a sense of humour. In a variation of "shaggy dog" stories, she tells several stories about dogs with names like Chip and Dale or dogs who are "dog napped." Like N. Scott Momaday, she recognizes that her people take the presence of dogs for granted but miss them when they are not around. In **"How She Was Given Her Name"** (*Sáanii,* 43), she tells the story of how a child was given the name "'Beep-beep' / because she liked to be a roadrunner / and she liked having people try to catch her." Naming is a serious subject; however, Tapahonso recognizes that even traditions can evoke laughter.

Not all of Tapahonso's poetry is pleasant, however. She is aware of the racism that permeates the Southwest and rears its ugly head in those towns closest to the reservations. She knows of deaths for no reason, of alcoholism bred by despair, and of children who suffer. In **"Hard to Take"** (*Seasonal Woman,* 17) she describes the cashier at Foodway and salesladies at Merle Norman who insult or ignore Navajo customers, and in **"Pay Up or Else"** in the same volume (28) her narrative poem tells of the murder of Vincent Watchman at Thriftway for ninety-seven cents. In **"Uncle's Journey"** (*Sáanii,* 71-76) and in **"The Snakeman"** in the same collection (79-83), children learn about death, but they also learn of the "other worlds" of the dead. Uncle becomes a star, and the little girl visits her parents at the cemetery and talks to her mother every night.

Tapahonso also has a sense of who she is as a "westerner." Tony Lamas, pickups, country western clothing and music, and strong black Hills Brothers coffee all appear in her poetry and stories. These are elements of contemporary Navajo life that represent changes occurring within the context of the still-existing strong traditions of her people. **"Raisin Eyes"** (*Seasonal Woman,* 40) is often reprinted and is one of the most frequently requested poems at Tapahonso's readings. It tells of the modern Navajo woman trapped by her attraction to Navajo cowboys:

> These Navajo cowboys with raisin eyes
> and pointed boots are just bad news
> but it's so hard to remember that
> all the time.

(p. 41)

In **"The Way It Is,"** Tapahonso explains the superimposition of new traditions of roadside vendors, video games, and carnivals on traditional Navajo life. Ice cubes and portable toilets exist side-by-side with celebrations of feast days and frybread. Pick-up trucks and motorbikes have replaced horses for many families, but amidst these differences, some things never change. When she leaves the reservation to return to Kansas in **"The Weekend is Over,"** she stops to buy strong coffee and mutton and green chile along with sweet blue corn Navajo cake to remember the taste of Dinetah as her car marks the miles away from her "home" (*Sáanii,* 3-4).

The Navajo phrase *taahooajii twiitaaye* encompasses a philosophy of the "total environment: the weather, the land, and the individual, and ensures that all tasks associated with the economic well-being of the family are shared by all able family members" (McAuley, 14).

Tapahonso remembers the advice she was given: "Remember who you are" (*Sáanii,* 91). She writes in **"What I Am"** of carrying pollen to Paris and watching it drift down from the top of the Eiffel Tower to the plaza below: "It was while I stood on top of the Eiffel Tower that I understood that who I am is my mother, her mother, and my great-grandmother" (92). It is this strong matrilineal line that gives Luci Tapahonso strength and identifies her place among her people. She knows her heritage, and it is knowledge she will pass on to her daughters to give them the accumulated strength of generations of Navajo women. Herding sheep has been replaced by a different economic system for many Navajo people just as oil lamps have given way to electricity. In the past Luci Tapahonso might have stayed in the shadows of the red rocks of the reservation to pass on the stories of Changing Woman; today she has a wider audience.

Tapahonso writes of hozho, beauty that comes from a state of balance with all things living and non-breathing. By adhering to the old stories and songs, by transforming them so that a new generation continues the beliefs, and by chanting her poems as prayers, Tapahonso maintains that balance in her own life. Tapahonso's culture is dynamic and changing, always in the process of being recreated using new forms and new stories.

Bibliography

By Luci Tapahonso

Bah's Baby Brother is Born. (Washington: National Organization on Fetal Alcohol Syndrome, 1994).

A Breeze Swept Through. (Los Angeles: West End Press, 1987).

"Come into the Shade." *Open Places, City Spaces: Contemporary Writers on the Changing Southwest.* Ed. Judy Nolte Temple. (Tucson: University of Arizona Press, 1994), pp. 73-85.

Dine ABC Book. (New York: MacMillan, 1995).

Hayoolkal: An Anthology of Navajo Writers. (Tucson: University of Arizona Press, 1995).

"The Kaw River Rushes Eastward." *A Circle of Nations: Voices and Visions of American Indians.* Ed. John Gattuso. (Hillsboro: Beyond Words, 1993), pp. 106-110.

One More Shiprock Night. (San Antonio: Tejas Art Press, 1981).

Sáanii Dahataal. (Tucson: University of Arizona Press, 1993).

Seasonal Woman. (Santa Fe: Tooth of Time Press, 1981).

"Singing in Navajo, Writing in English: The Poetics of Four Navajo Writers." *Culturefront* 2, 2 (Summer 1993): 36-41, 74.

This is how they were placed for us. Kansas City, MO: Midwest Centre for the Literary Arts, 1994.

"The Way It Is." In *Sign Language: Contemporary Southwest Native America.* [Photographs by Skeet McAuley; organized by the Amon Carter Museum, Fort Worth, TX] (New York: Aperture, 1989), pp. 37-45.

SECONDARY SOURCES

Alarcón, Norma, 1988. "Tapahonso, Luci, *A Breeze Swept Through.*" *Small Press Review* 5: 45.

Alexander, Floyce, 1983. "A New Voice Among the Navajo." Rev. of *Seasonal Woman. Greenfield Review* 11, 1: 191-93.

Balassi, William, John F. Crawford, and Annie O. Eysturoy, eds., 1990. *This Is About Vision: Interviews with Southwestern Writers.* [Interview by John Crawford and Annie O. Eysturoy in 1988.] Albuquerque: University of New Mexico Press, pp. 195-202.

Baldinger, Jo Ann, 1992. "Navajo Poet: Tapahonso Holds Home in Her Heart." *New Mexico Magazine* 70, 8: 31-35.

Bruchac, Joseph, 1984. "A MELUS Interview: Luci Tapahonso." *MELUS* 11, 4: 85-91.

Bruchac, Joseph, 1987. "For What It Is: An Interview with Luci Tapahonso." *Survival This Way: Interviews with American Indian Poets.* Tucson: University of Arizona Press, pp. 271-85.

Gill, Sam D, 1983. "Navajo Views of Their Origin." *Handbook of North American Indians 10: Southwest.* Edited by Alfonso Ortiz. Washington: Smithsonian Institution: 502-505.

Heimbrecht, Breinig and Klaus Losch, 1994. "Interview." *Facing America.* Eds. Wolfgang Binder and Heimbrecht Breinig. Middletown, CT: Wesleyan University Press, 1994; Berlin: Elefanten-Press, pp. 114-30, 333-46.

Moulin, Sylvie, 1991. "Nobody Is an Orphan: Interview with Luci Tapahonso." *Studies in American Indian Literatures* 3, 3: 14-18.

Penner, Andrea Millenson, 1993. "At Once, Gentle and Powerful: Voices of the Landscape in the Poetry of Luci Tapahonso." MA Thesis. Northern Arizona University, Skeet, Jennifer. "Interview." *Maazo* (Spring 1985): 35.

Tsosie, Rebecca, 1988. "Changing Women: The Cross-Currents of American Indian Feminine Identity." *American Indian Culture and Research Journal* 12, 1: 1-37.

Witherspoon, Gary, 1983. "Language and Reality in Navajo Worldview." *Handbook of North American Indians* 10: Southwest. Edited by Alfonso Ortiz. Washington: Smithsonian Institution: 570-78.

Worth, Sol and John Adair, 1972. *Through Navajo Eyes: An Exploration in Film Communication and Anthropology.* Bloomington: Indiana University Press.

FURTHER READING

Biographies

Lincoln, Kenneth. "Luci Tapahonso." In *Native American Women: A Biographical Dictionary,* edited by Gretchen Bataille and Laurie Lisa, pp. 303-05. New York: Routledge, 2001.
 Offers a biographical sketch of Tapahonso.

Sonneborn, Liz. "Luci Tapahonso." In *A to Z of Native American Women,* pp. 171-72. New York: Facts on File, Inc., 1998.
 Provides a brief sketch of Tapahonso's life and work.

Criticism

Roemer, Kenneth M. Review of *Sáanii Dahataal/The Women Are Singing: Poems and Stories* by Luci Tapahonso. *American Indian Quarterly* 17, no. 3 (summer 1993): 430-32.
 Favorable assessment of *Sáanii Dahataal.*

Tapahonso, Luci. Preface to *Blue Horses Rush In: Poems and Stories,* pp. ix-xv. Tucson: The University of Arizona Press, 1997.
 Recounts the writing of the poems and stories in this collection.

Tapahonso, Luci, and Sylvie Moulin. "Nobody Is an Orphan: Interview with Luci Tapahonso." *SAIL: Studies in American Indian Literatures* 3, no. 3 (fall 1991): 14-18.
 Interview in which Tapahonso discusses the influence of Navajo traditions on her writing.

Additional coverage of Tapahonso's life and career is contained in the following sources published by Thomson Gale: *Contemporary Authors,* **Vol. 145;** *Contemporary Authors New Revision Series,* **Vols. 72, 127;** *Dictionary of Literary Biography,* **Vol. 175;** *Literature Resource Center***; and** *Native North American Literature.*

Andrea Zanzotto
1921-

Italian poet.

INTRODUCTION

Andrea Zanzotto is considered one of the most important twentieth-century Italian and European poets. His poetry records the profound social and cultural changes that transformed postwar Italy, from the fall of Fascism in the 1940s to the advent of mass culture in the 1970s. Renowned for its experimental language and distinctive style, Zanzotto's poetry examines scientific discoveries, philosophical debates, artistic developments, and the events of contemporary history on an international stage.

BIOGRAPHICAL INFORMATION

Zanzotto was born on October 10, 1921, in Pieve di Soligo in the Veneto region of Italy. He grew up during the Fascist years and was a member of the Partisan Resistance after earning a degree in literature from the University of Padua in 1942. He published his first collection of poems, *Dietro il paesaggio* (*Behind the Landscape*) in 1951; in 1959, he married his wife, Marisa. The couple has two sons, Giovanni and Fabio. Zanzotto teaches at a public school in his hometown, a position he has held for over forty years. Zanzotto's poetry has received many awards, including the Premio Viareggio in 1979, the Premio Librex-Montale for poetry in 1983, and the Premio di poesia Pandolfo in 1998.

MAJOR POETIC WORKS

Zanzotto's first book of poetry, *Dietro il paesaggio,* is a combination of forty-five poems written from 1940 to 1948. This collection has been praised for its intellectual depth, experimental energy, and revitalization of Italian poetic traditions. In this first work, Zanzotto refers to the land as a sort of alter ego, using recurring symbols such as the moon, sun, child, and mother to reflect the changeability and flux of the seasons. In 1954, Zanzotto continued the themes expressed in *Dietro il paesaggio* with the publication of his second collection, *Elegia e altri versi* (*Elegy and Other Verses*). His third book, *Vocativo* (*Vocative*, 1957), is stylisti-

cally more complex than his previous works and focuses on a concern with the landscape and the nature of subjectivity and language. *Vocativo* is made up of two sections, the first titled "Come una bucolica" ("Like a Bucolic") and the second "Prima persona" ("First Person"). The experience of the war and his participation in the Resistance movement seem to have greatly influenced this work. "I compagni corsi avanti" ("The Comrades Who Have Gone Ahead") is a poem dedicated to his deceased comrades. Also evident in this collection is Zanzotto's growing mistrust of language as an authentic instrument for depicting reality. That mistrust is carried over into *IX Ecloghe* (*IX Ecologues,* 1962), a collection of twenty-eight poems written between 1957 and 1960. In this work, Zanzotto questions the legitimacy of the lyric form and depicts the landscape as a object of satire.

With the publication of *La Beltà* (*Beauty,* 1968), Zanzotto broke with the style of his earlier works. The forty-one poems contained in this collection broaden his investigation of linguistic truth and provide numerous linguistic experimentations. The poems in *La Beltà,* which mirror the frustration and anger of the 1960s, often defy accepted standards of language and force the reader to abandon normal reading habits. Zanzotto's linguistic experimentation became even more pronounced in his later works. For example, the trilogy consisting of *Il galateo in bosco* (*A Code of Manners in the Forest,* 1978), *Fosfeni* (*Phosphenes,* 1983), and *Idioma* (*Idiom,* 1986) has been described and one of the most significant poetic and linguistic experiments in twentieth-century Italian literature. However, Zanzotto's best known experimentation with language occurs in the poetry he wrote for Federico Fellini's film *Casanova.* The poems from this film are published in *Filò: per il Casanova di Fellini* (*The Peasant's Wake: For Fellini's Casanova,* 1976). This collection contains one of Zanzotto's most significant poems, *Filò,* which is written in the vernacular of his hometown Pieve di Soligo. In this poem, Zanzotto comments on the cinema as a new visual, global language.

CRITICAL RECEPTION

Zanzotto's reputation has grown in recent years, particularly with the publication of *La Beltà.* According to critic P. R. J. Hainsworth, Zanzotto's earlier verse was "admired for its seriousness and its formal, severely literary qualities," but it was his highly original and experimental *La Beltà* that "produced a poetry that excited, that was modernistic, difficult, even bewildering, but not facilely experimental or scandalous." Although he is not as well known in America, in Italy he is widely recognized as one of Italy's greatest living poets and has the unparalleled respect of his peers. As John P. Welle notes, the critical acclaim of Zanzotto's poetry "is particularly noteworthy given the arduous nature of Zanzotto's verse," which is often cited as inaccessible and ambiguous. However, Thomas Harrison contends that Zanzotto's poems "are often as unseemly as they are wonderfully beautiful. But when they work—and they do with astonishing regularity—they bear witness to that horizon of significance that is always addressed, though rarely so directly, by the greatest art."

PRINCIPAL WORKS

Poetry

Dietro il paesaggio [*Behind the Landscape*] 1951
Elegia e altri versi [*Elegy and Other Verses*] 1954
Vocativo [*Vocative*] 1957
IX Ecloghe [*IX Ecologues*] 1962
La Beltà [*Beauty*] 1968
Gli sguardi i fatti e senhal [*The Glances, the Facts, and Senhal*] 1969
A che valse? Versi, 1938-1942 [*What For? Verses, 1938-1942*] 1970; published as *Poesie, 1938-1973*, 1974
Pasque [*Easters*] 1973
Selected Poetry of Andrea Zanzotto 1975
Filò: per il Casanova di Fellini [*The Peasant's Wake: For Fellini's Casanova*] 1976
*Il galateo in bosco [*A Code of Manners in the Forest*] 1978
*Fosfeni [*Phosphenes*] 1983
*Idioma [*Idiom*] 1986
Meteo 1996

These works comprise a recognized but unnamed trilogy.

CRITICISM

P. R. J. Hainsworth (essay date 1982)

SOURCE: Hainsworth, P. R. J. "The Poetry of Andrea Zanzotto." *Italian Studies* 37 (1982): 101-21.

[*In the following essay, Hainsworth provides an overview of Zanzotto's career, examines the development of his poetry, and comments on the growth of his reputation in recent years.*]

Andrea Zanzotto, Vittorio Sereni, Pier Paolo Pasolini, Franco Fortini and Mario Luzi are all poets who grew up and began to write under Fascism but who have published their more important work since the war. During the 1960s they seemed to risk being eclipsed by the massive presences of Montale and Ungaretti on the one hand and by the flamboyant performances of the then young *Gruppo 63* on the other: hence the somewhat slighting appellation, *la generazione di mezzo,* that was then sometimes given to them.

If that perspective has been upturned, it has been for many reasons. But one important factor has been the progress of Zanzotto's work and an accompanying growth in his reputation in recent years. His first four books[1]—*Dietro il paesaggio* (1951), *Elegia e altri versi* (1954), *Vocativo* (1957) and *IX Ecloghe* (1962)—had gradually modulated a somewhat individual but not strikingly unusual hermeticism into an almost neoclassical mode, and each had been judiciously admired for its seriousness and its formal, severely literary qualities.[2] Yet more tumultuous energies were also discernible (or certainly are in retrospect) in *IX Ecloghe.* These energies were released in *La Beltà* (1968). Here Zanzotto produced a poetry that excited, that was modernistic, difficult, even bewildering, but not facilely experimental or scandalous, a poetry which opened itself to an amalgam of conflicting linguistic registers and yet which was still in some sense literary or poetic and within which the earlier poet could still be seen. However disturbing *La Beltà* might be, it was generally felt that Zanzotto had shown himself a much more important figure than he had previously been thought to be.[3] Since 1968 Zanzotto has published *A che valse?* (1972), which contains poems from the period 1938-42, and a further five books of new poems—*Gli sguardi, i fatti e senhal* (1969), *Pasque* (1973), *Filò* (1976) and *Il Galateo in Bosco* (1978)—the last of which is apparently intended as the first volume in a trilogy. This more recent work, in which Zanzotto has developed the novel manner of *La Beltà,* although in some compositions he flaunts more traditional, even archaic skills, has only increased his standing. Some doubt has been expressed about the political implications of his assault on 'normal' language, as have reservations about the opacity of some poems,[4] but Contini's qualification of him as 'il più importante poeta italiano dopo Montale'[5] is at the very least an index of the interest and respect which his work has aroused in Italy, if not abroad.[6]

What follows is intended as a general introduction to Zanzotto's later poetry, although it gives particular weight to *La Beltà*. It rests on two assumptions. The first is that Zanzotto's work is as intelligible, if as difficult, as the modern tradition from which it emerges. I do not mean that all possible or warranted meanings can be described, but simply that it is possible to indicate the nature of the enterprise in which Zanzotto is engaged and to discuss at least some of the significances of its products. The second assumption is that Zanzotto's more recent work is indeed worth the candle. It is so partly for simple reasons of texture. Breadth and richness of lexicon, morphological and syntactic adventurousness, fluid but baroque verse forms, unconventional, often percussive rhythms—all these features combine to give an impression of exuberance and substantiality which much hermetic and post-hermetic verse in Italy does not give. But it is also a poetry which is alive to its own existence and to the questions that its existence raises. To investigate these questions, as it does, becomes a pursuit of what may be called 'integrity' or 'reality'. The term used does not perhaps matter, since, whatever we call it, 'it' lies somewhere outside language. What does matter is that the pursuit of 'it' should be continued in the face of a world that seems perversely hostile to any such endeavour. The wager is that the negative forces may themselves be undermined if they are recognized, if, that is, instead of being rejected or repressed, they are admitted into poetry. This struggle to open and to be open may make Zanzotto's work puzzling and contradictory, but it also makes it exciting and, whatever the cost, increasingly affirmative.

In some ways Zanzotto fits into a familiar pattern. Like Pascoli, Leopardi and others before them, he is a poet whose life and work are closely bound up with a specific place, and yet, like his famous predecessors, he is no mere provincial poet. The place in question is Pieve di Soligo, a sprawling, largely modern village set on a broad shelf of hills above the valley of the Piave just before the mountains proper begin. Zanzotto was born there in 1921 and for most of his life has lived and worked there as a schoolteacher. It is Pieve di Soligo and the countryside around it, cut off from the main centres of Italy, cut off even from the larger towns of the Veneto, with a landscape, culture and to some extent a dialect of its own, which has always been a focus, perhaps the focus, of his work: it is, as it were, a centre from which primal experiences of illumination and of poetry have sprung and to which they return, both metaphorically and, it would seem, in actuality.

Initially it was the countryside, seen in its idyllic aspect, that most asserted its presence and demanded poetic attention.[7] Such an attention is given by Zanzotto in his earlier books of poetry. Whilst the landscape has held its importance, other aspects of the locality have also made themselves felt. *Filò* is written in dialect, and generally the language, stories and customs of the region have been alluded to more and more. In *Il Galateo in Bosco* the scope has widened, or rather deepened, to include more of its contradictory past and of traces of that past in the present. The hills around the Piave, especially the Montello, saw some of the worst fighting of the First World War in Italy. Yet the woods of the

Montello, to which the title alludes and which were largely destroyed in the fighting, were previously a place of *ville* and *villeggiature,* a civilized retreat celebrated by local poets, such as a certain Niccolò Zotti, whose *Oda rusticale* of 1683 is quoted by Zanzotto: and it was on the Montello that the original *Galateo* was written in 1552. Behind that Renaissance world lies a primitive Mediterranean culture and behind that again lies the world before man, evidence for which hides in the rocks and earth in disturbing conjunction with the remains of the recent and not so recent human dead.

If the past has had to be sought out, the present has demanded to be let in. The periphery may constitute an insecure coign of vantage from which to consider in poetry, as Zanzotto has done, wars, waste, injustice, mass media and other collective nightmares and achievements. But whereas Pieve di Soligo could reasonably be made a protected retreat in *Dietro il paesaggio,* more and more account has been taken in later books of the rift between literary images of the idyllic (however much renewed) and actual existence in a modern village. The 'buona gente senza più dialetto', as they are called in **'Fuisse'** (*Vocativo*), have come to live a technological and consumerist life largely directed by dubious economic and political forces. As a result the idyll may become bizarrely comical, as in **'Profezie o memorie o giornali murali XVI'** (*Beltà*) in which Nino, Zanzotto's (almost) ideal peasant, is imagined encountering technological language and technological dreams:

Così dura sul naufragio e si carena per il futuro
congettura forme inalbera e sventola piani di ricerca
Nino il ducàzio,
motorizza elettronizza televisivizza,
mette in sintonia con l'iper con l'ultra,
ottiene mandati patenti primati.

Alternatively the idyll may be twisted into the despairing satire of **'La Pasqua a Pieve di Soligo'** (*Pasque*):

su, bambine, è primizia e gemma, la luna lo attesta,
vanno in amore benzine ed essenze, ogni stecco va in
      festa,

e Pieve di Soligo ai nostri piedi formicola,
pascola comunioni e focacce, per campi e selve svi-
      cola,

e Pieve di Soligo vuota boccali di bianco e di rosso
      così
che rosso-passio e bianco-surrexit sarà presto voto D.
      C.

Even the private 'gabbia sospesa' imagined by Montale in 'Notizie dall'Amiata' is seen in **'Biglia'** (*Pasque*) to have now usually taken the form of a weekend villa, that is, of a parasitic growth on the remaining life of a depopulated region. The modern world is not, it would seem, to be shut out. At best there may be moments when the old idyll may be glimpsed, but increasingly the glimpses occur only in poetry.

The excavation of a buried but undead past and the recognition of a modern world which is distant only in a geographical sense, if at all, form part of a process of discovery, of laying bare, which is also cultural and intellectual. Zanzotto has of course expressed a special sympathy with other writers from the Veneto, such as Giacomo Noventa and Giovanni Comisso,[8] but his range has always been wider. *Dietro il paesaggio* draws not only upon the earlier Quasimodo and the hermetic idiom in general but also, as has been noted,[9] upon Eluard, Lorca and Rimbaud. Since *Dietro il paesaggio* other presences have been exposed, the more patently with each collection. Dante, Tasso, Ariosto and increasingly Petrarch and the Petrarchists have been particularly significant, and from outside Italy Hölderlin, Blanchot, Bataille, Nietzsche, Husserl, Heidegger and Lacan.[10] As these last names indicate, phenomenology, literary theory, psychology and linguistics are fields which Zanzotto refuses to relegate to prose. Instead they have been ransacked for ideas, phrases and terms which are referred to or quoted verbatim, often in distorted form, in the poems themselves. The provincial poet is also the European intellectual, much as were Leopardi and Manzoni before him, but, unlike them, he is an intellectual who announces, parodies and examines his intellectuality on almost every page that he writes. As a result, if, from one point of view, Zanzotto fits into a pattern and hence to a degree reaffirms a tradition, from another he seems to stand outside the tradition, and to call into question the very notions of literature and poetry. The laying bare may seem to become a laying waste.

In fact the commitment to something which has to be called *poesia* is total. The aim is not so much to destroy as to renew, even if, in Nietzschean fashion, the renewal is involved with destruction and often seems completely at risk. Making a metaphor of his geographical position (as he has often done), Zanzotto has said that the poet is someone on the edge of things, whose work goes against and beyond approved limits.

> Non c'è poesia che non abbia a che fare con l'emarginazione, e, appunto quando vi è coinvolta in pieno, questa forza da cui viene la poesia tocca 'il margine', il limite, e forse va al di là di tutto quello che si poteva sospettare all'inizio. Per questo il fare poetico rimane nella sua cenciosa e discutibile autonomia a istituire un polo opposto e necessario a tutte le istituzioni umane che hanno rapporto con il potere storico.[11]

Poetry then can only come into being at a point where social and intellectual institutions, however advanced, do not function. Poetry must always go further: as **'Oltranza oltraggio'**, the opening poem of *La Beltà,* suggests, the desire is and has to be to go *oltre,* to risk the outrage, to risk the loss in the hope of finding what is really there.

The going *oltre* is true of Zanzotto's own poetry. Any mode of writing and any frame of thought which might seem to attain consistency in his work have so far proved inconclusive. There is no finality because any resolution, however positive it may appear, institutionalizes and so excludes the elusive *poesia*. Hence, for example, if Lacan is appropriated (and he is most in evidence in *La Beltà*), the appropriation is already the object of ironic comment in **'La Pasqua a Pieve di Soligo'** (*Pasque*):

> oui, je lis SCILICET, la revue paraissant trois fois l'an
> à Paris, sous la direction du docteur J. Lacan;
>
> oui, je veux savoir ce qu'en pense l'école freudienne
> de Paris,
> peut-être par là arriverai-je à étouffer mes soucis.

So, on the larger scale, each of Zanzotto's books tends to move forward from the last, developing suggestions and implications of earlier work and often commenting explicitly upon it as if earlier poems had been written by someone else. Of course there are constants: indeed it is possible to see each book as a fresh raid on an identical inarticulate darkness in the hope of bringing to light what is hidden. But it is the forward urgency which is most apparent, particularly in the period stretching from *Dietro il paesaggio* (1951) to *La Beltà* (1968). Here, at least in retrospect, an almost linear progression is discernible, the most important stages of which it is worth charting in order both to show the continuity between Zanzotto's earlier and later work and also to clarify the point of departure in *La Beltà.*

Dietro il paesaggio centres on a somewhat hermetic, somewhat surreal landscape. Although there are allusions to the actual countryside of Pieve di Soligo, depiction gives way to an exploration of significance, of what it is that the phenomenal landscape points to as existing behind itself. But such an exploration becomes also an exploration of the language of landscape and in particular of the poetic language. Hence certain traditional elements of Italian poetry—especially certain substantives, such as *acqua, ghiaccio, monte, albero, luna, valle*—are privileged in the verse because they constitute another world, discoverable in and through poetry, which is more real than the phenomenal world in some sense, and which is yet there, 'dietro il paesaggio'. What is to be complained of is the loss of that world (for example in **'Montana'**); what is to be celebrated is the marriage of the self with it ('è cresciuta la gioia / di chi non sa parlare / che per conoscere / il proprio oscuro matrimonio / con il cielo e le selve'; **'Nella valle'**) or a joyful, childlike immersion in it ('Leggeri ormai sono i sogni, / da tutti amato / con essi sto nel mio paese, / mi sento goloso di zucchero'; **'Nel mio paese'**). Such a movement can also involve a return to the mother, as in **'Perché siamo'**:

> O mamma, piccolo è il tuo tempo,
> tu mi vi porti perch'io mi consoli
> e là v'è l'erba di novembre,
> là v'è la franca salute dell'acqua,
> sani come acqua siamo noi.

Yet the mother is herself a figuration of the landscape, just as the landscape is a figuration of her. For the world posited in these poems is one in which the 'I' can find joy and security, in which language, the world and the self come together in a totality where one is a feature of the other. A wholeness is regained. At the same time what is all too clear in the writing is an objectifying consciousness which may address this real or authentic world (using, to do so, a *tu* of perhaps Montalian descent), but which, by that very token, sets it apart: the consciousness has to make poems *about* a world which it cannot itself enter. The problem, as it now seems with hindsight, is that the real or authentic self may be as much, if not more, in that excluded consciousness as in the world which is addressed.

Elegia e altri versi do not really alter the position. But in the two following books an attempt is made to investigate and to uncover the more authentic self and a more authentic language associated with it. However, from the beginning of the second part of ***Vocativo*** a sense of crisis becomes apparent. The possibility emerges that the landscape is merely a function of the 'I' and so has only an illusory significance, or conversely that the self is alien and unintelligible:

> Un senso che non muove ad un'immagine,
> un colore disgiunto da un'idea,
> un'ansia senza testimoni
> o una pace perfetta ma precaria:
> questo è l'io che mi désti, madre e che ora
> appena riconosco, né parola
> né forma né ombra?

> **('Da un'altezza nuova')**

At best the ambiguous reality that is still assumed to be there may be fertile, if empty:

> il ricchissimo nihil
> che incombe e esalta, dove
> beatificanti fiori e venti gelidi
> s'aprono dopo il terrore.

> **('Da un'altezza nuova')**

But more commonly, as the title *Vocativo* suggests, there can only be an invocation of aid from that reality in the face of the actual terror of existence:

> Dai mattini orribili tu liberami
> dalla luce infinita che non leva a sé le mie scomposte

passioni, i gesti invano ripetuti,
> ai mattini toglimi, ai risvegli
> nel raggiante terrore,
> tu risveglio perpetuo su te stesso.

> **('Impossibilità della parola')**

In *IX Ecloghe* the pursuit of authenticity takes more explicitly the form of a discussion, of a contradictory and unresolved kind, about the nature of poetry. Though the discussion is partly general, several times there is an attempt to write in a poem about the poem which is actually being written. If that contradiction could become more than a mere clash of words, then subject and object, the 'I' which speaks and the 'I' which is spoken, might be brought together in the unity which appears to be denied them. Of course it is recognized from the very first poem, **'Un libro di Ecloghe'**, that the struggle must fail, because there must always be a knower who is unknown: 'pronome che da sempre a farsi nome attende, / mozza scala di Jacob, "io": l'ultimo reso unico'. One possibility is, therefore, renunciation of the enterprise: hence in the following poem, **'Ecloga I'**, the voice *b* which responds to the complaints of the voice *a* asking for the impossible to be achieved, can only recommend a surrender to the conventions accepted by previous poets:

> Come per essi, basterà la tua
> confessione, immodesta, amorosa,
> e quasi vera e più che vera
> come il canone detta.

Yet, as these lines show, there is also present an unreasonable conviction that in the conventions of poetry, in its language, even in the expression of doubts about the reality of poetry or of the self, something of value occurs which has to be continued at whatever cost to logic or common sense:

> E così sia: ma io
> credo con altrettanta
> forza in tutto il mio nulla,
> perciò non ti ho perduto
> o, più ti perdo e più ti perdi,
> più mi sei simile, più m'avvicini.

> **('Così siamo')**

It is on this basis that particularly in the later eclogues Zanzotto is able to go on celebrating poetry as a salvation from the evils of life, attaining sometimes a distinctly mystical note (as at the end of **'Ecloga VII'**: 'Perché la luce non ha che la luce / a esplicarla nel suo / attimo'). But perhaps the paradoxes come a little too easily: for the book as a whole is dominated by a consciousness that is as strict as that of ***Dietro il paesaggio,*** however much it may try to enunciate itself in the poems.

In one important respect there is a development which anticipates ***La Beltà***. In the earlier books Zanzotto had remained within the broad ambit of the hermetic idiom.

In *IX Ecloghe* the range of language expands, scientific, technical and literary Latinisms being especially noticeable. If an opening in this direction indicates a desire to avoid the immediate, the 'natural', in favour of an underlying latinate literariness, the actual presence of a new range of language sometimes creates a certain sense of freedom, as if the limits of the controlling consciousness have at least been exceeded. The extreme example of this freedom is **'13 settembre 1959 (Variante)'**, which, taking as its point of departure the 'Animula vagula blandula' of the Emperor Hadrian, begins as follows:

> Luna puella pallidula,
> Luna flora eremitica,
> Luna unica selenita,
> distonia vita traviata,
> atonia vita evitata,
> mataia, matta morula,
> vampirisma, paralisi,
> glabro latte, polarizzato zucchero.

Through the mysterious Latinisms, following one on the other in incantatory assonance, greater powers of language are activated here than the 'I' can direct. The attempt to understand has to be relinquished, if by understanding is meant a mastery of the objects of attention within a preestablished system, be it ever so paradoxical. But the real paradox is that here a poem is created which is as 'authentic' and as 'poetic' as anything which Zanzotto had so far written, and as rich in significance: for all their obscurity the words of the poem carry a complex range of meanings and associations that is in fairly sharp contrast with the monochord of some of the lines quoted above.

What therefore suggests itself is the possibility that words signify irrespective of structures of meaning that the speaker might predispose, indeed might signify more if such structures can be resisted. Characteristically, Zanzotto considers the question in theoretical terms in **'Ecloghe VIII'** and **'IX'**. In the latter he examines the problem in the context of schoolteaching, reflecting on the way in which the two contrasting positions (of 'structured' and 'free' knowledge) are assumed by the teacher and the pupils. It is, however, in **'Ecloga VIII'** that he states the conclusion towards which this new development points:

> tutto conosce
> maestramente l'arte dell'esistere.
> Ora mi sarà inutile
> dirti e dire, poi che tutto dice
> di te, per me.

In other words there is no privileged language or consciousness: everything is significant of the self, of reality and of poetry: everything speaks.

'Tutto dice' might well serve as the motto, albeit an ambiguous one, of Zanzotto's later work. It is a

principle and a mystery to which he returns in one way or another in all the books from *La Beltà* onwards, although not always to elicit the same implications. Hence from this point I shall largely abandon a chronological description in order to deal better with Zanzotto's multiform and recursive progress.

Immediately in *La Beltà* Zanzotto makes a leap from the recognition of *IX Ecloghe* that everything speaks to an attempt to activate such a total significance. The first task (one might say) is to avoid a special language or perspective which gives a factitious order to things or to words by implicitly asserting that not everything speaks, but only a specific form of words or a specific speaker. So long as a particular idiom (for instance the hermetic) is privileged in poetry, then the poet will be guilty of such a falsification. Hence Zanzotto admits into *La Beltà* any and every register of language, from that of *fumetti* to the most literary, scientific or psychoanalytic terminology, and readily distorts language semantically, phonologically and syntactically, no matter what fragmentation or conflation of linguistic units may ensue. **'Sì ancora la neve'**, for example, opens as follows:

> Che sarà della neve
> che sarà di noi?
> Una curva sul ghiaccio
> e poi e poi . . . ma i pini, i pini
> tutti uscenti alla neve, e fin l'ultima età
> circondata da pini. Sic et simpliciter?
> E perché si è—il mondo pinoso il mondo nevoso—
> perché si è fatto bambucci-ucci, odore di cristianucci,
> perché si è fatto noi, roba per noi?

Here the barriers between one register and another are down, and, since there is no hierarchy of language, there is no reason for exclusion: for to exclude suggests a privileging of what is included. Instead the text becomes omnivorous: the aim is to include as much of language as possible, to include (if it could be brought about) everything. The qualitative yields to the quantitative.

Not only is the hierarchy of registers within language undermined, but so too is that perspective which sees language as a whole to be privileged with respect to other sign-systems or to what (if anything) lies beyond those systems. Language undergoes a de-grading—some would say a degradation—to become one sign-system among many. In *Pasque* and *Il Galateo in Bosco* non-linguistic signs of various kinds are introduced which interfere with language,[12] or else, together with language, point to what has not been said in spite of the omnivorousness of the text. Rather than being closed systems, the poems seem to aspire to a maximum involvement with what is outside them, because as **'Per lumina, per limina'** (*Pasque*) concludes, there is 'l'insegnamento mutuo / di tutto a tutto': a teaching, but also a signalling of everything to everything.

The risk is readily run that the result will simply bewilder or be no more than a chaotic homologue of what is perceived as social and cultural chaos. Reproaches of this type can obviously be made, although critics such as Stefano Agosti have admired the way in which language proliferates in such poems as **'Sì, ancora la neve'**, to produce 'un vuoto di senso in cui si risolve la realtà: una *béance*',[13] as if the signifiers sprang freely from each other irrespective of any scheme of meaning. Yet, although the poems may disconcert and may well be obscure, the direction of the enterprise is not towards nonsense. Unlike the *Novissimi*,[14] who tried in their earlier work to divest language of all institutional meanings in favour of a non-sense that they saw as the only possible, if negative, authenticity, Zanzotto follows the path of sense taken by most important poets since Mallarmé: the project is to stimulate the signifying powers of language rather than to neutralize them, to produce, perhaps, a plethora of meanings rather than an absence of meaning—even if one of those meanings may be the meaninglessness or the absence of meaning of reality.

What further impedes a collapse into mere logorrhoea is the ineliminable presence of a subjective consciousness which, in some way, shapes the material and which cannot, or will not, surrender itself. As had already been intimated in *IX Ecloghe,* the desire is to unify what are plausibly and conventionally seen as irreconcilable opposites: the knower and the known, the speaker and the spoken, the subject and the object might in poetry come together so that the fracture of being to which we are condemned is healed. In *La Beltà* in particular it is implicitly recognized that it is inadequate simply to say that everything speaks: the speaker of that statement must include his own speaking within the totality that speaks and his knowledge of that inclusion. Indeed the 'I' is so present that it would be possible to invert the terms and to describe the process which occurs as rather self-expression, the extension of the self into everything rather than its dissolution. Whatever way we put it, the presence of that consciousness restricts the range of signification in the texts, and implants what we may call themes or tendencies, although one of these themes may well be the question of how meaning is created and what it is, as I believe is the case in **'Sì, ancora la neve'**.

But there are of course further complications. If everything does speak, it may only be to a certain consciousness. To the 'normal' consciousness, especially to one which looks with horror at the modern world, nothing may speak, and the phrase 'tutto dice' may point to a desideratum beyond the bounds of normal language and awareness: it may be that it is useless to assert that everything speaks if we are deaf, or if the only language we know is doomed to falsify the universal speech.

Here Zanzotto's long-standing interest in the child and childishness is relevant. Like Pascoli, Zanzotto posits a difference between the 'normal' and the 'childish'. The child, whether seen as the actual human infant or as a metaphor for a mentality, becomes particularly in *La Beltà* and *Pasque* an index of everything speaking and hence of the wholeness to which poet and poem aspire.

Two prose pieces are illuminating in this respect. Writing in 1965 about Giacomo Noventa,[15] Zanzotto discusses *putèl,* that is the Veneto word (from *putellus*) used by Noventa to indicate child-language, the child itself and the state of being a child. To return to *putèl* is to return to an uninhibiting awareness of language, 'come nell'infante che arrivi a sentirsi parlare, che avverta in sé il parlare'. If, negatively, this means a loss of adult knowledge, positively, it means a recovery: 'Il *putèl* redivivo e ferito attraverso lo sconcio, riappare come quel puer che è fantasma iniziale della stessa poesia, o meglio se ci si vuole ricollegare a frequenti affermazioni del Noventa saggista . . . è manifestazione del "venir fuori" dell'essere'. In this manifestation of being, values which are beyond direct affirmation and under continual threat are somehow reaffirmed: 'Il *putèl* iniziale è dunque, soprattutto, pienezza di responsabilità'.

Zanzotto is also aware how tenuous is the alternative which Noventa's *putèl* counterposes to the violence of history. In an article of 1973[16] he admits that the child in actuality is involved in the horrors of population explosions, of genetic programming, of generalized neurosis, as well as of environmental pollution and what Zanzotto calls 'avvelenate città-lager': hence it is hard for him to retain 'la figura quasi carismatica che aveva, in quanto "dono" o sorprendente irruzione'. And yet the child, like the poet, cannot be ignored: both are open to a future which may in a sense be present but unspoken. 'Poesia ed infanzia di quel non-detto vengono a parlarci; il rischio che esso sia terribile, entro un orizzonte in cui rivelazione e apocalisse potrebbero, etimologicamente, coincidere, non può giustificare una mancanza di ascolto.' What is perhaps more important is that they both are open to a necessary wonder in the face of the world: 'Si ritrovano, come è sempre avvenuto, nello stupore che fonda il sempre nuovo sentirsi nuovi, aperti al trauma dell'ammirazione-angoscia, capaci di tutto riorganizzare intorno a un nucleo di risveglio'.

To a degree the poems themselves follow out this 'poetica del fanciullino'. By deforming words in a childish way ('bambucci-ucci', 'pini-ini' in 'Sì, ancora la neve', for example), by imitating the cadences and apparent nonsense of nursery-rhymes and generally by impeding the 'normal' communicative functioning of language, a kind of discourse is achieved which often does seem to be in the process of becoming articulate, as if something were coming into being which as yet lacks definition. But on the whole the poems go beyond the prose. Rather as the idea that everything speaks is taken up as a theme as well as pointing to a poetic practice, so too childhood is taken up thematically: again an attempt is made to practise what is preached and to preach what is practised in order to attain the impossible unity of being. And again Zanzotto is willing to be contradictory: for there is always at work an ironic intelligence which threatens to parody its own project, although, on the other hand, it may well be that this very instability in the poetry is precisely what makes it new, something apart from 'normal' or 'adult' schemes, even those elaborated by Zanzotto himself.

The important poem, **'L'elegia in petèl'** (*Beltà*), is exemplary in this connexion. *Petèl* is presumably a variant on *putèl*, although Zanzotto explains in a note[17] that it has specific connotations: 'Nello stesso dialetto si dice *petèl* la lingua vezzeggiativa con cui le mamme si rivolgono ai bambini piccoli, e che vorrebbe coincidere con quella in cui si esprimono gli stessi (è l' "Ammensprache" dei linguisti). Il vocabolo copre appunto tutti e due i significati ed ha anche un certo valore dispregiativo'. *Petèl* is actually introduced into the poem in a pair of lines near the beginning ('Mama e nona te dà ate e cuco e pepi e memela. / Bono ti, ca, co nona. Béi bumba bona. È fet foa e upi')[18] and in another pair near the end (quoted below): but the poem as a whole is (understandably) not in this half-language. Rather than attempting simply a return to childhood, the poem attempts to bring together beginning (*petèl*) and ending (*elegia*) in a totality which embraces both ('l'elegia in petèl'). Hence the lines in *petèl* are juxtaposed with versions of lines written by Hölderlin when he was on the brink of madness: opening encounters closure, the pre-rational the postrational. And yet the poem points to, rather than is, what it calls 'la non scrivibile e inevitata elegia in petèl', because it consists of opposing words, not opposing realities: 'ma non c'è il latte petèl, qui, non il patibolo, / mi ripeto, qui no; mai stata origine mai disiezione'. What there is outside the poem is a silence and a space that the poem cannot infringe, and yet which it characterizes in language in various ways in a struggle to embrace the whole. All these elements in turn become the object of ironic reflection ('ma tutto fa brodo'): but this affirmation of total significance is itself denied in another ironic citation (from an advertising jingle): 'ma non è vero che tutto fa brodo'. The potentially infinite series of *ma* are then brought to an end as follows:

> ma: e rinascono i ma: ma
> Scardanelli faccia la pagina per Tallémant des Réaux,
> Scardanelli sia compilato con passi dell'Histoire d'O.
>
> Ta bon ciatu? Ada ciòl e úna e tée e mana papa.
> Te bata cheto, te bata: e po mama e nana.
> 'Una volta ho interrogato la Musa'.

A form of poetry (Scardanelli being the name Hölderlin appended to the poems of his madness) merges with the 'historiettes' of Tallemant (rather than Zanzotto's Tallémant) des Réaux and the pornography of the *Histoire d'O*. This 'decadence' also merges with childhood, and not merely in the two lines of *petèl*: for the babbling succession of *ma* suggests childish language too, perhaps even a half-ludicrous rebirth. The final line, which is also a quotation from Hölderlin ('Einst hab ich die Muse gefragt' from the *Hymnische Entwürfe*) is a last comment on the poem, summarizing its contradictions and alluding to the 'real' poem, which has not been written.

Even where there is little direct reference to childhood, the issue of beginnings, of coming into existence, of movement from the hidden and unnamed into the manifest and nameable is often raised—for example in **'Ampolla (cisti) e fuori'** (*Beltà*) where the question regards precisely *la beltà*. The extreme point which Zanzotto has reached in his exploration of origins would appear to be **'Pasqua di maggio'** (*Pasque*). In this long and ambitious poem there is an attempt to go metaphorically beyond the infant into an intra-uterine or egg-like state, that is, to exemplify and reflect upon the biological proliferation of seeds, eggs and other ovoid formations and the proliferation of meanings in an 'ovular' manner in language. At the same time the poem recognizes that both pullulations may be futile, the more so in a scientifically programmed and yet disastrous world. In these conditions the traditional view of Easter as a time of rebirth becomes not merely invalid but almost unimaginable, except as an impossibility, an Easter in May, which may through a poem become imaginable again. There the forces of destruction may lose their terror and their energies become in some sense good—although this poem, **'Pasqua di maggio'**, like **'L'elegia in petèl'**, suggests that it may not be in its words that the impossible occurs.

Cognate with Zanzotto's exploration of the language and metaphor of childhood seems to be his interest in dialect; for dialect may be the lost language of childhood, more intimate and mysterious than the national language and yet more a language than the *petèl* of **'L'elegia'**. Zanzotto's main poems in dialect to date are contained in *Filò*.[19] They were written as a result of a request from Federico Fellini (published here as a preface) for some verse for his *Casanova*. The scenes for which the verse was intended show archetypal female figures, and Fellini suggested that the appropriate language would be a Venetian which had been revitalized, if necessary through the mixing of elements from different periods and the invention of neologisms, so that the eventual effect might resemble that of the *petèl* included in **'L'elegia'**. What Zanzotto provided are the **'Recitativo veneziano'** and the **'Cantilena londinese'** which occupy the first part of the book. But, characteristically, these two poems gave rise to a third, the actual **'Filò'** ('filò: veglia di contadini, nelle stalle durante l'inverno, ma anche interminabile discorso che serve a far passare il tempo e a nient'altro'),[20] which takes up the rest of the book and which is itself written in the dialect of the Soligo valley, as Zanzotto explains in an essay on dialect appended to the poem. **'Filò'** is a string of reflections on the cinema, the earth, earthquakes and the earth-mother, but also on the problems of writing in dialect in all three poems. As is apparent, the diversity of lexicon and register characteristic of Zanzotto's later work is here muted: the more primary language is also the more impoverished, as, of course, the poem itself recognizes:

> Vecio parlar che tu à inte'l tó saór
> un s'cip de lat de la Eva,
> vecio parlar che no so pi,
> che me se á descuní
> dì par dì 'nte la boca (e no tu me basta);
> che tu sé canbià co la me fazha
> co la me pèl ano par an;
> parlar porét, da poreti, ma s'cèt
> ma fis, ma tóch cofà 'na branca
> de fien 'pena segà dal faldin (parché no bàstetu?).[21]

It would appear, then, that for the moment at least the limitations of dialect exclude its becoming the main language of poetry. Hence, although Zanzotto includes one poem in dialect, **'E pò, muci'**, in *Il Galateo in Bosco,* which was the book written after *Filò,* he prefers generally there to introduce words or phrases from dialect into an overall Italianate language in order to gain particular effects (see, for example, the last line of the first citation from '(Stracaganasse o castagne secche)' below).

As two ways of approaching the problem of how everything speaks or might speak, dialect and *petèl,* at least in isolation, fail, as Zanzotto recognizes they must fail. At best they can point to a reality which remains unattainable, inarticulable, in Lacan's sense of the word, 'impossible',[22] because it will not be penetrated by the 'outrage' of language (see **'Oltranza, oltraggio'**) or embraced within it (as is recognized in **'L'elegia in petèl'**). Yet in, or through, the failure of these two modes, as of any other that could be imagined, may come the only possible success. At the end of 'Retorica su: lo sbandamento, il principio **"resistenza" III'** (*Beltà*), Zanzotto asks: 'Una riga tremante Hölderlin fammi scrivere. / Sì? Nel fascino tutto conversa converge?'. The trembling line, the line which cannot itself be held in focus, but which has the mysterious power of fascination, may be the point of convergence of everything in speech. Some activation of language may occur which releases forces too powerful for the schemes of classification with which we construct a false reality, and the other reality from which we are barred may be revealed, if only for a moment. Instead of a poem about reality, the poem in its unassimilable otherness may perhaps *be* reality.

It is towards such an activation of language that Zanzotto's insistence on paradox and contradiction in the verbal texture of so many poems seems to be directed, because it is in paradox and contradiction that the barriers created by false consciousness are at their weakest. Sometimes the effect is negative: in lines such as 'Levigatissima spigolosissima / tu te tibi a te per te / ledeva illesa . . .' (**'Ampolla (cisti) e fuori'**) the antithetical terms, as it were, eliminate each other to leave a vacuum, the *béance* of which Agosti speaks. At other points the semantic conflict is more complex, as in the concluding lines of **'Possibili prefazi o riprese o conclusioni V'** (*Beltà*):

> Ma di fatto lascio la presa, non esorto
> alle storie alle scienze alle lingue.
> Indulgo e d'altro il mio stato faccio pingue,
> torno nel giro delle lievi lusinghe
> torno al brevissimo che appena appena so.
>
> 'Non far fuori'   'Far fuori'

Here the chiasma of double meanings created by the negative and positive of 'far fuori' in its two senses of 'to bring out' and 'to kill' may create at some point of intersection (indicated on the page by the space in the line) a pressure of signification which it is impossible to divert into familiar interpretative channels. And here, as always, the doubt is that the paradox may be no more, and no less, than a manner, or word-play.

In *Pasque* and *Il Galateo in Bosco* contradiction and conflict are extended beyond the individual poem, to give rise, at least in *Pasque,* to strangely formalistic patterns. **'La Pasqua a Pieve di Soligo'**, which itself concludes with the discrepant comments of a series of voices, is negated in the following poem, **'Codicillo'**. **'Pasqua di maggio'**, which is the 'positive' correlative of the 'negative' **'Pasqua a Pieve di Soligo'**, also concludes with divergent voices and is itself negated in **'Attoniti, amanti'**. In *Il Galateo,* perhaps developing a possibility suggested in two poems of *Pasque* entitled **'Feria sexta in Parasceve'** and **'Feria sexta in Parasceve (Variante)'**, sequences of poems appear all of which, it would seem, are different attempts on the same poem or the same reality. For example, in the sequence of five poems on illumination with the unusual but not unintelligible titles **'(Ill Ill)'**, **'Ill Ill'**, **'(ILL) (ILL)'**, **'(ILL ILL)'**, and **'ILL ILL'**, there is a fluid movement from something which cannot be spoken in the first poem to a positive enunciation in the last. Each poem negates the preceding and yet by including all five versions Zanzotto negates that negation. The process by which the affirmation comes to be made is implicitly recognized as being as important or as poetic as the affirmation itself. Here, as elsewhere in *Il Galateo,* contradiction becomes an impressive collusion of fixity and flux, in which the latter takes precedence.

The dissatisfaction with any single formulation and the readiness to build up schemes of contradiction within and across poems are features of Zanzotto's work which suggest links with a poet with whom he may seem to have little in common. In fact Petrarch can be discerned in the distance behind Zanzotto's early poetry, if mediated by the hermetic *koiné*, and increasingly he has been brought forward, as if he too represented some repressed zone which has had to be slowly returned to the light. In many senses Zanzotto is a Petrarchist, and in some poems explicitly so.

Included in *IX Ecloghe* is **'Notificazione di presenza'**, an ironic sonnet, Petrarchan in articulation, which anticipates the remarkable **'Ipersonetto'** of *Il Galateo*. Zanzotto's note explains: 'È un componimento formato da 14 sonetti che tengono ognuno il posto di un verso in un sonetto. Più una premessa e una postilla. È questo un particolare omaggio a coloro che, come Gaspara e il Monsignore del *Galateo*, scrissero sonetti abitando nel Bosco'.[23] These poems may indeed recall Della Casa, but Zanzotto does seem also to reach back to Petrarch himself in his virtuoso manipulations of the conventions in order to point up the falsity of language, as in the last sonnet:

> Falso pur io, clone di tanto falso,
> od aborto, e peggiore in ciò del padre,
> accalco detti in fatto ovver misfatto:
>
> così ancora di te mi sono avvalso,
> di te sonetto, righe infami e ladre—
> mandala in cui di frusto in frusto accatto.

Petrarch (the father referred to here?) would have recognized the problem and the linguistic game which it gives rise to.

Recently Zanzotto has tended to see Petrarch as an emblematic figure. In 1976 he commented on the role which Petrarch and the Petrarchists may claim for themselves:

> Il poeta—il letterato—che secondo un luogo comune sembra gridare pace pace pace soltanto perché non se ne disturbino i melanconici e incantevoli *otia*, di fatto insinua che solo l'autorità sfuggente di una inerme e ansiosa consapevolezza originata da un costante, non evitato rapporto col limite, e in apparenza rivolta soltanto a smussare mediare ovattare, può forse rendere meno costrittive le maglie rigidissime dei vettori della violenza che fa la storia, può sviare un poco questa storia dal suo bestialismo, forse felicemente snaturarla.[24]

This favourable reinterpretation of Petrarchist abstraction has obviously a relevance for Zanzotto's own practice and for his own poetry, particularly in *Pasque*

and *Il Galateo in Bosco,* in which the ethical dimension of the search for authenticity has become more explicit and more dominant than it was in *La Beltà.*

Zanzotto's neo-Petrarchism—as it might be called—has a polemical aspect which is most apparent in certain poems of *Pasque.* **'I misteri della pedagogia'**, for example, is a mocking, not quite despairing consideration of the difficulties which Zanzotto himself faces as a teacher of Dante in a *centro di lettura*: but the scope of the poem embraces the whole question of teaching (compare **'Ecloga IX'**) and the possible, or impossible, functioning of poetry in existing institutions. More important is the stridently virtuoso **'Pasqua a Pieve di Soligo'**, written, according to Zanzotto's note, in homage to Cendrars's 'Les Pâques à New York', but certainly surpassing it in power. It is a summation, in the form of an Easter meditation, of Zanzotto's negative vision; in it all that can be seen, said or thought is judged inauthentic and destructive, but even the reality of violence is elusive, since language itself is flawed:

> E mi sfuggono intanto questi pseudoalessandrini
> —demodizzati, a gradini, da Cendrars a Pasolini—
>
> l'alessandrino baciato non va più
> nemmeno per snobbarti non che per sviolinarti Gesù.

Consciousness of falsehood and a readiness to speak knowing that speech to be false, as in **'Ipersonetto'**, constitute the one slight positive that can be affirmed.

La Beltà however had already suggested a less hopeless alternative. In 'Retorica su: lo sbandamento, il principio **"resistenza" IV'**, Zanzotto substitutes for false versions of History, whether Marxist or idealist, the possibility of egalitarian wholeness:

> E ho mangiato anche quel giorno
> —dopo il sangue—
> e mangio tutti i giorni
> —dopo l'insegnamento—
> una zuppa gustosa, fagioli.
> Posso farlo e devo.
> Tutti possono e devono.
> Bello. Fagiolo. Fiore.

And towards the end of the poem he elaborates further:

> Va' corri. Spera una zuppa di fagioli
> spera arrivare possedere entrare
> nel templum-tempus.
> Contemplare. Tempo ottimo e massimo.

What he seems to be suggesting here is perhaps mystical, perhaps it is even a re-evocation of pauperizing Christianity: for a renunciation of false desires in favour of a 'zuppa di fagioli' is related to an entry into real time, perhaps into sacred time (the 'templum-tempus' deriving from Heidegger according to the note) which can and must be opposed to the delusions of History, in all senses of the word. In this sacred time perhaps the dilemmas that arise from the principle that 'tutto dice' and its extensions in *petèl* and dialect come to a resolution which is not a false closure of the issue. It may itself be a metaphor and point to an impossibility: but here the 'impossible' is not unimaginable, merely at the antipodes of any materialism.

The eighteen 'Profezie o memorie o giornali murali' evince something of a similar outlook. In the figure of the farmer Nino, Zanzotto celebrates the virtues of a peasant civilization which survive in the face of modernity—friendliness, modesty, obstinacy, poverty, pleasure in sex and wine. But on the whole he hesitates in *La Beltà* to explore further the path he takes in **'Retorica'** and even in the 'Profezie' the affection is shot with irony. It is in *Il Galateo in Bosco* that the positive is affirmed more strongly, perhaps most impressively in **'(Stracaganasse o castagne secche)'**. In this poem authenticity is imagined as bringing together buried and present selves in a pig-like closeness with the earth:

> A questo mio bisavolo-me ed a me
> prima che arrivi il guardiano
> a strapparci di bocca la lurida cibaria
> a impedirci il raspare e il rosicchiare
> > tra i piedi sporchi della Grande Terra
> > sia concesso ancora qualche scasso o scrostatura
> > (cionpo gobo zhòt zhabòt zhalèch . . .).

A few lines later there is a picture of the two figures eating a celebratory meal at which there is a necessary absence of nourishment and, in consequence, the possibility of a symbiosis between 'us' and the much-pillaged wood:

> e poi ci metteremo a tavola di fronte a una
> sfarinata, magra di vitamine, a un pasto di stracaga-
> > nasse;
> davanti a un bicchiere di vin piccolo
> guardandoci l'un l'altro come sacre immagini
> attenderemo il sàtori
>
> > e allora il bosco tutto
> > con le unghie rotte e le gengive scotte
> > potremo insieme rovistare e rapinare
> > ma senza dargli rovina
>
> > > nemmeno in una stilla, in una trina.

It is this vision, ascetic and humorous at the same time, that is the object of much of *Il Galateo*: that is, a non-horrific recuperation of a horrific past hidden in the wood (in the past, in the self, in language and in the real wood of the Montello) in order to derive from it a life that can be regulated by a shifting system of conventions. But the regulation will not be to exploit, to dominate or even to defend: it will simply give ever-changing form to the multiplicities of meaning or being

which the wood will provide. The 'I' may still insist on being heard, but now it is in metaphors of biological dissolution and rebirth, at the level of insects, bacteria and other minimal animal and plant life, that it comes into being or loses being and that its happiness can be imagined.

Il Galateo in Bosco no more resolves the problems than previous books had done, but in the midst of its hostility to History and its continuing doubts it does project this minimal positiveness of morality and of being in some remarkable, if difficult, poems. Particularly here Zanzotto seems to have written a poetry which satisfies the criteria he laid down in 1974:

> La poesia allora avvenga come avvengono, prima di una colpa o di un merito, le nascite. Sia tollerata se non altro perché pone il problema e l'inquietudine del nascere, anche nella più sfatta e grigia crepuscolarità o depressione, anche quando sembra non parlare 'umanamente' o perdere il tempo. Grazie a questa gentile tolleranza—o perfino distratta tolleranza—la poesia passerà avanti, e per lunghi capziosi viziosi (anche) giri arriverà ad essere 'utile', a *servire a tutti* nel modo più incerto ma fraterno, nel modo più dimesso ma vero, *senza aver servito nessuno.*[25]

It remains to be seen which way he will turn next, particularly in his current state of celebrity.

Notes

1. Publishing details of Zanzotto's books of poetry are as follows: *Dietro il paesaggio* (Milan, Mondadori, 1951); *Elegia e altri versi* (Milan, La Meridiana, 1954); *Vocativo* (Milan, Mondadori, 1957); *IX Ecloghe* (Milan, Mondadori, 1962); *La Beltà* (Milan, Mondadori, 1968); *Gli sguardi, i fatti e senhal* (Pieve di Soligo, Bernardi, 1969); *A che valse?* (Milano, Scheiwiller, 1970); *Pasque* (Milan, Mondadori, 1973); *Filò* (Venice, Edizioni del Ruzante, 1976); *Il Galateo in Bosco* (Milan, Mondadori, 1978). To these are to be added: the pamphlet *Mistieròi* (Feltre, Edizioni Castaldi, undated); the anthology Andrea Zanzotto, *Poesie (1938-1972)*, edited by Stefano Agosti (Milan, Mondadori, 1973); and the bilingual anthology *Selected Poetry of Andrea Zanzotto,* edited and translated by Ruth Feldman and Brian Swann (Princeton, Princeton University Press, 1975). Apart from a large number of critical articles, Zanzotto has also published *Sull'altopiano (prose 1942-54)* (Venice, Neri Pozza, 1964).

2. See for example G. Barberi Squarotti, 'Zanzotto o gli schemi dell'astrazione' in his *Poesia e narrativa del secondo Novecento* (Milan, 1961), pp. 116-23 (written in 1958).

3. See especially the important review by Montale, originally in the *Corriere della sera* of 1 June 1968, now in Eugenio Montale, *Sulla poesia* (Milan, 1976), pp. 337-49.

4. See W. Siti, 'Per Zanzotto: Possibili prefazi', *Nuovi argomenti,* new series, 32 (1973), 127-42, and B. Pento, 'Le verbalità informali', *Otto/Novecento,* 3 (1979), 399-406.

5. *Il Galateo in Bosco,* p. 5. The preface is by Contini.

6. For a bibliography of critical writing on Zanzotto, see G. Nuvoli, *Zanzotto,* 'Il Castoro', 148 (Florence, 1979), 129-30.

7. See A. Zanzotto, 'Autoritratto', *L'approdo letterario,* 77-78 (1977), 272-76.

8. For Noventa see below; for Comisso see '(Che sotto l'alta guida)' in *Il Galateo in Bosco.*

9. See Nuvoli, *Zanzotto,* pp. 28-31, and Agosti, introduction to *Poesie (1938-1972),* pp. 10-11.

10. But note Montale's comment in *Sulla poesia,* p. 339: 'Tuttavia cercare le fonti di Zanzotto sarebbe come individuare un ago nel pagliaio'.

11. A. Zanzotto, 'Poesia?' *Il Verri,* sixth series, 1 (September 1976), 110-13 (but dated 1974).

12. 'Microfilm' (*Pasque*) is almost a concrete poem plus its own commentary. For a discussion of this experiment (?), see Nuvoli, *Zanzotto,* pp. 85-86.

13. Agosti, introduction to *Poesie (1938-1972),* p. 20; compare his 'Zanzotto o la conquista del dire' in *Il testo poetico: Teoria e pratiche d'analisi,* (Milan, 1972); also L. Milone, 'Per una storia del linguaggio poetico di Andrea Zanzotto', *Studi novecenteschi,* 3, 8-9 (July-November 1974), 207-35. (The whole of this issue is devoted to Zanzotto.)

14. For Zanzotto's hostility to the more publicity-conscious groups of the 1960s see his 'Parole, comportamenti, gruppi' in the same issue of *Studi novecenteschi,* pp. 349-55. See also Siti, 'Per Zanzotto'.

15. 'Noventa tra i moderni', *Comunità,* 130 (1965), 74-79, and republished as 'Il *putèl* nel poeta Noventa', in *I metodi attuali della critica in Italia,* edited by M. Corti and C. Segre (Turin, 1970), pp. 153-58.

16. 'Infanzie, poesie, scuoletta (appunti)', *Strumenti critici,* 20 (February 1973), 52-77.

17. *La Beltà,* p. 112.

18. The same note comments: 'Non vale la pena di tradurre i versi in *petèl,* i quali si chiudono nella loro presenza di "lingua a due" o di "lingua privata", anche se alcune parole, vicine ai primi suoni emessi da tutti i bambini, al di qua della lingua, indicano qualcosa di diametralmente opposto, e perduto'.

19. *Mistieròi* is also in dialect.

20. *Filò,* p. 58 n.

21. 'Vecchio dialetto che hai nel tuo sapore / un gocciolo del latte di Eva, / vecchio dialetto che non so più, / che mi ti sei estenuato / giorno per giorno nella bocca (e non mi basti); / che sei cambiato con la mia faccia / con la mia pelle anno per anno; / parlare povero, da poveri, ma schietto / ma fitto, ma denso come una manciata / di fieno appena tagliato dalla falce (perché non basti?).' (This translation is printed opposite the original.)

22. For a discussion of this aspect of Lacan's thought, see M. Bowie, 'Jacques Lacan' in *Structuralism and Since: From Lévi-Strauss to Derrida,* edited by J. Sturrock (Oxford, 1979), pp. 116-53, especially pp. 125-28 and 132-34.

23. *Il Galateo in Bosco,* p. 115.

24. Francesco Petrarca, *Rime,* introduction and notes by G. Bezzola, with an essay by Andrea Zanzotto, 'Petrarca fra il palazzo e la cameretta' (Milan, 1976), p. 15.

25. 'Poesia?', p. 113.

Thomas Harrison (essay date 1984)

SOURCE: Harrison, Thomas. "Andrea Zanzotto: From the Language of the World to the World of Language." *Poesis* 5, no. 3 (1984): 68-85.

[*In the following essay, Harrison compares the traditional nature of Zanzotto's early verse with his more original later works.*]

Since the death of Eugenio Montale, Italy possesses once again a single, *altissimo poeta.* His name is Andrea Zanzotto, presented to English readers in **Selected Poetry of Andrea Zanzotto,** edited and translated by Ruth Feldman and Brian Swann (Princeton: Princeton University Press, 1975). While eight years have done little for his American reputation, in Italy they have earned him the unparalleled respect of his peers. Although among the eldest of the contemporary Italian poets (born 1921), Zanzotto is still, as Stefano Agosti puts it, the man "whom the new poets recognize . . . . as their 'youngest' traveling companion, thanks to the increasingly daring and original vivacity of his experimentation, which is always renewed, always ahead."[1] Every move of this pioneer is carefully mapped out by the new avant-gardes also clearing a way through the bush. But Zanzotto's tracks mark *Holzwege,* to use an image from Heidegger dear also to the poet—lanes leading away from all thoroughfares, twisting, deadend woodland trails, journey-ways that are ends in themselves. Much may be learned from Zanzotto but he cannot be followed. He steps out alone.

Zanzotto's singularity is all the more striking when one considers the "traditional" nature of his early verse. The critical consensus is that, as with Yeats, Zanzotto's work divides into a first, "unoriginal" phase and a second in which it "comes of age." Difficult as it may be to characterize the so-called second phase, contemporary critics have no problem with the first (considered to extend roughly from 1938-1968). They call it "hermetic" (today a disparaging term) and leave it at that. But Zanzotto has always been of age. More like Picasso than like Yeats, he has written perfect poems along every step of the way. It is true that what he has done in the last fifteen years is more daring than anything he or any other poet wrote in the decades immediately following the war. Yet his extravagance occasionally waxes complacent. His early poetry, on the other hand, is committed, profound, and beautifully labored. Were a judgment required, one might say that Zanzotto's greatest poems belong to neither a first nor a second but to a "middle" phase, a middle that could be chronologically situated around *La Beltà* and *Pasque* (1968 and 1974), but that actually informs his best poems at every stage. In fact, an overview of Zanzotto's career from the very beginning up to the recently issued *Fosfeni* might even dispel the notion of a Zanzotto I and a Zanzotto II and rather reveal a conceptual continuity that "guides" his stylistic transformations. To interpolate a theoretical structure into a succession of individual poems is, of course, to perform an injustice, but it is just such creative injustice that Zanzotto's intellectual poetry elicits. Here I propose such a theoretical matrix to his work, and add it to the structural and thematic matrices already provided by, respectively, Gino Rizzo ("Afterword" to *Selected Poetry*) and Stefano Agosti ("Introduction" to *Poesie: 1938-1973,* Milan: Mondadori, 1974).

From the start, Zanzotto has been an "ontological" poet. His prime concern has been not the individual self, social and sexual mores, or political organization, but the nature of reality—the question preceding all questions. His poetry does not focus on a particular dimension of human experience but on experience as a whole, on experience *as* experience. In his introduction to *Selected Poetry* Glauco Cambon observes that Zanzotto is on a "quest for a valid perception of reality."[2] His poetic dynamic tends to be centripetal rather than centrifugal—from a circle of questions in to specifics, not from a nucleus of interest out to universals. If Zanzotto is truly committed to the psyche, love, wisdom, and nature, the commitment is to eventual results of his inquiry rather than to guiding hypotheses. His poetry chooses skepsis over knowledge. Its takes its place in that modernistic tradition of ontological uncertainty that

moves from Mallarmé, through expressionism and surrealism to Ungaretti and Montale, Stevens and Ammons, but that excludes more "definitive" poets such as Pound, Williams, and even Eliot and Ashbery.

But there is another, stricter sense in which Zanzotto's poetry is ontological. It explicitly addresses the issue of the onto-logical tie—of thing and thought, of reality and understanding, of world and language. In fact, one can read the shift from the first to the second phase of his poetry as involving a reassessment of the terms of the relation. In the early poetry, Zanzotto hearkens to the language of the world. This is the traditional endeavor to make one's language correspond to reality, as articulated, for instance, by Baudelaire's "Correspondences" and developed with subtle variations from Rimbaud through the surrealists, Ungaretti, and Montale. One adapts one's language to "the essence of things," whether through symbolism, unconsciousness, dream, or negative definition. In the later poetry, Zanzotto seeks the world of language. The understanding of reality as a linguistic phenomenon has no real poetic tradition (although Hölderlin, Mallarmé, Rilke, and Stevens would all deserve a place within it). If one had to identify "sources" for Zanzotto's ontological shift, one would recognize theoretical influences, notably Heidegger, Husserl, Lacan, and even Derrida. The conceptual groundwork for Zanzotto's later, "grammatological" poetry is the understanding of language as the "horizon" of the world.

Zanzotto's beginnings are metaphysical. His poems of the Forties aim to penetrate the phenomenal surface of nature, to move *Behind the Landscape (Dietro il paesaggio),* his first collection of 1951. The structure of experience is clearly that of subject and object, self and world, even if the two are continually running into each other. Attempting to speak the world, the poet is a universal and Orphic I:

> Se in te mi esprime il risveglio
> se io tutto avvampo e sono mente,
> io tuo seno, realtà:
>
> . . . . .
>
> e tutto da te riconosco
>
>   (**"Dal cielo,"** p. 138)

> *If the awakening expresses me in you*
> *if all of me blazes and is mind,*
> *I your breast, reality:*
>
> . . . . .
>
> *and I acknowledge everything from you*

Transcendent as it may be, this rich, terrestrial world "teaches" the poet and is wakened by him:

> Uccelli che parlate il mio dialetto
> là dal prato che balza ad inebriarmi,

là dietro il focolare e tra la siepe,

("Lorna," p. 56)

Birds that speak my dialect
there in the meadow that leaps to make me drunk,
there behind the hearth and inside the hedge,

Ho raccolto la foglia di colore
e la ciliega dimenticata
sul colle meno visibile;

("Declivio su Lorna," p. 54)

I have gathered the colored leaf
and the forgotten cherry
on the least visible hill;

To speak reality is to speak himself. Or is it? The poet's desire to coincide with the landscape seems rather to react to a primal severance, as between a child and his parents (and Zanzotto often addresses nature as "mother" and "father"). Close as he is, the child can never reappropriate the parent. He must "turn his back" on the illusory embrace:

Ormai la primula e il calore
ai piedi e il verde acume del mondo

I tappetti scoperti
le logge vibrate dal vento ed il sole
tranquillo baco di spinosi boschi;
il mio male lontano, la sete distinta
come un'altra vita nel petto

Qui non resta che cingersi intorno il paesaggio
qui volgere le spalle.

("Ormai," p. 12)

By now the primrose and the warmth
at one's feet and the green insight of the world

Uncovered carpets
the loggias shaken by wind and sun
quiet larva of thorny woods
my distant pain, thirst distinct
as another life in the breast
Here all that's left is to lock the landscape around the
* self*
to turn one's back.

The wish for an Orphic communion with the universe is founded in distance and irreparable solitude:

Or che mi cinge tutta la tua distanza
sto inerme dentro un'unica sera

. . . . .

Io sono spazio frequentato
dal tuo sole deserto

("Distanza," p. 18)

Now that I'm surrounded by all your distance
I stand unarmed within a single evening

. . . . .

I am frequented space
deserted by your sun

The estrangement is sometimes an anguish reminiscent of Trackl or Lorca: "I have wept away my whole face / all night I wept into the fountain" (p. 42). Even when speaking for **"Primal Landscapes,"** Zanzotto posits the longing for union at the very bottom of things:

Dal mio corpo la coltre di neve
rimuovi, padre, e il sole
sei che brusco mi anima:

. . . . .

tu modesto signore
di Lorna che creasti e che ti crea,
tu artefice
di me, di un mai sopito amore.

("I paesaggi primi," p. 112)

From my body, father, you remove
the blanket of snow, and you are
the sudden sun that quickens me:

. . . . .

you modest lord
of Lorna which you created and which creates you,
you maker
of me, of a never-resting love.

This early poetry is thoroughly **Vocative,** as he entitles his third collection (1957). Between 1951 and 1957 stands the equally significant **Elegy and Other Verses** (1954), in which what is "behind the landscape" seem to be entirely hidden: invoked but never evoked. This Orpheus begins to recognize himself as on one side of the divide. His endeavor to correspond with the world through language seems unsuccessful:

O miei mozzi trastulli
pensieri in cui mi credo e vedo,
ingordo vocativo
decerebrato anelito

. . . . .

Io parlo in questa
lingua che passerà

. . . . .

Anni perduti sotto la rotta vampa
pomeridiana dei cicloni,
anni dove l'attesa mi dissolse,
dove straziato il ritorno invocai;

("Caso vocativo," pp. 90-92)

Oh my mulitated toys
thoughts in which I believe and see myself,

voracious vocative
decerebrated yearning

. . . . .

I speak in this tongue that will pass.

. . . . .

Years lost under the broken afternoon blaze of cy-
    clones,
years when waiting dissolved me,
when tormented I invoked return;

And Zanzotto continues to invoke this return to oneness, even if it is not clear just how it is to be effected:

> Dalla viscosa confusione
> dall'immondo calore
> sempre invano accenna sempre torna
> tuo figlio, o madre, per le curve
> strade, per infiniti avvolgimenti.
>
> **("Altrui e mia,"** p. 79)

> *From viscous confusion*
> *from foul heat*
> *always in vain your son beckons,*
> *always returns, mother, through winding*
> *streets, through endless twistings.*

The return seems to have no other destination than its
own point of departure, that is, reality as "viscous
confusion." In the pivotal poem of this collection,
"From a New Height" ("Da un'altezza nuova"), Zanzotto reaches new conclusions about his poetic project:
there is no real communion of self and world, no appropriation of transcendent meanings, no retrieval of es-
sences, but only severance, fragmentation, and silence.
In the manner of Montale's famous poem of 1925, "Non
chiederci la parola"—"Do not demand of us the word
that would square off / this unformed soul of ours on
every side / . . . Only this can we tell you: / what we
are *not,* what we do *not* want"—Zanzotto here admits
to **"The Impossibility of the Word"** (another poem in
Vocative):

> Ancora, madre, a te mi volgo,
> non chiedermi del vero,
> non di questo precluso
> estremo verde ch'io ignorai
> per tanti anni e che maggio mi tende
> ora sfuggendo; alla mia inquinata
> mente, alla mia disfatta pace.
>
> (p. 114)

> *Again, mother, I turn to you,*
> *don't ask the truth of me*
> *nor this closed*
> *extreme green I ignored*
> *so many years and which May now fleeing*
> *offers to me; to my polluted*
> *mind, my shattered peace.*

A series of metaphysical questions, beginning with the
"why" of poetic speech, receive no reply:

> Madre, donde il mio dirti,
> perché mi taci come il verde altissimo
> il ricchissimo nihil
> che incombe ed esalta, dove
> beatificantí fiori e venti gelidi
> s'aprono dopo il terrore. . . .
>
> (p. 114)

> *Mother, whence my speaking to you,*
> *why do you keep silent like the high green*
> *the rich nihil that impends and exalts, where*
> *beautifying flowers and icy winds*
> *open after the terror . . .*

The poet's remoteness resounds in monologue. Being—
the mother, the *altissimo verde*—has come to be
understood in the most paradoxical terms: a *ricchissimo
nihil,* like the self which, despite its vitality, can find no
words:

> Un senso che non muove ad un'imagine,
> un colore disgiunto da un'idea,
> un'ansia senza testimoni
> o una pace perfetta ma precaria:
> questo è l'io che mi desti, madre, e che ora
> appena riconosco, né parola
> né forma né ombra?
>
> (p. 116)

> *A sense that does not move to an image,*
> *a color detached from an idea,*
> *an unwitnessed anxiety*
> *or a peace perfect but precarious:*
> *is this the I you gave me, mother, that now*
> *I scarcely recognize, not word*
> *not shape not shadow?*

If he has been deluding himself about the power of
poetry, Zanzotto now redefines his terms:

> Al vero—al negro bollore dei monti—
>
> . . . . .
>
> ritorno e non so
> non so tacere.
>
> (p. 116)

> *To truth—to the black seethe of mountains—*
>
> . . . . .
>
> *I return and do not know*
> *do not know to keep silent*

There is nothing one can meaningfully say about this
"boil" of reality—except that this anxiety "always
multiplying / in every crease" (p. 116) engenders the
poetic quest. The *ricchissimo nihil,* the longing and lack

at the basis of poetic vision, seems to be the only proper domain of poetry. Zanzotto begins to abandon the project of reading the book of nature. "Sappiate scrivere ma non leggere," he recommends ten years later (*learn how to write but not how to read*, p. 244).

In fact, in *IX Eclogues and other Verses* (1962), language is not sought in reality as much as it is explored from within, in its own process of producing significance. Unidentified interlocutors A and B, sometimes even C and D and Polyphemus, engage in openended dialogic exchanges in which "death-rattle and dung become human studies" (p. 146). The external world is considered impenetrable: Man, a "vague term, / improper light," is a "phenomenological boil" (p. 166). The "anancasma called life" (p. 206)—anancasma being the obsessive repetition of a thought or gesture—is a "universal non-presence, / uniqueness and multiplicity" (p. 174), composed of "radiant / monads, throngs, corymb-like boils" (p. 168).

It is not until his next volume (usually thought to inaugurate the "second phase") that Zanzotto truly begins to develop language into an autonomous sphere of signification. In the introduction to *Poesie,* Stefano Agnosti speaks of Zanzotto's recognition, in *La Beltà* (1968), of the disjunction between signifier and signified. Gino Rizzo, in the afterword, reinterprets the division as that of sign and object: "While it lasted, Surrealism and, in Italy, various generations of 'hermetic' poets—Montale foremost, but also the Zanzotto of before **'From a New Height'**—could *avoid* the impasse by resorting to oneiric language" (p. 309). Vocative and symbolistic language, too presents means of overleaping the distance from sign to object (or signifier to signified). Zanzotto's new understanding of the "problem of meaning," or of the ontological relation, shifts the responsibility from the occlusiveness of nature to the inadequacy of the means of expression. It is not reality that does not divulge its names but names that do not divulge reality:

> Hölderlin: "siamo un segno senza significato"
> Ma dove le due serie entrano in contatto?
> Ma è vero? E che sarà di noi?
>
> ("**Si ancora la neve,**" p. 214)

> *Hölderlin: "we are a sign without signification"*
> *But where do the two series enter into contract?*
> *But is it true? And what will become of us?*

If it is true that phenomena are no more than problematic signs, then what will become of poetry? One possibility is that it will opt for an abstract language, as did the *Duino Elegies*; another is that it will pursue the concrete to the limit. Zanzotto does both (another reason to align him, as Cambon does, with Wallace Stevens). Realizing that the signified is not pre-given, he proliferates his signifiers at large:

> cose e cosine
> scienze lingue e profezie
> cronaca bianca nera azzurra
> di stimoli anime e dei,
> libido e cupido e la loro
> prestidigitazione finissima
>
> (p. 214)

> *things and thingies*
> *sciences tongues and prophecies*
> *white black blue news*
> *of stimuli souls and gods.*
> *libido and cupidity and their*
> *very subtle sleight of hand*

The poet no longer demands ultimate coherence; he "lets things be," as Heidegger would say, in their irreducible complexity. The arch-dichotomy of self and world splits into countless differences and repetitions (anancasma), all harbored in a language capable of infinite possibilities of meaning:

> Quante perfezioni, quante
> quante totalità, Pungendo aggiunge.
> E poi astrazioni astrificazioni formulazioni d'astri
> assideramento, attraverso sidera e coelos
> assideramenti assimilazioni
>
> ("**La perfezione della neve,**" p. 210)

> *How many perfections, how*
> *how many totalities. Stinging it adds.*
> *And then abstractions astrifications astral formations*
> *assideration, across sidera and coelos*
> *assiderations assimilations*

Zanzotto stops seeking a translucent signifier; he now "produces" a signified. He no longer aims at turning a pronoun into a noun (as he characterizes his work in the Fifties, p. 86), but at finding a pronoun for nouns, at abstracting from particulars. While his end remains the same—to discover the meaning of reality—his means change. The expositional ideal—Michelangelo's "Non ha l'ottimo artista"—gets replaced by a compositional one. As Cambon notes, "monody has made way for polytonalism, elegy for satire; classicism has been replaced by 'glossalalia,' a Babelic verve that is apt to incorporate dialect as well as functional or dislocated quotations from Heidegger, Hölderlin, and Dante along with ominous statements by nuclear strategist Herman Kahn and onomatopoeic babblings of baby-talk" (p. xxii). Philosophically, the metaphysical distinctions between reality and language, world and self, essence and appearance give way to hermeneutic infinity.

"**La perfezione della neve**" continues: "nel perfezionato procederei / più in là del grande abbaglio, del pieno e del vuoto" (*I would proceed in the perfected / further beyond the blinding dazzle, the full and the empty* (p. 210). The perfection of sense requires a procession beyond the blindness of conceptual opposites ("del pieno e del vuoto"). The *ricchissimo nihil* admits of no objectification. As in Heidegger's philosophy of *a-letheia*—a strong presence in Zanzotto's work from the late Sixties through to today—the real is to be viewed as sense-informing rather than sense-informed. To "recreate" the advent of sense, Zanzotto involves language in a self-generating process, in a "radial movement-lack" (p. 210).

As can be observed even in his titles, in the Seventies Zanzotto elaborates the "meta" of his linguistic thrust. With its insistent refrain of "più in là" *(further on),* one of the most remarkable poems in **La Beltà** is **"Oltranza oltraggio"** (translatable only by **"Outrance Outrage"**). In *Pasque* (1974)—*Easters,* though also to be read as *Passovers*—his lexis becomes replete with neologisms, superlatives, and prefix/suffix accretions ("supradeterminations"); his titles coin words of excess (**"Supraexistences,"** p. 286). In his penultimate book, **Il Galateo in Bosco** (*A Code of Manners in the Forest,* 1978), "beyondness" will lead him to **"Gnessuluogo"** (**"Nowhere,"** in dialect) and to the **"Ipersonnetto"** (**"Hypersonnet"**).

The **"Hypersonnet"** represents as it were the self-exceeding of form, of linguistic structure. The fourteen "verses" (plus *premessa* and *postilla*) that compose this hypersonnet are all complete sonnets. Strictly rhymed according to the Petrarchan convention, they even sophisticate the already complex genre by means of *rime care* (codice-godi-nodi-modici / grifi-schifi-scientifico-mirifico). On one level, as critics have recognized, the cycle presents a manneristic parody of classicism; but on another, deeper level it attempts to marshal as many signifying techniques as possible. Formal coherence is informed by the most disgregated content; archaic diction is mixed with physics and clinical psychology. As in **La Beltà** and Pasque, phenomena are accumulated in parataxis:

> Modi e moti cosi soavemente
> ed infinitamenta lievi / sadici
> dondolii, fibre e febbri, troppo radi
> o fitti per qualunque fede o mente
>
> (**Il Galateo in Bosco,** p. 62)

> *Modes and motions so softly*
> *and infinitely delicate / sadistic,*
> *rockings, fibers and fevers, too scarce*
> *or thick for any faith or mind*

In this sense typical of Zanzotto's latest poetry, the **"Hypersonnet"** presents merely hypothetical surfaces. Instead of reflecting a pre-constituted reality, it analyzes and develops the syntactic elements upon which comprehension is predicated. Thus it is that many of the titles in *Galateo* are bracketed by parentheses and immediately followed by alternatives. Here, for instance, are the titles of seven contiguous poems: 1. **"(Sotto l'alta guida)(traiettorie, mosche),"** 2. **"(Sotto l'alta guida),"** 3. **"(Sotto l'alta guida), (Abbondanze),"** 4. **"(Che sotto l'alta guida),"** 5. **"Che sotto l'alta guida,"** 6. **"( )   ) (," 7. "((   )."** Zanzotto suggests that no word is a proper name, that no sense can be reduced to a code. His gloss on the title of this collection makes it clear that codes are precisely what are to be overcome:

> A Code of Manners in a Forest . . . : the
> very subtle rules supporting symbiosis
> and cohabitation, and the reticules of
> the symbolic, from language to gestures
> and maybe even to perception itself:
> hung like spiderwebs or buried, veiled
> like filigree above / within the boil of
> power-plays that is reality. Especially
> the sonnets relate to these improbable
> formulations of codes and subcodes among
> what is in no way codifiable
>
> (*Galateo,* p. 111)

An immanent critique of codified language, Zanzotto's poetry of the Seventies and Eighties is both a setting apart *(krisis)* and a putting back together. It seeks semantic originality. With **La Beltà,** Montale observes, Zanzotto takes a "dive into that pre-expression which precedes the articulate word" (**Galateo,** p. 5). Gino Rizzo, too, in his reading of the same poem that seems to have inspired Montale (**"Elegia in Petel"**), gives the "pre-language of the *in-fans*" and the "irretrievable beginning of the 'mother tongue" the status of *desideratum.* Given the much more extensive linguistic experimentation that has followed **La Beltà,** one might just as well speak of post-expression. To want to get beneath language is to be already beyond it. Whether conceived as an origin—"Never has there been an origin," writes Zanzotto in the same elegy (p. 240)—or as a transcendent end to be achieved by poetry, Zanzotto's goal is unlimited significance. His deconstructions clear the way for a "codeless" language. His metonymic universe appears to be an organic and never completed "system" of anaphoric associations, echoes, and differentiations. It renders the sign—whether a neologism, a line from the poets, a philosophical phrase, an onomatopoeic cartoon utterance, or a road indication—absolute and infinite, arranged in a mosaic-like construction. "What is poetry," asks Zanzotto in a recent interview, "if not a set of echoes, or voices which remain in the air or in us? And, almost unaware of it, we repeat them."[3] What has often been interpreted as satire—baroque mannerisms and mass-media slogans—is actually an effort to compile an encyclopedia of expression, to authenticate even the most "inauthentic" statements.

Thus it is not surprising that the key word of the just-issued **Fosfeni** (the second of a trilogy begun with

Galateo) is "logos." The leitmotiv of every other poem and apostrophized in the concluding three, logos includes "every insistent and benign force of connection, communication, interrelation that traverses reality fantasy words and even tends to 'offer' them, to put them into relation with a foundation (?)" (*Fosfeni,* p. 79). Here is a vision of the ontological originality of language comparable to Heidegger's mediations on *legein, Rede,* and *Sprache.* Indeed, in a statement of poetics accompanying his very latest poems (to appear in November in *The Favorite Malice: Ontology and Reference in Contemporary Italian Poetry,* edited and translated by T. Harrison), Zanzotto wonders whether the world—including matter, the psyche, and all forms of life—cannot be conceived as "pangraphy." Zanzotto would let himself "be spoken" by such infinite semiosis. Of course, the risk of madness, of incomprehensibility, stands in direct proportion to the hyperbolic aim of the project. Accordingly, like the *ricchissimo nihil,* like *A Code of Manners in a Forest, Fosfeni* has a studiedly duplicitous meaning. Emphasizing the blindness implicit in such visions, Zanzotto defines *Fosfeni* as "sign-vortexes and luminous points that can be noticed when keeping one's eyes closed (or while pressing them) or even in pathological situations" (*Fosfeni,* p. 79). The poet eclipses the visible world to peer into the "ground" of all meaning-constellations.

In their attempt to disclose the infinity of the world of language, Zanzotto's latest poems are often as unseemly as they are wonderfully beautiful. But when they work—and they do with astonishing regularity—they bear witness to that horizon of significance that is always addressed, though rarely so directly, by the greatest art.

Notes

1. Thomas J. Harrison, ed., *The Favorite Malice: Ongology and Reference in Contemporary Italian Poetry* (New York: Out of London Press, forthcoming, 1983), p. 286.
2. Page xx. Unless otherwise specified, henceforth all page numbers refer to this bilingual edition of Zanzotto's poems. Occasionally the translations have been modified.
3. Giuliana Massini and Bruno Rivalta, *Sulla Poesia: Conversazioni nelle Scuole* (Parma: Pratiche, 1981), p. 88.

John P. Welle (essay date 1987)

SOURCE: Welle, John P. "The Poetry of the Mandala: Writing and Subjectivity." In *The Poetry of Andrea Zanzotto,* pp. 91-112. Rome: Bulzoni Editore, 1987.

[*In the following essay, Welle examines Zanzotto's fascination with mental processes and psychoanalysis in his poetry.*]

Il Galateo in Bosco constitutes a catalog of codifying practices, signifying behaviors, and discursive positions that inscribe the subject within the symbolic order. At the center of this textual forest, the speaking subject—the one who says "I"—finds itself bewildered by the proliferation of codes and subcodes, the infinite paths of warring philosophies and ideologies, the Heideggerian "Holzwege" that lead in every direction. This confused "I"—"pronome che da sempre a farsi nome attende" (*IX Ecloghe* 7)—forms the fulcrum of Zanzotto's universe: the meeting ground of nature and culture, the balancing point between *galateo* and *bosco.* Zanzotto's depiction of subjectivity provides an important narrative element in his contemporary *Canzoniere.* Just as the poet reflects on the language and the literary tradition within which he writes (and within which he is written), so too he depicts various stages in the development of individual consciousness. Furthermore, the verbalization of these events reveals that the subject itself is an effect of discourse. In exploring the relationship between subjectivity and the discourse which expresses it, Zanzotto adopts the mandala archetype as a symbol of unity and wholeness. The text's various themes, which heretofore have been dealt with separately, come together in the portrayal of subjectivity.

Interested in psychoanalysis since his university days, Zanzotto has always shown a fascination with mental states and processes. In fact, much of his previous work deals with the construction of the self through the act of writing. In *Vocativo* (1957), for example, the poems **"Prima persona"** and **"Esistere psichicamente"** evince his interest in psychological phenomena[1]. With *La Beltà* (1968) references to Jacques Lacan become explicit. The following passage testifies to Zanzotto's familiarity with a psychoanalytical theory that has relevance for *Il Galateo in Bosco*:

> Lo stadio psicologico detto "dello specchio"
> come costitutivo della funzione dell'io
>
> (*La Beltà* 42)

In *Pasque* (1973) Zanzotto once again makes reference to the writings of this important French interpreter of Freud:

> oui, je lis SCILICET, la revue paraissant trois fois l'an
> à Paris, sous la direction du docteur J. Lacan;
>
> oui, je veux savoir ce qu'en pense l'école freudienne
>   de Paris
> peut-être par là arriverai-je à étouffer mes soucis;
>
> (*Pasque* 60)

In *Il Galateo in Bosco* Zanzotto's interest in psychoanalysis takes the form of an anamnesis[2]. A verbalization of the history of the self, anamnesis constitutes one of the fundamental techniques of the "talking cure."

The text's initial composition sets the anamnesis in motion as it opens onto the primordial communicative gestures between mother and unborn child:

> Dolcezza. Carezza. Piccoli schiaffi in quiete.
>
> *(Galateo* 13)

At the root of the subject lies an experience that is preverbal. The inner rhyme between the first two words of the text ("Dolcezza. Carezza") suggests the profound intimacy and love that binds the mother and her fetus. In answer to the mother's caress, the child's small slaps, "Piccoli schiaffi in quiete," symbolize the stirrings of a capacity for communication that will soon find expression in language. This brief exchange encapsulates the primordial bond of affection established between the *infans* and the mother while the child is still in the womb.

Zanzotto's passion for this primordial word, this umbilical code connecting mother and child, takes many forms in his work. From the **"Elegia in petèl"** of *La Beltà,* a remarkable poem that explores baby talk, to the dialect poems of *Filò,* which seek to reach the "Mother" through a "perpetual orality," Zanzotto shows a keen interest in the origins of poetry in childhood and the relationship between language, writing, and subjectivity. In *Il Galateo in Bosco* the portrayal of subjectivity begins in the first two lines of the initial poem. The original harmony between the mother and child gives way to another state: "Diteggiata fredda sul vetro" (*Galateo* 13). The "cold finger marks on the glass" evoke a child in front of a frost-covered window. The image of the window constitutes a re-occurring motif in a number of Zanzotto's poems and short-stories[3].

The "cold finger marks on the glass" continue the movement of hands begun in the first line with the baby's "piccoli schiaffi in quiete." Yet, the cold state of the child in front of the glass contrasts sharply with the warmth and sweetness of the fetus in the womb. The glass does not respond to the child's gestures as the mother did, but simply records what the child has fingered upon its surface. In the formative stages of consciousness, then, separation follows an original period of harmony. The glass closes like a curtain upon the early scene: the child has suddenly become distinct from the mother. At the same time, "ditteggiata" suggests that the child has imprinted its finger marks on a glass surface. This minimal gesture, together with the "piccoli schiaffi in quiete," represents the first budding of a capacity for communication, a potential for self-expression, a primitive kind of "writing." With this subtle movement of hands in the womb and upon the surface of the glass, Zanzotto introduces into *Il Galateo in Bosco* the link between writing and subjectivity which is explored throughout his poetry, prose, and criticism[4].

Moreover, the child in front of the glass brings to mind Lacan's celebrated theory of the mirror stage. The mirror stage constitutes that moment when the subject first forms a self-image. As Lacan explains:

> We have only to understand the mirror stage *as an identification* . . . namely, the transformation that takes place in the subject when he assumes an image. . . . This jubilant assumption of his specular image by the child at the *infans* stage . . . would seem to exhibit in an exemplary situation the symbolic matrix in which the *I* is precipitated in a primordial form. . . .
>
> *(Écrits* 2)

According to Lacan, the child upon seeing his reflection projects an image of bodily unity with which he subjectively identifies. This important turning point in the development of the subject marks a fundamental moment in the history of every person.

After beginning with a fetus in the womb, the first poem presents a child separated from the mother. This poem also re-enacts the process through which a child acquires language. In attempting to reproduce the child's playful manipulation of words, Zanzotto gives free reign to the signifier:

> Botteghino paradisiaco. Vendita biglietti. Ingresso vero.
> Chiavistelli, chiavistelle a grande offerta.
> Chiave di circo-colori-cocchio circo. Bandiere.
> Nel giocattolato fresco paese, giocattolo circo.
> Piccolissimo circo. Linguine che lambono. Inguini. Bifide
> trifide bandiere, battaglie. Biglie. Bottiglie.
> Oh che come un fiotto di fiotti bandiere balza tutto il circo-cocò.
>
> *(Galateo* 13)

The rush and tumble of words cascading over the page, "Bifide / trifide bandiere, battaglie. Biglie. Bottiglie," captures the jubilation of the infant in the primordial stages of ego formation. In this highly lyrical passage, "Oh che come un fiotto di fiotti bandiere balza tutto il circo-cocò," Zanzotto enacts, rather than describes, the infant's pleasure in playing with sounds. The nonsense word "cocò" (a fragment from the Italian ditty "ambarabà cici cocò"), together with references to "giocattolo" and "circo," evinces the level of language on which the poet is operating. The phonetic similarity between different signifiers ("battaglie. Biglie. Bottiglie") leads the poem forward as the sign is frequently reduced to a joyful playing of sounds. Zanzotto attempts to mimetically inscribe within his text the signifieds of experience, rather than the signifiers that the child may actually use. At the same time, phrases like "Botteghino paradisiaco," "Ingresso vero," "Chiavistelli, chiavistelle," "Linguine che lambono," "Inguini," and "Biglie. Bottiglie" carry a wealth of sexual connotations. The child's passage from a preverbal to a verbal condition results from an intricate nexus of muscle movements, perceptions, and desires: "Chiave di circo-colori-cocchio circo."

This poem reconstructs the primal process through which subjectivity comes into being. The child's playing with language makes possible the development of memory and personal history. Furthermore, the child's birth into language represents an entrance into what Lacan calls the "symbolic order." This web of affiliations—"i reticoli del simbolico" as Zanzotto states in a note (*Galateo* 111)—precedes the existence of the subject who, in developing an ego or individual identity, assumes a particular position within a network of sexual, familial, and societal relations.

In addition to the fetus in the womb, the allusion to the mirror stage, and the child's birth into language, the initial poem offers a series of hints that concern the poet's biography:

> Dolcezza. Carezza. Piccoli schiaffi in quiete.
>   Diteggiata fredda sul vetro.
> Bandiere piccoli intensi venti / vetri.
>   Bandiere, interessi giusti e palesi.
> Esse accarezzano libere inquiete. Legate leggiere.
> Esse bandiere, come-mai? Come-qui?
> Battaglie lontane. Battaglie in album, nel medagliere.
> Paesi. Antichissimi. Giovani scavi, scavare nel cielo,
>   bandiere.
>
> (*Galateo* 13)

Zanzotto begins to excavate the terrain of his own infancy. These lines—"Battaglie lontane. Battaglie in album, nel medagliere"—point to the presence of the Great War in the poet's earliest memory. Zanzotto was born in 1921 and, as was discussed in Chapter Two, the tragic war-time experiences of the people of his village have played an important part in his development. A still-faintly reverberating cannon fire seems to have almost ruffled the maternal waters from which this baby was to emerge. By the same token, references to "interessi giusti e palesi" indicate the pristine state of the child's earliest desires. The phrases "come-mai? Come-qui?" moreover, can be read in a Heideggerian vein. These questions represent the question that precedes all other questions: Why is there something instead of nothing at all? In Zanzotto's poem of origins these questions express the wonder and grace that surround the child's entrance into the world.

The initial poem of *Il Galateo in Bosco* introduces the geological substratum of the subject upon which all subsequent development is built. This poem sets in motion a discourse involving memory, subjectivity, language, and poetry. For Zanzotto all of these elements are bound up inextricably in the child's earliest experiences[5]. Zanzotto portrays the passage from a preverbal to a verbal state by giving free rein to the signifier. He also constructs a montage of early memory traces. Whereas the circus referred to in the first part of this poem would seem to be an analogy for the child's interaction with the world around him, "il circo" mentioned in the final stanza may refer to an actual circus that the poet remembers from his early boyhood:

> Partiva il circo la mattina presto—
> furtivo, con un trepestio di pecorelle.
> Io perché (fatti miei), stavo già desto.
> Io sapevo dell'alba in partenza, delle
>   pecorelle del circo sotto le stelle.
>
> (*Galateo* 14)

In these lines—"Io perché (fatti miei), stavo già desto"—the crucial pronoun first appears. The initial section of this composition, then, which opens with a fetus in the womb and a child before a pane of glass, portrays the matrix in which an identity can be formulated. It also illustrates the child's ludic relationship to language. In the final section (which begins with the lines quoted above), the use of the imperfect ("stavo," "sapevo") reveals that the subject has already been constituted. While in the first section Zanzotto presents a montage of movements, perceptions, and childlike wordplay, in the final stanza he presents the memories of an individual consciousness: "Io sapevo dell'alba in partenza."

Throughout *Il Galateo in Bosco* Zanzotto traces the path of this fractured subject born into the symbolic order through the play of language in early infancy. In the book's seventh poem, Zanzotto returns to the thematic presences of the initial composition:

> Vorrei bucarmi di ogni chimica rovina
> per accogliere tutti, in anteprima,
> nello specchio medicato d'infinitudini e desii
> di quel circo i fermenti gli enzimi
>
> (*Galateo* 27)

The "specchio medicato" referred to here provides further evidence of the Lacanian underpinnings of Zanzotto's portrayal of subjectivity. The "specchio medicato d'infinitudini e desii" is nothing other than the subject's own sense of self: an identity fractured and patched together again. The mirror stage constitutes an on-going source of alienation and unrealizable desires in the life of the individual.

Zanzotto's text recapitulates the essential conditions of human psychology according to Lacan. Subsequent to separation from the mother, the child projects a separate identity formed upon a fictional image of wholeness. The very genesis of the subject, therefore, produces a fundamental alienation: the irretrievable harmony that once existed between mother and child stimulates a continual search for a lost totality. According to Lacanian theory, the subject carries within itself the seeds of its own unhappiness: a discrepancy between what it is and what it thinks itself to be. Lacan describes this discrepancy in the subject as a rift, a "lack," "an organic insufficiency in . . . natural reality" (4).

The search for a lost object impels Zanzotto's unstable "I." The rift upon which subjectivity rests is subtly referred to in the ending of the first poem: "Partenza il 19, S. Giuseppe, / a raso a raso il bosco, la brinata, le crepe" (*Galateo* 14). The Lacanian overtones to "le crepe" recall similar allusions in Zanzotto's notes. In describing the topography of the Montello, for example, the poet depicts the forest's underlying geological substratum as a "fault":

> La topografia della zona . . . è esatta. In più è segnata la Linea degli Ossari che ad est va fino al mare Adriatico, ad ovest (nord-ovest) continua attraverso il territorio italiano e poi francese, fino alla Manica. Linee su cui l'Europa, ancora oggi, mette in gioco la sua esistenza, e segnalazione di una faglia: che nel Montello si sovrappone alla faglia Periadriatica della crosta terrestre . . .
>
> (*Galateo* 111)

The Periadriatic fault beneath the Montello forest resembles the "fault" at the origins of human identity. The lines which define Europe's existence are superimposed over the lines which define the existence of the individual subject. Lacan's concept of "lack"—a loss suffered by the subject as a result of being separated from the mother at birth—informs Zanzotto's portrayal of subjectivity. The subject senses a continual "lack" because it believes itself to be a fragment of something larger, something whole. The harmony between mother and child in the book's first line, "Dolcezza. Carezza. Piccoli schiaffi in quiete," symbolizes the unity that will be disrupted definitively in the poem's second line. This "natural fault" will determine the subject's entire future development.

In the seventh composition the story of the "I" continues as the poet considers his parents, the circumstances of his birth, and the green world into which he was born:

> Arteria aperta il Piave, né calmo né placido
> ma soltanto gaiamente sollecito oltre i beni i mali e simili
>
> . . . . .
>
> Padre e madre, in quel nume forse uniti
>   tra quell'incoercibile sanguinare
>   ed il verde e l'argenteizzare altrettanto incoercibili,
> in quel grandore dove tutti i silenzi sono possibili
> voi mi combinaste, sotto quelle caterve di
> os-ossa, ben catalogate, nemmeno geroglifici, ostie
> rivomitate ma come in un più alto, in un aldilà d'erbe
>   e d'enzimi erbosi assunte,
>   in un fuori-luogo che su me s'inclina e domina
>   un poco creandomi, facendomi assurgere a
>
> (*Galateo* 28)

Before he came into the world, the poet existed in "that grandeur where all silences are possible . . . beneath those masses of bo-bones, well-catalogued." The beauty of that sublime moment of personal beginning along the riverbank is tempered by the child's waking to find a world littered with the remnants of war: the "os-ossa" symbolize unholy relics of human destruction which cause the poet to stutter in naming them[6].

The lyrical description of Zanzotto's personal origins breaks off in mid-sentence. The fragmented syntax of the incompleted phrase "assurgere a," as well as the cleavage in the spatial organization of the page, communicates the end of an original idyllic state, the eruption of a fault, the formation of an organic insufficiency in reality:

> in un fuori-luogo che su me s'inclina e domina
>   un poco creandomi, facendomi assurgere a
> Così che suono a parlamento
> per le balbuzie e le più ardue rime,
>
> . . . . .
>
> io mi avvicendo, vado per ossari, e cari stinchi e teschi
> mi trascino dietro dolcissimamente, senza o con flauto magico
>
> (*Galateo* 28)

The subject's original communion with the river and the parents has been broken off. The fractured "I," damaged irreparably in its separation from the mother, rotates various selves within itself ("io mi avvicendo"). Furthermore, as the "symbolic" overtakes the "imaginary" ("in un fuori luogo che su me s'inclina e domina / un poco creandomi"), the subject becomes entangled in a web of language. The subject coagulates between two extremes of linguistic experience: between "le balbuzie e le più ardue rime."

Throughout the fifty-two poems of *Il Galateo in Bosco* the fractured subject seeks to become whole and to assume a stable identity. In the book's eighth composition, **"Stati maggiori contrapposti, loro piani,"** the bewildered I-protagonist wanders among a carnival world of phantasms. This poem expresses a crisis, a breakdown in the subject's sense of reality:

> Ed ero come riflesso
> o meglio fratto in ognuna delle facce
> di un cubo a quattro dimensioni
>   di un lunapark formato a tesseract
>   mai mai nella stessa positura
>   mai mai nella stessa pastura mentale
>
> (*Galateo* 29)

The same poem describes the psychological make-up of the subject as a goal which is never reached:

> Galatei-Poesie quali pure scomparizioni
>   che mi lasciano
>   solo come una meta I mai raggiunta. . . .
>
> (*Galateo* 30)

The impossibility of reaching the goal of a balanced identity results from, in Lacan's terms, the fundamental illusion of unity stemming from the mirror stage.

In *Il Galateo in Bosco* the numerous permutations of the subject present a string of what Lacan would call "imaginary identifications." As human beings grow up, they make imaginary identifications with various objects. In this way, a fictive sense of unitary selfhood develops. In the following passage, Zanzotto's consciousness of this process comes through clearly:

> ti risalgo, identità,   che
> fai sgambetto al rotto sentiero
> calchi la serpe come in un'icona—di
> identità in identità risulti risalti—
> identità dilavate spolpate, ma pur sempre infetuate di
> me—
>
>   . . . . .
>
> e io madre dell'identità
> nell'identità del nostro noi che si
> differenzia enzia furiosamente mi ripeto
> e ripeto-vi
>
>   (*Galateo* 49-50)

Here, the linguistic status of person ("mi ripeto / e ripeto-vi") is depicted as the very foundation of subjectivity. A fundamental property of language makes possible different identities: "nell'identità del nostro noi che si / differenzia enzia." These "persons" are nothing more than positions within discourse. Zanzotto's interests in linguistics and psychoanalysis converge at this point: the subject is itself an effect of discourse and depends upon linguistic structures.

In commenting on his interest in Lacanian psychoanalysis, Zanzotto renders explicit the ideas concerning subjectivity and discourse implicit in *Il Galateo in Bosco*:

> . . . per lunghissimi anni ho avuto a che fare con la realtà psicanalitica e psichiatrica perché "desideravo guarire" di alcuni gravi disturbi che mi affliggevano. . . . Forse è vero, come ha detto Michel David, che in me si era sviluppato un certo inconsapevole lacanismo. . . . Il trasformarsi di ogni discorso, anzi di "tutto" in mero significante, anzi in lettera; il sospetto che l'io fosse una produzione grammaticalizzata dell'immaginario, un punto di fuga e non una realtà. . . .
>
>   ("Perché mi piace il dottor vampiro" 76)

Il Galateo in Bosco expresses Zanzotto's fears that the subject is a product of grammatical structures, a fantasm, a "punto di fuga e non una realtà." The subject formulated in this text includes within itself its past permutations as well as its future imagined alterations.

The suffering and anguish that these interior fluctuations bring about is particularly prevalent in **"Ipersonetto."** In **"(Sonetto di furtività e traversie),"** for example, Zanzotto suggests the Protean malleability of the subject and the difficulty of representing the essence of its innumerable transfigurations:

> . . . come di plurime
> serpi sospinte a traversie, di tossiche
> invenzioni onde al niente si va appresso:
>
> così quanto imprendibile a me stesso
> a tutto, a tutti, com'è il tutto, io fossi,
> furtività per dossi orme echi oscuri.
>
>   (*Galateo* 69)

In a later poem, **"(Stracaganasse o castagne secche),"** the poet sets up a meeting between various aspects of his own identity. He imagines a reunion in which he sits down to eat with one of his former selves:

> A questo mio bisavolo-me ed a me
> prima che arrivi il guardiano
>
>   . . . . .
>
> tra i piedi sporchi della Grande Terra
>   sia concesso ancora qualche scasso o scrostatura
>
>   . . . . .
>
> ma arriverà una domenica gran sagra
>   di paese a rasobosco, martellata di campane
>
>   . . . . .
>
> e poi ci metteremo a tavola di fronte a una
>   sfarinata, magra di vitamine, a un pasto di stracaganasse;
>   davanti ad un bicchiere di vin piccolo
>   guardandoci l'un l'altro come sacre immagini
>   attenderemo il sàtori
>
>   (*Galateo* 80-81)

The "great-grandfather-me" and the "me" sit down to eat dried chestnuts and to drink wine at a country festival. They look each other squarely in the eye and radiate wholeness like "sacred images." Together they will await "sàtori," the final illumination:

> e allora il bosco tutto
> con le unghie rotte e le gengive scotte
> potremo insieme rovistare e rapinare
> ma senza dargli rovina
>   nemmeno in una stilla, in una trina
>
>   (*Galateo* 81)

This final illumination, this "sàtori," resembles the longed-for totality first imagined during the formation of the ego during the mirror stage. The fractured subject, re-united with one of its former permutations, finds itself in deep concord with the *bosco*. Although driven by violent desires ("potremo insieme rovistare e rapinare"), the subject in this instance is in sympathy with nature: "senza dargli rovina / nemmeno in una stilla, in una trina."

The moment of balanced harmony depicted in this poem temporarily soothes the wounds of the alienated subject. Similar moments of an envisioned oneness occur at various points in the text as the subject seeks to become whole. This desire for a stable identity is best expressed in **"Postilla."** The final poem in the sonnet series and the central composition of *Il Galateo in Bosco*, **"Postilla."** treats the symbiotic relationship between the subject and the discourse which expresses it. Like a hemostatic that arrests a bleeding wound, the rigid structure of the Petrarchan sonnet furnishes a necessary focal point for a subject suffering from a debilitating sense of disintegration. Far more than a stylistic tour de force, **"Postilla."** demonstrates how the book's various themes contribute to one narrative totality. In this respect, **"Postilla."** forms a microcosm of the text and rewards thorough analysis.

> Postilla
> (Sonetto infamia e mandala)
> a F. Fortini
>
> Somma di sommi d'irrealtà, paese
> che a zero smotta e pur genera a vista
> vermi mutanti in dèi, così che acquista
> nel suo perdersi, e inventa e inforca imprese,
>
> vanno da falso a falso tue contese,
> ma in sì variata ed infinita lista
> che quanto in falso qui s'intigna e intrista
> là col vero via guizza a nozze e intese.
>
> Falso pur io, clone di tanto falso,
> od aborto, e peggiore in ciò del padre,
> accalco detti in fatto ovver misfatto:
>
> così ancora di te mi sono avvalso,
> di te sonetto, righe infami e ladre—
> mandala in cui di frusto in frusto accatto.

(Galateo 74)

Repeated five times, "falso" is the poem's key word. The figure of antithesis, which both posits and negates, also expresses the theme of falsehood. The following diagram illustrates the various pairs of opposites that Zanzotto unites in **"Postilla"**:

paese che a zero smotta	e pur genera
vermi	dèi
in falso qui	là col vero
s'intigna e intrista	via guizza a nozze
io	te
aborto	padre
detti	fatto
fatto	misfatto
righe infami e ladre	mandala

Antithesis expresses the contrast between true and false as Zanzotto simultaneously maligns and praises the sonnet. The contrasting pairs outlined above are carefully counterbalanced to indicate an underlying unity.

The key word "falso" brings about the fusion of opposites. Zanzotto first applies the word "falso" to the sonnet and then extends it to the *io* as the poem moves toward a unification of these two elements. In the first quattrain, the sonnet is evoked and described in the third person: "così che acquista / nel suo perdersi, e inventa e inforca imprese." In the second quattrain, the poet engages the sonnet in direct address, bringing it within closer range of his poetic voice: "vanno da falso a falso tue contese." The *io* appears in the first tercet and through the word "falso" identifies itself with the theme of falsehood. This connection also suggests a possible affiliation between the subject and the sonnet form: "Falso pur io, clone di tanto falso." In the final tercet, the sonnet and the subject merge in a strophe that fuses the diverse elements of poem and poet as the speaker's voice both blames and praises the sonnet to which and through which he speaks:

> così ancora di te mi sono avvalso,
> di te sonetto, righe infami e ladre—
> mandala in cui di frusto in frusto accatto.

As the poem unfolds, the subject admits to deriving nourishment from the sonnet. The I-protagonist acknowledges its symbiotic relationship to the sonnet form which encompasses it. The poem's movement toward synthesis can be seen in the following diagram:

I	sonnet described	third person	"nel suo perdersi"
II	sonnet addressed	second person	"tue contese"
III	speaker appears	first person	"Falso pur io"
IV	fusion of speaker and sonnet	first and second person	"di te mi sono avvalso, di te sonetto"

Once again, antithesis brings about a coalescence of converse statements. In the process of blaming and praising the sonnet, the subject becomes nourished and grows strong.

Furthermore, the alliterative figure in the last tercet creates a rich semantic ambiguity: "così ancora di te mi sono avvalso / di te sonetto. . . ." Here the semantic boundaries between words become blurred momentarily. Indeed, the repetition of the prepositional phrase "di te" in both verses, coupled with the syllable "son" in the words "sono" and "sonetto," creates an alliterative figure that privileges the signifier over the signified. For a moment it seems that "sonetto" may be the first person conjugation of a non-existent verb, "sonettare"[7]. The phonetic similarity between the phrases "di te mi sono" and "di te sonetto" expresses the culmination of opposities as *io* and *tu* blend into each other in a striving for oneness. The phrase "di te sonetto" forms a polyvalent construction that can be read in two ways: "of you sonnet," and, "of you I sonnetize." This moment of symbiosis between the subject and the sonnet recalls the persistent dream of lost unity that permeates the text.

The coupling of opposites, which indicates an underlying unity, is not limited to **"Postilla"** but constitutes the ruling procedure of the entire book whose title is itself an oxymoron. *Il Galateo in Bosco* connects diverse categories of experience typically considered to be separate entities. Zanzotto engages in numerous binary operations that unite pairs of diverse elements into a single component. Thus, he creates brief moments of harmony, minimal epiphanies of equilibrium that bridge the gap between the imaginary and the symbolic, between nature and culture, between subjectivity and the discourse which makes it possible.

In **"Postilla,"** this equilibrium is alluded to in the poem's subtitle, "(Sonetto infamia e mandala)." The lack of the preposition "di" brings "infamia" and "mandala" together in an unexpected fashion. Zanzotto deviates from a grammatical and stylistic norm: "di" represents the most frequently occurring preposition in the text and the most frequently used preposition in the language (Rosiello 132). This grammatical violation adds two signs together to produce a novel sum: "infamia e mandala = sonetto." This final sonnet is not a poem about baseness and about the mandala: it is not "un sonetto di." Rather, it is both of these at the same time: this sonnet wants to be a mandala.

A design containing concentric geometric figures, mandala means "magic circle" in Sanskrit. Hindus and Buddhists regard the mandala as a representation of the cosmos symbolizing the universe in its totality and wholeness. Jung's explanation of mandala symbolism sheds light on Zanzotto's use of this archetype:

> As a rule a mandala occurs in conditions of psychic dissociation or disorientation. . . . the *severe pattern* imposed by a circular image of this kind compensates the disorder and confusion of the psychic state— namely, through the construction of a central point to which everything is related, or by a concentric arrangement of the disordered multiplicity and of contradictory and irreconcilable elements. This is evidently an *attempt at self-healing* on the part of Nature, which does not spring from conscious reflection but from an instinctive impulse.
>
> (*Mandala Symbolism* 3-4)

Subjectivity as envisioned in *Il Galateo in Bosco* constitutes a pattern of psychic disorientation. An antidote to the "disordered multiplicity" of the subject, **"Postilla"** functions as a mandala-sonnet. This poem provides, in Jung's words, "a central point to which everything is related."

"Postilla" creates a small corner of the universe structured in perfect order. The fractured *io-scrivente* of the text becomes re-integrated, temporarily, within the

boundaries of the sonnet form: "mandala in cui di frusto in frusto accatto." Following Jung who named the mandala the "archetype of wholeness," we might title Zanzotto's **"Postilla"** the "sonnet of wholeness." Furthermore, this sonnet provides a dense index of the text's main themes, which conjoin in the depiction of subjectivity. The theme of biological interdependence, for example, is expressed through references to nourishment in the poem's final lines:

> così ancora di te mi sono avvalso,
> di te sonetto, righe infami e ladre—
> mandala in cui di frusto in frusto accatto.

Just as various animals live off the flesh of other creatures, so too the subject feeds off various objects with which it identifies.

"Postilla" also encapsulates Zanzotto's treatment of the Italian literary experience. As Chapter Four demonstrates, this sonnet contains Petrarchan overtones and a key reference to Dante. In addition, Zanzotto's concern with language as a problematic instrument for portraying reality expresses itself here through the key word "falso." Finally, through the caustic exchange between the "I" and the sonnet form that encloses it, Zanzotto focuses on the relationship between discourse and subjectivity: "di te mi sono avvalso, / di te sonetto." The mandala-sonnet brings opposites together "in simbiosi e convivenze" (*Galateo* 111) as it seeks to bridge the splits in the poet's identity and in reality. A therapeutic use of poetry, **"Postilla"** supplies the sustenance that allows the poet to maintain a fragile equilibrium.

In its use of the mandala archetype, **"Postilla"** resembles a protective circle, a central point of energy, a psychic refuge. Inaugurated in the initial poem with the child who leaves fingermarks on a pane of glass, the interrelationship between writing and subjectivity culminates in this central composition. As in the first poem, so too in **"Postilla,"** the subject reveals itself, sustains itself, and heals itself through a ludic manipulation of language. This summary of the text's thematic orientation can be elucidated in the following manner. Although the subject produces the sonnet, the sonnet makes possible the production of the subject. In other words, "It is the world of words that creates the world of things. . . . Man speaks, then, but it is because the symbol has made him man" (Lacan 65). Doubtful of its own reality and fearful of being a mere effect of grammar, the subject sustains itself through discourse and grows strong in the act of writing. The subject rebels against the tyranny of the symbolic order by manipulating language in a playful manner. In this way, the subject rediscovers and reclaims the position of autonomy which it enjoyed in early childhood as the imagined master of the signifier. The mandala-sonnet emerges from this grand exercise of poetic recreation to form a protective circle which holds psychic disintegration at bay.

In its role as healing circle, the mandala archetype constitutes the controlling symbol of *Il Galateo in Bosco*. In "Postilla," the mandala-sonnet reconciles a fractured subject. In "Diffrazioni, eritemi," a poem that occurs at an earlier point in the volume, Zanzotto also adopts the mandala as an image of cohesion:

> eventi
> degni comunque di minuziosissimo riguardo
> se si collocheranno   nella giusta costellazione
> nel mandala
>
> (*Galateo* 21)

In presenting fragmentary elements of the Montello's history, this poem typifies Zanzotto's attempt to connect the past and the present. Furthermore, the events "degni comunque di minuziosissimo riguardo" involve not only the story of an individual subject, i.e., the poet's personal history, but also the history of his native region[8]. The historical events and folk legends portrayed in "Diffrazioni, eritemi" depict both the history of the Montello and the collective memory of the people who live there. What began as a personal anamnesis—an attempt to recover the origins of the poet's personhood—widens into a broader exploration of the roots and identity of an entire community.

These past and present events would make more sense, however, if they could be rearranged in the correct pattern, if they could be seen as part of a mandala. If the Montello could be grasped in its totality, if its history could be seen as in a wide-angle lens—"ripresa col grandangolare / quasi a fish-eye" (*Galateo* 18)—then, perhaps, this amazing forest of human artifacts and natural codes might deliver up its secrets. This attempt to recuperate fragments of a personal and collective history into a mandala-like pattern explains the non-linear narrative motion of *Il Galateo in Bosco*: "Pretesa di narrazione e di ripresa, rubata / a grandangolo" (*Galateo* 18). By pointing to the mandala image in "Diffrazioni, eritemi," and by placing the mandala-sonnet in the center of the volume, Zanzotto has given a mandala structure to *Il Galateo in Bosco*. This text is circular in conception with meanings emanating out from its nucleus, i.e., from the "I" which struggles to obtain a cohesive identity amid the incessant metamorphoses of nature and the ossified layers of convention which constitute culture.

Zanzotto's anamnesis gives birth to a complex synthesis of disintegration and cohesiveness, a set of troubling images of fragmentation and wholeness. The story of the "I," which begins in the initial poem with the unborn child in the mother's womb, progresses through the text but reaches no fixed conclusion. Zanzotto's narrative moves toward closure without imposing it: the end point resembles the beginning. In the book's penultimate and final compositions the outer rings of the mandala are similar to the inner rings: the concluding poems recall the introductory poems.

In the text's penultimate composition, **"Inverno in bosco—osterie—cippi,"** Zanzotto offers a self-reflexive comment on the personal and collective anamnesis about to end:

> Figure o meglio vuoti di memoria
>   incongruità specifiche, mossa più mossa
>   della luce mai usabile, né sotto il moggio né là
>   sul vertice donde accecherà.
>
> . . . . .
>
>   Così nel morto tepore dei boschi
>   rimembranze battono battono la battaglia
>   del solstizio d'inverno (osteoporosi)
> di colore in colore distinsero le distruzioni
>   come io qui da dietro la feritoia—
>   ne diedi menzione—
>   senza mai ritrovarmi a nessun appuntamento
>
> (*Galateo* 106-07)

A verbalization of the history of the self, Zanzotto's story is built upon "vuoti di memoria" and "incongruità specifiche." The "mossa più mossa" that make up the narrative reflect a "luce mai usabile." The poet recapitulates the history of his own consciousness without ever reaching a definitive integration: "ne diedi menzione—/ senza mai ritrovarmi a nessun appuntamento."

The narrative movement comes to an end in the text's final poem as the subject futilely dismisses the ambitious project of depicting an elusive essence. Images of disintegration prepare the *io* for a return to its starting point:

> Nella sempre rinviata essenza
>   . . . . .
>
>   secondo quello schema
>   che si è coerentemente svolto
>   e finalmente è giunto al sodo
>   nel cranio nettato allo shampoo, residuato,
>   . . . . .
>
> Bah, qualcosa d'altro che te cranietà voltità
>   da te grifo per grifo, bruchio per bruchìo . . .
>   . . . . .
>
> . . . . frangersi
> di cartilagini in iridi di ritmi
>   ire viticci spire—
>
> (*Galateo* 108-109)

The consciousness depicted in this poem belongs to the same being who, in the text's opening lines, was awakened from the profound sleep of interuterine life.

Il Galateo in Bosco tells the story of how this "pronoun always waiting to become a noun" assumes an identity based on prevailing codes. Just as the book's initial poem portrays the child's passage from the "imaginary" into the "symbolic," so too the final poem depicts the reintegration of culture and nature as the "I" returns full circle to its origins. Zanzotto concludes his anamnesis by restoring the subject to the same mysterious sleep and the same fecund darkness from whence it sprang:

> nero autoscatto
> di spore   sopori.
> Resta in pace o bel Bosco
>
> . . . . .
>
> (*Galateo* 109)

The movement of the text's final lines may be summarized by a phrase with which Zanzotto describes the hypnotic effects of nursery rhymes and lullabies. These elemental forms of poetry lull the child to sleep in a happy transition between "veglia dormiveglia sonno sogni (nulla)" ("Infanzie, poesie, scuoletta" 55). The fifty-two poems of *Il Galateo in Bosco* take the reader on a cyclical voyage between the awakening of the child in the volume's opening lines and the drowsiness of the forest drifting toward peaceful oblivion in the conclusion. The subject, then, the "autoscatto" whose presence was first signified by "cold finger marks on the glass," and whose emergence gave rise to a narrative concerning the interrelationship of language, writing, and subjectivity, now returns to its point of departure in "quel grandore / dove tutti i silenzi sono possibili."

Notes

1. For a discussion of Zanzotto's portrayal of subjectivity in his early works, see David, p. 585; Giacomini; and Allen, "Zanzotto's *Grammaticalismo*: Positions and Performance."

2. Zanzotto uses the psychoanalytic technique of anamnesis in other works as well. In describing "La Pasqua a Pieve di Soligo" from *Pasque,* he states: "È un tentativo di anamnesi e una specie di bilancio che tuttavia resta in sospeso" (Listri 192). Also, in her analysis of the points of intersection between *Mistieròi* and Zanzotto's other works, Nuvoli emphasizes the significant role that memory plays throughout: ". . . la sequenza: volontà di tuffarsi nella memoria / visione nella memoria / risveglio e ritorno alla realtà purificato dalla memoria, non è difficile da rinvenire sin dagli inizi della produzione zanzottiana" ("Mistieròi" 343).

3. Nuvoli explicates the significance of the window imagery in *Mistieròi* and documents the reoccurrences of this motif in *Sull'altopiano.* See "Mistieròi," especially pp. 345-346, note 7.

4. The poem "Microfilm" in *Pasque* is the clearest example of Zanzotto's previous treatment of writing and subjectivity. For an analysis of this poem, see Balduino, "Zanzotto e l'ottica della contraddizione." For Zanzotto's comments on the relationship between language, writing, and subjectivity, see Andrea Zanzotto, "Postfazione," *Età d'uomo,* by Michel Leiris; "Fiches Leiris"; "Infanzie, poesie, scuoletta (appunti)"; "Parole, comportamenti, gruppi (appunti)"; and "(Ontology?) (Reference?)." See also Bandini, "Scheda per *Sull'altopiano.*"

5. Zanzotto describes the confluence of these various elements as follows: "Voce materna, voci dell'ambiente, voci-colore, figure o immagini del mondo e dell'io emergenti restano fuse in un'impalpabile unità di fondo risolta nelle apparizioni della poesia-linguaggio" ("Infanzie, poesie, scuoletta" 54).

6. Zanzotto explored this theme of personal origins in "Sul Piave: nel quarantesimo anniversario della Battaglia del Solstizio" in *IX Ecloghe.* This poem contains the same three elements which comprise the later poem, i.e., the river Piave, the parents, and the First World War.

> Fiume fedele
>
> . . . . .
>
> crescesti questi sedimenti
> da cui prendemmo forma e forza a vivere
>
> . . . . .
>
> sulla tua riva sinistra mia madre patí sola,
> a destra combatteva mio padre ed io non ero.
>
> (*IX Ecloghe* 37)

7. In "E la madre-norma," which like "Postilla" is also dedicated to Franco Fortini, Zanzotto coins the verb "poemizzare" to depict the relationship between the subject and the poem which expresses it:

> Fino all'ultimo sangue
> io che sono l'esangue
>
> . . . . .
>
> torno a capo ogni volta ogni volta poemizzo
> e mi poemizzo a ogni cosa e insieme
>
> (*La Beltà* 106)

8. In commenting on "Diffrazioni, eritemi," Zanzotto remarks on the relationship between poetry, history, and the collective memory: "Quando qualcuno scrive dei versi, molto spesso è trascinato proprio da una corrente sotterranea di memoria sua personale che però, a guardare bene, è anche

memoria d'altri, della gente che ha intorno, una memoria strana, collettiva. A volte è molto diffi-cile distinguere la memoria vera e propria dalla fantasticheria . . ." (Massini and Rivalta 74).

Works Cited

Allen, Beverly. "Zanzotto's *Grammaticalismo*: Posi-tions and Performance." Stanford Italian Review 4 (1984): 209-244.

Balduino, Armando. "Scheda bibliografica per Zanzotto critico." *Studi novecenteschi* 4 (1974): 341-48.

———. "Zanzotto e l'ottica della contraddizione (impressioni e divagazioni su *Pasque*)." *Studi nove-centeschi* 4 (1974): 281-313.

David, Michel. *La psicoanalisi nella cultura italiana.* Torino: Boringhieri, 1966.

Giacomini, Amedeo. "Da *Dietro il paesaggio* alle *IX Ecloghe*: l'io grammaticale nella poesia di Andrea Zan-zotto." *Studi novecenteschi* 4 (1974): 185-205.

Listri, Pier Francesco. "Uno sguardo dalla periferia. In-tervista con Andrea Zanzotto." *L'Approdo letterario* 18 (1972): 185-92.

Massini, Giuliana and Bruno Rivalta, eds. *Sulla poesia: Conversazioni nella scuole.* Parma: Pratiche editrice, 1981.

Nuvoli, Giuliana. "Mistieròi." *Strumenti critici* 13 (1979): 335-48.

Zanzotto, Andrea. *La Beltà.* Milano: Mondadori, 1968.

———. "Fiches Leiris." *Il Verri* 18 (1980): 92-101.

———. "Infanzie, poesie, scuoletta (appunti)." *Stru-menti critici* 20 (1973): 52-77.

———. *IX Ecloghe.* Milano: Mondadori, 1962.

———. "(Ontology?) (Reference?)." *The Favorite Mal-ice.* Ed. trans. Thomas J. Harrison. New York: Out of London Press, 1983. 133-136.

———. "Parole, comportamenti, gruppi (appunti)." *Studi novecenteschi* 4 (1974): 349-355.

———. "Postfazione." *Età d'uomo.* By Michel Leiris. Trans. Andrea Zanzotto. 1966. Milano: Mondadori, 1980. 327-36.

Beverly Allen (essay date 1988)

SOURCE: Allen, Beverly. "Gatherings of Poetry and Mushrooms: A Landscape Elegy." In *Andrea Zanzotto: The Language of Beauty's Apprentice,* pp. 98-117. Berkeley: University of California Press, 1988.

[*In the following essay, Allen explains the significance of three of Zanzotto's major collections of poetry: El-egia e altri versi,* Vocativo, *and* IX Ecloghe, *collections which Allen considers to be largely overlooked by liter-ary critics.*]

Ce soir, du haut d'une tour, l'immense
forêt sous les nuées basses et la pluie,
la guerre en atteint les limites, du
sud-ouest à l'est, un grondement sourd.

Bataille, *Sur Nietzsche*

[This evening, from the top of a tower,
the immense forest beneath low clouds
and rain, the war reaches its edge,
from southwest to east, a dull rumbling.]
Solo d'un lauro tal selva verdeggia

Petrarch

[Only with the laurel does such a forest shine green.]

This chapter and the two that follow are concerned with three books that titularly lend themselves to a grouping under the rubric of Poetry. *Elegia e altri versi* (1954), *Vocativo* (1957), and *IX Ecloghe* (1962) each have an independent significance in the itinerary of Zanzotto's poetics, a fact well recognized by much critical writ-ing.[1] But we would draw attention to them as a group, for a moment, in order to consider them as a tripartite unity of engagement with the notion of Poetry under-taken by Zanzotto during the 1950s and early 1960s. It is an engagement in which Zanzotto subjects his processes of textual production to a detailed critique by a self-awareness that shows up as the flesh and bones—sometimes lively, sometimes moribund—of Poetry.

Lest our grouping be found surprisingly exclusive, let us briefly consider the titles of Zanzotto's first five published books. The first presents the metaphor of the landscape and an implicit subjective situation with which we are by now familiar. The fifth, which remains outside the realm of our study, presents a metaphysics of aesthetics not unknown to readers of Leopardi. Both *Dietro il paesaggio* (the first book) and *La beltà* (the fifth) may therefore be seen by virtue of the images their titles conjure up to be indirect references to some aspects of poetic discourse: namely, metaphor in general and precedent poets in particular. The case with the three intervening titles, however, is distinctly more direct: each is a literal reference to a specific kind of poetic utterance. In fact, each names itself, in turn, as elegy, vocative, and eclogue. These three books delineate a period of extreme textual self-referentiality when Zanzotto's themes converge toward an examina-tion of their existence in a singularly poetic discourse.

Further, in these three books in particular, an attempt is made at a readable though not exactly literal self-definition of a "space," as Zanzotto calls it, which stands not only in opposition but actually in contradiction to the "space" of historical narrative. The poetic discourse in the *Elegia e altri versi,* in *Vocativo,* and in the *IX Ecloghe* accedes to conscious (and verbalized) responsibility as the "mondo Autre" that Zanzotto evidently felt pressed to chart during the 1950s.[2] The connections between grammar and history suggested in these books are connections of opposition or contradiction and, also, of subversion. The rapport of opposition or contradiction exists between the spaces of poetry and history; the subversion, as we shall see especially in *Vocativo,* is that of poetry by itself effected through a thematic voiding of certain aspects of standard and traditional grammatical usage. This voiding is less a negative procedure, however, than an unrelenting and unrepentant investigation of essentially two grammatical constructs: (1) the division of being into subjectivity and objectivity as determined by personal pronouns (along with the concomitant ontological confusion of any linguistically aware identity calling itself by the first person singular) and (2) the multifaceted referential ambiguity engendered by any textual use of the vocative case.

As we consider these three volumes, our analysis will concentrate on three central issues. Concerning *Elegia e altri versi,* we shall take a cue from critical neglect; of all of Zanzotto's works, this is the one about which the least has been written. This relative silence may imply that critical attention subsumes *Elegia* to *Dietro il paesaggio* as a kind of *coda* that would have appeared with the main *corpus* had the landscape's door not shut so soon, giving the elegy a semblance of separateness. We are curious to know, on the one hand, to what extent there may be validity in seeing this work as a kind of postscript to *Dietro il paesaggio* and, on the other, to what extent it distances itself from the first book. Our look at *Vocativo* will next bring us to considerations which will utilize some tools borrowed from the study of linguistics. For example, we shall analyze the extent to which the vocative case may be considered, in linguistic terms, a performative speech act—namely, one which might be classified as illocutionary—in an attempt to see how Zanzotto's use of that particular device holds implications about the nature of poetic discourse itself.

Finally, as we turn to the *IX Ecloghe,* we shall trace both the guise salvaged by a textual subjectivity for itself and the use made by this surviving subjectivity of poetic patterns bearing traditional implications. We shall also try to discern the ways in which those patterns are broken in a subversion of the very implications they inevitably carry.

> O natura, o natura,
> perché non rendi poi
> quel che prometti allor?
>
> Leopardi, "A Silvia"

> [Oh nature, oh nature,
> why did you not give then
> what you had promised before?]

In his 1973 anthology of Zanzotto's work, Stefano Agosti includes only four texts from *Elegia e altri versi.*[3] This sparse selection is justifiable in a proportional economy of representation, since Zanzotto's second published book, in its entirety, consists of only thirty-one pages. But even in his extremely helpful and otherwise thorough Introduction, Agosti foregoes any mention whatsoever of *Elegia e altri versi.* This lapsus, we should note, is not Agosti's alone. In two of the most detailed critical texts tracing the path of Zanzotto's poetic discourse from *Dietro il paesaggio* up to or through *La beltà,* both Amedeo Giacomini and Luigi Milone completely ignore the little book that nonetheless did appear in 1954.[4] It would seem that, in a bit of a rush to arrive at the perhaps more weighty matters of such issues as grammar, subjectivity, trauma, and the ascendance of medicoscientific lexicon in Zanzotto's work, critics have been distracted from the little book that arrived in second place. But to ignore *Elegia e altri versi* might be to miss Zanzotto's *Secretum*: there is an old saying about small packages. . . .

In any case, such critical distraction with regard to *Elegia e altri versi* is understandable to some extent because several aspects of the *Elegia* texts suggest an almost automatic association with *Dietro il paesaggio.* Thematically, for example, the discourse in *Elegia* is still sylvan, or in the town, or on the mountain: the landscape remains the essential metaphor. Moreover, what the thematic landscape setting does include, as was the case in the first book, is the play or interaction of subjectivity and otherness, or *io* and *tu* or its variants. Furthermore, the *Elegia* metaphors of seasons, as well as those of silence, the sun, and descent, are all familiar to a reader of *Dietro il paesaggio,* and, even stylistically, the most evident rapport between the two books is one of similarity, though not homogeneity. A significant stylistic difference between Zanzotto's first book and his second occurs, for example, in the versification. *Elegia e altri versi* contains no persistently short verse schemes and in this differs from *Dietro il paesaggio.* And except for the first, in quatrains of unrhymed hendecasyllables, all of its texts are composed in free verse. We may thus note a lesser degree of emphasis on traditional formal patterns of versification than exists in the first book, a lesser presence of rhythmic regularity, and a greater presence of long breaths, slow lines, run on in streams. Yet for all its other reminders of *Dietro il paesaggio, Elegia e altri versi* is defined by its author as a separate entity from the first work; its independence as a published unit perhaps merits more attention that has yet been paid it.

* * *

When asked how he determines what for him comprises a book, or how he decides when a book is ready for publication, Zanzotto speaks of the drawers in his desk at home in Pieve di Soligo.[5] These drawers serve as repositories for Zanzotto's works-in-progress. At any given time, there are many texts at many stages of "completion" in Zanzotto's desk drawers, where they grow almost on their own, like mushrooms in a forest, at different rates and with different appearances depending on climatic conditions and the engendering agents.

At some point, it occurs to Zanzotto that there are certain relations between some of the texts coming to fruition in his drawers. We know from the end results that these are not always relations of correspondence. They are, as often as not, relations of opposition, variation, contiguity, substitution. Notably, thematic patterns tend to be foremost among associative characteristics, however, and it may perhaps be assumed that such patterns contribute to Zanzotto's intuition of which texts should eventually come together under the same cover. Thus, a book begins to take on definition for Zanzotto in a manner more aptly characterized as layered than as linear. Such second-stage multi-level genesis—this drawing-from-the-drawers—demonstrates a significant authorial "stance" which is actually more a sitting back, a refusal to stand.

Evidently, Zanzotto's texts exist independently of a certain degree of traditional authorial intention—the intention that might envision them as filling a spot in a predetermined structure before they have even come onto a page. On the contrary, their eventual formal assemblage seems to have almost hidden beginnings, as if their author were not conscious of their silent growing together. The texts themselves gradually appear to him in a pattern that seems, for one reason or another, to appropriate the ontology of an interdependent unity which will in turn make a certain set of texts separate from all others: the book. Those poems sit in the drawers like unconscious desires or instincts that, more or less displaced, come into conscious structures independently of subjective will, producing readable symptoms in the book. The drawer-maturation of his texts, in any case, supports Zanzotto's own attitude as participant in, rather than director of, the processes of textual production.

This fact may be surprising to a reader acquainted with Zanzotto's *opus,* for the stylistic commitments of each of his volumes would seem to imply, on the contrary, a very conscious effort at control. What we learn from the story of the drawers, however, is that Zanzotto is not an experimental poet moving from one controlled and documented attempt at innovation to another with specific results always in mind. Instead, he exercises selectivity at various moments in the process of text-production in response only to the exigencies of his own ambiguous rapport with the signs in which his enunciation is simultaneously actuated and trapped. To the extent that each of the books resulting from various moments of this involvement is unique, each may be

seen as the record of its own peculiarity. Further, what we call a moment is not necessarily temporally exclusive: several moments might occur simultaneously and later be situated by the author in a topical rather than a chronological pattern (as seems to be the case with the synchrony of inscription and the diachrony of publication dates of *Dietro il paesaggio* and *A che vale?*). To a great extent, and unavoidably, in any case, the books are chronologically determined. But how many texts lie in the drawer past the gestation period of their synchronic siblings? How many texts of *Vocativo* were already in the drawers at the time of *Dietro il paesaggio*? *Elegia e altri versi* itself could be a bridge built when its author already had one foot on either side of a ravine. The possibility that several books may begin to appear to their author as units more or less simultaneously is the case recently: *Il galateo in bosco, Fosfeni,* and *Idioma* are three books that Zanzotto says have matured more or less in tandem, presenting themselves as a triptych whose panels we readers are now able to view in any order we please.[6]

Whereas Zanzotto assumes a consciously passive attitude at early stages in the structural determination of the books, there is nonetheless—in fact, all the more—a great deal of significance in the divisions into books that Zanzotto's work finally takes, for it is with this division that the beginnings of our readings are set. The criteria that determine which texts appear to him not only as being independent at an initial stage (that of the individual poem) but, at a later moment, interrelated (as units of a book) first become readable in the very book groupings which result. With these, at least the beginnings of our readings are encouraged to mime Zanzotto's own.

This leads us back to a tautological assertion of the evident: *Elegia e altri versi* could have been appended to *Dietro il paesaggio* without seeming an inappropriate swelling had Zanzotto recognized it as part of the first book, but he did not. *Elegia e altri versi* exists as a separate entity and thus exhibits a conscious authorial determination it is our purpose to examine.

We would like to suggest that *Elegia e altri versi* shows its differentiation from *Dietro il paesaggio* in two main respects: the first is related to a thematics of narration and the second to a thematics of technique or style. Not only is the independent existence of *Elegia* after *Dietro* retrospectively meaning-productive as a kind of ending to the story in the first book, it is also significant as the beginning of a textual engagement with the potential meaning of poetry itself, a beginning that is already more than a prophecy to be fulfilled at some later date, a beginning that, in a flurry of critical distraction, has been somewhat overlooked.

* * *

Whereas the most immediate comparison is *Elegia e altri versi* with *Dietro il paesaggio,* we have already made another when we hinted that the *Elegia* is something of a *Secretum* in its author's *opus.* This simile holds to the extent that both are *libelli* in a production usually more voluminous and both contain secrets. In the *Elegia* the secret is a kind of confession of a depression into which the *io* has been induced in his dealings with otherness—a marked departure from the exalted ascents and descents of the first book. But a tenuous simile could also be made with the *Canzoniere* on the basis of Zanzotto's efficacious use of the turning point of thought initiated by Petrarch in his sonnets. Such a pivot is most often effected by Zanzotto in the *Elegia* with a *ma* [but] that suddenly creates a neatly proportioned thought progression in verse forms which themselves are far removed from the delicate divisions of Petrarch's octaves and sestets. **"Storie dell'Arsura II"** [**"Stories of the Drought II"**] and **"Elegia"** [**"Elegy"**] are cases in point.[7]

But if we wish to trace the story of *Dietro il paesaggio* beyond its own seasons and landscapes, our Petrarchan simile would have to be made, more appropriately, with the *Trionfi.* It is in his *Trionfi* that Petrarch tells us what becomes of Laura after the narrative of the *Canzoniere* and how the love-death story of the vulgate fragments finally ends. This general scheme is remarkably like what happens to the *Dietro* story in *Elegia,* where we read a kind of second ending in a mode very different from the first. For example, at the end of *Dietro il paesaggio,* the *io* finds a conjugal resolution, the *proprio oscuro matrimonio con il cielo e la selva,* to some aspects at least of the subject-object division which to a certain extent torments but which mostly discombobulates him.

The second ending presented by *Elegia e altri versi* is much less assuring than that union. In the *Elegia,* while the objectivity of *tu* is given several identities, its sudden, central occurrence as *Tu, morte,* to which we shall turn shortly, has a striking ring of finality. This death is associated, by means of the multiple identities of *tu,* with other instances of alterity as perceived subjectively. *Tu* is love, for example, in **"Martire, Primavera"** [**"Martyrdom, Springtime"**], where we find:

> Tanti scoscesi terrori
> e pietrose distanze violando
> rompi tu solo al petto, amore.[8]

> [Violating so many steep terrors
> and rocky distances,
> you alone break into the breast, love.]

Elsewhere, *tu* is some aspect of the landscape or the sky. In **"Partenza per il Vaud"** [**"Departure for Vaud"**], for example, we read:

> Riposo potrò chiamarti, cielo? E vento
> te, piangere concorde di pendici e di liane
> verso il freddo Montello, parallele
> ombre e certezze della mia giornata?[9]

> [Might I call you repose, sky? And you,
> wind, the slopes' and lianas' concordant crying
> toward the cold Montello, parallel
> shadows and certainties of my day?]

Finally, in **"Storie dell'Arsura I,"** *tu* is the town itself: *Da tanto a te, Soligo, mi conformo* [I've resembled you for a long time, Soligo].[10] But in a metaphoric current that returns more often to the season than to the landscape (in one of the significant variations on the metaphoric structure of *Dietro il paesaggio*), the season is most often winter, and the other evoked in central position is, as we mentioned above, primarily death.

These metaphorical attributions braid together at the center of *Elegia e altri versi.* There, **"Storie dell'Arsura I & II"** establishes first a season of drought that, for lack of water in a river bed, also implies silence (by itself a threat to the *io*'s identity inasmuch as it suggests the absence of any interlocution). The imagery then moves from a faraway *Pasqua dell'Angelo* [*Angel's Easter*] sun to the unhappy sun of a winter noonday, testimony that there is nothing *dietro.* This winter scene is one side of the *Elegia*'s central conjunction of winter setting and final alterity. Here is section II, one side, so to speak, of this braiding:

> Dai miei poveri giorni mi svio,
> salgo con lena primaverile
> verso i boschi di Lorna
> e benefiche valli e grato verde
> d'aprile acerbamente sogno.
> Nulla per dorsi spenti
> e per cavi torpori mattutini
> nulla dietro il ventaglio del meriggio
> che soffocate sere scopre
> per tramiti gessosi e stecchi e brividi.
> Negli altri anni a queste ore
> sulle mie pene invernali
> grande e madido il bosco
> era cresciuto, mansueto limo
> aveva popolato il mio cortile.
> Ma ora un sole infelice mi fa scuotere il capo,
> or si fende la creta, sbigottito è il ruscello,
> e le tue care labbra
> sento umide solo
> per un'avara dimenticanza
> dell'immenso risucchio dell'arsura.[11]

> [From my poor days I stray,
> I go up with springtime breath
> toward Lorna's woods
> and I bitterly dream
> of April's generous valleys and welcome green.
> Nothing on the spent ridges
> and in hollow morning torpors
> nothing behind the fan of noontide
> that exposes suffocated evenings
> on chalky pathways, twigs, and tremblings.

In other years at these hours
the woods had grown
large and damp
upon my winter pains, gentle mire
had populated my courtyard.
But now an unhappy sun makes me shake my head,
now the clay cracks, the river takes fright,
and your precious lips
I feel moist only
because of my greedy forgetfulness
of the draught's immense whirlpool.]

The misleading humidity of this text's final kiss depends on subjective forgetfulness. The following text, the other surface in the interfacing where winter and death meet in one place, begins with memory, a major theme of *Elegia e altri versi,* as the title itself implies. This poem is **"Ore calanti I, II, III"** [**"Declining hours I, II, III"**]; we cite its first section here for the identification of the intimate other, the *tu,* as death, a perhaps logical conclusion in the gnosiology or cognitive phenomenology of subjectivity, but one at which *Dietro il paesaggio* never arrives:

Quale lento riflesso, quale vitrea memoria
di sè ai prati affranti va tentando
questo scorcio di maggio calante?

E a me tu sempre nell'angolo oscuro
della mia sorte distruggi quel lume

Tace il fianco beato del colle,
guarda incerto il papavero
le dissolte forze delle erbe

Prati affranti, affranti di tante acque,
grilli residui dello spazio vinto,
e non raggiungeranno il crudo azzurro
nè il felice giro dei monti

Tu, mia morte, fredda riporti
e cara quest'ombra di maggio
ed una sera divenuta un raggio
che triste si sfibra a illimpidirsi.[12]

[What slow reflection, what vitreous self-memory
is this tag end of waning May
trying for on the crushed fields?

And in the dark corner of my fate
you always destroy that light for me.

The blissful flank of the hill falls silent,
the poppy gazes uncertain
at the dissolved strength of the grass.

Crushed fields, crushed by so many waters,
left-over crickets of the vanquished space,
and they will not reach the raw azure
nor the happy circle of the mountains.

You, my death, bring back cold
and dear this May shadow
and an evening become a ray
that for sadness dims to transparency.]

This is the innovation and the quiet depression of the *Elegia*: the *io*'s recognition of the ultimate alterity as that which is closest to him, that which is his interlocutor in a setting that hides—or promises—nothing.

Going *dietro* here, unlike in *Dietro il paesaggio,* takes on figurative significance as an effort of memory, elegy, sad recollection, and singing about something behind not a surface or evidence, but a moment of time, the present. The constant and varied identification of *tu* as so many different things is implicitly subsumed in the identity of *tu* with death. The implications of the shifting identity of the other and its central appearance as a final alterity associate all alterity with a fruitless stasis, as if all chance for differentiation need flirt with annihilation, as if all were already over and the most that could now be expected were some internalized accounts of what had already happened. Take, for example, lines in which the dependence on the past is evident grammatically as well as thematically as *Ormai m'apparve il senso dell'estate* [By now the meaning of summer appeared to me], *Di tutto ho vuotato le mie mani* [I have emptied my hands of everything], *Arrischiata luce / prati che v'induceste / lungi nel grembo di una sera* [Daring light / fields that led you deep / into the lap of an evening].[13]

In **"Martire, Primavera"** the season is more promising, but the identity of *tu* is left in an ambiguity of spring / death that corresponds, as it did in the **"Elegia pasquale"** of *Dietro il paesaggio,* to the events preceding Easter renewal. Here are some excerpts:

Il monte scende, paese diviene,
qui con te cede il monte
[. . .]
Tu sei custode e causa
dei pochi nostri pensieri d'infermi
chiusi nel denso maggio
da calve piogge e ghiacci di Golgota
[. . .]
Nessuna svolta di tante strade
si attarda per te
per rifarti tra noi
altro dal ferreo stupore
dall'oscuro limite ove esisti
E noi ti proteggiamo
dall'essere ciò che ora sei.[14]

[The mountain descends, becomes a village
here with you the mountain gives way
[. . .]
You are custodian and cause
of our few sickly thoughts
closed in the thick May
of bald rains and Golgotha freezes
[. . .]
Of so many streets not one turn
tarries for you
to bring you back among us
as anything other than the ironclad stupor
of the dark border where you exist

And we protect you
from being what you now are.]

In the book's final poem, the **"Elegia"** proper, we find, at last, the ambiguous but death-related *tu* merging with memory:

Pullula invano la sera di dolente
verde e di tardi monti,
la tua terra si vela di amori profondi,
fiumi e vallate divengono memoria;[15]

[The evening swarms in vain
with mournful green and lingering mountains,
your land mists over with deep loves,
rivers and valleys become memory;]

Next, in a difficult winter wedding of an architecture signalling accomplishment (the past) and a landscape emblematizing presence (the present), the joining of what is over with what is now may suggest that the present is as much done with as the past, or that the past is as present, subjectively, as the present:

sta la mia sorte con te, con la tua
che già di grigie note punge i capelli stanchi,
e fervono i pianeti dal calore d'arancio
oltre mozze rovine pei cieli invernali,
celebra il vuoto dei cortili scoperti
le ardue nozze delle colonne e dei colli.[16]

my fate rests with you, with yours
that already plucks grey notes on tired hairs,
and the orange-colored planets blaze
beyond mutilated ruins in the winter skies,
the uncovered courtyards' void celebrates
the arduous marriage of the columns and the hills.

This nuptial bed is a deathbed. A subjectivity comforted by traditional signals of goodwill is distracted from its watch just as terror is about to take hold by the very signs (*una stella di pace*) its vigil remarks:

Questo è il talamo tuo che precorre la selva
quello è il vitreo giaciglio della brina,
e Vespero, natura umana,
e una stella di pace e di volontà buona
tocca i primi terrori, soggiace
alla fosca vigilia che in sè già ci distrae.[17]

[This is your bridal bed, it foretells the woods,
that is the hoarfrost's vitreous pallet,
and Vespers, human nature,
and a star of peace and goodwill
touch the first terrors, succumb
to the dark vigil which itself already distracts us.]

A second *Vespero* occurs in the second stanza of **"Elegia."** The canonical evening hour and its (Christmas) star recur as death signals of an alterity itself distracted to the point of being lost even to memory (*le tue spalle cui preme l'oblio*), an otherness that now ignores the signrich landscape:

Tu stai, nè più cura hai dell'umile
palpito ovino che ha la tua strada
se da notte a notte la guardi languire,
la tua nuca non cura
me e l'oriente ove vibra
l'illusorio vigore del frumento;
le tue spalle cui preme l'oblio
la tua mente che infrange altra legge
già da tanto giacquero, e trema e s'abbassa
l'oro natalizio della stella
di Vespero tra i capelli
tuoi che nota furtiva la morte.[18]

[You hold still and no longer care about the humble
ovine pulsating in your street
when night after night you watch it languish,
the nape of your neck doesn't care about
me and the east where
the wheat's illusory vigor vibrates;
your shoulders, where oblivion presses,
your mind, that another law breaks,
have already lain low for so long, and the evening
  star's natal gold
that stealthily takes note of death
trembles and settles
in your hair.]

With the elimination of temporal differentiation, and with the other's refusal of the landscape and even its illusory promise, the *io* becomes insensitive to the other's speech and to his own vision, thus blocking two channels of communication. This occurs along with what amounts to a renunciation of seasons as well in a generalized refusal of one system of signification after another.

The third line group of **"Elegia"** shows how in this situation nonetheless, and by means of an obstinate Petrarchan reversal, the *io* conducts a stubborn, if fruitless, nighttime search. In a synesthetic suggestion of great subjective dismay (*l'alba nera con acide palpebre*), the *io*'s insomniac quest for memory leads only to a dark dawn and to the *incipit,* long anticipating the more notorious instances in ***La beltà,*** of a lexicon of pathology:

Non puoi dirmi la ruvida pioggia
che di sè ci stordiva
e che improvvisi spazi e primavere
ci rovesciò vive negli occhi,
non puoi dirmi la grandine fresca
che in fuga volò dalla nube
a pettinare paesi frettolosi,
nè l'erba grande nei giardini
nè i grandi pomi dell'agosto,
nulla puoi dirmi nulla so nulla vedo;
ma di quel cibo ora il seme perduto
lungo cieche ansie notturne ricerco
nel campo dissestato e le ore vanno e nera
sarà più l'alba che i grumi dei monti,
l'alba nera con acide palpebre
ci secernerà nella valle del mondo.

E da ghiacci orgogliosi a iride levando
spoglierà il vento le nari,
le viscere stente, la tosse,
e tra poco lo stretto petroso
focolare che ignora la fiamma
rabbrividirà di lumache e di crete
cerule all'orlo della solitudine,
gemerà di stanchezza la campana
che offesa trapela dal cielo,
l'iride irrisa tremerà
tremerà nell'inverno
su chine e chine avide di paesi.[19]

[You cannot tell me the coarse rain
that was deafening us with itself
and that spilled sudden spaces
and living springtimes into our eyes,
you cannot tell me the cool hail
that in flight flew from the cloud
to comb hurried villages,
nor the grass tall in the garden
nor the big August apples,
you can tell me nothing I know nothing I see nothing
but now I seek that food's lost seed
along blind nocturnal anxieties
in the ruined field and the hours pass and the dawn
will be blacker than the mountains' clots,
the black dawn whose eyelids are acid
will secrete us into the valley of the world.

And, rising from proud ice to rainbows,
the wind will strip our nostrils,
our weakened viscera, our cough,
and soon the narrow rocky
fireplace that knows no flame
will shiver on the edge of solitude
with snails and cerulean clay,
the bell oozing offended from the sky
will moan with fatigue,
the scorned rainbow will tremble
will tremble in the winter
upon slopes and slopes that are yearning for villages.]

Next, the final stanza of **"Elegia,"** and of *Elegia e altri versi* brings a past gloss for these predictions:

Ho coinvolto sole e luna nella mia sorte,
ho seguito le aperte promesse dei fiori
e la stagione che tutto presume, la bocca
rossa, gli occhi e il profilo che stimola e schiara
il mutevole margine delle radure
ed il pesco boschivo,
ho seguito la tua
piccola casa dall'ombra
riconosciuta familiare
anche tra i denti raggianti impetuosi
delle estati che saranno,
tra i pensieri implacati
tra le moltitudini e i giorni. Ma stanche
ora le mani sul parapetto a luci
di logge s'esalano, inverno
senza requie logora presagi
e moti d'alberi tristi lungi affila.[20]

[I have implicated sun and moon in my fate,
I have followed the open promises of flowers

and the season that presumes everything, the red
mouth, the eyes, and the profile that excites and
  brightens
the changeable border of the glade
and the forest peach tree,
I have followed your
little house from the shadow
familiar to me
even among the gleaming impetuous teeth
of summers to come,
among relentless thoughts
among multitudes and days. But tired
now my hands breathe forth their last
to loggia lights on the parapet, and winter
unremittingly wears out omens
and sharpens long sad movements of trees.]

The anaphora here is a familiar one to readers of *Dietro il paesaggio*'s penultimate, namesake poem. A pattern of titular repetition ("**Elegia**" in *Elegia e altri versi,* "**Dietro il paesaggio**" in *Dietro il paesaggio*) is carried over in the rhetoric of this text to the inexact repetition in the preterit anaphora, *Ho coinvolto . . . / ho seguito,* and, later, an exact repetition, *ho seguito.* Within "Elegia" itself, this anaphora resembles the series of negative assertions in the third stanza: *Non puoi dirmi / . . . non puoi dirmi . . . / nulla puoi dirmi.*

In a multi-level play of similarity (titular, rhetorical, inter-stanzaic) that presages the poem's thematic conclusion, both the third and the final stanzas are serial in structure: the third lists what the *tu* cannot say; the fifth lists what the *io* has done. This is a seriality of progressive accession to silence at first objective (*non puoi dirmi*) and then, we would suggest, subjective. In the final line group, we find familiar images of sun, moon, flowers, seasons, the woman in the landscape, the *tu,* the house, the shadow; these are the signs that were the readable promise in *Dietro il paesaggio,* but here they are relegated to the past tense by a subjectivity whose silence perhaps consists of no longer finding anything to read. This second ending finds a final *Ma* that speaks the conclusive subjective alienation: the signs were there (all that was *riconosciuta familiare*); the future will vampirize them in its own historical version (*anche tra i denti raggianti impetuosi / delle estati che saranno*). But now, *ora,* the signs are worn out, and what was once the edge of *dietro* is now simply *tristi,* like a Sibelius waltz.

A note on verse groupings: since the four preceding stanzas alternate in length between sixteen and twelve verses, one might expect that the fifth would contain sixteen lines and thus preserve the pattern of alternation. Such is not the case: this final stanza contains seventeen verses. The extra line, the shortest, occurs in an anticipated central position in the line group. There, we find what might appropriately have been a fifteen-syllable verse—a length not at all uncommon in this text—*ho seguito la tua piccola casa dall'ombra,* broken into two lines. This break creates the shortest verse in the entire text (prompting us to identify it as the "extra" one) as well as a marked enjambement that leaves *tua* at the end of the verse, like an unreachable jewel glimmering at the bottom of a deep pond: *ho seguito la tua / piccola casa dall'ombra* (vv. 63-64). Even in this listing of past signs and subjective efforts at reading them, even in a moment of elegy for the passing of those signs and those efforts, the central, magnetic presence of the other is the fulcrum on which everything turns. The *tua,* simultaneously the familiar and the strange other (*dall'ombra / riconosciuta familiare*), would persist at an edge somewhere between woodland and shadow, but all is past.

Then, in the final four and one half lines, the turn of the thought swings on a Petrarchan *ma*: logical resistance as sign of resignation. The (writing) hands are tired; the setting is a parapet or windowsill, not an adventure-promising precipice. The elegy of past desire, of the search, of the other, of what was behind the landscape now draws to a close in the signless, sad dead of winter.

* * *

In a narrative economy, as we mentioned earlier, *Elegia e altri versi* may be seen to resemble Petrarch's *Trionfi* since both present a kind of second ending of a story written earlier and appearing elsewhere. Both, moreover, present a final association of alterity with death, a story of desire thwarted by mortality (though in Zanzotto's *Elegia* the death is subjective, *la mia morte*). Both show the transposition of signs once readable in a context that reserved some promise of fulfillment to a context of the willful evocation of a past standing as witness that promises were not fulfilled. Both present a subjective discourse about an absent object.

But here is precisely where the analogy breaks down. Petrarch ends his story of his love for Laura with a triumph, the victory parade of death which sweeps her away where he could not. Whatever the philosophical or theological implications, the vehicle he uses is one borrowed from returning conquerors. To the victor go the spoils, and the honor, and the vindictive last laugh. To the victor, especially, goes power over the vanquished: Petrarch's triumph is to show death victorious in his place.

Zanzotto's little *Elegia* stands in stark contrast to such triumphal sentiments. The mode is the sad lament of elegy rather than the glaring trumpetings of the *trionfo.* Zanzotto's tone is minimal, not grandiose. His verses are irregular; there is not even a rhyming vestige of drumbeats here. His sentiment is regret, not pride or vindictiveness. In the circumstances of the *Elegia,* the loser is not the other but the longing subject, alone.

Our initial question here, however, was not how *Elegia e altri versi* resembles or differs from Petrarch's several works, but how it distinguishes itself from *Dietro il paesaggio* to the extent that published manifestation of authorial intention determines the *Elegia* as a separate book. From our brief readings, we have already noted several significant points of differentiation. The condensation of the multiple identities of the other to a central, finalizing identity as death occurs only in *Elegia e altri versi,* for example. Furthermore, if *Dietro il paesaggio* may be considered as primarily formed upon a metaphor of landscape, and secondarily upon one of season, *Elegia e altri versi* would seem to present the inverse situation, for in this work seasonal metaphors take precedence over those of landscape. The shift from the implied (though at times contradicted) stasis of landscape to the temporality of seasons emphasizes the thematic importance of time in the second book. The very choice of elegy as the mode of expression implies a temporality that situates the subject in a present, taking most of its definition from the past via the function of memory. In *Elegia e altri versi,* moreover, the future barely exists. This is quite a different ontological situation from the one even of the **"Elegia pasquale"** in *Dietro il paesaggio,* where the present views itself essentially as a dividing line between a determinate past and a projected different kind of time to come.[21] Signs have foregone their projective referents and now depend more on a regressive pattern of signifieds.

A temporality circumscribed by memory is one of the marks of elegy; it is the earmark distinguishing Zanzotto's second published book from his first. The shift from a dependence on metaphor and narration to one of the oldest modalities of traditional poetic utterance has the consequences mentioned above and also leads to the oft-remarked grammaticalism in Zanzotto's following works, as we shall see. Thus, in *Elegia e altri versi* we may find the beginning of Zanzotto's simultaneously serious and ludic manipulation not only of the fragments of his myriad predecessors—the *operazioni decontestualizzanti* of *Dietro il paesaggio* as described by Luigi Milone[22]—but of the bones of poetry itself, of the privileged space it claims for itself in language. In other words, Zanzotto is now playing very seriously with the signifying possibilities of traditional forms or modes that he uses as semantic elements in a lexicon where signs now quite intentionally include all the implications associated with those modes.

This plunge into the realms of poetic modalities hallowed as far back as the Greeks suits very well Zanzotto's avowed purpose of creating *un mondo Autre.*[23] In the case of elegy, there can be no thematic claim of superiority or victory. There is memory and regret, but not exhortation or triumph. The elegiac mode, with its more or less resigned lamentations, creates a space for itself which traditionally has existed in counterpoint and even opposition to the discourse of history; the telling of subjective regret for the past is never the telling of the presumed fact of the past.

Elegy thus seconds the anti-historicism of Zanzotto's notion of poetic discourse in general, where words are not just symbols of facts or events but are themselves events, factual in their equivalence only to themselves. These poetic signs are manipulated in ways outlawed by everyday usage in attempts to find new and consequently always contemporary possibilities of meaning based on an eventfulness of the signs themselves. Such a technique does not carve in some figurative slab of marble what generations to come, limited by the letter, will read as the truth of any given time. The simultaneous multiplicity of signification that Zanzotto taps in his production of poetic texts exists instead as a vantage point from which history is revealed as but another discourse—one bent on a kind of persuasion, perhaps, or captured by its own desire to capture a past for a captive present, but a discourse nonetheless, and thus like all discourse susceptible to whatever analysis and scrutiny may obtain, and as feeble as any signs held in the shackles of narrative exclusivity, of one version of "truth."

The ending in *Elegia e altri versi* is, therefore, like all endings, simultaneously a beginning. With this book, Zanzotto begins his involvement with the semantic potential of poetry per se—of poetry, that is, as apart from other kinds of discourse, as traditionally, originally, an other kind of speech. He recognizes the internal alterity of his own poetic discourse; as *tu* dies to its old existence as the unattainable, it appears here as the very letter of a subjective *terminus*. This recognition continues in the following two books, turning around one facet or another of itself first with *Vocativo* and then with *IX Ecloghe,* both evident banner-titles in Zanzotto's rummagings through traditional poetic practice. In the book of eclogues, as we shall see, the notion of poetic discourse is problematized far beyond the degree present in the *Elegia.* But it is only after these three volumes of Poetry, so to speak, that Zanzotto's *beltà* will appear at stage center.

As concerns the *Elegia e altri versi* itself, we may conclude that, even though Zanzotto's most impressive stylistic innovations of the three Poetry books perhaps occur only midway through *Vocativo,* his little book of elegy may be seen as a first movement toward a textualized consciousness of poetic utterance as an antihistorical space, one in which subjectivity, though bound in this *libellum* perhaps more than anywhere else to temporality, may engage in a speech which, by beginning to make of itself the event it describes, takes its significance from a very different realm than that of linear narrative. The elegy elegizes the exaltation of poetry and therefore of itself; in so doing, it perpetuates the possibility both of elegy and of poetic utterance. It would hardly be possible to imagine anything more self-referential.

Notes

1. See, for example, the articles on Zanzotto in *Studi novecenteschi* 4, nos. 8/9 (July-November 1974); Giorgio Bàrberi-Squarotti, *Poesia e narrativa del secondo novecento,* 170-177, and Stefano Agosti, Introduction to *Andrea Zanzotto Poesie* (Milan: Mondadori, 1973), 9-27, as well as the critical anthology included in the same book, 28-32.

2. Personal communication. Interview of July 1978 conducted in Pieve di Soligo and published in the *Stanford Italian Review,* 4, no. 2 (Fall 1984): 253-265.

3. Stefano Agosti, ed., *Andrea Zanzotto Poesie.*

4. Amedeo Giacomini, "Da *Dietro il paesaggio* alle *IX Ecloghe,*" and Luigi Milone, "Per una storia."

5. Personal communication, August 1976, in Pieve di Soligo. What follows is a reconstruction based on my recollection of one of my conversations with Zanzotto.

6. Personal communication, July 1978. *Il galateo in bosco* appeared in 1978, *Fosfeni,* 1983, and *Idioma,* in 1986.

7. For a more detailed discussion of the innovative aspects of the turning points of thought in Petrarch's sonnets, see "The Petrarchan Sonnet: The Turn of the Thought," submitted by this writer in partial fulfillment of the requirements for the Master of Arts degree in Italian, Department of Italian, Columbia University, New York, 1972.

8. Zanzotto, *Elegia e altri versi* (Milan: Edizioni della Meridiana, 1954), 24.

9. Ibid., 11.

10. Ibid., 13, v. 14.

11. Ibid., 14.

12. Ibid., 15.

13. These are the initial lines of sections III, IV, and V, respectively, of "Ore calanti," in *Elegia e altri versi,* 17-19.

14. "Martire, Primavera," in Zanzotto, *Elegia e altri versi,* 22-23.

15. "Elegia," in Zanzotto, *Elegia e altri versi,* 27.

16. Ibid.

17. Ibid.

18. Ibid., 28.

19. Ibid., 28-29.

20. Ibid., 29-30.

21. See our discussion of "Elegia pasquale," chap. I.

22. Milone, "Per una storia," 209.

23. Interview of July 1978. See note #2 above.

John P. Welle (essay date spring 1992)

SOURCE: Welle, John P. "Dante and Poetic *Communio* in Zanzotto's Pseudo-Trilogy." *Lectura Dantis,* no. 10 (spring 1992): 34-58.

[*In the following essay, Welle examines Zanzotto's use of* communio, *or poetic "borrowing," particularly the influence of Dante on his* Il galateo in bosco, Fosfeni, *and* Idioma.]

In the post-Montalean era, Andrea Zanzotto has become widely recognized as one of Italy's greatest living poets and one of her most important voices in this century. This critical consensus is particularly noteworthy given the arduous nature of Zanzotto's verse. The often cited inaccessibility or frequently encountered ambiguity in Zanzotto's poetry stems, in part, from his widespread and idiosyncratic appropriation of other poets. The first critic to comment on this aspect of Zanzotto's style, Eugenio Montale once warned that "cercare le fonti di Zanzotto sarebbe come individuare un ago nel pagliaio" ("La poesia di Zanzotto" 339). While Zanzotto's exaggerated or "hyper" literariness contributes to the difficulty of his work, his innovative transformation of familiar poetic sources provides precious clues to the possible meanings of his texts.

Zanzotto himself has frequently commented on poetic imitation and borrowing, on the relationships that develop between poets, and on his own affinity with the "fathers" of the Italian tradition, Dante and Petrarch.[1] It is, therefore, of the greatest interest to observe Zanzotto's attitude toward one of the most frequently discussed issues in current literary criticism—intertextuality (*Gli sguardi* 43-44):

> tutti coloro che abbiano avuto certe esperienze poetiche, si trovano, grandi o piccoli, precedenti o successivi, entro una sola corrente profonda, rientrante in se stessa come l'omerico fiume Oceano, rapiti in essa, testimoni di essa, più o meno consapevolmente non importa. Né importano "plagi", imitazioni, o altri tipi di contatti tra autori, che non sono mai casuali, mentre importa che vi sia questa *communio,* questa circolazione, questo dare e ricevere, questo rubacchiare in una specie di ipnotica cleptomania, od arrivare a punti che possono essere contemporaneamente d'incontro e di scontro.

Moving beyond the "anxiety" associated with Harold Bloom's Oedipal theory of poetic influence, Zanzotto places the emphasis on *communio.* Rather than concentrating on the "weak" and the "strong" in matters of influence and imitation, on the "fathers" who came first and the "sons" who followed later, Zanzotto suggests that we consider poetry as a shared activity, as a dialogic form of human expression, and as an ongoing circulation of interrelated voices.

Zanzotto's concept of poetic *communio* sheds light on his poetics of "borrowing" in general and on his imitation of Dante in particular. Heretofore, in discussing Zanzotto's use of literary fragments, critics have tended to focus on the poet's imitation of Petrarch and Petrarchism.[2] Although many critics have alluded to the more apparent Dantean qualities of Zanzotto's verse, i.e. plurilingualism, linguistic inventiveness, and poetic difficulty, frequently in a passing manner, no one has yet undertaken a systematic study of what Gino Rizzo has called "the dialectical tension of Zanzotto's confrontation with Dante's universe" (318).[3] To be sure, Zanzotto, like Montale before him, has had a profound and lengthy engagement with Dante.[4] Needless to say, such an overarching and comprehensive analysis of all of Zanzotto's borrowings from Dante in the fifteen volumes that he has written to date would require a book.

In the present context, convinced as I am that the significance of Zanzotto's literary borrowing continues to be misconstrued, I intend to trace the trajectory of Dantean allusions in the poet's recent masterpiece, the trilogy or "pseudo-trilogy", consisting of *Il Galateo in Bosco* (1978), *Fosfeni* (1983), and *Idioma* (1986). Although Zanzotto's poetic duel with Petrarch occurs chiefly in the series of sonnets at the center of *Il Galateo in Bosco,* his "incontro-scontro" with Dante spans the length of the entire pseudo-trilogy. This is not surprising given that the trilogy framework in itself represents the Dantean reference *par excellence* and also provides a backdrop for other Dantean echoes, themes, and allusions. Rather than providing a series of close readings of all the poems that contain Dantean references, my study will focus on a number of key texts and will attempt to link Zanzotto's borrowings from Dante with the broader intentions, themes, and organizing principles of the work as a whole.

In characterizing Dante's reception in contemporary Italian literature, Zygmunt Barański describes the general trends which help locate Zanzotto's Dantean borrowings within a broader context ("Power of Influence" 347):

> In a situation in which Dante holds a position of some authority and notoriety, it is feasible that each writer might try to come to terms with him in a personal man-

ner and to bend him to his or her own ends, while, at the same time and possibly at a deeper level, revealing and utilizing culturally determined common attitudes and borrowings.

Here Barański moves the discussion on Dantean imitation beyond the heretofore dominant and somewhat confining concentration on the specifically marked quotation. In examining the Dantean elements in Zanzotto's pseudo-trilogy, we shall attempt to demonstrate how the poet "comes to terms with Dante in a personal manner". Toward this end, we shall analyze Zanzotto's idiosyncratic rewriting of specifically marked Dantean passages. Moreover, mindful of Barański's assertion that Dante's presence "at a deeper level" may also be "culturally determined", we shall also interpret those Dantean allusions that, while more general than the specifically marked quotation, are nevertheless essential to Zanzotto's strategy for tapping the rich Dantean vein in the Italian memory deposit.[5]

The Trilogy as Pseudo-Trilogy

Before we turn to the texts, a word of explanation is in order with regard to the trilogy structure. Zanzotto commented on the Dantean elements in the pseudo-trilogy in a private letter (summer of 1990): "Il riferimento dantesco esiste, ma il mio è un 'campo rotante' con l'ultimo lavoro (*Idioma*) che costituisce il (perno) centro, centro vuoto eppure super-denso, grazie al suo nucleo dialettale. Siamo all'opposto della perfetta continuazione simbolica dantesca, col suo itinerario lineare. Ma sto delirando, ora, nel mettermi in sia pur lontano paragone col padre Dante!" The poet's comments here contribute to our understanding of his intentions in providing a trilogy structure and are consonant with his other statements on this matter.[6] As Zanzotto himself suggests, and as various critics have pointed out,[7] his discourse is fractured, discontinuous, interrupted, and elliptical while Dante's is linear, symmetrical, and highly layered with interrelated symbols. The three volumes in Zanzotto's pseudo-trilogy form a discontinuous poetic whole and represent "momenti non cronologici di uno stesso lavoro, che rinviano l'uno all'altro a partire da qualunque di essi" (*Idioma* 113). The references to Dante, therefore, participate in what Zanzotto calls "un campo rotante" that shifts from volume to volume. At the opposite extreme from "father Dante", Zanzotto's poetry is circular rather than linear in orientation with meanings emanating outward from concentrically organized but scattered and rotating thematic nuclei.

In light of Zanzotto's statements regarding the "campo rotante" of his pseudo-trilogy, and since we intend to privilege the Dantean moments in his work, we must guard against the temptation to view his individual volumes as corresponding to the individual *cantiche* in

Dante's *Commedia*. This, I take it, is the purpose of Zanzotto's comment in his letter cited earlier ("il riferimento dantesco esiste ma il mio è un 'campo rotante' . . .") and also the point of his notes on the trilogy form quoted above ("momenti non cronologici di uno stesso lavoro"). I would add to these statements only that their sincerity seems to be borne out by a reading of the pseudo-trilogy from a Dantean perspective. In other words, the reader who progresses through the individual volumes in the order in which they were published, *Il Galateo in Bosco, Fosfeni, Idioma,* will happen upon radically resemanticized Dantean quotations and will also enter into and pass out of intermittent, re-occurring, Dantean "thematic zones". These thematic zones include a highly original treatment of such Dantean themes as the descent to the underworld, the desire for purgation, the journey toward the logos, and meditations on Paradise.

The Descent to the Underworld in *Idioma*

Because the individual volumes constitute, in Zanzotto's words, "momenti non cronologici di uno stesso lavoro che rinviano l'uno all'altro a partire da qualunque di essi", we might consider ourselves authorized to enter the pseudo-trilogy from any vantage point we might choose. Since Dante's journey begins with a descent to the underworld, let us commence our examination with an analysis of Zanzotto's treatment of this theme. One of the clearest treatments occurs in the final volume, *Idioma.* In the poem **"da Dittico e fistole"**, the allusion to a guide and the plea for guidance recall the relationship between Dante and Beatrice. Instead of calling her by name, Zanzotto implores "la Diversa", ("the Other"; *Idioma* 29):

> Sì eri la Diversa nel più sfacciato e arduo senso . . .
>   Ma guidami ancora—e ti perdonerò
>   le tue noncolpe—oltre i meandri di Rio Bo.
>   Guidami come mascherina di un cinema
>   infero,
>   là dove s'impara nell'ultimo flash di ne-
>   crosi
>   dove nidifichi il mai scattato fotogramma
>   oggi-sposi.
>   Su quelle rive intasate di radici e schemi di
>   ogni suicidio
>   tra latta e plastica, ad un nero che è stinto
>   per troppa forza, monco per eccesso di zelo,
>   guidami: su al punto bianco-pus che ben
>   sai tu,
>   là dove sta scritto che ogni OPUS è zero
>   più pus.

Addressed to Beatrice in the guise of "la Diversa", the plea for guidance is repeated three times. In the space of a few lines, Zanzotto suggests Beatrice's allure and eternal unavailability. The blinding light which accompanies her, "nell'ultimo flash di necrosi", is an apt depiction of her visual radiance in contemporary terms.

So too, the line, "dove nidifichi il mai scattato foto-gramma oggi-sposi", continues the emphasis on visual technology while introducing a veiled reference to sexual attraction through the phrase, "oggi-sposi". The fact that the "fotogramma oggi-sposi" remains in the realm of fantasy ("mai scattato") suits Beatrice's nature as an inviting but unreachable woman/symbol.

While the gender of the noun "la Diversa", the "masche-rina" image, and the "oggi-sposi" phrase suggest a famous female guide, the Latin words "OPUS" and "in-fero" may remind us that before Dante's descent to Hell a similar journey had been described by Beatrice's Dantean counterpart, Virgil.[8] Seen from this perspective, Zanzotto's descent to the underworld through the infernal cinema constitutes a contemporary approach to a traditional literary *topos*.[9] In fact, the fertile ambiguity that accompanies Zanzotto's rewriting of the *descensus ad inferos* would seem to be characteristic of twentieth-century Dantean "imitation" in general. Making a persuasive case for the uncertainty surrounding many contemporary adaptations of Dante, Barański ("Power of Influence" 351-354) argues that

> borrowings present themselves as "infernal" or they evoke an episode or a character in general terms rather than particular aspects of these, so that they necessarily provoke different specific memories in different read-ers, but at the same time can elicit commonly-held general ones. In fact, it is at times difficult to establish the precise provenance of some of these debts, because they have become so vague, contaminated, and cor-rupted. . . . What is significant are the possible textual effects caused by a recognition of these Dantesque echoes, and not speculations on their origins in each writer. The ambiguity which can surround a *dantismo* is an important feature of Dante's fortune in the twentieth century.

Building on the rich ambiguity of the Dantean situation, Zanzotto's Latin words illustrate his attempt to cast a wide net to evoke not only Dante and Beatrice but also Virgil and the classical poets who visited Avernus.

In the lines cited above from *Idioma,* Zanzotto's "Inferno-Avernus" relays images of a dark place where hope has been lost. The "roots and plans" of suicides choke these desperate banks littered with tin and plastic. Appealing to be guided as if by an usher through an infernal cinema, Zanzotto reactivates specifically marked Dantean elements in comparing a movie theatre to the underworld as we read in the second section of the poem (*Idioma* 30; emphasis added):

> Prego, sopporta questo che non è insulto ma ancora
>   forse sussulto
> di fronte a un sillogismo violato. E tu nel favolistico
> cinema dove m'infilai per uno sgorbio quasi mistico
> dà ancora *acqua e schiuma* all'incendiata pellicola;
> nel gran *fumo che attossica,* nel nebbione
>   infero . . .

Zanzotto uses "infero" twice in this poem: once in as-sociation with the cinema and once in association with a thick fog. In these lines, in addition to the hellish "nebbione", we also note the presence of such infernal Dantean elements as "acqua e schiuma" and "fumo che attossica". Smoke and fog are everpresent in Dante's *Inferno*; Zanzotto's adaptation contributes to the Dantean qualitites of his pseudo-trilogy. Remember the juxtapostion of smoke, water, and foam in *Inferno* XXIV: "qual *fummo* in aere e in *acqua* la *schiuma*" (50). The verb "attossica" also has an infernal ring to it and its use by Zanzotto is particularly efficacious: a similar form occurs only once in the *Inferno* (at VI. 84): "se 'l ciel li addolcia o lo 'nferno li *attosca*".

Zanzotto's infernal cinema cannot help but trigger as-sociations of a Dantean descent to the underworld.[10] These associations are further reinforced by specific Dantean words and phrases. At the same time, the poem also brings to mind two other famous "infernal cinemas" from contemporary Italian culture: Pasolini's *La divina mimesis* and Fellini's *La città delle donne.* As is well known, Pasolini's "rewriting" of the first four cantos of Dante opens with the poet-protagonist lost in the "'selva' della realtà del 1963" when he finds himself "davanti al cinema Splendid . . . o Splendore o Smer-aldo?" and glimpses "una luce felice e cattiva: tra i due portali del cinema" (*La divina mimesis* 5-6). Numerous critics have written on the Dantean qualities of Fellini's films.[11] Gian Piero Brunetta, for example, has referred to Fellini's *oeuvre* as the filmmaker's "Divina Comme-dia cinematografica" (78). Zanzotto himself has written on the Dantean allusions in *La città delle donne.* His description takes on greater significance in light of his own poetic treatment of this theme: "Tutto il film sem-brerebbe . . . la fase finale di uno stralunato 'descensus ad Superos' oppure 'ascensus ad Inferos'. . . . I richi-ami danteschi . . . diventano inevitabili e senza enfasi, ma per essere, appunto, buttati via. E ce ne sono qui ad ogni crocicchio, interferenza, occasione" ("Ipotesi" 21-22). Zanzotto's unexpected reversal of the "destina-tions" parallels his own equally "stralunato" descent-ascent in the pseudo-trilogy. Like *La divina mimesis* and *La città delle donne,* Zanzotto's own "cinema inf-ero" from *Idioma* resurrects the same inevitable Dantean qualities associated with any descent to the underworld. However, because it happens in a movie theatre, Zanzotto's descent has a feeling of immediacy and veracity.[12]

Let us now turn to the first volume in the pseudo-trilogy, *Il Galateo in Bosco,* and survey Zanzotto's infernal references. His **"Sonetto del Linneo e Dioscoride"**, as the title suggests, contains a specific borrowing that frames the text within a Dantean system of reference. Dioscorides, as Zanzotto reminds the reader in a note, is "il buono accoglitor del quale" (*Galateo* 115). He serves the poet as a Dantean character who, by virtue of a treatise he wrote, is associated with the study of plants, "recensore di tutte le qualità, a tutti i livelli, delle piante" (*Galateo* 115). Hence he is paired with "Linnaeus", Carl von Linné, the great Swedish botanist of the eighteenth century. Zanzotto writes: "di Linneo l'occhio invidio e Dïoscoride / tanto fecondo è il far vostro, e il costume / molteplice e l'aspetto . . ." (*Galateo* 68). Momentarily bewildered by the foliage and the thick underbrush of his textual forest, Zanzotto envies the clear and well-ordered vision of the two great botanists, Dioscorides and Linnaeus, who function primarily as references to scientific attempts to describe nature.[13] On one level, *Il Galateo in Bosco* poeticizes the biological codes that govern all life forms. Lexical items from botany, agriculture, zoology, geology, and human anatomy underline the interdependence of all animate and inanimate things. Dioscorides serves Zanzotto's purpose in that his name is associated with the classification of plants. A secondary but no less important feature of Dioscorides, however, is that he constitutes one ring in a long chain of Dantean associations. By incorporating Dioscorides into his text, therefore, Zanzotto not only celebrates his contribution to science but also evokes Dante as a repository of knowledge, a constant point of reference.

Zanzotto's own statements on the importance of literary *communio*, on the give and take between poets, and on the circulation / exchange of common poetic experiences lead us to weigh all of his literary echoes, however faint their reverberations might register on a first reading. Having noted Zanzotto's coupling of Linnaeus with an explicitly Dantean Dioscoride in his **"Sonetto del Linneo e Dioscoride"**, we may recall Pound's interest in the great botanist: "to walk with Mozart, Agassiz and *Linnaeus* / 'neath overhanging air under sun-beat" (*Canto* CXIII. 9-10); "Night under wind mid garofani, / the petals are almost still / Mozart, *Linnaeus*, Sulmona, / When one's friends hate each other / how can there be peace in the world?" (*Canto* CXV); "And I have learned more from Jules / (Jules Laforgue) since then / deeps in him, / and *Linnaeus*" (*Canto* CXVI). Zanzotto's allusion to Linnaeus in conjunction with Dioscorides brings the American poet to mind within a Dantean frame of reference. In this way, **"Sonetto del Linneo e Dioscoride"** resembles the infernal cinema poem from *Idioma*. In both instances, the Dantean connotations are enriched by the presence of other poets who have had a similarly deep rapport with Dante.

INFERNO XIII IN *IL GALATEO IN BOSCO*

Zanzotto's "rewritings" of *Inferno* illustrate the wide-ranging inclusiveness of his method of citation; the carefully organized pattern of the "infernal" borrowings sheds light on the "campo rotante" as a structural principle. Both aspects of Zanzotto's technique can be better understood when we consider the relationship between the "infernal cinema" poem from *Idioma,* **"da Dittico e fistole"**, and three of the poems from the first volume in the pseudo-trilogy that contain allusions to *Inferno* XIII. For example, the reference in **"da Dittico e fistole"** to "rive intasate di radici e schemi di ogni suicidio" forges a link with Pier della Vigna and the wood of the suicides. This link, while it is implied in *Idioma,* is explicit in *Il Galateo in Bosco.* In the poem **"Questioni di etichetta e anche cavalleresche"**, we note a specific reference to the wood of the suicides and the harpies (my italics; *Galateo* 82-83):

> comunque, pettegolezzi e trepestii tanti di piante
> da *selva dei suicidi* o
> *delle arpie* o della battaglia massaia beccaia
> Pace dunque al qualunque baco parassita
> che si credette *fabbro* di seta garantita . . .

The reference to the silk worm as "fabbro" may trigger memories of the Dantean undercurrent in Eliot's famous dedication. Recalling the passage from *Purgatorio* XXVI and Guinizzelli's praise of Arnaut as the "miglior fabbro del parlar materno", Eliot was not only honoring Pound as the "better craftsman" but was also alluding to Dante's own technique of citation, imitation, and rewriting.[14] Given the profound shift in direction that Pound and Eliot gave to Dante's reception in the twentieth century,[15] as well as the considerable but still relatively undervalued influence of their own poetry and criticism on postwar Italian poets,[16] we should not be surprised to find this minimal but typically Zanzottean reference to the two greatest modern imitators of Dante.[17] Thus, by weaving "fabbro" into the context of the "selva dei suicidi o / delle arpie", Zanzotto demonstrates his interest in poetry as *communio*. Rather than staging a contest between "fathers" and "sons", Zanzotto offers us the example of the silk worm, a parasite who turns his food into a silken cocoon: like the silk worm, and not unlike Dante, Pound, and Eliot, Zanzotto spins diverse fragments of the literary tradition into a seamless poetic garment.

The wood of the suicides appears for the third time in **"Sonetto di sterpi e limiti"**, also from *Il Galateo in Bosco,* as Pier della Vigna's plight sets the stage for a significant "incontro-scontro" involving Dante, Montale, and Zanzotto. With tongue firmly in cheek, Zanzotto conjures forth allusions to Dante's wood of the suicides, where the bodies of those who took their own lives have been turned to bushes or trees. Before examining Zanzotto's reworking of this scene, however, let us review the original Dantean passage in which Pier della Vigna blurts out his indignation as Dante-pilgrim breaks a bough (my italics; *Inferno* XIII. 35-39):

> ricominciò a dir: "Perché mi *scerpi*?
> non hai tu spirto di pietade alcuno?

Uomini fummo, e or siam fatti *sterpi*:
ben dovrebb' essser la tua man più pia,
se state fossimo anime di *serpi*".

Now let us examine the Zanzottean text with its playful adaptation of some eminently Dantean (and Montalean) signifiers (emphasis added, *Galateo* 67):

Sguiscio gentil che fra mezzo erbe *serpi*,
difficil *guizzo* che un enigma orienta,
che nulla enigma orienta, e pur spaventa
il cor che in *serpi* vede mutar *sterpi*;
nausea, che da una debil quiete *scerpi*
me nel vacuo onde ogni erba qui s'imprenta,
però che in vie e vie di *serpi* annienta
luci ed arbusti, in sfrigolio di *serpi* . . .

Giorgio Orelli (62) has noted that the phrase "Sguiscio gentil" in the incipit of this sonnet recalls the Dantean "spirito gentil". In the changing emphasis from "spirito" to "sguiscio" we glimpse a key to Zanzotto's method. He decontextualizes a famous Dantean reference, empties it of its previous meaning, and puts it to his own ironic use. What Gino Rizzo has observed with regard to *La Beltà* is also true for the pseudo-trilogy: "Zanzotto resemanticizes Dante drastically: i.e. in a way not dissimilar from Dante's own resemanticization of Virgil. Even when he recalls Dante, say, at the phonematic level, the semantic context is such as to oppose assimilation" (320).

The poet has obviously structured this sonnet around the famous Dantean rhyme words *scerpi: sterpi: serpi*. By recombining these elements in a radically different context, Zanzotto forces heavily charged signifiers to assume new signifieds. Here, as elsewhere, the poet's borrowing of Dantean references seems to be filtered through another poet. Rather than recalling Virgil's descent to the underworld, Pasolini's *La divina mimesis*, Fellini's "stralunato descensus ad Superos", or Pound and Eliot, this time the connotations suggest Montale. As a number of critics have pointed out, albeit with different conclusions,[18] Montale used the rhyme *sterpi: serpi* in the opening quattrain of "Merriggiare pallido e assorto": "ascoltare tra i pruni e gli *sterpi* / schiocchi di merli, frusci di *serpi* . . ." (*L'opera in versi* 28). Montale uses "sterpi" and "serpi" in a straightforward manner that, while activating the memory of Dante, does not distract the reader from the poet's more immediate aims, i.e. to convey the spiritual torpor and *ennui* of an existential situation. Zanzotto, however, is more emphatic in calling attention to the Dantean signifiers and repeats "serpi" four times.

In light of the poet's concept of poetic *communio*, it is not insignificant that while evoking Dante's wood of the suicides Zanzotto also stirs memories of Montale. The association is further strengthened through the word "guizzo" which occurs eight times in Montale. On one level, the Dantean-Montalean echoes cause a comic effect resulting from the mixture of a high style with a "low" subject matter: whereas Dante's "spirito gentil" refers to the noble qualities required by the medieval lover, Zanzotto's "sguiscio gentil" refers to the wriggling action of the snakes. Seen from this perspective, **"Sonetto di sterpi e limiti"** constitutes a technical *tour de force* and also indicates the poet's sense of humor, a sense of humor that caused Pasolini to compare Zanzotto with Joyce and Gadda.[19]

It is interesting to note that Zanzotto also calls attention to *Inferno* XIII by evoking Torquato Tasso's imitation of this very same canto: "Ora è stato tastato tutto il bassorilievo il manufatto / di quella cubità estrapolata dalla / Selva Incantata Gerusalemme Liberata, XIII" (*Galateo* 30). In the next poem, Zanzotto repeats the reference to Tasso: "questo simulacro da Selva Incantata / della Gerusalemme Liberata" (*Galateo* 31). Now, canto XIII of the *Gerusalemme* represents Tasso's "rewriting" of *Inferno* XIII: Dante's "selva dei suicidi" provides a model to be transformed into Tasso's "selva incantata". Zanzotto underscores once again his notion of poetic *communio*. The Tasso imitation provides Zanzotto with another example of the intertextual relations typical of the Western poetic tradition. From the classical poets through Dante and Petrarch to Ariosto and Tasso, from the epic to the lyric, from T. S. Eliot to Andrea Zanzotto, whether "selva oscura", "selva incantata", "sacred wood", or "galateo in bosco", the forest has remained a privileged literary locus.[20] The wood of the suicides, therefore, functions in Zanzotto's text as a Dantean reminder of the numerous forests that have sprung from the literary imagination.

As these references to Dante's "selva dei suicidi" would suggest, Zanzotto's "bosco" is built upon layers of literary sedimentation. In fact, Zanzotto has described *Il Galateo in Bosco* as consisting of "quotations of quotations": "Il libro è tutto giocato su citazioni di citazioni, che si richiamano di componimento in componimento specie nei sonetti. Si tratta dunque di 'sentieri nel bosco' non solo in riferimento ad un bosco reale (il Montello), non solo simbolici, ma anche letterari" (cited by Nuvoli, 13-14). Zanzotto's comments here situate the Dantean allusions of *Il Galateo in Bosco* within an overall strategy of literary borrowing. Dramatizing the critical commonplace that poetry most often speaks of itself while pretending to speak of other things, Zanzotto frames his discourse within a literary context. This is particularly true, as he states above, with respect to "Ipersonetto", the sonnet series at the center of *Il Galateo in Bosco*. The Dantean echoes, then, on one level, contribute to the text's literary and cultural density and help to produce a keenly felt, self-reflexive literariness, a literariness which has become one of Zanzotto's trademarks.

And yet, it is precisely this quality of "literariness" which seems to have lulled critics into overlooking other issues at stake in Zanzotto's poetics of borrowing. By following the references to Dante's *Canto* XIII, for example, we discover that these allusions are not merely "hyperliterary" but that they reveal a structural principle involving the organization of the pseudo-trilogy: they link four different poems from two volumes in a "campo rotante" of Dantean references. Moreover, these texts also dramatize Zanzotto's concept of poetic *communio*: they point to a shared tradition of borrowing that connects Dante, Tasso, Montale, and Zanzotto. Granted, Dante is only one of many sources from which Zanzotto draws in *Il Galateo in Bosco*. However, as we shall see, Dante remains the dominant and most frequently cited figure in the pseudo-trilogy as a whole. Dante's re-occurring presence influences the direction, shape, and final significance of the entire project.[21] Zanzotto's carefully orchestrated "re-writing" of Dante provides a unifying element that links the individual microtexts and draws together the three volumes into a unitary albeit discontinuous poetic whole. For this reason, only when we have perceived the general contours of the entire work, and have weighed the cumulative effects of Dante's presence within it, can we reach a greater appreciation of Zanzotto's pseudo-trilogy as an extended reading of Dante's *Commedia*.

THE JOURNEY TO THE LOGOS IN *FOSFENI*

Dante's second canticle enters into Zanzotto's scheme chiefly through the theme of purgation and a purgatorial-like journey up a mountainside, elements which are developed extensively in *Fosfeni*. While *Il Galateo in Bosco* uncovers the rich humus of the Montello forest, and excavates the local remains from various epochs (pre-historic, the Renaissance, the First World War), the second book in the pseudo-trilogy, *Fosfeni,* focuses on the mountainous landscape to the north of the poet's place of birth. The craggy peaks of the Dolomites with their ice, fogs, and reflected light provide the background for a Dantean ascent toward the logos. Let us begin with a consideration of the purgatorial aspects of that ascent.

The theme of purgation is introduced in the volume's opening poem, **"Come ultime cene"**. Here in the darkness of a late winter or early spring night, "Sete notturna di marzo" (*Fosfeni* 11), the fields seem reduced to a complete stasis. In this state of brute materiality, "ogni volontà di levitazione" has been stripped, shaved down to the nub. From this zero point, the poet looks closely into the darkness and ascertains a desire for purification: "strade cui ogni più minima cosa accorse a morire / per esssere più casta più *degna* un istante / per essere un faro / o un luccichio di niente-vetro". The purgation theme begins here, on these "roads". Even the brute forces of nature contain an impulse to move toward the light, to become light, "per essere un faro".

In introducing the theme of purgation, Zanzotto brings to mind the overture of *Purgatorio,* where Dante sets forth the dynamics of purification that propel souls to climb the mount of Purgatory, the "secondo regno / dove l'umano spirito si purga / e di salire al ciel diventa *degno*" (I. 4-6). Dante treats the human soul which purifies itself to become worthy of the ascent up the mountain of Purgatory; Zanzotto personifies the brute elements of nature, "ogni più minima cosa". Once again, Zanzotto's adaptation of a Dantean element is filtered through his own sensibility. Zanzotto poeticizes material forces, personifies them, and at times will endow them with mythic and religious symbolism. The title of this composition, **"Come ultime cene"**, with its recollection of the Last Supper, indicates the poet's gravitation toward religious imagery as does the volume of poetry that Zanzotto published before the pseudo-trilogy, *Pasque* (1973).[22]

However, although Zanzotto makes use of religious elements associated with Dante, he distances himself from organized religion in general and from Christianity in particular. As Ardizzone points out with reference to *Fosfeni,* "Il cammino è verso il *logos* e il *logos* viene rivelato come *eros*" (11). The phenomenological rather than theological nature of Zanzotto's journey becomes more clear as we examine the following passage from "Silicio, carbonio, castellieri". Here Zanzotto focuses on the communicative properties or the "logos" to be found in silicon chips and in carbon.[23] These lines also include a specific reference to Christianity (*Fosfeni* 15-17):

> pareva giusto coltivare
> logos in carbonio logos in silicio . . .
> Ma di là dove tutto è rauco d'ombre e sfondamenti
> chiama il désir piraña, la charitas
> sempre in rogo, la concupiscenza
>   di cieli dei cieli—la peggiore—
>   chiama la gran religione di amore . . .
> Ma con queste falcate collinari andrò
>   fino ai primi rapporti con ghiacci senza fine
> con vertigini infidamente divinatrici
> predicando ogni non-religione
> ogni conversione oppure conversazione,
> non predicando, non predicando, cadendo ne andrò.

"Preaching every non-religion", Zanzotto-pilgrim will follow the curves of the hills towards the mountains with their "ghiacci senza fine". Gazing toward the north and the snow-capped Dolomites, Zanzotto fantasizes a Dantean journey, an ascent-descent, "cadendo ne andrò". Zanzotto's "descensus ad Superos" is definitely a journey with a twist, since he borrows imagery and symbols from Dante and Christianity while putting them towards a different, purely poetic purpose. As is to be expected in the waning decades of the twentieth century, "la gran religione di amore", celebrated by Dante in the *Comedy,* does not command the same allegiance from Zanzotto whose pseudo-trilogy, as well as *La Beltà,*

Pasque, and much of his earlier work, contains reversals or curiously ambiguous negations of familiar Christian situations and beliefs.[24]

Now let us simply take note of a few lines in *Fosfeni* that carry Purgatorial connotations: "dove fu giusto e senza sottintesi il soffrire" (45); "io tetra vestale / di questo fuoco malocchio / e carro trionfale" (47); "dove più digiuna è la montagna" (62), and "non pentirsi . . . troppo" (74). While these lines out of context convey only a hint of their possible referentiality to Dante, I would argue that they have a cumulative effect that magnifies their individual weight. In still other texts a specific Dantean intertextuality buttresses a situation that can be considered Purgatorial in a general way. The poem **"Da Ghène"**, for example, begins with a vague purgatorial echo, and then develops closer associations with that canticle. The opening line, "Impossibile *accedere* alla dolce ruina", may bring to mind the Dantean line "Come degnasti d'*accedere* al monte?" (XXX. 74). The poem goes on to introduce other purgatorial themes of transcendence, imperfection, forgiveness, purification, and restoration (*Fosfeni* 43-44):

> Impossibile accedere alla dolce ruina
> dell'osteria immota sull'angolo
> delle due vie . . .
> Nessuna temporalità nei
> muri . . .
> Intravedonsi pannelli e pareti sfondate
> reggonsi travi e coppi a far tetto
>   così che l'imperfetto
>   del tutto vi si sposta . . .
>   lievissima sipariette o porta inferi
>   o porta di limbo-vignetta . . .
>   sintesi d'ogni colorazione
>   d'ogni perdonazione, d'ogni ristoro . . .
>   ma non v'è mistero che duri
>   che in calcine e malte sfritte non si purifichi
>   per occhi appena divaganti
>   o buttati giù col ruscello . . .

Here the references to a "porta inferi" or a "porta di limbo-vignetta" send out signals generally Dantean in nature. By now the shift of focus from the human spirit in Dante to material elements in Zanzotto should not surprise us. Zanzotto finds profound but barely perceptible changes taking place in the walls of an *osteria* and personifies the material elements involved. Here, as in other poems, "qualcosa si altera stupendamente" (*Fosfeni* 65) as material elements such as lime and mortar participate in a process of purification.

The theme of vision, developed extensively throughout *Fosfeni,* is touched on in the passage above in a very Dantean way. In fact, it is precisely this theme that has lead Giorgio Luzzi to comment on one of the qualities of *Fosfeni* that makes it similar to the *Purgatorio.* Luzzi has related Zanzotto's three local "saints" or female deities in *Fosfeni,* Eurosia, Lùcia, and Barbara,[25] to the female presences in Dante's *Purgatorio.* Luzzi makes this connection by virtue of the theme of vision (90):

> Una serie di epifanie soteriche femminili pervade questo secondo tempo della "trilogia", connettendosi per un verso al livello complesso della visione-vista . . . ma permettendo per altre vie di supporre anche una sorta di relazione con le grandi apparizioni femminili nel *Purgatorio* dantesco (Lucia, Lia, Rachele, Matelda e, naturalmente, Beatrice).

THE PARADISE EFFECT OF *FOSFENI*

Le Paradis n'est pas artificiel / but is jagged

Ezra Pound, *Canto XCII*

Fosfeni contains various elements reminiscent of *Paradiso.* As Romano Luperini has noted ("Gel" 7):

> Il titolo del libro suggerisce la centralità di un altro campo semantico—quello della luce—strettamente legato a quello visivo. Di nuovo siamo introdotti in un sistema luminoso di segni (di luminarie, di stelle, di barbagli), attraverso il quale si esprime—come nel *Paradiso* dantesco o nelle *Occasioni* di Montale—la forza del logos, la ricerca di un senso.

Linking *Fosfeni* with Dante's final canticle, Zanzotto's emphases can be seen in the following minimal catalogue. On light and stars: "magistero stellare / Stellarità delle cose" (42); "ogni fucina . . . è come / la sua orrida parente, la stella" (48); "io camaleontizzato, trasecolato / in lumini di mutanti alfabeti" (49); "della stella che si degnò di noi nella sera . . ." (72); "la / più terribile stellarità" (75); a Paradise-like transcendence of limits: "e mi apriste in incalcolabili avanti" (20); "preparo il terreno a liquidi cristalli / vibrantissimi, trascoloranti, trasecolanti / verso tutte le tinte e i limiti" (46); utterances regarding ineffability: "Esso crepa di memoria e di stupore / e in memoria e stupore si ritira e ricuce" (71); and specific borrowings[26] from the *Paradiso*: "menti emerse per meriti speciali / a battesimi, in crani Traiani" (49). Other elements in *Fosfeni* which convey a sense of Dante's *Paradiso* include a reappearing mysterious (if not quite mystic) rose: "Come una candida gelata evapora / galaverna stigia / eppure rosa futuribile di spilla in spilla" (57). This passage demonstrates Zanzotto's method of resemanticizing Dantean phrases and also provides a close-up view of the dynamics of the "campo rotante".

The individual Dantean components of Hell, Purgatory, and Paradise are not circumscribed within individual poems or volumes. Rather, they have been scattered throughout the entire work and are nevertheless closely interrelated. The infernal river Styx, or, more precisely, a "Stygian hoar frost", is intimately connected to a "rosa futuribile". This rose is the Zanzottean substitute for the "candida rosa" from *Paradiso* XXXI: the adjective "candida" used by Zanzotto in conjunction with the noun "galaverna" associates the infernal waters with the rose of paradise.

Conclusion

Just as the "galaverna stigia" and the "rosa futuribile" in *Fosfeni* form a poetic connection between Hell and Paradise so too the pseudo-trilogy contains the complete trajectory of the Dantean journey. Although in his letter cited earlier Zanzotto downplays the Dantean model ("il riferimento dantesco esiste ma . . ."), traces of all three *cantiche* can be found in the pseudo-trilogy. While our thesis regarding Dante's central role in Zanzotto's poetics of *communio* has led us to focus on Dantean allusions in his recent poetic masterpiece, a similar analysis of the poet's critical writings[27] would reveal an equally intense "confrontation with Dante's universe", to adopt Rizzo's phrase cited earlier. To be sure, Zanzotto's critical insights into other poets are frequently framed with reference to Dante.[28] This is particularly true of Zanzotto's writings on Montale.[29] Discussing Montale's later poetry and the absence of a "paradise" in his work, Zanzotto comments on the significance of this poetic "non-place" ("La freccia" 50-51):

> Si sa che, forse, il fine ultimo della poesia è il paradiso, e che un'esperienza paradisiaca, "il paradisiaco", è il miraggio più o meno confessato di ogni poeta, miraggio dalle più diverse coloriture, ma terribilmente *uno* nel suo carattere. Pochi toccarono questo non-luogo dell'esperienza, anche se ogni testo, perfino il più "infernale" ha un qualche rapporto con questo non-luogo. Dante, o Ariosto, ebbero e diedero paradisi. . . . Si ostinò Pound in questa ricerca, per arrivare, dal baratro del suo silenzio del tardo periodo, alle conclusioni allucinate ma delusive del testamentario canto CXX, credo il suo ultimo (I have tried to write Paradise—Do not move—let the wind speak—that's [sic] paradise). E concludeva dicendo tra l'altro "Let the Gods forgive—what I have made". . . . Ebbene, Montale è sull'opposto versante. Sa di non poter scrivere alcun paradiso, sa di averlo talvolta sfiorato, sa comunque di non esservi mai stato.

According to Zanzotto, Montale, due to his artistic temperament and no doubt to historical circumstances as well, is not among those who "tried to write Paradise". On the other hand, Dante, Ariosto, and Pound (to a lesser degree), form part of a "community" of poets who, in Zanzotto's terms, "ebbero e diedero paradisi".

"Il fine ultimo della poesia è il paradiso". Even if it remains a deeply cherished illusion, "anca si paradisi no ghe n'é" (*Idioma* 52), this re-occurring "mirage" shapes our experience of poetry so much so that, "ogni testo perfino il più 'infernale' ha un qualche rapporto con questo non-luogo". These remarks were occasioned by Zanzotto's interpretation of Montale framed in Dantean terms, but they also pertain to the textual dynamics of the "campo rotante". In the pseudo-trilogy, Zanzotto's "Inferno", "Purgatorio", and "Paradiso" are all "non-places". They have been constructed, rather, as poetic locations or textual sites whose individual significance emerges only in relation to the other absent sites.

The same thing could be said for the individual volumes in Zanzotto's pseudo-trilogy. The extreme abstraction, brilliant light, and visual effulgence of the logos in *Fosfeni* is counterposed by the blood-soaked humus and the powerfully negative *tenebrae* of *Il Galateo in Bosco*. In a similar fashion, if the logos of *Fosfeni* exists in a state of dynamic tension with the non-logos of *Il Galateo in Bosco*, *Idioma* constitutes the middle ground, hinge, or center of the "OPUS". *Il Galateo in Bosco* portrays the Montello forest to Zanzotto's south; *Fosfeni* depicts the mountains to Zanzotto's north; *Idioma* celebrates the poet's native town, Pieve di Soligo, and its inhabitants.[30] The third book completes the "trilogy" not by explaining what may be unclear in the preceding volumes, but by its further development of common themes and by its repetition of familiar patterns.[31] By virtue of its division into three sections, for example, *Idioma* mirrors the "trilogy" structure of the work as a whole. Moreover, the sense of community implied in the other volumes in part by way of literary references, i.e. through a wide-ranging poetic *communio* anchored in Dantean imitation, becomes tangible and familiar in *Idioma* as the poet explores the ordinary, daily affairs of the actual community in which he lives. Thus, in providing a sense of closure, *Idioma* brings Zanzotto's experimental discourse to pause momentarily within a familiar, quotidian realm that nevertheless opens onto the eternal.[32]

Notes

1. Zanzotto describes his relationship to the tradition as follows: "I must say that I have undergone, or rather enjoyed, the influence mostly of the fathers of our Italian poetry: Petrarch on the one hand, Dante on the other. This is a constant which I find unavoidable. Authors who haven't been close, who haven't referred either to Dante or to Petrarch are rare. It's somewhat more difficult to put Dante and Petrarch together, though" (cited by Allen, "Interview" 253). See also Camon; Massini; Sillanpoa; and Zanzotto "Intervento".

2. In addition to Zanzotto's own articles on Petrarch, "Petrarca fra il palazzo e la cameretta", and "Una stanza piena di libri", see also Falchetta, Hainsworth, Conti Bertini (97-100), Paltrinieri "Atti", and chapter four in Welle *The Poetry*. For an illuminating study of Zanzotto's interest in Leopardi, see Pezzin.

3. Written in 1975 and therefore prior to the publication of the pseudo-trilogy, Rizzo's illuminating discussion of Zanzotto's relationship to Dante remains the most in-depth treatment of the subject

to date. Bàrberi Squarotti comments ("L'ultimo trentennio") on Zanzotto's Dantean borrowings in *IX Ecloghe, La Beltà,* and *Pasque* (cf. especially 259-63). For an interesting analysis of some of the Dantean echoes in Zanzotto's "Ipersonetto", see Viola. See also Conti Bertini, and Scorrano.

4. Interestingly enough, in the interview with Allen cited above, after characterizing his own bipolar relationship with Petrarch and Dante, Zanzotto goes on to discuss Dante's importance for twentieth-century literature in general and for Montale in particular: "Dante . . . has been at the heart of twentieth-century Italian culture. He has influenced a great many authors. One need only think of Montale himself, although he also had a close rapport with Petrarch. (Let's not forget that even Montale finds himself in this bipolarity.) Dante influenced important writers of the Anglo-Saxon world, from Joyce to Pound to Eliot, and is a necessary reference especially now, when Italy is tossed about in a linguistic storm, because he is a truly total creator. He creates his language phoneme by phoneme; he continuously poses the problem of language with every word he abandons on paper" (255). The bibliography of criticism on Montale's relationship to Dante, while too extensive to detail here, can be found in studies by Barański ("Dante and Montale"), Luperini, Barile, and Pipa. For a discussion of Montale's "Petrarchism", hinted at by Zanzotto in the comments above, see O'Neill.

5. In describing his position in contemporary Italian literature, Zanzotto comments on the notion of the "memory deposit": "I have searched for an almost impossible linkage between tradition and the avant-garde, between the memory deposit constituted by our literary past—which, as is well known, is enormous—and attempts at experimentation" (cited in Allen, "Interview" 253). On Dante's presence in the Italian collective memory, see Contini.

6. In reference to *Il Galateo in Bosco,* Zanzotto states: "La raccolta apre quella che impropriamente si potrebbe dire una trilogia" (*Galateo* 111); so too with regard to *Fosfeni* Zanzotto qualifies the trilogy structure with these remarks: "La presente raccolta rappresenterebbe dunque la seconda parte di una assai improbabile trilogia" (*Fosfeni* 79).

7. See Agosti, Paltrinieri ("L'affabilità"), Tassoni ("Discorso"), and Viola.

8. Similar to his longstanding interest in Dante and Petrarch, Zanzotto has had a deep rapport with Virgil. This relationship finds expression in Zanzotto's book of Virgilian imitations, *IX Ecloghe.*

For an analysis of Virgil's presence in this book, see Allen's *Andrea Zanzotto.* Moreover, *Idioma* contains an explicit reference to Virgil's fourth eclogue in the poem "San Gal sora la son": "ciascuno come / dentro la sua propria Egloga Quarta" (20). For some interesting remarks by Zanzotto on Virgil and on the Latin poet's poetics of imitation, see "Zanzotto: un'Arcadia".

9. Within this context, Ezra Pound's comments come to mind regarding the *descensus ad inferos*: "For such as are interested in the question of sources, it may be well to write, once and for all, that there is nothing particularly new in describing the journey of a living man through Hell, or even of his translation into Paradise. . . . The description of such journeys may be regarded as a confirmed literary habit of the race" (*Spirit of Romance* 16). For a treatment of this theme in modern Italian poetry up to and including Montale, see Bàrberi Squarotti (*Gli inferi*).

10. Once again Barański's general characterization of twentieth-century Italian *dantismo* sheds light on the issue at hand: Dante "is actively engaged in influencing and shaping a writer's expressive possibilities, because situations, phrases, even single words have become, regardless of anything else they might mean, references to Dante. . . . The going on a journey, certain acts of barbarity, particular landscapes, characters, encounters, etc., words such as *inferno, purgatorio,* even *limbo,* all tend to evoke irresistibly the presence of Dante whatever an author's more specific intentions might be" ("Power" 348-349).

11. See Barański ("Power" 48), Lewalski, and my own "Fellini's Use".

12. Like *Gli sguardi i fatti e senhal* (a long poem on the television coverage of the American moonlanding) and *Filò,* a major dialect poem inspired by Zanzotto's collaboration with Fellini on *Casanova* (1976), the pseudo-trilogy contains a number of interesting poems on television and cinema. For example, the "cinema infero" finds an interesting parallel in the expression "perfetto aldilà / in elisie Tivù" (*Idioma* 31). Zanzotto has commented on this aspect of his work: "Il riferimento alla fotografia ed al cinema rientra spesso nelle mie poesie, perchè appartiene alla nostra esperienza quotidiana; tutti gli apparecchietti della civiltà tecnologica hanno ormai condizionato la nostra quotidianità, ma possono anche fornirci delle chiavi di espressione più complete" (cited in Massini 104). For a discussion of this element see my "Zanzotto: il poeta del cosmorama".

13. Zanzotto mentions Dioscorides in commenting on the garden-like or forest-like qualities of Petrarch's *Canzoniere*: "Basterà solo accennare alle metafore

che la struttura stessa del *Canzoniere* può sugger-ire in modo fin troppo facile: appunto un giardino curato fisicamente in ogni splendida minuzia, una selva (selvetta o infinità) in cui ogni pianta pare confondersi nelle altre, elemento sostituibile, men-tre vista da vicino rivela le sue caratteristiche di 'essenza' e individuo nell'essenza, di venatura, di freschezza, di 'qualità' dioscoridea che la rendono inconfondibile con le altre, anche le più simili" ("Petrarca fra il palazzo" 9).

14. On Dante's poetics of imitation, see Barolini. For a finely nuanced analysis of the Pound-Eliot crux as it relates to Dante, see Menocal. See also Frec-cero who, in discussing Eliot's characterization of Pound as "il miglior fabbro", suggests that "the is-sue of Dante's 'influence' may well be a mask for contemporary rivalry" (4).

15. Mario Praz's ground breaking article of 1937, "T. S. Eliot e Dante", underlines the fundamental importance of Pound and Eliot for the modernist re-reading of Dante: "Pound sapeva dare al suo Dante quel calore di vita vissuta che si cercherebbe invano nelle pagine di tanti studiosi ortodossi. E se la relazione di Eliot verso Dante è fuori del co-mune sentiero del culto dantesco, ciò si deve si-curamente al modo in cui egli scoprì Dante per via di Pound" (240). For Dante's reception in the Modernist period, and the fundamental role played by Pound and Eliot, see the various essays edited by McDougal.

16. Reiterating in 1988 a critical insight first made in 1971, Luciano Anceschi states: "basterà testimoni-are ancora una volta che la fortuna di Pound e di Eliot come poeti, ma anche come grandi 'fabbri' è stata largamente e intensamente vivace in Italia, direi in modo molto più incisivo e resistente di quel che la critica abbia registrato finora" (10). For a number of significant studies and testimoni-als concerning Eliot's influence on contemporary Italian poetry, see "T. S. Eliot e l'Italia", a special issue of *Nuova corrente* edited by Stefano Ver-dino. See also Sanguineti, Caretti, and Barile. While much remains to be said concerning Pound's possible influence on postwar Italian poetry, I find Mario Luzi's recent comments to be highly suggestive: "La sanzione di attualità po-etica data da Pound all'opera dantesca è di un va-lore incalcolabile. . . . La spinta impressa dalle fresche, fervide, sia pure un po' avventurose elu-cubrazioni di Pound . . . ha assecondato quel ritorno di Dante al ruolo di maestro non più mitico ma effettivo di scrittura e di *poiesis* che le condiz-ioni del tempo e della cultura hanno portato con sé. E agisce in tutti i migliori poeti imperanti oggi

in Italia" (cited by Singh, "Il Dante di Eliot" 167). For a current overview of the American poet's legacy, see Singh, *Ezra Pound Centenary.*

17. Among the testimonials included in Verdino, we find an interesting comment by Zanzotto. Respond-ing to an inquiry about his possible rapport with Eliot, Zanzotto replies: "Eliot ha contato anche per me, come, penso, per la maggior parte di quelli della mia generazione. Ma sono vaghe e sotterra-nee irruzioni e vene. Non c'è stata una fase 'eliotiana' per me. . . . Mi piacerebbe ricercare le tracce sepolte del mio Eliot (waste land= 'paese guasto': 'In mezzo mar siede un paese guasto, / diss'egli allora, che s'apella Creta . . .' XIV Inf.). Il paese guasto è sempre più guasto" (19).

18. See Pipa; Almansi; and Barański ("A Note"). Eli-ot's influence on Zanzotto is discussed by Pezzin (cf. pp. 67-78).

19. In his review of *La Beltà* (269), Pasolini writes: "Il libro di Zanzotto è spiritoso e pieno di un hu-mour degno di Gadda, di Joyce: questo humour si manifesta stilisticamente—ad apertura di pagina—come mescolanza, a frequenza altissima, di stile comico e sublime".

20. See Noferi, Ardizzone, Tassoni, ("Vari elementi"), Paltrinieri ("Atti"), as well as chapter four in my book.

21. In analyzing *La Beltà,* Paltrinieri ("L'affabilità" 21) offers some observations which are useful for our reading of the pseudo-trilogy: "la pagina della *Beltà* riesce ostica a una prima e anche a una sec-onda, terza lettura; e il libro intero uno dei più 'petrosi' di Zanzotto. Ma se la concrezione del testo produce un *surplus* di significati, a volte in-attingibili—quasi un cortocircuito—ripetiamo che il senso, nonostante lacune e coaguli, si illumina nella totalità conoscitiva dei micro—e del mac-rotesto: e al lettore di Zanzotto giova non perdere mai la visione d'assieme". For a similar conclu-sion on the relationship between the parts and the whole in *Il Galateo in Bosco,* see Testa.

22. In discussing Zanzotto's "poesia minerale", Maria Luisa Ardizzone has noted his tendency to endow material elements with a mythical or religious symbolism: "tra ciò che è in divenire e l'atto, es-senza del nutrirsi, vivono *Le pasque* di Andrea Zanzotto. Esse sembrano sostituire al mistero del rito, quello biologico, genetico. O forse è meglio considerare che lo riconducono a una matrice che riprende il mito della ri-generazione, della ri-nascita alle sue radici, aggiornandolo in base alle nostre conoscenze odierne" (8).

23. Zanzotto describes the logos in the following terms: "Sotto il nome di logos va qui ogni forza insistente e benigna di raccordo, comunicazione,

interlegame che attraversa le realtà le fantasie le parole, e tende anche a 'donarle', e metterle in rapporto con un fondamento (?)" (*Fosfeni* 79).

24. In commenting on this aspect of the poet's work, Abati has observed "la convergenza in Zanzotto tanto di correnti culturali cristiane quanto di altre matrici socialistiche" ("Itinerario" 4). Ossola, noting the poet's method of proceeding through negation, borrows a phrase from George Bataille to characterize Zanzotto's poetry as a "summa ateologica" (479). On Zanzotto's "nihilism", see Sommavilla; for a different interpretation of the philosophical-religious vein in Zanzotto, one more along the lines suggested by Abati's comments above, see Turoldo.

25. See, for example, the poem "Vocabilità, fotoni": "Dispersa entro una vocabilità dolcissima / Eurosia, genio dei chicchi / di grandine, dispersa ivi Barbara / fotoricettiva delle radicolarità del fulmine / emerge ora Lùcia dal terremotato / cristallo delle diafanità" (*Fosfeni* 63).

26. For a discussion of Zanzotto's rewriting of *Paradiso* VI: 141: "mendicando sua vita a frusto a frusto", see chapter four of my *Poetry of Andrea Zanzotto.*

27. The first of a projected series of three volumes of Zanzotto's critical writings has recently been published by Mondadori with the title *Fantasie di avvicinamento.*

28. Zanzotto's remarks on Virgil illustrate this aspect of his Dantean *forma mentis*: "Virgilio appare dunque, oggi più che mai, come 'degli altri poeti onore e lume' per aver fatto intravedere l'accidentatissimo cammino della ricerca poetica, da lui depressa a livello della 'imitazione' in tutte le sue opere, come riconquista di una autonomia: che è poi rivalsa, ritorno simbolico ad una Heimat, ad una prima patria storica psichica e culturale, sede di ogni *affectus animi* fondante la vita. Resta sempre in Virgilio all'orizzonte il poderetto e quasi l'orto, ben diverso dagli Eden connessi più nettamente alla base religiosa del fatto poetico . . ." ("Zanzotto: un'Arcadia").

29. Zanzotto's essays on Montale include the following, "Il diario senza fine dell'ultimo Montale", "La freccia dei diari", "In margine a *Satura*", "Sviluppo di una situazione montaliana (Escatologia-Scatologia)", and "Il diario senza fine dell'ultimo Montale".

30. "C'è una reale corrispondenza geografica che è sottintesa ai miei scritti. *Il Galateo in Bosco* è connivente col Montello che io vedo verdeggiare riccamente a sud e mi rappresenta e simboleggia i grovigli di umano e non umano, storia e natura; a

nord invece comincio a vedere le sagome astratte delle Dolomiti che mi portano ad un mondo rarefatto, sospeso. . . . Poi esiste come ombelico del mondo e centralità quotidiana la realtà del paesetto dove abito. Essa mi appare come composta di frammenti di vario genere, ognuno con una sua spiccata unicità eppure fusi tutti insieme, storia formata da una sommessa coralità che però è disturbata, vira verso il falsetto. Il paese è come un giardino qua e là devastato, mappa e palinsesto, gesti fissati in un eterno istante, ammicchi di occhi, aprirsi improvviso di stradine che sono sempre qui eppure svoltano sull'altrove. Su questa tripartizione è basata quella che ho annunciato come una pseudo-trilogia, che forse non riuscirà mai a comporsi e in ogni caso corrisponde a tre rami di un albero che non c'è" ("Intervento" 175-176).

31. For example, in a poem in dialect dedicated to Eugenio Montale and occasioned by his eightieth birthday, Zanzotto refers to sending verses to his great predecessor: "Par questo, asséi difizhil no basta che stranbo / me par mandarte, Eusebio, par casa versi" ("Per questo, assai difficile oltre che bizzarro / mi sembra, Eusebio, mandarti versi in casa": *Idioma* 64). In another dialect poem, dedicated to the memory of Pier Paolo Pasolini, Zanzotto describes their friendship, their shared values, and their reading of each other's work: "Se se à parlà, pi avanti, se se à ledést; / zherte òlte 'von tasést o se à sticà" ("Più avanti, ci siamo parlati, ci siamo letti; / certe volte abbiamo taciuto o abbiamo litigato": *Idioma* 67). Zanzotto's sending verses to Montale and his exchange of work with Pasolini flow from his sense of poetry as a form of *communio*. By virtue of their location in the central section of *Idioma,* the nucleus of the entire pseudo-trilogy, the two poems can be considered emblematic. In meeting these two poets again in the final volume of the trilogy, we begin to gain a firmer grasp of how the three volumes may be interrelated. The emphasis in the dialect poems on the exchange of verses, therefore, can be said to mirror a parallel but different kind of poetic sharing that occurs through the hyperliterary references of *Il Galateo in Bosco* and the Dantean allusions of *Fosfeni.*

32. Although the word "paradiso" appears intermittently throughout the three volumes, it is in *Idioma* that it receives particular emphasis. Each of the three sections contains a "paradise" poem, all of which differ significantly from the Paradise effects of *Fosfeni.* These poems include "Genti", which plays on the etymological roots of "paradiso" as "enclosure" and "garden"; "Andar a cucire" ("Si no 'l te fèsse 'n paradiso . . ."), which portrays the traditional Christian notion of paradise; and "Docile, riluttante", the last compo-

sition in the volume: "Quanto quanto qui distilla / e si distillò quale paradiso / perfino dolorosamente nel suo insistere muto / ora è soltanto lieto, e non distrattamente, / ma i suoi valori li compie e li ritira / e li riacconsente un posto più in là" (*Idioma* 108).

Works Cited

Dante is quoted from the *vulgata* of Petrocchi.

The writings of Zanzotto are quoted from the following texts: "Il diario senza fine dell'ultimo Montale", *Corriere della sera,* 11 settembre 1983; *Fantasie di avvicinamento,* Milano, Mondadori, 1991; *Filò: per il* Casanova *di Fellini,* Venezia, Ruzante, 1976 (and Milano, Mondadori, 1988³); *Fosfeni,* Milano, Mondadori, 1983; "La freccia dei diari", in *La poesia di Montale,* Atti del convegno internazionale, Milano, Librex, 1982, pp. 49-53; *Il Galateo in Bosco,* Milano, Mondadori, 1978; *Idioma,* Milano, Mondadori, 1986; "In margine a *Satura*", *Nuovi argomenti* 23-24 (luglio-dicembre 1971), pp. 215-220; "Intervento", *Ateneo veneto* 18 (1980), pp. 170-78; "Ipotesi attorno alla *Città delle donne*", in *La città delle donne,* by Federico Fellini, Milano, Garzanti, 1980, pp. 19-31; *IX Ecloghe,* Milano, Mondadori, 1962; *Pasque,* Milano, Mondadori, 1973; "Petrarca fra il palazzo e la cameretta", in Francesco Petrarca, *Rime,* ed. Guido Bezzola, Milano, Rizzoli, 1976, pp. 5-16; *Gli sguardi i fatti e senhal,* Pieve di Soligo, Bernardi, 1969 (& Milano, Mondadori, 1990); "Una stanza piena di libri", *Il Giorno,* 14 July 1974 (rpt. in *Francesco Petrarca: nel VI centenario della morte,* Bologna, Boni, 1976, pp. 81-85; "Sviluppo di una situazione montaliana (Escatologia-Scatologia)", in *Omaggio a Montale,* ed. Silvio Ramat, Milano, Mondadori, 1966, pp. 157-164; "Testimonianze", *Nuova corrente* 36 (gennaio-giugno 1989), p. 19; "Zanzotto: un'Arcadia attraversata dal dubbio", *Tuttolibri,* 19 settembre 1981.

OTHER WORKS CITED

Abati, Velio, "Itinerario di ricerca", *L'immaginazione* 37-38 (gennaio-febbraio 1987), p. 4.

Agosti, Stefano, ed., "Introduzione alla poesia di Zanzotto", in Andrea Zanzotto, *Poesie (1938-1972),* Milano, Mondadori, 1980, pp. 7-25.

Allen, Beverly, *Andrea Zanzotto: The Language of Beauty's Apprentice,* Berkeley, U of California Press, 1988.

"Interview with Andrea Zanzotto", *Stanford Italian Review* 4 (1984), pp. 253-265.

Almansi, Guido & Bruce Merry, *Eugenio Montale: The Private Language of Poetry.* Edinburgh, Edinburgh UP, 1977.

Anceschi, Luciano, "Testimonianze", *Nuova Corrente* 36 (gennaio-giugno 1989), pp. 9-15.

Ardizzone, Maria Luisa, "La poesia "minerale" di Andrea Zanzotto", *Forum Italicum* 23 (1989), pp. 3-17.

Barański, Zygmunt, "Dante and Montale: The Threads of Influence", in *Dante Comparisons,* ed. Eric Haywood & Barry Jones, Dublin, Irish Academic Press, 1985, pp. 11-48.

Id., "A Note on Montale's Presumed Dantism in "Meriggiare pallido e assorto"", *Italica* 56 (1979), pp. 394-402.

Id., "The Power of Influence: Aspects of Dante's Presence in Twentieth-Century Italian Culture", *Strumenti critici* n.s. 1 (settembre 1986), pp. 343-376.

Bàrberi Squarotti, Giorgio, *Gli inferi e il labirinto: da Pascoli a Montale,* Bologna, Cappelli, 1974.

Id., "L'ultimo trentennio", in *Dante nella letteratura italiana del Novecento,* ed. Silvio Zennaro, Roma, Bonacci, 1979, pp. 245-277.

Barile, Laura, *Adorate mie larve: Montale e la poesia anglosassone,* Bologna, Il Mulino, 1990.

Barolini, Teodolinda, *Dante's Poets: Textuality and Truth in the* Comedy, Princeton, Princeton UP, 1984.

Bloom, Harold, *The Anxiety of Influence: A Theory of Poetry,* New York, Oxford UP, 1973.

Brunetta, Gianpiero, *Buio in sala: cent'anni di passioni dello spettatore cinematografico,* Venezia, Marsilio, 1989.

Camon, Ferdinando. "Andrea Zanzotto", in *Il mestiere di poeta,* 1965, Milano, Garzanti, 1982, pp. 169-81.

Caretti, Laura, *T. S. Eliot in Italia,* Bari, Adriatica, 1968.

Conti Bertini, Lucia, *Andrea Zanzotto o la sacra menzogna,* Venezia, Marsilio editore, 1984.

Contini, Gianfranco, "Un'interpretazione di Dante", in *Varianti e altra linguistica,* Torino, Einaudi, 1970, pp. 369-405.

Falchetta, Piero, *Oculus Pudens: vent' anni di poesia di Andrea Zanzotto (1957-1978),* Padova, Francisci, 1983.

Freccero, John, "Virgil, Sweet Father", in *Dante Among the Moderns,* ed. Stuart Y. McDougal, Chapel Hill, U of North Carolina Press, 1985, pp. 3-10.

Hainsworth, P. R. J., "The Poetry of Andrea Zanzotto", *Italian Studies* 37 (1982), pp. 101-121.

Lewalski, Barbara K., "Federico Fellini's *Purgatorio*", in *Federico Fellini: Essays in Criticism,* ed. Peter E. Bondanella, New York, Oxford UP, 1978, pp. 113-120.

Luperini, Romano, "Gel", *Alfabeta* 52 (settembre 1983), pp. 7-8.

Id., *Montale o l'identità negata,* Napoli, Liguori, 1984.

Luzzi, Giorgio, ed., Andrea Zanzotto, *Poesie (1938-1986),* Torino, L'Arzanà, 1987.

Massini, Giuliana & Bruno Rivalta, eds., *Sulla poesia: conversazioni nelle scuole,* Parma, Pratiche, 1981.

McDougal, Stuart Y., ed. *Dante Among the Moderns,* Chapel Hill, U of North Carolina Press, 1985.

Menocal, Maria Rosa, *Writing in Dante's Cult of Truth from Borges to Boccaccio,* Durham, Duke UP, 1991.

Montale, Eugenio, *L'opera in versi,* ed. R. Bettarini & G. F. Contini, Torino, Einaudi, 1980.

Id., "La poesia di Zanzotto", in *Sulla poesia,* ed. Giorgio Zampa, Milano, Mondadori, 1976, pp. 337-341.

Noferi, Adelia, "Il bosco: traversata di un luogo simbolico," *Paradigma* 8 (1988), pp. 35-66.

Nuvoli, Giuliana, *Andrea Zanzotto,* Firenze, La nuova Italia, 1979.

O'Neill, Tom, "Montale's Fishy Petrarchism", *Modern Language Notes* 106 (January 1991), pp. 78-106.

Orelli, Giorgio, "Un sonetto di Zanzotto", *Il piccolo Hans,* n. 23 (1979), pp. 61-70.

Ossola, Carlo, ""Un oeil immense artificiel": Il sogno "pineale" della scrittura (Da Baudelaire a D'Annunzio e a Zanzotto)", *Lettere italiane* 35 (1983), pp. 457-479.

Paltrinieri, Mara, "L'affabilità di Zanzotto", *Il verri* n. 1-2 (March-June 1987), pp. 19-38.

Ead., "Atti di polistilismo in Zanzotto", *Lingua e stile* 21 (March 1986), pp. 149-73.

Pasolini, Pier Paolo, "*La beltà* (appunti)", *Nuovi argomenti* 21 n.s. (gennaio-marzo 1970; rpt. in *Il portico della morte,* ed. Cesare Segre, Roma, Associazione Fondo P. P. Pasolini, 1988, pp. 267-270).

Id., *La divina mimesis,* Torino. Einaudi, 1975.

Pezzin, Claudio, *Zanzotto e Leopardi,* Verona, Cierre, 1988.

Pipa, Arshi, *Montale and Dante,* Minneapolis, U of Minnesota Press, 1968.

Pound, Ezra, *The Cantos,* London, Faber & Faber, 1987[4].

Praz, Mario, "T. S. Eliot e Dante", *Letteratura* 1 (1937; rpt. in *Machiavelli in Inghilterra ed altri saggi,* Roma, Tumminelli, 1942).

Rizzo, Gino, "Zanzotto, "fabbro del parlar materno"", in Andrea Zanzotto, *Selected Poetry,* ed. & trans. Ruth Feldman & Brian Swann, Princeton, Princeton UP, 1975, pp. 307-323.

Sanguineti, Edoardo, *Interpretazione di Malebolge,* Firenze, Olschki, 1961.

Scorrano, Luigi, *Modi ed esempi di dantismo novecentesco,* Lecce, Adriatica, 1976.

Sillanpoa, Wallace P., "An Interview with Andrea Zanzotto", *Yale Italian Studies* 2 (1978), pp. 297-307.

Singh, Ghanshyam, "Il Dante di Eliot", *Nuova corrente* 36 (gennaio-giugno 1989), pp. 157-74.

Singh, Ghanshyam, ed., *Ezra Pound Centenary,* Udine, Campanotto, 1990.

Sommavilla, Guido, *Peripezie dell'epica contemporanea,* Milano, Jaca Book, 1980.

Tassoni, Luigi, "Discorso interdetto ed elaborazione del senso: riflessioni sulla "trilogia" di Zanzotto", *Paradigma* 8 (1988), pp. 217-37.

Id., "Vari elementi nella selva di Zanzotto", *Paradigma* 5 (1983), pp. 205-226.

Testa, Enrico, *Il libro di poesia: tipologie e analisi macrotestuali,* Genova, Il melangolo, 1983.

Turoldo, Davide Maria, "Postfazione", in Andrea Zanzotto, *Mistieròi / Mistirús,* tr. into Friulian Amedeo Giacomini, Milano, Vanni Scheiwiller, 1984.

Verdino, Stefano, ed., "T. S. Eliot e l'Italia", *Nuova corrente* 36 (gennaio-giugno 1989).

Viola, Italo, "Nuove petrose", *Il piccolo Hans,* n. 25 (1980), pp. 44-70.

Welle, John P., "Fellini's Use of Dante in *La dolce vita*", *Studies in Medievalism* 2 (Summer 1983), pp. 53-65.

Id., *The Poetry of Andrea Zanzotto: A Critical Study of Il Galateo in Bosco,* Roma, Bulzoni, 1987.

Id., "Zanzotto: il poeta del cosmorama," *Cinema & Cinema* 14 (1987), pp. 51-55.

Vivienne Hand (essay date 1994)

SOURCE: Hand, Vivienne. "Undermining Logocentric Thought: *La Beltà* (1961-7)." In *Zanzotto,* pp. 130-54. Edinburgh: Edinburgh University Press, 1994.

[*In the following essay, Hand contends that Zanzotto's* La Beltà, *like Neo-Avant-garde poetry, attempts to "destroy meaning."*]

'Since the death of Eugenio Montale, Italy possesses once again a single "altissimo poeta"' ('very great poet'). This is how Thomas Harrison begins an article on Zanzotto in *The Empty Set* published in 1985, and statements of this sort, emphasizing the poet's singularity, are commonly found in critical studies of Zanzotto's later works, beginning with *LB* [*La Beltà*].

While it is easy to state that Zanzotto is original, it is a more difficult task to justify his originality. Critics, however, have attempted to do so when writing on **LB**. For two main reasons **LB** is posited as being like, but fundamentally very different from, Neo-Avant-garde poetry: Zanzotto's schizoid style is not programmatic, but rather the result of a neurosis; whereas the Neo-Avant-garde aimed at destroying all meaning, Zanzotto produced poetry with a plethora of meanings (see especially Corti 427; Forti 1971, 361; Agosti 1972, 211-12; and Bandini 1982, 9756).

These reasons, however, are not ones that I accept. **LB** is like Neo-Avant-garde poetry precisely in those areas where former critics draw distinctions: Zanzotto *is* attempting to destroy meaning, and he sets about doing it in a programmatic way.

Alfredo Giuliani in *I novissimi: poesie per gli anni '60*—the first major publication to draw attention to the group—outlined the main features of *Novissimi* poetry. He claimed that the effect of the new poetry would be shock and provocation, and that this was to be achieved in three ways: through an interruption of the imaginative process, an abandonment of traditional syntax, and a systematic use of violent images. The new poetry was also to have no definite meaning: the reader, rather than being traditionally 'entertained' was to assist in the process of lending meaning to the poem.

Except in one of these areas—the use of violent images—Giuliani's description of Neo-Avant-garde poetry could equally be applied to Zanzotto's **LB**. Radical distinctions between Zanzotto and the *Novissimi* can only be drawn in the field of declared intentions. The *Novissimi* movement was a politicized one. When Sanguineti, Curi, Balestrini and Giuliani established themselves in centres of cultural power—newspapers, radio, television, universities—they were intent upon destroying an institutionalized culture by attacking the linguistic norm through which it operated.

Zanzotto has never been a politicized writer. It is for personal reasons that he breaks linguistic rules in **LB** and these reasons, although serious, are not as aggressive as those of the *Novissimi*. In the light of his previous discoveries about language, and in view of contemporary theories of semiology, Zanzotto is questioning the functioning of language, and *inviting* his readers to do the same.

I emphasize 'inviting', for **LB** is also less dogmatic than the poetry of the *Novissimi*. Not only did the latter dismiss convention as a vice (seeming not to realize, as Zanzotto once observed, that their own poetry, through time, was destined to become conventional), they were also intolerant of contemporaries who did not conform to Neo-Avant-garde principles. An example in point

was their *jeu de massacre* organized in *Il Verri* (their literary journal) against the *Officina* group that was lead by Pasolini. Pasolini, before the formation of the Neo-Avant-garde, had expounded a new form of poetry which he labelled *Neosperimentalismo* ('Neo-Experimentalism')—a movement born from the failure of Neo-Realist culture and which laid many of the foundations for the Neo-Avant-garde. It too was advocating the principle of innovation, yet the *Novissimi* attacked it because of its difference from their own ideology in one particular area: it operated within terms of moral and civil commitment, and was therefore still linked to immediate postwar tenets.

This intolerance of ideologies other than one's own is not typical of Zanzotto who partly for that reason has never identified himself with any literary movement. Broadly speaking, what Zanzotto has done is to set traditionalism against experimentalism. However, **LB**'s promotion of the second in favour of the first, which gives rise to its similarities with Neo-Avant-garde poetry, is accompanied by a *crise de conscience,* as it were, and a major part of the collection is concerned with the poet presenting reasons for the validity of both schools of thought. It is this obedience to his conscience which lends integrity to his poetry.

Agosti, writing on Zanzotto's **VCT** [**Vocativo**] (1949-56), claimed that Zanzotto was anticipating Saussure's theory of the sign as presented in his *Cours de linguistique générale*. Agosti observed that the latter book only assumed a particular influence on European thought at the beginning of the 1960s. **LB** was written between 1961 and 1967 (mostly, as Zanzotto explains in a note to the collection, between 1964 and 1967) and by this time Zanzotto has obviously read Saussure. Indeed, I shall attempt to illustrate how **LB** not only displays an awareness of Saussurian thought, but is also to some extent prefiguring Derrida whose theory of language involves a re-reading of Saussure. I use the term 'prefiguring' since a question of influence is highly unlikely given that Derrida's work only began to be published in 1967.

Saussure, in his *Cours de linguistique générale* proposed that a linguistic sign consisted of two elements: a signifier (a sound or its written substitute) and a signified (a concept). The sign, composed of these two elements, is both 'arbitrary' and 'differential'. It is 'arbitrary' for two reasons. First, because there is no reason why a certain sound and its written substitute (for example, 'hat') should correspond to one particular concept (the concept of a "hat") and not to some other concept. Apart from special cases such as onomatopoeia, the relationship between the signifier and the signified is in no way motivated or natural or inevitable. Rather, it is the product of linguistic convention. Second, the sign is arbitrary because there is no necessary relationship between the sign as a whole (comprising signifier and signified) and the reality to which it refers. There is an essential division between the world of language and the world of reality.

The sign is differential because it acquires meaning only by virtue of its differences from other signs. In other words, a sound-image has meaning not 'in itself' but only because one differentiates it from other related sound-images (one differentiates 'hat' from 'cat' or 'mat'); just as one differentiates one concept from other related concepts (one differentiates "hat" from "coat" or "dress"). This shows how Saussure was aware of the chaotic continua of sound-images on the one hand, and concepts on the other. Nevertheless, he acknowledged that the linguistic system, by providing certain sound-images for certain concepts, sorted out the chaos. Within the linguistic system, signifier and signified are inseparably linked like the two sides of one sheet of paper.

It is this last idea about the linguistic system sorting out the chaotic continua of sound-images and concepts that is the point of contention for Derrida. In his *La Voix et le Phénomène (Speech and Phenomenon)* Derrida claims that if, as Saussure says, every sign is what it is only because it is not all the other signs, then every sign would seem to be made up of a potentially endless network of differences. In other words, if in the linguistic system, one sound-image has to ward off other related sound-images in order to be itself, then, according to Derrida, it is only true to say that the latter are contained within the former and form part of its identity. Consequently, signifiers refer only to other signifiers, not to things or entities beyond themselves; and meaning is a quality which is never free, never separable from the signifier which 'invokes' it. Derrida argues that language is self-referential, incapable of pointing beyond itself. He identifies Saussure with the *logocentric* tradition, that is, a tradition wherein writers and readers see the word and texts as *centred* by definite meaning in accordance with their belief in a *logos*—a God or some ultimate truth—which acts as a foundation for all of their language and thought. The logocentric tradition, Derrida then observes, is one which favours a system of hierarchies (the word being a derivative of the Word of God or some ultimate authority) which governs not only the linguistic system but also the whole of the cultural system. These ideas form the basic premisses of Derrida's theory of *différance*.

Zanzotto's ideas in *LB* lean more toward Derridean than Saussurian thought. He does acknowledge the arbitrary and differential nature of the sign, and here his reasoning could be identified as Saussurian. Nevertheless, unlike Saussure, he never concedes that the linguistic system sorts out the chaotic continua of signifiers and signifieds. If anything, Zanzotto, like Derrida,

is presenting the idea that the linguistic system is a false convention, and he attempts to undermine it by thwarting the reader's attempts to posit meaning. This subversion of meaning constitutes one of the ways in which Zanzotto tries to overthrow traditional, logocentric reading habits. Such a subversive practice is to be found in the majority of the poems in *LB* but there are a number of poems where Zanzotto debates the validity of his own revolutionary thought.

Toward the beginning of the collection, in **'Sí, ancora la neve' ('Yes, The Snow Again')**, Zanzotto quotes from a variant of Hölderlin's 'Mnemosyne': "'siamo un segno senza significato'" ("'we are a sign without a signified'"). He then follows this quotation with a question of his own: 'ma dove le due serie entrano in contatto?' ('but where do the two series come into contact?'). Hölderlin was probably not even using the terms 'segno' and 'significato' with linguistic implications in mind: the line from 'Mnemosyne' in the original reads 'Ein Zeichen sind wir deutungslos' ('We are a sign without meaning').

However, given that *LB* is largely about language, and that its approach to the subject is a modern one, it would seem reasonable to assume that Hölderlin's line is being incorporated into a contemporary, Saussurian context. This is also implied by the question which Zanzotto directs at the citation from 'Mnemosyne'. Here he indicates two series of phenomena which do not 'come into contact'. The line is evocative of what Saussure called the arbitrariness of the linguistic sign. Zanzotto is suggesting one of two things: the disjunction between signifier and signified ('we are a sign without a signified'), or the disjunction between sign and reality—Saussure's two reasons for the sign's arbitrary nature.

But it is more likely the first of Saussure's reasons for the sign's arbitrariness which Zanzotto is alluding to in his quotation from Hölderlin: the essential disjunction between signifiers and signifieds or, to put it more simply, between words and concepts. If one were to choose between Saussure's two discoveries, this is, after all, the more far-reaching one in that from it developed the notion of differentiality, acknowledged, importantly, in some poems of *LB,* as I show later.

If words do not refer to the concepts that they are normally considered to refer to, then the poet who wants to conjure up concepts and say something about them, is a poet *malgré lui*. Such a poet must deal with the *impossibility* of writing. It is for this reason that in some of Zanzotto's poems one encounters the negation of words as soon as they are written on the page. It is a gesture which amounts to the erasing of the signifier because of its inability to signify:

storia—storiella

story—fib

. . . te ne vai; oh stagione.
Non sei la stagione

. . . you vanish; oh season. / You are not the season

e me e non-me

and me and non-me

vivi al superlativo
morti al superlativo

('Alla stagione')

superlatively alive / superlatively dead

('To The Season')

Là origini—Mai c'è stata origine

There beginnings—There never was a beginning

Nessuno si è qui soffermato—Anzi moltissimi

No one has lingered here—On the contrary too many
have

L'assenza degli dèi, sta scritto, ricamato, ci
aiuterà
      —non ci
         aiuterà—
tanto l'assenza non è assenza gli dèi non dèi
l'aiuto non è aiuto

The gods' absence, it is written, embroidered, will help
us /—will not help us—/ after all, absence is not
absence gods not gods / help is not help

. . . storie storielle

('L'elegia in petèl')

. . . stories fibs.

('The Elegy in Petèl')

It is obvious, however, that if the poet is to remain a poet and write something productive, he must find a way out of his dilemma. Zanzotto, in the first poem of the collection, **'Oltranza oltraggio' ('Outrance Outrage')** reveals an attempt to resolve his predicament. He suggests that the authentic poem may still be written, but for the time being it is 'further ahead' not 'here'. The dominant motif of this poem is 'ti fai piú in là' ('you move further ahead'), and the reflexive verb here refers to poetry itself, for as has already become apparent in previous chapters, in Zanzotto 'tu' and poetry are always coterminous, excepting two occa-

sions: in the 'Prima persona' section of *VCT* where 'tu' referred to the 'real' self, as opposed to the linguistically determined self ('io'); and when the 'tu' occasionally refers to a person who is generally named in the poem.

A variant of the 'ti fai piú in là' motif is repeated in line 7: 'sei piú in là' ('you are further ahead'); and in line 13 it occurs again in the original: 'ti fai piú in là'. How Zanzotto may continue to write—and the repetition of the motif displays his urgency to do so—is suggested by the title of the piece: by going beyond all conventional conceptions of poetry, thereby creating outrage ('oltraggio') on the part of the reader.

Zanzotto's logic is quite clear. He feels it is untruthful to continue to write poetry where language aims to have a referential function. To write poems in that way is to conform to a logocentric and, consequently, false tradition. The authentic poem can only be one in which that tradition is subverted. However, the task of subversion is a difficult one, for Zanzotto knows that all readers conform to logocentrism: they will assume, for example, that words are referring to specific concepts even when, in the intentions of the poet, they are not; they will search for meaning and give meaning both to individual words and to the poem as a whole. The only manner, therefore, in which Zanzotto can subvert this tradition is by attempting to undermine some of the reader's logocentric reading habits, by attempting to dislodge his complacency. This is exactly what Zanzotto sets out to do in a number of poems in *LB*. His project is undoubtedly pursued with sincerity, although his attitude toward the reader is tongue-in-cheek.

Various methods are adopted: sometimes Zanzotto thwarts the reader's attempts to find *any* meaning in a poem; on other occasions he deliberately *confuses* the meaning of both individual words and poems as a whole; he also undermines the hierarchic structures regulating linguistic and cultural systems; and finally, he invalidates the reader's preconceptions of a poem as an artefact that is carefully constructed.

Each of these areas is explored individually here, and in the order in which they are presented above, although from such a systematic approach, one may get the impression that 'themes' are being examined. This impression derives from the fact that my critical method conforms to the tradition that the poet is subverting. Zanzotto does not inject his own writing with themes. This allows for a *comparison* with the Neo-Avant-garde rather than the distinction that is posited by Corti. Furthermore, since the aim of the collection is clearly subversive, Zanzotto's schizoid style *is* often programmatic, just as his point of departure *is* often destructive. Forti and Agosti present the opposite viewpoint (that Zanzotto's schizoid style is unprogrammatic and his point of departure is only creative), intending thereby to dissociate Zanzotto from the Neo-Avant-garde tradition. But **LB** is like that tradition precisely because of its subversive techniques.

There are a number of ways in which Zanzotto subverts the reader's attempts to give meaning to a poem. In **'Adorazioni, richieste, acufeni' ('Adorations, Requests, Buzzings in the Ears')** he pokes fun at the reader who is attempting to fix the traditional connection between title and content. Alluding to the first he begins by asking

> . . . e che cosa
> è stato tutto questo chiedere?
> Questo voler adorare?

. . . and what / was all this asking? / This wanting to adore?

He then continues to suggest that he wants to clarify the connection, only to interrupt these 'clarifications' with teasing and flippant remarks:

> Questo voler adorare? Ma che è questa storia
> dell'adorare?
> Adorate adorate. Fischi negli orecchi

This wanting to adore? But what is this story about adoring? / Adore adore. Whistlings in the ears

> Eccomi, ben chiedere lungo chiedere,
> eccomi, bell'adorare
> —avevi un bell'adorare, tu!—

Here I am, asking in earnest asking at length, / here I am, fine adoration /—a fine adoration you had!—

The poem ends by anticipating the reader's bewilderment:

> . . . Nonsense, pare?
> Nonsense e nottinere?

. . . Nonsense, it seems? / Nonsense and blacknights?

On other occasions Zanzotto places emphasis upon sound, and the pleasure which sound and its oral articulation, irrespective of sense, can afford. He calls it a 'Danza orale danza / del muscolío di tutta la bocca' (**'Profezie V'**) ('Oral dance a dance / of the muscles in the whole mouth') (**'Prophecies V'**), and it is prevalent both in the 'petèl' monologues (to be considered later) and in sequences such as the following:

> tutte sanissime e strette in solido

all very healthy and packed *in solido*

> mille linguine e a-lingue a-labbra
> argento neve nulla e anche meno
> oppure neve e poi a-neve a-nulla

(**'Profezie V'**)

a thousand little tongues and non-tongues non-lips / silver snow nothing and even less / or rather snow and then non-snow non-nothing

> . . . Là ero a perdifiato
> là. E tutta la mia fifa nel fifaus:
> tutto fronzuto trotterellante di verdi visioni

. . . There I was at breakneck speed / there. And all of my funk in the frethouse: / all leafy trotting along with green visions

> e—oh i frutti, che frutti, fruttame

and—oh the fruits, what fruits, fruitage

> Perfidia, perfido, perfidamente

(**'Possibili prefazi II'**)

Malice, malicious, maliciously

(**'Possible prefaces II'**)

Here pleasure can be derived from abundant alliteration; from the creation of compounds allowing two accents ('a-lingue a-labbra', 'a-neve a-nulla'); and from the variety of stress present in a sequence of noun-adjective-adverb produced from one stem ('Perfidia, perfido, perfidamente').

Zanzotto's intertextuality or, what previous critics have called, his 'culturalismo' (his allusions to and citations from other literary sources) also hampers the reader who is looking for meaning—an idea not pursued by the critics so far. If one has no knowledge of the literature evoked, one cannot bring that knowledge to bear on the poems, and is left with the feeling of having suffered a loss.

I am not concerned here with drawing up a list of Zanzotto's literary allusions for such a list has been compiled by a number of critics (see Corti 427; Rossi 1973, 115; Antonielli 628; Montale 339, who between them detect echoes from Dante to Borges). Rather, using as examples the poems **'Possibili prefazi X'** and **'Profezie IX'**, I consider the *problems* these allusions create.

'Possibili prefazi X' opens with a translation of the title of an article by Lacan: '1.—Lo stadio psicologico detto "dello specchio" / come costitutivo della funzione dell'io' ('1.—The psychological phase called "The Mirror Stage" / as a constituent of the function of the self'). Zanzotto gives the source of this reference in his notes to the poem, but how he is using it only becomes clear from an examination of the poem.

From a first reading it is obvious that the poem is an eulogy of Hölderlin—a salute to a personal 'hero'. Zanzotto speaks of the 'homage' he feels, his 'imitation' of Hölderlin, his desire to reflect him, be a specular 'image':

Da qui basterebbe ora, in reattivo,
l'onesta imitazione l'omaggio convinto

From here the honest imitation the convinced homage /
would suffice now, as a psychological test

7—Si fa degno, in quella lontananza,
anche questo speculare mancamento

7—In that distance, even this / specular failing becomes
worthy

10—E divago, nel mancamento, alla ricerca di
un'immagine

10—And I stray, in the failing, looking for an image.

A quotation from Hölderlin—'Mit Unterthänigkeit'
('With awe')—is cited three times in the poem (twice
in translation as 'Con soggezione'). It is the phrase that
Hölderlin placed before his signature ('Scardanelli') to
the later poems written during the period of his madness. Zanzotto's devotion to Hölderlin is very much
linked to his fixation with romantic eccentrics.

Where in all of this does Lacan fit? In his 'Mirror Stage'
article Lacan argues that a child, generally from the age
of six months, can recognize as such his own image in
a mirror. Although still in a primordial form, the child's
'I', on the assumption of this specular image, begins to
take on its function as subject in the world. The specular image becomes a 'je-idéal' ('ideal-I') and will later
be the source of *secondary* identifications. Lacan
stresses the point that the 'je-idéal' situates the ego in a
fictional direction: the subject in its process of coming-
into-being, attempts to synthesize the real I with the 'je-
idéal', but the synthesis can never be fully achieved.

Hölderlin, it seems, is Zanzotto's 'je-idéal' in the form
of a *secondary* identification. However, the allusion in
the note to the article by Lacan points to a strong element of irony in the poem: Zanzotto is acknowledging
that his identification with Hölderlin is only a *continuation* of the ego's first process of situating itself in a
fictional direction. His identification, in other words, is
an illusory one.

The poem is of greater interest when one examines how
Zanzotto *uses* theories of Lacan than when one attempts
to decode it through Lacanian thought. Its emphasis
shifts from the greatness of Hölderlin to the impoverished figure of Zanzotto himself. What is really being
stressed is the I's inferiority, its inability to synthesize
with the 'je-idéal'. This idea is presented toward the
end of the poem. Here Zanzotto claims that if his
coveted image were truly a reflection of himself, it
would have an ego, like his own, the size of a fly:

10—E divago, nel mancamento, alla ricerca di
un'immagine,

immaginina mia come una mosca, io

10—And I stray, in the defect, looking for an image, /
my little image like a fly, I.

A smaller intertextual problem is present in **'Profezie
IX'**. In his notes Zanzotto talks about the theme of the
poem: '"L'Urkind", the original child (in a Husserlian
sense too), tries to focus itself in an Ego that can never
be fully specified'. The echo back to Lacan does not
escape the attentive reader of **'Possibili prefazi X'** who
has consulted the 'Mirror Stage' article. However, this
echo is less fertile than another which occurs at the end
of the poem where Dante and baby-talk fuse:

con tanta pappa-pappo,
con tanti dindi-sissi,
Ego-nepios, o Ego, miserrimo al centro del
mondo tondo

with so much pap and chink, / with so many ting-a-ling
collars with bells, / Ego-infant, oh Ego, most miserable
at the centre of the round world.

The reader who misses the allusion to Dante ('Pappo e
dindi', *Purgatorio* xi, 105) not indicated by Zanzotto in
his notes to the poem, will only see in these lines Zanzotto's attempt to echo the language and cadence of
nursery rhymes—indicated by him at the beginning of
the poem (and also a feature of 'Sí, ancora la neve':
'bambucci-ucci', 'pini-ini' ('baby-wabies', 'piney-
winies')):

Bimbo, bimbo!
Secondo cantilena, volta la carta, volta la carta

Baby, baby! / As in the lullaby, turn the page, turn the
page.

The reader who sees the allusion to Dante can also
recognize a mixture of high and low cultures, and go on
to examine the reason behind it.

Earlier I observed that Zanzotto can hope to deflate, but
not defeat the logocentric tradition. My own criticism
so far has borne witness to this: I hunted for meaning
(consulting Lacan, for example); or I arrived at the
conclusion that the meaning of the poem is the *absence
of meaning* (as in 'Adorazioni, richieste, acufeni') or
again, that its meaning *is* the prevalence of sound over
sense (as in **'Profezie V'** and **'Possibili prefazi II'**).
What Zanzotto has succeeded in doing is to make me
aware that I am being estranged from my logocentric
reading habits.

A more interesting way in which Zanzotto does this is
by suggesting differing interpretations for words and
poems, thereby preventing the reader from seeing them
as 'centred' by definite meaning.

Two methods are used to decentralize words. Sometimes
Zanzotto in his notes to the poems indicates ambiguity
in his use of certain terms: '"ninine": potrebbe essere

un singolare friulano (fanciulla), sentito come plurale e conglobante ogni cosa piccola e graziosa' (note to **'Profezie XIII'**) ('"ninine": it could be a rare word from the Friuli area (meaning a little girl), felt as a plural here, and incorporating every small and graceful thing'); '"base": forse, secondo fantascienza, su un pianeta-exemplar' (note to **'Profezie XV'**) ('base': perhaps, in accordance with science fiction, on an exemplary planet').

On other occasions within the poems he uses polysemy as is the case in the following example where 'fonte' is meant in the sense of 'origin', but where the onomatopoeia underscores an allusion to Palazzeschi's 'La fontana malata' ('The Sick Fountain'):

> E che messaggi ha la fonte di messaggi?
> Ed esiste la fonte, o non sono
> che io-tu-questi-quaggiú
> questi cloffete clocchete ch ch
>
> **('Sí, ancora la neve')**

And what messages does the source of messages have? / And does the source exist, or is it only / I-you-these-down here / these gutter splutter squirt spirt.

Here 'fonte' has not one meaning, but two: 'source' both in a literal and figurative sense—one related to the other through (Saussurian) 'difference'.

Zanzotto often plays with the Saussurian idea that language is a differential phenomenon: poems are constructed through a linking together of related sound-images and concepts. Generally the result is a variety of meanings. Such is the case in **'Possibili prefazi I'**, **'Profezie V'**, and **'La perfezione della neve'** (**'The Snow's Perfection'**). **'La perfezione della neve'** provides the best example. Here are the first sixteen lines of the poem, followed by my indication as to how they are 'structured'. I use the word 'structured' with some reservation since a sequence such as that quoted below has more of an extempore than a conscious construction (an issue I return to later). However, there seems little ground for accepting the opinions of some critics that psychoanalysis is involved in a sequence like this: to say that here one has an example of the Freudian preconscious (Corti 427), or the Lacanian unconscious (Siti 1973, 132; Milone 229) is to make shaky speculations that cannot be proven.

> Quante perfezioni, quante
> quante totalità. Pungendo aggiunge.
> E poi astrazioni astrificazioni formulazione
>   d'astri
> assideramento, attraverso sidera e coelos
> assideramenti assimilazioni—
> nel perfezionato procederei
> piú in là del grande abbaglio, del pieno e del
>   vuoto,
> ricercherei procedimenti
> risaltando, evitando
> dubbiose tenebrose; saprei direi.
> Ma come ci soffolce, quanta è l'ubertà nivale

> come vale: a valle del mattino a valle
> a monte della luce plurifonte.
> Mi sono messo di mezzo a questo movimento-
>   mancamento radiale
> ahi il primo brivido del salire, del capire,
> partono in ordine, sfidano: ecco tutto

How many perfections, how many / how many totalities. Stinging it adds. / And then abstractions astrifications formulations of stars / frostbite, across stars and skies / frostbites assimilations—/ I would proceed into the perfected / beyond the great dazzle, beyond the full and the empty, / I would search for proceedings / jumping once more, avoiding / the dubious the dark; I'd know I'd say. / But how it supports us, how great is the snowy fertility / how much it is worth: downstream from the morning downstream / upstream from the multi-sourced light. / I have placed myself in the midst of this radial movement-cum-defect / ah the first thrill of ascending, of understanding, / they fall into a sequence, they challenge: that's all there's to it.

The following relationships are at work in this sequence:

'perfezioni' ('perfections') 'totalità' ('totalities'): semantic contiguity

'astrazioni astrificazioni' ('abstractions astrifications'): phonic or orthographic relationship

'astri' ('stars') 'assideramento' ('frostbite'): semantic contiguity (Zanzotto in a note explains 'assideramento' as a neologism created from '"sideratus": colpito da un (maligno) influsso di un'astro' ('"sideratus": struck down by the evil influence of a star'))

'assideramento' ('frostbite') 'sidera' ('stars'): etymological relationship

'sidera e coelos' ('stars and skies'): same semantic field

'assideramenti assimilazioni' ('frostbites assimilations'): phonic relationship

'pieno' ('full') 'vuoto' ('empty'): antonyms

'dubbiose' ('dubious') 'tenebrose' ('dark'): semantic contiguity

'nivale' ('snowy') 'vale' ('it is worth') 'valle' ('valley'): phonic or orthographic relationships

'a valle' ('upstream') 'a monte' ('downstream'): antonyms.

As Zanzotto himself states in the final line of this section, the words of his poem fall into sequences and challenge the reader: 'partono in ordine, sfidano: ecco tutto'. They 'challenge' him to give a definite meaning to the poem, faced as he is by a number of meanings. For example, one could interpret the poem as a metapoetic discourse, dealing with the *fact* that words only function by virtue of their differences from other words. If one considers description to be more important than structure, the poem could be said to be depicting a snow scene, the 'Quante perfezioni' and 'astrazioni' referring to thousands of starry, molecular flakes. Yet again, the snow with its illusory presence (suggested in phrases such as 'del pieno e del vuoto', 'questo movimento-mancamento') could be said to be functioning as a symbol for the 'absence' inherent in words. One could even choose to pursue the poem's intertextual features—the words 'soffolce' and 'l'ubertà' of line 11 being taken directly from Dante (*Paradiso* xxiii, 130), and the 'grande abbaglio' of line 7 evoking the blinding light of *Paradiso*.

Rizzo thinks that Zanzotto authorizes the reader to paraphrase the poems in any way he wishes, but, in fact, a poem like **'La perfezione della neve'** encourages the reader to discover a plethora of meanings (as in Mallarmé's poetry, as Hainsworth has noted (1982, 111)) which cannot be hierarchized in terms of importance.

The hierarchies involved in language and culture are also swept by the board. The following examples show Zanzotto inverting the hierarchies of grammatical law:

> Fa' di (ex-de-ob etc.)—sistere
>
> > **('Al mondo')**

> Try to (ex-des-res etc.)—ist
>
> > **('To The World')**

> L'archi-, trans, iper, iper, (amore) (statuto del trauma)
>
> > **('Possibili prefazi IV')**

> The archi-, trans, hyper, hyper (love) (the trauma statute).

In **'Al mondo'** the morpheme '-sistere' is elevated to the role of a word *per se,* and expression is compressed to resemble a mathematical equation where prefixes within the parentheses are meant to be added to the morpheme outside. In **'Possibili prefazi *IV*'** it is the prefix that is now raised to the status of a word, while 'real' words, by being placed in parentheses, have their importance reduced.

Culture in *LB* is to be understood in the sense of history and literature—two issues carried over from *IXE* [*IX Ecloghe*]. History is discussed in 'Retorica su: lo sbandamento, il principio **"resistenza" (I-II-III-IV-V-VI)'** ('Rhetoric on: Disbandment, the **"Resistance" Principle (I-II-III-IV-V-VI)'**) (henceforth **'Retorica su'**). Considering Italy's part in the Second World War, the poet audaciously remarks that the staple peasant diet—'una zuppa gustosa' ('a tasty soup')—played a much greater part in keeping men alive and 'resistant' than did the rhetoric of politicians, called an 'opera-fascino' ('spell-work'):

> E ho mangiato anche quel giorno
> —dopo il sangue—
> e mangio tutti i giorni
> —dopo l'insegnamento—
> una zuppa gustosa, fagioli.

> Posso farlo e devo.
> Tutti possono e devono.
> Bello. Fagiolo. Fiore.

And even that day I ate /—after the blood—/ and everyday I eat /—after teaching—/ a tasty soup, of beans. / I can and must do it. / Everyone can and must. / Nice. Bean. Flower.

In other words, a small, unrecorded historical event—what Zanzotto calls in a note to the poem, a 'microstoria' or 'storiella'—is being elevated above the rhetoric of history.

'L'elegia in petèl' launches a simultaneous attack on hierarchical attitudes to language and literature. The title of the poem alludes to two contrasting 'languages'—an elegiac one and 'petèl'. The elegy has associations with death and an end, and it is the death of language that is being lamented in the poem, exemplified again (as Zanzotto explains in a note) by a fragment from the demented Hölderlin. This fragment comes significantly at the end of the poem: "'Una volta ho interrogato la Musa'" ("'Once I questioned my Muse'").

'Petèl' has associations with birth and beginnings. In another note to the poem Zanzotto explains it as the dialect word in Pieve di Soligo for the endearing nonsense talk used by mothers to their babies in which they try to approximate the language of the child. Examples from the poem are as follows:

> 'Mama e nona te dà ate e cuco e pepi e memela. Bono ti, ca, co nona. Béi bumba bona. È fet foa e upi'.

> Ta bon ciatu? Ada ciòl e úna e tée e mana papa. Te bata cheto, te bata: e po mama e nana.

Hölderlin's alienated speech and the baby's 'petèl' are being highlighted by Zanzotto for the following reasons. Broadly speaking, both languages are unintelligible: Hölderlin's line, 'Once I questioned my Muse', makes *grammatical* sense, but given that it was uttered in a state of insanity, its import can never be fully ascertained. A primordial meaning may be present in 'petèl', but it is a meaning intuited only by mothers: 'petèl' is a 'lingua privata' ('private language') or 'lingua a due' ('language for two') (as Zanzotto underlines in another note to the poem) that does not even translate into standard Italian.

Moreover, Hölderlin's quotation and the 'petèl' sequences are marginal utterances with respect to the norm. The language of the child *precedes* the norm (displaying a freedom of speech as yet unconstrained by rules of grammar, syntax, or meaning); the language of the madman *goes beyond* it. Consequently, Zanzotto, by using these languages, and by even highlighting them in the title, is attempting to raise what is generally considered to be nonsensical and marginal to the status of literature. 'Tutto fa brodo' ('Anything goes'), as he says in the poem using, as he explains in a note, a part of an advertisement jingle—'non è vero che tutto fa brodo' ('it isn't true that anything goes' (literally, 'it isn't true that everything makes broth'))—to emphasize this process—recurrent in the collection—of including what the norm would 'normally' exclude. This is the reason for Zanzotto's much debated 'plurilinguismo'. By using many different lexical registers that are not normally considered to constitute the language of literature, Zanzotto is re-evaluating the notion of literature and deflating our traditional preconceptions of it.

The jingle above merits further attention. **'L'elegia in petèl'** is claiming to be a 'brodo' ('broth'); **'Possibili prefazi X'** calls itself a 'minestra' ('soup'). They are indelicate metaphors, and intentionally so. But they also reinforce the hotchpotch element that characterizes many of the poems in the collection. This is another of Zanzotto's revolutionary tactics, one which explodes the age-old notion of the poem as a perfected artefact. Many of his poems contain notes for poems: 'Dire, molte cose, di stagione, usando l'infinito' ('To say, many things, about the season, using the infinitive'); 'e l'uso dell'infinito' ('and the use of the infinitive') (**'Alla stagione'**). Others are presented as a series of notes, where lines are preceded by either arabic numerals or letters of the alphabet indicating point number one, point two, point a, point b, and so on. It is a 'modo piuttosto rozzo' ('rather rough method') in the words of the poet himself (see **'Possibili prefazi X'** in which this quotation occurs, and **'Possibili prefazi VIII'**, **'Possibili prefazi IX'**, and **'Profezie XVIII'**).

The self-generating language that I emphasized earlier when discussing **'La perfezione della neve'** brings an element of improvisation to the fore. Zanzotto, rather than choosing his own words and organizing them in a deliberate structure, lets words beget words by themselves. They precipitate forth, breeding off each other, and giving the impression that the main concern of some poems is to remain in a state of being born, as it were,—never to come to a literal 'end' (**'Profezie IX'** claims to be 'renitente all'omega' ('unwilling to reach the omega')). This is yet another reason why the collection displays an interest in baby-talk and nursery rhymes: there is echolalia in the first; and nursery rhymes, when recited, generally end with a return to the beginning. In both the repetition is gratuitous but pleasurable. (It is interesting to note that there is a reference to baby-talk in the canto from Dante's *Paradiso* that Zanzotto quoted from in **'La perfezione della neve'** (see *Paradiso* xxiii, 121-2)).

'Sí, ancora la neve' is the best example of a poem which prolongs its duration by breeding off itself. Apart from cases of direct repetition (as in the examples below, under 1) this is achieved by a process of constantly modifying language in the following ways:

by reversing the order of words (2), or changing the gender of adjectives (3); by adding prefixes or suffixes to a constant stem (4); and by repeating a sequence, with one or more words linked or added to the repetition (5).

1 e poi e poi . . . ma i pini, i pini (4)
. . .—il mondo pinoso il mondo nevoso— (7)
E il pino. E i pini-ini-ini per profili
e profili mai scissi mai cuciti (100-1)

and then and then . . . but the pines, the pines / . . .— the piney world the snowy world—. . . / And the pine. And the piney-winey-inies by profiles / and the profiles never split never sewn

. . . bambucci-ucci, odore di cristianucci (8)
. . . i bambucci-ucci (42)

. . . waddler-toddlers, smell of wee Christian men / . . . waddler-toddlers

Buona neve, buone ombre, glissate glissate (28)

Good snow, good shadows, glide glide

. . . sniff sniff
gnam gnam yum yum slurp slurp (48-9)

E l'avanguardia ha trovato, ha trovato? (90)

And the Avant-garde, has it found, has it found?

2 E tu perché, perché tu? (15)

And you, why, why you?

. . . davanti
dietro . . .
dietro davanti (102-4)

. . . in front / behind . . . / behind in front

3 . . . evaso o morto
evasa o morta (26-7)

. . . escaped or dead / escaped or dead

. . . piú o meno truffaldini (52)
piú o meno truffaldine (54)

. . . more or less swindling / more or less swindling

4 . . . in persona ed ex-persona
un solo possibile ed ex-possibile? (10-11)

. . . in person and ex-person / a one and only possible and ex-possible?

. . .—per una minima o semiminima
biscroma semibiscroma nanobiscroma

cose e cosine (73-5)

. . .—for a minim or semi-minim / demisemiquaver semidemisemiquaver minidemisemiquaver / things and thingies

5 Che sarà della neve (1)
   ma che sarà della neve dei pini (22)

What will become of the snow / but what will become of the snow of the pines

E perché si è . . .
perché si è fatto . . .
perché si è fatto noi, roba per noi? (7-9)

And why has it . . . / why has it become . . . / why has it become us, stuff for us?

However, there is a more constant method employed by Zanzotto to defer the conclusion of a poem—the stringing together of words or phrases by means of simple conjunctions: 'agganciare catene di e, di o' (**Possibili prefazi V'**) ('to hook together chains of ands, of ors'). Sometimes this phrase is to be interpreted literally—in **'Sí, ancora la neve'** where there is an abundance of 'e's, and in **'Profezie IX'** where there is an abundance of 'o's. Mostly, however, it has a figurative meaning, for the 'catene di e' (also called 'innesti' ('graftings')) denote verbal repetition (where words, ideas, but also sound, are repeated); and the 'catene di o' (also called 'clivaggi' ('cleavages')) denote verbal opposition—the use of antitheses.

Repetition and opposition of this verbal kind also help to defer the conclusion of a poem: when Zanzotto uses the first, the poem moves *forward* by repeating the words, ideas, or sounds that have come *before,* so that *progression* is really a form of *regression.* When Zanzotto uses the second, the juxtapositioning of opposites prevents the poem from attaining a linear discourse or, what he himself calls, an 'andatura rettilinea' ('straight walk') (**Profezie V'**). **'Profezie V'** and **'Profezie X'** show the 'innesti' and 'clivaggi' simultaneously at work. They become much more readily apparent if isolated in the form of the charts that follow.

Earlier I emphasized the point that although Zanzotto's attitude is often facetious, his revolutionary tactics are pursued with sincerity. This sincerity is reinforced by the attacks that he launches (especially in the sequence 'Possibili prefazi') on one of his earlier collections of landscape poetry—*DIP* [*Dietro il paesaggio*]. *DIP* (as demonstrated in Chapter 1) adhered to a tradition—Hermeticism—and never doubted or even questioned the logocentrism of words, so that consequently it was full of the themes and messages that one expects in traditional poetry. It is precisely these themes and the language of the collection that Zanzotto now ruthlessly ironizes. This, I believe, is the target, not exterior powers—consumerist society and an industrial civilization—that have made lyricism no longer possible (Forti 1971, 360).

Zanzotto now calls his love of the rustic a 'perfidious' one, full of green visions and a childish enthusiasm ('e—oh i frutti'; 'e—oh i collicelli'):

Quell'io che già tra selve e tra pastori.
Perfido, perfido

That I who already among woods and shepherds. / Malicious, malicious tutto fronzuto trotterellante di verdi visioni

e le debolezze e la grazia di fioretti e germogli
e—oh i frutti, che frutti, fruttame
e—oh i collicelli, morbido da portare al naso da fiutare
assimilare come faceva quel vecchio: io

(**'Possibili prefazi II'**)

SEMANTIC
'Profezie x' ('Ammirata, eminente erba di Dolle') ('Dolle's admired, eminent grass')

Repetition ('innesti')	Opposition ('clivaggi')
luna nuova o mondata appieno (6–7) new moon / or fully cleansed	sereno o follia di piove (7–8) fine weather / or madness of rain
equivale corrisponde consuona (10) is equivalent to corresponds harmonizes	Eccitavi, addormivi? (8) Were you excited, falling asleep?
Repetition ('innesti')	Opposition ('clivaggi')
E come oso rivolger(mi) a (te), metter(ti) in rapporto con (me) (25) And how do I dare turn (myself) to (you), put (you) in relation to (me)	
	Salire o scendere muovere o giacere con te (9) Ascending or descending moving / or lying with you
	di realtà e di fantasma? (15) real and fantastic?
	Ostensione immediata e rapina (16) Immediate showing and robbery
	sulla via che da tutto svia (19) on the road which leads astray from everything
	muta . . . sai il dicibile e . . . lo fai (20) silent . . . you know the sayable and . . . you say it
	crittogamie fanerogamie (23) crytogamia phanerogamia

SEMANTIC	
'Profezie v' ('Chiamarlo giro o andatura rettilinea') ('To Call it a Circle or a Straight Walk')	
Repetition ('innesti')	Opposition ('clivaggi')
abbacina . . . sfavillanti (11) dazzles . . . sparkling	giro o andatura rettilinea (1) circle or straight walk
leccano l'idillio succhiano dall'idillio (12–13) they lick the idyll / they suck from the idyll	lievi o grosse (7) light or large
l'idillia la piccola cosa la cosina (14–15) the idyll the little thing / the thingy	seduzioni censure (9) seductions censorships
Danza orale danza del muscolío di tutta la bocca (16–17) Oral dance dance / of the muscles in the whole mouth	innesti clivaggi (9) graftings cleavages
	in stagione o fuori stagione (10) in season or out of season
	mille linguine e a-lingue (20) a thousand little tongues and non-tongues
	neve nulla e poi a-neve a-nulla (21–2) snow nothing / and then non-snow non-nothing

all leafy and trotting along with green visions / and the frailties and the gracefulness of florets and buds / and—oh the fruits, what fruits, fruitage / and—oh the little hills, soft to bring to one's nose to smell / to assimilate as that old I did.He ridicules the way in which, in the vein of Éluard, the landscape was assimilated to woman and love, suggested by the terms 'assimilare' above and 'similitudini' and 'similitudine' below:

>   . . . un pleonastico straboccante
>   canzoniere epistolario d'amore

. . . a pleonastic overflowing / collection of love lyrics love letters

>   grande libro verissimo verosimile e simile,
>   grembo di tutte le similitudini: gremito di una
>   sola similitudine
>   sola similitudine

great most true book likely and alike, / womb of all similitudes: packed with one single similitude

>   non le chantage mais le chant des choses,
>   con crismi eluardiani fortemente amorosi

>   ('**Possibili prefazi IV**')

not the singing but the song of things, / with strongly loving Éluardian chrisms.

Whereas in **DIP** a love for the moon indicated a romantic commitment to Nature (see page 1), the poem '**Profezie III**' is in praise of Nino, an eighty-year-old selenographer of Zanzotto's region who holds sessions at his home during which he and his friends study the moon in a *practical* way:

>   Nino, la piú bella profezia
>   non può mettere boccio che nei clinami di Dolle,
>   dove tu, duca per diritto divino
>   e per universa investitura,
>   frughi gli arcani del tempo e della natura,
>   . . . . .
>
>   . . . nelle tue cantine
>   presto ci troveremo in compagnia—che sum
>   mit!—
>   sceltissima e con cento e cento 'ombre'
>   conosceremo sempre piú profonde
>   le profondità del tuo valore

>   ('**Profezie III**')

Nino, the loveliest prophecy / can only bud on the slopes of Dolle, / where you, duke by divine right / and by universal investiture, / search the mysteries of time and nature, / . . . / . . . in your cellars / we will soon find ourselves in the most select company /—what a summit!—and with hundreds and hundreds of glasses of wine / we will more profoundly acquire an ever deepening knowledge / of the depths of your worth.

'**Possibili prefazi IX**' actually quotes from **DIP** where Zanzotto was expressing his communion with the land—a feeling now dismissed as pretentious and laughable. Leopardi's 'A Silvia' ('To Sylvia') is sacrilegiously echoed, whereas in **DIP** the poet was fervently imitated as part of an attempt to restore the importance of past poetry:

>   Nel risibile giaccio, nella pretesa.
>   Astuzia di far posto al pretendente
>   al promesso: 'non sa parlare—che per
>   conoscere—
>   il proprio oscuro matrimonio—con il cielo e le
>   selve'.
>   Natura natura che non realizzi poi
>   quel che prospetti allor, quale puzzo, purezza di
>   natura

How ludicrous, how pretentious I am. / How cunning to make room for what was expected / and promised: 'he cannot speak—but to acknowledge—/ his own dark marriage—with the sky and the woods'. / Oh Nature nature, you who afterwards does not carry out / what you previously advance, what a stink, the purity of nature.

Attention is now diverted from the beauty of the landscape and focused instead upon the beauty of language: the archaic title, *La Beltà* is a reference to the first as something now obsolete, and an allusion simultaneously to the second. Beautiful effects can, as Zanzotto says, 'perhaps' issue from the word if it is used, as I have shown it to be used in this collection, as a many-sided crystal, a 'lingua-rubino' ('ruby-language') generating more words and a number of meanings:

> non sta il punto di equilibrio mai là: non apporsi
> accingersi
> a te bella, beltà

the point of equilibrium never lies there: not in an affixing a wrapping of oneself / around you, oh lovely, oh beautiful one

> non sta nel cammino esemplare
> di un Soligo

it doesn't lie in the exemplary path / of a Soligo

> non sta in quell'apprensione superante
> fumi e refoulements favori e guizzi

it's not to be found in that overwhelming apprehension / mists and repressions favours and flickers

> ma forse sta nel rubino

but perhaps it's to be found in the ruby

> lingua-rubino
>
> ('**Possibili prefazi VII**')

ruby-language.

The qualifying 'forse' in the quotation above surprisingly implies that Zanzotto has doubts. And the doubts are not limited to doubts about whether his self-generating language is a 'beautiful' one. The very fact that Zanzotto writes not one poem but five denouncing the values of **DIP** makes the reader suspect that he cannot completely discredit his early Hermeticism. These suspicions are well-founded for there are intermittent suggestions in the 'Possibili prefazi' sequence and sometimes elsewhere that Zanzotto has not severed his links with Hermeticism; that he cannot help feeling in spite of himself that **DIP**'s poems were authentic and relevant.

Some poems display a loving closeness to Nature:

> B—Petali verzure oro Asolo ovunque:
> intanto per questa sera
> non turbare l'assetto.
>
> ('**Possibili prefazi IX**')

B—Petals greenery gold Asolo everywhere: / in the meantime just for this evening / do not disturb the order.

And **DIP**'s Éluardian woman who was part of the landscape (epitomizing the poetry 'behind' or within it) and over which Zanzotto once sentimentally 'drooled', is now pursued and invoked when in danger of vanishing:

> azzurro
> piú azzurro sui monti, ricche
> d'infinito le colline dove
> cercavo te sbavavo scalciavo.
> E mi torni con spessori
> di nascite e d'amori, nel terrore
> del tuo svanire, che non è terrore
>
> ('**Profezie XI**')

blue / more blue on the mountains, the hills / are rich with the infinite where / I used search drool and kick for you. / And you come back to me with the thickness / of births and loves, amidst the terror / which isn't terror, of your vanishing.

Indeed in '**Retorica su**' Zanzotto finds fault with some of **LB**'s revolutionary poems for he sees them draw near to the forbidding area of politics. Part 3 of this poem condemns political rhetoric: it has a dangerous ability to arouse heated emotion, and to bewitch. It confuses reality with its contradictory arguments, and it signifies nothing while pouring out words:

> Oh retorico amore
> opera-fascino

Oh rhetorical love / spell-work

> Ardeva il fascino e la realtà
> conversando convergendo
> horeb ardevi tutto d'arbusti
> tutto arbusto horeb il mondo ardeva

The spell burned and reality / conversing converging / horeb you burned full of burning bushes / all a bush horeb the world burned

> questa espressione è la punta di diamante
> del retorizzamento, lo scolice della
> sacramentale contraddizione

this expression is the diamond point / of rhetorical speech, the scolex of / sacramental contradiction

> una sola parola che diceva
> e diceva il dire
> e diceva il che. E. Congiungere. Con.
>
> ('**Retorica su**')

one word alone which spoke / and it spoke the speaking / and it spoke the why and the wherefore. And. To join up. With.

The passage, as indicated, ends with the words 'E. Congiungere. Con.' Zanzotto is tacitly acknowledging that his revolutionary poems bear an affinity with political rhetoric. They too have often functioned on the rhetorical principles of 'contradiction' and 'addition'. The language of these poems was called a 'lingua-rubino' ('**Possibili prefazi VII**'); now political rhetoric is called a 'punta di diamante'. In the section above Zanzotto is condemning political rhetoric for its ability to fascinate; in the sixth and final section of **'Retorica su'** he avows to his own use of language for the very same purpose:

> Quelle sarebbero state le parole finali
> ma . . . Ancora il fascino?
> Il fascino e il principio

Those would have been the last words / but . . . Fascination still? / Fascination and the beginning.

The poem ends with an indication that it has not ended as such, reinforcing thereby this principle of fascination:

> L'azione sbanda si riprende
> sbanda glissa e

The action scatters picks itself up again / scatters glides and.

Zanzotto, it would seem, is accusing himself of a degree of untruthful sensationalism. This sensationalism undoubtedly had a large part to play in his provocation of 'outrage' in the logocentric reader, as is testified by a line from **'Profezie I'**: 'non mancare allo show, né poi allo show dei piccoli oltraggi' ('Do not miss the show, nor the show of the little outrages').

The use of paradox and contradiction in *LB* is therefore not limited to individual poems. The poet's impudent parody of a logocentric tradition is occasionally beset with recantations and doubts. The fact that these doubts are strewn through the work and not bundled together into one of its sequences, helps only to intensify the impression of conflict. This conflict of ideas then intentionally jars with the architectural structure of the work as a whole (Agosti 1972, 217), to create yet another form of paradox.

Paradox is what is upheld in the end. Zanzotto refuses to make sense of his contrary allegiances to a traditional poetry with logocentric persuasions and to a revolutionary poetry destroying the concept of a logos. The variance is left in Zanzotto's mind in just the same manner as it is left in the book—in the disparate form of a 'collage':

> No, non respingo, non accetto.
> Lo sottopongo come tanti a
> un—creduto possibile—collage

> **('Possibili prefazi IX')**

No, I do not reject, I do not accept. / I submit it like so many others for / a—believed to be possible—collage.

The last poem in the collection reinforces this idea:

> . . . torno
> senza arte né parte: ma attivante

> **('E la madre-norma')**

> . . . I return / with neither art nor part: but activating

> **('And the Mother-Norm')**

To adhere exclusively to one school of thought necessarily implies the rejection of another. Zanzotto is 'attivante' because he refuses to be biased: more creatively 'free' on account of his tolerance. Paradox, in the collection, points toward poetical freedom.

All the same, paradox, of its nature, is opposed to logocentrism, since a serious commitment to it must necessarily include a paradoxical sense of the paradoxical. The doubter cannot be sure even of his doubt, of the validity of his word doubting his word. In this sense Zanzotto is paradoxically consistent.

Select Bibliography

EDITIONS OF ZANZOTTO'S WORKS

POETRY

Dietro il paesaggio (Milan: Mondadori, 1951).

Elegia e altri versi (Milan: La Meridiana, 1954).

Vocativo (Milan: Mondadori, 1957).

IX Ecloghe (Milan: Mondadori, 1962).

La Beltà (Milan: Mondadori, 1968).

Gli sguardi i fatti e senhal (Pieve di Soligo: Tipografia Bernardi, 1969), republished, Milan: Mondadori, 1990.

A che valse? (Milan: Scheiwiller, 1970).

Pasque (Milan: Mondadori, 1973).

Filò (Venice: Edizioni del Ruzante, 1976).

Il Galateo in bosco (Milan: Mondadori, 1978).

Mistieròi (Feltre: Castaldi, 1979), now included in *Idioma*.

Fosfeni (Milan: Mondadori, 1983).

Idioma (Milan: Mondadori, 1986).

PROSE

Sull'altopiano (prose 1942-54) (Venice: Neri-Pozza, 1964), now included in *Racconti e prose*.

Racconti e prose (Milan: Mondadori, 1990).

SELECTED EDITIONS

Poesie (1938-1972), ed. S. Agosti (Milan: Mondadori, 1973).

Selected Poetry of Andrea Zanzotto (a bilingual anthology), ed. and trans. R. Feldman and B. Swann (Surrey: Princeton University Press, 1975).

Abbreviations

DIP: Dietro il paesaggio (*Behind the Landscape*) *DIP* 1, *DIP* 2 and *DIP* 3 indicate the three sections into which the book is divided.

IXE: IX Ecloghe (*IX Eclogues*)

LB: La Beltà (*Beauty*)

'Possibili prefazi': 'Possibili prefazi o riprese o conclusioni' ('Possible prefaces or refrains or conclusions')

'Profezie': 'Profezie o memorie o giornali murali' ('Prophecies or memories or placards')

VCT: Vocativo (*Vocative*)

With the exception of *Filò* and *Idioma,* the emphases in the quotations from poetry and prose are all mine, as are all the English translations. I have tried to keep the translation of Zanzotto's works and their punctuation as close as possible to the Italian. These translations are literal, and in no way attempt to reproduce the literary qualities of the originals.

Dana Renga (essay date 1999)

SOURCE: Renga, Dana. "Irony and the Aesthetics of Nostalgia: Fellini, Zanzotto and Casanova's Redemption." *Quaderni D'Italianistica* 20, nos. 1-2 (1999): 159-90.

[*In the following essay, Renga examines the importance of Zanzotto's poetry in Federico Fellini's film* Casanova.]

I.

This essay is about the encounter of a poet and a film-maker, and their mutual interest in an aesthetics of nostalgia that might be neither regressive nor reactionary but, rather, critical and ironic. Nearly two years after beginning production on *Fellini's Casanova,* Federico Fellini wrote to Andrea Zanzotto, soliciting his collaboration on his most recent film. "Dear Andrea, . . . I'm writing to you now, a bit hesitant, because deep down I do not really know what I want and hate to bother you. My intention is confused, I have no idea whether my proposal is achievable" (*Peasants Wake* 5). Fellini asked the famous poet from Pieve di Soligo—who would return to assist the director with *E la nave va*—to compose Venetian dialect poetry as background to two of the most visually and verbally poignant sequences of the film: the ritual of the Venetian Carnival which frames the film and Casanova's encounter with the circus giantess Angelì in London. Despite his evident aversion to and possible distrust of the film-world,[1] Zanzotto expresses his im-mediate interest in the project (Sillanpao 296), an attraction that stems from Zanzotto's growing concern in experimenting with dialect as well as his admiration of Fellini's work, especially his sophisticated and complex use of the soundtrack.[2]

Fellini and Zanzotto are members of the same generation, a generation that matured as Fascism developed and grew stronger; their birthdays are just one year apart, 1920 and 1921 respectively. In their life's work,[3] they both went on to explore and actively contest fascism both as a political regime and, in Foucault's terminology, a mentality. As Foucault explains in the preface to Deleuze and Guattari's *Anti-Oedipus: Capitalism and Schizophrenia,* Fascism is "not only historical fascism, the fascism of Hitler and Mussolini—which was able to mobilize and use the desire of the masses so effectively—but also the fascism in us all, in our heads and in our everyday behavior, the fascism that causes us to love power, to desire the very thing that dominates and exploits us" (xiii). Fellini's films and Zanzotto's poetic texts destabilize fascistic constructions of power—whether they be political, social, or gender based—and in doing so offer up alternatives that are devoid of the necessary signifiers that could aid in constructing a "fascist" consciousness. Fellini's most obvious deconstruction of a collective fascist consciousness can be found in his film *Amarcord,* a film that looks back—as is clear from the title meaning "I Remember"—on the fascist experience in terms of personal lore and obscured memory. Zanzotto's specific recollections of fascism are fewer and connected with war. The landscapes of his earlier collections such as *Dietro il paesaggio,* represent a country grown tired by the devastation of the war. **"The Infirm Love of Day"** gives space to that which has survived the war, yet still remembers its tragedies and impressions: "The cemeteries dark deluges / have gathered the smell of rubble" (*Selected Poetry* 61).

Yet as artists, Zanzotto and Fellini both combat fascistic oppression on multiple levels that have to do with the survival, re-emergence and expansion of totalitarian and dehumanizing tendencies even after the collapse of "historical" fascisms and the emergence of a postmodern society. They share, for example, a profound interest in how, in contemporary society, the individual becomes controlled by consumer media. This theme and concern emerge in the moral and intellectual depravity of Fellini's Roman jet-setters of *La Dolce Vita* as well as his later depiction of the hyper-media cosmos of *Ginger and Fred.* In Zanzotto's ironic prologue to the poem **"Yes, the Snow Again,"** the child abandons any interest in ontology, play and wonder, choosing to latch on to the material products that can be obtained at the local drug store: "'Are you glad you came into this world?' Child: 'Yes, because there's the 5 and 10'" (**II.** *Selected Poetry* 215). Fellini and Zanzotto's interest in the ontological impact of the contemporary hyper-consumerist postmodern age is particularly evident in the representation of Casanova's character. Zanzotto points this out while answering Sillanpao's inquiry regarding reading the film as a "rebuttal to the consumer sex of contemporary cinema" (304). Zanzotto explains his allegiance with Fellini, continuing that he felt Fellini was right to create an archetypal character rather than a "human-historical personage." Zanzotto feels that Casanova's character is bound to the present, and instead of interpreting him as the representative of love/*eros,* Zanzotto feels that he approximates more closely death/*Thanatos.* He explains that death in this sense is productive as "it holds *eros* in counterpoise," continuing that in the film "there is a luxuriant filiation of images charged with so many nuclei of mythologies in formation" (Sillanpao 305). Fellini as well sees his project as a study not specifically in death, but in non-life, and he explains that he wants to tell the story of: "un uomo che non è mai nato, le avventure di uno zombi . . . un <italiano> imprigionato nella ventre della madre" (*Fare un film* 176). Both Fellini and Zanzotto view Casanova as a work in formation, whose ontology has explicit repercussions into the world of the present. Fellini and Zanzotto's encounter with Casanova represents an attempt to revisit a cultural emblem, revitalizing it and offering fresh perspectives on the problems of cultural, linguistic as well as gender representation in a postmodern era.

II.

The name "Casanova" resonates with multiple descriptive adjectives: lover, seducer, philanderer, womanizer, don juan. The exploits of an important literary and cultural figure of the Enlightenment are often thus boiled down to an over-stereotyped and free-floating sexual prototype.[4] *Fellini's Casanova* deals directly with these multiple associations, grappling with these images in an attempt to furnish some dimension of depth to the cliché while at the same time exploiting it and deriding it. Fellini chooses to re-represent Casanova as an artist in exile in search of a more profound meaning for his chaotic existence and who ultimately most secretly desires to return "home." In the course of this problematic portrayal, Fellini explores several of the recurrent themes so common to his opus, particularly the role played by memory and myth in constructing the historical subject, including the idea of the mythical female who acts as both a terrifying agent of castration and a source of artistic inspiration. In fact, Fellini's treatment of Casanova is so self-conscious that the historical adventurer ends up being an icon for Fellini's ultimate concern, the complex processes of aesthetic self-representation. Furthermore, Casanova's proverbial voyeurism, his eroticism of the gaze and the look, make him a perfect (if uncanny) embodiment of the scopophiliac aesthetics of cinema.

Criticism of Fellini's film has focused primarily on the director's "love/hate" relationship with the historical Casanova, which resulted in, as many reviewers have pointed out, a highly negative and subversive depiction of the legendary lover.[5] Despite Fellini's strong apparent prejudice against both the historical Casanova and age of the Enlightenment to which Casanova belonged,[6] Fellini's interests, as a few insightful critics have noted,[7] are not that shallow. Although Fellini's representation has been judged reductive and static, this is far from a legitimate description of the film. Indeed, Casanova's character illumines a space of activity and self-evolution that not only challenges century-old associations of gender determinations, but also offers a reevaluation of the character's place within a literary as well as a cultural tradition. Fellini's success in his interpretation is due in part to his ability to reinvent Casanova.[8] His choice of Donald Sutherland to interpret the role of the Latin lover is the first, and possibly most evident, step towards a self-conscious deconstruction of the stereotype. When Fellini is asked by an American producer from Universal Studios why he chose to make Casanova into a "zombie," the director comments:

> Looking at the big face of that fine megabucks American, who made a pile of films with Gary Cooper, Joan Crawford, Huston, Billy Wilder . . . I didn't know what to answer. I stammered something about the amniotic sac, Casanova locked in the amniotic sac of a prison-mother, mother-Mediterranean-lagoon-Venice, and of a birth continuously postponed, never achieved: 'Casanova—I concluded, blurting it out—was never born. His is a non-life, understand?'
>
> (*Federico Fellini: Comments on Film* 205)

Fellini's image of Casanova as a non-evolving, non-developing character becomes chrystallized in the face, gestures and voice of Sutherland, an actor who interprets a character lost among the backdrop of an historical timeframe of which he cannot, despite various attempts at self-proclamation, become a part. Fellini chose Sutherland not only because he contrasts so conspicuously with the American stars mentioned above, but also precisely because his physical attributes so obviously contradicted the image of the cultural icon: "The true motive of my choice is precisely the 'lunar' face of Sutherland, totally estranged from the conventional image that people have of Casanova: the Italian with dark, magnetic eyes, raven hair, swarthy complexion, the classic type of Latin lover, in short, his archetype. And therefore the operation that I want to perform with Casanova, of estrangement, or overturning the traditional model, is precisely this."[9] Rather than reinforcing the prototypical gender icon of Italian masculinity embodied by Casanova in the popular imagination, Fellini chooses to defamiliarize the character as much as possible. Donald Sutherland's Casanova searches for a sense of life and identity not through his proverbial "male" qualities, but instead through his multiple defining encounters with figures of maternity and womanhood to which Fellini alludes in the passage quoted above.

Fellini's rendition of Casanova is one of multiple possible models of representation of the "original" literary figure. In *Simulations,* Jean Baudrillard explains the implications inherent in simulating a copy of an original source that does not really exist. Fellini's postmodern depiction, being itself a replication of a non-existing original model, is not less "real" than its original. Baudrillard explains: "All the possible interpretations, even the most contradictory—all are true, in the sense that their truth is exchangeable, in the image of the models from which they proceed, in a generalized cycle . . . [and] . . . in fact power, genuine power, no longer exists, and hence there is no risk of seizing it or taking it over" (32-33). Fellini's depiction is in effect based less on the historical figure of Giacomo Casanova (1725-1798) than on the constellation of imaginary clichéd meanings that has been constructed around his mythic image. It is precisely this distance and difference from the "original source" that allows for a deconstructive reading of Fellini's text, a reading that details insight and promotes reflection into a self-consciously estranged reproduction. This perspective discloses the shortsightedness of those critics who have attacked the film's lack of realism and/or absence of an historically valid interpretation of the literary figure. In addition, and most importantly, Fellini's film is also remarkable from a gender perspective, for it points to the fallacy of gender and power relations that were traditionally associated with Casanova as a cultural icon. Fallacies of male power, virility and absolute reason become apparent as Fellini's reproduction weakens the "authorial" role of previous models, whether the model is the historical figure himself, or the aura of masculinity and rationality that has been attached to the famous name for multiple generations. Thus, the film implicitly articulates a critique of Enlightenment rationality as based on an exclusively masculinist reason that, like Casanova in his popular mythic image, objectifies, seduces, exploits and finally debases all that is feminine.

The film's beauty and originality lie precisely in the self-conscious artifice of the multiple simulations that are presented throughout the work. These "reproductions" might be evidenced in the physical and intellectual qualities of the artist himself or also in the explicitly unrealistic replicas of the many locales visited during the exile's travels to Venice, Paris, Parma, London, Rome, Switzerland, Dresden, Wurtëmberg or Dux. The film demands an acknowledgment of these forms as illusory in order for the viewer to perceive the infinite distance from "historical" truth and meaning. This semiotic duplicity is presented at the very beginning of the film, as the viewer is warned early on to avoid a literal reading of Fellini's representation of

Casanova's character, not to mention of the screen's visual and verbal signs. At the beginning of the Venetian Carnival sequence, the initial verbal utterance directly contradicts the visual image. The title scene is composed of a reflected image of Venice in the waters of the canal, a likeness that is accompanied by Nina Rota's eerie and unstable soundtrack. The title "*Fellini's Casanova*"[10] is then superimposed on the reflection on the water. The title signifies the artist's re-appropriation of the historical Casanova, but the image and sound also suggest that this re-interpretation is as unstable and inconstant as the fluidity of water. The camera then cuts to the evidently artificial recreation of Venice that includes an improbably compressed representation of the Rialto, St. Mark's and the Campanile. Immediately after the music fades and before the title disappears, the words "true form, true essence"—the beginning of Andrea Zanzotto's dialect poem **"Recitativo Veneziano"**—are heard off-screen. It is an ironic juxtaposition, for obviously the set design of the Grand Canal is far from an accurate historical representation. The viewer is cautioned to question notions of "essence" and "truth." Fellini's "truth" then resides precisely within the very process of simulation, and in Benjaminian terms, the farther that the copy is distanced from its initial source, the less obliged it is to depend on the semiotic coding that shaped the original's form.[11] In the seemingly utterly artificial world of *Fellini's Casanova,* the rational scientific character so typical of Enlightenment philosophy is replaced by the vision of a self-doubting and unstable protagonist, realism is replaced by the hyperreal, and mythic stereotype is destabilized and reinterpreted. Ironically, it will be precisely the artifice of Fellini's re-creation that will allow life and form to be given to what would otherwise be a vapid caricature.

Casanova's first appearance in the film alludes precisely to this sense of duplicity and questionable self-identity that Fellini explores so profoundly throughout his film. During the chaos of the carnival sequence, the viewer hardly notices a man masked as Pierrot—a descendent of the *Commedia dell'arte* character Pedrolino—who appears three times throughout the sequence. By choosing to dress as Pierrot, Casanova presents himself as a clown, someone who is forever unlucky in love, and is often the victim of mockery and derision. Hence, the Latin lover himself performs a type of auto-critique, thus preparing the viewer for a less virile and masculine and more vulnerable and powerless version of his own image. This image is furthered when Casanova is shown in his cell of the Piombi prison—he is unclean and discontent, with his costume still hanging from his back. Despite his multiple boastings to the high court, he is unable to present himself as a serious literary or scientific figure, and his tattered and torn costume reminds the viewer of his own vulnerability. Casanova's initial visual ambiguity has much to do with the rapid pace of the Venetian carnival sequence—which lasts less than 4 minutes and is comprised of 44 shots—as the Pierrot figure is present in only six shots. In his initial appearance, Pierrot brings a scimitar to the doge so that he may "cut the placenta," so beginning the ritual of birth accompanied by the rise of a goddess head out of the Venetian lagoon. He is then seen standing amongst the crowd, and finally he is delivered a letter. In the visual pandemonium of quick cuts—the average shot lasts about 5 seconds—chaotic camera movement, alternating camera angles, objects such as masks that literally intrude into the foreground of the frame and flamboyant use of color and extras, the viewer is not meant to notice this character's presence, let alone ponder his significance.

It is not until the next sequence, at the beginning of Casanova's encounter with the nun Maddelena, that Pierrot removes his mask, exposing against the lightning-filled sky in striking profile the physical attributes least associated with the mythical icon of Casanova: a pallid gaunt face, hollow eye sockets with small unimposing eyes and a generous sloping forehead. This presentation points towards Fellini's interest in "unmasking" the cultural figure, while at the same time cautioning the viewer to avoid literal interpretations of visual and verbal cues. Fellini's film begins with an unmasking, but as in Pirandello, illusion and reality are often conflated as the removal of one mask signifies the appropriation of another, as self-identity is both unstable and continually in flux. Pirandello comments on mask as symbol, proposing the instability and fluctuation of individual identity and discussing the difference between personal projection and appearance:

> Ciascuno si racconcia la maschera come può—la maschera esteriore. Perché dentro poi c'è l'altra, che spesso non s'accorda con quella di fuori. E niente è vero! Vero il mare, sì, vera la montagna; vero il sasso; vero un filo d'erba; ma l'uomo? Sempre mascherato, senza volerlo, senza saperlo, di quello tal cosa ch'egli in buon fede si figura d'essere: *bello, buono, grazioso, generoso, infelice,* ecc."

(*L'umorismo* 156)

Pirandello's discussion of ontological multiplicity mirrors the construction of many of Fellini's male protagonists including *La strada*'s Zampanò, *La dolce vita*'s Marcello, *8?*'s Guido and of course, Casanova.

Elements of uncertainty and self-reservation are reinforced by the mise-enscène of Casanova's "seduction" of Maddelena, a sequence that follows immediately the Carnival scene and is filled with elements of voyeurism and performance. The setting for their tryst is replete with disjointed and blurred mirrors and the architecture is itself disordered, as the small hideaway is composed of a long hallway and a main circular entry way connected to another circular bed chamber. Casanova's image is reflected in the thousands of mirrors, which become themselves fractured and divided, echoing the disarray of Casanova's psyche. A further element that adds to the multi-faceted interpretation of the lovers' acrobatics is the presence of Maddalena's lover, the Ambassador De Bernis, who has been hiding behind the bed-chamber the whole time, watching the two through the eye of a painted fish. After their performance, and subsequent "approval" by the Ambassador, Casanova attempts to assert his intellectual qualities, but, as Marcus points out, an extreme close-up "of the empty socket confirms our worst suspicions—the voyeuristic eye that rivets itself on Casanova's erotic performance is 'blind' to the artist's higher gifts of intellect and taste" ("Adaptation by Self-Projection" 213). In just the first few moments of the film, Casanova has come across as the fool Pierrot, a sought-after and over-amplified sexual performer as well as a dismissed diplomat, scientist and engineer. None of these incarnations should be taken at face value, as each one merely alludes to one of the multiple qualities of Casanova's character.

The manipulation of point-of-view, the presence of the multiple mirrors as well as Casanova's clear and self-conscious positioning as spectacle in the Maddalena encounter constructs Casanova's sexuality as essentially scopophiliac. As such, it conspicuously doubles the scopophilia of narrative cinema as defined by Laura Mulvey. In "Visual Pleasure and Narrative Cinema," Mulvey discusses scopophilia in mainstream cinema as a system of repression and projection on the part of the audience, allowing for a projection of their own "voyeuristic fantasies" (17) onto the actors while simultaneously identifying with the projected "male" image and fetishizing the female protagonist. In that Casanova's performance is so deliberately staged, the audience has no possibility of either identification or fetishization, and therefore Fellini's film deconstructs Mulvey's notion of identification, and instead places the viewer in the position of critic.

The aesthetics of Fellini's film reinforce the character's multiplicity and artificiality as the film's visual images and verbal cues are consistently presented as being in discord with realist cinema. *Fellini's Casanova* is laden with various sophisticated technical devices that rupture the formal conventions of cinematic realism. The film foregrounds dream sequences, narrative voice-overs, flashbacks, intrinsic editing as well as a highly repetitive musical score, which turns from diegetic to extra-diegetic with hardly a warning. All of these elements interact so subtly that traditional rendering of space by film and of film language itself are transcended at virtually every moment. Films, or parts of films, which rupture formal cinematic coding are described by Gilles Deleuze in *Cinema 1: The Movement Image* as "Any-space-whatevers":

We have passed . . . from physical space to spiritual space which restores a physics (or metaphysics) to us. The first space is cell-like and closed, but the second is not different, it is the same in so far as it has merely discovered the spiritual opening which overcomes all its formal obligations and material constraints by a theoretical or practical evasion . . . *Space is no longer determined, it has become the any-space-whatever which is identical to the power of the spirit,* to the perpetually renewed spiritual decision; it is this decision which constitutes the effect, or the "auto-effection," and which takes upon itself the linking of parts.

(117)

Rather than draw attention to the film's lack of realism, these technical elements allude to a space of heightened signification. Examples of these multiple filmic elements include ornate costumes, markedly simulated set designs, obsessive reliance on an unstable first person point-of-view narrative and repeated use of allegorical symbols such as the Venetian goddess head, the mechanical bird or the various forms of water throughout the film.[12] Such elements should be classified as more than simply "Felliniesque" as these manifold technical devices enhance the rhetorical nature of the film, and overdetermine the aesthetic investigation into the compound building-blocks that constitute the "spirit"—to borrow Deleuze's terminology—of a man who is essentially an artist in exile.

III.

Loss, nostalgia and exile are passionately foregrounded in the scene of Casanova's famous escape from the Piombi prison. It is here, as Marcus notes, that the sense of artistic "nostalgia" can be felt at its strongest. Marcus states that this is "the richest source of that nostalgia which so typifies the film's poetic mood" ("Portrait of the Artist" 32). Upon escaping the prison, Casanova is forced to abandon Venice, his home, and to be in continual exile. This scene aligns the audience with Casanova's perspective not only through his voice-over narration, thematizing his grief, but also through the point of view shot as he surveys the city. At this moment Casanova is now a definitive exile, robbed of his primary counter of self, the city of Venice. In the film Casanova actually spends one evening of "real time" in the city of Venice before he is put in prison, in the rest of the film, Venice is literally behind him. The source for the nostalgic tone of this scene, however, is problematic as although Casanova does yearn for his metaphorical homeland throughout the film, the notion of "nostalgia" itself becomes deconstructed as the idea of origin itself is undermined—and with it originality. This is apparent in the film as there is nothing "real" to be nostalgic for: Fellini's Venice is perpetually represented as artifice and simulation, a simulacrum that is so distanced from the model that there is no chance of reapproximation. Baudrillard explains the role of nostalgia and origin in *Simulations*:

When the real is no longer what it used to be, nostalgia assumes its full meaning. There is a proliferation of myths of origin and signs of reality; of second-hand truth, objectivity and authenticity. There is an escalation of the true, of the lived experience; a resurrection of the figurative where the object and substance have disappeared. And there is a panic-stricken production of the real and the referential.

(12)

The city that Casanova mourns is represented in terms of lack, lack of original presence, suggested in fact by Casanova from the rooftop as non-recognition when he does not recognize his object of sight: "I had never before seen Venice from so high a vantage point, and I found it hard to recognize my beloved city, which I was being forced to abandon, forever." Casanova's exile marks the beginning of his journey through a figurative landscape of metaphor and symbol. Casanova, and with him Fellini, strive to regain the lost origin through various forms of aesthetic re-representation whether they be recollection, voice-over, flashback, dream, and subconscious symbolism.

One of the most subtle ways in which the thematics of nostalgia is furthered by the Piombi escape scene is by the score, strangely and for the only time in the film composed of the film's main musical themes. As Casanova peruses Venice from the rooftop, the music begins. An instrumental motif is heard that was previously present in the opening credits and which will return to be the theme music of Rosalba, the automaton whom Casanova calls his perfect creation. As the shot of Casanova's point of view begins, the tune becomes combined with an instrumental version of the second poem that Zanzotto composed at Fellini's request for the film, **"Cantilena londinese."** These two main musical themes accompany Casanova's encounters with some of the film's most important female protagonists. In each case the themes help qualify Casanova's personal and artistic journey as a painful return—to refer to the etymology of "nostalgia" itself—towards a sense of past identity, continually approximating that sense of "home" which Casanova yearns to re-accomplish throughout his journeys.[13]

The emotional yearning present in the Piombi escape sequence can be understood by reviewing what Fellini intended the **"Cantilena"** to achieve. A brief history of the inclusion of Zanzotto's two poems within the film will be helpful in illustrating their effects upon the protagonist. In a letter to Zanzotto, Fellini first describes the effect he wants to accompany the appearance and subsequent disappearance of the goddess-head in **"Recitativo veneziano"**:

Like every ritual that, in order to become a liberating element, needs to feed on an enkindled psychic force expressed in verbal or mimetic formulas, so too the emergence, the appearance of the dark female simu-lacrum, should be accompanied by proprietary prayers, repeated pleas, seductive sounds . . . a gamut of uneasy skepticism to exercise the dreaded failure of the event.

(*Peasant's Wake* 4-5)

He continues to describe the desired consequences of the encounter with Angelì, the giantess, who sings **"Cantilena londinese."**: "The locations, the situations, the atmosphere in which the meeting takes place, the very aspect of this extraordinary female incarnation make up that mosaic of childish shudders, painful, fabulous and terrifying, which most emblematically defines Casanova's neurotic relationship with women, i.e., with something obscure, engulfing, overwhelming" (5). The effect Fellini desires for the dialect poetry is to verbalize Casanova's impossible relationship with the female, qualifying his seemingly linear journey through the bodies of his female conquests as a circular attempt to return to the infantile and the guttural. As a result, the functions of Casanova's female conquests were to appear much more dubious than they seemed as their characters become shrouded in doubt, fear and loss.

Zanzotto is a follower of both Heidegger and Hölderlin and as such adheres to many of their insights into the nature of the written word. In "Hölderlin and the Es-sence of Poetry" in Heidegger states: "Poetry is the establishment of being by means of the word" (281). Zanzotto's poetry, both dialect and otherwise, explores universal origins of language and (being the Lacanian that Zanzotto is) as such human "Being" regardless of the contemporary desire to objectify existence as an historical fact. In the same essay, Heidegger suggests that it is possible to discern the "essence of poetry" (270) within Hölderlin's poems. Heidegger states that Hölderlin, through his poetry, ". . . determines a new time. It is the time of the gods that have fled *and* the time of the god that is coming. It is the time of *need,* because it lies under a double lack and a double Not: the No-more of the gods that have fled and the Not-yet of the god that is coming" (289). Heidegger's poet is a displayer of meaning in a godless world, someone who has the ability to demonstrate manifold layers of universal and historical Being and to subsequently show this investigation to the public. The poet operates in a world without order—whether divine or otherwise—with the intention of writing in order to let things be in their complexity.

Like Hölderlin, Zanzotto writes in a godless era, but, as is also the case with Hölderlin, he is not a pessimist. Within Zanzotto's poetry nothing is fixed, most of all his use of language, but that does not mean that all will lead towards chaos. Rather, the human element of being in the world, at a number of levels, finds a way to exist within the pandemonium of over-signification. Zanzotto

expresses his sentiments regarding the individual's rela-tion to the excessively crowded contemporary world that teems with an overabundance of ciphers and symbols in a prose statement that acts as an introduc-tion to his poetry in *The Favorite Malice*:

It seems that for quite a while it has no longer been a question of word or silence or of related betrayals: there's too much stuff that sizzles and cracks, on pyres or not, . . . or else just *sits there,* not having anything to do with, at a stalemate with, the <full moon> impudence . . . Today it seems that everything has gone into gelatin, an excellent one, made of chicken, or perhaps the plasma of daily drippings of blood . . . It feels as if we are in gel, not in Cocitus or in Swanson: in something that is more . . . Comfortable?

(135-136)

Zanzotto then determines that the philosophical debate regarding the relationship between silence and the word is no longer an issue that can be studied in contemporary culture. The above mentioned "gelatin" has infiltrated the space in between these two components, and as such all possible forms including history, philosophy, biography, pop culture etc. become part of this relativ-ized substance.

Zanzotto's "gel" approximates Baudrillard's discussion of the negotiability of truth in postmodern culture that is inundated with hyperreal simulation. Baudrillard's discussion in *Simulations* posits that the motivations of, consequences for and truths behind such seemingly disparate phenomenon as ethnology, Disneyland, Water-gate, media culture and war are all relativized. In the postmodern world of the hyperreal there is no original source or symbol that is motivated by or that motivates the model, all is interconnected without origin or destination. Zanzotto's idea of "gel," as well, is made up of every possible source, whether from the past, present or future, as does his poetry. Zanzotto's poetic lexicon, however, attempts to navigate through the impasse of the hyperreal, seeking out origins presumed lost and unretrievable. Hierarchical distinction has no place within Zanzotto's poetic glossary, as within his lyrics he proposes a relative cosmos that leads towards awareness and integration, not sublimation and fragmen-tation. In his poetry he combines the incongruous, whether languages, grammatical structures, allusions, citations or symbolism, yet, much as within Fellini's films, where the viewer/reader would expect to find disorder, there is instead a comfortable zone of ontologi-cal exploration foregrounded by redolent aesthetics.

The choice of dialect over codified language in the poems commissioned for the film strengthens the effect, exemplifying a desired return through the postmodern "gel" towards the pre-symbolic. In a sort of afterward to his poem **"Filò"** Zanzotto expresses his thoughts on the signification of dialect:

Dialect, all things considered, is an absolute freedom, capable of tracing consistent/mutable limits . . . [it] . . . poses itself like a "first mystery," which escapes every possible contemplation as well as every objectifying detachment . . . Dialect is felt as coming from a place where no writing exists . . . nor "grammar": the location, therefore, of a logos that remains always *erchómenos* (coming), which never freezes in a slice of event, which remains almost infantile even in its speaking, which, at any rate, is far from any throne.

(88-90)

For Zanzotto, dialect implies a space of non-signification, the inconstant nature of the linguistic subject, of a type of primordial existence before the advent of grammatical codification. As Zanzotto makes explicit in one of his most well known poems, **"L'elegia in petèl"** from *La beltà,* dialect alludes to a wish to return to the pre-symbolic[14] and the elusive feminine,[15] an image which has a strong presence not only in *Fellini's Casanova* but also in *Amarcord, La Dolce Vita, 8?* and *The City of Women.*

Julia Kristeva's notion of a linguistic "Revolution" in "Revolution in Poetic Language" could be applied to Zanzotto's use of language, in particular his employment of dialect. Kristeva argues that specific types of modern poetic language penetrate and undermine the ideological, social and/or political constraints of contemporary society. In going "through" language rather than analyzing it psychoanalytically or scientifically, it is possible to tap the "Semiotic *Chora*" which is "neither model nor copy, the *chora* precedes and underlies figuration and thus specularization, and is analogous only to vocal or kinetic rhythm" (453). The *chora* is inherently maternal, a womb-like space of creation and destruction; it is, like Zanzotto's dialect, a domain of pre-language and the pre-symbolic that continually threatens to override the symbolic order, and therefore must be regulated and kept in check by the very symbolic order that it threatens. When poetic language succeeds in liberating the *chora,* the subject becomes aware of society's restrictions, and rather than being governed by civilization and its laws and symbolic structures, she/he becomes a "subject in process," aware of her/his place within the social order and therefore capable of resisting governing discourses of power.

As dialect is predominantly an unrecorded form of communication with no prior written referent, it is emblematic of the poet's desire to reconcile the self with the world of unconstrained signifiers—which in Fellini and Casanova frequently proliferate in the sexual domain. Zanzotto's poetry speaks of a world of overabundance and excessive signification. Within such a universe it would seem possible that individuality could become lost. Instead, it is within the inconstant nature of the world and language that poetic subjectivity is avowed.

Zanzotto pronounces the constitution of being regardless of the multifaceted presence of the other; reconciliation with the world/word of and in desiring language is the perfect receptacle for the affirmation of the ontological principle. Hence, the multi-faceted presence of Zanzotto's dialect poetry within Fellini's film helps qualify Casanova's personal and artistic journey as a "painful return" through the overabundantly loaded present towards a sense of past identity that continually approximates that sense of "home" which Casanova yearns to re-accomplish throughout his travels. What Casanova yearns for, however, is not his actual home, the city of Venice itself, but an imaginary homeland, or rather a homeland of the imaginary. Throughout the film Venice is represented as an intangible and unreachable entity, continuously exemplified as a city of artifice and reflection, conjured up in dreams and flashbacks. What Casanova truly seeks is Kristeva's semiotic *chora,* the place of absolute being with the (m)other, and that is the place of his true "origin."

IV.

Casanova's imaginary homeland, or "Venice," is often displaced onto the female characters and icons of the film. Frank Burke discusses the relationship between Casanova's much sought after women and his nostalgia for his own birthplace, concluding that Casanova is performing a "process of substitution as home becomes woman becomes Casanova's seemingly endless pursuit and loss/abandonment of women." (224) These multiple references to female characters and/or icons and their subsequent loss include the goddess head from the Venetian carnival episode that reappears at the end of the film as mysteriously as it disappears in the opening sequence. As the carnival sequence comes to a close, the immense emblem representing the tie between Venus/Venice or *eros*/homeland sinks out of sight, lost, but not forgotten. There is also the giantess Angelì whom Casanova encounters at the circus in London who is herself in a type of exile from the mountains around Venice, and who sings Zanzotto's lullaby **"Cantilena londinese."** Then, when Casanova encounters his mother at the opera in Dresden, he asks after news of their Venetian relatives, a question that is left unanswered. Finally, there is also the ultimate female experience, according to Fellini at least, that is captured in the automaton Rosalba. This encounter alludes to the Pygmalion myth, and therefor to the goddess Venus, and so Casanova's relationship with Rosalba allows him to attempt again to approximate a representation of his birthplace.

I will now go on to analyze these revealing and moving sequences in which Casanova has his most profound experiences with questions of femininity and sexuality: These relationships are constructed to reinforce unusual, strange or foreign elements in Casanova's habitual eroticism, as these figures are often associated with castration, regression and lost innocence and youth. These elements all contribute to de-eroticize the typically voyeuristic dimension that characterizes Casanova's exploits, with the aging Casanova rejecting the scopophilic elements he indulged in earlier in so many escapades. Thanks to these key experiences, it becomes clear that sexual desire is deeply implicated with questions about individual origin and absolute power.

A central instance linking many aspects of the visual and poetic tropes of the film is the appearance of the circus performer Angelì, who sings **"Cantilena londinese."** Angelì is associated with the goddess head at the beginning of the film. Both disappear as mysteriously as they appear to Casanova. Both represent love and earth. The head is addressed as both Venice and Venus, and Bondanella points out that this coupling ". . . establishes the link in Fellini's film between Casanova's birthplace (Venice) and the ancient goddess of love (Venus)" (310). The head is called "vera figura," and "vera natura" and is described as "futuro nostro." Both figures have childlike qualities as well, as Angelì is shown with her dolls, and in Zanzotto's poem **"Recitativo veneziano"** the goddess head is referred to as "putina perla, putina unica" who promises future gifts: ". . . chissà dopo / cossa che la ne dona." Most importantly, both are figures of loss in that the goddess head disappears in the beginning of the film, and Angelì withdraws herself from Casanova's life as enigmatically as she entered it. Fellini's goddess head represents a Venice that, like Thomas Mann's some years later, is in decline, approximating its demise and literally fighting to remain above the water. This perception of Venice is echoed in Fellini's letter to Zanzotto, in which Fellini describes "the kind of sub-aqueous iconography that characterizes the film," as "the placental, amniotic image of a decomposed and shifting Venice of algae, mossiness and musty dank darkness" (*Peasants Wake* 6). Fellini, and with him Zanzotto, present an image of a city that resists advancement and assists in postponing its own birth. Much like Casanova himself, who continuously searches out his own origins throughout the film in order to revert to earlier stages before the advent of symbolic implication, and not solely systematically advancing in his life, the goddess head is wedded to aqueous images of degeneration and regression.

The goddess head as described in Zanzotto's dialect poem represents the very moment when language itself becomes aware of its inability to last, endure and promote consistent meanings and reactions. In "The Symbolic Order" from "The Function and Field of Speech in Psychoanalysis," Lacan discusses the problematic relationship between the spoken word and that which it references:

> Through the word—already a presence made of absence—absence itself gives itself a name in that moment of origin . . . And from this pair of sounds modulated on presence and absence . . . there is born the world of meaning of a particular language in wwhich the world of things will come to be arranged. Through that which becomes embodied only by being the trace of a nothingness and whose support cannot thereafter be impaired, the concept, saving the duration of what passes by, engenders the thing.

(65)

A discussion of the scene in which the goddess head appears to the city will assist in illustrating the connection between language acquisition and the symbolic implication of the goddess head. As the head is slowly raised from the water, its significance as a crucial symbolic icon for the city of Venice is made clear. As the reader of **"Recitativo Veneziano"** begins reciting Zanzotto's poem in the film, the crowd collaborates and cheers him on. In stating "we are you, you are we," the evident desire of the Venetians to create a future sense of cultural identity based on the representative of eros/motherland is made clear. Visually, the scene weds the fate of the onlookers to that of the goddess head by repeatedly cutting from the head as it is raised from the pale green waters of the canal to the crowds of observers—in the brief scene, the camera swwitches between the goddess head and the spectators nine times. Upon realizing that the attempt to raise the head is doomed, the camera zooms out from a medium shot of the goddess head, and then in the following scene a similar zoom of the crowd on the Rialto is present, strengthening the connection between the emblem and the mass. As the crowds disperse, one woman exclaims "It's a disaster, an evil omen! Make the sign of the cross, bless yourselves . . . We'll never see her again!" In this way the woman reiterates not only the goddess head's symbolic signification, but also her spiritual consequence. Finally, after she sinks below the waters, there is a concluding shot of her bright white eyes that stand out amongst the murky blue-green backdrop of the sea. There are no sounds from above the surface, and all that can be heard are the bubbles she emits as she settles into her subaqueous realm. In Lacanian terms the silence that engenders this brief moment represents the inability of word or image to hold onto and maintain a specific referent. The Venetians hoped that the manifestation of the goddess head would create direction in their lives through both becoming and governing the citizens. After her non-birth, the film moves to a realm of non-language and non-narrative, conscious of the inability to promote unilateral significance. The Venetian dialect in which the poem is written tells of the desire to resist linguistic integration into hegemonic language systems. Fellini's film then advances the notion of reflection rather than action as the failed event once more reiterates the overall thematics of the film: the continual postponing of progress and advancement in positivist terms. In addition, this failed birth and the collapse of the head is actually a type of beheading and hence once again a figure of castration as well as an allusion to the darkest side of the Enlightenment.

Angelì is initially presented as a figure of both salvation and castration for Casanova. Her presence saves him after his inability to perform sexually resulting in an over-staged suicide attempt in the Thames. Angelì disrupts the pomp of his suicide attempt with a slight laugh, and this introductory act of her verbal utterance heightens the concept of her words being more important than her physical appearance throughout the film. Her presence in this sequence also serves to disrupt and contrast the traditional Italian literary canon, as she diverts Casanova's attention from his citation of Tasso's verses on death: "Deh, vien morte soave, ai miei lamenti, / vieni pietosa e con pietosa mano / copri questi occhi e queste membra algenti" (*Il Casanova* 148). Tasso, and with him Orazio, Dante, Petrarca, and Ariosto (all authors that Casanova hopes to converse with in his afterlife) are all forgotten as Casanova shifts his focus to Angelì, whose literary ramifications have no place in the traditional canon of Italian literature. Thus, Angelì represents a form of castration of the Italian canon in that her presence "cuts off" Casanova's interest in his so-called fathers. Castration is a leitmotif associated with Angelì: she publicly humiliates, disempowers and emasculates Casanova, for example, when she beats him at arm wrestling after he begs her to let him win. She is also shown in flashback in a large cage-like wrestling ring, where she swiftly defeats every man who challenges her to a match. Metacinematically, she is also associated with castration when Casanova searches for her by entering the great whale "Mona"—meaning literally "cunt"—a name borrowed from Zanzotto's **"Recitativo Veneziano"** in the opening sequence of the film. During Casanova's quest, images of the *vagina dentata*[16] are projected on the side of the great whale, thematicizing a mythical fear of female sexuality as something that consumes the man, a trope that is reinforced as a close-up on the last of these images appears literally to call Casanova's name, beckoning the protagonist into its snare. Casanova's encounter with such a castrating image of female power comes only briefly after he has been already publicly "castrated" by the Charpillon women, who threaten to publicize his most recent lack of virility. This encounter then leaves him feeling worthless, and almost leads him to take his own life. The whale Mona, and with her Angelì, are constructed as universal figures of woman. Mona is all that creates and destroys in the world. She is a "burier", a white sugar mountain, a furnace where all—including all of the men that line up to enter into her—is consumed. The circus announcer tells us that "Out of Mona explodes the world with the trees and the clouds and the races of man and Mona has come out of Mona as well." Through Mona the female gender is endowed with absolute power (including self-generation), castration and control. Just before Angelì defeats Casanova in

arm wrestling, he notes her accent and asks after her origins. She states that she is a Venetian, from the mountains, and we later find that she too is in a type of exile from the mountains around Venice, as she has been sold by her husband "like a circus animal." The arm wrestling scene is crucial in constructing Angelì's identity for the spectator. Up until that scene, and during part of it, she is cloaked in mystery. She is a veiled woman, and her physical identity does not become apparent until she speaks for the first time, asking "what are you trying to do" when Casanova begs her to let him retain his honor. Thus, her physical presence and female power for Casanova as well as the viewer are strictly tied to her origins, and not to her sexuality, as was the case with many of Casanova's previous conquests.

A close textual examination of the scene which includes Zanzotto's **"Cantilena londinese"** will assist in illustrating my point. This scene is comprised of seventeen shots and is constructed in a way that emphasizes what could be called the "spectacularity" of the film. As Casanova opens the tent to begin spying on Angelì, **"Cantilena londinese"** begins. Angelì is constructed as an unaware spectacle for the viewer as well as for Casanova. The sequence includes point of view shots from Casanova's perspective as Angelì prepares for and takes her bath. The presence of the dolls throughout the sequence simultaneously reinforces the theme of the song which is a lament for lost innocence and youth and contributes to de-eroticizing the act of voyeurism. A parallel could also be drawn between the audience, Casanova, and the dolls themselves, who are all positioned to be "looking" at Angelì in the tub: all three act as voyeurs with Angelì as object. As evident in the comparison between two of the shots, Casanova then leaves the opening of the tent, and with his exit the audience adopts his former perspective. Through this manipulation of perspectives culminating in a close-up on Angelì's face, the viewer is implicated as voyeur and as such is forced to rethink Casanova's experience. Formerly constructed as sexual performer *par excellence* in the scene with the Monaca and in the competition for the best sexual performer, Casanova now inexplicably walks away from a spectacle that has the makings of a sexual adventure. Consequently, the viewer, too, questions whether we have understood his motivations. Mulvey argues that film is a medium which creates and reinforces desire through objectifying the threatening female characters.[17] The logic of Mulvey's theory of castration anxiety does not comply with the film's montage as this scene is constructed so that the viewer experiences voyeurism as a self-reflexive and de-eroticized act. This scene is constructed to reinforce a foreign element in Casanova's habitual eroticism. The aging Casanova rejects the scopophilic elements which he earlier indulged in so many escapades, especially in his first sexual exploit with the Monaca. As he leaves the tent and falls into a deep sleep, the audience senses that sexual desire is deeply implicated with questions of individual origin and thwarted fantasies of absolute power.

The desired regression inherent in Casanova's contemplation has as its source Zanzotto's lullaby **"Cantilena londinese,"** which is sung in Casanova's dialect and accentuates the nostalgia attached to the loss of innocence and youth. The lullaby combines nursery rhymes with poignant images of sexual and emotional maturation with a desire to regress to the simple life of a little girl. The poetic subject desires to return to childhood before "le nosse," symbolizing lost innocence that, in Lacanian terms, signifies language acquisition after entering into a hegemonic system (the symbolic) that leads towards social integration into pre-established norms. Angelì sings roughly one-third of Zanzotto's lullaby within the film, and her diegetic song is composed of multiple verses taken from the majority of the nine stanzas of the original poem. The original dialect poem is divided into four primary sections, each comprised of two stanzas except for the first section that includes an extra introductory stanza paraphrasing the nursery rhyme that inspired the poem. The initial stanza of each section is 5-17 lines in length and describes either the activity, physical qualities or emotional distress of the poetic subject while the second stanza is a two to four line lament, ending in the refrain "che jeri la jera putéa" ("of the girl who was a child only yesterday"). The style and vocabulary are simple and contained, with minimal punctuation—in the 67 line poem there are only six dashes, five commas and one period, question mark and quotation—while the verses are replete with anaphora, alliteration, hyperbaton and general repetition of both individual words and phrases. These stylistic qualities endow the poem with a highly lyrical and sonorous quality, and Zanzotto himself explains his motivations for these specific stylistic selections: "As soon as Fellini let me see the film, which at that point was only filled with blocks of sound, my ear immediately sensed the initial phonic-rhythmic motifs coming into being. Thus, the sing-song motif, no? . . . Finally, certain phonic-rhythmic suggestions came to me after long walks in the marshlands around Venice . . . hints of sounds which then became lodged among my daily sounds back on dry land" (Sillanpao 301-2). The lullaby then was inspired by Fellini's visual interpretation of Casanova's encounter with Angelì as well as originating specifically from the *terra materna* that Casanova perpetually searches out.

The nursery rhyme that begins the poem is a slightly revised popular lullaby, composed of many untranslatable neologisms. The content of the first section of the poem flows well with the introductory rhyme as it addresses the images previously associated with Annamaria: innocent childish games of needlepoint and dress-

up. The second section, however, includes multiple innuendoes of sexual maturation as well as voyeurism as the poetic subject is constructed as an object of desire for an external viewer. The stanza begins with a question "Pin pidin / cossa gastu visto?" ("Pin pidin / what have you seen?") that is answered in an eight line response highlighting the physical attributes of a young girl on the verge of corporeal development. Interestingly, variants of the word "questo" begin or are present in seven of the eight lines,[18] heightening the physical presence of the young girl's material qualities. She is initially portrayed as vulnerable as she is presented in the diminutive without any clothes on: "'Sta piavoleta nuda" ("This naked little doll"). Further references to her soft skin—"'sta pele lissa" ("this silk-smooth skin"),—her breasts—"'ste rosete" ("these rosettes") and "'ste suchete" ("these little pumpkins")—and her sexual organs—"'sti pissigheti de rissi" ("these tiny curls that tickle") and "'sta sfeseta" ("this little slit")—accentuate her exposure to an external eye. The thematics of looking are reinforced as the young girl is described as actively gazing at her soon to be lover: "'sti oceti che te varda fissi / e che sa dir 'te vói ben'" ("these eyes that watch you intently too / and seem to be saying 'I love you'". Although the girl is described as in control of the gaze, this is not the case as the repetitive external description allows her no objectivity. Rather, the initial question of the stanza, "cossa gastu visto?," is never answered as her gaze is appropriated by the object of her apparent declaration of love, similarly to the way Casanova's gaze becomes appropriated by the audience within the film. The final stanza of this section references the young girl's nuptials, immediately followed by the refrain of lament of forfeited purity: "che jeri la jera putéa." Thus, sexual maturation directly leads to social integration and deprived youth.

In the third section of the poem, rather than being described externally, the poetic subject is given a voice to express her despondency and dissolution following her initiation into the sexual world of the symbolic. As she is initiated into the world of language she acquires her own voice in order to question the construction of her own ontology. The poem states: "te serco inte'l fogo inte'l giasso / te serco e no ghe riesso / te serco e no ghe la fasso." ("I search for you in ice and fire / I search for you but never find you / I search for you and can't go on"). What is being searched for is the origin of the self and of one's own language. Within Zanzotto's poetry as well as Fellini's film, self-realization cannot be boiled down to sexual conquest on behalf of an over-stereotyped sexual prototype. Rather the poetic/filmic subject must travel through a landscape obscured by symbols and interpretations, continually approximating the unattainable, yet never abandoned, objective. The apparent resignation within the search ("te serco e no ghe la fasso") is annulled through repetition, and the journey of the poetic subject does not end when the destination appears obscured. Rather than symbolizing finality and escape, sleep and death are both presented within the stanza as a form of regression and anticipated return: "chi mi fa dormir / chi mi fa morir / tuta pa'l me amor / chi me fa tornar." ("who makes me sleep / who makes me die / all for my love / who makes me return"). These sentiments can be evidenced within the film during Casanova's encounter with and abandonment by Angelì.

Two stanzas later, in the fourth section, the seemingly futile search continues through, within and behind the signifier: "te serco drento inte'l masso / te serco fora dal masso / te serco te serco e indrío sbrisso" ("I search for you in the bouquet / I search for you outside of the bouquet / I search and I search for you and I slip behind.") These lines reference Zanzotto's first collection of poetry, *Dietro il paesaggio,* in which the poet searches for sense and meaning not within the signifier, but behind it as he investigates the ontology of experience as a continual process of creation and renewal within the natural world. The "mazzo," or "bouquet" of the search references the unfulfilled promises associated with the wedding bouquet, while the following four lines, all beginning with "chi," longingly remind the reader of the delusion and disappointment associated with the expulsion from the presymbolic. The last four lines of the poem intimate a return to the realm of fairy tale, play and the make-believe: "i xe zoghessi de la piavoleta / le xe le nosse e caprissi di chéa / di chéa / che jeri le jera putèa." (this is the make-believe of the little doll / the wedding and the whims of the girl / of the girl / who yesterday was a child at play." The search is not relinquished, for the poem takes on an utopian dimension, as the games of the present may attempt to re-approximate the innocence of the child expressed by the imperfect "jera/was." The poetic subject—either within the lullaby, Angelì or Casanova—continues to travel through the world of language, continually approximating the illusory "homeland" of Kristeva's semiotic *chora.*

The lullaby has a profoundly ironic and estranging effect upon Casanova. The thematics of nostalgia, regret and loss inherent in the lullaby belong as much to Angelì's narrative as to Casanova's. Casanova identifies with the young girl of the lullaby whose uncomplicated actions and simple desires ironically contradict many of Casanova's extravagant sexual scenarios and convoluted orations. Rather than represent the traditionally "masculine" qualities of sexual and literary imperialism associated with the myth of Casanova, the "Cantilena" succeeds in feminizing the cultural figure. Zanzotto's poem is an example of *l'écriture féminine* in that it literally tells the story of the female body. In writing the body, the lullaby gives voice and space to an arbitrary and evolving subject-in-process rather than a rational and finalized gender stereotype. As Hélène Cix-

ous explains in "The Laugh of the Medusa," in writing herself, the subject "will return to the body which has been more that confiscated from her, which has been turned into the uncanny stranger on display" (350). Casanova's performative sexuality has no place in his encounter with Angelì, rather the feminized protagonist gives up his position as voyeur, allowing himself instead to sleep, dream and regress.

It is in the Angelì scene accompanied by Zanzotto's poem that Casanova seems, albeit temporarily, to transcend the limited meaning of his erotic nature so aptly described by his friend Egard in the tavern. After entering the great whale Mona, Casanova runs into Egard and tells this seemingly belligerent friend that he "prefers to travel in the real world." Egard's response reaffirms the above-mentioned notion of the linear nature of Casanova's exploits: "But your travels take you through the bodies of women and that gets you nowhere." Thanks to his encounter with Angelì, Casanova is not depicted as a sexual conqueror *per se*; rather he is allowed a brief moment to contemplate the nature of his own ontology. It is precisely within Casanova's interaction with Angelì that the human element of being in the world, at a number of levels, seeks to find a way to exist within the pandemonium of oversignification of visual and verbal systems.

V.

Casanova's ultimate distance from his own origins is most poignantly demonstrated in his surprise encounter with his own mother at the opera in Dresden.[19] As the opera ends, Casanova bows to the royal box, and becomes as Marcus states, "transfixed by this image of inaccessible glamour" ("Adaptation by Self-Projection" 215). As the opera house suddenly empties and the lighting fades, the massive candelabra fall and are ritually spent, and Casanova remains in the opera house, the final witness to what could be looked at as the end of yet another failure in his proclaimed political, social, scientific and/or literary career. The thematics of disappointment following Casanova's sexual relations is not uncommon in the film, in fact more often than not Casanova's sexual exploits are followed by feelings of inadequacy (in his relationship with Maddalena the nun and her lover De Bernis), loss (for example is his relationship with his "true love" Henriette, who abandons him shortly after their meeting), embarrassment (following his impotence with the Charpillon women) or, in the case of the orgy in Dresden, melancholy.

After Casanova finds himself to be completely alone in the opera house his mother surreally appears in one of the boxes, whispering his name and laughing dissonantly. Their conversation is disquieting and uncanny in that the distance and difference between mother and son are repeatedly emphasized. Not only does he barely recognize her—Casanova states "Mama, can it be you?"—in addition the audience soon discovers that Casanova has not even bothered to look her up, knowing full well where she currently resides. Their conversation as well further demonstrates Casanova's current sense of self-doubt and rejection as he attempts to explain to his mother that he is in Dresden on business: "I am here on business, a project of mine, the minister himself is very interested in, an entirely new invention of mine. Excellent . . ." His confident statement is decidedly interrupted and ridiculed by his mother who counters: "Ah you haven't changed I see, always bragging about your ridiculous ideas." Visually Fellini puts Casanova in his place as well, as his mother is shot from a low angle in extreme close-up, while he is presented through a medium shot at low angle. His mother then is one more in a long string of critics to question Casanova's "higher talents." Casanova's reunion with his mother does not bring him closer to that sense of self-identity and home that he has continuously sought out throughout the film. Rather, the mother becomes an enigma that perhaps holds an interpretive key to Casanova's long and complex relation with the female other. This difference is thematized by her multilingual discourse—she speaks French, Italian as well as German—that at some points in their conversation is unintelligible to Casanova. As he poses more questions to her about her deceased husband, current residence and their relatives in Venice, Casanova becomes visually and verbally different. He is no longer the braggart, pompous adventurer of many previous encounters such as at the dinner parties at either the Marquise D'Urfé's salon in Paris or at Du Bois' residence in Parma. Rather, his voice is strained and tinged with concern and his gaze is concerted and contemplative.

Her ultimate and unbridgeable distance is most powerfully demonstrated when Casanova carries her to her coach on his back, in an image that deconstructs the notion of stable parental "foundation."[20] This image also alludes to the extremely uncanny nature of Casanova's relationship to not only his mother, but also to Annamaria, Rosalba, Angelì and the goddess head—all of which painfully remind him of his homeland. His mother is both "familiar and old—established in the mind and . . . alienated only through the process of repression" (Freud. "The Uncanny" 241). Their final visual exchange forces Casanova to confront his own repressed fears of death and old age as her concluding image reminds Casanova of his approaching fate: through the clouded glass of the carriage, his mother appears much older than her years, yet with her curled white hair, pale skin and concave eyesockets she resembles Casanova remarkably. When she does take leave of Casanova, her carriage disappears into a snowy, barren and dismal landscape while her son is left to look on after her, seemingly moved by their chance meeting. This final visual image is accented by the presence of the subtle, whistling wind that will reappear after Casanova's "seduction" of Rosalba as well as in the final sequence of the film. This representation shares many affinities with not only Casanova's point-of-view shot as he searches for Angelì amidst the remains of the vague and dreary deserted circus, but also during his final vision of a frozen and oneiric Venice. Following Casanova's encounters with the most significant female agents in his life, the visual imagery of the film links with his psyche, echoing his feelings of coldness, introspection and loneliness. Through this process of externalization, Fellini allows Casanova to project his feelings to the viewer, creating sense and giving meaning to his continual struggle for approval and acceptance.

As Casanova ages and that sexual prowess which had always classified his reputation—regardless of his continual and oftentimes failed desire to assert his more dignified attributes—degenerates, he turns towards a third type of female entity to achieve sexual and emotional fulfillment. The first type is represented by the women who were lost as soon as than they were attained. It is these, who abandoned him, who apparently had the greatest emotional and psychological impact upon him: Henriette, Isabella, Angelì, his mother. The second type of sexual encounter which did not have such an effect, had an undeniably scopophiliac flavor: as is clear in his encounters with Maddelena the nun, in Mdm. D'Urfé's impregnation ritual, in the sexual competition in Rome and the orgy with the acting troupe in Dresden. The ultimate female experience, according to Fellini at least, is captured in the automaton Rosalba. Of course this encounter alludes to the Pygmalion myth. After dancing with Rosalba—his final "seduction" in the film—Casanova wonders whether she had an incestuous relationship with her creator.[21] This "uncanny" relationship does not simply serve to reinforce Casanova's narcissism and desire to continually objectify his sexual conquests as has been commonplace with many of his earlier relationships. More importantly, his relationship with Rosalba—who could be thought of as the ideal object—allows Casanova to attempt again to approximate a representation of his birthplace. Pygmalion's statue, which was later brought to life by Venus, was of Venus herself, and this intertextual reference reinforces the protagonist's desire to re-create the idea of Venus/Venice that has eluded him throughout his exile.

Casanova's relationship with Rosalba represents his desire to regress to an earlier existential condition in order to ward off his own death. His choice to recite Petrarch's sonnet 292 to the doll as he places her on the bed is telling of his desire to prolong his ever-fleeting mortality. Casanova recites only the first 7 lines of the sonnet, those which praise Laura's beauty that turns the poet's temporal world into a heavenly paradise: "Gli occhi di ch'io parlai sí caldamente, / e le braccia, e le mani, e i piedi, e 'l viso, / che m'avean sí da me stesso diviso, / e fatto singular da l'altra gente; / le crespe chiome d'òr puro lucente, / e 'l lampeggiar de l'angelica riso / che solean fare in terra un paradiso." Were he to continue his recitation, line 8 of the sonnet resonates with morbidity as all of Laura's beauty has turned to dust after her death: "poco polvere son, che nulla sente." The final two tercets reinforce Laura's demise, addressing the plight of the poet left alone to continually mourn her loss throughout his desperate, hopeless existence. In his relationship with Rosalba, Casanova is able to adopt the verses of Petrarca that suit him, and ignore those that evoke his own mortality. In the *Canzoniere* Petrarca's Laura is the object that mediates the poet's desire. As a signifier she enables him to investigate that which he consistently seeks: himself projected in language by means of aesthetic creation. Along the same lines, Casanova's relationship with Rosalba allows him to project himself as an artist and breather of life into another being. This becomes clear during their sexual encounter as Rosalba comes to occupy the cinematic position typically held exclusively by Casanova. In his sexual encounters with Maddelena, Annamaria and Mdm. D'Urfé, the camera is positioned below Casanova, and he is shown from a low angle, framed in the center of the screen. Moreover, during these encounters, he is utterly isolated from his counterpart, and after the sexual act is almost never shown in the same frame with her. Rosalba, however, with Casanova's help, adopts his former position as well as relation with the camera. This scene thus becomes a mirror image of many of the other sexual scenes throughout the film. Here after the sexual act, the two are united in the same frame, for the only time in the film, suggesting a more intimately bound relationship between Casanova and his sexual "conquest." Casanova moves on to study his indistinct and blurred reflection for the first time throughout the film in the cracked and dusty mirror, an act that intimates a rare sense of self-contemplation and regret rather than self-promotion. In his old age, the protagonist has finally seemed to acquire both a sense of humanity and a degree of self-reflection.

Of course, Casanova's relationship with Rosalba brings out one of the most ironic elements of the film: his attempt to hold onto his ever-fleeting mortality through his re-found virility only points towards his impending death. The following scenes strengthen this trope as he has aged considerably, is depicted alone, is relegated to eating in the kitchen with the servants at the Castle of Waldentsein and is ridiculed by both his peers and a group of young courtiers. Casanova's encounter with Rosalba, like many of the female simulacra throughout the film, results not in Casanova's integration and realization, but in estrangement and difference. Paul de Man defines these qualities of irony in "The Rhetoric of Temporality:"

> The act of irony, as we now understand it, reveals the existence of a temporality that is definitely not organic, in that it relates to its source only in terms of distance and difference and allows for no end, for no totality. Irony divides the flow of temporal experience into a past that is pure mystification and a future that remains harassed forever by a relapse within the inauthentic.
>
> (222)

In his relationships with Rosalba, Annamaria and his mother—all characters connected to his imaginary homeland—Casanova realizes, albeit temporarily, the temporal division that presents his past/Venice/the womb as a mystified distant space of the pre-symbolic and his future/death/desired return as a journey through the present that is over-laden with signs and symbols of loss.

VI.

Throughout the film Casanova constantly searches for the "elusive feminine," which could give meaning to his life and facilitate his integration into a cosmic order. His search leads him to travel continuously and performatively through the bodies of women. And this, as his friend Egard states, gets him nowhere. In the scenes accompanied by the film's main musical themes, reflective rather than physical experience is heightened, as though to suggest that it is a privileged means of returning the artist to the spiritual home from which he has been exiled. The last few episodes of the film at the Castle of Dux reinforce Casanova's sense of exile, as he is simultaneously ridiculed and ignored. In the final sequence of the film Casanova recounts a dream infused with images of repressed desires of acceptance and homecoming. It is here that he finds himself face to face with an image of himself as an exile and an aging man who looks back on a representation of his life as an eternal attempt to create himself by distance from his origins, and as Marcus writes, celebrates the act of the artist as creator ("Portrait of the Artist" 33).

In the last moments of the film, Casanova is allowed a final return to Venice, his birthplace. The setting is the same as the opening Carnival sequence, only the space is deserted, the waters of the lagoon are frozen over and the only sound is that of the wind. The silence that fills the scene alludes to a constructed space of memory, regret and nostalgia. The Venetian goddess head is also present in Casanova's final dream, buried but not forever lost, a crystallized memory resisting extinction beneath the unstable ice, much like Zanzotto's beloved dialect as expressed in the poetry of *Filò*. Next, four groups of various personages from Casanova's life—most of whom are women whom he either seduced or lost, including Henriette—all evade him in a series of seven shots. Although Casanova attempts vaguely to follow these manifestations of the unattainable other as they depart, he concludes by watching impotently as these illusory forms surreally disappear or float off-screen. Rather than show rage, embarrassment or despair at their departure (his typical reactions to previous abandonments) Casanova accepts their loss, focusing his attentions on an elaborately decorated gold carriage pulled by four white horses that carries both his mother and the pope (his surrogate father figure) into the center of the frozen canal. Both as signifier and metaphor this carriage is quite different from the carriage that took Casanova's mother from him in the earlier scene. Rather than embodying the coldness and loneliness of imminent death and unbridgeable distance, this carriage originates from the realm of fairy tale and therefore symbolizes happy endings and fulfilled desires. In a scene redolent of the central thematics of Fellini's cinema, Casanova has been given "approval" by both his mother and the pope to dance with Rosalba. Rosalba magically appears in front of the Rialto, in roughly the same location from which the last set of imaginary women vanished. When Casanova encounters Rosalba, her theme music begins, and she turns towards him, beckoning him to dance with her. The musical tone of the final scene intimates a return to the presymbolic. It constructs a poetic space in which the fragmented self transcends objectification, and is capable of existing without asserting itself by objectifying the female other.

Casanova follows Rosalba in her dance and as the pair twirls together on the frozen ice, there is an abrupt cut to an extreme close-up of Casanova's red watering eyes and tensely knit brow that reunites the spectator (both Casanova and the film viewer) with the particular memory. Marcus reads this scene as Casanova's appropriation of the performative and sexual voyeurism that he is previously associated with, and she concludes that Casanova finally realizes that what counts is not the external voyeuristic eye, but rather "the self's view of the self" ("Adaptation by Self-Projection" 224). In addition, and I would argue more importantly, this sequence comments on the possibilities of cinematic invention. Through Casanova's dream/memory, cinema is demonstrated as capable of constructing a poetic space of the imaginary, a poetic space of absolute belonging and re-established homeland. This is clear as the film cuts back to Casanova and Rosalba's dance, and rather than controlling their actions, Casanova forfeits his own creative power, becoming, with Rosalba, himself manipulated by some unseen source as they spin motionless and frozen on an hidden axis. Casanova is now represented as both statue and Pygmalion, only now he chooses not to sculpt out his life as he would like it to be, but rather to accept it as it is, with all of his shortcomings and failures.

Ironically, Casanova has finally found himself to be truly at "home" in a visual space replete with simulacra. Rather than attest to the hopelessness of integra-tion and completion in such a (dis)simulated order, the city of Venice, the goddess-head, Casanova's mother as well as his multiple female conquests including Rosalba all assist in creating, constructing and enforcing a new aura of spirituality and self-acknowledgment rather than delusion. As he approaches his death, Casanova travels within his dreams and memories through the postmodern age of the inauthentic. It is here that he becomes a true ironic subject as he is made aware of the distance between his present self as he approaches annihilation and his subconscious dreams, desires and fears. Rather than reject an image of himself which could be interpreted as an egotistical last attempt to objectify and control his female counterpart, Casanova finally recognizes that the objective of his life-long exhausting search for his origins, although unattainable in the actual present, may be achieved within his own consciousness.

Zanzotto, in *Filò,* links the Venetian goddess head with Angelì, describing the association as a "vera mama," who "fursi che spèta un sposo tant eterno / cofà éla—e che l'è éla Logoz ercomeuoz" (who waits perhaps for a bridegroom / eternal like her—and that is her—, *logos erchomenos*). In the final moments of the film, Casanova is at last ultimately linked with a representation of the eternal feminine—Rosalba, the Goddess Head, His Mother, Venice—that has so often eluded him throughout his life's work and exhaustive journeys. Rather than attempt to manage and make sense of the manifold symbols peppering the screen, the protagonist joins them in their own eternal "becoming," capable of being with the other without the need to dominate or exploit. In this final moment of self-acceptance, Casanova's nostalgia has finally led to the creation of his true aesthetics.

Notes

1. Zanzotto's poem *Filò* actually begins "I'm not talking about movies—/ I'd like to talk about movies—/ I get carried away by movies—/ I'm scared by movies—/ because they fill our brains with bubbles and buds / and almost a poisonous color" (*Peasants Wake* 55). All translations from Zanzotto's collection *Filò* are taken from J. Welle and R. Feldman's translation published as *Peasants Wake for Fellini's 'Casanova' and Other Poems.* Occasionally the translations have been modified.

2. The obvious linguistic challenge of writing not in his own dialect of the Soligo valley, but in a mixed dialect in an historical as well as a geographical sense—Fellini writes that he desires Zanzotto to "restore some freshness to [the Venetian dialect], render it more alive, penetrating, mercurial, keen" (*Peasants Wake* 5)—was also a deciding factor in his cooperation.

3. Zanzotto also actively fought against Fascism during the war as a member of the Partisan Resistance.

4. To the futurist leader F. T. Marinetti, for example, "Casanova" was, along with Cagliostro and D'Annunzio, an emblem of virility, seduction, and aggressiveness, and thus essentially a proto-fascist figure ("Futurismo e fascismo" in *Teorie e invenzione Futurista*).

5. M. Marcus's "Adaptation by Self-Projection" includes multiple references to negative reviews of Fellini's film. They include Andrew Sarris' "*Fellini's Casanova*: Venice on Ice," *Time* 107, May 17, 1976, Stephen Farber's "Casanova: Love's Labors Lost," *New West* 2, January 31, 1977 and Christopher Porterfield's "Waxwork Narcissus," *Time* 109, February 21, 1977.

6. Fellini discusses his feelings towards Casanova's *Memoirs* as well as the '700 in *Fare un film*: "Ma perchè questo soffocante interminabile librone piace tanto agli intellettuali? . . . [T]utte le volte che ho provato a sfogliare le *Memorie* a un certo punto ho dovuto smettere, mi veniva quasi da tossire sperduto e abbondonato in quel polveroso deserto cartaceo" (85); "Dal punto di vista figurativo, il Settecento è il secolo più esaurito, esausto e svenato da tutte le parti. Restituire l'originalità, una nuova seduzione, una visione nuova di questo secolo è sul piano figurativo un'impresa disperata" (175).

7. See M. Marcus, "Portrait of the Artist" and "Adaptation by Self-projection", P. Bondanella's section on this film in *The Cinema of Federico Fellini*, F. Burke's section on this film in *Fellini's Films: From Postwar to Postmodern* and Kevin Moore's article "*Fellini's Casanova* or the Fate of Formalism."

8. In *Fellini's Films: From Postwar to Postmodern*, Burke discusses the differences in representation between the historical figure and Fellini's cinematic invention: "Casanova is not a person or a representation of one: he, like everything else in the film, is an ungrounded fiction produced entirely by his and Fellini's texts" (224).

9. *Il cinema di Federico Fellini* (32), as quoted in M. Marcus. "Adaptation by Self-projection" (206).

10. All references will be to the English dubbed version of the film.

11. "[T]he technique of reproduction detaches the reproduced object from the domain of tradition . . . Aura is tied to presence; there can be no replica of it . . . [T]he singularity of the shot in the studio is that the camera is substituted for the public. Consequently, the aura that envelops the actor vanishes, and with it the aura of the figure he portrays" ("The Work of Art in the Age on Mechanical Reproduction" *Illuminations* 221 and 229).

12. Fellini himself affirms that in part because of his collaboration with costume designer and prop coordinator Danilo Donati, he considers *Fellini's Casanova* and *Satyricon* to be his two most "attractive" films from a visual point of view (*Comments on Film* 187-188).

13. The first page of the original script establishes Casanova's character as melancholic, as his initial voice-over, although omitted from the film, relates his feelings for his city: "I have all four temperaments: the phlegmatic, the sanguine, the choleric, the melancholic . . . Above all I loved my city, ancient and bright, cruel and tender, yielding" (*Fellini's Casanova* 1).

14. In this poem Zanzotto problematicizes the possibility of grasping universal linguistic origins: "Là origini—Mai c'è stata origine" (176).

15. Zanzotto includes a nursery rhyme written in *petèl*, the dialect which mothers speak to their children: "Mama e nona te dà ate e cuco e pepi e memela" (176).

16. Bondanella discusses the importance of the projections of the *vagina dentata* in *The Cinema of Federico Fellini*. He states: "This link of the projection of male sexual fantasies (or fears) to the Enlightenment equivalent of the cinema cannot help but recall Fellini's views on the feminine qualities of the cinema" (315).

17. In "Visual Pleasure and Narrative Cinema" L. Mulvey states:

> In psychological terms, the female figure poses a deeper problem. She . . . connotes something that the look circles around but disavows: her lack of a penis implying the threat of castration and hence unpleasure . . . The male unconscious has two alternatives of escape from this castration anxiety: preoccupation with the re-enactment of original trauma (. . . demystifying her mystery), counterbalanced by the devaluation, punishment or saving of the guilty object . . . or else complete disavowal of castration by the substitution of a fetish object or turning the represented figure itself into a fetish so that it becomes reassuring rather than dangerous.
>
> (21)

18. "'Sta" or "questa" is used four times, "'ste" or "queste" once, "'sto" or "questo" once and "'sti" or "questi" twice.

19. This sequence immediately follows a circus-like orgy whose staging is so elaborate that it almost downplays the sexual act, highlighting instead the performative and theatrical nature of the event. One performance follows another, and as the orgy comes to a close, the scene cuts to the end of the opera in Dresden, staged by the same characters that earlier occupied Casanova's bed chamber.

The music reinforces the evident comparison between the two sequences as a sound bridge is employed, and the equivalent melody associated with Casanova's phallic bird becomes the diegetic music of the opera. Of course, the Wagnerian grandiosity of the mise-en-scène of the opera sequence ironically contradicts the earlier squalor of the orgy sequence, and Casanova literally is put in his place, forced to occupy one of the least prominent sections of the theater.

20. Frank Burke points out: "The notion of maternal origin or 'roots' is visually reversed by the image of Casanova's mother up off the ground, piggyback, 'grounded' by her son" (226).

21. An obvious reference to Freud's "The Uncanny" is present in the Rosalba sequence as the relationship between Rosalba, a beautiful life-size doll, and Casanova is strikingly similar to Freud's retelling of Hoffman's "The Sand-Man." In the story the young man Nathaniel falls madly in love with Olympia, a life-size mechanical doll partially created by the man Nathaniel fears the most—the optician Coppola.

Works Cited

Baudrillard, Jean. *Simulations,* trans. P. Foss, P. Patton and P. Beitchman. New York: Semiotext(e) Foreign Agents Series, 1983.

Benjamin, Walter. "The Work of Art in the Age of Mechanical Reproduction." *Illuminations.* New York: Schocken Books, 1969.

Bondanella, Peter. *The Cinema of Federico Fellini.* Princeton: Princeton University Press, 1992.

Burke, Frank. *Fellini's Films: From Postwar to Postmodern.* New York: Twain Publishers, 1996.

Cixous, Hélène. "The Laugh of the Medusa." *Literary Theory: An Anthology.* Oxford: Blackwell Publishers, 1998.

Deleuze, Gilles. *Cinema 1: The Movement Image.* Trans. H. Tomlinson and B. Habberjam. Minneapolis: University of Minnesota Press, 1991.

De Maria, Luciano ed., "Futurismo e fascismo." *Teorie e invenzione futurista.* Milano: Mondadori, 1968.

Fellini, Federico. *Fare un film.* Torino: Giulio Einaudi editore, 1980.

———. *Il Casanova di Federico Fellini.* Bologna: Cappelli editore, 1977. Translated as *Fellini's Casanova,* trans. C. Cremasco. Portsmouth: Heinemann, 1997.

Freud, Sigmund. "The 'Uncanny'." *The Standard Edition of the Complete Psychological Works of Sigmund Freud, Volume XVII.* Trans. J. Strachey. London: The Hogarth Press, 1953-1974.

Grazzini, Giovanni, ed. *Federico Fellini: Comments on Film.* Trans. J. Henry. Fresno: The Press at California State University, Fresno, 1988.

Harrison, Thomas, ed. *The Favorite Malice Ontology and Reference in Contemporary Italian Poetry.* Trans. Thomas Harrison. New York: Out of London Press, 1983.

Heidegger, Martin. *Existence and Being.* Washington D.C.: Henry Regnery Company, 1967.

Kristeva, Julia. "Revolution in Poetic Language." *Literary Theory: An Anthology.* Oxford: Blackwell Publishers, 1998.

Lacan, Jacques. "Function and Field of Speech and Language in Psychoanalysis." *Ècrits.* New York: W.W. Norton & Co., 1977.

de Man, Paul. "The Rhetoric of Temporality." *Blindness and Insight: Essays in the Rhetoric of Contemporary Criticism.* Minneapolis: University of Minnesota Press, 1983.

Marcus, Millicent. "Fellini's Casanova: Portrait of the Artist." *Quarterly Review of Film Studies,* 5:1 (1980): 19-34.

———. "Fellini's Casanova: Adaptation by Self-Projection" in *Filmmaking by the Book, Italian Cinema and Literary Adaptation.* Baltimore and London: The Johns Hopkins University Press, 1993.

Moore, Kevin. "*Fellini's Casanova* or the Fate of Formalism." *Film Quarterly,* 27:2 (1999): 125-141.

Mulvey, Laura. *Visual and Other Pleasures.* Bloomington: Indiana University Press, 1989.

Pirandello, Luigi. *L'umorismo.* Milano:Arnoldo Mondadori editori, 1992.

Sillanpao, W. P.. "An Interview with Andrea Zanzotto." *Yale Italian Studies,* Fall 2:4 (1978): 297-301.

Zanzotto, Andrea. *Andrea Zanzotto Poesie (1938-1986).* Milano: Arnoldo Mondadori Editore. 1993.

———. *Filò Per il Casanova di Federico Fellini.* Milano: Arnoldo Mondadori editore, 1988.

———. *Peasant's Wake for Fellini's 'Casanova' and Other Poems.* Trans. J. Welle and R. Feldman. Urbana and Chicago: University of Illinois, 1997.

Nicola Gardini (essay date fall 2001)

SOURCE: Gardini, Nicola. "Linguistic Dilemma and Intertextuality in Contemporary Italian Poetry: The Case of Andrea Zanzotto." *Forum Italicum* 35, no. 2 (fall 2001): 432-41.

[*In the following essay, Gardini examines Zanzotto's poetical language, contending that his "final and greatest achievement is an enlargement of the scope of poetry itself through a voracious absorption and manipulation of all available languages."*]

A recurring feature of contemporary Italian poetry, especially of war-time and post-war Italian poetry, is the poet's own meditation on the status and power of his or her language. This results in a constant activity of self-criticism and self-definition, as can be seen in the works of the most outstanding poets of the century: Giuseppe Ungaretti, Eugenio Montale, Mario Luzi, Andrea Zanzotto, Pier Paolo Pasolini, Giovanni Giudici, and Amelia Rosselli. What is striking about these poets' theoretical exploration of literary language as compared to that of other poets from the near past, such as Pascoli or D'Annunzio, is that their new critical awareness not only pinpoints problems of poetics ("what language shall I choose for my potry?"), but also raises a far more unsetting question: "Is there a language of poetry?," ultimately meaning "Is poetry possible at all?" or, as Montale put it, "Will poetry survive the universe of mass-media?"[1]

What is at stake is either a triumphal conquest of the realm of the uppercase Poetry and, as a consequence, an affirmation of the self through it, or a catastrophic defeat of human language as such. Poetry is generally felt to be a quest for language itself, not for a code, and ultimately coincides with the poet's quest for his right to speak, that is his linguistic legitimacy or motivation to speak. This quest is more than a negative awareness of the mutability and the mortality of human language, which is central to the linguistic thought of Western authors, from Horace to Beckett. Nor can this quest be explained away simply in terms of resistance to Fascist censure and political repression—much as Fascism impinged upon freedom of speech and prompted poets to hermetic obscurity, reticence and self-effacement.[2] What an Italian contemporary poet has had to come to terms with, especially after 1945, is an unprecedented mass of conflicting codes, due to both a problematic relation with tradition and to a general adulteration of all given values. This is one of the main reasons why in the 20th century numerous poets resorted to dialect. Not only does dialect seem unscathed from semantic corruption and still capable to express eternal values, but it is generally felt to be an immediately recognizable medium of linguistic originality, i.e. a mark and warrant of poetry. This need for linguistic and formal self-identification originated from the fall of the traditional opposition between the language of poetry and the language of prose. In the 19th century Leopardi is a salient case in point. As is evident in his letters and notebooks, Leopardi's early concerns about lyric poetry are based on, and linked with, a firm acceptance of the classical dualism of prose and poetry. His will to restore one presupposed the necessity to reform also the other: the *Canti,* on the one hand, and, on the other, the *Operette morali*—two different realisations of two complementary but not interchangeable ideas of style and language.[3] The same is true of Manzoni's twofold attempt to reform traditional lyricism in the *Inni sacri* and to create a new linguistic model for prose literature in the *Promessi sposi.*[4] In the 20th century such dualism turns into widespread erosion of all generic specificity and categories. Now the antithetical term of poetry is poetry itself. This is part of a general crisis concerning not just literary writing as such, but the very notion of national consciousness.

The hegemonic power of the English language has contributed significantly to the general crisis and reformation of other national languages, in particular the Italian language. Authors all around the world have given up their native languages for English, and not just where English remains a colonial bequest, in the hope of gaining prestige or at least being more widely read. Not since Latin has there been such a common tongue as English now is. This is true above all of prose, i.e. of fiction or criticism, inherently connected with "narrative" and "communication." Yet even the language of poetry, embedded as it is in the physical body of expression, has called into question, if sometimes unconsciously, the inalienability of its national identity, as is visible, for example, in the practice of Amelia Rosselli's bilingualism. Montale himself purported to give his own poetic language the semantic and sonorous concentration of English one-syllable words.[5] He considered such untranslatable poets as Browning and Hopkins his ideal models. Montale's liking for English poetry is a rather unique instance within the frame of twentieth-century poetry, but doubtless reflects a general tendency of contemporary Italian poets to find their models in foreign traditions, mainly the French one of Baudelaire, Rimbaud and especially Mallarmé.[6] Indeed, the present century witnesses an unprecedented impact of foreign traditions on Italian literature. Montale himself declared that Italy did not have any significant poet after Leopardi, so that a 20th century Italian poet could rely on no recent predecessor, unless he or she looked elsewhere outside Italy.[7]

Tradition (*tradizione*) is thus supplanted by translation (*traduzione*), in the sense of both intellectual adaptation and verbal displacement. Linguistic propagation is no longer a vertical movement, but a horizontal shift between contiguous systems. The metaphorical implications of such a spatial reversal deserves specific analysis. For now I shall limit myself to suggesting that the making of contemporary lyricism is grounded on the dramatic collapse of historical hierarchies and stylistic oppositions. Temporal distance vanishes and makes room for a novel juxtaposition of divergent exemplars. For instance, Leopardi becomes as influential as Mallarmé, Dante or Petrarch.[8] On the other hand, Dante and Petrarch cease to be the patrons of two incompatible ideals of style, as was the case throughout the centuries.[9] To be sure, Dante's presence is more prominent in the poetry where Petrarch's presence is less recognizable (primarily in the Pasolini *oeuvre,* where the paradigm of the *Commedia* legitimates an idea of thorough realism, linguistic experimentation and inexhaustible mimesis). Montale's linguistic richness and sensuality in his first three books certainly, via D'Annunzio and Pascoli, leads back to Dante.[10] But his metrical and formalistic rigour in some sections of *La bufera* deliberately recall Petrarch's stylistic exactitude and, along with this, a rarer version of Dante, the poet of *La vita nova.*[11] Luzi, like all other hermetic poets, clearly harks back to Leopardi and Petrarch, but his indebtedness to Dante's lesson is conspicuous and this is evident as well in some of his critical writings.[12] Opposition gives way to coexistence of alternative options: restoration and reformation; destruction and construction, or dispersion and concentration, for example. Again, Montale is a salient case in point. At a time when Futurism called into question all conventions and rules, Montale started off "under the sign" of metrical and formal regularity. On the other hand, his writing was in itself a rather daring compromise between the old and the new, as is evident in his vocabulary and stylistic devices like rhymes, stanzas, rhythms, and above all in the creation of what he called his counter-eloquence.

Such combination of conflicting modes and forms is brought to an extreme by Montale's most radical, intelligent, and authoritative inheritor, Andrea Zanzotto. In Zanzotto's writing, the central questions I very rapidly highlighted—i.e. the linguistic crisis of poetry, the quest for a poetic language and a continuous swing between integration and disintegration—take on most alarming features and tones. His need of a language for poetry brought him, at the beginning of his career, to adopt the style, by then used-up and even passé, of the hermetic poetry of the Thirties. Hence the cold, abstract and even enigmatic vocabulary of his early poems. His first collection of verse, **Dietro il paesaggio** (1951), supported by such outstanding patrons as Ungaretti and Montale, was published in 1951. A mysterious solitude of the self, unable to express its presence in the "here and now" and almost dissolving into the natural forms of a mute and unintelligible countryside, is the constitutive theme of those poems. Suffering becomes the overpowering element in the next collections. The traditional aspect of Zanzotto's early texts cracks up and falls (**IX Ecloghe,** 1962). Words are scattered, raped, broken, and made up, and lines are misplaced, twisted, splayed, fragmented. All idea of syntactical order collapses. The self gives up all hope of being fully reflected in natural language or of identifying natural language with the barbaric expressions of neo-capitalistic everyday language, which is compromised with the worst crimes against mankind and guilty of destroying the identity of beauty and truth (especially in **La Beltà,** 1968). Zanzotto's idea of the self finds the closest and ultimate representation of its mutilated and impoverished state in the destruction of conventional language, i.e. tradition,

communication, all disciplines of human knowledge. His poetry comes into being by way of demolition. From this point on, his writing is a sea of flotsam and jetsam, from which occasionally emerge desperate yet obstinate islands of regularity. These are tragic attempts to retrieve an illusion of order and beauty, and to sustain belief in an ideal of linguistic and aesthetic integrity. Thus, destruction gives way to stylistic restoration: Zanzotto then resorts to a prestigious and normative form like the sonnet (in **Il galateo in bosco,** 1978); or he uses native dialect (**Idioma,** 1986). He even turns to the imitation of infantile sing-song (called "petèl," in **La Beltà**). Zanzotto has thus become a fierce guardian of folklore and oral culture, drawing the attention of an exceptional film director like Fellini, who asked Zanzotto to compose rhymes for some pagan rituals portrayed in his film *Casanova* (**Filò,** 1976).

Zanzotto's poetry, while protesting against cultural oblivion and anthropological decadence, has become a repository of local memory through a process of cultural archaeology which resembles Seamus Heaney's activity of digging. Its starting point was a compelling need of poetical language. Its final and greatest achievement is an enlargement of the scope of poetry itself through a voracious absorption and manipulation of all available languages. Zanzotto could not find a satisfactory system. He created a new one out of the debris of all given systems. His original distance has turned into a radical proximity to the physical matter of human thought and imagination. His unrelenting experimentation is a startling sign of his presence and loyalty toward reality.

One of Zanzotto's new poems, **"Altri papaveri"** (included in one of his latest volumes of verse, *Meteo,* published in 1996), is highly representative of Zanzotto's entire work. Not only does this poem provide a coherent continuation of Zanzotto's discourse on war, as explored in one of his most important books, **Il galateo in bosco,** but it also proves to be a great poetic achievement per se, illustrating of the poet's linguistic creativity, intertextual discourse and civil engagement.

"Altri Papaveri"

Fieri di una fierezza e foia barbara
sovrabbondanti con ogni petalo
rosso + rosso + rosso + rosso
    coup de dés maledetto
    sanguinose potenze dilaganti,
    quasi ognuno di voi a coprire un prato intero—
da che
da che mondi stragiferi
stragiferi papaveri
    qui vi accampaste avvampando,
    sfacciato forno del rosso
    che in misteriche chiazze
    non cessa di accedere sgorgar su
    straventando i soliti maggi grigioblù?

Come i calabroni si fanno sempre più enormi
    CRABRO CRABRO
e quasi difformi da ogni destino
e le limacce budella a stravento su verzure:
via! via! è tempo di toglier via questa primavera
di pozze di sangue da tiri di cecchino
Correre Correre
coprendosi in affanno teste e braccia e corpi orbi
correre correre per chi
corre e corre sotto calabroni e cecchini
e in orridi papaveri finì

                  (incerti frammenti 1993-95)

"Other Poppies"

Fierce with a barbaric fierceness and flirtation
overflowing with every petal
red + red + red + red
    cursed coup de dés
    bloody powers spreading,
    as though each of you covered a whole
meadow—
from what
from what slaughter-bearer world
slaughter-bearer poppies
    did you camp out here blazing,
    brazen furnace of redness
    that in mystery splatters
    incessantly approximates regurgitates
    overblowing the usual greyblue Mays?

As the giant hornets become increasingly huge
    CRABRO CRABRO
and almost unlike any destiny
and slugs guts blown over greenery:
flee! flee! it's time to end this spring
of pools of blood from sniper fire
Run Run
breathlessly covering your heads and arms and blind
  bodies
run run for the one
who runs and runs under hornets and snipers
and died among horrendous poppies.

                (uncertain fragments 1993-95)

The occasion of the poem was the war in Sarajevo. From his home in Pieve, Zanzotto could hear the planes departing from nearby NATO bases for missions in Bosnia. The inventive imagery of the text, then, mirrors a real situation: pools of blood, hornets and snipers were broadcast by Italian television virtually every day. Sickened by people's passive acquiescence to horror and destruction, Zanzotto turns out to bring these images back to their original ambiguity and negativity by a process of verbal and even typographic deformation and defamiliarisation. A clear clue of such a process is, in the final stanza, the use of the Latin noun "crabro" for "calabrone" (*hornet*). The subtext is Vergil's *Georgics* IV mentioning bees and hornets in a context of death-rebirth symbology. Vergil has exerted a constant influence on Zanzotto from the beginning, especially in the role of a bucolic poet. Here Vergil ceases to represent an idea of accomplished and self-content poetry, as fixed by his idyllic shepherds, and comes to represent just the opposite. Thus all hope of redemption and success for the modern poet vanishes. The symbolic space of a retrieved Arcadia collapses under the weight of lethal forces, as represented by huge hornets, that are in themselves a reversal of the classical imagery of bees for bards, as found in Plato, in Vergil himself, and still in D'Annunzio and Montale. Linguistic monstrosity and aberration ultimately stand as congruous embodiments of the deranged reality that the poem sets out to represent, as always in Zanzotto and as appears here from the Mallarmé quote "coup de dés." Typical of Zanzotto's style is such a nonchalant citation of central and problematic notions from other authors—notions that instructors, teachers and students of literature take plenty of time to explain and sometimes dismiss as broad enough to become dissertation topics. The point here is that the crisis of the outer world, as mirrored by the destructiveness of war, reflects a dilemma that is always hanging over the poet's head: the impossibility of "speaking" the world and yet the desperate attempt to "speak" it, a sort of throw of dice by which the poet hopes to outdo human language and in fact bets himself. To this notion of linguistic impotence also refers the line "quasi difformi da ogni destino," whose real meaning can be understood only in relation with its subtext: "stella difforme et fato sol qui reo," a line from Petrarch (*RVF* 187, 12). Petrarch here states that Laura underwent an unfavourable destiny in that she did not find a poet good enough to sing praises of her. Likewise, Zanzotto here claims, however covertly, not to be good enough to express verbally the deformity of the world, which is also suggested by the adjective "difformi," meaning only "unfavourable," "inimical" in Pe-trarch. This is another feature of Zanzotto's style: to appropri-ate words and phrases from his beloved poets, and use them in the ancient meaning while stressing the allusive power of the pure signifier.

This poem is entirely centred around the image of pop-pies and redness, which are self-evident metaphors for blood and massacre. The equivalence between murdered warriors and poppies is as old as Vergil: "Volvitur Eury-alus leto, pulchrosque per artus / it cruor inque umeros cervix conlapsa recumbit: / purpureos veluti cum flos succisus aratro / languescit moriens lassove papavera collo / demisere caput, pluvia cum forte gravantur" (*Aeneid* IX, 433-437). Whereas the Latin poet empha-sises the similarity between the frailty of the flower and the tenderness of the youths massacred, Zanzotto insists on the color of the flower. In this respect, he shows more affinity with another poet, Gabriele D'Annunzio. Poppies are recurrent in the D'Annunzio oeuvre. Two passages appear to be Zanzotto's direct subtext. The in-cipit of *Laus vitae*, included in *Maia*: "Papaveri, sangue fulgente—/ qual sangue d'eroi e d'amanti / innanzi a periglio mortale . . ." (ll. 1-3) And, even more closely, a central section of *Ditirambo I,* included in *Alcyone*: "Vidi campo di rossi / papaveri vasto al mio sguardo / come letto di strage, / come flutto ancor caldo / sgorgato da un'ecatombe" (ll. 69-73). Literal and thematic resemblance notwithstanding, Zanzotto here is subverting his subtext. For D'Annunzio, bleeding and slaughter are still images of primitive vitality and force (as is suggested by the titles *Laus vitae* and *Ditirambo,* which is a traditional song in honour of Dyonisus). On the contrary, Zanzotto sees in carnage only the terrible and hopeless atrocity of war. D'Annunzio's *Ditirambo I* is subtitled by the dedication *Romae frugiferae dic.,* "dedicated to crop-bearer Rome." Zanzotto polemically responds to D'Annunzio's sensuous cult of life by making up the adjective "stragifero," "slaughter-bearer" (ironically enough, "strage" is already in D'Annunzio's passage), as opposed to *frugiferae,* and thus making a very strong point of his discord from a whole line of Italian contemporary poetry viewing war in positive terms.[13] In the end, this poem appears to be a compendium of poetic modes, a *mise en abyme* of Zanzotto's heterogeneous inspiration: Mallarmé, Vergil, Petrarch, D'Annunzio, and the dialect, while formal and visual innovations are tributes to the graphic devices of avanguarde and, ultimately, again to Mallarmé's *coup de dés*. The conclusive line, though, still seems to envisage an idea of order: it is a hendecasyllable, albeit not a typical one (nor are the other hendecasyllabic lines typical hendecasyllables: ll. 1, 3, 5, 17). The ending word should not be a masculine rhyme (*rima tronca*) in a traditional Italian line. The most similar to this I can think of is a conclusive line by Carducci: "L'acqua che tenue tra i sassi fluì" (*Mezzogiorno alpino,* included in *Rime e ritmi*). But "rime tronche" (masculine rhymes) are also common in poets of "canzonette," Arcadian poets of the XVI and XVII century. Whether this explicit is to be attributed to the model of one of these poets or that of Carducci himself, Zanzotto here overtly imitates the lyric diction of lighter poetry and thus seems to give himself another possibility of untroubled song ("canto") for the future.

In closing, how can one answer the question I put at the beginning, "Is there a language of poetry?" Zanzotto's starting point was a compelling need for poetical language. His final and greatest achievement is an enlargement of the scope of poetry itself through a voracious absorption and manipulation of all available languages. What, at the outset, was perceived to be an impossibility of natural language has turned into a virtual infinity of linguistic options. Will, then, poetry survive the universe of mass-media? Zanzotto himself, in a recent talk, stated that he will explore new possibilities of self-expression by means of identification with lesser forms of existence: flowers, fossils, minerals; i.e. those living forms where time still maintains a hint of the eternal.

Notes

1. See Montale's Nobel speech: Eugenio Montale, "È ancora possibile la poesia?," *Sulla poesia,* ed. Giorgio Zampa (Milano: Mondadori, 1976) 5-14.

2. Sergio Solmi, one of Montale's most important critics and, in his own right, a protagonist of the war-time literary scene, wrote: "In una situazione confusa e incoerente, dove i veli delle vecchie ipocrisie stavano andando all'aria, e nuove ne sorgevano ben più clamorose, svelanti il loro fondo di inequivocabile cinismo, incapaci come ci sentivamo di uniformarci ai modelli di vita elaborati e consolidati da chiese e tradizioni sociali, gruppi e ideologie correnti [i.e. Fascism], il bisogno d'uno stile ci sembrò l'ultima insopprimibile esigenza, l'ultima garanzia di autenticità della nostra reazione al mondo attorniante [. . .] Certo, la nostra giovanile esperienza fu in gran parte negativa: l'urto era stato troppo forte. Comunque, non avremmo potuto durarci a lungo. A un certo momento, sentimmo la necessità di ricostruire un mondo saldo intorno a noi. Verso i vent'anni, su di un panorama di deserto, cominciammo a riconoscere i nostri veri maestri e compagni, ad acquistare un senso vivo della tradizione, della nostra dimensione nel tempo: *anche se il sopraggiungere della dittatura doveva smorzare tante possibilità di piena estrinsecazione* [my emphasis]": Sergio Solmi, *Scrittori negli anni* (Milano: Il Saggiatore, 1963) 280-281.

3. See at least *Zibaldone* 3417.

4. Incidentally, in the XIX century, poetry also provided authors with a prestigious means to acquire fame. As Carlo Dionisotti stated, "[a]ppena occorre ricordare che nella letteratura italiana nessuno mai era giunto al principato per sola virtù di prosa: neppure vi sarebbe giunto, dopo il Monti, l'autore dei *Promessi sposi,* se il riconoscimento della sua abilità poetica non avesse bilanciato il successo popolare del romanzo: Carlo Dionisotti, *Appunti sui moderni* (Bologna: Il Mulino, 1988) 90-91.

5. On Montale's indebtedness to English, see Nicola Gardini, "Corno inglese," *Poesia* 127 (1999): 11-14.

6. On Mallarmé's influence on Italian poetry, see Nicola Gardini "Stéphane Mallarmé cent'anni dopo," *Poesia* 120 (1998): 36-38.

7. See Eugenio Montale, *Sulla poesia* (Milano: Mondadori, 1976) 108.

8. On Leopardi's influence on twentieth-century Italian poetry, see Gilberto Lonardi, *Leopardismo,* 2nd ed. (Firenze: Sansoni, 1990); Nicola Gardini, "La

tradizione assente," *Lezioni leopardiane,* ed. Marco Dondero and Marida Gaeta (Roma: Fahrenheit, 2000 pp. 71-98).

9. The Dante/Petrarch opposition is the core of Gianfranco Contini's interpretation of Italian poetry: see Gianfranco Contini, *Varianti e altra linguistica* (Torino: Einaudi, 1970). Contini's ideas are to be found also throughout Pasolini's critical writings: see Pier Paolo Pasolini, *Passione e ideologia* (Torino: Einaudi, 1985).

10. See Piero Bonfiglioli, "Dante Pascoli Montale," *Materiali critici per Giovanni Pascoli,* ed. Mario Petrucciani, Marta Bruscia, and Gianfranco Mariani (Roma: Edizioni dell'Ateneo, 1971) 72-90.

11. See Giuseppe Savoca, "Sul petrarchismo di Montale," *Per la lingua di Montale,* ed. Giuseppe Savoca (Firenze: Olschki, 1989) 53-70; on Montale's indebtedness to Dante's *Vita nuova,* see Gilberto Lonardi, "Beatrice e Antibeatrice," *Il vecchio e il giovane* (Bologna: Zanichelli, 1980) 57-66.

12. Mario Luzi, *Dante e Leopardi o della modernità* (Roma: Editori Riuniti, 1992).

13. On the problematic image and significance of war (in particular of WWI) in contemporary Italian poetry, see Andrea Cortellessa, *Le notti chiare erano tutte un'alba* (Milano: Bruno Mondadori, 1998).

FURTHER READING

Criticism

Cambon, Glauco. Foreword to *Selected Poetry of Andrea Zanzotto,* edited by Ruth Feldman and Brian Swann, pp. xiii-xxii. Princeton, N.J.: Princeton University Press, 1975.

Provides a general overview of Zanzotto's poetry.

Additional coverage of Zanzotto's life and career is contained in the following sources published by Thomson Gale: *Contemporary Authors,* **Vol. 208;** *Contemporary World Writers,* **Ed. 2;** *Dictionary of Literary Biography,* **Vol. 128;** *Encyclopedia of World Literature in the 20th Century,* **Ed. 3.; and** *Literature Resource Center.*

How to Use This Index

The main references

Calvino, Italo
1923-1985 .... CLC **5, 8, 11, 22, 33, 39,**
73; SSC 3, 48

---

list all author entries in the following Gale Literary Criticism series:

AAL = *Asian American Literature*
BG = *The Beat Generation: A Gale Critical Companion*
BLC = *Black Literature Criticism*
BLCS = *Black Literature Criticism Supplement*
CLC = *Contemporary Literary Criticism*
CLR = *Children's Literature Review*
CMLC = *Classical and Medieval Literature Criticism*
DC = *Drama Criticism*
HLC = *Hispanic Literature Criticism*
HLCS = *Hispanic Literature Criticism Supplement*
HR = *Harlem Renaissance: A Gale Critical Companion*
LC = *Literature Criticism from 1400 to 1800*
NCLC = *Nineteenth-Century Literature Criticism*
NNAL = *Native North American Literature*
PC = *Poetry Criticism*
SSC = *Short Story Criticism*
TCLC = *Twentieth-Century Literary Criticism*
WLC = *World Literature Criticism, 1500 to the Present*
WLCS = *World Literature Criticism Supplement*

The cross-references

See also CA 85-88, 116; CANR 23, 61;
DAM NOV; DLB 196; EW 13; MTCW 1, 2;
RGSF 2; RGWL 2; SFW 4; SSFS 12

---

list all author entries in the following Gale biographical and literary sources:

AAYA = *Authors & Artists for Young Adults*
AFAW = *African American Writers*
AFW = *African Writers*
AITN = *Authors in the News*
AMW = *American Writers*
AMWR = *American Writers Retrospective Supplement*
AMWS = *American Writers Supplement*
ANW = *American Nature Writers*
AW = *Ancient Writers*
BEST = *Bestsellers*
BPFB = *Beacham's Encyclopedia of Popular Fiction: Biography and Resources*
BRW = *British Writers*
BRWS = *British Writers Supplement*
BW = *Black Writers*
BYA = *Beacham's Guide to Literature for Young Adults*
CA = *Contemporary Authors*
CAAS = *Contemporary Authors Autobiography Series*
CABS = *Contemporary Authors Bibliographical Series*
CAD = *Contemporary American Dramatists*
CANR = *Contemporary Authors New Revision Series*
CAP = *Contemporary Authors Permanent Series*
CBD = *Contemporary British Dramatists*
CCA = *Contemporary Canadian Authors*
CD = *Contemporary Dramatists*
CDALB = *Concise Dictionary of American Literary Biography*
CDALBS = *Concise Dictionary of American Literary Biography Supplement*
CDBLB = *Concise Dictionary of British Literary Biography*

CMW = *St. James Guide to Crime & Mystery Writers*
CN = *Contemporary Novelists*
CP = *Contemporary Poets*
CPW = *Contemporary Popular Writers*
CSW = *Contemporary Southern Writers*
CWD = *Contemporary Women Dramatists*
CWP = *Contemporary Women Poets*
CWRI = *St. James Guide to Children's Writers*
CWW = *Contemporary World Writers*
DA = *DISCovering Authors*
DA3 = *DISCovering Authors 3.0*
DAB = *DISCovering Authors: British Edition*
DAC = *DISCovering Authors: Canadian Edition*
DAM = *DISCovering Authors: Modules*
   DRAM: *Dramatists Module;* **MST:** *Most-studied Authors Module;*
   MULT: *Multicultural Authors Module;* **NOV:** *Novelists Module;*
   POET: *Poets Module;* **POP:** *Popular Fiction and Genre Authors Module*
DFS = *Drama for Students*
DLB = *Dictionary of Literary Biography*
DLBD = *Dictionary of Literary Biography Documentary Series*
DLBY = *Dictionary of Literary Biography Yearbook*
DNFS = *Literature of Developing Nations for Students*
EFS = *Epics for Students*
EXPN = *Exploring Novels*
EXPP = *Exploring Poetry*
EXPS = *Exploring Short Stories*
EW = *European Writers*
FANT = *St. James Guide to Fantasy Writers*
FW = *Feminist Writers*
GFL = *Guide to French Literature,* Beginnings to 1789, 1798 to the Present
GLL = *Gay and Lesbian Literature*
HGG = *St. James Guide to Horror, Ghost & Gothic Writers*
HW = *Hispanic Writers*
IDFW = *International Dictionary of Films and Filmmakers: Writers and Production Artists*
IDTP = *International Dictionary of Theatre: Playwrights*
LAIT = *Literature and Its Times*
LAW = *Latin American Writers*
JRDA = *Junior DISCovering Authors*
MAICYA = *Major Authors and Illustrators for Children and Young Adults*
MAICYAS = *Major Authors and Illustrators for Children and Young Adults Supplement*
MAWW = *Modern American Women Writers*
MJW = *Modern Japanese Writers*
MTCW = *Major 20th-Century Writers*
NCFS = *Nonfiction Classics for Students*
NFS = *Novels for Students*
PAB = *Poets: American and British*
PFS = *Poetry for Students*
RGAL = *Reference Guide to American Literature*
RGEL = *Reference Guide to English Literature*
RGSF = *Reference Guide to Short Fiction*
RGWL = *Reference Guide to World Literature*
RHW = *Twentieth-Century Romance and Historical Writers*
SAAS = *Something about the Author Autobiography Series*
SATA = *Something about the Author*
SFW = *St. James Guide to Science Fiction Writers*
SSFS = *Short Stories for Students*
TCWW = *Twentieth-Century Western Writers*
WLIT = *World Literature and Its Times*
WP = *World Poets*
YABC = *Yesterday's Authors of Books for Children*
YAW = *St. James Guide to Young Adult Writers*

Literary Criticism Series
Cumulative Author Index

Baraka, Amiri 1934- .... **BLC 1; CLC 1, 2, 3, 5, 10, 14, 33, 115; DC 6; PC 4; WLCS**
See Jones, LeRoi
See also AFAW 1, 2; AMWS 2; BW 2, 3; CA 21-24R; CABS 3; CAD; CANR 27, 38, 61, 133; CD 5; CDALB 1941-1968; CP 7; CPW; DA; DA3; DAC; DAM MST, MULT, POET, POP; DFS 3, 11, 16; DLB 5, 7, 16, 38; DLBD 8; EWL 3; MTCW 1, 2; PFS 9; RGAL 4; TUS; WP

Baratynsky, Evgenii Abramovich
1800-1844 .... **NCLC 103**
See also DLB 205

Barbauld, Anna Laetitia
1743-1825 .... **NCLC 50**
See also DLB 107, 109, 142, 158; RGEL 2

Barbellion, W. N. P. .... **TCLC 24**
See Cummings, Bruce F(rederick)

Barber, Benjamin R. 1939- .... **CLC 141**
See also CA 29-32R; CANR 12, 32, 64, 119

Barbera, Jack (Vincent) 1945- .... **CLC 44**
See also CA 110; CANR 45

Barbey d'Aurevilly, Jules-Amedee
1808-1889 .... **NCLC 1; SSC 17**
See also DLB 119; GFL 1789 to the Present

Barbour, John c. 1316-1395 .... **CMLC 33**
See also DLB 146

Barbusse, Henri 1873-1935 .... **TCLC 5**
See also CA 105; 154; DLB 65; EWL 3; RGWL 2, 3

Barclay, Alexander c. 1475-1552 .... **LC 109**
See also DLB 132

Barclay, Bill
See Moorcock, Michael (John)

Barclay, William Ewert
See Moorcock, Michael (John)

Barea, Arturo 1897-1957 .... **TCLC 14**
See also CA 111; 201

Barfoot, Joan 1946- .... **CLC 18**
See also CA 105

Barham, Richard Harris
1788-1845 .... **NCLC 77**
See also DLB 159

Baring, Maurice 1874-1945 .... **TCLC 8**
See also CA 105; 168; DLB 34; HGG

Baring-Gould, Sabine 1834-1924 ... **TCLC 88**
See also DLB 156, 190

Barker, Clive 1952- .... **CLC 52, 205; SSC 53**
See also AAYA 10, 54; BEST 90:3; BPFB 1; CA 121; 129; CANR 71, 111, 133; CPW; DA3; DAM POP; DLB 261; HGG; INT CA-129; MTCW 1, 2; SUFW 2

Barker, George Granville
1913-1991 .... **CLC 8, 48**
See also CA 9-12R; 135; CANR 7, 38; DAM POET; DLB 20; EWL 3; MTCW 1

Barker, Harley Granville
See Granville-Barker, Harley
See also DLB 10

Barker, Howard 1946- .... **CLC 37**
See also CA 102; CBD; CD 5; DLB 13, 233

Barker, Jane 1652-1732 .... **LC 42, 82**
See also DLB 39, 131

Barker, Pat(ricia) 1943- ...... **CLC 32, 94, 146**
See also BRWS 4; CA 117; 122; CANR 50, 101; CN 7; DLB 271; INT CA-122

Barlach, Ernst (Heinrich)
1870-1938 .... **TCLC 84**
See also CA 178; DLB 56, 118; EWL 3

Barlow, Joel 1754-1812 .... **NCLC 23**
See also AMWS 2; DLB 37; RGAL 4

Barnard, Mary (Ethel) 1909- .... **CLC 48**
See also CA 21-22; CAP 2

Barnes, Djuna 1892-1982 .... **CLC 3, 4, 8, 11, 29, 127; SSC 3**
See Steptoe, Lydia
See also AMWS 3; CA 9-12R; 107; CAD; CANR 16, 55; CWD; DLB 4, 9, 45; EWL 3; GLL 1; MTCW 1, 2; RGAL 4; TUS

Barnes, Jim 1933- .... **NNAL**
See also CA 108; 175; CAAE 175; CAAS 28; DLB 175

Barnes, Julian (Patrick) 1946- . **CLC 42, 141**
See also BRWS 4; CA 102; CANR 19, 54, 115; CN 7; DAB; DLB 194; DLBY 1993; EWL 3; MTCW 1

Barnes, Peter 1931-2004 .... **CLC 5, 56**
See also CA 65-68; CAAS 12; CANR 33, 34, 64, 113; CBD; CD 5; DFS 6; DLB 13, 233; MTCW 1

Barnes, William 1801-1886 .... **NCLC 75**
See also DLB 32

Baroja (y Nessi), Pio 1872-1956 .... **HLC 1; TCLC 8**
See also CA 104; EW 9

Baron, David
See Pinter, Harold

Baron Corvo
See Rolfe, Frederick (William Serafino Austin Lewis Mary)

Barondess, Sue K(aufman)
1926-1977 .... **CLC 8**
See Kaufman, Sue
See also CA 1-4R; 69-72; CANR 1

Baron de Teive
See Pessoa, Fernando (Antonio Nogueira)

Baroness Von S.
See Zangwill, Israel

Barres, (Auguste-)Maurice
1862-1923 .... **TCLC 47**
See also CA 164; DLB 123; GFL 1789 to the Present

Barreto, Afonso Henrique de Lima
See Lima Barreto, Afonso Henrique de

Barrett, Andrea 1954- .... **CLC 150**
See also CA 156; CANR 92

Barrett, Michele .... **CLC 65**

Barrett, (Roger) Syd 1946- .... **CLC 35**

Barrett, William (Christopher)
1913-1992 .... **CLC 27**
See also CA 13-16R; 139; CANR 11, 67; INT CANR-11

Barrett Browning, Elizabeth
1806-1861 ... **NCLC 1, 16, 61, 66; PC 6, 62; WLC**
See also BRW 4; CDBLB 1832-1890; DA; DA3; DAB; DAC; DAM MST, POET; DLB 32, 199; EXPP; PAB; PFS 2, 16; TEA; WLIT 4; WP

Barrie, J(ames) M(atthew)
1860-1937 .... **TCLC 2, 164**
See also BRWS 3; BYA 4, 5; CA 104; 136; CANR 77; CDBLB 1890-1914; CLR 16; CWRI 5; DA3; DAB; DAM DRAM; DFS 7; DLB 10, 141, 156; EWL 3; FANT; MAICYA 1, 2; MTCW 1; SATA 100; SUFW; WCH; WLIT 4; YABC 1

Barrington, Michael
See Moorcock, Michael (John)

Barrol, Grady
See Bograd, Larry

Barry, Mike
See Malzberg, Barry N(athaniel)

Barry, Philip 1896-1949 .... **TCLC 11**
See also CA 109; 199; DFS 9; DLB 7, 228; RGAL 4

Bart, Andre Schwarz
See Schwarz-Bart, Andre

Barth, John (Simmons) 1930- ... **CLC 1, 2, 3, 5, 7, 9, 10, 14, 27, 51, 89; SSC 10**
See also AITN 1, 2; AMW; BPFB 1; CA 1-4R; CABS 1; CANR 5, 23, 49, 64, 113; CN 7; DAM NOV; DLB 2, 227; EWL 3; FANT; MTCW 1; RGAL 4; RGSF 2; RHW; SSFS 6; TUS

Barthelme, Donald 1931-1989 ... **CLC 1, 2, 3, 5, 6, 8, 13, 23, 46, 59, 115; SSC 2, 55**
See also AMWS 4; BPFB 1; CA 21-24R; 129; CANR 20, 58; DA3; DAM NOV; DLB 2, 234; DLBY 1980, 1989; EWL 3; FANT; LMFS 2; MTCW 1, 2; RGAL 4; RGSF 2; SATA 7; SATA-Obit 62; SSFS 17

Barthelme, Frederick 1943- ...... **CLC 36, 117**
See also AMWS 11; CA 114; 122; CANR 77; CN 7; CSW; DLB 244; DLBY 1985; EWL 3; INT CA-122

Barthes, Roland (Gerard)
1915-1980 .... **CLC 24, 83; TCLC 135**
See also CA 130; 97-100; CANR 66; DLB 296; EW 13; EWL 3; GFL 1789 to the Present; MTCW 1, 2; TWA

Bartram, William 1739-1823 .... **NCLC 145**
See also ANW; DLB 37

Barzun, Jacques (Martin) 1907- ..... **CLC 51, 145**
See also CA 61-64; CANR 22, 95

Bashevis, Isaac
See Singer, Isaac Bashevis

Bashkirtseff, Marie 1859-1884 .... **NCLC 27**

Basho, Matsuo
See Matsuo Basho
See also PFS 18; RGWL 2, 3; WP

Basil of Caesaria c. 330-379 .... **CMLC 35**

Basket, Raney
See Edgerton, Clyde (Carlyle)

Bass, Kingsley B., Jr.
See Bullins, Ed

Bass, Rick 1958- .... **CLC 79, 143; SSC 60**
See also ANW; CA 126; CANR 53, 93; CSW; DLB 212, 275

Bassani, Giorgio 1916-2000 .... **CLC 9**
See also CA 65-68; 190; CANR 33; CWW 2; DLB 128, 177, 299; EWL 3; MTCW 1; RGWL 2, 3

Bastian, Ann .... **CLC 70**

Bastos, Augusto (Antonio) Roa
See Roa Bastos, Augusto (Antonio)

Bataille, Georges 1897-1962 .... **CLC 29; TCLC 155**
See also CA 101; 89-92; EWL 3

Bates, H(erbert) E(rnest)
1905-1974 .... **CLC 46; SSC 10**
See also CA 93-96; 45-48; CANR 34; DA3; DAB; DAM POP; DLB 162, 191; EWL 3; EXPS; MTCW 1, 2; RGSF 2; SSFS 7

Bauchart
See Camus, Albert

Baudelaire, Charles 1821-1867 . **NCLC 6, 29, 55, 155; PC 1; SSC 18; WLC**
See also DA; DA3; DAB; DAC; DAM MST, POET; DLB 217; EW 7; GFL 1789 to the Present; LMFS 2; PFS 21; RGWL 2, 3; TWA

Baudouin, Marcel
See Peguy, Charles (Pierre)

Baudouin, Pierre
See Peguy, Charles (Pierre)

Baudrillard, Jean 1929- .... **CLC 60**
See also DLB 296

Baum, L(yman) Frank 1856-1919 .. **TCLC 7, 132**
See also AAYA 46; BYA 16; CA 108; 133; CLR 15; CWRI 5; DLB 22; FANT; JRDA; MAICYA 1, 2; MTCW 1, 2; NFS 13; RGAL 4; SATA 18, 100; WCH

Baum, Louis F.
See Baum, L(yman) Frank
Baumbach, Jonathan 1933- .... **CLC 6, 23**
See also CA 13-16R; CAAS 5; CANR 12, 66; CN 7; DLBY 1980; INT CANR-12; MTCW 1
Bausch, Richard (Carl) 1945- .... **CLC 51**
See also AMWS 7; CA 101; CAAS 14; CANR 43, 61, 87; CSW; DLB 130
Baxter, Charles (Morley) 1947- . **CLC 45, 78**
See also CA 57-60; CANR 40, 64, 104, 133; CPW; DAM POP; DLB 130; MTCW 2
Baxter, George Owen
See Faust, Frederick (Schiller)
Baxter, James K(eir) 1926-1972 .... **CLC 14**
See also CA 77-80; EWL 3
Baxter, John
See Hunt, E(verette) Howard, (Jr.)
Bayer, Sylvia
See Glassco, John
Baynton, Barbara 1857-1929 .... **TCLC 57**
See also DLB 230; RGSF 2
Beagle, Peter S(oyer) 1939- .... **CLC 7, 104**
See also AAYA 47; BPFB 1; BYA 9, 10, 16; CA 9-12R; CANR 4, 51, 73, 110; DA3; DLBY 1980; FANT; INT CANR-4; MTCW 1; SATA 60, 130; SUFW 1, 2; YAW
Bean, Normal
See Burroughs, Edgar Rice
Beard, Charles A(ustin)
1874-1948 .... **TCLC 15**
See also CA 115; 189; DLB 17; SATA 18
Beardsley, Aubrey 1872-1898 .... **NCLC 6**
Beattie, Ann 1947- ..... **CLC 8, 13, 18, 40, 63, 146; SSC 11**
See also AMWS 5; BEST 90:2; BPFB 1; CA 81-84; CANR 53, 73, 128; CN 7; CPW; DA3; DAM NOV, POP; DLB 218, 278; DLBY 1982; EWL 3; MTCW 1, 2; RGAL 4; RGSF 2; SSFS 9; TUS
Beattie, James 1735-1803 .... **NCLC 25**
See also DLB 109
Beauchamp, Kathleen Mansfield 1888-1923
See Mansfield, Katherine
See also CA 104; 134; DA; DA3; DAC; DAM MST; MTCW 2; TEA
Beaumarchais, Pierre-Augustin Caron de
1732-1799 .... **DC 4; LC 61**
See also DAM DRAM; DFS 14, 16; EW 4; GFL Beginnings to 1789; RGWL 2, 3
Beaumont, Francis 1584(?)-1616 .. **DC 6; LC 33**
See also BRW 2; CDBLB Before 1660; DLB 58; TEA
Beauvoir, Simone (Lucie Ernestine Marie Bertrand) de 1908-1986 .... **CLC 1, 2, 4, 8, 14, 31, 44, 50, 71, 124; SSC 35; WLC**
See also BPFB 1; CA 9-12R; 118; CANR 28, 61; DA; DA3; DAB; DAC; DAM MST, NOV; DLB 72; DLBY 1986; EW 12; EWL 3; FW; GFL 1789 to the Present; LMFS 2; MTCW 1, 2; RGSF 2; RGWL 2, 3; TWA
Becker, Carl (Lotus) 1873-1945 ..... **TCLC 63**
See also CA 157; DLB 17
Becker, Jurek 1937-1997 .... **CLC 7, 19**
See also CA 85-88; 157; CANR 60, 117; CWW 2; DLB 75, 299; EWL 3
Becker, Walter 1950- .... **CLC 26**
Beckett, Samuel (Barclay)
1906-1989 .. **CLC 1, 2, 3, 4, 6, 9, 10, 11, 14, 18, 29, 57, 59, 83; DC 22; SSC 16, 74; TCLC 145; WLC**
See also BRWC 2; BRWR 1; BRWS 1; CA 5-8R; 130; CANR 33, 61; CBD; CDBLB 1945-1960; DA; DA3; DAB; DAC; DAM DRAM, MST, NOV; DFS 2, 7, 18; DLB

13, 15, 233; DLBY 1990; EWL 3; GFL 1789 to the Present; LATS 1:2; LMFS 2; MTCW 1, 2; RGSF 2; RGWL 2, 3; SSFS 15; TEA; WLIT 4
Beckford, William 1760-1844 .... **NCLC 16**
See also BRW 3; DLB 39, 213; HGG; LMFS 1; SUFW
Beckham, Barry (Earl) 1944- .... **BLC 1**
See also BW 1; CA 29-32R; CANR 26, 62; CN 7; DAM MULT; DLB 33
Beckman, Gunnel 1910- .... **CLC 26**
See also CA 33-36R; CANR 15, 114; CLR 25; MAICYA 1, 2; SAAS 9; SATA 6
Becque, Henri 1837-1899 .... **DC 21; NCLC 3**
See also DLB 192; GFL 1789 to the Present
Becquer, Gustavo Adolfo
1836-1870 .... **HLCS 1; NCLC 106**
See also DAM MULT
Beddoes, Thomas Lovell 1803-1849 .. **DC 15; NCLC 3, 154**
See also DLB 96
Bede c. 673-735 .... **CMLC 20**
See also DLB 146; TEA
Bedford, Denton R. 1907-(?) .... **NNAL**
Bedford, Donald F.
See Fearing, Kenneth (Flexner)
Beecher, Catharine Esther
1800-1878 .... **NCLC 30**
See also DLB 1, 243
Beecher, John 1904-1980 .... **CLC 6**
See also AITN 1; CA 5-8R; 105; CANR 8
Beer, Johann 1655-1700 .... **LC 5**
See also DLB 168
Beer, Patricia 1924- .... **CLC 58**
See also CA 61-64; 183; CANR 13, 46; CP 7; CWP; DLB 40; FW
Beerbohm, Max
See Beerbohm, (Henry) Max(imilian)
Beerbohm, (Henry) Max(imilian)
1872-1956 .... **TCLC 1, 24**
See also BRWS 2; CA 104; 154; CANR 79; DLB 34, 100; FANT
Beer-Hofmann, Richard
1866-1945 .... **TCLC 60**
See also CA 160; DLB 81
Beg, Shemus
See Stephens, James
Begiebing, Robert J(ohn) 1946- .... **CLC 70**
See also CA 122; CANR 40, 88
Begley, Louis 1933- .... **CLC 197**
See also CA 140; CANR 98; DLB 299
Behan, Brendan (Francis)
1923-1964 .... **CLC 1, 8, 11, 15, 79**
See also BRWS 2; CA 73-76; CANR 33, 121; CBD; CDBLB 1945-1960; DAM DRAM; DFS 7; DLB 13, 233; EWL 3; MTCW 1, 2
Behn, Aphra 1640(?)-1689 .. **DC 4; LC 1, 30, 42; PC 13; WLC**
See also BRWS 3; DA; DA3; DAB; DAC; DAM DRAM, MST, NOV, POET; DFS 16; DLB 39, 80, 131; FW; TEA; WLIT 3
Behrman, S(amuel) N(athaniel)
1893-1973 .... **CLC 40**
See also CA 13-16; 45-48; CAD; CAP 1; DLB 7, 44; IDFW 3; RGAL 4
Belasco, David 1853-1931 .... **TCLC 3**
See also CA 104; 168; DLB 7; RGAL 4
Belcheva, Elisaveta Lyubomirova
1893-1991 .... **CLC 10**
See Bagryana, Elisaveta
Beldone, Phil "Cheech"
See Ellison, Harlan (Jay)
Beleno
See Azuela, Mariano
Belinski, Vissarion Grigoryevich
1811-1848 .... **NCLC 5**
See also DLB 198

Belitt, Ben 1911- .... **CLC 22**
See also CA 13-16R; CAAS 4; CANR 7, 77; CP 7; DLB 5
Belknap, Jeremy 1744-1798 .... **LC 115**
See also DLB 30, 37
Bell, Gertrude (Margaret Lowthian)
1868-1926 .... **TCLC 67**
See also CA 167; CANR 110; DLB 174
Bell, J. Freeman
See Zangwill, Israel
Bell, James Madison 1826-1902 .... **BLC 1; TCLC 43**
See also BW 1; CA 122; 124; DAM MULT; DLB 50
Bell, Madison Smartt 1957- ...... **CLC 41, 102**
See also AMWS 10; BPFB 1; CA 111, 183; CAAE 183; CANR 28, 54, 73, 134; CN 7; CSW; DLB 218, 278; MTCW 1
Bell, Marvin (Hartley) 1937- .... **CLC 8, 31**
See also CA 21-24R; CAAS 14; CANR 59, 102; CP 7; DAM POET; DLB 5; MTCW 1
Bell, W. L. D.
See Mencken, H(enry) L(ouis)
Bellamy, Atwood C.
See Mencken, H(enry) L(ouis)
Bellamy, Edward 1850-1898 ..... **NCLC 4, 86, 147**
See also DLB 12; NFS 15; RGAL 4; SFW 4
Belli, Gioconda 1948- .... **HLCS 1**
See also CA 152; CWW 2; DLB 290; EWL 3; RGWL 3
Bellin, Edward J.
See Kuttner, Henry
Bello, Andres 1781-1865 .... **NCLC 131**
See also LAW
Belloc, (Joseph) Hilaire (Pierre Sebastien Rene Swanton) 1870-1953 .... **PC 24; TCLC 7, 18**
See also CA 106; 152; CLR 102; CWRI 5; DAM POET; DLB 19, 100, 141, 174; EWL 3; MTCW 1; SATA 112; WCH; YABC 1
Belloc, Joseph Peter Rene Hilaire
See Belloc, (Joseph) Hilaire (Pierre Sebastien Rene Swanton)
Belloc, Joseph Pierre Hilaire
See Belloc, (Joseph) Hilaire (Pierre Sebastien Rene Swanton)
Belloc, M. A.
See Lowndes, Marie Adelaide (Belloc)
Belloc-Lowndes, Mrs.
See Lowndes, Marie Adelaide (Belloc)
Bellow, Saul 1915- . **CLC 1, 2, 3, 6, 8, 10, 13, 15, 25, 33, 34, 63, 79, 190, 200; SSC 14; WLC**
See also AITN 2; AMW; AMWC 2; AMWR 2; BEST 89:3; BPFB 1; CA 5-8R; CABS 1; CANR 29, 53, 95, 132; CDALB 1941-1968; CN 7; DA; DA3; DAB; DAC; DAM MST, NOV, POP; DLB 2, 28, 299; DLBD 3; DLBY 1982; EWL 3; MTCW 1, 2; NFS 4, 14; RGAL 4; RGSF 2; SSFS 12; TUS
Belser, Reimond Karel Maria de 1929-
See Ruyslinck, Ward
See also CA 152
Bely, Andrey .... **PC 11; TCLC 7**
See Bugayev, Boris Nikolayevich
See also DLB 295; EW 9; EWL 3; MTCW 1
Belyi, Andrei
See Bugayev, Boris Nikolayevich
See also RGWL 2, 3
Bembo, Pietro 1470-1547 .... **LC 79**
See also RGWL 2, 3
Benary, Margot
See Benary-Isbert, Margot

Benary-Isbert, Margot 1889-1979 .... **CLC 12**
See also CA 5-8R; 89-92; CANR 4, 72;
CLR 12; MAICYA 1, 2; SATA 2; SATA-
Obit 21

Benavente (y Martinez), Jacinto
1866-1954 .... **DC 26; HLCS 1; TCLC 3**
See also CA 106; 131; CANR 81; DAM
DRAM, MULT; EWL 3; GLL 2; HW 1,
2; MTCW 1, 2

Benchley, Peter (Bradford) 1940- .. **CLC 4, 8**
See also AAYA 14; AITN 2; BPFB 1; CA
17-20R; CANR 12, 35, 66, 115; CPW;
DAM NOV, POP; HGG; MTCW 1, 2;
SATA 3, 89

Benchley, Robert (Charles)
1889-1945 .... **TCLC 1, 55**
See also CA 105; 153; DLB 11; RGAL 4

Benda, Julien 1867-1956 .... **TCLC 60**
See also CA 120; 154; GFL 1789 to the
Present

Benedict, Ruth (Fulton)
1887-1948 .... **TCLC 60**
See also CA 158; DLB 246

Benedikt, Michael 1935- .... **CLC 4, 14**
See also CA 13-16R; CANR 7; CP 7; DLB
5

Benet, Juan 1927-1993 .... **CLC 28**
See also CA 143; EWL 3

Benet, Stephen Vincent 1898-1943 ..... **PC 64;**
SSC 10; TCLC 7
See also AMWS 11; CA 104; 152; DA3;
DAM POET; DLB 4, 48, 102, 249, 284;
DLBY 1997; EWL 3; HGG; MTCW 1;
RGAL 4; RGSF 2; SUFW; WP; YABC 1

Benet, William Rose 1886-1950 ..... **TCLC 28**
See also CA 118; 152; DAM POET; DLB
45; RGAL 4

Benford, Gregory (Albert) 1941- ..... **CLC 52**
See also BPFB 1; CA 69-72, 175; CAAE
175; CAAS 27; CANR 12, 24, 49, 95,
134; CSW; DLBY 1982; SCFW 2; SFW
4

Bengtsson, Frans (Gunnar)
1894-1954 .... **TCLC 48**
See also CA 170; EWL 3

Benjamin, David
See Slavitt, David R(ytman)

Benjamin, Lois
See Gould, Lois

Benjamin, Walter 1892-1940 .... **TCLC 39**
See also CA 164; DLB 242; EW 11; EWL
3

Ben Jelloun, Tahar 1944-
See Jelloun, Tahar ben
See also CA 135; CWW 2; EWL 3; RGWL
3; WLIT 2

Benn, Gottfried 1886-1956 .. **PC 35; TCLC 3**
See also CA 106; 153; DLB 56; EWL 3;
RGWL 2, 3

Bennett, Alan 1934- .... **CLC 45, 77**
See also BRWS 8; CA 103; CANR 35, 55,
106; CBD; CD 5; DAB; DAM MST;
MTCW 1, 2

Bennett, (Enoch) Arnold
1867-1931 .... **TCLC 5, 20**
See also BRW 6; CA 106; 155; CDBLB
1890-1914; DLB 10, 34, 98, 135; EWL 3;
MTCW 2

Bennett, Elizabeth
See Mitchell, Margaret (Munnerlyn)

Bennett, George Harold 1930-
See Bennett, Hal
See also BW 1; CA 97-100; CANR 87

Bennett, Gwendolyn B. 1902-1981 .... **HR 2**
See also BW 1; CA 125; DLB 51; WP

Bennett, Hal .... **CLC 5**
See Bennett, George Harold
See also DLB 33

Bennett, Jay 1912- .... **CLC 35**
See also AAYA 10; CA 69-72; CANR 11,
42, 79; JRDA; SAAS 4; SATA 41, 87;
SATA-Brief 27; WYA; YAW

Bennett, Louise (Simone) 1919- .... **BLC 1;**
CLC 28
See also BW 2, 3; CA 151; CDWLB 3; CP
7; DAM MULT; DLB 117; EWL 3

Benson, A. C. 1862-1925 .... **TCLC 123**
See also DLB 98

Benson, E(dward) F(rederic)
1867-1940 .... **TCLC 27**
See also CA 114; 157; DLB 135, 153;
HGG; SUFW 1

Benson, Jackson J. 1930- .... **CLC 34**
See also CA 25-28R; DLB 111

Benson, Sally 1900-1972 .... **CLC 17**
See also CA 19-20; 37-40R; CAP 1; SATA
1, 35; SATA-Obit 27

Benson, Stella 1892-1933 .... **TCLC 17**
See also CA 117; 154, 155; DLB 36, 162;
FANT; TEA

Bentham, Jeremy 1748-1832 .... **NCLC 38**
See also DLB 107, 158, 252

Bentley, E(dmund) C(lerihew)
1875-1956 .... **TCLC 12**
See also CA 108; DLB 70; MSW

Bentley, Eric (Russell) 1916- .... **CLC 24**
See also CA 5-8R; CAD; CANR 6, 67;
CBD; CD 5; INT CANR-6

ben Uzair, Salem
See Horne, Richard Henry Hengist

Beranger, Pierre Jean de
1780-1857 .... **NCLC 34**

Berdyaev, Nicolas
See Berdyaev, Nikolai (Aleksandrovich)

Berdyaev, Nikolai (Aleksandrovich)
1874-1948 .... **TCLC 67**
See also CA 120; 157

Berdyayev, Nikolai (Aleksandrovich)
See Berdyaev, Nikolai (Aleksandrovich)

Berendt, John (Lawrence) 1939- ...... **CLC 86**
See also CA 146; CANR 75, 93; DA3;
MTCW 1

Beresford, J(ohn) D(avys)
1873-1947 .... **TCLC 81**
See also CA 112; 155; DLB 162, 178, 197;
SFW 4; SUFW 1

Bergelson, David (Rafailovich)
1884-1952 .... **TCLC 81**
See Bergelson, Dovid
See also CA 220

Bergelson, Dovid
See Bergelson, David (Rafailovich)
See also EWL 3

Berger, Colonel
See Malraux, (Georges-)Andre

Berger, John (Peter) 1926- .... **CLC 2, 19**
See also BRWS 4; CA 81-84; CANR 51,
78, 117; CN 7; DLB 14, 207

Berger, Melvin H. 1927- .... **CLC 12**
See also CA 5-8R; CANR 4; CLR 32;
SAAS 2; SATA 5, 88; SATA-Essay 124

Berger, Thomas (Louis) 1924- .. **CLC 3, 5, 8,**
11, 18, 38
See also BPFB 1; CA 1-4R; CANR 5, 28,
51, 128; CN 7; DAM NOV; DLB 2;
DLBY 1980; EWL 3; FANT; INT CANR-
28; MTCW 1, 2; RHW; TCWW 2

Bergman, (Ernst) Ingmar 1918- ...... **CLC 16,**
72
See also CA 81-84; CANR 33, 70; CWW
2; DLB 257; MTCW 2

Bergson, Henri(-Louis) 1859-1941 . **TCLC 32**
See also CA 164; EW 8; EWL 3; GFL 1789
to the Present

Bergstein, Eleanor 1938- .... **CLC 4**
See also CA 53-56; CANR 5

Berkeley, George 1685-1753 .... **LC 65**
See also DLB 31, 101, 252

Berkoff, Steven 1937- .... **CLC 56**
See also CA 104; CANR 72; CBD; CD 5

Berlin, Isaiah 1909-1997 .... **TCLC 105**
See also CA 85-88; 162

Bermant, Chaim (Icyk) 1929-1998 ... **CLC 40**
See also CA 57-60; CANR 6, 31, 57, 105;
CN 7

Bern, Victoria
See Fisher, M(ary) F(rances) K(ennedy)

Bernanos, (Paul Louis) Georges
1888-1948 .... **TCLC 3**
See also CA 104; 130; CANR 94; DLB 72;
EWL 3; GFL 1789 to the Present; RGWL
2, 3

Bernard, April 1956- .... **CLC 59**
See also CA 131

Bernard of Clairvaux 1090-1153 .. **CMLC 71**
See also DLB 208

Berne, Victoria
See Fisher, M(ary) F(rances) K(ennedy)

Bernhard, Thomas 1931-1989 ..... **CLC 3, 32,**
61; DC 14; TCLC 165
See also CA 85-88; 127; CANR 32, 57; CD-
WLB 2; DLB 85, 124; EWL 3; MTCW 1;
RGWL 2, 3

Bernhardt, Sarah (Henriette Rosine)
1844-1923 .... **TCLC 75**
See also CA 157

Bernstein, Charles 1950- .... **CLC 142,**
See also CA 129; CAAS 24; CANR 90; CP
7; DLB 169

Bernstein, Ingrid
See Kirsch, Sarah

Beroul fl. c. 1150- .... **CMLC 75**

Berriault, Gina 1926-1999 .... **CLC 54, 109;**
SSC 30
See also CA 116; 129; 185; CANR 66; DLB
130; SSFS 7,11

Berrigan, Daniel 1921- .... **CLC 4**
See also CA 33-36R, 187; CAAE 187;
CAAS 1; CANR 11, 43, 78; CP 7; DLB 5

Berrigan, Edmund Joseph Michael, Jr.
1934-1983
See Berrigan, Ted
See also CA 61-64; 110; CANR 14, 102

Berrigan, Ted .... **CLC 37**
See Berrigan, Edmund Joseph Michael, Jr.
See also DLB 5, 169; WP

Berry, Charles Edward Anderson 1931-
See Berry, Chuck
See also CA 115

Berry, Chuck .... **CLC 17**
See Berry, Charles Edward Anderson

Berry, Jonas
See Ashbery, John (Lawrence)
See also GLL 1

Berry, Wendell (Erdman) 1934- ... **CLC 4, 6,**
8, 27, 46; PC 28
See also AITN 1; AMWS 10; ANW; CA
73-76; CANR 50, 73, 101, 132; CP 7;
CSW; DAM POET; DLB 5, 6, 234, 275;
MTCW 1

Berryman, John 1914-1972 ... **CLC 1, 2, 3, 4,**
6, 8, 10, 13, 25, 62; PC 64
See also AMW; CA 13-16; 33-36R; CABS
2; CANR 35; CAP 1; CDALB 1941-1968;
DAM POET; DLB 48; EWL 3; MTCW 1,
2; PAB; RGAL 4; WP

Bertolucci, Bernardo 1940- ...... **CLC 16, 157**
See also CA 106; CANR 125

Berton, Pierre (Francis Demarigny)
1920-2004 .... **CLC 104**
See also CA 1-4R; CANR 2, 56; CPW;
DLB 68; SATA 99

Bertrand, Aloysius 1807-1841 .... **NCLC 31**
See Bertrand, Louis oAloysiusc

Bertrand, Louis oAloysiusc
See Bertrand, Aloysius
See also DLB 217

Bertran de Born c. 1140-1215 .... **CMLC 5**

Besant, Annie (Wood) 1847-1933 ..... **TCLC 9**
See also CA 105; 185

Bessie, Alvah 1904-1985 .... **CLC 23**
See also CA 5-8R; 116; CANR 2, 80; DLB 26

Bestuzhev, Aleksandr Aleksandrovich
1797-1837 .... **NCLC 131**
See also DLB 198

Bethlen, T. D.
See Silverberg, Robert

Beti, Mongo .... **BLC 1; CLC 27**
See Biyidi, Alexandre
See also AFW; CANR 79; DAM MULT; EWL 3; WLIT 2

Betjeman, John 1906-1984 ...... **CLC 2, 6, 10, 34, 43**
See also BRW 7; CA 9-12R; 112; CANR 33, 56; CDBLB 1945-1960; DA3; DAB; DAM MST, POET; DLB 20; DLBY 1984; EWL 3; MTCW 1, 2

Bettelheim, Bruno 1903-1990 .... **CLC 79; TCLC 143**
See also CA 81-84; 131; CANR 23, 61; DA3; MTCW 1, 2

Betti, Ugo 1892-1953 .... **TCLC 5**
See also CA 104; 155; EWL 3; RGWL 2, 3

Betts, Doris (Waugh) 1932- ..... **CLC 3, 6, 28; SSC 45**
See also CA 13-16R; CANR 9, 66, 77; CN 7; DLB 218; DLBY 1982; INT CANR-9; RGAL 4

Bevan, Alistair
See Roberts, Keith (John Kingston)

Bey, Pilaff
See Douglas, (George) Norman

Bialik, Chaim Nachman
1873-1934 .... **TCLC 25**
See also CA 170; EWL 3

Bickerstaff, Isaac
See Swift, Jonathan

Bidart, Frank 1939- .... **CLC 33**
See also CA 140; CANR 106; CP 7

Bienek, Horst 1930- .... **CLC 7, 11**
See also CA 73-76; DLB 75

Bierce, Ambrose (Gwinett)
1842-1914(?) ..... **SSC 9, 72; TCLC 1, 7, 44; WLC**
See also AAYA 55; AMW; BYA 11; CA 104; 139; CANR 78; CDALB 1865-1917; DA; DA3; DAC; DAM MST; DLB 11, 12, 23, 71, 74, 186; EWL 3; EXPS; HGG; LAIT 2; RGAL 4; RGSF 2; SSFS 9; SUFW 1

Biggers, Earl Derr 1884-1933 .... **TCLC 65**
See also CA 108; 153; DLB 306

Billiken, Bud
See Motley, Willard (Francis)

Billings, Josh
See Shaw, Henry Wheeler

Billington, (Lady) Rachel (Mary)
1942- .... **CLC 43**
See also AITN 2; CA 33-36R; CANR 44; CN 7

Binchy, Maeve 1940- .... **CLC 153**
See also BEST 90:1; BPFB 1; CA 127; 134; CANR 50, 96, 134; CN 7; CPW; DA3; DAM POP; INT CA-134; MTCW 1; RHW

Binyon, T(imothy) J(ohn) 1936- .... **CLC 34**
See also CA 111; CANR 28

Bion 335B.C.-245B.C. .... **CMLC 39**

Bioy Casares, Adolfo 1914-1999 ... **CLC 4, 8, 13, 88; HLC 1; SSC 17**
See Casares, Adolfo Bioy; Miranda, Javier; Sacastru, Martin
See also CA 29-32R; 177; CANR 19, 43, 66; CWW 2; DAM MULT; DLB 113; EWL 3; HW 1, 2; LAW; MTCW 1, 2

Birch, Allison .... **CLC 65**

Bird, Cordwainer
See Ellison, Harlan (Jay)

Bird, Robert Montgomery
1806-1854 .... **NCLC 1**
See also DLB 202; RGAL 4

Birkerts, Sven 1951- .... **CLC 116**
See also CA 128; 133, 176; CAAE 176; CAAS 29; INT CA-133

Birney, (Alfred) Earle 1904-1995 .. **CLC 1, 4, 6, 11; PC 52**
See also CA 1-4R; CANR 5, 20; CP 7; DAC; DAM MST, POET; DLB 88; MTCW 1; PFS 8; RGEL 2

Biruni, al 973-1048(?) .... **CMLC 28**

Bishop, Elizabeth 1911-1979 ..... **CLC 1, 4, 9, 13, 15, 32; PC 3, 34; TCLC 121**
See also AMWR 2; AMWS 1; CA 5-8R; 89-92; CABS 2; CANR 26, 61, 108; CDALB 1968-1988; DA; DA3; DAC; DAM MST, POET; DLB 5, 169; EWL 3; GLL 2; MAWW; MTCW 1, 2; PAB; PFS 6, 12; RGAL 4; SATA-Obit 24; TUS; WP

Bishop, John 1935- .... **CLC 10**
See also CA 105

Bishop, John Peale 1892-1944 ..... **TCLC 103**
See also CA 107; 155; DLB 4, 9, 45; RGAL 4

Bissett, Bill 1939- .... **CLC 18; PC 14**
See also CA 69-72; CAAS 19; CANR 15; CCA 1; CP 7; DLB 53; MTCW 1

Bissoondath, Neil (Devindra)
1955- .... **CLC 120**
See also CA 136; CANR 123; CN 7; DAC

Bitov, Andrei (Georgievich) 1937- ... **CLC 57**
See also CA 142; DLB 302

Biyidi, Alexandre 1932-
See Beti, Mongo
See also BW 1, 3; CA 114; 124; CANR 81; DA3; MTCW 1, 2

Bjarme, Brynjolf
See Ibsen, Henrik (Johan)

Bjoernson, Bjoernstjerne (Martinius)
1832-1910 .... **TCLC 7, 37**
See also CA 104

Black, Robert
See Holdstock, Robert P.

Blackburn, Paul 1926-1971 .... **CLC 9, 43**
See also BG 2; CA 81-84; 33-36R; CANR 34; DLB 16; DLBY 1981

Black Elk 1863-1950 .... **NNAL; TCLC 33**
See also CA 144; DAM MULT; MTCW 1; WP

Black Hawk 1767-1838 .... **NNAL**

Black Hobart
See Sanders, (James) Ed(ward)

Blacklin, Malcolm
See Chambers, Aidan

Blackmore, R(ichard) D(oddridge)
1825-1900 .... **TCLC 27**
See also CA 120; DLB 18; RGEL 2

Blackmur, R(ichard) P(almer)
1904-1965 .... **CLC 2, 24**
See also AMWS 2; CA 11-12; 25-28R; CANR 71; CAP 1; DLB 63; EWL 3

Black Tarantula
See Acker, Kathy

Blackwood, Algernon (Henry)
1869-1951 .... **TCLC 5**
See also CA 105; 150; DLB 153, 156, 178; HGG; SUFW 1

Blackwood, Caroline 1931-1996 .... **CLC 6, 9, 100**
See also BRWS 9; CA 85-88; 151; CANR 32, 61, 65; CN 7; DLB 14, 207; HGG; MTCW 1

Blade, Alexander
See Hamilton, Edmond; Silverberg, Robert

Blaga, Lucian 1895-1961 .... **CLC 75**
See also CA 157; DLB 220; EWL 3

Blair, Eric (Arthur) 1903-1950 .... **TCLC 123**
See Orwell, George
See also CA 104; 132; DA; DA3; DAB; DAC; DAM MST, NOV; MTCW 1, 2; SATA 29

Blair, Hugh 1718-1800 .... **NCLC 75**

Blais, Marie-Claire 1939- .... **CLC 2, 4, 6, 13, 22**
See also CA 21-24R; CAAS 4; CANR 38, 75, 93; CWW 2; DAC; DAM MST; DLB 53; EWL 3; FW; MTCW 1, 2; TWA

Blaise, Clark 1940- .... **CLC 29**
See also AITN 2; CA 53-56; CAAS 3; CANR 5, 66, 106; CN 7; DLB 53; RGSF 2

Blake, Fairley
See De Voto, Bernard (Augustine)

Blake, Nicholas
See Day Lewis, C(ecil)
See also DLB 77; MSW

Blake, Sterling
See Benford, Gregory (Albert)

Blake, William 1757-1827 . **NCLC 13, 37, 57, 127; PC 12, 63; WLC**
See also AAYA 47; BRW 3; BRWR 1; CD-BLB 1789-1832; CLR 52; DA; DA3; DAB; DAC; DAM MST, POET; DLB 93, 163; EXPP; LATS 1:1; LMFS 1; MAI-CYA 1, 2; PAB; PFS 2, 12; SATA 30; TEA; WCH; WLIT 3; WP

Blanchot, Maurice 1907-2003 .... **CLC 135**
See also CA 117; 144; 213; DLB 72, 296; EWL 3

Blasco Ibanez, Vicente 1867-1928 . **TCLC 12**
See also BPFB 1; CA 110; 131; CANR 81; DA3; DAM NOV; EW 8; EWL 3; HW 1, 2; MTCW 1

Blatty, William Peter 1928- .... **CLC 2**
See also CA 5-8R; CANR 9, 124; DAM POP; HGG

Bleeck, Oliver
See Thomas, Ross (Elmore)

Blessing, Lee 1949- .... **CLC 54**
See also CAD; CD 5

Blight, Rose
See Greer, Germaine

Blish, James (Benjamin) 1921-1975 . **CLC 14**
See also BPFB 1; CA 1-4R; 57-60; CANR 3; DLB 8; MTCW 1; SATA 66; SCFW 2; SFW 4

Bliss, Frederick
See Card, Orson Scott

Bliss, Reginald
See Wells, H(erbert) G(eorge)

Blixen, Karen (Christentze Dinesen)
1885-1962
See Dinesen, Isak
See also CA 25-28; CANR 22, 50; CAP 2; DA3; DLB 214; LMFS 1; MTCW 1, 2; SATA 44; SSFS 20

Bloch, Robert (Albert) 1917-1994 .... **CLC 33**
See also AAYA 29; CA 5-8R, 179; 146; CAAE 179; CAAS 20; CANR 5, 78; DA3; DLB 44; HGG; INT CANR-5; MTCW 1; SATA 12; SATA-Obit 82; SFW 4; SUFW 1, 2

Blok, Alexander (Alexandrovich)
1880-1921 .... **PC 21; TCLC 5**
See also CA 104; 183; DLB 295; EW 9; EWL 3; LMFS 2; RGWL 2, 3

Blom, Jan
  See Breytenbach, Breyten
Bloom, Harold 1930- .... **CLC 24, 103**
  See also CA 13-16R; CANR 39, 75, 92,
  133; DLB 67; EWL 3; MTCW 1; RGAL
  4
Bloomfield, Aurelius
  See Bourne, Randolph S(illiman)
Bloomfield, Robert 1766-1823 ..... **NCLC 145**
  See also DLB 93
Blount, Roy (Alton), Jr. 1941- .... **CLC 38**
  See also CA 53-56; CANR 10, 28, 61, 125;
  CSW; INT CANR-28; MTCW 1, 2
Blowsnake, Sam 1875-(?) .... **NNAL**
Bloy, Leon 1846-1917 .... **TCLC 22**
  See also CA 121; 183; DLB 123; GFL 1789
  to the Present
Blue Cloud, Peter (Aroniawenrate)
  1933- .... **NNAL**
  See also CA 117; CANR 40; DAM MULT
Bluggage, Oranthy
  See Alcott, Louisa May
Blume, Judy (Sussman) 1938- .... **CLC 12, 30**
  See also AAYA 3, 26; BYA 1, 8, 12; CA 29-
  32R; CANR 13, 37, 66, 124; CLR 2, 15,
  69; CPW; DA3; DAM NOV, POP; DLB
  52; JRDA; MAICYA 1, 2; MAICYAS 1;
  MTCW 1, 2; SATA 2, 31, 79, 142; WYA;
  YAW
Blunden, Edmund (Charles)
  1896-1974 .... **CLC 2, 56**
  See also BRW 6; CA 17-18; 45-48; CANR
  54; CAP 2; DLB 20, 100, 155; MTCW 1;
  PAB
Bly, Robert (Elwood) 1926- .... **CLC 1, 2, 5,
  10, 15, 38, 128; PC 39**
  See also AMWS 4; CA 5-8R; CANR 41,
  73, 125; CP 7; DA3; DAM POET; DLB
  5; EWL 3; MTCW 1, 2; PFS 6, 17; RGAL
  4
Boas, Franz 1858-1942 .... **TCLC 56**
  See also CA 115; 181
Bobette
  See Simenon, Georges (Jacques Christian)
Boccaccio, Giovanni 1313-1375 ... **CMLC 13,
  57; SSC 10**
  See also EW 2; RGSF 2; RGWL 2, 3; TWA
Bochco, Steven 1943- .... **CLC 35**
  See also AAYA 11; CA 124; 138
Bode, Sigmund
  See O'Doherty, Brian
Bodel, Jean 1167(?)-1210 .... **CMLC 28**
Bodenheim, Maxwell 1892-1954 .... **TCLC 44**
  See also CA 110; 187; DLB 9, 45; RGAL 4
Bodenheimer, Maxwell
  See Bodenheim, Maxwell
Bodker, Cecil 1927-
  See Bodker, Cecil
Bodker, Cecil 1927- .... **CLC 21**
  See also CA 73-76; CANR 13, 44, 111;
  CLR 23; MAICYA 1, 2; SATA 14, 133
Boell, Heinrich (Theodor)
  1917-1985 ..... **CLC 2, 3, 6, 9, 11, 15, 27,
  32, 72; SSC 23; WLC**
  See Boll, Heinrich
  See also CA 21-24R; 116; CANR 24; DA;
  DA3; DAB; DAC; DAM MST, NOV;
  DLB 69; DLBY 1985; MTCW 1, 2; SSFS
  20; TWA
Boerne, Alfred
  See Doeblin, Alfred
Boethius c. 480-c. 524 .... **CMLC 15**
  See also DLB 115; RGWL 2, 3
Boff, Leonardo (Genezio Darci)
  1938- .... **CLC 70; HLC 1**
  See also CA 150; DAM MULT; HW 2

Bogan, Louise 1897-1970 .... **CLC 4, 39, 46,
  93; PC 12**
  See also AMWS 3; CA 73-76; 25-28R;
  CANR 33, 82; DAM POET; DLB 45, 169;
  EWL 3; MAWW; MTCW 1, 2; PFS 21;
  RGAL 4
Bogarde, Dirk
  See Van Den Bogarde, Derek Jules Gaspard
  Ulric Niven
  See also DLB 14
Bogosian, Eric 1953- .... **CLC 45, 141**
  See also CA 138; CAD; CANR 102; CD 5
Bograd, Larry 1953- .... **CLC 35**
  See also CA 93-96; CANR 57; SAAS 21;
  SATA 33, 89; WYA
Boiardo, Matteo Maria 1441-1494 .... **LC 6**
Boileau-Despreaux, Nicolas 1636-1711 . **LC 3**
  See also DLB 268; EW 3; GFL Beginnings
  to 1789; RGWL 2, 3
Boissard, Maurice
  See Leautaud, Paul
Bojer, Johan 1872-1959 .... **TCLC 64**
  See also CA 189; EWL 3
Bok, Edward W(illiam)
  1863-1930 .... **TCLC 101**
  See also CA 217; DLB 91; DLBD 16
Boker, George Henry 1823-1890 . **NCLC 125**
  See also RGAL 4
Boland, Eavan (Aisling) 1944- .. **CLC 40, 67,
  113; PC 58**
  See also BRWS 5; CA 143, 207; CAAE
  207; CANR 61; CP 7; CWP; DAM POET;
  DLB 40; FW; MTCW 2; PFS 12
Boll, Heinrich
  See Boell, Heinrich (Theodor)
  See also BPFB 1; CDWLB 2; EW 13; EWL
  3; RGSF 2; RGWL 2, 3
Bolt, Lee
  See Faust, Frederick (Schiller)
Bolt, Robert (Oxton) 1924-1995 .... **CLC 14**
  See also CA 17-20R; 147; CANR 35, 67;
  CBD; DAM DRAM; DFS 2; DLB 13,
  233; EWL 3; LAIT 1; MTCW 1
Bombal, Maria Luisa 1910-1980 .... **HLCS 1;
  SSC 37**
  See also CA 127; CANR 72; EWL 3; HW
  1; LAW; RGSF 2
Bombet, Louis-Alexandre-Cesar
  See Stendhal
Bomkauf
  See Kaufman, Bob (Garnell)
Bonaventura .... **NCLC 35**
  See also DLB 90
Bond, Edward 1934- .... **CLC 4, 6, 13, 23**
  See also AAYA 50; BRWS 1; CA 25-28R;
  CANR 38, 67, 106; CBD; CD 5; DAM
  DRAM; DFS 3, 8; DLB 13; EWL 3;
  MTCW 1
Bonham, Frank 1914-1989 .... **CLC 12**
  See also AAYA 1; BYA 1, 3; CA 9-12R;
  CANR 4, 36; JRDA; MAICYA 1, 2;
  SAAS 3; SATA 1, 49; SATA-Obit 62;
  TCWW 2; YAW
Bonnefoy, Yves 1923- . **CLC 9, 15, 58; PC 58**
  See also CA 85-88; CANR 33, 75, 97;
  CWW 2; DAM MST, POET; DLB 258;
  EWL 3; GFL 1789 to the Present; MTCW
  1, 2
Bonner, Marita .... **HR 2**
  See Occomy, Marita (Odette) Bonner
Bonnin, Gertrude 1876-1938 .... **NNAL**
  See Zitkala-Sa
  See also CA 150; DAM MULT
Bontemps, Arna(ud Wendell)
  1902-1973 ..... **BLC 1; CLC 1, 18; HR 2**
  See also BW 1; CA 1-4R; 41-44R; CANR
  4, 35; CLR 6; CWRI 5; DA3; DAM
  MULT, NOV, POET; DLB 48, 51; JRDA;
  MAICYA 1, 2; MTCW 1, 2; SATA 2, 44;
  SATA-Obit 24; WCH; WP

Boot, William
  See Stoppard, Tom
Booth, Martin 1944-2004 .... **CLC 13**
  See also CA 93-96; 188; 223; CAAE 188;
  CAAS 2; CANR 92
Booth, Philip 1925- .... **CLC 23**
  See also CA 5-8R; CANR 5, 88; CP 7;
  DLBY 1982
Booth, Wayne C(layson) 1921- .... **CLC 24**
  See also CA 1-4R; CAAS 5; CANR 3, 43,
  117; DLB 67
Borchert, Wolfgang 1921-1947 .... **TCLC 5**
  See also CA 104; 188; DLB 69, 124; EWL
  3
Borel, Petrus 1809-1859 .... **NCLC 41**
  See also DLB 119; GFL 1789 to the Present
Borges, Jorge Luis 1899-1986 ... **CLC 1, 2, 3,
  4, 6, 8, 9, 10, 13, 19, 44, 48, 83; HLC 1;
  PC 22, 32; SSC 4, 41; TCLC 109;
  WLC**
  See also AAYA 26; BPFB 1; CA 21-24R;
  CANR 19, 33, 75, 105, 133; CDWLB 3;
  DA; DA3; DAB; DAC; DAM MST,
  MULT; DLB 113, 283; DLBY 1986;
  DNFS 1, 2; EWL 3; HW 1, 2; LAW;
  LMFS 2; MSW; MTCW 1, 2; RGSF 2;
  RGWL 2, 3; SFW 4; SSFS 17; TWA;
  WLIT 1
Borowski, Tadeusz 1922-1951 .... **SSC 48;
  TCLC 9**
  See also CA 106; 154; CDWLB 4; DLB
  215; EWL 3; RGSF 2; RGWL 3; SSFS
  13
Borrow, George (Henry)
  1803-1881 .... **NCLC 9**
  See also DLB 21, 55, 166
Bosch (Gavino), Juan 1909-2001 ..... **HLCS 1**
  See also CA 151; 204; DAM MST, MULT;
  DLB 145; HW 1, 2
Bosman, Herman Charles
  1905-1951 .... **TCLC 49**
  See Malan, Herman
  See also CA 160; DLB 225; RGSF 2
Bosschere, Jean de 1878(?)-1953 ... **TCLC 19**
  See also CA 115; 186
Boswell, James 1740-1795 ... **LC 4, 50; WLC**
  See also BRW 3; CDBLB 1660-1789; DA;
  DAB; DAC; DAM MST; DLB 104, 142;
  TEA; WLIT 3
Bottomley, Gordon 1874-1948 ..... **TCLC 107**
  See also CA 120; 192; DLB 10
Bottoms, David 1949- .... **CLC 53**
  See also CA 105; CANR 22; CSW; DLB
  120; DLBY 1983
Boucicault, Dion 1820-1890 .... **NCLC 41**
Boucolon, Maryse
  See Conde, Maryse
Bourdieu, Pierre 1930-2002 .... **CLC 198**
  See also CA 130; 204
Bourget, Paul (Charles Joseph)
  1852-1935 .... **TCLC 12**
  See also CA 107; 196; DLB 123; GFL 1789
  to the Present
Bourjaily, Vance (Nye) 1922- .... **CLC 8, 62**
  See also CA 1-4R; CAAS 1; CANR 2, 72;
  CN 7; DLB 2, 143
Bourne, Randolph S(illiman)
  1886-1918 .... **TCLC 16**
  See also AMW; CA 117; 155; DLB 63
Bova, Ben(jamin William) 1932- ...... **CLC 45**
  See also AAYA 16; CA 5-8R; CAAS 18;
  CANR 11, 56, 94, 111; CLR 3, 96; DLBY
  1981; INT CANR-11; MAICYA 1, 2;
  MTCW 1; SATA 6, 68, 133; SFW 4
Bowen, Elizabeth (Dorothea Cole)
  1899-1973 . **CLC 1, 3, 6, 11, 15, 22, 118;
  SSC 3, 28, 66; TCLC 148**
  See also BRWS 2; CA 17-18; 41-44R;
  CANR 35, 105; CAP 2; CDBLB 1945-

1960; DA3; DAM NOV; DLB 15, 162; EWL 3; EXPS; FW; HGG; MTCW 1, 2; NFS 13; RGSF 2; SSFS 5; SUFW 1; TEA; WLIT 4

Bowering, George 1935- .... **CLC 15, 47**
See also CA 21-24R; CAAS 16; CANR 10; CP 7; DLB 53

Bowering, Marilyn R(uthe) 1949- .... **CLC 32**
See also CA 101; CANR 49; CP 7; CWP

Bowers, Edgar 1924-2000 .... **CLC 9**
See also CA 5-8R; 188; CANR 24; CP 7; CSW; DLB 5

Bowers, Mrs. J. Milton 1842-1914
See Bierce, Ambrose (Gwinett)

Bowie, David .... **CLC 17**
See Jones, David Robert

Bowles, Jane (Sydney) 1917-1973 ..... **CLC 3, 68**
See Bowles, Jane Auer
See also CA 19-20; 41-44R; CAP 2

Bowles, Jane Auer
See Bowles, Jane (Sydney)
See also EWL 3

Bowles, Paul (Frederick) 1910-1999 . **CLC 1, 2, 19, 53; SSC 3**
See also AMWS 4; CA 1-4R; 186; CAAS 1; CANR 1, 19, 50, 75; CN 7; DA3; DLB 5, 6, 218; EWL 3; MTCW 1, 2; RGAL 4; SSFS 17

Bowles, William Lisle 1762-1850 . **NCLC 103**
See also DLB 93

Box, Edgar
See Vidal, (Eugene Luther) Gore
See also GLL 1

Boyd, James 1888-1944 .... **TCLC 115**
See also CA 186; DLB 9; DLBD 16; RGAL 4; RHW

Boyd, Nancy
See Millay, Edna St. Vincent
See also GLL 1

Boyd, Thomas (Alexander) 1898-1935 .... **TCLC 111**
See also CA 111; 183; DLB 9; DLBD 16

Boyd, William 1952- .... **CLC 28, 53, 70**
See also CA 114; 120; CANR 51, 71, 131; CN 7; DLB 231

Boyesen, Hjalmar Hjorth 1848-1895 .... **NCLC 135**
See also DLB 12, 71; DLBD 13; RGAL 4

Boyle, Kay 1902-1992 .... **CLC 1, 5, 19, 58, 121; SSC 5**
See also CA 13-16R; 140; CAAS 1; CANR 29, 61, 110; DLB 4, 9, 48, 86; DLBY 1993; EWL 3; MTCW 1, 2; RGAL 4; RGSF 2; SSFS 10, 13, 14

Boyle, Mark
See Kienzle, William X(avier)

Boyle, Patrick 1905-1982 .... **CLC 19**
See also CA 127

Boyle, T. C.
See Boyle, T(homas) Coraghessan
See also AMWS 8

Boyle, T(homas) Coraghessan 1948- .... **CLC 36, 55, 90; SSC 16**
See Boyle, T. C.
See also AAYA 47; BEST 90:4; BPFB 1; CA 120; CANR 44, 76, 89, 132; CN 7; CPW; DA3; DAM POP; DLB 218, 278; DLBY 1986; EWL 3; MTCW 2; SSFS 13, 19

Boz
See Dickens, Charles (John Huffam)

Brackenridge, Hugh Henry 1748-1816 .... **NCLC 7**
See also DLB 11, 37; RGAL 4

Bradbury, Edward P.
See Moorcock, Michael (John)
See also MTCW 2

Bradbury, Malcolm (Stanley) 1932-2000 .... **CLC 32, 61**
See also CA 1-4R; CANR 1, 33, 91, 98; CN 7; DA3; DAM NOV; DLB 14, 207; EWL 3; MTCW 1, 2

Bradbury, Ray (Douglas) 1920- .... **CLC 1, 3, 10, 15, 42, 98; SSC 29, 53; WLC**
See also AAYA 15; AITN 1, 2; AMWS 4; BPFB 1; BYA 4, 5, 11; CA 1-4R; CANR 2, 30, 75, 125; CDALB 1968-1988; CN 7; CPW; DA; DA3; DAB; DAC; DAM MST, NOV, POP; DLB 2, 8; EXPN; EXPS; HGG; LAIT 3, 5; LATS 1:2; LMFS 2; MTCW 1, 2; NFS 1; RGAL 4; RGSF 2; SATA 11, 64, 123; SCFW 2; SFW 4; SSFS 1, 20; SUFW 1, 2; TUS; YAW

Braddon, Mary Elizabeth 1837-1915 .... **TCLC 111**
See also BRWS 8; CA 108; 179; CMW 4; DLB 18, 70, 156; HGG

Bradfield, Scott (Michael) 1955- .... **SSC 65**
See also CA 147; CANR 90; HGG; SUFW 2

Bradford, Gamaliel 1863-1932 .... **TCLC 36**
See also CA 160; DLB 17

Bradford, William 1590-1657 .... **LC 64**
See also DLB 24, 30; RGAL 4

Bradley, David (Henry), Jr. 1950- .... **BLC 1; CLC 23, 118**
See also BW 1, 3; CA 104; CANR 26, 81; CN 7; DAM MULT; DLB 33

Bradley, John Ed(mund, Jr.) 1958- . **CLC 55**
See also CA 139; CANR 99; CN 7; CSW

Bradley, Marion Zimmer 1930-1999 .... **CLC 30**
See Chapman, Lee; Dexter, John; Gardner, Miriam; Ives, Morgan; Rivers, Elfrida
See also AAYA 40; BPFB 1; CA 57-60; 185; CAAS 10; CANR 7, 31, 51, 75, 107; CPW; DA3; DAM POP; DLB 8; FANT; FW; MTCW 1, 2; SATA 90, 139; SATA-Obit 116; SFW 4; SUFW 2; YAW

Bradshaw, John 1933- .... **CLC 70**
See also CA 138; CANR 61

Bradstreet, Anne 1612(?)-1672 ...... **LC 4, 30; PC 10**
See also AMWS 1; CDALB 1640-1865; DA; DA3; DAC; DAM MST, POET; DLB 24; EXPP; FW; PFS 6; RGAL 4; TUS; WP

Brady, Joan 1939- .... **CLC 86**
See also CA 141

Bragg, Melvyn 1939- .... **CLC 10**
See also BEST 89:3; CA 57-60; CANR 10, 48, 89; CN 7; DLB 14, 271; RHW

Brahe, Tycho 1546-1601 .... **LC 45**
See also DLB 300

Braine, John (Gerard) 1922-1986 . **CLC 1, 3, 41**
See also CA 1-4R; 120; CANR 1, 33; CD-BLB 1945-1960; DLB 15; DLBY 1986; EWL 3; MTCW 1

Braithwaite, William Stanley (Beaumont) 1878-1962 .... **BLC 1; HR 2; PC 52**
See also BW 1; CA 125; DAM MULT; DLB 50, 54

Bramah, Ernest 1868-1942 .... **TCLC 72**
See also CA 156; CMW 4; DLB 70; FANT

Brammer, William 1930(?)-1978 ...... **CLC 31**
See also CA 77-80

Brancati, Vitaliano 1907-1954 .... **TCLC 12**
See also CA 109; DLB 264; EWL 3

Brancato, Robin F(idler) 1936- .... **CLC 35**
See also AAYA 9; BYA 6; CA 69-72; CANR 11, 45; CLR 32; JRDA; MAICYA 2; MAICYAS 1; SAAS 9; SATA 97; WYA; YAW

Brand, Dionne 1953- .... **CLC 192**
See also BW 2; CA 143; CWP

Brand, Max
See Faust, Frederick (Schiller)
See also BPFB 1; TCWW 2

Brand, Millen 1906-1980 .... **CLC 7**
See also CA 21-24R; 97-100; CANR 72

Branden, Barbara .... **CLC 44**
See also CA 148

Brandes, Georg (Morris Cohen) 1842-1927 .... **TCLC 10**
See also CA 105; 189; DLB 300

Brandys, Kazimierz 1916-2000 .... **CLC 62**
See also EWL 3

Branley, Franklyn M(ansfield) 1915-2002 .... **CLC 21**
See also CA 33-36R; 207; CANR 14, 39; CLR 13; MAICYA 1, 2; SAAS 16; SATA 4, 68, 136

Brant, Beth (E.) 1941- .... **NNAL**
See also CA 144; FW

Brant, Sebastian 1457-1521 .... **LC 112**
See also DLB 179; RGWL 2, 3

Brathwaite, Edward Kamau 1930- .... **BLCS; CLC 11; PC 56**
See also BW 2, 3; CA 25-28R; CANR 11, 26, 47, 107; CDWLB 3; CP 7; DAM POET; DLB 125; EWL 3

Brathwaite, Kamau
See Brathwaite, Edward Kamau

Brautigan, Richard (Gary) 1935-1984 .... **CLC 1, 3, 5, 9, 12, 34, 42; TCLC 133**
See also BPFB 1; CA 53-56; 113; CANR 34; DA3; DAM NOV; DLB 2, 5, 206; DLBY 1980, 1984; FANT; MTCW 1; RGAL 4; SATA 56

Brave Bird, Mary .... **NNAL**
See Crow Dog, Mary (Ellen)

Braverman, Kate 1950- .... **CLC 67**
See also CA 89-92

Brecht, (Eugen) Bertolt (Friedrich) 1898-1956 ..... **DC 3; TCLC 1, 6, 13, 35; WLC**
See also CA 104; 133; CANR 62; CDWLB 2; DA; DA3; DAB; DAC; DAM DRAM, MST; DFS 4, 5, 9; DLB 56, 124; EW 11; EWL 3; IDTP; MTCW 1, 2; RGWL 2, 3; TWA

Brecht, Eugen Berthold Friedrich
See Brecht, (Eugen) Bertolt (Friedrich)

Bremer, Fredrika 1801-1865 .... **NCLC 11**
See also DLB 254

Brennan, Christopher John 1870-1932 .... **TCLC 17**
See also CA 117; 188; DLB 230; EWL 3

Brennan, Maeve 1917-1993 ... **CLC 5; TCLC 124**
See also CA 81-84; CANR 72, 100

Brent, Linda
See Jacobs, Harriet A(nn)

Brentano, Clemens (Maria) 1778-1842 .... **NCLC 1**
See also DLB 90; RGWL 2, 3

Brent of Bin Bin
See Franklin, (Stella Maria Sarah) Miles (Lampe)

Brenton, Howard 1942- .... **CLC 31**
See also CA 69-72; CANR 33, 67; CBD; CD 5; DLB 13; MTCW 1

Breslin, James 1930-
See Breslin, Jimmy
See also CA 73-76; CANR 31, 75; DAM NOV; MTCW 1, 2

Breslin, Jimmy .... **CLC 4, 43**
See Breslin, James
See also AITN 1; DLB 185; MTCW 2

Bresson, Robert 1901(?)-1999 .... **CLC 16**
See also CA 110; 187; CANR 49

Brown, William Hill 1765-1793 .... **LC 93**
See also DLB 37

Brown, William Wells 1815-1884 ...... **BLC 1;
DC 1; NCLC 2, 89**
See also DAM MULT; DLB 3, 50, 183,
248; RGAL 4

Browne, (Clyde) Jackson 1948(?)- ... **CLC 21**
See also CA 120

Browne, Thomas 1605-1682 .... **LC 111**
See also BW 2; DLB 151

Browning, Robert 1812-1889 . **NCLC 19, 79;
PC 2, 61; WLCS**
See also BRW 4; BRWC 2; BRWR 2; CD-
BLB 1832-1890; CLR 97; DA; DA3;
DAB; DAC; DAM MST, POET; DLB 32,
163; EXPP; LATS 1:1; PAB; PFS 1, 15;
RGEL 2; TEA; WLIT 4; WP; YABC 1

Browning, Tod 1882-1962 .... **CLC 16**
See also CA 141; 117

Brownmiller, Susan 1935- .... **CLC 159**
See also CA 103; CANR 35, 75; DAM
NOV; FW; MTCW 1, 2

Brownson, Orestes Augustus
1803-1876 .... **NCLC 50**
See also DLB 1, 59, 73, 243

Bruccoli, Matthew J(oseph) 1931- ... **CLC 34**
See also CA 9-12R; CANR 7, 87; DLB 103

Bruce, Lenny .... **CLC 21**
See Schneider, Leonard Alfred

Bruchac, Joseph III 1942- .... **NNAL**
See also AAYA 19; CA 33-36R; CANR 13,
47, 75, 94; CLR 46; CWRI 5; DAM
MULT; JRDA; MAICYA 2; MAICYAS 1;
MTCW 1; SATA 42, 89, 131

Bruin, John
See Brutus, Dennis

Brulard, Henri
See Stendhal

Brulls, Christian
See Simenon, Georges (Jacques Christian)

Brunetto Latini c. 1220-1294 .... **CMLC 73**

Brunner, John (Kilian Houston)
1934-1995 .... **CLC 8, 10**
See also CA 1-4R; 149; CAAS 8; CANR 2,
37; CPW; DAM POP; DLB 261; MTCW
1, 2; SCFW 2; SFW 4

Bruno, Giordano 1548-1600 .... **LC 27**
See also RGWL 2, 3

Brutus, Dennis 1924- ... **BLC 1; CLC 43; PC
24**
See also AFW; BW 2, 3; CA 49-52; CAAS
14; CANR 2, 27, 42, 81; CDWLB 3; CP
7; DAM MULT, POET; DLB 117, 225;
EWL 3

Bryan, C(ourtlandt) D(ixon) B(arnes)
1936- .... **CLC 29**
See also CA 73-76; CANR 13, 68; DLB
185; INT CANR-13

Bryan, Michael
See Moore, Brian
See also CCA 1

Bryan, William Jennings
1860-1925 .... **TCLC 99**
See also DLB 303

Bryant, William Cullen 1794-1878 . **NCLC 6,
46; PC 20**
See also AMWS 1; CDALB 1640-1865;
DA; DAB; DAC; DAM MST, POET;
DLB 3, 43, 59, 189, 250; EXPP; PAB;
RGAL 4; TUS

Bryusov, Valery Yakovlevich
1873-1924 .... **TCLC 10**
See also CA 107; 155; EWL 3; SFW 4

Buchan, John 1875-1940 .... **TCLC 41**
See also CA 108; 145; CMW 4; DAB;
DAM POP; DLB 34, 70, 156; HGG;
MSW; MTCW 1; RGEL 2; RHW; YABC
2

Buchanan, George 1506-1582 .... **LC 4**
See also DLB 132

Buchanan, Robert 1841-1901 .... **TCLC 107**
See also CA 179; DLB 18, 35

Buchheim, Lothar-Guenther 1918- .... **CLC 6**
See also CA 85-88

Buchner, (Karl) Georg
1813-1837 .... **NCLC 26, 146**
See also CDWLB 2; DLB 133; EW 6;
RGSF 2; RGWL 2, 3; TWA

Buchwald, Art(hur) 1925- .... **CLC 33**
See also AITN 1; CA 5-8R; CANR 21, 67,
107; MTCW 1, 2; SATA 10

Buck, Pearl S(ydenstricker)
1892-1973 .... **CLC 7, 11, 18, 127**
See also AAYA 42; AITN 1; AMWS 2;
BPFB 1; CA 1-4R; 41-44R; CANR 1, 34;
CDALBS; DA; DA3; DAB; DAC; DAM
MST, NOV; DLB 9, 102; EWL 3; LAIT
3; MTCW 1, 2; RGAL 4; RHW; SATA 1,
25; TUS

Buckler, Ernest 1908-1984 .... **CLC 13**
See also CA 11-12; 114; CAP 1; CCA 1;
DAC; DAM MST; DLB 68; SATA 47

Buckley, Christopher (Taylor)
1952- .... **CLC 165**
See also CA 139; CANR 119

Buckley, Vincent (Thomas)
1925-1988 .... **CLC 57**
See also CA 101; DLB 289

Buckley, William F(rank), Jr. 1925- . **CLC 7,
18, 37**
See also AITN 1; BPFB 1; CA 1-4R; CANR
1, 24, 53, 93, 133; CMW 4; CPW; DA3;
DAM POP; DLB 137; DLBY 1980; INT
CANR-24; MTCW 1, 2; TUS

Buechner, (Carl) Frederick 1926- . **CLC 2, 4,
6, 9**
See also AMWS 12; BPFB 1; CA 13-16R;
CANR 11, 39, 64, 114; CN 7; DAM NOV;
DLBY 1980; INT CANR-11; MTCW 1, 2

Buell, John (Edward) 1927- .... **CLC 10**
See also CA 1-4R; CANR 71; DLB 53

Buero Vallejo, Antonio 1916-2000 ... **CLC 15,
46, 139; DC 18**
See also CA 106; 189; CANR 24, 49, 75;
CWW 2; DFS 11; EWL 3; HW 1; MTCW
1, 2

Bufalino, Gesualdo 1920-1996 .... **CLC 74**
See also CA 209; CWW 2; DLB 196

Bugayev, Boris Nikolayevich
1880-1934 .... **PC 11; TCLC 7**
See Bely, Andrey; Belyi, Andrei
See also CA 104; 165; MTCW 1

Bukowski, Charles 1920-1994 ... **CLC 2, 5, 9,
41, 82, 108; PC 18; SSC 45**
See also CA 17-20R; 144; CANR 40, 62,
105; CPW; DA3; DAM NOV, POET;
DLB 5, 130, 169; EWL 3; MTCW 1, 2

Bulgakov, Mikhail (Afanas'evich)
1891-1940 ..... **SSC 18; TCLC 2, 16, 159**
See also BPFB 1; CA 105; 152; DAM
DRAM, NOV; DLB 272; EWL 3; NFS 8;
RGSF 2; RGWL 2, 3; SFW 4; TWA

Bulgya, Alexander Alexandrovich
1901-1956 .... **TCLC 53**
See Fadeev, Aleksandr Aleksandrovich;
Fadeev, Alexandr Alexandrovich; Fadeyev,
Alexander
See also CA 117; 181

Bullins, Ed 1935- ... **BLC 1; CLC 1, 5, 7; DC
6**
See also BW 2, 3; CA 49-52; CAAS 16;
CAD; CANR 24, 46, 73, 134; CD 5;
DAM DRAM, MULT; DLB 7, 38, 249;
EWL 3; MTCW 1, 2; RGAL 4

Bulosan, Carlos 1911-1956 .... **AAL**
See also CA 216; RGAL 4

**Bulwer-Lytton, Edward (George Earle
Lytton)** 1803-1873 .... **NCLC 1, 45**
See also DLB 21; RGEL 2; SFW 4; SUFW
1; TEA

Bunin, Ivan Alexeyevich 1870-1953 ... **SSC 5;
TCLC 6**
See also CA 104; EWL 3; RGSF 2; RGWL
2, 3; TWA

Bunting, Basil 1900-1985 ...... **CLC 10, 39, 47**
See also BRWS 7; CA 53-56; 115; CANR
7; DAM POET; DLB 20; EWL 3; RGEL
2

Bunuel, Luis 1900-1983 ... **CLC 16, 80; HLC
1**
See also CA 101; 110; CANR 32, 77; DAM
MULT; HW 1

Bunyan, John 1628-1688 ..... **LC 4, 69; WLC**
See also BRW 2; BYA 5; CDBLB 1660-
1789; DA; DAB; DAC; DAM MST; DLB
39; RGEL 2; TEA; WCH; WLIT 3

Buravsky, Alexandr .... **CLC 59**

Burckhardt, Jacob (Christoph)
1818-1897 .... **NCLC 49**
See also EW 6

Burford, Eleanor
See Hibbert, Eleanor Alice Burford

Burgess, Anthony . **CLC 1, 2, 4, 5, 8, 10, 13,
15, 22, 40, 62, 81, 94**
See Wilson, John (Anthony) Burgess
See also AAYA 25; AITN 1; BRWS 1; CD-
BLB 1960 to Present; DAB; DLB 14, 194,
261; DLBY 1998; EWL 3; MTCW 1;
RGEL 2; RHW; SFW 4; YAW

Burke, Edmund 1729(?)-1797 .... **LC 7, 36;
WLC**
See also BRW 3; DA; DA3; DAB; DAC;
DAM MST; DLB 104, 252; RGEL 2;
TEA

Burke, Kenneth (Duva) 1897-1993 ... **CLC 2,
24**
See also AMW; CA 5-8R; 143; CANR 39,
74; DLB 45, 63; EWL 3; MTCW 1, 2;
RGAL 4

Burke, Leda
See Garnett, David

Burke, Ralph
See Silverberg, Robert

Burke, Thomas 1886-1945 .... **TCLC 63**
See also CA 113; 155; CMW 4; DLB 197

Burney, Fanny 1752-1840 .... **NCLC 12, 54,
107**
See also BRWS 3; DLB 39; NFS 16; RGEL
2; TEA

Burney, Frances
See Burney, Fanny

Burns, Robert 1759-1796 ... **LC 3, 29, 40; PC
6; WLC**
See also AAYA 51; BRW 3; CDBLB 1789-
1832; DA; DA3; DAB; DAC; DAM MST,
POET; DLB 109; EXPP; PAB; RGEL 2;
TEA; WP

Burns, Tex
See L'Amour, Louis (Dearborn)
See also TCWW 2

Burnshaw, Stanley 1906- .... **CLC 3, 13, 44**
See also CA 9-12R; CP 7; DLB 48; DLBY
1997

Burr, Anne 1937- .... **CLC 6**
See also CA 25-28R

Burroughs, Edgar Rice 1875-1950 . **TCLC 2,
32**
See also AAYA 11; BPFB 1; BYA 4, 9; CA
104; 132; CANR 131; DA3; DAM NOV;
DLB 8; FANT; MTCW 1, 2; RGAL 4;
SATA 41; SCFW 2; SFW 4; TUS; YAW

Burroughs, William S(eward)
1914-1997 .. **CLC 1, 2, 5, 15, 22, 42, 75, 109; TCLC 121; WLC**
See Lee, William; Lee, Willy
See also AAYA 60; AITN 2; AMWS 3; BG 2; BPFB 1; CA 9-12R; 160; CANR 20, 52, 104; CN 7; CPW; DA; DA3; DAB; DAC; DAM MST, NOV, POP; DLB 2, 8, 16, 152, 237; DLBY 1981, 1997; EWL 3; HGG; LMFS 2; MTCW 1, 2; RGAL 4; SFW 4

Burton, Sir Richard F(rancis)
1821-1890 .... **NCLC 42**
See also DLB 55, 166, 184

Burton, Robert 1577-1640 .... **LC 74**
See also DLB 151; RGEL 2

Buruma, Ian 1951- .... **CLC 163**
See also CA 128; CANR 65

Busch, Frederick 1941- ... **CLC 7, 10, 18, 47, 166**
See also CA 33-36R; CAAS 1; CANR 45, 73, 92; CN 7; DLB 6, 218

Bush, Barney (Furman) 1946- .... **NNAL**
See also CA 145

Bush, Ronald 1946- .... **CLC 34**
See also CA 136

Bustos, F(rancisco)
See Borges, Jorge Luis

Bustos Domecq, H(onorio)
See Bioy Casares, Adolfo; Borges, Jorge Luis

Butler, Octavia E(stelle) 1947- .. **BLCS; CLC 38, 121**
See also AAYA 18, 48; AFAW 2; AMWS 13; BPFB 1; BW 2, 3; CA 73-76; CANR 12, 24, 38, 73; CLR 65; CPW; DA3; DAM MULT, POP; DLB 33; LATS 1:2; MTCW 1, 2; NFS 8; SATA 84; SCFW 2; SFW 4; SSFS 6; YAW

Butler, Robert Olen, (Jr.) 1945- ...... **CLC 81, 162**
See also AMWS 12; BPFB 1; CA 112; CANR 66; CSW; DAM POP; DLB 173; INT CA-112; MTCW 1; SSFS 11

Butler, Samuel 1612-1680 .... **LC 16, 43**
See also DLB 101, 126; RGEL 2

Butler, Samuel 1835-1902 .... **TCLC 1, 33; WLC**
See also BRWS 2; CA 143; CDBLB 1890-1914; DA; DA3; DAB; DAC; DAM MST, NOV; DLB 18, 57, 174; RGEL 2; SFW 4; TEA

Butler, Walter C.
See Faust, Frederick (Schiller)

Butor, Michel (Marie Francois)
1926- .... **CLC 1, 3, 8, 11, 15, 161**
See also CA 9-12R; CANR 33, 66; CWW 2; DLB 83; EW 13; EWL 3; GFL 1789 to the Present; MTCW 1, 2

Butts, Mary 1890(?)-1937 .... **TCLC 77**
See also CA 148; DLB 240

Buxton, Ralph
See Silverstein, Alvin; Silverstein, Virginia B(arbara Opshelor)

Buzo, Alex
See Buzo, Alexander (John)
See also DLB 289

Buzo, Alexander (John) 1944- .... **CLC 61**
See also CA 97-100; CANR 17, 39, 69; CD 5

Buzzati, Dino 1906-1972 .... **CLC 36**
See also CA 160; 33-36R; DLB 177; RGWL 2, 3; SFW 4

Byars, Betsy (Cromer) 1928- .... **CLC 35**
See also AAYA 19; BYA 3; CA 33-36R, 183; CAAE 183; CANR 18, 36, 57, 102; CLR 1, 16, 72; DLB 52; INT CANR-18; JRDA; MAICYA 1, 2; MAICYAS 1; MTCW 1; SAAS 1; SATA 4, 46, 80; SATA-Essay 108; WYA; YAW

Byatt, A(ntonia) S(usan Drabble)
1936- .... **CLC 19, 65, 136**
See also BPFB 1; BRWC 2; BRWS 4; CA 13-16R; CANR 13, 33, 50, 75, 96, 133; DA3; DAM NOV, POP; DLB 14, 194; EWL 3; MTCW 1, 2; RGSF 2; RHW; TEA

Byrd, Willam II 1674-1744 .... **LC 112**
See also DLB 24, 140; RGAL 4

Byrne, David 1952- .... **CLC 26**
See also CA 127

Byrne, John Keyes 1926-
See Leonard, Hugh
See also CA 102; CANR 78; INT CA-102

Byron, George Gordon (Noel)
1788-1824 ..... **DC 24; NCLC 2, 12, 109, 149; PC 16; WLC**
See also BRW 4; BRWC 2; CDBLB 1789-1832; DA; DA3; DAB; DAC; DAM MST, POET; DLB 96, 110; EXPP; LMFS 1; PAB; PFS 1, 14; RGEL 2; TEA; WLIT 3; WP

Byron, Robert 1905-1941 .... **TCLC 67**
See also CA 160; DLB 195

C. 3. 3.
See Wilde, Oscar (Fingal O'Flahertie Wills)

Caballero, Fernan 1796-1877 .... **NCLC 10**

Cabell, Branch
See Cabell, James Branch

Cabell, James Branch 1879-1958 .... **TCLC 6**
See also CA 105; 152; DLB 9, 78; FANT; MTCW 1; RGAL 4; SUFW 1

Cabeza de Vaca, Alvar Nunez
1490-1557(?) .... **LC 61**

Cable, George Washington
1844-1925 .... **SSC 4; TCLC 4**
See also CA 104; 155; DLB 12, 74; DLBD 13; RGAL 4; TUS

Cabral de Melo Neto, Joao
1920-1999 .... **CLC 76**
See Melo Neto, Joao Cabral de
See also CA 151; DAM MULT; DLB 307; LAW; LAWS 1

Cabrera Infante, G(uillermo) 1929- . **CLC 5, 25, 45, 120; HLC 1; SSC 39**
See also CA 85-88; CANR 29, 65, 110; CD-WLB 3; CWW 2; DA3; DAM MULT; DLB 113; EWL 3; HW 1, 2; LAW; LAWS 1; MTCW 1, 2; RGSF 2; WLIT 1

Cade, Toni
See Bambara, Toni Cade

Cadmus and Harmonia
See Buchan, John

Caedmon fl. 658-680 .... **CMLC 7**
See also DLB 146

Caeiro, Alberto
See Pessoa, Fernando (Antonio Nogueira)

Caesar, Julius .... **CMLC 47**
See Julius Caesar
See also AW 1; RGWL 2, 3

Cage, John (Milton, Jr.)
1912-1992 .... **CLC 41; PC 58**
See also CA 13-16R; 169; CANR 9, 78; DLB 193; INT CANR-9

Cahan, Abraham 1860-1951 .... **TCLC 71**
See also CA 108; 154; DLB 9, 25, 28; RGAL 4

Cain, G.
See Cabrera Infante, G(uillermo)

Cain, Guillermo
See Cabrera Infante, G(uillermo)

Cain, James M(allahan) 1892-1977 .. **CLC 3, 11, 28**
See also AITN 1; BPFB 1; CA 17-20R; 73-76; CANR 8, 34, 61; CMW 4; DLB 226; EWL 3; MSW; MTCW 1; RGAL 4

Caine, Hall 1853-1931 .... **TCLC 97**
See also RHW

Caine, Mark
See Raphael, Frederic (Michael)

Calasso, Roberto 1941- .... **CLC 81**
See also CA 143; CANR 89

Calderon de la Barca, Pedro
1600-1681 .... **DC 3; HLCS 1; LC 23**
See also EW 2; RGWL 2, 3; TWA

Caldwell, Erskine (Preston)
1903-1987 ... **CLC 1, 8, 14, 50, 60; SSC 19; TCLC 117**
See also AITN 1; AMW; BPFB 1; CA 1-4R; 121; CAAS 1; CANR 2, 33; DA3; DAM NOV, POP; DLB 9, 86; EWL 3; MTCW 1, 2; RGAL 4; RGSF 2; TUS

Caldwell, (Janet Miriam) Taylor (Holland)
1900-1985 .... **CLC 2, 28, 39**
See also BPFB 1; CA 5-8R; CANR 5; DA3; DAM NOV, POP; DLBD 17; RHW

Calhoun, John Caldwell
1782-1850 .... **NCLC 15**
See also DLB 3, 248

Calisher, Hortense 1911- ..... **CLC 2, 4, 8, 38, 134; SSC 15**
See also CA 1-4R; CANR 1, 22, 117; CN 7; DA3; DAM NOV; DLB 2, 218; INT CANR-22; MTCW 1, 2; RGAL 4; RGSF 2

Callaghan, Morley Edward
1903-1990 ..... **CLC 3, 14, 41, 65; TCLC 145**
See also CA 9-12R; 132; CANR 33, 73; DAC; DAM MST; DLB 68; EWL 3; MTCW 1, 2; RGEL 2; RGSF 2; SSFS 19

Callimachus c. 305B.C.-c.
240B.C. .... **CMLC 18**
See also AW 1; DLB 176; RGWL 2, 3

Calvin, Jean
See Calvin, John
See also GFL Beginnings to 1789

Calvin, John 1509-1564 .... **LC 37**
See Calvin, Jean

Calvino, Italo 1923-1985 .... **CLC 5, 8, 11, 22, 33, 39, 73; SSC 3, 48**
See also AAYA 58; CA 85-88; 116; CANR 23, 61, 132; DAM NOV; DLB 196; EW 13; EWL 3; MTCW 1, 2; RGSF 2; RGWL 2, 3; SFW 4; SSFS 12

Camara Laye
See Laye, Camara
See also EWL 3

Camden, William 1551-1623 .... **LC 77**
See also DLB 172

Cameron, Carey 1952- .... **CLC 59**
See also CA 135

Cameron, Peter 1959- .... **CLC 44**
See also AMWS 12; CA 125; CANR 50, 117; DLB 234; GLL 2

Camoens, Luis Vaz de 1524(?)-1580
See Camoes, Luis de
See also EW 2

Camoes, Luis de 1524(?)-1580 . **HLCS 1; LC 62; PC 31**
See Camoens, Luis Vaz de
See also DLB 287; RGWL 2, 3

Campana, Dino 1885-1932 .... **TCLC 20**
See also CA 117; DLB 114; EWL 3

Campanella, Tommaso 1568-1639 .... **LC 32**
See also RGWL 2, 3

Campbell, John W(ood, Jr.)
1910-1971 .... **CLC 32**
See also CA 21-22; 29-32R; CANR 34; CAP 2; DLB 8; MTCW 1; SCFW; SFW 4

Campbell, Joseph 1904-1987 .... **CLC 69; TCLC 140**
See also AAYA 3; BEST 89:2; CA 1-4R; 124; CANR 3, 28, 61, 107; DA3; MTCW 1, 2

Campbell, Maria 1940- .... **CLC 85; NNAL**
See also CA 102; CANR 54; CCA 1; DAC

Campbell, (John) Ramsey 1946- ..... **CLC 42; SSC 19**
See also AAYA 51; CA 57-60, 228; CAAE 228; CANR 7, 102; DLB 261; HGG; INT CANR-7; SUFW 1, 2

Campbell, (Ignatius) Roy (Dunnachie) 1901-1957 .... **TCLC 5**
See also AFW; CA 104; 155; DLB 20, 225; EWL 3; MTCW 2; RGEL 2

Campbell, Thomas 1777-1844 .... **NCLC 19**
See also DLB 93, 144; RGEL 2

Campbell, Wilfred .... **TCLC 9**
See Campbell, William

Campbell, William 1858(?)-1918
See Campbell, Wilfred
See also CA 106; DLB 92

Campion, Jane 1954- .... **CLC 95**
See also AAYA 33; CA 138; CANR 87

Campion, Thomas 1567-1620 .... **LC 78**
See also CDBLB Before 1660; DAM POET; DLB 58, 172; RGEL 2

Camus, Albert 1913-1960 ...... **CLC 1, 2, 4, 9, 11, 14, 32, 63, 69, 124; DC 2; SSC 9, 76; WLC**
See also AAYA 36; AFW; BPFB 1; CA 89-92; CANR 131; DA; DA3; DAB; DAC; DAM DRAM, MST, NOV; DLB 72; EW 13; EWL 3; EXPN; EXPS; GFL 1789 to the Present; LATS 1:2; LMFS 2; MTCW 1, 2; NFS 6, 16; RGSF 2; RGWL 2, 3; SSFS 4; TWA

Canby, Vincent 1924-2000 .... **CLC 13**
See also CA 81-84; 191

Cancale
See Desnos, Robert

Canetti, Elias 1905-1994 .. **CLC 3, 14, 25, 75, 86; TCLC 157**
See also CA 21-24R; 146; CANR 23, 61, 79; CDWLB 2; CWW 2; DA3; DLB 85, 124; EW 12; EWL 3; MTCW 1, 2; RGWL 2, 3; TWA

Canfield, Dorothea F.
See Fisher, Dorothy (Frances) Canfield

Canfield, Dorothea Frances
See Fisher, Dorothy (Frances) Canfield

Canfield, Dorothy
See Fisher, Dorothy (Frances) Canfield

Canin, Ethan 1960- .... **CLC 55; SSC 70**
See also CA 131; 135

Cankar, Ivan 1876-1918 .... **TCLC 105**
See also CDWLB 4; DLB 147; EWL 3

Cannon, Curt
See Hunter, Evan

Cao, Lan 1961- .... **CLC 109**
See also CA 165

Cape, Judith
See Page, P(atricia) K(athleen)
See also CCA 1

Capek, Karel 1890-1938 .... **DC 1; SSC 36; TCLC 6, 37; WLC**
See also CA 104; 140; CDWLB 4; DA; DA3; DAB; DAC; DAM DRAM, MST, NOV; DFS 7, 11; DLB 215; EW 10; EWL 3; MTCW 1; RGSF 2; RGWL 2, 3; SCFW 2; SFW 4

Capote, Truman 1924-1984 . **CLC 1, 3, 8, 13, 19, 34, 38, 58; SSC 2, 47; TCLC 164; WLC**
See also AMWS 3; BPFB 1; CA 5-8R; 113; CANR 18, 62; CDALB 1941-1968; CPW; DA; DA3; DAB; DAC; DAM MST, NOV; POP; DLB 2, 185, 227; DLBY 1980, 1984; EWL 3; EXPS; GLL 1; LAIT 3; MTCW 1, 2; NCFS 2; RGAL 4; RGSF 2; SATA 91; SSFS 2; TUS

Capra, Frank 1897-1991 .... **CLC 16**
See also AAYA 52; CA 61-64; 135

Caputo, Philip 1941- .... **CLC 32**
See also AAYA 60; CA 73-76; CANR 40, 135; YAW

Caragiale, Ion Luca 1852-1912 ...... **TCLC 76**
See also CA 157

Card, Orson Scott 1951- .... **CLC 44, 47, 50**
See also AAYA 11, 42; BPFB 1; BYA 5, 8; CA 102; CANR 27, 47, 73, 102, 106, 133; CPW; DA3; DAM POP; FANT; INT CANR-27; MTCW 1, 2; NFS 5; SATA 83, 127; SCFW 2; SFW 4; SUFW 2; YAW

Cardenal, Ernesto 1925- .... **CLC 31, 161; HLC 1; PC 22**
See also CA 49-52; CANR 2, 32, 66; CWW 2; DAM MULT, POET; DLB 290; EWL 3; HW 1, 2; LAWS 1; MTCW 1, 2; RGWL 2, 3

Cardinal, Marie 1929-2001 .... **CLC 189**
See also CA 177; CWW 2; DLB 83; FW

Cardozo, Benjamin N(athan) 1870-1938 .... **TCLC 65**
See also CA 117; 164

Carducci, Giosue (Alessandro Giuseppe) 1835-1907 .... **PC 46; TCLC 32**
See also CA 163; EW 7; RGWL 2, 3

Carew, Thomas 1595(?)-1640 . **LC 13; PC 29**
See also BRW 2; DLB 126; PAB; RGEL 2

Carey, Ernestine Gilbreth 1908- ...... **CLC 17**
See also CA 5-8R; CANR 71; SATA 2

Carey, Peter 1943- .... **CLC 40, 55, 96, 183**
See also CA 123; 127; CANR 53, 76, 117; CN 7; DLB 289; EWL 3; INT CA-127; MTCW 1, 2; RGSF 2; SATA 94

Carleton, William 1794-1869 .... **NCLC 3**
See also DLB 159; RGEL 2; RGSF 2

Carlisle, Henry (Coffin) 1926- .... **CLC 33**
See also CA 13-16R; CANR 15, 85

Carlsen, Chris
See Holdstock, Robert P.

Carlson, Ron(ald F.) 1947- .... **CLC 54**
See also CA 105, 189; CAAE 189; CANR 27; DLB 244

Carlyle, Thomas 1795-1881 ..... **NCLC 22, 70**
See also BRW 4; CDBLB 1789-1832; DA; DAB; DAC; DAM MST; DLB 55, 144, 254; RGEL 2; TEA

Carman, (William) Bliss 1861-1929 ... **PC 34; TCLC 7**
See also CA 104; 152; DAC; DLB 92; RGEL 2

Carnegie, Dale 1888-1955 .... **TCLC 53**
See also CA 218

Carossa, Hans 1878-1956 .... **TCLC 48**
See also CA 170; DLB 66; EWL 3

Carpenter, Don(ald Richard) 1931-1995 .... **CLC 41**
See also CA 45-48; 149; CANR 1, 71

Carpenter, Edward 1844-1929 .... **TCLC 88**
See also CA 163; GLL 1

Carpenter, John (Howard) 1948- ... **CLC 161**
See also AAYA 2; CA 134; SATA 58

Carpenter, Johnny
See Carpenter, John (Howard)

Carpentier (y Valmont), Alejo 1904-1980 . **CLC 8, 11, 38, 110; HLC 1; SSC 35**
See also CA 65-68; 97-100; CANR 11, 70; CDWLB 3; DAM MULT; DLB 113; EWL 3; HW 1, 2; LAW; LMFS 2; RGSF 2; RGWL 2, 3; WLIT 1

Carr, Caleb 1955- .... **CLC 86**
See also CA 147; CANR 73, 134; DA3

Carr, Emily 1871-1945 .... **TCLC 32**
See also CA 159; DLB 68; FW; GLL 2

Carr, John Dickson 1906-1977 .... **CLC 3**
See Fairbairn, Roger
See also CA 49-52; 69-72; CANR 3, 33, 60; CMW 4; DLB 306; MSW; MTCW 1, 2

Carr, Philippa
See Hibbert, Eleanor Alice Burford

Carr, Virginia Spencer 1929- .... **CLC 34**
See also CA 61-64; DLB 111

Carrere, Emmanuel 1957- .... **CLC 89**
See also CA 200

Carrier, Roch 1937- .... **CLC 13, 78**
See also CA 130; CANR 61; CCA 1; DAC; DAM MST; DLB 53; SATA 105

Carroll, James Dennis
See Carroll, Jim

Carroll, James P. 1943(?)- .... **CLC 38**
See also CA 81-84; CANR 73; MTCW 1

Carroll, Jim 1951- .... **CLC 35, 143**
See also AAYA 17; CA 45-48; CANR 42, 115; NCFS 5

Carroll, Lewis ..... **NCLC 2, 53, 139; PC 18; WLC**
See Dodgson, Charles L(utwidge)
See also AAYA 39; BRW 5; BYA 5, 13; CD-BLB 1832-1890; CLR 2, 18; DLB 18, 163, 178; DLBY 1998; EXPN; EXPP; FANT; JRDA; LAIT 1; NFS 7; PFS 11; RGEL 2; SUFW 1; TEA; WCH

Carroll, Paul Vincent 1900-1968 ...... **CLC 10**
See also CA 9-12R; 25-28R; DLB 10; EWL 3; RGEL 2

Carruth, Hayden 1921- ..... **CLC 4, 7, 10, 18, 84; PC 10**
See also CA 9-12R; CANR 4, 38, 59, 110; CP 7; DLB 5, 165; INT CANR-4; MTCW 1, 2; SATA 47

Carson, Anne 1950- .... **CLC 185; PC 64**
See also AMWS 12; CA 203; DLB 193; PFS 18

Carson, Ciaran 1948- .... **CLC 201**
See also CA 153; CA-Brief 112; CANR 113; CP 7

Carson, Rachel
See Carson, Rachel Louise
See also AAYA 49; DLB 275

Carson, Rachel Louise 1907-1964 .... **CLC 71**
See Carson, Rachel
See also AMWS 9; ANW; CA 77-80; CANR 35; DA3; DAM POP; FW; LAIT 4; MTCW 1, 2; NCFS 1; SATA 23

Carter, Angela (Olive) 1940-1992 ...... **CLC 5, 41, 76; SSC 13; TCLC 139**
See also BRWS 3; CA 53-56; 136; CANR 12, 36, 61, 106; DA3; DLB 14, 207, 261; EXPS; FANT; FW; MTCW 1, 2; RGSF 2; SATA 66; SATA-Obit 70; SFW 4; SSFS 4, 12; SUFW 2; WLIT 4

Carter, Nick
See Smith, Martin Cruz

Carver, Raymond 1938-1988 ..... **CLC 22, 36, 53, 55, 126; PC 54; SSC 8, 51**
See also AAYA 44; AMWS 3; BPFB 1; CA 33-36R; 126; CANR 17, 34, 61, 103; CPW; DA3; DAM NOV; DLB 130; DLBY 1984, 1988; EWL 3; MTCW 1, 2; PFS 17; RGAL 4; RGSF 2; SSFS 3, 6, 12, 13; TCWW 2; TUS

Cary, Elizabeth, Lady Falkland 1585-1639 .... **LC 30**

Cary, (Arthur) Joyce (Lunel) 1888-1957 .... **TCLC 1, 29**
See also BRW 7; CA 104; 164; CDBLB 1914-1945; DLB 15, 100; EWL 3; MTCW 2; RGEL 2; TEA

Casal, Julian del 1863-1893 .... **NCLC 131**
See also DLB 283; LAW

Casanova de Seingalt, Giovanni Jacopo 1725-1798 .... **LC 13**

Casares, Adolfo Bioy
See Bioy Casares, Adolfo
See also RGSF 2

Chomsky, (Avram) Noam 1928- ..... **CLC 132**
See also CA 17-20R; CANR 28, 62, 110, 132; DA3; DLB 246; MTCW 1, 2

Chona, Maria 1845(?)-1936 .... **NNAL**
See also CA 144

Chopin, Kate .... **SSC 8, 68; TCLC 127; WLCS**
See Chopin, Katherine
See also AAYA 33; AMWR 2; AMWS 1; BYA 11, 15; CDALB 1865-1917; DA; DAB; DLB 12, 78; EXPN; EXPS; FW; LAIT 3; MAWW; NFS 3; RGAL 4; RGSF 2; SSFS 17; TUS

Chopin, Katherine 1851-1904
See Chopin, Kate
See also CA 104; 122; DA3; DAC; DAM MST, NOV

Chretien de Troyes c. 12th cent. - . **CMLC 10**
See also DLB 208; EW 1; RGWL 2, 3; TWA

Christie
See Ichikawa, Kon

Christie, Agatha (Mary Clarissa) 1890-1976 .. **CLC 1, 6, 8, 12, 39, 48, 110**
See also AAYA 9; AITN 1, 2; BPFB 1; BRWS 2; CA 17-20R; 61-64; CANR 10, 37, 108; CBD; CDBLB 1914-1945; CMW 4; CPW; CWD; DA3; DAB; DAC; DAM NOV; DFS 2; DLB 13, 77, 245; MSW; MTCW 1, 2; NFS 8; RGEL 2; RHW; SATA 36; TEA; YAW

Christie, Philippa .... **CLC 21**
See Pearce, Philippa
See also BYA 5; CANR 109; CLR 9; DLB 161; MAICYA 1; SATA 1, 67, 129

Christine de Pizan 1365(?)-1431(?) .... **LC 9**
See also DLB 208; RGWL 2, 3

Chuang Tzu c. 369B.C.-c. 286B.C. .... **CMLC 57**

Chubb, Elmer
See Masters, Edgar Lee

Chulkov, Mikhail Dmitrievich 1743-1792 .... **LC 2**
See also DLB 150

Churchill, Caryl 1938- .... **CLC 31, 55, 157; DC 5**
See Churchill, Chick
See also BRWS 4; CA 102; CANR 22, 46, 108; CBD; CWD; DFS 12, 16; DLB 13; EWL 3; FW; MTCW 1; RGEL 2

Churchill, Charles 1731-1764 .... **LC 3**
See also DLB 109; RGEL 2

Churchill, Chick
See Churchill, Caryl
See also CD 5

Churchill, Sir Winston (Leonard Spencer) 1874-1965 .... **TCLC 113**
See also BRW 6; CA 97-100; CDBLB 1890-1914; DA3; DLB 100; DLBD 16; LAIT 4; MTCW 1, 2

Chute, Carolyn 1947- .... **CLC 39**
See also CA 123; CANR 135

Ciardi, John (Anthony) 1916-1986 . **CLC 10, 40, 44, 129**
See also CA 5-8R; 118; CAAS 2; CANR 5, 33; CLR 19; CWRI 5; DAM POET; DLB 5; DLBY 1986; INT CANR-5; MAICYA 1, 2; MTCW 1, 2; RGAL 4; SAAS 26; SATA 1, 65; SATA-Obit 46

Cibber, Colley 1671-1757 .... **LC 66**
See also DLB 84; RGEL 2

Cicero, Marcus Tullius 106B.C.-43B.C. .... **CMLC 3**
See also AW 1; CDWLB 1; DLB 211; RGWL 2, 3

Cimino, Michael 1943- .... **CLC 16**
See also CA 105

Cioran, E(mil) M. 1911-1995 .... **CLC 64**
See also CA 25-28R; 149; CANR 91; DLB 220; EWL 3

Cisneros, Sandra 1954- .... **CLC 69, 118, 193; HLC 1; PC 52; SSC 32, 72**
See also AAYA 9, 53; AMWS 7; CA 131; CANR 64, 118; CWP; DA3; DAM MULT; DLB 122, 152; EWL 3; EXPN; FW; HW 1, 2; LAIT 5; LATS 1:2; LLW 1; MAI-CYA 2; MTCW 2; NFS 2; PFS 19; RGAL 4; RGSF 2; SSFS 3, 13; WLIT 1; YAW

Cixous, Helene 1937- .... **CLC 92**
See also CA 126; CANR 55, 123; CWW 2; DLB 83, 242; EWL 3; FW; GLL 2; MTCW 1, 2; TWA

Clair, Rene .... **CLC 20**
See Chomette, Rene Lucien

Clampitt, Amy 1920-1994 .... **CLC 32; PC 19**
See also AMWS 9; CA 110; 146; CANR 29, 79; DLB 105

Clancy, Thomas L., Jr. 1947-
See Clancy, Tom
See also CA 125; 131; CANR 62, 105; DA3; INT CA-131; MTCW 1, 2

Clancy, Tom .... **CLC 45, 112**
See Clancy, Thomas L., Jr.
See also AAYA 9, 51; BEST 89:1, 90:1; BPFB 1; BYA 10, 11; CANR 132; CMW 4; CPW; DAM NOV, POP; DLB 227

Clare, John 1793-1864 .. **NCLC 9, 86; PC 23**
See also DAB; DAM POET; DLB 55, 96; RGEL 2

Clarin
See Alas (y Urena), Leopoldo (Enrique Garcia)

Clark, Al C.
See Goines, Donald

Clark, (Robert) Brian 1932- .... **CLC 29**
See also CA 41-44R; CANR 67; CBD; CD 5

Clark, Curt
See Westlake, Donald E(dwin)

Clark, Eleanor 1913-1996 .... **CLC 5, 19**
See also CA 9-12R; 151; CANR 41; CN 7; DLB 6

Clark, J. P.
See Clark Bekederemo, J(ohnson) P(epper)
See also CDWLB 3; DLB 117

Clark, John Pepper
See Clark Bekederemo, J(ohnson) P(epper)
See also AFW; CD 5; CP 7; RGEL 2

Clark, Kenneth (Mackenzie) 1903-1983 .... **TCLC 147**
See also CA 93-96; 109; CANR 36; MTCW 1, 2

Clark, M. R.
See Clark, Mavis Thorpe

Clark, Mavis Thorpe 1909-1999 ...... **CLC 12**
See also CA 57-60; CANR 8, 37, 107; CLR 30; CWRI 5; MAICYA 1, 2; SAAS 5; SATA 8, 74

Clark, Walter Van Tilburg 1909-1971 .... **CLC 28**
See also CA 9-12R; 33-36R; CANR 63, 113; DLB 9, 206; LAIT 2; RGAL 4; SATA 8

Clark Bekederemo, J(ohnson) P(epper) 1935- .... **BLC 1; CLC 38; DC 5**
See Clark, J. P.; Clark, John Pepper
See also BW 1; CA 65-68; CANR 16, 72; DAM DRAM, MULT; DFS 13; EWL 3; MTCW 1

Clarke, Arthur C(harles) 1917- .... **CLC 1, 4, 13, 18, 35, 136; SSC 3**
See also AAYA 4, 33; BPFB 1; BYA 13; CA 1-4R; CANR 2, 28, 55, 74, 130; CN 7; CPW; DA3; DAM POP; DLB 261; JRDA; LAIT 5; MAICYA 1, 2; MTCW 1, 2; SATA 13, 70, 115; SCFW 4; SFW 4; SSFS 4, 18; YAW

Clarke, Austin 1896-1974 .... **CLC 6, 9**
See also CA 29-32; 49-52; CAP 2; DAM POET; DLB 10, 20; EWL 3; RGEL 2

Clarke, Austin C(hesterfield) 1934- .. **BLC 1; CLC 8, 53; SSC 45**
See also BW 1; CA 25-28R; CAAS 16; CANR 14, 32, 68; CN 7; DAC; DAM MULT; DLB 53, 125; DNFS 2; RGSF 2

Clarke, Gillian 1937- .... **CLC 61**
See also CA 106; CP 7; CWP; DLB 40

Clarke, Marcus (Andrew Hislop) 1846-1881 .... **NCLC 19**
See also DLB 230; RGEL 2; RGSF 2

Clarke, Shirley 1925-1997 .... **CLC 16**
See also CA 189

Clash, The
See Headon, (Nicky) Topper; Jones, Mick; Simonon, Paul; Strummer, Joe

Claudel, Paul (Louis Charles Marie) 1868-1955 .... **TCLC 2, 10**
See also CA 104; 165; DLB 192, 258; EW 8; EWL 3; GFL 1789 to the Present; RGWL 2, 3; TWA

Claudian 370(?)-404(?) .... **CMLC 46**
See also RGWL 2, 3

Claudius, Matthias 1740-1815 .... **NCLC 75**
See also DLB 97

Clavell, James (duMaresq) 1925-1994 .... **CLC 6, 25, 87**
See also BPFB 1; CA 25-28R; 146; CANR 26, 48; CPW; DA3; DAM NOV, POP; MTCW 1, 2; NFS 10; RHW

Clayman, Gregory .... **CLC 65**

Cleaver, (Leroy) Eldridge 1935-1998 .... **BLC 1; CLC 30, 119**
See also BW 1, 3; CA 21-24R; 167; CANR 16, 75; DA3; DAM MULT; MTCW 2; YAW

Cleese, John (Marwood) 1939- .... **CLC 21**
See Monty Python
See also CA 112; 116; CANR 35; MTCW 1

Cleishbotham, Jebediah
See Scott, Sir Walter

Cleland, John 1710-1789 .... **LC 2, 48**
See also DLB 39; RGEL 2

Clemens, Samuel Langhorne 1835-1910
See Twain, Mark
See also CA 104; 135; CDALB 1865-1917; DA; DA3; DAB; DAC; DAM MST, NOV; DLB 12, 23, 64, 74, 186, 189; JRDA; LMFS 1; MAICYA 1, 2; NCFS 4; NFS 20; SATA 100; SSFS 16; YABC 2

Clement of Alexandria 150(?)-215(?) .... **CMLC 41**

Cleophil
See Congreve, William

Clerihew, E.
See Bentley, E(dmund) C(lerihew)

Clerk, N. W.
See Lewis, C(live) S(taples)

Cleveland, John 1613-1658 .... **LC 106**
See also DLB 126; RGEL 2

Cliff, Jimmy .... **CLC 21**
See Chambers, James
See also CA 193

Cliff, Michelle 1946- .... **BLCS; CLC 120**
See also BW 2; CA 116; CANR 39, 72; CD-WLB 3; DLB 157; FW; GLL 2

Clifford, Lady Anne 1590-1676 .... **LC 76**
See also DLB 151

Clifton, (Thelma) Lucille 1936- .... **BLC 1; CLC 19, 66, 162; PC 17**
See also AFAW 2; BW 2, 3; CA 49-52; CANR 2, 24, 42, 76, 97; CLR 5; CP 7; CSW; CWP; CWRI 5; DA3; DAM MULT, POET; DLB 5, 41; EXPP; MAICYA 1, 2; MTCW 1, 2; PFS 1, 14; SATA 20, 69, 128; WP

Conrad, Robert Arnold
See Hart, Moss
Conroy, (Donald) Pat(rick) 1945- ... **CLC 30, 74**
See also AAYA 8, 52; AITN 1; BPFB 1; CA 85-88; CANR 24, 53, 129; CPW; CSW; DA3; DAM NOV, POP; DLB 6; LAIT 5; MTCW 1, 2
Constant (de Rebecque), (Henri) Benjamin 1767-1830 .... **NCLC 6**
See also DLB 119; EW 4; GFL 1789 to the Present
Conway, Jill K(er) 1934- .... **CLC 152**
See also CA 130; CANR 94
Conybeare, Charles Augustus
See Eliot, T(homas) S(tearns)
Cook, Michael 1933-1994 .... **CLC 58**
See also CA 93-96; CANR 68; DLB 53
Cook, Robin 1940- .... **CLC 14**
See also AAYA 32; BEST 90:2; BPFB 1; CA 108; 111; CANR 41, 90, 109; CPW; DA3; DAM POP; HGG; INT CA-111
Cook, Roy
See Silverberg, Robert
Cooke, Elizabeth 1948- .... **CLC 55**
See also CA 129
Cooke, John Esten 1830-1886 .... **NCLC 5**
See also DLB 3, 248; RGAL 4
Cooke, John Estes
See Baum, L(yman) Frank
Cooke, M. E.
See Creasey, John
Cooke, Margaret
See Creasey, John
Cooke, Rose Terry 1827-1892 ...... **NCLC 110**
See also DLB 12, 74
Cook-Lynn, Elizabeth 1930- .... **CLC 93; NNAL**
See also CA 133; DAM MULT; DLB 175
Cooney, Ray .... **CLC 62**
See also CBD
Cooper, Anthony Ashley 1671-1713 .. **LC 107**
See also DLB 101
Cooper, Dennis 1953- .... **CLC 203**
See also CA 133; CANR 72, 86; GLL 1; St. James Guide to Horror, Ghost, and Gothic Writers.
Cooper, Douglas 1960- .... **CLC 86**
Cooper, Henry St. John
See Creasey, John
Cooper, J(oan) California (?)- .... **CLC 56**
See also AAYA 12; BW 1; CA 125; CANR 55; DAM MULT; DLB 212
Cooper, James Fenimore 1789-1851 .... **NCLC 1, 27, 54**
See also AAYA 22; AMW; BPFB 1; CDALB 1640-1865; DA3; DLB 3, 183, 250, 254; LAIT 1; NFS 9; RGAL 4; SATA 19; TUS; WCH
Cooper, Susan Fenimore 1813-1894 .... **NCLC 129**
See also ANW; DLB 239, 254
Coover, Robert (Lowell) 1932- ...... **CLC 3, 7, 15, 32, 46, 87, 161; SSC 15**
See also AMWS 5; BPFB 1; CA 45-48; CANR 3, 37, 58, 115; CN 7; DAM NOV; DLB 2, 227; DLBY 1981; EWL 3; MTCW 1, 2; RGAL 4; RGSF 2
Copeland, Stewart (Armstrong) 1952- .... **CLC 26**
Copernicus, Nicolaus 1473-1543 .... **LC 45**
Coppard, A(lfred) E(dgar) 1878-1957 .... **SSC 21; TCLC 5**
See also BRWS 8; CA 114; 167; DLB 162; EWL 3; HGG; RGEL 2; RGSF 2; SUFW 1; YABC 1
Coppee, Francois 1842-1908 .... **TCLC 25**
See also CA 170; DLB 217

Coppola, Francis Ford 1939- ... **CLC 16, 126**
See also AAYA 39; CA 77-80; CANR 40, 78; DLB 44
Copway, George 1818-1869 .... **NNAL**
See also DAM MULT; DLB 175, 183
Corbiere, Tristan 1845-1875 .... **NCLC 43**
See also DLB 217; GFL 1789 to the Present
Corcoran, Barbara (Asenath) 1911- .... **CLC 17**
See also AAYA 14; CA 21-24R, 191; CAAE 191; CAAS 2; CANR 11, 28, 48; CLR 50; DLB 52; JRDA; MAICYA 2; MAIC-YAS 1; RHW; SAAS 20; SATA 3, 77; SATA-Essay 125
Cordelier, Maurice
See Giraudoux, Jean(-Hippolyte)
Corelli, Marie .... **TCLC 51**
See Mackay, Mary
See also DLB 34, 156; RGEL 2; SUFW 1
Corinna c. 225B.C.-c. 305B.C. ...... **CMLC 72**
Corman, Cid .... **CLC 9**
See Corman, Sidney
See also CAAS 2; DLB 5, 193
Corman, Sidney 1924-2004
See Corman, Cid
See also CA 85-88; 225; CANR 44; CP 7; DAM POET
Cormier, Robert (Edmund) 1925-2000 .... **CLC 12, 30**
See also AAYA 3, 19; BYA 1, 2, 6, 8, 9; CA 1-4R; CANR 5, 23, 76, 93; CDALB 1968-1988; CLR 12, 55; DA; DAB; DAC; DAM MST, NOV; DLB 52; EXPN; INT CANR-23; JRDA; LAIT 5; MAICYA 1, 2; MTCW 1, 2; NFS 2, 18; SATA 10, 45, 83; SATA-Obit 122; WYA; YAW
Corn, Alfred (DeWitt III) 1943- .... **CLC 33**
See also CA 179; CAAE 179; CAAS 25; CANR 44; CP 7; CSW; DLB 120, 282; DLBY 1980
Corneille, Pierre 1606-1684 ... **DC 21; LC 28**
See also DAB; DAM MST; DLB 268; EW 3; GFL Beginnings to 1789; RGWL 2, 3; TWA
Cornwell, David (John Moore) 1931- .... **CLC 9, 15**
See le Carre, John
See also CA 5-8R; CANR 13, 33, 59, 107, 132; DA3; DAM POP; MTCW 1, 2
Cornwell, Patricia (Daniels) 1956- . **CLC 155**
See also AAYA 16, 56; BPFB 1; CA 134; CANR 53, 131; CMW 4; CPW; CSW; DAM POP; DLB 306; MSW; MTCW 1
Corso, (Nunzio) Gregory 1930-2001 . **CLC 1, 11; PC 33**
See also AMWS 12; BG 2; CA 5-8R; 193; CANR 41, 76, 132; CP 7; DA3; DLB 5, 16, 237; LMFS 2; MTCW 1, 2; WP
Cortazar, Julio 1914-1984 ... **CLC 2, 3, 5, 10, 13, 15, 33, 34, 92; HLC 1; SSC 7, 76**
See also BPFB 1; CA 21-24R; CANR 12, 32, 81; CDWLB 3; DA3; DAM MULT, NOV; DLB 113; EWL 3; EXPS; HW 1, 2; LAW; MTCW 1, 2; RGSF 2; RGWL 2, 3; SSFS 3, 20; TWA; WLIT 1
Cortes, Hernan 1485-1547 .... **LC 31**
Corvinus, Jakob
See Raabe, Wilhelm (Karl)
Corwin, Cecil
See Kornbluth, C(yril) M.
Cosic, Dobrica 1921- .... **CLC 14**
See also CA 122; 138; CDWLB 4; CWW 2; DLB 181; EWL 3
Costain, Thomas B(ertram) 1885-1965 .... **CLC 30**
See also BYA 3; CA 5-8R; 25-28R; DLB 9; RHW
Costantini, Humberto 1924(?)-1987 . **CLC 49**
See also CA 131; 122; EWL 3; HW 1

Costello, Elvis 1954- .... **CLC 21**
See also CA 204
Costenoble, Philostene
See Ghelderode, Michel de
Cotes, Cecil V.
See Duncan, Sara Jeannette
Cotter, Joseph Seamon Sr. 1861-1949 .... **BLC 1; TCLC 28**
See also BW 1; CA 124; DAM MULT; DLB 50
Couch, Arthur Thomas Quiller
See Quiller-Couch, Sir Arthur (Thomas)
Coulton, James
See Hansen, Joseph
Couperus, Louis (Marie Anne) 1863-1923 .... **TCLC 15**
See also CA 115; EWL 3; RGWL 2, 3
Coupland, Douglas 1961- .... **CLC 85, 133**
See also AAYA 34; CA 142; CANR 57, 90, 130; CCA 1; CPW; DAC; DAM POP
Court, Wesli
See Turco, Lewis (Putnam)
Courtenay, Bryce 1933- .... **CLC 59**
See also CA 138; CPW
Courtney, Robert
See Ellison, Harlan (Jay)
Cousteau, Jacques-Yves 1910-1997 .. **CLC 30**
See also CA 65-68; 159; CANR 15, 67; MTCW 1; SATA 38, 98
Coventry, Francis 1725-1754 .... **LC 46**
Coverdale, Miles c. 1487-1569 .... **LC 77**
See also DLB 167
Cowan, Peter (Walkinshaw) 1914-2002 .... **SSC 28**
See also CA 21-24R; CANR 9, 25, 50, 83; CN 7; DLB 260; RGSF 2
Coward, Noel (Peirce) 1899-1973 . **CLC 1, 9, 29, 51**
See also AITN 1; BRWS 2; CA 17-18; 41-44R; CANR 35, 132; CAP 2; CDBLB 1914-1945; DA3; DAM DRAM; DFS 3, 6; DLB 10, 245; EWL 3; IDFW 3, 4; MTCW 1, 2; RGEL 2; TEA
Cowley, Abraham 1618-1667 .... **LC 43**
See also BRW 2; DLB 131, 151; PAB; RGEL 2
Cowley, Malcolm 1898-1989 .... **CLC 39**
See also AMWS 2; CA 5-8R; 128; CANR 3, 55; DLB 4, 48; DLBY 1981, 1989; EWL 3; MTCW 1, 2
Cowper, William 1731-1800 ..... **NCLC 8, 94; PC 40**
See also BRW 3; DA3; DAM POET; DLB 104, 109; RGEL 2
Cox, William Trevor 1928-
See Trevor, William
See also CA 9-12R; CANR 4, 37, 55, 76, 102; DAM NOV; INT CANR-37; MTCW 1, 2; TEA
Coyne, P. J.
See Masters, Hilary
Cozzens, James Gould 1903-1978 . **CLC 1, 4, 11, 92**
See also AMW; BPFB 1; CA 9-12R; 81-84; CANR 19; CDALB 1941-1968; DLB 9, 294; DLBD 2; DLBY 1984, 1997; EWL 3; MTCW 1, 2; RGAL 4
Crabbe, George 1754-1832 .... **NCLC 26, 121**
See also BRW 3; DLB 93; RGEL 2
Crace, Jim 1946- .... **CLC 157; SSC 61**
See also CA 128; 135; CANR 55, 70, 123; CN 7; DLB 231; INT CA-135
Craddock, Charles Egbert
See Murfree, Mary Noailles
Craig, A. A.
See Anderson, Poul (William)
Craik, Mrs.
See Craik, Dinah Maria (Mulock)
See also RGEL 2

Denmark, Harrison
See Zelazny, Roger (Joseph)
Dennis, John 1658-1734 .... **LC 11**
See also DLB 101; RGEL 2
Dennis, Nigel (Forbes) 1912-1989 ...... **CLC 8**
See also CA 25-28R; 129; DLB 13, 15, 233;
EWL 3; MTCW 1
Dent, Lester 1904-1959 .... **TCLC 72**
See also CA 112; 161; CMW 4; DLB 306;
SFW 4
De Palma, Brian (Russell) 1940- ...... **CLC 20**
See also CA 109
De Quincey, Thomas 1785-1859 ..... **NCLC 4,
87**
See also BRW 4; CDBLB 1789-1832; DLB
110, 144; RGEL 2
Deren, Eleanora 1908(?)-1961
See Deren, Maya
See also CA 192; 111
Deren, Maya .... **CLC 16, 102**
See Deren, Eleanora
Derleth, August (William)
1909-1971 .... **CLC 31**
See also BPFB 1; BYA 9, 10; CA 1-4R; 29-
32R; CANR 4; CMW 4; DLB 9; DLBD
17; HGG; SATA 5; SUFW 1
Der Nister 1884-1950 .... **TCLC 56**
See Nister, Der
Der Stricker c. 1190-c. 1250 .... **CMLC 75**
de Routisie, Albert
See Aragon, Louis
Derrida, Jacques 1930-2004 .... **CLC 24, 87**
See also CA 124; 127; CANR 76, 98, 133;
DLB 242; EWL 3; LMFS 2; MTCW 1;
TWA
Derry Down Derry
See Lear, Edward
Dersonnes, Jacques
See Simenon, Georges (Jacques Christian)
Desai, Anita 1937- .... **CLC 19, 37, 97, 175**
See also BRWS 5; CA 81-84; CANR 33,
53, 95, 133; CN 7; DA3; DAB;
DAM NOV; DLB 271; DNFS 2; EWL 3;
FW; MTCW 1, 2; SATA 63, 126
Desai, Kiran 1971- .... **CLC 119**
See also BYA 16; CA 171; CANR 127
de Saint-Luc, Jean
See Glassco, John
de Saint Roman, Arnaud
See Aragon, Louis
Desbordes-Valmore, Marceline
1786-1859 .... **NCLC 97**
See also DLB 217
Descartes, Rene 1596-1650 .... **LC 20, 35**
See also DLB 268; EW 3; GFL Beginnings
to 1789
Deschamps, Eustache 1340(?)-1404 .. **LC 103**
See also DLB 208
De Sica, Vittorio 1901(?)-1974 .... **CLC 20**
See also CA 117
Desnos, Robert 1900-1945 .... **TCLC 22**
See also CA 121; 151; CANR 107; DLB
258; EWL 3; LMFS 2
Des Roches, Catherine 1542-1587 ..... **LC 117**
Destouches, Louis-Ferdinand
1894-1961 .... **CLC 9, 15**
See Celine, Louis-Ferdinand
See also CA 85-88; CANR 28; MTCW 1
de Tolignac, Gaston
See Griffith, D(avid Lewelyn) W(ark)
Deutsch, Babette 1895-1982 .... **CLC 18**
See also BYA 3; CA 1-4R; 108; CANR 4,
79; DLB 45; SATA 1; SATA-Obit 33
Devenant, William 1606-1649 .... **LC 13**
Devkota, Laxmiprasad 1909-1959 . **TCLC 23**
See also CA 123

De Voto, Bernard (Augustine)
1897-1955 .... **TCLC 29**
See also CA 113; 160; DLB 9, 256
De Vries, Peter 1910-1993 ..... **CLC 1, 2, 3, 7,
10, 28, 46**
See also CA 17-20R; 142; CANR 41; DAM
NOV; DLB 6; DLBY 1982; MTCW 1, 2
Dewey, John 1859-1952 .... **TCLC 95**
See also CA 114; 170; DLB 246, 270;
RGAL 4
Dexter, John
See Bradley, Marion Zimmer
See also GLL 1
Dexter, Martin
See Faust, Frederick (Schiller)
See also TCWW 2
Dexter, Pete 1943- .... **CLC 34, 55**
See also BEST 89:2; CA 127; 131; CANR
129; CPW; DAM POP; INT CA-131;
MTCW 1
Diamano, Silmang
See Senghor, Leopold Sedar
Diamond, Neil 1941- .... **CLC 30**
See also CA 108
Diaz del Castillo, Bernal
1496-1584 .... **HLCS 1; LC 31**
See also LAW
di Bassetto, Corno
See Shaw, George Bernard
Dick, Philip K(indred) 1928-1982 ... **CLC 10,
30, 72; SSC 57**
See also AAYA 24; BPFB 1; BYA 11; CA
49-52; 106; CANR 2, 16, 132; CPW;
DA3; DAM NOV, POP; DLB 8; MTCW
1, 2; NFS 5; SCFW; SFW 4
Dickens, Charles (John Huffam)
1812-1870 .... **NCLC 3, 8, 18, 26, 37, 50,
86, 105, 113; SSC 17, 49; WLC**
See also AAYA 23; BRW 5; BRWC 1, 2;
BYA 1, 2, 3, 13, 14; CDBLB 1832-1890;
CLR 95; CMW 4; DA; DA3; DAB; DAC;
DAM MST, NOV; DLB 21, 55, 70, 159,
166; EXPN; HGG; JRDA; LAIT 1, 2;
LATS 1:1; LMFS 1; MAICYA 1, 2; NFS
4, 5, 10, 14, 20; RGEL 2; RGSF 2; SATA
15; SUFW 1; TEA; WCH; WLIT 4; WYA
Dickey, James (Lafayette)
1923-1997 .... **CLC 1, 2, 4, 7, 10, 15, 47,
109; PC 40; TCLC 151**
See also AAYA 50; AITN 1, 2; AMWS 4;
BPFB 1; CA 9-12R; 156; CABS 2; CANR
10, 48, 61, 105; CDALB 1968-1988; CP
7; CPW; CSW; DA3; DAM NOV, POET,
POP; DLB 5, 193; DLBD 7; DLBY 1982,
1993, 1996, 1997, 1998; EWL 3; INT
CANR-10; MTCW 1, 2; NFS 9; PFS 6,
11; RGAL 4; TUS
Dickey, William 1928-1994 .... **CLC 3, 28**
See also CA 9-12R; 145; CANR 24, 79;
DLB 5
Dickinson, Charles 1951- .... **CLC 49**
See also CA 128
Dickinson, Emily (Elizabeth)
1830-1886 ... **NCLC 21, 77; PC 1; WLC**
See also AAYA 22; AMW; AMWR 1;
CDALB 1865-1917; DA; DA3; DAB;
DAC; DAM MST, POET; PAB; PFS 1, 2, 3, 4, 5,
6, 8, 10, 11, 13, 16; RGAL 4; SATA 29;
TUS; WP; WYA
Dickinson, Mrs. Herbert Ward
See Phelps, Elizabeth Stuart
Dickinson, Peter (Malcolm de Brissac)
1927- .... **CLC 12, 35**
See also AAYA 9, 49; BYA 5; CA 41-44R;
CANR 31, 58, 88, 134; CLR 29; CMW 4;
DLB 87, 161, 276; JRDA; MAICYA 1, 2;
SATA 5, 62, 95, 150; SFW 4; WYA; YAW
Dickson, Carr
See Carr, John Dickson

Dickson, Carter
See Carr, John Dickson
Diderot, Denis 1713-1784 .... **LC 26**
See also EW 4; GFL Beginnings to 1789;
LMFS 1; RGWL 2, 3
Didion, Joan 1934- . **CLC 1, 3, 8, 14, 32, 129**
See also AITN 1; AMWS 4; CA 5-8R;
CANR 14, 52, 76, 125; CDALB 1968-
1988; CN 7; DA3; DAM NOV; DLB 2,
173, 185; DLBY 1981, 1986; EWL 3;
MAWW; MTCW 1, 2; NFS 3; RGAL 4;
TCWW 2; TUS
di Donato, Pietro 1911-1992 .... **TCLC 159**
See also CA 101; 136; DLB 9
Dietrich, Robert
See Hunt, E(verette) Howard, (Jr.)
Difusa, Pati
See Almodovar, Pedro
Dillard, Annie 1945- .... **CLC 9, 60, 115**
See also AAYA 6, 43; AMWS 6; ANW; CA
49-52; CANR 3, 43, 62, 90, 125; DA3;
DAM NOV; DLB 275, 278; DLBY 1980;
LAIT 4, 5; MTCW 1, 2; NCFS 1; RGAL
4; SATA 10, 140; TUS
Dillard, R(ichard) H(enry) W(ilde)
1937- .... **CLC 5**
See also CA 21-24R; CAAS 7; CANR 10;
CP 7; CSW; DLB 5, 244
Dillon, Eilis 1920-1994 .... **CLC 17**
See also CA 9-12R, 182; 147; CAAE 182;
CAAS 3; CANR 4, 38, 78; CLR 26; MAI-
CYA 1, 2; MAICYAS 1; SATA 2, 74;
SATA-Essay 105; SATA-Obit 83; YAW
Dimont, Penelope
See Mortimer, Penelope (Ruth)
Dinesen, Isak ..... **CLC 10, 29, 95; SSC 7, 75**
See Blixen, Karen (Christentze Dinesen)
See also EW 10; EWL 3; EXPS; FW; HGG;
LAIT 3; MTCW 1; NCFS 2; NFS 9;
RGSF 2; RGWL 2, 3; SSFS 3, 6, 13;
WLIT 2
Ding Ling .... **CLC 68**
See Chiang, Pin-chin
See also RGWL 3
Diphusa, Patty
See Almodovar, Pedro
Disch, Thomas M(ichael) 1940- ... **CLC 7, 36**
See Disch, Tom
See also AAYA 17; BPFB 1; CA 21-24R;
CAAS 4; CANR 17, 36, 54, 89; CLR 18;
CP 7; DA3; DLB 8; HGG; MAICYA 1, 2;
MTCW 1, 2; SAAS 15; SATA 92; SCFW;
SFW 4; SUFW 2
Disch, Tom
See Disch, Thomas M(ichael)
See also DLB 282
d'Isly, Georges
See Simenon, Georges (Jacques Christian)
Disraeli, Benjamin 1804-1881 ... **NCLC 2, 39,
79**
See also BRW 4; DLB 21, 55; RGEL 2
Ditcum, Steve
See Crumb, R(obert)
Dixon, Paige
See Corcoran, Barbara (Asenath)
Dixon, Stephen 1936- .... **CLC 52; SSC 16**
See also AMWS 12; CA 89-92; CANR 17,
40, 54, 91; CN 7; DLB 130
Dixon, Thomas 1864-1946 .... **TCLC 163**
See also RHW
Djebar, Assia 1936- .... **CLC 182**
See also CA 188; EWL 3; RGWL 3; WLIT
2
Doak, Annie
See Dillard, Annie
Dobell, Sydney Thompson
1824-1874 .... **NCLC 43**
See also DLB 32; RGEL 2

Doblin, Alfred .... **TCLC 13**
See Doeblin, Alfred
See also CDWLB 2; EWL 3; RGWL 2, 3

Dobroliubov, Nikolai Aleksandrovich
See Dobrolyubov, Nikolai Alexandrovich
See also DLB 277

Dobrolyubov, Nikolai Alexandrovich
1836-1861 .... **NCLC 5**
See Dobroliubov, Nikolai Aleksandrovich

Dobson, Austin 1840-1921 .... **TCLC 79**
See also DLB 35, 144

Dobyns, Stephen 1941- .... **CLC 37**
See also AMWS 13; CA 45-48; CANR 2,
18, 99; CMW 4; CP 7

Doctorow, E(dgar) L(aurence)
1931- .... **CLC 6, 11, 15, 18, 37, 44, 65,
113**
See also AAYA 22; AITN 2; AMWS 4;
BEST 89:3; BPFB 1; CA 45-48; CANR
2, 33, 51, 76, 97, 133; CDALB 1968-
1988; CN 7; CPW; DA3; DAM NOV,
POP; DLB 2, 28, 173; DLBY 1980; EWL
3; LAIT 3; MTCW 1, 2; NFS 6; RGAL 4;
RHW; TUS

Dodgson, Charles L(utwidge) 1832-1898
See Carroll, Lewis
See also CLR 2; DA; DA3; DAB; DAC;
DAM MST, NOV, POET; MAICYA 1, 2;
SATA 100; YABC 2

Dodsley, Robert 1703-1764 .... **LC 97**
See also DLB 95; RGEL 2

Dodson, Owen (Vincent) 1914-1983 .. **BLC 1;
CLC 79**
See also BW 1; CA 65-68; 110; CANR 24;
DAM MULT; DLB 76

Doeblin, Alfred 1878-1957 .... **TCLC 13**
See Doblin, Alfred
See also CA 110; 141; DLB 66

Doerr, Harriet 1910-2002 .... **CLC 34**
See also CA 117; 122; 213; CANR 47; INT
CA-122; LATS 1:2

Domecq, H(onorio Bustos)
See Bioy Casares, Adolfo

Domecq, H(onorio) Bustos
See Bioy Casares, Adolfo; Borges, Jorge
Luis

Domini, Rey
See Lorde, Audre (Geraldine)
See also GLL 1

Dominique
See Proust, (Valentin-Louis-George-Eugene)
Marcel

Don, A
See Stephen, Sir Leslie

Donaldson, Stephen R(eeder)
1947- .... **CLC 46, 138**
See also AAYA 36; BPFB 1; CA 89-92;
CANR 13, 55, 99; CPW; DAM POP;
FANT; INT CANR-13; SATA 121; SFW
4; SUFW 1, 2

Donleavy, J(ames) P(atrick) 1926- .... **CLC 1,
4, 6, 10, 45**
See also AITN 2; BPFB 1; CA 9-12R;
CANR 24, 49, 62, 80, 124; CBD; CD 5;
CN 7; DLB 6, 173; INT CANR-24;
MTCW 1, 2; RGAL 4

Donnadieu, Marguerite
See Duras, Marguerite

Donne, John 1572-1631 ... **LC 10, 24, 91; PC
1, 43; WLC**
See also BRW 1; BRWC 1; BRWR 2; CD-
BLB Before 1660; DA; DAB; DAC;
DAM MST, POET; DLB 121, 151; EXPP;
PAB; PFS 2, 11; RGEL 3; TEA; WLIT 3;
WP

Donnell, David 1939(?)- .... **CLC 34**
See also CA 197

Donoghue, Denis 1928- .... **CLC 209**
See also CA 17-20R; CANR 16, 102

Donoghue, P. S.
See Hunt, E(verette) Howard, (Jr.)

Donoso (Yanez), Jose 1924-1996 ... **CLC 4, 8,
11, 32, 99; HLC 1; SSC 34; TCLC 133**
See also CA 81-84; 155; CANR 32, 73; CD-
WLB 3; CWW 2; DAM MULT; DLB 113;
EWL 3; HW 1, 2; LAW; LAWS 1; MTCW
1, 2; RGSF 2; WLIT 1

Donovan, John 1928-1992 .... **CLC 35**
See also AAYA 20; CA 97-100; 137; CLR
3; MAICYA 1, 2; SATA 72; SATA-Brief
29; YAW

Don Roberto
See Cunninghame Graham, Robert
(Gallnigad) Bontine

Doolittle, Hilda 1886-1961 . **CLC 3, 8, 14, 31,
34, 73; PC 5; WLC**
See H. D.
See also AMWS 1; CA 97-100; CANR 35,
131; DA; DAC; DAM MST, POET; DLB
4, 45; EWL 3; FW; GLL 1; LMFS 2;
MAWW; MTCW 1, 2; PFS 6; RGAL 4

Doppo, Kunikida .... **TCLC 99**
See Kunikida Doppo

Dorfman, Ariel 1942- .... **CLC 48, 77, 189;
HLC 1**
See also CA 124; 130; CANR 67, 70, 135;
CWW 2; DAM MULT; DFS 4; EWL 3;
HW 1, 2; INT CA-130; WLIT 1

Dorn, Edward (Merton)
1929-1999 .... **CLC 10, 18**
See also CA 93-96; 187; CANR 42, 79; CP
7; DLB 5; INT CA-93-96; WP

Dor-Ner, Zvi .... **CLC 70**

Dorris, Michael (Anthony)
1945-1997 .... **CLC 109; NNAL**
See also AAYA 20; BEST 90:1; BYA 12;
CA 102; 157; CANR 19, 46, 75; CLR 58;
DA3; DAM MULT, NOV; DLB 175;
LAIT 5; MTCW 2; NFS 3; RGAL 4;
SATA 75; SATA-Obit 94; TCWW 2; YAW

Dorris, Michael A.
See Dorris, Michael (Anthony)

Dorsan, Luc
See Simenon, Georges (Jacques Christian)

Dorsange, Jean
See Simenon, Georges (Jacques Christian)

Dorset
See Sackville, Thomas

Dos Passos, John (Roderigo)
1896-1970 ... **CLC 1, 4, 8, 11, 15, 25, 34,
82; WLC**
See also AMW; BPFB 1; CA 1-4R; 29-32R;
CANR 3; CDALB 1929-1941; DA; DA3;
DAB; DAC; DAM MST, NOV; DLB 4,
9, 274; DLBD 1, 15; DLBY 1996; EWL
3; MTCW 1, 2; NFS 14; RGAL 4; TUS

Dossage, Jean
See Simenon, Georges (Jacques Christian)

Dostoevsky, Fedor Mikhailovich
1821-1881 .. **NCLC 2, 7, 21, 33, 43, 119;
SSC 2, 33, 44; WLC**
See Dostoevsky, Fyodor
See also AAYA 40; DA; DA3; DAB; DAC;
DAM MST, NOV; EW 7; EXPN; NFS 3,
8; RGSF 2; RGWL 2, 3; SSFS 8; TWA

Dostoevsky, Fyodor
See Dostoevsky, Fedor Mikhailovich
See also DLB 238; LATS 1:1; LMFS 1, 2

Doty, M. R.
See Doty, Mark (Alan)

Doty, Mark
See Doty, Mark (Alan)

Doty, Mark (Alan) 1953(?)- .... **CLC 176; PC
53**
See also AMWS 11; CA 161, 183; CAAE
183; CANR 110

Doty, Mark A.
See Doty, Mark (Alan)

Doughty, Charles M(ontagu)
1843-1926 .... **TCLC 27**
See also CA 115; 178; DLB 19, 57, 174

Douglas, Ellen .... **CLC 73**
See Haxton, Josephine Ayres; Williamson,
Ellen Douglas
See also CN 7; CSW; DLB 292

Douglas, Gavin 1475(?)-1522 .... **LC 20**
See also DLB 132; RGEL 2

Douglas, George
See Brown, George Douglas
See also RGEL 2

Douglas, Keith (Castellain)
1920-1944 .... **TCLC 40**
See also BRW 7; CA 160; DLB 27; EWL
3; PAB; RGEL 2

Douglas, Leonard
See Bradbury, Ray (Douglas)

Douglas, Michael
See Crichton, (John) Michael

Douglas, (George) Norman
1868-1952 .... **TCLC 68**
See also BRW 6; CA 119; 157; DLB 34,
195; RGEL 2

Douglas, William
See Brown, George Douglas

Douglass, Frederick 1817(?)-1895 ..... **BLC 1;
NCLC 7, 55, 141; WLC**
See also AAYA 48; AFAW 1, 2; AMWC 1;
AMWS 3; CDALB 1640-1865; DA; DA3;
DAC; DAM MST, MULT; DLB 1, 43, 50,
79, 243; FW; LAIT 2; NCFS 2; RGAL 4;
SATA 29

Dourado, (Waldomiro Freitas) Autran
1926- .... **CLC 23, 60**
See also CA 25-28R; 179; CANR 34, 81;
DLB 145, 307; HW 2

Dourado, Waldomiro Freitas Autran
See Dourado, (Waldomiro Freitas) Autran

Dove, Rita (Frances) 1952- . **BLCS; CLC 50,
81; PC 6**
See also AAYA 46; AMWS 4; BW 2; CA
109; CAAS 19; CANR 27, 42, 68, 76, 97,
132; CDALBS; CP 7; CSW; CWP; DA3;
DAM MULT, POET; DLB 120; EWL 3;
EXPP; MTCW 1; PFS 1, 15; RGAL 4

Doveglion
See Villa, Jose Garcia

Dowell, Coleman 1925-1985 .... **CLC 60**
See also CA 25-28R; 117; CANR 10; DLB
130; GLL 2

Dowson, Ernest (Christopher)
1867-1900 .... **TCLC 4**
See also CA 105; 150; DLB 19, 135; RGEL
2

Doyle, A. Conan
See Doyle, Sir Arthur Conan

Doyle, Sir Arthur Conan
1859-1930 . **SSC 12, 83; TCLC 7; WLC**
See Conan Doyle, Arthur
See also AAYA 14; BRWS 2; CA 104; 122;
CANR 131; CDBLB 1890-1914; CMW
4; DA; DA3; DAB; DAC; DAM MST,
NOV; DLB 18, 70, 156, 178; EXPS;
HGG; LAIT 2; MSW; MTCW 1, 2; RGEL
2; RGSF 2; RHW; SATA 24; SCFW 2;
SFW 4; SSFS 2; TEA; WCH; WLIT 4;
WYA; YAW

Doyle, Conan
See Doyle, Sir Arthur Conan

Doyle, John
See Graves, Robert (von Ranke)

Doyle, Roddy 1958(?)- .... **CLC 81, 178**
See also AAYA 14; BRWS 5; CA 143;
CANR 73, 128; CN 7; DA3; DLB 194

Doyle, Sir A. Conan
See Doyle, Sir Arthur Conan

102; DLBD 2; DLBY 1986, 1997; EWL
3; EXPN; EXPS; LAIT 2; LATS 1:1;
LMFS 2; MTCW 1, 2; NFS 4, 8, 13;
RGAL 4; RGSF 2; SSFS 2, 5, 6, 12; TUS

Fauset, Jessie Redmon
1882(?)-1961 .. **BLC 2; CLC 19, 54; HR
2**
See also AFAW 2; BW 1; CA 109; CANR
83; DAM MULT; DLB 51; FW; LMFS 2;
MAWW

Faust, Frederick (Schiller)
1892-1944(?) .... **TCLC 49**
See Austin, Frank; Brand, Max; Challis,
George; Dawson, Peter; Dexter, Martin;
Evans, Evan; Frederick, John; Frost, Fred-
erick; Manning, David; Silver, Nicholas
See also CA 108; 152; DAM POP; DLB
256; TUS

Faust, Irvin 1924- .... **CLC 8**
See also CA 33-36R; CANR 28, 67; CN 7;
DLB 2, 28, 218, 278; DLBY 1980

Faustino, Domingo 1811-1888 ...... **NCLC 123**

Fawkes, Guy
See Benchley, Robert (Charles)

Fearing, Kenneth (Flexner)
1902-1961 .... **CLC 51**
See also CA 93-96; CANR 59; CMW 4;
DLB 9; RGAL 4

Fecamps, Elise
See Creasey, John

Federman, Raymond 1928- .... **CLC 6, 47**
See also CA 17-20R, 208; CAAE 208;
CAAS 8; CANR 10, 43, 83, 108; CN 7;
DLBY 1980

Federspiel, J(uerg) F. 1931- .... **CLC 42**
See also CA 146

Feiffer, Jules (Ralph) 1929- ...... **CLC 2, 8, 64**
See also AAYA 3; CA 17-20R; CAD; CANR
30, 59, 129; CD 5; DAM DRAM; DLB 7,
44; INT CANR-30; MTCW 1; SATA 8,
61, 111

Feige, Hermann Albert Otto Maximilian
See Traven, B.

Feinberg, David B. 1956-1994 .... **CLC 59**
See also CA 135; 147

Feinstein, Elaine 1930- .... **CLC 36**
See also CA 69-72; CAAS 1; CANR 31,
68, 121; CN 7; CP 7; CWP; DLB 14, 40;
MTCW 1

Feke, Gilbert David .... **CLC 65**

Feldman, Irving (Mordecai) 1928- ..... **CLC 7**
See also CA 1-4R; CANR 1; CP 7; DLB
169

Felix-Tchicaya, Gerald
See Tchicaya, Gerald Felix

Fellini, Federico 1920-1993 .... **CLC 16, 85**
See also CA 65-68; 143; CANR 33

Felltham, Owen 1602(?)-1668 .... **LC 92**
See also DLB 126, 151

Felsen, Henry Gregor 1916-1995 ..... **CLC 17**
See also CA 1-4R; 180; CANR 1; SAAS 2;
SATA 1

Felski, Rita .... **CLC 65**

Fenno, Jack
See Calisher, Hortense

Fenollosa, Ernest (Francisco)
1853-1908 .... **TCLC 91**

Fenton, James Martin 1949- .... **CLC 32, 209**
See also CA 102; CANR 108; CP 7; DLB
40; PFS 11

Ferber, Edna 1887-1968 .... **CLC 18, 93**
See also AITN 1; CA 5-8R; 25-28R; CANR
68, 105; DLB 9, 28, 86, 266; MTCW 1,
2; RGAL 4; RHW; SATA 7; TCWW 2

Ferdowsi, Abu'l Qasem 940-1020 . **CMLC 43**
See also RGWL 2, 3

Ferguson, Helen
See Kavan, Anna

Ferguson, Niall 1964- .... **CLC 134**
See also CA 190

Ferguson, Samuel 1810-1886 .... **NCLC 33**
See also DLB 32; RGEL 2

Fergusson, Robert 1750-1774 .... **LC 29**
See also DLB 109; RGEL 2

Ferling, Lawrence
See Ferlinghetti, Lawrence (Monsanto)

Ferlinghetti, Lawrence (Monsanto)
1919(?)- ..... **CLC 2, 6, 10, 27, 111; PC 1**
See also CA 5-8R; CANR 3, 41, 73, 125;
CDALB 1941-1968; CP 7; DA3; DAM
POET; DLB 5, 16; MTCW 1, 2; RGAL 4;
WP

Fern, Fanny
See Parton, Sara Payson Willis

Fernandez, Vicente Garcia Huidobro
See Huidobro Fernandez, Vicente Garcia

Fernandez-Armesto, Felipe .... **CLC 70**

Fernandez de Lizardi, Jose Joaquin
See Lizardi, Jose Joaquin Fernandez de

Ferre, Rosario 1938- ...... **CLC 139; HLCS 1;
SSC 36**
See also CA 131; CANR 55, 81, 134; CWW
2; DLB 145; EWL 3; HW 1, 2; LAWS 1;
MTCW 1; WLIT 1

Ferrer, Gabriel (Francisco Victor) Miro
See Miro (Ferrer), Gabriel (Francisco
Victor)

Ferrier, Susan (Edmonstone)
1782-1854 .... **NCLC 8**
See also DLB 116; RGEL 2

Ferrigno, Robert 1948(?)- .... **CLC 65**
See also CA 140; CANR 125

Ferron, Jacques 1921-1985 .... **CLC 94**
See also CA 117; 129; CCA 1; DAC; DLB
60; EWL 3

Feuchtwanger, Lion 1884-1958 .... **TCLC 3**
See also CA 104; 187; DLB 66; EWL 3

Feuerbach, Ludwig 1804-1872 ..... **NCLC 139**
See also DLB 133

Feuillet, Octave 1821-1890 .... **NCLC 45**
See also DLB 192

Feydeau, Georges (Leon Jules Marie)
1862-1921 .... **TCLC 22**
See also CA 113; 152; CANR 84; DAM
DRAM; DLB 192; EWL 3; GFL 1789 to
the Present; RGWL 2, 3

Fichte, Johann Gottlieb
1762-1814 .... **NCLC 62**
See also DLB 90

Ficino, Marsilio 1433-1499 .... **LC 12**
See also LMFS 1

Fiedeler, Hans
See Doeblin, Alfred

Fiedler, Leslie A(aron) 1917-2003 ..... **CLC 4,
13, 24**
See also AMWS 13; CA 9-12R; 212; CANR
7, 63; CN 7; DLB 28, 67; EWL 3; MTCW
1, 2; RGAL 4; TUS

Field, Andrew 1938- .... **CLC 44**
See also CA 97-100; CANR 25

Field, Eugene 1850-1895 .... **NCLC 3**
See also DLB 23, 42, 140; DLBD 13; MAI-
CYA 1, 2; RGAL 4; SATA 16

Field, Gans T.
See Wellman, Manly Wade

Field, Michael 1915-1971 .... **TCLC 43**
See also CA 29-32R

Field, Peter
See Hobson, Laura Z(ametkin)
See also TCWW 2

Fielding, Helen 1958- .... **CLC 146**
See also CA 172; CANR 127; DLB 231

Fielding, Henry 1707-1754 .... **LC 1, 46, 85;
WLC**
See also BRW 3; BRWR 1; CDBLB 1660-
1789; DA; DA3; DAB; DAC; DAM
DRAM, MST, NOV; DLB 39, 84, 101;
NFS 18; RGEL 2; TEA; WLIT 3

Fielding, Sarah 1710-1768 .... **LC 1, 44**
See also DLB 39; RGEL 2; TEA

Fields, W. C. 1880-1946 .... **TCLC 80**
See also DLB 44

Fierstein, Harvey (Forbes) 1954- ..... **CLC 33**
See also CA 123; 129; CAD; CD 5; CPW;
DA3; DAM DRAM, POP; DFS 6; DLB
266; GLL

Figes, Eva 1932- .... **CLC 31**
See also CA 53-56; CANR 4, 44, 83; CN 7;
DLB 14, 271; FW

Filippo, Eduardo de
See de Filippo, Eduardo

Finch, Anne 1661-1720 .... **LC 3; PC 21**
See also BRWS 9; DLB 95

Finch, Robert (Duer Claydon)
1900-1995 .... **CLC 18**
See also CA 57-60; CANR 9, 24, 49; CP 7;
DLB 88

Findley, Timothy (Irving Frederick)
1930-2002 .... **CLC 27, 102**
See also CA 25-28R; 206; CANR 12, 42,
69, 109; CCA 1; CN 7; DAC; DAM MST;
DLB 53; FANT; RHW

Fink, William
See Mencken, H(enry) L(ouis)

Firbank, Louis 1942-
See Reed, Lou
See also CA 117

Firbank, (Arthur Annesley) Ronald
1886-1926 .... **TCLC 1**
See also BRWS 2; CA 104; 177; DLB 36;
EWL 3; RGEL 2

Fish, Stanley
See Fish, Stanley Eugene

Fish, Stanley E.
See Fish, Stanley Eugene

Fish, Stanley Eugene 1938- .... **CLC 142**
See also CA 112; 132; CANR 90; DLB 67

Fisher, Dorothy (Frances) Canfield
1879-1958 .... **TCLC 87**
See also CA 114; 136; CANR 80; CLR 71,;
CWRI 5; DLB 9, 102, 284; MAICYA 1,
2; YABC 1

Fisher, M(ary) F(rances) K(ennedy)
1908-1992 .... **CLC 76, 87**
See also CA 77-80; 138; CANR 44; MTCW
1

Fisher, Roy 1930- .... **CLC 25**
See also CA 81-84; CAAS 10; CANR 16;
CP 7; DLB 40

Fisher, Rudolph 1897-1934 ..... **BLC 2; HR 2;
SSC 25; TCLC 11**
See also BW 1, 3; CA 107; 124; CANR 80;
DAM MULT; DLB 51, 102

Fisher, Vardis (Alvero) 1895-1968 .... **CLC 7;
TCLC 140**
See also CA 5-8R; 25-28R; CANR 68; DLB
9, 206; RGAL 4; TCWW 2

Fiske, Tarleton
See Bloch, Robert (Albert)

Fitch, Clarke
See Sinclair, Upton (Beall)

Fitch, John IV
See Cormier, Robert (Edmund)

Fitzgerald, Captain Hugh
See Baum, L(yman) Frank

FitzGerald, Edward 1809-1883 ...... **NCLC 9,
153**
See also BRW 4; DLB 32; RGEL 2

Fitzgerald, F(rancis) Scott (Key)
1896-1940 ... **SSC 6, 31, 75; TCLC 1, 6, 14, 28, 55, 157; WLC**
See also AAYA 24; AITN 1; AMW; AMWC 2; AMWR 1; BPFB 1; CA 110; 123; CDALB 1917-1929; DA; DA3; DAB; DAC; DAM MST, NOV; DLB 4, 9, 86, 219, 273; DLBD 1, 15, 16; DLBY 1981, 1996; EWL 3; EXPN; EXPS; LAIT 3; MTCW 1, 2; NFS 2, 19, 20; RGAL 4; RGSF 2; SSFS 4, 15; TUS

Fitzgerald, Penelope 1916-2000 . **CLC 19, 51, 61, 143**
See also BRWS 5; CA 85-88; 190; CAAS 10; CANR 56, 86, 131; CN 7; DLB 14, 194; EWL 3; MTCW 2

Fitzgerald, Robert (Stuart)
1910-1985 .... **CLC 39**
See also CA 1-4R; 114; CANR 1; DLBY 1980

FitzGerald, Robert D(avid)
1902-1987 .... **CLC 19**
See also CA 17-20R; DLB 260; RGEL 2

Fitzgerald, Zelda (Sayre)
1900-1948 .... **TCLC 52**
See also AMWS 9; CA 117; 126; DLBY 1984

Flanagan, Thomas (James Bonner)
1923-2002 .... **CLC 25, 52**
See also CA 108; 206; CANR 55; CN 7; DLBY 1980; INT CA-108; MTCW 1; RHW

Flaubert, Gustave 1821-1880 .... **NCLC 2, 10, 19, 62, 66, 135; SSC 11, 60; WLC**
See also DA; DA3; DAB; DAC; DAM MST, NOV; DLB 119, 301; EW 7; EXPS; GFL 1789 to the Present; LAIT 2; LMFS 1; NFS 14; RGSF 2; RGWL 2, 3; SSFS 6; TWA

Flavius Josephus
See Josephus, Flavius

Flecker, Herman Elroy
See Flecker, (Herman) James Elroy

Flecker, (Herman) James Elroy
1884-1915 .... **TCLC 43**
See also CA 109; 150; DLB 10, 19; RGEL 2

Fleming, Ian (Lancaster) 1908-1964 . **CLC 3, 30**
See also AAYA 26; BPFB 1; CA 5-8R; CANR 59; CDBLB 1945-1960; CMW 4; CPW; DA3; DAM POP; DLB 87, 201; MSW; MTCW 1, 2; RGEL 2; SATA 9; TEA; YAW

Fleming, Thomas (James) 1927- ...... **CLC 37**
See also CA 5-8R; CANR 10, 102; INT CANR-10; SATA 8

Fletcher, John 1579-1625 .... **DC 6; LC 33**
See also BRW 2; CDBLB Before 1660; DLB 58; RGEL 2; TEA

Fletcher, John Gould 1886-1950 .... **TCLC 35**
See also CA 107; 167; DLB 4, 45; LMFS 2; RGAL 4

Fleur, Paul
See Pohl, Frederik

Flieg, Helmut
See Heym, Stefan

Flooglebuckle, Al
See Spiegelman, Art

Flora, Fletcher 1914-1969
See Queen, Ellery
See also CA 1-4R; CANR 3, 85

Flying Officer X
See Bates, H(erbert) E(rnest)

Fo, Dario 1926- .... **CLC 32, 109; DC 10**
See also CA 116; 128; CANR 68, 114, 134; CWW 2; DA3; DAM DRAM; DLBY 1997; EWL 3; MTCW 1, 2

Fogarty, Jonathan Titulescu Esq.
See Farrell, James T(homas)

Follett, Ken(neth Martin) 1949- .... **CLC 18**
See also AAYA 6, 50; BEST 89:4; BPFB 1; CA 81-84; CANR 13, 33, 54, 102; CMW 4; CPW; DA3; DAM NOV, POP; DLB 87; DLBY 1981; INT CANR-33; MTCW 1

Fondane, Benjamin 1898-1944 ..... **TCLC 159**

Fontane, Theodor 1819-1898 .... **NCLC 26**
See also CDWLB 2; DLB 129; EW 6; RGWL 2, 3; TWA

Fontenot, Chester .... **CLC 65**

Fonvizin, Denis Ivanovich
1744(?)-1792 .... **LC 81**
See also DLB 150; RGWL 2, 3

Foote, Horton 1916- .... **CLC 51, 91**
See also CA 73-76; CAD; CANR 34, 51, 110; CD 5; CSW; DA3; DAM DRAM; DFS 20; DLB 26, 266; EWL 3; INT CANR-34

Foote, Mary Hallock 1847-1938 .. **TCLC 108**
See also DLB 186, 188, 202, 221

Foote, Samuel 1721-1777 .... **LC 106**
See also DLB 89; RGEL 2

Foote, Shelby 1916- .... **CLC 75**
See also AAYA 40; CA 5-8R; CANR 3, 45, 74, 131; CN 7; CPW; CSW; DA3; DAM NOV, POP; DLB 2, 17; MTCW 2; RHW

Forbes, Cosmo
See Lewton, Val

Forbes, Esther 1891-1967 .... **CLC 12**
See also AAYA 17; BYA 2; CA 13-14; 25-28R; CAP 1; CLR 27; DLB 22; JRDA; MAICYA 1, 2; RHW; SATA 2, 100; YAW

Forche, Carolyn (Louise) 1950- .... **CLC 25, 83, 86; PC 10**
See also CA 109; 117; CANR 50, 74; CP 7; CWP; DA3; DAM POET; DLB 5, 193; INT CA-117; MTCW 1; PFS 18; RGAL 4

Ford, Elbur
See Hibbert, Eleanor Alice Burford

Ford, Ford Madox 1873-1939 ... **TCLC 1, 15, 39, 57**
See Chaucer, Daniel
See also BRW 6; CA 104; 132; CANR 74; CDBLB 1914-1945; DA3; DAM NOV; DLB 34, 98, 162; EWL 3; MTCW 1, 2; RGEL 2; TEA

Ford, Henry 1863-1947 .... **TCLC 73**
See also CA 115; 148

Ford, Jack
See Ford, John

Ford, John 1586-1639 .... **DC 8; LC 68**
See also BRW 2; CDBLB Before 1660; DA3; DAM DRAM; DFS 7; DLB 58; IDTP; RGEL 2

Ford, John 1895-1973 .... **CLC 16**
See also CA 187; 45-48

Ford, Richard 1944- .... **CLC 46, 99, 205**
See also AMWS 5; CA 69-72; CANR 11, 47, 86, 128; CN 7; CSW; DLB 227; EWL 3; MTCW 1; RGAL 4; RGSF 2

Ford, Webster
See Masters, Edgar Lee

Foreman, Richard 1937- .... **CLC 50**
See also CA 65-68; CAD; CANR 32, 63; CD 5

Forester, C(ecil) S(cott) 1899-1966 . **CLC 35; TCLC 152**
See also CA 73-76; 25-28R; CANR 83; DLB 191; RGEL 2; RHW; SATA 13

Forez
See Mauriac, Francois (Charles)

Forman, James
See Forman, James D(ouglas)

Forman, James D(ouglas) 1932- .... **CLC 21**
See also AAYA 17; CA 9-12R; CANR 4, 19, 42; JRDA; MAICYA 1, 2; SATA 8, 70; YAW

Forman, Milos 1932- .... **CLC 164**
See also CA 109

Fornes, Maria Irene 1930- .... **CLC 39, 61, 187; DC 10; HLCS 1**
See also CA 25-28R; CAD; CANR 28, 81; CD 5; CWD; DLB 7; HW 1, 2; INT CANR-28; LLW 1; MTCW 1; RGAL 4

Forrest, Leon (Richard)
1937-1997 .... **BLCS; CLC 4**
See also AFAW 2; BW 2; CA 89-92; 162; CAAS 7; CANR 25, 52, 87; CN 7; DLB 33

Forster, E(dward) M(organ)
1879-1970 ...... **CLC 1, 2, 3, 4, 9, 10, 13, 15, 22, 45, 77; SSC 27; TCLC 125; WLC**
See also AAYA 2, 37; BRW 6; BRWR 2; BYA 12; CA 13-14; 25-28R; CANR 45; CAP 1; CDBLB 1914-1945; DA; DA3; DAB; DAC; DAM MST, NOV; DLB 34, 98, 162, 178, 195; DLBD 10; EWL 3; EXPN; LAIT 3; LMFS 1; MTCW 1, 2; NCFS 1; NFS 3, 10, 11; RGEL 2; RGSF 2; SATA 57; SUFW 1; TEA; WLIT 4

Forster, John 1812-1876 .... **NCLC 11**
See also DLB 144, 184

Forster, Margaret 1938- .... **CLC 149**
See also CA 133; CANR 62, 115; CN 7; DLB 155, 271

Forsyth, Frederick 1938- .... **CLC 2, 5, 36**
See also BEST 89:4; CA 85-88; CANR 38, 62, 115; CMW 4; CN 7; CPW; DAM NOV, POP; DLB 87; MTCW 1, 2

Forten, Charlotte L. 1837-1914 .... **BLC 2; TCLC 16**
See Grimke, Charlotte L(ottie) Forten
See also DLB 50, 239

Fortinbras
See Grieg, (Johan) Nordahl (Brun)

Foscolo, Ugo 1778-1827 .... **NCLC 8, 97**
See also EW 5

Fosse, Bob .... **CLC 20**
See Fosse, Robert Louis

Fosse, Robert Louis 1927-1987
See Fosse, Bob
See also CA 110; 123

Foster, Hannah Webster
1758-1840 .... **NCLC 99**
See also DLB 37, 200; RGAL 4

Foster, Stephen Collins
1826-1864 .... **NCLC 26**
See also RGAL 4

Foucault, Michel 1926-1984 . **CLC 31, 34, 69**
See also CA 105; 113; CANR 34; DLB 242; EW 13; EWL 3; GFL 1789 to the Present; GLL 1; LMFS 2; MTCW 1, 2; TWA

Fouque, Friedrich (Heinrich Karl) de la Motte 1777-1843 .... **NCLC 2**
See also DLB 90; RGWL 2, 3; SUFW 1

Fourier, Charles 1772-1837 .... **NCLC 51**

Fournier, Henri-Alban 1886-1914
See Alain-Fournier
See also CA 104; 179

Fournier, Pierre 1916- .... **CLC 11**
See Gascar, Pierre
See also CA 89-92; CANR 16, 40

Fowles, John (Robert) 1926- . **CLC 1, 2, 3, 4, 6, 9, 10, 15, 33, 87; SSC 33**
See also BPFB 1; BRWS 1; CA 5-8R; CANR 25, 71, 103; CDBLB 1960 to Present; CN 7; DA3; DAB; DAC; DAM MST; DLB 14, 139, 207; EWL 3; HGG; MTCW 1, 2; RGEL 2; RHW; SATA 22; TEA; WLIT 4

Fox, Paula 1923- .... **CLC 2, 8, 121**
See also AAYA 3, 37; BYA 3, 8; CA 73-76; CANR 20, 36, 62, 105; CLR 1, 44, 96; DLB 52; JRDA; MAICYA 1, 2; MTCW 1; NFS 12; SATA 17, 60, 120; WYA; YAW

Garrigue, Jean 1914-1972 .... **CLC 2, 8**
See also CA 5-8R; 37-40R; CANR 20

Garrison, Frederick
See Sinclair, Upton (Beall)

Garrison, William Lloyd
1805-1879 .... **NCLC 149**
See also CDALB 1640-1865; DLB 1, 43, 235

Garro, Elena 1920(?)-1998 .. **HLCS 1; TCLC 153**
See also CA 131; 169; CWW 2; DLB 145; EWL 3; HW 1; LAWS 1; WLIT 1

Garth, Will
See Hamilton, Edmond; Kuttner, Henry

Garvey, Marcus (Moziah, Jr.)
1887-1940 .... **BLC 2; HR 2; TCLC 41**
See also BW 1; CA 120; 124; CANR 79; DAM MULT

Gary, Romain .... **CLC 25**
See Kacew, Romain
See also DLB 83, 299

Gascar, Pierre .... **CLC 11**
See Fournier, Pierre
See also EWL 3

Gascoigne, George 1539-1577 .... **LC 108**
See also DLB 136; RGEL 2

Gascoyne, David (Emery)
1916-2001 .... **CLC 45**
See also CA 65-68; 200; CANR 10, 28, 54; CP 7; DLB 20; MTCW 1; RGEL 2

Gaskell, Elizabeth Cleghorn
1810-1865 .... **NCLC 5, 70, 97, 137; SSC 25**
See also BRW 5; CDBLB 1832-1890; DAB; DAM MST; DLB 21, 144, 159; RGEL 2; RGSF 2; TEA

Gass, William H(oward) 1924- . **CLC 1, 2, 8, 11, 15, 39, 132; SSC 12**
See also AMWS 6; CA 17-20R; CANR 30, 71, 100; CN 7; DLB 2, 227; EWL 3; MTCW 1, 2; RGAL 4

Gassendi, Pierre 1592-1655 .... **LC 54**
See also GFL Beginnings to 1789

Gasset, Jose Ortega y
See Ortega y Gasset, Jose

Gates, Henry Louis, Jr. 1950- ... **BLCS; CLC 65**
See also BW 2, 3; CA 109; CANR 25, 53, 75, 125; CSW; DA3; DAM MULT; DLB 67; EWL 3; MTCW 1; RGAL 4

Gautier, Theophile 1811-1872 .. **NCLC 1, 59; PC 18; SSC 20**
See also DAM POET; DLB 119; EW 6; GFL 1789 to the Present; RGWL 2, 3; SUFW; TWA

Gawsworth, John
See Bates, H(erbert) E(rnest)

Gay, John 1685-1732 .... **LC 49**
See also BRW 3; DAM DRAM; DLB 84, 95; RGEL 2; WLIT 3

Gay, Oliver
See Gogarty, Oliver St. John

Gay, Peter (Jack) 1923- .... **CLC 158**
See also CA 13-16R; CANR 18, 41, 77; INT CANR-18

Gaye, Marvin (Pentz, Jr.)
1939-1984 .... **CLC 26**
See also CA 195; 112

Gebler, Carlo (Ernest) 1954- .... **CLC 39**
See also CA 119; 133; CANR 96; DLB 271

Gee, Maggie (Mary) 1948- .... **CLC 57**
See also CA 130; CANR 125; CN 7; DLB 207

Gee, Maurice (Gough) 1931- .... **CLC 29**
See also AAYA 42; CA 97-100; CANR 67, 123; CLR 56; CN 7; CWRI 5; EWL 3; MAICYA 2; RGSF 2; SATA 46, 101

Geiogamah, Hanay 1945- .... **NNAL**
See also CA 153; DAM MULT; DLB 175

Gelbart, Larry (Simon) 1928- .... **CLC 21, 61**
See Gelbart, Larry
See also CA 73-76; CANR 45, 94

Gelbart, Larry 1928-
See Gelbart, Larry (Simon)
See also CAD; CD 5

Gelber, Jack 1932-2003 ...... **CLC 1, 6, 14, 79**
See also CA 1-4R; 216; CAD; CANR 2; DLB 7, 228

Gellhorn, Martha (Ellis)
1908-1998 .... **CLC 14, 60**
See also CA 77-80; 164; CANR 44; CN 7; DLBY 1982, 1998

Genet, Jean 1910-1986 . **DC 25; CLC 1, 2, 5, 10, 14, 44, 46; TCLC 128**
See also CA 13-16R; CANR 18; DA3; DAM DRAM; DFS 10; DLB 72; DLBY 1986; EW 13; EWL 3; GFL 1789 to the Present; GLL 1; LMFS 2; MTCW 1, 2; RGWL 2, 3; TWA

Gent, Peter 1942- .... **CLC 29**
See also AITN 1; CA 89-92; DLBY 1982

Gentile, Giovanni 1875-1944 .... **TCLC 96**
See also CA 119

Gentlewoman in New England, A
See Bradstreet, Anne

Gentlewoman in Those Parts, A
See Bradstreet, Anne

Geoffrey of Monmouth c.
1100-1155 .... **CMLC 44**
See also DLB 146; TEA

George, Jean
See George, Jean Craighead

George, Jean Craighead 1919- .... **CLC 35**
See also AAYA 8; BYA 2, 4; CA 5-8R; CANR 25; CLR 1; 80; DLB 52; JRDA; MAICYA 1, 2; SATA 2, 68, 124; WYA; YAW

George, Stefan (Anton) 1868-1933 . **TCLC 2, 14**
See also CA 104; 193; EW 8; EWL 3

Georges, Georges Martin
See Simenon, Georges (Jacques Christian)

Gerald of Wales c. 1146-c. 1223 ... **CMLC 60**

Gerhardi, William Alexander
See Gerhardie, William Alexander

Gerhardie, William Alexander
1895-1977 .... **CLC 5**
See also CA 25-28R; 73-76; CANR 18; DLB 36; RGEL 2

Gerson, Jean 1363-1429 .... **LC 77**
See also DLB 208

Gersonides 1288-1344 .... **CMLC 49**
See also DLB 115

Gerstler, Amy 1956- .... **CLC 70**
See also CA 146; CANR 99

Gertler, T. .... **CLC 34**
See also CA 116; 121

Gertsen, Aleksandr Ivanovich
See Herzen, Aleksandr Ivanovich

Ghalib .... **NCLC 39, 78**
See Ghalib, Asadullah Khan

Ghalib, Asadullah Khan 1797-1869
See Ghalib
See also DAM POET; RGWL 2, 3

Ghelderode, Michel de 1898-1962 ..... **CLC 6, 11; DC 15**
See also CA 85-88; CANR 40, 77; DAM DRAM; EW 11; EWL 3; TWA

Ghiselin, Brewster 1903-2001 .... **CLC 23**
See also CA 13-16R; CAAS 10; CANR 13; CP 7

Ghose, Aurabinda 1872-1950 .... **TCLC 63**
See Ghose, Aurobindo
See also CA 163

Ghose, Aurobindo
See Ghose, Aurabinda
See also EWL 3

Ghose, Zulfikar 1935- .... **CLC 42, 200**
See also CA 65-68; CANR 67; CN 7; CP 7; EWL 3

Ghosh, Amitav 1956- .... **CLC 44, 153**
See also CA 147; CANR 80; CN 7; WWE 1

Giacosa, Giuseppe 1847-1906 .... **TCLC 7**
See also CA 104

Gibb, Lee
See Waterhouse, Keith (Spencer)

Gibbon, Edward 1737-1794 .... **LC 97**
See also BRW 3; DLB 104; RGEL 2

Gibbon, Lewis Grassic .... **TCLC 4**
See Mitchell, James Leslie
See also RGEL 2

Gibbons, Kaye 1960- .... **CLC 50, 88, 145**
See also AAYA 34; AMWS 10; CA 151; CANR 75, 127; CSW; DA3; DAM POP; DLB 292; MTCW 1; NFS 3; RGAL 4; SATA 117

Gibran, Kahlil 1883-1931 . **PC 9; TCLC 1, 9**
See also CA 104; 150; DA3; DAM POET, POP; EWL 3; MTCW 2

Gibran, Khalil
See Gibran, Kahlil

Gibson, William 1914- .... **CLC 23**
See also CA 9-12R; CAD 2; CANR 9, 42, 75, 125; CD 5; DA; DAB; DAC; DAM DRAM, MST; DFS 2; DLB 7; LAIT 2; MTCW 2; SATA 66; YAW

Gibson, William (Ford) 1948- ... **CLC 39, 63, 186, 192; SSC 52**
See also AAYA 12, 59; BPFB 2; CA 126; 133; CANR 52, 90, 106; CN 7; CPW; DA3; DAM POP; DLB 251; MTCW 2; SCFW 2; SFW 4

Gide, Andre (Paul Guillaume)
1869-1951 ..... **SSC 13; TCLC 5, 12, 36; WLC**
See also CA 104; 124; DA; DA3; DAB; DAC; DAM MST, NOV; DLB 65; EW 8; EWL 3; GFL 1789 to the Present; MTCW 1, 2; RGSF 2; RGWL 2, 3; TWA

Gifford, Barry (Colby) 1946- .... **CLC 34**
See also CA 65-68; CANR 9, 30, 40, 90

Gilbert, Frank
See De Voto, Bernard (Augustine)

Gilbert, W(illiam) S(chwenck)
1836-1911 .... **TCLC 3**
See also CA 104; 173; DAM DRAM, POET; RGEL 2; SATA 36

Gilbreth, Frank B(unker), Jr.
1911-2001 .... **CLC 17**
See also CA 9-12R; SATA 2

Gilchrist, Ellen (Louise) 1935- .. **CLC 34, 48, 143; SSC 14, 63**
See also BPFB 2; CA 113; 116; CANR 41, 61, 104; CN 7; CPW; CSW; DAM POP; DLB 130; EWL 3; EXPS; MTCW 1, 2; RGAL 4; RGSF 2; SSFS 9

Giles, Molly 1942- .... **CLC 39**
See also CA 126; CANR 98

Gill, Eric 1882-1940 .... **TCLC 85**
See Gill, (Arthur) Eric (Rowton Peter Joseph)

Gill, (Arthur) Eric (Rowton Peter Joseph)
1882-1940
See Gill, Eric
See also CA 120; DLB 98

Gill, Patrick
See Creasey, John

Gillette, Douglas .... **CLC 70**

Gilliam, Terry (Vance) 1940- .... **CLC 21, 141**
See Monty Python
See also AAYA 19, 59; CA 108; 113; CANR 35; INT CA-113

Gillian, Jerry
See Gilliam, Terry (Vance)

Gombrowicz, Witold 1904-1969 .... **CLC 4, 7, 11, 49**
See also CA 19-20; 25-28R; CANR 105; CAP 2; CDWLB 4; DAM DRAM; DLB 215; EW 12; EWL 3; RGWL 2, 3; TWA

Gomez de Avellaneda, Gertrudis
1814-1873 .... **NCLC 111**
See also LAW

Gomez de la Serna, Ramon
1888-1963 .... **CLC 9**
See also CA 153; 116; CANR 79; EWL 3; HW 1, 2

Goncharov, Ivan Alexandrovich
1812-1891 .... **NCLC 1, 63**
See also DLB 238; EW 6; RGWL 2, 3

Goncourt, Edmond (Louis Antoine Huot) de
1822-1896 .... **NCLC 7**
See also DLB 123; EW 7; GFL 1789 to the Present; RGWL 2, 3

Goncourt, Jules (Alfred Huot) de
1830-1870 .... **NCLC 7**
See also DLB 123; EW 7; GFL 1789 to the Present; RGWL 2, 3

Gongora (y Argote), Luis de
1561-1627 .... **LC 72**
See also RGWL 2, 3

Gontier, Fernande 19(?)- .... **CLC 50**

Gonzalez Martinez, Enrique
See Gonzalez Martinez, Enrique
See also DLB 290

Gonzalez Martinez, Enrique
1871-1952 .... **TCLC 72**
See Gonzalez Martinez, Enrique
See also CA 166; CANR 81; EWL 3; HW 1, 2

Goodison, Lorna 1947- .... **PC 36**
See also CA 142; CANR 88; CP 7; CWP; DLB 157; EWL 3

Goodman, Paul 1911-1972 ..... **CLC 1, 2, 4, 7**
See also CA 19-20; 37-40R; CAD; CANR 34; CAP 2; DLB 130, 246; MTCW 1; RGAL 4

GoodWeather, Harley
See King, Thomas

Googe, Barnabe 1540-1594 .... **LC 94**
See also DLB 132; RGEL 2

Gordimer, Nadine 1923- ...... **CLC 3, 5, 7, 10, 18, 33, 51, 70, 123, 160, 161; SSC 17, 80; WLCS**
See also AAYA 39; AFW; BRWS 2; CA 5-8R; CANR 3, 28, 56, 88, 131; CN 7; DA; DA3; DAB; DAC; DAM MST, NOV; DLB 225; EWL 3; EXPS; INT CANR-28; LATS 1:2; MTCW 1, 2; NFS 4; RGEL 2; RGSF 2; SSFS 2, 14, 19; TWA; WLIT 2; YAW

Gordon, Adam Lindsay
1833-1870 .... **NCLC 21**
See also DLB 230

Gordon, Caroline 1895-1981 . **CLC 6, 13, 29, 83; SSC 15**
See also AMW; CA 11-12; 103; CANR 36; CAP 1; DLB 4, 9, 102; DLBD 17; DLBY 1981; EWL 3; MTCW 1, 2; RGAL 4; RGSF 2

Gordon, Charles William 1860-1937
See Connor, Ralph
See also CA 109

Gordon, Mary (Catherine) 1949- .... **CLC 13, 22, 128; SSC 59**
See also AMWS 4; BPFB 2; CA 102; CANR 44, 92; CN 7; DLB 6; DLBY 1981; FW; INT CA-102; MTCW 1

Gordon, N. J.
See Bosman, Herman Charles

Gordon, Sol 1923- .... **CLC 26**
See also CA 53-56; CANR 4; SATA 11

Gordone, Charles 1925-1995 .. **CLC 1, 4; DC 8**
See also BW 1, 3; CA 93-96; 180; 150; CAAE 180; CAD; CANR 55; DAM DRAM; DLB 7; INT CA-93-96; MTCW 1

Gore, Catherine 1800-1861 .... **NCLC 65**
See also DLB 116; RGEL 2

Gorenko, Anna Andreevna
See Akhmatova, Anna

Gorky, Maxim .... **SSC 28; TCLC 8; WLC**
See Peshkov, Alexei Maximovich
See also DAB; DFS 9; DLB 295; EW 8; EWL 3; MTCW 2; TWA

Goryan, Sirak
See Saroyan, William

Gosse, Edmund (William)
1849-1928 .... **TCLC 28**
See also CA 117; DLB 57, 144, 184; RGEL 2

Gotlieb, Phyllis (Fay Bloom) 1926- .. **CLC 18**
See also CA 13-16R; CANR 7, 135; DLB 88, 251; SFW 4

Gottesman, S. D.
See Kornbluth, C(yril) M.; Pohl, Frederik

Gottfried von Strassburg fl. c.
1170-1215 .... **CMLC 10**
See also CDWLB 2; DLB 138; EW 1; RGWL 2, 3

Gotthelf, Jeremias 1797-1854 .... **NCLC 117**
See also DLB 133; RGWL 2, 3

Gottschalk, Laura Riding
See Jackson, Laura (Riding)

Gould, Lois 1932(?)-2002 .... **CLC 4, 10**
See also CA 77-80; 208; CANR 29; MTCW 1

Gould, Stephen Jay 1941-2002 .... **CLC 163**
See also AAYA 26; BEST 90:2; CA 77-80; 205; CANR 10, 27, 56, 75, 125; CPW; INT CANR-27; MTCW 1, 2

Gourmont, Remy(-Marie-Charles) de
1858-1915 .... **TCLC 17**
See also CA 109; 150; GFL 1789 to the Present; MTCW 2

Gournay, Marie le Jars de
See de Gournay, Marie le Jars

Govier, Katherine 1948- .... **CLC 51**
See also CA 101; CANR 18, 40, 128; CCA 1

Gower, John c. 1330-1408 .... **LC 76; PC 59**
See also BRW 1; DLB 146; RGEL 2

Goyen, (Charles) William
1915-1983 .... **CLC 5, 8, 14, 40**
See also AITN 2; CA 5-8R; 110; CANR 6, 71; DLB 2, 218; DLBY 1983; EWL 3; INT CANR-6

Goytisolo, Juan 1931- .... **CLC 5, 10, 23, 133; HLC 1**
See also CA 85-88; CANR 32, 61, 131; CWW 2; DAM MULT; EWL 3; GLL 2; HW 1, 2; MTCW 1, 2

Gozzano, Guido 1883-1916 .... **PC 10**
See also CA 154; DLB 114; EWL 3

Gozzi, (Conte) Carlo 1720-1806 .... **NCLC 23**

Grabbe, Christian Dietrich
1801-1836 .... **NCLC 2**
See also DLB 133; RGWL 2, 3

Grace, Patricia Frances 1937- .... **CLC 56**
See also CA 176; CANR 118; CN 7; EWL 3; RGSF 2

Gracian y Morales, Baltasar
1601-1658 .... **LC 15**

Gracq, Julien .... **CLC 11, 48**
See Poirier, Louis
See also CWW 2; DLB 83; GFL 1789 to the Present

Grade, Chaim 1910-1982 .... **CLC 10**
See also CA 93-96; 107; EWL 3

Graduate of Oxford, A
See Ruskin, John

Grafton, Garth
See Duncan, Sara Jeannette

Grafton, Sue 1940- .... **CLC 163**
See also AAYA 11, 49; BEST 90:3; CA 108; CANR 31, 55, 111, 134; CMW 4; CPW; CSW; DA3; DAM POP; DLB 226; FW; MSW

Graham, John
See Phillips, David Graham

Graham, Jorie 1951- .... **CLC 48, 118; PC 59**
See also CA 111; CANR 63, 118; CP 7; CWP; DLB 120; EWL 3; PFS 10, 17

Graham, R(obert) B(ontine) Cunninghame
See Cunninghame Graham, Robert (Gallnigad) Bontine
See also DLB 98, 135, 174; RGEL 2; RGSF 2

Graham, Robert
See Haldeman, Joe (William)

Graham, Tom
See Lewis, (Harry) Sinclair

Graham, W(illiam) S(idney)
1918-1986 .... **CLC 29**
See also BRWS 7; CA 73-76; 118; DLB 20; RGEL 2

Graham, Winston (Mawdsley)
1910-2003 .... **CLC 23**
See also CA 49-52; 218; CANR 2, 22, 45, 66; CMW 4; CN 7; DLB 77; RHW

Grahame, Kenneth 1859-1932 ...... **TCLC 64, 136**
See also BYA 5; CA 108; 136; CANR 80; CLR 5; CWRI 5; DA3; DAB; DLB 34, 141, 178; FANT; MAICYA 1, 2; MTCW 2; NFS 20; RGEL 2; SATA 100; TEA; WCH; YABC 1

Granger, Darius John
See Marlowe, Stephen

Granin, Daniil 1918- .... **CLC 59**
See also DLB 302

Granovsky, Timofei Nikolaevich
1813-1855 .... **NCLC 75**
See also DLB 198

Grant, Skeeter
See Spiegelman, Art

Granville-Barker, Harley
1877-1946 .... **TCLC 2**
See Barker, Harley Granville
See also CA 104; 204; DAM DRAM; RGEL 2

Granzotto, Gianni
See Granzotto, Giovanni Battista

Granzotto, Giovanni Battista
1914-1985 .... **CLC 70**
See also CA 166

Grass, Günter (Wilhelm) 1927- ... **CLC 1, 2, 4, 6, 11, 15, 22, 32, 49, 88, 207; WLC**
See Grass, Guenter (Wilhelm)
See also BPFB 2; CA 13-16R; CANR 20, 75, 93, 133; CDWLB 2; CWW 2; DA; DA3; DAB; DAC; DAM MST, NOV; DLB 75, 124; EW 13; EWL 3; MTCW 1, 2; RGWL 2, 3; TWA

Gratton, Thomas
See Hulme, T(homas) E(rnest)

Grau, Shirley Ann 1929- .... **CLC 4, 9, 146; SSC 15**
See also CA 89-92; CANR 22, 69; CN 7; CSW; DLB 2, 218; INT CA-89-92; CANR-22; MTCW 1

Gravel, Fern
See Hall, James Norman

Graver, Elizabeth 1964- .... **CLC 70**
See also CA 135; CANR 71, 129

Graves, Richard Perceval
1895-1985 .... **CLC 44**
See also CA 65-68; CANR 9, 26, 51

Grove, Frederick Philip .... **TCLC 4**
See Greve, Felix Paul (Berthold Friedrich)
See also DLB 92; RGEL 2

Grubb
See Crumb, R(obert)

Grumbach, Doris (Isaac) 1918- . **CLC 13, 22, 64**
See also CA 5-8R; CAAS 2; CANR 9, 42, 70, 127; CN 7; INT CANR-9; MTCW 2

Grundtvig, Nicolai Frederik Severin
1783-1872 .... **NCLC 1**
See also DLB 300

Grunge
See Crumb, R(obert)

Grunwald, Lisa 1959- .... **CLC 44**
See also CA 120

Gryphius, Andreas 1616-1664 .... **LC 89**
See also CDWLB 2; DLB 164; RGWL 2, 3

Guare, John 1938- .... **CLC 8, 14, 29, 67; DC 20**
See also CA 73-76; CAD; CANR 21, 69, 118; CD 5; DAM DRAM; DFS 8, 13; DLB 7, 249; EWL 3; MTCW 1, 2; RGAL 4

Guarini, Battista 1537-1612 .... **LC 102**

Gubar, Susan (David) 1944- .... **CLC 145**
See also CA 108; CANR 45, 70; FW; MTCW 1; RGAL 4

Gudjonsson, Halldor Kiljan 1902-1998
See Halldor Laxness
See also CA 103; 164

Guenter, Erich
See Eich, Gunter

Guest, Barbara 1920- .... **CLC 34; PC 55**
See also BG 2; CA 25-28R; CANR 11, 44, 84; CP 7; CWP; DLB 5, 193

Guest, Edgar A(lbert) 1881-1959 ... **TCLC 95**
See also CA 112; 168

Guest, Judith (Ann) 1936- .... **CLC 8, 30**
See also AAYA 7; CA 77-80; CANR 15, 75; DA3; DAM NOV, POP; EXPN; INT CANR-15; LAIT 5; MTCW 1, 2; NFS 1

Guevara, Che .... **CLC 87; HLC 1**
See Guevara (Serna), Ernesto

Guevara (Serna), Ernesto
1928-1967 .... **CLC 87; HLC 1**
See Guevara, Che
See also CA 127; 111; CANR 56; DAM MULT; HW 1

Guicciardini, Francesco 1483-1540 ..... **LC 49**

Guild, Nicholas M. 1944- .... **CLC 33**
See also CA 93-96

Guillemin, Jacques
See Sartre, Jean-Paul

Guillen, Jorge 1893-1984 . **CLC 11; HLCS 1; PC 35**
See also CA 89-92; 112; DAM MULT, POET; DLB 108; EWL 3; HW 1; RGWL 2, 3

Guillen, Nicolas (Cristobal)
1902-1989 .... **BLC 2; CLC 48, 79; HLC 1; PC 23**
See also BW 2; CA 116; 125; 129; CANR 84; DAM MST, MULT, POET; DLB 283; EWL 3; HW 1; LAW; RGWL 2, 3; WP

Guillen y Alvarez, Jorge
See Guillen, Jorge

Guillevic, (Eugene) 1907-1997 .... **CLC 33**
See also CA 93-96; CWW 2

Guillois
See Desnos, Robert

Guillois, Valentin
See Desnos, Robert

Guimaraes Rosa, Joao 1908-1967 .... **HLCS 2**
See Rosa, Joao Guimaraes
See also CA 175; LAW; RGSF 2; RGWL 2, 3

Guiney, Louise Imogen
1861-1920 .... **TCLC 41**
See also CA 160; DLB 54; RGAL 4

Guinizelli, Guido c. 1230-1276 ...... **CMLC 49**

Guiraldes, Ricardo (Guillermo)
1886-1927 .... **TCLC 39**
See also CA 131; EWL 3; HW 1; LAW; MTCW 1

Gumilev, Nikolai (Stepanovich)
1886-1921 .... **TCLC 60**
See Gumilyov, Nikolay Stepanovich
See also CA 165; DLB 295

Gumilyov, Nikolay Stepanovich
See Gumilev, Nikolai (Stepanovich)
See also EWL 3

Gump, P. Q.
See Card, Orson Scott

Gunesekera, Romesh 1954- .... **CLC 91**
See also BRWS 10; CA 159; CN 7; DLB 267

Gunn, Bill .... **CLC 5**
See Gunn, William Harrison
See also DLB 38

Gunn, Thom(son William)
1929-2004 . **CLC 3, 6, 18, 32, 81; PC 26**
See also BRWS 4; CA 17-20R; 227; CANR 9, 33, 116; CDBLB 1960 to Present; CP 7; DAM POET; DLB 27; INT CANR-33; MTCW 1; PFS 9; RGEL 2

Gunn, William Harrison 1934(?)-1989
See Gunn, Bill
See also AITN 1; BW 1, 3; CA 13-16R; 128; CANR 12, 25, 76

Gunn Allen, Paula
See Allen, Paula Gunn

Gunnars, Kristjana 1948- .... **CLC 69**
See also CA 113; CCA 1; CP 7; CWP; DLB 60

Gunter, Erich
See Eich, Gunter

Gurdjieff, G(eorgei) I(vanovich)
1877(?)-1949 .... **TCLC 71**
See also CA 157

Gurganus, Allan 1947- .... **CLC 70**
See also BEST 90:1; CA 135; CANR 114; CN 7; CPW; CSW; DAM POP; GLL 1

Gurney, A. R.
See Gurney, A(lbert) R(amsdell), Jr.
See also DLB 266

Gurney, A(lbert) R(amsdell), Jr.
1930- .... **CLC 32, 50, 54**
See Gurney, A. R.
See also AMWS 5; CA 77-80; CAD; CANR 32, 64, 121; CD 5; DAM DRAM; EWL 3

Gurney, Ivor (Bertie) 1890-1937 ... **TCLC 33**
See also BRW 6; CA 167; DLBY 2002; PAB; RGEL 2

Gurney, Peter
See Gurney, A(lbert) R(amsdell), Jr.

Guro, Elena (Genrikhovna)
1877-1913 .... **TCLC 56**
See also DLB 295

Gustafson, James M(oody) 1925- ... **CLC 100**
See also CA 25-28R; CANR 37

Gustafson, Ralph (Barker)
1909-1995 .... **CLC 36**
See also CA 21-24R; CANR 8, 45, 84; CP 7; DLB 88; RGEL 2

Gut, Gom
See Simenon, Georges (Jacques Christian)

Guterson, David 1956- .... **CLC 91**
See also CA 132; CANR 73, 126; DLB 292; MTCW 2; NFS 13

Guthrie, A(lfred) B(ertram), Jr.
1901-1991 .... **CLC 23**
See also CA 57-60; 134; CANR 24; DLB 6, 212; SATA 62; SATA-Obit 67

Guthrie, Isobel
See Grieve, C(hristopher) M(urray)

Guthrie, Woodrow Wilson 1912-1967
See Guthrie, Woody
See also CA 113; 93-96

Guthrie, Woody .... **CLC 35**
See Guthrie, Woodrow Wilson
See also DLB 303; LAIT 3

Gutierrez Najera, Manuel
1859-1895 .... **HLCS 2; NCLC 133**
See also DLB 290; LAW

Guy, Rosa (Cuthbert) 1925- .... **CLC 26**
See also AAYA 4, 37; BW 2; CA 17-20R; CANR 14, 34, 83; CLR 13; DLB 33; DNFS 1; JRDA; MAICYA 1, 2; SATA 14, 62, 122; YAW

Gwendolyn
See Bennett, (Enoch) Arnold

H. D. .... **CLC 3, 8, 14, 31, 34, 73; PC 5**
See Doolittle, Hilda

H. de V.
See Buchan, John

Haavikko, Paavo Juhani 1931- .. **CLC 18, 34**
See also CA 106; CWW 2; EWL 3

Habbema, Koos
See Heijermans, Herman

Habermas, Juergen 1929- .... **CLC 104**
See also CA 109; CANR 85; DLB 242

Habermas, Jurgen
See Habermas, Juergen

Hacker, Marilyn 1942- ...... **CLC 5, 9, 23, 72, 91; PC 47**
See also CA 77-80; CANR 68, 129; CP 7; CWP; DAM POET; DLB 120, 282; FW; GLL 2; PFS 19

Hadewijch of Antwerp fl. 1250- ... **CMLC 61**
See also RGWL 3

Hadrian 76-138 .... **CMLC 52**

Haeckel, Ernst Heinrich (Philipp August)
1834-1919 .... **TCLC 83**
See also CA 157

Hafiz c. 1326-1389(?) .... **CMLC 34**
See also RGWL 2, 3

Hagedorn, Jessica T(arahata)
1949- .... **CLC 185**
See also CA 139; CANR 69; CWP; RGAL 4

Haggard, H(enry) Rider
1856-1925 .... **TCLC 11**
See also BRWS 3; BYA 4, 5; CA 108; 148; CANR 112; DLB 70, 156, 174, 178; FANT; LMFS 1; MTCW 2; RGEL 2; RHW; SATA 16; SCFW 1, 2; SFW 4; SUFW 1; WLIT 4

Hagiosy, L.
See Larbaud, Valery (Nicolas)

Hagiwara, Sakutaro 1886-1942 .... **PC 18; TCLC 60**
See Hagiwara Sakutaro
See also CA 154; RGWL 3

Hagiwara Sakutaro
See Hagiwara, Sakutaro
See also EWL 3

Haig, Fenil
See Ford, Ford Madox

Haig-Brown, Roderick (Langmere)
1908-1976 .... **CLC 21**
See also CA 5-8R; 69-72; CANR 4, 38, 83; CLR 31; CWRI 5; DLB 88; MAICYA 1, 2; SATA 12

Haight, Rip
See Carpenter, John (Howard)

Hailey, Arthur 1920- .... **CLC 5**
See also AITN 2; BEST 90:3; BPFB 2; CA 1-4R; CANR 2, 36, 75; CCA 1; CN 7; CPW; DAM NOV, POP; DLB 88; DLBY 1982; MTCW 1, 2

Hailey, Elizabeth Forsythe 1938- ..... **CLC 40**
See also CA 93-96; 188; CAAE 188; CAAS 1; CANR 15, 48; INT CANR-15

Harris, George Washington
1814-1869 .... **NCLC 23**
See also DLB 3, 11, 248; RGAL 4

Harris, Joel Chandler 1848-1908 ..... **SSC 19;**
TCLC 2
See also CA 104; 137; CANR 80; CLR 49;
DLB 11, 23, 42, 78, 91; LAIT 2; MAI-
CYA 1, 2; RGSF 2; SATA 100; WCH;
YABC 1

Harris, John (Wyndham Parkes Lucas)
Beynon 1903-1969
See Wyndham, John
See also CA 102; 89-92; CANR 84; SATA
118; SFW 4

Harris, MacDonald .... **CLC 9**
See Heiney, Donald (William)

Harris, Mark 1922- .... **CLC 19**
See also CA 5-8R; CAAS 3; CANR 2, 55,
83; CN 7; DLB 2; DLBY 1980

Harris, Norman .... **CLC 65**

Harris, (Theodore) Wilson 1921- .... **CLC 25,**
159
See also BRWS 5; BW 2, 3; CA 65-68;
CAAS 16; CANR 11, 27, 69, 114; CD-
WLB 3; CN 7; CP 7; DLB 117; EWL 3;
MTCW 1; RGEL 2

Harrison, Barbara Grizzuti
1934-2002 .... **CLC 144**
See also CA 77-80; 205; CANR 15, 48; INT
CANR-15

Harrison, Elizabeth (Allen) Cavanna
1909-2001
See Cavanna, Betty
See also CA 9-12R; 200; CANR 6, 27, 85,
104, 121; MAICYA 2; SATA 142; YAW

Harrison, Harry (Max) 1925- .... **CLC 42**
See also CA 1-4R; CANR 5, 21, 84; DLB
8; SATA 4; SCFW 2; SFW 4

Harrison, James (Thomas) 1937- ...... **CLC 6,**
14, 33, 66, 143; SSC 19
See Harrison, Jim
See also CA 13-16R; CANR 8, 51, 79; CN
7; CP 7; DLBY 1982; INT CANR-8

Harrison, Jim
See Harrison, James (Thomas)
See also AMWS 8; RGAL 4; TCWW 2;
TUS

Harrison, Kathryn 1961- .... **CLC 70, 151**
See also CA 144; CANR 68, 122

Harrison, Tony 1937- .... **CLC 43, 129**
See also BRWS 5; CA 65-68; CANR 44,
98; CBD; CD 5; CP 7; DLB 40, 245;
MTCW 1; RGEL 2

Harriss, Will(ard Irvin) 1922- .... **CLC 34**
See also CA 111

Hart, Ellis
See Ellison, Harlan (Jay)

Hart, Josephine 1942(?)- .... **CLC 70**
See also CA 138; CANR 70; CPW; DAM
POP

Hart, Moss 1904-1961 .... **CLC 66**
See also CA 109; 89-92; CANR 84; DAM
DRAM; DFS 1; DLB 7, 266; RGAL 4

Harte, (Francis) Bret(t)
1836(?)-1902 ... **SSC 8, 59; TCLC 1, 25;**
WLC
See also AMWS 2; CA 104; 140; CANR
80; CDALB 1865-1917; DA; DA3; DAC;
DAM MST; DLB 12, 64, 74, 79, 186;
EXPS; LAIT 2; RGAL 4; RGSF 2; SATA
26; SSFS 3; TUS

Hartley, L(eslie) P(oles) 1895-1972 ... **CLC 2,**
22
See also BRWS 7; CA 45-48; 37-40R;
CANR 33; DLB 15, 139; EWL 3; HGG;
MTCW 1, 2; RGEL 2; RGSF 2; SUFW 1

Hartman, Geoffrey H. 1929- .... **CLC 27**
See also CA 117; 125; CANR 79; DLB 67

Hartmann, Sadakichi 1869-1944 ... **TCLC 73**
See also CA 157; DLB 54

Hartmann von Aue c. 1170-c.
1210 .... **CMLC 15**
See also CDWLB 2; DLB 138; RGWL 2, 3

Hartog, Jan de
See de Hartog, Jan

Haruf, Kent 1943- .... **CLC 34**
See also AAYA 44; CA 149; CANR 91, 131

Harvey, Caroline
See Trollope, Joanna

Harvey, Gabriel 1550(?)-1631 .... **LC 88**
See also DLB 167, 213, 281

Harwood, Ronald 1934- .... **CLC 32**
See also CA 1-4R; CANR 4, 55; CBD; CD
5; DAM DRAM, MST; DLB 13

Hasegawa Tatsunosuke
See Futabatei, Shimei

Hasek, Jaroslav (Matej Frantisek)
1883-1923 .... **SSC 69; TCLC 4**
See also CA 104; 129; CDWLB 4; DLB
215; EW 9; EWL 3; MTCW 1, 2; RGSF
2; RGWL 2, 3

Hass, Robert 1941- ... **CLC 18, 39, 99; PC 16**
See also AMWS 6; CA 111; CANR 30, 50,
71; CP 7; DLB 105, 206; EWL 3; RGAL
4; SATA 94

Hastings, Hudson
See Kuttner, Henry

Hastings, Selina .... **CLC 44**

Hathorne, John 1641-1717 .... **LC 38**

Hatteras, Amelia
See Mencken, H(enry) L(ouis)

Hatteras, Owen .... **TCLC 18**
See Mencken, H(enry) L(ouis); Nathan,
George Jean

Hauptmann, Gerhart (Johann Robert)
1862-1946 .... **SSC 37; TCLC 4**
See also CA 104; 153; CDWLB 2; DAM
DRAM; DLB 66, 118; EW 8; EWL 3;
RGSF 2; RGWL 2, 3; TWA

Havel, Vaclav 1936- ..... **CLC 25, 58, 65, 123;**
DC 6
See also CA 104; CANR 36, 63, 124; CD-
WLB 4; CWW 2; DA3; DAM DRAM;
DFS 10; DLB 232; EWL 3; LMFS 2;
MTCW 1, 2; RGWL 3

Haviaras, Stratis .... **CLC 33**
See Chaviaras, Strates

Hawes, Stephen 1475(?)-1529(?) .... **LC 17**
See also DLB 132; RGEL 2

Hawkes, John (Clendennin Burne, Jr.)
1925-1998 .. **CLC 1, 2, 3, 4, 7, 9, 14, 15,**
27, 49
See also BPFB 2; CA 1-4R; 167; CANR 2,
47, 64; CN 7; DLB 2, 7, 227; DLBY
1980, 1998; EWL 3; MTCW 1, 2; RGAL
4

Hawking, S. W.
See Hawking, Stephen W(illiam)

Hawking, Stephen W(illiam) 1942- . **CLC 63,**
105
See also AAYA 13; BEST 89:1; CA 126;
129; CANR 48, 115; CPW; DA3; MTCW
2

Hawkins, Anthony Hope
See Hope, Anthony

Hawthorne, Julian 1846-1934 .... **TCLC 25**
See also CA 165; HGG

Hawthorne, Nathaniel 1804-1864 ... **NCLC 2,**
10, 17, 23, 39, 79, 95; SSC 3, 29, 39;
WLC
See also AAYA 18; AMW; AMWC 1;
AMWR 1; BPFB 2; BYA 3; CDALB
1640-1865; DA; DA3; DAB; DAC; DAM
MST, NOV; DLB 1, 74, 183, 223, 269;
EXPN; EXPS; HGG; LAIT 1; NFS 1, 20;
RGAL 4; RGSF 2; SSFS 1, 7, 11, 15;
SUFW 1; TUS; WCH; YABC 2

Hawthorne, Sophia Peabody
1809-1871 .... **NCLC 150**
See also DLB 183, 239

Haxton, Josephine Ayres 1921-
See Douglas, Ellen
See also CA 115; CANR 41, 83

Hayaseca y Eizaguirre, Jorge
See Echegaray (y Eizaguirre), Jose (Maria
Waldo)

Hayashi, Fumiko 1904-1951 .... **TCLC 27**
See Hayashi Fumiko
See also CA 161

Hayashi Fumiko
See Hayashi, Fumiko
See also DLB 180; EWL 3

Haycraft, Anna (Margaret) 1932-
See Ellis, Alice Thomas
See also CA 122; CANR 85, 90; MTCW 2

Hayden, Robert E(arl) 1913-1980 ..... **BLC 2;**
CLC 5, 9, 14, 37; PC 6
See also AFAW 1, 2; AMWS 2; BW 1, 3;
CA 69-72; 97-100; CABS 2; CANR 24,
75, 82; CDALB 1941-1968; DA; DAC;
DAM MST, MULT, POET; DLB 5, 76;
EWL 3; EXPP; MTCW 1, 2; PFS 1;
RGAL 4; SATA 19; SATA-Obit 26; WP

Haydon, Benjamin Robert
1786-1846 .... **NCLC 146**
See also DLB 110

Hayek, F(riedrich) A(ugust von)
1899-1992 .... **TCLC 109**
See also CA 93-96; 137; CANR 20; MTCW
1, 2

Hayford, J(oseph) E(phraim) Casely
See Casely-Hayford, J(oseph) E(phraim)

Hayman, Ronald 1932- .... **CLC 44**
See also CA 25-28R; CANR 18, 50, 88; CD
5; DLB 155

Hayne, Paul Hamilton 1830-1886 . **NCLC 94**
See also DLB 3, 64, 79, 248; RGAL 4

Hays, Mary 1760-1843 .... **NCLC 114**
See also DLB 142, 158; RGEL 2

Haywood, Eliza (Fowler)
1693(?)-1756 .... **LC 1, 44**
See also DLB 39; RGEL 2

Hazlitt, William 1778-1830 ...... **NCLC 29, 82**
See also BRW 4; DLB 110, 158; RGEL 2;
TEA

Hazzard, Shirley 1931- .... **CLC 18**
See also CA 9-12R; CANR 4, 70, 127; CN
7; DLB 289; DLBY 1982; MTCW 1

Head, Bessie 1937-1986 ...... **BLC 2; CLC 25,**
67; SSC 52
See also AFW; BW 2, 3; CA 29-32R; 119;
CANR 25, 82; CDWLB 3; DA3; DAM
MULT; DLB 117, 225; EWL 3; EXPS;
FW; MTCW 1, 2; RGSF 2; SSFS 5, 13;
WLIT 2; WWE 1

Headon, (Nicky) Topper 1956(?)- ..... **CLC 30**

Heaney, Seamus (Justin) 1939- ..... **CLC 5, 7,**
14, 25, 37, 74, 91, 171; PC 18; WLCS
See also BRWR 1; BRWS 2; CA 85-88;
CANR 25, 48, 75, 91, 128; CDBLB 1960
to Present; CP 7; DA3; DAB; DAM
POET; DLB 40; DLBY 1995; EWL 3;
EXPP; MTCW 1, 2; PAB; PFS 2, 5, 8,
17; RGEL 2; TEA; WLIT 4

Hearn, (Patricio) Lafcadio (Tessima Carlos)
1850-1904 .... **TCLC 9**
See also CA 105; 166; DLB 12, 78, 189;
HGG; RGAL 4

Hearne, Samuel 1745-1792 .... **LC 95**
See also DLB 99

Hearne, Vicki 1946-2001 .... **CLC 56**
See also CA 139; 201

Hearon, Shelby 1931- .... **CLC 63**
See also AITN 2; AMWS 8; CA 25-28R;
CANR 18, 48, 103; CSW

Hesse, Hermann 1877-1962 ... **CLC 1, 2, 3, 6, 11, 17, 25, 69; SSC 9, 49; TCLC 148; WLC**
　See also AAYA 43; BPFB 2; CA 17-18; CAP 2; CDWLB 2; DA; DA3; DAB; DAC; DAM MST, NOV; DLB 66; EW 9; EWL 3; EXPN; LAIT 1; MTCW 1, 2; NFS 6, 15; RGWL 2, 3; SATA 50; TWA

Hewes, Cady
　See De Voto, Bernard (Augustine)

Heyen, William 1940- .... **CLC 13, 18**
　See also CA 33-36R, 220; CAAE 220; CAAS 9; CANR 98; CP 7; DLB 5

Heyerdahl, Thor 1914-2002 .... **CLC 26**
　See also CA 5-8R; 207; CANR 5, 22, 66, 73; LAIT 4; MTCW 1, 2; SATA 2, 52

Heym, Georg (Theodor Franz Arthur)
　1887-1912 .... **TCLC 9**
　See also CA 106; 181

Heym, Stefan 1913-2001 .... **CLC 41**
　See also CA 9-12R; 203; CANR 4; CWW 2; DLB 69; EWL 3

Heyse, Paul (Johann Ludwig von)
　1830-1914 .... **TCLC 8**
　See also CA 104; 209; DLB 129

Heyward, (Edwin) DuBose
　1885-1940 .... **HR 2; TCLC 59**
　See also CA 108; 157; DLB 7, 9, 45, 249; SATA 21

Heywood, John 1497(?)-1580(?) .... **LC 65**
　See also DLB 136; RGEL 2

Heywood, Thomas 1573(?)-1641 .... **LC 111**
　See also DLB 62; DAM DRAM; LMFS 1; RGEL 2; TWA

Hibbert, Eleanor Alice Burford
　1906-1993 .... **CLC 7**
　See Holt, Victoria
　See also BEST 90:4; CA 17-20R; 140; CANR 9, 28, 59; CMW 4; CPW; DAM POP; MTCW 2; RHW; SATA 2; SATA-Obit 74

Hichens, Robert (Smythe)
　1864-1950 .... **TCLC 64**
　See also CA 162; DLB 153; HGG; RHW; SUFW

Higgins, Aidan 1927- .... **SSC 68**
　See also CA 9-12R; CANR 70, 115; CN 7; DLB 14

Higgins, George V(incent)
　1939-1999 .... **CLC 4, 7, 10, 18**
　See also BPFB 2; CA 77-80; 186; CAAS 5; CANR 17, 51, 89, 96; CMW 4; CN 7; DLB 2; DLBY 1981, 1998; INT CANR-17; MSW; MTCW 1

Higginson, Thomas Wentworth
　1823-1911 .... **TCLC 36**
　See also CA 162; DLB 1, 64, 243

Higgonet, Margaret ed. .... **CLC 65**

Highet, Helen
　See MacInnes, Helen (Clark)

Highsmith, (Mary) Patricia
　1921-1995 .... **CLC 2, 4, 14, 42, 102**
　See Morgan, Claire
　See also AAYA 48; BRWS 5; CA 1-4R; 147; CANR 1, 20, 48, 62, 108; CMW 4; CPW; DA3; DAM NOV, POP; DLB 306; MSW; MTCW 1, 2

Highwater, Jamake (Mamake)
　1942(?)-2001 .... **CLC 12**
　See also AAYA 7; BPFB 2; BYA 4; CA 65-68; 199; CAAS 7; CANR 10, 34, 84; CLR 17; CWRI 5; DLB 52; DLBY 1985; JRDA; MAICYA 1, 2; SATA 32, 69; SATA-Brief 30

Highway, Tomson 1951- ...... **CLC 92; NNAL**
　See also CA 151; CANR 75; CCA 1; CD 5; DAC; DAM MULT; DFS 2; MTCW 2

Hijuelos, Oscar 1951- .... **CLC 65; HLC 1**
　See also AAYA 25; AMWS 8; BEST 90:1; CA 123; CANR 50, 75, 125; CPW; DA3; DAM MULT, POP; DLB 145; HW 1, 2; LLW 1; MTCW 2; NFS 17; RGAL 4; WLIT 1

Hikmet, Nazim 1902(?)-1963 .... **CLC 40**
　See also CA 141; 93-96; EWL 3

Hildegard von Bingen 1098-1179 . **CMLC 20**
　See also DLB 148

Hildesheimer, Wolfgang 1916-1991 .. **CLC 49**
　See also CA 101; 135; DLB 69, 124; EWL 3

Hill, Geoffrey (William) 1932- ...... **CLC 5, 8, 18, 45**
　See also BRWS 5; CA 81-84; CANR 21, 89; CDBLB 1960 to Present; CP 7; DAM POET; DLB 40; EWL 3; MTCW 1; RGEL 2

Hill, George Roy 1921-2002 .... **CLC 26**
　See also CA 110; 122; 213

Hill, John
　See Koontz, Dean R(ay)

Hill, Susan (Elizabeth) 1942- ...... **CLC 4, 113**
　See also CA 33-36R; CANR 29, 69, 129; CN 7; DAB; DAM MST, NOV; DLB 14, 139; HGG; MTCW 1; RHW

Hillard, Asa G. III .... **CLC 70**

Hillerman, Tony 1925- .... **CLC 62, 170**
　See also AAYA 40; BEST 89:1; BPFB 2; CA 29-32R; CANR 21, 42, 65, 97, 134; CMW 4; CPW; DA3; DAM POP; DLB 206, 306; MSW; RGAL 4; SATA 6; TCWW 2; YAW

Hillesum, Etty 1914-1943 .... **TCLC 49**
　See also CA 137

Hilliard, Noel (Harvey) 1929-1996 ... **CLC 15**
　See also CA 9-12R; CANR 7, 69; CN 7

Hillis, Rick 1956- .... **CLC 66**
　See also CA 134

Hilton, James 1900-1954 .... **TCLC 21**
　See also CA 108; 169; DLB 34, 77; FANT; SATA 34

Hilton, Walter (?)-1396 .... **CMLC 58**
　See also DLB 146; RGEL 2

Himes, Chester (Bomar) 1909-1984 .. **BLC 2; CLC 2, 4, 7, 18, 58, 108; TCLC 139**
　See also AFAW 2; BPFB 2; BW 2; CA 25-28R; 114; CANR 22, 89; CMW 4; DAM MULT; DLB 2, 76, 143, 226; EWL 3; MSW; MTCW 1, 2; RGAL 4

Himmelfarb, Gertrude 1922- .... **CLC 202**
　See also CA 49-52; CANR 28, 66, 102;

Hinde, Thomas .... **CLC 6, 11**
　See Chitty, Thomas Willes
　See also EWL 3

Hine, (William) Daryl 1936- .... **CLC 15**
　See also CA 1-4R; CAAS 15; CANR 1, 20; CP 7; DLB 60

Hinkson, Katharine Tynan
　See Tynan, Katharine

Hinojosa(-Smith), Rolando (R.)
　1929- .... **HLC 1**
　See Hinojosa-Smith, Rolando
　See also CA 131; CAAS 16; CANR 62; DAM MULT; DLB 82; HW 1, 2; LLW 1; MTCW 2; RGAL 4

Hinton, S(usan) E(loise) 1950- .. **CLC 30, 111**
　See also AAYA 2, 33; BPFB 2; BYA 2, 3; CA 81-84; CANR 32, 62, 92, 133; CDALBS; CLR 3, 23; CPW; DA; DA3; DAB; DAC; DAM MST, NOV; JRDA; LAIT 5; MAICYA 1, 2; MTCW 1, 2; NFS 5, 9, 15, 16; SATA 19, 58, 115; WYA; YAW

Hippius, Zinaida (Nikolaevna) .... **TCLC 9**
　See Gippius, Zinaida (Nikolaevna)
　See also DLB 295; EWL 3

Hiraoka, Kimitake 1925-1970
　See Mishima, Yukio
　See also CA 97-100; 29-32R; DA3; DAM DRAM; GLL 1; MTCW 1, 2

Hirsch, E(ric) D(onald), Jr. 1928- .... **CLC 79**
　See also CA 25-28R; CANR 27, 51; DLB 67; INT CANR-27; MTCW 1

Hirsch, Edward 1950- .... **CLC 31, 50**
　See also CA 104; CANR 20, 42, 102; CP 7; DLB 120

Hitchcock, Alfred (Joseph)
　1899-1980 .... **CLC 16**
　See also AAYA 22; CA 159; 97-100; SATA 27; SATA-Obit 24

Hitchens, Christopher (Eric)
　1949- .... **CLC 157**
　See also CA 152; CANR 89

Hitler, Adolf 1889-1945 .... **TCLC 53**
　See also CA 117; 147

Hoagland, Edward 1932- .... **CLC 28**
　See also ANW; CA 1-4R; CANR 2, 31, 57, 107; CN 7; DLB 6; SATA 51; TCWW 2

Hoban, Russell (Conwell) 1925- ... **CLC 7, 25**
　See also BPFB 2; CA 5-8R; CANR 23, 37, 66, 114; CLR 3, 69; CN 7; CWRI 5; DAM NOV; DLB 52; FANT; MAICYA 1, 2; MTCW 1, 2; SATA 1, 40, 78, 136; SFW 4; SUFW 2

Hobbes, Thomas 1588-1679 .... **LC 36**
　See also DLB 151, 252, 281; RGEL 2

Hobbs, Perry
　See Blackmur, R(ichard) P(almer)

Hobson, Laura Z(ametkin)
　1900-1986 .... **CLC 7, 25**
　See Field, Peter
　See also BPFB 2; CA 17-20R; 118; CANR 55; DLB 28; SATA 52

Hoccleve, Thomas c. 1368-c. 1437 ...... **LC 75**
　See also DLB 146; RGEL 2

Hoch, Edward D(entinger) 1930-
　See Queen, Ellery
　See also CA 29-32R; CANR 11, 27, 51, 97; CMW 4; DLB 306; SFW 4

Hochhuth, Rolf 1931- .... **CLC 4, 11, 18**
　See also CA 5-8R; CANR 33, 75; CWW 2; DAM DRAM; DLB 124; EWL 3; MTCW 1, 2

Hochman, Sandra 1936- .... **CLC 3, 8**
　See also CA 5-8R; DLB 5

Hochwaelder, Fritz 1911-1986 .... **CLC 36**
　See Hochwalder, Fritz
　See also CA 29-32R; 120; CANR 42; DAM DRAM; MTCW 1; RGWL 3

Hochwalder, Fritz
　See Hochwaelder, Fritz
　See also EWL 3; RGWL 2

Hocking, Mary (Eunice) 1921- .... **CLC 13**
　See also CA 101; CANR 18, 40

Hodgins, Jack 1938- .... **CLC 23**
　See also CA 93-96; CN 7; DLB 60

Hodgson, William Hope
　1877(?)-1918 .... **TCLC 13**
　See also CA 111; 164; CMW 4; DLB 70, 153, 156, 178; HGG; MTCW 2; SFW 4; SUFW 1

Hoeg, Peter 1957- .... **CLC 95, 156**
　See also CA 151; CANR 75; CMW 4; DA3; DLB 214; EWL 3; MTCW 2; NFS 17; RGWL 3; SSFS 18

Hoffman, Alice 1952- .... **CLC 51**
　See also AAYA 37; AMWS 10; CA 77-80; CANR 34, 66, 100; CN 7; CPW; DAM NOV; DLB 292; MTCW 1, 2

Hoffman, Daniel (Gerard) 1923- . **CLC 6, 13, 23**
　See also CA 1-4R; CANR 4; CP 7; DLB 5

Hoffman, Eva 1945- .... **CLC 182**
　See also CA 132

Housman, Laurence 1865-1959 .... **TCLC 7**
  See also CA 106; 155; DLB 10; FANT;
  RGEL 2; SATA 25

Houston, Jeanne (Toyo) Wakatsuki
  1934- .... **AAL**
  See also AAYA 49; CA 103; CAAS 16;
  CANR 29, 123; LAIT 4; SATA 78

Howard, Elizabeth Jane 1923- ..... **CLC 7, 29**
  See also CA 5-8R; CANR 8, 62; CN 7

Howard, Maureen 1930- .... **CLC 5, 14, 46, 151**
  See also CA 53-56; CANR 31, 75; CN 7;
  DLBY 1983; INT CANR-31; MTCW 1, 2

Howard, Richard 1929- .... **CLC 7, 10, 47**
  See also AITN 1; CA 85-88; CANR 25, 80;
  CP 7; DLB 5; INT CANR-25

Howard, Robert E(rvin)
  1906-1936 .... **TCLC 8**
  See also BPFB 2; BYA 5; CA 105; 157;
  FANT; SUFW 1

Howard, Warren F.
  See Pohl, Frederik

Howe, Fanny (Quincy) 1940- .... **CLC 47**
  See also CA 117; 187; CAAE 187; CAAS
  27; CANR 70, 116; CP 7; CWP; SATA-
  Brief 52

Howe, Irving 1920-1993 .... **CLC 85**
  See also AMWS 6; CA 9-12R; 141; CANR
  21, 50; DLB 67; EWL 3; MTCW 1, 2

Howe, Julia Ward 1819-1910 .... **TCLC 21**
  See also CA 117; 191; DLB 1, 189, 235;
  FW

Howe, Susan 1937- .... **CLC 72, 152; PC 54**
  See also AMWS 4; CA 160; CP 7; CWP;
  DLB 120; FW; RGAL 4

Howe, Tina 1937- .... **CLC 48**
  See also CA 109; CAD; CANR 125; CD 5;
  CWD

Howell, James 1594(?)-1666 .... **LC 13**
  See also DLB 151

Howells, W. D.
  See Howells, William Dean

Howells, William D.
  See Howells, William Dean

Howells, William Dean 1837-1920 ... **SSC 36; TCLC 7, 17, 41**
  See also AMW; CA 104; 134; CDALB
  1865-1917; DLB 12, 64, 74, 79, 189;
  LMFS 1; MTCW 2; RGAL 4; TUS

Howes, Barbara 1914-1996 .... **CLC 15**
  See also CA 9-12R; 151; CAAS 3; CANR
  53; CP 7; SATA 5

Hrabal, Bohumil 1914-1997 ...... **CLC 13, 67; TCLC 155**
  See also CA 106; 156; CAAS 12; CANR
  57; CWW 2; DLB 232; EWL 3; RGSF 2

Hrotsvit of Gandersheim c. 935-c.
  1000 .... **CMLC 29**
  See also DLB 148

Hsi, Chu 1130-1200 .... **CMLC 42**

Hsun, Lu
  See Lu Hsun

Hubbard, L(afayette) Ron(ald)
  1911-1986 .... **CLC 43**
  See also CA 77-80; 118; CANR 52; CPW;
  DA3; DAM POP; FANT; MTCW 2; SFW
  4

Huch, Ricarda (Octavia)
  1864-1947 .... **TCLC 13**
  See also CA 111; 189; DLB 66; EWL 3

Huddle, David 1942- .... **CLC 49**
  See also CA 57-60; CAAS 20; CANR 89;
  DLB 130

Hudson, Jeffrey
  See Crichton, (John) Michael

Hudson, W(illiam) H(enry)
  1841-1922 .... **TCLC 29**
  See also CA 115; 190; DLB 98, 153, 174;
  RGEL 2; SATA 35

Hueffer, Ford Madox
  See Ford, Ford Madox

Hughart, Barry 1934- .... **CLC 39**
  See also CA 137; FANT; SFW 4; SUFW 2

Hughes, Colin
  See Creasey, John

Hughes, David (John) 1930- .... **CLC 48**
  See also CA 116; 129; CN 7; DLB 14

Hughes, Edward James
  See Hughes, Ted
  See also DA3; DAM MST, POET

Hughes, (James Mercer) Langston
  1902-1967 ..... **BLC 2; CLC 1, 5, 10, 15, 35, 44, 108; DC 3; HR 2; PC 1, 53; SSC 6; WLC**
  See also AAYA 12; AFAW 1, 2; AMWR 1;
  AMWS 1; BW 1, 3; CA 1-4R; 25-28R;
  CANR 1, 34, 82; CDALB 1929-1941;
  CLR 17; DA; DA3; DAB; DAC; DAM
  DRAM, MST, MULT, POET; DFS 6, 18;
  DLB 4, 7, 48, 51, 86, 228; EWL 3; EXPP;
  EXPS; JRDA; LAIT 3; LMFS 2; MAI-
  CYA 1, 2; MTCW 1, 2; PAB; PFS 1, 3, 6,
  10, 15; RGAL 4; RGSF 2; SATA 4, 33;
  SSFS 4, 7; TUS; WCH; WP; YAW

Hughes, Richard (Arthur Warren)
  1900-1976 .... **CLC 1, 11**
  See also CA 5-8R; 65-68; CANR 4; DAM
  NOV; DLB 15, 161; EWL 3; MTCW 1;
  RGEL 2; SATA 8; SATA-Obit 25

Hughes, Ted 1930-1998 . **CLC 2, 4, 9, 14, 37, 119; PC 7**
  See Hughes, Edward James
  See also BRWC 2; BRWR 2; BRWS 1; CA
  1-4R; 171; CANR 1, 33, 66, 108; CLR 3;
  CP 7; DAB; DAC; DLB 40, 161; EWL 3;
  EXPP; MAICYA 1, 2; MTCW 1, 2; PAB;
  PFS 4, 19; RGEL 2; SATA 49; SATA-
  Brief 27; SATA-Obit 107; TEA; YAW

Hugo, Richard
  See Huch, Ricarda (Octavia)

Hugo, Richard F(ranklin)
  1923-1982 .... **CLC 6, 18, 32**
  See also AMWS 6; CA 49-52; 108; CANR
  3; DAM POET; DLB 5, 206; EWL 3; PFS
  17; RGAL 4

Hugo, Victor (Marie) 1802-1885 .... **NCLC 3, 10, 21; PC 17; WLC**
  See also AAYA 28; DA; DA3; DAB; DAC;
  DAM DRAM, MST, NOV, POET; DLB
  119, 192, 217; EFS 2; EW 6; EXPN; GFL
  1789 to the Present; LAIT 1, 2; NFS 5,
  20; RGWL 2, 3; SATA 47; TWA

Huidobro, Vicente
  See Huidobro Fernandez, Vicente Garcia
  See also DLB 283; EWL 3; LAW

Huidobro Fernandez, Vicente Garcia
  1893-1948 .... **TCLC 31**
  See Huidobro, Vicente
  See also CA 131; HW 1

Hulme, Keri 1947- .... **CLC 39, 130**
  See also CA 125; CANR 69; CN 7; CP 7;
  CWP; EWL 3; FW; INT CA-125

Hulme, T(homas) E(rnest)
  1883-1917 .... **TCLC 21**
  See also BRWS 6; CA 117; 203; DLB 19

Humboldt, Wilhelm von
  1767-1835 .... **NCLC 134**
  See also DLB 90

Hume, David 1711-1776 .... **LC 7, 56**
  See also BRWS 3; DLB 104, 252; LMFS 1;
  TEA

Humphrey, William 1924-1997 .... **CLC 45**
  See also AMWS 9; CA 77-80; 160; CANR
  68; CN 7; CSW; DLB 6, 212, 234, 278;
  TCWW 2

Humphreys, Emyr Owen 1919- .... **CLC 47**
  See also CA 5-8R; CANR 3, 24; CN 7;
  DLB 15

Humphreys, Josephine 1945- ..... **CLC 34, 57**
  See also CA 121; 127; CANR 97; CSW;
  DLB 292; INT CA-127

Huneker, James Gibbons
  1860-1921 .... **TCLC 65**
  See also CA 193; DLB 71; RGAL 4

Hungerford, Hesba Fay
  See Brinsmead, H(esba) F(ay)

Hungerford, Pixie
  See Brinsmead, H(esba) F(ay)

Hunt, E(verette) Howard, (Jr.)
  1918- .... **CLC 3**
  See also AITN 1; CA 45-48; CANR 2, 47,
  103; CMW 4

Hunt, Francesca
  See Holland, Isabelle (Christian)

Hunt, Howard
  See Hunt, E(verette) Howard, (Jr.)

Hunt, Kyle
  See Creasey, John

Hunt, (James Henry) Leigh
  1784-1859 .... **NCLC 1, 70**
  See also DAM POET; DLB 96, 110, 144;
  RGEL 2; TEA

Hunt, Marsha 1946- .... **CLC 70**
  See also BW 2, 3; CA 143; CANR 79

Hunt, Violet 1866(?)-1942 .... **TCLC 53**
  See also CA 184; DLB 162, 197

Hunter, E. Waldo
  See Sturgeon, Theodore (Hamilton)

Hunter, Evan 1926- .... **CLC 11, 31**
  See McBain, Ed
  See also AAYA 39; BPFB 2; CA 5-8R;
  CANR 5, 38, 62, 97; CMW 4; CN 7;
  CPW; DAM POP; DLB 306; DLBY 1982;
  INT CANR-5; MSW; MTCW 1; SATA
  25; SFW 4

Hunter, Kristin
  See Lattany, Kristin (Elaine Eggleston)
  Hunter

Hunter, Mary
  See Austin, Mary (Hunter)

Hunter, Mollie 1922- .... **CLC 21**
  See McIlwraith, Maureen Mollie Hunter
  See also AAYA 13; BYA 6; CANR 37, 78;
  CLR 25; DLB 161; JRDA; MAICYA 1,
  2; SAAS 7; SATA 54, 106, 139; SATA-
  Essay 139; WYA; YAW

Hunter, Robert (?)-1734 .... **LC 7**

Hurston, Zora Neale 1891-1960 .... **BLC 2; CLC 7, 30, 61; DC 12; HR 2; SSC 4, 80; TCLC 121, 131; WLCS**
  See also AAYA 15; AFAW 1, 2; AMWS 6;
  BW 1, 3; BYA 12; CA 85-88; CANR 61;
  CDALBS; DA; DA3; DAC; DAM MST,
  MULT, NOV; DFS 6; DLB 51, 86; EWL
  3; EXPN; EXPS; FW; LAIT 3; LATS 1:1;
  LMFS 2; MAWW; MTCW 1, 2; NFS 3;
  RGAL 4; RGSF 2; SSFS 1, 6, 11, 19;
  TUS; YAW

Husserl, E. G.
  See Husserl, Edmund (Gustav Albrecht)

Husserl, Edmund (Gustav Albrecht)
  1859-1938 .... **TCLC 100**
  See also CA 116; 133; DLB 296

Huston, John (Marcellus)
  1906-1987 .... **CLC 20**
  See also CA 73-76; 123; CANR 34; DLB
  26

Hustvedt, Siri 1955- .... **CLC 76**
  See also CA 137

Hutten, Ulrich von 1488-1523 .... **LC 16**
  See also DLB 179

Huxley, Aldous (Leonard)
  1894-1963 .... **CLC 1, 3, 4, 5, 8, 11, 18, 35, 79; SSC 39; WLC**
  See also AAYA 11; BPFB 2; BRW 7; CA
  85-88; CANR 44, 99; CDBLB 1914-1945;
  DA; DA3; DAB; DAC; DAM MST, NOV;

Johnson, Benjamin F., of Boone
See Riley, James Whitcomb
Johnson, Charles (Richard) 1948- .... **BLC 2; CLC 7, 51, 65, 163**
See also AFAW 2; AMWS 6; BW 2, 3; CA 116; CAAS 18; CANR 42, 66, 82, 129; CN 7; DAM MULT; DLB 33, 278; MTCW 2; RGAL 4; SSFS 16
Johnson, Charles S(purgeon)
1893-1956 .... **HR 3**
See also BW 1, 3; CA 125; CANR 82; DLB 51, 91
Johnson, Denis 1949- . **CLC 52, 160; SSC 56**
See also CA 117; 121; CANR 71, 99; CN 7; DLB 120
Johnson, Diane 1934- .... **CLC 5, 13, 48**
See also BPFB 2; CA 41-44R; CANR 17, 40, 62, 95; CN 7; DLBY 1980; INT CANR-17; MTCW 1
Johnson, E. Pauline 1861-1913 .... **NNAL**
See also CA 150; DAC; DAM MULT; DLB 92, 175
Johnson, Eyvind (Olof Verner)
1900-1976 .... **CLC 14**
See also CA 73-76; 69-72; CANR 34, 101; DLB 259; EW 12; EWL 3
Johnson, Fenton 1888-1958 .... **BLC 2**
See also BW 1; CA 118; 124; DAM MULT; DLB 45, 50
Johnson, Georgia Douglas (Camp)
1880-1966 .... **HR 3**
See also BW 1; CA 125; DLB 51, 249; WP
Johnson, Helene 1907-1995 .... **HR 3**
See also CA 181; DLB 51; WP
Johnson, J. R.
See James, C(yril) L(ionel) R(obert)
Johnson, James Weldon 1871-1938 .. **BLC 2; HR 3; PC 24; TCLC 3, 19**
See also AFAW 1, 2; BW 1, 3; CA 104; 125; CANR 82; CDALB 1917-1929; CLR 32; DA3; DAM MULT, POET; DLB 51; EWL 3; EXPP; LMFS 2; MTCW 1, 2; PFS 1; RGAL 4; SATA 31; TUS
Johnson, Joyce 1935- .... **CLC 58**
See also BG 3; CA 125; 129; CANR 102
Johnson, Judith (Emlyn) 1936- .... **CLC 7, 15**
See Sherwin, Judith Johnson
See also CA 25-28R; 153; CANR 34
Johnson, Lionel (Pigot)
1867-1902 .... **TCLC 19**
See also CA 117; 209; DLB 19; RGEL 2
Johnson, Marguerite Annie
See Angelou, Maya
Johnson, Mel
See Malzberg, Barry N(athaniel)
Johnson, Pamela Hansford
1912-1981 .... **CLC 1, 7, 27**
See also CA 1-4R; 104; CANR 2, 28; DLB 15; MTCW 1, 2; RGEL 2
Johnson, Paul (Bede) 1928- .... **CLC 147**
See also BEST 89:4; CA 17-20R; CANR 34, 62, 100
Johnson, Robert .... **CLC 70**
Johnson, Robert 1911(?)-1938 .... **TCLC 69**
See also BW 3; CA 174
Johnson, Samuel 1709-1784 .... **LC 15, 52; WLC**
See also BRW 3; BRWR 1; CDBLB 1660-1789; DA; DAB; DAC; DAM MST; DLB 39, 95, 104, 142, 213; LMFS 1; RGEL 2; TEA
Johnson, Uwe 1934-1984 .. **CLC 5, 10, 15, 40**
See also CA 1-4R; 112; CANR 1, 39; CD-WLB 2; DLB 75; EWL 3; MTCW 1; RGWL 2, 3
Johnston, Basil H. 1929- .... **NNAL**
See also CA 69-72; CANR 11, 28, 66; DAC; DAM MULT; DLB 60

Johnston, George (Benson) 1913- .... **CLC 51**
See also CA 1-4R; CANR 5, 20; CP 7; DLB 88
Johnston, Jennifer (Prudence)
1930- .... **CLC 7, 150**
See also CA 85-88; CANR 92; CN 7; DLB 14
Joinville, Jean de 1224(?)-1317 ..... **CMLC 38**
Jolley, (Monica) Elizabeth 1923- ..... **CLC 46; SSC 19**
See also CA 127; CAAS 13; CANR 59; CN 7; EWL 3; RGSF 2
Jones, Arthur Llewellyn 1863-1947
See Machen, Arthur
See also CA 104; 179; HGG
Jones, D(ouglas) G(ordon) 1929- ..... **CLC 10**
See also CA 29-32R; CANR 13, 90; CP 7; DLB 53
Jones, David (Michael) 1895-1974 .... **CLC 2, 4, 7, 13, 42**
See also BRW 6; BRWS 7; CA 9-12R; 53-56; CANR 28; CDBLB 1945-1960; DLB 20, 100; EWL 3; MTCW 1; PAB; RGEL 2
Jones, David Robert 1947-
See Bowie, David
See also CA 103; CANR 104
Jones, Diana Wynne 1934- .... **CLC 26**
See also AAYA 12; BYA 6, 7, 9, 11, 13, 16; CA 49-52; CANR 4, 26, 56, 120; CLR 23; DLB 161; FANT; JRDA; MAICYA 1, 2; SAAS 7; SATA 9, 70, 108; SFW 4; SUFW 2; YAW
Jones, Edward P. 1950- .... **CLC 76**
See also BW 2, 3; CA 142; CANR 79, 134; CSW
Jones, Gayl 1949- ...... **BLC 2; CLC 6, 9, 131**
See also AFAW 1, 2; BW 2, 3; CA 77-80; CANR 27, 66, 122; CN 7; CSW; DA3; DAM MULT; DLB 33, 278; MTCW 1, 2; RGAL 4
Jones, James 1921-1977 ...... **CLC 1, 3, 10, 39**
See also AITN 1, 2; AMWS 11; BPFB 2; CA 1-4R; 69-72; CANR 6; DLB 2, 143; DLBD 17; DLBY 1998; EWL 3; MTCW 1; RGAL 4
Jones, John J.
See Lovecraft, H(oward) P(hillips)
Jones, LeRoi .... **CLC 1, 2, 3, 5, 10, 14**
See Baraka, Amiri
See also MTCW 2
Jones, Louis B. 1953- .... **CLC 65**
See also CA 141; CANR 73
Jones, Madison (Percy, Jr.) 1925- ...... **CLC 4**
See also CA 13-16R; CAAS 11; CANR 7, 54, 83; CN 7; CSW; DLB 152
Jones, Mervyn 1922- .... **CLC 10, 52**
See also CA 45-48; CAAS 5; CANR 1, 91; CN 7; MTCW 1
Jones, Mick 1956(?)- .... **CLC 30**
Jones, Nettie (Pearl) 1941- .... **CLC 34**
See also BW 2; CA 137; CAAS 20; CANR 88
Jones, Peter 1802-1856 .... **NNAL**
Jones, Preston 1936-1979 .... **CLC 10**
See also CA 73-76; 89-92; DLB 7
Jones, Robert F(rancis) 1934-2003 .... **CLC 7**
See also CA 49-52; CANR 2, 61, 118
Jones, Rod 1953- .... **CLC 50**
See also CA 128
Jones, Terence Graham Parry
1942- .... **CLC 21**
See Jones, Terry; Monty Python
See also CA 112; 116; CANR 35, 93; INT CA-116; SATA 127
Jones, Terry
See Jones, Terence Graham Parry
See also SATA 67; SATA-Brief 51

Jones, Thom (Douglas) 1945(?)- ..... **CLC 81; SSC 56**
See also CA 157; CANR 88; DLB 244
Jong, Erica 1942- .... **CLC 4, 6, 8, 18, 83**
See also AITN 1; AMWS 5; BEST 90:2; BPFB 2; CA 73-76; CANR 26, 52, 75, 132; CN 7; CP 7; CPW; DA3; DAM NOV, POP; DLB 2, 5, 28, 152; FW; INT CANR-26; MTCW 1, 2
Jonson, Ben(jamin) 1572(?)-1637 . **DC 4; LC 6, 33, 110; PC 17; WLC**
See also BRW 1; BRWC 1; BRWR 1; CD-BLB Before 1660; DA; DAB; DAC; DAM DRAM, MST, POET; DFS 4, 10; DLB 62, 121; LMFS 1; RGEL 2; TEA; WLIT 3
Jordan, June (Meyer)
1936-2002 .. **BLCS; CLC 5, 11, 23, 114; PC 38**
See also AAYA 2; AFAW 1, 2; BW 2, 3; CA 33-36R; 206; CANR 25, 70, 114; CLR 10; CP 7; CWP; DAM MULT, POET; DLB 38; GLL 2; LAIT 5; MAICYA 1, 2; MTCW 1; SATA 4, 136; YAW
Jordan, Neil (Patrick) 1950- .... **CLC 110**
See also CA 124; 130; CANR 54; CN 7; GLL 2; INT CA-130
Jordan, Pat(rick M.) 1941- .... **CLC 37**
See also CA 33-36R; CANR 121
Jorgensen, Ivar
See Ellison, Harlan (Jay)
Jorgenson, Ivar
See Silverberg, Robert
Joseph, George Ghevarughese .... **CLC 70**
Josephson, Mary
See O'Doherty, Brian
Josephus, Flavius c. 37-100 .... **CMLC 13**
See also AW 2; DLB 176
Josiah Allen's Wife
See Holley, Marietta
Josipovici, Gabriel (David) 1940- ...... **CLC 6, 43, 153**
See also CA 37-40R; 224; CAAE 224; CAAS 8; CANR 47, 84; CN 7; DLB 14
Joubert, Joseph 1754-1824 .... **NCLC 9**
Jouve, Pierre Jean 1887-1976 .... **CLC 47**
See also CA 65-68; DLB 258; EWL 3
Jovine, Francesco 1902-1950 .... **TCLC 79**
See also DLB 264; EWL 3
Joyce, James (Augustine Aloysius)
1882-1941 .... **DC 16; PC 22; SSC 3, 26, 44, 64; TCLC 3, 8, 16, 35, 52, 159; WLC**
See also AAYA 42; BRW 7; BRWC 1; BRWR 1; BYA 11, 13; CA 104; 126; CD-BLB 1914-1945; DA; DA3; DAB; DAC; DAM MST, NOV, POET; DLB 10, 19, 36, 162, 247; EWL 3; EXPN; EXPS; LAIT 3; LMFS 1, 2; MTCW 1, 2; NFS 7; RGSF 2; SSFS 1, 19; TEA; WLIT 4
Jozsef, Attila 1905-1937 .... **TCLC 22**
See also CA 116; CDWLB 4; DLB 215; EWL 3
Juana Ines de la Cruz, Sor
1651(?)-1695 ...... **HLCS 1; LC 5; PC 24**
See also DLB 305; FW; LAW; RGWL 2, 3; WLIT 1
Juana Inez de La Cruz, Sor
See Juana Ines de la Cruz, Sor
Judd, Cyril
See Kornbluth, C(yril) M.; Pohl, Frederik
Juenger, Ernst 1895-1998 .... **CLC 125**
See Junger, Ernst
See also CA 101; 167; CANR 21, 47, 106; DLB 56
Julian of Norwich 1342(?)-1416(?) . **LC 6, 52**
See also DLB 146; LMFS 1

Julius Caesar 100B.C.-44B.C.
   See Caesar, Julius
   See also CDWLB 1; DLB 211
Junger, Ernst
   See Juenger, Ernst
   See also CDWLB 2; EWL 3; RGWL 2, 3
Junger, Sebastian 1962- .... **CLC 109**
   See also AAYA 28; CA 165; CANR 130
Juniper, Alex
   See Hospital, Janette Turner
Junius
   See Luxemburg, Rosa
Just, Ward (Swift) 1935- .... **CLC 4, 27**
   See also CA 25-28R; CANR 32, 87; CN 7;
   INT CANR-32
Justice, Donald (Rodney)
   1925-2004 .... **CLC 6, 19, 102; PC 64**
   See also AMWS 7; CA 5-8R; CANR 26,
   54, 74, 121, 122; CP 7; CSW; DAM
   POET; DLBY 1983; EWL 3; INT CANR-
   26; MTCW 2; PFS 14
Juvenal c. 60-c. 130 .... **CMLC 8**
   See also AW 2; CDWLB 1; DLB 211;
   RGWL 2, 3
Juvenis
   See Bourne, Randolph S(illiman)
K., Alice
   See Knapp, Caroline
Kabakov, Sasha .... **CLC 59**
Kabir 1398(?)-1448(?) .... **LC 109; PC 56**
   See also RGWL 2, 3
Kacew, Romain 1914-1980
   See Gary, Romain
   See also CA 108; 102
Kadare, Ismail 1936- .... **CLC 52, 190**
   See also CA 161; EWL 3; RGWL 3
Kadohata, Cynthia 1956(?)- ..... **CLC 59, 122**
   See also CA 140; CANR 124
Kafka, Franz 1883-1924 ... **SSC 5, 29, 35, 60;
   TCLC 2, 6, 13, 29, 47, 53, 112; WLC**
   See also AAYA 31; BPFB 2; CA 105; 126;
   CDWLB 2; DA; DA3; DAB; DAC; DAM
   MST, NOV; DLB 81; EW 9; EWL 3;
   EXPS; LATS 1:1; LMFS 2; MTCW 1, 2;
   NFS 7; RGSF 2; RGWL 2, 3; SFW 4;
   SSFS 3, 7, 12; TWA
Kahanovitsch, Pinkhes
   See Der Nister
Kahn, Roger 1927- .... **CLC 30**
   See also CA 25-28R; CANR 44, 69; DLB
   171; SATA 37
Kain, Saul
   See Sassoon, Siegfried (Lorraine)
Kaiser, Georg 1878-1945 .... **TCLC 9**
   See also CA 106; 190; CDWLB 2; DLB
   124; EWL 3; LMFS 2; RGWL 2, 3
Kaledin, Sergei .... **CLC 59**
Kaletski, Alexander 1946- .... **CLC 39**
   See also CA 118; 143
Kalidasa fl. c. 400-455 .... **CMLC 9; PC 22**
   See also RGWL 2, 3
Kallman, Chester (Simon)
   1921-1975 .... **CLC 2**
   See also CA 45-48; 53-56; CANR 3
Kaminsky, Melvin 1926-
   See Brooks, Mel
   See also CA 65-68; CANR 16
Kaminsky, Stuart M(elvin) 1934- ..... **CLC 59**
   See also CA 73-76; CANR 29, 53, 89;
   CMW 4
Kamo no Chomei 1153(?)-1216 .... **CMLC 66**
   See also DLB 203
Kamo no Nagaakira
   See Kamo no Chomei
Kandinsky, Wassily 1866-1944 .... **TCLC 92**
   See also CA 118; 155
Kane, Francis
   See Robbins, Harold

Kane, Henry 1918-
   See Queen, Ellery
   See also CA 156; CMW 4
Kane, Paul
   See Simon, Paul (Frederick)
Kanin, Garson 1912-1999 .... **CLC 22**
   See also AITN 1; CA 5-8R; 177; CAD;
   CANR 7, 78; DLB 7; IDFW 3, 4
Kaniuk, Yoram 1930- .... **CLC 19**
   See also CA 134; DLB 299
Kant, Immanuel 1724-1804 ..... **NCLC 27, 67**
   See also DLB 94
Kantor, MacKinlay 1904-1977 .... **CLC 7**
   See also CA 61-64; 73-76; CANR 60, 63;
   DLB 9, 102; MTCW 2; RHW; TCWW 2
Kanze Motokiyo
   See Zeami
Kaplan, David Michael 1946- .... **CLC 50**
   See also CA 187
Kaplan, James 1951- .... **CLC 59**
   See also CA 135; CANR 121
Karadzic, Vuk Stefanovic
   1787-1864 .... **NCLC 115**
   See also CDWLB 4; DLB 147
Karageorge, Michael
   See Anderson, Poul (William)
Karamzin, Nikolai Mikhailovich
   1766-1826 .... **NCLC 3**
   See also DLB 150; RGSF 2
Karapanou, Margarita 1946- .... **CLC 13**
   See also CA 101
Karinthy, Frigyes 1887-1938 .... **TCLC 47**
   See also CA 170; DLB 215; EWL 3
Karl, Frederick R(obert)
   1927-2004 .... **CLC 34**
   See also CA 5-8R; 226; CANR 3, 44
Karr, Mary 1955- .... **CLC 188**
   See also AMWS 11; CA 151; CANR 100;
   NCFS 5
Kastel, Warren
   See Silverberg, Robert
Kataev, Evgeny Petrovich 1903-1942
   See Petrov, Evgeny
   See also CA 120
Kataphusin
   See Ruskin, John
Katz, Steve 1935- .... **CLC 47**
   See also CA 25-28R; CAAS 14, 64; CANR
   12; CN 7; DLBY 1983
Kauffman, Janet 1945- .... **CLC 42**
   See also CA 117; CANR 43, 84; DLB 218;
   DLBY 1986
Kaufman, Bob (Garnell) 1925-1986 . **CLC 49**
   See also BG 3; BW 1; CA 41-44R; 118;
   CANR 22; DLB 16, 41
Kaufman, George S. 1889-1961 ...... **CLC 38;
   DC 17**
   See also CA 108; 93-96; DAM DRAM;
   DFS 1, 10; DLB 7; INT CA-108; MTCW
   2; RGAL 4; TUS
Kaufman, Moises 1964- .... **DC 26**
   CA 211; MTFW
Kaufman, Sue .... **CLC 3, 8**
   See Barondess, Sue K(aufman)
Kavafis, Konstantinos Petrou 1863-1933
   See Cavafy, C(onstantine) P(eter)
   See also CA 104
Kavan, Anna 1901-1968 .... **CLC 5, 13, 82**
   See also BRWS 7; CA 5-8R; CANR 6, 57;
   DLB 255; MTCW 1; RGEL 2; SFW 4
Kavanagh, Dan
   See Barnes, Julian (Patrick)
Kavanagh, Julie 1952- .... **CLC 119**
   See also CA 163
Kavanagh, Patrick (Joseph)
   1904-1967 .... **CLC 22; PC 33**
   See also BRWS 7; CA 123; 25-28R; DLB
   15, 20; EWL 3; MTCW 1; RGEL 2

Kawabata, Yasunari 1899-1972 ..... **CLC 2, 5,
   9, 18, 107; SSC 17**
   See Kawabata Yasunari
   See also CA 93-96; 33-36R; CANR 88;
   DAM MULT; MJW; MTCW 2; RGSF 2;
   RGWL 2, 3
Kawabata Yasunari
   See Kawabata, Yasunari
   See also DLB 180; EWL 3
Kaye, M(ary) M(argaret)
   1908-2004 .... **CLC 28**
   See also CA 89-92; 223; CANR 24, 60, 102;
   MTCW 1, 2; RHW; SATA 62; SATA-Obit
   152
Kaye, Mollie
   See Kaye, M(ary) M(argaret)
Kaye-Smith, Sheila 1887-1956 .... **TCLC 20**
   See also CA 118; 203; DLB 36
Kaymor, Patrice Maguilene
   See Senghor, Leopold Sedar
Kazakov, Iurii Pavlovich
   See Kazakov, Yuri Pavlovich
   See also DLB 302
Kazakov, Yuri Pavlovich 1927-1982 . **SSC 43**
   See Kazakov, Iurii Pavlovich; Kazakov,
   Yury
   See also CA 5-8R; CANR 36; MTCW 1;
   RGSF 2
Kazakov, Yury
   See Kazakov, Yuri Pavlovich
   See also EWL 3
Kazan, Elia 1909-2003 .... **CLC 6, 16, 63**
   See also CA 21-24R; 220; CANR 32, 78
Kazantzakis, Nikos 1883(?)-1957 .... **TCLC 2,
   5, 33**
   See also BPFB 2; CA 105; 132; DA3; EW
   9; EWL 3; MTCW 1, 2; RGWL 2, 3
Kazin, Alfred 1915-1998 ..... **CLC 34, 38, 119**
   See also AMWS 8; CA 1-4R; CAAS 7;
   CANR 1, 45, 79; DLB 67; EWL 3
Keane, Mary Nesta (Skrine) 1904-1996
   See Keane, Molly
   See also CA 108; 114; 151; CN 7; RHW
Keane, Molly .... **CLC 31**
   See Keane, Mary Nesta (Skrine)
   See also INT CA-114
Keates, Jonathan 1946(?)- .... **CLC 34**
   See also CA 163; CANR 126
Keaton, Buster 1895-1966 .... **CLC 20**
   See also CA 194
Keats, John 1795-1821 ...... **NCLC 8, 73, 121;
   PC 1; WLC**
   See also AAYA 58; BRW 4; BRWR 1; CD-
   BLB 1789-1832; DA; DA3; DAB; DAC;
   DAM MST, POET; DLB 96, 110; EXPP;
   LMFS 1; PAB; PFS 1, 2, 3, 9, 17; RGEL
   2; TEA; WLIT 3; WP
Keble, John 1792-1866 .... **NCLC 87**
   See also DLB 32, 55; RGEL 2
Keene, Donald 1922- .... **CLC 34**
   See also CA 1-4R; CANR 5, 119
Keillor, Garrison .... **CLC 40, 115**
   See Keillor, Gary (Edward)
   See also AAYA 2; BEST 89:3; BPFB 2;
   DLBY 1987; EWL 3; SATA 58; TUS
Keillor, Gary (Edward) 1942-
   See Keillor, Garrison
   See also CA 111; 117; CANR 36, 59, 124;
   CPW; DA3; DAM POP; MTCW 1, 2
Keith, Carlos
   See Lewton, Val
Keith, Michael
   See Hubbard, L(afayette) Ron(ald)
Keller, Gottfried 1819-1890 .... **NCLC 2; SSC
   26**
   See also CDWLB 2; DLB 129; EW; RGSF
   2; RGWL 2, 3
Keller, Nora Okja 1965- .... **CLC 109**
   See also CA 187

Kingsley, Charles 1819-1875 .... **NCLC 35**
See also CLR 77; DLB 21, 32, 163, 178, 190; FANT; MAICYA 2; MAICYAS 1; RGEL 2; WCH; YABC 2

Kingsley, Henry 1830-1876 .... **NCLC 107**
See also DLB 21, 230; RGEL 2

Kingsley, Sidney 1906-1995 .... **CLC 44**
See also CA 85-88; 147; CAD; DFS 14, 19; DLB 7; RGAL 4

Kingsolver, Barbara 1955- . **CLC 55, 81, 130**
See also AAYA 15; AMWS 7; CA 129; 134; CANR 60, 96, 133; CDALBS; CPW; CSW; DA3; DAM POP; DLB 206; INT CA-134; LAIT 5; MTCW 2; NFS 5, 10, 12; RGAL 4

Kingston, Maxine (Ting Ting) Hong
1940- .... **AAL; CLC 12, 19, 58, 121; WLCS**
See also AAYA 8, 55; AMWS 5; BPFB 2; CA 69-72; CANR 13, 38, 74, 87, 128; CDALBS; CN 7; DA3; DAM MULT, NOV; DLB 173, 212; DLBY 1980; EWL 3; FW; INT CANR-13; LAIT 5; MAWW; MTCW 1, 2; NFS 6; RGAL 4; SATA 53; SSFS 3

Kinnell, Galway 1927- ..... **CLC 1, 2, 3, 5, 13, 29, 129; PC 26**
See also AMWS 3; CA 9-12R; CANR 10, 34, 66, 116; CP 7; DLB 5; DLBY 1987; EWL 3; INT CANR-34; MTCW 1, 2; PAB; PFS 9; RGAL 4; WP

Kinsella, Thomas 1928- .... **CLC 4, 19, 138**
See also BRWS 5; CA 17-20R; CANR 15, 122; CP 7; DLB 27; EWL 3; MTCW 1, 2; RGEL 2; TEA

Kinsella, W(illiam) P(atrick) 1935- . **CLC 27, 43, 166**
See also AAYA 7, 60; BPFB 2; CA 97-100, 222; CAAE 222; CAAS 7; CANR 21, 35, 66, 75, 129; CN 7; CPW; DAC; DAM NOV, POP; FANT; INT CANR-21; LAIT 5; MTCW 1, 2; NFS 15; RGSF 2

Kinsey, Alfred C(harles)
1894-1956 .... **TCLC 91**
See also CA 115; 170; MTCW 2

Kipling, (Joseph) Rudyard 1865-1936 . **PC 3; SSC 5, 54; TCLC 8, 17, 167; WLC**
See also AAYA 32; BRW 6; BRWC 1, 2; BYA 4; CA 105; 120; CANR 33; CDBLB 1890-1914; CLR 39, 65; CWRI 5; DA; DA3; DAB; DAC; DAM MST, POET; DLB 19, 34, 141, 156; EWL 3; EXPS; FANT; LAIT 3; LMFS 1; MAICYA 1, 2; MTCW 1, 2; RGEL 2; RGSF 2; SATA 100; SFW 4; SSFS 8; SUFW 1; TEA; WCH; WLIT 4; YABC 2

Kirk, Russell (Amos) 1918-1994 .. **TCLC 119**
See also AITN 1; CA 1-4R; 145; CAAS 9; CANR 1, 20, 60; HGG; INT CANR-20; MTCW 1, 2

Kirkham, Dinah
See Card, Orson Scott

Kirkland, Caroline M. 1801-1864 . **NCLC 85**
See also DLB 3, 73, 74, 250, 254; DLBD 13

Kirkup, James 1918- .... **CLC 1**
See also CA 1-4R; CAAS 4; CANR 2; CP 7; DLB 27; SATA 12

Kirkwood, James 1930(?)-1989 .... **CLC 9**
See also AITN 2; CA 1-4R; 128; CANR 6, 40; GLL 2

Kirsch, Sarah 1935- .... **CLC 176**
See also CA 178; CWW 2; DLB 75; EWL 3

Kirshner, Sidney
See Kingsley, Sidney

Kis, Danilo 1935-1989 .... **CLC 57**
See also CA 109; 118; 129; CANR 61; CDWLB 4; DLB 181; EWL 3; MTCW 1; RGSF 2; RGWL 2, 3

Kissinger, Henry A(lfred) 1923- ..... **CLC 137**
See also CA 1-4R; CANR 2, 33, 66, 109; MTCW 1

Kivi, Aleksis 1834-1872 .... **NCLC 30**

Kizer, Carolyn (Ashley) 1925- ... **CLC 15, 39, 80**
See also CA 65-68; CAAS 5; CANR 24, 70, 134; CP 7; CWP; DAM POET; DLB 5, 169; EWL 3; MTCW 2; PFS 18

Klabund 1890-1928 .... **TCLC 44**
See also CA 162; DLB 66

Klappert, Peter 1942- .... **CLC 57**
See also CA 33-36R; CSW; DLB 5

Klein, A(braham) M(oses)
1909-1972 .... **CLC 19**
See also CA 101; 37-40R; DAB; DAC; DAM MST; DLB 68; EWL 3; RGEL 2

Klein, Joe
See Klein, Joseph

Klein, Joseph 1946- .... **CLC 154**
See also CA 85-88; CANR 55

Klein, Norma 1938-1989 .... **CLC 30**
See also AAYA 2, 35; BPFB 2; BYA 6, 7, 8; CA 41-44R; 128; CANR 15, 37; CLR 2, 19; INT CANR-15; JRDA; MAICYA 1, 2; SAAS 1; SATA 7, 57; WYA; YAW

Klein, T(heodore) E(ibon) D(onald)
1947- .... **CLC 34**
See also CA 119; CANR 44, 75; HGG

Kleist, Heinrich von 1777-1811 ...... **NCLC 2, 37; SSC 22**
See also CDWLB 2; DAM DRAM; DLB 90; EW 5; RGSF 2; RGWL 2, 3

Klima, Ivan 1931- .... **CLC 56, 172**
See also CA 25-28R; CANR 17, 50, 91; CDWLB 4; CWW 2; DAM NOV; DLB 232; EWL 3; RGWL 2, 3

Klimentev, Andrei Platonovich
See Klimentov, Andrei Platonovich

Klimentov, Andrei Platonovich
1899-1951 .... **SSC 42; TCLC 14**
See also Platonov, Andrei Platonovich; Platonov, Andrey Platonovich
See also CA 108

Klinger, Friedrich Maximilian von
1752-1831 .... **NCLC 1**
See also DLB 94

Klingsor the Magician
See Hartmann, Sadakichi

Klopstock, Friedrich Gottlieb
1724-1803 .... **NCLC 11**
See also DLB 97; EW 4; RGWL 2, 3

Kluge, Alexander 1932- .... **SSC 61**
See also CA 81-84; DLB 75

Knapp, Caroline 1959-2002 .... **CLC 99**
See also CA 154; 207

Knebel, Fletcher 1911-1993 .... **CLC 14**
See also AITN 1; CA 1-4R; 140; CAAS 3; CANR 1, 36; SATA 36; SATA-Obit 75

Knickerbocker, Diedrich
See Irving, Washington

Knight, Etheridge 1931-1991 ... **BLC 2; CLC 40; PC 14**
See also BW 1, 3; CA 21-24R; 133; CANR 23, 82; DAM POET; DLB 41; MTCW 2; RGAL 4

Knight, Sarah Kemble 1666-1727 .... **LC 7**
See also DLB 24, 200

Knister, Raymond 1899-1932 .... **TCLC 56**
See also CA 186; DLB 68; RGEL 2

Knowles, John 1926-2001 ... **CLC 1, 4, 10, 26**
See also AAYA 10; AMWS 12; BPFB 2; BYA 3; CA 17-20R; 203; CANR 40, 74, 76, 132; CDALB 1968-1988; CLR 98; CN 7; DA; DAC; DAM MST, NOV; DLB 6; EXPN; MTCW 1, 2; NFS 2; RGAL 4; SATA 8, 89; SATA-Obit 134; YAW

Knox, Calvin M.
See Silverberg, Robert

Knox, John c. 1505-1572 .... **LC 37**
See also DLB 132

Knye, Cassandra
See Disch, Thomas M(ichael)

Koch, C(hristopher) J(ohn) 1932- .... **CLC 42**
See also CA 127; CANR 84; CN 7; DLB 289

Koch, Christopher
See Koch, C(hristopher) J(ohn)

Koch, Kenneth (Jay) 1925-2002 .... **CLC 5, 8, 44**
See also CA 1-4R; 207; CAD; CANR 6, 36, 57, 97, 131; CD 5; CP 7; DAM POET; DLB 5; INT CANR-36; MTCW 2; PFS 20; SATA 65; WP

Kochanowski, Jan 1530-1584 .... **LC 10**
See also RGWL 2, 3

Kock, Charles Paul de 1794-1871 . **NCLC 16**

Koda Rohan
See Koda Shigeyuki

Koda Rohan
See Koda Shigeyuki
See also DLB 180

Koda Shigeyuki 1867-1947 .... **TCLC 22**
See Koda Rohan
See also CA 121; 183

Koestler, Arthur 1905-1983 ... **CLC 1, 3, 6, 8, 15, 33**
See also BRWS 1; CA 1-4R; 109; CANR 1, 33; CDBLB 1945-1960; DLBY 1983; EWL 3; MTCW 1, 2; NFS 19; RGEL 2

Kogawa, Joy Nozomi 1935- ...... **CLC 78, 129**
See also AAYA 47; CA 101; CANR 19, 62, 126; CN 7; CWP; DAC; DAM MST, MULT; FW; MTCW 2; NFS 3; SATA 99

Kohout, Pavel 1928- .... **CLC 13**
See also CA 45-48; CANR 3

Koizumi, Yakumo
See Hearn, (Patricio) Lafcadio (Tessima Carlos)

Kolmar, Gertrud 1894-1943 .... **TCLC 40**
See also CA 167; EWL 3

Komunyakaa, Yusef 1947- .. **BLCS; CLC 86, 94, 207; PC 51**
See also AFAW 2; AMWS 13; CA 147; CANR 83; CP 7; CSW; DLB 120; EWL 3; PFS 5, 20; RGAL 4

Konrad, George
See Konrad, Gyorgy

Konrad, Gyorgy 1933- .... **CLC 4, 10, 73**
See also CA 85-88; CANR 97; CDWLB 4; CWW 2; DLB 232; EWL 3

Konwicki, Tadeusz 1926- .... **CLC 8, 28, 54, 117**
See also CA 101; CAAS 9; CANR 39, 59; CWW 2; DLB 232; EWL 3; IDFW 3; MTCW 1

Koontz, Dean R(ay) 1945- .... **CLC 78, 206**
See also AAYA 9, 31; BEST 89:3, 90:2; CA 108; CANR 19, 36, 52, 95; CMW 4; CPW; DA3; DAM NOV, POP; DLB 292; HGG; MTCW 1; SATA 92; SFW 4; SUFW 2; YAW

Kopernik, Mikolaj
See Copernicus, Nicolaus

Kopit, Arthur (Lee) 1937- ...... **CLC 1, 18, 33**
See also AITN 1; CA 81-84; CABS 3; CD 5; DAM DRAM; DFS 7, 14; DLB 7; MTCW 1; RGAL 4

Kopitar, Jernej (Bartholomaus)
1780-1844 .... **NCLC 117**

Kops, Bernard 1926- .... **CLC 4**
See also CA 5-8R; CANR 84; CBD; CN 7; CP 7; DLB 13

Kornbluth, C(yril) M. 1923-1958 .... **TCLC 8**
See also CA 105; 160; DLB 8; SFW 4

Korolenko, V. G.
See Korolenko, Vladimir Galaktionovich

Lagerkvist, Par .... **SSC 12**
See Lagerkvist, Paer (Fabian)
See also DLB 259; EW 10; EWL 3; MTCW
2; RGSF 2; RGWL 2, 3

Lagerloef, Selma (Ottiliana Lovisa)
1858-1940 .... **TCLC 4, 36**
See Lagerlof, Selma (Ottiliana Lovisa)
See also CA 108; MTCW 2; SATA 15

Lagerlof, Selma (Ottiliana Lovisa)
See Lagerloef, Selma (Ottiliana Lovisa)
See also CLR 7; SATA 15

La Guma, (Justin) Alex(ander)
1925-1985 . **BLCS; CLC 19; TCLC 140**
See also AFW; BW 1, 3; CA 49-52; 118;
CANR 25, 81; CDWLB 3; DAM NOV;
DLB 117, 225; EWL 3; MTCW 1, 2;
WLIT 2; WWE 1

Laidlaw, A. K.
See Grieve, C(hristopher) M(urray)

Lainez, Manuel Mujica
See Mujica Lainez, Manuel
See also HW 1

Laing, R(onald) D(avid) 1927-1989 . **CLC 95**
See also CA 107; 129; CANR 34; MTCW 1

Laishley, Alex
See Booth, Martin

Lamartine, Alphonse (Marie Louis Prat) de
1790-1869 .... **NCLC 11; PC 16**
See also DAM POET; DLB 217; GFL 1789
to the Present; RGWL 2, 3

Lamb, Charles 1775-1834 ..... **NCLC 10, 113;
WLC**
See also BRW 4; CDBLB 1789-1832; DA;
DAB; DAC; DAM MST; DLB 93, 107,
163; RGEL 2; SATA 17; TEA

Lamb, Lady Caroline 1785-1828 ... **NCLC 38**
See also DLB 116

Lamb, Mary Ann 1764-1847 .... **NCLC 125**
See also DLB 163; SATA 17

Lame Deer 1903(?)-1976 .... **NNAL**
See also CA 69-72

Lamming, George (William) 1927- ... **BLC 2;
CLC 2, 4, 66, 144**
See also BW 2, 3; CA 85-88; CANR 26,
76; CDWLB 3; CN 7; DAM MULT; DLB
125; EWL 3; MTCW 1, 2; NFS 15; RGEL
2

L'Amour, Louis (Dearborn)
1908-1988 .... **CLC 25, 55**
See Burns, Tex; Mayo, Jim
See also AAYA 16; AITN 2; BEST 89:2;
BPFB 2; CA 1-4R; 125; CANR 3, 25, 40;
CPW; DA3; DAM NOV, POP; DLB 206;
DLBY 1980; MTCW 1, 2; RGAL 4

Lampedusa, Giuseppe (Tomasi) di
.... **TCLC 13**
See Tomasi di Lampedusa, Giuseppe
See also CA 164; EW 11; MTCW 2; RGWL
2, 3

Lampman, Archibald 1861-1899 ... **NCLC 25**
See also DLB 92; RGEL 2; TWA

Lancaster, Bruce 1896-1963 .... **CLC 36**
See also CA 9-10; CANR 70; CAP 1; SATA
9

Lanchester, John 1962- .... **CLC 99**
See also CA 194; DLB 267

Landau, Mark Alexandrovich
See Aldanov, Mark (Alexandrovich)

Landau-Aldanov, Mark Alexandrovich
See Aldanov, Mark (Alexandrovich)

Landis, Jerry
See Simon, Paul (Frederick)

Landis, John 1950- .... **CLC 26**
See also CA 112; 122; CANR 128

Landolfi, Tommaso 1908-1979 .... **CLC 11, 49**
See also CA 127; 117; DLB 177; EWL 3

Landon, Letitia Elizabeth
1802-1838 .... **NCLC 15**
See also DLB 96

Landor, Walter Savage
1775-1864 .... **NCLC 14**
See also BRW 4; DLB 93, 107; RGEL 2

Landwirth, Heinz 1927-
See Lind, Jakov
See also CA 9-12R; CANR 7

Lane, Patrick 1939- .... **CLC 25**
See also CA 97-100; CANR 54; CP 7; DAM
POET; DLB 53; INT CA-97-100

Lang, Andrew 1844-1912 .... **TCLC 16**
See also CA 114; 137; CANR 85; CLR 101;
DLB 98, 141, 184; FANT; MAICYA 1, 2;
RGEL 2; SATA 16; WCH

Lang, Fritz 1890-1976 .... **CLC 20, 103**
See also CA 77-80; 69-72; CANR 30

Lange, John
See Crichton, (John) Michael

Langer, Elinor 1939- .... **CLC 34**
See also CA 121

Langland, William 1332(?)-1400(?) ..... **LC 19**
See also BRW 1; DA; DAB; DAC; DAM
MST, POET; DLB 146; RGEL 2; TEA;
WLIT 3

Langstaff, Launcelot
See Irving, Washington

Lanier, Sidney 1842-1881 . **NCLC 6, 118; PC
50**
See also AMWS 1; DAM POET; DLB 64;
DLBD 13; EXPP; MAICYA 1; PFS 14;
RGAL 4; SATA 18

Lanyer, Aemilia 1569-1645 .... **LC 10, 30, 83;
PC 60**
See also DLB 121

Lao-Tzu
See Lao Tzu

Lao Tzu c. 6th cent. B.C.-3rd cent.
B.C. .... **CMLC 7**

Lapine, James (Elliot) 1949- .... **CLC 39**
See also CA 123; 130; CANR 54, 128; INT
CA-130

Larbaud, Valery (Nicolas)
1881-1957 .... **TCLC 9**
See also CA 106; 152; EWL 3; GFL 1789
to the Present

Lardner, Ring
See Lardner, Ring(gold) W(ilmer)
See also BPFB 2; CDALB 1917-1929; DLB
11, 25, 86, 171; DLBD 16; RGAL 4;
RGSF 2

Lardner, Ring W., Jr.
See Lardner, Ring(gold) W(ilmer)

Lardner, Ring(gold) W(ilmer)
1885-1933 .... **SSC 32; TCLC 2, 14**
See Lardner, Ring
See also AMW; CA 104; 131; MTCW 1, 2;
TUS

Laredo, Betty
See Codrescu, Andrei

Larkin, Maia
See Wojciechowska, Maia (Teresa)

Larkin, Philip (Arthur) 1922-1985 ... **CLC 3,
5, 8, 9, 13, 18, 33, 39, 64; PC 21**
See also BRWS 1; CA 5-8R; 117; CANR
24, 62; CDBLB 1960 to Present; DA3;
DAB; DAM MST, POET; DLB 27; EWL
3; MTCW 1, 2; PFS 3, 4, 12; RGEL 2

La Roche, Sophie von
1730-1807 .... **NCLC 121**
See also DLB 94

La Rochefoucauld, Francois
1613-1680 .... **LC 108**

Larra (y Sanchez de Castro), Mariano Jose
de 1809-1837 .... **NCLC 17, 130**

Larsen, Eric 1941- .... **CLC 55**
See also CA 132

Larsen, Nella 1893(?)-1963 .... **BLC 2; CLC
37; HR 3**
See also AFAW 1, 2; BW 1; CA 125; CANR
83; DAM MULT; DLB 51; FW; LATS
1:1; LMFS 2

Larson, Charles R(aymond) 1938- ... **CLC 31**
See also CA 53-56; CANR 4, 121

Larson, Jonathan 1961-1996 .... **CLC 99**
See also AAYA 28; CA 156

La Sale, Antoine de c. 1386-1460(?) . **LC 104**
See also DLB 208

Las Casas, Bartolome de
1474-1566 .... **HLCS; LC 31**
See Casas, Bartolome de las
See also LAW

Lasch, Christopher 1932-1994 .... **CLC 102**
See also CA 73-76; 144; CANR 25, 118;
DLB 246; MTCW 1, 2

Lasker-Schueler, Else 1869-1945 ... **TCLC 57**
See Lasker-Schuler, Else
See also CA 183; DLB 66, 124

Lasker-Schuler, Else
See Lasker-Schueler, Else
See also EWL 3

Laski, Harold J(oseph) 1893-1950 . **TCLC 79**
See also CA 188

Latham, Jean Lee 1902-1995 .... **CLC 12**
See also AITN 1; BYA 1; CA 5-8R; CANR
7, 84; CLR 50; MAICYA 1, 2; SATA 2,
68; YAW

Latham, Mavis
See Clark, Mavis Thorpe

Lathen, Emma .... **CLC 2**
See Hennissart, Martha; Latsis, Mary J(ane)
See also BPFB 2; CMW 4; DLB 306

Lathrop, Francis
See Leiber, Fritz (Reuter, Jr.)

Latsis, Mary J(ane) 1927-1997
See Lathen, Emma
See also CA 85-88; 162; CMW 4

Lattany, Kristin
See Lattany, Kristin (Elaine Eggleston)
Hunter

Lattany, Kristin (Elaine Eggleston) Hunter
1931- .... **CLC 35**
See also AITN 1; BW 1; BYA 3; CA 13-
16R; CANR 13, 108; CLR 3; CN 7; DLB
33; INT CANR-13; MAICYA 1, 2; SAAS
10; SATA 12, 132; YAW

Lattimore, Richmond (Alexander)
1906-1984 .... **CLC 3**
See also CA 1-4R; 112; CANR 1

Laughlin, James 1914-1997 .... **CLC 49**
See also CA 21-24R; 162; CAAS 22; CANR
9, 47; CP 7; DLB 48; DLBY 1996, 1997

Laurence, (Jean) Margaret (Wemyss)
1926-1987 . **CLC 3, 6, 13, 50, 62; SSC 7**
See also BYA 13; CA 5-8R; 121; CANR
33; DAC; DAM MST; DLB 53; EWL 3;
FW; MTCW 1, 2; NFS 11; RGEL 2;
RGSF 2; SATA-Obit 50; TCWW 2

Laurent, Antoine 1952- .... **CLC 50**

Lauscher, Hermann
See Hesse, Hermann

Lautreamont 1846-1870 .. **NCLC 12; SSC 14**
See Lautreamont, Isidore Lucien Ducasse
See also GFL 1789 to the Present; RGWL
2, 3

Lautreamont, Isidore Lucien Ducasse
See Lautreamont
See also DLB 217

Lavater, Johann Kaspar
1741-1801 .... **NCLC 142**
See also DLB 97

Laverty, Donald
See Blish, James (Benjamin)

Lavin, Mary 1912-1996 . **CLC 4, 18, 99; SSC 4, 67**
See also CA 9-12R; 151; CANR 33; CN 7; DLB 15; FW; MTCW 1; RGEL 2; RGSF 2

Lavond, Paul Dennis
See Kornbluth, C(yril) M.; Pohl, Frederik

Lawes Henry 1596-1662 .... **LC 113**
See also DLB 126

Lawler, Ray
See Lawler, Raymond Evenor
See also DLB 289

Lawler, Raymond Evenor 1922- .... **CLC 58**
See Lawler, Ray
See also CA 103; CD 5; RGEL 2

Lawrence, D(avid) H(erbert Richards)
1885-1930 .... **PC 54; SSC 4, 19, 73; TCLC 2, 9, 16, 33, 48, 61, 93; WLC**
See Chambers, Jessie
See also BPFB 2; BRW 7; BRWR 2; CA 104; 121; CANR 131; CDBLB 1914-1945; DA; DA3; DAB; DAC; DAM MST, NOV, POET; DLB 10, 19, 36, 98, 162, 195; EWL 3; EXPP; EXPS; LAIT 2, 3; MTCW 1, 2; NFS 18; PFS 6; RGEL 2; RGSF 2; SSFS 2, 6; TEA; WLIT 4; WP

Lawrence, T(homas) E(dward)
1888-1935 .... **TCLC 18**
See Dale, Colin
See also BRWS 2; CA 115; 167; DLB 195

Lawrence of Arabia
See Lawrence, T(homas) E(dward)

Lawson, Henry (Archibald Hertzberg)
1867-1922 .... **SSC 18; TCLC 27**
See also CA 120; 181; DLB 230; RGEL 2; RGSF 2

Lawton, Dennis
See Faust, Frederick (Schiller)

Layamon fl. c. 1200- .... **CMLC 10**
See Laȝamon
See also DLB 146; RGEL 2

Laye, Camara 1928-1980 ..... **BLC 2; CLC 4, 38**
See Camara Laye
See also AFW; BW 1; CA 85-88; 97-100; CANR 25; DAM MULT; MTCW 1, 2; WLIT 2

Layton, Irving (Peter) 1912- .... **CLC 2, 15, 164**
See also CA 1-4R; CANR 2, 33, 43, 66, 129; CP 7; DAC; DAM MST, POET; DLB 88; EWL 3; MTCW 1, 2; PFS 12; RGEL 2

Lazarus, Emma 1849-1887 ...... **NCLC 8, 109**

Lazarus, Felix
See Cable, George Washington

Lazarus, Henry
See Slavitt, David R(ytman)

Lea, Joan
See Neufeld, John (Arthur)

Leacock, Stephen (Butler)
1869-1944 .... **SSC 39; TCLC 2**
See also CA 104; 141; CANR 80; DAC; DAM MST; DLB 92; EWL 3; MTCW 2; RGEL 2; RGSF 2

Lead, Jane Ward 1623-1704 .... **LC 72**
See also DLB 131

Leapor, Mary 1722-1746 .... **LC 80**
See also DLB 109

Lear, Edward 1812-1888 ..... **NCLC 3; PC 65**
See also AAYA 48; BRW 5; CLR 1, 75; DLB 32, 163, 166; MAICYA 1, 2; RGEL 2; SATA 18, 100; WCH; WP

Lear, Norman (Milton) 1922- .... **CLC 12**
See also CA 73-76

Leautaud, Paul 1872-1956 .... **TCLC 83**
See also CA 203; DLB 65; GFL 1789 to the Present

Leavis, F(rank) R(aymond)
1895-1978 .... **CLC 24**
See also BRW 7; CA 21-24R; 77-80; CANR 44; DLB 242; EWL 3; MTCW 1, 2; RGEL 2

Leavitt, David 1961- .... **CLC 34**
See also CA 116; 122; CANR 50, 62, 101, 134; CPW; DA3; DAM POP; DLB 130; GLL 1; INT CA-122; MTCW 2

Leblanc, Maurice (Marie Emile)
1864-1941 .... **TCLC 49**
See also CA 110; CMW 4

Lebowitz, Fran(ces Ann) 1951(?)- ... **CLC 11, 36**
See also CA 81-84; CANR 14, 60, 70; INT CANR-14; MTCW 1

Lebrecht, Peter
See Tieck, (Johann) Ludwig

le Carre, John .... **CLC 3, 5, 9, 15, 28**
See Cornwell, David (John Moore)
See also AAYA 42; BEST 89:4; BPFB 2; BRWS 2; CDBLB 1960 to Present; CMW 4; CN 7; CPW; DLB 87; EWL 3; MSW; MTCW 2; RGEL 2; TEA

Le Clezio, J(ean) M(arie) G(ustave)
1940- .... **CLC 31, 155**
See also CA 116; 128; CWW 2; DLB 83; EWL 3; GFL 1789 to the Present; RGSF 2

Leconte de Lisle, Charles-Marie-Rene
1818-1894 .... **NCLC 29**
See also DLB 217; EW 6; GFL 1789 to the Present

Le Coq, Monsieur
See Simenon, Georges (Jacques Christian)

Leduc, Violette 1907-1972 .... **CLC 22**
See also CA 13-14; 33-36R; CANR 69; CAP 1; EWL 3; GFL 1789 to the Present; GLL 1

Ledwidge, Francis 1887(?)-1917 .... **TCLC 23**
See also CA 123; 203; DLB 20

Lee, Andrea 1953- .... **BLC 2; CLC 36**
See also BW 1, 3; CA 125; CANR 82; DAM MULT

Lee, Andrew
See Auchincloss, Louis (Stanton)

Lee, Chang-rae 1965- .... **CLC 91**
See also CA 148; CANR 89; LATS 1:2

Lee, Don L. .... **CLC 2**
See Madhubuti, Haki R.

Lee, George W(ashington)
1894-1976 .... **BLC 2; CLC 52**
See also BW 1; CA 125; CANR 83; DAM MULT; DLB 51

Lee, (Nelle) Harper 1926- . **CLC 12, 60, 194; WLC**
See also AAYA 13; AMWS 8; BPFB 2; BYA 3; CA 13-16R; CANR 51, 128; CDALB 1941-1968; CSW; DA; DA3; DAB; DAC; DAM MST, NOV; DLB 6; EXPN; LAIT 3; MTCW 1, 2; NFS 2; SATA 11; WYA; YAW

Lee, Helen Elaine 1959(?)- .... **CLC 86**
See also CA 148

Lee, John .... **CLC 70**

Lee, Julian
See Latham, Jean Lee

Lee, Larry
See Lee, Lawrence

Lee, Laurie 1914-1997 .... **CLC 90**
See also CA 77-80; 158; CANR 33, 73; CP 7; CPW; DAB; DAM POP; DLB 27; MTCW 1; RGEL 2

Lee, Lawrence 1941-1990 .... **CLC 34**
See also CA 131; CANR 43

Lee, Li-Young 1957- .... **CLC 164; PC 24**
See also CA 153; CANR 118; CP 7; DLB 165; LMFS 2; PFS 11, 15, 17

Lee, Manfred B(ennington)
1905-1971 .... **CLC 11**
See Queen, Ellery
See also CA 1-4R; 29-32R; CANR 2; CMW 4; DLB 137

Lee, Nathaniel 1645(?)-1692 .... **LC 103**
See also DLB 80; RGEL 2

Lee, Shelton Jackson 1957(?)- .. **BLCS; CLC 105**
See Lee, Spike
See also BW 2, 3; CA 125; CANR 42; DAM MULT

Lee, Spike
See Lee, Shelton Jackson
See also AAYA 4, 29

Lee, Stan 1922- .... **CLC 17**
See also AAYA 5, 49; CA 108; 111; CANR 129; INT CA-111

Lee, Tanith 1947- .... **CLC 46**
See also AAYA 15; CA 37-40R; CANR 53, 102; DLB 261; FANT; SATA 8, 88, 134; SFW 4; SUFW 1, 2; YAW

Lee, Vernon .... **SSC 33; TCLC 5**
See Paget, Violet
See also DLB 57, 153, 156, 174, 178; GLL 1; SUFW 1

Lee, William
See Burroughs, William S(eward)
See also GLL 1

Lee, Willy
See Burroughs, William S(eward)
See also GLL 1

Lee-Hamilton, Eugene (Jacob)
1845-1907 .... **TCLC 22**
See also CA 117

Leet, Judith 1935- .... **CLC 11**
See also CA 187

Le Fanu, Joseph Sheridan
1814-1873 .... **NCLC 9, 58; SSC 14**
See also CMW 4; DA3; DAM POP; DLB 21, 70, 159, 178; HGG; RGEL 2; RGSF 2; SUFW 1

Leffland, Ella 1931- .... **CLC 19**
See also CA 29-32R; CANR 35, 78, 82; DLBY 1984; INT CANR-35; SATA 65

Leger, Alexis
See Leger, (Marie-Rene Auguste) Alexis Saint-Leger

Leger, (Marie-Rene Auguste) Alexis Saint-Leger 1887-1975 .. **CLC 4, 11, 46; PC 23**
See Perse, Saint-John; Saint-John Perse
See also CA 13-16R; 61-64; CANR 43; DAM POET; MTCW 1

Leger, Saintleger
See Leger, (Marie-Rene Auguste) Alexis Saint-Leger

Le Guin, Ursula K(roeber) 1929- ..... **CLC 8, 13, 22, 45, 71, 136; SSC 12, 69**
See also AAYA 9, 27; AITN 1; BPFB 2; BYA 5, 8, 11, 14; CA 21-24R; CANR 9, 32, 52, 74, 132; CDALB 1968-1988; CLR 3, 28, 91; CN 7; CPW; DA3; DAB; DAC; DAM MST, POP; DLB 8, 52, 256, 275; EXPS; FANT; FW; INT CANR-32; JRDA; LAIT 5; MAICYA 1, 2; MTCW 1, 2; NFS 6, 9; SATA 4, 52, 99, 149; SCFW; SFW 4; SSFS 2; SUFW 1, 2; WYA; YAW

Lehmann, Rosamond (Nina)
1901-1990 .... **CLC 5**
See also CA 77-80; 131; CANR 8, 73; DLB 15; MTCW 2; RGEL 2; RHW

Leiber, Fritz (Reuter, Jr.)
1910-1992 .... **CLC 25**
See also BPFB 2; CA 45-48; 139; CANR 2, 40, 86; DLB 8; FANT; HGG; MTCW 1, 2; SATA 45; SATA-Obit 73; SCFW 2; SFW 4; SUFW 1, 2

Longfellow, Henry Wadsworth
1807-1882 .... **NCLC 2, 45, 101, 103; PC 30; WLCS**
See also AMW; AMWR 2; CDALB 1640-1865; CLR 99; DA; DA3; DAB; DAC; DAM MST, POET; DLB 1, 59, 235; EXPP; PAB; PFS 2, 7, 17; RGAL 4; SATA 19; TUS; WP

Longinus c. 1st cent. - .... **CMLC 27**
See also AW 2; DLB 176

Longley, Michael 1939- .... **CLC 29**
See also BRWS 8; CA 102; CP 7; DLB 40

Longus fl. c. 2nd cent. - .... **CMLC 7**

Longway, A. Hugh
See Lang, Andrew

Lonnbohm, Armas Eino Leopold 1878-1926
See Leino, Eino
See also CA 123

Lonnrot, Elias 1802-1884 .... **NCLC 53**
See also EFS 1

Lonsdale, Roger ed. .... **CLC 65**

Lopate, Phillip 1943- .... **CLC 29**
See also CA 97-100; CANR 88; DLBY 1980; INT CA-97-100

Lopez, Barry (Holstun) 1945- .... **CLC 70**
See also AAYA 9; ANW; CA 65-68; CANR 7, 23, 47, 68, 92; DLB 256, 275; INT CANR-7, -23; MTCW 1; RGAL 4; SATA 67

Lopez Portillo (y Pacheco), Jose
1920-2004 .... **CLC 46**
See also CA 129; 224; HW 1

Lopez y Fuentes, Gregorio
1897(?)-1966 .... **CLC 32**
See also CA 131; EWL 3; HW 1

Lorca, Federico Garcia
See Garcia Lorca, Federico
See also DFS 4; EW 11; PFS 20; RGWL 2, 3; WP

Lord, Audre
See Lorde, Audre (Geraldine)
See also EWL 3

Lord, Bette Bao 1938- .... **AAL; CLC 23**
See also BEST 90:3; BPFB 2; CA 107; CANR 41, 79; INT CA-107; SATA 58

Lord Auch
See Bataille, Georges

Lord Brooke
See Greville, Fulke

Lord Byron
See Byron, George Gordon (Noel)

Lorde, Audre (Geraldine)
1934-1992 .. **BLC 2; CLC 18, 71; PC 12**
See Domini, Rey; Lord, Audre
See also AFAW 1, 2; BW 1, 3; CA 25-28R; 142; CANR 16, 26, 46, 82; DA3; DAM MULT, POET; DLB 41; FW; MTCW 1, 2; PFS 16; RGAL 4

Lord Houghton
See Milnes, Richard Monckton

Lord Jeffrey
See Jeffrey, Francis

Loreaux, Nichol .... **CLC 65**

Lorenzini, Carlo 1826-1890
See Collodi, Carlo
See also MAICYA 1, 2; SATA 29, 100

Lorenzo, Heberto Padilla
See Padilla (Lorenzo), Heberto

Loris
See Hofmannsthal, Hugo von

Loti, Pierre .... **TCLC 11**
See Viaud, (Louis Marie) Julien
See also DLB 123; GFL 1789 to the Present

Lou, Henri
See Andreas-Salome, Lou

Louie, David Wong 1954- .... **CLC 70**
See also CA 139; CANR 120

Louis, Adrian C. .... **NNAL**
See also CA 223

Louis, Father M.
See Merton, Thomas (James)

Louise, Heidi
See Erdrich, Louise

Lovecraft, H(oward) P(hillips)
1890-1937 .... **SSC 3, 52; TCLC 4, 22**
See also AAYA 14; BPFB 2; CA 104; 133; CANR 106; DA3; DAM POP; HGG; MTCW 1, 2; RGAL 4; SCFW; SFW 4; SUFW

Lovelace, Earl 1935- .... **CLC 51**
See also BW 2; CA 77-80; CANR 41, 72, 114; CD 5; CDWLB 3; CN 7; DLB 125; EWL 3; MTCW 1

Lovelace, Richard 1618-1657 .... **LC 24**
See also BRW 2; DLB 131; EXPP; PAB; RGEL 2

Lowe, Pardee 1904- .... **AAL**

Lowell, Amy 1874-1925 ... **PC 13; TCLC 1, 8**
See also AAYA 57; AMW; CA 104; 151; DAM POET; DLB 54, 140; EWL 3; EXPP; LMFS 2; MAWW; MTCW 2; RGAL 4; TUS

Lowell, James Russell 1819-1891 ... **NCLC 2, 90**
See also AMWS 1; CDALB 1640-1865; DLB 1, 11, 64, 79, 189, 235; RGAL 4

Lowell, Robert (Traill Spence, Jr.)
1917-1977 .... **CLC 1, 2, 3, 4, 5, 8, 9, 11, 15, 37, 124; PC 3; WLC**
See also AMW; AMWC 2; AMWR 2; CA 9-12R; 73-76; CABS 2; CANR 26, 60; CDALBS; DA; DA3; DAB; DAC; DAM MST, NOV; DLB 5, 169; EWL 3; MTCW 1, 2; PAB; PFS 6, 7; RGAL 4; WP

Lowenthal, Michael (Francis)
1969- .... **CLC 119**
See also CA 150; CANR 115

Lowndes, Marie Adelaide (Belloc)
1868-1947 .... **TCLC 12**
See also CA 107; CMW 4; DLB 70; RHW

Lowry, (Clarence) Malcolm
1909-1957 .... **SSC 31; TCLC 6, 40**
See also BPFB 2; BRWS 3; CA 105; 131; CANR 62, 105; CDBLB 1945-1960; DLB 15; EWL 3; MTCW 1, 2; RGEL 2

Lowry, Mina Gertrude 1882-1966
See Loy, Mina
See also CA 113

Loxsmith, John
See Brunner, John (Kilian Houston)

Loy, Mina .... **CLC 28; PC 16**
See Lowry, Mina Gertrude
See also DAM POET; DLB 4, 54; PFS 20

Loyson-Bridet
See Schwob, Marcel (Mayer Andre)

Lucan 39-65 .... **CMLC 33**
See also AW 2; DLB 211; EFS 2; RGWL 2, 3

Lucas, Craig 1951- .... **CLC 64**
See also CA 137; CAD; CANR 71, 109; CD 5; GLL 2

Lucas, E(dward) V(errall)
1868-1938 .... **TCLC 73**
See also CA 176; DLB 98, 149, 153; SATA 20

Lucas, George 1944- .... **CLC 16**
See also AAYA 1, 23; CA 77-80; CANR 30; SATA 56

Lucas, Hans
See Godard, Jean-Luc

Lucas, Victoria
See Plath, Sylvia

Lucian c. 125-c. 180 .... **CMLC 32**
See also AW 2; DLB 176; RGWL 2, 3

Lucretius c. 94B.C.-c. 49B.C. .... **CMLC 48**
See also AW 2; CDWLB 1; DLB 211; EFS 2; RGWL 2, 3

Ludlam, Charles 1943-1987 .... **CLC 46, 50**
See also CA 85-88; 122; CAD; CANR 72, 86; DLB 266

Ludlum, Robert 1927-2001 .... **CLC 22, 43**
See also AAYA 10, 59; BEST 89:1, 90:3; BPFB 2; CA 33-36R; 195; CANR 25, 41, 68, 105, 131; CMW 4; CPW; DA3; DAM NOV, POP; DLBY 1982; MSW; MTCW 1, 2

Ludwig, Ken .... **CLC 60**
See also CA 195; CAD

Ludwig, Otto 1813-1865 .... **NCLC 4**
See also DLB 129

Lugones, Leopoldo 1874-1938 .... **HLCS 2; TCLC 15**
See also CA 116; 131; CANR 104; DLB 283; EWL 3; HW 1; LAW

Lu Hsun .... **SSC 20; TCLC 3**
See Shu-Jen, Chou
See also EWL 3

Lukacs, George .... **CLC 24**
See Lukacs, Gyorgy (Szegeny von)

Lukacs, Gyorgy (Szegeny von) 1885-1971
See Lukacs, George
See also CA 101; 29-32R; CANR 62; CDWLB 4; DLB 215, 242; EW 10; EWL 3; MTCW 2

Luke, Peter (Ambrose Cyprian)
1919-1995 .... **CLC 38**
See also CA 81-84; 147; CANR 72; CBD; CD 5; DLB 13

Lunar, Dennis
See Mungo, Raymond

Lurie, Alison 1926- ..... **CLC 4, 5, 18, 39, 175**
See also BPFB 2; CA 1-4R; CANR 2, 17, 50, 88; CN 7; DLB 2; MTCW 1; SATA 46, 112

Lustig, Arnost 1926- .... **CLC 56**
See also AAYA 3; CA 69-72; CANR 47, 102; CWW 2; DLB 232, 299; EWL 3; SATA 56

Luther, Martin 1483-1546 .... **LC 9, 37**
See also CDWLB 2; DLB 179; EW 2; RGWL 2, 3

Luxemburg, Rosa 1870(?)-1919 ..... **TCLC 63**
See also CA 118

Luzi, Mario 1914- .... **CLC 13**
See also CA 61-64; CANR 9, 70; CWW 2; DLB 128; EWL 3

L'vov, Arkady .... **CLC 59**

Lydgate, John c. 1370-1450(?) .... **LC 81**
See also BRW 1; DLB 146; RGEL 2

Lyly, John 1554(?)-1606 .... **DC 7; LC 41**
See also BRW 1; DAM DRAM; DLB 62, 167; RGEL 2

L'Ymagier
See Gourmont, Remy(-Marie-Charles) de

Lynch, B. Suarez
See Borges, Jorge Luis

Lynch, David (Keith) 1946- ...... **CLC 66, 162**
See also AAYA 55; CA 124; 129; CANR 111

Lynch, James
See Andreyev, Leonid (Nikolaevich)

Lyndsay, Sir David 1485-1555 .... **LC 20**
See also RGEL 2

Lynn, Kenneth S(chuyler)
1923-2001 .... **CLC 50**
See also CA 1-4R; 196; CANR 3, 27, 65

Lynx
See West, Rebecca

Lyons, Marcus
See Blish, James (Benjamin)

Lyotard, Jean-Francois
1924-1998 .... **TCLC 103**
See also DLB 242; EWL 3

Lyre, Pinchbeck
See Sassoon, Siegfried (Lorraine)

Maillet, Antonine 1929- .... **CLC 54, 118**
See also CA 115; 120; CANR 46, 74, 77, 134; CCA 1; CWW 2; DAC; DLB 60; INT CA-120; MTCW 2

Maimonides 1135-1204 .... **CMLC 76**
See also DLB 115

Mais, Roger 1905-1955 .... **TCLC 8**
See also BW 1, 3; CA 105; 124; CANR 82; CDWLB 3; DLB 125; EWL 3; MTCW 1; RGEL 2

Maistre, Joseph 1753-1821 .... **NCLC 37**
See also GFL 1789 to the Present

Maitland, Frederic William
1850-1906 .... **TCLC 65**

Maitland, Sara (Louise) 1950- .... **CLC 49**
See also CA 69-72; CANR 13, 59; DLB 271; FW

Major, Clarence 1936- ... **BLC 2; CLC 3, 19, 48**
See also AFAW 2; BW 2, 3; CA 21-24R; CAAS 6; CANR 13, 25, 53, 82; CN 7; CP 7; CSW; DAM MULT; DLB 33; EWL 3; MSW

Major, Kevin (Gerald) 1949- .... **CLC 26**
See also AAYA 16; CA 97-100; CANR 21, 38, 112; CLR 11; DAC; DLB 60; INT CANR-21; JRDA; MAICYA 1, 2; MAIC-YAS 1; SATA 32, 82, 134; WYA; YAW

Maki, James
See Ozu, Yasujiro

Makine, Andrei 1957- .... **CLC 198**
See also CA 176; CANR 103

Malabaila, Damiano
See Levi, Primo

Malamud, Bernard 1914-1986 .. **CLC 1, 2, 3, 5, 8, 9, 11, 18, 27, 44, 78, 85; SSC 15; TCLC 129; WLC**
See also AAYA 16; AMWS 1; BPFB 2; BYA 15; CA 5-8R; 118; CABS 1; CANR 28, 62, 114; CDALB 1941-1968; CPW; DA; DA3; DAB; DAC; DAM MST, NOV, POP; DLB 2, 28, 152; DLBY 1980, 1986; EWL 3; EXPS; LAIT 4; LATS 1:1; MTCW 1, 2; NFS 4, 9; RGAL 4; RGSF 2; SSFS 8, 13, 16; TUS

Malan, Herman
See Bosman, Herman Charles; Bosman, Herman Charles

Malaparte, Curzio 1898-1957 .... **TCLC 52**
See also DLB 264

Malcolm, Dan
See Silverberg, Robert

Malcolm, Janet 1934- .... **CLC 201**
See also CA 123; CANR 89; NCFS 1

Malcolm X .... **BLC 2; CLC 82, 117; WLCS**
See Little, Malcolm
See also LAIT 5; NCFS 3

Malherbe, Francois de 1555-1628 .... **LC 5**
See also GFL Beginnings to 1789

Mallarme, Stephane 1842-1898 ...... **NCLC 4, 41; PC 4**
See also DAM POET; DLB 217; EW 7; GFL 1789 to the Present; LMFS 2; RGWL 2, 3; TWA

Mallet-Joris, Francoise 1930- .... **CLC 11**
See also CA 65-68; CANR 17; CWW 2; DLB 83; EWL 3; GFL 1789 to the Present

Malley, Ern
See McAuley, James Phillip

Mallon, Thomas 1951- .... **CLC 172**
See also CA 110; CANR 29, 57, 92

Mallowan, Agatha Christie
See Christie, Agatha (Mary Clarissa)

Maloff, Saul 1922- .... **CLC 5**
See also CA 33-36R

Malone, Louis
See MacNeice, (Frederick) Louis

Malone, Michael (Christopher)
1942- .... **CLC 43**
See also CA 77-80; CANR 14, 32, 57, 114

Malory, Sir Thomas 1410(?)-1471(?) . **LC 11, 88; WLCS**
See also BRW 1; BRWR 2; CDBLB Before 1660; DA; DAB; DAC; DAM MST; DLB 146; EFS 2; RGEL 2; SATA 59; SATA-Brief 33; TEA; WLIT 3

Malouf, (George Joseph) David
1934- .... **CLC 28, 86**
See also CA 124; CANR 50, 76; CN 7; CP 7; DLB 289; EWL 3; MTCW 2

Malraux, (Georges-)Andre
1901-1976 .... **CLC 1, 4, 9, 13, 15, 57**
See also BPFB 2; CA 21-22; 69-72; CANR 34, 58; CAP 2; DA3; DAM NOV; DLB 72; EW 12; EWL 3; GFL 1789 to the Present; MTCW 1, 2; RGWL 2, 3; TWA

Malthus, Thomas Robert
1766-1834 .... **NCLC 145**
See also DLB 107, 158; RGEL 2

Malzberg, Barry N(athaniel) 1939- ... **CLC 7**
See also CA 61-64; CAAS 4; CANR 16; CMW 4; DLB 8; SFW 4

Mamet, David (Alan) 1947- .. **CLC 9, 15, 34, 46, 91, 166; DC 4, 24**
See also AAYA 3, 60; AMWS 14; CA 81-84; CABS 3; CANR 15, 41, 67, 72, 129; CD 5; DA3; DAM DRAM; DFS 2, 3, 6, 12, 15; DLB 7; EWL 3; IDFW 4; MTCW 1, 2; RGAL 4

Mamoulian, Rouben (Zachary)
1897-1987 .... **CLC 16**
See also CA 25-28R; 124; CANR 85

Mandelshtam, Osip
See Mandelstam, Osip (Emilievich)
See also EW 10; EWL 3; RGWL 2, 3

Mandelstam, Osip (Emilievich)
1891(?)-1943(?) .... **PC 14; TCLC 2, 6**
See Mandelshtam, Osip
See also CA 104; 150; MTCW 2; TWA

Mander, (Mary) Jane 1877-1949 ... **TCLC 31**
See also CA 162; RGEL 2

Mandeville, Bernard 1670-1733 .... **LC 82**
See also DLB 101

Mandeville, Sir John fl. 1350- ...... **CMLC 19**
See also DLB 146

Mandiargues, Andre Pieyre de .... **CLC 41**
See Pieyre de Mandiargues, Andre
See also DLB 83

Mandrake, Ethel Belle
See Thurman, Wallace (Henry)

Mangan, James Clarence
1803-1849 .... **NCLC 27**
See also RGEL 2

Maniere, J.-E.
See Giraudoux, Jean(-Hippolyte)

Mankiewicz, Herman (Jacob)
1897-1953 .... **TCLC 85**
See also CA 120; 169; DLB 26; IDFW 3, 4

Manley, (Mary) Delariviere
1672(?)-1724 .... **LC 1, 42**
See also DLB 39, 80; RGEL 2

Mann, Abel
See Creasey, John

Mann, Emily 1952- .... **DC 7**
See also CA 130; CAD; CANR 55; CD 5; CWD; DLB 266

Mann, (Luiz) Heinrich 1871-1950 ... **TCLC 9**
See also CA 106; 164, 181; DLB 66, 118; EW 8; EWL 3; RGWL 2, 3

Mann, (Paul) Thomas 1875-1955 . **SSC 5, 80, 82; TCLC 2, 8, 14, 21, 35, 44, 60; WLC**
See also BPFB 2; CA 104; 128; CANR 133; CDWLB 2; DA; DA3; DAB; DAC; DAM MST, NOV; DLB 66; EW 9; EWL 3; GLL 1; LATS 1:1; LMFS 1; MTCW 1, 2; NFS 17; RGSF 2; RGWL 2, 3; SSFS 4, 9; TWA

Mannheim, Karl 1893-1947 .... **TCLC 65**
See also CA 204

Manning, David
See Faust, Frederick (Schiller)
See also TCWW 2

Manning, Frederic 1882-1935 .... **TCLC 25**
See also CA 124; 216; DLB 260

Manning, Olivia 1915-1980 .... **CLC 5, 19**
See also CA 5-8R; 101; CANR 29; EWL 3; FW; MTCW 1; RGEL 2

Mano, D. Keith 1942- .... **CLC 2, 10**
See also CA 25-28R; CAAS 6; CANR 26, 57; DLB 6

Mansfield, Katherine .... **SSC 9, 23, 38, 81; TCLC 2, 8, 39, 164; WLC**
See Beauchamp, Kathleen Mansfield
See also BPFB 2; BRW 7; DAB; DLB 162; EWL 3; EXPS; FW; GLL 1; RGEL 2; RGSF 2; SSFS 2, 8, 10, 11; WWE 1

Manso, Peter 1940- .... **CLC 39**
See also CA 29-32R; CANR 44

Mantecon, Juan Jimenez
See Jimenez (Mantecon), Juan Ramon

Mantel, Hilary (Mary) 1952- .... **CLC 144**
See also CA 125; CANR 54, 101; CN 7; DLB 271; RHW

Manton, Peter
See Creasey, John

Man Without a Spleen, A
See Chekhov, Anton (Pavlovich)

Manzano, Juan Francisco
1797(?)-1854 .... **NCLC 155**

Manzoni, Alessandro 1785-1873 ... **NCLC 29, 98**
See also EW 5; RGWL 2, 3; TWA

Map, Walter 1140-1209 .... **CMLC 32**

Mapu, Abraham (ben Jekutiel)
1808-1867 .... **NCLC 18**

Mara, Sally
See Queneau, Raymond

Maracle, Lee 1950- .... **NNAL**
See also CA 149

Marat, Jean Paul 1743-1793 .... **LC 10**

Marcel, Gabriel Honore 1889-1973 . **CLC 15**
See also CA 102; 45-48; EWL 3; MTCW 1, 2

March, William 1893-1954 .... **TCLC 96**
See also CA 216

Marchbanks, Samuel
See Davies, (William) Robertson
See also CCA 1

Marchi, Giacomo
See Bassani, Giorgio

Marcus Aurelius
See Aurelius, Marcus
See also AW 2

Marguerite
See de Navarre, Marguerite

Marguerite d'Angouleme
See de Navarre, Marguerite
See also GFL Beginnings to 1789

Marguerite de Navarre
See de Navarre, Marguerite
See also RGWL 2, 3

Margulies, Donald 1954- .... **CLC 76**
See also AAYA 57; CA 200; DFS 13; DLB 228

Marie de France c. 12th cent. - ..... **CMLC 8; PC 22**
See also DLB 208; FW; RGWL 2, 3

Marie de l'Incarnation 1599-1672 ...... **LC 10**

Marier, Captain Victor
See Griffith, D(avid Lewelyn) W(ark)

Mariner, Scott
See Pohl, Frederik

Matheson, Richard (Burton) 1926- .. **CLC 37**
See also AAYA 31; CA 97-100; CANR 88, 99; DLB 8, 44; HGG; INT CA-97-100; SCFW 2; SFW 4; SUFW 2

Mathews, Harry 1930- .... **CLC 6, 52**
See also CA 21-24R; CAAS 6; CANR 18, 40, 98; CN 7

Mathews, John Joseph 1894-1979 .. **CLC 84; NNAL**
See also CA 19-20; 142; CANR 45; CAP 2; DAM MULT; DLB 175

Mathias, Roland (Glyn) 1915- .... **CLC 45**
See also CA 97-100; CANR 19, 41; CP 7; DLB 27

Matsuo Basho 1644-1694 .... **LC 62; PC 3**
See Basho, Matsuo
See also DAM POET; PFS 2, 7

Mattheson, Rodney
See Creasey, John

Matthews, (James) Brander
1852-1929 .... **TCLC 95**
See also DLB 71, 78; DLBD 13

Matthews, (James) Brander
1852-1929 .... **TCLC 95**
See also CA 181; DLB 71, 78; DLBD 13

Matthews, Greg 1949- .... **CLC 45**
See also CA 135

Matthews, William (Procter III)
1942-1997 .... **CLC 40**
See also AMWS 9; CA 29-32R; 162; CAAS 18; CANR 12, 57; CP 7; DLB 5

Matthias, John (Edward) 1941- .... **CLC 9**
See also CA 33-36R; CANR 56; CP 7

Matthiessen, F(rancis) O(tto)
1902-1950 .... **TCLC 100**
See also CA 185; DLB 63

Matthiessen, Peter 1927- ... **CLC 5, 7, 11, 32, 64**
See also AAYA 6, 40; AMWS 5; ANW; BEST 90:4; BPFB 2; CA 9-12R; CANR 21, 50, 73, 100; CN 7; DA3; DAM NOV; DLB 6, 173, 275; MTCW 1, 2; SATA 27

Maturin, Charles Robert
1780(?)-1824 .... **NCLC 6**
See also BRWS 8; DLB 178; HGG; LMFS 1; RGEL 2; SUFW

Matute (Ausejo), Ana Maria 1925- .. **CLC 11**
See also CA 89-92; CANR 129; CWW 2; EWL 3; MTCW 1; RGSF 2

Maugham, W. S.
See Maugham, W(illiam) Somerset

Maugham, W(illiam) Somerset
1874-1965 .. **CLC 1, 11, 15, 67, 93; SSC 8; WLC**
See also AAYA 55; BPFB 2; BRW 6; CA 5-8R; 25-28R; CANR 40, 127; CDBLB 1914-1945; CMW 4; DA; DA3; DAB; DAC; DAM DRAM, MST, NOV; DLB 10, 36, 77, 100, 162, 195; EWL 3; LAIT 3; MTCW 1, 2; RGEL 2; RGSF 2; SATA 54; SSFS 17

Maugham, William Somerset
See Maugham, W(illiam) Somerset

Maupassant, (Henri Rene Albert) Guy de
1850-1893 . **NCLC 1, 42, 83; SSC 1, 64; WLC**
See also BYA 14; DA; DA3; DAB; DAC; DAM MST; DLB 123; EW 7; EXPS; GFL 1789 to the Present; LAIT 2; LMFS 1; RGSF 2; RGWL 2, 3; SSFS 4; SUFW; TWA

Maupin, Armistead (Jones, Jr.)
1944- .... **CLC 95**
See also CA 125; 130; CANR 58, 101; CPW; DA3; DAM POP; DLB 278; GLL 1; INT CA-130; MTCW 2

Maurhut, Richard
See Traven, B.

Mauriac, Claude 1914-1996 .... **CLC 9**
See also CA 89-92; 152; CWW 2; DLB 83; EWL 3; GFL 1789 to the Present

Mauriac, Francois (Charles)
1885-1970 .... **CLC 4, 9, 56; SSC 24**
See also CA 25-28; CAP 2; DLB 65; EW 10; EWL 3; GFL 1789 to the Present; MTCW 1, 2; RGWL 2, 3; TWA

Mavor, Osborne Henry 1888-1951
See Bridie, James
See also CA 104

Maxwell, William (Keepers, Jr.)
1908-2000 .... **CLC 19**
See also AMWS 8; CA 93-96; 189; CANR 54, 95; CN 7; DLB 218, 278; DLBY 1980; INT CA-93-96; SATA-Obit 128

May, Elaine 1932- .... **CLC 16**
See also CA 124; 142; CAD; CWD; DLB 44

Mayakovski, Vladimir (Vladimirovich)
1893-1930 .... **TCLC 4, 18**
See Maiakovskii, Vladimir; Mayakovsky, Vladimir
See also CA 104; 158; EWL 3; MTCW 2; SFW 4; TWA

Mayakovsky, Vladimir
See Mayakovski, Vladimir (Vladimirovich)
See also EW 11; WP

Mayhew, Henry 1812-1887 .... **NCLC 31**
See also DLB 18, 55, 190

Mayle, Peter 1939(?)- .... **CLC 89**
See also CA 139; CANR 64, 109

Maynard, Joyce 1953- .... **CLC 23**
See also CA 111; 129; CANR 64

Mayne, William (James Carter)
1928- .... **CLC 12**
See also AAYA 20; CA 9-12R; CANR 37, 80, 100; CLR 25; FANT; JRDA; MAICYA 1, 2; MAICYAS 1; SAAS 11; SATA 6, 68, 122; SUFW 2; YAW

Mayo, Jim
See L'Amour, Louis (Dearborn)
See also TCWW 2

Maysles, Albert 1926- .... **CLC 16**
See also CA 29-32R

Maysles, David 1932-1987 .... **CLC 16**
See also CA 191

Mazer, Norma Fox 1931- .... **CLC 26**
See also AAYA 5, 36; BYA 1, 8; CA 69-72; CANR 12, 32, 66, 129; CLR 23; JRDA; MAICYA 1, 2; SAAS 1; SATA 24, 67, 105; WYA; YAW

Mazzini, Guiseppe 1805-1872 .... **NCLC 34**

McAlmon, Robert (Menzies)
1895-1956 .... **TCLC 97**
See also CA 107; 168; DLB 4, 45; DLBD 15; GLL 1

McAuley, James Phillip 1917-1976 .. **CLC 45**
See also CA 97-100; DLB 260; RGEL 2

McBain, Ed
See Hunter, Evan
See also MSW

McBrien, William (Augustine)
1930- .... **CLC 44**
See also CA 107; CANR 90

McCabe, Patrick 1955- .... **CLC 133**
See also BRWS 9; CA 130; CANR 50, 90; CN 7; DLB 194

McCaffrey, Anne (Inez) 1926- .... **CLC 17**
See also AAYA 6, 34; AITN 2; BEST 89:2; BPFB 2; BYA 5; CA 25-28R, 227; CAAE 227; CANR 15, 35, 55, 96; CLR 49; CPW; DA3; DAM NOV, POP; DLB 8; JRDA; MAICYA 1, 2; MTCW 1, 2; SAAS 11; SATA 8, 70, 116, 152; SATA-Essay 152; SFW 4; SUFW 2; WYA; YAW

McCall, Nathan 1955(?)- .... **CLC 86**
See also AAYA 59; BW 3; CA 146; CANR 88

McCann, Arthur
See Campbell, John W(ood, Jr.)

McCann, Edson
See Pohl, Frederik

McCarthy, Charles, Jr. 1933-
See McCarthy, Cormac
See also CANR 42, 69, 101; CN 7; CPW; CSW; DA3; DAM POP; MTCW 2

McCarthy, Cormac ...... **CLC 4, 57, 101, 204**
See McCarthy, Charles, Jr.
See also AAYA 41; AMWS 8; BPFB 2; CA 13-16R; CANR 10; DLB 6, 143, 256; EWL 3; LATS 1:2; TCWW 2

McCarthy, Mary (Therese)
1912-1989 .. **CLC 1, 3, 5, 14, 24, 39, 59; SSC 24**
See also AMW; BPFB 2; CA 5-8R; 129; CANR 16, 50, 64; DA3; DLB 2; DLBY 1981; EWL 3; FW; INT CANR-16; MAWW; MTCW 1, 2; RGAL 4; TUS

McCartney, (James) Paul 1942- . **CLC 12, 35**
See also CA 146; CANR 111

McCauley, Stephen (D.) 1955- .... **CLC 50**
See also CA 141

McClaren, Peter .... **CLC 70**

McClure, Michael (Thomas) 1932- ... **CLC 6, 10**
See also BG 3; CA 21-24R; CAD; CANR 17, 46, 77, 131; CD 5; CP 7; DLB 16; WP

McCorkle, Jill (Collins) 1958- .... **CLC 51**
See also CA 121; CANR 113; CSW; DLB 234; DLBY 1987

McCourt, Frank 1930- .... **CLC 109**
See also AMWS 12; CA 157; CANR 97; NCFS 1

McCourt, James 1941- .... **CLC 5**
See also CA 57-60; CANR 98

McCourt, Malachy 1931- .... **CLC 119**
See also SATA 126

McCoy, Horace (Stanley)
1897-1955 .... **TCLC 28**
See also AMWS 13; CA 108; 155; CMW 4; DLB 9

McCrae, John 1872-1918 .... **TCLC 12**
See also CA 109; DLB 92; PFS 5

McCreigh, James
See Pohl, Frederik

McCullers, (Lula) Carson (Smith)
1917-1967 .... **CLC 1, 4, 10, 12, 48, 100; SSC 9, 24; TCLC 155; WLC**
See also AAYA 21; AMW; AMWC 2; BPFB 2; CA 5-8R; 25-28R; CABS 1, 3; CANR 18, 132; CDALB 1941-1968; DA; DA3; DAB; DAC; DAM MST, NOV; DFS 5, 18; DLB 2, 7, 173, 228; EWL 3; EXPS; FW; GLL 1; LAIT 3, 4; MAWW; MTCW 1, 2; NFS 6, 13; RGAL 4; RGSF 2; SATA 27; SSFS 5; TUS; YAW

McCulloch, John Tyler
See Burroughs, Edgar Rice

McCullough, Colleen 1938(?)- .. **CLC 27, 107**
See also AAYA 36; BPFB 2; CA 81-84; CANR 17, 46, 67, 98; CPW; DA3; DAM NOV, POP; MTCW 1, 2; RHW

McCunn, Ruthanne Lum 1946- .... **AAL**
See also CA 119; CANR 43, 96; LAIT 2; SATA 63

McDermott, Alice 1953- .... **CLC 90**
See also CA 109; CANR 40, 90, 126; DLB 292

McElroy, Joseph 1930- .... **CLC 5, 47**
See also CA 17-20R; CN 7

McEwan, Ian (Russell) 1948- .... **CLC 13, 66, 169**
See also BEST 90:4; BRWS 4; CA 61-64; CANR 14, 41, 69, 87, 132; CN 7; DAM NOV; DLB 14, 194; HGG; MTCW 1, 2; RGSF 2; SUFW 2; TEA

Moore, Marianne (Craig)
1887-1972 .... CLC 1, 2, 4, 8, 10, 13, 19, 47; PC 4, 49; WLCS
See also AMW; CA 1-4R; 33-36R; CANR 3, 61; CDALB 1929-1941; DA; DA3; DAB; DAC; DAM MST, POET; DLB 45; DLBD 7; EWL 3; EXPP; MAWW; MTCW 1, 2; PAB; PFS 14, 17; RGAL 4; SATA 20; TUS; WP

Moore, Marie Lorena 1957- .... CLC 165
See Moore, Lorrie
See also CA 116; CANR 39, 83; CN 7; DLB 234

Moore, Thomas 1779-1852 .... NCLC 6, 110
See also DLB 96, 144; RGEL 2

Moorhouse, Frank 1938- .... SSC 40
See also CA 118; CANR 92; CN 7; DLB 289; RGSF 2

Mora, Pat(ricia) 1942- .... HLC 2
See also AMWS 13; CA 129; CANR 57, 81, 112; CLR 58; DAM MULT; DLB 209; HW 1, 2; LLW 1; MAICYA 2; SATA 92, 134

Moraga, Cherrie 1952- ...... CLC 126; DC 22
See also CA 131; CANR 66; DAM MULT; DLB 82, 249; FW; GLL 1; HW 1, 2; LLW 1

Morand, Paul 1888-1976 .... CLC 41; SSC 22
See also CA 184; 69-72; DLB 65; EWL 3

Morante, Elsa 1918-1985 .... CLC 8, 47
See also CA 85-88; 117; CANR 35; DLB 177; EWL 3; MTCW 1, 2; RGWL 2, 3

Moravia, Alberto .... CLC 2, 7, 11, 27, 46; SSC 26
See Pincherle, Alberto
See also DLB 177; EW 12; EWL 3; MTCW 2; RGSF 2; RGWL 2, 3

More, Hannah 1745-1833 ...... NCLC 27, 141
See also DLB 107, 109, 116, 158; RGEL 2

More, Henry 1614-1687 .... LC 9
See also DLB 126, 252

More, Sir Thomas 1478(?)-1535 ... LC 10, 32
See also BRWC 1; BRWS 7; DLB 136, 281; LMFS 1; RGEL 2; TEA

Moreas, Jean .... TCLC 18
See Papadiamantopoulos, Johannes
See also GFL 1789 to the Present

Moreton, Andrew Esq.
See Defoe, Daniel

Morgan, Berry 1919-2002 .... CLC 6
See also CA 49-52; 208; DLB 6

Morgan, Claire
See Highsmith, (Mary) Patricia
See also GLL 1

Morgan, Edwin (George) 1920- .... CLC 31
See also BRWS 9; CA 5-8R; CANR 3, 43, 90; CP 7; DLB 27

Morgan, (George) Frederick
1922-2004 .... CLC 23
See also CA 17-20R; 224; CANR 21; CP 7

Morgan, Harriet
See Mencken, H(enry) L(ouis)

Morgan, Jane
See Cooper, James Fenimore

Morgan, Janet 1945- .... CLC 39
See also CA 65-68

Morgan, Lady 1776(?)-1859 .... NCLC 29
See also DLB 116, 158; RGEL 2

Morgan, Robin (Evonne) 1941- .... CLC 2
See also CA 69-72; CANR 29, 68; FW; GLL 1; MTCW 1; SATA 80

Morgan, Scott
See Kuttner, Henry

Morgan, Seth 1949(?)-1990 .... CLC 65
See also CA 185; 132

Morgenstern, Christian (Otto Josef Wolfgang) 1871-1914 .... TCLC 8
See also CA 105; 191; EWL 3

Morgenstern, S.
See Goldman, William (W.)

Mori, Rintaro
See Mori Ogai
See also CA 110

Mori, Toshio 1910-1980 .... SSC 83
See also AAL; CA 116; DLB 312; RGSF 2

Moricz, Zsigmond 1879-1942 .... TCLC 33
See also CA 165; DLB 215; EWL 3

Morike, Eduard (Friedrich)
1804-1875 .... NCLC 10
See also DLB 133; RGWL 2, 3

Mori Ogai 1862-1922 .... TCLC 14
See Ogai
See also CA 164; DLB 180; EWL 3; RGWL 3; TWA

Moritz, Karl Philipp 1756-1793 .... LC 2
See also DLB 94

Morland, Peter Henry
See Faust, Frederick (Schiller)

Morley, Christopher (Darlington)
1890-1957 .... TCLC 87
See also CA 112; 213; DLB 9; RGAL 4

Morren, Theophil
See Hofmannsthal, Hugo von

Morris, Bill 1952- .... CLC 76
See also CA 225

Morris, Julian
See West, Morris L(anglo)

Morris, Steveland Judkins 1950(?)-
See Wonder, Stevie
See also CA 111

Morris, William 1834-1896 . NCLC 4; PC 55
See also BRW 5; CDBLB 1832-1890; DLB 18, 35, 57, 156, 178, 184; FANT; RGEL 2; SFW 4; SUFW

Morris, Wright 1910-1998 .. CLC 1, 3, 7, 18, 37; TCLC 107
See also AMW; CA 9-12R; 167; CANR 21, 81; CN 7; DLB 2, 206, 218; DLBY 1981; EWL 3; MTCW 1, 2; RGAL 4; TCWW 2

Morrison, Arthur 1863-1945 .... SSC 40; TCLC 72
See also CA 120; 157; CMW 4; DLB 70, 135, 197; RGEL 2

Morrison, Chloe Anthony Wofford
See Morrison, Toni

Morrison, James Douglas 1943-1971
See Morrison, Jim
See also CA 73-76; CANR 40

Morrison, Jim .... CLC 17
See Morrison, James Douglas

Morrison, Toni 1931- ..... BLC 3; CLC 4, 10, 22, 55, 81, 87, 173, 194
See also AAYA 1, 22; AFAW 1, 2; AMWC 1; AMWS 3; BPFB 2; BW 2, 3; CA 29-32R; CANR 27, 42, 67, 113, 124; CDALB 1968-1988; CLR 99; CN 7; CPW; DA; DA3; DAB; DAC; DAM MST, MULT, NOV, POP; DLB 6, 33, 143; DLBY 1981; EWL 3; EXPN; FW; LAIT 2, 4; LATS 1:2; LMFS 2; MAWW; MTCW 1, 2; NFS 1, 6, 8, 14; RGAL 4; RHW; SATA 57, 144; SSFS 5; TUS; YAW

Morrison, Van 1945- .... CLC 21
See also CA 116; 168

Morrissy, Mary 1957- .... CLC 99
See also CA 205; DLB 267

Mortimer, John (Clifford) 1923- ..... CLC 28, 43
See also CA 13-16R; CANR 21, 69, 109; CD 5; CDBLB 1960 to Present; CMW 4; CN 7; CPW; DA3; DAM DRAM, POP; DLB 13, 245, 271; INT CANR-21; MSW; MTCW 1, 2; RGEL 2

Mortimer, Penelope (Ruth)
1918-1999 .... CLC 5
See also CA 57-60; 187; CANR 45, 88; CN 7

Mortimer, Sir John
See Mortimer, John (Clifford)

Morton, Anthony
See Creasey, John

Morton, Thomas 1579(?)-1647(?) .... LC 72
See also DLB 24; RGEL 2

Mosca, Gaetano 1858-1941 .... TCLC 75

Moses, Daniel David 1952- .... NNAL
See also CA 186

Mosher, Howard Frank 1943- .... CLC 62
See also CA 139; CANR 65, 115

Mosley, Nicholas 1923- .... CLC 43, 70
See also CA 69-72; CANR 41, 60, 108; CN 7; DLB 14, 207

Mosley, Walter 1952- .... BLCS; CLC 97, 184
See also AAYA 57; AMWS 13; BPFB 2; BW 2; CA 142; CANR 57, 92; CMW 4; CPW; DA3; DAM MULT, POP; DLB 306; MSW; MTCW 2

Moss, Howard 1922-1987 . CLC 7, 14, 45, 50
See also CA 1-4R; 123; CANR 1, 44; DAM POET; DLB 5

Mossgiel, Rab
See Burns, Robert

Motion, Andrew (Peter) 1952- .... CLC 47
See also BRWS 7; CA 146; CANR 90; CP 7; DLB 40

Motley, Willard (Francis)
1909-1965 .... CLC 18
See also BW 1; CA 117; 106; CANR 88; DLB 76, 143

Motoori, Norinaga 1730-1801 .... NCLC 45

Mott, Michael (Charles Alston)
1930- .... CLC 15, 34
See also CA 5-8R; CAAS 7; CANR 7, 29

Mountain Wolf Woman 1884-1960 . CLC 92; NNAL
See also CA 144; CANR 90

Moure, Erin 1955- .... CLC 88
See also CA 113; CP 7; CWP; DLB 60

Mourning Dove 1885(?)-1936 .... NNAL
See also CA 144; CANR 90; DAM MULT; DLB 175, 221

Mowat, Farley (McGill) 1921- .... CLC 26
See also AAYA 1, 50; BYA 2; CA 1-4R; CANR 4, 24, 42, 68, 108; CLR 20; CPW; DAC; DAM MST; DLB 68; INT CANR-24; JRDA; MAICYA 1, 2; MTCW 1, 2; SATA 3, 55; YAW

Mowatt, Anna Cora 1819-1870 ..... NCLC 74
See also RGAL 4

Moyers, Bill 1934- .... CLC 74
See also AITN 2; CA 61-64; CANR 31, 52

Mphahlele, Es'kia
See Mphahlele, Ezekiel
See also AFW; CDWLB 3; DLB 125, 225; RGSF 2; SSFS 11

Mphahlele, Ezekiel 1919- ... BLC 3; CLC 25, 133
See Mphahlele, Es'kia
See also BW 2, 3; CA 81-84; CANR 26, 76; CN 7; DA3; DAM MULT; EWL 3; MTCW 2; SATA 119

Mqhayi, S(amuel) E(dward) K(rune Loliwe)
1875-1945 .... BLC 3; TCLC 25
See also CA 153; CANR 87; DAM MULT

Mrozek, Slawomir 1930- .... CLC 3, 13
See also CA 13-16R; CAAS 10; CANR 29; CDWLB 4; CWW 2; DLB 232; EWL 3; MTCW 1

Mrs. Belloc-Lowndes
See Lowndes, Marie Adelaide (Belloc)

Mrs. Fairstar
See Horne, Richard Henry Hengist

M'Taggart, John M'Taggart Ellis
See McTaggart, John McTaggart Ellis

MST, MULT, NOV, POP; DLB 173; EWL
3; FW; MTCW 1, 2; NFS 4, 7; RGAL 4;
TUS

Neff, Debra .... **CLC 59**

Neihardt, John Gneisenau
1881-1973 .... **CLC 32**
See also CA 13-14; CANR 65; CAP 1; DLB
9, 54, 256; LAIT 2

Nekrasov, Nikolai Alekseevich
1821-1878 .... **NCLC 11**
See also DLB 277

Nelligan, Emile 1879-1941 .... **TCLC 14**
See also CA 114; 204; DLB 92; EWL 3

Nelson, Willie 1933- .... **CLC 17**
See also CA 107; CANR 114

Nemerov, Howard (Stanley)
1920-1991 .... **CLC 2, 6, 9, 36; PC 24;
TCLC 124**
See also AMW; CA 1-4R; 134; CABS 2;
CANR 1, 27, 53; DAM POET; DLB 5, 6;
DLBY 1983; EWL 3; INT CANR-27;
MTCW 1, 2; PFS 10, 14; RGAL 4

Neruda, Pablo 1904-1973 .. **CLC 1, 2, 5, 7, 9,
28, 62; HLC 2; PC 4, 64; WLC**
See also CA 19-20; 45-48; CANR 131; CAP
2; DA; DA3; DAB; DAC; DAM MST,
MULT, POET; DLB 283; DNFS 2; EWL
3; HW 1; LAW; MTCW 1, 2; PFS 11;
RGWL 2, 3; TWA; WLIT 1; WP

Nerval, Gerard de 1808-1855 ... **NCLC 1, 67;
PC 13; SSC 18**
See also DLB 217; EW 6; GFL 1789 to the
Present; RGSF 2; RGWL 2, 3

Nervo, (Jose) Amado (Ruiz de)
1870-1919 .... **HLCS 2; TCLC 11**
See also CA 109; 131; DLB 290; EWL 3;
HW 1; LAW

Nesbit, Malcolm
See Chester, Alfred

Nessi, Pio Baroja y
See Baroja (y Nessi), Pio

Nestroy, Johann 1801-1862 .... **NCLC 42**
See also DLB 133; RGWL 2, 3

Netterville, Luke
See O'Grady, Standish (James)

Neufeld, John (Arthur) 1938- .... **CLC 17**
See also AAYA 11; CA 25-28R; CANR 11,
37, 56; CLR 52; JRDA; MAICYA 1, 2; SAAS 3;
SATA 6, 81, 131; SATA-Essay 131; YAW

Neumann, Alfred 1895-1952 .... **TCLC 100**
See also CA 183; DLB 56

Neumann, Ferenc
See Molnar, Ferenc

Neville, Emily Cheney 1919- .... **CLC 12**
See also BYA 2; CA 5-8R; CANR 3, 37,
85; JRDA; MAICYA 1, 2; SAAS 2; SATA
1; YAW

Newbound, Bernard Slade 1930-
See Slade, Bernard
See also CA 81-84; CANR 49; CD 5; DAM
DRAM

Newby, P(ercy) H(oward)
1918-1997 .... **CLC 2, 13**
See also CA 5-8R; 161; CANR 32, 67; CN
7; DAM NOV; DLB 15; MTCW 1; RGEL
2

Newcastle
See Cavendish, Margaret Lucas

Newlove, Donald 1928- .... **CLC 6**
See also CA 29-32R; CANR 25

Newlove, John (Herbert) 1938- .... **CLC 14**
See also CA 21-24R; CANR 9, 25; CP 7

Newman, Charles 1938- .... **CLC 2, 8**
See also CA 21-24R; CANR 84; CN 7

Newman, Edwin (Harold) 1919- ...... **CLC 14**
See also AITN 1; CA 69-72; CANR 5

Newman, John Henry 1801-1890 . **NCLC 38,
99**
See also BRWS 7; DLB 18, 32, 55; RGEL
2

Newton, (Sir) Isaac 1642-1727 ...... **LC 35, 53**
See also DLB 252

Newton, Suzanne 1936- .... **CLC 35**
See also BYA 7; CA 41-44R; CANR 14;
JRDA; SATA 5, 77

New York Dept. of Ed. .... **CLC 70**

Nexo, Martin Andersen
1869-1954 .... **TCLC 43**
See also CA 202; DLB 214; EWL 3

Nezval, Vitezslav 1900-1958 .... **TCLC 44**
See also CA 123; CDWLB 4; DLB 215;
EWL 3

Ng, Fae Myenne 1957(?)- .... **CLC 81**
See also BYA 11; CA 146

Ngema, Mbongeni 1955- .... **CLC 57**
See also BW 2; CA 143; CANR 84; CD 5

Ngugi, James T(hiong'o) . **CLC 3, 7, 13, 182**
See Ngugi wa Thiong'o

Ngugi wa Thiong'o
See Ngugi wa Thiong'o
See also DLB 125; EWL 3

Ngugi wa Thiong'o 1938- ... **BLC 3; CLC 36,
182**
See Ngugi, James T(hiong'o); Ngugi wa
Thiong'o
See also AFW; BRWS 8; BW 2; CA 81-84;
CANR 27, 58; CDWLB 3; DAM MULT,
NOV; DNFS 2; MTCW 1, 2; RGEL 2;
WWE 1

Niatum, Duane 1938- .... **NNAL**
See also CA 41-44R; CANR 21, 45, 83;
DLB 175

Nichol, B(arrie) P(hillip) 1944-1988 . **CLC 18**
See also CA 53-56; DLB 53; SATA 66

Nicholas of Cusa 1401-1464 .... **LC 80**
See also DLB 115

Nichols, John (Treadwell) 1940- ...... **CLC 38**
See also AMWS 13; CA 9-12R, 190; CAAE
190; CAAS 2; CANR 6, 70, 121; DLBY
1982; LATS 1:2; TCWW 2

Nichols, Leigh
See Koontz, Dean R(ay)

Nichols, Peter (Richard) 1927- .... **CLC 5, 36,
65**
See also CA 104; CANR 33, 86; CBD; CD
5; DLB 13, 245; MTCW 1

Nicholson, Linda ed. .... **CLC 65**

Ni Chuilleanain, Eilean 1942- .... **PC 34**
See also CA 126; CANR 53, 83; CP 7;
CWP; DLB 40

Nicolas, F. R. E.
See Freeling, Nicolas

Niedecker, Lorine 1903-1970 ..... **CLC 10, 42;
PC 42**
See also CA 25-28; CAP 2; DAM POET;
DLB 48

Nietzsche, Friedrich (Wilhelm)
1844-1900 .... **TCLC 10, 18, 55**
See also CA 107; 121; CDWLB 2; DLB
129; EW 7; RGWL 2, 3; TWA

Nievo, Ippolito 1831-1861 .... **NCLC 22**

Nightingale, Anne Redmon 1943-
See Redmon, Anne
See also CA 103

Nightingale, Florence 1820-1910 ... **TCLC 85**
See also CA 188; DLB 166

Nijo Yoshimoto 1320-1388 .... **CMLC 49**
See also DLB 203

Nik. T. O.
See Annensky, Innokenty (Fyodorovich)

Nin, Anais 1903-1977 ..... **CLC 1, 4, 8, 11, 14,
60, 127; SSC 10**
See also AITN 2; AMWS 10; BPFB 2; CA
13-16R; 69-72; CANR 22, 53; DAM
NOV, POP; DLB 2, 4, 152; EWL 3; GLL
2; MAWW; MTCW 1, 2; RGAL 4; RGSF
2

Nisbet, Robert A(lexander)
1913-1996 .... **TCLC 117**
See also CA 25-28R; 153; CANR 17; INT
CANR-17

Nishida, Kitaro 1870-1945 .... **TCLC 83**

Nishiwaki, Junzaburo
See Nishiwaki, Junzaburo
See also CA 194

Nishiwaki, Junzaburo 1894-1982 .... **PC 15**
See Nishiwaki, Junzaburo; Nishiwaki
Junzaburo
See also CA 194; 107; MJW; RGWL 3

Nishiwaki Junzaburo
See Nishiwaki, Junzaburo
See also EWL 3

Nissenson, Hugh 1933- .... **CLC 4, 9**
See also CA 17-20R; CANR 27, 108; CN
7; DLB 28

Nister, Der
See Der Nister
See also EWL 3

Niven, Larry .... **CLC 8**
See Niven, Laurence Van Cott
See also AAYA 27; BPFB 2; BYA 10; DLB
8; SCFW 2

Niven, Laurence Van Cott 1938-
See Niven, Larry
See also CA 21-24R, 207; CAAE 207;
CAAS 12; CANR 14, 44, 66, 113; CPW;
DAM POP; MTCW 1, 2; SATA 95; SFW
4

Nixon, Agnes Eckhardt 1927- .... **CLC 21**
See also CA 110

Nizan, Paul 1905-1940 .... **TCLC 40**
See also CA 161; DLB 72; EWL 3; GFL
1789 to the Present

Nkosi, Lewis 1936- .... **BLC 3; CLC 45**
See also BW 1, 3; CA 65-68; CANR 27,
81; CBD; CD 5; DAM MULT; DLB 157,
225; WWE 1

Nodier, (Jean) Charles (Emmanuel)
1780-1844 .... **NCLC 19**
See also DLB 119; GFL 1789 to the Present

Noguchi, Yone 1875-1947 .... **TCLC 80**

Nolan, Christopher 1965- .... **CLC 58**
See also CA 111; CANR 88

Noon, Jeff 1957- .... **CLC 91**
See also CA 148; CANR 83; DLB 267;
SFW 4

Norden, Charles
See Durrell, Lawrence (George)

Nordhoff, Charles Bernard
1887-1947 .... **TCLC 23**
See also CA 108; 211; DLB 9; LAIT 1;
RHW 1; SATA 23

Norfolk, Lawrence 1963- .... **CLC 76**
See also CA 144; CANR 85; CN 7; DLB
267

Norman, Marsha 1947- . **CLC 28, 186; DC 8**
See also CA 105; CABS 3; CAD; CANR
41, 131; CD 5; CSW; CWD; DAM
DRAM; DFS 2; DLB 266; DLBY 1984;
FW

Normyx
See Douglas, (George) Norman

Norris, (Benjamin) Frank(lin, Jr.)
1870-1902 .... **SSC 28; TCLC 24, 155**
See also AAYA 57; AMW; AMWC 2; BPFB
2; CA 110; 160; CDALB 1865-1917; DLB
12, 71, 186; LMFS 2; NFS 12; RGAL 4;
TCWW 2; TUS

Okri, Ben 1959- .... **CLC 87**
See also AFW; BRWS 5; BW 2, 3; CA 130;
138; CANR 65, 128; CN 7; DLB 157,
231; EWL 3; INT CA-138; MTCW 2;
RGSF 2; SSFS 20; WLIT 2; WWE 1

Olds, Sharon 1942- .. **CLC 32, 39, 85; PC 22**
See also AMWS 10; CA 101; CANR 18,
41, 66, 98, 135; CP 7; CPW; CWP; DAM
POET; DLB 120; MTCW 2; PFS 17

Oldstyle, Jonathan
See Irving, Washington

Olesha, Iurii
See Olesha, Yuri (Karlovich)
See also RGWL 2

Olesha, Iurii Karlovich
See Olesha, Yuri (Karlovich)
See also DLB 272

Olesha, Yuri (Karlovich) 1899-1960 . **CLC 8;**
SSC 69; TCLC 136
See Olesha, Iurii; Olesha, Iurii Karlovich;
Olesha, Yury Karlovich
See also CA 85-88; EW 11; RGWL 3

Olesha, Yury Karlovich
See Olesha, Yuri (Karlovich)
See also EWL 3

Oliphant, Mrs.
See Oliphant, Margaret (Oliphant Wilson)
See also SUFW

Oliphant, Laurence 1829(?)-1888 .. **NCLC 47**
See also DLB 18, 166

Oliphant, Margaret (Oliphant Wilson)
1828-1897 .... **NCLC 11, 61; SSC 25**
See Oliphant, Mrs.
See also BRWS 10; DLB 18, 159, 190;
HGG; RGEL 2; RGSF 2

Oliver, Mary 1935- .... **CLC 19, 34, 98**
See also AMWS 7; CA 21-24R; CANR 9,
43, 84, 92; CP 7; CWP; DLB 5, 193;
EWL 3; PFS 15

Olivier, Laurence (Kerr) 1907-1989 . **CLC 20**
See also CA 111; 150; 129

Olsen, Tillie 1912- ... **CLC 4, 13, 114; SSC 11**
See also AAYA 51; AMWS 13; BYA 11;
CA 1-4R; CANR 1, 43, 74, 132;
CDALBS; CN 7; DA; DA3; DAB; DAC;
DAM MST; DLB 28, 206; DLBY 1980;
EWL 3; EXPS; FW; MTCW 1, 2; RGAL
4; RGSF 2; SSFS 1; TUS

Olson, Charles (John) 1910-1970 .. **CLC 1, 2,**
5, 6, 9, 11, 29; PC 19
See also AMWS 2; CA 13-16; 25-28R;
CABS 2; CANR 35, 61; CAP 1; DAM
POET; DLB 5, 16, 193; EWL 3; MTCW
1, 2; RGAL 4; WP

Olson, Toby 1937- .... **CLC 28**
See also CA 65-68; CANR 9, 31, 84; CP 7

Olyesha, Yuri
See Olesha, Yuri (Karlovich)

Olympiodorus of Thebes c. 375-c.
430 .... **CMLC 59**

Omar Khayyam
See Khayyam, Omar
See also RGWL 2, 3

Ondaatje, (Philip) Michael 1943- .... **CLC 14,**
29, 51, 76, 180; PC 28
See also CA 77-80; CANR 42, 74, 109, 133;
CN 7; CP 7; DA3; DAB; DAC; DAM
MST; DLB 60; EWL 3; LATS 1:2; LMFS
2; MTCW 2; PFS 8, 19; TWA; WWE 1

Oneal, Elizabeth 1934-
See Oneal, Zibby
See also CA 106; CANR 28, 84; MAICYA
1, 2; SATA 30, 82; YAW

Oneal, Zibby .... **CLC 30**
See Oneal, Elizabeth
See also AAYA 5, 41; BYA 13; CLR 13;
JRDA; WYA

O'Neill, Eugene (Gladstone)
1888-1953 ... **DC 20; TCLC 1, 6, 27, 49;**
WLC
See also AAYA 54; AITN 1; AMW; AMWC
1; CA 110; 132; CAD; CANR 131;
CDALB 1929-1941; DA; DA3; DAB;
DAC; DAM DRAM, MST; DFS 2, 4, 5,
6, 9, 11, 12, 16, 20; DLB 7; EWL 3; LAIT
3; LMFS 2; MTCW 1, 2; RGAL 4; TUS

Onetti, Juan Carlos 1909-1994 ... **CLC 7, 10;**
HLCS 2; SSC 23; TCLC 131
See also CA 85-88; 145; CANR 32, 63; CD-
WLB 3; CWW 2; DAM MULT, NOV;
DLB 113; EWL 3; HW 1, 2; LAW;
MTCW 1, 2; RGSF 2

O Nuallain, Brian 1911-1966
See O'Brien, Flann
See also CA 21-22; 25-28R; CAP 2; DLB
231; FANT; TEA

Ophuls, Max 1902-1957 .... **TCLC 79**
See also CA 113

Opie, Amelia 1769-1853 .... **NCLC 65**
See also DLB 116, 159; RGEL 2

Oppen, George 1908-1984 ..... **CLC 7, 13, 34;**
PC 35; TCLC 107
See also CA 13-16R; 113; CANR 8, 82;
DLB 5, 165

Oppenheim, E(dward) Phillips
1866-1946 .... **TCLC 45**
See also CA 111; 202; CMW 4; DLB 70

Opuls, Max
See Ophuls, Max

Orage, A(lfred) R(ichard)
1873-1934 .... **TCLC 157**
See also CA 122

Origen c. 185-c. 254 .... **CMLC 19**

Orlovitz, Gil 1918-1973 .... **CLC 22**
See also CA 77-80; 45-48; DLB 2, 5

O'Rourke, P(atrick) J(ake) 1947- .. **CLC 209**
See also CA 77-80; CANR 13, 41, 67, 111;
CPW; DLB 185; DAM POP

Orris
See Ingelow, Jean

Ortega y Gasset, Jose 1883-1955 ...... **HLC 2;**
TCLC 9
See also CA 106; 130; DAM MULT; EW 9;
EWL 3; HW 1, 2; MTCW 1, 2

Ortese, Anna Maria 1914-1998 .... **CLC 89**
See also DLB 177; EWL 3

Ortiz, Simon J(oseph) 1941- ... **CLC 45, 208;**
NNAL; PC 17
See also AMWS 4; CA 134; CANR 69, 118;
CP 7; DAM MULT, POET; DLB 120,
175, 256; EXPP; PFS 4, 16; RGAL 4

Orton, Joe ...... **CLC 4, 13, 43; DC 3; TCLC**
157
See Orton, John Kingsley
See also BRWS 5; CBD; CDBLB 1960 to
Present; DFS 3, 6; DLB 13; GLL 1;
MTCW 2; RGEL 2; TEA; WLIT 4

Orton, John Kingsley 1933-1967
See Orton, Joe
See also CA 85-88; CANR 35, 66; DAM
DRAM; MTCW 1, 2

Orwell, George ...... **SSC 68; TCLC 2, 6, 15,**
31, 51, 128, 129; WLC
See Blair, Eric (Arthur)
See also BPFB 3; BRW 7; BYA 5; CDBLB
1945-1960; CLR 68; DAB; DLB 15, 98,
195, 255; EWL 3; EXPN; LAIT 4, 5;
LATS 1:1; NFS 3, 7; RGEL 2; SCFW 2;
SFW 4; SSFS 4; TEA; WLIT 4; YAW

Osborne, David
See Silverberg, Robert

Osborne, George
See Silverberg, Robert

Osborne, John (James) 1929-1994 .... **CLC 1,**
2, 5, 11, 45; TCLC 153; WLC
See also BRWS 1; CA 13-16R; 147; CANR
21, 56; CDBLB 1945-1960; DA; DAB;
DAC; DAM DRAM, MST; DFS 4, 19;
DLB 13; EWL 3; MTCW 1, 2; RGEL 2

Osborne, Lawrence 1958- .... **CLC 50**
See also CA 189

Osbourne, Lloyd 1868-1947 .... **TCLC 93**

Osgood, Frances Sargent
1811-1850 .... **NCLC 141**
See also DLB 250

Oshima, Nagisa 1932- .... **CLC 20**
See also CA 116; 121; CANR 78

Oskison, John Milton
1874-1947 .... **NNAL; TCLC 35**
See also CA 144; CANR 84; DAM MULT;
DLB 175

Ossian c. 3rd cent. - .... **CMLC 28**
See Macpherson, James

Ossoli, Sarah Margaret (Fuller)
1810-1850 .... **NCLC 5, 50**
See Fuller, Margaret; Fuller, Sarah Margaret
See also CDALB 1640-1865; FW; LMFS 1;
SATA 25

Ostriker, Alicia (Suskin) 1937- .... **CLC 132**
See also CA 25-28R; CAAS 24; CANR 10,
30, 62, 99; CWP; DLB 120; EXPP; PFS
19

Ostrovsky, Aleksandr Nikolaevich
See Ostrovsky, Alexander
See also DLB 277

Ostrovsky, Alexander 1823-1886 .. **NCLC 30,**
57
See Ostrovsky, Aleksandr Nikolaevich

Otero, Blas de 1916-1979 .... **CLC 11**
See also CA 89-92; DLB 134; EWL 3

O'Trigger, Sir Lucius
See Horne, Richard Henry Hengist

Otto, Rudolf 1869-1937 .... **TCLC 85**

Otto, Whitney 1955- .... **CLC 70**
See also CA 140; CANR 120

Otway, Thomas 1652-1685 ... **DC 24; LC 106**
See also DAM DRAM; DLB 80; RGEL 2

Ouida .... **TCLC 43**
See De la Ramee, Marie Louise (Ouida)
See also DLB 18, 156; RGEL 2

Ouologuem, Yambo 1940- .... **CLC 146**
See also CA 111; 176

Ousmane, Sembene 1923- ... **BLC 3; CLC 66**
See Sembene, Ousmane
See also BW 1, 3; CA 117; 125; CANR 81;
CWW 2; MTCW 1

Ovid 43B.C.-17 .... **CMLC 7; PC 2**
See also AW 2; CDWLB 1; DA3; DAM
POET; DLB 211; RGWL 2, 3; WP

Owen, Hugh
See Faust, Frederick (Schiller)

Owen, Wilfred (Edward Salter)
1893-1918 ... **PC 19; TCLC 5, 27; WLC**
See also BRW 6; CA 104; 141; CDBLB
1914-1945; DA; DAB; DAC; DAM MST,
POET; DLB 20; EWL 3; EXPP; MTCW
2; PFS 10; RGEL 2; WLIT 4

Owens, Louis (Dean) 1948-2002 .... **NNAL**
See also CA 137, 179; 207; CAAE 179;
CAAS 24; CANR 71

Owens, Rochelle 1936- .... **CLC 8**
See also CA 17-20R; CAAS 2; CAD;
CANR 39; CD 5; CP 7; CWD; CWP

Oz, Amos 1939- ...... **CLC 5, 8, 11, 27, 33, 54;**
SSC 66
See also CA 53-56; CANR 27, 47, 65, 113;
CWW 2; DAM NOV; EWL 3; MTCW 1,
2; RGSF 2; RGWL 3

Paterson, A(ndrew) B(arton)
 1864-1941 .... **TCLC 32**
 See also CA 155; DLB 230; RGEL 2; SATA
 97

Paterson, Banjo
 See Paterson, A(ndrew) B(arton)

Paterson, Katherine (Womeldorf)
 1932- .... **CLC 12, 30**
 See also AAYA 1, 31; BYA 1, 2, 7; CA 21-
 24R; CANR 28, 59, 111; CLR 7, 50;
 CWRI 5; DLB 52; JRDA; LAIT 4; MAI-
 CYA 1, 2; MAICYAS 1; MTCW 1; SATA
 13, 53, 92, 133; WYA; YAW

Patmore, Coventry Kersey Dighton
 1823-1896 .... **NCLC 9; PC 59**
 See also DLB 35, 98; RGEL 2; TEA

Paton, Alan (Stewart) 1903-1988 ...... **CLC 4,**
 10, 25, 55, 106; TCLC 165; WLC
 See also AAYA 26; AFW; BPFB 3; BRWS
 2; BYA 1; CA 13-16; 125; CANR 22;
 CAP 1; DA; DA3; DAB; DAC; DAM
 MST, NOV; DLB 225; DLBD 17; EWL
 3; EXPN; LAIT 4; MTCW 1, 2; NFS 3,
 12; RGEL 2; SATA 11; SATA-Obit 56;
 TWA; WLIT 2; WWE 1

Paton Walsh, Gillian 1937- .... **CLC 35**
 See Paton Walsh, Jill; Walsh, Jill Paton
 See also AAYA 11; CANR 38, 83; CLR 2,
 65; DLB 161; JRDA; MAICYA 1, 2;
 SAAS 3; SATA 4, 72, 109; YAW

Paton Walsh, Jill
 See Paton Walsh, Gillian
 See also AAYA 47; BYA 1, 8

Patterson, (Horace) Orlando (Lloyd)
 1940- .... **BLCS**
 See also BW 1; CA 65-68; CANR 27, 84;
 CN 7

Patton, George S(mith), Jr.
 1885-1945 .... **TCLC 79**
 See also CA 189

Paulding, James Kirke 1778-1860 ... **NCLC 2**
 See also DLB 3, 59, 74, 250; RGAL 4

Paulin, Thomas Neilson 1949-
 See Paulin, Tom
 See also CA 123; 128; CANR 98; CP 7

Paulin, Tom .... **CLC 37, 177**
 See Paulin, Thomas Neilson
 See also DLB 40

Pausanias c. 1st cent. - .... **CMLC 36**

Paustovsky, Konstantin (Georgievich)
 1892-1968 .... **CLC 40**
 See also CA 93-96; 25-28R; DLB 272;
 EWL 3

Pavese, Cesare 1908-1950 .... **PC 13; SSC 19;**
 TCLC 3
 See also CA 104; 169; DLB 128, 177; EW
 12; EWL 3; PFS 20; RGSF 2; RGWL 2,
 3; TWA

Pavic, Milorad 1929- .... **CLC 60**
 See also CA 136; CDWLB 4; CWW 2; DLB
 181; EWL 3; RGWL 3

Pavlov, Ivan Petrovich 1849-1936 . **TCLC 91**
 See also CA 118; 180

Pavlova, Karolina Karlovna
 1807-1893 .... **NCLC 138**
 See also DLB 205

Payne, Alan
 See Jakes, John (William)

Paz, Gil
 See Lugones, Leopoldo

Paz, Octavio 1914-1998 . **CLC 3, 4, 6, 10, 19,**
 51, 65, 119; HLC 2; PC 1, 48; WLC
 See also AAYA 50; CA 73-76; 165; CANR
 32, 65, 104; CWW 2; DA; DA3; DAB;
 DAC; DAM MST, MULT, POET; DLB
 290; DLBY 1990, 1998; DNFS 1; EWL
 3; HW 1, 2; LAW; LAWS 1; MTCW 1, 2;
 PFS 18; RGWL 2, 3; SSFS 13; TWA;
 WLIT 1

p'Bitek, Okot 1931-1982 .... **BLC 3; CLC 96;**
 TCLC 149
 See also AFW; BW 2, 3; CA 124; 107;
 CANR 82; DAM MULT; DLB 125; EWL
 3; MTCW 1, 2; RGEL 2; WLIT 2

Peacock, Molly 1947- .... **CLC 60**
 See also CA 103; CAAS 21; CANR 52, 84;
 CP 7; CWP; DLB 120, 282

Peacock, Thomas Love
 1785-1866 .... **NCLC 22**
 See also BRW 4; DLB 96, 116; RGEL 2;
 RGSF 2

Peake, Mervyn 1911-1968 .... **CLC 7, 54**
 See also CA 5-8R; 25-28R; CANR 3; DLB
 15, 160, 255; FANT; MTCW 1; RGEL 2;
 SATA 23; SFW 4

Pearce, Philippa
 See Christie, Philippa
 See also CA 5-8R; CANR 4, 109; CWRI 5;
 FANT; MAICYA 2

Pearl, Eric
 See Elman, Richard (Martin)

Pearson, T(homas) R(eid) 1956- .... **CLC 39**
 See also CA 120; 130; CANR 97; CSW;
 INT CA-130

Peck, Dale 1967- .... **CLC 81**
 See also CA 146; CANR 72, 127; GLL 2

Peck, John (Frederick) 1941- .... **CLC 3**
 See also CA 49-52; CANR 3, 100; CP 7

Peck, Richard (Wayne) 1934- .... **CLC 21**
 See also AAYA 1, 24; BYA 1, 6, 8, 11; CA
 85-88; CANR 19, 38, 129; CLR 15; INT
 CANR-19; JRDA; MAICYA 1, 2; SAAS
 2; SATA 18, 55, 97; SATA-Essay 110;
 WYA; YAW

Peck, Robert Newton 1928- .... **CLC 17**
 See also AAYA 3, 43; BYA 1, 6; CA 81-84,
 182; CAAE 182; CANR 31, 63, 127; CLR
 45; DA; DAC; DAM MST; JRDA; LAIT
 3; MAICYA 1, 2; SAAS 1; SATA 21, 62,
 111; SATA-Essay 108; WYA; YAW

Peckinpah, (David) Sam(uel)
 1925-1984 .... **CLC 20**
 See also CA 109; 114; CANR 82

Pedersen, Knut 1859-1952
 See Hamsun, Knut
 See also CA 104; 119; CANR 63; MTCW
 1, 2

Peele, George .... **LC 115**
 See also BW 1; DLB 62, 167; RGEL 2

Peeslake, Gaffer
 See Durrell, Lawrence (George)

Peguy, Charles (Pierre)
 1873-1914 .... **TCLC 10**
 See also CA 107; 193; DLB 258; EWL 3;
 GFL 1789 to the Present

Peirce, Charles Sanders
 1839-1914 .... **TCLC 81**
 See also CA 194; DLB 270

Pellicer, Carlos 1897(?)-1977 .... **HLCS 2**
 See also CA 153; 69-72; DLB 290; EWL 3;
 HW 1

Pena, Ramon del Valle y
 See Valle-Inclan, Ramon (Maria) del

Pendennis, Arthur Esquir
 See Thackeray, William Makepeace

Penn, Arthur
 See Matthews, (James) Brander

Penn, William 1644-1718 .... **LC 25**
 See also DLB 24

PEPECE
 See Prado (Calvo), Pedro

Pepys, Samuel 1633-1703 ... **LC 11, 58; WLC**
 See also BRW 2; CDBLB 1660-1789; DA;
 DA3; DAB; DAC; DAM MST; DLB 101,
 213; NCFS 4; RGEL 2; TEA; WLIT 3

Percy, Thomas 1729-1811 .... **NCLC 95**
 See also DLB 104

Percy, Walker 1916-1990 .... **CLC 2, 3, 6, 8,**
 14, 18, 47, 65
 See also AMWS 3; BPFB 3; CA 1-4R; 131;
 CANR 1, 23, 64; CPW; CSW; DA3;
 DAM NOV, POP; DLB 2; DLBY 1980,
 1990; EWL 3; MTCW 1, 2; RGAL 4;
 TUS

Percy, William Alexander
 1885-1942 .... **TCLC 84**
 See also CA 163; MTCW 2

Perec, Georges 1936-1982 .... **CLC 56, 116**
 See also CA 141; DLB 83, 299; EWL 3;
 GFL 1789 to the Present; RGWL 3

Pereda (y Sanchez de Porrua), Jose Maria
 de 1833-1906 .... **TCLC 16**
 See also CA 117

Pereda y Porrua, Jose Maria de
 See Pereda (y Sanchez de Porrua), Jose
 Maria de

Peregoy, George Weems
 See Mencken, H(enry) L(ouis)

Perelman, S(idney) J(oseph)
 1904-1979 .. **CLC 3, 5, 9, 15, 23, 44, 49;**
 SSC 32
 See also AITN 1, 2; BPFB 3; CA 73-76;
 89-92; CANR 18; DAM DRAM; DLB 11,
 44; MTCW 1, 2; RGAL 4

Peret, Benjamin 1899-1959 .... **PC 33; TCLC**
 20
 See also CA 117; 186; GFL 1789 to the
 Present

Peretz, Isaac Leib
 See Peretz, Isaac Loeb
 See also CA 201

Peretz, Isaac Loeb 1851(?)-1915 ...... **SSC 26;**
 TCLC 16
 See Peretz, Isaac Leib
 See also CA 109

Peretz, Yitzkhok Leibush
 See Peretz, Isaac Loeb

Perez Galdos, Benito 1843-1920 ..... **HLCS 2;**
 TCLC 27
 See Galdos, Benito Perez
 See also CA 125; 153; EWL 3; HW 1;
 RGWL 2, 3

Peri Rossi, Cristina 1941- .. **CLC 156; HLCS**
 2
 See also CA 131; CANR 59, 81; CWW 2;
 DLB 145, 290; EWL 3; HW 1, 2

Perlata
 See Peret, Benjamin

Perloff, Marjorie G(abrielle)
 1931- .... **CLC 137**
 See also CA 57-60; CANR 7, 22, 49, 104

Perrault, Charles 1628-1703 .... **LC 2, 56**
 See also BYA 4; CLR 79; DLB 268; GFL
 Beginnings to 1789; MAICYA 1, 2;
 RGWL 2, 3; SATA 25; WCH

Perry, Anne 1938- .... **CLC 126**
 See also CA 101; CANR 22, 50, 84; CMW
 4; CN 7; CPW; DLB 276

Perry, Brighton
 See Sherwood, Robert E(mmet)

Perse, St.-John
 See Leger, (Marie-Rene Auguste) Alexis
 Saint-Leger

Perse, Saint-John
 See Leger, (Marie-Rene Auguste) Alexis
 Saint-Leger
 See also DLB 258; RGWL 3

Persius 34-62 .... **CMLC 74**
 See also AW 2; DLB 211; RGWL 2, 3

Perutz, Leo(pold) 1882-1957 .... **TCLC 60**
 See also CA 147; DLB 81

Peseenz, Tulio F.
 See Lopez y Fuentes, Gregorio

Pesetsky, Bette 1932- .... **CLC 28**
 See also CA 133; DLB 130

Prager, Emily 1952- .... **CLC 56**
See also CA 204
Pratchett, Terry 1948- .... **CLC 197**
See also AAYA 19, 54; BPFB 3; CA 143;
CANR 87, 126; CLR 64; CN 7; CPW;
CWRI 5; FANT; SATA 82, 139; SFW 4;
SUFW 2
Pratolini, Vasco 1913-1991 .... **TCLC 124**
See also CA 211; DLB 177; EWL 3; RGWL
2, 3
Pratt, E(dwin) J(ohn) 1883(?)-1964 . **CLC 19**
See also CA 141; 93-96; CANR 77; DAC;
DAM POET; DLB 92; EWL 3; RGEL 2;
TWA
Premchand .... **TCLC 21**
See Srivastava, Dhanpat Rai
See also EWL 3
Preseren, France 1800-1849 .... **NCLC 127**
See also CDWLB 4; DLB 147
Preussler, Otfried 1923- .... **CLC 17**
See also CA 77-80; SATA 24
Prevert, Jacques (Henri Marie)
1900-1977 .... **CLC 15**
See also CA 77-80; 69-72; CANR 29, 61;
DLB 258; EWL 3; GFL 1789 to the
Present; IDFW 3, 4; MTCW 1; RGWL 2,
3; SATA-Obit 30
Prevost, (Antoine Francois)
1697-1763 .... **LC 1**
See also EW 4; GFL Beginnings to 1789;
RGWL 2, 3
Price, (Edward) Reynolds 1933- ... **CLC 3, 6,**
13, 43, 50, 63; SSC 22
See also AMWS 6; CA 1-4R; CANR 1, 37,
57, 87, 128; CN 7; CSW; DAM NOV;
DLB 2, 218, 278; EWL 3; INT CANR-
37; NFS 18
Price, Richard 1949- .... **CLC 6, 12**
See also CA 49-52; CANR 3; DLBY 1981
Prichard, Katharine Susannah
1883-1969 .... **CLC 46**
See also CA 11-12; CANR 33; CAP 1; DLB
260; MTCW 1; RGEL 2; RGSF 2; SATA
66
Priestley, J(ohn) B(oynton)
1894-1984 .... **CLC 2, 5, 9, 34**
See also BRW 7; CA 9-12R; 113; CANR
33; CDBLB 1914-1945; DA3; DAM
DRAM, NOV; DLB 10, 34, 77, 100, 139;
DLBY 1984; EWL 3; MTCW 1, 2; RGEL
2; SFW 4
Prince 1958- .... **CLC 35**
See also CA 213
Prince, F(rank) T(empleton)
1912-2003 .... **CLC 22**
See also CA 101; 219; CANR 43, 79; CP 7;
DLB 20
Prince Kropotkin
See Kropotkin, Peter (Aleksieevich)
Prior, Matthew 1664-1721 .... **LC 4**
See also DLB 95; RGEL 2
Prishvin, Mikhail 1873-1954 .... **TCLC 75**
See Prishvin, Mikhail Mikhailovich
Prishvin, Mikhail Mikhailovich
See Prishvin, Mikhail
See also DLB 272; EWL 3
Pritchard, William H(arrison)
1932- .... **CLC 34**
See also CA 65-68; CANR 23, 95; DLB
111
Pritchett, V(ictor) S(awdon)
1900-1997 ... **CLC 5, 13, 15, 41; SSC 14**
See also BPFB 3; BRWS 3; CA 61-64; 157;
CANR 31, 63; CN 7; DA3; DAM NOV;
DLB 15, 139; EWL 3; MTCW 1, 2;
RGEL 2; RGSF 2; TEA
Private 19022
See Manning, Frederic

Probst, Mark 1925- .... **CLC 59**
See also CA 130
Prokosch, Frederic 1908-1989 ...... **CLC 4, 48**
See also CA 73-76; 128; CANR 82; DLB
48; MTCW 2
Propertius, Sextus c. 50B.C.-c.
16B.C. .... **CMLC 32**
See also AW 2; CDWLB 1; DLB 211;
RGWL 2, 3
Prophet, The
See Dreiser, Theodore (Herman Albert)
Prose, Francine 1947- .... **CLC 45**
See also CA 109; 112; CANR 46, 95, 132;
DLB 234; SATA 101, 149
Proudhon
See Cunha, Euclides (Rodrigues Pimenta)
da
Proulx, Annie
See Proulx, E(dna) Annie
Proulx, E(dna) Annie 1935- ...... **CLC 81, 158**
See also AMWS 7; BPFB 3; CA 145;
CANR 65, 110; CN 7; CPW 1; DA3;
DAM POP; MTCW 2; SSFS 18
Proust, (Valentin-Louis-George-Eugene)
Marcel 1871-1922 ..... **SSC 75; TCLC 7,**
13, 33, 161; WLC
See also AAYA 58; BPFB 3; CA 104; 120;
CANR 110; DA; DA3; DAB; DAC; DAM
MST, NOV; DLB 65; EW 8; EWL 3; GFL
1789 to the Present; MTCW 1, 2; RGWL
2, 3; TWA
Prowler, Harley
See Masters, Edgar Lee
Prus, Boleslaw 1845-1912 .... **TCLC 48**
See also RGWL 2, 3
Pryor, Richard (Franklin Lenox Thomas)
1940- .... **CLC 26**
See also CA 122; 152
Przybyszewski, Stanislaw
1868-1927 .... **TCLC 36**
See also CA 160; DLB 66; EWL 3
Pteleon
See Grieve, C(hristopher) M(urray)
See also DAM POET
Puckett, Lute
See Masters, Edgar Lee
Puig, Manuel 1932-1990 .... **CLC 3, 5, 10, 28,**
65, 133; HLC 2
See also BPFB 3; CA 45-48; CANR 2, 32,
63; CDWLB 3; DA3; DAM MULT; DLB
113; DNFS 1; EWL 3; GLL 1; HW 1, 2;
LAW; MTCW 1, 2; RGWL 2, 3; TWA;
WLIT 1
Pulitzer, Joseph 1847-1911 .... **TCLC 76**
See also CA 114; DLB 23
Purchas, Samuel 1577(?)-1626 .... **LC 70**
See also DLB 151
Purdy, A(lfred) W(ellington)
1918-2000 .... **CLC 3, 6, 14, 50**
See also CA 81-84; 189; CAAS 17; CANR
42, 66; CP 7; DAC; DAM MST, POET;
DLB 88; PFS 5; RGEL 2
Purdy, James (Amos) 1923- .... **CLC 2, 4, 10,**
28, 52
See also AMWS 7; CA 33-36R; CAAS 1;
CANR 19, 51, 132; CN 7; DLB 2, 218;
EWL 3; INT CANR-19; MTCW 1; RGAL
4
Pure, Simon
See Swinnerton, Frank Arthur
Pushkin, Aleksandr Sergeevich
See Pushkin, Alexander (Sergeyevich)
See also DLB 205
Pushkin, Alexander (Sergeyevich)
1799-1837 .... **NCLC 3, 27, 83; PC 10;**
SSC 27, 55; WLC
See Pushkin, Aleksandr Sergeevich
See also DA; DA3; DAB; DAC; DAM
DRAM, MST, POET; EW 5; EXPS; RGSF
2; RGWL 2, 3; SATA 61; SSFS 9; TWA

P'u Sung-ling 1640-1715 .... **LC 49; SSC 31**
Putnam, Arthur Lee
See Alger, Horatio, Jr.
Puttenham, George 1529-1590 .... **LC 116**
See also DLB 281
Puzo, Mario 1920-1999 .... **CLC 1, 2, 6, 36,**
107
See also BPFB 3; CA 65-68; 185; CANR 4,
42, 65, 99, 131; CN 7; CPW; DA3; DAM
NOV, POP; DLB 6; MTCW 1, 2; NFS 16;
RGAL 4
Pygge, Edward
See Barnes, Julian (Patrick)
Pyle, Ernest Taylor 1900-1945
See Pyle, Ernie
See also CA 115; 160
Pyle, Ernie .... **TCLC 75**
See Pyle, Ernest Taylor
See also DLB 29; MTCW 2
Pyle, Howard 1853-1911 .... **TCLC 81**
See also AAYA 57; BYA 2, 4; CA 109; 137;
CLR 22; DLB 42, 188; DLBD 13; LAIT
1; MAICYA 1, 2; SATA 16, 100; WCH;
YAW
Pym, Barbara (Mary Crampton)
1913-1980 .... **CLC 13, 19, 37, 111**
See also BPFB 3; BRWS 2; CA 13-14; 97-
100; CANR 13, 34; CAP 1; DLB 14, 207;
DLBY 1987; EWL 3; MTCW 1, 2; RGEL
2; TEA
Pynchon, Thomas (Ruggles, Jr.)
1937- ...... **CLC 2, 3, 6, 9, 11, 18, 33, 62,**
72, 123, 192; SSC 14; WLC
See also AMWS 2; BEST 90:2; BPFB 3;
CA 17-20R; CANR 22, 46, 73; CN 7;
CPW 1; DA; DA3; DAB; DAC; DAM
MST, NOV, POP; DLB 2, 173; EWL 3;
MTCW 1, 2; RGAL 4; SFW 4; TUS
Pythagoras c. 582B.C.-c. 507B.C. . **CMLC 22**
See also DLB 176

Q
See Quiller-Couch, Sir Arthur (Thomas)
Qian, Chongzhu
See Ch'ien, Chung-shu
Qian, Sima 145B.C.-c. 89B.C. .... **CMLC 72**
Qian Zhongshu
See Ch'ien, Chung-shu
See also CWW 2
Qroll
See Dagerman, Stig (Halvard)
Quarles, Francis 1592-1644 .... **LC 117**
See also DLB 126; RGEL 2
Quarrington, Paul (Lewis) 1953- ..... **CLC 65**
See also CA 129; CANR 62, 95
Quasimodo, Salvatore 1901-1968 .... **CLC 10;**
PC 47
See also CA 13-16; 25-28R; CAP 1; DLB
114; EW 12; EWL 3; MTCW 1; RGWL
2, 3
Quatermass, Martin
See Carpenter, John (Howard)
Quay, Stephen 1947- .... **CLC 95**
See also CA 189
Quay, Timothy 1947- .... **CLC 95**
See also CA 189
Queen, Ellery .... **CLC 3, 11**
See Dannay, Frederic; Davidson, Avram
(James); Deming, Richard; Fairman, Paul
W.; Flora, Fletcher; Hoch, Edward
D(entinger); Kane, Henry; Lee, Manfred
B(ennington); Marlowe, Stephen; Powell,
(Oval) Talmage; Sheldon, Walter J(ames);
Sturgeon, Theodore (Hamilton); Tracy,
Don(ald Fiske); Vance, John Holbrook
See also BPFB 3; CMW 4; MSW; RGAL 4
Queen, Ellery, Jr.
See Dannay, Frederic; Lee, Manfred
B(ennington)

Queneau, Raymond 1903-1976 ..... **CLC 2, 5, 10, 42**
See also CA 77-80; 69-72; CANR 32; DLB 72, 258; EW 12; EWL 3; GFL 1789 to the Present; MTCW 1, 2; RGWL 2, 3

Quevedo, Francisco de 1580-1645 .... **LC 23**

Quiller-Couch, Sir Arthur (Thomas)
1863-1944 .... **TCLC 53**
See also CA 118; 166; DLB 135, 153, 190; HGG; RGEL 2; SUFW 1

Quin, Ann (Marie) 1936-1973 .... **CLC 6**
See also CA 9-12R; 45-48; DLB 14, 231

Quincey, Thomas de
See De Quincey, Thomas

Quindlen, Anna 1953- .... **CLC 191**
See also AAYA 35; CA 138; CANR 73, 126; DA3; DLB 292; MTCW 2

Quinn, Martin
See Smith, Martin Cruz

Quinn, Peter 1947- .... **CLC 91**
See also CA 197

Quinn, Simon
See Smith, Martin Cruz

Quintana, Leroy V. 1944- ...... **HLC 2; PC 36**
See also CA 131; CANR 65; DAM MULT; DLB 82; HW 1, 2

Quintilian c. 35-40-c. 96. .... **CMLC 77**
See also AW 2; DLB 211; RGWL 2, 3

Quiroga, Horacio (Sylvestre)
1878-1937 .... **HLC 2; TCLC 20**
See also CA 117; 131; DAM MULT; EWL 3; HW 1; LAW; MTCW 1; RGSF 2; WLIT 1

Quoirez, Francoise 1935- .... **CLC 9**
See Sagan, Francoise
See also CA 49-52; CANR 6, 39, 73; MTCW 1, 2; TWA

Raabe, Wilhelm (Karl) 1831-1910 . **TCLC 45**
See also CA 167; DLB 129

Rabe, David (William) 1940- .. **CLC 4, 8, 33, 200; DC 16**
See also CA 85-88; CABS 3; CAD; CANR 59, 129; CD 5; DAM DRAM; DFS 3, 8, 13; DLB 7, 228; EWL 3

Rabelais, Francois 1494-1553 .... **LC 5, 60; WLC**
See also DA; DAB; DAC; DAM MST; EW 2; GFL Beginnings to 1789; LMFS 1; RGWL 2, 3; TWA

Rabinovitch, Sholem 1859-1916
See Aleichem, Sholom
See also CA 104

Rabinyan, Dorit 1972- .... **CLC 119**
See also CA 170

Rachilde
See Vallette, Marguerite Eymery; Vallette, Marguerite Eymery
See also EWL 3

Racine, Jean 1639-1699 .... **LC 28, 113**
See also DA3; DAB; DAM MST; DLB 268; EW 3; GFL Beginnings to 1789; LMFS 1; RGWL 2, 3; TWA

Radcliffe, Ann (Ward) 1764-1823 ... **NCLC 6, 55, 106**
See also DLB 39, 178; HGG; LMFS 1; RGEL 2; SUFW; WLIT 3

Radclyffe-Hall, Marguerite
See Hall, (Marguerite) Radclyffe

Radiguet, Raymond 1903-1923 ...... **TCLC 29**
See also CA 162; DLB 65; EWL 3; GFL 1789 to the Present; RGWL 2, 3

Radnoti, Miklos 1909-1944 .... **TCLC 16**
See also CA 118; 212; CDWLB 4; DLB 215; EWL 3; RGWL 2, 3

Rado, James 1939- .... **CLC 17**
See also CA 105

Radvanyi, Netty 1900-1983
See Seghers, Anna
See also CA 85-88; 110; CANR 82

Rae, Ben
See Griffiths, Trevor

Raeburn, John (Hay) 1941- .... **CLC 34**
See also CA 57-60

Ragni, Gerome 1942-1991 .... **CLC 17**
See also CA 105; 134

Rahv, Philip .... **CLC 24**
See Greenberg, Ivan
See also DLB 137

Raimund, Ferdinand Jakob
1790-1836 .... **NCLC 69**
See also DLB 90

Raine, Craig (Anthony) 1944- .. **CLC 32, 103**
See also CA 108; CANR 29, 51, 103; CP 7; DLB 40; PFS 7

Raine, Kathleen (Jessie) 1908-2003 .. **CLC 7, 45**
See also CA 85-88; 218; CANR 46, 109; CP 7; DLB 20; EWL 3; MTCW 1; RGEL 2

Rainis, Janis 1865-1929 .... **TCLC 29**
See also CA 170; CDWLB 4; DLB 220; EWL 3

Rakosi, Carl .... **CLC 47**
See Rawley, Callman
See also CA 228; CAAS 5; CP 7; DLB 193

Ralegh, Sir Walter
See Raleigh, Sir Walter
See also BRW 1; RGEL 2; WP

Raleigh, Richard
See Lovecraft, H(oward) P(hillips)

Raleigh, Sir Walter 1554(?)-1618 .... **LC 31, 39; PC 31**
See Ralegh, Sir Walter
See also CDBLB Before 1660; DLB 172; EXPP; PFS 14; TEA

Rallentando, H. P.
See Sayers, Dorothy L(eigh)

Ramal, Walter
See de la Mare, Walter (John)

Ramana Maharshi 1879-1950 .... **TCLC 84**

Ramoacn y Cajal, Santiago
1852-1934 .... **TCLC 93**

Ramon, Juan
See Jimenez (Mantecon), Juan Ramon

Ramos, Graciliano 1892-1953 .... **TCLC 32**
See also CA 167; DLB 307; EWL 3; HW 2; LAW; WLIT 1

Rampersad, Arnold 1941- .... **CLC 44**
See also BW 2, 3; CA 127; 133; CANR 81; DLB 111; INT CA-133

Rampling, Anne
See Rice, Anne
See also GLL 2

Ramsay, Allan 1686(?)-1758 .... **LC 29**
See also DLB 95; RGEL 2

Ramsay, Jay
See Campbell, (John) Ramsey

Ramuz, Charles-Ferdinand
1878-1947 .... **TCLC 33**
See also CA 165; EWL 3

Rand, Ayn 1905-1982 ...... **CLC 3, 30, 44, 79; WLC**
See also AAYA 10; AMWS 4; BPFB 3; BYA 12; CA 13-16R; 105; CANR 27, 73; CDALBS; CPW; DA; DA3; DAC; DAM MST, NOV, POP; DLB 227, 279; MTCW 1, 2; NFS 10, 16; RGAL 4; SFW 4; TUS; YAW

Randall, Dudley (Felker) 1914-2000 . **BLC 3; CLC 1, 135**
See also BW 1, 3; CA 25-28R; 189; CANR 23, 82; DAM MULT; DLB 41; PFS 5

Randall, Robert
See Silverberg, Robert

Ranger, Ken
See Creasey, John

Rank, Otto 1884-1939 .... **TCLC 115**

Ransom, John Crowe 1888-1974 .. **CLC 2, 4, 5, 11, 24; PC 61**
See also AMW; CA 5-8R; 49-52; CANR 6, 34; CDALBS; DA3; DAM POET; DLB 45, 63; EWL 3; EXPP; MTCW 1, 2; RGAL 4; TUS

Rao, Raja 1909- .... **CLC 25, 56**
See also CA 73-76; CANR 51; CN 7; DAM NOV; EWL 3; MTCW 1, 2; RGEL 2; RGSF 2

Raphael, Frederic (Michael) 1931- ... **CLC 2, 14**
See also CA 1-4R; CANR 1, 86; CN 7; DLB 14

Ratcliffe, James P.
See Mencken, H(enry) L(ouis)

Rathbone, Julian 1935- .... **CLC 41**
See also CA 101; CANR 34, 73

Rattigan, Terence (Mervyn)
1911-1977 .... **CLC 7; DC 18**
See also BRWS 7; CA 85-88; 73-76; CBD; CDBLB 1945-1960; DAM DRAM; DFS 8; DLB 13; IDFW 3, 4; MTCW 1, 2; RGEL 2

Ratushinskaya, Irina 1954- .... **CLC 54**
See also CA 129; CANR 68; CWW 2

Raven, Simon (Arthur Noel)
1927-2001 .... **CLC 14**
See also CA 81-84; 197; CANR 86; CN 7; DLB 271

Ravenna, Michael
See Welty, Eudora (Alice)

Rawley, Callman 1903-2004
See Rakosi, Carl
See also CA 21-24R; CANR 12, 32, 91

Rawlings, Marjorie Kinnan
1896-1953 .... **TCLC 4**
See also AAYA 20; AMWS 10; ANW; BPFB 3; BYA 3; CA 104; CANR 74; CLR 63; DLB 9, 22, 102; DLBD 17; JRDA; MAICYA 1, 2; MTCW 2; RGAL 4; SATA 100; WCH; YABC 1; YAW

Ray, Satyajit 1921-1992 .... **CLC 16, 76**
See also CA 114; 137; DAM MULT

Read, Herbert Edward 1893-1968 ..... **CLC 4**
See also BRW 6; CA 85-88; 25-28R; DLB 20, 149; EWL 3; PAB; RGEL 2

Read, Piers Paul 1941- .... **CLC 4, 10, 25**
See also CA 21-24R; CANR 38, 86; CN 7; DLB 14; SATA 21

Reade, Charles 1814-1884 .... **NCLC 2, 74**
See also DLB 21; RGEL 2

Reade, Hamish
See Gray, Simon (James Holliday)

Reading, Peter 1946- .... **CLC 47**
See also BRWS 8; CA 103; CANR 46, 96; CP 7; DLB 40

Reaney, James 1926- .... **CLC 13**
See also CA 41-44R; CAAS 15; CANR 42; CD 5; CP 7; DAC; DAM MST; DLB 68; RGEL 2; SATA 43

Rebreanu, Liviu 1885-1944 .... **TCLC 28**
See also CA 165; DLB 220; EWL 3

Rechy, John (Francisco) 1934- ...... **CLC 1, 7, 14, 18, 107; HLC 2**
See also CA 5-8R; 195; CAAE 195; CAAS 4; CANR 6, 32, 64; CN 7; DAM MULT; DLB 122, 278; DLBY 1982; HW 1, 2; INT CANR-6; LLW 1; RGAL 4

Redcam, Tom 1870-1933 .... **TCLC 25**

Reddin, Keith .... **CLC 67**
See also CAD

Redgrove, Peter (William)
1932-2003 .... **CLC 6, 41**
See also BRWS 6; CA 1-4R; 217; CANR 3, 39, 77; CP 7; DLB 40

Redmon, Anne .... **CLC 22**
See Nightingale, Anne Redmon
See also DLBY 1986

Reed, Eliot
See Ambler, Eric

Reed, Ishmael 1938- ..... **BLC 3; CLC 2, 3, 5, 6, 13, 32, 60, 174**
See also AFAW 1, 2; AMWS 10; BPFB 3; BW 2, 3; CA 21-24R; CANR 25, 48, 74, 128; CN 7; CP 7; CSW; DA3; DAM MULT; DLB 2, 5, 33, 169, 227; DLBD 8; EWL 3; LMFS 2; MSW; MTCW 1, 2; PFS 6; RGAL 4; TCWW 2

Reed, John (Silas) 1887-1920 .... **TCLC 9**
See also CA 106; 195; TUS

Reed, Lou .... **CLC 21**
See Firbank, Louis

Reese, Lizette Woodworth 1856-1935 . **PC 29**
See also CA 180; DLB 54

Reeve, Clara 1729-1807 .... **NCLC 19**
See also DLB 39; RGEL 2

Reich, Wilhelm 1897-1957 .... **TCLC 57**
See also CA 199

Reid, Christopher (John) 1949- .... **CLC 33**
See also CA 140; CANR 89; CP 7; DLB 40; EWL 3

Reid, Desmond
See Moorcock, Michael (John)

Reid Banks, Lynne 1929-
See Banks, Lynne Reid
See also AAYA 49; CA 1-4R; CANR 6, 22, 38, 87; CLR 24; CN 7; JRDA; MAICYA 1, 2; SATA 22, 75, 111; YAW

Reilly, William K.
See Creasey, John

Reiner, Max
See Caldwell, (Janet Miriam) Taylor (Holland)

Reis, Ricardo
See Pessoa, Fernando (Antonio Nogueira)

Reizenstein, Elmer Leopold
See Rice, Elmer (Leopold)
See also EWL 3

Remarque, Erich Maria 1898-1970 . **CLC 21**
See also AAYA 27; BPFB 3; CA 77-80; 29-32R; CDWLB 2; DA; DA3; DAB; DAC; DAM MST, NOV; DLB 56; EWL 3; EXPN; LAIT 3; MTCW 1, 2; NFS 4; RGWL 2, 3

Remington, Frederic 1861-1909 ..... **TCLC 89**
See also CA 108; 169; DLB 12, 186, 188; SATA 41

Remizov, A.
See Remizov, Aleksei (Mikhailovich)

Remizov, A. M.
See Remizov, Aleksei (Mikhailovich)

Remizov, Aleksei (Mikhailovich) 1877-1957 .... **TCLC 27**
See Remizov, Alexey Mikhaylovich
See also CA 125; 133; DLB 295

Remizov, Alexey Mikhaylovich
See Remizov, Aleksei (Mikhailovich)
See also EWL 3

Renan, Joseph Ernest 1823-1892 . **NCLC 26, 145**
See also GFL 1789 to the Present

Renard, Jules(-Pierre) 1864-1910 .. **TCLC 17**
See also CA 117; 202; GFL 1789 to the Present

Renault, Mary .... **CLC 3, 11, 17**
See Challans, Mary
See also BPFB 3; BYA 2; DLBY 1983; EWL 3; GLL 1; LAIT 1; MTCW 2; RGEL 2; RHW

Rendell, Ruth (Barbara) 1930- .. **CLC 28, 48**
See Vine, Barbara
See also BPFB 3; BRWS 9; CA 109; CANR 32, 52, 74, 127; CN 7; CPW; DAM POP; DLB 87, 276; INT CANR-32; MSW; MTCW 1, 2

Renoir, Jean 1894-1979 .... **CLC 20**
See also CA 129; 85-88

Resnais, Alain 1922- .... **CLC 16**

Revard, Carter (Curtis) 1931- .... **NNAL**
See also CA 144; CANR 81; PFS 5

Reverdy, Pierre 1889-1960 .... **CLC 53**
See also CA 97-100; 89-92; DLB 258; EWL 3; GFL 1789 to the Present

Rexroth, Kenneth 1905-1982 .... **CLC 1, 2, 6, 11, 22, 49, 112; PC 20**
See also BG 3; CA 5-8R; 107; CANR 14, 34, 63; CDALB 1941-1968; DAM POET; DLB 16, 48, 165, 212; DLBY 1982; EWL 3; INT CANR-14; MTCW 1, 2; RGAL 4

Reyes, Alfonso 1889-1959 .... **HLCS 2; TCLC 33**
See also CA 131; EWL 3; HW 1; LAW

Reyes y Basoalto, Ricardo Eliecer Neftali
See Neruda, Pablo

Reymont, Wladyslaw (Stanislaw) 1868(?)-1925 .... **TCLC 5**
See also CA 104; EWL 3

Reynolds, John Hamilton 1794-1852 .... **NCLC 146**
See also DLB 96

Reynolds, Jonathan 1942- .... **CLC 6, 38**
See also CA 65-68; CANR 28

Reynolds, Joshua 1723-1792 .... **LC 15**
See also DLB 104

Reynolds, Michael S(hane) 1937-2000 .... **CLC 44**
See also CA 65-68; 189; CANR 9, 89, 97

Reznikoff, Charles 1894-1976 .... **CLC 9**
See also AMWS 14; CA 33-36; 61-64; CAP 2; DLB 28, 45; WP

Rezzori (d'Arezzo), Gregor von 1914-1998 .... **CLC 25**
See also CA 122; 136; 167

Rhine, Richard
See Silverstein, Alvin; Silverstein, Virginia B(arbara Opshelor)

Rhodes, Eugene Manlove 1869-1934 .... **TCLC 53**
See also CA 198; DLB 256

R'hoone, Lord
See Balzac, Honore de

Rhys, Jean 1890-1979 .... **CLC 2, 4, 6, 14, 19, 51, 124; SSC 21, 76**
See also BRWS 2; CA 25-28R; 85-88; CANR 35, 62; CDBLB 1945-1960; CD-WLB 3; DA3; DAM NOV; DLB 36, 117, 162; DNFS 2; EWL 3; LATS 1:1; MTCW 1, 2; RGEL 2; RGSF 2; RHW; TEA; WWE 1

Ribeiro, Darcy 1922-1997 .... **CLC 34**
See also CA 33-36R; 156; EWL 3

Ribeiro, Joao Ubaldo (Osorio Pimentel) 1941- .... **CLC 10, 67**
See also CA 81-84; CWW 2; EWL 3

Ribman, Ronald (Burt) 1932- .... **CLC 7**
See also CA 21-24R; CAD; CANR 46, 80; CD 5

Ricci, Nino (Pio) 1959- .... **CLC 70**
See also CA 137; CANR 130; CCA 1

Rice, Anne 1941- .... **CLC 41, 128**
See Rampling, Anne
See also AAYA 9, 53; AMWS 7; BEST 89:2; BPFB 3; CA 65-68; CANR 12, 36, 53, 74, 100, 133; CN 7; CPW; CSW; DA3; DAM POP; DLB 292; GLL 2; HGG; MTCW 2; SUFW 2; YAW

Rice, Elmer (Leopold) 1892-1967 ...... **CLC 7, 49**
See Reizenstein, Elmer Leopold
See also CA 21-22; 25-28R; CAP 2; DAM DRAM; DFS 12; DLB 4, 7; MTCW 1, 2; RGAL 4

Rice, Tim(othy Miles Bindon) 1944- .... **CLC 21**
See also CA 103; CANR 46; DFS 7

Rich, Adrienne (Cecile) 1929- ... **CLC 3, 6, 7, 11, 18, 36, 73, 76, 125; PC 5**
See also AMWR 2; AMWS 1; CA 9-12R; CANR 20, 53, 74, 128; CDALBS; CP 7; CSW; CWP; DA3; DAM POET; DLB 5, 67; EWL 3; EXPP; FW; MAWW; MTCW 1, 2; PAB; PFS 15; RGAL 4; WP

Rich, Barbara
See Graves, Robert (von Ranke)

Rich, Robert
See Trumbo, Dalton

Richard, Keith .... **CLC 17**
See Richards, Keith

Richards, David Adams 1950- .... **CLC 59**
See also CA 93-96; CANR 60, 110; DAC; DLB 53

Richards, I(vor) A(rmstrong) 1893-1979 .... **CLC 14, 24**
See also BRWS 2; CA 41-44R; 89-92; CANR 34, 74; DLB 27; EWL 3; MTCW 2; RGEL 2

Richards, Keith 1943-
See Richard, Keith
See also CA 107; CANR 77

Richardson, Anne
See Roiphe, Anne (Richardson)

Richardson, Dorothy Miller 1873-1957 .... **TCLC 3**
See also CA 104; 192; DLB 36; EWL 3; FW; RGEL 2

Richardson (Robertson), Ethel Florence Lindesay 1870-1946
See Richardson, Henry Handel
See also CA 105; 190; DLB 230; RHW

Richardson, Henry Handel .... **TCLC 4**
See Richardson (Robertson), Ethel Florence Lindesay
See also DLB 197; EWL 3; RGEL 2; RGSF 2

Richardson, John 1796-1852 .... **NCLC 55**
See also CCA 1; DAC; DLB 99

Richardson, Samuel 1689-1761 ...... **LC 1, 44; WLC**
See also BRW 3; CDBLB 1660-1789; DA; DAB; DAC; DAM MST, NOV; DLB 39; RGEL 2; TEA; WLIT 3

Richardson, Willis 1889-1977 .... **HR 3**
See also BW 1; CA 124; DLB 51; SATA 60

Richler, Mordecai 1931-2001 .... **CLC 3, 5, 9, 13, 18, 46, 70, 185**
See also AITN 1; CA 65-68; 201; CANR 31, 62, 111; CCA 1; CLR 17; CWRI 5; DAC; DAM MST, NOV; DLB 53; EWL 3; MAICYA 1, 2; MTCW 1, 2; RGEL 2; SATA 44, 98; SATA-Brief 27; TWA

Richter, Conrad (Michael) 1890-1968 .... **CLC 30**
See also AAYA 21; BYA 2; CA 5-8R; 25-28R; CANR 23; DLB 9, 212; LAIT 1; MTCW 1, 2; RGAL 4; SATA 3; TCWW 2; TUS; YAW

Ricostranza, Tom
See Ellis, Trey

Riddell, Charlotte 1832-1906 .... **TCLC 40**
See Riddell, Mrs. J. H.
See also CA 165; DLB 156

Riddell, Mrs. J. H.
See Riddell, Charlotte
See also HGG; SUFW

Ridge, John Rollin 1827-1867 ...... **NCLC 82;**
NNAL
See also CA 144; DAM MULT; DLB 175
Ridgeway, Jason
See Marlowe, Stephen
Ridgway, Keith 1965- .... **CLC 119**
See also CA 172
Riding, Laura .... **CLC 3, 7**
See Jackson, Laura (Riding)
See also RGAL 4
Riefenstahl, Berta Helene Amalia 1902-2003
See Riefenstahl, Leni
See also CA 108; 220
Riefenstahl, Leni .... **CLC 16, 190**
See Riefenstahl, Berta Helene Amalia
Riffe, Ernest
See Bergman, (Ernst) Ingmar
Riggs, (Rolla) Lynn
1899-1954 .... **NNAL; TCLC 56**
See also CA 144; DAM MULT; DLB 175
Riis, Jacob A(ugust) 1849-1914 ..... **TCLC 80**
See also CA 113; 168; DLB 23
Riley, James Whitcomb 1849-1916 .... **PC 48;**
TCLC 51
See also CA 118; 137; DAM POET; MAI-
CYA 1, 2; RGAL 4; SATA 17
Riley, Tex
See Creasey, John
Rilke, Rainer Maria 1875-1926 .... **PC 2;**
TCLC 1, 6, 19
See also CA 104; 132; CANR 62, 99; CD-
WLB 2; DA3; DAM POET; DLB 81; EW
9; EWL 3; MTCW 1, 2; PFS 19; RGWL
2, 3; TWA; WP
Rimbaud, (Jean Nicolas) Arthur
1854-1891 ... **NCLC 4, 35, 82; PC 3, 57;**
WLC
See also DA; DA3; DAB; DAC; DAM
MST, POET; DLB 217; EW 7; GFL 1789
to the Present; LMFS 2; RGWL 2, 3;
TWA; WP
Rinehart, Mary Roberts
1876-1958 .... **TCLC 52**
See also BPFB 3; CA 108; 166; RGAL 4;
RHW
Ringmaster, The
See Mencken, H(enry) L(ouis)
Ringwood, Gwen(dolyn Margaret) Pharis
1910-1984 .... **CLC 48**
See also CA 148; 112; DLB 88
Rio, Michel 1945(?)- .... **CLC 43**
See also CA 201
Rios, Alberto (Alvaro) 1952- .... **PC 57**
See also AMWS 4; CA 113; CANR 34, 79;
CP 7; DLB 122; HW 2; PFS 11
Ritsos, Giannes
See Ritsos, Yannis
Ritsos, Yannis 1909-1990 .... **CLC 6, 13, 31**
See also CA 77-80; 133; CANR 39, 61; EW
12; EWL 3; MTCW 1; RGWL 2, 3
Ritter, Erika 1948(?)- .... **CLC 52**
See also CD 5; CWD
Rivera, Jose Eustasio 1889-1928 ... **TCLC 35**
See also CA 162; EWL 3; HW 1, 2; LAW
Rivera, Tomas 1935-1984 .... **HLCS 2**
See also CA 49-52; CANR 32; DLB 82;
HW 1; LLW 1; RGAL 4; SSFS 15;
TCWW 2; WLIT 1
Rivers, Conrad Kent 1933-1968 .... **CLC 1**
See also BW 1; CA 85-88; DLB 41
Rivers, Elfrida
See Bradley, Marion Zimmer
See also GLL 1
Riverside, John
See Heinlein, Robert A(nson)

Rizal, Jose 1861-1896 .... **NCLC 27**
Roa Bastos, Augusto (Antonio)
1917- .... **CLC 45; HLC 2**
See also CA 131; CWW 2; DAM MULT;
DLB 113; EWL 3; HW 1; LAW; RGSF 2;
WLIT 1
Robbe-Grillet, Alain 1922- .... **CLC 1, 2, 4, 6,**
8, 10, 14, 43, 128
See also BPFB 3; CA 9-12R; CANR 33,
65, 115; CWW 2; DLB 83; EW 13; EWL
3; GFL 1789 to the Present; IDFW 3, 4;
MTCW 1, 2; RGWL 2, 3; SSFS 15
Robbins, Harold 1916-1997 .... **CLC 5**
See also BPFB 3; CA 73-76; 162; CANR
26, 54, 112; DA3; DAM NOV; MTCW 1,
2
Robbins, Thomas Eugene 1936-
See Robbins, Tom
See also CA 81-84; CANR 29, 59, 95; CN
7; CPW; CSW; DA3; DAM NOV, POP;
MTCW 1, 2
Robbins, Tom .... **CLC 9, 32, 64**
See Robbins, Thomas Eugene
See also AAYA 32; AMWS 10; BEST 90:3;
BPFB 3; DLBY 1980; MTCW 2
Robbins, Trina 1938- .... **CLC 21**
See also CA 128
Roberts, Charles G(eorge) D(ouglas)
1860-1943 .... **TCLC 8**
See also CA 105; 188; CLR 33; CWRI 5;
DLB 92; RGEL 2; RGSF 2; SATA 88;
SATA-Brief 29
Roberts, Elizabeth Madox
1886-1941 .... **TCLC 68**
See also CA 111; 166; CLR 100; CWRI 5;
DLB 9, 54, 102; RGAL 4; RHW; SATA
33; SATA-Brief 27; WCH
Roberts, Kate 1891-1985 .... **CLC 15**
See also CA 107; 116
Roberts, Keith (John Kingston)
1935-2000 .... **CLC 14**
See also BRWS 10; CA 25-28R; CANR 46;
DLB 261; SFW 4
Roberts, Kenneth (Lewis)
1885-1957 .... **TCLC 23**
See also CA 109; 199; DLB 9; RGAL 4;
RHW
Roberts, Michele (Brigitte) 1949- .... **CLC 48,**
178
See also CA 115; CANR 58, 120; CN 7;
DLB 231; FW
Robertson, Ellis
See Ellison, Harlan (Jay); Silverberg, Robert
Robertson, Thomas William
1829-1871 .... **NCLC 35**
See Robertson, Tom
See also DAM DRAM
Robertson, Tom
See Robertson, Thomas William
See also RGEL 2
Robeson, Kenneth
See Dent, Lester
Robinson, Edwin Arlington
1869-1935 .... **PC 1, 35; TCLC 5, 101**
See also AMW; CA 104; 133; CDALB
1865-1917; DA; DAC; DAM MST,
POET; DLB 54; EWL 3; EXPP; MTCW
1, 2; PAB; PFS 4; RGAL 4; WP
Robinson, Henry Crabb
1775-1867 .... **NCLC 15**
See also DLB 107
Robinson, Jill 1936- .... **CLC 10**
See also CA 102; CANR 120; INT CA-102
Robinson, Kim Stanley 1952- .... **CLC 34**
See also AAYA 26; CA 126; CANR 113;
CN 7; SATA 109; SCFW 2; SFW 4
Robinson, Lloyd
See Silverberg, Robert

Robinson, Marilynne 1944- ...... **CLC 25, 180**
See also CA 116; CANR 80; CN 7; DLB
206
Robinson, Mary 1758-1800 .... **NCLC 142**
See also DLB 158; FW
Robinson, Smokey .... **CLC 21**
See Robinson, William, Jr.
Robinson, William, Jr. 1940-
See Robinson, Smokey
See also CA 116
Robison, Mary 1949- .... **CLC 42, 98**
See also CA 113; 116; CANR 87; CN 7;
DLB 130; INT CA-116; RGSF 2
Rochester
See Wilmot, John
See also RGEL 2
Rod, Edouard 1857-1910 .... **TCLC 52**
Roddenberry, Eugene Wesley 1921-1991
See Roddenberry, Gene
See also CA 110; 135; CANR 37; SATA 45;
SATA-Obit 69
Roddenberry, Gene .... **CLC 17**
See Roddenberry, Eugene Wesley
See also AAYA 5; SATA-Obit 69
Rodgers, Mary 1931- .... **CLC 12**
See also BYA 5; CA 49-52; CANR 8, 55,
90; CLR 20; CWRI 5; INT CANR-8;
JRDA; MAICYA 1, 2; SATA 8, 130
Rodgers, W(illiam) R(obert)
1909-1969 .... **CLC 7**
See also CA 85-88; DLB 20; RGEL 2
Rodman, Eric
See Silverberg, Robert
Rodman, Howard 1920(?)-1985 .... **CLC 65**
See also CA 118
Rodman, Maia
See Wojciechowska, Maia (Teresa)
Rodo, Jose Enrique 1871(?)-1917 .... **HLCS 2**
See also CA 178; EWL 3; HW 2; LAW
Rodolph, Utto
See Ouologuem, Yambo
Rodriguez, Claudio 1934-1999 .... **CLC 10**
See also CA 188; DLB 134
Rodriguez, Richard 1944- .... **CLC 155; HLC**
2
See also AMWS 14; CA 110; CANR 66,
116; DAM MULT; DLB 82, 256; HW 1,
2; LAIT 5; LLW 1; NCFS 3; WLIT 1
Roelvaag, O(le) E(dvart) 1876-1931
See Rolvaag, O(le) E(dvart)
See also CA 117; 171
Roethke, Theodore (Huebner)
1908-1963 .... **CLC 1, 3, 8, 11, 19, 46,**
101; PC 15
See also AMW; CA 81-84; CABS 2;
CDALB 1941-1968; DA3; DAM POET;
DLB 5, 206; EWL 3; EXPP; MTCW 1, 2;
PAB; PFS 3; RGAL 4; WP
Rogers, Carl R(ansom)
1902-1987 .... **TCLC 125**
See also CA 1-4R; 121; CANR 1, 18;
MTCW 1
Rogers, Samuel 1763-1855 .... **NCLC 69**
See also DLB 93; RGEL 2
Rogers, Thomas Hunton 1927- .... **CLC 57**
See also CA 89-92; INT CA-89-92
Rogers, Will(iam Penn Adair)
1879-1935 .... **NNAL; TCLC 8, 71**
See also CA 105; 144; DA3; DAM MULT;
DLB 11; MTCW 2
Rogin, Gilbert 1929- .... **CLC 18**
See also CA 65-68; CANR 15
Rohan, Koda
See Koda Shigeyuki
Rohlfs, Anna Katharine Green
See Green, Anna Katharine
Rohmer, Eric .... **CLC 16**
See Scherer, Jean-Marie Maurice

Rulfo, Juan 1918-1986 .. **CLC 8, 80; HLC 2; SSC 25**
See also CA 85-88; 118; CANR 26; CD-WLB 3; DAM MULT; DLB 113; EWL 3; HW 1, 2; LAW; MTCW 1, 2; RGSF 2; RGWL 2, 3; WLIT 1

Rumi, Jalal al-Din 1207-1273 ...... **CMLC 20; PC 45**
See also RGWL 2, 3; WP

Runeberg, Johan 1804-1877 .... **NCLC 41**

Runyon, (Alfred) Damon
1884(?)-1946 .... **TCLC 10**
See also CA 107; 165; DLB 11, 86, 171; MTCW 2; RGAL 4

Rush, Norman 1933- .... **CLC 44**
See also CA 121; 126; CANR 130; INT CA-126

Rushdie, (Ahmed) Salman 1947- .... **CLC 23, 31, 55, 100, 191; SSC 83; WLCS**
See also BEST 89:3; BPFB 3; BRWS 4; CA 108; 111; CANR 33, 56, 108, 133; CN 7; CPW 1; DA3; DAB; DAC; DAM MST, NOV, POP; DLB 194; EWL 3; FANT; INT CA-111; LATS 1:2; LMFS 2; MTCW 1, 2; RGEL 2; RGSF 2; TEA; WLIT 4; WWE 1

Rushforth, Peter (Scott) 1945- .... **CLC 19**
See also CA 101

Ruskin, John 1819-1900 .... **TCLC 63**
See also BRW 5; BYA 5; CA 114; 129; CD-BLB 1832-1890; DLB 55, 163, 190; RGEL 2; SATA 24; TEA; WCH

Russ, Joanna 1937- .... **CLC 15**
See also BPFB 3; CA 5-28R; CANR 11, 31, 65; CN 7; DLB 8; FW; GLL 1; MTCW 1; SCFW 2; SFW 4

Russ, Richard Patrick
See O'Brian, Patrick

Russell, George William 1867-1935
See A.E.; Baker, Jean H.
See also BRWS 8; CA 104; 153; CDBLB 1890-1914; DAM POET; EWL 3; RGEL 2

Russell, Jeffrey Burton 1934- .... **CLC 70**
See also CA 25-28R; CANR 11, 28, 52

Russell, (Henry) Ken(neth Alfred)
1927- .... **CLC 16**
See also CA 105

Russell, William Martin 1947-
See Russell, Willy
See also CA 164; CANR 107

Russell, Willy .... **CLC 60**
See Russell, William Martin
See also CBD; CD 5; DLB 233

Russo, Richard 1949- .... **CLC 181**
See also AMWS 12; CA 127; 133; CANR 87, 114

Rutherford, Mark .... **TCLC 25**
See White, William Hale
See also DLB 18; RGEL 2

Ruyslinck, Ward .... **CLC 14**
See Belser, Reimond Karel Maria de

Ryan, Cornelius (John) 1920-1974 ..... **CLC 7**
See also CA 69-72; 53-56; CANR 38

Ryan, Michael 1946- .... **CLC 65**
See also CA 49-52; CANR 109; DLBY 1982

Ryan, Tim
See Dent, Lester

Rybakov, Anatoli (Naumovich)
1911-1998 .... **CLC 23, 53**
See Rybakov, Anatolii (Naumovich)
See also CA 126; 135; 172; SATA 79; SATA-Obit 108

Rybakov, Anatolii (Naumovich)
See Rybakov, Anatoli (Naumovich)
See also DLB 302

Ryder, Jonathan
See Ludlum, Robert

Ryga, George 1932-1987 .... **CLC 14**
See also CA 101; 124; CANR 43, 90; CCA 1; DAC; DAM MST; DLB 60

S. H.
See Hartmann, Sadakichi

S. S.
See Sassoon, Siegfried (Lorraine)

Sa'adawi, al- Nawal
See El Saadawi, Nawal
See also AFW; EWL 3

Saadawi, Nawal El
See El Saadawi, Nawal
See also WLIT 2

Saba, Umberto 1883-1957 .... **TCLC 33**
See also CA 144; CANR 79; DLB 114; EWL 3; RGWL 2, 3

Sabatini, Rafael 1875-1950 .... **TCLC 47**
See also BPFB 3; CA 162; RHW

Sabato, Ernesto (R.) 1911- .... **CLC 10, 23; HLC 2**
See also CA 97-100; CANR 32, 65; CD-WLB 3; CWW 2; DAM MULT; DLB 145; EWL 3; HW 1, 2; LAW; MTCW 1, 2

Sa-Carneiro, Mario de 1890-1916 . **TCLC 83**
See also DLB 287; EWL 3

Sacastru, Martin
See Bioy Casares, Adolfo
See also CWW 2

Sacher-Masoch, Leopold von
1836(?)-1895 .... **NCLC 31**

Sachs, Hans 1494-1576 .... **LC 95**
See also CDWLB 2; DLB 179; RGWL 2, 3

Sachs, Marilyn (Stickle) 1927- .... **CLC 35**
See also AAYA 2; BYA 6; CA 17-20R; CANR 13, 47; CLR 2; JRDA; MAICYA 1, 2; SAAS 2; SATA 3, 68; SATA-Essay 110; WYA; YAW

Sachs, Nelly 1891-1970 .... **CLC 14, 98**
See also CA 17-18; 25-28R; CANR 87; CAP 2; EWL 3; MTCW 2; PFS 20; RGWL 2, 3

Sackler, Howard (Oliver)
1929-1982 .... **CLC 14**
See also CA 61-64; 108; CAD; CANR 30; DFS 15; DLB 7

Sacks, Oliver (Wolf) 1933- .... **CLC 67, 202**
See also CA 53-56; CANR 28, 50, 76; CPW; DA3; INT CANR-28; MTCW 1, 2

Sackville, Thomas 1536-1608 .... **LC 98**
See also DAM DRAM; DLB 62, 132; RGEL 2

Sadakichi
See Hartmann, Sadakichi

Sa'dawi, Nawal al-
See El Saadawi, Nawal
See also CWW 2

Sade, Donatien Alphonse Francois
1740-1814 .... **NCLC 3, 47**
See also EW 4; GFL Beginnings to 1789; RGWL 2, 3

Sade, Marquis de
See Sade, Donatien Alphonse Francois

Sadoff, Ira 1945- .... **CLC 9**
See also CA 53-56; CANR 5, 21, 109; DLB 120

Saetone
See Camus, Albert

Safire, William 1929- .... **CLC 10**
See also CA 17-20R; CANR 31, 54, 91

Sagan, Carl (Edward) 1934-1996 .... **CLC 30, 112**
See also AAYA 2; CA 25-28R; 155; CANR 11, 36, 74; CPW; DA3; MTCW 1, 2; SATA 58; SATA-Obit 94

Sagan, Francoise .... **CLC 3, 6, 9, 17, 36**
See Quoirez, Francoise
See also CWW 2; DLB 83; EWL 3; GFL 1789 to the Present; MTCW 2

Sahgal, Nayantara (Pandit) 1927- .... **CLC 41**
See also CA 9-12R; CANR 11, 88; CN 7

Said, Edward W. 1935-2003 .... **CLC 123**
See also CA 21-24R; 220; CANR 45, 74, 107, 131; DLB 67; MTCW 2

Saigyō 1118-1190 .... **CMLC 77**
See also DLB 203; RGWL 3

Saint, H(arry) F. 1941- .... **CLC 50**
See also CA 127

St. Aubin de Teran, Lisa 1953-
See Teran, Lisa St. Aubin de
See also CA 118; 126; CN 7; INT CA-126

Saint Birgitta of Sweden c.
1303-1373 .... **CMLC 24**

Sainte-Beuve, Charles Augustin
1804-1869 .... **NCLC 5**
See also DLB 217; EW 6; GFL 1789 to the Present

Saint-Exupery, Antoine (Jean Baptiste Marie Roger) de 1900-1944 .... **TCLC 2, 56; WLC**
See also BPFB 3; BYA 3; CA 108; 132; CLR 10; DA3; DAM NOV; DLB 72; EW 12; EWL 3; GFL 1789 to the Present; LAIT 3; MAICYA 1, 2; MTCW 1, 2; RGWL 2, 3; SATA 20; TWA

St. John, David
See Hunt, E(verette) Howard, (Jr.)

St. John, J. Hector
See Crevecoeur, Michel Guillaume Jean de

Saint-John Perse
See Leger, (Marie-Rene Auguste) Alexis Saint-Leger
See also EW 10; EWL 3; GFL 1789 to the Present; RGWL 2

Saintsbury, George (Edward Bateman)
1845-1933 .... **TCLC 31**
See also CA 160; DLB 57, 149

Sait Faik .... **TCLC 23**
See Abasiyanik, Sait Faik

Saki .... **SSC 12; TCLC 3**
See Munro, H(ector) H(ugh)
See also BRWS 6; BYA 11; LAIT 2; MTCW 2; RGEL 2; SSFS 1; SUFW

Sala, George Augustus 1828-1895 . **NCLC 46**

Saladin 1138-1193 .... **CMLC 38**

Salama, Hannu 1936- .... **CLC 18**
See also EWL 3

Salamanca, J(ack) R(ichard) 1922- .. **CLC 4, 15**
See also CA 25-28R; 193; CAAE 193

Salas, Floyd Francis 1931- .... **HLC 2**
See also CA 119; CAAS 27; CANR 44, 75, 93; DAM MULT; DLB 82; HW 1, 2; MTCW 2

Sale, J. Kirkpatrick
See Sale, Kirkpatrick

Sale, Kirkpatrick 1937- .... **CLC 68**
See also CA 13-16R; CANR 10

Salinas, Luis Omar 1937- ... **CLC 90; HLC 2**
See also AMWS 13; CA 131; CANR 81; DAM MULT; DLB 82; HW 1, 2

Salinas (y Serrano), Pedro
1891(?)-1951 .... **TCLC 17**
See also CA 117; DLB 134; EWL 3

Salinger, J(erome) D(avid) 1919- .. **CLC 1, 3, 8, 12, 55, 56, 138; SSC 2, 28, 65; WLC**
See also AAYA 2, 36; AMW; AMWC 1; BPFB 3; CA 5-8R; CANR 39, 129; CDALB 1941-1968; CLR 18; CN 7; CPW 1; DA; DA3; DAB; DAC; DAM MST, NOV, POP; DLB 2, 102, 173; EWL 3; EXPN; LAIT 4; MAICYA 1, 2; MTCW 1, 2; NFS 1; RGAL 4; RGSF 2; SATA 67; SSFS 17; TUS; WYA; YAW

Salisbury, John
See Caute, (John) David

Sallust c. 86B.C.-35B.C. .... **CMLC 68**
  See also AW 2; CDWLB 1; DLB 211;
  RGWL 2, 3
Salter, James 1925- .. **CLC 7, 52, 59; SSC 58**
  See also AMWS 9; CA 73-76; CANR 107;
  DLB 130
Saltus, Edgar (Everton) 1855-1921 . **TCLC 8**
  See also CA 105; DLB 202; RGAL 4
Saltykov, Mikhail Evgrafovich
  1826-1889 .... **NCLC 16**
  See also DLB 238:
Saltykov-Shchedrin, N.
  See Saltykov, Mikhail Evgrafovich
Samarakis, Andonis
  See Samarakis, Antonis
  See also EWL 3
Samarakis, Antonis 1919-2003 .... **CLC 5**
  See Samarakis, Andonis
  See also CA 25-28R; 224; CAAS 16; CANR
  36
Sanchez, Florencio 1875-1910 .... **TCLC 37**
  See also CA 153; DLB 305; EWL 3; HW 1;
  LAW
Sanchez, Luis Rafael 1936- .... **CLC 23**
  See also CA 128; DLB 305; EWL 3; HW 1;
  WLIT 1
Sanchez, Sonia 1934- .... **BLC 3; CLC 5, 116;
  PC 9**
  See also BW 2, 3; CA 33-36R; CANR 24,
  49, 74, 115; CLR 18; CP 7; CSW; CWP;
  DA3; DAM MULT; DLB 41; DLBD 8;
  EWL 3; MAICYA 1, 2; MTCW 1, 2;
  SATA 22, 136; WP
Sancho, Ignatius 1729-1780 .... **LC 84**
Sand, George 1804-1876 ..... **NCLC 2, 42, 57;
  WLC**
  See also DA; DA3; DAB; DAC; DAM
  MST, NOV; DLB 119, 192; EW 6; FW;
  GFL 1789 to the Present; RGWL 2, 3;
  TWA
Sandburg, Carl (August) 1878-1967 . **CLC 1,
  4, 10, 15, 35; PC 2, 41; WLC**
  See also AAYA 24; AMW; BYA 1, 3; CA
  5-8R; 25-28R; CANR 35; CDALB 1865-
  1917; CLR 67; DA; DA3; DAB; DAC;
  DAM MST, POET; DLB 17, 54, 284;
  EWL 3; EXPP; LAIT 2; MAICYA 1, 2;
  MTCW 1, 2; PAB; PFS 3, 6, 12; RGAL
  4; SATA 8; TUS; WCH; WP; WYA
Sandburg, Charles
  See Sandburg, Carl (August)
Sandburg, Charles A.
  See Sandburg, Carl (August)
Sanders, (James) Ed(ward) 1939- .... **CLC 53**
  See Sanders, Edward
  See also BG 3; CA 13-16R; CAAS 21;
  CANR 13, 44, 78; CP 7; DAM POET;
  DLB 16, 244
Sanders, Edward
  See Sanders, (James) Ed(ward)
  See also DLB 244
Sanders, Lawrence 1920-1998 .... **CLC 41**
  See also BEST 89:4; BPFB 3; CA 81-84;
  165; CANR 33, 62; CMW 4; CPW; DA3;
  DAM POP; MTCW 1
Sanders, Noah
  See Blount, Roy (Alton), Jr.
Sanders, Winston P.
  See Anderson, Poul (William)
Sandoz, Mari(e Susette) 1900-1966 .. **CLC 28**
  See also CA 1-4R; 25-28R; CANR 17, 64;
  DLB 9, 212; LAIT 2; MTCW 1, 2; SATA
  5; TCWW 2
Sandys, George 1578-1644 .... **LC 80**
  See also DLB 24, 121
Saner, Reg(inald Anthony) 1931- .... **CLC 9**
  See also CA 65-68; CP 7

Sankara 788-820 .... **CMLC 32**
Sannazaro, Jacopo 1456(?)-1530 .... **LC 8**
  See also RGWL 2, 3
Sansom, William 1912-1976 . **CLC 2, 6; SSC
  21**
  See also CA 5-8R; 65-68; CANR 42; DAM
  NOV; DLB 139; EWL 3; MTCW 1;
  RGEL 2; RGSF 2
Santayana, George 1863-1952 .... **TCLC 40**
  See also AMW; CA 115; 194; DLB 54, 71,
  246, 270; DLBD 13; EWL 3; RGAL 4;
  TUS
Santiago, Danny .... **CLC 33**
  See James, Daniel (Lewis)
  See also DLB 122
**Santillana, Íñigo López de Mendoza,
  Marqués de** 1398-1458 .... **LC 111**
  See also DLB 286
Santmyer, Helen Hooven
  1895-1986 .... **CLC 33; TCLC 133**
  See also CA 1-4R; 118; CANR 15, 33;
  DLBY 1984; MTCW 1; RHW
Santoka, Taneda 1882-1940 .... **TCLC 72**
Santos, Bienvenido N(uqui)
  1911-1996 ... **AAL; CLC 22; TCLC 156**
  See also CA 101; 151; CANR 19, 46; DAM
  MULT; EWL; RGAL 4; SSFS 19
Sapir, Edward 1884-1939 .... **TCLC 108**
  See also CA 211; DLB 92
Sapper .... **TCLC 44**
  See McNeile, Herman Cyril
Sapphire
  See Sapphire, Brenda
Sapphire, Brenda 1950- .... **CLC 99**
Sappho fl. 6th cent. B.C.- ... **CMLC 3, 67; PC
  5**
  See also CDWLB 1; DA3; DAM POET;
  DLB 176; PFS 20; RGWL 2, 3; WP
Saramago, Jose 1922- ..... **CLC 119; HLCS 1**
  See also CA 153; CANR 96; CWW 2; DLB
  287; EWL 3; LATS 1:2
Sarduy, Severo 1937-1993 .... **CLC 6, 97;
  HLCS 2; TCLC 167**
  See also CA 89-92; 142; CANR 58, 81;
  CWW 2; DLB 113; EWL 3; HW 1, 2;
  LAW
Sargeson, Frank 1903-1982 .... **CLC 31**
  See also CA 25-28R; 106; CANR 38, 79;
  EWL 3; GLL 2; RGEL 2; RGSF 2; SSFS
  20
Sarmiento, Domingo Faustino
  1811-1888 .... **HLCS 2**
  See also LAW; WLIT 1
Sarmiento, Felix Ruben Garcia
  See Dario, Ruben
Saro-Wiwa, Ken(ule Beeson)
  1941-1995 .... **CLC 114**
  See also BW 2; CA 142; 150; CANR 60;
  DLB 157
Saroyan, William 1908-1981 ... **CLC 1, 8, 10,
  29, 34, 56; SSC 21; TCLC 137; WLC**
  See also CA 5-8R; 103; CAD; CANR 30;
  CDALBS; DA; DA3; DAB; DAC; DAM
  DRAM, MST, NOV; DFS 17; DLB 7, 9,
  86; DLBY 1981; EWL 3; LAIT 4; MTCW
  1, 2; RGAL 4; RGSF 2; SATA 23; SATA-
  Obit 24; SSFS 14; TUS
Sarraute, Nathalie 1900-1999 .... **CLC 1, 2, 4,
  8, 10, 31, 80; TCLC 145**
  See also BPFB 3; CA 9-12R; 187; CANR
  23, 66, 134; CWW 2; DLB 83; EW 12;
  EWL 3; GFL 1789 to the Present; MTCW
  1, 2; RGWL 2, 3
Sarton, (Eleanor) May 1912-1995 ..... **CLC 4,
  14, 49, 91; PC 39; TCLC 120**
  See also AMWS 8; CA 1-4R; 149; CANR
  1, 34, 55, 116; CN 7; CP 7; DAM POET;
  DLB 48; DLBY 1981; EWL 3; FW; INT
  CANR-34; MTCW 1, 2; RGAL 4; SATA
  36; SATA-Obit 86; TUS

Sartre, Jean-Paul 1905-1980 . **CLC 1, 4, 7, 9,
  13, 18, 24, 44, 50, 52; DC 3; SSC 32;
  WLC**
  See also CA 9-12R; 97-100; CANR 21; DA;
  DA3; DAB; DAC; DAM DRAM, MST,
  NOV; DFS 5; DLB 72, 296; EW 12; EWL
  3; GFL 1789 to the Present; LMFS 2;
  MTCW 1, 2; RGSF 2; RGWL 2, 3; SSFS
  9; TWA
Sassoon, Siegfried (Lorraine)
  1886-1967 .... **CLC 36, 130; PC 12**
  See also BRW 6; CA 104; 25-28R; CANR
  36; DAB; DAM MST, NOV, POET; DLB
  20, 191; DLBD 18; EWL 3; MTCW 1, 2;
  PAB; RGEL 2; TEA
Satterfield, Charles
  See Pohl, Frederik
Satyremont
  See Peret, Benjamin
Saul, John (W. III) 1942- .... **CLC 46**
  See also AAYA 10; BEST 90:4; CA 81-84;
  CANR 16, 40, 81; CPW; DAM NOV,
  POP; HGG; SATA 98
Saunders, Caleb
  See Heinlein, Robert A(nson)
Saura (Atares), Carlos 1932-1998 .... **CLC 20**
  See also CA 114; 131; CANR 79; HW 1
Sauser, Frederic Louis
  See Sauser-Hall, Frederic
Sauser-Hall, Frederic 1887-1961 ...... **CLC 18**
  See Cendrars, Blaise
  See also CA 102; 93-96; CANR 36, 62;
  MTCW 1
Saussure, Ferdinand de
  1857-1913 .... **TCLC 49**
  See also DLB 242
Savage, Catharine
  See Brosman, Catharine Savage
Savage, Richard 1697(?)-1743 .... **LC 96**
  See also DLB 95; RGEL 2
Savage, Thomas 1915-2003 .... **CLC 40**
  See also CA 126; 132; 218; CAAS 15; CN
  7; INT CA-132; SATA-Obit 147; TCWW
  2
Savan, Glenn 1953-2003 .... **CLC 50**
  See also CA 225
Sax, Robert
  See Johnson, Robert
Saxo Grammaticus c. 1150-c.
  1222 .... **CMLC 58**
Saxton, Robert
  See Johnson, Robert
Sayers, Dorothy L(eigh) 1893-1957 . **SSC 71;
  TCLC 2, 15**
  See also BPFB 3; BRWS 3; CA 104; 119;
  CANR 60; CDBLB 1914-1945; CMW 4;
  DAM POP; DLB 10, 36, 77, 100; MSW;
  MTCW 1, 2; RGEL 2; SSFS 12; TEA
Sayers, Valerie 1952- .... **CLC 50, 122**
  See also CA 134; CANR 61; CSW
Sayles, John (Thomas) 1950- .... **CLC 7, 10,
  14, 198**
  See also CA 57-60; CANR 41, 84; DLB 44
Scammell, Michael 1935- .... **CLC 34**
  See also CA 156
Scannell, Vernon 1922- .... **CLC 49**
  See also CA 5-8R; CANR 8, 24, 57; CP 7;
  CWRI 5; DLB 27; SATA 59
Scarlett, Susan
  See Streatfeild, (Mary) Noel
Scarron, Paul 1610-1660 .... **LC 116**
  See also GFL Beginnings to 1789; RGWL
  2, 3
Scarron 1847-1910
  See Mikszath, Kalman
Schaeffer, Susan Fromberg 1941- ..... **CLC 6,
  11, 22**
  See also CA 49-52; CANR 18, 65; CN 7;
  DLB 28, 299; MTCW 1, 2; SATA 22

Schama, Simon (Michael) 1945- ..... **CLC 150**
See also BEST 89:4; CA 105; CANR 39, 91

Schary, Jill
See Robinson, Jill

Schell, Jonathan 1943- .... **CLC 35**
See also CA 73-76; CANR 12, 117

Schelling, Friedrich Wilhelm Joseph von
1775-1854 .... **NCLC 30**
See also DLB 90

Scherer, Jean-Marie Maurice 1920-
See Rohmer, Eric
See also CA 110

Schevill, James (Erwin) 1920- .... **CLC 7**
See also CA 5-8R; CAAS 12; CAD; CD 5

Schiller, Friedrich von 1759-1805 ...... **DC 12;**
NCLC 39, 69
See also CDWLB 2; DAM DRAM; DLB 94; EW 5; RGWL 2, 3; TWA

Schisgal, Murray (Joseph) 1926- .... **CLC 6**
See also CA 21-24R; CAD; CANR 48, 86; CD 5

Schlee, Ann 1934- .... **CLC 35**
See also CA 101; CANR 29, 88; SATA 44; SATA-Brief 36

Schlegel, August Wilhelm von
1767-1845 .... **NCLC 15, 142**
See also DLB 94; RGWL 2, 3

Schlegel, Friedrich 1772-1829 .... **NCLC 45**
See also DLB 90; EW 5; RGWL 2, 3; TWA

Schlegel, Johann Elias (von)
1719(?)-1749 .... **LC 5**

Schleiermacher, Friedrich
1768-1834 .... **NCLC 107**
See also DLB 90

Schlesinger, Arthur M(eier), Jr.
1917- .... **CLC 84**
See also AITN 1; CA 1-4R; CANR 1, 28, 58, 105; DLB 17; INT CANR-28; MTCW 1, 2; SATA 61

Schlink, Bernhard 1944- .... **CLC 174**
See also CA 163; CANR 116

Schmidt, Arno (Otto) 1914-1979 ...... **CLC 56**
See also CA 128; 109; DLB 69; EWL 3

Schmitz, Aron Hector 1861-1928
See Svevo, Italo
See also CA 104; 122; MTCW 1

Schnackenberg, Gjertrud (Cecelia)
1953- .... **CLC 40; PC 45**
See also CA 116; CANR 100; CP 7; CWP; DLB 120, 282; PFS 13

Schneider, Leonard Alfred 1925-1966
See Bruce, Lenny
See also CA 89-92

Schnitzler, Arthur 1862-1931 ..... **DC 17; SSC**
15, 61; TCLC 4
See also CA 104; CDWLB 2; DLB 81, 118; EW 8; EWL 3; RGSF 2; RGWL 2, 3

Schoenberg, Arnold Franz Walter
1874-1951 .... **TCLC 75**
See also CA 109; 188

Schonberg, Arnold
See Schoenberg, Arnold Franz Walter

Schopenhauer, Arthur 1788-1860 . **NCLC 51,**
157
See also DLB 90; EW 5

Schor, Sandra (M.) 1932(?)-1990 ..... **CLC 65**
See also CA 132

Schorer, Mark 1908-1977 .... **CLC 9**
See also CA 5-8R; 73-76; CANR 7; DLB 103

Schrader, Paul (Joseph) 1946- .... **CLC 26**
See also CA 37-40R; CANR 41; DLB 44

Schreber, Daniel 1842-1911 .... **TCLC 123**

Schreiner, Olive (Emilie Albertina)
1855-1920 .... **TCLC 9**
See also AFW; BRWS 2; CA 105; 154; DLB 18, 156, 190, 225; EWL 3; FW; RGEL 2; TWA; WLIT 2; WWE 1

Schulberg, Budd (Wilson) 1914- .. **CLC 7, 48**
See also BPFB 3; CA 25-28R; CANR 19, 87; CN 7; DLB 6, 26, 28; DLBY 1981, 2001

Schulman, Arnold
See Trumbo, Dalton

Schulz, Bruno 1892-1942 .. **SSC 13; TCLC 5,**
51
See also CA 115; 123; CANR 86; CDWLB 4; DLB 215; EWL 3; MTCW 2; RGSF 2; RGWL 2, 3

Schulz, Charles M(onroe)
1922-2000 .... **CLC 12**
See also AAYA 39; CA 9-12R; 187; CANR 6, 132; INT CANR-6; SATA 10; SATA-Obit 118

Schumacher, E(rnst) F(riedrich)
1911-1977 .... **CLC 80**
See also CA 81-84; 73-76; CANR 34, 85

Schumann, Robert 1810-1856 ...... **NCLC 143**

Schuyler, George Samuel 1895-1977 .... **HR 3**
See also BW 2; CA 81-84; 73-76; CANR 42; DLB 29, 51

Schuyler, James Marcus 1923-1991 .. **CLC 5,**
23
See also CA 101; 134; DAM POET; DLB 5, 169; EWL 3; INT CA-101; WP

Schwartz, Delmore (David)
1913-1966 ... **CLC 2, 4, 10, 45, 87; PC 8**
See also AMWS 2; CA 17-18; 25-28R; CANR 35; CAP 2; DLB 28, 48; EWL 3; MTCW 1, 2; PAB; RGAL 4; TUS

Schwartz, Ernst
See Ozu, Yasujiro

Schwartz, John Burnham 1965- .... **CLC 59**
See also CA 132; CANR 116

Schwartz, Lynne Sharon 1939- .... **CLC 31**
See also CA 103; CANR 44, 89; DLB 218; MTCW 2

Schwartz, Muriel A.
See Eliot, T(homas) S(tearns)

Schwarz-Bart, Andre 1928- .... **CLC 2, 4**
See also CA 89-92; CANR 109; DLB 299

Schwarz-Bart, Simone 1938- . **BLCS; CLC 7**
See also BW 2; CA 97-100; CANR 117; EWL 3

Schwerner, Armand 1927-1999 .... **PC 42**
See also CA 9-12R; 179; CANR 50, 85; CP 7; DLB 165

Schwitters, Kurt (Hermann Edward Karl
Julius) 1887-1948 .... **TCLC 95**
See also CA 158

Schwob, Marcel (Mayer Andre)
1867-1905 .... **TCLC 20**
See also CA 117; 168; DLB 123; GFL 1789 to the Present

Sciascia, Leonardo 1921-1989 .. **CLC 8, 9, 41**
See also CA 85-88; 130; CANR 35; DLB 177; EWL 3; MTCW 1; RGWL 2, 3

Scoppettone, Sandra 1936- .... **CLC 26**
See Early, Jack
See also AAYA 11; BYA 8; CA 5-8R; CANR 41, 73; GLL 1; MAICYA 2; MAICYAS 1; SATA 9, 92; WYA; YAW

Scorsese, Martin 1942- .... **CLC 20, 89, 207**
See also AAYA 38; CA 110, 114; CANR 46, 85

Scotland, Jay
See Jakes, John (William)

Scott, Duncan Campbell
1862-1947 .... **TCLC 6**
See also CA 104; 153; DAC; DLB 92; RGEL 2

Scott, Evelyn 1893-1963 .... **CLC 43**
See also CA 104; 112; CANR 64; DLB 9, 48; RHW

Scott, F(rancis) R(eginald)
1899-1985 .... **CLC 22**
See also CA 101; 114; CANR 87; DLB 88; INT CA-101; RGEL 2

Scott, Frank
See Scott, F(rancis) R(eginald)

Scott, Joan .... **CLC 65**

Scott, Joanna 1960- .... **CLC 50**
See also CA 126; CANR 53, 92

Scott, Paul (Mark) 1920-1978 ...... **CLC 9, 60**
See also BRWS 1; CA 81-84; 77-80; CANR 33; DLB 14, 207; EWL 3; MTCW 1; RGEL 2; RHW; WWE 1

Scott, Ridley 1937- .... **CLC 183**
See also AAYA 13, 43

Scott, Sarah 1723-1795 .... **LC 44**
See also DLB 39

Scott, Sir Walter 1771-1832 .... **NCLC 15, 69,**
110; PC 13; SSC 32; WLC
See also AAYA 22; BRW 4; BYA 2; CD-BLB 1789-1832; DA; DAB; DAC; DAM MST, NOV, POET; DLB 93, 107, 116, 144, 159; HGG; LAIT 1; RGEL 2; RGSF 2; SSFS 10; SUFW 1; TEA; WLIT 3; YABC 2

Scribe, (Augustin) Eugene 1791-1861 . **DC 5;**
NCLC 16
See also DAM DRAM; DLB 192; GFL 1789 to the Present; RGWL 2, 3

Scrum, R.
See Crumb, R(obert)

Scudery, Georges de 1601-1667 .... **LC 75**
See also GFL Beginnings to 1789

Scudery, Madeleine de 1607-1701 .. **LC 2, 58**
See also DLB 268; GFL Beginnings to 1789

Scum
See Crumb, R(obert)

Scumbag, Little Bobby
See Crumb, R(obert)

Seabrook, John
See Hubbard, L(afayette) Ron(ald)

Seacole, Mary Jane Grant
1805-1881 .... **NCLC 147**
See also DLB 166

Sealy, I(rwin) Allan 1951- .... **CLC 55**
See also CA 136; CN 7

Search, Alexander
See Pessoa, Fernando (Antonio Nogueira)

Sebald, W(infried) G(eorg)
1944-2001 .... **CLC 194**
See also BRWS 8; CA 159; 202; CANR 98

Sebastian, Lee
See Silverberg, Robert

Sebastian Owl
See Thompson, Hunter S(tockton)

Sebestyen, Igen
See Sebestyen, Ouida

Sebestyen, Ouida 1924- .... **CLC 30**
See also AAYA 8; BYA 7; CA 107; CANR 40, 114; CLR 17; JRDA; MAICYA 1, 2; SAAS 10; SATA 39, 140; WYA; YAW

Sebold, Alice 1963(?)- .... **CLC 193**
See also AAYA 56; CA 203

Second Duke of Buckingham
See Villiers, George

Secundus, H. Scriblerus
See Fielding, Henry

Sedges, John
See Buck, Pearl S(ydenstricker)

Sedgwick, Catharine Maria
1789-1867 .... **NCLC 19, 98**
See also DLB 1, 74, 183, 239, 243, 254; RGAL 4

Seelye, John (Douglas) 1931- .... **CLC 7**
See also CA 97-100; CANR 70; INT CA-97-100; TCWW 2

Sheldon, Alice Hastings Bradley
  1915(?)-1987
  See Tiptree, James, Jr.
  See also CA 108; 122; CANR 34; INT CA-108; MTCW 1
Sheldon, John
  See Bloch, Robert (Albert)
Sheldon, Walter J(ames) 1917-1996
  See Queen, Ellery
  See also AITN 1; CA 25-28R; CANR 10
Shelley, Mary Wollstonecraft (Godwin)
  1797-1851 ...... **NCLC 14, 59, 103; WLC**
  See also AAYA 20; BPFB 3; BRW 3; BRWC 2; BRWS 3; BYA 5; CDBLB 1789-1832; DA; DA3; DAB; DAC; DAM MST, NOV; DLB 110, 116, 159, 178; EXPN; HGG; LAIT 1; LMFS 1, 2; NFS 1; RGEL 2; SATA 29; SCFW; SFW 4; TEA; WLIT 3
Shelley, Percy Bysshe 1792-1822 .. **NCLC 18, 93, 143; PC 14; WLC**
  See also BRW 4; BRWR 1; CDBLB 1789-1832; DA; DA3; DAB; DAC; DAM MST, POET; DLB 96, 110, 158; EXPP; LMFS 1; PAB; PFS 2; RGEL 2; TEA; WLIT 3; WP
Shepard, Jim 1956- .... **CLC 36**
  See also CA 137; CANR 59, 104; SATA 90
Shepard, Lucius 1947- .... **CLC 34**
  See also CA 128; 141; CANR 81, 124; HGG; SCFW 2; SFW 4; SUFW 2
Shepard, Sam 1943- .... **CLC 4, 6, 17, 34, 41, 44, 169; DC 5**
  See also AAYA 1, 58; AMWS 3; CA 69-72; CABS 3; CAD; CANR 22, 120; CD 5; DA3; DAM DRAM; DFS 3, 6, 7, 14; DLB 7, 212; EWL 3; IDFW 3, 4; MTCW 1, 2; RGAL 4
Shepherd, Michael
  See Ludlum, Robert
Sherburne, Zoa (Lillian Morin)
  1912-1995 .... **CLC 30**
  See also AAYA 13; CA 1-4R; 176; CANR 3, 37; MAICYA 1, 2; SAAS 18; SATA 3; YAW
Sheridan, Frances 1724-1766 .... **LC 7**
  See also DLB 39, 84
Sheridan, Richard Brinsley
  1751-1816 .... **DC 1; NCLC 5, 91; WLC**
  See also BRW 3; CDBLB 1660-1789; DA; DAB; DAC; DAM DRAM, MST; DFS 15; DLB 89; WLIT 3
Sherman, Jonathan Marc .... **CLC 55**
Sherman, Martin 1941(?)- .... **CLC 19**
  See also CA 116; 123; CAD; CANR 86; CD 5; DFS 20; DLB 228; GLL 1; IDTP
Sherwin, Judith Johnson
  See Johnson, Judith (Emlyn)
  See also CANR 85; CP 7; CWP
Sherwood, Frances 1940- .... **CLC 81**
  See also CA 146; 220; CAAE 220
Sherwood, Robert E(mmet)
  1896-1955 .... **TCLC 3**
  See also CA 104; 153; CANR 86; DAM DRAM; DFS 11, 15, 17; DLB 7, 26, 249; IDFW 3, 4; RGAL 4
Shestov, Lev 1866-1938 .... **TCLC 56**
Shevchenko, Taras 1814-1861 .... **NCLC 54**
Shiel, M(atthew) P(hipps)
  1865-1947 .... **TCLC 8**
  See Holmes, Gordon
  See also CA 106; 160; DLB 153; HGG; MTCW 2; SFW 4; SUFW
Shields, Carol (Ann) 1935-2003 ...... **CLC 91, 113, 193**
  See also AMWS 7; CA 81-84; 218; CANR 51, 74, 98, 133; CCA 1; CN 7; CPW; DA3; DAC; MTCW 2

Shields, David (Jonathan) 1956- ...... **CLC 97**
  See also CA 124; CANR 48, 99, 112
Shiga, Naoya 1883-1971 ..... **CLC 33; SSC 23**
  See Shiga Naoya
  See also CA 101; 33-36R; MJW; RGWL 3
Shiga Naoya
  See Shiga, Naoya
  See also DLB 180; EWL 3; RGWL 3
Shilts, Randy 1951-1994 .... **CLC 85**
  See also AAYA 19; CA 115; 127; 144; CANR 45; DA3; GLL 1; INT CA-127; MTCW 2
Shimazaki, Haruki 1872-1943
  See Shimazaki Toson
  See also CA 105; 134; CANR 84; RGWL 3
Shimazaki Toson .... **TCLC 5**
  See Shimazaki, Haruki
  See also DLB 180; EWL 3
Shirley, James 1596-1666 .... **DC 25; LC 96**
  See also DLB 58; RGEL 2
Sholokhov, Mikhail (Aleksandrovich)
  1905-1984 .... **CLC 7, 15**
  See also CA 101; 112; DLB 272; EWL 3; MTCW 1, 2; RGWL 2, 3; SATA-Obit 36
Shone, Patric
  See Hanley, James
Showalter, Elaine 1941- .... **CLC 169**
  See also CA 57-60; CANR 58, 106; DLB 67; FW; GLL 2
Shreve, Susan
  See Shreve, Susan Richards
Shreve, Susan Richards 1939- .... **CLC 23**
  See also CA 49-52; CAAS 5; CANR 5, 38, 69, 100; MAICYA 1, 2; SATA 46, 95, 152; SATA-Brief 41
Shue, Larry 1946-1985 .... **CLC 52**
  See also CA 145; 117; DAM DRAM; DFS 7
Shu-Jen, Chou 1881-1936
  See Lu Hsun
  See also CA 104
Shulman, Alix Kates 1932- .... **CLC 2, 10**
  See also CA 29-32R; CANR 43; FW; SATA 7
Shuster, Joe 1914-1992 .... **CLC 21**
  See also AAYA 50
Shute, Nevil .... **CLC 30**
  See Norway, Nevil Shute
  See also BPFB 3; DLB 255; NFS 9; RHW; SFW 4
Shuttle, Penelope (Diane) 1947- .... **CLC 7**
  See also CA 93-96; CANR 39, 84, 92, 108; CP 7; CWP; DLB 14, 40
Shvarts, Elena 1948- .... **PC 50**
  See also CA 147
Sidhwa, Bapsy (N.) 1938- .... **CLC 168**
  See also CA 108; CANR 25, 57; CN 7; FW
Sidney, Mary 1561-1621 .... **LC 19, 39**
  See Sidney Herbert, Mary
Sidney, Sir Philip 1554-1586 . **LC 19, 39; PC 32**
  See also BRW 1; BRWR 2; CDBLB Before 1660; DA; DA3; DAB; DAC; DAM MST, POET; DLB 167; EXPP; PAB; RGEL 2; TEA; WP
Sidney Herbert, Mary
  See Sidney, Mary
  See also DLB 167
Siegel, Jerome 1914-1996 .... **CLC 21**
  See Siegel, Jerry
  See also CA 116; 169; 151
Siegel, Jerry
  See Siegel, Jerome
  See also AAYA 50
Sienkiewicz, Henryk (Adam Alexander Pius)
  1846-1916 .... **TCLC 3**
  See also CA 104; 134; CANR 84; EWL 3; RGSF 2; RGWL 2, 3

Sierra, Gregorio Martinez
  See Martinez Sierra, Gregorio
Sierra, Maria (de la O'LeJarraga) Martinez
  See Martinez Sierra, Maria (de la O'LeJarraga)
Sigal, Clancy 1926- .... **CLC 7**
  See also CA 1-4R; CANR 85; CN 7
Siger of Brabant 1240(?)-1284(?) . **CMLC 69**
  See also DLB 115
Sigourney, Lydia H.
  See Sigourney, Lydia Howard (Huntley)
  See also DLB 73, 183
Sigourney, Lydia Howard (Huntley)
  1791-1865 .... **NCLC 21, 87**
  See Sigourney, Lydia H.; Sigourney, Lydia Huntley
  See also DLB 1
Sigourney, Lydia Huntley
  See Sigourney, Lydia Howard (Huntley)
  See also DLB 42, 239, 243
Siguenza y Gongora, Carlos de
  1645-1700 .... **HLCS 2; LC 8**
  See also LAW
Sigurjonsson, Johann
  See Sigurjonsson, Johann
Sigurjonsson, Johann 1880-1919 ... **TCLC 27**
  See also CA 170; DLB 293; EWL 3
Sikelianos, Angelos 1884-1951 .... **PC 29; TCLC 39**
  See also EWL 3; RGWL 2, 3
Silkin, Jon 1930-1997 .... **CLC 2, 6, 43**
  See also CA 5-8R; CAAS 5; CANR 89; CP 7; DLB 27
Silko, Leslie (Marmon) 1948- .... **CLC 23, 74, 114; NNAL; SSC 37, 66; WLCS**
  See also AAYA 14; AMWS 4; ANW; BYA 12; CA 115; 122; CANR 45, 65, 118; CN 7; CP 7; CPW 1; CWP; DA; DA3; DAC; DAM MST, MULT, POP; DLB 143, 175, 256, 275; EWL 3; EXPP; EXPS; LAIT 4; MTCW 2; NFS 4; PFS 9, 16; RGAL 4; RGSF 2; SSFS 4, 8, 10, 11
Sillanpaa, Frans Eemil 1888-1964 ... **CLC 19**
  See also CA 129; 93-96; EWL 3; MTCW 1
Sillitoe, Alan 1928- .. **CLC 1, 3, 6, 10, 19, 57, 148**
  See also AITN 1; BRWS 5; CA 9-12R, 191; CAAE 191; CAAS 2; CANR 8, 26, 55; CDBLB 1960 to Present; CN 7; DLB 14, 139; EWL 3; MTCW 1, 2; RGEL 2; RGSF 2; SATA 61
Silone, Ignazio 1900-1978 .... **CLC 4**
  See also CA 25-28; 81-84; CANR 34; CAP 2; DLB 264; EW 12; EWL 3; MTCW 1; RGSF 2; RGWL 2, 3
Silone, Ignazione
  See Silone, Ignazio
Silver, Joan Micklin 1935- .... **CLC 20**
  See also CA 114; 121; INT CA-121
Silver, Nicholas
  See Faust, Frederick (Schiller)
  See also TCWW 2
Silverberg, Robert 1935- .... **CLC 7, 140**
  See also AAYA 24; BPFB 3; BYA 7, 9; CA 1-4R, 186; CAAE 186; CAAS 3; CANR 1, 20, 36, 85; CLR 59; CN 7; CPW; DAM POP; DLB 8; INT CANR-20; MAICYA 1, 2; MTCW 1, 2; SATA 13, 91; SATA-Essay 104; SCFW 2; SFW 4; SUFW 2
Silverstein, Alvin 1933- .... **CLC 17**
  See also CA 49-52; CANR 2; CLR 25; JRDA; MAICYA 1, 2; SATA 8, 69, 124
Silverstein, Shel(don Allan)
  1932-1999 .... **PC 49**
  See also AAYA 40; BW 3; CA 107; 179; CANR 47, 74, 81; CLR 5, 96; CWRI 5; JRDA; MAICYA 1, 2; MTCW 2; SATA 33, 92; SATA-Brief 27; SATA-Obit 116

Stephens, James 1882(?)-1950 .... **SSC 50; TCLC 4**
See also CA 104; 192; DLB 19, 153, 162; EWL 3; FANT; RGEL 2; SUFW

Stephens, Reed
See Donaldson, Stephen R(eeder)

Steptoe, Lydia
See Barnes, Djuna
See also GLL 1

Sterchi, Beat 1949- .... **CLC 65**
See also CA 203

Sterling, Brett
See Bradbury, Ray (Douglas); Hamilton, Edmond

Sterling, Bruce 1954- .... **CLC 72**
See also CA 119; CANR 44, 135; SCFW 2; SFW 4

Sterling, George 1869-1926 .... **TCLC 20**
See also CA 117; 165; DLB 54

Stern, Gerald 1925- .... **CLC 40, 100**
See also AMWS 9; CA 81-84; CANR 28, 94; CP 7; DLB 105; RGAL 4

Stern, Richard (Gustave) 1928- ... **CLC 4, 39**
See also CA 1-4R; CANR 1, 25, 52, 120; CN 7; DLB 218; DLBY 1987; INT CANR-25

Sternberg, Josef von 1894-1969 .... **CLC 20**
See also CA 81-84

Sterne, Laurence 1713-1768 .... **LC 2, 48; WLC**
See also BRW 3; BRWC 1; CDBLB 1660-1789; DA; DAB; DAC; DAM MST, NOV; DLB 39; RGEL 2; TEA

Sternheim, (William Adolf) Carl 1878-1942 .... **TCLC 8**
See also CA 105; 193; DLB 56, 118; EWL 3; RGWL 2, 3

Stevens, Mark 1951- .... **CLC 34**
See also CA 122

Stevens, Wallace 1879-1955 . **PC 6; TCLC 3, 12, 45; WLC**
See also AMW; AMWR 1; CA 104; 124; CDALB 1929-1941; DA; DA3; DAB; DAC; DAM MST, POET; DLB 54; EWL 3; EXPP; MTCW 1, 2; PAB; PFS 13, 16; RGAL 4; TUS; WP

Stevenson, Anne (Katharine) 1933- ... **CLC 7, 33**
See also BRWS 6; CA 17-20R; CAAS 9; CANR 9, 33, 123; CP 7; CWP; DLB 40; MTCW 1; RHW

Stevenson, Robert Louis (Balfour) 1850-1894 ...... **NCLC 5, 14, 63; SSC 11, 51; WLC**
See also AAYA 24; BPFB 3; BRW 5; BRWC 1; BRWR 1; BYA 1, 2, 4, 13; CD-BLB 1890-1914; DA; DA3; DAB; DAC; DAM MST, NOV; DLB 18, 57, 141, 156, 174; DLBD 13; HGG; JRDA; LAIT 1, 3; MAICYA 1, 2; NFS 11, 20; RGEL 2; RGSF 2; SATA 100; SUFW; TEA; WCH; WLIT 4; WYA; YABC 2; YAW

Stewart, J(ohn) I(nnes) M(ackintosh) 1906-1994 .... **CLC 7, 14, 32**
See Innes, Michael
See also CA 85-88; 147; CAAS 3; CANR 47; CMW 4; MTCW 1, 2

Stewart, Mary (Florence Elinor) 1916- .... **CLC 7, 35, 117**
See also AAYA 29; BPFB 3; CA 1-4R; CANR 1, 59, 130; CMW 4; CPW; DAB; FANT; RHW; SATA 12; YAW

Stewart, Mary Rainbow
See Stewart, Mary (Florence Elinor)

Stifle, June
See Campbell, Maria

Stifter, Adalbert 1805-1868 .. **NCLC 41; SSC 28**
See also CDWLB 2; DLB 133; RGSF 2; RGWL 2, 3

Still, James 1906-2001 .... **CLC 49**
See also CA 65-68; 195; CAAS 17; CANR 10, 26; CSW; DLB 9; DLBY 01; SATA 29; SATA-Obit 127

Sting 1951-
See Sumner, Gordon Matthew
See also CA 167

Stirling, Arthur
See Sinclair, Upton (Beall)

Stitt, Milan 1941- .... **CLC 29**
See also CA 69-72

Stockton, Francis Richard 1834-1902
See Stockton, Frank R.
See also CA 108; 137; MAICYA 1, 2; SATA 44; SFW 4

Stockton, Frank R. .... **TCLC 47**
See Stockton, Francis Richard
See also BYA 4, 13; DLB 42, 74; DLBD 13; EXPS; SATA-Brief 32; SSFS 3; SUFW; WCH

Stoddard, Charles
See Kuttner, Henry

Stoker, Abraham 1847-1912
See Stoker, Bram
See also CA 105; 150; DA; DA3; DAC; DAM MST, NOV; HGG; SATA 29

Stoker, Bram . **SSC 62; TCLC 8, 144; WLC**
See Stoker, Abraham
See also AAYA 23; BPFB 3; BRWS 3; BYA 5; CDBLB 1890-1914; DAB; DLB 304; LATS 1:1; NFS 18; RGEL 2; SUFW; TEA; WLIT 4

Stolz, Mary (Slattery) 1920- .... **CLC 12**
See also AAYA 8; AITN 1; CA 5-8R; CANR 13, 41, 112; JRDA; MAICYA 1, 2; SAAS 3; SATA 10, 71, 133; YAW

Stone, Irving 1903-1989 .... **CLC 7**
See also AITN 1; BPFB 3; CA 1-4R; 129; CAAS 3; CANR 1, 23; CPW; DA3; DAM POP; INT CANR-23; MTCW 1, 2; RHW; SATA 3; SATA-Obit 64

Stone, Oliver (William) 1946- .... **CLC 73**
See also AAYA 15; CA 110; CANR 55, 125

Stone, Robert (Anthony) 1937- ... **CLC 5, 23, 42, 175**
See also AMWS 5; BPFB 3; CA 85-88; CANR 23, 66, 95; CN 7; DLB 152; EWL 3; INT CANR-23; MTCW 1

Stone, Ruth 1915- .... **PC 53**
See also CA 45-48; CANR 2, 91; CP 7; CSW; DLB 105; PFS 19

Stone, Zachary
See Follett, Ken(neth Martin)

Stoppard, Tom 1937- ... **CLC 1, 3, 4, 5, 8, 15, 29, 34, 63, 91; DC 6; WLC**
See also BRWC 1; BRWR 2; BRWS 1; CA 81-84; CANR 39, 67, 125; CBD; CD 5; CDBLB 1960 to Present; DA; DA3; DAB; DAC; DAM DRAM, MST; DFS 2, 5, 8, 11, 13, 16; DLB 13, 233; DLBY 1985; EWL 3; LATS 1:2; MTCW 1, 2; RGEL 2; TEA; WLIT 4

Storey, David (Malcolm) 1933- . **CLC 2, 4, 5, 8**
See also BRWS 1; CA 81-84; CANR 36; CBD; CD 5; CN 7; DAM DRAM; DLB 13, 14, 207, 245; EWL 3; MTCW 1; RGEL 2

Storm, Hyemeyohsts 1935- ... **CLC 3; NNAL**
See also CA 81-84; CANR 45; DAM MULT

Storm, (Hans) Theodor (Woldsen) 1817-1888 .... **NCLC 1; SSC 27**
See also CDWLB 2; DLB 129; EW; RGSF 2; RGWL 2, 3

Storni, Alfonsina 1892-1938 . **HLC 2; PC 33; TCLC 5**
See also CA 104; 131; DAM MULT; DLB 283; HW 1; LAW

Stoughton, William 1631-1701 .... **LC 38**
See also DLB 24

Stout, Rex (Todhunter) 1886-1975 ..... **CLC 3**
See also AITN 2; BPFB 3; CA 61-64; CANR 71; CMW 4; DLB 306; MSW; RGAL 4

Stow, (Julian) Randolph 1935- ... **CLC 23, 48**
See also CA 13-16R; CANR 33; CN 7; DLB 260; MTCW 1; RGEL 2

Stowe, Harriet (Elizabeth) Beecher 1811-1896 .... **NCLC 3, 50, 133; WLC**
See also AAYA 53; AMWS 1; CDALB 1865-1917; DA; DA3; DAB; DAC; DAM MST, NOV; DLB 1, 12, 42, 74, 189, 239, 243; EXPN; JRDA; LAIT 2; MAICYA 1, 2; NFS 6; RGAL 4; TUS; YABC 1

Strabo c. 64B.C.-c. 25 .... **CMLC 37**
See also DLB 176

Strachey, (Giles) Lytton 1880-1932 .... **TCLC 12**
See also BRWS 2; CA 110; 178; DLB 149; DLBD 10; EWL 3; MTCW 2; NCFS 4

Stramm, August 1874-1915 .... **PC 50**
See also CA 195; EWL 3

Strand, Mark 1934- .. **CLC 6, 18, 41, 71; PC 63**
See also AMWS 4; CA 21-24R; CANR 40, 65, 100; CP 7; DAM POET; DLB 5; EWL 3; PAB; PFS 9, 18; RGAL 4; SATA 41

Stratton-Porter, Gene(va Grace) 1863-1924
See Porter, Gene(va Grace) Stratton
See also ANW; CA 137; CLR 87; DLB 221; DLBD 14; MAICYA 1, 2; SATA 15

Straub, Peter (Francis) 1943- ... **CLC 28, 107**
See also BEST 89:1; BPFB 3; CA 85-88; CANR 28, 65, 109; CPW; DAM POP; DLBY 1984; HGG; MTCW 1, 2; SUFW 2

Strauss, Botho 1944- .... **CLC 22**
See also CA 157; CWW 2; DLB 124

Strauss, Leo 1899-1973 .... **TCLC 141**
See also CA 101; 45-48; CANR 122

Streatfeild, (Mary) Noel 1897(?)-1986 .... **CLC 21**
See also CA 81-84; 120; CANR 31; CLR 17, 83; CWRI 5; DLB 160; MAICYA 1, 2; SATA 20; SATA-Obit 48

Stribling, T(homas) S(igismund) 1881-1965 .... **CLC 23**
See also CA 189; 107; CMW 4; DLB 9; RGAL 4

Strindberg, (Johan) August 1849-1912 ... **DC 18; TCLC 1, 8, 21, 47; WLC**
See also CA 104; 135; DA; DA3; DAB; DAC; DAM DRAM, MST; DFS 4, 9; DLB 259; EW 7; EWL 3; IDTP; LMFS 2; MTCW 2; RGWL 2, 3; TWA

Stringer, Arthur 1874-1950 .... **TCLC 37**
See also CA 161; DLB 92

Stringer, David
See Roberts, Keith (John Kingston)

Stroheim, Erich von 1885-1957 ..... **TCLC 71**

Strugatskii, Arkadii (Natanovich) 1925-1991 .... **CLC 27**
See Strugatsky, Arkadii Natanovich
See also CA 106; 135; SFW 4

Strugatskii, Boris (Natanovich) 1933- .... **CLC 27**
See Strugatsky, Boris (Natanovich)
See also CA 106; SFW 4

Strugatsky, Arkadii Natanovich
See Strugatskii, Arkadii (Natanovich)
See also DLB 302

Strugatsky, Boris (Natanovich)
See Strugatskii, Boris (Natanovich)
See also DLB 302

Strummer, Joe 1953(?)- .... **CLC 30**

Strunk, William, Jr. 1869-1946 ...... **TCLC 92**
See also CA 118; 164; NCFS 5

Stryk, Lucien 1924- .... **PC 27**
See also CA 13-16R; CANR 10, 28, 55,
110; CP 7

Stuart, Don A.
See Campbell, John W(ood, Jr.)

Stuart, Ian
See MacLean, Alistair (Stuart)

Stuart, Jesse (Hilton) 1906-1984 ... **CLC 1, 8,
11, 14, 34; SSC 31**
See also CA 5-8R; 112; CANR 31; DLB 9,
48, 102; DLBY 1984; SATA 2; SATA-
Obit 36

Stubblefield, Sally
See Trumbo, Dalton

Sturgeon, Theodore (Hamilton)
1918-1985 .... **CLC 22, 39**
See Queen, Ellery
See also AAYA 51; BPFB 3; BYA 9, 10;
CA 81-84; 116; CANR 32, 103; DLB 8;
DLBY 1985; HGG; MTCW 1, 2; SCFW;
SFW 4; SUFW

Sturges, Preston 1898-1959 .... **TCLC 48**
See also CA 114; 149; DLB 26

Styron, William 1925- .... **CLC 1, 3, 5, 11, 15,
60; SSC 25**
See also AMW; AMWC 2; BEST 90:4;
BPFB 3; CA 5-8R; CANR 6, 33, 74, 126;
CDALB 1968-1988; CN 7; CPW; CSW;
DA3; DAM NOV, POP; DLB 2, 143, 299;
DLBY 1980; EWL 3; INT CANR-6;
LAIT 2; MTCW 1, 2; NCFS 1; RGAL 4;
RHW; TUS

Su, Chien 1884-1918
See Su Man-shu
See also CA 123

Suarez Lynch, B.
See Bioy Casares, Adolfo; Borges, Jorge
Luis

Suassuna, Ariano Vilar 1927- .... **HLCS 1**
See also CA 178; DLB 307; HW 2; LAW

Suckert, Kurt Erich
See Malaparte, Curzio

Suckling, Sir John 1609-1642 . **LC 75; PC 30**
See also BRW 2; DAM POET; DLB 58,
126; EXPP; PAB; RGEL 2

Suckow, Ruth 1892-1960 .... **SSC 18**
See also CA 193; 113; DLB 9, 102; RGAL
4; TCWW 2

Sudermann, Hermann 1857-1928 .. **TCLC 15**
See also CA 107; 201; DLB 118

Sue, Eugene 1804-1857 .... **NCLC 1**
See also DLB 119

Sueskind, Patrick 1949- .... **CLC 44, 182**
See Suskind, Patrick

Suetonius c. 70-c. 130 .... **CMLC 60**
See also AW 2; DLB 211; RGWL 2, 3

Sukenick, Ronald 1932-2004 ..... **CLC 3, 4, 6,
48**
See also CA 25-28R; 209; 229; CAAE 209;
CAAS 8; CANR 32, 89; CN 7; DLB 173;
DLBY 1981

Suknaski, Andrew 1942- .... **CLC 19**
See also CA 101; CP 7; DLB 53

Sullivan, Vernon
See Vian, Boris

Sully Prudhomme, Rene-Francois-Armand
1839-1907 .... **TCLC 31**
See also GFL 1789 to the Present

Su Man-shu .... **TCLC 24**
See Su, Chien
See also EWL 3

Sumarokov, Aleksandr Petrovich
1717-1777 .... **LC 104**
See also DLB 150

Summerforest, Ivy B.
See Kirkup, James

Summers, Andrew James 1942- .... **CLC 26**

Summers, Andy
See Summers, Andrew James

Summers, Hollis (Spurgeon, Jr.)
1916- .... **CLC 10**
See also CA 5-8R; CANR 3; DLB 6

**Summers, (Alphonsus Joseph-Mary
Augustus) Montague**
1880-1948 .... **TCLC 16**
See also CA 118; 163

Sumner, Gordon Matthew .... **CLC 26**
See Police, The; Sting

Sun Tzu c. 400B.C.-c. 320B.C. ...... **CMLC 56**

Surrey, Henry Howard 1517-1574 ...... **PC 59**
See also BRW 1; RGEL 2

Surtees, Robert Smith 1805-1864 .. **NCLC 14**
See also DLB 21; RGEL 2

Susann, Jacqueline 1921-1974 .... **CLC 3**
See also AITN 1; BPFB 3; CA 65-68; 53-
56; MTCW 1, 2

Su Shi
See Su Shih
See also RGWL 2, 3

Su Shih 1036-1101 .... **CMLC 15**
See Su Shi

Suskind, Patrick .... **CLC 182**
See Sueskind, Patrick
See also BPFB 3; CA 145; CWW 2

Sutcliff, Rosemary 1920-1992 .... **CLC 26**
See also AAYA 10; BYA 1, 4; CA 5-8R;
139; CANR 37; CLR 1, 37; CPW; DAB;
DAC; DAM MST, POP; JRDA; LATS
1:1; MAICYA 1, 2; MAICYAS 1; RHW;
SATA 6, 44, 78; SATA-Obit 73; WYA;
YAW

Sutro, Alfred 1863-1933 .... **TCLC 6**
See also CA 105; 185; DLB 10; RGEL 2

Sutton, Henry
See Slavitt, David R(ytman)

Suzuki, D. T.
See Suzuki, Daisetz Teitaro

Suzuki, Daisetz T.
See Suzuki, Daisetz Teitaro

Suzuki, Daisetz Teitaro
1870-1966 .... **TCLC 109**
See also CA 121; 111; MTCW 1, 2

Suzuki, Teitaro
See Suzuki, Daisetz Teitaro

Svevo, Italo .... **SSC 25; TCLC 2, 35**
See Schmitz, Aron Hector
See also DLB 264; EW 8; EWL 3; RGWL
2, 3

Swados, Elizabeth (A.) 1951- .... **CLC 12**
See also CA 97-100; CANR 49; INT CA-
97-100

Swados, Harvey 1920-1972 .... **CLC 5**
See also CA 5-8R; 37-40R; CANR 6; DLB
2

Swan, Gladys 1934- .... **CLC 69**
See also CA 101; CANR 17, 39

Swanson, Logan
See Matheson, Richard (Burton)

Swarthout, Glendon (Fred)
1918-1992 .... **CLC 35**
See also AAYA 55; CA 1-4R; 139; CANR
1, 47; LAIT 5; SATA 26; TCWW 2; YAW

Swedenborg, Emanuel 1688-1772 ..... **LC 105**

Sweet, Sarah C.
See Jewett, (Theodora) Sarah Orne

Swenson, May 1919-1989 ...... **CLC 4, 14, 61,
106; PC 14**
See also AMWS 4; CA 5-8R; 130; CANR
36, 61, 131; DA; DAB; DAC; DAM MST,
POET; DLB 5; EXPP; GLL 2; MTCW 1,
2; PFS 16; SATA 15; WP

Swift, Augustus
See Lovecraft, H(oward) P(hillips)

Swift, Graham (Colin) 1949- ...... **CLC 41, 88**
See also BRWC 2; BRWS 5; CA 117; 122;
CANR 46, 71, 128; CN 7; DLB 194;
MTCW 2; NFS 18; RGSF 2

Swift, Jonathan 1667-1745 ..... **LC 1, 42, 101;
PC 9; WLC**
See also AAYA 41; BRW 3; BRWC 1;
BRWR 1; BYA 5, 14; CDBLB 1660-1789;
CLR 53; DA; DA3; DAB; DAC; DAM
MST, NOV, POET; DLB 39, 95, 101;
EXPN; LAIT 1; NFS 6; RGEL 2; SATA
19; TEA; WCH; WLIT 3

Swinburne, Algernon Charles
1837-1909 ... **PC 24; TCLC 8, 36; WLC**
See also BRW 5; CA 105; 140; CDBLB
1832-1890; DA; DA3; DAB; DAC; DAM
MST, POET; DLB 35, 57; PAB; RGEL 2;
TEA

Swinfen, Ann .... **CLC 34**
See also CA 202

Swinnerton, Frank Arthur
1884-1982 .... **CLC 31**
See also CA 108; DLB 34

Swithen, John
See King, Stephen (Edwin)

Sylvia
See Ashton-Warner, Sylvia (Constance)

Symmes, Robert Edward
See Duncan, Robert (Edward)

Symonds, John Addington
1840-1893 .... **NCLC 34**
See also DLB 57, 144

Symons, Arthur 1865-1945 .... **TCLC 11**
See also CA 107; 189; DLB 19, 57, 149;
RGEL 2

Symons, Julian (Gustave)
1912-1994 .... **CLC 2, 14, 32**
See also CA 49-52; 147; CAAS 3; CANR
3, 33, 59; CMW 4; DLB 87, 155; DLBY
1992; MSW; MTCW 1

Synge, (Edmund) J(ohn) M(illington)
1871-1909 .... **DC 2; TCLC 6, 37**
See also BRW 6; BRWR 1; CA 104; 141;
CDBLB 1890-1914; DAM DRAM; DFS
18; DLB 10, 19; EWL 3; RGEL 2; TEA;
WLIT 4

Syruc, J.
See Milosz, Czeslaw

Szirtes, George 1948- .... **CLC 46; PC 51**
See also CA 109; CANR 27, 61, 117; CP 7

Szymborska, Wislawa 1923- ... **CLC 99, 190;
PC 44**
See also CA 154; CANR 91, 133; CDWLB
4; CWP; CWW 2; DA3; DLB 232; DLBY
1996; EWL 3; MTCW 2; PFS 15; RGWL
3

T. O., Nik
See Annensky, Innokenty (Fyodorovich)

Tabori, George 1914- .... **CLC 19**
See also CA 49-52; CANR 4, 69; CBD; CD
5; DLB 245

Tacitus c. 55-c. 117 .... **CMLC 56**
See also AW 2; CDWLB 1; DLB 211;
RGWL 2, 3

Tagore, Rabindranath 1861-1941 .... **PC 8;
SSC 48; TCLC 3, 53**
See also CA 104; 120; DA3; DAM DRAM,
POET; EWL 3; MTCW 1, 2; PFS 18;
RGEL 2; RGSF 2; RGWL 2, 3; TWA

Taine, Hippolyte Adolphe
1828-1893 .... **NCLC 15**
See also EW 7; GFL 1789 to the Present
Talayesva, Don C. 1890-(?) .... **NNAL**
Talese, Gay 1932- .... **CLC 37**
See also AITN 1; CA 1-4R; CANR 9, 58;
DLB 185; INT CANR-9; MTCW 1, 2
Tallent, Elizabeth (Ann) 1954- .... **CLC 45**
See also CA 117; CANR 72; DLB 130
Tallmountain, Mary 1918-1997 .... **NNAL**
See also CA 146; 161; DLB 193
Tally, Ted 1952- .... **CLC 42**
See also CA 120; 124; CAD; CANR 125;
CD 5; INT CA-124
Talvik, Heiti 1904-1947 .... **TCLC 87**
See also EWL 3
Tamayo y Baus, Manuel
1829-1898 .... **NCLC 1**
Tammsaare, A(nton) H(ansen)
1878-1940 .... **TCLC 27**
See also CA 164; CDWLB 4; DLB 220;
EWL 3
Tam'si, Tchicaya U
See Tchicaya, Gerald Felix
Tan, Amy (Ruth) 1952- . **AAL; CLC 59, 120, 151**
See also AAYA 9, 48; AMWS 10; BEST
89:3; BPFB 3; CA 136; CANR 54, 105,
132; CDALBS; CN 7; CPW 1; DA3;
DAM MULT, NOV, POP; DLB 173;
EXPN; FW; LAIT 3, 5; MTCW 2; NFS
1, 13, 16; RGAL 4; SATA 75; SSFS 9;
YAW
Tandem, Felix
See Spitteler, Carl (Friedrich Georg)
Tanizaki, Jun'ichiro 1886-1965 ... **CLC 8, 14, 28; SSC 21**
See Tanizaki Jun'ichiro
See also CA 93-96; 25-28R; MJW; MTCW
2; RGSF 2; RGWL 2
Tanizaki Jun'ichiro
See Tanizaki, Jun'ichiro
See also DLB 180; EWL 3
Tannen, Deborah F. 1945- .... **CLC 206**
See also CA 118; CANR 95
Tanner, William
See Amis, Kingsley (William)
Tao Lao
See Storni, Alfonsina
Tapahonso, Luci 1953- .... **NNAL; PC 65**
See also CA 145; CANR 72, 127; DLB 175
Tarantino, Quentin (Jerome)
1963- .... **CLC 125**
See also AAYA 58; CA 171; CANR 125
Tarassoff, Lev
See Troyat, Henri
Tarbell, Ida M(inerva) 1857-1944 . **TCLC 40**
See also CA 122; 181; DLB 47
Tarkington, (Newton) Booth
1869-1946 .... **TCLC 9**
See also BPFB 3; BYA 3; CA 110; 143;
CWRI 5; DLB 9, 102; MTCW 2; RGAL
4; SATA 17
Tarkovskii, Andrei Arsen'evich
See Tarkovsky, Andrei (Arsenyevich)
Tarkovsky, Andrei (Arsenyevich)
1932-1986 .... **CLC 75**
See also CA 127
Tartt, Donna 1963- .... **CLC 76**
See also AAYA 56; CA 142
Tasso, Torquato 1544-1595 .... **LC 5, 94**
See also EFS 2; EW 2; RGWL 2, 3
Tate, (John Orley) Allen 1899-1979 .. **CLC 2, 4, 6, 9, 11, 14, 24; PC 50**
See also AMW; CA 5-8R; 85-88; CANR
32, 108; DLB 4, 45, 63; DLBD 17; EWL
3; MTCW 1, 2; RGAL 4; RHW
Tate, Ellalice
See Hibbert, Eleanor Alice Burford

Tate, James (Vincent) 1943- ..... **CLC 2, 6, 25**
See also CA 21-24R; CANR 29, 57, 114;
CP 7; DLB 5, 169; EWL 3; PFS 10, 15;
RGAL 4; WP
Tate, Nahum 1652(?)-1715 .... **LC 109**
See also DLB 80; RGEL 2
Tauler, Johannes c. 1300-1361 ...... **CMLC 37**
See also DLB 179; LMFS 1
Tavel, Ronald 1940- .... **CLC 6**
See also CA 21-24R; CAD; CANR 33; CD
5
Taviani, Paolo 1931- .... **CLC 70**
See also CA 153
Taylor, Bayard 1825-1878 .... **NCLC 89**
See also DLB 3, 189, 250, 254; RGAL 4
Taylor, C(ecil) P(hilip) 1929-1981 .... **CLC 27**
See also CA 25-28R; 105; CANR 47; CBD
Taylor, Edward 1642(?)-1729 . **LC 11; PC 63**
See also AMW; DA; DAB; DAC; DAM
MST, POET; DLB 24; EXPP; RGAL 4;
TUS
Taylor, Eleanor Ross 1920- .... **CLC 5**
See also CA 81-84; CANR 70
Taylor, Elizabeth 1932-1975 ..... **CLC 2, 4, 29**
See also CA 13-16R; CANR 9, 70; DLB
139; MTCW 1; RGEL 2; SATA 13
Taylor, Frederick Winslow
1856-1915 .... **TCLC 76**
See also CA 188
Taylor, Henry (Splawn) 1942- .... **CLC 44**
See also CA 33-36R; CAAS 7; CANR 31;
CP 7; DLB 5; PFS 10
Taylor, Kamala (Purnaiya) 1924-2004
See Markandaya, Kamala
See also CA 77-80; 227; NFS 13
Taylor, Mildred D(elois) 1943- .... **CLC 21**
See also AAYA 10, 47; BW 1; BYA 3, 8;
CA 85-88; CANR 25, 115; CLR 9, 59,
90; CSW; DLB 52; JRDA; LAIT 3; MAI-
CYA 1, 2; SAAS 5; SATA 135; WYA;
YAW
Taylor, Peter (Hillsman) 1917-1994 .. **CLC 1, 4, 18, 37, 44, 50, 71; SSC 10**
See also AMWS 5; BPFB 3; CA 13-16R;
147; CANR 9, 50; CSW; DLB 218, 278;
DLBY 1981, 1994; EWL 3; EXPS; INT
CANR-9; MTCW 1, 2; RGSF 2; SSFS 9;
TUS
Taylor, Robert Lewis 1912-1998 .... **CLC 14**
See also CA 1-4R; 170; CANR 3, 64; SATA
10
Tchekhov, Anton
See Chekhov, Anton (Pavlovich)
Tchicaya, Gerald Felix 1931-1988 .. **CLC 101**
See Tchicaya U Tam'si
See also CA 129; 125; CANR 81
Tchicaya U Tam'si
See Tchicaya, Gerald Felix
See also EWL 3
Teasdale, Sara 1884-1933 .... **PC 31; TCLC 4**
See also CA 104; 163; DLB 45; GLL 1;
PFS 14; RGAL 4; SATA 32; TUS
Tecumseh 1768-1813 .... **NNAL**
See also DAM MULT
Tegner, Esaias 1782-1846 .... **NCLC 2**
Fujiwara no Teika 1162-1241 .... **CMLC 73**
See also DLB 203
Teilhard de Chardin, (Marie Joseph) Pierre
1881-1955 .... **TCLC 9**
See also CA 105; 210; GFL 1789 to the
Present
Temple, Ann
See Mortimer, Penelope (Ruth)
Tennant, Emma (Christina) 1937- .. **CLC 13, 52**
See also BRWS 9; CA 65-68; CAAS 9;
CANR 10, 38, 59, 88; CN 7; DLB 14;
EWL 3; SFW 4

Tenneshaw, S. M.
See Silverberg, Robert
Tenney, Tabitha Gilman
1762-1837 .... **NCLC 122**
See also DLB 37, 200
Tennyson, Alfred 1809-1892 ... **NCLC 30, 65, 115; PC 6; WLC**
See also AAYA 50; BRW 4; CDBLB 1832-
1890; DA; DA3; DAB; DAC; DAM MST,
POET; DLB 32; EXPP; PAB; PFS 1, 2, 4,
11, 15, 19; RGEL 2; TEA; WLIT 4; WP
Teran, Lisa St. Aubin de .... **CLC 36**
See St. Aubin de Teran, Lisa
Terence c. 184B.C.-c. 159B.C. ...... **CMLC 14; DC 7**
See also AW 1; CDWLB 1; DLB 211;
RGWL 2, 3; TWA
Teresa de Jesus, St. 1515-1582 .... **LC 18**
Terkel, Louis 1912-
See Terkel, Studs
See also CA 57-60; CANR 18, 45, 67, 132;
DA3; MTCW 1, 2
Terkel, Studs .... **CLC 38**
See Terkel, Louis
See also AAYA 32; AITN 1; MTCW 2; TUS
Terry, C. V.
See Slaughter, Frank G(ill)
Terry, Megan 1932- .... **CLC 19; DC 13**
See also CA 77-80; CABS 3; CAD; CANR
43; CD 5; CWD; DFS 18; DLB 7, 249;
GLL 2
Tertullian c. 155-c. 245 .... **CMLC 29**
Tertz, Abram
See Sinyavsky, Andrei (Donatevich)
See also RGSF 2
Tesich, Steve 1943(?)-1996 .... **CLC 40, 69**
See also CA 105; 152; CAD; DLBY 1983
Tesla, Nikola 1856-1943 .... **TCLC 88**
Teternikov, Fyodor Kuzmich 1863-1927
See Sologub, Fyodor
See also CA 104
Tevis, Walter 1928-1984 .... **CLC 42**
See also CA 113; SFW 4
Tey, Josephine .... **TCLC 14**
See Mackintosh, Elizabeth
See also DLB 77; MSW
Thackeray, William Makepeace
1811-1863 .... **NCLC 5, 14, 22, 43; WLC**
See also BRW 5; BRWC 2; CDBLB 1832-
1890; DA; DA3; DAB; DAC; DAM MST,
NOV; DLB 21, 55, 159, 163; NFS 13;
RGEL 2; SATA 23; TEA; WLIT 3
Thakura, Ravindranatha
See Tagore, Rabindranath
Thames, C. H.
See Marlowe, Stephen
Tharoor, Shashi 1956- .... **CLC 70**
See also CA 141; CANR 91; CN 7
Thelwell, Michael Miles 1939- .... **CLC 22**
See also BW 2; CA 101
Theobald, Lewis, Jr.
See Lovecraft, H(oward) P(hillips)
Theocritus c. 310B.C.- .... **CMLC 45**
See also AW 1; DLB 176; RGWL 2, 3
Theodorescu, Ion N. 1880-1967
See Arghezi, Tudor
See also CA 116
Theriault, Yves 1915-1983 .... **CLC 79**
See also CA 102; CCA 1; DAC; DAM
MST; DLB 88; EWL 3
Theroux, Alexander (Louis) 1939- .... **CLC 2, 25**
See also CA 85-88; CANR 20, 63; CN 7

Tolstoy, Count Leo
See Tolstoy, Leo (Nikolaevich)
Tomalin, Claire 1933- .... **CLC 166**
See also CA 89-92; CANR 52, 88; DLB
155
Tomasi di Lampedusa, Giuseppe 1896-1957
See Lampedusa, Giuseppe (Tomasi) di
See also CA 111; DLB 177; EWL 3
Tomlin, Lily .... **CLC 17**
See Tomlin, Mary Jean
Tomlin, Mary Jean 1939(?)-
See Tomlin, Lily
See also CA 117
Tomline, F. Latour
See Gilbert, W(illiam) S(chwenck)
Tomlinson, (Alfred) Charles 1927- .... **CLC 2,
4, 6, 13, 45; PC 17**
See also CA 5-8R; CANR 33; CP 7; DAM
POET; DLB 40
Tomlinson, H(enry) M(ajor)
1873-1958 .... **TCLC 71**
See also CA 118; 161; DLB 36, 100, 195
Tonna, Charlotte Elizabeth
1790-1846 .... **NCLC 135**
See also DLB 163
Tonson, Jacob fl. 1655(?)-1736 .... **LC 86**
See also DLB 170
Toole, John Kennedy 1937-1969 ..... **CLC 19,
64**
See also BPFB 3; CA 104; DLBY 1981;
MTCW 2
Toomer, Eugene
See Toomer, Jean
Toomer, Eugene Pinchback
See Toomer, Jean
Toomer, Jean 1894-1967 .. **BLC 3; CLC 1, 4,
13, 22; HR 3; PC 7; SSC 1, 45; WLCS**
See also AFAW 1, 2; AMWS 3, 9; BW 1;
CA 85-88; CDALB 1917-1929; DA3;
DAM MULT; DLB 45, 51; EWL 3; EXPP;
EXPS; LMFS 2; MTCW 1, 2; NFS 11;
RGAL 4; RGSF 2; SSFS 5
Toomer, Nathan Jean
See Toomer, Jean
Toomer, Nathan Pinchback
See Toomer, Jean
Torley, Luke
See Blish, James (Benjamin)
Tornimparte, Alessandra
See Ginzburg, Natalia
Torre, Raoul della
See Mencken, H(enry) L(ouis)
Torrence, Ridgely 1874-1950 .... **TCLC 97**
See also DLB 54, 249
Torrey, E(dwin) Fuller 1937- .... **CLC 34**
See also CA 119; CANR 71
Torsvan, Ben Traven
See Traven, B.
Torsvan, Benno Traven
See Traven, B.
Torsvan, Berick Traven
See Traven, B.
Torsvan, Berwick Traven
See Traven, B.
Torsvan, Bruno Traven
See Traven, B.
Torsvan, Traven
See Traven, B.
Tourneur, Cyril 1575(?)-1626 .... **LC 66**
See also BRW 2; DAM DRAM; DLB 58;
RGEL 2
Tournier, Michel (Edouard) 1924- .... **CLC 6,
23, 36, 95**
See also CA 49-52; CANR 3, 36, 74; CWW
2; DLB 83; EWL 3; GFL 1789 to the
Present; MTCW 1, 2; SATA 23
Tournimparte, Alessandra
See Ginzburg, Natalia

Towers, Ivar
See Kornbluth, C(yril) M.
Towne, Robert (Burton) 1936(?)- ..... **CLC 87**
See also CA 108; DLB 44; IDFW 3, 4
Townsend, Sue .... **CLC 61**
See Townsend, Susan Lilian
See also AAYA 28; CA 119; 127; CANR
65, 107; CBD; CD 5; CPW; CWD; DAB;
DAC; DAM MST; DLB 271; INT CA-
127; SATA 55, 93; SATA-Brief 48; YAW
Townsend, Susan Lilian 1946-
See Townsend, Sue
Townshend, Pete
See Townshend, Peter (Dennis Blandford)
Townshend, Peter (Dennis Blandford)
1945- .... **CLC 17, 42**
See also CA 107
Tozzi, Federigo 1883-1920 .... **TCLC 31**
See also CA 160; CANR 110; DLB 264;
EWL 3
Tracy, Don(ald Fiske) 1905-1970(?)
See Queen, Ellery
See also CA 1-4R; 176; CANR 2
Trafford, F. G.
See Riddell, Charlotte
Traherne, Thomas 1637(?)-1674 .... **LC 99**
See also BRW 2; DLB 131; PAB; RGEL 2
Traill, Catharine Parr 1802-1899 .. **NCLC 31**
See also DLB 99
Trakl, Georg 1887-1914 .... **PC 20; TCLC 5**
See also CA 104; 165; EW 10; EWL 3;
LMFS 2; MTCW 2; RGWL 2, 3
Tranquilli, Secondino
See Silone, Ignazio
Transtroemer, Tomas Gosta
See Transtromer, Tomas (Goesta)
Transtromer, Tomas (Gosta)
See Transtromer, Tomas (Goesta)
See also CWW 2
Transtromer, Tomas (Goesta)
1931- .... **CLC 52, 65**
See Transtromer, Tomas (Gosta)
See also CA 117; 129; CAAS 17; CANR
115; DAM POET; DLB 257; EWL 3; PFS
21
Transtromer, Tomas Gosta
See Transtromer, Tomas (Goesta)
Traven, B. 1882(?)-1969 .... **CLC 8, 11**
See also CA 19-20; 25-28R; CAP 2; DLB
9, 56; EWL 3; MTCW 1; RGAL 4
Trediakovsky, Vasilii Kirillovich
1703-1769 .... **LC 68**
See also DLB 150
Treitel, Jonathan 1959- .... **CLC 70**
See also CA 210; DLB 267
Trelawny, Edward John
1792-1881 .... **NCLC 85**
See also DLB 110, 116, 144
Tremain, Rose 1943- .... **CLC 42**
See also CA 97-100; CANR 44, 95; CN 7;
DLB 14, 271; RGSF 2; RHW
Tremblay, Michel 1942- .... **CLC 29, 102**
See also CA 116; 128; CCA 1; CWW 2;
DAC; DAM MST; DLB 60; EWL 3; GLL
1; MTCW 1, 2
Trevanian .... **CLC 29**
See Whitaker, Rod(ney)
Trevor, Glen
See Hilton, James
Trevor, William .. **CLC 7, 9, 14, 25, 71, 116;
SSC 21, 58**
See Cox, William Trevor
See also BRWS 4; CBD; CD 5; CN 7; DLB
14, 139; EWL 3; LATS 1:2; MTCW 2;
RGEL 2; RGSF 2; SSFS 10
Trifonov, Iurii (Valentinovich)
See Trifonov, Yuri (Valentinovich)
See also DLB 302; RGWL 2, 3

Trifonov, Yuri (Valentinovich)
1925-1981 .... **CLC 45**
See Trifonov, Iurii (Valentinovich); Tri-
fonov, Yury Valentinovich
See also CA 126; 103; MTCW 1
Trifonov, Yury Valentinovich
See Trifonov, Yuri (Valentinovich)
See also EWL 3
Trilling, Diana (Rubin) 1905-1996 . **CLC 129**
See also CA 5-8R; 154; CANR 10, 46; INT
CANR-10; MTCW 1, 2
Trilling, Lionel 1905-1975 ..... **CLC 9, 11, 24;
SSC 75**
See also AMWS 3; CA 9-12R; 61-64;
CANR 10, 105; DLB 28, 63; EWL 3; INT
CANR-10; MTCW 1, 2; RGAL 4; TUS
Trimball, W. H.
See Mencken, H(enry) L(ouis)
Tristan
See Gomez de la Serna, Ramon
Tristram
See Housman, A(lfred) E(dward)
Trogdon, William (Lewis) 1939-
See Heat-Moon, William Least
See also CA 115; 119; CANR 47, 89; CPW;
INT CA-119
Trollope, Anthony 1815-1882 .... **NCLC 6, 33,
101; SSC 28; WLC**
See also BRW 5; CDBLB 1832-1890; DA;
DA3; DAB; DAC; DAM MST; NOV;
DLB 21, 57, 159; RGEL 2; RGSF 2;
SATA 22
Trollope, Frances 1779-1863 .... **NCLC 30**
See also DLB 21, 166
Trollope, Joanna 1943- .... **CLC 186**
See also CA 101; CANR 58, 95; CPW;
DLB 207; RHW
Trotsky, Leon 1879-1940 .... **TCLC 22**
See also CA 118; 167
Trotter (Cockburn), Catharine
1679-1749 .... **LC 8**
See also DLB 84, 252
Trotter, Wilfred 1872-1939 .... **TCLC 97**
Trout, Kilgore
See Farmer, Philip Jose
Trow, George W. S. 1943- .... **CLC 52**
See also CA 126; CANR 91
Troyat, Henri 1911- .... **CLC 23**
See also CA 45-48; CANR 2, 33, 67, 117;
GFL 1789 to the Present; MTCW 1
Trudeau, G(arretson) B(eekman) 1948-
See Trudeau, Garry B.
See also AAYA 60; CA 81-84; CANR 31;
SATA 35
Trudeau, Garry B. .... **CLC 12**
See Trudeau, G(arretson) B(eekman)
See also AAYA 10; AITN 2
Truffaut, Francois 1932-1984 ... **CLC 20, 101**
See also CA 81-84; 113; CANR 34
Trumbo, Dalton 1905-1976 .... **CLC 19**
See also CA 21-24R; 69-72; CANR 10;
DLB 26; IDFW 3, 4; YAW
Trumbull, John 1750-1831 .... **NCLC 30**
See also DLB 31; RGAL 4
Trundlett, Helen B.
See Eliot, T(homas) S(tearns)
Truth, Sojourner 1797(?)-1883 ...... **NCLC 94**
See also DLB 239; FW; LAIT 2
Tryon, Thomas 1926-1991 .... **CLC 3, 11**
See also AITN 1; BPFB 3; CA 29-32R; 135;
CANR 32, 77; CPW; DA3; DAM POP;
HGG; MTCW 1
Tryon, Tom
See Tryon, Thomas
Ts'ao Hsueh-ch'in 1715(?)-1763 .... **LC 1**
Tsushima, Shuji 1909-1948
See Dazai Osamu
See also CA 107

Weininger, Otto 1880-1903 .... **TCLC 84**
Weinstein, Nathan
   See West, Nathanael
Weinstein, Nathan von Wallenstein
   See West, Nathanael
Weir, Peter (Lindsay) 1944- .... **CLC 20**
   See also CA 113; 123
Weiss, Peter (Ulrich) 1916-1982 .. **CLC 3, 15,**
   51; TCLC 152
   See also CA 45-48; 106; CANR 3; DAM
   DRAM; DFS 3; DLB 69, 124; EWL 3;
   RGWL 2, 3
Weiss, Theodore (Russell)
   1916-2003 .... **CLC 3, 8, 14**
   See also CA 9-12R, 189; 216; CAAE 189;
   CAAS 2; CANR 46, 94; CP 7; DLB 5
Welch, (Maurice) Denton
   1915-1948 .... **TCLC 22**
   See also BRWS 8, 9; CA 121; 148; RGEL
   2
Welch, James (Phillip) 1940-2003 ..... **CLC 6,**
   14, 52; NNAL; PC 62
   See also CA 85-88; 219; CANR 42, 66, 107;
   CN 7; CP 7; CPW; DAM MULT, POP;
   DLB 175, 256; LATS 1:1; RGAL 4;
   TCWW 2
Weldon, Fay 1931- . **CLC 6, 9, 11, 19, 36, 59,**
   122
   See also BRWS 4; CA 21-24R; CANR 16,
   46, 63, 97; CDBLB 1960 to Present; CN
   7; CPW; DAM POP; DLB 14, 194; EWL
   3; FW; HGG; INT CANR-16; MTCW 1,
   2; RGEL 2; RGSF 2
Wellek, Rene 1903-1995 .... **CLC 28**
   See also CA 5-8R; 150; CAAS 7; CANR 8;
   DLB 63; EWL 3; INT CANR-8
Weller, Michael 1942- .... **CLC 10, 53**
   See also CA 85-88; CAD; CD 5
Weller, Paul 1958- .... **CLC 26**
Wellershoff, Dieter 1925- .... **CLC 46**
   See also CA 89-92; CANR 16, 37
Welles, (George) Orson 1915-1985 .. **CLC 20,**
   80
   See also AAYA 40; CA 93-96; 117
Wellman, John McDowell 1945-
   See Wellman, Mac
   See also CA 166; CD 5
Wellman, Mac .... **CLC 65**
   See Wellman, John McDowell; Wellman,
   John McDowell
   See also CAD; RGAL 4
Wellman, Manly Wade 1903-1986 ... **CLC 49**
   See also CA 1-4R; 118; CANR 6, 16, 44;
   FANT; SATA 6; SATA-Obit 47; SFW 4;
   SUFW
Wells, Carolyn 1869(?)-1942 .... **TCLC 35**
   See also CA 113; 185; CMW 4; DLB 11
Wells, H(erbert) G(eorge) 1866-1946 . **SSC 6,**
   70; TCLC 6, 12, 19, 133; WLC
   See also AAYA 18; BPFB 3; BRW 6; CA
   110; 121; CDBLB 1914-1945; CLR 64;
   DA; DA3; DAB; DAC; DAM MST, NOV;
   DLB 34, 70, 156, 178; EWL 3; EXPS;
   HGG; LAIT 3; LMFS 2; MTCW 1, 2;
   NFS 17, 20; RGEL 2; RGSF 2; SATA 20;
   SCFW 4; SFW 4; SSFS 3; SUFW; TEA;
   WCH; WLIT 4; YAW
Wells, Rosemary 1943- .... **CLC 12**
   See also AAYA 13; BYA 7, 8; CA 85-88;
   CANR 48, 120; CLR 16, 69; CWRI 5;
   MAICYA 1, 2; SAAS 1; SATA 18, 69,
   114; YAW
Wells-Barnett, Ida B(ell)
   1862-1931 .... **TCLC 125**
   See also CA 182; DLB 23, 221
Welsh, Irvine 1958- .... **CLC 144**
   See also CA 173; DLB 271

Welty, Eudora (Alice) 1909-2001 .. **CLC 1, 2,**
   5, 14, 22, 33, 105; SSC 1, 27, 51; WLC
   See also AAYA 48; AMW; AMWR 1; BPFB
   3; CA 9-12R; 199; CABS 1; CANR 32,
   65, 128; CDALB 1941-1968; CN 7; CSW;
   DA; DA3; DAB; DAC; DAM MST, NOV;
   DLB 2, 102, 143; DLBD 12; DLBY 1987,
   2001; EWL 3; EXPS; HGG; LAIT 3;
   MAWW; MTCW 1, 2; NFS 13, 15; RGAL
   4; RGSF 2; RHW; SSFS 2, 10; TUS
Wen I-to 1899-1946 .... **TCLC 28**
   See also EWL 3
Wentworth, Robert
   See Hamilton, Edmond
Werfel, Franz (Viktor) 1890-1945 ... **TCLC 8**
   See also CA 104; 161; DLB 81, 124; EWL
   3; RGWL 2, 3
Wergeland, Henrik Arnold
   1808-1845 .... **NCLC 5**
Wersba, Barbara 1932- .... **CLC 30**
   See also AAYA 2, 30; BYA 6, 12, 13; CA
   29-32R, 182; CAAE 182; CANR 16, 38;
   CLR 3, 78; DLB 52; JRDA; MAICYA 1,
   2; SAAS 2; SATA 1, 58; SATA-Essay 103;
   WYA; YAW
Wertmueller, Lina 1928- .... **CLC 16**
   See also CA 97-100; CANR 39, 78
Wescott, Glenway 1901-1987 .. **CLC 13; SSC**
   35
   See also CA 13-16R; 121; CANR 23, 70;
   DLB 4, 9, 102; RGAL 4
Wesker, Arnold 1932- .... **CLC 3, 5, 42**
   See also CA 1-4R; CAAS 7; CANR 1, 33;
   CBD; CD 5; CDBLB 1960 to Present;
   DAB; DAM DRAM; DLB 13; EWL 3;
   MTCW 1; RGEL 2; TEA
Wesley, John 1703-1791 .... **LC 88**
   See also DLB 104
Wesley, Richard (Errol) 1945- .... **CLC 7**
   See also BW 1; CA 57-60; CAD; CANR
   27; CD 5; DLB 38
Wessel, Johan Herman 1742-1785 .... **LC 7**
   See also DLB 300
West, Anthony (Panther)
   1914-1987 .... **CLC 50**
   See also CA 45-48; 124; CANR 3, 19; DLB
   15
West, C. P.
   See Wodehouse, P(elham) G(renville)
West, Cornel (Ronald) 1953- .... **BLCS; CLC**
   134
   See also CA 144; CANR 91; DLB 246
West, Delno C(loyde), Jr. 1936- .... **CLC 70**
   See also CA 57-60
West, Dorothy 1907-1998 .. **HR 3; TCLC 108**
   See also BW 2; CA 143; 169; DLB 76
West, (Mary) Jessamyn 1902-1984 ... **CLC 7,**
   17
   See also CA 9-12R; 112; CANR 27; DLB
   6; DLBY 1984; MTCW 1, 2; RGAL 4;
   RHW; SATA-Obit 37; TCWW 2; TUS;
   YAW
West, Morris
   See West, Morris L(anglo)
   See also DLB 289
West, Morris L(anglo) 1916-1999 ..... **CLC 6,**
   33
   See West, Morris
   See also BPFB 3; CA 5-8R; 187; CANR
   24, 49, 64; CN 7; CPW; MTCW 1, 2
West, Nathanael 1903-1940 .. **SSC 16; TCLC**
   1, 14, 44
   See also AMW; AMWR 2; BPFB 3; CA
   104; 125; CDALB 1929-1941; DA3; DLB
   4, 9, 28; EWL 3; MTCW 1, 2; NFS 16;
   RGAL 4; TUS
West, Owen
   See Koontz, Dean R(ay)

West, Paul 1930- .... **CLC 7, 14, 96**
   See also CA 13-16R; CAAS 7; CANR 22,
   53, 76, 89; CN 7; DLB 14; INT CANR-
   22; MTCW 2
West, Rebecca 1892-1983 ... **CLC 7, 9, 31, 50**
   See also BPFB 3; BRWS 3; CA 5-8R; 109;
   CANR 19; DLB 36; DLBY 1983; EWL
   3; FW; MTCW 1, 2; NCFS 4; RGEL 2;
   TEA
Westall, Robert (Atkinson)
   1929-1993 .... **CLC 17**
   See also AAYA 12; BYA 2, 6, 7, 8, 9, 15;
   CA 69-72; 141; CANR 18, 68; CLR 13;
   FANT; JRDA; MAICYA 1, 2; MAICYAS
   1; SAAS 2; SATA 23, 69; SATA-Obit 75;
   WYA; YAW
Westermarck, Edward 1862-1939 . **TCLC 87**
Westlake, Donald E(dwin) 1933- . **CLC 7, 33**
   See also BPFB 3; CA 17-20R; CAAS 13;
   CANR 16, 44, 65, 94; CMW 4; CPW;
   DAM POP; INT CANR-16; MSW;
   MTCW 2
Westmacott, Mary
   See Christie, Agatha (Mary Clarissa)
Weston, Allen
   See Norton, Andre
Wetcheek, J. L.
   See Feuchtwanger, Lion
Wetering, Janwillem van de
   See van de Wetering, Janwillem
Wetherald, Agnes Ethelwyn
   1857-1940 .... **TCLC 81**
   See also CA 202; DLB 99
Wetherell, Elizabeth
   See Warner, Susan (Bogert)
Whale, James 1889-1957 .... **TCLC 63**
Whalen, Philip (Glenn) 1923-2002 .... **CLC 6,**
   29
   See also BG 3; CA 9-12R; 209; CANR 5,
   39; CP 7; DLB 16; WP
Wharton, Edith (Newbold Jones)
   1862-1937 ... **SSC 6; TCLC 3, 9, 27, 53,**
   129, 149; WLC
   See also AAYA 25; AMW; AMWC 2;
   AMWR 1; BPFB 3; CA 104; 132; CDALB
   1865-1917; DA; DA3; DAB; DAC; DAM
   MST, NOV; DLB 4, 9, 12, 78, 189; DLBD
   13; EWL 3; EXPS; HGG; LAIT 2, 3;
   LATS 1:1; MAWW; MTCW 1, 2; NFS 5,
   11, 15, 20; RGAL 4; RGSF 2; RHW;
   SSFS 6, 7; SUFW; TUS
Wharton, James
   See Mencken, H(enry) L(ouis)
Wharton, William (a pseudonym) . **CLC 18,**
   37
   See also CA 93-96; DLBY 1980; INT CA-
   93-96
Wheatley (Peters), Phillis
   1753(?)-1784 ... **BLC 3; LC 3, 50; PC 3;**
   WLC
   See also AFAW 1, 2; CDALB 1640-1865;
   DA; DA3; DAC; DAM MST, MULT,
   POET; DLB 31, 50; EXPP; PFS 13;
   RGAL 4
Wheelock, John Hall 1886-1978 .... **CLC 14**
   See also CA 13-16R; 77-80; CANR 14;
   DLB 45
Whim-Wham
   See Curnow, (Thomas) Allen (Monro)
White, Babington
   See Braddon, Mary Elizabeth
White, E(lwyn) B(rooks)
   1899-1985 .... **CLC 10, 34, 39**
   See also AITN 2; AMWS 1; CA 13-16R;
   116; CANR 16, 37; CDALBS; CLR 1, 21;
   CPW; DA3; DAM POP; DLB 11, 22;
   EWL 3; FANT; MAICYA 1, 2; MTCW 1,
   2; NCFS 5; RGAL 4; SATA 2, 29, 100;
   SATA-Obit 44; TUS

White, Edmund (Valentine III)
1940- .... **CLC 27, 110**
See also AAYA 7; CA 45-48; CANR 3, 19,
36, 62, 107, 133; CN 7; DA3; DAM POP;
DLB 227; MTCW 1, 2

White, Hayden V. 1928- .... **CLC 148**
See also CA 128; CANR 135; DLB 246

White, Patrick (Victor Martindale)
1912-1990 ...... **CLC 3, 4, 5, 7, 9, 18, 65,
69; SSC 39**
See also BRWS 1; CA 81-84; 132; CANR
43; DLB 260; EWL 3; MTCW 1; RGEL
2; RGSF 2; RHW; TWA; WWE 1

White, Phyllis Dorothy James 1920-
See James, P. D.
See also CA 21-24R; CANR 17, 43, 65,
112; CMW 4; CN 7; CPW; DA3; DAM
POP; MTCW 1, 2; TEA

White, T(erence) H(anbury)
1906-1964 .... **CLC 30**
See also AAYA 22; BPFB 3; BYA 4, 5; CA
73-76; CANR 37; DLB 160; FANT;
JRDA; LAIT 1; MAICYA 1, 2; RGEL 2;
SATA 12; SUFW 1; YAW

White, Terence de Vere 1912-1994 ... **CLC 49**
See also CA 49-52; 145; CANR 3

White, Walter
See White, Walter F(rancis)

White, Walter F(rancis) 1893-1955 ... **BLC 3;
HR 3; TCLC 15**
See also BW 1; CA 115; 124; DAM MULT;
DLB 51

White, William Hale 1831-1913
See Rutherford, Mark
See also CA 121; 189

Whitehead, Alfred North
1861-1947 .... **TCLC 97**
See also CA 117; 165; DLB 100, 262

Whitehead, E(dward) A(nthony)
1933- .... **CLC 5**
See also CA 65-68; CANR 58, 118; CBD;
CD 5

Whitehead, Ted
See Whitehead, E(dward) A(nthony)

Whiteman, Roberta J. Hill 1947- ...... **NNAL**
See also CA 146

Whitemore, Hugh (John) 1936- .... **CLC 37**
See also CA 132; CANR 77; CBD; CD 5;
INT CA-132

Whitman, Sarah Helen (Power)
1803-1878 .... **NCLC 19**
See also DLB 1, 243

Whitman, Walt(er) 1819-1892 .. **NCLC 4, 31,
81; PC 3; WLC**
See also AAYA 42; AMW; AMWR 1;
CDALB 1640-1865; DA; DA3; DAB;
DAC; DAM MST, POET; DLB 3, 64,
224, 250; EXPP; LAIT 2; LMFS 1; PAB;
PFS 2, 3, 13; RGAL 4; SATA 20; TUS;
WP; WYAS 1

Whitney, Phyllis A(yame) 1903- .... **CLC 42**
See also AAYA 36; AITN 2; BEST 90:3;
CA 1-4R; CANR 3, 25, 38, 60; CLR 59;
CMW 4; CPW; DA3; DAM POP; JRDA;
MAICYA 1, 2; MTCW 2; RHW; SATA 1,
30; YAW

Whittemore, (Edward) Reed, Jr.
1919- .... **CLC 4**
See also CA 9-12R; 219; CAAE 219; CAAS
8; CANR 4, 119; CP 7; DLB 5

Whittier, John Greenleaf
1807-1892 .... **NCLC 8, 59**
See also AMWS 1; DLB 1, 243; RGAL 4

Whittlebot, Hernia
See Coward, Noel (Peirce)

Wicker, Thomas Grey 1926-
See Wicker, Tom
See also CA 65-68; CANR 21, 46

Wicker, Tom .... **CLC 7**
See Wicker, Thomas Grey

Wideman, John Edgar 1941- ... **BLC 3; CLC
5, 34, 36, 67, 122; SSC 62**
See also AFAW 1, 2; AMWS 10; BPFB 4;
BW 2, 3; CA 85-88; CANR 14, 42, 67,
109; CN 7; DAM MULT; DLB 33, 143;
MTCW 2; RGAL 4; RGSF 2; SSFS 6, 12

Wiebe, Rudy (Henry) 1934- .. **CLC 6, 11, 14,
138**
See also CA 37-40R; CANR 42, 67, 123;
CN 7; DAC; DAM MST; DLB 60; RHW

Wieland, Christoph Martin
1733-1813 .... **NCLC 17**
See also DLB 97; EW 4; LMFS 1; RGWL
2, 3

Wiene, Robert 1881-1938 .... **TCLC 56**

Wieners, John 1934- .... **CLC 7**
See also BG 3; CA 13-16R; CP 7; DLB 16;
WP

Wiesel, Elie(zer) 1928- .... **CLC 3, 5, 11, 37,
165; WLCS**
See also AAYA 7, 54; AITN 1; CA 5-8R;
CAAS 4; CANR 8, 40, 65, 125; CDALBS;
CWW 2; DA; DA3; DAB; DAC; DAM
MST, NOV; DLB 83, 299; DLBY 1987;
EWL 3; INT CANR-8; LAIT 4; MTCW
1, 2; NCFS 4; NFS 4; RGWL 3; SATA
56; YAW

Wiggins, Marianne 1947- .... **CLC 57**
See also BEST 89:3; CA 130; CANR 60

Wigglesworth, Michael 1631-1705 .... **LC 106**
See also DLB 24; RGAL 4

Wiggs, Susan .... **CLC 70**
See also CA 201

Wight, James Alfred 1916-1995
See Herriot, James
See also CA 77-80; SATA 55; SATA-Brief
44

Wilbur, Richard (Purdy) 1921- ..... **CLC 3, 6,
9, 14, 53, 110; PC 51**
See also AMWS 3; CA 1-4R; CABS 2;
CANR 2, 29, 76, 93; CDALBS; CP 7;
DA; DAB; DAC; DAM MST, POET;
DLB 5, 169; EWL 3; EXPP; INT CANR-
29; MTCW 1, 2; PAB; PFS 11, 12, 16;
RGAL 4; SATA 9, 108; WP

Wild, Peter 1940- .... **CLC 14**
See also CA 37-40R; CP 7; DLB 5

Wilde, Oscar (Fingal O'Flahertie Wills)
1854(?)-1900 .... **DC 17; SSC 11, 77;
TCLC 1, 8, 23, 41; WLC**
See also AAYA 49; BRW 5; BRWC 1, 2;
BRWR 2; BYA 15; CA 104; 119; CANR
112; CDBLB 1890-1914; DA; DA3;
DAB; DAC; DAM DRAM, MST, NOV;
DFS 4, 8, 9; DLB 10, 19, 34, 57, 141,
156, 190; EXPS; FANT; LATS 1:1; NFS
20; RGEL 2; RGSF 2; SATA 24; SSFS 7;
SUFW; TEA; WCH; WLIT 4

Wilder, Billy .... **CLC 20**
See Wilder, Samuel
See also DLB 26

Wilder, Samuel 1906-2002
See Wilder, Billy
See also CA 89-92; 205

Wilder, Stephen
See Marlowe, Stephen

Wilder, Thornton (Niven)
1897-1975 .. **CLC 1, 5, 6, 10, 15, 35, 82;
DC 1, 24; WLC**
See also AAYA 29; AITN 2; AMW; CA 13-
16R; 61-64; CAD; CANR 40, 132;
CDALBS; DA; DA3; DAB; DAC; DAM
DRAM, MST, NOV; DFS 1, 4, 16; DLB
4, 7, 9, 228; DLBY 1997; EWL 3; LAIT
3; MTCW 1, 2; RGAL 4; RHW; WYAS 1

Wilding, Michael 1942- ...... **CLC 73; SSC 50**
See also CA 104; CANR 24, 49, 106; CN
7; RGSF 2

Wiley, Richard 1944- .... **CLC 44**
See also CA 121; 129; CANR 71

Wilhelm, Kate .... **CLC 7**
See Wilhelm, Katie (Gertrude)
See also AAYA 20; BYA 16; CAAS 5; DLB
8; INT CANR-17; SCFW 2

Wilhelm, Katie (Gertrude) 1928-
See Wilhelm, Kate
See also CA 37-40R; CANR 17, 36, 60, 94;
MTCW 1; SFW 4

Wilkins, Mary
See Freeman, Mary E(leanor) Wilkins

Willard, Nancy 1936- .... **CLC 7, 37**
See also BYA 5; CA 89-92; CANR 10, 39,
68, 107; CLR 5; CWP; CWRI 5; DLB 5,
52; FANT; MAICYA 1, 2; MTCW 1;
SATA 37, 71, 127; SATA-Brief 30; SUFW
2

William of Malmesbury c. 1090B.C.-c.
1140B.C. .... **CMLC 57**

William of Ockham 1290-1349 ..... **CMLC 32**

Williams, Ben Ames 1889-1953 ..... **TCLC 89**
See also CA 183; DLB 102

Williams, C(harles) K(enneth)
1936- .... **CLC 33, 56, 148**
See also CA 37-40R; CAAS 26; CANR 57,
106; CP 7; DAM POET; DLB 5

Williams, Charles
See Collier, James Lincoln

Williams, Charles (Walter Stansby)
1886-1945 .... **TCLC 1, 11**
See also BRWS 9; CA 104; 163; DLB 100,
153, 255; FANT; RGEL 2; SUFW 1

Williams, Ella Gwendolen Rees
See Rhys, Jean

Williams, (George) Emlyn
1905-1987 .... **CLC 15**
See also CA 104; 123; CANR 36; DAM
DRAM; DLB 10, 77; IDTP; MTCW 1

Williams, Hank 1923-1953 .... **TCLC 81**
See Williams, Hiram King

Williams, Helen Maria
1761-1827 .... **NCLC 135**
See also DLB 158

Williams, Hiram Hank
See Williams, Hank

Williams, Hiram King
See Williams, Hank
See also CA 188

Williams, Hugo (Mordaunt) 1942- ... **CLC 42**
See also CA 17-20R; CANR 45, 119; CP 7;
DLB 40

Williams, J. Walker
See Wodehouse, P(elham) G(renville)

Williams, John A(lfred) 1925- . **BLC 3; CLC
5, 13**
See also AFAW 2; BW 2, 3; CA 53-56; 195;
CAAE 195; CAAS 3; CANR 6, 26, 51,
118; CN 7; CSW; DAM MULT; DLB 2,
33; EWL 3; INT CANR-6; RGAL 4; SFW
4

Williams, Jonathan (Chamberlain)
1929- .... **CLC 13**
See also CA 9-12R; CAAS 12; CANR 8,
108; CP 7; DLB 5

Williams, Joy 1944- .... **CLC 31**
See also CA 41-44R; CANR 22, 48, 97

Williams, Norman 1952- .... **CLC 39**
See also CA 118

Williams, Sherley Anne 1944-1999 ... **BLC 3;
CLC 89**
See also AFAW 2; BW 2, 3; CA 73-76; 185;
CANR 25, 82; DAM MULT, POET; DLB
41; INT CANR-25; SATA 78; SATA-Obit
116

Williams, Shirley
See Williams, Sherley Anne

Wolfram von Eschenbach c. 1170-c. 1220 .... **CMLC 5**
See Eschenbach, Wolfram von
See also CDWLB 2; DLB 138; EW 1; RGWL 2

Wolitzer, Hilma 1930- .... **CLC 17**
See also CA 65-68; CANR 18, 40; INT CANR-18; SATA 31; YAW

Wollstonecraft, Mary 1759-1797 .... **LC 5, 50, 90**
See also BRWS 3; CDBLB 1789-1832; DLB 39, 104, 158, 252; FW; LAIT 1; RGEL 2; TEA; WLIT 3

Wonder, Stevie .... **CLC 12**
See Morris, Steveland Judkins

Wong, Jade Snow 1922- .... **CLC 17**
See also CA 109; CANR 91; SATA 112

Woodberry, George Edward 1855-1930 .... **TCLC 73**
See also CA 165; DLB 71, 103

Woodcott, Keith
See Brunner, John (Kilian Houston)

Woodruff, Robert W.
See Mencken, H(enry) L(ouis)

Woolf, (Adeline) Virginia 1882-1941 .. **SSC 7, 79; TCLC 1, 5, 20, 43, 56, 101, 123, 128; WLC**
See also AAYA 44; BPFB 3; BRW 7; BRWC 2; BRWR 1; CA 104; 130; CANR 64, 132; CDBLB 1914-1945; DA; DA3; DAB; DAC; DAM MST, NOV; DLB 36, 100, 162; DLBD 10; EWL 3; EXPS; FW; LAIT 3; LATS 1:1; LMFS 1; MTCW 1, 2; NCFS 2; NFS 8, 12; RGEL 2; RGSF 2; SSFS 4, 12; TEA; WLIT 4

Woollcott, Alexander (Humphreys) 1887-1943 .... **TCLC 5**
See also CA 105; 161; DLB 29

Woolrich, Cornell .... **CLC 77**
See Hopley-Woolrich, Cornell George
See also MSW

Woolson, Constance Fenimore 1840-1894 .... **NCLC 82**
See also DLB 12, 74, 189, 221; RGAL 4

Wordsworth, Dorothy 1771-1855 . **NCLC 25, 138**
See also DLB 107

Wordsworth, William 1770-1850 .. **NCLC 12, 38, 111; PC 4; WLC**
See also BRW 4; BRWC 1; CDBLB 1789-1832; DA; DA3; DAB; DAC; DAM MST, POET; DLB 93, 107; EXPP; LATS 1:1; LMFS 1; PAB; PFS 2; RGEL 2; TEA; WLIT 3; WP

Wotton, Sir Henry 1568-1639 .... **LC 68**
See also DLB 121; RGEL 2

Wouk, Herman 1915- .... **CLC 1, 9, 38**
See also BPFB 2, 3; CA 5-8R; CANR 6, 33, 67; CDALBS; CN 7; CPW; DA3; DAM NOV, POP; DLBY 1982; INT CANR-6; LAIT 4; MTCW 1, 2; NFS 7; TUS

Wright, Charles (Penzel, Jr.) 1935- .. **CLC 6, 13, 28, 119, 146**
See also AMWS 5; CA 29-32R; CAAS 7; CANR 23, 36, 62, 88, 135; CP 7; DLB 165; DLBY 1982; EWL 3; MTCW 1, 2; PFS 10

Wright, Charles Stevenson 1932- ..... **BLC 3; CLC 49**
See also BW 1; CA 9-12R; CANR 26; CN 7; DAM MULT, POET; DLB 33

Wright, Frances 1795-1852 .... **NCLC 74**
See also DLB 73

Wright, Frank Lloyd 1867-1959 .... **TCLC 95**
See also AAYA 33; CA 174

Wright, Jack R.
See Harris, Mark

Wright, James (Arlington) 1927-1980 .... **CLC 3, 5, 10, 28; PC 36**
See also AITN 2; AMWS 3; CA 49-52; 97-100; CANR 4, 34, 64; CDALBS; DAM POET; DLB 5, 169; EWL 3; EXPP; MTCW 1, 2; PFS 7, 8; RGAL 4; TUS; WP

Wright, Judith (Arundell) 1915-2000 .... **CLC 11, 53; PC 14**
See also CA 13-16R; 188; CANR 31, 76, 93; CP 7; CWP; DLB 260; EWL 3; MTCW 1, 2; PFS 8; RGEL 2; SATA 14; SATA-Obit 121

Wright, L(auarli) R. 1939- .... **CLC 44**
See also CA 138; CMW 4

Wright, Richard (Nathaniel) 1908-1960 ... **BLC 3; CLC 1, 3, 4, 9, 14, 21, 48, 74; SSC 2; TCLC 136; WLC**
See also AAYA 5, 42; AFAW 1, 2; AMW; BPFB 3; BW 1; BYA 2; CA 108; CANR 64; CDALB 1929-1941; DA; DA3; DAB; DAC; DAM MST, MULT, NOV; DLB 76, 102; DLBD 2; EWL 3; EXPN; LAIT 3, 4; MTCW 1, 2; NCFS 1; NFS 1, 7; RGAL 4; RGSF 2; SSFS 3, 9, 15, 20; TUS; YAW

Wright, Richard B(ruce) 1937- .... **CLC 6**
See also CA 85-88; CANR 120; DLB 53

Wright, Rick 1945- .... **CLC 35**

Wright, Rowland
See Wells, Carolyn

Wright, Stephen 1946- .... **CLC 33**

Wright, Willard Huntington 1888-1939
See Van Dine, S. S.
See also CA 115; 189; CMW 4; DLBD 16

Wright, William 1930- .... **CLC 44**
See also CA 53-56; CANR 7, 23

Wroth, Lady Mary 1587-1653(?) .... **LC 30; PC 38**
See also DLB 121

Wu Ch'eng-en 1500(?)-1582(?) .... **LC 7**

Wu Ching-tzu 1701-1754 .... **LC 2**

Wulfstan c. 10th cent. -1023 .... **CMLC 59**

Wurlitzer, Rudolph 1938(?)- .... **CLC 2, 4, 15**
See also CA 85-88; CN 7; DLB 173

Wyatt, Sir Thomas c. 1503-1542 . **LC 70; PC 27**
See also BRW 1; DLB 132; EXPP; RGEL 2; TEA

Wycherley, William 1640-1716 .... **LC 8, 21, 102**
See also BRW 2; CDBLB 1660-1789; DAM DRAM; DLB 80; RGEL 2

Wyclif, John c. 1330-1384 .... **CMLC 70**
See also DLB 146

Wylie, Elinor (Morton Hoyt) 1885-1928 .... **PC 23; TCLC 8**
See also AMWS 1; CA 105; 162; DLB 9, 45; EXPP; RGAL 4

Wylie, Philip (Gordon) 1902-1971 ... **CLC 43**
See also CA 21-22; 33-36R; CAP 2; DLB 9; SFW 4

Wyndham, John .... **CLC 19**
See Harris, John (Wyndham Parkes Lucas) Beynon
See also DLB 255; SCFW 2

Wyss, Johann David Von 1743-1818 .... **NCLC 10**
See also CLR 92; JRDA; MAICYA 1, 2; SATA 29; SATA-Brief 27

Xenophon c. 430B.C.-c. 354B.C. ... **CMLC 17**
See also AW 1; DLB 176; RGWL 2, 3

Xingjian, Gao 1940-
See Gao Xingjian
See also CA 193; RGWL 3

Yakamochi 718-785 .... **CMLC 45; PC 48**

Yakumo Koizumi
See Hearn, (Patricio) Lafcadio (Tessima Carlos)

Yamada, Mitsuye (May) 1923- .... **PC 44**
See also CA 77-80

Yamamoto, Hisaye 1921- .... **AAL; SSC 34**
See also CA 214; DAM MULT; LAIT 4; SSFS 14

Yamauchi, Wakako 1924- .... **AAL**
See also CA 214

Yanez, Jose Donoso
See Donoso (Yanez), Jose

Yanovsky, Basile S.
See Yanovsky, V(assily) S(emenovich)

Yanovsky, V(assily) S(emenovich) 1906-1989 .... **CLC 2, 18**
See also CA 97-100; 129

Yates, Richard 1926-1992 .... **CLC 7, 8, 23**
See also AMWS 11; CA 5-8R; 139; CANR 10, 43; DLB 2, 234; DLBY 1981, 1992; INT CANR-10

Yau, John 1950- .... **PC 61**
See also CA 154; CANR 89; CP 7; DLB 234

Yeats, W. B.
See Yeats, William Butler

Yeats, William Butler 1865-1939 . **PC 20, 51; TCLC 1, 11, 18, 31, 93, 116; WLC**
See also AAYA 48; BRW 6; BRWR 1; CA 104; 127; CANR 45; CDBLB 1890-1914; DA; DA3; DAB; DAC; DAM DRAM, MST, POET; DLB 10, 19, 98, 156; EWL 3; EXPP; MTCW 1, 2; NCFS 3; PAB; PFS 1, 2, 5, 7, 13, 15; RGEL 2; TEA; WLIT 4; WP

Yehoshua, A(braham) B. 1936- .. **CLC 13, 31**
See also CA 33-36R; CANR 43, 90; CWW 2; EWL 3; RGSF 2; RGWL 3

Yellow Bird
See Ridge, John Rollin

Yep, Laurence Michael 1948- .... **CLC 35**
See also AAYA 5, 31; BYA 7; CA 49-52; CANR 1, 46, 92; CLR 3, 17, 54; DLB 52; FANT; JRDA; MAICYA 1, 2; MAICYAS 1; SATA 7, 69, 123; WYA; YAW

Yerby, Frank G(arvin) 1916-1991 ..... **BLC 3; CLC 1, 7, 22**
See also BPFB 3; BW 1, 3; CA 9-12R; 136; CANR 16, 52; DAM MULT; DLB 76; INT CANR-16; MTCW 1; RGAL 4; RHW

Yesenin, Sergei Alexandrovich
See Esenin, Sergei (Alexandrovich)

Yesenin, Sergey
See Esenin, Sergei (Alexandrovich)
See also EWL 3

Yevtushenko, Yevgeny (Alexandrovich) 1933- ...... **CLC 1, 3, 13, 26, 51, 126; PC 40**
See Evtushenko, Evgenii Aleksandrovich
See also CA 81-84; CANR 33, 54; DAM POET; EWL 3; MTCW 1

Yezierska, Anzia 1885(?)-1970 .... **CLC 46**
See also CA 126; 89-92; DLB 28, 221; FW; MTCW 1; RGAL 4; SSFS 15

Yglesias, Helen 1915- .... **CLC 7, 22**
See also CA 37-40R; CAAS 20; CANR 15, 65, 95; CN 7; INT CANR-15; MTCW 1

Yokomitsu, Riichi 1898-1947 .... **TCLC 47**
See also CA 170; EWL 3

Yonge, Charlotte (Mary) 1823-1901 .... **TCLC 48**
See also CA 109; 163; DLB 18, 163; RGEL 2; SATA 17; WCH

York, Jeremy
See Creasey, John

York, Simon
See Heinlein, Robert A(nson)

Yorke, Henry Vincent 1905-1974 ..... **CLC 13**
See Green, Henry
See also CA 85-88; 49-52

Yosano Akiko 1878-1942 .... **PC 11; TCLC 59**
See also CA 161; EWL 3; RGWL 3

PC Cumulative Nationality Index

Nationality Index

PC-65 Title Index

449

Title Index

ISBN 0-7876-8699-9